FOURTH EDITION

WORLDS TOGETHER, WORLDS APART

Volume 2

NORTH POLAR REGION
ARCTIC OCEAN
NORTH AMERICA
ASIA
GREENLAND
North Pole
ARCTIC CIRCLE
NORTH AMERICA
SOUTH AMERICA
CENTRAL AMERICA
NORTH PACIFIC OCEAN
SOUTH PACIFIC OCEAN
NORTH ATLANTIC OCEAN
SOUTH ATLANTIC OCEA
GULF OF MEXICO
CARIBBEAN SEA
Hudson Bay
Hawaii
POLYNESIA
TROPIC OF CANCER
EQUATOR
TROPIC OF CAPRICORN
ANTARCTIC CIRCLE
ANTARCTIC PENINSULA
WEDDELL SEA
Marie Byrd Land
ANTA
Longitude West of Greenwich
GLOBAL SATELLITE MOSAIC
The beauty and complexity of Earth's landscapesnabove and below the oceansnis revealed with the Global Satellite Mosaic. The mosaic was produced for the National Geographic Society by NASA's Jet Propulsion Laboratory, using more than 500 satellite images from the National Oceanic and Atmospheric Administration. The cloud-free images show Earth in its natural colors as it would be seen from space. One can easily identify the world's major glaciers, deserts, mountain ranges, and rain forests. For example, follow the green ribbon of lush vegetation along the Nile into the stark, dry Sahara. The mountain ranges seem to rise off the map thanks to digital elevation databases from the Department of Defense. The deepest areas of the ocean realm are colored dark blue in contrast to the light blue areas highlighting continental shelves, submarine ridges, and underwater mountains.
BIOSPHERE
Thousands of satellite images are combined to show a picture of biospheric productivity. In the oceans, red, yellow, and green indicate waters rich in phytoplankton. On land green areas show high-potential plant productivity; tan areas suffer from productivity limitations due to aridity and temperature.
THE
SATE

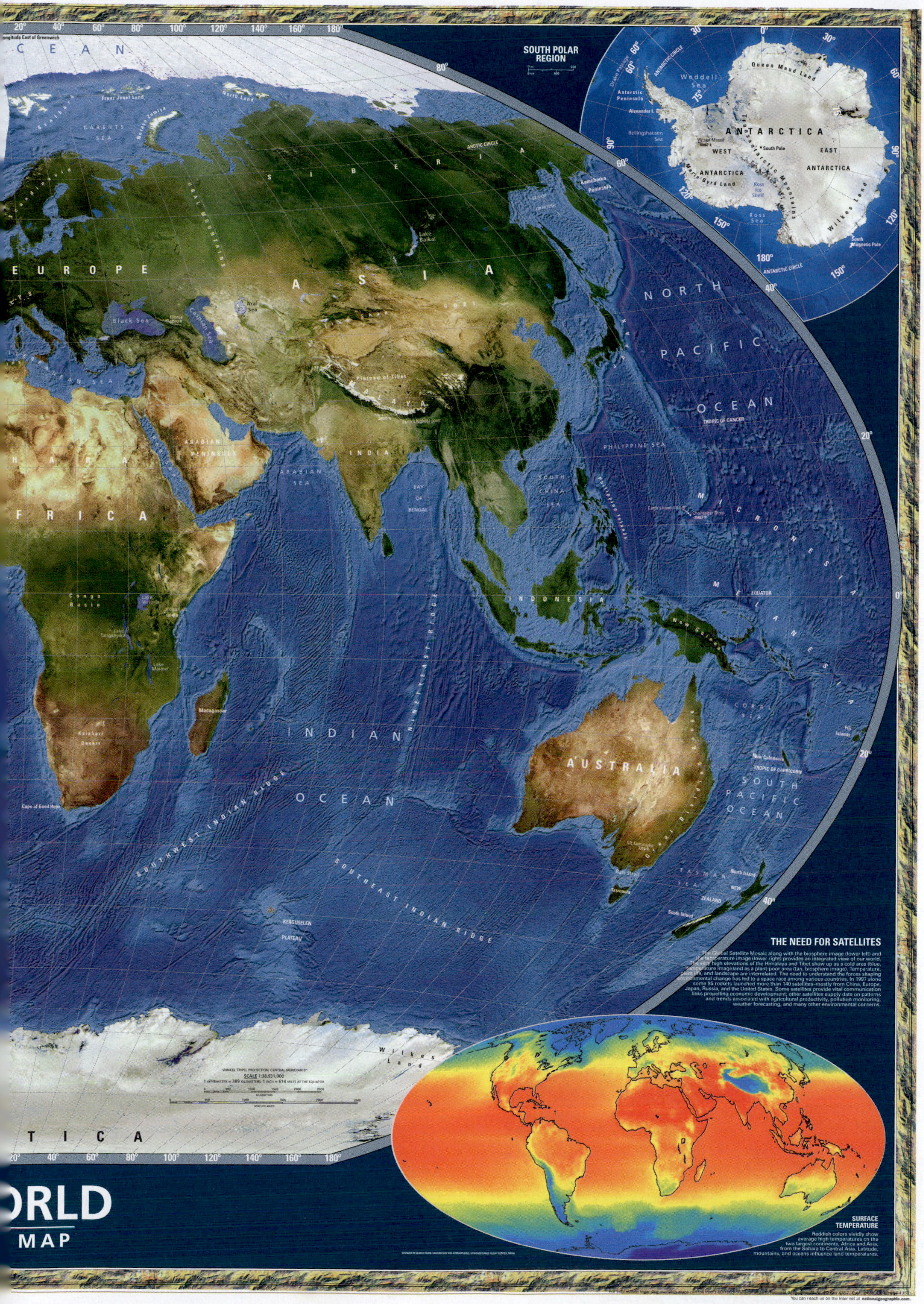
SOUTH POLAR REGION
ANTARCTICA
Queen Maud Land
Weddell Sea
Antarctic Peninsula
WEST ANTARCTICA
EAST ANTARCTICA
South Pole
Ross Ice Shelf
Ross Sea
Wilkes Land
ANTARCTIC CIRCLE
EUROPE
ASIA
SIBERIA
URAL MOUNTAINS
Black Sea
Caspian Sea
Aral Sea
Lake Baikal
Franz Josef Land
BARENTS SEA
ARCTIC CIRCLE
Plateau of Tibet
ARABIAN PENINSULA
ARABIAN SEA
INDIA
BAY OF BENGAL
SOUTH CHINA SEA
PHILIPPINE SEA
NORTH PACIFIC OCEAN
TROPIC OF CANCER
MICRONESIA
MELANESIA
EQUATOR
INDONESIA
AFRICA
Congo Basin
Madagascar
Kalahari Desert
Cape of Good Hope
INDIAN OCEAN
NINETYEAST RIDGE
SOUTHWEST INDIAN RIDGE
SOUTHEAST INDIAN RIDGE
KERGUELEN PLATEAU
AUSTRALIA
TROPIC OF CAPRICORN
SOUTH PACIFIC OCEAN
TASMAN SEA
NEW ZEALAND
North Island
South Island
Wilkes Land
ANTARCTICA
ORLD
MAP
THE NEED FOR SATELLITES
The Global Satellite Mosaic along with the biosphere image (lower left) and the temperature image (lower right) provides an integrated view of our world. The very high elevations of the Himalaya and Tibet show up as a cold area (blue, temperature image)and as a plant-poor area (tan, biosphere image). Temperature, plant life, and landscape are interrelated. The need to understand the forces shaping environmental change has led to a space race among various countries. In 1997 alone some 85 rockets launched more than 140 satellites–mostly from China, Europe, Japan, Russia, and the United States. Some satellites provide vital communication links propelling economic development; other satellites supply data on patterns and trends associated with agricultural productivity, pollution monitoring, weather forecasting, and many other environmental concerns.
SURFACE TEMPERATURE
Reddish colors vividly show average high temperatures on the two largest continents, Africa and Asia, from the Sahara to Central Asia. Latitude, mountains, and oceans influence land temperatures.

Political World

NORTH POLAR REGION

Human boundaries

The world is divided into 192 independent nations, with colors on the map showing the extents of national sovereignty. International boundaries only occasionally mark true cultural boundaries, however; they're a complex artifact of colonialism, conquest, religious conversion, and conflict. The political map is a useful but all too-neat construct for a bewilderingly complicated world.

SOUTH POLAR REGION

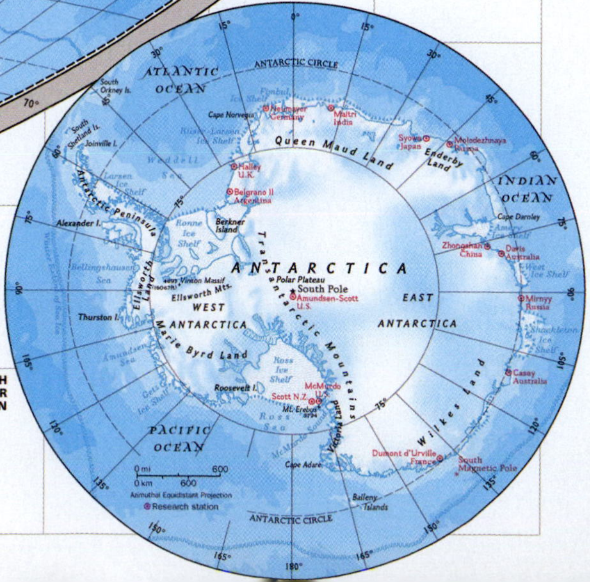

FOURTH EDITION

WORLDS TOGETHER, WORLDS APART

Volume 2: From 1000 CE to the Present

Robert **Tignor** • Jeremy **Adelman** • Stephen **Aron**
Stephen **Kotkin** • Suzanne **Marchand** • Gyan **Prakash** • Michael **Tsin**

W. W. Norton & Company
New York • London

W. W. Norton & Company has been independent since its founding in 1923, when William Warder Norton and Mary D. Herter Norton first published lectures delivered at the People's Institute, the adult education division of New York City's Cooper Union. The firm soon expanded its program beyond the Institute, publishing books by celebrated academics from America and abroad. By midcentury, the two major pillars of Norton's publishing program—trade books and college texts—were firmly established. In the 1950s, the Norton family transferred control of the company to its employees, and today—with a staff of four hundred and a comparable number of trade, college, and professional titles published each year—W. W. Norton & Company stands as the largest and oldest publishing house owned wholly by its employees.

Printed in the United States of America.

Editor: Jon Durbin
Associate Editor: Justin Cahill
Editorial Assistant: Penelope Lin
Project Editor: Diane Cipollone
Managing Editor, College: Marian Johnson
Copyeditor: Nancy Green
Editor, E-media: Tacy Quinn
Associate Editor, E-media: Lorraine Klimowich
Assistant Editor, E-media: Stefani Wallace
Photo Editor: Evan Luberger
Marketing Manager, History: Sarah England
Production Manager: Andy Ensor
Permissions Manager: Megan Jackson
Permissions Clearing: Bethany Salminen
Design Director: Rubina Yeh
Book Designer: Jillian Burr
Cartographer: Mapping Specialists
Composition: Cenveo® Publisher Services
Manufacturing: Courier, Kendallville

The Library of Congress has cataloged the one-volume edition as follows:

Tignor, Robert L.
Worlds together, worlds apart : a history of the world from the beginnings of humankind to the present / by Robert Tignor, Jeremy Adelman, Stephen Aron, Peter Brown, Benjamin Elman, Stephen Kotkin, Xinru Liu, Suzanne Marchand, Holly Pittman, Gyan Prakash, Brent Shaw, and Michael Tsin. — Fourth edition.
pages cm
Includes bibliographical references and index.
ISBN 978-0-393-92207-3 (hardcover : alk. paper) — ISBN 978-0-393-12376-0 (pbk. : alk. paper)
1. World history. I. Title.
D21.T53 2013
909—dc23

2013038525

This edition: ISBN 978-0-393-92209-7 (pbk.)

W. W. Norton & Company, Inc., 500 Fifth Avenue, New York, NY 10110-0017
wwnorton.com

W. W. Norton & Company Ltd., Castle House, 75/76 Wells Street, London W1T 3QT
1 2 3 4 5 6 7 8 9 0

CONTENTS IN BRIEF

CONTENTS

Chapter 14
CULTURES OF SPLENDOR AND POWER, 1500–1780 518

Chapter 16

ALTERNATIVE VISIONS OF THE NINETEENTH CENTURY 594

Chapter 17

NATIONS AND EMPIRES, 1850–1914 628

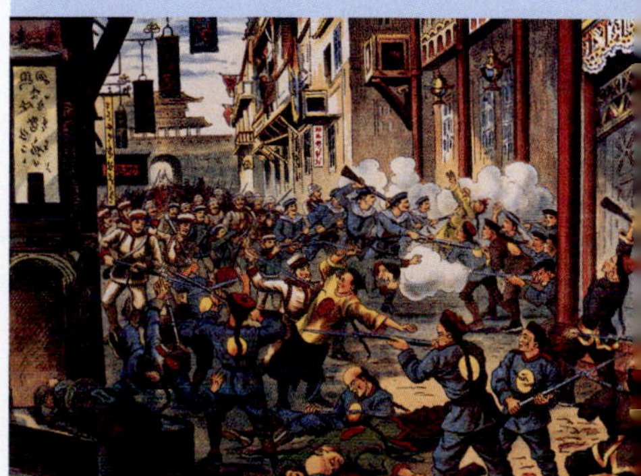

CURRENT TRENDS IN WORLD HISTORY

ANALYZING GLOBAL DEVELOPMENTS

PRIMARY SOURCES

Chapter 10

Chapter 11

Chapter 12

Chapter 13

Chapter 14

Chapter 15

Chapter 16

Chapter 17

Chapter 18

Chapter 19

Chapter 20

Chapter 21

MAPS

PREFACE

Worlds Together, Worlds Apart has set the standard for three editions for those instructors who want to teach a globally integrated world history survey course. Just as the dynamic field of world history evolves, so too has *Worlds Together, Worlds Apart*. Building on the success of the first three editions, the Fourth Edition of *Worlds Together, Worlds Apart* continues to offer a highly coherent, cutting-edge survey of the field built around world history stories of significance that make it possible for students to readily make connections and comparisons across time and place and make the teaching of the course more manageable for instructors (e.g., the building of the Silk Road, the spread of the Black Death across Afro-Eurasia, the impact of New World silver on global trade, and alternative ways to organize societies during the rise of nineteenth-century capitalism). The new Fourth Edition has been further shortened and fully updated, and features a robust new suite of pedagogical and media tools designed to help students master core content, develop history skills, and make connections across time and place. In particular, more than any previous edition, *Worlds Together, Worlds Apart* provides an array of digital media that offers the materials faculty need to address their course goals—in the classroom and online—while providing students activities to develop core skills in reading comprehension, writing, and historical analysis.

HIGHLIGHTS OF THE NEW FEATURES OF THE FOURTH EDITION

- **Streamlined presentation with new pedagogical tools** make the text even more accessible.
  - Each chapter has been **shortened** to further highlight the global stories.
  - **The new robust suite of pedagogical features** is designed to make it easier for students to master core content and to readily make connections and comparisons.
    - The ***Before You Read This Chapter*** pedagogy includes new **Global Storylines** that highlight the chapter themes and new **Focus Questions** that focus on the core objectives students must understand to get a good grade on a quiz or exam.
    - The ***After You Read This Chapter*** pedagogy includes a new **Tracing the Global Storylines** feature, which serves as a chapter summary by showing the chapter themes in action in each region of the world. Bright new **Global Timelines** highlight by region the major developments in world history in the period. Refreshed **Key Terms** and **Study Questions** help students review core material.
- **Cutting-edge scholarship enables students to think like world historians.**
  - New ***Analyzing Global Developments*** features empower students to do historical analysis the way historians do: using historical data or comparative information. Each new *Analyzing Global Developments* feature highlights a major topic in world history, such as comparing the development of writing across cultures, quantifying the destruction caused by the Black Death, and measuring the impact of the Atlantic slave trade in human and economic costs.
  - New ***Current Trends in World History*** features showcase cutting-edge scholarship that is driving the field of world history. These brief essays with analysis questions focus on major research topics in the field, such as the environment, transnational developments, gender, and trade in global commodities, to let students

see the range of topics and ways that world historians think about and conduct their research. Examples include "Climate Change at the End of the Third Millennium BCE in Mesopotamia, Egypt, and the Indus Valley"; "Big Military Forces in Early Empires"; "Empires, Allies, and Frontiers in the Han and Roman Empires"; "Corn and the Rise of Slave-Supplying Kingdoms in West Africa"; "Stimulants, Sociability, and Coffee Houses"; and "Population Movements: Filling Up The Empty Spaces" and "Spread of Capitalism in the Early Twentieth Century."

  - **Completely rewritten coverage of South and East Asia in early world history** builds more social and cultural material into the narrative and makes each period of history in these regions more distinctive.

- **Robust map and primary source programs** build students' history skills.
  - **The updated, stellar map program** includes global and regional maps designed to highlight the main story in each chapter. Enhanced map captions ask students a series of questions to help them learn how to read maps and connect the content back to the narrative. Most maps have been simplified and made easier to read so that students can identify major developments more readily.
  - **A wealth of carefully selected primary sources empower students to carry out historical analysis.**
    - **More than 100 primary sources are integrated into the main text (five to six per chapter)**, each carefully chosen to highlight the chapter's main theme in a different region of the world.
    - ***Worlds Together, Worlds Apart: A Companion Reader,*** edited by Kenneth Pomeranz (University of Chicago), Laura Mitchell, and James Givens (both of University of California, Irvine) is an impressive collection of over 150 primary source documents carefully chosen to align with each chapter in *Worlds Together, Worlds Apart*. The reader also includes mini-casebooks on (1) women and power in the ancient world; (2) the Mongols and warfare; (3) the Atlantic world slave trade; and (4) rubber as a global commodity.
    - The **online world history reader on Norton StudySpace** includes 100 additional primary sources with headnotes and study questions.

- **Norton Coursepacks** allow you to bring strong assessment and lecture tools directly into your Learning Management System (LMS).
  - Available at no cost to professors or students in a variety of formats (including Blackboard, Moodle, and Angel), Norton Coursepacks include chapter-based assignments, test banks and quizzes, interactive learning tools, and selected content from StudySpace, the student Web site.
  - Content unique to the *Worlds Together, Worlds Apart* Coursepack includes new **Guided Reading Exercises**, new **Story Maps**, new **Map Exercises**, and new **Chrono-Quiz** (see below for more information).

Since work began on *Worlds Together, Worlds Apart*, world history has gained even more prominence in college classrooms and historical studies. Courses in the history of the world now abound, often replacing the standard surveys of European history and western civilization overviews. Graduate history students receive training in world history, and journals routinely publish studies in this field. A new generation of textbooks was needed to help students and instructors make sense of this vast, complex, and rapidly evolving field. We believe that *Worlds Together, Worlds Apart* remains the most cutting-edge, engaging, readable, and useful text available for all students of world history. We also believe that this text, one that has advanced the teaching of this field, could have only grown out of the highly collaborative effort of a team of scholars and teachers rather than the more typical single- or two-author efforts. Indeed, the idea to build each chapter around stories of world history significance and the execution of this model grew out of our monthly team meetings and our joint writing efforts during the development stage. As a team-driven text, *Worlds Together, Worlds Apart* also has the advantage of area experts to make sure the material is presented accurately, which is always a challenge for the single- or two-author texts, especially in world history. Finally, our book also reads with a single voice due to the extraordinary efforts of our general editor, and leader, Robert Tignor, who with every edition makes the final major sweep through the text to make sure that the voice, style, and level of detail are consistent throughout. Building on these distinctive strengths, we have worked hard and thoughtfully to make the Fourth Edition of *Worlds Together, Worlds Apart* the best one so far. While there are many exciting additions to the main text and support package, we have made every effort to remain true to our original vision.

OUR GUIDING PRINCIPLES

Five principles inform this book, guiding its framework and the organization of its individual chapters. The first is that

world history is global history. There are many fine histories of the individual regions of the world, which we have endeavored to make good use of. But unlike the authors of many other so-called world histories, we have chosen not to deal with the great regions and cultures of the world as separate units, reserving individual chapters to East Asia, South Asia, Southwest Asia, Europe, Africa, and the Americas. Our goal is to place each of these regions in its largest geographical context. Accordingly, we have written chapters that are truly global in that most major regions of the world are discussed in each one. We achieved these globally integrated chapters by building each around a significant world history story or theme. There are a number of wonderful examples throughout the book, including the peopling of the earth (Chapter 1), the building of the Silk Road (Chapter 6), the rise of universal religions (Chapters 8 and 9), the Black Death (Chapter 11), the effects of New World silver on the economies of the world (Chapter 13), alternative visions to nineteenth-century capitalism (Chapter 15), the rise of nation-states and empires (Chapter 16), and so on. It would be misleading, of course, to say that the context is the world, because none of these regions, even the most highly developed commercially, enjoyed commercial or cultural contact with peoples all over the globe before Columbus's voyage to the Americas and the sixteenth century. But the peoples living in the Afro-Eurasian landmass, probably the single most important building block for our study, were deeply influenced by one another, as were the more scattered peoples living in the Americas and in Africa below the Sahara. Products, ideas, and persons traveled widely across the large land units of Eurasia, Africa, and the Americas. Indeed, Afro-Eurasia was not divided or thought of as divided into separate landmasses until recent times. It is in this sense that our world history is global.

The second principle informing this work is **the importance of chronology in framing world history**. Rather than telling the story of world history by analyzing separate geographical areas, we have elected to frame the chapters around significant world history themes and periods that transcended regional and cultural boundaries—moments or periods of meaningful change in the way that human beings organized their lives. Some of these changes were dramatic and affected many people. Environments changed; the earth became drier and warmer; humans learned to domesticate plants and animals; technological innovations in warfare, political organization, and commercial activities occurred; and new religious and cultural beliefs spread far and wide. These changes swept across large landmasses, paying scant heed to preexisting cultural and geographical unity. They affected peoples living in widely dispersed societies. In other cases, changes occurred in only one locality while other places retained their traditions or took alternative routes. Chronology helps us understand the ways in which the world has, and has not, shared a common history.

The third principle is **historical and geographical balance**. Ours is not a history focused on the rise of the West. We seek to pay attention to the global histories of all peoples and not to privilege those developments that led directly into European history as if the rest of the history of the world was but a prelude to the rise of western civilization. We deal with peoples living outside Europe on their own terms and try to see world history from their perspective. Even more significantly, while we describe societies that obviously influenced Europe's historical development, we do so in a context very different from that which western historians have stressed. Rather than simply viewing these cultures in terms of their role in western development, we seek to understand them in their own terms and to illuminate the ways they influenced other parts of the world. From our perspective, it is historically inaccurate to annex Mesopotamia and Egypt to western civilization, because these territories lay well outside Europe and had a large influence on Africa, South Asia, and East Asia as well as on Europe. Indeed, our presentation of Europe in the period leading up to and including the founding of the Roman Empire is different from many of the standard treatments. The Europeans we describe are rather rough, wild-living, warring peoples living on the fringes of the settled parts of the world and looked down on by more politically stable communities. They hardly seem to be made of the stuff that will catapult Europeans to world leadership a millennium later—indeed, they were very different people from those who, as the result of myriad intervening and contingent events, founded the nineteenth- and twentieth-century empires whose ruins are still all around us.

Our fourth principle is **an emphasis on connections and what we call disconnections across societal and cultural boundaries**. World history is not the history of separate regions of the world at different periods of time. It is the history of the connections among peoples living often at great distances from one another, and it is also the history of the resistances of peoples living within and outside societies to connections that threatened to put them in subordinate positions or to rob them of their independence.

A stress on connections inevitably foregrounds those elements within societies that promoted long-distance ties. Merchants are important, as are military men and political potentates seeking to expand their polities. So are scholars and religious leaders, particularly those who believed that they had universalistic messages with which to convert others to their visions. Perhaps most important of all in pre-modern world history, certainly the most understudied, are the nomadic pastoral peoples, who were often the agents for the transmission of products, peoples, and ideas across long and harsh distances. They exploded onto the scene of settled societies at critical junctures, erasing old cultural and geographical barriers and producing new unities, as the Arabs did in the seventh century CE and the Mongols in the thirteenth century. *Worlds Together, Worlds Apart* is not intended to convey the message that the history of the world is a story of increasing integration. What for one ruling group brought benefits in the form of increased workforces, material prosperity, and political stability often meant enslavement, political subordination, and loss of territory for other groups. The historian's task, then, is not only to represent the different experiences of increased connectedness, describing worlds that came together, but also to be attentive to the opposite trends, describing peoples and communities that remained apart.

The fifth and final principle is that **world history is a narrative of big themes and high-level comparisons.** *Worlds Together, Worlds Apart* is not a book of record. Indeed, in a work that covers the whole of the historical record of humankind from the beginnings of history to the present, the notion that no event or individual worthy of attention would be excluded is the height of folly. We have sought to offer clear themes and interpretations in order to synthesize the vast body of data that often overwhelms histories of the world. Our aspiration is to identify the main historical forces that have moved history, to highlight those monumental innovations that have changed the way humans lived, and to describe the creation and evolution of those bedrock institutions, many of which, of course, endure. In this regard, self-conscious cross-cultural comparisons of developments, institutions, and even founding figures receive attention to make students aware that some common institutions, such as slavery, did not have the same features in every society. Or, in the opposite fashion, the seemingly diverse terms that were used, say, to describe learned and religious men in different parts of the world—monks in Europe, ulama in Islam, Brahmans in India, and scholar-gentries in China—often meant much the same thing in very different settings. We have constructed *Worlds Together, Worlds Apart* around big ideas, stories, and themes rather than filling the book with names and dates that encourage students only to memorize rather than understand world history concepts.

OUR MAJOR THEMES

The primary organizing framework of *Worlds Together, Worlds Apart*—one that runs through the chapters and connects the different parts of the volume—is the theme of **interconnection and divergence**. While describing movements that facilitated global connectedness, this book also shows how different regions developed their own ways of handling or resisting connections and change. Throughout history, different regions and different population groups often stood apart from the rest of the world until touched by traders or explorers or missionaries or soldiers. Some of these regions welcomed global connections. Others sought to change the nature of their connections with the outside world, and yet others resisted efforts to bring them into the larger world. All, however, were somehow affected by their experience of connection. Yet, the history of the world is not simply one of increasing globalization, in which all societies eventually join a common path to the present. Rather, it is a history of the ways in which, as people became linked, their experience of these global connections diverged.

Besides the central theme of interconnection and divergence, other themes also stand out in *Worlds Together, Worlds Apart*. First, the book discusses **how the recurring efforts of people to cross religious, political, and cultural borders brought the world together.** Merchants and educated men and women traded goods and ideas. Whole communities, in addition to select groups, moved to safer or more promising environments. **The transregional crossings of ideas, goods, and peoples produced transformations and conflicts**—a second important theme. Finally, the movement of ideas, peoples, products, and germs over long distances upset the balance of power across the world and within individual societies. Such movements changed the relationship of different population groups with other peoples and areas of the world and led over time to dramatic shifts in the ascendancy of regions. **Changes in power arrangements within and between regions explain which parts of the world and regional groups benefited from integration and which resisted it.** These three themes (exchange and migration, conflict and resistance, and alterations in the balance of power) weave themselves through every chapter of this work. While we highlight major themes throughout, we tell the stories of the people caught in these currents of exchange, conflict, and changing power relations, paying particular attention to the role that gender and the environment play in shaping the evolution of societies.

The history of the world is not a single, sweeping narrative. On the contrary, the last 5,000 years have produced multiple histories, moving along many paths and trajectories. Sometimes these histories merge, intertwining themselves in substantial ways. Sometimes they disentangle themselves and simply stand apart. Much of the time, however, they are simultaneously together and apart. In place of a single narrative, the usual one being the rise of the

West, this book maps the many forks in the road that confronted the world's societies at different times and the surprising turns and unintended consequences that marked the choices that peoples and societies made, including the unanticipated and dramatic rise of the West in the nineteenth century. Formulated in this way, world history is the unfolding of many possible histories, and readers of this book should come away with a reinforced sense of the unpredictability of the past, the instability of the present, and the uncertainty of the future.

OVERVIEW OF VOLUME ONE

Volume One of *Worlds Together, Worlds Apart* deals with the period from the beginnings of human history through the Mongol invasions of the thirteenth century and the spread of the Black Death across Afro-Eurasia. It is divided into eleven chapters, each of which marks a distinct historical period. Hence, each chapter has an overarching theme or small set of themes that hold otherwise highly diverse material together.

Chapter 1, "Becoming Human," presents biological and cultural perspectives on the way that early hominoids became truly human. We believe that this chapter is important in establishing the global context of world history. We believe too that our chapter is unique in its focus on how humans became humans, so we discuss how early humans became bipedal and how they developed complex cognitive processes such as language and artistic abilities. Recent research indicates that *Homo sapiens* originated in Africa, probably no more than 200,000 years ago. These early men and women walked out of the African landmass sometime between 120,000 and 50,000 years ago, gradually populating all regions of the world. What is significant in this story is that the different population groups around the world, the so-called races of humankind, have only recently broken off from one another. Also in this chapter, we describe the domestication of plants and animals and the founding of the first village settlements around the globe.

Chapter 2, "Rivers, Cities, and First States, 4000–2000 BCE," covers the period during which five of the great river basins experienced extraordinary breakthroughs in human activity. On the flood plains of the Tigris and Euphrates in Mesopotamia, the Nile in Egypt, the Indus valley in modern-day northern India and Pakistan, and the Yellow and Yangzi rivers in China, men and women mastered annual floods and became expert in seeding and cultivating foodstuffs. In these areas, populations became dense. Riverine cultures had much in common. They had highly developed hierarchical political, social, and cultural systems, priestly and bureaucratic classes, and organized religious and cultural systems. But they also differed greatly, and these differences were passed from generation to generation. The development of these major complex societies certainly is a turning point in world history.

Extensive climatic and technological changes serve as major turning points for **Chapter 3, "Nomads, Territorial States, and Microsocieties, 2000–1200 BCE."** Drought, environmental degradation, and political instability brought the first riverine societies to a crashing end around 2000 BCE. When aridity forced tribal and nomadic peoples living on the fringes of the settled populations to move closer to settled areas, they brought with them an insurmountable military advantage. They had become adept at yoking horses to war chariots, and hence they were in a position to subjugate or intermarry with the peoples in the settled polities in the river basins. Around 2000 BCE these peoples established new territorial kingdoms in Mesopotamia, Egypt, the Indus valley, and China, which gave way a millennium later (1000 BCE) to even larger, militarily and politically more powerful states. In the Americas, the Mediterranean, sub-Saharan Africa, and the Pacific worlds, microsocieties arose as an alternative form of polity in which peoples lived in much smaller-scale societies that showcased their own unique and compelling features.

Chapter 4, "First Empires and Common Cultures in Afro-Eurasia, 1200–350 BCE," describes the different ways in which larger-scale societies grew and became unified. In the case of the world's first empires, the neo-Assyrian and Persian, political power was the main unifying element. Both states established different models that future empires would emulate. The Assyrians used brutal force to intimidate and subjugate different groups within their societies and neighboring states. The Persians followed a pattern that relied less on coercion and more on tributary relationships, while reveling in cultural diversity. The Zhou state in China offered yet a third way of political unity, basing its rule on the doctrine of the mandate of heaven, which legitimated its rulers' succession as long as they were able to maintain stability and order. Vedic society in South Asia offers a dramatically different model in which religion and culture were the main unifying forces. Religion moves to the forefront of the narrative in other ways in this chapter. The birth of monotheism occurred in the Zoroastrian and Hebrew faiths and the beginnings of Buddhism. All three religions endure today.

The last millennium before the common era witnessed some of the most monumental developments in human history. In the six and half centuries discussed in **Chapter 5, "Worlds Turned Inside Out, 1000–350 BCE,"** teachers and thinkers, rather than kings, priests, and warriors, came to the fore. Men like Confucius, the Buddha, Plato, and Aristotle, to name only the best known of this brilliant group, offered new insights into the natural world and provided new guidelines for how to govern justly and live ethically. In this era, small-scale societies, benefiting from more intimate relationships, took the place of the first great empires, now in decline. These highly individualistic cultures developed new strategies for political organization, even including experimenting with a democratic polity. In Africa, the Bantu peoples spread across sub-Saharan Africa, and the Sudanic peoples of Meroe created a society that blended Egyptian and sub-Saharan influences. These were all dynamic hybrid societies building on existing knowledge. Equally dramatic transformations occurred in the Americas, where the Olmec and Chavín peoples were creating hierarchical societies of the like never before seen in their part of the world.

Chapter 6, "Shrinking the Afro-Eurasian World, 350 BCE–250 CE," describes three major forces that simultaneously integrated large segments of the Afro-Eurasian landmass culturally and economically. First, Alexander and his armies changed the political and cultural landscape of North Africa and Southwest and South Asia. Culturally, Alexander spread Hellenism through North Africa and Southwest and central Asia, making it the first cultural system to achieve a transregional scope. Second, it was in the post-Alexander world that these commercial roads were stabilized and intensified. For the first time, a trading network, known as the Silk Road, stretching from Palmyra in the West to central Asia in the East, came into being. Buddhism was the first religion to seize on the Silk Road's more formal existence as its followers moved quickly with the support of the Mauryan Empire to spread their ideas into central Asia. Finally, we witness the growth of a "silk road of the seas" as new technologies and bigger ships allowed for a dramatic expansion in maritime trade from South Asia all the way to Egypt and East Africa.

Chapter 7, "Han Dynasty China and Imperial Rome, 300 BCE–300 CE," compares Han China and the Roman Empire, the two political, economic, and cultural systems that dominated much of the Afro-Eurasian landmass from 200 BCE to 200 CE. Both the Han Dynasty and the Roman Empire ruled effectively in their own way, providing an instructive comparative case study. Both left their imprint on Afro-Eurasia, and rulers for centuries afterward tried to revive these glorious polities and use them as models of greatness. This chapter also discusses the effect of state sponsorship on religion, as Christianity came into existence in the context of the late Roman Empire and Buddhism was introduced to China during the decline of the Han.

Out of the crumbling Roman Empire new polities and a new religion emerged, the major topic of **Chapter 8, "The Rise of Universal Religions, 300–600 CE."** The Byzantine Empire, claiming to be the successor state to the Roman Empire, embraced Christianity as its state religion. The Tang rulers patronized Buddhism to such a degree that Confucian statesmen feared it had become the state religion. Both Buddhism and Christianity enjoyed spectacular success in the politically fragmented post-Han era in China and in the feudal world of western Europe. These dynamic religions represent a decisive transformation in world history. Christianity enjoyed its eventual successes through state sponsorship via the Roman and Byzantine empires and by providing spiritual comfort and hope during the chaotic years of Rome's decline. Buddhism grew through imperial sponsorship and significant changes to its fundamental beliefs, when adherents to the faith deified Buddha and created notions of an afterlife. In Africa a wide range of significant developments and a myriad of cultural practices existed; yet large common cultures also arose. The Bantu peoples spread throughout the southern half of the landmass, spoke closely related languages, and developed similar political institutions based on the prestige of individuals of high achievement. In the Americas the Olmecs established their own form of the city-state, while the Mayans owed their success to a decentralized common culture built around a strong religious belief system and a series of spiritual centers.

In **Chapter 9, "New Empires and Common Cultures, 600–1000 CE,"** in a relatively remote corner of the Arabian Peninsula another world religion, Islam, exploded with world-changing consequences. The rise of Islam provides a contrast to the way in which universalizing religions and political empires interacted. Islam and empire arose in a fashion quite different from Christianity and the Roman Empire. Christianity took over an already existing empire—the Roman—after suffering persecution at its hands for several centuries. In contrast, Islam created an empire almost at the moment of its emergence. By the time the Abbasid Empire came into being in the middle of the eighth century, Islamic armies, political leaders, and clerics exercised power over much of the Afro-Eurasian landmass from southern Spain, across North Africa, all the way to central Asia. The Tang Empire in China, however, served as a counterweight to Islam's power both politically and intellectually. Confucianism enjoyed a spectacular recovery in this period. With the Tang rulers, Confucianism slowed the spread of Buddhism and further reinforced China's development along different, more secular pathways. Japan and Korea also enter world history at this time, as tributary states to Tang China and as hybrid cultures that mixed Chinese customs and practices with their own. The Christian world split in this period between the western Latin church and the eastern Byzantine church. Both branches of Christianity played a role in unifying societies, especially in western Europe, which lacked strong political rule.

In the three centuries from 1000 to 1300 (**Chapter 10, "Becoming 'the World,' 1000–1300 CE"**) Afro-Eurasia experienced an unprecedented rise in prosperity and population that even spread into West and East Africa. Just as importantly, the world in this period divided into regional zones that are recognizable today. And trade grew rapidly.

A view of the major trading cities of this time demonstrates how commerce transformed cultures. Sub-Saharan Africa also underwent intense regional integration via the spread of the Mande-speaking peoples and the Mali Empire. The Americas witnessed their first empire in the form of the Chimu peoples in the Andes. This chapter ends with the Mongol conquests of the twelfth and thirteenth centuries, which brought massive destruction. The Mongol Empire, however, once in place, promoted long-distance commerce, scholarly exchange, and travel on an unprecedented scale. The Mongols brought Eurasia, North Africa, and many parts of sub-Saharan Africa into a new connectedness. The Mongol story also underscores the important role that nomads played throughout the history of the early world.

The Black Death brought Afro-Eurasia's prosperity and population growth to a catastrophic end as discussed in **Chapter 11, "Crises and Recovery in Afro-Eurasia, 1300s–1500s."** The dying and destruction of the fourteenth century saw traditional institutions give way and forced peoples to rebuild their cultures. The polities that came into being at this time and the intense religious experimentation that took place effected a sharp break with the past. The bubonic plague wiped out as much as two-thirds of the population in many of the densely settled locations of Afro-Eurasia. Societies were brought to their knees by the Mongols' depredations as well as by biological pathogens. In the face of one of humanity's grimmest periods, peoples and societies demonstrated tremendous resilience as they looked for new ways to rebuild their communities, some turning inward and others seeking inspiration, conquests, and riches elsewhere. Volume One concludes on the eve of the "Columbian Exchange," the moment when "old" worlds discovered "new" ones and a vast series of global interconnections and divergences commenced.

OVERVIEW OF VOLUME TWO

The organizational structure for Volume Two reaffirms the commitment to write a decentered, global history of the world. Christopher Columbus is not the starting point, as he is in so many modern world histories. Rather, we begin in the eleventh and twelfth centuries with two major developments in world history: the Mongols and the Black Death. The first, set forth in **Chapter 10, "Becoming 'the World,' 1000–1300 CE,"** describes a world that was divided for the first time into regions that are recognizable today. This world experienced rapid population growth, as is shown by a simple look at the major trading cities from Asia in the East to the Mediterranean in the West. Yet nomadic peoples remain a force as revealed in the Mongol invasions of Afro-Eurasia.

Chapter 11, "Crises and Recovery in Afro-Eurasia, 1300s–1500s," describes how the Mongol warriors, through their conquests and the integration of the Afro-Eurasian world, spread the bubonic plague, which brought death and depopulation to much of Afro-Eurasia. Both these stories set the stage for the modern world and are clear-cut turning points in world history. The primary agents of world connection described in this chapter were dynasts, soldiers, clerics, merchants, and adventurers who rebuilt the societies that disease and political collapse had destroyed.

The Mongols joined the two hemispheres, as we describe in **Chapter 12, "Contact, Commerce, and Colonization, 1450s–1600,"** bringing the peoples and products of the Western Hemisphere into contact and conflict with Eurasia and Africa. It is the collision between the Eastern and Western Hemispheres that sets in motion modern world history and marks a distinct divide or turning point between the pre-modern and the modern. Here, too, disease and increasing trade linkages were vital. Unprepared for the advanced military technology and the disease pool of European and African peoples, the Amerindian population experienced a population decline even more devastating than that caused by the Black Death.

Europeans sailed across the Atlantic Ocean to find a more direct, less encumbered route to Asia and came upon lands, peoples, and products that they had not expected. One item, however, that they had sought in every part of the world and that they found in abundance in the Americas was precious metal. In **Chapter 13, "Worlds Entangled, 1600–1750,"** we discuss how New World silver from Mexico and Peru became the major currency of global commerce, oiling the long-distance trading networks that had been revived after the Black Death. The effect of New World silver on the world economy was so great that it, even more than the Iberian explorations of the New World, brought the hemispheres together and marks the true genesis of modern world history. Sugar also linked the economies and polities of western Europe, Africa, and the Americas and was a powerful force in a triangular trade centered on the Atlantic Ocean. This trade involved the shipment of vast numbers of African captives to the Americas, where they toiled on sugar, tobacco, cotton, and rice slave plantations.

Chapter 14, "Cultures of Splendor and Power, 1500–1780," discusses the Ottoman scientists, Safavid and Mughal artists, and Chinese literati, as well as European thinkers, whose notable achievements were rooted in their own cultures but tempered by awareness of the intellectual activities of others. In this chapter, we look closely at how culture is created as a historical process and describe how the massive increase in wealth during this period, growing out of global trade, led to one of the great periods of cultural flourishing in world history.

Around 1800, transformations reverberated outward from the Atlantic world and altered economic and political relationships in the rest of the world. In **Chapter 15, "Reordering the World, 1750–1850,"** we discuss how political revolutions in the Americas and Europe, new ideas about how to trade and organize labor, and a powerful rhetoric of freedom and universal rights underlay the beginning of "a great divide" between peoples of European descent and those who were not. These forces of laissez-faire capitalism, industrialization, the nation-state, and republicanism not only attracted diverse groups around the world; they also threatened groups that put forth alternative visions. Ideas of freedom, as manifested in trading relations, labor, and political activities, clashed with a traditional world based on inherited rights and statuses and further challenged the way men and women had lived in earlier times. These political, intellectual, and economic reorderings changed the way people around the world saw themselves and thus represent something quite novel in world history.

These new ways of envisioning the world did not go unchallenged, as **Chapter 16, "Alternative Visions of the Nineteenth Century,"** makes clear. Here, intense resistance to evolving modernity reflected the diversity of peoples and their hopes for the future. Wahabbism in Islam, the strongman movement in Africa, Indian resistance in America and Mexico, socialism and communism in Europe, the Taiping Rebellion in China, and the Indian mutiny in South Asia catapulted to historical prominence prophets and leaders whose visions often drew on earlier traditions and led these individuals to resist rapid change.

Chapter 17, "Nations and Empires, 1850–1914," discusses the political, economic, military, and ideological power that thrust Europe and North America to the fore of global events and led to an era of nationalism and modern imperialism, new forces in world history. Yet this period of seeming European supremacy was to prove short-lived.

As **Chapter 18, "An Unsettled World, 1890–1914,"** demonstrates, even before World War I shattered Europe's moral certitude, many groups at home (feminists, Marxists, and unfulfilled nationalists) and abroad (anticolonial nationalists) had raised a chorus of complaints about European and North American dominance. As in Chapter 14, we look at the processes by which specific cultural movements rose and reflected the concerns of individual societies. Yet here, too, syncretistic movements emerged in many cultures and reflected the sway of global imperialism, which by then had become a dominant force.

Chapter 19, "Of Masses and Visions of the Modern, 1910–1939," briefly covers World War I and then discusses how, from the end of World War I until World War II, different visions of being modern competed around the world. It is the development of modernism and its effects on multiple cultures that integrate the diverse developments discussed in this chapter. In the decades between the world wars, proponents of liberal democracy struggled to defend their views and often to impose their will on authoritarian rulers and anticolonial nationalists.

Chapter 20, "The Three-World Order, 1940–1975," presents World War II and describes how new adversaries arose after the war. A three-world order came into being—the First World, led by the United States and extolling capitalism, the nation-state, and democratic government; the Second World, led by the Soviet Union and favoring authoritarian polities and economies; and the Third World, made up of former colonies seeking an independent status for themselves in world affairs. The rise of this three-world order dominates the second half of the twentieth century and constitutes another major theme of world history.

In **Chapter 21, "Globalization, 1970–2000,"** we explain that, at the end of the cold war, the modern world, while clearly more unified than before, still had profound cultural differences and political divisions. At the beginning of the twenty-first century, capital, commodities, peoples, and ideas move rapidly over long distances. But cultural tensions and political impasses continue to exist. It is the rise of this form of globalism that represents a vital new element as humankind heads into a new century and millennium.

We close with an **Epilogue**, which tracks developments since the turn of the millennium. These last few years have brought profound changes to the world order, yet we hope readers of *Worlds Together, Worlds Apart* will see more clearly how this most recent history is, in fact, entwined with trends of much longer duration that are the chief focus of this book.

MEDIA & PRINT ANCILLARIES

The Fourth Edition of *Worlds Together, Worlds Apart* is supported by an array of digital media with tools faculty need to meet course goals—in the classroom and online—and activities for students to develop core skills in reading comprehension, writing and historical analysis.

FOR STUDENTS

Free and open StudySpace Web site includes:

- **Chapter Quizzes.** Quiz feedback is aligned to student learning outcomes and chapter Focus Questions, accompanied by page references.
- **Flashcards** clarify key terms and events with brief descriptions and definitions.
- **iMaps** allow students to view layers of information on each map.
- **Map Worksheets** provide each map without labels for offline relabeling and quizzing.
- 100 **primary source documents and images** are included.
- **World History Tours,** powered by Google Earth, are dynamic, interactive primary source exercises that trace global developments over time.
- **Ebook links** tie the online text to all study and review materials.

FOR INSTRUCTORS

Classroom Presentation Tools

- **Chapter maps** and images are available as PowerPoint slides and JPG image files
- **Lecture slides** provide bullet points from the chapter outlines. Map and image files are inserted into the presentation.
- **New *Story Maps*** break complex maps into a sequence of five annotated screens that focus on the story behind the geography. Ten maps include such topics as "The Silk Road," "The Spread of the Black Death," and "Population Growth and the Economy."

Instructor's Manual (Grace Chee, West Los Angeles College, and Alice Roberti, Santa Rosa Junior College)

The Instructor's Manual for *Worlds Together, Worlds Apart*, Fourth Edition, is designed to help instructors prepare lectures and exams. The Instructor's Manual contains detailed chapter outlines, lecture outlines, lecture ideas, classroom activities, and lists of recommended books, films, and Web sites. It is available in print and downloadable formats.

Test Bank (Aaron Gulyas and Brian Harding, both of Mott Community College)

The Test Bank contains approximately 1,400 multiple-choice, true/false, and essay questions. All test questions are now aligned with Bloom's Taxonomy for greater ease of assessment (available in print, PDF, Word, and Examview formats).

Free Norton Coursepack (downloadable in Blackboard, D2L, and Moodle; additional formats can be provided upon request) includes:

- **NEW Guided Reading Exercises,** keyed to each chapter's *Focus Questions*, instill the three-step Note-Summarize-Assess pedagogy. Each chapter has three exercises, which are built around actual passages from the text. Feedback will provide model responses with direct page references. **(Coursepack Only)**
- **NEW *Story Maps*** break complex maps into a sequence of five annotated screens that focus on the *story* behind the *geography*. Ten maps include such topics as "The Silk Road," "The Spread of the Black Death," and "Population Growth and the Economy." **(Coursepack Only)**
- **NEW 35 Map Exercises** can be assigned for assessment. These activities ask students a series of questions about historical events that must be answered by clicking on the map to record the answer. **(Coursepack Only)**
- **NEW Chrono-Quiz.** Addressing reviewer feedback, the ever-popular *Chrono-Sequencer* is now available as an assessment activity that will report to the school's native LMS. **(Coursepack Only)**
- **Chapter Outlines and Quizzes.** Quiz feedback is aligned to student learning outcomes and chapter Focus Questions, accompanied by page references.
- **World History Tours,** powered by Google Earth, are dynamic, interactive primary source exercises that trace global developments over time.
- **iMaps** allow students to view layers of information on each map.
- **Map Worksheets** provide each map without labels for offline relabeling and quizzing.
- **Flashcards** align key terms and events with brief descriptions and definitions.
- **100 primary-source documents and images are included.**
- **Ebook links** tie the online text to all study and review materials.

ACKNOWLEDGMENTS

Worlds Together, Worlds Apart would never have happened without the full support of Princeton University. In a highly unusual move, and one for which we are truly grateful, the university helped underwrite this project with financial support from its 250th Anniversary Fund for undergraduate teaching and by allowing release time for the authors from campus commitments.

The history department's support of the effort over many years has been exceptional. Four chairs made funds and departmental support available, including the department's incomparable administrative talents. We would be remiss if we did not single out the department manager, Judith Hanson, who provided us with assistance whenever we needed it. We also thank Eileen Kane, who provided help in tracking down references and illustrations and in integrating changes into the manuscript. We also would like to thank Pamela Long, who made all of the complicated arrangements for ensuring that we were able to discuss matters in a leisurely and attractive setting. Sometimes that meant arranging for long-distance conference calls. She went even further and proofread the entire manuscript, finding many errors that we had all overlooked.

We drew shamelessly on the expertise of the departmental faculty, and although it might be wise simply to include a roster of the Princeton history department, that would do an injustice to those of whom we took most advantage. So here they are: Mariana Candido, Robert Darnton, Sheldon Garon, Anthony Grafton, Molly Greene, David Howell, Harold James, William Jordan, Emmanuel Kreike, Michael Mahoney, Arno Mayer, Kenneth Mills, John Murrin, Susan Naquin, Willard Peterson, Theodore Rabb, Bhavani Raman, Stanley Stein, and Richard Turits. When necessary, we went outside the history department, getting help from L. Carl Brown, Michael Cook, Norman Itzkowitz, Martin Kern, Thomas Leisten, Heath Lowry, and Peter Schaefer. Two departmental colleagues—Natalie Z. Davis and Elizabeth Lunbeck—were part of the original team but had to withdraw because of other commitments. Their contributions were vital, and we want to express our thanks to them. David Gordon, now at Bowdoin College, used portions of the text while teaching an undergraduate course at the University of Durban in South Africa and shared comments with us. Shamil Jeppie, like David Gordon a graduate of the Princeton history department, now teaching at the University of Cape Town in South Africa, read and commented on various chapters.

Beyond Princeton, we have also benefited from exceptionally gifted and giving colleagues who have assisted this book in many ways. Colleagues at Louisiana State University, the University of Florida, the University of North Carolina, the University of Pennsylvania, and the University of California at Los Angeles, where Suzanne Marchand, Michael Tsin, Holly Pittman, and Stephen Aron, respectively, are now teaching, pitched in whenever we turned to them. Especially helpful have been the contributions of James Gelvin, Naomi Lamoreaux, Gary Nash, and Joyce Appleby at UCLA; Michael Bernstein at Tulane University; and Maribel Dietz, John Henderson, Christine Kooi, David Lindenfeld, Reza Pirbhai, and Victor Stater at Louisiana State University. It goes without saying that none of these individuals bears any responsibility for factual or interpretive errors that the text may contain. Xinru Liu would like to thank her Indian mentor, Romila Thapar, who changed the way we think about Indian history.

The quality and range of reviews on this project were truly exceptional. The final version of the manuscript was greatly influenced by the thoughts and ideas of numerous instructors. We wish to particularly thank our consulting reviewers, who read multiple versions of the manuscript from start to finish.

First Edition Consultants

Hugh Clark, Ursinus College
Jonathan Lee, San Antonio College
Pamela McVay, Ursuline College
Tom Sanders, United States Naval Academy

Second Edition Consultants

Jonathan Lee, San Antonio College
Pamela McVay, Ursuline College
Steve Rapp, Georgia State University
Cliff Rosenberg, City University of New York

First Edition Reviewers

Lauren Benton, New Jersey Institute of Technology
Ida Blom, University of Bergen, Norway
Ricardo Duchesne, University of New Brunswick
Major Bradley T. Gericke, United States Military Academy
John Gillis, Rutgers University
David Kenley, Marshall University
John Kicza, Washington State University
Matthew Levinger, Lewis and Clark College
James Long, Colorado State University
Adam McKeown, Columbia University
Mark McLeod, University of Delaware
John Mears, Southern Methodist University
Michael Murdock, Brigham Young University
David Newberry, University of North Carolina, Chapel Hill
Tom Pearcy, Slippery Rock State University
Oliver B. Pollak, University of Nebraska, Omaha
Ken Pomeranz, University of California, Irvine
Major David L. Ruffley, United States Air Force Academy
William Schell, Murray State University
Major Deborah Schmitt, United States Air Force Academy
Sarah Shields, University of North Carolina, Chapel Hill
Mary Watrous-Schlesinger, Washington State University

Second Edition Reviewers

William Atwell, Hobart and William Smith Colleges
Susan Besse, City University of New York

Tithi Bhattacharya, Purdue University
Mauricio Borrerero, St. John's University
Charlie Briggs, Georgia Southern University
Antoinne Burton, University of Illinois, Urbana-Champaign
Jim Cameron, St. Francis Xavier University
Kathleen Comerford, Georgia Southern University
Duane Corpis, Georgia State University
Denise Davidson, Georgia State University
Ross Doughty, Ursinus College
Alison Fletcher, Kent State University
Phillip Gavitt, Saint Louis University
Brent Geary, Ohio University
Henda Gilli-Elewy, California State Polytechnic University, Pomona
Fritz Gumbach, John Jay College
William Hagen, University of California, Davis
Laura Hilton, Muskingum College
Jeff Johnson, Villanova University
David Kammerling-Smith, Eastern Illinois University
Jonathan Lee, San Antonio College
Dorothea Martin, Appalachian State University
Don McGuire, State University of New York, Buffalo
Pamela McVay, Ursuline College
Joel Migdal, University of Washington
Anthony Parent, Wake Forest University
Sandra Peacock, Georgia Southern University
David Pietz, Washington State University
Jared Poley, Georgia State University
John Quist, Shippensburg State University
Steve Rapp, Georgia State University
Paul Rodell, Georgia Southern University
Ariel Salzman, Queen's University
Bill Schell, Murray State University
Claire Schen, State University of New York, Buffalo
Jonathan Skaff, Shippensburg State University
David Smith, California State Polytechnic University, Pomona
Neva Specht, Appalachian State University
Ramya Sreeniva, State University of New York, Buffalo
Charles Stewart, University of Illinois, Urbana-Champaign
Rachel Stocking, Southern Illinois University, Carbondale
Heather Streets, Washington State University
Tim Teeter, Georgia Southern University
Charlie Wheeler, University of California, Irvine
Owen White, University of Delaware
James Wilson, Wake Forest University

Third Edition Reviewers

Henry Antkiewicz, Eastern Tennessee State University
Anthony Barbieri-Low, University of California, Santa Barbara
Andrea Becksvoort, University of Tennessee, Chattanooga
Hayden Bellonoit, United States Naval Academy
John Bloom, Shippensburg University
Kathryn Braund, Auburn University
Catherine Candy, University of New Orleans
Karen Carter, Brigham Young University
Stephen Chappell, James Madison University
Jessey Choo, University of Missouri, Kansas City
Timothy Coates, College of Charleston
Gregory Crider, Wingate University
Denise Davidson, Georgia State University
Jessica Davidson, James Madison University
Sal Diaz, Santa Rosa, Junior College
Todd Dozier, Baton Rouge Community College
Richard Eaton, University of Arizona
Lee Farrow, Auburn University, Montgomery
Bei Gao, College of Charleston
Behrooz Ghamari-Tabrizi, University of Illinois, Urbana-Champaign
Steven Gish, Auburn University, Montgomery
Jeffrey Hamilton, Baylor University
Barry Hankins, Baylor University
Brian Harding, Mott Community College
Tim Henderson, Auburn University, Montgomery
Marjorie Hilton, University of Redlands
Richard Hines, Washington State University
Lisa Holliday, Appalachian State University
Jonathan Lee, San Antonio College
David Kalivas, University of Massachusetts, Lowell
Christopher Kelley, Miami University, Ohio
Kenneth Koons, Virginia Military Institute
Michael Kulikowski, Pennsylvania State University
Benjamin Lawrence, University of California, Davis
Lu Liu, University of Tennessee, Knoxville
David Longfellow, Baylor University
Harold Marcuse, University of California, Santa Barbara
Dorothea Martin, Appalachian State University
David Mayes, Sam Houston State University
James Mokhiber, University of New Orleans
Mark Munzinger, Radford College
David Murphree, Virginia Tech University
Joshua Nadel, North Carolina Central University
Wing Chung Nq, University of Texas, San Antonio
Robert Norrell, University of Tennessee, Knoxville
Chandrika Paul, Shippensburg University
Beth Pollard, San Diego State University
Timothy Pytell, California State University, San Bernardino
Stephen Rapp, Professional Historian
Alice Roberti, Santa Rosa Junior College
Aviel Roshwald, Georgetown University

James Sanders, Utah State University
Lynn Sargeant, California State University, Fullerton
William Schell, Murray State University
Michael Seth, James Madison University
Barry Stentiford, Grambling State University
Gabrielle Sutherland, Baylor University
Lisa Tran, California State University, Fullerton
Michael Vann, California State University, Sacramento
Peter Von Sivers, University of Utah
Andrew Wackerfuss, Georgetown University
Ted Weeks, Southern Illinois University, Carbondale
Angela White, Indiana University of Pennsylvania
Jennifer Williams, Nichols State University
Andrew Wise, State University of New York, Buffalo
Eloy Zarate, Pasadena City College
William Zogby, Mohawk Valley Community College

Fourth Edition Reviewers

Andrea Becksvoort, University of Tennessee at Chattanooga
Hayden Bellenoit, United States Naval Academy
Volker Benkert, Arizona State University
Gayle Brunelle, California State University, Fullerton
Jessica Clark, California State University, Chico
Brian Harding, Mott Community College
Emily Hill, Queen's University at Kingston
Laura Hilton, Muskingum University
Dennis Laumann, University of Memphis
Elaine MacKinnon, University of West Georgia
Ronald Mellor, University of California, Los Angeles
Carol Miller, Tallahassee Community College
Greg O'Malley, University of California, Santa Cruz
David Ortiz, Jr., University of Arizona
Charles Parker, Saint Louis University
Juanjuan Peng, Georgia Southern University
Dana Rabin, University of Illinois, Urbana-Champaign
Matthew Rothwell, University of Southern Indiana
Teo Ruiz, University of California, Los Angeles
Jeffrey Shumway, Brigham Young University
Lisa Tran, California State University, Fullerton
Lela Urquhart, Georgia State University

We also want to thank Nancy Khalek (Ph.D. Princeton University), who now teaches at Brown University. Nancy was our jack-of-all-trades who helped in any way she could. She attended all the monthly meetings during the development of the early volume. She provided critiques of the manuscript, helped with primary research, worked on the photo program and pedagogical features, and contributed content to the student Web site. She was invaluable. For the Third Edition, Nancy authored a number of the new digital World History Tours powered by Google Maps. For the Fourth Edition, we want to thank Beth Pollard (San Diego State University) and Cliff Rosenberg (CUNY-City College) for their substantial help with creating the exciting new Analyzing Global Developments features. We also want to send a special thanks to Jon Lee (San Antonio College). Jon has worn many different hats on this project over the years. On this exciting new edition, Jon updated all the pedagogical features in the main text. He also read and critiqued all the new feature elements and the newly revised materials on South and East Asia in Volume 1. We would also like to thank Grace Chee (West Los Angeles College) and Alice Roberti (Santa Rosa Junior College) for authoring the Instructor's Manual. Finally, we'd like to thank Aaron Gulyas and Brian Harding (both of Mott Community College) for thoroughly revising the test bank.

For the Fourth Edition we have some familiar and new friends at Norton to thank. Chief among them is Jon Durbin, who once again played a major role in bringing this edition to publication. Sarah England has put together a creative marketing plan for the book. Jillian Burr is responsible for the book's beautiful and effective new design. Justin Cahill and Penelope Lin have been invaluable with their work on the maps, illustrations, and new feature boxes. Steve Hoge, Tacy Quinn, and Stefani Wallace have done a masterful job strengthening the media support materials to meet the ever more complex classroom and assessment needs of instructors. Lorraine Klimowich has strategically strengthened the Instructor's Manual and Test Bank. Diane Cipollone, our project editor, and Andrew Ensor, our production manager, have done a great job getting the book published on time with a very tight schedule. Nancy Green did a fine job with the copyediting, turning the chapters around quickly to meet our schedule. A special shout out goes to Debra Morton-Hoyt and her team of cover designers. *Worlds Together, Worlds Apart* has always been incredibly creative and distinctive looking, and the Fourth Edition covers are even more eye-catching and memorable than the first three editions. Bravo!

Finally, we must recognize that while this project often kept us apart from family members, their support held our personal worlds together.

ABOUT THE AUTHORS

ROBERT TIGNOR (Ph.D. Yale University) is Professor Emeritus and the Rosengarten Professor of Modern and Contemporary History at Princeton University and the three-time chair of the history department. With Gyan Prakash, he introduced Princeton's first course in world history nearly twenty years ago. Professor Tignor has taught graduate and undergraduate courses in African history and world history and written extensively on the history of twentieth-century Egypt, Nigeria, and Kenya. Besides his many research trips to Africa, Professor Tignor has taught at the University of Ibadan in Nigeria and the University of Nairobi in Kenya.

JEREMY ADELMAN (D.Phil. Oxford University) is currently the Director of the Council for International Teaching and Research at Princeton University and the Walter S. Carpenter III Professor of Spanish Civilization and Culture. He has written and edited five books, including *Republic of Capital: Buenos Aires and the Legal Transformation of the-Atlantic World,* which won the best book prize in Atlantic history from the American Historical Association, and most-recently *Sovereignty and Revolution in the Iberian Atlantic.* Professor Adelman is the recent recipient of a Guggenheim Memorial Foundation Fellowship and the Frederick Burkhardt Award from the American Council of Learned Societies.

STEPHEN ARON (Ph.D. University of California, Berkeley) is professor of history at the University of California, Los Angeles, and executive director of the Institute for the Study of the American West, Autry National Center. A specialist in frontier and Western American history, Aron is the author of *How the West Was Lost: the Transformation of Kentucky from Daniel Boone to Henry Clay* and *American Confluence: the Missouri Frontier from Borderland to Border State.* He is currently editing the multi-volume *Autry History of the American West* and writing a book with the tentative title *Can We All Just Get Along: An Alternative History of the American West.*

STEPHEN KOTKIN (Ph.D. University of California, Berkeley) is professor of European and Asian history as well as international affairs at Princeton University. He formerly directed Princeton's program in Russian and Eurasian studies (1996–2009). He is the author of *Magnetic Mountain: Stalinism as a Civilization, Uncivil Society: 1989 and the Implosion of the Communist Establishment,* and *Armageddon Averted: the Soviet Collapse, 1970–2000.* He is a coeditor of *Mongolia in the Twentieth Century: Landlocked Cosmopolitan.* Professor Kotkin has twice been a visiting professor in Japan.

SUZANNE MARCHAND (Ph.D. University of Chicago) is professor of European and intellectual history at Louisiana State University, Baton Rouge. Professor Marchand also spent a number of years teaching at Princeton University. She is the author of *Down from Olympus: Archaeology and Philhellenism in Germany, 1750–1970* and *German Orientalism in the Age of Empire: Religion, Race and Scholarship.*

GYAN PRAKASH (Ph.D. University of Pennsylvania) is professor of modern Indian history at Princeton University and a member of the Subaltern Studies Editorial Collective. He is the author of *Bonded Histories: Genealogies of Labor Servitude in Colonial India, Another Reason: Science and the Imagination of Modern India,* and *Mumbai Fables.* Professor Prakash edited *After Colonialism: Imperial Histories and Postcolonial Displacements* and *Noir Urbanisms,* coedited *the Space of the Modern City* and *Utopia/Dystopia,* and has written a number of articles on colonialism and history writing. He is currently working on a history of the city of Bombay. With Robert Tignor, he introduced the modern world history course at Princeton University.

MICHAEL TSIN (Ph.D. Princeton) is associate professor of history and international studies at the University of North Carolina at Chapel Hill. He previously taught at the University of Illinois at Chicago, Princeton University, Columbia University, and the University of Florida. Professor Tsin's primary interests include the histories of modern China and colonialism. He is the author of *Nation, Governance, and Modernity in China: Canton, 1900–1927.* He is currently writing a social history of the reconfiguration of Chinese identity in the twentieth century.

THE GEOGRAPHY OF THE ANCIENT AND MODERN WORLDS

Today, we believe the world to be divided into continents, and most of us think that it was always so. Geographers usually identify six inhabited continents: Africa, North America, South America, Europe, Asia, and Australia. Inside these continents they locate a vast number of subcontinental units, such as East Asia, South Asia, Southeast Asia, the Middle East, North Africa, and sub-Saharan Africa. Yet this geographical understanding would have been completely alien to premodern men and women, who did not think that they inhabited continents bounded by large bodies of water. Lacking a firm command of the seas, they saw themselves living on contiguous landmasses, and they thought these territorial bodies were the main geographical units of their lives. Hence, in this volume we have chosen to use a set of geographical terms, the main one being Afro-Eurasia, that more accurately reflect the world that the premoderns believed that they inhabited.

The most interconnected and populous landmass of premodern times was Afro-Eurasia. The term Eurasia is widely used in general histories, but we think it is in its own ways inadequate. The preferred term from our perspective must be Afro-Eurasia, for the interconnected

landmass of premodern and indeed much of modern times included large parts of Europe and Asia and significant regions in Africa. The major African territories that were regularly joined to Europe and Asia were Egypt, North Africa, and even parts of sub-Saharan Africa.

Only gradually and fitfully did the divisions of the world that we take for granted today take shape. The peoples inhabiting the northwestern part of the Afro-Eurasian landmass did not see themselves as European Christians, and hence as a distinctive cultural entity, until the Middle Ages drew to a close in the twelfth and thirteenth centuries. Islam did not arise and extend its influence throughout the middle zone of the Afro-Eurasian landmass until the eighth and ninth centuries. And, finally, the peoples living in what we today term the Indian subcontinent did not feel a strong sense of their own cultural and political unity until the Delhi Sultanate of the thirteenth and fourteenth centuries and the Mughal Empire, which emerged at the beginning of the sixteenth century, brought political unity to that vast region. As a result, we use the terms South Asia, Vedic society, and India in place of Indian subcontinent for the premodern part of our narrative, and we use Southwest Asia and North Africa to refer to what today is designated as the Middle East. In fact, it is only in the period from 1000 to 1300 that some of the major cultural areas that are familiar to us today truly crystallized.

FOURTH EDITION

WORLDS TOGETHER, WORLDS APART

Volume 2

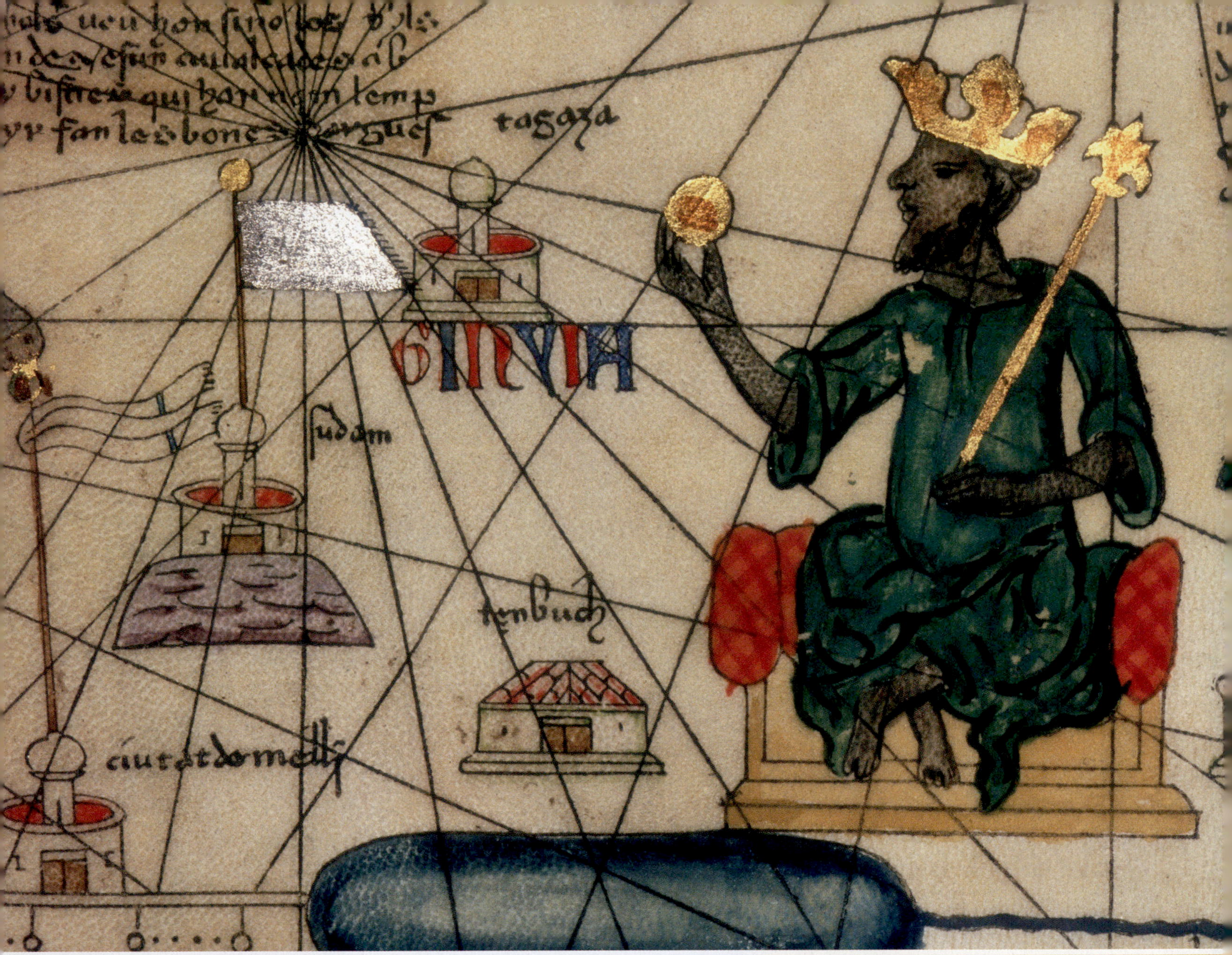

BEFORE YOU READ THIS CHAPTER

GLOBAL STORYLINES

- Trade routes shift from land to sea, transforming coastal cities into global trading hubs and elevating Afro-Eurasian trade to unprecedented levels.
- Intensified trade, linguistic, and religious integration generate the foundational cultural spheres that we recognize today: China, India, Islam, and Europe.
- The rise of the Mongol Empire integrates the world's foundational cultural spheres.

CHAPTER OUTLINE

FOCUS QUESTIONS

- What factors led to the explosion of global trade between 1000 and 1300?
- What institutions and beliefs linked the peoples of the world's four major cultural spheres?
- To what extent do political, economic, and cultural integration occur in the America and sub-Saharan Africa during this era?
- How did Mongol conquest reshape Afro-Eurasian landscapes?

10

Becoming "The World," 1000–1300 CE

In the late 1270s two Christian monks, Bar Sāwmā and Markōs, voyaged into the heart of Islam. They were not Europeans. They were Uighurs, a Turkish people of central Asia, many of whom had converted to Christianity centuries earlier. Sent by the mighty Mongol ruler Kubilai Khan as he prepared to become the first emperor of China's Yuan dynasty, the monks were supposed to worship at the temple in Jerusalem. But the Great Khan also had political ambitions. He was eager to conquer Jerusalem, held by the Muslims. Accordingly, he dispatched the monks as agents to make alliances with Christian kings in the area and to gather intelligence about his potential enemy in Palestine.

By 1280, conflict and conquest had transformed many parts of the world. But friction was simply one manifestation of cultures brushing up against one another. More important was trade. Indeed, Bar Sāwmā and Markōs lingered at the magnificent trading hub of Kashgar in what is now western China, where caravan routes converged in a market for jade, exotic spices, and precious silks. Later, at Baghdad, the monks parted ways. Bar Sāwmā visited Constantinople (where the king gave him gold and silver), Rome (where he met with the pope at the shrine of Saint Peter), and

Paris (where he saw that city's vibrant university) before deciding to return to China, where the Christians of the east awaited his reports. In the end, neither monk ever returned. Yet their voyages exemplified the crisscrossing of people, money, and goods along the trade routes and sea-lanes that connected the world's regions. For just as religious conflict was a hallmark of this age, so was a surge in trade, migration, and global exchange.

The period brought to a climax many centuries of human development, and it ushered in a new, very long cycle of cultural interaction from which emerge three interrelated themes. First, trade was shifting from land-based routes to sea-based routes. Coastal trading cities began to dramatically expand. Second, intensified trade and linguistic and religious integration generated the world's four major cultural "spheres," whose inhabitants were linked by shared institutions and beliefs: China, India, Islam, and Europe. Not all cultures turned into "spheres," though. In the Americas and sub-Saharan Africa there was not the same impulse to integrate regions, which remained more fragmented but thrived nonetheless. Third, the rise of the Mongol Empire represented the peak in the long history of ties and tensions between settled and mobile peoples. From China to Persia and as far as eastern Europe, the Mongols ruled over much land in the world's major cultural spheres.

COMMERCIAL CONNECTIONS

Revolutions at Sea

By the tenth century, sea routes were eclipsing land networks for long-distance trade. Improved navigational aids, refinements in shipbuilding, better mapmaking, and new legal arrangements and accounting practices made shipping easier and slashed the costs of seaborne trade. The numbers testify to the power of the maritime revolution: while a porter could carry about 10 pounds over long distances, and animal-drawn wagons could move 100 pounds of goods over small distances, the Arab dhows plying the Indian Ocean were capable of transporting up to 5 tons of cargo. (**Dhows** are ships with triangle-shaped sails, called lateens, that allow best use of the monsoon trade winds on the Arabian Sea and the Indian Ocean.) As a result some coastal ports, like Mogadishu in eastern Africa, became vast transshipment centers for a thriving trade across the Indian Ocean.

A new navigational instrument spurred this boom: the needle **compass**. This Chinese invention initially identified promising locations for houses and tombs, but eleventh-century sailors from Guangzhou (anglicized as Canton) used it to find their way on the high seas. The device spread rapidly. Not only did it allow sailing under cloudy skies, but it also improved mapmaking. And it made all the oceans, including the Atlantic, easier to navigate.

Now shipping became less dangerous. Navigators relied on lateen-rigged dhows between the Indian Ocean and the Red Sea, heavy junks in the South China seas, and Atlantic "cogs," which linked Genoa to locations as distant as the Azores and Iceland. They also enjoyed the protection of political authorities, such as the Song dynasts in China, in guiding the trading fleets in and out of harbors. The Fatimid caliphate in Egypt, for instance, profited from maritime trade and defended merchant fleets from pirates. Armed convoys of ships escorted commercial fleets and regularized the ocean traffic. The system soon spread

Dhow. *This modern dhow in the harbor of Zanzibar displays the characteristic triangle sail. The triangle sail can make good use of the trade monsoon and thus has guided dhows on the Arabian Sea since ancient times.*

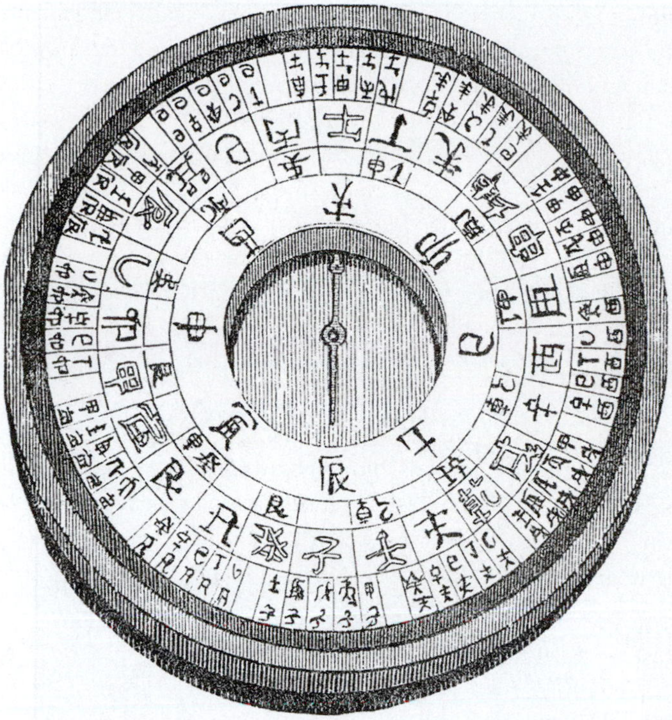

Antique Chinese Compass. *Chinese sailors from Canton started to use needle compasses in the eleventh century. By the thirteenth century, needle compasses were widely used on ships in the Indian Ocean and were starting to appear in the Mediterranean.*

to North Africa and southern Spain. Most of these shipping firms were family-based, and they sent young men of the family, sometimes servants or slaves, to work in India. Wives in Cairo could expect gifts from their husbands to arrive with the fleet.

Changes in navigation ushered in the demise of overland routes. Silk Road merchants eventually gave up using camel trains, caravansaries (inns for travelers), and oasis hubs as they switched to the sea-lanes. The shift took centuries, but overland routes and camels were no match for multiple-masted cargo ships.

Commercial Contacts

The opening of the sea-lanes also tapped into changes in world agriculture (see Map 10.1). By 1000 CE, major innovations in irrigation techniques, carried out over many centuries and in numerous locations, yielded enormous returns. New strains of cereals—and in the Americas, the refinement of maize—led to grain cultivation in vast areas that had been too cold or arid to sustain it previously. Clover, alfalfa, and other newly domesticated grasses became fodder for healthier, stronger, and fatter animals. Agriculture pushed into new regions, buoying population growth and surpluses that now could be shipped over great distances.

Global Commercial Hubs

Long-distance trade spawned the growth of commercial cities. These urban hubs became cosmopolitan nerve centers of an increasingly integrated world. Beginning in the late tenth century, regional centers became major anchorages of the maritime trade: in the west, the Egyptian port cities of Alexandria and Cairo; in the east, the Chinese city of Quanzhou; in the Malaysian Archipelago, the city of Melaka; and near the tip of the Indian peninsula, the port of Kollan (often anglicized as Quilon). These hubs thrived under the political stability of powerful dynasts who recognized that the free-for-all of trade and market life would generate wealth for them. Yemeni rulers, for instance, offered shelter to fleets in return for taxes collected on cargoes; so did Egyptian rulers for fleets moving through the Red Sea.

THE EGYPTIAN ANCHORAGE Cairo and Alexandria were the Mediterranean's main maritime commercial centers. Cairo was home to numerous Muslim and Jewish trading firms, and Alexandria was their lookout post on the Mediterranean.

Silk yarn and textiles were the most popular commodities in the global trade involving Egypt. It was through Alexandria that Europeans acquired silks from China, especially the coveted *zaytuni* (satin) fabric from Quanzhou. Spanish silks also passed through Alexandria, heading to eastern Mediterranean markets. But the new commercial hubs handled much more. Goods from the Mediterranean included olive oil, glassware, flax, corals, and metals. Gemstones and aromatic perfumes poured in from India. Also changing hands were minerals and chemicals for dyeing or tanning, and raw materials such as timber and bamboo. The real novelties were paper and books. Hand-copied Bibles, Talmuds, Qurans, legal and moral works, grammars in various languages, and Arabic books became the first best sellers of the Mediterranean.

Fleets in the Mediterranean and Red Sea were so effective, in part based on armed convoys provided by the caliphs, that ships arrived on schedule and were relied on for postal service. When an Egyptian trader in Kollam, India, around 1100, was delayed on his journey home, he was able to send a consoling message to his wife in Cairo. He apologized for his absence but promised gifts including pearl bracelets, red silk garments, a bronze basin, a ewer, and a slave girl: "I shall send them, if God wills it, with somebody who is traveling home" (Goitein, "New Light," 179).

The Islamic legal system also promoted a favorable business environment. Consider how legal specialists got around the rule that might have brought commerce to a halt—the *sharia*'s (see Chapter 9) prohibition against earning interest on loans. With the clerics' blessing, Muslim traders formed partnerships between those who had capital to lend and those who needed

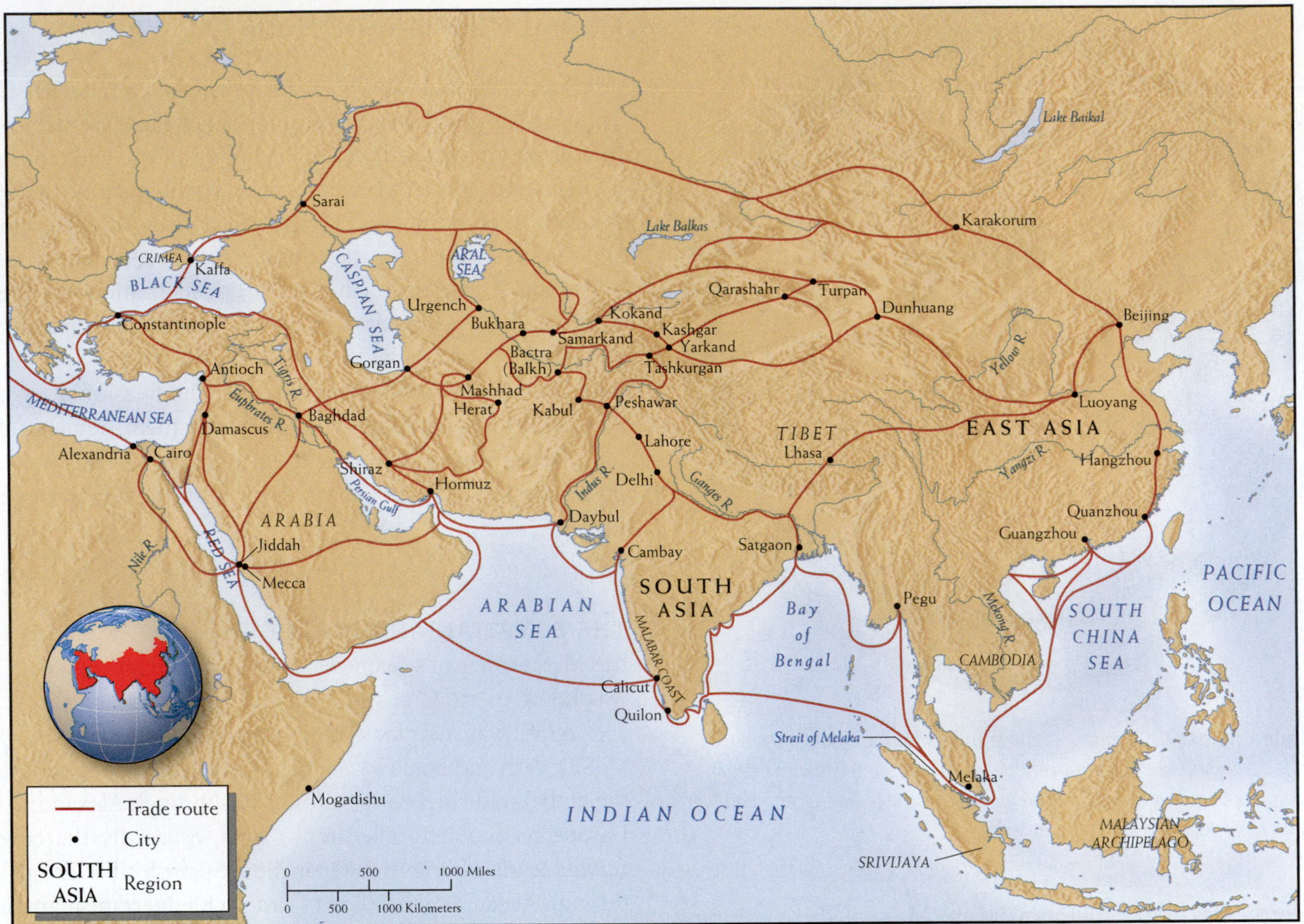

MAP 10.1 | Afro-Eurasian Trade, 1000–1300

During the early second millennium, Afro-Eurasian merchants increasingly turned to the Indian Ocean to transport their goods. Locate the global hubs of Kollam, Alexandria, Cairo, Melaka, and Quanzhou on this map.

- What regions do each of these global hubs represent?
- Based on the map, why would sea travel have been preferable to overland travel?
- According to the text, what revolutions in maritime travel facilitated this development?

money to expand their businesses. These partnerships enabled owners of capital to entrust their money or commodities to agents who, after completing their work, returned the investment and a share of the profits to the owners—and kept the rest as their reward. The English word "risk" derives from the Arabic *rizq*, the extra allowance paid to merchants in lieu of interest.

THE ANCHORAGE OF QUANZHOU In China, Quanzhou was as busy as Cairo and Alexandria. The Song government set up offices of Seafaring Affairs in its three major ports: Canton, Quanzhou, and an area near present-day Shanghai in the Yangzi delta. In return for a portion of the taxes, these offices registered cargoes, sailors, and traders, while guards kept a keen eye on the traffic.

All foreign traders were guests of the governor, who doubled as the Chief of Seafaring Affairs. Part of his mandate was to summon favorable winds for shipping. Every year, the governor took his place on a high perch facing the harbor, in front of a rock cliff filled with inscriptions that recorded the wind-calling rituals. Traders of every origin witnessed the rite, then joined the dignitaries for a sumptuous banquet.

Ships departing from Quanzhou and other Chinese ports were junks—large, flat-bottomed ships with internal sealed bulkheads and stern-mounted rudders. Their multiple watertight compartments increased stability; the largest ones boasted four decks, six masts, and a dozen sails and could carry 500 men. Those departing Quanzhou headed for Srivijaya (Java) in the Malay Archipelago, navigating through the Strait of Melaka, a choke

Mazu. *Many Quanzhou sailors sought protection at the shrine of the goddess Mazu. According to legend, before assuming godhood Mazu had performed many miracles. Her temple became prominent after 1123, when Quanzhou's governor survived a storm at sea while returning from Korea. After that, sailors and their families burned incense for the goddess and prayed for her aid in keeping them safe at sea.*

point between the South China Sea and the Indian Ocean. The final destination was Kollam on the coast of southwest India. Traders heading farther west in Arab-dominated seas unloaded their cargo and boarded small Arabian dhows.

Arabs, Persians, Jews, and Indians, as well as Chinese, traded at Quanzhou, and some stayed on to manage their businesses. Perhaps as many as 100,000 Muslims lived there during the Song dynasty. And traders could become power brokers in their own right. Although most foreign merchants did not reside apart from the rest of the city, they had their own buildings for religious worship. A mosque from this period is still standing on a busy street. Hindu traders living in Quanzhou worshipped in a Buddhist shrine where statues of Hindu deities stood alongside those of Buddhist gods.

THE CROSSROADS OF AFRO-EURASIA: MELAKA Because of its strategic location and proximity to Malayan tropical produce, Melaka became a key cosmopolitan city. Indian, Javanese, and Chinese merchants and sailors spent months in such ports selling their goods, purchasing return cargo, and waiting for the winds to change so they could reach their next destination. During peak season, Southeast Asian ports teemed with colorfully dressed foreign sailors, local Javanese artisans who produced finely textured batik handicrafts, and money-grubbing traders. The latter converged from all over Asia to flood the markets with their merchandise and to search for pungent herbs, aromatic spices, and agrarian staples such as quick-ripening strains of rice to ship out.

THE TIP OF INDIA In the tenth century, the Chola dynasty in south India supported a nerve center of maritime trade between China and the Red Sea and the Mediterranean. Although the Chola golden age lasted only about two generations, trade continued to flourish. Many Muslim traders settled in Malabar, on the southwest coast of the Indian peninsula, and Kollam became a major cosmopolitan hub. Dhows arrived, laden not only with goods from the Red Sea and Africa but also with traders, sojourners, and fugitives. Chinese junks unloaded silks and porcelain, and picked up passengers and commodities for East Asian markets. Sailors and traders strictly observed the customs of this trading port, for it was good business to respect others' norms and values while doing business with them.

Muslims, the largest foreign community, lived in their own neighborhoods. They shipped horses from Arab countries to India and the southeast islands, where kings viewed them as symbols of royalty. Because the animals could not survive well in those climates, the demand was constant. There was even trade in elephants and cattle from tropical countries, though most goods were spices, perfumes, and textiles. Traders knew each other well, and personal relationships were key. When striking a deal with a local merchant, a Chinese trader would mention his Indian neighbor in Quanzhou and that family's residence in Quilon. Global commercial hubs relied on friendship and family to keep their businesses thriving across religious and regional divides.

SUB-SAHARAN AFRICA COMES TOGETHER

During this period sub-Saharan Africa's relationship to the rest of the world changed dramatically. Before 1000 CE sub-Saharan Africa had never been a world entirely apart, but now its integration became much stronger. Africans and outsiders were determined to overcome the sea, river, and desert barriers that had blocked sub-Saharan peoples from participating in long-distance trade and intellectual exchanges (see Map 10.2). Increasingly, interior hinterlands found themselves touched by the commercial and migratory impulses emanating from the Indian Ocean and Arabian Sea transformations.

West Africa and the Mande-Speaking Peoples

Once the camel bridged the Sahara Desert (see Chapter 9), the flow of commodities and ideas linked sub-Saharan Africa to North Africa and Southwest Asia. As the savanna region became increasingly connected to developments in Afro-Eurasia, Mande-speaking peoples emerged as the primary agents for integration within and beyond West Africa. Exploiting their expertise in commerce and political organization, the Mande edged out rivals.

The Mande, or Mandinka, homeland was a vast area, 1,000 miles wide, between the bend in the Senegal River to the west and the bend of the Niger River to the east, stretching more than 2,000 miles from the Senegal River in the north to the Bandama River in the south. This was where the kingdom of Ghana had arisen (see Chapter 9) and where Ghana's successor state—the Mandinka state of Mali, discussed below—emerged around 1100.

The Mande-speaking peoples were constantly on the go and marvelously adaptable. By the eleventh century they were spreading their cultural, commercial, and political hegemony from the high savanna grasslands southward into the woodlands and tropical rain forests stretching to the Atlantic Ocean. Those dwelling in the rain forests organized small-scale societies led by local councils, while those in the savanna lands developed centralized forms of government under sacred kingships. These peoples believed that their kings had descended from the gods and that they enjoyed the gods' blessing.

As the Mande broadened their territory to the Atlantic coast, they gained access to tradable items that residents of the interior were eager to have—notably kola nuts and malaguetta peppers, for which the Mande exchanged iron products and textile manufactures. By 1300 the Mandinka merchants had followed the Senegal River to its outlet on the coast and then pushed their commercial frontiers farther inland and down the coast. Thus, even before European explorers and traders arrived in the mid-fifteenth century, West African peoples had created dynamic networks linking the hinterlands with coastal trading hubs.

From the eleventh century to the late fifteenth century, the most vigorous businesses were those that spanned the Sahara Desert. The Mande-speaking peoples, with their far-flung commercial networks and highly dispersed populations, dominated this trade as well. Here one of the most prized commodities was salt, mined in the northern Sahel around the city of Taghaza; it was in demand on both sides of the Sahara. Another valuable commodity was gold, mined within the Mande homeland and borne by camel caravans to the far northern side of the Sahara, where traders exchanged it for various manufactures. Equally important in West African commerce were slaves, who were shipped to the settled Muslim communities of North Africa and Egypt.

The Empire of Mali

As booming trade spawned new political organizations, the empire of Mali became the Mande successor state to the kingdom of Ghana. Founded in the twelfth century, it exercised political sway over a vast area for three centuries.

The Mali Empire represented the triumph of horse warriors, and its origins are enshrined in an epic, *The Epic of Sundiata*, involving the dynasty's founder, the legendary Sundiata. Sundiata might well have actually existed. Arab historian Ibn Khaldun referred to him by name and reported that he was "their [Mali's] greatest king" (Levtzion and Pouwels, p. 64). His triumph, which occurred in the thirteenth century, marked the victory of new cavalry forces over traditional foot soldiers. Horses—which had always existed in some parts of Africa—now became prestige objects of the savanna peoples, symbols of state power. (See Primary Source: An African Epic.)

Under the Mali Empire, commerce was in full swing. With Mande trade routes extending to the Atlantic Ocean and spanning the Sahara Desert, West Africa was no longer an isolated periphery of the central Muslim lands. Mali's most famous sovereign, Mansa Musa (r. 1312–1332), made a celebrated hajj, or pilgrimage to Mecca, in 1325–1326, traveling through Cairo and impressing crowds with the size of his retinue and his displays of wealth, especially many dazzling items made of gold.

MAP 10.2 | Sub-Saharan Africa, 1300

Increased commercial contacts influenced the religious and political dimensions of sub-Saharan Africa at this time. Compare this map to Map 9.3 (p. 331).

- Where had strong Islamic communities emerged by 1300?
- According to this map, what types of activity were affecting the Mande homeland?
- To what extent had sub-Saharan Africa "come together"?

PRIMARY SOURCE

An African Epic

The traditional story of the founding of the kingdom of Mali was passed down orally from generation to generation by griots, counselors, and other official historians to the royal family. Only in 1960 was it finally written down in French. The narrative recounts the life of Sundiata, the heroic founder of the Mali state. The following passage provides insight into the role of the narrator (the griot) in the Malian kingdom, as well as some of the qualities of good and bad rulers.

Griots know the history of kings and kingdoms and that is why they are the best counsellors of kings. Every king wants to have a singer to perpetuate his memory, for it is the griot who rescues the memories of kings from oblivion, as men have short memories.

Kings have prescribed destinies just like men, and seers who probe the future know it. They have knowledge of the future, whereas we griots are depositories of the knowledge of the past. But whoever knows the history of a country can read its future.

Other peoples use writing to record the past, but this invention has killed the faculty of memory among them. They do not feel the past any more, for writing lacks the warmth of the human voice. . . .

I, Djeli Mamoudou Kouyaté, am the result of a long tradition. For generations we have passed on the history of kings from father to son. The narrative was passed on to me without alteration and I deliver it without alteration, for I received it free from all untruth.

Listen now to the story of Sundiata, the Na'Kamma, the man who had a mission to accomplish.

At the time when Sundiata was preparing to assert his claim over the kingdom of his fathers, Soumaoro was the king of kings, the most powerful king in all the lands of the setting sun. The fortified town of Sosso was the bulwark of fetishism against the word of Allah. For a long time Soumaoro defied the whole world. Since his accession to the throne of Sosso he had defeated nine kings whose heads served him as fetishes in his macabre chamber. Their skins served as seats and he cut his footwear from human skin. Soumaoro was not like other men, for the jinn had revealed themselves to him and his power was beyond measure. So his countless sofas [soldiers] were very brave since they believed their king to be invincible. But Soumaoro was an evil demon and his reign had produced nothing but bloodshed. Nothing was taboo for him. His greatest pleasure was publicly to flog venerable old men. He had defiled every family and everywhere in his vast empire there were villages populated by girls whom he had forcibly abducted from their families without marrying them.

QUESTIONS FOR ANALYSIS

- What are you able to understand about the function of the griot after reading this passage?
- What makes this kind of oral history reliable? What makes it unreliable?
- Soumaoro, the adversary of Sundiata, exemplified the characteristics of a bad ruler. What were they? Can you tell, indirectly, what the characteristics of a good ruler (like Sundiata) were?

Source: Sundiata: An Epic of Old Mali, *compiled by D. T. Niane (Harlow, UK: Longman Group, 1965), pp. 40–41.*

Mansa Musa's visit to Cairo was a sensation in its time. The stopover in one of Islam's primary cities astonished the Egyptian elite and awakened much of the world to the fact that Islam had spread far below the Sahara and that a sub-Saharan state could mount such an ostentatious display. Mansa Musa spared no expense to impress his hosts. He sent ahead an enormous gift of 50,000 dinars (a unit of money widely used in the Islamic world at this time), and his entourage included soldiers, wives, consorts, and as many as 12,000 slaves, many wearing rich brocades woven of Persian silks. And there was gold—a lot of it. He brought immense quantities and distributed it lavishly during his three-month stay. Preceding his retinue as it crossed the desert were 500 slaves, each carrying a golden staff. The caravan also included around 100 camels, each bearing two 300-pound sacks of gold.

The Mali Empire boasted two of West Africa's largest cities. Jenne, an ancient entrepôt, was a vital assembly point for caravans laden with salt, gold, and slaves preparing for journeys west to the Atlantic coast and north over the Sahara. The city had originated as an urban settlement around 200 BCE; by 1000 CE most substantial structures were made of brick. Around the city ran an impressive wall over eleven feet thick at its base and extending over a mile in length. More spectacular was the city of Timbuktu; founded around 1100 as a seasonal

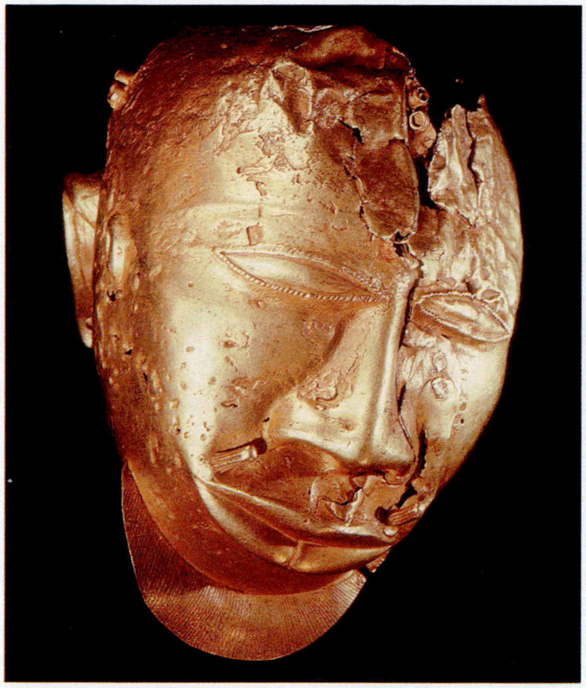

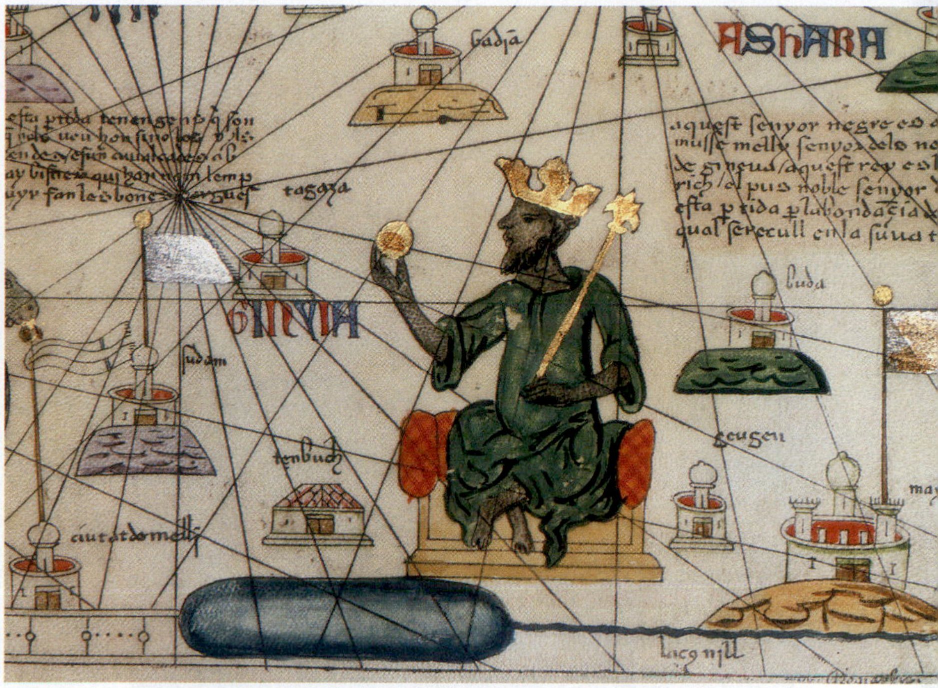

West African Asante Gold. *Although this gold head from the kingdom of Asante (left) was made in the eighteenth century, it shows the artistic abilities of the West African peoples. The head probably belonged to the Asante ruler, known as the Asantehene, and symbolized his power and wealth. This 1375 picture (right) shows the king of Mali on his throne, surrounded by images of gold.*

camp for nomads, it grew in size and importance under the patronage of various Malian kings. By the fourteenth century it was a thriving commercial and religious center famed for its two large mosques, which are still standing. Timbuktu was also renowned for its intellectual vitality. Here, West African Muslim scholars congregated to debate the tenets of Islam and to ensure that the faithful, even when distant from the Muslim heartland, practiced their religion with no taint of pagan observances. These clerics acquired treatises on Islam from all over the world for their personal libraries, remnants of which remain to this day.

East Africa and the Indian Ocean

Africa's eastern and southern regions were also integrated into long-distance trading systems. Because of monsoon winds, East Africa was a logical end point for much of the Indian Ocean trade. Swahili peoples living along that coast became brokers for trade from the Arabian Peninsula, the Persian Gulf territories, and the western coast of India. Merchants in the city of Kilwa on the coast of present-day Tanzania brought ivory, slaves, gold, and other items from the interior and shipped them to destinations around the Indian Ocean.

The most valued commodity in the trade was gold. Shona-speaking peoples grew rich by mining the ore in the highlands between the Limpopo and Zambezi rivers. By the year 1000, the Shona had founded up to fifty small religious and political centers, each one erected from stone to display its power over the peasant villages surrounding it. Around 1100 one of these centers, Great Zimbabwe, stood supreme among the Shona. Built on the fortunes made from gold, its most impressive landmark was a massive elliptical building made of stone fitted so expertly that it needed no grouting. The buildings of Great Zimbabwe probably housed the king and may also have contained smelters for melting down gold.

The Trans-Saharan and Indian Ocean Slave Trade

African slaves were as valuable as African gold in shipments to the Mediterranean and Indian Ocean markets. There had been a lively trade in African slaves (mainly from Nubia) into pharaonic Egypt well before the Common Era. After Islam spread into Africa and sailing techniques improved, the slave trade across the Sahara Desert and Indian Ocean boomed.

Although the Quran attempted to mitigate the severity of slavery, requiring Muslim slave owners to treat their slaves kindly

Great Zimbabwe. *These walls surrounded the city of Great Zimbabwe, which was a center of the gold trade between the East African coastal peoples and traders sailing on the Indian Ocean. Great Zimbabwe flourished during the thirteenth, fourteenth, and fifteenth centuries.*

and praising manumission as an act of piety, nonetheless the African slave trade flourished under Islam.

Africans became slaves during this period much as they had before: some were prisoners of war; others were considered criminals and sold into slavery as punishment. Their duties were varied. Some slaves were pressed into military service, rising in a few instances to positions of high authority. Others with seafaring skills worked as crewmen on dhows or as dockworkers. Still others, mainly women, were domestic servants, and many became concubines of Muslim political figures and businessmen. Slaves also did forced labor on plantations, the most oppressive being the agricultural estates of lower Iraq. There, slaves endured fearsome discipline and revolted in the ninth century in one of the great slave wars documented in world history. Yet in this era plantation-slave labor like that which later became prominent in the Americas was the exception, not the rule. Slaves were more prized as additions to family labor or as status symbols for their owners.

Slave Market. *Slaves were a common commodity in the marketplaces of the Islamic world. Turkish conquests during the years from 1000 to 1300 put many prisoners on the slave market.*

ISLAM IN A TIME OF POLITICAL FRAGMENTATION

Islam underwent the same burst of expansion, prosperity, and cultural diversification that swept through the rest of Afro-Eurasia (see Map 10.3 and Map 10.4). Whereas prosperity fostered greater integration in other regions, the peoples of Islam remained politically fractured. As in China, efforts to unite under a common rulership failed, giving way to defeats by marauding outsiders. The attempt to uphold centralized rule ended cataclysmically in 1258 with the Mongol sacking of Baghdad. Unlike China, Muslim leaders were unable to reunite after their collapse.

Becoming the "Middle East"

Islam responded to political fragmentation by undergoing major changes, many prompted by contacts and conflicts with neighbors. Commercial networks, sustained by Muslim merchants, carried the word of the Quran far and wide. As Islam spread, it attracted more converts.

Decisive in the spread of Islam was a popular form of the religion, highly mystical and communal, called **Sufism**. The

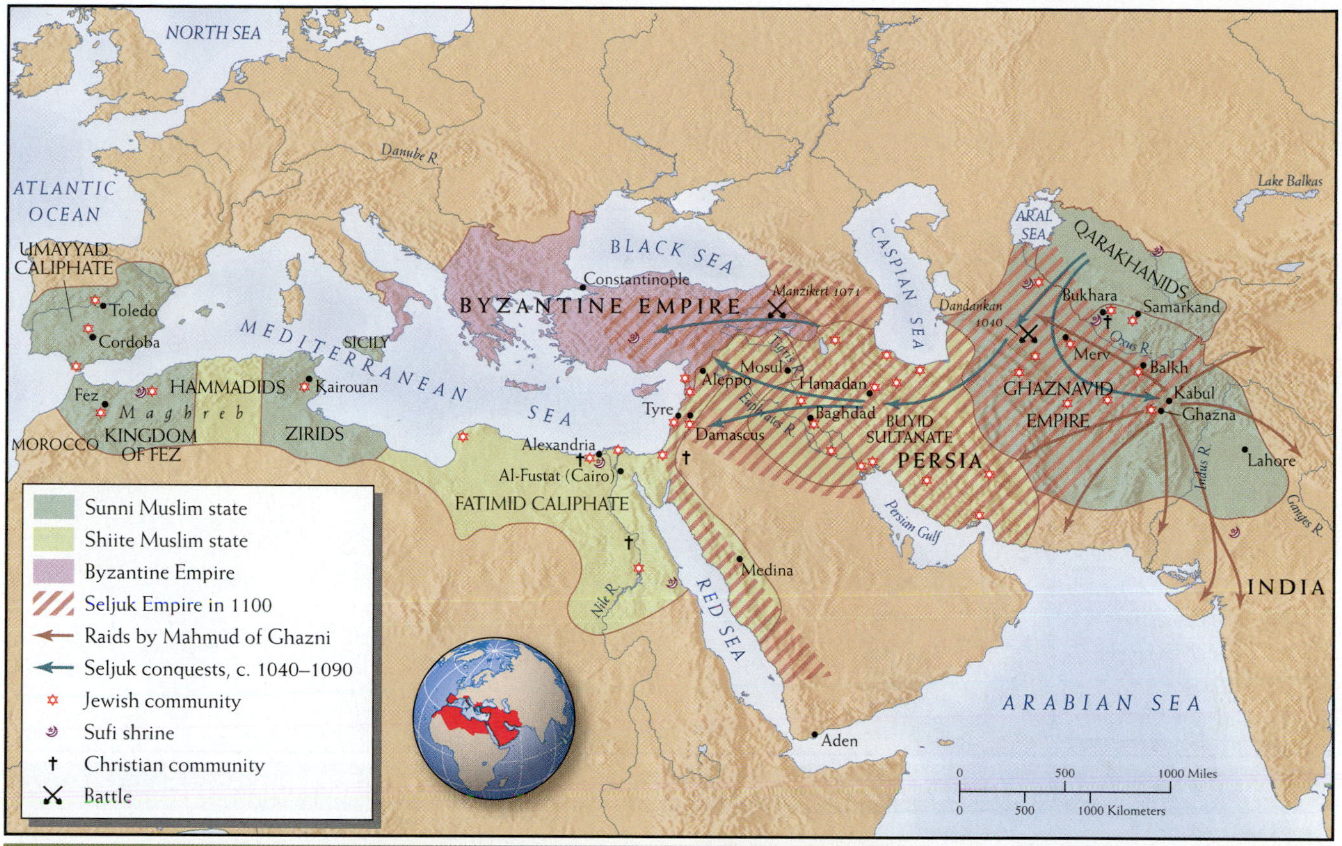

MAP 10.3 | Islam between 900 and 1200

The Muslim world experienced political disintegration in the first centuries of the second millennium.

- According to the map key, what were the two major types of Muslim states in this period and what were the two major empires?
- What were the sources of instability in this period according to the map?
- As Islam continued to expand in this period, what challenges did it face?

term *Sufi* comes from the Arabic word for wool (*suf*), which many of the early mystics wrapped themselves in to mark their penitence. Seeking closer union with God, they also performed ecstatic rituals such as repeating over and over again the name of God. In time, groups of devotees gathered to read aloud the Quran and other religious tracts. Although many clerics despised the Sufis and loathed their seeming lack of theological rigor, the movement spread with astonishing speed. Sufism's emotional content and strong social bonds, sustained in Sufi brotherhoods, made its appeal to common people irresistible. Sufi missionaries carried the universalizing faith to India, across the Sahara Desert, and to many other distant locations. It was from within these brotherhoods that Islam became truly a religion for the people.

Sufism had an intellectual and artistic dynamism that complemented its missionizing zeal. This was especially true of poetry, where the mystics' desire to experience God's love found ready expression. Most admired of Islam's mystical love poets

Dervishes. *Today, the whirling dance of dervishes is a tourist attraction, as shown in this picture from the Jerash Cultural Festival in Jordan. Though Sufis in the early second millennium* CE *were not this neatly dressed, the whirling dance was an important means of reaching union with God.*

MAP 10.4 | Islamic and Hindu States and the Byzantine Empire between 1200 and 1300

Islam continued to expand after the thirteenth century.

- Where were its largest and most important gains according to the map?
- How did other religions fare under Islamic rule in this period?
- How was Islam able to continue to expand in this period?

was Jalal al-Din Rumi, spiritual founder of the Medlevi Sufi order that became famous for the ceremonial dancing of its whirling devotees, known as dervishes. Rumi, who wrote in Persian, celebrated all forms of love, spiritual and sexual, and preached a universalistic religious message:

> What is to be done of Muslims? For I do not recognize myself.
>
> I am neither Christian, nor Jew, nor Gabr (Zoroastrian), nor Muslim.

Another Sufi mystic and advocate of the universality of religions, the Spanish Muslim poet Ibn Arabi, wrote in Arabic:

> My heart has been of every form; it is a pasture for gazelles and a convent for Christian monks.
>
> And a temple for idols and the pilgrim's kaaba, and the tables of the Torah and the book of the Quran.

As trade increased and more converts appeared in the Islamic lands, urban and peasant populations came to understand the faith practiced by the political, commercial, and scholarly upper classes even while they remained attached to their Sufi brotherhood ways. Islam became even more accommodating, embracing Persian literature, Turkish ruling skills, and Arabic-language contributions in law, religion, literature, and science. In this way the world acquired a "core" region centered in what we now call the Middle East united by a shared faith and pulsating with religious and commercial energies.

Afro-Eurasian Merchants

By the thirteenth century, as the old Islamic heartland became the crossroads for commercial networks, Muslim merchants were the world's premier traders. A universal religion, an imagined political unity projected by the Abbasid caliphate, the spread of the Arabic language, and Islamic law allowed entrepreneurs of varied backgrounds to flourish. Muslim traders were joined by Armenian, Indian, and Jewish merchants, building on family connections all across Afro-Eurasia. (See Primary Source: The Merchants of Egypt.)

PRIMARY SOURCE

The Merchants of Egypt

The most comprehensive collection of eleventh- and twelfth-century commercial materials from the Islamic world comes from a repository connected to the Jewish synagogue in Cairo. (It was the custom of the Jewish community to preserve, in a special storeroom, all texts that mention God.) These papers, a rich source of information about the Jewish community in Egypt at that time, touch on all manner of activities: cultural, religious, judicial, political, and commercial. The following letter is addressed to Joseph ibn 'Awkal, one of Egypt's leading merchants in the eleventh century.

Dear and beloved elder and leader, may God prolong your life, never take away your rank, and increase his favors and benefactions to you.

I inform you, my elder, that I have arrived safely. I have written you a letter before, but have seen no answer. Happy preoccupations—I hope. In that letter I provided you with all the necessary information.

I loaded nine pieces of antimony (kohl), five in baskets and four in complete pieces, on the boat of Ibn Jubār—may God keep it; these are for you personally, sent by Mūsā Ibn al-Majjānī. On this boat, I have in partnership with you—may God keep you—a load of cast copper, a basket with (copper) fragments, and two pieces of antimony. I hope God will grant their safe arrival. Kindly take delivery of everything, my lord.

I have also sent with Banāna a camel load for you from Ibn al-Majjānī and a camel load for me in partnership with you—may God keep you. He also carries another partnership of mine, namely, with 'Ammā r Ibn Yijū, four small jugs (of oil).

With Abū Zayd I have a shipload of tin in partnership with Salāma al-Mahdawī. Your share in this partnership with him is fifty pounds. I also have seventeen small jugs of s[oap]. I hope they arrive safely. They belong to a man [called . . .] r b. Salmūn, who entrusted them to me at his own risk. Also a bundle of hammered copper, belonging to [a Muslim] man from the Maghreb, called Abū Bakr Ibn Rizq Allah. Two other bundles, on one is written Abraham, on the other M[. . .]. I agreed with the shipowner that he would transport the goods to their destination. I wish my brother Abū Nasr—may God preserve him—to take care of all the goods and carry them to his place until I shall arrive, if God wills.

Please sell the tin for me at whatever price God may grant and leave its "purse" (the money received for it) until my arrival. I am ready to travel, but must stay until I can unload the tar and oil from the ships.

Please take care of this matter and take from him the price of five skins (filled with oil). The account is with Salāma.

Al-Sabbāgh of Tripoli has bribed Bu 'l-'Alā the agent, and I shall unload my goods soon.

Kindest regards to your noble self and to my master [. . . and] Abu 'l-Fadl, may God keep them.

QUESTIONS FOR ANALYSIS

- List all the different kinds of commodities that the letter talks about.
- How many different people are named as owners, partners, dealers, and agents?
- What does the letter reveal about the ties among merchants and about how they conducted their business?

Source: Letters of Medieval Jewish Traders, *translated with introductions and notes by S. D. Goitein (Princeton, NJ: Princeton University Press, 1973), pp. 85–87.*

Diversity and Uniformity in Islam

Not until the ninth and tenth centuries did Muslims become a majority within their own Abbasid Empire (see Chapter 9). From the outset, Muslim rulers and clerics had to deal with large non-Muslim populations, even as these groups were converting to Islam. Rulers through the ***dhimma* system** accorded non-Muslims religious toleration as long as the non-Muslims accepted Islam's political dominion. Jewish, Christian, and Zoroastrian communities were free to choose their own religious leaders and to settle internal disputes in their own religious courts. They did, however, have to pay a special tax, the *jizya*, and be deferential to their rulers. The dhimma system spared the Islamic world some of the religious conflict that afflicted other areas, and it made Islamic cities hospitable environments for traders from around the world.

While tolerant, Islam was an expansionist, universalizing faith. Intense proselytizing carried the sacred word to new frontiers and, in the process, reinforced the spread of Islamic institutions that supported commercial exchange. There were also moments of intense religious passion within Islam's frontiers, especially when Muslim rulers feared that Christian minorities would align with the Europeans pressing on their borders. Ugly incidents left some Christian churches in flames. Pressures to convert to Islam were unremitting at this time. After a surge of conversions to Islam from the ninth century onward, the Christian Copts of Egypt shrank to a small community and never recovered their numbers.

Political Integration and Disintegration

Just as the Islamic faith was increasing its reach from Africa to India and ultimately to Southeast Asia, its political institutions began to fragment. From 950 to 1050, it appeared that Shiism would be the vehicle for uniting the Islamic world. The Fatimid Shiites had established their authority over Egypt and much of North Africa (see Chapter 9), and the Abbasid state in Baghdad fell under the sway of a Shiite family. Each group created universities, in Cairo and Baghdad, respectively, ensuring that leading centers of higher learning were Shiite. But divisions also sapped Shiism, as Sunni Muslims began to challenge Shiite power and establish their own strongholds. The last of the Shiite Fatimid rulers gave way to a new Sunni regime in Egypt. In Baghdad, the Shiite Buyid family surrendered to a group of Sunni strongmen.

The new strongmen were mainly Turks. Their people had been migrating into the Islamic heartland from the Asian steppes since the eighth century, bringing superior military skills and an intense devotion to Sunni Islam. Once established in Baghdad, they founded outposts in Syria and Palestine, and then moved into Anatolia after defeating Byzantine forces in 1071. But this Turkish state also crumbled, as tribesmen quarreled for preeminence. By the thirteenth century the Islamic heartland had fractured into three regions. In the east (central Asia, Iran, and eastern Iraq), the remnants of the old Abbasid state persevered. Caliphs succeeded one another, still claiming to speak for all of Islam yet deferring to their Turkish military commanders. Even in the core of the Islamic world—Egypt, Syria, and the Arabian Peninsula—where Arabic was the primary tongue, military men of non-Arab origin held the reins of power. Farther west in North Africa, Arab rulers prevailed, but the influence of Berbers, some from the northern Sahara, was extensive. Islam was a vibrant faith, but its polities were splintered.

What Was Islam?

Buoyed by Arab dhows on the high seas and carried on the backs of camels, following commercial networks, Islam had been transformed from Muhammad's original goal of creating a religion for Arab peoples. By 1300, its influence spanned Afro-Eurasia and enjoyed multitudes of non-Arabic converts. It attracted urbanites and rural peasants alike, as well as its original audience of desert nomads. Its extraordinary universal appeal generated an intense Islamic cultural flowering around 1000 CE.

Some people worried about the preservation of Islam's true nature as, for example, Arabic ceased to be the language of many Islamic believers. True, the devout read and recited the Quran in its original tongue, as the religion mandated. But Persian was now the language of Muslim philosophy and art, and Turkish was the language of law and administration. Moreover, Jerusalem and Baghdad no longer stood alone as Islamic cultural capitals. Other cities, housing universities and other centers of learning, promoted alternative, vernacular versions of Islam. In fact, some of the most dynamic thought came from Islam's fringes.

At the same time, diversity fostered cultural blossoming in all fields of high learning. Indicative of the prominence of the Islamic faith and the Arabic language in thought was the legendary Ibn Rushd (1126–1198). Known as Averroës in the western world, where scholars pored over his writings, he wrestled with the same theological issues that troubled western scholars. Steeped in the writings of Aristotle, Ibn Rushd became Islam's most thoroughgoing advocate for the use of reason in understanding the universe. His knowledge of Aristotle was so great that it influenced the thinking of the Christian world's leading philosopher and theologian, Thomas Aquinas (1225–1274). Above all, Ibn Rushd believed that faith and reason could be compatible. He also argued for a social hierarchy in which learned men would command influence akin to Confucian scholars in China or Greek philosophers in Athens. Ibn Rushd believed that the proper forms of reasoning had to be entrusted to the educated class—in the case of Islam, the *ulama*—which would serve the common people.

Equally powerful works appeared in Persian, which by now was expressing the most sophisticated ideas of culture and religion. Best representing the new Persian ethnic pride was Abu al-Qasim Firdawsi (920–1020), a devout Muslim who believed in the importance of pre-Islamic Sasanian traditions. In the epic poem *Shah Namah*, or *Book of Kings*, he celebrated the origins of Persian culture and narrated the history of the Iranian highland peoples from the dawn of time to the Muslim conquest. As part of his effort to extol a pure Persian culture, Firdawsi attempted to compose his entire poem in Persian unblemished by other languages, even avoiding Arabic words.

By the fourteenth century, Islam had achieved what early converts would have considered unthinkable. No longer a religion of a minority of peoples living among Christian, Zoroastrian, and Jewish communities, it had become the people's faith. The agents of conversion were mainly Sufi saints and Sufi

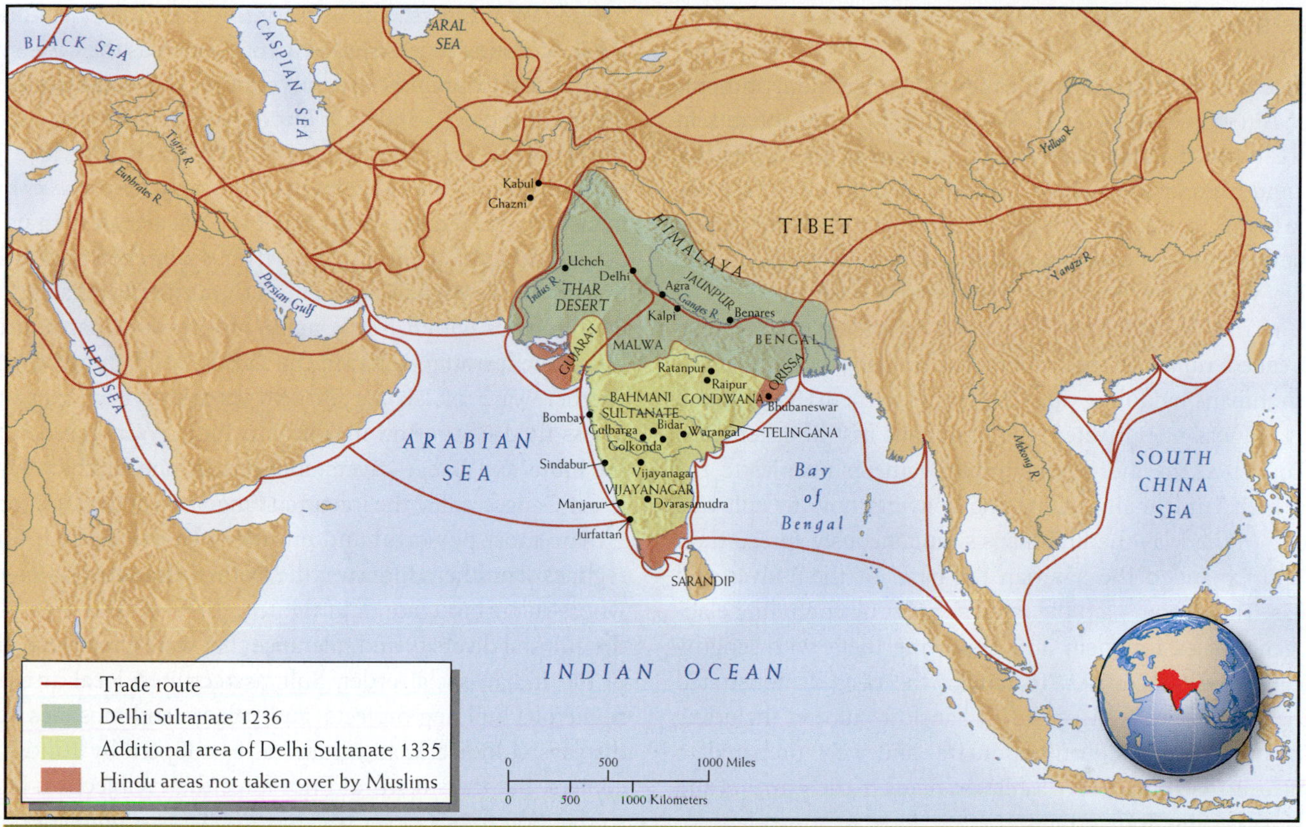

MAP 10.5 | South Asia in 1300

As the fourteenth century began, India was a blend of many cultures. Politically, the Turkish Muslim regime of the Delhi Sultanate dominated the region. Use the map key to identify the areas dominated by the Delhi Sultanate.

- How do you suppose the trade routes helped to spread the Muslims' influence in India?
- Now use the key to find the Hindu areas. Based on your reading, what factors accounted for Hinduism's continued appeal despite the Muslims' political power?

brotherhoods—not the *ulama,* whose exhortations had little impact on common people. The Sufis had carried their faith far and wide to North African Berbers, to Anatolian villagers, and to West African animists who believed that things in nature have souls. Ibn Rushd worried about the growing appeal of what he considered an "irrational" piety. But his message failed, because he did not appreciate that Islam's expansionist powers rested on its appeal to common folk. While the *sharia* was the core of Islam for the educated and scholarly classes, Sufism spoke to ordinary men and women.

During this period, Islam became one of the four cultural spheres that would play a major role in world history, laying the foundation for what would become known as the Middle East up through the middle of the twentieth century. Islam became the majority religion of most of the inhabitants of Southwest Asia and North Africa, Arabic became the everyday language for most people, and the Turks began to establish themselves as the dominant rulership force, ultimately creating the Ottoman empire, which would last into the twentieth century. The region became integral in transregional trade and the creation and maintenance of knowledge.

INDIA AS A CULTURAL MOSAIC

Trade and migration affected India, just as it did the rest of Asia and Africa. As in the case of Islam, India's growing cultural interconnections and increasing prosperity produced little political integration. Under the canopy of Hinduism it remained a cultural mosaic; Islamic faith now joined others to make the region even more diverse (see Map 10.5). India illustrates how cross-cultural integration can just as easily preserve diversity as promote internal unity.

Rajas and Sultans

India became an intersection for the trade, migration, and culture of Afro-Eurasian peoples. With 80 million inhabitants in 1000 CE, it had the second-largest population in the region, not far behind China's 120 million. Turks spilled into India as they had the Islamic heartlands, bringing their newfound Islamic beliefs. But the newcomers encountered an ethnic and religious mix that they would add to without upsetting the balance.

Before the Turks arrived, India was splintered among rival chiefs called ***rajas***. These leaders gained support from high-caste Brahmans by doling out land grants to them. Since much of the land was uncultivated, the Brahmans first built temples, then converted the indigenous hunter-gatherer peoples to the Hindu faith, and finally taught the converts how to cultivate the land. In this way the Brahmans simultaneously spread their faith and expanded the agrarian tax base for themselves and the rajas. They also repaid the rajas' support by compiling elaborate genealogies for them and endowing them with lengthy and legitimizing ancestries. In return, the rajas demonstrated that they, too, were well versed in Sanskrit culture, including equestrian skills and courtly etiquette, and were prepared to patronize artists and poets. Ultimately, many of the warriors and their heirs became Indian rajas.

Invasions and Consolidations

When the Turkish warlords began entering India, the rajas had neither the will nor resources to resist them after centuries of fighting off invaders. The Turks introduced their own customs while accepting local social structures, such as the caste system. Concerned to promote Islamic culture, the Turks constructed grandiose mosques and built impressive libraries where scholars could toil and share their wisdom with the court. Previous invaders from central Asia had reinforced the rajas' power base through intermarriage. But the Turks upset the balance of the raja kingdoms. Mahmud of Ghazna (971–1030) launched many expeditions from the Afghan heartland into northern India and, eager to win status within Islam, made his capital, Ghazni, a center of Islamic learning. Later, in the 1180s, Muhammad Ghuri led another wave of Islamic Turkish invasions from Afghanistan across the Delhi region in northern India. Wars raged between the Indus and Ganges rivers until one by one, all the way to the lower Ganges valley, the fractured kingdoms of the rajas toppled.

The most powerful and enduring of the Turkish Muslim regimes of northern India was the **Delhi Sultanate** (1206–1526), whose rulers brought political integration but also strengthened the cultural diversity and tolerance that were already a hallmark of the Indian social order. Sultans recruited local artisans for numerous building projects, and palaces and mosques became displays of Indian architectural tastes adopted by Turkish newcomers. But the sultans did not force their subjects to convert, so that South Asia never became an Islamic-dominant country. Nor did they display much interest in the flourishing commercial life along the Indian coast, permitting these areas to develop on their own and allowing Persian Zoroastrian traders to settle on the coast around modern-day Mumbai (Bombay). Farther south, the Malabar coast became the preserve of Arab traders.

Lodi Gardens. *The Lodi dynasty was the last Delhi sultanate. Lodi Gardens, the cemetery of Lodi sultans, placed central Asian Islamic architecture in an Indian landscape, thereby creating a scene of "heaven on the earth."*

Hindu Temple. *When Buddhism started to decline in India, Hinduism was on the rise. Numerous Hindu temples were built, many of them adorned with ornate carvings like this small tenth-century temple in Bhubaneshwar, east India.*

What Was India?

During the eleventh, twelfth, and thirteenth centuries India became the most diverse and, in some respects, most tolerant region in Afro-Eurasia. It is from this era that India arises as an impressive but fragile mosaic of cultures, religions, and ethnicities.

When the Turks arrived, the local Hindu population, having had much experience with foreign invaders and immigrants, assimilated these intruders as they had done earlier peoples. Before long, the newcomers thought of themselves as Indians who, however, retained their Islamic beliefs and steppe ways. They continued to wear their distinctive trousers and robes and flaunted their horse-riding skills. At the same time, the local population embraced some of their conquerors' ways, donning the tunics and trousers that characterized Central Asian peoples.

Diversity and cultural mixing became most visible in the multiple languages that flourished in India. Although the sultans spoke Turkish languages, they regarded Persian literature as a high cultural achievement and made Persian their courtly and administrative language. Meanwhile, most of their Hindu subjects spoke local languages, followed their caste regulations, and practiced diverse forms of Hindu worship. The rulers did what Muslim rulers did with Christian and Jewish communities living in their midst: they collected the *jizya* tax and permitted communities to worship as they saw fit and to administer their own communal law. Ultimately, Islam proved in India that it did not have to be a conquering religion to prosper. As rulers, sultans granted lands to *ulama* (Islamic scholars) and Sufi saints, much as Hindu rajas had earlier granted lands to Brahmans. These scholars and saints in turn attracted followers, who enjoyed the benefits of membership in a community of believers.

Although the newcomers and the locals remained loyal to their own religious traditions, nonetheless their customs began to merge. Sultans maintained their steppe lifestyle and equestrian culture and took delight in the fact that their subjects adopted central Asian–style clothing. Within only a few decades, once the subject peoples realized that sultans and Islam were there to stay, they embraced the fashions of the court. In turn, their Muslim rulers understood that ruling effectively meant mastering the local language. Before long, court scholars and Sufi holy men were writing and teaching proficiently in local dialects. In time, these dialects, mixed with Persian and Arabic words, gave rise to a common language, Hindavi, or Hindustani, the root of Urdu and Hindi.

This exchange of skills among diverse communities was not confined to governance and religion. It spilled over into the economic arena as well. The foreign artisans who had arrived with their rulers brought silk textiles, rugs, and appliances to irrigate gardens that the leading families of Delhi cherished. Soon the artisans' talents were influencing local manufacturing techniques. Native-born Indians learned from Muslims how to extract long filaments from silk cocoons and were themselves weaving fine silk textiles.

Although Buddhism had been in decline in India for centuries, it, too, became part of the cultural intermixing of these centuries. As Vedic Brahmanism evolved into Hinduism (see Chapter 8), it absorbed many Buddhist doctrines and practices, such as *ahimsa* (non-killing) and vegetarianism. The two religions became so similar that Hindus simply considered the Buddha to be one of their deities—an incarnation of the great god Vishnu. Many Buddhist moral teachings mixed with and became Hindu stories. Artistic motifs reflected a similar process of adoption and adaptation. Goddesses, some beautiful and others fierce, appeared alongside Buddhas, Vishnus, and Sivas as their consorts. The Turkish invaders' destruction of major monasteries in the thirteenth century deprived Buddhism of local spiritual leaders. Lacking dynastic support, Buddhists in India were more easily assimilated into the Hindu population or converted to Islam.

Once the initial disruptive effects of the Turkish invasions were absorbed, India remained a highly diverse and tolerant region during this period. Most importantly, it also emerged as one of the four major cultural spheres, enjoying a tremendous level of integration as Turkish-Muslim rulership and their traditions and practices were successfully intermixed into the native Hindu society, leading to a more integrated and peaceful India.

Vishnu. *In addition to the Buddha, the four-armed Vishnu has nine other avatars, some of whom are portrayed at his feet in this tenth-century sandstone sculpture.*

SONG CHINA: INSIDERS VERSUS OUTSIDERS

The preeminent world power in 1000 CE was still China, despite its recent turmoil. Once dampened, the turbulence yielded to a long era of stability and splendor, a combination that made China a regional engine of Afro-Eurasian prosperity.

In 907 CE the Tang dynasty splintered into regional kingdoms, mostly led by military generals. In 960 CE one of these generals, Zhao Kuangyin, ended the fragmentation, reunified China, and assumed the mandate of heaven for the Song dynasty (960–1279).

The following three centuries witnessed many economic and political successes, but northern nomadic tribes kept the Song from completely securing their reign (see Map 10.6 and Map 10.7). Their efforts to deter these warriors were ultimately unsuccessful, and in 1127 the Song lost control of northern China to the Jurchen (ancestors of the Manchu, who would rule China from the seventeenth until the twentieth century). After reconstituting their dynasty in southern China, their empire's most economically robust region, the Song enjoyed another century and a half of rule before falling to the Mongols.

China's Economic Progress

China, like India and the Islamic world, participated in Afro-Eurasia's powerful long-distance trade. Chinese merchants were as energetic as their Muslim and Indian counterparts. Yet China's commercial successes could not have occurred without the country's strong agrarian base—especially its vast wheat, millet, and rice fields, which fed a population that reached 120 million. Agriculture benefited from breakthroughs in metalworking that produced stronger iron plows, which the Song harnessed to sturdy water buffalo to extend the farming frontier. In 1078, for example, total Song iron production reached between 75,000 and 150,000 tons, roughly the equivalent of European iron production in the early eighteenth century. The Chinese piston-driven bellows used to provide forced air for furnaces were a marvel, and of a size unsurpassed until the nineteenth century.

Manufacturing also flourished. In the early tenth century, Chinese alchemists mixed saltpeter with sulfur and charcoal to produce a product that would burn and could be deployed on the battlefield: gunpowder. Song entrepreneurs were soon inventing a remarkable array of incendiary devices that flowed from their mastery of techniques for controlling explosions and high heat. Moreover, artisans produced increasingly light,

MAP 10.6 | East Asia in 1000

Several states emerged in East Asia between 1000 and 1300, but none were as strong as the Song dynasty in China. Using the key to the map, try to identify the factors that contributed to the Song state's economic dynamism.

- What external factors kept the Song dynasty from completely securing their reign?
- What factors drove the Chinese commercial revolution in this period?

durable, and exquisitely beautiful porcelains. Before long, their porcelain (now called "china") was the envy of all Afro-Eurasia. Also flowing from the artisans' skillful hands were vast amounts of clothing and handicrafts, made from the fibers grown by Song farmers. In effect, the Song Chinese oversaw the world's first manufacturing revolution, producing finished goods on a large scale for consumption far and wide.

Money and Inflation

Expanding commerce transformed the role of money and its wide circulation. By now the Song government was annually minting nearly two million strings of currency, each containing 1,000 copper coins. In fact, as the economy grew, the supply of metal currency could not match the demand. One result was East Asia's thirst for gold from East Africa. At the same time, merchant guilds in northwestern Shanxi developed the first letters of exchange, called "flying cash." These letters linked northern traders with their colleagues in the south. Before long, printed money had eclipsed coins. Even the government collected more than half its tax revenues in cash rather than grain and cloth. The government also issued more notes to pay its bills—a practice that ultimately contributed to the world's first case of runaway inflation.

New Elites

Song emperors ushered in a period of social and cultural vitality. They built on Tang institutions by expanding a central bureaucracy

MAP 10.7 | East Asia in 1200

- The Song dynasty regularly dealt with "barbarian" neighbors. What were the major "barbarian" tribes during this period?
- Approximately what percentage of Song China was lost to the Jin in 1126?
- How did the "barbarian" tribes affect the Han Chinese identity in this period?

of scholar-officials chosen even more extensively through competitive civil service examinations. Zhao Kuangyin, or Emperor Taizu (r. 960–976 CE), himself administered the final test for all who had passed the highest-level palace examination. In subsequent dynasties, the emperor was the nation's premier examiner, symbolically demanding oaths of allegiance from successful candidates. By 1100 these ranks of learned men had accumulated sufficient power to become China's new ruling elite.

The expansion of the civil service examination system was crucial to a shift in power from the still powerful hereditary aristocracy to a less wealthy but more highly schooled class of scholar officials. Consider the career of the Northern Song reformer Wang Anshi (1021–1086), who ascended to power from a commoner family outside of Hangzhou in the south. He owed his success to gaining high marks in Song state examinations—a not insignificant achievement, for in nearby Fujian province

Wang Anshi. *He owed his rise from a commoner family to a powerful position as a reformer to the Song state examinations.*

alone, of the roughly 18,000 candidates who gathered triennially to take the provincial examination, over 90 percent failed! After gaining the emperor's ear, Wang eventually challenged the political and cultural influence of the old Tang dynasty elites from the northwest.

Negotiating with Neighbors

As the Song flourished, nomads on the outskirts eyed the Chinese successes closely. To the north, Khitan, Tungusic, Tangut, and Jurchen nomadic societies formed their own dynasties and adopted Chinese institutions. Located within the "greater China," as defined by the Han and Tang dynasties, these non-Chinese nomads saw China proper as an object both of conquest and emulation.

In military power the Song dynasts were relatively weak. Despite their sophisticated weapons, they could not match their enemies on the steppe when the latter united against them. Steel tips improved the arrows that their soldiers shot from their crossbows, and flame throwers and "crouching tiger catapults" sent incendiary bombs streaking into their enemies' ranks. But none of these breakthroughs was secret. Warrior neighbors on the steppe mastered the new arts of war more fully than did the Song dynasts themselves.

China's strength as a manufacturing powerhouse made economic diplomacy an option, so the Song relied on "gifts" and generous trade agreements with the borderlanders. For example, after losing North China to the Khitan Liao dynasty, the Song agreed to make annual payments of 100,000 ounces of silver and 200,000 bolts of silk. The treaty allowed them to live in relative peace for more than a century. Securing peace meant emptying the state coffers and then printing more paper money. The resulting inflation added economic instability to military weakness, making the Song an easy target when Jurchen invaders made their final assault.

What Was China?

Paradoxically, the increasing exchange between outsiders and insiders within China hardened the lines that divided them and gave residents of China's interior a highly developed sense of themselves as a distinctive people possessing a superior culture. Exchanges with outsiders nurtured a "Chinese" identity among those who considered themselves true insiders and referred to themselves as Han. Driven south from their ancient homeland in the eleventh century, they grew increasingly suspicious and resentful toward the outsiders living in their midst. They called these outsiders "barbarians" and treated them accordingly.

Vital in crystallizing this sense of a distinct Chinese identity was print culture. Of all Afro-Eurasian societies in 1300, the Chinese were the most advanced in their use of printing and book publishing and circulation. Moreover, their books established classical Chinese as the lingua franca of educated classes in East Asia. The Song government used its plentiful supply of

Chinese and Barbarian. *After losing the north, the Han Chinese grew resentful of outsiders. They drew a dividing line between their own agrarian society and the nomadic warriors, calling them "barbarians." Such identities were not fixed, however. Chinese and so-called barbarians were mutually dependent.*

paper to print books, especially medical texts, and to distribute calendars. The private publishing industry also expanded. Printing houses throughout the country produced Confucian classics, works on history, philosophical treatises, and literature—all of which figured in the civil examinations. Buddhist publications, too, were available everywhere.

China's resources, its huge population base coupled with a strong agrarian economy, and its strong foreign trade and diplomatic relations made it the most wealthy among the four major cultural spheres; its common language and its transfer of power to nonhereditary Confucian scholars made it the most unified.

CHINA'S NEIGHBORS ADAPT TO CHANGE

Feeling the pull of China's economic and political gravity, cultures around China consolidated their own internal political authority and defined their own identities in order to keep from being swallowed up, while increasing their commercial transactions.

The Rise of Warriors in Japan

Japan, like China, laid many political and cultural foundations for its later development in the three centuries between 1000 and 1300. Not only did its leaders distance themselves from Chinese influences during this period, but they also developed a strong sense of their islands' distinctive identity. Even so, the long-standing dominance of Chinese ways remained apparent at virtually every level of Japanese society, and was most pronounced at the imperial court in the capital city of Heian, present-day Kyoto. The city itself, founded in 795 CE, was modeled after the Chinese capital city of Chang'an. Three and a half miles from north to south and three miles from east to west, Heian-kyo, meaning the place of peace and tranquility, was surrounded by a moat and divided into squares by broad intersecting city-long roads, with the imperial court located in the north central part of the city. Although the city itself was not of imposing grandeur, those who resided in it admired its attractive gates, recessed courtyards, well-maintained and reposeful gardens, and its bustling streets and shops. To serve at the imperial court entailed a demanding knowledge of correct etiquette and ethics, based mostly on Chinese practices. Courtiers were obligated to wear the right colored robes, to carry swords of the correct length, and to know the proper salutations for greeting other members of the imperial bureaucracy.

The Tale of Genji best captures life at the Heian court. Written by Lady Murasaki Shikibu (c. 976–c. 1031), it is possibly the worlds' first novel, certainly the first novel to be written by a woman. *The Tale of Genji* reveals the imperial court's outward dedication to official rituals and values, as well as its rivalries, infighting, and sordid affairs—the stuff of court politics seemingly everywhere in the world, Yet, even this work, so preoccupied with the imperial center where Chinese institutions and values were dominant, reveals Japan's quest to create its own identity, for the work was written in the native Japanese script. (See Primary Source: The Tale of Genji.)

Outside Kyoto, however, a less China-centered way of life existed and began to impose itself on the center. Here, local notables, mainly military leaders and large landowners, began to challenge the imperial court for dominance. In 1185 one such rising clan leader, Minamoto-no-Yoritomo, supported by a large group of loyal followers in the eastern part of Japan, 300 miles away from Kyoto, consolidated his own administration there and soon extended his control over the entire country. Yoritomo was the first of many such military men who would dominate Japanese politics. As he and his successors elected to keep the Japanese emperors and their court at Kyoto in office even while stripping them of real power, Japan continued to have an emperor residing at the imperial city of Kyoto right down to 1868 when the Meiji restoration took place (see Chapter 17).

The emergence of Yoritomo marked the arrival of an important new social group in Japanese society—the warriors, or samurai. Heian aristocrats, disdaining the military and even abolishing the conscription system used to raise imperial armies, had thus allowed trained warriors, affiliated with kinship groups, to gather strength in the provinces. In lightweight leather armor, these expert horsemen defended their private estates with remarkable long-range bowmanship and superbly crafted single-edged long steel swords, lethal for close combat in warfare. The warriors also brought with them an idealization of their martial ethics, with an emphasis on loyalty, self-discipline, and a simple life tied to the land, which helped to shape Japanese society until recent times.

By the beginning of the fourteenth century, Japan had multiple sources of political and cultural power: an endangered and declining aristocracy; an imperial family with prestige but little authority; powerful landowning notables based in the provinces; and a rising and increasingly ambitious class of samurai. There was, in short, a combustible mix of refined high culture in the capital versus a warrior ethos in the provinces. Such a mix produced social intrigue in politics and led different provincial factions to vie with one another for preeminence.

Southeast Asia: A Maritime Mosaic

Southeast Asia, like India, now became a crossroads of Afro-Eurasian influences. Its sparse population of probably around 10 million in 1000 CE—tiny compared with that of China and

PRIMARY SOURCE

The Tale of Genji

Lacking a written language of their own, Heian aristocrats adopted classical Chinese as the official written language while continuing to speak Japanese. Men at the court took great pains to master the Chinese literary forms, but Japanese court ladies were not expected to do so. Lady Murasaki Shikibu, the author of* The Tale of Genji*, hid her knowledge of Chinese, fearing that she would be criticized. In the meantime, the Japanese developed a native syllabary (a table of syllables) based on Chinese written graphs. Using this syllabary, Murasaki kept a diary in Japanese that gave vivid accounts of Heian court life. Her story—possibly the world's first novel—relates the adventures of a dashing young courtier named Genji. In the passage below, Genji evidently speaks for Murasaki in explaining why fiction can be as truthful as a work of history in capturing human life and its historical significance.

Genji . . . smiled, and went on: "But I have a theory of my own about what this art of the novel is, and how it came into being. To begin with, it does not simply consist in the author's telling a story about the adventures of some other person. On the contrary, it happens because the storyteller's own experience of men and things, whether for good or ill—not only what he has passed through himself, but even events which he has only witnessed or been told of—has moved him to an emotion so passionate that he can no longer keep it shut up in his heart. Again and again something in his own life or in that around him will seem to the writer so important that he cannot bear to let it pass into oblivion. There must never come a time, he feels, when men do not know about it. That is my view of how this art arose.

"Clearly then, it is no part of the storyteller's craft to describe only what is good or beautiful. Sometimes, of course, virtue will be his theme, and he may then make such play with it as he will. But he is just as likely to have been struck by numerous examples of vice and folly in the world around him, and about them he has exactly the same feelings as about the pre-eminently good deeds which he encounters: they are more important and must all be garnered in. Thus anything whatsoever may become the subject of a novel, provided only that it happens in this mundane life and not in some fairyland beyond our human ken.

"The outward forms of this art will not of course be everywhere the same. At the court of China and in other foreign lands both the genius of the writers and their actual methods of composition are necessarily very different from ours; and even here in Japan the art of storytelling has in course of time undergone great changes. There will, too, always be a distinction between the lighter and the more serious forms of fiction. . . . So too, I think, may it be said that the art of fiction must not lose our allegiance because, in the pursuit of the main purpose to which I have alluded above, it sets virtue by the side of vice, or mingles wisdom with folly. Viewed in this light the novel is seen to be not, as is usually supposed, a mixture of useful truth with idle invention, but something which at every stage and in every part has a definite and serious purpose."

QUESTIONS FOR ANALYSIS

- According to this passage, what motivates an author to write a story (i.e., fiction)?
- Genji feels it is appropriate for a writer to address not only "what is good or beautiful" but also "vice and folly." What explanation does he give? Do you agree?

Source: Sources of Japanese Tradition, *compiled by Ryūsaku Tsunoda, Wm. Theodore de Bary, and Donald Keene (New York: Columbia University Press, 1964), vol. 1, pp. 177–79.*

India—was not immune to the foreign influences riding the sea-lanes into the archipelago. The Malay Peninsula became home to many trading ports and stopovers for traders shuttling between India and China, because it connected the Bay of Bengal and the Indian Ocean with the South China Sea (see Map 10.8).

"INDO-CHINESE" INFLUENCES Indian influence had been prominent both on the Asian mainland and in island portions of Southeast Asia since 800 CE, but Islamic expansion into the islands after 1200 gradually superseded these influences. Only Bali and a few other islands far to the east of Malaya preserved their Brahmanic-Vedic religious origins. Elsewhere in Java and Sumatra, Islam became the dominant religion. In Vietnam and northern portions of mainland Southeast Asia, Chinese cultural influences and northern schools of Mahayana Buddhism were especially prominent.

Heiji Rebellion. *This illustration from the Kamakura period depicts a battle during the Heiji Rebellion, which was fought between rival subjects of the cloistered emperor Go-Shirakawa in 1159. Riding in full armor on horseback, the fighters on both sides are armed with devastating long bows.*

MAINLAND BUFFER KINGDOMS During this period Cambodian, Burmese, and Thai peoples founded powerful mixed polities along the Mekong, Salween, Chao Phraya, and Irriwaddy river basins of the Asian mainland. Important Vedic and Buddhist kingdoms emerged here as political buffers between the strong states in China and India and brought stability and further commercial prosperity to the region.

Consider the kingdom that ruled Angkor in present-day Cambodia. With their capital in Angkor, the Khmers (889–1431) created the most powerful and wealthy empire in Southeast Asia. Countless water reservoirs enabled them to flourish on the great plain to the west of the Mekong River after the loss of eastern territories. Public works and magnificent temples dedicated to the revived Vedic gods from India went hand in hand with the earlier influence of Indian Buddhism. Eventually the Khmer kings united adjacent kingdoms and extended Khmer influence to the Thai and Burmese states along the Chaophraya and Irriwaddy rivers.

One of the greatest temple complexes in Angkor exemplified the Khmers' heavy borrowing from Vedic Indian architecture. Angkor aspired to represent the universe in the magnificence of its buildings. As signs of the ruler's power, the pagodas, pyramids, and terra-cotta friezes (ornamented walls) presented the life of the gods on earth. The crowning structure of the royal

Angkor Wat. *Mistaken by later European explorers as a remnant of Alexander the Great's conquests, the enormous temple complexes built by the Khmer people in Angkor borrowed their intricate layout and stupa (a moundlike structure containing religious relics) architecture from the Brahmanist Indian temples of the time. As the capital, Angkor was a microcosm of the world for the Khmer, who aspired to represent the macrocosm of the universe in the magnificence of Angkor's buildings and their geometric layout.*

MAP 10.8 | Southeast Asia, 1000–1300

Cross-cultural influences affected Southeast Asian societies during this period.

- What makes Southeast Asia unique geographically compared to other regions of the world?
- Based on the map, why were the kingdoms of Southeast Asia exposed to so many cross-cultural influences?
- In this chapter, the term "mosaic" describes both South and Southeast Asia. Compare Map 10.5 with this map, and explain how the mosaic of Southeast Asia differed from the mosaic of India.

palace was the magnificent temple of **Angkor Wat**, possibly the largest religious structure ever built. In ornate detail and with great artistry, its buildings and statues represented the revival of the Hindu pantheon within the Khmer royal state.

CHRISTIAN EUROPE

In the far western corner of Afro-Eurasia, people were building a culture revealingly different. Although their numbers were small compared with the rest of Afro-Eurasia in 1000 CE (36 million in Europe, compared to 80 million in India and 120 million in China), their population would soar to 80 million before the arrival of the Black Death in the fourteenth century.

This was a region of strong contrasts. On the one hand, the period 1000–1300 witnessed an intense localization of politics because there was no successor to the Roman Empire or Charlemagne's (see Chapter 9). On the other hand, the territory united under a shared sense of its place in the world. Some inhabitants even began to believe in the existence of something

MAP 10.9 | Latin Christendom in 1300

Catholic Europe expanded geographically and integrated culturally during this era.

- According to this map, into what areas did western Christendom successfully expand?
- What factors contributed to the growth of a widespread common culture and shared ideas?
- How did long-distance trade shape the history of the region during this time?

called "Europe" and increasingly referred to themselves as "Europeans" (see Map 10.9).

Western and Northern Europe

The collapse of Charlemagne's empire had exposed much of northern Europe to invasion, principally from the Vikings, and left the peasantry with no central authority to protect them from local warlords. Armed with deadly weapons, these strongmen collected taxes, imposed forced labor, and became the unchallenged rulers of society. Within this growing warrior aristocracy, northern France led the way. The Franks (later called Frenchmen) were the trendsetters of eleventh- and twelfth-century western Europe.

The most important change was the peasantry's subjugation to the knightly class. Previously, well-to-do peasants had carried arms as "free" men. The moment the farmers lost the right to carry arms, they were no longer free. They slipped back to being mere agricultural laborers. Each peasant toiled under the authority of a lord, who controlled every detail of his or her life. This was the basis of a system known as **feudalism**.

The Bayeux Tapestry. *This tapestry was prepared by a queen and her ladies to celebrate the victories of William, known as the Conqueror because of his successful invasion of England in 1066. It shows the fascination of the entire "feudal" class, even women, with war, on which they depended—great horses, tightly meshed chain mail, long shields, and the stirrups that made such cavalry warfare possible.*

Assured of control of the peasantry, feudal lords watched over an agrarian breakthrough—which fueled a commercial transformation that drew Europe into the rest of the global trading networks. Lordly protection and more advanced metal tools like axes and plows, combined with heavier livestock to pull plows through the root-infested sods of northern Europe, led to massive deforestation. Above this clearing activity stood the castle. Its threatening presence ensured that the peasantry stayed within range of the collector of rents for the lords and of tithes (shares of crops, earmarked as "donations") for the church. In this blunt way, feudalism harnessed agrarian energy to its own needs. The population of western Europe as a whole leaped forward, most spectacularly in the north. As a result, northern Europe, from England to Poland, ceased to be an underdeveloped "barbarian" appendage of the Mediterranean.

Olavinilinna Castle. *This castle in Finland was the easternmost extension of a "western" feudal style of rule through great castles. It was built at the very end of the Baltic, to keep away the Russians of Novgorod.*

Eastern Europe

Nowhere did pioneering peasants develop more land than in the wide-open spaces of eastern Europe, the region's land of opportunity. Between 1100 and 1200, some 200,000 farmers emigrated from Flanders (in modern Belgium), Holland, and northern Germany to eastern frontiers. Well-watered landscapes, covered with vast forests, filled up what are now Poland, the Czech Republic, Hungary, and the Baltic states. "Little Europes," whose castles, churches, and towns echoed the landscape of France, now replaced economies that had been based on gathering honey, hunting, and the slave trade. For a thousand miles along the Baltic Sea, forest clearings dotted with new farmsteads and small towns edged inward from the coast up the river valleys.

The social structure here was a marriage of convenience between migrating peasants and local elites. The area offered the promise of freedom from the feudal lords' arbitrary justice and imposition of forced labor. Even the harsh landscape of the eastern Baltic (where the sea froze every year and impenetrable forests blocked settlers from the coast) was preferable to life in the feudal west. For their part, the elites of eastern Europe—the nobility of Poland, Bohemia, and Hungary and the princes of the Baltic—wished to live well, in the "French" style. But they could do so only if they attracted manpower to their lands by offering newcomers a liberty that they had no hope of enjoying in the west.

The Russian Lands

In Russian lands, western settlers and knights met an eastern brand of Christian devotion. This world looked toward Byzantium, not Rome. Russia was a giant borderland between the steppes of Eurasia and the booming feudalisms of Europe. Its cities lay at the crossroads of overland trade and migration, and Kiev became one of the region's greatest cities. Standing on a bluff above the Dnieper River, it straddled newly opened trade routes. With a population exceeding 20,000, including merchants from eastern and western Europe and the Middle East, Kiev was larger than Paris—larger even than the much-diminished city of Rome.

Kiev looked south to the Black Sea and to Constantinople. Under Iaroslav the Wise (1016–1054), it became a small-scale Constantinople on the Dnieper. A stone church called St. Sophia stood (as in Constantinople) beside the imperial palace. With its distinctive "Byzantine" domes, it was a miniature Hagia Sophia (see Chapter 8). Its highest dome towered a hundred feet above the floor, and its splendid mosaics depicting Byzantine saints echoed the religious art of Constantinople. But the message was political as well, for the ruler of Kiev was cast in the mold of the emperor of Constantinople. He now took the title *tsar* from the ancient Roman name given to the emperor, Caesar. From this time onward, *tsar* was the title of rulers in Russia.

The Russian form of Christianity replicated the Byzantine style of churches all along the great rivers leading to the trading cities of the north and northeast. These were not agrarian centers, but hubs of expanding long-distance trade. (See Primary Source: The Birch Bark Letters of Novgorod.) Each city became a small-scale Kiev, and a smaller-scale echo of Constantinople. The Orthodox religion looked to Byzantium's Hagia Sophia rather than the Catholic faith associated with the popes in Rome. Russian Christianity remained the Christianity of a borderland—vivid oases of high culture set against the backdrop of vast forests and widely scattered settlements.

What Was Christian Europe?

Catholicism became a universalizing faith that transformed the region becoming known as "Europe." The Christianity of post-Roman Europe had been a religion of monks, and its most dynamic centers were great monasteries. Members of the laity were expected to revere and support their monks, nuns, and clergy, but not to imitate them. By 1200, all this had changed. The internal colonization of western Europe—the clearing of woods and founding of villages—ensured that parish churches arose in all but the wildest landscapes. Their spires were visible and their bells were audible from one valley to the next. Church graveyards were the only places where good Christians could be buried; criminals' and outlaws' bodies piled up in "heathen" graves outside the cemetery walls.

Now the clergy reached more deeply into the private lives of the laity. Marriage and divorce, previously considered family matters, became a full-time preoccupation of the church. And sin was no longer an offense that just "happened"; it was a matter that every person could do something about. Regular confession to a priest became obligatory for all Catholic, western Christians. The followers of Francis of Assisi (1182–1226) emerged as an order of preachers who brought a message of repentance. They did not tell their audiences to enter the monastery. Instead, their listeners were to weep, confess their sins to local priests, and strive to be better Christians. Franciscans instilled in the hearts of all believers a Europe-wide Catholicism based on daily remorse and daily contemplation of the sufferings of Christ and his mother, Mary. From Ireland

Saint Sophia Cathedral, Novgorod. *The cathedral of Novgorod (like that of Kiev) was called Hagia Sophia. It was a deliberate imitation of the Hagia Sophia of Constantinople, showing Russia's roots in a glorious Roman/Byzantine past that had nothing to do with western Europe.*

PRIMARY SOURCE

The Birch Bark Letters of Novgorod

The city of Novgorod was a vibrant trading center with a diverse population. From 1951 onward, Russian archaeologists in Novgorod have excavated almost a thousand letters and accounts scratched on birch bark and preserved in the sodden, frequently frozen ground. Reading them, we realize how timeless people's basic concerns can be.

First, we meet the merchants. Many letters are notes by creditors of the debts owed to them by trading partners. The sums are often expressed in precious animal furs. They contain advice to relatives or to partners in other cities:

> Giorgii sends his respects to his father and mother: Sell the house and come here to Smolensk or to Kiev: for the bread is cheap there.

Then we meet neighborhood disputes:

> From Anna to Klemiata: Help me, my lord brother, in my matter with Konstantin. . . . [For I asked him,] "Why have you been so angry with my sister and her daughter. You called her a cow and her daughter a whore. And now Fedor has thrown them both out of the house."

There are even glimpses of real love. A secret marriage is planned:

> Mikiti to Ulianitza: Come to me. I love you, and you me. Ignato will act as witness.

And a poignant note from a woman was discovered in 1993:

> I have written to you three times. What is it that you hold against me, that you did not come to see me this Sunday? I regarded you as I would my own brother. Did I really offend you by that which I sent to you? If you had been pleased you would have torn yourself away from company and come to me. Write to me. If in my clumsiness I have offended you and you should spurn me, then let God be my judge. I love you.

QUESTIONS FOR ANALYSIS

- What does the range of people writing on birch bark tell us about these people?
- Think of the messages you send to friends and relatives today. Even if texting and e-mailing seem centuries distant from writing on birch bark, can you relate in any way to these ancient letter-writers?

Source: A. V. Artsikhovskii and V. I. Borkovski, Novgorodskie Gramoty na Bereste, *11 vols. (Moscow: Izd-vo Akademii nauk SSSR, 1951–2004), document nos. 424, 531, 377, and 752.*

to Riga and Budapest, Catholic Christians came to share a common piety.

UNIVERSITIES AND INTELLECTUALS Vital to the creation of Europe's Christian identity was the emergence of universities, for it was during this era that Europe acquired its first class of intellectuals. Since the late twelfth century, scholars had gathered in Paris, where they formed a *universitas*—a term borrowed from merchant communities, where it denoted a type of union. Those who belonged to the *universitas* enjoyed protection by their fellows and freedom to continue their trade. Similarly protected by their own "union," the scholars of Paris began wrestling with the new learning from Arab lands. When the bishop of Paris forbade this undertaking, they simply moved to the Left Bank of the Seine, so as to place the river between themselves and the bishop's officials, who lived around the cathedral of Notre Dame.

The scholars' ability to organize themselves gave them an advantage that their Arab contemporaries lacked. For all his genius, Ibn Rushd had to spend his life courting the favor of individual monarchs to protect him from conservative fellow Muslims, who frequently burned his books. Ironically, European scholars congregating in Paris could quietly absorb the most persuasive elements of Arabic thought, like Ibn Rushd's. Yet they endeavored to prove that Christianity was the only religion that fully met the aspirations of all rational human beings. Such was the message of the great intellectual Thomas Aquinas, who wrote *Summa contra Gentiles* (Summary of Christian Belief against Non-Christians) in 1264.

The Europe of 1300 was more culturally unified than in previous centuries. It was permeated by Catholicism, and its leading intellectuals extolled the virtues of Christian learning. Such a confident region was not, however, a tolerant place for heretics, Jews, or Muslims.

Christian Europe on the Move: The Crusades and Iberia

By the tenth and eleventh centuries, western Christianity was on the move, spreading into Scandinavia, southern Italy, the Baltic, and eastern Europe. Its ambitions to reconquer Spain and Portugal (which had been under Islamic control since the eighth century CE) demonstrated one of the effects of feudal power: the lords' self-confidence, their belief in their military capability, and their pious sense of destiny were all inflated. Besides, the wealth of the east was irresistible to those whose piety entwined with an appetite for plunder. Yet the two Christendoms formed an uneasy alliance to roll back the expanding frontiers of Islam. Europeans zealously took war outside their own borders.

CRUSADES In the late eleventh century, western Europeans launched a wave of attacks known as the **Crusades**. The First Crusade began in 1095, when Pope Urban II appealed to the warrior nobility of France to put their violence to good use: they should combine their role as pilgrims to Jerusalem with that of soldiers, and free Jerusalem from Muslim rule. What the clergy proposed was a novel kind of war. Whereas previously war had been a dirty business and a source of sin, now the clergy told the knights that good and just wars were possible. Such wars could cancel out the sins of those who waged them.

Starting in 1097, an armed host of around 60,000 men moved all the way from northwestern Europe to Jerusalem. This was a huge crowd. But it was divided. Knights in heavy armor led, as they did in Europe. But in the eastern Mediterranean they depended on poor masses who joined the movement to help besiege cities and construct a network of castles as the Christian knights drove their frontier forward. Later Crusaders brought their wives, especially those from the upper class. As in many colonial societies away from the homeland, these women felt freer. Eleanor of Aquitaine, for example, led her own army. Also, queens were crucial in opening up to the local populations. Consider the Armenian queen, Melisende (r. 1131–1152): regarded as wise and experienced in affairs of the state, she was popular with local Christians. As a result, the society of the Crusader states remained more open to women and the lower classes than in Europe. Above all, the Crusades could not have happened without the sailors and merchants of Italy. It was the fleets of Venice, Genoa, and Pisa that transported the later Crusaders and supplied their kingdom.

There were five Crusades in all, spread out over two centuries. None of the coalitions, in the end, created permanent Christian kingdoms in the lands they "reconquered." Only a small proportion of Crusaders remained in Southwest Asia, and those who did met their match in Muslim armies. (See Current Trends in World History: The Crusades from Dual Perspectives.)

Crusader. *Kneeling, this Crusader promises to serve God (as he would serve a feudal lord) by going to fight on a Crusade (as he would fight for any lord to whom he had sworn loyalty). The two kinds of loyalty—to God and to one's lord—were deliberately confused in Crusader ideas. Both were about war. But fighting for God was unambiguously good, while fighting for a lord was not always so clear-cut.*

Part of the problem was that few Crusaders had any intention of becoming colonists. Only a small proportion remained to defend the Kingdom of Jerusalem after the First Crusade. Most knights returned home, their epic pilgrimage completed. The remaining fragile network of Crusader lordships could barely threaten the Islamic heartlands.

Muslim leaders, however, did not see the Frankish knights as a threat. For them, the Crusades were irrelevant. And as far as the average Muslim of the region was concerned, the Crusaders hardly mattered at all. Jerusalem and Palestine had always been fringe areas in the Middle East. Real prosperity and the capital cities of Muslim kingdoms lay inland, away from the coast—at Cairo, Damascus, and Baghdad. The assaults' long-term effect was to harden Muslim feelings against the Franks and the millions of non-western Christians who had previously lived peacefully in Egypt and Syria. Muslims viewed the Crusaders as brave but uncivilized warriors. A neighboring Muslim wrote: "The Franks possess none of the virtues of men except courage. . . . Nobody counts for them except knights." Their lack of medical knowledge shocked this observer. He noted that they would rather chop off a man's leg than administer ointments, as Muslim doctors would have advised.

Other campaigns of Christian expansion, like the Iberian efforts to drive out the Muslims, were more successful. Beginning with the capture of Toledo in 1061, the Christian kings of northern Spain slowly pushed back the Muslims. Eventually they reached the heart of Andalusia in southern Iberia and conquered Seville, adding more than 100,000 square miles of territory to Christian Europe. Another force from northern France crossed Italy to conquer Muslim-held Sicily, ensuring Christian rule in the strategically located mid-Mediterranean island. Unlike the Crusaders' fragile foothold at the edge of the Middle East, these two conquests turned the tide in relations between Christian and Muslim power.

Christianity—in particular the rise of the Roman Catholic Church, the spread of universities, and the fight against the Muslims in their native and spiritual homelands—would be the force that would create the fourth cultural sphere known as Europe, whose peoples would become known as European, at the western end of the Afro-Eurasian landmass.

THE AMERICAS

During this period, the Americas were untouched by the connections reverberating across Afro-Eurasia. After all, navigators still could not cross the large oceans that separated the Americas from other lands. Yet, here, too, commercial and expansionist impulses fostered closer contact among peoples who lived there.

Andean States

Growth and prosperity in the Andean region gave rise to South America's first empire. Known as the Chimú Empire, it developed early in the second millennium in the fertile Moche Valley bordering the Pacific Ocean (see Map 10.10). Ultimately the Moche people expanded their influence across numerous valleys and ecological zones, from pastoral highlands to rich valley floodplains to the fecund fishing grounds of the Pacific Coast. As their geographical reach grew, so did their wealth.

Andean States. *The image to the left shows what remains of Chan Chan. The city covered fifteen square miles and was divided into neighborhoods for nobles, artisans, and commoners, with the elites living closest to the hub of governmental and spiritual power. The buildings of Tiahuanaco (below) were made of giant, hand-hewn stones assembled without mortar. Engineers had not discovered the principle of curved arches and keystones and instead relied on massive slabs atop gateways. Gateways were important symbolic features, for they were places where people acknowledged the importance of sun and moon gods.*

CURRENT TRENDS IN WORLD HISTORY

The Crusades from Dual Perspectives

World history promotes comparative historical study, and when two cultures come together, as they did in the European crusades, their meeting offers unique opportunities to see how different societies view one another, and it provides a clear sense for their own self-identity. Such a confrontation took place during the crusades between European Christians and Muslims between 1095-1272.

In 1095, Pope Urban II called for the First Crusade in the following words:

> Oh, race of Franks, race from across the mountains, race chosen and beloved by God, as shines forth in very many of your works, set apart from all nations by the situation of your country, as well as by your Catholic faith and the honor of the Holy Church! To you our discourse is addressed, and for you our exhortation is intended. We wish you to know what a grievous cause has led us to your country, what peril, threatening you and all the faithful, has brought us.

The "grievous cause" was the occupation of the Holy City of Jerusalem by the Islamic empire. Formed within the complex relationship between the Byzantine Empire and the western Christian papacy and kingdoms of Europe, the religious motivation behind the Crusades became the subject of many literary renditions of the tumultuous events. It also generated emotionally stirring and polemical (argumentative) writing, depicting either a Muslim or Christian enemy (depending on the work's author).

Polemics are often passionate, harsh, and emotional. They also inspire and reinforce the conviction of fellow believers, with little concern for accuracy. Thus authors of polemic in the time of the Crusades were usually too biased or too misinformed to present accurate portraits of their enemies. But occasionally, firsthand accounts in the form of chronicles and histories offer us unique glimpses into Christian-Muslim relations in the age of the Crusades.

Consider Usāmah ibn Munqidh (1095–1188), the learned ruler of the city of Shaizar in western Syria. Skirmishes, truces, and the ransoming of prisoners were part of his daily life, and Usāmah socialized with his Frankish neighbors as much as he fought with them. He offers a dismissive opinion of his enemies. Basically, they struck him as "animals possessing the virtues of courage and fighting, but nothing else." In particular, their medical practice appalled him. More strange, the Franks allowed their wives to walk about freely and to talk to strangers unaccompanied by male guardians. How could men be at once so brave and yet so lacking in a proper, Arab sense of honor, which would lead a man to protect his women? Unlike other Muslim authors of his time, however, Usāmah does not refer to the Franks in derogatory terms such as "infidels" or "devils." In fact, he occasionally refers to some of them as his companions and writes of a Frank who called him "my brother" (*An Arab-Syrian Gentleman and Warrior in the Time of the Crusades,* 16).

Christian authors had similar interests in documenting the customs of their enemies in battle. Jean de Joinville

---

The Chimú regime lasted until Incan armies invaded in the 1460s and incorporated the Pacific state into their own immense empire.

A THRIVING LOWLAND ECONOMY The Chimú economy was successful because it was highly commercialized. Agriculture was its base, and complex irrigation systems turned the arid coast into a string of fertile oases capable of feeding an increasingly dispersed population. Cotton became a lucrative export to distant markets along the Andes. Parades of llamas and porters lugged these commodities up and down the steep mountain chains that are the spine of South America. As in China, a well-trained bureaucracy oversaw the construction and maintenance of canals, with a hierarchy of provincial administrators watching over commercial hinterlands.

Between 850 and 900 CE, the Moche peoples founded their biggest city, Chan Chan, with a core population of 30,000 inhabitants. A sprawling walled metropolis, covering nearly ten square miles with extensive roads circulating through neighborhoods, it boasted ten huge palaces at its center. Protected by thick walls thirty feet high, these opulent residence halls bespoke the rulers' power. Within the compound, emperors erected mortuary monuments for storing their accumulated riches: fine cloth, gold and silver objects, splendid *Spondylus* shells, and other luxury goods. Around the compound spread neighborhoods for nobles and artisans; farther out stood rows of commoners' houses.

AN INVENTIVE HIGHLAND STATE The Andes also saw its first highland empires during this period. On the shores

(1224/1225–1317) was a chronicler of medieval France. During one crusade, while in the service of the king, Joinville had occasion to note the Muslims' social behavior:

> Whenever the Sultan was in the camp, the men of the personal Guard were quartered all round his lodging, and appointed to guard his person. At the door of the Sultan's lodging there was a little tent for the Sultan's door-keepers, and for his musicians, who had Arabian horns and drums and kettledrums; and they used to make such a din at daybreak and at nightfall that people near them could not hear one another speak, and that they could be heard plainly all through the camp. The musicians never dared sound their instruments in the daytime unless by the order of the Chief of the Guard. Thus it was, that whenever the Sultan had a proclamation to make he used to send for the Chief of the Guard, and give him the order; and then the Chief would cause all the Sultan's instruments to be sounded; and thereupon all the host would come to hear the Sultan's commands.

Jeane de Joinville. *Joinville dictating his memoir of St. Louis, in which he described the Seventh Crusade.*

Although scholars regard such literary renditions with caution, they are useful for gleaning personal details that other types of works omit. The colorful accounts by authors such as Usāmah ibn Munqidh and Joinville are invaluable resources for the social history of the Crusaders.

QUESTIONS FOR ANALYSIS

- What customs or practices of their opponents did the Muslim and the Christian writers select to write about? Why?
- What aspects of the other side's customs does the writer seem to see as good or praiseworthy? What does that tell us about their perceptions of the strangers they encountered?
- If a historian is to use polemical written sources like this to analyze societies in the past, what can he or she say is trustworthy about them?

Explore Further

Hodgson, Natasha, *Women, Crusading and the Holy Land in Historical Narrative* (2007).

Maalouf, Amin, *The Crusades Through Arab Eyes*, trans. Jon Rothschild (1984).

Peters, Edward (ed.), *The First Crusade: The Chronicle of Fulcher of Chartres and Other Source Materials* (1971).

of the plateau lake Titicaca, the people of Tiahuanaco forged a high-altitude state. Though neither as large nor as wealthy as the Chimú Empire, its residents converted the inhospitable highlands into an environment where farmers and herders thrived. There is evidence of long-distance trade with neighbors in semitropical valleys, and even signs of highlanders migrating to the lowlands to produce agrarian staples for their kin in the mountains. Dried fish and cotton came from the coast; fruits and vegetables came from lowland valleys. Trade sustained an enormous urban population of up to 115,000 people. Looming over the skyline of Tiahuanaco was an imposing pyramid of massive sandstone blocks. Its advanced engineering system conveyed water to the summit, from which an imitation rainfall coursed down the carefully carved sides—an awesome spectacle of engineering prowess in such an arid region.

Connections to the North

Additional hubs of regional trade developed farther north, showing once again that even in areas of relative geographic isolation, cultures could flourish and interact within expanding regional spheres. The Toltecs and the Cahokians are superb examples.

THE TOLTECS IN MESOAMERICA By 1000 CE, Mesoamerica had seen the rise and fall of several complex societies. Caravans of porters worked the intricate roads that connected the coast of the Gulf of Mexico to the Pacific, and the southern lowlands of Central America to the arid regions of modern Texas (see Map 10.11). The region's heartland was the rich valley of central Mexico. Here the Toltecs filled the political

MAP 10.10 | Andean States

Although the Andes region of South America was isolated from Afro-Eurasian developments before 1500, it was not stagnant. Indeed, political and cultural integration brought the peoples of this region closer together.

- Where are the areas of the Chimú Empire and Tiahuanaco influence on the map?
- What kinds of ecological niches did they govern?
- According to your reading, how did each polity encourage greater cultural and economic integration?

vacuum left by the decline of Teotihuacán (see Chapter 8) and tapped into the commercial network radiating from the valley.

The Toltecs were a combination of migrant groups, refugees from the south, and farmers from the north. They settled northwest of Teotihuacán as the city waned, making their capital at Tula. They relied on a maize-based economy supplemented by beans, squash, and dog, deer, and rabbit meat. Their rulers made sure that enterprising merchants provided them with status goods such as ornamental pottery, rare shells and stones, and precious skins and feathers.

Tula was a commercial hub, a political capital, and a ceremonial center. While its layout differed from Teotihuacán's, many features revealed borrowings from other Mesoamerican peoples. Temples consisted of giant pyramids topped by colossal stone soldiers, and ball courts where subjects and conquered peoples alike played their ritual sport were found everywhere. The architecture and monumental art reflected the mixed and migratory origins of the Toltecs: a combination of Mayan and Teotihuacáno influences. At its height, the Toltec capital teemed with 60,000 people, a huge metropolis by contemporary European standards.

THE CAHOKIANS IN NORTH AMERICA Cities took shape at the hubs of trading networks all across North America. The largest was **Cahokia**, along the Mississippi River near modern-day East St. Louis. A city of about 15,000, it approximated the size of London at the time. Farmers and hunters settled in the region around 600 CE, attracted by its rich soil, its woodlands for fuel and game, and its access to the trading artery of the Mississippi. Eventually, fields of maize and other crops fanned out toward the horizon. The hoe replaced the trusty digging stick, and satellite towns erected granaries to hold the increased yields.

Now Cahokia became a commercial center for regional and long-distance trade. The hinterlands produced staples for Cahokia's urban consumers, and in return its crafts rode inland on the backs of porters and to distant markets in canoes. The city's woven fabrics and ceramics were especially desirable. In exchange, traders brought mica from the Appalachian Mountains, seashells and sharks' teeth from the Gulf of Mexico, and copper from the upper Great Lakes. Cahokia became more than an importer and

MAP 10.11 | Commercial Hubs in Mesoamerica and North America, 1000

Both Cahokia and Tula were commercial hubs of vibrant regional trade networks.

- Where are Cahokia and Tula on the map?
- According to the map, what kinds of goods circulated through these cities?
- How much political influence on the surrounding region do you think each city had?

exporter: it was the exchange hub for an entire regional network trading in salt, tools, pottery, woven stuffs, jewelry, and ceremonial goods.

Dominating Cahokia's urban landscape were enormous mounds (hence their nickname, "mound people"). These earthen monuments reveal a sophisticated design and careful maintenance: their builders applied layers of sand and clay to prevent the foundations from drying and cracking. It was from these artificial hills that the people paid homage to spiritual forces. Building this kind of infrastructure without draft animals, hydraulic tools, or even wheels was labor-intensive, so the Cahokians recruited neighboring people to help. A palisade around the city protected the metropolis from marauders.

Ultimately the city outgrew its environment, and its success bred its downfall. As woodlands fell to the axe and arable soil lost nutrients, timber and food became scarce. Because the city lacked a means to ship bulky items over long distances—in contrast to the sturdy dhows of the Arabian Sea and the bulky junks of the China Sea—its river canoes could carry only limited cargoes. Cahokia's commercial networks met their limits. When the creeks that fed its water system could not keep up with demand, engineers changed their course, but to no avail. By 1350 the city was practically empty. Nevertheless, Cahokia was a remarkable center of exchange while it lasted. It represented the growing networks of trade and migration, and the ability of North Americans to organize vibrant commercial societies.

Toltec Temple. *Tula, the capital of the Toltec Empire, carried on the Mesoamerican tradition of locating ceremonial architecture at the center of the city. The Pyramid of the Morning Star cast its shadow over all other buildings. And above them stood columns of the Atlantes, carved Toltec god-warriors, the figurative pillars of the empire itself. The walls of this pyramid were likely embellished with images of snakes and skulls. The north face of the pyramid has the image of a snake devouring a human.*

Cahokia Mounds. *This is all that is left of what was once a large city organized around temple mounds in what today is Illinois. The largest of the temples, known as Monks' Mound, was likely a burial site, with four separate terraces for crowds to gather. Centuries of neglect and erosion have taken their toll on what was once the largest human-made earthen mound in North America.*

THE MONGOL TRANSFORMATION OF AFRO-EURASIA

The world's sea-lanes grew crowded with ships; ports buzzed with activity. Commercial networks were clearly one way to integrate the world. But just as long-distance trade connected people, so could conquerors—as we have seen throughout the history of the world. Transformative conquerors now came from the Inner Eurasian steppes, the same place that centuries earlier had unleashed horse-riding warriors such as the Xiongnu (see Chapters 6 and 7).

Like the Xiongnu and the Kushans before them, the Mongols not only conquered but intensified trade and cultural exchange. By consolidating a latticework of states across northern and central Asia, they created an empire that straddled east and west (see Map 10.12). It was unstable and not as durable as other dynasties. It did not even have a shared faith; the mother of the conquering emperors, Hulagu and Kubilai Khan, was a devout Christian, reflecting Nestorian missionaries' centuries-long efforts to convert the nomads. Many Europeans prayed that the entire empire would convert. But it did not; the Mongols were a religious patchwork of Afro-Eurasian belief systems. Yet they brought far-flung parts of the world together as they conquered territories much larger than their own.

Who Were the Mongols?

The **Mongols** were a combination of forest and prairie peoples. Residing in circular, felt-covered tents, which they shared with some of their animals, they lived by hunting and livestock herding. They changed campgrounds with the seasons. Life on the steppes was such a constant struggle that only the strong survived. Their food, primarily animal products, provided high levels of protein, which built up their muscle mass and their strength. Always on the march, their society resembled a perpetual standing army with bands of well-disciplined military units led by commanders chosen for their skill.

MILITARY SKILLS Mongol archers were uniquely skilled. Wielding heavy recurved compound bows made of sinew, wood, and horns, they were deadly accurate at over 200 yards—even at full gallop. Their small but sturdy horses, capable of withstanding extreme cold, bore saddles with high supports in front and back, enabling the warriors to maneuver at high speeds. With their feet secure in iron stirrups, the archers could rise in their saddles to aim their arrows without stopping. These expert horsemen often remained in the saddle all day and night, even sleeping while their horses continued on. Each warrior kept many horses, replacing tired mounts with fresh ones so that the armies could cover up to seventy miles per day.

KINSHIP NETWORKS AND SOCIAL ROLES Mongol tribes solidified their conquests by extending kinship networks, building an empire out of an expanding confederation of familial tribes. The tents or households were interrelated mostly by marriage: they were alliances sealed by the exchange of daughters. Conquering men married conquered women, and conquered men were selected to marry the conquerors' women. Chinggis Khan may have had more than 500 wives, most of them daughters of tribes that he conquered or that allied with him.

Mongol Warriors. *This miniature painting is one of the illustrations for History by Rashid al Din, the most outstanding scholar under the Mongol regimes. Note the relatively small horses and strong bows used by the Mongol soldiers.*

Women in Mongol society were responsible for child-rearing, shearing and milking livestock, and processing pelts for clothing. But they also took part in battles. Kubilai Khan's niece Khutulun became famous for besting men in wrestling matches and claiming their horses as spoils. Although women were often bought and sold, Mongol wives had the right to own property and to divorce. Elite women even played important political roles. Consider Sorghaghtani Beki, Kubilai Khan's mother, who helped to engineer her sons' rule. Illiterate herself, she made sure that each son acquired a second language to aid in administering conquered lands. She gathered Confucian scholars to prepare Kubilai Khan to rule China. Chabi, Kubilai's senior wife, followed a similar pattern, offering patronage to Tibetan monks who set about converting the Mongol elite in China to Tibetan Buddhism.

Conquest and Empire

The nomads' need for grazing lands contributed to their desire to conquer the splendors of distant fertile belts and rich cities. As they acquired new lands, they increasingly craved control of richer agricultural and urban areas nearby to increase their wealth and power through tribute. The Mongols depended on settled peoples for grain and manufactured goods—including iron for tools, wagons, weapons, bridles, and stirrups—and their first expansionist forays followed caravan routes.

The expansionist thrust began in 1206 under a united cluster of tribes. A gathering of clan heads acclaimed one of those present as Chinggis (Genghis) Khan, or Supreme Ruler. Chinggis (c. 1155–1227) launched a series of conquests southward across the Great Wall of China, and westward to Afghanistan and Persia. The Mongols also invaded Korea in 1231. The armies of Chinggis's son reached both the Pacific Ocean and the Adriatic Sea. His grandsons founded dynasties in China, in Persia, and on the southern Eurasian steppes. One of them, Kubilai Khan, enlisted thousands of Koryo men and ships for ill-fated invasions of Japan. Thus, a realm took shape that touched all four of Afro-Eurasia's main worlds.

Mongol raiders ultimately built a permanent empire by incorporating conquered peoples and some of their ways. Their feat of unification was far more surprising and sudden than the ties developed incrementally by traders and travelers on ships. Now, Afro-Eurasian regions were connected by land and by sea, in historically unparalleled ways.

Mongols in China

Mongol forces under Chinggis Khan entered northern China at the beginning of the thirteenth century, defeating the Jin army, which was no match for the Mongols' superior cavalry on the North China plain. But below the Yangzi River, where the climate and weather changed, the Mongol horsemen fell ill from diseases such as malaria, and their horses perished from the heat. To conquer the semitropical south, the Mongols took to boats and fought along rivers and canals. **Kubilai Khan** (1215–1294) seized the grandest prize of all—southern China—after 1260. His cavalry penetrated the higher plateaus of southwest China and then attacked South China's economic heartland from the west. The Southern Song army fell before his warriors brandishing the latest gunpowder-based weapons (which the Mongols had borrowed from Chinese inventors only to be used against them).

KHANATE OF THE GOLDEN HORDE
URAL MOUNTAINS
BALTIC SEA
POLAND
Leigritz
Moscow
RUSSIAN PRINCIPALITIES
Kiev
UKRAINE
Buda
Pest
New Sarai
Old Sarai
Lake Balkas
ARAL SEA
BLACK SEA
CAUCASUS MTS.
CASPIAN SEA
Constantinople
BYZANTINE EMPIRE
Tabriz
Samarkand
KHANATE OF T
Balkh
HINDU KUSH MTS.
Aleppo
MEDITERRANEAN SEA
Damascus
Baghdad
Herat
IL-KHANATE
Jerusalem
HIMALAY
SULTANAT OF DELH
RED SEA
ARABIA
INDIAN OCEAN

MAP 10.12 | Mongol Campaigns and Conquests, 1200–1300

Mongol campaigns and conquests brought Afro-Eurasian worlds together as never before. Trace the outline of the entire area of Mongol influence shaded on this map.

- What cultural groups did the Mongol armies conquer, partially conquer, or invade?
- How many different Khanates did the Mongols establish across Eurasia, and what were they?
- What role did geography play in limiting the spread of their influence?

ANALYZING GLOBAL DEVELOPMENTS

Growth in the World Population to 1340

The world experienced considerable human population growth during the first millennium of the Common Era in spite of occasional downturns, such as in Asia and Europe between 200 CE and 600 CE that were the result of climate change, movement of peoples, and the decline of the Roman and Han Empires. Overall, however, an upward trajectory occurred though it averaged out to a mere .06 percent per year. For the period from 1750 to 1950 that percentage has increased to a little more than .5 percent per year, and since 1950 the number has risen to 1.75 percent per year. Even so, as we will see in the next chapter, the major populations in the Afro-Eurasian landmass were terrified by the loss of life that accompanied the spread of the Black Death across this immense area. Since the Afro-Eurasian recovery from the Black Death, the world's population has been on a steady increase, spectacularly so in the twentieth century, the result of more abundant food supplies, more accurate knowledge of the spread of diseases and a resulting control of epidemic diseases, and a general rise in the standards of living.

Regional Human Population (in millions)						
Year	**Asia**	**Europe**	**Africa**	**Americas**	**Oceania**	**World**
400 BCE	97	30	17	8	1	**153**
1 CE	172	41	26	12	1	**252**
200	160	55	30	11	1	**257**
600	136	31	24	16	1	**208**
1000	154	41	39	18	1	**253**
1200	260	64	48	26	2	**400**
1340	240	88	80	32	2	**442**

Source: Massimo Livi-Bacci, A Concise History of World Population *(Malden, MA: Wiley-Blackwell, 2012), p. 25.*

QUESTIONS FOR ANALYSIS

- Why was the rate of population growth so limited in premodern times?
- Comparing the population size of the regions in 1340, what do the numbers tell us about where the largest share of wealth and power resided? How does this compare to earlier moments in the chart?
- Why was the population of the Americas in 1340 so small considering its large territorial size?
- Why were the peoples living in the Afro-Eurasian landmass so vulnerable to epidemic diseases in the fourteenth century?
- How do changes in global population relate to the developments tracked in this chapter: a maritime revolution, a more integrally connected Africa; a thriving Abbasid caliphate; and an expanding Mongol Empire?

THE FALL OF HANGZHOU Hangzhou, the last Song capital, succumbed in 1276. Rather than see the invaders pillage the city and their emperors' tombs, the Southern Song bowed to the inevitable. Kubilai Khan's most able commander, Bayan, led his crack Mongol forces in seizing town after town, ever closer to the capital. The Empress Dowager tried to buy them off, proposing substantial tribute payments, but Bayan kept his eye on the prize: Hangzhou, which fell under Mongol control but survived reasonably intact. Bayan escorted the emperor and the Empress Dowager to Beijing, where Kubilai treated them with honor. Within three years, Song China's defeat was complete. With all of South China in their grip, the Mongols established the Yuan dynasty with a new capital at Dadu ("Great Capital," present-day Beijing).

Although it fell to Mongol control, Hangzhou was still one of the greatest cities in the world when it was visited by the Venetian traveler Marco Polo in the 1280s and by the Muslim traveler Ibn Battuta in the 1340s. Both men agreed that neither Europe nor the Islamic world had anything like it. (See Current Trends in World History: The Travels of Marco Polo and Ibn Battuta.)

OUTSIDERS TAKE CONTROL The Mongol conquest both north and south changed the political and social landscape. But Mongol rule did not impose rough steppe-land ways on the "civilized" urbanite Chinese. Non-Chinese outsiders—a mixed and varied group of Mongols, Tanguts, Khitan, Jurchen, Muslims, Tibetans, Persians, Turks, Nestorians, Jews, Armenians—took political control. They were a conquering elite that ruled over a vast Han majority. The result was a divided ruling system in which incumbent Chinese elites governed locally, while newcomers managed the central dynastic polity and collected taxes for the Mongols.

Mongols on Horseback. *Even after the Mongols became the rulers of China, the emperors remembered their steppe origin and maintained the skills of horse-riding nomads. This detail from a thirteenth/fourteenth-century silk painting shows Kubilai Khan hunting.*

Mongol Reverberations in Southeast Asia

Southeast Asia also felt the whiplash of conquest. Circling Song defenses in southern China, the Mongols galloped southwest and conquered states in Yunnan and in Burma. From there, in the 1270s, the armies headed directly back east into the soft underbelly of the Song state. In this sweep, portions of mainland Southeast Asia became annexed to China for the first time. Even the distant Khmer regime felt repercussions when the Mongol fleet, which grew out of the conquered Song navy, passed by on its way to attack Java (unsuccessfully) in 1293. Kubilai Khan used the conquered Chinese fleets to push his expansionism onto the high seas—meeting with failure during the unsuccessful 1274 and 1281 invasions of Japan from Korea. The ill-fated Javanese expedition was his last.

The Fall of Baghdad

In the thirteenth century, Mongol tribesmen streamed out of the steppes, crossing the whole of Asia and entering the eastern parts of Europe. Mongke Khan, a grandson of Chinggis, made clear the Mongol aspiration for world domination: he appointed his brother Kubilai to rule over China, Tibet, and the northern parts of India; and he commanded another brother, Hulagu, to conquer Iran, Syria, Egypt, Byzantium, and Armenia.

When Hulagu reached Baghdad in 1258, he encountered a feeble foe and a city that was a shadow of its former glorious self. Merely 10,000 horsemen faced his army of 200,000 soldiers, who were eager to acquire the booty of a wealthy city. Even before the battle had taken place, Baghdadi poets were composing elegies for their dead and mourning the defeat of Islam.

The slaughter was vast. Hulagu himself boasted of taking the lives of at least 200,000 people. The Mongols pursued their adversaries everywhere. They hunted them in wells, latrines, and sewers and followed them into the upper floors of buildings, killing them on rooftops until, as an Iraqi Arab historian observed, "blood poured from the gutters into the streets. . . . The same happened in the mosques" (Lewis, pp. 82–83). In a few weeks of sheer terror, the venerable Abbasid caliphate was demolished. Hulagu's forces showed no mercy to the caliph himself, who was rolled up in a carpet and trampled to death by horses, his blood soaked up by the rug so it would leave no mark on the ground. With Baghdad crushed, the Mongol armies pushed on to Syria, slaughtering Muslims along the way.

In the end, the Egyptian Mamluks stemmed the advancing Mongol armies and prevented Egypt from falling into their hands. The Mongol Empire had reached its outer limits. Better at conquering than governing, the Mongols struggled to rule their vast possessions in makeshift states. Bit by bit, they yielded control to local administrators and dynasts who governed as their surrogates. There was also chronic feuding among the Mongol dynasts themselves. In China and in Persia, Mongol rule collapsed in the fourteenth century.

Mongol conquest reshaped Afro-Eurasia's social landscape. Islam would never again have a unifying authority like the caliphate or a powerful center like Baghdad. China, too, was divided and changed, but in other ways. The Mongols introduced Persian, Islamic, and Byzantine influences on China's architecture, art, science, and medicine. The Yuan policy of benign tolerance also brought elements from Christianity, Judaism, Zoroastrianism, and Islam into the Chinese mix. The Mongol thrust led to a great opening, as fine goods, traders, and technology flowed from China to the rest of the world in ensuing centuries. Finally, the Mongol conquests, somewhat like those of Alexander the Great in an earlier age (see Chapter 5), encouraged an Afro-Eurasian interconnectedness, but on a scale that the huge landmass had not known before and would not experience again for hundreds of years. Out of conquest and warfare would come centuries of trade, migration, and increasing contacts among Africa, Europe, and Asia.

CURRENT TRENDS IN WORLD HISTORY

The Travels of Marco Polo and Ibn Battuta

Travelers are one of the most important resources for world historians because they create firsthand accounts of foreign rulers, their societies, and their cultures through their diaries, letters, and books. Recall from the start of the chapter our two Turkish-Christian monks, Bar Sāwmā and Markōs, whom Kubilai Khan sent to learn more about the Muslims and Europeans prior to the Mongol invasions across the Afro-Eurasian landmass. At nearly the same time they were setting out on their travels, Marco Polo, one of the most famous European travelers, was setting out to visit China and the Mongol emperor, creating one of the most widely read travel narratives in world history. It also helped motivate the search for the most direct route to China and Southeast Asia. Only fifty years later, Ibn Battuta would travel most of the known Islamic world, leaving an invaluable portrait of much of North Africa, Southwest Asia, and South Asia.

Polo and Battuta encountered a world linked by trade routes that often had as their ultimate destination the imperial court of the Great Khan in China. These two men, and less celebrated travelers, observed worlds that were highly localized and yet culturally unified.

In 1271, Marco Polo (1254–1324), the son of an enterprising Venetian merchant, set out with his father and uncle on a journey to East Asia. Making their way along the fabled Silk Road across central Asia, after a three-and-a-half-year journey the Polos arrived in Xanadu, the summer capital of the Mongol Empire. There they remained for more than two decades. When they returned to Venice in 1295, fellow townsmen greeted them with astonishment, believing that the Polos had perished years before. So, too, Marco Polo's published account of his travels generated an incredulous reaction. Some of his European readers considered his tales of eastern wonders to be mere fantasy, yet others found their appetites for Asian splendor whetted by his descriptions.

A half-century after Polo began his travels, the Moroccan-born scholar Muhammad ibn Abdullah ibn Battuta (1304–1369) embarked on a journey of his own. Then just twenty-one, he vowed to visit the whole of the Islamic world without traveling the same road twice. It was an ambitious goal, for Islam's domain extended from one end of the Afro-Eurasian landmass to the other and far into Africa as well. On his journey, Ibn Battuta eventually covered some 75,000 miles. Along his way, he claimed to have met at least sixty rulers, and in his book he recorded the names of more than 2,000 persons whom he knew personally.

The writings of Marco Polo and Ibn Battuta provide a wealth of information on the well-traversed lands of Africa, Europe, and Asia. What they and other travelers observed was the extreme diversity of Afro-Eurasian peoples, reflecting numerous ethnicities, political formations, and religious faiths. In addition, they observed that the vast majority of people lived deeply localized lives, primarily seeking to obtain the basic necessities of everyday life. Yet, they were also aware the same societies welcomed trade and cultural exchange. In fact, they wrote most eloquently about how each of the four major cultural systems of the landmass—Christian, Muslim, Indian, and Chinese—struggled

CONCLUSION

Between 1000 and 1300, Afro-Eurasia was forming large cultural spheres. As trade and migration spanned longer distances, these spheres prospered and became more integrated. In central Afro-Eurasia, Islam was firmly established, its merchants, scholars, and travelers acting as commercial and cultural intermediaries joining the landmass together, as they spread their universalizing faith. As seaborne trade expanded, India, too, became a commercial crossroads. Merchants in its port cities welcomed traders arriving from Arab lands to the west, from China, and from Southeast Asia. China also boomed, pouring its manufactures into trading networks that reached throughout Afro-Eurasia and even into Africa. Christian Europe had two centers, both of which were at war with Islam. In the east, Byzantium was a formidable empire with a resplendent and unconquerable capital city, Constantinople, in many ways the pride of Christianity. In the west, the Catholic papacy had risen from the ashes of the Roman Empire and sought to extend its ecclesiastical authority over Rome's territories in western Europe.

Trade helped outline the parts of the world. The prosperity it brought also supported new classes of people—thinkers, writers, and naturalists—who clarified what it meant to belong to the regions of Afro-Eurasia. By 1300, learned priests and writers had begun to reimagine these regions as more than just territories: they were maturing into cultures with definable geographic boundaries. Increasingly these intellectuals delivered their messages to commoners as well as to rulers.

Neither the Americas nor sub-Saharan Africa saw the same degree of integration, but trade and migration in these areas had profound effects. Certain African cultures flourished as they encountered the commercial energy of trade on the Indian

to define itself. Interestingly, if Ibn Battuta and Marco Polo had been able to travel in the "unknown" worlds—the African hinterlands, the Americas, and Oceania—they would have witnessed to varying degrees similar phenomena and challenges.

QUESTIONS FOR ANALYSIS

- To what extent were travelers like Marco Polo and Ibn Battuta connecting new worlds as opposed to following routes that had already been established by others?
- What were the different incentives that impelled Marco Polo and Ibn Battuta to undertake their journeys of exploration? And what might that tell us about how and why greatly divergent worlds contact each other?
- Why were the Polos and Ibn Battuta able to undertake very long-range journeys? What enables travelers like these to function and to strengthen connections across the globe?

Marco Polo. *This medieval painting shows the caravan of Marco Polo's father and uncle crossing Asia.*

Explore Further

Ibn Battuta, *The Travels of Ibn Battuta,* translated by H. A. R. Bigg (2002).

Polo, Marco, *The Travels of Marco Polo,* edited by Manuel Komroff, translated by William Marsden (1926).

Ocean. Africans' trade with one another linked coastal and interior regions in an ever more integrated world. American peoples also built cities that dominated cultural areas and thrived through trade. American cultures shared significant features: reliance on trade, maize, and the exchange of goods such as shells and precious feathers. And larger areas honored the same spiritual centers.

By 1300, trade, migration, and conflict were connecting Afro-Eurasian worlds in unprecedented ways. When Mongol armies swept into China, into Southeast Asia, and into the heart of Islam, they applied a thin, surface-like coating of political integration to these widespread regions and built on existing trade links. At the same time, most people's lives remained quite local, driven by the need for subsistence and governed by spiritual and governmental representatives acting at the behest of distant authorities. Still, locals noticed the evidence of cross-cultural exchanges everywhere—in the clothing styles of provincial elites, such as Chinese silks in Paris or Quetzal plumes in northern Mexico; in enticements to move (and forced removals) to new frontiers; in the news of faraway conquests or advancing armies. Worlds were coming together within themselves and across territorial boundaries, while remaining apart as they sought to maintain their own identity and traditions. In Afro-Eurasia especially, as the movement of goods and peoples shifted from ancient land routes to sea-lanes, these contacts were more frequent and far-reaching. Never before had the world seen so much activity connecting its parts. Nor within them had there been so much shared cultural similarity—linguistic, religious, legal, and military. By the time the Mongol Empire arose, the regions composing the globe were those that we now recognize as the cultural spheres of today's world.

AFTER YOU READ THIS CHAPTER

Review and research on **STUDYSPACE:** wwnorton.com/studyspace

TRACING THE GLOBAL STORYLINES

FOCUS ON: *Foundational Cultural Spheres*

The Islamic World

- Islam undergoes a burst of expansion, prosperity, and cultural diversification but remains politically fractured.
- Arab merchants and Sufi mystics spread Islam over great distances and make it more appealing to other cultures, helping to transform Islam into a foundational world.
- Islam travels across the Sahara Desert; the powerful gold- and slave-supplying empire of Mali arises in West Africa.

China

- The Song dynasty reunites China after three centuries of fragmented rulership, reaching into the past to reestablish a sense of a "true" Chinese identity as the Han, through a widespread print culture and denigration of outsiders.
- Breakthroughs in iron metallurgy allow agricultural expansion to support 120 million people and undergird Han commercial success.
- China undergoes the world's first manufacturing revolution: gunpowder, porcelain, and handicrafts are produced on a large scale for widespread consumption.

India

- India remains a mosaic under the canopy of Hinduism despite cultural interconnections and increasing prosperity.
- The invasion of Turkish Muslims leads to the Delhi Sultanate, which rules over India for three centuries, strengthening cultural diversity and tolerance.

Christian Europe

- Catholicism becomes a "mass" faith and helps to create a common European cultural identity.
- An emphasis on religious education spawns numerous universities and a new intellectual elite.
- Feudalism causes a fundamental reordering of the elite-peasant relationship, leading to agricultural and commercial expansion.
- Europe's growing confidence is manifest in the Crusades and Reconquista, an effort to drive Islam out of Christian lands.

CHRONOLOGY

Sub-Saharan Africa
The Americas
The Islamic World
South Asia
East Asia
Southeast Asia
Europe

Kingdom of Mali emerges (King Mansa Musa 1312–1332) **1100**

Great Zimbabwe flourishes **1100**

Cahokia flourishes as a commercial hub in North America **1000**

Moche people found city of Chan Chan in South America **900**

Toltecs dominate valley of Mexico **900–1100**

Chimú Empire in South America **1000–1460**

Turkish migrants and armies spread into Islamic world's heartland **1000**

Central Asian invasions begin **1000**

Reconquista of the Iberian Peninsula **1061–1492**

Crusades **1095–1272**

1000 1100

KEY TERMS

Angkor Wat *p. 383*
Cahokia *p. 392*
compass *p. 360*
Crusades *p. 388*
Delhi Sultanate *p. 374*
dhimma system *p. 371*
dhows *p. 360*
feudalism *p. 384*
Kubilai Khan *p. 395*
Mongols *p. 394*
rajas *p. 374*
Sufism *p. 368*

STUDY QUESTIONS

1. **List** the four major cultural regions in Afro-Eurasia, and briefly explain the defining characteristics of each. What did the various people and groups in these geographic areas all have in common that distinguished them from others?
2. **Explain** the role of global commercial hubs in India, China, and Egypt in fostering commercial contacts across Afro-Eurasia. How did they reflect revolutions in maritime transportation?
3. **Which areas** of sub-Saharan Africa were parts of the larger Afro-Eurasian world by 1300? How did contact with other regions shape political and cultural developments in sub-Saharan Africa?
4. **Describe** the cultural diversity within the Islamic world during this era. How did diverse Islamic communities achieve a uniform regional identity?
5. **Analyze** the impact of Muslim Turkish invaders on India. To what extent did India remain distinct from the Islamic world in this era?
6. **Describe** how the Song dynasty reacted to the military strength of its nomadic pastoral neighbors. How did these relationships foster a distinct Chinese identity?
7. **Compare and contrast** cultural and political developments in Korea, Japan, and Southeast Asia during this era. How did other regional cultures influence these societies?
8. **Describe** how Christianity expanded its geographic reach during this era. How did this expansion affect Latin Christianity in western Europe and Orthodox Christianity in eastern Europe?
9. **Analyze** the extent to which peoples in the Americas established closer contact with each other. How extensive were these contacts compared with those in the Afro-Eurasian world?
10. **Describe** the empire that the Mongols created in the thirteenth century. How did their policies promote greater contact among the various regions of Afro-Eurasia?

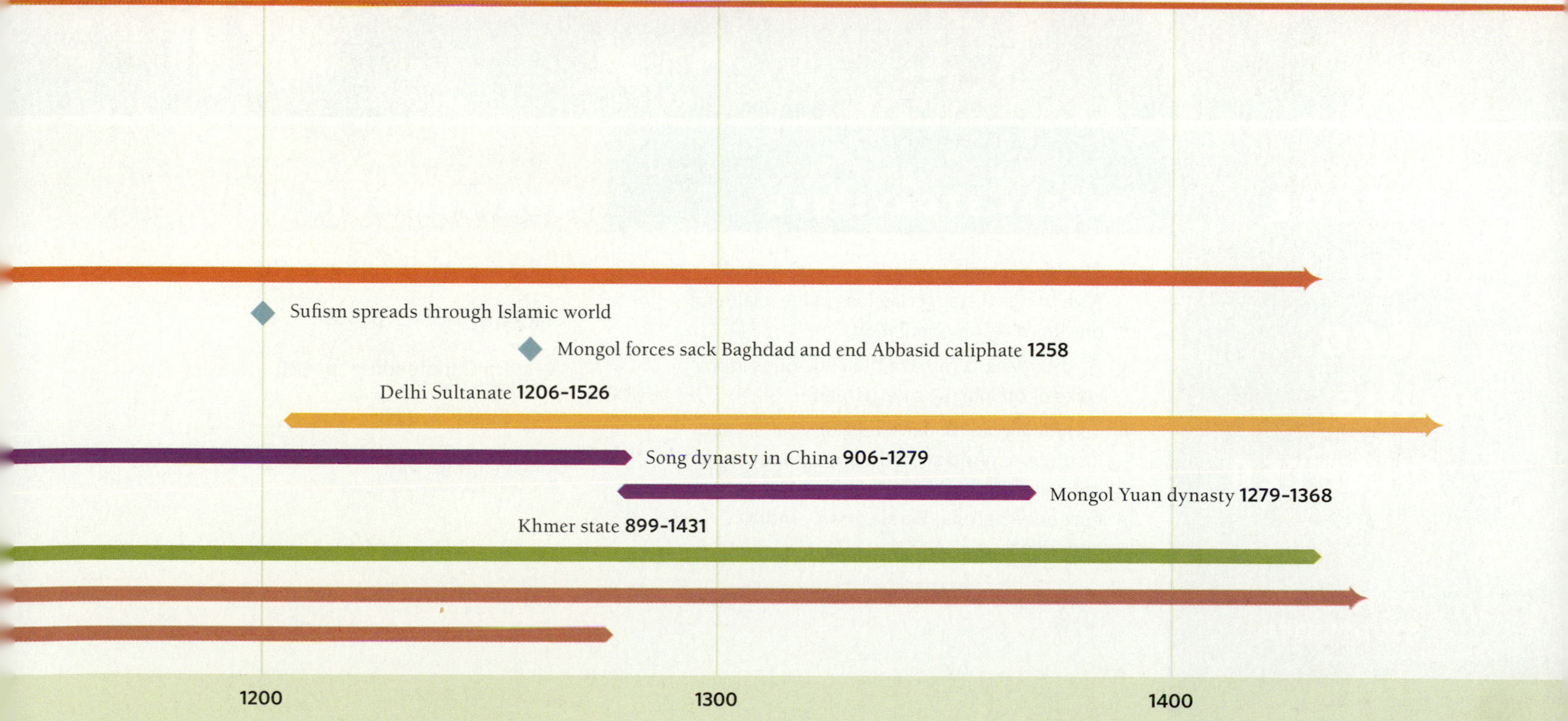

BEFORE YOU READ THIS CHAPTER

wwnorton.com/
STUDYSPACE

GLOBAL STORYLINES

- The Black Death spreading out of Inner Asia brings a staggering loss of life, claiming one-third of the population.
- Afro-Eurasians remake their societies in the wake of the plague's devastation.
- Something old remains: religious beliefs and institutions. And something new appears: radically different imperial dynasties in Europe, Anatolia, Persia (Iran), India, and China.

CHAPTER OUTLINE

11

Crises and Recovery in Afro-Eurasia, 1300–1500

FOCUS QUESTIONS

- How did Afro-Eurasian societies cope with the long-term repercussions from Mongol invasions and the Black Death?
- How were Afro-Eurasian states after the Black Death similar to and different from their predecessors?
- To what extent did the major cultural regions of Afro-Eurasia sustain their traditions and institutions under new political dynasties?
- How did state decisions regarding trade and expansion in Europe and China during this era shape world history?

When Mongol armies besieged the Genoese trading outpost of Caffa on the Black Sea in 1346, they not only damaged trading links between East Asia and the Mediterranean but also unleashed a devastating disease: the bubonic plague. Defeated Genoese merchants and soldiers withdrew, inadvertently taking the germs with them aboard their ships. By the time they arrived in Messina, Sicily, half the passengers were dead. The rest were dying. People waiting on shore for the ships' trade goods were horrified at the sight and turned the ships away. Desperately, the captains went to the next port, only to face the same fate. Despite these efforts at isolation, Europeans could not keep the plague (called the Black Death) from reaching their shores. As it spread from port to port it eventually contaminated all of Europe, killing nearly two-thirds of the population.

This story illustrates the disruptive effects of the Mongol invasions on Afro-Eurasian societies. Although the invasions ushered in an age of intensified cultural and political contact, the channels of exchange—the land trails and sea-lanes of human voyagers—became accidental conduits for deadly microbes. These germs devastated societies far more decisively than did Mongol warfare. They were the real "murderous hordes" of world history, infecting people from every community, class, and culture. So staggering was the Black Death's toll that population densities did not recover for 200 years. Most severely affected were regions that the Mongols had brought together: settlements and commercial hubs along the old Silk Road and around the Mediterranean Sea and the South China Sea. While segments of the Indian Ocean trading world experienced death and disruption, South Asian societies, which had escaped the Mongol conquest, also escaped the dying and political disruptions associated with the Black Death.

During the fourteenth and fifteenth centuries—following population loss, political crises, and social disorders—peoples struggled to remake their societies. This chapter explores the ways in which Afro-Eurasian peoples restored what they thought was valuable from the old while discarding what they felt had failed them, in favor of radically new institutions and ideas. Considering how grievously people suffered and how many had died, it is surprising that so much of the old (particularly religious beliefs and institutions) survived, though in modified forms. What was truly new and would prove enduring was a group of imperial dynasties that emerged all across Afro-Eurasia: national monarchies in Europe, Ottoman sultans in Anatolia, Safavids in Persia, Mughals in India, and Ming dynasts in China. The aftermath of Mongol rule and of the Black Death witnessed the transformation of the political setting in Afro-Eurasia. Focusing on the formation of new states with highly centralized forms of rulership, this chapter explores how societies coped with the long-term impact of the Mongol invasions and the Black Death.

Plague Victim. *The plague was highly contagious and after a series of grotesque symptoms, quickly resulted in death. Here the physician and his helper (left) cover their noses, most likely in attempt to block out the unbearable stench emanating from the patient's boils.*

COLLAPSE AND INTEGRATION

Although the Mongol invasions overturned political systems, the plague devastated society itself. Rulers could explain to their people the assaults of "barbarians," but it was much harder to make sense of an invisible enemy. Many concluded that mass death was God's wish. However, the upheaval gave ruling groups the opportunity to consolidate power by making dynastic matches through marriage, establishing new armies and taxes, and creating new systems to administer their states.

The Black Death

The spread of the Black Death out of inner Asia was the fourteenth century's most significant historical development (see Map 11.1). The disease stemmed from a combination of bubonic, pneumonic, and septicemic plague strains, and it caused a staggering loss of life. Among infected populations, death rates ranged from 25 to 65 percent.

How did the **Black Death** spread so far? One explanation may lie in climatic changes. A drying up of the central Asian steppe borderlands, where bubonic plague had existed for centuries, may have forced rodents out of their usual dwelling places and pressed pastoral peoples, who carried the strains, to move closer to settled agricultural communities. So, it is thought, began the migration of microbes. But what spread the germs across Afro-Eurasia was the Mongols' trading network. The first outbreak in a heavily populated region occurred in the 1320s in southwestern China. From there, the disease spread through China and then took its death march along the major trade routes. The main avenue of transmission was across central Asia to the Crimea and the Black Sea, and from there by ship to the Mediterranean Sea and the Italian city-states.

Secondary routes were by sea: one from China to the Red Sea, and another across the Indian Ocean, through the Persian Gulf, and into the Fertile Crescent and Iraq. All routes terminated at the Italian port cities, where ships with dead and dying men aboard arrived in 1347. From there, what Europeans called the Pestilence or the Great Mortality engulfed the western end of the landmass.

The Black Death struck an expanding Afro-Eurasian population, made vulnerable because its members had no immunities to the disease and because its major realms were thoroughly connected through trading networks. Rodents, mainly rats, carried the plague bacilli that caused the disease. Fleas transmitted the bacilli from rodent to rodent, as well as to humans. The epidemic was terrifying, for its causes were unknown at the time. Infected victims died quickly—sometimes overnight—and in great agony, coughing up blood and oozing pus and blood from ugly black sores the size of eggs. Some European sages attributed the ravaging of their societies to an unusual alignment of Saturn, Jupiter, and Mars. Many believed that God was angry with mankind. One Florentine historian compared the plague to the biblical Flood and believed that the end of mankind was imminent.

The Black Death wrought devastation throughout much of the landmass. The Chinese population plunged from around 120 million to 80 million over the course of a century. Europe saw its numbers shrink by two-thirds. When farmers were afflicted, food production collapsed. Famine then followed and killed off the weak survivors. Cities were the hardest hit. The population of London before the Black Death arrived was 100,000. Its numbers were reduced to 37,500 between 1346 and 1353. Refugees from the cities fled their homes, seeking security and food in the countryside. The shortage of food and other necessities led to rapidly rising prices, work stoppages, and unrest. Political leaders added to their unpopularity by repressing the unrest. The great Arab historian Ibn Khaldun (1332–1406), who lost his mother and father and a number of his teachers to the Black Death in Tunis, underscored the sense of desolation: "Cities and buildings were laid waste, roads and way signs were obliterated, settlements and mansions became empty, dynasties and tribes grew weak," he wrote. "The entire world changed."

Rebuilding States

Starting in the late fourteenth century, Afro-Eurasians began the task of reconstructing both their political order and their trading networks. (By then the plague had died down, though it continued to afflict peoples for centuries.) However, the rebuilding of military and civil administrations—no easy task—also required political legitimacy. Rulers needed to revive confidence in themselves and their polities, which they did by fostering beliefs and rituals that confirmed their legitimacy and by increasing their control over subjects.

The basis for power was the **dynasty**—the hereditary ruling family that passed control from one generation to the next. Dynasties sought to establish their legitimacy in three ways. First, ruling families insisted that their power derived from a divine calling: Ming emperors in China claimed for themselves what previous dynasts had asserted—the "mandate of heaven"—while European monarchs claimed to rule by "divine right." Either way, ruling households asserted that they were closer to the gods than to commoners. Second, leaders squelched squabbling among potential heirs by establishing clear rules about succession to the throne. Many European countries tried to standardize succession by passing titles to the eldest male heir, but in practice there were countless complications and quarrels. In the Islamic world, successors could be designated by the incumbent or elected by the community; here, too, struggles over succession were frequent. Third, ruling families elevated their power through conquest or alliance—by ordering armies to forcibly extend their domains, or by marrying their royal offspring to rulers of other states or members of other elite households. Once it established legitimacy, the typical royal family would consolidate power by enacting coercive laws and punishments and sending emissaries to govern far-flung territories. It would also establish standing armies and new administrative structures to collect taxes and to oversee building projects that proclaimed royal power.

The innovative state-building that occurred in the wake of the plague's devastation would not have been as successful had it not drawn on older traditions. In China, the Ming renounced the Mongol legacy by emphasizing their role in restoring Han rulership and by rejecting the Mongol eagerness to expand. In Europe, a cultural flourishing based largely on ancient Greek and Roman models gave rise to thinkers who proposed novel views of governance. The peoples of the Islamic world held fiercely to their religion as two successor states—the Ottoman Empire and the Safavid state—absorbed numerous Turkish-speaking groups. A third Islamic state—the Mughal Empire—drew on local traditions of religious and cultural tolerance as it built a new regime on the foundations of the weakened Delhi Sultanate (see Chapter 10). Many of these regimes lasted for centuries, promoting political institutions and cultural values that became deeply embedded in the fabric of their societies.

ISLAMIC DYNASTIES

The devastation of the Black Death following hard on the heels of the Mongol destruction of Islam's most important city and capital of the Abbasid Empire, Baghdad (see Chapter 10), eliminated

SCANDINAVIA
1349
NORTH SEA
BALTIC SEA
Novgorod
Moscow
MUSCOVY
1351
Edinburgh
(1350)
BRITAIN
Dublin
(1349)
Oxford
(1348)
London
(1348)
Lübeck
(1349)
Danzig
Bremen
(1349)
Cologne
(1349)
Amiens
(1348)
Paris
(1348)
EUROPE
Cracow
Kiev
KHANATE OF THE
GOLDEN HORDE
New Sarai
Rostov
ARAL
SEA
CASPIAN
SEA
Buda
(1349)
Venice
(1347)
Bordeaux
(1348)
Genoa
(1347)
Avignon
(1347)
Florence
(1347)
Pisa
(1347)
Siena
(1347)
Marseille
Barcelona
(1348)
Madrid
Lisbon
(1349)
SPAIN
1348
Naples
Palermo
(1347)
Messina
(1347)
Constantinople
(1347)
BLACK
SEA
Caffa
(1346)
Trebizond
ANATOLIA
Tabriz
Maraghah
Bukhara
Silk route
Athens
(1347)
Ceuta
Fez
Algiers
Tunis
Marrakesh
(1349)
MEDITERRANEAN
SEA
Tripoli
(1348)
Aleppo
(1347)
Damascus
(1347)
Jerusalem
(1347)
Baghdad
(1347)
Isfahan
PERSIA
IL-KHANA
Shiraz
Basra
Hormuz
Persian Gulf
Alexandria
(1347)
Cairo
(1347)
Medina
Mecca
(1348)
ARABIA
RED SEA
Aden
(1351)
ARABI
AFRICA
Mogadishu
INDI
ATLANTIC
OCEAN
Progress of bubonic plague
Trade routes
Known areas of major outbreaks
Modern Chinese provincial names for regions affected by outbreak of plague

MAP 11.1 | The Spread of the Black Death

The Black Death was an Afro-Eurasian pandemic of the fourteenth century.

- What was the origin point of the Black Death?
- What were the main trade routes that allowed the Black Death to spread across Afro-Eurasia?
- Can you explain why certain parts of Afro-Eurasia were more severely affected than others?

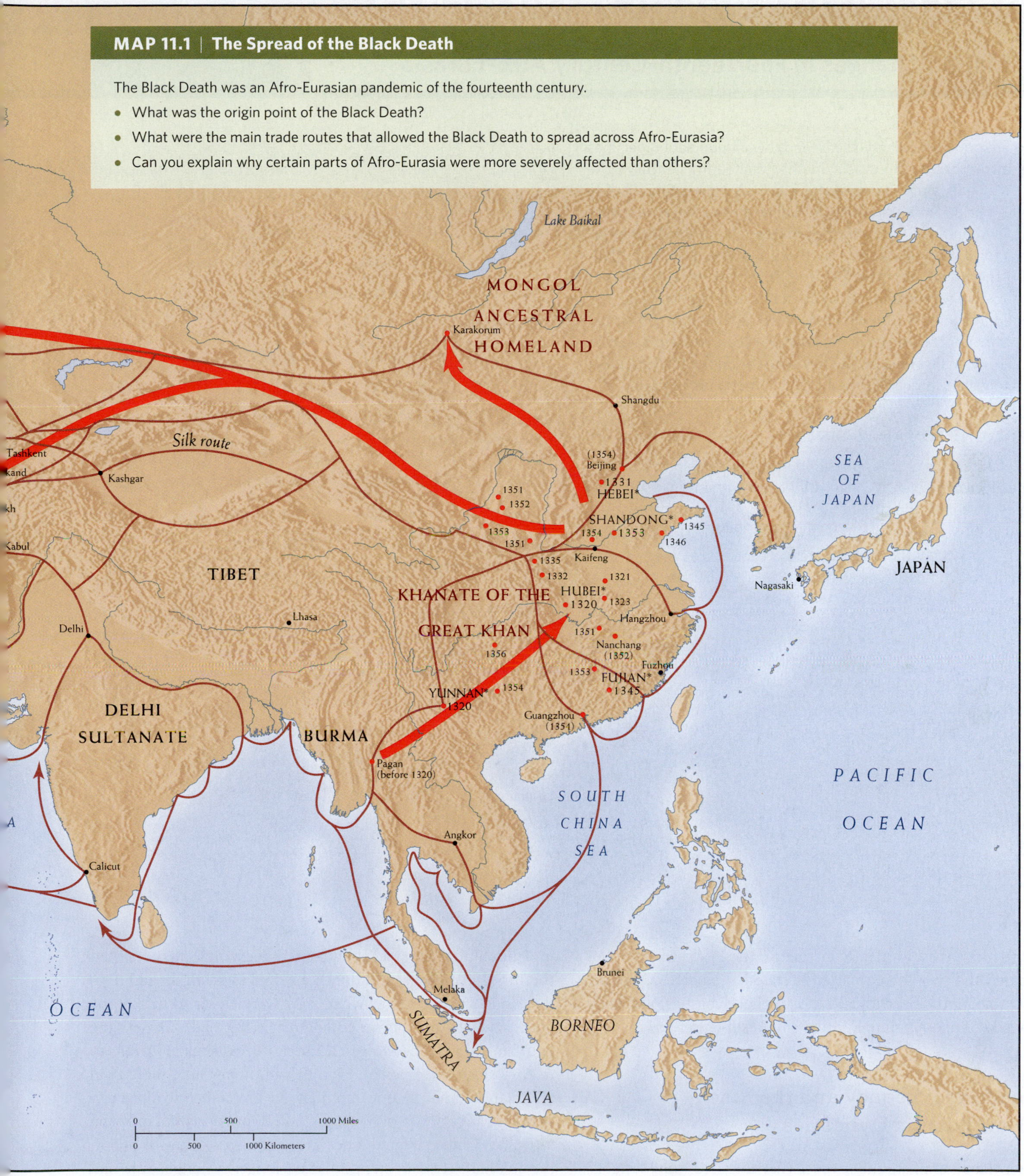

ANALYZING GLOBAL DEVELOPMENTS

Population Changes in Fourteenth-Century Afro-Eurasia

Famine, warfare, and disease led to vast population declines all across Afro-Eurasia in the fourteenth century. The Mongols were instrumental players in spreading disease across the landmass, starting in China and moving westward along land and sea-based trading routes toward the Mediterranean World, and ultimately northern Europe (see Map 11-1). While the effects of these destructive forces were felt across the Afro-Eurasian landmass, some states and regions were less affected than others. The population data in the table come from the best historical studies of the last forty years and are based on painstaking archival research. They serve as one of the best ways for us to gain historical insight into this tumultuous century.

QUESTIONS FOR ANALYSIS

- In what regions or cities does population loss seem to have been lower? Higher? Why might those variations in death rates have been the case?
- How do the losses in urban areas compare with the losses in the region where those urban areas are located? What might that comparison suggest about the impact of fourteenth-century disasters on urban versus other populations?
- Why do you think that the population decline was more severe and widespread in Europe than in Asia?
- In what ways was the great loss of population in Europe and China a turning point in their histories?

Location	Population Figures	Across the Fourteenth Century	% Change
By Regions			
Europe	80 m in 1346	30 m in 1353	−60%
Asia	230 m in 1300	235 m in 1400	+2%
Islam	(regional data are not available)		
By Countries			
Spain	6 m in 1346	2.5 m in 1353	−60%
Italy	10 m in 1346	4.5 m in 1363	−55%
France	18 m in 1346	7.2 m in 1353	−60%
England	6 m in 1346	2.25 m in 1353	−62.5%
China	115 m in 1200	75 m in 1400	−35%
Japan	9.75 m in 1300	12.5 m in 1400	+28%
Korea	3 m in 1300	3.5 m in 1400	+17%
India	91 m in 1300	97 m in 1400	+6.5%
By Cities			
London	100,000 in 1346	37,000 in 1353	−62.5%
Florence	92,000 in 1346	37,250 in 1353	−59.5%
Siena	50,000 in 1346	20,000 in 1353	−60%
Bologna	50,000 in 1346	27,500 in 1353	−45%
Cairo	500,000 in 1300	300,000 in 1400	−40%
Damascus	80,000 in 1300	50,000 in 1400	−37%

Sources: Ole J. Benedictow, The Black Death, 1346–1353: The Complete History *(2004); Michael Dols,* The Black Death in the Middle East *(1974); Colin McEvedy and Richard Jones,* Atlas of World Population History *(1978). Ping-ti Ho,* Studies on the Population of China, 1368–1953 *(1959).*

Islam's old political order. Nonetheless, these two catastrophes prepared the way for new Islamic states to emerge. Of these, the Ottoman, the Safavid, and the Mughal dynasties ultimately grew powerful enough to become empires themselves.

The Mongol Legacy and the Rise of New Islamic Dynasties

Rather than assimilate the peoples they defeated, the Mongols, whose numbers were always small, often assimilated themselves into the cultures they had conquered. For example, they adopted the Turkish language, and they converted to Islam. In addition, the Mongols fared better when they were closer to the steppe grasses, where their horses could graze. They had a harder time in urban centers. The Mongol Il-khans in Persia made Maraghah in Azerbaijan their capital, even though it was little more than an enlarged military encampment, in preference to the great administrative center of Baghdad. Still, Mongol armies in Persia as well as China suffered a decline in prowess (Mongol rule in the southern Russian steppes lasted longer). Mongol rule had always had two components. One was an ability to terrorize opponents into voluntarily submitting by such tactics as parading the heads of resisters on pikes. But this strategy began to lose effectiveness and sometimes even backfired. The other Mongol tactic had involved borrowing skills from across the empire and promoting the exchange of technologies and knowledge. But new groups aspiring to rule could do this, too.

Muslim peoples had no respite following the Mongol conquests. The Black Death reached Baghdad by 1347, perhaps carried there by an Azerbaijani army that besieged the city. By the next year, the plague had overtaken Egypt, Syria, and Cyprus; one report from Tunis records the deaths of more than 1,000 people a day in that North African city. Animals, too, were afflicted. One Egyptian writer commented: "The country was not far from being ruined. . . . One found in the desert the bodies of savage animals with the bubos under their arms. It was the same with horses, camels, asses, and all the beasts in general, including birds, even the ostriches." In the eastern Mediterranean, the plague left much of the Islamic world in a state of near political and economic collapse.

As new polities emerged from this economic and demographic crisis, they had to build from the ground floor. Warrior chiefs and religious leaders vied to fill the political vacuum. After Mongol power waned, the new rulers—notably the Ottomans in Anatolia and the Safavids in western Persia—operated out of strategic locations in the Islamic heartland and gradually rebuilt state institutions.

Through migration, warfare, and the eventual consolidation of post-Mongol states, Islam's domain expanded. Prior to the Mongol invasions, the political, economic, and cultural centers of the Islamic world were in Egypt, Syria, and Iraq. Most of these territories' inhabitants spoke Arabic, the language of the Prophet Muhammad—hence the language of Islamic devotion and theology. These areas, along with the Arabian Peninsula, contained Islam's most holy cities: Mecca, Medina, Jerusalem, Damascus, Cairo, Baghdad, and various other cities in Iraq. Even before the Mongol invasions, Turks had migrated into these regions and Persian had become a rival language of Islamic poetry and philosophy. Yet it was the Mongol invasions, which brought devastation to Persia and Iraq and an influx of nomadic peoples, that enabled a new Islamic world to appear. (See Primary Source: Qalandar Dervishes in the Islamic World.)

THREE ISLAMIC EMPIRES This new Islamic world, now including large numbers of Turkish- and Persian-speaking populations, occupied a vast geographical triangle. It stretched from Anatolia in the west to Khurasan in the east and to the southern apex at Baghdad. Of course, the old Arabic-speaking Islamic world remained vital, still at the heart of Islam geographically, but it now had to cede authority to the new rulers and religious men.

The Ottomans, the Safavids, and the Mughals emerged as the dominant states in the old Islamic world in the early sixteenth century. They exploited the rich agrarian resources of the Indian Ocean regions and the Mediterranean Sea basin, and they benefited from a brisk seaborne and overland trade. By the mid-sixteenth century the Mughals controlled the northern Indus River valley; the Safavids occupied Persia; and the Ottomans ruled Anatolia, the Arab world, and much of southern and eastern Europe.

Despite sharing core Islamic beliefs, each empire had unique political features. The most powerful, the **Ottoman Empire**, occupied the pivotal area between Europe and Asia. The Ottomans embraced a Sunni view of Islam, while adopting traditional Byzantine ways of governance and trying new ways of integrating the diverse peoples of their expanding territories. The Safavids, though adherents of the Shiite vision of Islam, were at the same time ardently devoted to the pre-Islamic traditions of Persia (present-day Iran). An internally cohesive people, their rulers were not so effective at expanding beyond their Persian base. The Mughals ruled over the wealthy but divided realm that is much of today's India, Pakistan, and Bangladesh; here they carried even further the region's religious and political traditions of assimilating Islamic and pre-Islamic Indian ways. Their wealth and the decentralization of their domain made the Mughals constant targets for internal dissent and eventually for external aggression.

The Rise of the Ottoman Empire

Although the Mongols considered Anatolia to be a borderland region of little economic importance, their military forays against the Anatolian Seljuk Turkish state in the late thirteenth century opened up the region to new political forces. The ultimate victors here were the Ottoman Turks. They transformed themselves from warrior bands roaming the borderlands between Islamic and Christian worlds into rulers of a settled state and, finally, into sovereigns of a far-flung, highly bureaucratic empire (see Map 11.2).

Under their chief, Osman (r. 1299–1326), the Turkish Ottomans formalized a stern and disciplined warrior ethos, and they triumphed over many rivals by assimilating the techniques of settled administration from their neighbors. Other warrior bands, which lived off the land and fought for booty under charismatic military leaders, had little regard for artisans, merchants, bureaucrats, and clerics. By contrast, the Ottomans realized that the consolidation of power depended on attracting just these groups. In time, not only did the Ottoman state (based in Bursa in western Anatolia) win the favor of Islamic clerics, but it also became the champion of Sunni Islam throughout the Islamic world.

By the mid-fourteenth century, the Ottomans had expanded into the Balkans, becoming the most powerful force in the

PRIMARY SOURCE

Qalandar Dervishes in the Islamic World

The Qalandar dervish order sprang up in Damascus, Syria, and Egypt in the thirteenth century and spread rapidly throughout the Islamic world. In reaction to the period's widespread unrest, its members renounced the world and engaged in highly individualistic practices as they moved from place to place. The educated elite, however, criticized them as ignorant hypocrites living on alms obtained from gullible common folk. One of their practices was chiromancy, or palm-reading. In this excerpt Giovan Antonio Manavino, a European observer of Ottoman society, gives an obviously biased account of the Qalandars, whom he called the torlaks.

Dressed in sheepskins, the *torlaks* [Qalandars] are otherwise naked, with no headgear. Their scalps are always clean-shaven and well rubbed with oil as a precaution against the cold. They burn their temples with an old rag so that their faces will not be damaged by sweat. Illiterate and unable to do anything manly, they live like beasts, surviving on alms only. For this reason, they are to be found around taverns and public kitchens in cities. If, while roaming the countryside, they come across a well-dressed person, they try to make him one of their own, stripping him naked. Like Gypsies in Europe, they practice chiromancy, especially for women who then provide them with bread, eggs, cheese, and other foods in return for their services.

Amongst them there is usually an old man whom they revere and worship like God. When they enter a town, they gather around the best house of the town and listen in great humility to the words of this old man, who, after a spell of ecstasy, foretells the descent of a great evil upon the town. His disciples then implore him to fend off the disaster through his good services. The old man accepts the plea of his followers, though not without an initial show of reluctance, and prays to God, asking him to spare the town the imminent danger awaiting it. This time-honored trick earns them considerable sums of alms from ignorant and credulous people.

QUESTIONS FOR ANALYSIS

- Describe the way the Qalandar dervishes dressed, where they congregated, and how they obtained food. How did their lifestyle reflect the turmoil of the times?
- Why do you think the Qalandars chose individualistic practices rather than communal living?
- Why do you think Manavino is so critical of the Qalandars?

Source: Ahmet T. Karamustafa, "Dervish Groups in the Ottoman Empire, 1450–1550" from God's Unruly Friends: Dervish Groups in the Islamic Later Middle Period, 1200–1550, *pp. 6–7. Oneworld Publications, Oxford, 2006. Reprinted with the permission of Oneworld Publications.*

eastern Mediterranean and western Asia. The state controlled a vast territory, stretching in the west to the Moroccan border, in the north to Hungary and Moldavia, in the south through the Arabian Peninsula, and in the east to the Iraqi-Persian border. At the top of the Ottomans' elaborate hierarchy stood the sultan. Below him was a military and civilian bureaucracy, whose task was to demand obedience and revenue from subjects. The bureaucracy's vigilance enabled the sultan to expand his realm, which in turn forced him to invest in an even larger bureaucracy.

THE CONQUEST OF CONSTANTINOPLE The empire's spectacular expansion was primarily a military affair. To recruit followers, the Ottomans promised wealth and glory to new subjects. This was an expensive undertaking, but territorial expansion generated vast financial and administrative rewards. Moreover, by spreading the spoils of conquest and lucrative administrative positions, rulers bought off potentially discontented subordinates. Still, without military might, the Ottomans would not have enjoyed the successes associated with the brilliant reigns of Murad II (r. 1421–1451) and his aptly named successor, Mehmed the Conqueror (r. 1451–1481).

Mehmed's most spectacular triumph was the conquest of Constantinople, an ambition for Muslim rulers ever since the birth of Islam. Mehmed left no doubt that this was his primary goal: shortly after his coronation he vowed to capture the capital of the Byzantine Empire, a city of immense strategic and commercial importance. He knew this feat would require a large

MAP 11.2 | The Ottoman Empire, 1300–1566

This map charts the expansion of the Ottoman state from the time of its founder, Osman, through the reign of Suleiman, the empire's most illustrious ruler.

- Identify the earliest part of the empire under Osman. Then identify all the areas of conquest under Suleiman. Against whom did the Ottomans fight between the years 1326 and 1566?
- What were the geographic limits of the empire?
- According to your reading, how did Ottoman rulers promote unity among such a diverse population?

and well-armed fighting force, for the heavily fortified city had kept Muslims at bay for almost a century. First he built a fortress of his own, on the European bank of the Bosporus strait, to prevent European vessels from reaching the capital. Then, by promising his soldiers free access to booty and portraying the city's conquest as a holy cause, he amassed a huge army that outnumbered the defending force of 7,000 by more than tenfold. For forty days his troops bombarded Constantinople's massive walls with artillery that included enormous cannons built by Hungarian and Italian engineers. On May 29, 1453, Ottoman troops overwhelmed the surviving soldiers and took the ancient Roman and Christian capital of Byzantium—which Mehmed promptly renamed Istanbul.

Although Christians generally portrayed the "fall" of Constantinople as an insult and a disaster, in fact the Muslim conquest had cultural benefits for western Europe. Many Christian survivors fled to ports in the west, bringing with them classical and Arabic manuscripts previously unknown in Europe. The well-educated, Greek-speaking émigrés generally became teachers and translators, thereby helping to revive Europeans' interest in classical antiquity and spreading knowledge of ancient Greek (which had virtually died out in medieval times).

The Fall of Constantinople. *The use of heavy artillery in the fifty-three-day siege of Constantinople was instrumental to the Ottoman victory. At the center of this Turkish miniature is one such cannon, possibly of Hungarian origin, which required hundreds of men and oxen to transport and secure outside the city walls.*

These manuscripts and teachers would play a vital role in Europe's Renaissance.

The Ottomans followed their capture of Constantinople with other military successes that put many of Christian Europe's great cities in peril. Their forces sacked Athens in 1458, then took Bosnia in 1463. In 1480 the Ottomans launched an invasion of Italy. They captured one port city; but Mehmed II's death, and fights between his sons for control of the empire, prevented further conquests in Italy. The Ottomans then turned to the Balkans and central Europe, invading Hungary in 1492 and Croatia in 1493. Their inroads so frightened the French king that he decided to invade Italy himself in order to lead his own crusade against the Ottomans.

Meanwhile, Mehmed made Istanbul the Ottoman capital, adopting Byzantine administrative practices to unify his enlarged state and incorporating many of Byzantium's powerful families into it. From Istanbul, Mehmed and his successors would continue their expansion, eventually seizing all of Greece and the Balkan region. As a result, Ottoman navies increasingly controlled sea-lanes in the eastern Mediterranean, curtailing European access to the rich ports that handled the lucrative caravan trade. By the late fifteenth century, Ottoman forces menaced another of Christendom's great capitals, Vienna, and European merchants feared that never again would they obtain the riches of Asia via the traditional overland route.

THE TOOLS OF EMPIRE BUILDING Having penetrated the heartland of Christian Byzantium, under Selim (r. 1512–1520) and Suleiman (r. 1520–1566), the Ottomans turned their expansionist designs to the Arab world. During the latter's reign the Ottomans reached the height of their territorial expansion, with Suleiman himself leading thirteen major military campaigns and many minor engagements. An exceptional military leader, Suleiman was an equally gifted administrator. His subjects called him "the Lawgiver" and "the Magnificent" in recognition of his attention to civil bureaucratic efficiency and justice for his people. His fame spread to Europe, where he was known as "the Great Turk." Under Suleiman's administration, the Ottoman state ruled over 20 to 30 million people. By the time Suleiman died, the Ottoman Empire bridged Europe and the Arab world. Istanbul by then was a dynamic imperial hub, dispatching bureaucrats and military men to oversee a vast domain.

Ottoman dynastic power was, however, not only military; it also rested on a firm religious foundation. At the center of this empire were the sultans, who combined a warrior ethos with an unwavering devotion to Islam. Describing themselves as the "shadow of God" on earth, they claimed to be caretakers for the welfare of the Islamic faith. Throughout the empire, the sultans devoted substantial resources to the construction of elaborate mosques and to the support of Islamic schools. As self-appointed defenders of the faithful, the sultans assumed the role of protectors of the holy cities on the Arabian Peninsula and of Jerusalem, defending the realm's internal cohesion and constantly striving to extend the borders of Islam. Thus the Islamic faith helped to unite a diverse and sprawling imperial populace, with the sultan's power fusing the sacred and the secular.

ISTANBUL AND THE TOPKAPI PALACE Istanbul reflected the splendor of this awesome empire. After the Ottoman conquest, the sultans' engineers rebuilt the city's crumbling walls, while their architects redesigned homes, public buildings, baths, inns, and marketplaces to display the majesty of Islam's new imperial center. To crown his achievements, Suleiman ordered the construction of the Suleymaniye Mosque, which sat opposite the Hagia Sophia. That domed Byzantine cathedral was formerly the most sacred of Christian cathedrals, the largest house of worship in all of Christendom, but

The Suleymaniye Mosque. *Built by Sultan Suleiman to crown his achievements, the Suleymaniye Mosque was designed by the architect Sinan to dominate the city and to have four tall minarets from which the faithful were called to prayer.*

Suleiman had it turned into a mosque. Moreover, the Ottoman dynasts welcomed (indeed, forcibly transported) thousands of Muslims and non-Muslims to the city and revived Istanbul as a major trading center. Within twenty-five years of its conquest, its population more than tripled; by the end of the sixteenth century, 400,000 people regularly swarmed through its streets and knelt in its mosques, making it the world's largest city outside China.

Istanbul's **Topkapi Palace** reflected the Ottomans' view of governance, the sultans' emphasis on religion, and the continuing influence of Ottoman familial traditions—even in the administration of a far-flung empire. Laid out by Mehmed II, the palace complex reflected a vision of Istanbul as the center of the world. As a way to exalt the sultan's magnificent power, architects designed the complex so that the buildings containing the imperial household nestled behind layers of outer courtyards, in a mosaic of mosques, courts, and special dwellings for the sultan's harem.

The growing importance of Topkapi Palace as the command post of empire represented a crucial transition in the history of Ottoman rulers. Not only was the palace the place where future bureaucrats received their training; it was also the place where the chief bureaucrat, the grand vizier, carried out the day-to-day running of the empire. Whereas the early sultans had led their soldiers into battle personally and had met face-to-face with their kinsmen, the later rulers withdrew into the sanctity of the palace, venturing out only occasionally for grand ceremonies. Still, every Friday, subjects queued up outside the palace to introduce their petitions, ask for favors, and seek justice. If they were lucky, the sultans would be there to greet them—but they did so behind grated glass, issuing their decisions by tapping on the window. The palace thus projected a sense of majestic, distant wonder, a home fit for commanders of the faithful.

And Topkapi was indeed a home—for the increasingly sedentary sultan and his harem. Among his most cherished quarters were those set aside for women. At first, women's influence

The Topkapi Palace. *A view of the inner courtyard of the seraglio, where the sultan and his harem lived.*

in the Ottoman polity was slight. But as the realm consolidated, women became a powerful political force. The harem, like the rest of Ottoman society, had its own hierarchy of rank and prestige. At the bottom were slave women; at the top were the sultan's mother and his favorite consorts. As many as 10,000 to 12,000 women inhabited the palace, often in cramped quarters. Those who had the ruler's ear conspired to have him favor their own children, which made for widespread intrigue. When a sultan died, the entire retinue of women would be sent to a distant palace poignantly called the Palace of Tears, because the women who occupied it wept at the loss of the sultan and their own banishment from power.

DIVERSITY AND CONTROL The fact that the Ottoman Empire endured into the twentieth century owed much to the ruling elite's ability to win the favor of exceedingly diverse populations. After all, neither conquest nor conversion eliminated cultural differences in the empire's distant provinces. Thus, for example, the Ottomans' language policy was one of flexibility and tolerance. Although Ottoman Turkish was the official language of administration, Arabic was the primary language of the Arab provinces, the common tongue of street life. Within the empire's European corner, the sounds and cadences of various languages continued to prevail. From the fifteenth century onward, the Ottoman Empire was more multilingual than any of its rivals.

In politics, as in language, the Ottomans showed flexibility and tolerance. The imperial bureaucracy permitted extensive regional and religious autonomy. In fact, Ottoman military cadres perfected a technique for absorbing newly conquered territories into the empire by parceling them out as revenue-producing units among loyal followers and kin. Regional appointees could collect local taxes, part of which they earmarked for Istanbul and part of which they pocketed for themselves. (This was a common administrative device for many world dynasties ruling extensive domains.)

Like other empires, the Ottoman state was always in danger of losing control over its provincial rulers. Local rulers—the group that the imperial center allowed to rule locally—found that great distances enabled them to operate independently from central authority. These local authorities kept larger amounts of tax revenues than Istanbul deemed proper. So, to clip local autonomy, the Ottomans established a corps of infantry soldiers and bureaucrats (called janissaries) who owed direct allegiance to the sultan. The system at its high point involved a conscription of Christian youths from the empire's European lands. This conscription, called the *devshirme,* required each village to hand over a certain number of males between the ages of eight and eighteen. Uprooted from their families and villages, selected for their fine physiques and good looks, these young men were converted to Islam and sent to farms to build up their bodies and learn Turkish. A select few were moved on to Topkapi Palace to learn Ottoman military, religious, and administrative techniques. Some of these men—such as the architect Sinan, who designed the Suleymaniye Mosque—later enjoyed exceptional careers in the arts and sciences. Recipients of the best education available in the Islamic world, trained in Ottoman ways, instructed in the use of modern weaponry, and shorn of all family connections, the *devshirme* recruits were prepared to serve the sultan (and the empire as a whole) rather than the interests of any particular locality or ethnic group.

The *Devshirme*. *A miniature painting from 1558 depicts the* devshirme *system of taking non-Muslim children from their families in the Balkan Peninsula as a human tribute in place of cash taxes, which the poor region could not pay. The children were educated in Ottoman Muslim ways and prepared for service in the sultan's civil and military bureaucracy.*

The Ottomans thus artfully balanced the decentralizing tendencies of the outlying regions with the centralizing forces of the imperial capital. Relying on a careful mixture of faith, patronage, and tolerance, the sultans curried loyalty and secured political stability. Indeed, so strong and stable was the polity that the Ottoman Empire dominated the coveted and highly contested crossroads between Europe and Asia for many centuries.

The Safavid Empire in Iran

The Ottoman dynasts were not the only rulers to extend Islam's political domain. In Persia, too, a new empire arose in the aftermath of the Mongols. The legitimacy of the Safavid Empire, like that of the Ottoman, rested on an Islamic foundation. But the Shiism espoused by Safavid rulers was quite different from the Sunni faith of the Ottomans, and these contrasting religious visions shaped distinct political systems.

More so than in Anatolia, the Mongol conquest and decline brought terrible destruction and political instability to Persia. Initially, Mongol conquerors refused to embrace the majority population's Islamic faith. Instead, for over seven decades the Mongol rulers practiced a form of religious toleration. Various Mongol autocrats permitted Jews to serve the state as viziers (administrators) and employed Christians as auxiliary soldiers. But in 1295, the khan of the Persian state adopted Islam as the state religion. (A **khan** is a ruler who was acclaimed at an assembly of elites and supposedly descended from Chinggis Khan [see Chapter 10] on the male line; those not descended from Chinggis continually faced challenges to their legitimacy.) When the Mongol order slipped into decline soon after, no power arose to dominate the area. The region between Konya in eastern Anatolia and Tabriz in Persia and including Iraq fell into disorder, with warrior chieftains squabbling for preeminence. Adding to the volatility were various populist Islamic movements, some of which urged followers to withdraw from society or to parade around without clothing. Among the more prominent movements was a Sufi brotherhood led by Safi al-Din (1252–1334), which gained the backing of religious adherents and Turkish-speaking warrior bands. However, his successors, known as Safaviyeh or Safavids, embraced Shiism.

The Safavid aspirants to power rallied support from tribal groups in badly devastated parts of Persia by promising to restore good governance. They also steeped themselves in the separatist sacred tradition of Shiism. As a result, of the three great Islamic empires, the Safavid state became the most single-mindedly religious, persecuting those who did not follow its Shiite form of Islam. When the most dynamic of Safi al-Din's successors, Ismail (r. 1501–1524), took power in Tabriz, he required that the call to prayer announce that "there is no God but Allah, that Muhammad is His prophet, and that Ali is the successor of Muhammad." Rejecting his advisers' counsel to tolerate the Sunni creed of the vast majority of the city's population, Ismail made Shiism the official state religion. He offered the people a choice between conversion to Shiism or death, exclaiming at the moment of conquest that "with God's help, if the people utter one word of protest, I will draw the sword and leave not one of them alive." In 1502, Ismail proclaimed himself the first shah of the Safavid Empire. (**Shah** is the Persian word for king or leader, a title that many other cultures adopted as well.) Under Ismail and his successors, the Safavid shahs restored Persian sovereignty over the entire region traditionally regarded as the homeland of Persian speakers (see Map 11.3).

In the hands of the Safavids, Islam assumed an extreme and often militant form. The Safavids revived the traditional Persian idea that rulers were ordained by God, believing the shahs to

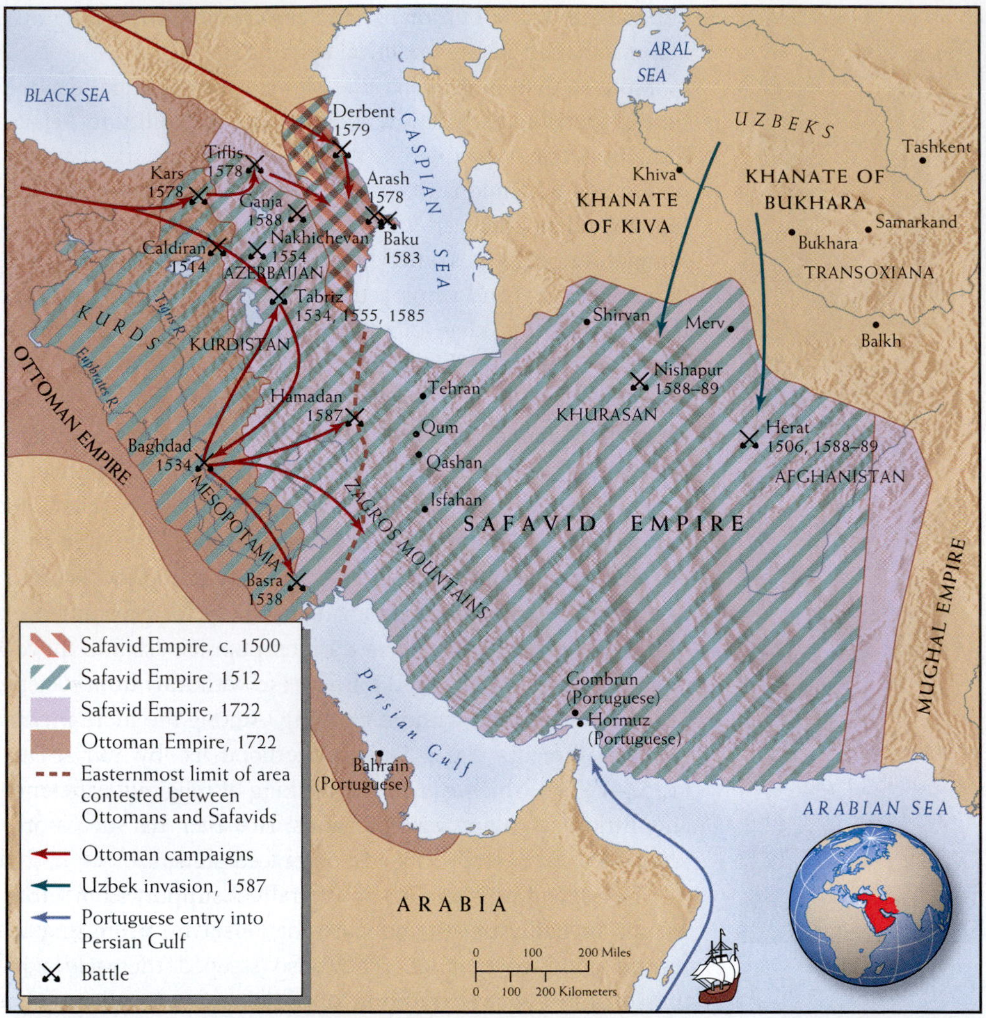

MAP 11.3 | The Safavid Empire, 1500–1722

The Safavid Empire rose to prominence alongside the Ottoman state.

- Locate the area where it originated. With which empire did the Safavids fight the most battles?
- Why were most of the battles limited to the regions of Azerbaijan, Kurdistan, and Mesopotamia?
- What were the geographical and political limits on the growth of the Safavid Empire?

be divinely chosen. Some Shiites even went so far as to affirm that there was no God but the shah. Moreover, Persian Shiism fostered an activist clergy who (in contrast to Sunni clerics) saw themselves as political and religious enforcers against any heretical authority. They compelled Safavid leaders to rule with a sacred purpose. Because the Safavids did not tolerate diversity, unlike the Ottomans, they never had as expansive an empire. Whatever territories they conquered, the Safavids ruled much more directly, based on central—and theocratic—authority. They also succeeded in transforming Iran, once a Sunni area, into a Shiite stronghold, a change that has endured down to the present.

The Delhi Sultanate and the Early Mughal Empire

A quarter century after the Safavids seized power in Persia, another Islamic dynasty, the Mughals, emerged in South Asia. Like the Ottomans and Safavids, the Mughals created a regime destined to last for many centuries. But unlike those other empires, the Mughals did not replace a Mongol regime. Instead, they erected their state on the foundations of the old Delhi Sultanate, which had come into existence in 1206. Although spared the devastating effects of the Mongols and the Black Death, nonetheless the peoples of India had to deal with an invading nomadic force every bit as destructive as the Mongols: the warriors of Tamerlane. His military forays crushed the Delhi Sultanate and opened the way for a new, even more powerful regime.

THE DECLINING DELHI SULTANATE In 1303, when Mongol forces had moved toward South Asia, the Delhi Sultanate was at its height. Its formidable military force extended imperial authority to most of the northern Indus River valley and cast a shadow over the political map of the south. The reigning sultan raised a sufficiently powerful army to drive the Mongols back toward Afghanistan. They never again disturbed the tranquility of the sultanate.

Although military strength was the foundation of the sultanate's power, it was also, ironically, a vulnerable institution. Toward the late fourteenth century, a decline in government revenues and a rise in expenditures combined to reduce resources for the military. Quarreling among nobles further weakened the sultanate and left it vulnerable to a Turkish, rather than Mongol, invader. This was a force led by Timur (Tamerlane), a Turkish warrior from central Asia. Sweeping down from the northwest, Timur's army sacked Delhi and pillaged and annexed the Punjab, an area around the headwaters of the Indus River. Thereafter death and destruction engulfed the city and much of the northern Indus River valley. Thousands were taken prisoner and carried off as

Raid on Delhi. *Timur's swift raid on Delhi in 1398 was notable for the death and destruction it caused. This sixteenth-century miniature captures the plunder and violence.*

slaves. Artisans and stonemasons who had constructed Delhi's beautiful buildings were carted away to work similar magic on the conqueror's city of Samarkand (in present-day Uzbekistan). Yet, with the approach of summer, a time when semiarid Delhi chokes with dust and the temperature hovers between 100 and 110 degrees Fahrenheit, Timur abandoned the scorching plains of northern India and returned home. Still, his conquest accelerated the fragmentation of the Delhi Sultanate.

RIVALRIES, RELIGIOUS REVIVAL, AND THE FIRST MUGHAL EMPEROR A wave of religious revival followed in the wake Timur's conquests. Bengal broke away from Delhi and soon embraced a Sufi form of mystical Islam, emphasizing personal union with God. Here, too, a special form of Hinduism, called Bhakti Hinduism, put down deep roots. Its devotees preached the doctrine of divine love. In the Punjab, previously a core area of the Delhi Sultanate, a new religion known as Sikhism came into being. **Sikhism** largely followed the teachings of Nanak (1469–1539). Although born a Hindu, he was inspired by Islamic ideals and called on his followers to renounce the caste system and to treat all believers as equal before God. (See Primary Source: Nanak's Teachings in India.)

Following Timur's attack, rival kingdoms and sultanates asserted their independence, leaving the Delhi Sultanate a mere shadow of its former self. It became just one of several competing powers in northern India, ruled first by the Sayyids and then by the Afghan dynasty of the Lodis. Surrounded by resurgent Hindu and Islamic polities, the weakened sultanate experienced something of a revival in the Lodi era. But the attempt by the last Lodi sultan to consolidate power by clipping the wings of the Afghan nobility provoked the governor of the Punjab to invite the Turkish prince Babur (the "Tiger") to India in 1526. A great-grandson of Timur, Babur traced his lineage to both the Turks and the Mongols (he was said to be a descendant of Chinggis Khan). For years, Babur had longed to conquer India. Massing an army of Turks and Afghans armed with matchlock cannons, he easily breached the wall of elephants put together by defenders of the sultan. Delhi fell, and the sultanate came to an end. Babur proclaimed himself emperor and spent the next few years snuffing out the remaining resistance to his rule (see Map 11.4). Thus he laid the foundation of the Mughal Empire, the third great Islamic dynasty (discussed in detail in Chapter 12).

By the sixteenth century, then, the Islamic heartland had seen the emergence of three new empires. Their differences were obvious, especially in the religious sphere. The Ottomans were Sunni Islam's most fervent champions, determined to eradicate the Shiite heresy on their border, where an equally determined Persian Safavid dynasty sought to expand the realm of Shiism. In contrast to these dynasties' sectarian religious commitments, the Mughals of India, drawing on well-established Indian traditions of religious and cultural tolerance, were open-minded toward non-Muslim believers and sectarian groups within the Muslim community. Yet, the political similarities of these imperial dynasties were equally clear-cut. Although these states did not hesitate to go to war against each other, they shared similar styles of rule. All established their legitimacy via military prowess, religious backing, and a loyal bureaucracy. This combination of spiritual and military weaponry enabled emperors, espousing Muhammad's preachings, to claim vast domains. Islam also bound together rulers and those whom they ruled. Moreover, their religious differences did not prevent the movement of goods, ideas, merchants, and scholars across

PRIMARY SOURCE

Nanak's Teachings in India

Nanak (1469–1539), generally recognized as the founder of Sikhism, lived in northern India and participated in the religious discussions that were prominent at the time. As in western Europe and Islamic Southwest Asia, this was a period of political turmoil and intense personal introspection. The following excerpts demonstrate Nanak's views on the failings of the age and his use of Islamic and Hindu ideas to elaborate a unique spiritual perspective. Nanak stressed the unity of God, an emphasis that reflected Islamic influences. Nonetheless, his insistence on the comparative unimportance of prophets ran counter to Islam, and his belief in rebirth was strictly Hindu.

There is but one God, whose name is true, the Creator, devoid of fear and enmity, immortal, unborn, self-existent; God the great and bountiful. Repeat His Name.

Numberless are the fools appallingly blind;
Numberless are the thieves and devourers of others' property;
Numberless are those who establish their sovereignty by force;
Numberless the cutthroats and murderers;
Numberless the liars who roam about lying;
Numberless the filthy who enjoy filthy gain;
Numberless the slandered who carry loads of calumny on their heads;
Nanak thus described the degraded.
So lowly am I, I cannot even once be a sacrifice unto Thee. Whatever pleaseth Thee is good.
O Formless One, Thou art ever secure.

The Hindus have forgotten God, and are going the wrong way.
They worship according to the instruction of Narad.
They are blind and dumb, the blindest of the blind.
The ignorant fools take stones and worship them.
O Hindus, how shall the stone which itself sinketh carry you across?

What power hath caste? It is the reality that is tested.
Poison may be held in the hand, but man dieth if he eat it.
The sovereignty of the True One is known in every age. He who obeyeth God's order shall become a noble in His court.

Those who have meditated on God as the truest of the true have done real worship and are contented;
They have refrained from evil, done good deeds, and practiced honesty;
They have lived on a little corn and water, and burst the entanglements of the world.
Thou art the great Bestower; ever Thou givest gifts which increase a quarterfold.
Those who have magnified the great God have found Him.

QUESTIONS FOR ANALYSIS

- Identify all the "numberless" groups that Nanak lists. What range of social classes do they represent? How does this enumeration reflect the tumultuous times?
- What criticisms of Hindu worship does Nanak raise?
- What lines reveal his belief in rebirth?
- How does Nanak expect true believers to behave?

Source: "Nanak's Teachings in India" from Sources of Indian Tradition, *ed. William Theodore de Bary, © 1958 Columbia University Press. Reprinted with permission of the publisher.*

political and religious boundaries—even across the most divisive boundary of all, that between Sunni Iraq and Shiite Persia.

WESTERN CHRISTENDOM

In western Afro-Eurasia, the period 1100–1300 was one of prosperity, population growth, and cultural flowering. Known as the High Middle Ages, this era saw spectacular advances in the arts, technology, learning, architecture, and banking. Expanding populations freed up laborers to move from the countryside to the cities. London, with a population of 100,000, was only one city to experience a housing crunch; in some of its poorer sections, up to twelve people slept in a single room. Though excluded from many crafts and professions, women made gains in retail trades, weaving, and food production. Wives often supervised shops or took goods to local fairs, where producers met to exchange their wares.

During the High Middle Ages, Europe's 80 million inhabitants remained largely rooted to their local communities, but

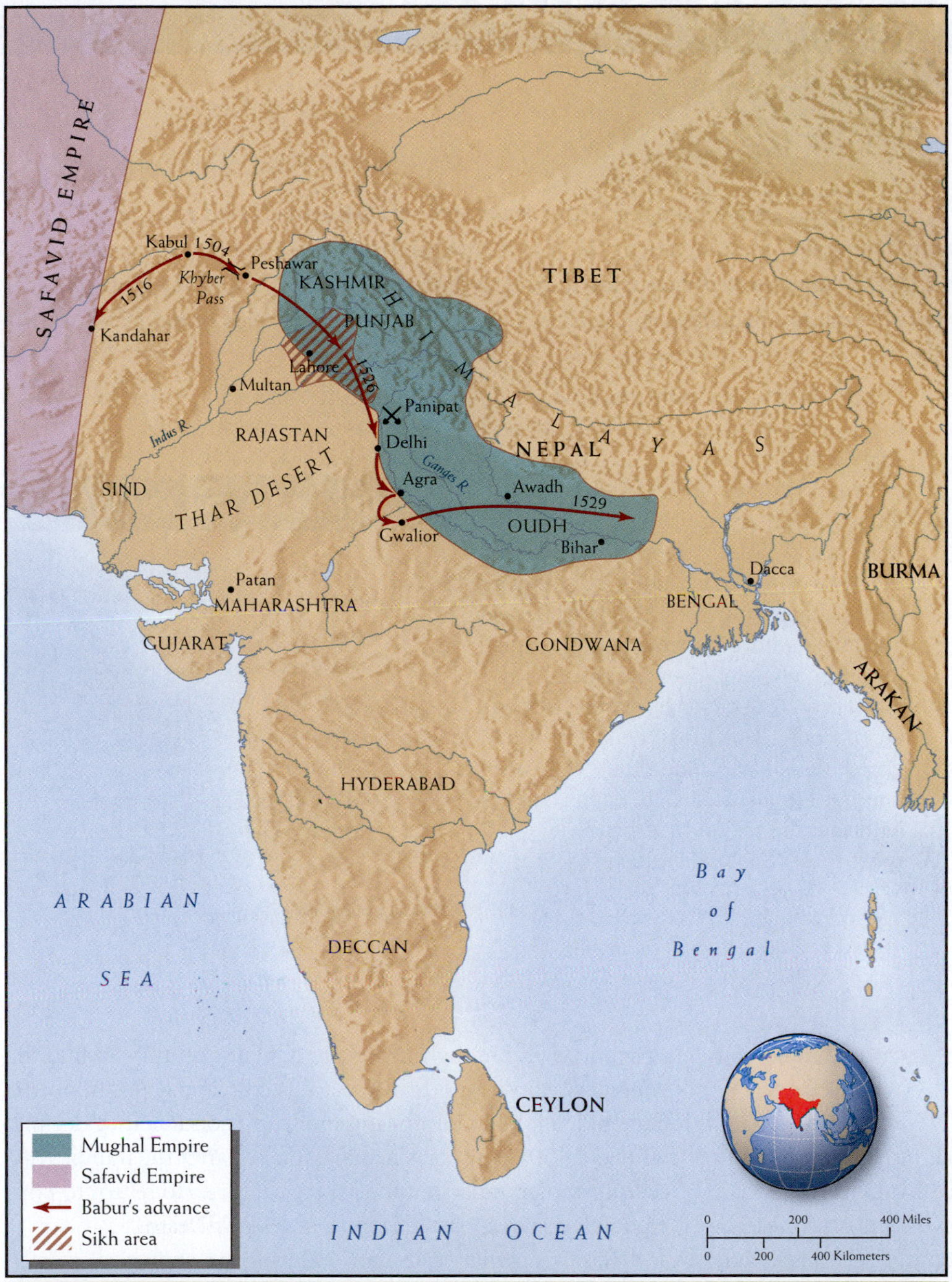

MAP 11.4 | The Mughal Empire, 1530

Compare the Mughal state with the other major Asian empires of this period, notably the Ottoman, Safavid, and Ming states (see Maps 11.2, 11.3, and 11.6).

- What geographic characteristic distinguished the Mughal state at this time from the others?
- Where in the landmass did the new state arise, and what effect do you think its place of origin had on the nature of Mughal rule?
- Based on their geographic location, to what religious traditions did the Mughals need to be sensitive?

growing wealth allowed some to widen their horizons. Bologna, Paris, Oxford, and Cambridge had universities (with medical, law, and theology faculties), and a few scholars had begun to appreciate the learning of Arabs and earlier Greeks and Romans. Thomas Aquinas (1225–1274), a leading philosopher and theologian, had laid out the main tenets of western Christianity and resolved questions of faith and reason to the satisfaction of clerical and secular intellectuals. Florentine bankers opened establishments in commercial port cities, and Greek shipbuilders expanded their trade. New devices like mechanical clocks and the compass improved the accuracy of measurements on sea and on land, while spinning wheels increased the pace of cloth production. But all of this prosperity, population growth, and innovation would be halted by the tragedies of the fourteenth century.

Reactions, Revolts, and Religion

Disastrous climatic changes struck first. Beginning around 1310, extremely harsh winters and rainy summers shortened the growing seasons and played havoc with harvests. Exhausted soils no longer supplied the resources to feed and clothe growing urban and rural populations. Nobles squeezed the peasantry hard in an effort to maintain their luxurious lifestyle. States raised taxes to balance their growing expenditures. In this context, Europe endured the first of several disasters: famine. It appeared in 1315 and did not let up for seven cruel years, by which time millions had died of starvation or of diseases against which the malnourished population had little resistance. But this was merely the prelude to a

PRIMARY SOURCE

Flagellants in England

Like the Qalandar dervishes in the Islamic realm (see p. 369), European Flagellants renounced the world and engaged in public self-punishment in reaction to the warfare, famines, and plagues of the fourteenth century. The Flagellants carried whips (flagella) with metal pieces run through knotted thongs, which they used to beat and whip themselves until they were bruised, swollen, and bloody. Robert of Avesbury here describes the actions of Flagellants in England during the reign of King Edward III.

In that same year of 1349, about Michaelmas [29 September], more than 120 men, for the most part from Zeeland or Holland, arrived in London from Flanders. These went barefoot in procession twice a day in the sight of the people, sometimes in St Paul's church and sometimes elsewhere in the city, their bodies naked except for a linen cloth from loins to ankle. Each wore a hood painted with a red cross at front and back and carried in his right hand a whip with three thongs. Each thong had a knot in it, with something sharp, like a needle, stuck through the middle of the knot so that it stuck out on each side, and as they walked one after the other they struck themselves with these whips on their naked, bloody bodies; four of them singing in their own tongue and the rest answering in the manner of the Christian litany. Three times in each procession they would all prostrate themselves on the ground, with their arms outstretched in the shape of a cross. Still singing, and beginning with the man at the end, each in turn would step over the others, lashing the man beneath him once with his whip, until all of those lying down had gone through the same ritual. Then each one put on his usual clothes and, always with their hoods on their heads and carrying their whips, they departed to their lodgings. It was said that they performed a similar penance every night.

QUESTIONS FOR ANALYSIS

- Describe how the Flagellants dressed, and identify the languages they spoke. What elements of Christianity did these characteristics display?
- Why do you think the Flagellants whipped themselves?
- How did the Flagellants differ from the Qalanders?

Source: Robertus de Avesbury, "Flagellants in England" from The Black Death, *Rosemary Horrox, trans./ed., pp. 153–54.*

century and more of warfare, epidemic disease, famine, and social unrest.

THE PLAGUE IN EUROPE In the wake of famine came the Black Death, starting around 1346 and ravaging the Italian Peninsula; then it seized France, the Low Countries (present-day Netherlands, Belgium, and Luxembourg), Germany, and England in its deathly grip. The overcrowded and unsanitary cities were particularly vulnerable. Bremen lost at least 8,000 souls, perhaps two-thirds of its population; Hamburg, another port city, at least as many. The poor, sleeping in crowded quarters, were especially at risk. But master bakers, bankers, and aristocrats died too, unless they were able to flee to the relatively safer countryside in time to escape infection. No one had seen dying on such a scale. Nearly two-thirds of Europe's total population perished between 1346 and 1353.

After 1353, the epidemic died down, having killed all those with no natural immunities and most of the original carriers of the disease, the European black rat. But the plague would return every seven years or so for the rest of the century, as well as sporadically through the entire fifteenth century, killing the young and those who had managed to escape exposure in the first epidemic. The European population continued to decline, until by 1450 many areas had only one-quarter the number of a century earlier. Indeed, it took three centuries to return to population levels that existed prior to the Black Death.

Disaster on this scale had enduring psychological, social, economic, and political effects. Many individuals turned to pleasure, even debauchery, determined to enjoy themselves before it came their turn to die. Others retreated into a personal spirituality, convinced that they needed to put their lives in order before passing on to the next life. Occasionally, eccentric groups took shape. The Beghards, or Brethren of the Free Speech, claimed to be in a state of grace that allowed them to do as they pleased—including adultery, free love, nudity, and murder. By contrast, the Flagellants were so sure that man had incurred God's wrath that they whipped themselves to atone for human sin. They also bullied communities that they visited, demanding to be housed, clothed, and fed. (See Primary Source: Flagellants in England.)

For many who survived the plague, Thomas Aquinas's rational Christianity no longer appealed, and disappointment with the clergy smoldered. Famished peasants resented priests and monks for living lives of luxury in violation of church tenets. In addition, they despaired at the absence of clergy when they were so greatly needed. In fact, many clerics had perished while attending to their parishioners. Others had fled to rural retreats far from the ravages of the Black Death, leaving their followers to fend for themselves.

THE CHURCH'S RESPONSE In the aftermath of famine and plague, religious authorities struggled to reclaim their power. The late medieval western church found itself divided at the top (at one point there were three popes) and challenged from below, both by individuals pursuing alternative kinds of spirituality and by increasing demands on the clergy and church administration. Facing challenges to its right to define religious doctrine and practices, the church identified all that was suspect and demanded strict obedience to the true faith. This entailed the persecution of heretics, Jews, Muslims, homosexuals, prostitutes, and "witches." But during this period the church also expanded its charitable and bureaucratic functions, providing alms to the urban poor and registering births, deaths, and economic transactions.

Persecution and administration cost money. Indeed, the needs as well as the extravagances of the clergy spurred certain questionable money-making tactics. One was the selling of indulgences (certificates that reduced one's time in purgatory, where souls continued the repentance that would eventually make them fit for heaven). This sort of unconventional fund raising, and the growing gap between the church's promises and its ability to bring Christianity into people's everyday lives, more than the persecutions, eventually sparked the Protestant Reformation (see Chapter 12).

A WEAKENING FEUDAL ORDER Just as the mayhem of the fourteenth and fifteenth centuries unleashed hostility toward the church, it also undermined the feudal order. Since the Roman era, peasant uprisings had occasionally erupted. But now they escalated into large-scale insurrections. In France and England, massive revolts signaled the peasants' resentment against lords who failed to protect them from marauding military bands, as well as their exasperation with feudal restrictions that now seemed—for the few survivors of plague and famine—too much to bear. In 1358 the French revolt, or **Jacquerie**, broke out (the term derived from "Jacques Bonhomme," a name that contemptuous masters used for all peasants). Armed with only knives and staves, the peasantry went on a rampage, killing hated nobles and clergy and burning and looting all the property they could get their hands on. At issue was the peasants' insistence that they should no longer be tied to their land or have to pay for the tools they used in farming.

Peasant Revolts. *Long before the French Revolution, European peasants vented their anger against their noble masters. Lacking armaments and supplies, they usually lost—as this image of the brutal suppression of the French Jacquerie of 1358 depicts.*

A better-organized uprising took place in England in 1381. Although the **English Peasants' Revolt** began as a protest against a tax levied to raise money for a war on France, it was also fueled by post-plague labor shortages: serfs demanded the freedom to move about, and free farm workers called for higher wages and lower rents. When landlords balked at these demands, aggrieved peasants assembled at the gates of London. The protesters demanded abolition of the feudal order, but the king ruthlessly suppressed them. Nonetheless, in both France and England a free peasantry gradually emerged as labor shortages made it impossible to keep peasants bound to the soil.

State Building and Economic Recovery

In the wake of famine, plague, and peasant uprisings, Europe's rulers tried to rebuild their polities and consolidate their power. Although their efforts at state building pale in comparison with those of the empires rising in Asia, one family, the Habsburgs, established a powerful and long-lasting dynasty. They provided emperors for the Holy Roman Empire from 1440 to 1806. Yet the Habsburg monarchs never succeeded in restoring an integrated empire to western Europe (as Chinese dynasts had done by claiming the mandate of heaven).

Moreover, language did not unite Europeans. While the written literary Chinese script remained a key administrative tool for China's dynasts, and in the Islamic world Arabic was the common language of faith, Persian the language of poetry,

MAP 11.5 | Europe, 1400–1500

Europe was a region divided by dynastic rivalries during the fifteenth century.

- Locate the most powerful regional dynasties on the map: Portugal, Castile, Aragon, France, England, and the Holy Roman Empire. In what country did the heaviest fighting occur?
- Why do you think one state was the scene for so many battles?
- On the basis of this map, predict which European territories and polities would become powerful in subsequent centuries, and which would not.

and Turkish the language of administration, in Europe Latin lost ground as rulers chose various regional dialects to be their official state language. In 1450 Europe had no central government, no official tongue, and only a few successful commercial centers, mostly in the Mediterranean basin (see Map 11.5). Feudalism had left a legacy of political fragmentation and enshrined privileges, which made the consolidation of a unified Christian Europe even more difficult to achieve.

Those who sought to rule the emerging states faced numerous obstacles. For example, rival claimants to the throne financed threatening private armies. Also, the clergy demanded and received privileges and often meddled in politics themselves.

The church's huge landholdings and exemptions from taxation made it, too, a formidable economic powerhouse. And once the printing press became available in the 1460s, printers circulated anonymous pamphlets criticizing the court and the clergy. Some states had consultative bodies—such as the Estates General in France, the Cortes in Spain, or Parliament in England—in which princes formally asked representatives of their people for advice and, in the case of the English Parliament, for consent to new forms of taxation. Such bodies gave no voice to most nonaristocratic men and no representation to women. But they did allow the collective expression of grievances against high-handed policies.

Out of the chaos of famine, disease, and warfare, the diverse peoples of Europe found a political way forward. This path involved the formation of centralized monarchies, much as the Ottomans, Safavids, Mughals, and Ming were accomplishing in Asia. (A **monarchy** is a political system in which one individual holds supreme power and passes that power on to his or her next of kin.) Often in competition with the new monarchies a sprinkling of city-states survived, in which a handful of wealthy and influential voters selected their leaders. Consolidation of these polities occurred sometimes through strategic marriages but more often through warfare, both between local princely families and with outsiders. Political stabilization was swiftest in southern Europe, where economies rebounded through trade with Southwest Asia. The stabilization of Italian city-states such as Venice and Florence, and of monarchical rule in Portugal and Spain, led to an economic and cultural flowering known as the Renaissance (see below).

Political Consolidation and Trade in Portugal

Portugal's fortunes demonstrate how political stabilization and the revival of trade entwined. After the chaos of the fourteenth century, Spain, England, and France followed the Portuguese example and established national monarchies. In Spain and Portugal, warfare against Muslims would help unite Christian territories, and Mediterranean trade would add valuable income to state coffers. In northern Europe, by contrast, lack of access to lucrative trade routes, in addition to internal feuding, regional warfare, and (after 1517) religious fragmentation, would delay recovery for decades.

Through the fourteenth century, Portuguese Christians devoted themselves to fighting the **Moors**, who were Muslim occupants of North Africa, the western Sahara, and the Iberian Peninsula. Decisive in this struggle was the Portuguese decision to cross the Strait of Gibraltar and seize the Moorish Moroccan fortresses at Ceuta in North Africa: their ships could now sail between the Mediterranean and the Atlantic without Muslim interference. With that threat diminished, the Portuguese perceived their neighbor, Castile (part of what is now Spain), as their chief foe. Under João I (r. 1385–1433) the Castilians were defeated, and the monarchy could seek new territories and trading opportunities in the North Atlantic and along the West African coasts. João's son Prince Henrique, known later as Henry the Navigator, further expanded the family's domain by supporting expeditions down the coast of Africa and offshore to the Atlantic islands of the Madeiras and the Azores. The west and central coasts of Africa and the islands of the North and South Atlantic, including the Cape Verde Islands, São Tomé, Principe, and Fernando Po, soon became Portuguese ports of call.

The Portuguese monarchs granted the Atlantic islands to nobles as hereditary possessions on condition that the grantees colonize them, and soon the colonizers were establishing lucrative sugar plantations. In gratitude, noble families and merchants threw their political weight behind the king. Subsequent monarchs continued to reduce local elites' authority and to ensure smooth succession for members of the royal family. This political consolidation enabled Portugal to thrive in the wake of the Black Death.

Dynasty Building and Reconquest in Spain

The road to dynasty in Spain was arduous. Medieval Spain comprised rival kingdoms that quarreled ceaselessly. Also, Spain lacked religious uniformity: Muslims, Jews, and Christians lived side by side in relative harmony, and Muslim armies still occupied strategic posts in the south. Over time, however, marriages and the formation of kinship ties among nobles and between royal lineages yielded a new political order. One by one, the major houses of the Spanish kingdoms intermarried, culminating in the fateful wedding of Isabella of Castile and Ferdinand of Aragon. Thus, Spain's two most important provinces were joined, and Spain became a state to be reckoned with.

THE UNION OF CASTILE AND ARAGON By the time Isabella and Ferdinand married in 1469, Spain was recovering from the miseries of the fourteenth century. This was more than a marriage of convenience. Castile was wealthy and populous; Aragon enjoyed an extended trading network in the Mediterranean. Together, the monarchs brought unruly nobles and distant towns under their domain. They topped off their achievements by marrying their children into other European royal families—especially the Habsburgs, central Europe's most powerful dynasty.

The new rulers also sent Christian armies south to push Muslim forces out of the Iberian Peninsula. By the mid-fifteenth century only Granada, a strategic lynchpin overlooking the straits between the Mediterranean and the Atlantic, remained in Muslim hands. After a long and costly siege, Christian forces captured the fortress there. This was a victory of enormous symbolic importance, as joyous as the fall of Constantinople was depressing. Many people in Spain thumped their chests in pride, unaware or unconcerned that at the same time Ottoman armies were conquering large sections of southeastern Europe.

THE INQUISITION AND WESTWARD EXPLORATION Just as the Safavid rulers had tried to stamp out all non-Shiite forms of Islam within their domains, so Isabella and Ferdinand sought to drive all non-Catholics out of Spain. Terrified by Ottoman incursions into Europe, in 1481 they launched the **Inquisition**, taking aim especially against *conversos*—converted Jews and Muslims, whom they suspected were Christians only in name. When Granada fell, the crown ordered the expulsion of all Jews from Spain; after 1499, a more tolerant attempt to convert the Moors by persuasion gave way to forced conversion—or emigration. All told, almost half a million people were forced to flee the Spanish kingdoms.

So strong was the tide of Spanish fervor by late 1491 that the monarchs listened now to a Genoese navigator whose pleas for patronage they had previously rejected. Christopher Columbus promised them unimaginable riches that could finance their military campaigns and bankroll a crusade to liberate Jerusalem from Muslim hands. Off he sailed with a royal patent that guaranteed the monarchs a share of all he discovered. Soon the Spanish economy was reorienting itself toward the Atlantic, and Spain's merchants, missionaries, and soldiers were preparing for conquest and profiteering in what had been, just a few years before, a blank space on the map.

The Struggles of France and England, and the Success of Small States

Warfare and strategic marriages allowed the Portuguese and Spanish monarchies to consolidate state power and to lay the foundations for revived commerce. But by no means were all states immediately successful. In France and England, the great age of European monarchy had yet to dawn.

When French forces finally pushed the English back across the English Channel in the Hundred Years' War (1337–1453), the French House of Valois began a slow process of consolidating royal power. Although diplomatic marriages helped the French crown expand its domain, two more centuries of royal initiatives and civil war were required to tame the powerful nobility. In England, even thirty years of civil war between the houses of Lancaster and York did not settle which one would take the throne. Both families in this War of the Roses ultimately lost out to the Tudors, who seized the throne in 1485. (See Current Trends in World History: Joan of Arc: A Charismatic Leader in a Time of Social Turmoil.)

Even where stable states did arise, they were fairly small compared to the Ottoman and Ming empires. In the mid-sixteenth century, Portugal and Spain, Europe's two most expansionist states, had populations of 1 million and 9 million, respectively. England, excluding Wales, was a mere 3 million in 1550. Only France, with 17 million, had a population close to the Ottoman Empire's 25 million. And these numbers paled in comparison with Ming China's population of nearly 200 million in 1550 and Mughal India's 110 million in 1600.

But in Europe, small was advantageous. Portugal's relatively small population meant that the crown had fewer groups to instill with loyalty. Also, in the world of finance, the most successful merchants were those inhabiting the smaller Italian city-states and, a bit later, the cities of the northern Netherlands. The Florentines developed sophisticated banking techniques, created extensive networks of agents throughout Europe and the Mediterranean, and served as bankers to the popes. Venetian merchants enjoyed a unique role in the exchange of silks and spices from the eastern Mediterranean. It was in these prosperous city-states that the Renaissance began.

European Identity and the Renaissance

Europe's political and economic revival included a powerful outpouring of cultural achievements, led by Italian scholars and artists and financed by bankers, churchmen, and nobles. Much later, scholars coined the word **Renaissance** ("rebirth") to characterize the expanded cultural production of the Italian city-states, France, the Low Countries, England, and the Holy Roman Empire in the period 1430–1550. What was being "reborn" were ancient Greek and Roman art and learning—knowledge that could illuminate a world of expanding horizons and support the rights of secular individuals to exert power in it. Although the Renaissance was largely funded by popes and Christian kings, it broke the medieval church's monopoly on answers to the big questions and opened the way for secular forms of learning and a more human-centered understanding of the cosmos.

THE ITALIAN RENAISSANCE The Renaissance, ironically, was all about the new: new exposure, that is, to the old—to classical texts and ancient art and architectural forms. Although some Greek and Roman texts were known in Europe and the Islamic world, the fall of Constantinople and the invention of the printing press made others accessible to western scholars for the first time. Scholars now realized that the pre-Christian Greeks and Romans had known more: about how to represent and care for the human body; about geography, astronomy, and architecture; about how to properly govern states and armies. It was no longer enough to understand Christian doctrine and to trust medieval authorities; one had to accurately retranslate the original sources, which required the learning of languages and of history. This dive backward into ancient Greece and Rome became known as **humanism**, which sums up the aspiration to know more about the human experience beyond what the Christian scriptures offered.

Wealthy families, powerful rulers, and the Catholic Church were the sponsors of Renaissance achievement. For example, by the 1480s the di Medici family had been patronizing art based on ancient models for three generations. The Medici were bankers, but also influential political players in Florence and Rome. The family contributed greatly to making Florence one of the showplaces of Renaissance art and architecture, as well as the center stage for early Renaissance philosophy. Cosimo di Medici (1389–1464) funded the completion of the sumptuous Duomo, or cathedral of Florence, topped by the architect Brunelleschi's masterful dome, the largest built since antiquity. Cosimo's grandson, Lorenzo the Magnificent, supported many of the great Renaissance artists, including Leonardo da Vinci, Sandro Botticelli, and Michelangelo Buonarotti.

The artists who flourished in Florence, Rome, and Venice embraced their own form of humanism. In their case, the return to ancient sources meant reviving the principles of the Roman architect Vitruvius and the imitation of nude classical sculpture. Their masterpieces, like Leonardo's *Last Supper* or Michelangelo's *David*, used the technique of perspective and classical treatments of the body to give vivacity and three-dimensionality to paintings and sculptures—even religious ones. Raphael's madonnas portrayed the Virgin Mary as a beautiful individual and not just as a symbol of chastity; similarly, Michelangelo's Sistine Chapel ceiling gave Adam the beautiful body of a Greek god so that viewers could appreciate the glory of the Creation. Of course, these artists also hoped to draw attention to their own achievements, and they were not disappointed. For soon northern European princes, too, sought out artists and humanists who could bring this inspiring new style to their courts.

THE RENAISSANCE SPREADS By the sixteenth century, increasing economic prosperity, the circulation of books and images, and interstate competition were spreading Renaissance culture throughout Europe. Philip II of Spain, for example, purchased more than 1,000 paintings during his reign; Henry IV of France and his queen, Marie de Medici, invested a fortune in renovating the Louvre, building a new royal residence at Fontainebleau, and hiring Peter Paul Rubens to paint grand canvases. Courtiers built up-to-date palaces and invited scholars to live on their estates; Dutch, German, and French merchants also patronized the arts. All wanted their sons to be educated in the humanistic manner. Some families and religious institutions offered women access to the new learning, and some men encouraged their sisters, daughters, and wives to expand their horizons. The well-educated nun Caritas Pirckheimer (1467–1532), for example, exchanged learned letters and books with male humanists in the German states. Studying Greek, Latin, and ancient rhetoric did not make the commercial elite

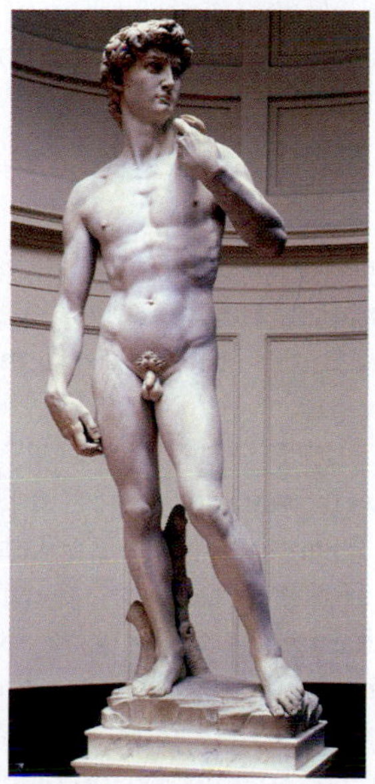

Renaissance Masterpieces. *Leonardo da Vinci's* The Last Supper (above) *depicts Christ's disciples reacting to his announcement that one of them will betray him. Michelangelo's* David (right) *stands over thirteen feet high and was conceived as an expression of Florentine civic ideals.*

CURRENT TRENDS IN WORLD HISTORY

Joan of Arc: A Charismatic Leader in a Time of Social Turmoil

The immense historical impact of a French peasant girl, Joan of Arc, demonstrates the importance of charismatic individuals—even women in male-dominated societies—during periods of social turmoil. As Europe endured plagues, famines, and war, its people sought help through the special talents of women, even in areas like warfare. Indeed, if not for Joan of Arc, the country we know today as France might not exist. Gender is also a useful approach to study the relations between men and women in a society. World historians use it as a comparative theme across cultures and time, which makes it an even more useful lens for historical analysis.

Appearing on the scene in 1429, as the English seemed to be winning the Hundred Years' War, she rallied the French against the English occupiers and turned the tide of the war. By giving religious sanction, as well as military succor, to the Valois monarch Charles VII, she made possible the consolidation of France and left Europe an inspiring image of the female warrior-saint.

The world of Joan's childhood was a chaotic one, in which English lords were laying claim to various French-speaking principalities. By 1420, Valois authority had been greatly eroded, and English armies were conquering more and more French towns. In 1428, the English laid siege to Orléans, a large town in north-central France. To contemporaries, it seemed a symbolic battle: as Orléans went, they thought, so the war would go—and so would God wish it to go.

This is the point at which the paths of a seventeen-year-old peasant girl and the monarch of France crossed. Beginning at about age thirteen, the shy girl had received visions of saints who instructed her to rescue Orléans and bring France's ruler to be crowned king at Reims Cathedral. (He had not been crowned there, in the tradition of all French kings, because the English armies controlled Reims, Paris, and northern France.) For five years Joan resisted, but at last she obeyed her celestial advisers. Granted an audience with Charles VII in 1429, Joan impressed him with her piety and her passionate devotion to the Valois crown. He concluded that God really had sent her to serve France's cause—and his own. Joan won command of 7,000 to 8,000 men; then, wearing a suit of armor and brandishing a sword, she marched to relieve Orléans. Joan directed the assault with brilliance and inspired the French forces; her charisma came not only from a tradition of female Christian "seers," but also from the peculiarity of her appearance (a young woman in male attire) and her appeal to French speakers who resented rule by English "outsiders." After driving the English from Orléans, she then pressed on to Reims; here, thanks to her military victories, Charles VII was crowned, fulfilling her visions. He was now king of France—and though the war continued, the tide now turned in favor of the French.

The tide for Joan, however, turned for the worse. Although she continued to direct the troops with remarkable savvy, she failed to force open the gates of Paris, and jealous courtiers around Charles began to question her divine authority. She was wounded, then taken prisoner. After a year in English captivity she faced the Inquisition and was found guilty of heresy, on the grounds that her visions were false and misleading. On May 30, 1431, she was burned at the stake

equal to the aristocrats, or women equal to men, but this sort of education did enable some non-nobles to obtain social influence and to criticize the ruling elites.

THE REPUBLIC OF LETTERS Since political and religious powers were not united in Europe (as they were in China and the Islamic world), scholars and artists could play one side against the other, or, alternatively, could suffer both clerical and political persecution. Michelangelo completed commissions for the Medici, for the Florentine Wool Guild, and for Pope Julius II. Peter Paul Rubens painted for the courts of France, Spain, England, and the Netherlands, as well as selling paintings on the open market. These two painters, renowned for showing a great deal of flesh, frequently offended conservative church officials, but their secular patrons kept them in oils. The Dutch scholar Desiderius Erasmus was able to ridicule the church because he had the patronage of English, Dutch, and French supporters. Fleeing persecution in Rome, the philosopher Giordano Bruno found a warm welcome in England—but made the mistake of thinking he was forgiven, and returned to Rome only to be burned at the stake.

The search for patrons and the flight from persecution, especially after the Reformation, made Europe's educated elite increasingly cosmopolitan (as it had in China and the Islamic empires). Scholars met one another in royal palaces and cultural centers such as Florence, Antwerp, and Amsterdam. Seeking specialized information or rare books, they formed what was known as "the republic of letters"—a network of correspondents who were more interested in individual knowledge or talent than in noble titles or clerical rank.

in the marketplace in the town of Rouen. Since that time she has stood as a heroic and charismatic martyr, and the French have often invoked her name to awaken patriotism against foreign threats.

The fact that this young, illiterate woman played such an important role in the history of European warfare and state formation testifies to the fact that male aristocrats, intellectuals, and clerics were not the only important actors. At the right place, at the right time, a woman could use courage, faith, and intelligence to make her visions prevail.

QUESTIONS FOR ANALYSIS

- What other heroic figures (male/female) does Joan of Arc remind you of and why?
- Why do you think Charles VII failed to rescue Joan of Arc from her English prison?

Explore Further

Pernoud, Régine and Marie-Véronique Clin, *Joan of Arc: Her Story*, trans. Jeremy Adams (1999).

COMPETING IDEAS OF GOVERNANCE Gradually, a network of educated men and women took shape that was not wholly dependent on either the church or the state. Thus these individuals acquired the means to challenge political, clerical, and aesthetic authority. Of course, they could also use their learning to defend the older elites: for example, numerous lawyers and scholars continued to work for the popes in defending the papacy. At the same time, in contrast, men like Erasmus and Martin Luther (the leading figure of the Reformation) looked to secular princes to support their critical scholarship.

Neither in Florence nor elsewhere did the Renaissance produce a consensus about who should rule. The Florentines pioneered a form of civic humanism under which all citizens were to devote themselves to defending the state against tyrants and foreign invaders; according to this view, the state would reward their civic virtue by ensuring their liberty. Yet it was also a Florentine, Niccolò Machiavelli, who wrote the most famous treatise on authoritarian power, *The Prince* (1513). Machiavelli argued that political leadership was not about obeying God's rules but about mastering the amoral means of modern statecraft. Holding and exercising power were ends in themselves, he claimed; civic virtue was merely a pretense on the part of those (like the Medici family he knew so well) who simply wanted to keep the upper hand.

The Renaissance produced a culture of critics who went back to classical ideas in order to go forward, to address the challenges and opportunities of an expanding world. This was not a movement that trickled down much to the common people, although they, too, surely were moved by the sight of the Duomo in Florence, or indirectly touched by the spread of printed books. The Renaissance transformed the European elite, however, making it more cosmopolitan and knitting together the artists and scholars who constituted "the republic of letters." By orienting the elite toward ancient models (for poetry, rhetoric, statecraft, geography, medicine, and architecture) instead of medieval ones, the Renaissance revolutionized European culture—even if it could not unify the states and peoples who cultivated it.

MING CHINA

Like the Europeans, the Chinese saw their stable worldview and political order crumble under the cataclysms of human and bacterial invasions. Moreover, like the Europeans, people in China had long regarded outsiders as "barbarians." Together, the Mongols and the Black Death upended the political and intellectual foundations of what had appeared to be the world's most integrated society. The Mongols brought the Yuan dynasty to power; then the plague devastated China and prepared the way for the emergence of the Ming dynasty.

Chaos and Recovery

China had been ripe for the plague's pandemic. Its population had increased significantly under the Song dynasty (960–1279) and subsequent Mongol rule. But by 1300, hunger and scarcity began to spread as resources stretched thin. A weakened population was especially vulnerable to plague. For seventy years, the Black Death ravaged China and shattered the Mongols' claim to a mandate from heaven. In 1331, plague may have killed 90 percent of the population in Bei Zhili (modern Hebei) province. From there it spread throughout other provinces, reaching Fujian and the coast at Shandong. By the 1350s, most of China's large cities suffered severe outbreaks.

The reign of the last Yuan Mongol rulers was a time of utter chaos. Even as the Black Death was engulfing large parts of China, bandit groups and dissident religious sects were undercutting the state's power. As in other realms devastated by the plague, popular religious movements foretold impending doom. Most prominent was the **Red Turban Movement**, which took its name from its soldiers' red headbands. This movement blended China's diverse cultural and religious traditions, including Buddhism, Daoism, and other faiths. Its leaders emphasized strict dietary restrictions, penance, and ceremonial rituals in which the sexes freely mixed, and made proclamations that the world was drawing to an end.

In these chaotic times, only a strong military movement capable of overpowering other groups could restore order. That intervention began at the hands of a poor young man who had trained in the Red Turban Movement: Zhu Yuanzhang. He was an orphan from a peasant household in an area devastated by disease and famine, and a former novice at a Buddhist monastery. At age twenty-four Zhu joined the Red Turbans, after which he rose quickly to become a distinguished commander. Eventually, his forces defeated the Yuan and drove the Mongols from China.

The Forbidden City. *The Yongle Emperor relocated the capital to Beijing, where he began the construction of the Forbidden City, or imperial palace. The palace was designed to inspire awe in all who saw it.*

It soon became clear that Zhu had a much grander design for all of China than the ambitions of most warlords. When he took the important city of Nanjing in 1356, he renamed it Yingtian ("In response to Heaven"). Buoyed by subsequent successful military campaigns, twelve years later Zhu (r. 1368–1398) proclaimed the founding of the Ming ("brilliant") dynasty. Soon thereafter, his troops met little resistance when they seized the Yuan capital of Beijing, causing the Mongol emperor to flee to his homeland in the steppe. It would, however, take Zhu almost another twenty years to reunify the entire country.

Centralization under the Ming

Zhu and successive Ming emperors had to rebuild a devastated society from the ground up. Although in the past China had experienced natural catastrophes, wars, and social dislocation, the plague's legacy was devastation on an unprecedented scale. It left the new rulers with the formidable challenge of rebuilding the great cities, restoring respect for ruling elites, and reconstructing the bureaucracy.

IMPERIAL GRANDEUR AND KINSHIP The rebuilding began under Zhu, the Hongwu ("expansive and martial") Emperor, whose extravagant capital at Nanjing reflected imperial grandeur. When the dynasty's third emperor, the Yongle ("perpetual happiness") Emperor, relocated the capital to Beijing, he flaunted an even more grandiose style. Construction here mobilized around 100,000 artisans and 1 million laborers. The city had three separate walled enclosures. Inside the outer city walls sprawled the imperial city; within its walls lay the palace city, the Forbidden City. Traffic within the walled sections navigated through boulevards leading to the different gates, above which imposing towers soared. The palace compound, where the imperial family resided, had more than 9,000 rooms. Anyone standing in the front courts, which measured more than 400 yards on a side and boasted marble terraces and carved railings, would gasp at the sense of awesome power. That was precisely the effect the Ming emperors wanted (just as the Ottoman sultans did in building Topkapi Palace).

Marriage and kinship buttressed the power of the Ming imperial household. The dynasty's founder married the adopted daughter of a leading Red Turban rebel (her father, according to legend, was a convicted murderer), thereby consolidating his power and eliminating a threat. Empress Ma, as she was known, became Hongwu's principal wife and was praised for her compassion. Emerging as the kinder face of the regime, she tempered the harsh and sometimes cruel disposition of her spouse. He had numerous other consorts as well, including Korean and Mongol women, who bore him twenty-six sons and sixteen daughters.

BUILDING A BUREAUCRACY Faced with the challenge of reestablishing order out of turmoil, Hongwu initially sought to

Chinese Irrigation. *Farmers in imperial China used sophisticated devices to extract water for irrigation, as depicted in this illustration from the Yuan Mongol period.*

rule through his many kinsmen—by giving imperial princes generous stipends, command of large garrisons, and significant autonomy in running their domains. However, when the princes' power began to threaten the court, Hongwu slashed their stipends, reduced their privileges, and took control of their garrisons. No longer dependent on these men, he established an imperial bureaucracy beholden only to him and to his successors. These officials won appointments through their outstanding performance on a reinstated civil service examination.

In addition, Hongwu took other steps to install a centralized system of rule. He assigned bureaucrats to oversee the manufacture of porcelain, cotton, and silk products, as well as tax collection. He reestablished the Confucian school system as a means of selecting a cadre of loyal officials (not unlike the Ottoman janissaries and administrators). He also set up local networks of villages to rebuild irrigation systems and to supervise reforestation projects to prevent flooding—with the astonishing result that the amount of land reclaimed nearly tripled within eight years. Historians estimate that Hongwu's reign oversaw the planting of about 1 billion trees, including 50 million sterculia, palm, and varnish trees around Nanjing. Their products served in building a maritime expedition fleet in the early fifteenth century. For water control, 40,987 reservoirs underwent repairs or new construction.

Now the imperial palace not only projected the image of a power center, it *was* the center of power. Every official received his appointment by the emperor through the Ministry of Personnel. Hongwu also eliminated the post of prime minister (he executed the man who held the post) and henceforth ruled directly. Ming bureaucrats literally lost their seats and had to kneel before the emperor. In one eight-day period, Hongwu reputedly reviewed over 1,600 petitions dealing with 3,392 separate matters. The drawback, of course, was that he had to keep tabs on this immense system, and his bureaucrats were not always up to the task. Indeed, Hongwu constantly juggled personal and impersonal forms of authority, sometimes fortifying the administration, sometimes undermining it lest it become too autonomous. In due course, he nurtured a bureaucracy far more extensive than those of the Islamic empires. The Ming thus established the most highly centralized system of government of all the monarchies of this period. (See Primary Source: The Hongwu Emperor's Proclamation.)

Religion under the Ming

The Ming's zeal extended to the religious pantheon as well. Citing the mandate of heaven, the emperor revised and strengthened the elaborate protocol of rites and ceremonies that had undergirded dynastic power for centuries. As well as underscoring the emperor's centrality, official rituals (such as those related to the gods of soil and grain) reinforced political and social hierarchies.

Under the guise of "community" gatherings, rites and sacrifices solidified the Ming order by portraying the rulers as the moral and spiritual benefactors of their subjects. On at least ninety occasions each year, the emperor engaged in sacrificial rites, providing symbolic communion between the human and the spiritual worlds. These lavish festivities reinforced the ruler's image as mediator between otherworldly affairs of the gods and worldly concerns of the empire's subjects. The message was clear: the gods were on the side of the Ming household.

Ming Deities. *A pantheon of deities worshipped during the Ming, demonstrating the rich religious culture of the period.*

PRIMARY SOURCE

The Hongwu Emperor's Proclamation

This proclamation by the founder of the Ming dynasty, the Hongwu Emperor (r. 1368–1398), reveals how he envisioned reconstructing the devastated country as his own personal project. He sought a return to austerity by denouncing the morally corrosive effect of money and material possessions, and he especially distrusted his officials. Although frustrated in his efforts, Hongwu nonetheless set the tone for the centralization of power in the person of the emperor.

To all civil and military officials:

I have told you to refrain from evil. Doing so would enable you to bring glory to your ancestors, your wives and children, and yourselves. With your virtue, you then could assist me in my endeavors to bring good fortune and prosperity to the people. You would establish names for yourselves in Heaven and on earth, and for thousands and thousands of years, you would be praised as worthy men.

However, after assuming your posts, how many of you really followed my instructions? Those of you in charge of money and grain have stolen them yourselves; those of you in charge of criminal laws and punishments have neglected the regulations. In this way grievances are not redressed and false charges are ignored. Those with genuine grievances have nowhere to turn; even when they merely wish to state their complaints, their words never reach the higher officials. Occasionally these unjust matters come to my attention. After I discover the truth, I capture and imprison the corrupt, villainous, and oppressive officials involved. I punish them with the death penalty or forced labor or have them flogged with bamboo sticks in order to make manifest the consequences of good or evil actions. . . .

Alas, how easily money and profit can bewitch a person! With the exception of the righteous person, the true gentleman, and the sage, no one is able to avoid the temptation of money. But is it really so difficult to reject the temptation of profit? The truth is people have not really tried.

Previously, during the final years of the Yuan dynasty, there were many ambitious men competing for power who did not treasure their sons and daughters but prized jade and silk, coveted fine horses and beautiful clothes, relished drunken singing and unrestrained pleasure, and enjoyed separating people from their parents, wives, and children. I also lived in that chaotic period. How did I avoid such snares? I was able to do so because I valued my reputation and wanted to preserve my life. Therefore I did not dare to do these evil things. . . .

In order to protect my reputation and to preserve my life, I have done away with music, beautiful girls, and valuable objects. Those who love such things are usually "a success in the morning, a failure in the evening." Being aware of the fallacy of such behavior, I will not indulge such foolish fancies. It is not really that hard to do away with these tempting things.

QUESTIONS FOR ANALYSIS

- What criticisms does Hongwu level against the Mongol Yuan, whose rule he overthrew?
- What crimes does he accuse his own officials of committing, and what punishments does he carry out?
- Why would this Chinese emperor issue a decree that focuses on defining moral behavior?

Source: Lily Hwa, "Proclamations of the Hongwu Emperor." Reprinted with the permission of The Free Press, a division of Simon & Schuster, Inc., from Chinese Civilization: A Sourcebook, *Second Edition, Revised and Expanded by Patricia Buckley Ebrey.*

As an example of religious rituals reinforcing hierarchies, the emperor sanctioned official cults that were either civil or military—and further distinguished as great, middle, or minor, as well as celestial, terrestrial, or human categories. Official cults, however, often conflicted with local faiths. In this regard, they revealed the limits of Ming centralism. Consider Dongyang, a hilly interior region. As was common in Ming China, the people of Dongyang supported Buddhist institutions. Guan Yu, a legendary martial hero killed centuries earlier, was enshrined in a local Buddhist monastery there. But he was also worshipped as part of a state cult. Herein lay the problem: the state cult and the Buddhist monastery were separate entities, and imperial law held that the demands of the state cult prevailed over those of the local monastery. So the state-appointed magistrates in Dongyang kept a watchful eye on local religious leaders, although the magistrates refrained from tampering directly in the monastery's affairs. Although the imperial government insisted that people honor their contributions to the state, Dongyang's residents delivered most of their funds to the Buddhist monks. So strong were local sentiments and contributions that even the officials siphoned revenues to the monastery.

MAP 11.6 | Ming China, 1500s

The Ming state was one of the largest empires at this time—and the most populous. It had a long seacoast and even longer internal borders.

- What were the two Ming capitals, and what were the three main seaport trading cities?
- According to the map, where did the Ming rulers expect the greatest threat to their security?
- How did the Ming rulers view foreign contact and exchange during this period?

Ming Rulership

Religious sources of political power were less essential for the Ming dynasty than for the Islamic dynasties. Conquest and defense helped establish the realm, and bureaucracy kept it functioning. The empire's large scale (see Map 11.6) required a remarkably complex administration. To many outsiders (especially Europeans, whose region was in a state of constant war), Ming stability and centralization appeared to be political wizardry.

In terms of the structures underlying Ming power, the usual dynastic dilemmas were present. The emperor wished to be seen as the special guardian of his subjects. He wanted their allegiance as well as their taxes and labor. But during hard times, poor farmers were reluctant to provide resources—taxes or services—to distant officials. For these reasons alone, Hongwu preferred to entrust management of the rural world to local leaders, whom he appointed as village chiefs, village elders, or tax captains. (In fact, a popular Chinese proverb was: "The mountain is high and the emperor is far away.") Within these communities, the dynasty created a social hierarchy based on age, sex, and kinship. While women's labor remained critical for the village economy, the government reinforced a gender hierarchy by promoting women's chastity and constructing commemorative arches for widows who refrained from remarrying. The Ming thus produced a more elaborate system for classifying and controlling its subjects than did the other Afro-Eurasian dynasties.

The Ming Empire, like the European and Islamic states, also faced periodic unrest and rebellion. Rebels often proclaimed their own brand of religious beliefs, just as local elites resented central authority. Outright terror helped stymie threats to central authority. In a massive wave of carnage, Hongwu slaughtered anyone who posed a threat to his authority, from the highest of ministers to the lowliest of scribes. From 1376 to 1393, four of his purges condemned close to 100,000 subjects to execution.

Yet, despite the emperor's immense power, the Ming Empire remained under-governed. Indeed, as the population multiplied, there were too few loyal officials to handle local affairs. By the sixteenth and early seventeenth centuries, for example, some 10,000 to 15,000 officials shouldered the responsibility of managing a population exceeding 200 million people. Nonetheless, Hongwu bequeathed to his descendants a set of tools for ruling that drew on subjects' direct loyalty to the emperor and on the intricate workings of an extensive bureaucracy. His legacy enabled his successors to balance local sources of power with centralizing ambitions.

Trade under the Ming

In the fourteenth century, China began its economic recovery from the devastation of disease and political turmoil. Gradually, political stability allowed trade to revive. Now the new dynasty's merchants reestablished China's preeminence in long-distance commercial exchange. Chinese silk and cotton textiles, as well as fine porcelains, ranked among the world's most coveted luxuries. Wealthy families from Lisbon to Kalabar loved to wash their hands in delicate Chinese bowls and to flaunt fine wardrobes made from bolts of Chinese dyed linens and smoothly spun silk. When a Chinese merchant ship sailed into port, trading partners and onlookers crowded the docks to watch the unloading of precious cargoes.

OVERSEAS TRADE: SUCCESS AND SUSPICION During the Ming period, Chinese traders based in ports such as Hangzhou, Quanzhou, and Guangzhou (Canton) were as energetic as their Muslim counterparts in the Indian Ocean. These ports were home to prosperous merchants and the point of convergence for vast sea-lanes. Leaving the mainland ports, Chinese vessels carried precious wares to offshore islands, the Pescadores, and Taiwan. From there, they sailed on to the ports of Kyūshū, the Ryūkyūs, Luzon, and maritime Southeast Asia. As entrepôts for global goods, East Asian ports flourished. Former fishing villages developed into major urban centers.

The Ming dynasty viewed overseas expansion with suspicion, however. Hongwu feared that too much contact with the outside world would cause instability and undermine his rule.

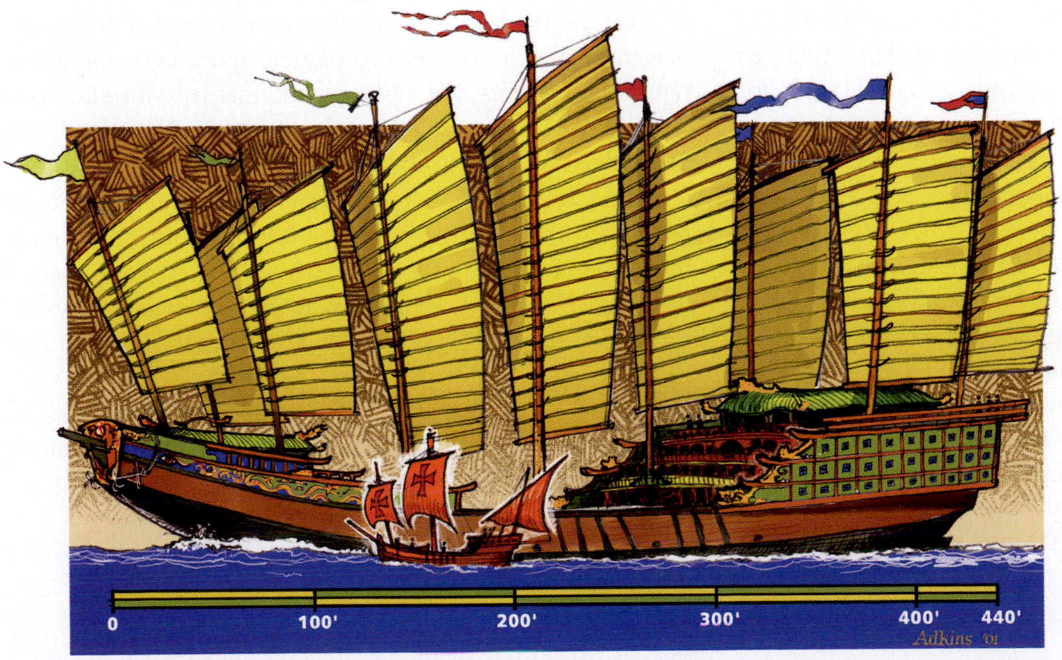

Zheng He's Ship. *A testament to centuries of experience in shipbuilding and maritime activities, the largest ship in Zheng He's armada in the early fifteenth century was about five times the length of Columbus's Santa Maria (pictured next to Zheng's ship) and had nine times the capacity in terms of tonnage. It had nine staggered masts and twelve silk sails, all designed to demonstrate the grandeur of the Ming Empire.*

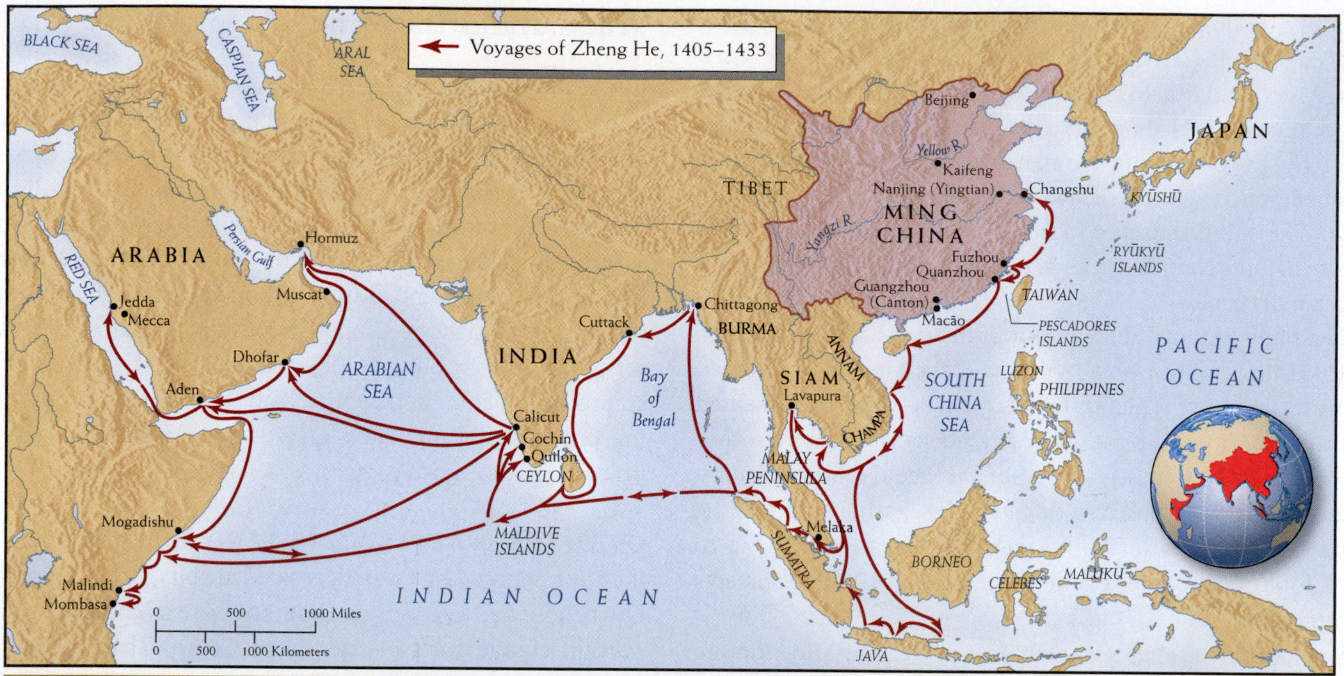

MAP 11.7 | Voyages of Zheng He, 1405–1433

Zheng He's voyages are some of the most famous in world history. Many have speculated about how history might be different if the Chinese emperors had allowed the voyages to continue.

- For how many years did Zheng's voyages go on?
- How far did Zheng go?
- Why did Chinese expeditions not have the same impact as European voyages of exploration toward the end of the fifteenth century?

In fact, he banned private maritime commerce in 1371. But enforcement was lax, and by the late fifteenth century maritime trade once again surged. Because much of the thriving business took place in defiance of official edicts, it led to constant friction between government officials and maritime traders. Although the Ming government ultimately agreed to issue licenses for overseas trade in the mid-sixteenth century, its policies continued to vacillate. To Ming officials, the sea represented problems of order and control rather than opportunities.

MARITIME EXPLORATION AND AFTERMATH One spectacular exception to the Ming's attitude toward maritime trade was a series of officially sponsored expeditions in the early fifteenth century. It was the ambitious Yongle Emperor who took the initiative. One of his loyal followers was a Muslim whom the Ming army had captured as a boy. The youth was castrated and sent to serve at the court (as a eunuch, he could not continue his family line and so theoretically owed sole allegiance to the emperor). Given the name **Zheng He** (1371–1433), he grew up to be an important military leader. The emperor entrusted him with venturing out to trade, collect tribute, and display China's power to the world.

From 1405 to 1433, Zheng He commanded the world's greatest armada and led seven naval expeditions. His larger ships stretched 400 feet in length (Columbus's *Santa Maria* was 85 feet), carried hundreds of sailors on four tiers of decks, and maneuvered with sophisticated rudders, nine masts, and watertight compartments. The first expedition set sail with a flotilla of 62 large ships and over 200 lesser ones. All 28,000 men aboard pledged to promote Ming glory.

Zheng He and his entourage aimed to establish tributary relations with far-flung territories—from Southeast Asia to the Indian Ocean ports, to the Persian Gulf, and to the east coast of Africa (see Map 11.7). These expeditions did not seek territorial expansion, but rather control of trade and tribute. Zheng traded for ivory, spices, ointments, exotic woods, and even some wildlife, including giraffes, zebras, and ostriches. He also used his considerable force to intervene in local affairs, exhibiting China's might in the process. If a community refused to pay tribute, Zheng's fleet would attack it. He encouraged rulers or envoys from Southeast Asia, India, Southwest Asia, and Africa to visit his homeland. When local rulers were uncooperative, Zheng might seize them and drag them all the way to China to face the emperor, as he did the rulers of Sumatra and Ceylon.

As spectacular as they were, Zheng's accomplishments could not survive the changing tides of events at home. Although many items gathered on his voyages delighted the court, most were not the stuff of everyday commerce. The expeditions were glamorous but expensive, and they came to an abrupt halt in 1433. Never again did the Ming undertake such large-scale maritime ventures. In fact, as early as 1424, when the Yongle Emperor died, the expeditions had already lost their most enthusiastic patron. Moreover, by the mid-fifteenth century, there was a revival of military threats from the north. At that time the Ming court was shocked to discover that during a tour of the frontiers, the emperor had been captured and held hostage by the Mongols. Recalling how the maritime-oriented Song dynasty had been overrun by invaders from the north (see Chapter 10), Ming officials withdrew imperial support for seagoing ventures and instead devoted their energies to overland ventures and defense.

Even though maritime commerce continued without official patronage, the abrupt withdrawal of imperial support led to the decline of Chinese naval power and opened the way for newcomers and rivals. Southeast Asians took advantage by constructing large oceangoing vessels, known as *jong*, which plied the regional trade routes from the fifteenth century to the early sixteenth century. These ships weighed an average of 350 to 500 tons (the largest weighed 1,000 tons) and carried 1,000 men on board. They transported cargoes and passengers not only to southern China, but also to the Indian Ocean as far west as Calicut and the Red Sea. Muslims also occupied the vacuum left by the Chinese, sailing west from ports such as Calicut across the Indian Ocean to Mombasa and Mogadishu, and east to Melaka (Malacca). In addition, Japanese pirates commandeered some of the trade. The Chinese decision to focus on internal trade and defending northern borders just at the time others began to look outward and overseas was, in a way, as monumental as that of Mehmed to take Constantinople, or that of Columbus to attempt a perilous westward voyage across "the Ocean Sea."

CONCLUSION

How could all the dying and devastation that came with the Black Death not have transformed the peoples of Afro-Eurasia? Much did change, but certain underlying ideals and institutions endured. What changed were mainly the political regimes, which took the blame for the catastrophes. The Delhi Sultanate, the Abbasid Empire, and the Yuan dynasty collapsed. In contrast, universal religions and wide-ranging cultural systems persisted even though they underwent vast transformations. The Ming dynasts in China set the stage for a long tenure by claiming as had previous rulers the mandate of heaven and stressing China's place at the center of their universe. A strict Shiite version of Islam emerged in Iran, while a fervent form of Sunni Islam found its champion in the Ottoman Empire. In Europe, national monarchies appeared in Spain, Portugal, France, and England. Yet Christianity, whose clerics had so often failed the dying and the disabled, swept back with renewed vigor.

The new states and empires had notable differences. These were evident in the ambition of a Ming warlord who established a new dynasty, the military expansionism of Turkish households bordering the Byzantine Empire, the unifying vision of Mughal rulers in northern India, and the desire of various European rulers to consolidate power. But interactions among peoples also mattered: an eagerness to reestablish and expand trade networks, and a desire to convert unbelievers to "the true faith"—be it a form of Islam, a variant of Hinduism, an exclusive Christianity, or a local type of Buddhism.

The dynasties all faced similar problems. They had to establish legitimacy, ensure smooth succession, deal with religious groups, and forge working relationships with nobles, townspeople, merchants, and peasants. Yet each state developed distinctive traits as a result of political innovation, traditional ways of ruling, and borrowing from neighbors. European monarchies achieved significant internal unity, often through warfare and in the context of a cultural Renaissance. Ottoman rulers perfected techniques for ruling an ethnically and religiously diverse empire: they moved military forces swiftly, allowed local communities a degree of political and religious autonomy, and trained a bureaucracy dedicated to the Ottoman and Sunni Islamic way of life. The Ming fashioned an imperial system based on a Confucian-trained bureaucracy and intense subordination to the emperor so that it could manage a mammoth population. The rising monarchies of Europe, the Shiite regime of the Safavids in Persia, and the Ottoman state all blazed with religious fervor and sought to eradicate or subordinate the beliefs of other groups.

The new states displayed unprecedented political and economic powers. All demonstrated military prowess, a desire for stable hierarchies and secure borders, and a drive to expand. Each legitimized its rule via dynastic marriage and succession, state-sanctioned religion, and administrative bureaucracies. Each supported vigorous commercial activity. The Islamic regimes, especially, engaged in long-distance commerce and, by conquest and conversion, extended their holdings.

For Europeans, the Ottoman conquests were decisive. They provoked Europeans to establish commercial connections to the east, south, and west. The consequences of their new toeholds would be momentous—just as the Chinese decision to turn *away* from overseas exploration and commerce marked a turning point in world history. Both decisions were instrumental in determining which worlds would come together and which would remain apart.

AFTER YOU READ THIS CHAPTER

Review and research on STUDYSPACE: wwnorton.com/studyspace

TRACING THE GLOBAL STORYLINES

FOCUS ON: *Rebuilding States*

Islamic Dynasties

- Ottoman, Safavid, and Mughal empires replace the Mongols.
- Ottomans overrun Constantinople and become the primary Sunni regime in the Islamic world.
- Safavids come to power in Iran as a Shiite state less tolerant of diversity than the Ottomans.
- Mughals replace the Delhi Sultanate in South Asia and continue to accommodate diverse religious beliefs.

China

- The Ming dynasty replaces the Mongol Yuan dynasty and rebuilds a strong state from the ground up.
- An elaborate, centralized bureaucracy oversees the revival of infrastructure and long-distance trade.

Western Christendom

- Devastation from the Black Death provokes revolt and extremist religious movements.
- New national monarchies appear in Portugal, Spain, France, and England.
- A rebirth of classical learning (the Renaissance) originates in Italian city-states and spreads throughout western Europe.

CHRONOLOGY

Islamic World
- Osman begins Ottoman Empire **1299**

South Asia

Europe
- Black Death reaches Italian port cities **1347**
- Peasant revolts in England and France **1358–1381**

East Asia
- Black Death begins in China **1320**
- Hongwu founds Ming dynasty **1368**

1300 | 1350

KEY TERMS

Black Death *p. 406*

dynasty *p. 407*

English Peasants' Revolt *p. 423*

humanism *p. 427*

Inquisition *p. 426*

Jacquerie *p. 423*

khan *p. 417*

monarchy *p. 425*

Moors *p. 425*

Ottoman Empire *p. 411*

Red Turban Movement *p. 430*

Renaissance *p. 426*

shah *p. 417*

Sikhism *p. 419*

Topkapi Palace *p. 415*

Zheng He *p. 436*

STUDY QUESTIONS

1. **Explain** how the Black Death, or bubonic plague, spread throughout Afro-Eurasia. What human activity facilitated its diffusion?
2. **Describe** the long-term consequences of bubonic plague for the Afro-Eurasian world. What were the plague's social, political, and economic ramifications in various parts of the landmass?
3. **Identify** the three main Islamic dynasties that emerged after the bubonic plague. How were they similar, and how were they different?
4. **Describe** how the Ming dynasty centralized its power in China in the fourteenth and fifteenth centuries. What political innovations did it pursue, and what traditions did it sustain?
5. **Describe** the goals of the Ming dynasty's maritime exhibitions. Why did the government later abandon them?
6. **Explain** why the bubonic plague undermined the feudal order of the Catholic Church. How did regional monarchs in Europe capitalize on this development?
7. **What were the key features** of the Renaissance in Europe? How did it spread and change?

Ottoman armies conquer Constantinople **1453**

Suleiman expands and consolidates Ottoman Empire **1520–1566**

Shah Ismail expands and consolidates Safavid Empire **1501–1524**

Timur sacks Delhi **1398**

Babur founds Mughal dynasty **1526**

Castile and Aragon unite to form Spain **1469**

Spain conquers Grenada **1492**

Tudor dynasty begins in England **1485**

Zheng He's voyages **1405–1433**

1400 | 1450 | 1500

BEFORE YOU READ THIS CHAPTER

wwnorton.com/
STUDYSPACE

GLOBAL STORYLINES

- European voyagers and colonizers "discover" the Americas (the so-called New World) and connect Afro-Eurasia with the Americas for the first time since the Ice Age.
- Not only do peoples move back and forth between Afro-Eurasia and the Americas; so do plants, animals, cultural products, and diseases—the Columbian exchange.
- Europeans create empires at great distances from their homelands, fail to enslave Native Americans, and bring in African captives as slave laborers, creating the Atlantic system.

CHAPTER OUTLINE

FOCUS QUESTIONS

- What was old and what was new in sixteenth-century world trade?
- How did the Portuguese attitude toward trade enable the Portuguese to exploit and dominate their trading partners?
- What did European conquerors adopt and change from the New World traditions they encountered?
- What military and maritime technologies advanced Portuguese exploration?
- What caused the political rivalries and religious rifts that divided Europe in the fifteenth and sixteenth centuries?
- Why did trade expand and wealth increase in sixteenth-century Asia?

12

Contact, Commerce, and Colonization, 1450–1600

In 1519, five ships under the command of Ferdinand Magellan set out from the Spanish mainland. Nearly three years later a single vessel returned, having successfully circumnavigated the globe. This achievement came at a high cost: four ships had been lost, and only 18 men out of 265 had staved off scurvy, starvation, and stormy seas to complete the journey. Magellan himself had died. But the survivors had become the first true world travelers. Unlike earlier adventurers who penetrated Eurasia and Africa, Magellan's transoceanic passage connected these worlds with others that, from an Afro-Eurasian viewpoint, had been apart—the Americas.

The voyages of Magellan and other European mariners intensified westerners' contact with Asia's vibrant commercial networks and gave Europeans access to a region they called the New World. Although Christopher Columbus did not intend to "discover" America when he went looking for Asia, his voyages convinced Europeans that there were still new territories to exploit and people to convert to Christianity. Moreover, in colonizing the Americas, Europeans drew on connections with West Africa. Indeed, African laborers became vital to agriculture and mining in the American colonies. Soon the New World's riches were prominent participants in the commercial circuits of Afro-Eurasia.

This chapter introduces the initial European conquest and colonization of the Americas. In the narrative of world history, few events surpass Columbus's voyages of discovery, which opened up worlds about which Afro-Eurasians had no previous knowledge. For the first time since the Ice Age migrations, peoples again moved from Afro-Eurasian landmasses to the Americas. So did animals, plants, commercial products, and—most momentous—deadly germs.

It was enormously significant that Europeans, rather than Asians or Africans, first stumbled upon the Americas and then exploited their resources. For Europeans, too, now became empire builders—but of a different nature. Their empires were overseas, far from the homeland. While the new colonies generated vast riches, they also brought unsettling changes to those who sought to make and maintain empires.

Despite the significance of Europeans' activity in the Americas, most Africans and Asians were barely aware of its importance to them. As the chapter demonstrates, Asian empires in Ottoman-controlled lands and in India and China continued to flourish after recovering from the Black Death. Nor was Europe's attention exclusively on the Americas, for its national monarchies competed for sway at home. Religious revolt in the form of the Protestant Reformation intensified these rivalries. In the wake of Columbus, the drive to build and protect empires across oceans—as well as religious conflicts abroad and at home—scattered peoples, shattered worlds, and created new cultural syntheses.

THE OLD TRADE AND THE NEW

Well before the products of the Americas entered the circuits of Afro-Eurasian trade, commerce had recovered from the destruction wrought by the Black Death. Just as political leaders had rebuilt states by mixing traditional and innovative ideas, merchant elites revived old trade patterns while establishing new networks. Increasingly, traffic across seas supplemented, if not supplanted, the overland transportation of goods. The Indian Ocean and China seas emerged as the focal points of Afro-Eurasia's maritime commerce. Across these waters moved an assortment of goods, coordinated by Arab, Persian, Indian, and Chinese merchants, who often settled in foreign lands. There they facilitated trade and mixed with locals.

European mariners and traders, searching for new routes to South and East Asia, began exploring the Atlantic coast of Africa. Lured by spices, silks, and slaves, and aided by new maritime technology, Portuguese expeditions made their way around Africa and onward to India. Meanwhile, Spanish monarchs sponsored Columbus's bid to reach Asia by sailing west across the Atlantic. Portuguese and Spanish ventures alike sought to convert "heathen" peoples to Christianity and to reap the riches abounding in Asian ports. Although Europeans still had little to offer would-be trading partners in Asia, their developing capability in overseas trade would lay the foundations for a new kind of global commerce.

The Revival of the Chinese Economy

China's economic dynamism was the crucial ingredient to Afro-Eurasia's global economic revival following the devastation wrought by the Black Death. Under the Ming dynasty, commerce rebounded and the Chinese achieved impressive economic expansion.

China's vast internal economy, not external trade, was the mainspring of the country's progress. After the Ming dynasty relocated its capital from Nanjing in the prosperous south to the northern city of Beijing, Chinese merchants, artisans, and farmers exploited the surging domestic market. Reconstruction of the Grand Canal now opened a major artery that allowed food and riches from the economically vibrant lower Yangzi area to reach the capital region of Beijing. Urban centers, such as Nanjing with a population approaching a million and Beijing at half a million, became massive and lucrative markets.

Along China's elaborate internal trading networks flowed silk and cotton textiles, rice, porcelain ceramics, paper, and many other products. The Ming's concern about the potentially disruptive effects of trade did not dampen this activity, and efforts to curb overseas commerce (following Zheng He's

Chinese Porcelain Box. *The shape, coloring, and texture of this Chinese porcelain writing box are a tribute to the exquisite craftsmanship that went into its production. This box was also a symbol of flourishing world trade and a typical example of what the French called "chinoiserie," the possession of which was a hallmark of taste and cultivation among the rich and the status-conscious in Europe.*

voyages; see Chapter 11) were largely unsuccessful. Merchants not only were tolerated but often thrived. And despite strictures on overseas trade, coastal cities remained active harbors.

Although the Chinese kept the best products for themselves, their silks and porcelain were esteemed across Afro-Eurasia. But what did foreign buyers have to trade with the Chinese? The answer was silver, which became essential to the Ming monetary system. Whereas their predecessors had used paper money, Ming consumers and traders mistrusted anything other than silver or gold for commercial dealings. Once the rulers adopted silver as a means of tax payment in the 1430s, it became the predominant medium for larger transactions.

However, China did not produce sufficient silver for its growing needs—a situation that foreigners learned to exploit. Indeed, silver and other precious metals were about the only commodities for which the Chinese would trade their precious manufactures. Through most of the sixteenth century, China's main source of silver was Japan, which one Florentine merchant called the "silver islands." Chinese and European merchants alike plied the routes from Japanese ports to the Chinese mainland.

After the 1570s, however, the Philippines, now under the control of the Spanish, became a gateway for silver coming from the New World. The Ming had developed a commercial fleet, which enabled their merchants to ship goods to Manila in exchange for silver (as well as firearms, sugar, potatoes, and tobacco). Despite official attempts to control trade, China became the final repository for much of the world's silver for roughly two hundred years. According to one estimate, one-third of all silver mined in the Americas wound up in Chinese hands. This influx fueled China's phenomenal economic expansion. New World silver also bought Europeans greater access to China's coveted goods.

The Revival of Indian Ocean Trade

China's economic expansion occurred within the revival of Indian Ocean trade. In fact, many of the same merchants seeking trade with China developed a brisk commerce that tied the whole of the Indian Ocean together. As a result, ports in East Africa and the Red Sea again enjoyed links with coastal cities of India, South Asia, and the Malay Peninsula. Muslims dominated this trade.

India was the geographic and economic center of these trade routes. With a population expanding as rapidly as China's, its large cities (such as Agra, Delhi, and Lahore) each boasted nearly half a million residents. India's manufacturing center, Bengal, exported silk and cotton textiles and rice throughout South and Southeast Asia. Like China, India had a favorable trade balance (meaning they were exporting more than they were importing) with Europe and West Asia, exporting textiles and pepper (a spice that Europeans prized) in exchange for silver.

In dealing with China, Indian merchants faced the same problem as Europeans and West Asians: they had to pay with silver. So they became as dependent on gaining access to silver as others who were courting Chinese commerce. But unlike Chinese merchants, Indian and Islamic traders in the region's commercial hubs did not obey one overarching political authority. This gave them considerable autonomy from political affairs and allowed them to occupy strategic positions in long-distance trade. Meanwhile, rulers all along the Indian Ocean enriched themselves with customs duties while flaunting their status with exotic goods. For glorifying sovereigns and worshipping deities, luxuries such as silks, porcelains, ivory, gold, silver, diamonds, spices, frankincense, myrrh, and incense were in high demand. Thus the Indian Ocean trade connected a vast array of consumers and producers long before Europeans arrived on the scene.

Of the many port cities supporting Indian Ocean commerce, none was more important than Melaka, located at a choke point between the Indian Ocean and the South China Sea. Melaka had no hinterland of farmers to support it, so it thrived exclusively as an entrepôt (a commercial hub for long-distance trade) for world traders, thousands of whom resided in the city or passed through it. Indeed, Melaka's merchants were a microcosm of the region's diverse commercial community. Arabs, Indians, Armenians, Jews, East Africans, Persians, and eventually western Europeans established themselves there to profit from the commerce that flowed in and out of the port.

Overland Commerce and Ottoman Expansion

In the fifteenth and sixteenth centuries, seaborne commerce eclipsed but did not eliminate overland caravan trading. In fact, along some routes, overland commerce thrived anew. One well-trafficked route linked the Baltic Sea, Muscovy, the Caspian Sea, the central Asian oases, and China. Other land routes carried goods to the ports of China and the Indian Ocean; from there, they crossed to the Ottoman Empire's heartland and went by land farther into Europe.

Of the many entrepôts that sprang up along caravan routes, none enjoyed more spectacular success than Aleppo in Syria. Thanks to its prime location at the end of caravan routes from India and Baghdad, Aleppo came to overshadow its Syrian rivals, Damascus and Homs. A vital supply point for Anatolia and the Mediterranean cities, Aleppo by the late sixteenth century was the most important commercial center in southwest Asia.

The Aleppans, like others within the Ottoman Empire, revered successful merchants. In popular stories such as *The Thousand and One Nights,* they celebrated these wealthy traders as shrewd men who amassed enormous wealth by mastering the intricacies of the caravan trade. Those close to the trade recognized how difficult the merchant's task was. The caravans gathered

Caravanserai. *As trade routes throughout the Ottoman Empire bustled with lucrative deals, roadside inns called caravanserais offered shrewd merchants and their helpers rest and refreshment. This illustration of a caravanserai comes from the 1581 travel journal of Venetian envoy Jacopo Soranzo.*

on the city's edge, where animals were hired, tents sewn, and saddles and packs arranged. Large caravans involved 600 to 1,000 camels and up to 400 men; smaller parties required no more than a dozen animals. Whatever the size, a good leader was essential. Only someone who knew the difficult desert routes and enjoyed the confidence of nomadic Bedouin tribes (which provided safe passage for a fee) could hope to make the journey profitable.

Ottoman authorities took a keen interest in the caravan trade, since the state gained considerable tax revenue from it. To facilitate the caravans' movement, the government maintained refreshment and military stations along the route. The largest had individual rooms to accommodate the chief merchants and could provide lodging for up to 800 travelers, as well as care for all their animals. But gathering so many traders, animals, and cargoes could also attract marauders, especially desert tribesmen. To stop the raids, authorities and merchants offered cash payments to tribal chieftains as "protection money." This was a small price to pay in order to protect the caravan trade, whose revenues ultimately supported imperial expansion.

EUROPEAN EXPLORATION AND EXPANSION

The Muslim conquest of Constantinople, Europe's gateway to the east (see Chapter 11), sent shock waves through Christendom and prompted Europeans to probe unexplored links to the east. That entailed looking south and west—and venturing across the seas. (See Map 12.1.) Taking the lead were the Portuguese, whose search for new routes to Asia led them first to Africa.

The Portuguese in Africa and Asia

Europeans had long believed that Africa was a storehouse of precious metals. In fact, a fourteenth-century map, the Catalan Atlas, depicted a single black ruler controlling a vast quantity of gold in the interior of Africa. Thus, as the price of gold skyrocketed during and after the Black Death, ambitious men decided to venture southward in search of this commodity and its twin, silver. These intrepid adventurers did not allow their fears of the world they anticipated encountering to overcome their ambitions. The first Portuguese sailors expected to find giants and Amazons, seas of darkness, and distant lands of savages and cannibals. After all, stories and myths had shaped their views of the places and peoples they would encounter.

NAVIGATION AND MILITARY ADVANCES Innovations in maritime technology and information from other mariners helped Portuguese sailors navigate the treacherous waters along the African coast. In the former category were new vessels. The carrack worked well on bodies of water like the Mediterranean; the caravel could nose in and out of estuaries and navigate unpredictable currents and winds. By using highly maneuverable caravels and perfecting the technique of tacking (sailing into the wind rather than before it), the Portuguese advanced far along the West African coast. In addition, newfound expertise with the compass and the astrolabe helped them determine latitude.

The Catalan Atlas. *This 1375 map shows the world as it was then known. Not only does it depict the location of continents and islands, but it also includes information on ancient and medieval tales, regional politics, astronomy, and astrology.*

The Portuguese also applied knowledge absorbed from ancient Greeks and Arabs and had assistance from Muslim mariners who shared their wide experience of Africa and the Indian Ocean.

The Portuguese success in the Indian Ocean was also partly the result of a revolution in military technology that owed much to borrowings from Asia. It began with the adaptation of a Chinese technology: gunpowder. The Ottomans used it to conquer Constantinople in 1453 with enormous cannons and 800-pound cannonballs. In 1492, Christians used cannons to breach the walls of Granada. Europeans also used smaller cannons, which were more mobile and propelled iron balls in relatively flat trajectories, to destroy old fortifications. When mounted against warships' gunwales, such cannons could bombard ports and rival navies—or merchant vessels—to shift the nature of ocean commerce toward military ends.

Within Europe the main beneficiaries of this revolution in warfare were the dynastic rulers, who could afford to equip large fighting forces with new armaments. Whereas in 1415 the English king had won the Battle of Agincourt against the French with fewer than 10,000 men, by 1492 the Spanish crown amassed a huge force of 60,000 Christian soldiers to drive the Moors out of Granada. Tactics shifted, too. In medieval Europe, a day of combat or a short siege of castles often settled matters. But by the mid-sixteenth century, battles often involved lengthy and inconclusive struggles. This way of war, more costly in money and manpower, gave an advantage to larger, centralized states.

SUGAR AND SLAVES Africa and the islands along its coast soon proved to be far more than a stop-off en route to India or a source of precious metals. Africa became a valued trading area, and its islands were prime locations for growing sugarcane—a crop that had exhausted the soils of Mediterranean islands, where it had been cultivated since the twelfth century. Along what they called the Gold Coast, the Portuguese established many fortresses and ports of call.

After seizing islands along the West African coast, the Portuguese introduced sugarcane cultivation on large plantations and exploited slave labor from the African mainland. The Madeira, Canary, and Cape Verde archipelagos in particular became laboratories for plantation agriculture, for their rainfall and fertile soils made them ideally suited for growing sugarcane. And because it took droves of workers to cultivate, harvest, and process sugarcane, a ready supply of slave labor enabled Portugal and Spain to build sizeable plantations in their first formal **colonies** (regions under the political control of another country). In the 1400s, these islands saw the beginnings of a system of plantation agriculture built on slavery that would travel across the Atlantic in the following century.

Caravel. *Caravels became the classic vessel for European exploration. They had many decks and plenty of portholes for cannons, could house a large crew, and had lots of storage for provisions, cargo, and booty.*

GREENLAND
FROBISHER 1576
ENGLAND
CARTIER 1534–1541
NEWFOUNDLAND (1497)
CABOT 1497–1498
NORTH AMERICA
PORTUGAL
SPAIN
Lisbon
Seville
Cadiz
Ceuta (1415)
AZORES
MADEIRA
ATLANTIC OCEAN
St. Augustine
SAN SALVADOR
COLUMBUS 1492
CANARY ISLANDS
CORTÉS 1519
Zacatecas
Havana (1492)
CUBA
YUCATAN
Tenochtitlán
DRAKE 1577–1580
AZTEC EMPIRE
COLUMBUS 1493–1494
HISPANIOLA (1482)
CAPE VERDE ISLANDS
FERNANDO
GOLD COAST
Elmina
Panama
VESPUCCI 1501–1502
MAGELLAN 1519
CABRAL 1500
DIAZ 1487–1488
PACIFIC OCEAN
Quito (1534)
SOUTH AMERICA
Lima (1535)
INCA EMPIRE
Cuzco
Potosí
Bahia
DRAKE 1577–1580
VASCO DA GAMA 1497–1498
SÃO TOMÉ
DEL CANO (after Magellan's death) 1521–1522
Rio de Janeiro
PIZARRO 1531
MAGELLAN AND DEL CANO 1520
Santiago
Buenos Aires (1535)
CABRAL 1500
Line of Tordesillas 1494
Cape Horn
Straits of Magellan
Portuguese exploration
Spanish exploration
English exploration
French exploration
Portuguese controlled islands
Spanish controlled islands
Portuguese controlled cities
Spanish controlled cities

MAP 12.1 | European Exploration, 1420–1580

In the fifteenth and sixteenth centuries, sailors from Portugal, Spain, England, and France explored and mapped the coastline of most of the world.

- What empire to the east prevented Europeans from expanding trade routes by land?
- Trace the voyages that started from Portugal, and then trace the voyages that started from Spain.
- Why did Portuguese explorers concentrate on Africa and the Indian Ocean, whereas their Spanish counterparts focused on the Americas?
- What does the map tell us about the different patterns of exploration in the New World versus those in the Indian Ocean and the South China Sea?

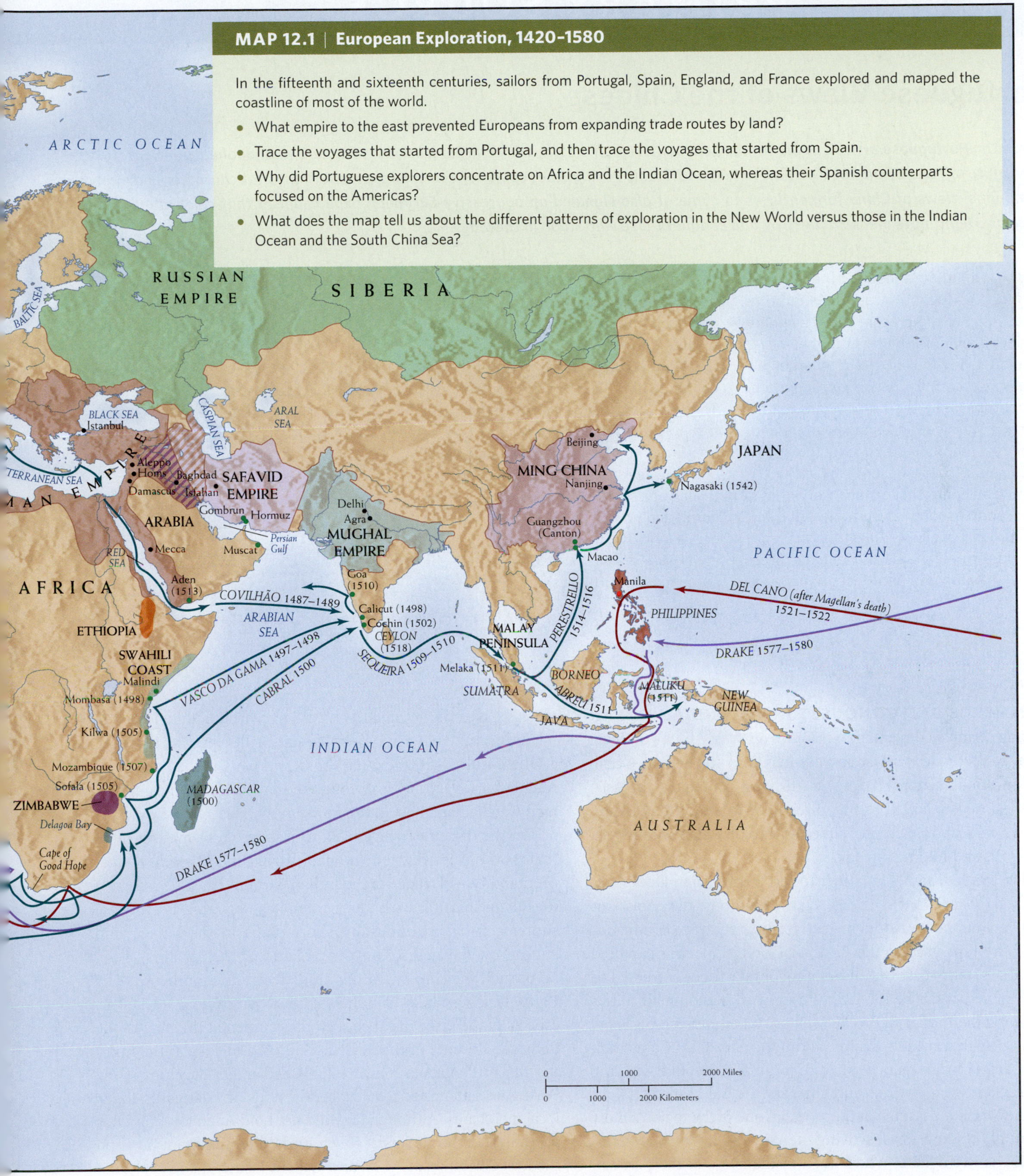

PRIMARY SOURCE

Portuguese Views of the Chinese

When the Portuguese arrived in China, they encountered an empire whose organizational structure and ideological orientation were quite different from their own. Written in 1517, this Portuguese report reflects misrepresentations that characterized many Europeans' views of China for centuries to come. It also signaled an aggressive European expansionism that celebrated brute force as a legitimate means to destroy and conquer those who stood in the way.

God grant that these Chinese may be fools enough to lose the country; because up to the present they have had no dominion, but little by little they have gone on taking the land from their neighbors; and for this reason the kingdom is great, because the Chinese are full of much cowardice, and hence they come to be presumptuous, arrogant, cruel; and because up to the present, being a cowardly people, they have managed without arms and without any practice of war, and have always gone on getting the land from their neighbors, and not by force but by stratagems and deceptions; and they imagine that no one can do them harm. They call every foreigner a savage; and their country they call the kingdom of God.

Whoever shall come now, let it be a captain with a fleet of ten or fifteen sail. The first thing will be to destroy the fleet if they should have one, which I believe they have not; let it be by fire and blood and cruel fear for this day, without sparing the life of a single person, every junk being burnt, and no one being taken prisoner, in order not to waste the provisions, because at all times a hundred Chinese will be found for one Portuguese.

QUESTIONS FOR ANALYSIS

- What do you think was the main purpose of this report?
- How could this observer's views be so inaccurate?
- What is the irony in the comment, "They call every foreigner a savage," followed by instructions to destroy, burn, and not spare "the life of a single person"?

Source: Letters from Canton, translated and edited by D. Ferguson, The Indian Antiquary *31 (January 1902), in J. H. Parry,* European Reconnaissance: Selected Documents *(New York: Walker, 1968), p. 140.*

COMMERCE AND CONQUEST IN THE INDIAN OCEAN

Having established plantation colonies on West Africa's outlying islands, Portuguese seafarers ventured into the Indian Ocean and inserted themselves into its thriving commerce. In Asia, Portugal never wanted to rule directly or to establish colonies. Rather, its seaborne empire aimed to exploit Asian commercial networks and trading systems.

The first Portuguese mariner to reach the Indian Ocean was Vasco da Gama (1469–1524). Like Columbus, da Gama was relatively unknown before his extraordinary voyage commanding four ships around the Cape of Good Hope. He explored Africa's eastern coast but did not encounter friendly traders or great riches. What he found was a network of commercial ties spanning the Indian Ocean, as well as skilled Muslim mariners who knew the currents, winds, and ports of call. Da Gama took on board a Muslim pilot at Malindi for instruction in navigating the Indian Ocean's winds and currents. He then sailed straight for the Malabar coast in southern India, one of the region's most important trading areas, arriving there in 1498.

To the Portuguese, who traded in the name of their crown, commercial access was worth fighting for. Da Gama was briefly taken hostage near Calicut, and though eventually allowed to take on a valuable cargo of spices and silks, he was incensed at the insult. While exiting from southern India, da Gama roughed up everyone he encountered, making sure local fishermen watched and spread the news.

On the difficult voyage back to Lisbon, da Gama lost more than half of his crew, but he had proved the feasibility—and profitability—of trade via the Indian Ocean. When he returned to Calicut in 1502 with a larger crew, he asserted Portuguese supremacy by boarding all twenty ships in the harbor and cutting off the noses, ears, and hands of their sailors. Then he burned the ships with the mutilated sailors on board. The Portuguese repeated their shows of force in strategic locations, especially the three naval choke points: Aden at the base of the Red Sea, Hormuz in the Persian Gulf, and Melaka at the tip of the Malay Peninsula. Once established in the key ports, the Portuguese attempted to take over the trade or, failing this, to tax local merchants. Although they did not hold Aden for long, they solidified control in Sofala, Kilwa, and other important ports on the East African coast, Goa and Calicut in India, and Macao in southern China. From these strongholds, the Portuguese soon commanded the most active sea-lanes of the Indian Ocean. (See Primary Source: Portuguese Views of the Chinese.)

To assert their domain over Indian Ocean trade (west of the Melaka Strait), the Portuguese introduced a pass system that required ships to pay for *cartazes*—documents identifying the ship's captain, size of the ship and crew, and its cargo. Indian Ocean rulers and merchants got cartazes for free, showing the limits of Portuguese control. Others calculated it was cheaper to pay than risk losses at sea from the Portuguese fleet. What made the Portuguese presence in the Indian Ocean world distinctive was that it did not interrupt the flow of luxuries among Asian and African elites; rather, the Portuguese naval captains simply kept a portion of the profits for themselves.

Over time, as Indian Ocean commodities made their way back to Lisbon, that city eclipsed Italian ports (such as Venice) that had previously been prime entrepôts for Asian goods. Even so, spices were less important in Europe than *within* the Indian Ocean world, where the Portuguese became an important player. Only with the discovery of the Americas and the conquest of Brazil did Portugal become an empire with large overseas colonies. For this to transpire, mariners would have to traverse the Atlantic Ocean itself.

THE ATLANTIC WORLD

Western European Christendom, in opening new sea-lanes in the Atlantic, set the stage for an epochal transformation in world history. New technologies aided European expansion, but diseases made the difference. In their encounters with the peoples of the Americas, Europeans introduced more than new cultures to this isolated world; they also brought devastating diseases such as smallpox, typhus, and cholera, for which Amerindian populations had no immunity. In the first years after Amerindians made contact with Europeans, their populations suffered a catastrophic decline. This decimation enabled Europeans to conquer and colonize the Americas as they could not do in Asia or Africa, where long-standing patterns of trade had resulted in the development of shared immunities.

The devastation of the Amerindian population also resulted in severe labor shortages. Thus began the large-scale introduction of slave laborers imported from Africa. After 1500, most of the people who made the Atlantic voyage were not Europeans but Africans. As a supplier of slave labor, Africa became the third corner in a triangular world order. Born of the links among the peoples and resources of Europe, Africa, and the Americas, this emerging "Atlantic system" enriched the Europeans. Through their access to the precious metals of the Americas, they now had something to offer their trading partners in Asia.

Crossing the Atlantic was a feat of monumental importance in world history. It did not occur, however, with an aim to discover new lands. Columbus had wanted to voyage into the "Ocean Sea" so as to open a more direct—and more lucrative—route to Japan and China. Fired by their victory at Granada, Ferdinand and Isabella had agreed to finance his trip, hoping for riches to bankroll a crusade to liberate Jerusalem from Muslim hands. Just as Columbus had no idea he would find a "New World," Spain's monarchs (not to mention its merchants, missionaries, and soldiers) never dreamed that soon they would be preparing for conquest and profiteering in what had been, just a few years before, a blank space on the map. (Thus the term **New World**, as applied to the Americas, reflects the Europeans' view that anything previously unknown to them was "new," even if it had existed and supported societies long before European explorers arrived on its shores.)

Although discovering the Americas was not Columbus's goal, it took scarcely a generation for Europeans to realize the significance of their accidental find. As news of Columbus's voyage spread through Europe, ambitious mariners prepared to sail west. By 1550, all of Europe's powers were scrambling, not just for a share of Indian Ocean action but also for spoils from the Atlantic. In the process, they began destroying the societies and dynasties of the New World. The devastation of its peoples coincided with a sharpening of European rivalries.

Westward Voyages of Columbus

Few figures in history embody their age more than Christopher Columbus. His three ships set sail from Spain in early 1492, stopped in the Canary Islands for supplies and repairs, and cast off into the unknown. When he stepped onto the beach of San Salvador (in the Bahamas) on October 12, 1492, Columbus ushered in a new era in world history. He did not, however, return with the precious Asian commodities he had sought. Columbus would search in vain over three subsequent voyages for the valuable products of the South China Sea and the Indian Ocean.

It is important to see Columbus as a man of his time. Like other expansion-minded Europeans, he aimed to Christianize the world while enriching himself and his backers. These goals—to save souls and to make money—drove the European colonization of the Americas and the formation of an Atlantic system. Still, it is noteworthy that Columbus's voyages aimed not to create something new but to generate revenues to cover the conquest of Granada and the reconquest of the Holy Land.

First Encounters

When Columbus made landfall in the Caribbean Sea, he unfurled the royal standard of Ferdinand and Isabella and claimed the "many islands filled with people innumerable" for Spain. It is

Columbus. *As Columbus made landfall and encountered Indians, he planted a cross to indicate the spiritual purpose of the voyage and read aloud a document proclaiming the sovereign authority of the king and queen of Spain. Quickly, he learned there was barter for precious stones and metals.*

fitting that the first encounter with Caribbean inhabitants, in this case the Tainos, drew blood. Columbus noted, "I showed them swords and they took them by the edge and through ignorance cut themselves." The Tainos had their own weapons but did not forge steel—and thus had no knowledge of such sharp edges.

For Columbus, the Tainos' naiveté in grabbing his sword symbolized the child-like primitivism of these people, whom he would mislabel "Indians" because he thought he had arrived off the coast of Asia. In Columbus's view the Tainos had no religion, but they did have at least some gold (found initially hanging as pendants from their noses). Likewise, Pedro Alvares Cabral, a Portuguese mariner whose trip down the coast of Africa in 1500 was blown off course across the Atlantic, wrote that the people of Brazil had all "the innocence of Adam." He also noted that they were ripe for conversion and that the soils "if rightly cultivated would yield everything." But, as with Africans and Asians, Europeans also developed a contradictory view of the peoples of the Americas. From the Tainos, Columbus learned of another people, the Caribs, who (according to his informants) were savage, warlike cannibals. For centuries, these contrasting images—innocents and savages—structured European (mis) understandings of the native peoples of the Americas.

We know less about what the Indians thought of Columbus or other Europeans on their first encounters. Certainly the Europeans' appearance and technologies inspired awe. The Tainos fled into the forest at the approach of European ships, which they thought were giant monsters; others thought they were floating islands. European metal goods, in particular weaponry, struck them as otherworldly. The strangely dressed white men seemed godlike to some, although many Indians soon abandoned this view. The natives found the newcomers different not for their skin color (only Europeans drew the distinction based on skin pigmentation), but for their hairiness. Indeed, the Europeans' beards, breath, and bad manners repulsed their Indian hosts. The newcomers' inability to live off the land also stood out.

In due course, the Indians realized that the strange, hairy people bearing metal weapons meant to stay and force the native population to labor for them. But by then, it was too late. The explorers had become **conquistadors** (conquerors).

First Conquests

After his first voyage, Columbus claimed that on Hispaniola (present-day Haiti and the Dominican Republic) "he had found what he was looking for"—gold. That was sufficient to persuade the Spanish crown to invest in larger expeditions, and to seek to conquer this promising new territory. Whereas Columbus first sailed with three small ships and 87 men, ten years later the Spanish outfitted an expedition with 2,500 men. Exploration now gave way to warfare, and to exploitation.

Between 1492 and 1519, the Spanish experimented with institutions of colonial rule over local populations on the Caribbean island that they renamed Hispaniola. Ultimately they created a model that the rest of the New World colonies would adapt. But the Spaniards faced problems that would recur. The first was Indian resistance. As early as 1494, starving Spaniards raided and pillaged Indian villages. When the Indians revolted, Spanish soldiers replied with punitive expeditions and began enslaving them to work in mines extracting gold. As the crown systematized grants (*encomiendas*) to the conquistadors for control over Indian labor, a rich class of *encomenderos* arose who enjoyed the fruits of the system. Although the placer gold mines soon ran dry, the model of granting favored settlers the right to coerce Indian labor endured. In return, those who received the labor rights paid special taxes on the precious metals that were extracted. Thus, both the crown and the *encomenderos* benefited from the extractive economy. The same cannot be said of the Indians, who perished in great numbers from disease, dislocation, malnutrition, and overwork.

It is no surprise that quarrels over spoils followed the conquests. The family of Columbus, in particular, had been granted a commercial monopoly on his discoveries, but some of the settlers challenged Columbus's authority. To prevent insurrection, the crown granted more *encomiendas* to other Spanish claimants. As special grants became a common feature of Spanish colonialism, less favored settlers grew disenchanted. When the Indians and the gold supplies began to disappear, many settlers pulled up their stakes and returned to Spain. Others looked for untapped territories that might yield precious metals.

Not all joined the rush for riches or celebrated the conquistadors and *encomenderos*. Dominican friars protested the abuse of the Indians, seeing them as potential converts who were equal to the Spaniards in the eyes of God. In 1511, Father Antonio Montesinos accused the settlers of barbarity: "By what right do you wage such detestable wars on these people who lived idly and peacefully in their own lands, where you have consumed infinite numbers of them with unheard-of murders and desolations?" Dissent and debate would be a permanent feature of Spanish colonialism in the New World.

The Aztec Empire and the Spanish Conquest

As Spanish colonists saw the bounty of Hispaniola dry up, they set out to discover and conquer new territories. Finding their way to the mainlands of the American landmasses, they encountered larger, more complex, and more militarized societies than those they had overrun in the Caribbean.

On the mainland, great civilizations had arisen centuries before, boasting large cities, monumental buildings, and riches based on wealthy agrarian societies. In both Mesoamerica, starting with the Olmecs (see Chapter 5), and the Andes, with the Chimú (see Chapter 10), large polities had laid the foundations for subsequent Aztec and Incan empires. The latter states were powerful. But they also represented the evolution of states and commercial systems untouched by Afro-Eurasian developments; as worlds apart, they were unprepared for the kind of assaults that European invaders had honed. In pre-Columbian Mesoamerica and then the Andes, warfare was more ceremonial, less inclined to wipe out enemies than to make them tributary subjects. As a result, the wealth of these empires made them irresistible to outside conquerors they never knew, and their habits of war made them vulnerable to conquests they could never foresee.

AZTEC SOCIETY In Mesoamerica, the ascendant Mexicas had created an empire known to us as "Aztec." Around Lake Texcoco, Mexica cities grew and formed a three-city league in 1430, which then expanded through the Central Valley of Mexico to incorporate neighboring peoples. Gradually the **Aztec Empire** united numerous small, independent states under a single monarch who ruled with the help of counselors, military leaders, and priests. By the late fifteenth century, the Aztec realm may have embraced 25 million people. Tenochtitlán, the primary city, situated on an immense island in Lake Texcoco, ranked among the world's largest.

Tenochtitlán spread in concentric circles, with the main religious and political buildings in the center and residences radiating outward. The city's outskirts connected a mosaic of floating gardens producing food for urban markets. Canals irrigated the land, waste served as fertilizer, and high-yielding produce found easy transport to markets. Entire households worked: men, women, and children all had roles in Aztec agriculture.

Extended kinship provided the scaffolding for Aztec statehood. Marriage of men and women from different villages solidified alliances and created clan-like networks. In Tenochtitlán, powerful families married their children to each other or found nuptial partners among the prominent families of other important cities. (Certain ruling houses in Europe were solidifying alliances in much the same way at this time; see Chapter 11.) Not only did this practice concentrate power in the great city, but it also ensured a pool of potential successors to the throne. Soon a lineage emerged to create a corps of "natural" rulers. Priests legitimized the new emperor in rituals to convey the image of a ruler close to the gods and to distinguish the elite from the lower orders.

Tenochtitlán. *At its height, the Aztec capital, Tenochtitlán, was as populous as Europe's largest city. As can be seen from this map, it spread in concentric circles, with the main religious and political buildings in the center and residences radiating outward.*

A hierarchy at the village level provided the bedrock for layers of increasingly centralized political authority. Local elders developed representative councils, which selected delegates to a committee that elected the dominant civil authority, the chief speaker. As Aztec power spread, the chief speaker became a full-blown emperor. He was, however, not supreme; instead, he jockeyed with rival religious and military power-wielders. Thus at the top of the Aztec social pyramid stood a small but antagonistic nobility. This hierarchically organized society held itself together through a shared understanding of the cosmos. The Aztecs believed that the universe was prone to unceasing cycles of disaster that would eventually end in apocalypse. Such an unstable cosmos exposed mortals to repeated creations and destructions of their world. The priesthood governed relationships between people and their deities. Their challenge was to balance a belief that history was destined to run in cycles with a faith that mortals could influence the gods, and their own fate, through religious rituals.

Ultimately Aztec power spread though much of Mesoamerica, but the empire's constant wars and conquests deprived it of stability. In successive military campaigns, the Aztecs subjugated their neighbors, feeding off plunder and then forcing subject peoples to pay tribute of crops, gold, silver, textiles, and other goods that financed Aztec grandeur. Such conquests also provided a constant supply of humans for sacrifice, because the Aztecs believed that the great god of the sun required human hearts to keep on burning and blood to replace that given by the gods to moisten the earth through rain. Priests escorted captured warriors up the temple steps and tore out their hearts, offering their lives and blood as a sacrifice to the sun god. Allegedly, between 20,000 and 80,000 men, women, and children were slaughtered in a single ceremony in 1487, with the four-person-wide line of victims stretching for over two miles. In this marathon of bloodletting, knife-wielding priests collapsed from exhaustion and surrendered their places to fresh executioners.

Those whom the Aztecs sought to dominate did not submit peacefully. From 1440, the empire faced constant turmoil as subject peoples rebelled against their oppressive overlords. Tlaxcalans and Tarascans along the Gulf of Mexico waged a relentless war for freedom, pinning down entire divisions of Aztec armies. To pacify the realm, the empire diverted more and more men and money into a mushrooming military. By the time the electoral committee chose Moctezuma II as emperor in 1502, divisions among elites and pressures from the periphery placed the Aztec Empire under extreme stress.

CORTÉS AND CONQUEST Not long after Moctezuma became emperor, news arrived from the coast of strange sightings of

Cortés Meets Mesoamerican Rulers. (Left) *This colonial image depicts the meeting of Cortés (second from right) and Moctezuma (seated on the left), with Doña Marina serving as an interpreter and informer for the Spanish conquistador. Notice at the bottom what are likely Aztec offerings for the newcomer.* (Right) *This detail from a twentieth-century Mexican mural depicts the meeting of Cortés and the king of Tlaxcala (enemy of the Aztecs). As Mexicans began to celebrate their mixed-blood heritage, Doña Marina (in the middle) became the symbolic mother of the first mestizos.*

The Conquest of the Aztecs. *Diego Rivera's twentieth-century representation of the fall of Tenochtitlan (left) emphasizes the helplessness of the Aztecs to the ruthless and technologically superior Spanish soldiers. Though the Aztecs outnumber the Spanish in this portrayal, their faces are obscured in postures of grief and suffering, unlike their counterparts in the sixteenth-century illustration of the same event (right). Painted by a converted Indian and based on indigenous oral histories, it shows the Aztec warriors in a glory of their own, as well as the cruel fact that they were force to fight other Indians who had sided with the Spanish.*

floating mountains (ships) bearing pale, bearded men and monsters (horses and dogs). Moctezuma consulted with his ministers and soothsayers, wondering if these men were the god Quetzalcoátl and his entourage. The people of Tenochtitlán saw omens of impending disaster. Moctezuma sank into despair, hesitating over what to do. He sent emissaries bearing jewels and prized feathers; later he sent sorcerers to confuse and bewitch the newcomers. But he did not prepare for any military engagement. After all, Mesoamericans had no idea of the interlopers' destructive potential in weaponry and germs.

Aboard one of the ships was Hernán Cortés (1485–1547), a former law student from one of the Spanish provinces. He would become the model conquistador, just as Columbus was the model explorer. For a brief time, Cortés was an *encomendero* in Hispaniola; but when news arrived of a potentially wealthier land to the west, he set sail with over 500 men, eleven ships, sixteen horses, and artillery.

When the expedition arrived near present-day Veracruz, Cortés acquired two translators, including the daughter of a local Indian noble family. The daughter, who became known as Doña Marina, was a "gift" to the triumphant Spaniards from the ruler of the Tabasco region (a rival to the Aztecs). Fluent in several languages, Doña Marina displayed such linguistic skills and personal charms that she soon came to Cortés's attention. She became his lover and ultimately revealed several Aztec plots against the tiny Spanish force. Doña Marina subsequently bore Cortés a son, who is considered one of the first mixed-blooded Mexicans (**mestizos**).

With the assistance of Doña Marina and other native allies, Cortés marched his troops to Tenochtitlán. Upon entering, he gasped in wonder that "this city is so big and so remarkable" that it was "almost unbelievable." One of his soldiers wrote, "It was all so wonderful that I do not know how to describe this first glimpse of things never heard of, seen or dreamed of before."

How was this tiny force to overcome an empire of many millions with an elaborate warring tradition? Crucial to Spanish conquest was their alliance, negotiated through translators, with Moctezuma's enemies—especially the Tlaxcalans. After decades of yearning for release from the Aztec yoke, the Tlaxcalans and other Mesoamerican peoples embraced Cortés's promise of help. The Spaniards' second advantage was their method of warfare. The Aztecs were seasoned fighters, but they fought to capture, not to kill. Nor were they familiar with gunpowder or sharp steel swords. Although outnumbered, the Spaniards killed their foe with abandon, using superior weaponry, horses, and war dogs. The Aztecs, still unsure who these strange men were, allowed Cortés to enter their city. With the aid of the Tlaxcalans and a handful of his own men, in 1519 Cortés captured Moctezuma, who became a puppet of the Spanish conqueror. (See Primary Source: Cortés Approaches Tenochtitlán.)

Within two years, the Aztecs realized that the newcomers were not gods and that Aztec warriors, too, could fight to kill.

PRIMARY SOURCE

Cortés Approaches Tenochtitlán

When the Spanish conquered the Aztec Empire, they defeated a mighty power. The capital, Tenochtitlán, was probably the same size as Europe's biggest city. Glimpsing Tenochtitlán in 1521, Hernán Cortés marveled at its magnificence. But to justify his acts, he claimed to be bringing civilization and Christianity to the Aztecs. Note the contrast between Cortés's admiration for Tenochtitlán and his condemnation of Indian beliefs and practices—as well as his claim that he abolished cannibalism, something the Aztecs did not practice (although they did sacrifice humans).

This great city of Tenochtitlán is built on the salt lake. . . . It has four approaches by means of artificial causeways. . . . The city is as large as Seville or Cordoba. Its streets . . . are very broad and straight, some of these, and all the others, are one half land, and the other half water on which they go about in canoes. . . . There are bridges, very large, strong, and well constructed, so that, over many, ten horsemen can ride abreast. . . . The city has many squares where markets are held. . . . There is one square, twice as large as that of Salamanca, all surrounded by arcades, where there are daily more than sixty thousand souls, buying and selling. . . . [I]n the service and manners of its people, their fashion of living was almost the same as in Spain, with just as much harmony and order; and considering that these people were barbarous, so cut off from the knowledge of God and other civilized peoples, it is admirable to see to what they attained in every respect. . . .

It happened . . . that a Spaniard saw an Indian . . . eating a piece of flesh taken from the body of an Indian who had been killed. . . . I had the culprit burned, explaining that the cause was his having killed that Indian and eaten him, which was prohibited by Your Majesty, and by me in Your Royal name. I further made the chief understand that all the people . . . must abstain from this custom. . . . I came . . . to protect their lives as well as their property, and to teach them that they were to adore but one God . . . that they must turn from their idols, and the rites they had practised until then, for these were lies and deceptions which the devil . . . had invented. . . . I, likewise, had come to teach them that Your Majesty, by the will of Divine Providence, rules the universe, and that they also must submit themselves to the imperial yoke, and do all that we who are Your Majesty's ministers here might order them. . . .

QUESTIONS FOR ANALYSIS

- What does Cortés's report tell us about the city of Tenochtitlán?
- Why does Cortés justify his actions to the degree he does?
- Cortés writes, "I came . . . to protect their lives as well as their property." Based on your reading of the chapter text, would you say he accomplished these objectives?

Source: Letters of Cortés, *translated by Francis A. MacNutt (New York: G. P. Putnam, 1908), pp. 244, 256–57.*

When Spanish troops massacred an unarmed crowd in Tenochtitlán's central square while Cortés was away, they provoked a massive uprising. The Spaniards led Moctezuma to one of the palace walls to plead with his people for a truce, but the Aztecs kept up their barrage of stones, spears, and arrows—striking and killing Moctezuma. Cortés returned to reassert control; but realizing this was impossible, he gathered his loot and escaped. Left behind were hundreds of Spaniards, many of whom were dragged up the temple steps and sacrificed by Aztec priests.

With the Tlaxcalans' help, Cortés regrouped. This time he chose to defeat the Aztecs completely. He ordered the building of boats to sail across Lake Texcoco to bombard the capital with artillery. Even more devastating was the spread of smallpox, brought by the Spanish, which ran through the soldiers and commoners like wildfire. Still, led by a new ruler, Cuauhtémoc, the Aztecs rallied and nearly drove the Spaniards from Tenochtitlán. In the end starvation, disease, and lack of artillery vanquished the Aztec forces. More died from disease than from fighting—the total number of Aztec casualties may have reached 240,000. As Spanish troops retook the capital, they found it in ruins, with a population too weak to resist. Cuauhtémoc himself faced execution, thereby ending the royal Mexica lineage. The Aztecs lamented their defeat in verse: "We have pounded our hands in despair against the adobe walls, for our inheritance, our city, is lost and dead." Cortés became governor of the new Spanish colony, renamed "New Spain." He promptly allocated *encomiendas* to his loyal followers and dispatched expeditions to conquer the more distant Mesoamerican provinces.

The Mexica experience taught the Spanish an important lesson: an effective conquest had to be swift—and it had to remove completely the symbols of legitimate authority. Their winning advantage, however, was disease. The Spaniards unintentionally introduced germs that made their subsequent efforts at military conquest much easier.

The Incas

The other great Spanish conquest occurred in the Andes, where Quechua-speaking rulers, called Incas, had established an impressive polity. From its base in the valley of Cuzco, the **Inca Empire** encompassed a population of 4 to 6 million. But the Incas were internally split. Lacking a clear inheritance system, the empire suffered repeated convulsions.

In the early sixteenth century, the struggle over who would succeed Huayna Capac, the Inca ruler, was especially fierce. Huascar, his "official" son, took Cuzco (the capital), while Atahualpa, his favored son, governed the province of present-day Ecuador. Open conflict might have been averted were it not for Huayna's premature death. His killer was probably smallpox, which swept down the trade routes from Mesoamerica into the Andes (much as the bubonic plague had earlier spread through Afro-Eurasian trade routes; see Chapter 11). With the father gone, Atahualpa declared war on his brother, crushed him, forced him to witness the execution of all his supporters, and then killed him and used his skull as a vessel for maize-beer.

Pizarro and the Incas. *This illustration is by the Andean native Guaman Poma, whose c. 1587 epic of the conquest of Peru depicted many of the barbarities of the Spanish. Here we see the conquistador Pizarro and a Catholic priest appealing to Atahualpa—before betraying and then killing him.*

When the Spaniards arrived in 1532 they found an internally divided empire, a situation they quickly learned to exploit. Francisco Pizarro, who led the Spanish campaign, had been inspired by Cortés's victory and yearned for his own glory. Commanding a force of about 600 men, he invited Atahualpa to confer at the town of Cajamarca. There he laid a trap. As columns of Inca warriors and servants covered with colorful plumage and plates of silver and gold entered the main square, the Spanish soldiers were awed. One recalled, "many of us urinated without noticing it, out of sheer terror." But Pizarro's plan worked. His guns and horses shocked the Inca forces. Atahualpa himself fell into Spanish hands, later to be decapitated. Pizarro's conquistadors overran Cuzco in 1533 and then vanquished the rest of the Inca forces, a process that took decades in some areas.

Meanwhile, Spaniards began arriving in droves at the new capital of Lima. They staked their own claims for *encomiendas*, outdoing each other with greed, and soon were at war with one another. In 1541, one faction assassinated Pizarro himself. Rival factions kept up a brutal war until the Spanish king issued new laws to prevent *encomiendas* from being heritable. This act sought to block the establishment of a powerful aristocracy, to deter uncontrollable civil war, and to reinforce loyalty to Madrid (since once an *encomendero* died, his title reverted to the crown).

The defeat of the New World's two great empires had enormous repercussions for world history. First, it meant that Europeans had their way with the human and material wealth of the Americas. Second, it gave Europeans a market for their own products—goods that found little favor in Afro-Eurasia. Finally, it opened a new frontier that the Europeans could colonize as staple-producing provinces. Now, following the Portuguese push into Africa and Asia (as well as a Russian push into northern Asia; see Chapter 13), the New World conquest introduced Europeans to a new scale of imperial expansion. The outcome, however, would destabilize Europe itself.

Environmental Consequences of the Conquest

The Spanish came to the Americas for gold and silver, but in the course of conquest and settlement they also learned about crops such as potatoes and corn that would fuel a population explosion across Afro-Eurasia. They brought with them first of all devastating diseases, but also horses, wheat, grapevines, and sugarcane. Historians call this hemispheric transfer of previously unknown plants, pathogens, people, and products in the wake of Columbus's voyages the **Columbian exchange**. Over

ANALYZING GLOBAL DEVELOPMENTS

The European Conquest of the Americas and Amerindian Mortality

If the fourteenth century was an age of dying across Afro-Eurasia, the sixteenth century saw even higher mortality rates in the Americas. As a result of European conquest, the exposure to virulent diseases, and the hyperexploitation of their labor under miserable conditions, the Native American populations saw their numbers reduced by 85 percent. The numbers themselves, however, are highly controversial and have sparked intense debates. Some scholars believe that no reliable numbers can be found for the population of the Americas when Europeans first arrived. Others have used a range of methods and data sources to establish population figures, including European firsthand accounts from that period, archaeological and anthropological evidence, estimates of the maximum population size of people the land can contain indefinitely (carrying capacity), and projections built backward from more recent censuses. These estimates vary widely from as little as 8 million to as high as more than 100 million.

Area	Population in 1492	Later Populations	Mortality Rates
The Americas	53.9 m	8 m in 1650	85%
The Caribbean			
Hispaniola	1.0 m	extinct by 1600	100%
The other islands	2.0 m	extinct by 1600	100%
Mexico	17.2 m	3.5 m in 1600	80%
The Andes	15.0 m	3.0 m in 1650	80%
Central America	5.63 m	1.12 m in 1700	80%
North America	3.79 m	1.5 m in 1700	60%
		250,000 in 1900	84%

QUESTIONS FOR ANALYSIS

- Imagine yourself a historical demographer. How would you attempt to estimate the population of the Americas in 1492?
- What effect did European conquest and Amerindian dying have on the polities and religious beliefs of the Native Americans?
- Why do you think Native American population growth never recovered from the initial encounter with Europeans as Afro-Eurasian population growth eventually recovered from the Black Death?

Sources: Suzanne Austin Alchon, A Pest in the Land: New World Epidemics in a Global Perspective *(2003); David Noble Cook,* Born to Die: Disease and New World Conquest, 1492 to 1650 *(1998); William M. Denevan,* The Native Populations of the Americas in 1492 *(1992); David Henige,* Numbers from Nowhere: The Amerindian Contact Population Debate *(1998); "La catastrophe demographique,"* L'histoire, *July–August, 2007, no. 322, p. 17; Thornton, Russell,* American Indian Holocaust: A Population History since 1492 *(1987), p. xvii.*

time, this exchange would transform the environments, economies, and diets of both the new and the old worlds.

The first and most profound effect of the Columbian exchange was a destructive one: the decimation of the Amerindian population by European diseases (see Analyzing Global Developments: The European Conquest of the Americas and Amerindian Mortality). For millennia, the isolated populations of the Americas had been cut off from Afro-Eurasian microbe migrations; in this sense, in contrast, the Amerindians were indeed "worlds apart."

Sickness spread from almost the moment the Spaniards arrived. One Spanish soldier noted, upon entering the conquered Aztec capital, "the streets were so filled with dead and sick people that our men walked over nothing but bodies." Native American accounts of the fall of Tenochtitlán recalled the smallpox epidemic more vividly than the fighting. Even worse, no sooner had smallpox done its work than Indians faced a second pandemic: measles. Then came pneumonic plague and influenza. As each wave retreated, it left a population more emaciated than before, even less prepared for the next wave. The scale of death remains unprecedented: imported pathogens wiped out up to 90 percent of the Indian population. A century after smallpox arrived on Hispaniola in 1519, no more than 5 to 10 percent of the island's population was left alive. Diminished and weakened by disease, Amerindians could not resist European settlement and colonization of the Americas. Thus were Europeans the unintended beneficiaries of a horrifying catastrophe.

As time passed, all sides adopted new forms of agriculture from one-another. Indians taught Europeans how to grow potatoes and corn, crops that would become staples all across Afro-Eurasia. The Chinese found that they could grow corn in areas too dry for rice and too wet for wheat, while corn replaced, at first by fits and starts, Africa's major food grains, sorghum, millet, and rice, to become the continent's principal food crop by the twentieth century. (See Current Trends in World History:

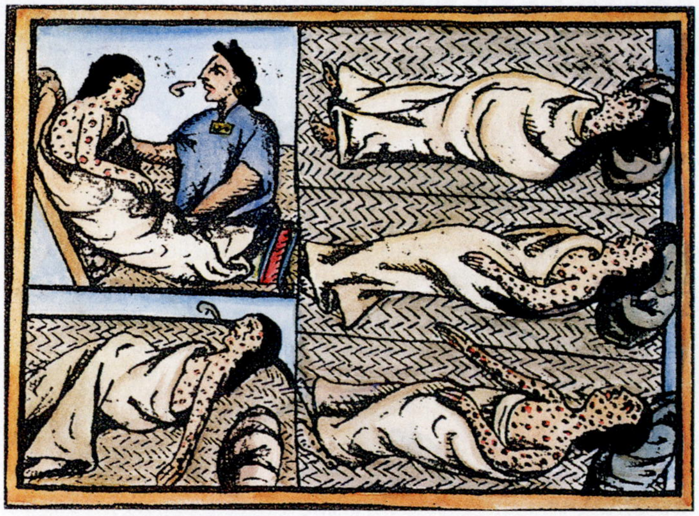

Disease and Decimation of Indians. *The real conqueror of Native Americans was not so much guns as germs. Even before Spanish soldiers seized the Aztec capital, germs had begun decimating the population. The first big killer was smallpox, recorded here by an Indian artist, covering the bodies of victims.*

Corn and the Rise of Slave-Supplying Kingdoms in West Africa.) Europeans also took away tomatoes, beans, cacao, peanuts, tobacco, and squash, while importing livestock such as cattle, swine, and horses to the New World. The environmental effects of the introduction of livestock to the Americas were manifold. In the highland regions north of the valley of central Mexico (where Native Americans had once maintained irrigated, highly productive agricultural estates), Spanish settlers opened up large herding ranches. An area that had once produced corn and squash now supported herds of sheep and cattle. Without natural predators, these animals reproduced with lightning speed, destroying entire landscapes with their hooves and their foraging.

As Europeans cleared trees and other vegetation for ranches, mines, or plantations, they undermined the habitats of many indigenous mammals and birds. On the islands of the West Indies, described by Columbus as "roses of the sea," the Spanish chopped down lush tropical and semitropical forests to make way for sugar plantations. Before long, nearly all of the islands' tall trees as well as many shrubs and ground plants were gone, and residents lamented the absence of birdsong. Over ensuing centuries, the flora and fauna of the Americas took on an increasingly European appearance—a process that the historian Alfred Crosby has called ecological imperialism.

Spain's Tributary Empire

Like the Europeans who sailed into the Indian Ocean to join existing commercial systems, the Spaniards sought to exploit the wealth of indigenous empires without fully dismantling them. Those Native Americans who survived the original encounters could be harnessed as a means to siphon tribute payments to the new masters. Spain could thereby extract wealth without extensive settlement. In Mexico and Peru, where the Inca Empire suffered the same fate as the Aztecs, conquistadors decapitated native communities but left much of their social and economic structure intact—including networks of tribute. But unlike the European penetration of the Indian Ocean, the occupation of the New World went beyond the control of commercial outposts. Instead, European colonialism in the Americas involved controlling large amounts of territory—and ultimately the entire landmass (see Map 12.2).

By fusing traditional tribute-taking with their own innovations, Spanish masters made villagers across their new American empire deliver goods and services. But because the Spanish authorities also bestowed *encomiendas*, those favored individuals could demand labor from their lands' Indian inhabitants—for mines, estates, and public works. Whereas Aztec and Inca rulers had used conscripted labor to build up their public wealth, the Spaniards did so for private gain.

Most Spanish migrants were men; only a few were women. One, Inés Suárez, reached the Indies only to find her husband, who had arrived earlier, dead. She then became mistress of the conquistador Pedro de Valdivia, and the pair worked as a conquering team. Initially, she joined an expedition to conquer Chile as Valdivia's domestic servant, but she soon became much more—nurse, caretaker, advisor, and guard, having uncovered several plots to assassinate her lover. Suárez even served as a diplomat between warring Indians and Spaniards in an effort to secure the conquest. Later, she helped to rule Chile as the wife of Rodrigo de Quiroga, governor of the province. Admittedly, hers

Silver. *Silver was an important discovery for Spanish conquerors in Mesoamerica and the Andes. Conquerors expanded the customs of Inca and Aztec labor drafts to force the natives to work in mines, often in brutal conditions.*

CURRENT TRENDS IN WORLD HISTORY

Corn and the Rise of Slave-Supplying Kingdoms in West Africa

New World varieties of corn spread rapidly throughout the Afro-Eurasian landmass soon after the arrival of Columbus in the Americas. Its hardiness and fast ripening qualities made it more desirable than many of the Old World grain products. In communities that consumed large quantities of meat, it became the main product fed to livestock.

Corn's impact on Africa was as substantial as it was in the rest of Eurasia. Seeds made their way to western regions more quickly than to the south of the Sahara along two routes. One was via European merchants calling into ports along the coast; the second was West African Muslims returning across the Sahara after participating in the pilgrimage. The first evidence of corn cultivation in sub-Saharan Africa comes from a Portuguese navigator who identified the crop being grown on the island of Cape Verde in 1540. By the early seventeenth century, corn was replacing millet and sorghum as the main grain being grown in many West African regions and was destined to transform the work routines and diets of the peoples living in the region's tropical rain forests all the way from present-day Sierra Leone in the east to Nigeria in the west. In many ways this area, which saw the rise of a group of powerful slave-supplying kingdoms in the eighteenth century, notably Asante, Dahomey, Oyo, and Benin, owed its prosperity to the cultivation of this New World crop. (See Chapter 14 for a fuller discussion of these states.)

The tropical rain forests of West and central Africa were thick with trees and ground cover in 1500. Clearing them so that they could support intensive agriculture was exhausting work, requiring enormous outlays of human energy and man-hours. Corn, a crop first domesticated in central Mexico 7,000 years ago, made this task possible. It added much-needed carbohydrates to the carbon-deficient diets of rain-forest dwellers. In addition, as a crop that matured more quickly than those that were indigenous to the region (millet, sorghum, and rice) and required less labor, it yielded two harvests in a single year. Farmers also cultivated cassava, another New World native, which in turn provided households with more carbohydrate calories. Yet corn did more than produce more food per unit of land and labor. Households put every part of the plant to use—grain, leaves, stalks, tassels, and roots were made to serve useful purposes.

Thus, at the very time that West African groups were moving southward into the rain forests, European navigators were arriving along the coast with new crops. Corn gave communities of cultivators the caloric energy to change their forest landscapes, expanding the arable areas. In a select few of these regions, enterprising clans emerged to dominate the political scene, creating centralized

was an exceptional story. More typical were women who foraged for food, tended wounded soldiers, and set up European-style settlements.

However, there were too few Spanish women to go around, so Spanish men consorted with local women. Although the crown did not approve the taking of concubines, the practice was widespread. From the onset of colonization, Spaniards also married into Indian families. After conquering the Incas, Pizarro himself wedded an Inca princess, thereby (or so he hoped) inheriting the mantle of local dynastic rule. As a result of intermarriages, mestizos became the fastest-growing segment of the population of Spanish America.

Spanish migrants and their progeny preferred towns to the countryside. Ports excepted, the major cities of Spanish America were the former centers of Indian empires. Mexico City took shape on the ruins of Tenochtitlán; Cuzco arose from the razed Inca capital. In their architecture, economy, and most intimate aspects, the Spanish colonies adopted as much as they transformed the worlds they encountered.

Silver

For the first Europeans in the Americas, the foremost measure of success was the gold and silver that they could hoard for themselves and their monarchs. But in plundering massive amounts of silver, the conquistadors introduced it to the world's commercial systems, an act that electrified them. In the twenty years after the fall of Tenochtitlán, conquistadors took more precious metals from Mexico and the Andes than all the gold accumulated by Europeans over the previous centuries.

Having looted Indian coffers, the Spanish entered the business of mining directly, opening the Andean Potosí mines in 1545. Between 1560 and 1685, Spanish America sent 25,000 to 35,000 tons of silver annually to Spain. From 1685 to 1810, this sum doubled. The two mother lodes were Potosí in present-day Bolivia and Zacatecas in northern Mexico. Silver brought bounty not only to the crown but also to a privileged group of families based in Spain's colonial capitals; thus private wealth funded the formation of local aristocracies.

Corn Plantation. *This nineteenth-century engraving by famed Italian explorer Savorgnan de Brazza shows women of the West African tribe Bateke working in corn plantations. De Brazza would later serve as the governor general of the French colony in the Congo.*

kingdoms like Asante in present-day Ghana, Dahomey in present-day Benin, and Oyo and Benin in present-day Nigeria. These elites transformed what had once been thinly settled environments into densely populated states, with elaborate bureaucracies, big cities, and large and powerful standing armies.

There was much irony in the rise of these states, which owed so much of their strength to the linking of the Americas with Afro-Eurasia. The armies that they created and the increased populations that the new crops allowed were part and parcel of the Atlantic slave trade. That which the Americas gave with one hand (new crops), it took back with the other (warfare, captives, and New World slavery).

QUESTIONS FOR ANALYSIS

- What were the major effects of growing corn in West Africa?
- How did the growing of corn reshape the history of the Atlantic world during this period?

Explore Further

McCann, James, *Maize and Grace: Africa's Encounter with a New World Crop, 1500–2000* (2005).

Colonial mines epitomized the Atlantic world's new economy. They relied on an extensive network of Indian labor, at first enslaved, subsequently drafted. Here again, the Spanish adopted Inca and Aztec practices of requiring labor from subjugated villages. Each year, under the traditional system, village elders selected a stipulated number of men to toil in the shafts, refineries, and smelters. Under the Spanish, the digging, hauling, and smelting taxed human limits to their capacity—and beyond. Those unfortunate enough to be sent underground pounded the rock walls with chisels and hammers, releasing silicon dust. Miners could not help but breathe in the toxic dust, which created lesions, and made simply inhaling seem like swallowing broken glass. (See Primary Source: Silver, the Devil, and Coca Leaf in the Andes.) But the miners' sufferings reaped huge profits, and significant consequences for the Europeans. The Spanish pumped so much New World silver into global commercial networks that they caused painful price inflation in Europe, and transformed Europe's relationship to all its trading partners, especially those in China and India.

PORTUGAL'S NEW WORLD COLONY

No sooner did Europeans—starting with the Portuguese and Spanish—venture into the seas than they carved them up to prevent a free-for-all. The Treaty of Tordesillas of 1494, drawn up by the pope, had foreseen that the non-European world—the Americas, Africa, and Asia—would be divided into spheres of interest between Spain and Portugal. Yet the treaty was unenforceable. No less interested in immediate riches than the Spanish, the Portuguese were disappointed by the absence of tributary populations and precious metals in the areas set aside for them. What they did find in Brazil, however, was abundant, fertile land on which favored persons received massive royal grants. These estate owners governed their plantations like feudal lords (see Chapter 10).

Coastal Enclaves

Hemmed in along the coast, the Portuguese created enclaves. Unlike the Spanish, they rarely intermarried with Indians, most

MAP 12.2 | The Spanish and Portuguese Empires in the Americas, 1492–1750

This map examines the growth of the Spanish and Portuguese empires in the Americas over two and a half centuries. Identify the natural resources that led the Spaniards and Portuguese to focus their empire-building where they did.

- What were the major export commodities from these colonized areas?
- Looking back to Map 12.1, why do you think Spanish settlement covered so much more area than Portuguese settlement?
- According to your reading, how did the production and export of silver and sugar shape the labor systems that evolved in both empires?

PRIMARY SOURCE

Silver, the Devil, and Coca Leaf in the Andes

When Spanish colonists forced thousands of Andean Indians to work in the silver mines of Potosí, they permitted the chewing of coca leaves (which are now used to extract cocaine). Chewing the leaves gave Indians a mild "high," alleviated their hunger, and blunted the pain of hard work and deteriorating lungs. The habit also spread to some Spaniards. In this document, Bartolomé Arzáns de Orsúa y Vela, a Spaniard born in Potosí in 1676, expresses how important coca was to Indian miners and how harmful it was for Spaniards who fell under its spell. By the time the author wrote his observations in the late seventeenth century, the use of the coca leaf had become widespread.

I wish to declare the unhappiness and great evil that, among so many felicities, this kingdom of Peru experiences in possessing the coca herb. . . . No Indian will go into the mines or to any other labor, be it building houses or working in the fields, without taking it in his mouth, even if his life depends on it. . . .

Among the Indians (and even the Spaniards by now) the custom of not entering the mines without placing this herb in the mouth is so well established that there is a superstition that the richness of the metal will be lost if they do not do so. . . .

The Indians being accustomed to taking this herb into their mouths, there is no doubt that as long as they have it there they lose all desire to sleep, and since it is extremely warming, they say that when the weather is cold they do not feel it if they have the herb in their mouths. In addition, they also say that it increases their strength and that they feel neither hunger nor thirst; hence these Indians cannot work without it.

When the herb is ground and placed in boiling water and if a person then takes a few swallows, it opens the pores, warms the body, and shortens labor in women; and this coca herb has many other virtues besides. But human perversity has caused it to become a vice, so that the devil (that inventor of vices) has made a notable harvest of souls with it, for there are many women who have taken it—and still take it—for the sin of witchcraft, invoking the devil and using it to summon him for their evil deeds. . . .

With such ferocity has the devil seized on this coca herb that—there is no doubt about it—when it becomes an addiction it impairs or destroys the judgment of its users just as if they had drunk wine to excess and makes them see terrible visions; demons appear before their eyes in frightful forms. In this city of Potosí it is sold publicly by the Indians who work in the mines, and so the harm arising from its continued abundance cannot be corrected; but neither is that harm remediable in other large cities of this realm, where the use and sale of coca have been banned under penalties as severe as that of excommunication and yet it is secretly bought and sold and used for casting spells and other like evils.

Would that our lord the king had ordered this noxious herb pulled up by the roots wherever it is found. . . . Great good would follow were it to be extirpated from this realm: the devil would be bereft of the great harvest of souls he reaps, God would be done a great service, and vast numbers of men and women would not perish (I refer to Spaniards, for no harm comes to the Indians from it).

QUESTIONS FOR ANALYSIS

- Why would the Spaniards ban the sale of the coca herb everywhere except Potosí?
- Why would Bartolomé believe that no harm would come to the Indians for taking the coca herb?
- How does this document reveal the central role of the Catholic Church in Spanish colonial thinking? Find several words and phrases that express this outlook.

Source: R. C. Padden, ed., "Claudia the Witch," pp. 117–21, from Tales of Potosí.

of whom had fled or had died from imported diseases. Failing to find established cities, the colonists remained in more dispersed settlements. By the late seventeenth century, Brazil's white population was 300,000.

The problem was where to find labor to work the rich lands. Because there was no centralized government to deal with the labor shortage, initially the Portuguese settlers tried to enlist the dispersed native population; but when recruitment became increasingly coercive, Indians turned on the settlers, whom they perceived to be interlopers. Some fought. Others fled to the vast interior. Reluctant to pursue the Indians inland, the Portuguese hugged their beachheads, extracting brazilwood (the source of a beautiful red dye) and sugar from their coastal enclaves.

Mission São Miguel. *The Jesuits were avid missionaries in the Spanish and Portuguese empires and often tried to shelter native peoples from conquistadors and labor recruiters. Missions, like this one, in the borderlands between Brazil and Spanish colonies were targets of attack from both sides.*

African slaves became the solution to this labor problem. What had worked for the Portuguese on sugarcane plantations in the Azores and other Atlantic islands now found application on their Brazilian plantations. Especially in the northeast, in the Bay of All Saints, the Atlantic world's first vast sugar-producing commercial center appeared.

Sugar Plantations

Along with silver, sugar emerged as the most valuable export from the Americas. It also was decisive in rearranging relations between peoples around the Atlantic. Cultivation of sugarcane had originated in India, spread to the Mediterranean region, and then reached the coastal islands of West Africa. The Portuguese transported the West African model to Brazil, and other Europeans took it to the Caribbean. By the early seventeenth century, sugar had become a major export from the New World. By the eighteenth century, its production required continuous and enormous transfers of labor from Africa, and its value surpassed that of silver as an export from the Americas to Europe.

Most Brazilian sugar plantations were fairly small, employing between 60 and 100 slaves. But they were efficient enough to create an alternative model of empire, one that resulted in full-scale colonization and dislocation of the existing population. The slaves lived in wretched conditions: their barracks were miserable, and their diets were insufficient to keep them alive under backbreaking work routines. Moreover, these slaves were disproportionately men. As they rapidly died off, the only way to ensure replenishment was to import more Africans. This model of settlement relied on the transatlantic flow of slaves.

Beginnings of the Transatlantic Slave Trade

Although African slaves were imported into the Americas starting in the fifteenth century, the first direct voyage carrying them from Africa to the Americas occurred in 1525. The transatlantic slave trade began modestly in support of one commodity, sugar. As European demand for sugar increased, the slave trade expanded. From the time of Columbus until 1820, more than five times as many Africans as Europeans moved to the Americas: approximately 2 million Europeans (voluntarily) and 12 million Africans (involuntarily) crossed the Atlantic—though the especially high mortality rate for Africans meant that only 10 million survived to reach New World shores.

First to master long-distance seafaring, the Portuguese also led the way in human cargo. Trade in slaves grew steadily throughout the sixteenth century, then surged in the seventeenth and eighteenth centuries (see Chapter 13). Initially, all European powers participated—Portuguese, Spanish, Dutch, English, and French. Eventually, New World merchants in both North and South America also established direct trade links with Africa.

Well before European merchants arrived off its western coast, Africa had known long-distance slave trading. In fact, the overall number of Africans sold into captivity in the Muslim world exceeded that of the Atlantic slave trade. Moreover, Africans maintained slaves themselves. African slavery, like its American counterpart, was a response to labor scarcities. In many parts of Africa, however, slaves did not face permanent servitude. Instead, they were assimilated into families, gradually losing their servile status and swelling the size and power of their adopted lineage-based groups.

With the additional European demand for slaves to work New World plantations alongside the ongoing Muslim slave trade, pressure on the supply of African slaves intensified. Only a narrow band stretching down the spine of the African landmass, from present-day Uganda and the highlands of Kenya to Zambia and Zimbabwe, escaped the impact of Asian and European slave traders.

Within Africa, the social and political consequences were not fully evident until the great age of the slave trade in the eighteenth century, but already some economic consequences were clear. The overwhelming trend was to further limit Africa's population. Indeed, African laborers fetched high enough prices to more than cover the costs of their capture and transportation across the Atlantic.

By the late sixteenth century, important pieces had fallen into place to create a new Atlantic world, one that could not have been imagined a century earlier. This was the three-cornered **Atlantic system**, with Africa supplying labor, the Americas land and minerals, and Europeans the technology and military power to hold the system together. In time, the wealth flows to Europe and the slave-based development of the Americas would alter the world balance of power.

THE TRANSFORMATION OF EUROPE

Instead of uniting Europeans, the Atlantic system deepened the region's internal divides. In particular, the growing wealth of the Spanish Empire added to the Habsburg dynasty's power and attracted the attention of jealous competitors. On top of the transformations wrought by transatlantic opportunities and rivalries, a split within the Roman Catholic Church (the Reformation, discussed below) led to profound religious rifts among states and brought additional divisions to the continent.

The Habsburgs and the Quest for Universal Empire in Europe

The European dream of a continent-wide empire, which had persisted since the fall of ancient Rome, found expression under the Habsburg dynasts. They were heirs to the eastern half of Charlemagne's empire. Here a loose confederation of principalities, the **Holy Roman Empire,** continued to obey an emperor elected by elite lower-level sovereigns (dukes, archbishops, and kings of individual states like Bavaria). After 1273, the emperor usually came from the Austrian house of Habsburg. The Holy Roman Empire included territory incorporated into the Netherlands, Germany, Austria, Belgium, Croatia, and parts of present-day Italy, Poland, and Switzerland. Although the realm was enormous, it never enjoyed effectively centralized power.

In 1519, the Habsburg prince Charles V was elected Holy Roman Emperor, and for a few decades he controlled a transatlantic empire larger than any before or since. As grandson of Spanish monarchs Isabella and Ferdinand and of Holy Roman Emperor Maximilian I, Charles inherited both Spain and its territories in the Americas, as well as the Habsburgs' traditional central European holdings. Overstretched by trying to keep such an ambitious empire intact, and unable to prevent some central European princes from embracing the new Protestant faith, Charles abdicated in 1556 and divided the realm between his younger brother Ferdinand and his son Philip. Ferdinand (r. 1556–1564) took the Austrian, German, and central European territories that straddled the Danube and became Holy Roman Emperor in 1556, enabling the Austrian Habsburgs to maintain dominance over central Europe.

Philip II (r. Spain 1556–1598) received Spain, Belgium, the Netherlands, southern Italy, and the New World possessions. Moreover, he inherited the Portuguese throne (from his mother), adding Portugal and its colonial possessions to his empire. This gave him a monopoly on Atlantic commerce. Yet the Spanish Habsburgs had to defend their empire against Dutch revolts, as well as confront Ottoman harassment on land and at sea. The size and wealth of Habsburg Spain continued to provoke enormous tension within Europe.

Conflict in Europe and the Demise of Universal Empire

As the situation on the European mainland grew tense, French, English, and Dutch elites envied the riches of Portuguese and Spanish colonial possessions. These rivals yearned for their own profitable colonies. But in their New World explorations, the French, English, and Dutch had not yet found gold and silver, nor had they discovered an easier route to Asia. Still, they managed to claim a share of the wealth of the Americas by stealing it on the high seas. Some of the plunderers were pirates who raided for their own benefit; others were privateers who stole with official sanction and shared the profits with their monarchs. Often the distinction between pirate and privateer was blurred.

The most famous raider was Sir Francis Drake, whom the English crown commissioned to plunder Spanish possessions. Circling the globe between 1577 and 1580, Drake plundered one Spanish port after another. His favorite hunting ground was the Caribbean, where Mesoamerican and Andean silver, loaded onto Spanish galleons (heavy, square-rigged ships used for war or commerce), made lucrative targets. Besides, the many islands provided natural shelter. Although Drake undertook his exploits for personal gain, Queen Elizabeth approved of his assaults on the Spanish Empire and rewarded him with a knighthood.

To retaliate against English plundering and to prevent Elizabeth from supporting the Dutch revolt, the Spanish sailed a mighty armada of 130 ships and almost 20,000 men into the English Channel. But England amassed even more vessels from its Royal Navy and private merchant fleet. The subsequent defeat of the Spanish Armada saw the burning and destruction of many prized battleships. Thereafter the conflict between a rising England and Spain continued in other seas, and Drake returned to privateering. When news of Drake's death in the Caribbean (from yellow fever) arrived in Madrid, the Spanish court erupted in jubilation. However, two months later an English fleet sailed into Spain's premier port of Cádiz, occupied the city for two weeks, burned 200 Spanish ships, and seized massive treasure from the Indies. Spain, the powerhouse of the Atlantic world, had been severely humbled. Two years later a despondent King Philip died. The dream of universal empire within Europe had failed, largely because Christendom continued to be at war with itself.

The Reformation

Like the Renaissance, the **Protestant Reformation** in Europe began as a movement devoted to returning to ancient sources—in this case, to biblical scriptures. Long before Martin Luther came on the scene, some scholars and believers had despaired of the Catholic Church's ability to satisfy their longings for deeper, more individualized religious experience. But interpreting Christian doctrine for oneself was still very dangerous in the fourteenth and fifteenth centuries, for the church feared that heresies and challenges to its authority would arise if laypersons were allowed to read the scriptures as they pleased. The church was right: for when Luther and his followers seized the right to read and interpret the Bible in a new way, they paved the way for a "Protestant" Reformation that split Christendom for good.

MARTIN LUTHER CHALLENGES THE CHURCH The opening challenge to the authority of the pope and the Catholic Church originated in Germany. Here a monk and a professor of theology, Martin Luther (1483–1546), used his knowledge of the Bible to criticize the church's ideas and practices. He sought no revolution but hoped to persuade church leaders to make reforms.

Beginning his career as a pious Catholic believer, Luther nonetheless believed that mortals were so given to sin that none would ever be worthy of salvation. In 1516, Luther found an answer to his quest for salvation in reading Paul's Letters to the Romans: since no human acts could be sufficient to earn admittance to heaven, individuals could only be saved by their faith in God's grace. God's free gift of forgiveness, Luther believed, did not depend on taking sacraments or performing good deeds. This faith, moreover, was something Christians could obtain just from reading the Bible—rather than by having a priest tell them what to believe. Finally, Luther concluded that Christians did not need specially appointed mediators to speak to God for them; all were, in his eyes, priests, equally bound by God's laws and obliged to minister to one another's spiritual needs.

These became the three main principles that launched Luther's reforming efforts: (1) belief that faith alone saves, (2) belief that the scriptures alone hold the key to Christian truth, and (3) belief in the priesthood of all believers. But other things motivated Luther as well: corrupt practices in the church, such as the keeping of mistresses by monks, priests, and even popes; and the selling of indulgences, certificates that would supposedly shorten the buyer's time in Purgatory. In the 1510s, clerics were hawking indulgences across Europe in an effort to raise money for the sumptuous new Saint Peter's basilica in Rome.

In 1517, Luther formulated ninety-five statements, or theses, and posted them on the doors to the Wittenberg cathedral, hoping to stir up his colleagues in debate. Before long his theses made him famous—and bolder in his criticisms. In a widely circulated pamphlet called *On the Freedom of the Christian Man* (1520), he upbraided "the Roman Church, which in past ages was the holiest of all" for having "become a den of murderers beyond

Protestant Reformation. *Following Luther's lead, many Reformers created inexpensive pamphlets to increase the circulation of their message. Pictured here is a woodcut from one such pamphlet, which shows Luther and his followers fending off the corrupt Pope Leo X.*

all other dens of murderers, a thieves' castle beyond all other thieves' castles, the head and empire of every sin, as well as of death and damnation." As Luther's ideas spread, a highly important "colleague" entered the debate: Pope Leo X.

The church and the Habsburg emperor, Charles V, demanded that Luther take back his criticisms and theological claims. When he refused, he was declared a heretic and narrowly avoided being burned at the stake. Luther wrote many more pamphlets attacking the church and the pope, whom he now described as the anti-Christ. In 1525, he attacked another aspect of Catholic doctrine by marrying a former nun, Katharina von Bora. In Luther's view, God approved of human sexuality within the bonds of marriage, and encouraging marriage for both the clergy and the laity was the only way to prevent illicit forms of sexual behavior. Luther also translated the New Testament from Latin into German so that laypersons could have direct access, without the clergy, to the word of God. This act spurred many other daring scholars across Europe to undertake translations of their own, and it encouraged the Protestant clergy to teach children (and adults) to read their national languages.

OTHER "PROTESTANT" REFORMERS Spread by printed books and ardent preachers in all the common languages of Europe, Luther's doctrines won widespread support. In fact, many German princes embraced the reformed faith to assert their independence from the Holy Roman Emperor. Those who followed the new faith identified themselves as "Protestants," and they promised that their reformed version of Christianity provided both an answer to individual spiritual needs and a new moral foundation for community life. The renewed Christian creed appealed to commoners as well as elites, especially in communities that resented rule by Catholic "outsiders" (like the Dutch, who resented being ruled by Philip II, a Habsburg prince who lived in Spain). Thus the reformed ideas took particularly firm hold in the German states, France, Switzerland, Scandinavia, the Low Countries, and England.

Some zealous reformers, like Jean Calvin (1509–1564) in France, modified Luther's ideas. To Luther's emphasis on the individual's relationship to God, Calvin added a focus on moral regeneration through church discipline and the autonomy of religious communities. He laid out the doctrine of predestination—the notion that each person is "predestined" for damnation or salvation even before birth. The "elect," he thought, should also be free to govern themselves, a doctrine that upheld radical political dissent (as in the case of Puritans in England) and the rule of the clergy (as in the Swiss city-state of Geneva). Calvinism proved especially popular in Switzerland, the Netherlands, northeastern France, and Scotland (where it was called Presbyterianism). In contrast, those who remained loyal to the original Protestant cause now described themselves as Lutherans.

In England, Henry VIII (r. 1509–1547) and his daughter Elizabeth (r. 1558–1603) crafted a moderate reformed religion—a "middle way"—called Anglicanism, which retained many Catholic practices and a hierarchy topped by bishops. (American followers would later call themselves Episcopalians, from the Latin word for bishop, *episcopus*). Although Anglican rule was imposed on Ireland, most nonelite Irishmen remained Catholic. The Scots maintained a fierce devotion to their Presbyterian Church, ensuring a measure of religious diversity within the British Isles. In England, as with the rest of Europe, more radical Protestant sects like Anabaptists and Quakers also developed. While all Protestants were opposed to Catholicism and distrustful of the papal hierarchy, these different communities sometimes developed animosities toward one another as well (see Map 12.3).

COUNTER-REFORMATION AND PERSECUTION The Catholic Church responded to Luther and Calvin by embarking on its own renovation, which became known as the **Counter-Reformation**. At the Council of Trent, whose twenty-five sessions stretched from 1545 to 1563, Catholic leaders reaffirmed numerous things: the church's doctrines, sacraments, acts of charity, papal supremacy, the clergy's distinctive role, and the insistence that priests, monks, and nuns remain celibate. But the council also enacted reforms to answer the Protestants' assaults on clerical corruption. In contrast to many of their predecessors, the popes who headed the Catholic Church late in the sixteenth century became renowned for their piety and asceticism. They also installed bishops and abbots who generally steered clear of unscrupulous practices. Taking on the Protestant theological challenge, Catholicism gave greater emphasis to individual spirituality. Like the Protestants, the reformed Catholics carried their message overseas—especially through an order established by Ignatius Loyola (1491–1556). Loyola founded a brotherhood of priests, the Society of Jesus, or **Jesuits**, dedicated to the revival of the Catholic Church. From bases in Lisbon, Rome, Paris, and elsewhere in Europe, the Jesuits opened missions as far as South and North America, India, Japan, and China.

Yet the Vatican continued to use repression and persecution to combat what it regarded as heretical beliefs. Priests in Augsburg performed public exorcisms, seeking to free Protestant parishioners from possession by "demons." The Index of Prohibited Books (a list of books and theological treatises banned by the Catholic Church) and the medieval Inquisition (from 1184) were weapons against those deemed to be the church's enemies. But the proliferation of printing presses and the spread of Protestantism made it impossible for the Catholic Counter-Reformation to turn back the tide leading toward increased autonomy from the papacy.

MAP 12.3 | Religious Divisions in Europe after the Reformation, 1590

The Protestant Reformation divided Europe religiously and politically.

- Within the formerly all-Catholic Holy Roman Empire, what Protestant groups took hold?
- Looking at the map, can you identify any geographic patterns in the distribution of Protestant communities?
- In what regions would you expect Protestant-Catholic tensions to be the most intense?

Both Catholics and Protestants persecuted witches. Between about 1500 and 1700, up to 100,000 people, mostly women, were accused of being witches. Many were tried, tortured, burned at the stake, or hanged. Older women, widows, and nurses were especially vulnerable to charges of cursing or poisoning babies. Other charges included killing livestock, causing hailstorms, and scotching marriage arrangements. People also believed that weak and susceptible women might have sex with the devil or be tempted to do his bidding. Clearly, by no means did the Reformation—or the Catholic response to it—make Europe a more tolerant society.

Religious Warfare in Europe

The religious revival led Europe into another round of ferocious wars. Their ultimate effect was to weaken the Holy Roman Empire and strengthen the English, French, and Dutch. Already in the 1520s, the circulation of books presenting Luther's ideas sparked peasant revolts across central Europe. Some peasants, hoping that Luther's assault on the church's authority would help liberate them, rose up against repressive feudal landlords. In contrast to earlier wars, in which one noble's retinue fought a rival's, the defense of the Catholic mass and the Protestant Bible brought crowds of simple folk to arms. Now wars between and within central European states raged for nearly forty years. In 1555, the exhausted Holy Roman Emperor Charles V was compelled to allow the German princes the right to choose Lutheranism or Catholicism as the official religion within their domains (Calvinism was still outlawed). However, this concession did not end Europe's religious wars.

Religious conflicts both weakened European dynasties and whetted their appetite for conquest abroad. Spain, with its massive empire and its silver mines in the New World, spent much of its new fortune waging war in Europe. Most debilitating was its costly effort to subdue recently acquired Dutch territories. After a series of wars spanning nearly a hundred years, Catholic Spain finally conceded the Protestant Netherlands its independence.

Wars took their toll on the Spanish Empire, which was soon wallowing in debts; not even the riches of its American silver mines could bail out the court. In the late 1550s, Philip II could not meet his obligations to creditors. Within two decades, Spain was declared bankrupt three times. Its decline opened the way for the Dutch and the English to extend their trading networks into Asia and the New World. Competition between the latter two bred trade wars, indicating that religious differences were not the only sources of inter-European strife.

Religious conflicts also sparked civil wars. In France, the divide between Catholics and Protestants exploded in the St. Bartholomew's Day Massacre of 1572. Catholic crowds rampaged through the streets of Paris murdering Huguenot (Protestant) men, women, and children and dumping their bodies into the Seine River; parades of rioters displayed Protestants' severed heads on pikes. The number of dead reached 3,000 in Paris and 10,000 in provincial towns. Slaughter on this scale did not break the Huguenots' spirit, but it did bring more disrepute to the monarchy for failing to ensure peace. This was the beginning of the end of the Valois dynasty. Another round of warfare exhausted the French and brought Henry of Navarre, a Protestant prince, to the throne. To become king, Henry IV converted to Catholicism. Shortly thereafter he issued the Edict of Nantes, a proclamation that declared France a Catholic country but also tolerated some Protestant worship.

St. Bartholomew's Day Massacre. *An important wedding between French Catholic and Huguenot families in Paris was scheduled for August 24, 1572, St. Bartholomew's Day; but instead of reconciliation, that day saw a massacre, as Catholics tried to stamp out Protestantism in France's capital city.*

As princes sought to resolve religious questions within their domains, states increasingly became identified with one or another form of Christian faith—and, for Protestants, with a national language. In this way, religious strife propelled forward the process of state building and the forming of national identities. At the same time, religious conflict fueled rivalries for wealth and territory overseas. Thus, Europe entered its age of overseas exploration as a collection of increasingly powerful yet irreconcilably competitive rival states, whose differences stemmed not just from language but from the ways they worshipped the Christian God.

Akbar Hears a Petition. *In keeping with the multiethnic and multireligious character of Akbar's empire, the image reflects the diversity of peoples seeking to have their petitions heard by the Mughal emperor.*

PROSPERITY IN ASIA

While Europe was experiencing religious warfare, Asian empires were expanding and consolidating their power, and trade was flourishing. If anything, the arrival of European sailors and traders in the Indian Ocean strengthened trading ties across the region and enhanced the political power and expansionist interests of Asia's imperial regimes. These regimes have left their mark on world history. The Ming dynasty's elegant manufactures enjoyed worldwide renown, and its ability to govern vast numbers of highly diverse peoples led outsiders to consider China the model imperial state. The Mughal ruler, Akbar, and the Ottoman sultan, Suleiman the Magnificent (see Chapter 11), were equally effective and esteemed rulers.

Mughal India and Commerce

The **Mughal Empire** became one of the world's wealthiest just when Europeans were establishing sustained connections with India. These connections, however, only touched the outer layer of Mughal India, one of Islam's greatest regimes. Established in 1526, it was a vigorous, centralized state whose political authority encompassed most of modern-day India. During the sixteenth century, it had a population of between 100 and 150 million.

The Mughals' strength rested on their military power (see Chapter 11). The dynasty's founder, Babur, had introduced horsemanship, artillery, and field cannons from central Asia, and gunpowder had secured his swift military victories over northern India. Under his grandson, Akbar (r. 1556–1605), the empire enjoyed expansion and consolidation that continued (under his own grandson, Aurangzeb) until it covered almost all of India (see Map 12.4). Known as the "Great Mughal," Akbar was skilled not only in military tactics but also in the art of alliance making. Deals with Hindu chieftains through favors and intermarriage also undergirded his empire.

Akbar's court benefited from commercial expansion in the Indian Ocean. Although the Mughals possessed no ocean navy, merchants from Mughal lands used overland routes and rivers to exchange Indian cottons, tobacco, saffron, betel leaf, sugar, and indigo for Iranian melons, dried fruits, nuts, silks, carpets, and precious metals, or for Russian pelts, leathers, walrus tusks, saddles, and chain-mail armor. Every year, Akbar ordered 1,000 new suits stitched of the most exquisite material. His harem preened in fine silks dripping with gold, brocades, and pearls. Carpets, mirrors, and precious metals adorned nobles' households and camps, while perfume and wine flowed freely. Soldiers, servants, and even horses and elephants sported elaborate attire.

During the sixteenth century, expanded trade with Europe brought more wealth to the Mughal polity, while the empire's

MAP 12.4 | **Expansion of the Mughal Empire, 1556–1707**

Under Akbar and Aurangzeb, the Mughal Empire expanded and dominated much of South Asia. Yet, by looking at the trading ports along the Indian coast, one can see the growing influence of Portuguese, Dutch, French, and English interests.

- Look at the dates for each port, and identify which traders came first and which came last.
- Compare this map with Map 12.1 (showing the earlier period 1420–1580): to what extent do the trading posts shown here reflect increased European influence in the region?
- How would these European outposts have affected Mughal policies?

strength limited European incursions. Although the Portuguese occupied Goa and Bombay on the Indian coast, they had little presence elsewhere and dared not antagonize the Mughal emperor. In 1578, Akbar recognized the credentials of a Portuguese ambassador and allowed a Jesuit missionary to enter his court. Thereafter, commercial ties between Mughals and Portuguese intensified, but the merchants were still restricted to a handful of ports. In the 1580s and 1590s, the Mughals ended the Portuguese monopoly on trade with Europe by allowing Dutch and English merchantmen to dock in Indian ports.

Akbar used the commercial boom to overhaul his revenue system. Until the 1560s, the Mughal state relied on a network of decentralized tribute collectors called *zamindars*. These collectors possessed rights to claim a share of the harvest while earmarking part of their earnings for the emperor. But the Mughals did not always receive their agreed share and the peasants resented the high levies, so local populations resisted. As flourishing trade bolstered the money supply, Akbar's officials monetized the tax assessment system and curbed the *zamindars'* power. After other centralizing reforms, increased imperial revenues helped finance military expeditions and the extravagant beautification of Akbar's court.

Such fiscal policies reinforced the empire's growing commercialization. To generate cash to pay taxes, peasants had to sell their produce in the market—so market towns and ports flourished. Meanwhile, in the countryside, dealers in grain and money helped peasants get their produce to market. Up to one-third the value of burgeoning rural produce filled state coffers. Now the *zamindars* evolved from private tribute lords into servants of the state, though they continued to pocket a share of the peasants' income.

Centered in northern India, the Mughal Empire used surrounding regions' wealth and resources—military, architectural, and artistic—to glorify the court. Over time, the enhanced wealth caused friction among Indian regions, and even between merchants and rulers. Yet as long as merchants relied on rulers for their commercial gains, and as long as rulers balanced local and imperial interests, the realm remained unified and kept Europeans on the outskirts of society.

Prosperity in Ming China

In the late sixteenth century, China also prospered from increased commerce. Like the Mughals, the Ming seemed unconcerned with the increasing appearance of foreigners, including Europeans bearing silver. As in India, the Ming confined European traders to port cities. Silver from the Americas did, however, circulate widely in China. It allowed employers to pay their workers with money rather than with produce or goods. It also contributed to soaring production in agriculture and handicrafts. Through the sixteenth century, rural industries in China flourished. A cotton boom, for example, made spinning and weaving China's largest industry.

One measure of greater prosperity under the Ming was its population surge. By the mid-seventeenth century, China's population probably accounted for more than one-third of the total world population. Although 90 percent of Chinese people lived in the countryside, large numbers filled the cities. Beijing, the Ming capital, grew to over 1 million; Nanjing, the secondary capital, nearly matched that number. Cities offered diversions ranging from literary and theatrical societies to schools of learning, religious societies, urban associations, and manufactures from all over the empire. The elegance and material prosperity of Chinese cities dazzled European visitors. One Jesuit missionary described Nanjing as surpassing all other cities "in beauty and grandeur. . . . It is literally filled with palaces and temples and towers and bridges. . . . There is a gaiety of spirit among the people who are well mannered and nicely spoken." (In contrast, see Primary Source: Commentary on Foreigners from a Ming Official.)

Urban prosperity fostered entertainment districts where people could indulge themselves anonymously and in relative freedom. Some Ming women found a place here as refined entertainers and courtesans, others as midwives, poets, sorcerers, and matchmakers. Female painters, mostly from scholar-official families, emulated males who used the home and garden for creative pursuits. The expanding book trade also accommodated women, who were writers as well as readers, not to mention literary characters and archetypes (especially of Confucian virtues). But Chinese women made their greatest fortunes inside the emperor's Forbidden City as healers, consorts, and power brokers.

To be sure, by the mid-sixteenth century Ming rule faced a variety of problems, from piracy along the coasts to ineptness in the state. Corruption and perceptions of social decay elicited even more criticism. Consider Wang Yangming, a government official and scholar of neo-Confucian thought who urged commitment to social action. Arguing for the unity of knowledge and action, he claimed that one's own thoughts and intuition, rather than observations and external principles (as earlier neo-Confucian thinkers had emphasized), could provide the answers to problems. His more radical followers suggested, against traditional belief, that women were equal to men intellectually and should receive full educations—a position that earned these radicals banishment from the elite establishment. But even as such new ideas and the state's weaknesses created discord, Ming society remained commercially vibrant. This vitality survived the dynasty's fall in 1644, laying the foundation for increased population growth and territorial expansion in subsequent centuries.

PRIMARY SOURCE

Commentary on Foreigners from a Ming Official

Although China had a long history of trade with the outside world, Ming officials were often hostile toward contact with foreigners. The bureaucrat He Ao (Ho Ao) wrote this commentary around 1520, portraying the Europeans (whom he called Feringis) as unruly, untrustworthy, and a threat to the country's security. Such sentiments were also common among officials in subsequent centuries, even as China thrived in the commercial exchanges of an increasingly connected world.

The Feringis are most cruel and crafty. Their arms are superior to those of other foreigners. Some years ago they came suddenly to the city of Canton, and the noise of their cannon shook the earth [these were cannon shots fired as a salute by the fleet of Fernão Peres]. Those who remained at the post-station [places where foreigners were lodged] disobeyed the law and had intercourse with others. Those who came to the Capital were proud and struggled [among themselves?] to become head. Now if we allow them to come and go and to carry on their trade, it will inevitably lead to fighting and bloodshed, and the misfortune of our South may be boundless.

In the time of our ancestors, foreigners came to bring tribute only at fixed periods, and the law provided for precautionary measures, therefore the foreigners who could come were not many. But some time ago the Provincial Treasurer, Wu T'ing-chü, saying that he needed spice to be sent to the Court, took some of their goods no matter when they came. It was due to what he did that foreigner ships have never ceased visiting our shores and that barbarians have lived scattered in our departmental cities. Prohibition and precaution having been neglected, the Feringis became more and more familiar with our fair ways. And thus availing themselves of the situation the Feringis came into our port.

I pray that all the foreign junks in our bay and the foreigners who secretly live (in our territory) be driven away, that private intercourse be prohibited and that our strategical defence be close, so that that part of our country will have peace.

QUESTIONS FOR ANALYSIS

- According to this document, what was the Chinese view of foreigners?
- How does this document compare to the earlier report from the European trader? (See Primary Source reading on p. 448.)
- In this translation, *intercourse* means "commerce" or "business." Find the two places where this term occurs. Does the context indicate a difference of opinion between officials and merchants in Ming China?

Source: T'ien-Tse Chang, Sino-Portuguese Trade from 1514 to 1644: A Synthesis of Portuguese and Chinese Sources *(Leyden: E. J. Brill, 1934), pp. 51–52. Reprinted by permission of Koninklijke Brill NV.*

Asian Relations with Europe

Europeans' overseas expansion had originally looked toward Asia, and now the products from their New World colonies enabled them to realize some of those dreams. The Portuguese led the way, being the first Europeans to join the overseas trading networks bridging East Africa and China. Before long, they became either important commercial intermediaries or collectors of customs duties from Asian traders. In 1557, the Portuguese arrival at Macao, a port along the southern coast of China, enabled them to penetrate China's expanding import-export trade. Within five years the number of Portuguese in Macao neared 1,000 (see Map 12.5).

True, Macao hosted many more Melakans, Indians, and Africans, who all enlivened the port. Moreover, although Ming authorities permitted a Portuguese presence there, the court refused to establish an official relationship with European traders. Like the Mughals, the Ming confined the merchants to a coastal enclave. In fact, in 1574 the Chinese built a wall at the isthmus connecting Macao with the mainland; this barrier, and the soldiers who guarded it, restricted Portuguese access to inland trade. Nonetheless the Portuguese became important shippers of China's prized porcelains and silks throughout Asia and beyond to Europe. They also dominated the silver trade from Japan.

Seeing how much the Portuguese were earning on Asian trade, the Spanish, English, and Dutch also ventured into Asian waters. With its monopoly on American silver, Spain enjoyed a competitive advantage. In 1565, the first Spanish trading galleon reached the Philippines; in 1571, after capturing Manila and making it a colonial capital, the Spanish established a brisk trade with China. Each year, ships from Spain's colonies in the Americas crossed the Pacific to Manila, bearing cargoes of silver. They returned carrying porcelain and silks for well-to-do

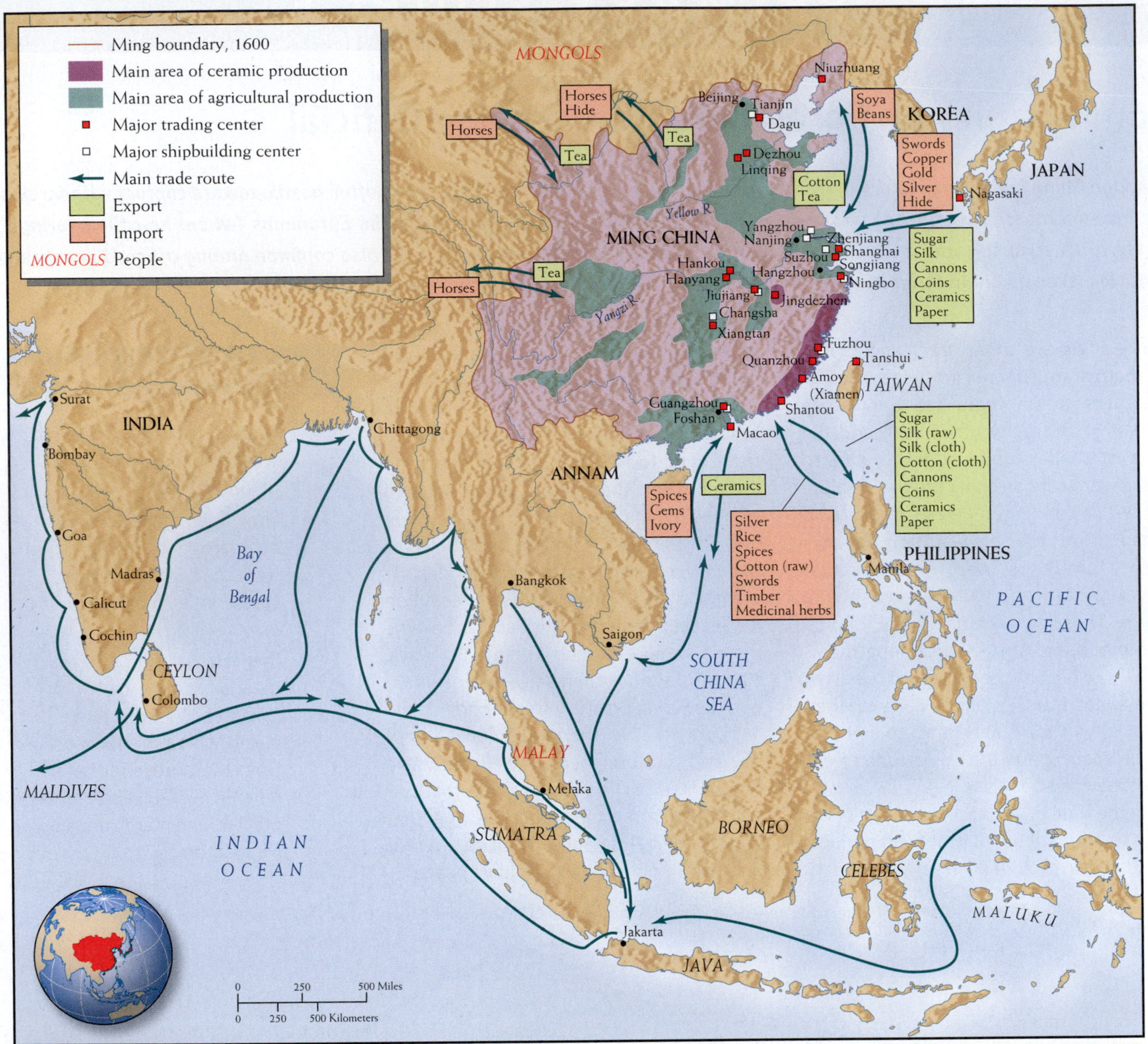

MAP 12.5 | Trade and Production in Ming China

The Ming Empire in the early seventeenth century was the world's most populous state and arguably its wealthiest.

- According to this map, what were the main items involved in China's export-import trade, and what were some of the regions that purchased its exports?
- In what way does the activity represented on this map indicate why China was the world's leading importer of silver at this time?
- Locate the major trading and shipbuilding centers, and then explain how important the export trade was to the Ming Empire's prosperity.

European consumers. Merchants in Manila also procured silks, tapestries, and feathers from the China seas for shipment to the Americas, where the mining elite eagerly awaited these imports.

The year 1571 was decisive in the history of the modern world, for in that year Spain inaugurated a trade circuit that made good on Magellan's earlier achievement. As Spanish ships circled the globe from the New World to China and from China back to Europe, the world became commercially interconnected. Silver solidified the linkage, being the only foreign commodity for which the Chinese had an insatiable demand. From the mother lodes of the Andes and Mesoamerica, silver made the commerce of the world go round.

Macao. *This Chinese painting depicts the Portuguese enclave of Macao on the southern border of China around 1800.*

Other Europeans, too, wanted their share of Asia's wealth. The English and the Dutch reached the South China Sea late in the sixteenth century. Captain James Lancaster made the first English voyage to the East Indies between 1591 and 1594. Five years later, 101 English subscribers pooled their funds and formed a joint-stock company (an association in which each member owned shares of capital). This English East India Company soon won a royal charter granting it exclusive rights to import East Indian goods. Soon the company displaced the Portuguese in the Arabian Sea and the Persian Gulf. Doing a brisk trade in indigo, saltpeter, pepper, and cotton textiles, the English East India Company eventually acquired control of ports on both coasts of India—Fort St. George (Madras; 1639), Bombay (1661), and Calcutta (1690).

It is tempting to see the Europeans' arrival in the South China Sea and the Indian Ocean as the beginning of the end of Asian autonomy. This was hardly the case, however. Through the sixteenth century, Europeans forged very weak connections to Asian societies. For the moment, the Europeans' increased presence enhanced the wealth and might of Asian dynasties.

CONCLUSION

In this multicentered world of the fifteenth century, Europe was a poor cousin. However, a new spirit of adventure and achievement animated its peoples, stirred up by the rediscovery of antiquity (the Renaissance), an ambitious mercantile elite, and the spiritual fervor of the Reformation and Counter-Reformation. Learning from Arab seamen, European sailors perfected techniques for sailing into dangerous waters. Desiring Asian luxury goods, European merchants and mariners were eager to exploit trade routes leading eastward. More important, Europe's location promoted expansion across the largely unknown Atlantic Ocean. With the Ottomans controlling Constantinople and the eastern Mediterranean, Atlantic sea-lanes offered an alternative route to Asia. As Europeans searched for routes around Islamic territory, they first sailed down the coast of Africa and then across the Atlantic.

Encountering the "New World" was an accident of monumental significance. In the Americas, Europeans found riches. Mountains of silver and rivers of gold gave them the currency they needed for dealing with Asian traders. Europeans also found opportunities for exchange, conquest, and colonization. Yet, establishing these transatlantic empires heightened tensions within Europe, as rivals fought over the spoils and a religious schism turned into a divisive political and spiritual struggle.

Thus two conquests characterize this age of increasing world interconnections. The Islamic conquest of Constantinople drove Europeans to find new links to Asia, thereby demonstrating Islam's pivotal role in shaping modern world history. In turn, the Spanish conquest of the Aztecs and the Incas gave Europeans access to silver, which bought them an increased presence in Asian trading networks.

American Indians also played an important role, as Europeans sought to conquer their lands, exploit their labor, and confiscate their gold and silver. Sometimes Indians worked with Europeans, sometimes under Europeans, sometimes against Europeans—and sometimes none were left to work at all. Then Europeans brought in African laborers, compounding the calamity of the encounter with the tragedy of slavery. Out of the catastrophe of contact, a new oceanic system arose to link Africa, America, and Europe. This was the Atlantic system. Unlike the tributary and trading orders of the Indian Ocean and China seas, the Atlantic Ocean supported a system of formal imperial control and settlement of distant colonies, and profoundly transformed the economies, agricultural practices, and environments across the globe. These catastrophes and exchanges would be foundational for the ways in which worlds connected and collided in the following centuries.

AFTER YOU READ THIS CHAPTER

Review and research materials on **StudySpace:** wwnorton.com/studyspace

TRACING THE GLOBAL STORYLINES

FOCUS ON: *Regional Impacts of European Colonization and Trade*

Europe

- Portugal creates a trading empire in the Indian Ocean and the South China Sea.
- Spain and Portugal establish colonies in the Americas, discover silver, and establish export-oriented plantation economies.
- As the balance of power in Europe shifts, the Protestant Reformation breaks out in northern and western Europe, splitting the Catholic Church.

The Americas

- Native Americans, lacking immunity to European diseases, perish everywhere.
- Spanish conquest and disease destroy the two great Native American empires in Mexico (the Aztecs) and Peru (the Incas).

Africa

- Trade in African captives fuels the Atlantic slave trade, which furnishes labor for European plantations in the Americas.

Asia

- Asian empires—the Mughals in India, the Ming in China, the Safavids in Iran, and the Ottomans in western Asia and the eastern Mediterranean—barely notice the Americas but profit economically from enhanced global trade.

CHRONOLOGY

Europe
- Luther begins Protestant Reformation **1517**

The Americas
- Columbus discovers the New World **1492**
- Cortés conquers Aztec Empire **1522**
- Pizarro conquers Inca Empire **1533**

South Asia
- Da Gama sails to India **1498**
- Portuguese establish bases around Indian Ocean **1508–1511**

East Asia

1500 | 1510 | 1520 | 1530 | 1540

KEY TERMS

Atlantic system *p. 462*
Aztec Empire *p. 451*
colonies *p. 445*
Columbian exchange *p. 455*
conquistadors *p. 450*
Counter-Reformation *p. 465*
Holy Roman Empire *p. 463*
Inca Empire *p. 455*
Jesuits *p. 465*
mestizos *p. 453*
Mughal Empire *p. 468*
New World *p. 449*
Protestant Reformation *p. 464*

STUDY QUESTIONS

1. **Describe** the new trade patterns in the Afro-Eurasian world during the fifteenth century. How similar and different were they from trade patterns during the Mongol period?
2. **Describe** how Spain created a vast empire in the Americas. How did the spread of lethal disease influence this outcome?
3. **Explain** the environmental consequences of the first contacts between Europeans and Amerindians. What consequences did the Columbian exchange have on regions both beyond the Atlantic world and within it?
4. **Compare and contrast** Spain's "tributary empire" in the Americas with Portugal's "seaborne empire" in the Indian ocean. Why did these empires pursue such different strategies?
5. **Explain** what conditions promoted the strengthening of regional dynasties in Europe in the sixteenth century as opposed to the growth of one large European empire.
6. **Explain** the transformation of the African slave trade during this period. What role did the growth of sugar plantations play?
7. **Compare and contrast** political and commercial developments in the Mughal and Ming dynasties during the sixteenth century. How did the expansion of global commerce affect each region?
8. **Evaluate** to what extent an increased European presence altered the political balance of power in Asia at this time. How did Asian dynasties react to increased European contacts?
9. **Explain** the role of silver in transforming global trade patterns during the sixteenth century. Which regions and dynasties benefited from the increased use of silver for monetary transactions?

Religious and dynastic wars **1520s–1570s**

Expansion and consolidation of Mughal dynasty **1556–1605**

Portuguese establish trading port in Macao **1557**

Spanish establish the port of Manila **1571**

1550 1560 1570 1580 1590 1600

BEFORE YOU READ THIS CHAPTER

wwnorton.com/
STUDYSPACE

GLOBAL STORYLINES

- Increased global trade brings the regions of the world more closely together, enriching some, destabilizing others, and provoking bitter rivalries.
- Silver and sugar are the major commodities of world trade.
- Western European states and Tsarist Russia expand their empires while the Ottoman, Safavid, Mughal, and Ming dynasties are shaken.

CHAPTER OUTLINE

13

Worlds Entangled, 1600–1750

FOCUS QUESTIONS

- How did global economic integration affect economic and political systems?
- How did European mercantilism and colonialism transform the Americas?
- How did the slave trade affect African societies?
- How did global trade affect the Asian dynasties?
- Why did Europe's economic and political centers shift northward?

In 1720, a financial panic engulfed Europe, making rich men into paupers and ruining many political careers. The panic arose from a speculative mania over anticipated profits from trade with the Americas. A group of British merchants established the South Sea Trading Company to compete with French firms and obtained privileged trading rights with all of Spanish America. Most coveted was the exclusive right to sell African slaves to Spanish colonies. As enthusiasm for such companies soared, eager investors sent share prices skyrocketing. But rumors of fantastic spoils gave way to word that the original investors were dumping their shares and that the companies were worthless. Then the speculative bubble burst. Share prices plummeted, nearly all the new companies went bankrupt, and many older firms collapsed. The so-called South Sea Bubble reflected the euphoria—and the perils—of global trade and investment.

From 1600 to 1750, global trading networks propelled commerce across the world's oceans. Sugar flowed from Brazil and the Caribbean, spices from Southeast Asia, cotton textiles from India, silks from China, and, increasingly, silver from Mesoamerica and the Andes. New World

CURRENT TRENDS IN WORLD HISTORY

Stimulants, Sociability, and Coffeehouses

While armies, travelers, missionaries, and diseases have breached the world's main political and cultural barriers, commodities have been the least respectful of the lines that separate communities. It has been difficult for ruling elites to curtail the desire of their populations to dress themselves in fine garments, to possess jewelry, and to consume satisfying food and drink no matter where these products may originate. The history of commodities, thus, is a core area for world historical research, for products span cultural barriers and connect peoples over long distances. As the world's trading networks expanded in the seventeenth and eighteenth centuries, merchants in Europe, Asia, Africa, and the Americas distributed many new commodities. By far the most popular were a group of stimulants—coffee, cocoa, sugar, tobacco, and tea—all of which (except for sugar) were addictive and also produced a sense of well-being. Previously, many of these products had been grown in isolated parts of the world: the coffee bean in Yemen, tobacco and cocoa in the New World, and sugar in Bengal. Yet, by the seventeenth century, in nearly every corner of the world, the well-to-do began to congregate in coffeehouses, consuming these new products and engaging in sociable activities.

Coffeehouses everywhere served as locations for social exchange, political discussions, and business activities. Yet they also varied from cultural area to cultural area, reflecting the values of the societies in which they arose.

The coffeehouse first appeared in Islamic lands late in the fifteenth century. As coffee consumption caught on among the wealthy and leisured classes in

Coffee. *Coffee drinkers at an Ottoman banquet (above) and in an English coffeehouse (left).*

silver was especially crucial to these networks: it gave Europeans a commodity to exchange with Asians, and it tilted the balance of wealth and power in a westerly direction across Afro-Eurasia.

Imperial expansion and transoceanic trade now brought the world together as never before. Europeans conquered and colonized more of the Americas, the demand for African slaves to work New World plantations leaped upward, and global trade intensified. Conquest, colonization, and commerce created riches for some but also provoked bitter rivalries. In the Americas, Spain and Portugal faced new competitors—primarily England and France. With religious tensions added to the mix, the stage was set for decades of bloody warfare in Europe and the Americas. At the same time, rulers in India, China, and Japan enlarged their empires, while Russia's tsars incorporated Siberian territories into their domain. Meanwhile, the Ottoman, Safavid, and Mughal dynasties, though resisting most European intrusions, found their stability profoundly shaken by the forces that entangled the world.

ECONOMIC AND POLITICAL EFFECTS OF GLOBAL COMMERCE

Global trade affected not only merchant groups and their sponsoring nations but also individual rulers and common people. Increasing economic ties brought new places and products into world markets: furs from French North America, sugar from the Caribbean, tobacco from British colonies on the American mainland, and coffee from Southeast Asia and the Middle East. (See Current Trends in World History: Stimulants, Sociability, and Coffeehouses.) Such products became so important that interruptions in availability sometimes destabilized economic and political systems. For example, gold and silver from the Americas were vital to the global networks (see Map 13.1). The supply of precious metals might fall when political disturbances caused work stoppages, or surge when new mines opened. Commodity prices could soar or drop, bringing prosperity to some and bankruptcy to others.

the Arabian Peninsula and the Ottoman Empire, local growers protected their advantage by monopolizing its cultivation and sale and refusing to allow any seeds or cuttings from the coffee tree to be taken abroad.

Despite some religious opposition, coffee spread into Egypt and throughout the Ottoman Empire in the sixteenth century. Ottoman bureaucrats, merchants, and artists assembled in coffeehouses to trade stories, read, listen to poetry, and play chess and backgammon. Indeed, so deeply connected were coffeehouses with literary and artistic pursuits that people referred to them as schools of knowledge.

From the Ottoman territories, the culture of coffee drinking spread to western Europe. The first coffeehouse in London opened in 1652, and within sixty years the city claimed no fewer than 500 such establishments. In fact, the Fleet Street area of London had so many that the English essayist Charles Lamb commented, "[T]he man must have a rare recipe for melancholy who can be dull in Fleet Street." Although coffeehouses attracted people from all levels of society, they especially appealed to the new mercantile and professional classes as locations where stimulating beverages like coffee, cocoa, and tea promoted lively conversations. Here, too, opponents claimed that excessive coffee drinking destabilized the thinking processes and even caused conversions to Islam. But against such opposition, the pleasures of coffee, tea, and cocoa prevailed. These bitter beverages in turn required liberal doses of the sweetener sugar. A smoke of tobacco topped off the experience. In this environment of pleasure, patrons of the coffeehouses indulged their addictions, engaged in gossip, conducted business, and talked politics.

QUESTIONS FOR ANALYSIS

- What factors drove the consumption of stimulants like coffee on a global scale?
- What other commodities from earlier in world history played a similar role? Were there differences in the underlying factors such as scale of consumption between the different periods?

Explore Further

Hattox, Ralph S., *Coffee and Coffeehouses: The Origins of a Social Beverage in the Medieval Near East* (1985).

Closer economic contact enhanced the power of certain states and destabilized others. It bolstered the legitimacy of England and France, and it prompted strong local support of new rulers in Japan and parts of sub-Saharan Africa. But also in England, France, Japan, Russia, and Africa, linkages led to civil wars and social unrest. In the Ottoman state, outlying provinces slipped from central control; the Safavid regime foundered and then ended; the Ming dynasty gave way to the Qing. In India, rivalries among princes and merchants eroded the Mughals' authority, compounding the instability caused by peasant uprisings.

Extracting Wealth: Mercantilism

Transformations in global relations began in the Atlantic, where the extraction and shipment of gold and silver siphoned wealth from the New World (the Americas) to the Old World (Afro-Eurasia). Mined by Indian and African workers and delivered into the hands of merchants and monarchs, silver from the Andes and Mesoamerica boosted the world's supply. In addition, a boom in gold production made Brazil the world's largest producer of that metal at this time.

American mining was so lucrative for Spain and Portugal that other European powers wanted a share in the bounty, so they, too, launched colonizing ventures in the New World. Although these latecomers found few precious minerals, they devised other ways to extract wealth, for the Americas had fertile lands on which to cultivate sugarcane, cotton, tobacco, indigo, and rice. The New World also had fur-bearing wildlife, whose pelts were prized in Europe. Better still from the colonizers' perspective, it was easy and inexpensive to produce and transport the New World crops and skins.

If silver quickened the pace of global trade, sugar transformed the European diet. First domesticated in Polynesia, sugar was not central to European diets before the New World plantations started exporting it. Previously, Europeans had used honey for sweetener, but they soon became insatiable consumers of sugar.

GREENLAND
ICELAND
ALASKA
DENMARK
NETHERLANDS
ENGLAND
Amsterdam
London
PORTUGAL
SPAIN
Lisbon
Seville
Cadiz
RUPERT'S LAND
Quebec
NEWFOUNDLAND
NOVA SCOTIA
NEW FRANCE
LOUISIANA
Boston
New York
Philadelphia
THIRTEEN COLONIES
New Orleans
VICEROYALTY OF NEW SPAIN
Zacatecas
MEXICO
Mexico City
Veracruz
Acapulco
Tobacco
Rice
Furs
Indigo
Meat
Timber
Grain
Taxes
From North America and Carribean
Sugar
Gold
Hides
Coffee
Diamonds
Calico
Taxes
From South America
Manufactures
Silk
Spices
Sugar
Coffee
Indigo
Cotton
Sugar
Indigo
Hides
Taxes
ATLANTIC OCEAN
CURAÇAO
Slaves
Cartagena
Panama
SURINAM
VICEROYALTY OF GRANADA
Quito
Lima
Potosí
VICEROYALTY OF PERU
DUTCH BRAZIL
Recife
Bahia
VICEROYALTY OF BRAZIL
Rio de Janeiro
Buenos Aires
PACIFIC OCEAN
Timbuktu
ASANTE
Accra
Lagos
FERNANDO P
Iron
Copper
Textiles
Cutlery
Firearms
Slaves
Tobacco
Sugar
Pepper
Spices
Silk
Coffee
Spices
Silk
Calico
Silk
Calico
Coffee
Pepper
Indigo
Drugs
Goa
China
India
Line of Tordesillas 1494

MAP 13.1 | Trade in Silver and Other Commodities, 1650–1750

The seventeenth and eighteenth centuries were the first centuries of true global commerce. Silver was the one item that was traded all over the world.

- Can you trace the flows of silver from the Americas around the globe (by following the thick red arrows) and identify the commodities that silver was exchanged for in different parts of the world?
- Does the map provide enough information for you to conclude which of these global empires was the wealthiest and most powerful?
- According to this map, how did increased trade shape European states' territorial ambitions?

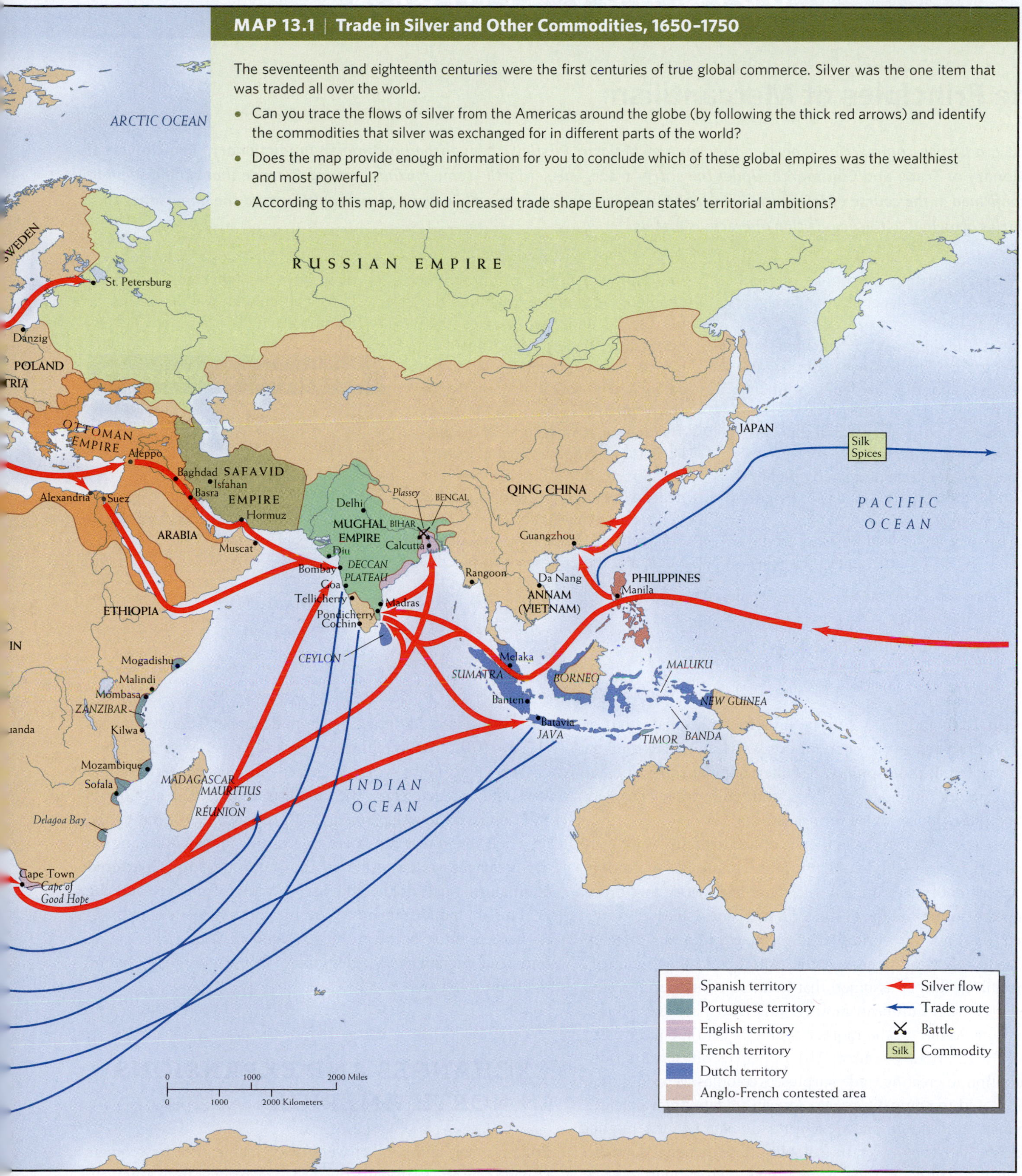

PRIMARY SOURCE

The Principles of Mercantilism

In 1757, a British commercial expert by the name of Malachy Postlewayt published a commercial dictionary,* The Universal Dictionary of Trade and Commerce. *Under the entry "trade," he set forth "some maxims relating to trade that should seem to be confirmed in the course of this work." The first five convey the economic philosophy of mercantilism and the importance that countries attached to the acquisition of precious metals.

I. That the lasting prosperity of the landed interest depends upon foreign commerce.

II. That the increase of the wealth, splendour, and power of Great Britain and Ireland depends upon exporting more in value of our native produce and manufactures than we import of commodities from other nations and bringing thereby money into the kingdom by means of freight by shipping.

III. That domestic and foreign trade, as they are the means of increasing national treasure, of breeding seamen, and of augmenting our mercantile and royal navies they necessarily become the means of our permanent prosperity and of the safety and preservation of our happy constitution.

IV. That the constant security of the public credit and the payment of interest and principal of the public creditors depend upon the prosperous state of our trade and navigation.

V. That gold and silver is the measure of trade, and that silver is a commodity and may be exported, especially in foreign coin as well as any other commodity.

Source: Malachy Postlewayt, The Universal Dictionary of Trade and Commerce, *vol. 2, p. 792.*

QUESTIONS FOR ANALYSIS

- According to this reading, whom does mercantilism serve?
- What are the key tenets of mercantilism?
- Why is silver more important than gold in trade?

Between 1690 and 1790, Europe imported 12 million tons of sugar—approximately one ton for every African enslaved in the Americas. Public tooth-pulling became a popular entertainment (for spectators!) in cities like Paris, and tooth decay became a leading cause of death for Europeans.

No matter what products they supplied, colonies were supposed to provide wealth for their "mother countries"—according to exponents of mercantilism, the economic theory that drove European empire-builders. The term **mercantilism** described a system that saw the world's wealth as fixed, meaning that any one country's wealth came at the expense of other countries. Mercantilism further assumed that overseas possessions existed solely to enrich European motherlands. Thus, colonies should ship more "value" to the mother country than they received in return. (See Primary Source: The Principles of Mercantilism.) In addition to creating trade surpluses, colonies were supposed to be closed to competitors, lest foreign traders drain precious resources from an empire's exclusive domain. As the mother country's monopoly over its colonies' trade generated wealth for royal treasuries, European states grew rich enough to wage almost unceasing wars against one another. Ultimately, mercantilists believed, as did the English philosopher Thomas Hobbes (1588–1679), that "wealth is power and power is wealth."

The mercantilist system required an alliance between the state and its merchants. Mercantilists understood economics and politics as interdependent, with the merchant needing the monarch to protect his interests and the monarch relying on the merchant's trade to enrich the state's treasury. **Chartered companies**, such as the (English) Virginia Company and the Dutch East India Company, were the most visible examples of the collaboration between the state and the merchant classes. European monarchs awarded these firms monopoly trading rights over vast areas.

EXCHANGES AND EXPANSIONS IN NORTH AMERICA

Entanglement and conflict were unavoidable once newcomers joined Spain and Portugal in the rush to reap riches from American colonies and to take a greater share of global commerce. As rulers in England, France, and Holland granted monopolies to merchant companies, they began to dominate the settlement and trade of new colonies in the Americas (see Map 13.2). Although the search for precious metals or water routes to Asia had initially spurred many of these enterprises, the new colonizers learned that only by exploiting other resources could their claims in the Americas generate profits. Also, differences among New World societies required rethinking the character of colonial regimes.

In their colonies along the Atlantic seaboard, the English established one model for new colonies in the Americas. Although these territories failed to yield precious metals or a waterway across the continent, they did boast land suitable for growing a variety of crops. Within the English domain, different climates and soils made for very different agricultural possibilities, but all the English colonies shared a common feature: population growth fed greater hunger for farmlands, which put pressure on Indian holdings. The result: a souring of relations between Amerindians and colonists, often ferocious wars between natives and newcomers, and, over the course of the seventeenth and eighteenth centuries, the dispossession of Indians from lands between the Atlantic Ocean and the Appalachian Mountains.

By contrast, Dutch and French colonies rested not on the expulsion of natives, but on dependence on them. Holland's North American venture, however, proved short-lived, as the English took over New Netherland and renamed it New York in 1664. French claims were more enduring and extended across a vast swath of the continent, encompassing eastern Canada, the Great Lakes, and the Mississippi Valley. But in much of this territory, the French presence remained limited to small numbers of missionaries and traders. The latter were especially dependent on Amerindians, though fragile ecological foundations did shift the balance of trade and power over time. Still, well into the eighteenth century, Amerindians in the middle of North America continued to control where Europeans lived and what they did.

Crucial to the trade between Europeans and Amerindians in the northern parts of North America was the beaver, an animal for which Indian peoples previously had little use. In response to the Europeans' interest, one local hunter proclaimed, "The beaver does everything perfectly well; it makes kettles, hatchets, swords, knives, bread; in short it makes everything." As long as there were beavers to be trapped, trade between the French and their Indian partners flourished.

The distinctive aspect of the fur trade was the Europeans' utter dependence on Indian know-how. After all, trapping required familiarity with the beaver's habits and habitats, which Europeans lacked. This reliance forced the French to adapt to Indian ways, which is evident in their pattern of exchange. Although the French wanted to export furs purely as a commercial venture, they were willing to permit exchanges with their Indian partners to go beyond material concerns. Responding to Indian desires to use trade as an instrument to cement familial bonds, the French gave gifts, participated in Indian diplomatic rituals, and even married into Indian families. As a result, *métis* (French-Indian offspring) played an important role in New France as interpreters, traders, and guides. Thus, the French colonization of the Americas—owing to their reliance on Indians as trading partners, military allies,

Woodlands Indians. *This late-sixteenth-century drawing by John White, a pioneer settler on Roanoke Island off the coast of North Carolina, depicts the Indian village of Secoton in eastern Virginia. In contrast to the great empires that the Spanish conquered in the valley of Mexico and in the Andes, the Indians whom English, French, and Dutch colonizers encountered in the woodlands of eastern North America generally lived in villages that were politically autonomous entities.*

MAP 13.2 | Colonies in North America, 1607–1763

France, England, and Spain laid claim to much of North America at this time.

- Where was each of these colonial powers strongest before the outbreak of the Seven Years' War in 1756? (See p. 514 for a discussion of the Seven Years' War.)
- Which empire gained the most North American territory, and who lost the most at the end of the war in 1763?
- How do you think Native American peoples reacted to the territorial arrangements agreed to by Spain, France, and England at the Peace of Paris, which ended the war?

and mates—rested more on cooperation than conquest, especially compared to the empires built by their Spanish and English rivals.

The beaver could do "everything perfectly well" as long as there were lots of beavers and the Indians' demand for European things was limited (as it generally was) to metal tools. But as French (as well as English) traders introduced guns into the exchange networks, they initiated an arms race among Indians. To get more guns, Indians had to collect more skins, which resulted in the depletion of beavers in heavily trapped areas. That, in turn, pushed Indians to expand their hunting/trapping zones, which heightened conflicts between groups now increasingly competing for hunting territories. Alcohol, too, became a potent weapon for Europeans. It gave them a commodity that Indians wanted badly enough to undermine long-standing understandings of the relationship between humans and animals and to overwhelm strictures against overhunting.

The advantages that Europeans gained from their guns, alcohol, germs, and other "weapons" of "ecological imperialism" were becoming more apparent in eastern North America over the course of the seventeenth and eighteenth centuries. But in the middle of the continent and to the west of French outposts, a different dynamic was playing out. On the Great Plains, some Indian peoples were also losing ground to newcomers, but here the winners were other Indian groups. On the northern plains, the Lakotas, who had migrated westward onto the grasslands, emerged as the most successful expansionists. Coming eastward, the Comanches reigned across a vast swath of the southern plains. These and other invaders displaced existing indigenous societies from some lands, added to their ranks by capturing and often enslaving large numbers of people (especially females), and enriched themselves by their raiding and through their control over trading. The effective realm of "Comancheria" included territory that the Spanish mapped as theirs and extended not only over other Indians in the area, but also over Spaniards.

There was considerable irony in the fact that Spanish colonizers had empowered the Plains Amerindians. The Spanish, after all, had brought horses to the Americas, and it was the acquisition of these animals that revolutionized Indian life and enabled the expansions that took place on the Great Plains. Recognizing the role that horses played in their conquests, the Spanish had tried to keep them out of Indian hands. They failed. Raiders targeted horses. Once introduced into Indian circuits, the animals dispersed and flourished on the grasses of the Plains. So did the Indians who had greatest access to horses and who most decisively adapted to equestrianism. On horseback, Indians could kill bison much more effectively, which encouraged some groups to forsake farming for hunting, and other groups, like the Lakotas and Comanches, to move on to the Plains and move around them in pursuit of buffalo. Astride horses, Indians also gained military superiority over more sedentary peoples, whose villages and cornfields were vulnerable to mobile forces.

Not all prospered, however, and certainly not all equally. The gains of nomadic equestrians often came at the expense

The Fur Trade. *For Europeans in northern North America, no commodity was as important as beaver skins. For the French especially, the fur trade determined the character of their colonial regime in North America. For Indians, it offered access to European goods, but overhunting depleted resources and provoked intertribal conflicts.*

Tobacco. *The cultivation of tobacco saved the Virginia colony from ruin and brought prosperity to increasing numbers of planters. The spread of tobacco plantations also pushed Indians off their lands and led planters to turn to Africa for a labor force.*

of those who remained wedded to a mixture of horticulture and hunting. Within horse cultures, new inequalities materialized. More successful raiders and hunters earned not only greater honor, but also acquired more horses—and with more horses usually came higher status and more wives. At the same time, the status of women generally declined in the transition from horticultural to hunting societies. Their burdens, however, did not, as there were now more buffalo waiting to be turned by women into the products that sustained Plains Indian life.

The Plantation Complex in the Caribbean

As late as 1670, the most populous English colony was not on the North American mainland, but on the Caribbean island of Barbados. Because sugar was so desirable, from the mid-seventeenth century onward the English- and French-controlled islands of the Caribbean replicated the Portuguese sugarcane plantations of Brazil. All was not sweet here, however. Because no colonial power held a monopoly, competition to control the region—and sugar production—was fierce. The resulting turbulence did not simply reflect imperial rivalry; it also reflected labor arrangements in the colonies. Because the native populations had been wiped out in Columbus's wake (see Chapter 12), owners of Caribbean estates looked to Africa to obtain workers for their plantations.

Sugar was a killing crop. So deadly was the hot, humid environment in which sugarcane flourished (as fertile for disease as for sugarcane), many sugar barons spent little time on their plantations. Management fell to overseers, who worked their slaves to death. Despite having immunities to yellow fever and malaria from their homeland's similar environment, Africans could not withstand the regimen. Inadequate food, atrocious living conditions, and filthy sanitation added to their miseries. Moreover, plantation managers treated their slaves as nonhumans: for example, on the first day all new slaves suffered branding with the planter's seal. One English gentleman commented that slaves were like cows, "as near as beasts may be, setting their souls aside."

More than disease and inadequate rations, the work itself decimated the enslaved. Average life expectancy was three years. Six days a week slaves rose before dawn, labored until noon, ate a short lunch, and then worked until dusk. At harvest time, sixteen-hour days saw hundreds of men, women, and children doubled over to cut the sugarcane and transport it to refineries,

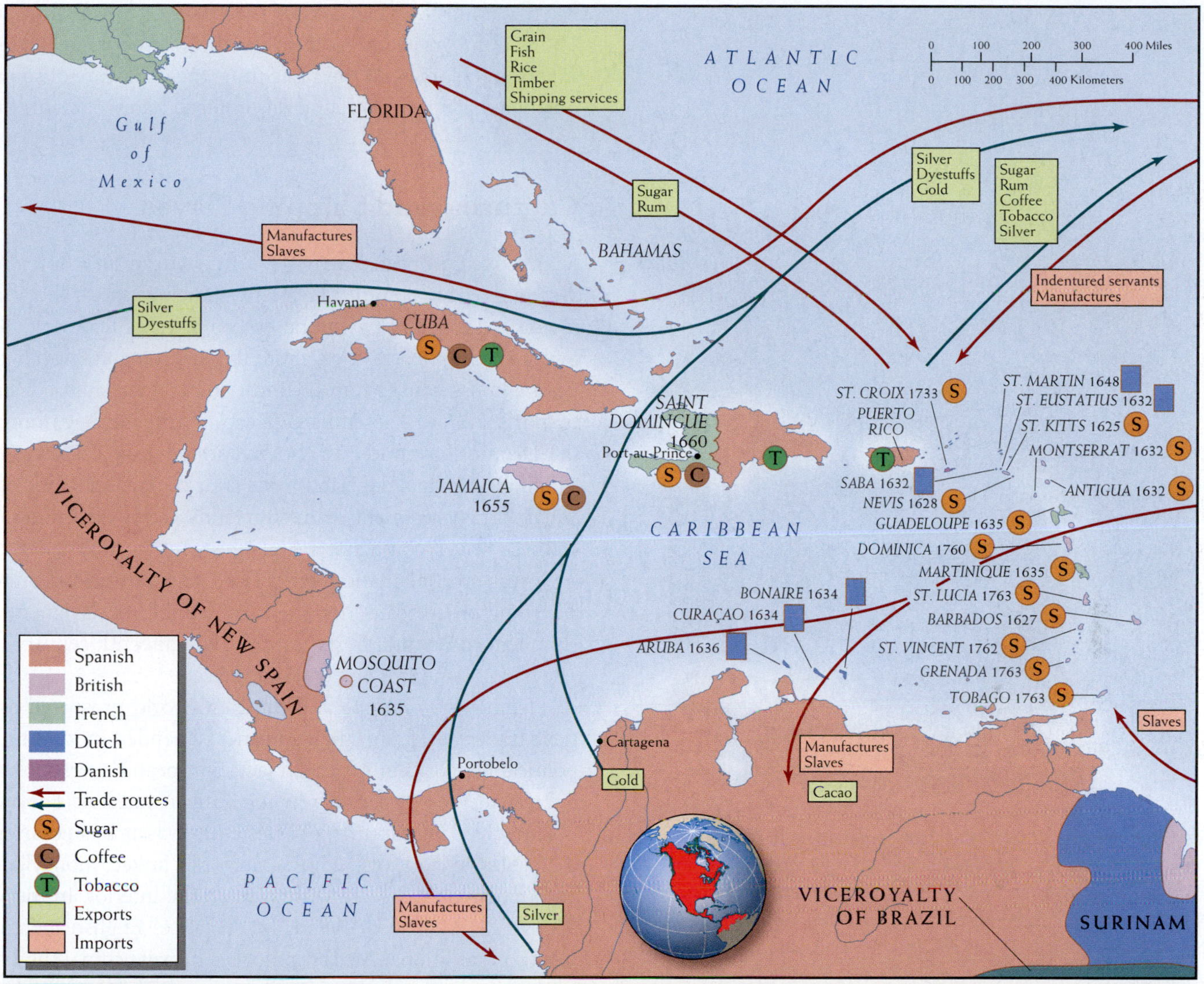

MAP 13.3 | Caribbean Colonies, 1625–1763

The Caribbean was a region of expanding trade in the seventeenth and eighteenth centuries.

- What were its major exports and imports?
- Who were its main colonizers and trading partners?
- According to your reading, how did the transformation of this region shape other societies in the Atlantic world?

sometimes seven days per week. Under this brutal schedule, slaves occasionally dropped dead from exhaustion.

Amid disease and toil, the enslaved resisted as they could. The most dramatic expression of resistance was violent revolt. In the early sixteenth century, in fact, slave revolts were so frequent in Panama that the crown banned all slave trade to the region. In the early seventeenth century, in parts of coastal Mexico, the viceroy negotiated an armistice with slaves to pacify the region. A more common form of resistance was flight. Seeking refuge from overseers, thousands of slaves took to the hills—for example, to the remote highlands of Caribbean islands or to Brazil's vast interior. Those who remained on the plantations resisted via foot dragging, pilfering, and sabotage.

Caribbean settlements and slaveholdings were not restricted to any single European power. But it was the latecomers—the Dutch, the English, and especially the French—who concentrated on the Antilles. The English took Jamaica from the Spanish and made it the premier site of Caribbean sugar by the 1740s. When the French seized half of Santo Domingo in the 1660s (renaming it Saint-Domingue, which is present-day

Slaves Cutting Cane. *Sugar was the preeminent agricultural export from the New World for centuries. Owners of sugarcane plantations relied almost exclusively on African slaves to produce the sweetener. Labor in the fields was especially harsh, as slaves worked in the blistering sun from dawn until dusk. This image shows how women and men toiled side by side.*

Haiti), they created one of the wealthiest societies based on slavery of all time. This French colony's exports eclipsed those of all the Spanish and English Antilles combined. The capital, Port-au-Prince, was one of the richest cities in the Atlantic world. The colony's merchants and planters built immense mansions worthy of the highest European nobles. Thus the Atlantic system benefited elite Europeans, who amassed new fortunes by exploiting the colonies' natural resources and the African slaves' labor.

THE SLAVE TRADE AND AFRICA

Although the slave trade began in the mid-fifteenth century, only in the seventeenth and eighteenth centuries did the numbers of human exports from Africa begin to soar (see Map 13.4). By 1820, four slaves had crossed the Atlantic for every European. Those numbers were essential to the prosperity of Europe's American colonies. At the same time, the departure of so many inhabitants depopulated and destabilized many parts of Africa.

Capturing and Shipping Slaves

Before the Europeans' arrival, Africa had an already existing system of slave commerce, mainly flowing across the Sahara to North Africa and Egypt and eastward to the Red Sea and the Swahili coast of East Africa. From the Red Sea and Swahili coast destinations, Muslim and Hindu merchants shipped slaves to ports around the Indian Ocean. From the beginnings of the Islamic slave trade, in the seventh century, no fewer than 9 million Africans departed from their homeland south of the Sahara for enslavement in Muslim lands. However, the number of these slaves could not match the volume destined for the Americas once plantation agriculture began to spread. Indeed, 12.8 million Africans departed for forcible enslavement and shipment to Atlantic ports from the late fifteenth century until 1867, when the last voyage took place.

Merchants in Europe and the New World prospered as the slave trade soared, but their fortunes depended on trading and political networks in Africa. In fact, European slavers took little interest in the happenings in the African interior. They were not involved in capturing slaves; this was a business left to their African partners, whose networks linked moneylenders and traders on the coast with allies in the interior. In the West African Bight (bay) of Biafra, for instance, English merchants relied on traditional African practices of pawnship—the use of human "pawns" to secure European commodities in advance of the delivery of slaves. According to custom, a secret male society called Ekpe enforced payments of promised slave deliveries. If a trader failed to deliver on his promise, his pawns (often members of his own kin group) were sold instead. By the mid-eighteenth century, Ekpe had powerful networks stretching deep into African hinterlands and supplying the slave trade in the port of Old Calabar.

Now the slave ports along the African coast became gruesome entrepôts. Indeed, high death rates occurred on the African side of the shipping; many slaves who perished did so before losing sight of Africa. Stuck in vast holding camps where disease and hunger were rampant, the slaves were then forced aboard vessels in cramped and wretched conditions. These ships waited for weeks to fill their holds while their human cargoes wasted away below deck. Crew members tossed dead Africans overboard as they loaded on other Africans from the shore. When the cargo was complete, the ships set sail. In their wake, crews continued to dump bodies. Most died of gastrointestinal diseases leading to dehydration. Smallpox and dysentery were also scourges.

PRIMARY SOURCE

Olaudah Equiano on the Atlantic Crossing

The most compelling description of the horrifying conditions that captives endured on the African coast as they awaited the arrival of slaving ships and the perils of the Atlantic crossing came from the pen of a former slave, Olaudah Equiano (c. 1745–1797). After purchasing his freedom and becoming a skilled writer, Equiano published* The Interesting Narrative of the Life of Olaudah Equiano, or Gustavus Vassa, the African. Written by Himself *(1789). An instantaneous best seller, within ten years the book saw nine English editions and appeared in American, Dutch, German, Russian, and French editions. Although some critics have questioned the authenticity of Equiano's birth and early life in Africa, the scholarly consensus remains that he was indeed born in Igboland (in the eastern part of present-day Nigeria) and made the voyage across the Atlantic after his capture at age nine.

The first object which saluted my eyes when I arrived on the coast was the sea, and a slave ship, which was then riding at anchor, and waiting for its cargo. These filled me with astonishment, which was soon converted into terror when I was carried on board. I was immediately handled and tossed up to see if I were sound by some of the crew; and I was now persuaded that I had gotten into a world of bad spirits, and that they were going to kill me. Their complexions too differing so much from ours, their long hair, and the language they spoke, (which was very different from any I had ever heard) united to confirm me in this belief. Indeed such were the horrors of my views and fears at the moment, that, if ten thousand worlds had been my own, I would have freely parted with them all to have exchanged my condition with that of the meanest slave in my own country. When I looked round the ship too and saw a large furnace or copper boiling, and a multitude of black people of every description chained together, every one of their countenances expressing dejection and sorrow, I no longer doubted of my fate; and, quite overpowered with horror and anguish, I fell motionless on the deck and fainted. When I recovered a little I found some black people about me, who I believed were some of those who brought me on board, and had been receiving their pay; they talked to me in order to cheer me, but all in vain. I asked them if we were not to be eaten by those white men with horrible looks, red faces, and loose hair. They told me I was not . . .

In a little time after, amongst the poor chained men, I found some of my own nation, which in a small degree gave ease to my mind. I inquired of these what was to be done with us; they gave me to understand we were to be carried to these white people's country to work for them. I then was a little revived, and thought, if it were no worse than working, my situation was not so desperate: but still I feared I should be put to death, the white people looked and acted, as I thought, in so savage a manner; for I had never seen among any people such instances of brutal cruelty; and this not only shewn towards us blacks, but also to some of the whites themselves. . . .

At last, when the ship we were in had got in all her cargo, they made ready with many fearful noises, and we were all put under deck, so that we could not see how they managed the vessel. But this disappointment was the least of my sorrow. The stench of the hold while we were on the coast was so intolerably loathsome, that it was dangerous to remain there for any time, and some of us had been permitted to stay on the deck for the fresh air; but now that the whole ship's cargo were confined together, it became absolutely pestilential. The closeness of the place, and the heat of the climate, added to the number in the ship, which was so crowded that each had scarcely room to turn himself, almost suffocated us. This produced copious perspirations, so that the air soon became unfit for respiration, from a variety of loathsome smells, and brought on a sickness among the slaves, of which many died, thus falling victims to the improvident avarice, as I may call it, of their purchasers. This wretched situation was again aggravated by the galling of the chains, now become insupportable; and the filth of the necessary tubs [latrines], into which the children often fell, and were almost suffocated. The shrieks of the women, and the groans of the dying, rendered the whole a scene of horror almost inconceivable.

QUESTIONS FOR ANALYSIS

- The slave trade involved capturing Africans from various parts of the interior of the continent. Which lines in the reading give evidence of this?
- Equiano's book came out in 1789 in the midst of a campaign to abolish the slave trade. Considering the formality of his language, what type of audience do you suppose he was seeking to reach?
- Why would this book describing the horrors of the slave trade have appeared only in the late 1700s, even though such brutal conditions had been existing for more than two centuries?

Source: Werner Sollors, ed., The Interesting Narrative of the Life of Olaudah Equiano, or Gustavus Vassa, the African, Written by Himself, *A Norton Critical Edition (New York: Norton, 2001), pp. 38–41.*

MAP 13.4 | The African Slave Trade, 1501–1867

The Atlantic slave trade flourished from the sixteenth to the nineteenth centuries, linking many parts of Africa with the Americas through enslavement and human trafficking on a massive scale. This map reflects recent estimates of the number of slaves transported during this period.

- What were the main areas of Africa from which the slaves were taken? What were the main areas that they were taken to in the Americas?
- What was the relationship between sugar cultivation in the Americas and the demand for African slave labor?
- How and where did the slave trade reshape African societies?

NORTH SEA
EUROPE
BLACK SEA
CASPIAN SEA
ARAL SEA
ASIA
MEDITERRANEAN SEA
ALGERIA
TUNISIA
MOROCCO
LIBYA
EGYPT
PERSIA
Persian Gulf
RED SEA
2 million (1700–1900)
SAHARA
ARABIA
1.32 million
YEMEN
SENEGAMBIA
SIERRA LEONE
WINDWARD COAST
GOLD COAST
BIGHT OF BENIN
BIGHT OF BIAFRA
AFRICA
ETHIOPIA
892,000
280,000
533,000
ARABIAN SEA
756,000
389,000
337,000
1.2 million
1.99 million
1.6 million
AMERICAS
12.57 million
(1501–1867)
5.7 million
WEST CENTRAL AFRICA
SWAHILI COAST
INDIAN OCEAN
SOUTHEAST AFRICA
200,000
MADAGASCAR
MASCARENE ISLANDS
359,000
0 500 1000 1500 Miles
0 500 1000 1500 Kilometers

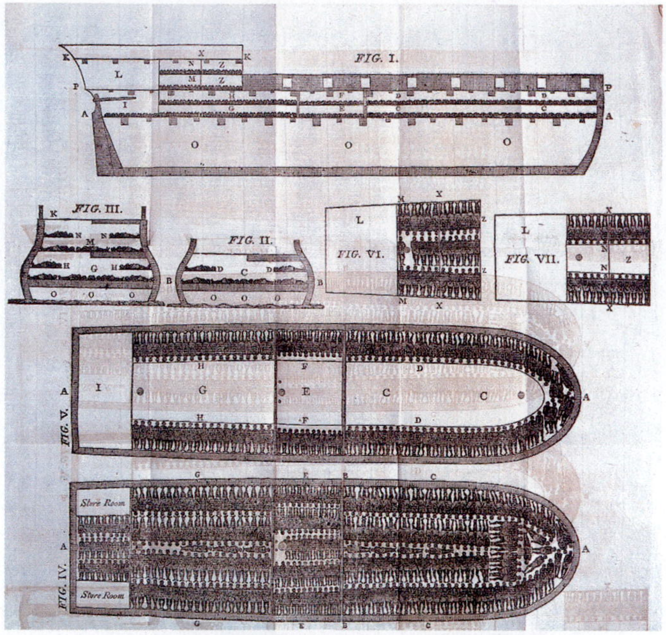

The Slave Trade. (Left) *Africans were captured in the interior and then bound and marched to the coast. Note that there is only one woman among the men (and a couple of children), reflecting the gender imbalance among those captured.* (Right) *After reaching the coast, the captured Africans would be crammed into the holds of slave vessels, where they suffered grievously from overcrowding and unsanitary conditions. Long voyages were especially deadly. If the winds failed or ships had to travel longer distances than usual, many of the captives would die en route to the slave markets across the ocean.*

Either way, death was slow and agonizing. Because high mortality led to lost profits, slavers learned to carry better food and more fresh water as the trade became more sophisticated. Still, when slave ships finally reached New World ports, they reeked of disease and excrement. (See Primary Source: Olaudah Equiano on the Atlantic Crossing.)

Slavery's Gender Imbalance

In moving so many Africans to the Americas, the slave trade played havoc with sex ratios in both places because most of the slaves shipped to the Americas were adult men. Although the numbers indicated Europeans' preferences for male laborers, they also reflected African slavers' desire to keep female slaves, primarily for household work. The gender imbalance made it difficult for slaves to reproduce in the Americas. So planters and slavers had to return to Africa to procure more captives—especially for the Caribbean islands, where slaves' death rates were so high.

Male slaves outnumbered females in the New World, but in the slave-supplying regions of Africa women outnumbered men. Female captives were especially prized in Africa because of their traditional role in the production of grains, leathers, and cotton. Moreover, the slave trade reinforced the traditional practice of polygyny—allowing relatively scarce men to take several wives. But in some states, notably the slave-supplying kingdom of Dahomey on the West African coast, women were able to assert power because of their large numbers and heightened importance. In fact, Dahomean women became so deeply involved in succession disputes that their intrigues could make the difference between winning and losing political power.

Within the Dahomean court the most powerful woman was the queen mother, the *kpojito*. Each new ruler selected his queen mother from among his predecessors' wives. Believing that she could communicate with the supernatural, the king and his courtiers consulted her before making important decisions. Indeed, queen mothers were so influential that in reality the king and the *kpojito* were joint rulers. Ultimately, though, the fact that powerful women rose to power in a few societies did not diminish the destabilizing effects of the Atlantic slave trade or the chaos that slave raiding and slave trading had on the relations among African states.

Africa's New Slave-Supplying Polities

Africans did not passively let captives fall into the arms of European slave buyers; instead, local political leaders and merchants were active suppliers. This activity promoted the growth of centralized polities, particularly in West African rain

ANALYZING GLOBAL DEVELOPMENTS

The Atlantic Trade in Slaves from Africa (1501-1900)

The world's leading slave traders were also the world's most important maritime powers during the period from 1501 to 1900. The following two tables focus on which countries transported these slaves and where they ended up. The Spanish and Portuguese established the first European empires in the Americas and created the model for the early slave trade. But northern European powers like Great Britain and France, reflecting their growing strength in maritime commerce, dominated the Atlantic slave trade between 1642 and 1808. In the final phase of the Atlantic slave trade, 1808–1867, the northern European powers and the United States disengaged from the trade, allowing the Portuguese and the Spanish once again to dominate the trade now centered largely on Cuba and Brazil.

In recent decades, scholars of the Atlantic slave trade have created the Trans-Atlantic Slave Trade Database, which can be accessed at the Voyages Web site (www.slavevoyages.org). Constructed from nearly 35,000 documented voyages during this period, this database incorporates roughly 80 percent of the slave ventures that set out for Africa to obtain slaves from all around the Atlantic world during this era. Through painstaking research, historians have been able to reconstruct the Atlantic world slave trade and offer a clear insight into the experiences of all those involved and the impact of this trade on the global economy during four centuries.

QUESTIONS FOR ANALYSIS

- Which countries were the most heavily invested in the Atlantic slave trade based on the data in the first table? How do you know?
- What was the relationship between the slave-trading countries and the colonies in the New World based on the entries in both tables?
- Why is the total number of slaves traded different from the number of slaves that disembarked? Did you expect the differences between these two numbers to be greater than they are? If so, why?

Source: David Eltis and David Richardson, Atlas of the Transatlantic Slave Trade *(2010).*

Number of Slaves Taken from Africa to Americas by Nationality of Vessels That Carried Them (1501-1867)

Vessel Nationality	Number of Slaves
Portugal/Brazil	5,849,300
Great Britain	3,259,900
France	1,380,970
Spain/Uruguay	1,060,900
Netherlands	555,300
United States	305,800
Baltic States	110,400
Total Atlantic World	**12,522,570**

Disembarkation of Slaves from Africa to the Americas (1501-1900)

Disembarking Country/Colony	Number of Slaves
Brazil (Portugal)	4.72 m
Smaller Caribbean Islands (mix)	1.75 m
Jamaica (Spain then Great Britain)	1.00 m
Saint-Domingue (Spain then France)	792,000
Cuba (Spain)	779,000
Spanish Caribbean Mainland	390,000
United States	389,000
Dutch Guiana	294,000
Amazonia	142,000
Total	**10,703,000**

forest areas. The trade also shifted control of wealth away from households owning large herds or lands to those who profited from the capture and exchange of slaves—urban merchants and warrior elites.

THE KONGO KINGDOM In some parts of Africa, the booming slave trade wreaked havoc as local leaders feuded over control of the traffic. In the Kongo kingdom, civil wars raged for over a century after 1665, and captured warriors were sold as slaves. As members of the royal family clashed, entire provinces saw their populations vanish. Most important to the conduct of war and the control of trade were firearms and gunpowder, which made the capturing of slaves highly efficient. Moreover, kidnapping became so prevalent

The Port of Loango. *Partly as a result of the profits of the slave trade, African rulers and merchants were able to create large and prosperous port cities such as Loango (pictured here), which was on the west coast of south-central Africa.*

that cultivators worked their fields bearing weapons, leaving their children behind in guarded stockades.

Some leaders of the Kongo kingdom fought back. Consider Queen Nzinga (1583–1663), a masterful diplomat and a shrewd military planner. Having converted to Christianity, she managed to keep the Portuguese slavers at bay during her long reign. Even after Portuguese forces defeated her troops in open battle, she conducted effective guerrilla warfare into her sixties.

Consider also the Christian visionary Dona Beatriz Kimpa Vita. Born in the Kongo in 1684 and baptized as a Christian, at age twenty she claimed to have received visions from St. Anthony of Padua. She believed that she died every Friday and was transported to heaven to converse with God, returning to earth on Monday to broadcast God's commands to believers. Her message aimed to end the Kongo civil wars and re-create a unified kingdom. Although she gained a large following, she failed to win the support of leading political figures. In 1706 she was captured and burned at the stake.

OYO, ASANTE, AND OTHER GROUPS As some African merchants and warlords sold other Africans, their commercial success enabled them to consolidate political power and grow wealthy. Their wealth financed additional weapons, with which they subdued neighbors and extended political control. Among the most durable new polities was the Asante state, which arose in the West African tropical rain forest in 1701 and expanded through 1750. This state benefited from its access to gold, which it used to acquire firearms (from European traders) to raid nearby communities for servile workers. From its capital city at Kumasi, the state eventually encompassed almost all of present-day Ghana. Main roads spread out from the capital like spokes of a wheel, each approximately twenty days' travel from the center. Through the Asante trading networks African traders bought, bartered, and sold slaves, who wound up in the hands of European merchants waiting in ports with vessels carrying manufactures and weaponry.

Also active in the slave trade—and enriched by it—was the Oyo Empire. This territory, which straddled the main trade routes, linked tropical rain forests with interior markets of the northern savannah areas. The empire's strength rested on its impressive army brandishing weapons secured from trade with Europeans. Deploying cavalry units in the savannah and infantry units in the rain forest, the Oyo's military campaigns became annual events, only suspended so that warriors could return home for their agricultural duties. Every dry season, Oyo armies marched on their neighbors to capture entire villages.

Slavery and the emergence of new political organizations enriched and empowered some Africans, but they cost Africa dearly. For the princes, warriors, and merchants who organized the slave trade, their business (like that of Amerindian fur suppliers) enabled them to obtain European goods—especially alcohol, tobacco, textiles, and guns. The Atlantic system also tilted wealth away from rural dwellers and village elders and increasingly toward port cities. Across the landmass, the slave trade thinned the population. True, Africa was spared a demographic catastrophe equal to the devastation of American Indians. The introduction of American food crops—notably maize and cassava, producing many more calories per acre than the old staples of millet and sorghum—blunted the trade's depopulating aspects. Yet some areas suffered grievously from three centuries of heavy involvement in the slave trade. The Atlantic trade enhanced the warrior class, who carried out raids for captives; the dislocations, internal power struggles, and economic hardships that followed precipitated the rise and fall of West African kingdoms.

ASIA IN THE SEVENTEENTH AND EIGHTEENTH CENTURIES

Global trading networks blossomed as vigorously in Asia as they did in the Americas. In Asia, however, the Europeans were less dominant. Although they could penetrate Asian markets with American silver, they could not conquer Asian empires or colonize vast portions of the region. Nor were they able to enslave Asian peoples as they had Africans. The Mughal Empire continued to grow, and the Qing dynasty, which had wrested control from the Ming, significantly expanded China's borders. China remained the richest state in the world, but in some places the balance of power was tilting in Europe's direction. Not only did the Ottomans' borders contract, but by the late eighteenth century Europeans had established economic and military dominance in parts of India and much of Southeast Asia.

The Dutch in Southeast Asia

In Southeast Asia the Dutch already enjoyed a dominant position by the seventeenth century. Although the Portuguese had seized the vibrant port city of Melaka in 1511 and the Spaniards had taken Manila in 1571, neither was able to monopolize the lucrative spice trade. To challenge them, the Dutch government persuaded its merchants to charter the Dutch East India Company (abbreviated as VOC) in 1602. Benefiting from Amsterdam's position as the most efficient money market with the lowest interest rates in the world, the VOC raised ten times the capital of its English counterpart—the royal chartered English East India Company. The advantages of chartered companies were evident in the VOC's scale of operation: at its peak the company had 257 ships and employed 12,000 persons. Throughout two centuries it sent ships manned by a total of one million men to Asia.

The VOC's main impact was in Southeast Asia, where spices, coffee, tea, and teak wood were key exports (see again Map 13.1). The company's objective was to secure a trade monopoly wherever it could, fix prices, and replace the native population with Dutch planters. In 1619, under the leadership of Jan Pieterszoon Coen (who once said that trade could not be conducted without war nor war without trade), the Dutch swept into the Javanese port of Jakarta (renamed Batavia by the Dutch). In defiance of local rulers and English rivals, the Dutch burned all the houses, drove out the population, and constructed a fortress from which to control the Southeast Asian trade. Two years later, Coen's forces took over a cluster of nutmeg-producing islands known as Banda. The traditional chiefs and almost the entire population were killed outright, left to starve, or taken into slavery. Dutch planters and their slaves replaced the decimated local population and sent their produce to the VOC. The motive for such rapacious action was the huge profit to be made by buying nutmeg at a low price in the Bandanese Islands and selling it at many times that price in Europe.

With their monopoly of nutmeg secured, the Dutch went after the market in cloves. Their strategy was to control production in one region and then destroy the rest, which entailed, once again, wars against producers and traders in other areas. Portuguese Melaka soon fell to the Dutch and became a VOC outpost. Although this aggressive expansion met widespread resistance from the local population and other merchants involved in the region's trade, by 1670 the Dutch controlled all of the lucrative spice trade from the Maluku islands.

Next, the VOC set its sights on pepper. In this gambit, it gained control of Bantam (present-day Banten), the largest pepper-exporting port. However, the Dutch had to share this commerce with Chinese and English competitors. Moreover, since there was no demand for European products in Asia, the Dutch had to participate more in inter-Asian trade as a way to reduce their need to make payments in precious metals. So they purchased, for example, calicoes (plain white cotton cloths) in India or copper in Japan for resale in Melaka and Java. They also diversified into trading silk, cotton, tea, and coffee, in addition to spices.

As a result of the Dutch enterprise, European outposts such as Dutch Batavia and Spanish Manila soon eclipsed old cosmopolitan cities such as Bantam. Indeed, as Europeans competed for supremacy in the borderlands of Southeast Asia, they made local societies serve their own ambitions and began replacing traditional networks with trade routes that primarily served European interests.

Transformations in Islam

Compared with Southeast Asia, the Islamic empires did not feel such direct effects of European intrusion. They did, however, face internal difficulties. While the Ottoman and Mughal empires remained resilient, the Safavid Empire fell into chaos.

Attack on Bantam. *This engraving depicts a Dutch attack on Bantam in the late seventeenth century as part of the VOC's effort to expand its empire in Southeast Asia.*

THE SAFAVID EMPIRE From its inception, the Safavid Empire had always required a powerful, religiously inspired ruler to enforce Shiite religious orthodoxy and to hold together the realm's tribal, pastoral, mercantile, and agricultural factions. The founding figure and his strongest successor had succeeded at this challenge. But when such a figure was not present, the state foundered. By 1722, after a series of weak rulers, it was under assault from within and without.

Internal turmoil was partly the result of a change in trade routes away from Persia and partly the result of tribal incursions against the central government. Such incursions were always a threat to political stability, but especially so when weak rulers sat on the throne. Meanwhile, neighboring Afghan clansmen invaded Safavid territory, overran the inept and divided armies, and besieged the capital at Isfahan (see Map 13.1). As the city's inhabitants perished from hunger and disease, some desperate survivors ate the corpses of the deceased. After the shah abdicated, the invaders executed thousands of officials and members of the royal household. The empire limped along until 1773, when a revolt toppled the last ruler from the throne.

THE OTTOMAN EMPIRE Having attained a high point under Suleiman (see Chapter 11), the Ottoman Empire, too, entered a period of territorial losses and a sense of decline. After Suleiman's reign, Ottoman armies and navies tried unsuccessfully to expand the empire's borders—losing, for example, on the western flank to the European Habsburgs. As military campaigns and a growing population strained the realm's limited resources, Ottoman intellectuals worried that the empire's glory was ebbing.

Even as the empire's strength waned, by the seventeenth century its sultans faced a commercially more connected world. Once New World silver entered Ottoman networks of commerce and money lending, its presence eventually destabilized the empire. Although early Ottoman rulers had avoided trade with the outside world, the lure of silver broke through state regulations. Now Ottoman merchants established black markets for commodities that eager European buyers paid for in silver—especially wheat, copper, and wool. Because these exports were illegal, their sale did not generate tax revenues to support the state's civilian and military administration. So Ottoman rulers had to rely on loans of silver from the merchants. Such financial dependence meant that rulers could ill afford to impose official rules on those who bankrolled them.

More silver and budget deficits were a recipe for inflation. Indeed, prices doubled and then tripled between 1550 and 1650. Runaway inflation caused hard-hit peasants in Anatolia, suffering from high food prices, shortages, and increasing taxes (used to pay off dynastic debts), to join together in uprisings that threatened the state's stability. By the time of Sultan Ibrahim's reign (1640–1648), the cycle of spending, taxing, borrowing, and inflation was so severe that his own officials murdered him. Moreover, disorder at the center of the empire was accompanied by difficulties in the provinces, where breakaway regimes appeared.

THE MAMLUKS IN OTTOMAN EGYPT The most threatening of the breakaway pressures occurred in Egypt beginning in the seventeenth century. In 1517, Egypt had become the Ottoman Empire's greatest conquest. As the wealthiest Ottoman territory, it was an important source of revenue, and its people shouldered heavy tax burdens.

The group that asserted Egypt's political and commercial autonomy from Istanbul were military men, known as **Mamluks** (Arabic for "owned" or "possessed"), who had ruled Egypt as an independent regime until the Ottoman conquest of the country (see Chapter 10). Although the Ottoman army had routed Mamluk forces on the battlefield in 1517, Ottoman governors in Egypt allowed the Mamluks to reform themselves. By the seventeenth century, these military men were nearly as powerful as their ancestors had been in the fifteenth century when they ruled Egypt independently. Turning the Ottoman administrator of Egypt into a mere figurehead, this new provincial elite kept much of the area's fiscal resources for themselves at the expense not only of the imperial coffers but also of the local peasantry. Mamluk households also enhanced their power by aligning with Egyptian merchants and catering to the Egyptian *ulama*.

THE OTTOMANS' KOPRULU REFORMS The Ottoman system also had elements of resilience—especially at the center, where decaying leadership provoked demands for reform from administrative elites. Late in the seventeenth century, the Koprulu family controlled the office of grand vizier and spearheaded changes to revitalize the empire. Mehmed Koprulu, the first to assume office, had been born into an obscure Albanian family. Taken as a slave in the *devshirme* (see Chapter 11), he slowly ascended the bureaucratic ladder and became grand vizier at age eighty. Pragmatic and incorruptible, Mehmed not only rooted out his corrupt peers but also balanced the budget and reversed the Ottoman armies' misfortunes. His death in 1661 did not halt the reforms, for he had groomed his son, Fazil Ahmed Koprulu, to continue them. The young grand vizier continued to trim the administration and strengthen the armies for another fifteen years.

Known as the Koprulu reforms, the changes in administration gave the state a new burst of energy and enabled the military to reacquire some of its lost possessions. Revenues again increased, and inflation decreased. Fired by revived expansionist ambitions, Istanbul decided to renew its assault on Christianity (see Chapter 11)—beginning with rekindled plans to seize Vienna under the leadership of Fazil Ahmed's brother-in-law, Kara Mustafa Pasha. Although the Ottomans gathered an enormous force outside the Habsburg capital in 1683, both sides suffered heavy losses and the Ottoman forces ultimately retreated. They planned to renew the assault months later, but the sultan, fearing disgrace, had Kara Mustafa strangled. Thereafter, the Ottomans halted their military advances. Worse still, under the treaty that ended the Austro-Ottoman

Siege of Vienna. *This seventeenth-century painting depicts the Ottoman siege of Vienna, which began on July 14, 1683, and ended on September 12. The city might have fallen if the Polish king, John III, had not answered the pope's plea to defend Christendom and sent an army to assist German and Austrian troops in defeating the Ottomans.*

Indian Cotton. *European traders were drawn to India by its famed cotton textiles. This image from c. 1800 shows a woman separating the cotton from the seeds; it captures the preindustrial technology of cotton production in India.*

war, the Ottomans lost major European territorial possessions, including Hungary.

Whereas in the sixteenth century rulers of the Ottoman Empire had wanted to create a self-contained and self-sufficient imperial economy, silver undermined this vision as it had elsewhere in the global economy. Indeed, the influx of silver opened Ottoman-controlled lands to trade with the rest of the world, producing intellectual ferment, breakaway regimes, widespread inflation, and social discontent.

THE MUGHAL EMPIRE In contrast to the Ottomans' setbacks, the Mughal Empire reached its height in the 1600s. The period saw Mughal rulers extend their domain over almost all of India and enjoy increased domestic and international trade. But they eventually had problems governing dispersed and resistant provinces, where many villages retained traditional religions and cultures.

Before the Mughals, India had never had a single political authority. Akbar and his successors had conquered territory in the north (see Chapter 12, Map 12.4), so now the Mughals turned to the south and gained control over most of that region by 1689. As the new provinces provided an additional source of resources, local lords, and warriors, the Mughal bureaucracy grew better at extracting services and taxes.

Imperial stability and prosperity did not depend entirely on the Indian Ocean trading system. Indeed, although the Mughals profited from seaborne trade, they never undertook overseas expansion. The main source of their wealth was land rents, which increased via incentives to bring new land into cultivation. Here peasants planted, in part, New World crops like maize and tobacco. But the imperial economy also benefited from Europeans' increased demand for Indian goods and services—such as a sixfold rise in the English East India Company's textile purchases within twenty years. Dutch trade with India saw similar trends. As precious metals flowed in from Japan and the New World to finance this booming trade, the imperial mint struck increasing numbers of silver coins, which fueled a cycle of greater trade and the use of **specie** (money in coin) for exchange.

Aurangzeb. *The last powerful Mughal emperor, Aurangzeb continued the conquest of the Indian subcontinent. Pictured in his old age, he is shown here with his courtiers.*

LOCAL AUTONOMY IN MUGHAL INDIA Mughals were victims of their own success. More than a century of imperial expansion, commercial prosperity, and agricultural development placed substantial resources in the hands of local and regional authorities. As a result, local warrior elites became more autonomous. By the late seventeenth century, many regional leaders were well positioned to resist Mughal authority.

As in the Ottoman Empire, then, distant provinces began to challenge central rulers. Under Aurangzeb (r. 1658–1707), as the Mughals pushed their frontier deep into southern India, they encountered fierce opposition from the Marathas in the northwestern Deccan plateau (see Map 13.1). To finance this expansion, Aurangzeb raised taxes on the peasants. Then resentment spread, and even the elite grew restive at the drain on imperial finances. Seeking support from the orthodox *ulama,* the monarch abandoned the toleration of heterodoxy and of non-Muslims that his predecessors had allowed. Ultimately, only the strong hand of Aurangzeb kept order in the empire.

When Aurangzeb died in 1707, a war of succession broke out. The revenue system eroded as local tax collectors pocketed more of the returns. Prosperous local elites rallied military forces of their own, annexing neighboring lands and chipping away at imperial authority. All this turmoil set the stage for successful peasant revolts.

Now the Indian peasants (like their counterparts in Ming China, Safavid Persia, and the Ottoman Empire) capitalized on weakening central authority to assert their independence. Many rose in rebellions; others took up banditry. Consider the revolt of the Jat peasant caste in northern India in the late seventeenth century: refusing to pay taxes, the Jat people killed a Mughal official and then seized lands and plundered the region. A half-century later, peasant cultivators of the Punjab turned their own closely knit community into a military power that stymied the Mughal forces. Peasants were also critical in the rise of the Marathas of western India, whose charismatic leader harnessed hatred of imperial oppression to fiercely resist Mughal control.

At this point the Mughal emperors had to accept diminished power over a loose unity of provincial "successor states." Most of these areas accepted Mughal control in name only, administering semiautonomous regimes through access to local resources. Yet India still flourished, and landed elites brought new territories into agrarian production. Cotton, for instance, supported a thriving textile industry as peasant households focused on weaving and cloth production. Much of their production was destined for export as the region deepened its integration into world trading systems.

PRIVATE COMMERCIAL ENTERPRISE The Mughals themselves paid scant attention to commercial matters, but local rulers welcomed Europeans into Indian ports. As more European ships arrived, these authorities struck deals with merchants from Portugal and, increasingly, from England and Holland. Some Indian merchants formed trading companies of their own to control the sale of regional produce to competing Europeans; others established intricate trading networks that reached as far north as Russia.

One of these companies built a trading and banking empire that demonstrated how local prosperity could undercut imperial power. This was the house of Jagat Seths, which at first specialized in shipping Bengal cloth through Asian and European merchants. Increasingly, however, most of their business in the provinces of Bengal and Bihar was tax-farming, whereby they collected taxes for the imperial coffers. (See Map 13.1.) The Jagat Seths maintained their own retinue of agents to gather levies from farmers while pocketing substantial profits for themselves. In this way, they and other mercantile houses grew richer and gained greater political influence over financially strapped emperors. Thus, even as global commercial entanglements enriched some in India, the effects undercut the Mughal dynasty.

From Ming to Qing in China

Like India, China prospered in the seventeenth and eighteenth centuries; but here, too, sizeable wealth undermined central control and contributed to the fall of a long-lasting dynasty. As in Mughal India, local power holders in China increasingly defied the Ming government. Moreover, because Ming sovereigns discouraged overseas commerce and forbade travel abroad, they did not reap the rewards of long-distance exchange. Rather, such profits went to traders and adventurers who evaded imperial edicts. Together, the persistence of local autonomy and the accelerating economic and social changes brought unprecedented challenges until finally, in 1644, the Ming dynasty collapsed.

ADMINISTRATIVE PROBLEMS How did a dynasty that in the early seventeenth century governed the world's most economically advanced society (and perhaps a third of the world's population) fall from power? As in the Ottoman Empire, responsibility often lay with the rulers. Consider the disastrous reign of Zhu Yijun, the Wanli Emperor (r. 1573–1620). This precocious youth ascended to the throne at age nine and, like his predecessors, grew up within the confines of the Forbidden City (see Chapter 11). The emperor was secluded despite being surrounded by a staff of 20,000 eunuchs and 3,000 women. The "Son of Heaven" rarely ventured outside the palace compound, and when he moved within it a large retinue accompanied him, led by eunuchs clearing his path with whips. His day was filled with state functions, for which he had to change clothes to suit each occasion—including formal headgear with curtain-like beads that forced him to move solemnly and deliberately.

Ming emperors like Wanli quickly discovered that despite the elaborate arrangements and ritual performances affirming their position as the Son of Heaven, they had scant control over the vast bureaucracy. An emperor frustrated with his officials could do little more than punish them or refuse to cooperate. Unable to change this system, Wanli avoided any involvement with managing the realm; he even refused to meet with officials or preside over state rituals. A mountain of reports and petitions piled up in his study unattended, while some of his bureaucrats exploited his neglect to accumulate wealth for themselves. During his long reign, Wanli's inaction as a ruler was in clear contrast to the ideal image of a wise and caring emperor.

ECONOMIC PROBLEMS The timing of administrative breakdown in the Ming government was unfortunate, because expanding opportunities for trade led many individuals to circumvent official rules. From the mid-sixteenth century, bands of supposedly Japanese pirates ravaged the Chinese coast. Indeed, the Ming government had difficulties regulating trade with Japan. Japanese missions, often armed and several hundred people strong, looted Chinese coastal villages. Yet, while Ming officials labeled all pirates as Japanese, many of the marauders were in fact Chinese.

Silver. *This seventeenth-century helmet from the Ming (1368–1633) or the Qing dynasties (1644–1911) features steel, gold, silver, and textiles, all of which were vital to the Chinese economy during this century. Silver was especially important, for its large influx from Japan and the Americas led to severe economic problems, political unrest, and the overthrow of Ming dynasty.*

Operating out of the empire's coastal towns, as well as from ports in Japan and Southeast Asia, these maritime adventurers deeply disturbed the Ming authorities. In tough times, the roving gangs terrorized sea-lanes and harbors. In better times, some functioned like mercantile groups: their leaders mingled with elites, foreign trade representatives, and imperial officials. What made these predators so resilient—and their business so lucrative—was their ability to move among the mosaic of East Asian cultures.

Just like in the Islamic empires, the influx of silver from the New World and Japan, while at first stimulating the Chinese economy, led to severe economic (and, eventually, political) dislocations. As noted in Chapter 12, Europeans used New World silver to pay for their purchases of Chinese goods. As a result, by the early seventeenth century silver imports exceeded domestic **bullion** production (uncoined gold or silver) by some twentyfold. Increasing **monetization** of the economy, which entailed silver becoming the primary medium of exchange, bolstered market activity and state revenues at the same time.

Yet the primacy of silver pressured peasants, who now needed that metal to pay their taxes and purchase goods. (See Primary Source: Huang Liuhong on Eliminating Authorized Silversmiths.) When silver supplies were abundant, the peasants faced inflationary prices. When supplies were scant, the peasants could not meet their obligations to state officials and merchants. The frustrated masses thus often seethed with resentment, which quickly turned to rebellion.

Market fluctuations abroad also affected the Chinese economy, introducing new sources of instability. After 1610, Dutch and English assaults on Spanish ships heading to Asia cut down on silver flows into China. Then, in 1639, Japanese authorities clamped down on foreign traders, a move that curbed the outflow of Japanese specie to China. All these blows to the Asian trading system destabilized China's money supply and weakened its economy.

THE COLLAPSE OF MING AUTHORITY By the seventeenth century, the Ming's administrative and economic difficulties were affecting their subjects' daily lives. This was particularly evident when the regime failed to cope with devastation caused by natural disasters, as in the northwestern province of Shaanxi. As the price of grain soared there, the poor and the hungry fanned out to find food by whatever means they could muster. To deal with the crisis, the government imposed heavier taxes and cut the military budget. Bands of dispossessed Chinese peasants and mutinous soldiers then vented their anger at local tax collectors and officials.

Now the cycle of rebellion and weakened central authority that played out in so many other places took its predictable toll. Outlaw armies grew large under charismatic leaders. Numerous

PRIMARY SOURCE

Huang Liuhong on Eliminating Authorized Silversmiths

The influx of silver into China had profound effects on its economy and government. For instance, silver became the medium for assessing taxes. In his magistrate's manual from around 1694, Huang Liuhong (Huang Liu-hung) indicated the problems that arose from involving authorized silversmiths in the payment process. The situation demonstrates how silver had become an integral part of the lives of the Chinese people.

The purpose of using an authorized silversmith in the collection of tax money is twofold. First, the quality of the silver delivered by the taxpayers must be up to standard. The authorized silversmith is expected to reject any substandard silver. Second, when the silver is delivered to the provincial treasury, it should be melted and cast into ingots to avoid theft while in transit. But, to get his commission, the authorized silversmith has to pay a fee and arrange for a guarantor. In addition, he has to pay bribes to the clerks of the revenue section and to absorb the operating expenses of his shop—rent, food, coal, wages for his employees, and so on. If he does not impose a surcharge on the taxpayers, how can he maintain his business?

There are many ways for an authorized silversmith to defraud the taxpayers. First, he can declare that the quality of the silver is not up to standard and a larger amount is required. Second, he can insist that all small pieces of silver have to be melted and cast into ingots; hence there will be wastage in the process of melting. Third, he may demand that all ingots, no matter how small they are, be stamped with his seal, and of course charge a stamping fee. Fourth, he may require a fee for each melting as a legitimate charge for the service. Fifth, he can procrastinate until the taxpayer becomes impatient and is willing to double the melting fee. Last, if the taxpayer seems naive or simple minded, the smith can purposely upset the melting container and put the blame on the taxpayer. All these tricks are prevalent, and little can be done to thwart them.

When the silver ingots are delivered to the provincial treasury, few of them are up to standard. The authorized silversmith often blames the taxpayers for bringing in silver of inferior quality although it would be easy for him to reject them at the time of melting. Powerful official families and audacious licentiates often put poor quality silver in sealed envelopes, which the authorized silversmith is not empowered to examine. Therefore, the use of an authorized silversmith contributes very little to the business of tax collection; it only increases the burden of small taxpayers. . . .

QUESTIONS FOR ANALYSIS

- What are the six ways that an authorized silversmith can defraud taxpayers?
- Why does the author suggest that the use of authorized silversmiths increases the burden of small taxpayers?
- What reasons would the Chinese state have for maintaining such a "flawed" system?

Source: Huang Liu-hung, "Elimination of Authorized Silversmiths" from A Complete Book Concerning Happiness and Benevolence: A Manual for Local Magistrates in Seventeenth Century China, *translated and edited by Djang Chu, pp. 190–91.*

mobile armies—the so-called roving bandits—took shape. The most famous rebel leader, the "dashing prince" Li Zicheng, arrived at the outskirts of Beijing in 1644. Only a few companies of soldiers and a few thousand eunuchs were there to defend the capital's twenty-one miles of walls, so Li Zicheng seized Beijing easily. Two days later, the emperor hanged himself. On the following day, the triumphant "dashing prince" rode into the capital and claimed the throne.

News of the fall of the Ming capital sent shock waves around the empire. One hundred and seventy miles to the northeast, where China meets Manchuria, the army's commander received the news within a matter of days. His task in the area was to defend the Ming against their menacing neighbor, a group that had begun to identify itself as Manchu. Immediately the commander's position became precarious. Caught between an advancing rebel army on the one side and the Manchus on the other, he made a fateful decision: he appealed for the Manchus' cooperation to fight the "dashing prince," promising his new allies that "gold and treasure" awaited them in the capital. Thus, without shedding a drop of blood, the Manchus joined the Ming forces. After years of coveting the Ming Empire, the Manchus were finally on their way to Beijing (see Map 13.5).

THE QING DYNASTY ASSERTS CONTROL Despite their small numbers, the Manchus overcame early resistance to their rule and oversaw an impressive expansion of their realm. The

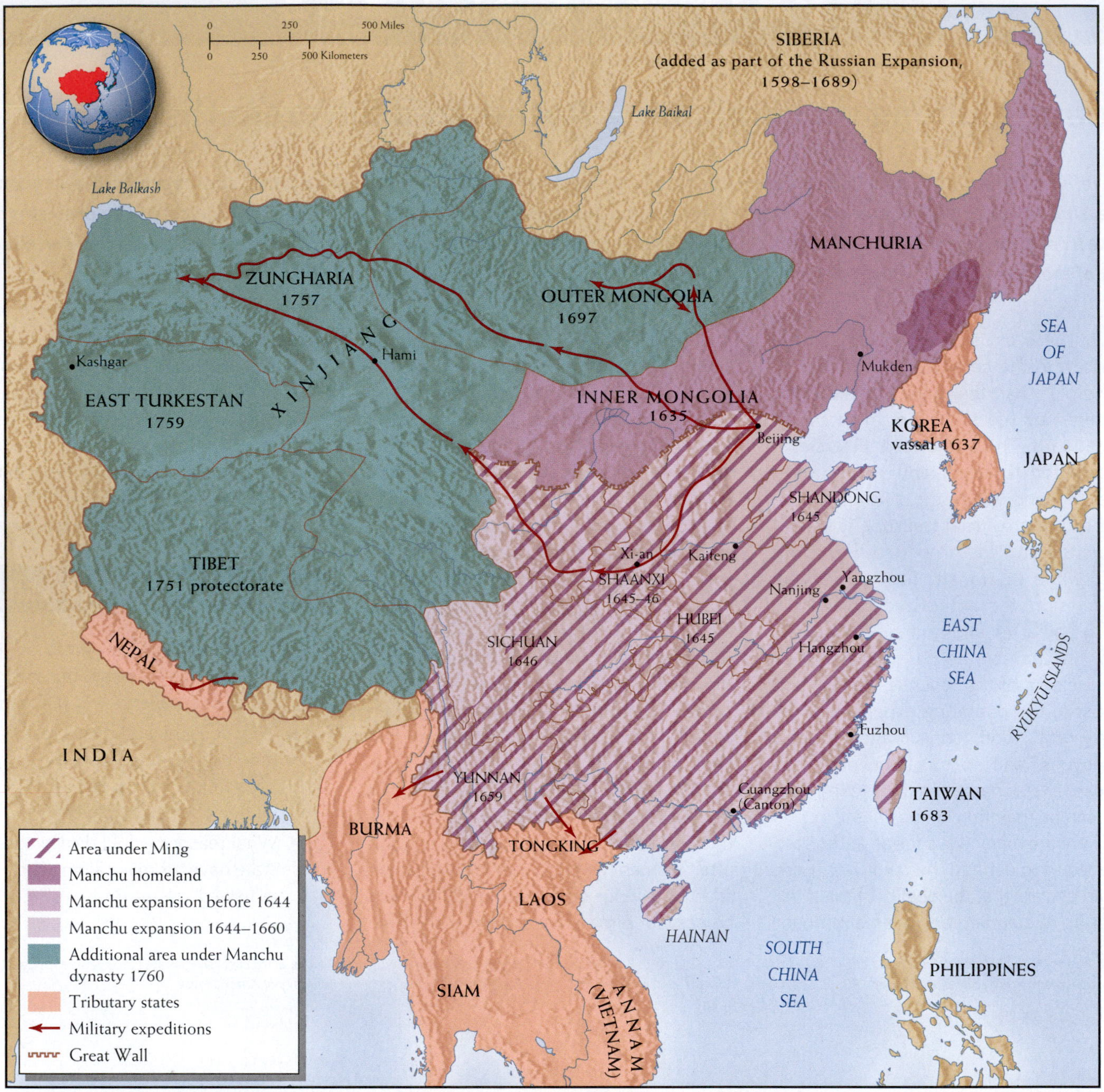

MAP 13.5 | From Ming to Qing China, 1644–1760

Qing China under the Manchus expanded its territory significantly during this period. Find the Manchu homeland and then the area of Manchu expansion after 1644, when the Manchus established the Qing dynasty.

- Where did the Qing dynasty expand?
- Based on the map, why do you think the Qing dynasty expanded so aggressively during this period?
- What does the location of Manchuria tell you about the historical origins of the Qing?

Manchus—the name was first used in 1635—were descendants of the Jurchens (see Chapter 10). They emerged as a force early in the seventeenth century, when their leader claimed the title of khan after securing the allegiance of various Mongol groups in northeastern Asia, paving the way for their eventual conquest of China.

When the Manchus defeated Li Zicheng and seized power in Beijing, they numbered around 1 million. Assuming control of a domain that included perhaps 250 million people, they were keenly aware of their minority status. Taking power was one thing; keeping it was another. But keep it they did. In fact, during the eighteenth century, the Manchu **Qing** ("pure") **dynasty** (1644–1911) incorporated new territories, experienced substantial population growth, and sustained significant economic growth. All this occurred without the kind of economic and political turmoil that rocked the societies of the Atlantic world.

The key to China's relatively stable economic and geographic expansion lay in its rulers' shrewd and flexible policies. The early Manchu emperors were able and diligent administrators. They also knew that to govern a diverse population they had to adapt to local ways. To promote continuity with previous practices, they respected Confucian codes and ethics and kept the classic texts as the basis of the prestigious civil service examinations (see Chapter 9). Social hierarchies of age, gender, and kin—indeed, the entire image of the family as the bedrock of social organization—endured. In some areas, like Taiwan, the Manchus added new territories to existing provinces. Elsewhere, they gave newly acquired territories, like Mongolia, Tibet, and Xinjiang, their own form of local administration. Imperial envoys in these regions administered through staffs of locals and relied on native institutions. Until the late nineteenth century, the Qing dynasty showed little interest in integrating those regions into "China proper."

At the same time, Qing rulers were determined to convey a clear sense of their own majesty and legitimacy. Rulers relentlessly promoted patriarchal values. Widows who remained "chaste" enjoyed public praise, and women in general were urged to lead a "virtuous" life serving male kin and family. To the majority Han population, the Manchu emperor represented himself as the worthy upholder of familial values and classical Chinese civilization; to the Tibetan Buddhists, the Manchu state offered imperial patronage. So, too, with Islamic subjects. Although the Islamic Uighurs, as well as other Muslim subjects, might have disliked the Manchus' easygoing religious attitude, they accepted the emperor's favors and generally endorsed his claim to rule.

However, insinuating themselves into an existing order and appeasing subject peoples did not satisfy the Manchu yearning to leave their imprint. They also introduced measures that emphasized their authority, their distinctiveness, and the submission of their mostly Han Chinese subjects. For example, Qing officials composed or translated important documents into Manchu and banned intermarriage between Manchu and Han (although this was difficult to enforce). Other edicts imposed Manchu ways. For example, the day after the Manchus entered Beijing, a decree required all Han males to follow the Manchu practice of shaving their foreheads and braiding their hair at the back in a queue. Although strong protests led to temporary shelving of the policy, a year later the Manchus reissued the order and gave their subjects the stark choice of shaving their hair or losing their heads. This time, the policy stood firm. In a similar vein, the Qing decreed that Han males adopt Manchu garb: instead of loose Ming-style robes, they had to wear high collars and tight jackets.

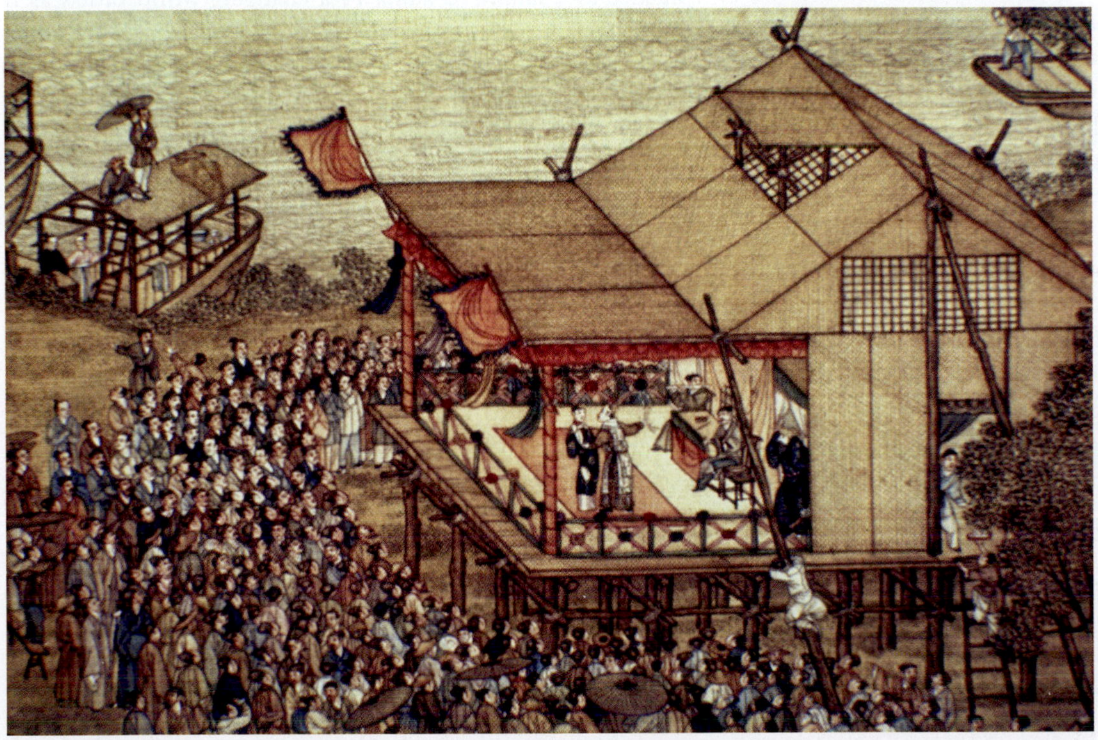

Qing Theater with Female Impersonators. *The Qing court banned women from performing in theaters, which led to the practice of using young boys in female roles.*

Nothing earned the regime's disapproval more than the urban elites' conspicuous consumption and indulgence in sensual pleasure. The Qing court regarded the "decadence" of the late Ming, symbolized by its famous actresses, as one of the Ming's principal failings. In 1723 the Qing banned female performers from the court, after which the practice spread to commercial theaters, with young boys taking female roles on stage. The Qing also tried to further regulate commercial theater by excluding women from the audience. The popularity of female impersonators on stage, however, brought a new cachet to homosexual relationships. A gulf began to open between the government's aspirations and its ability to police society. For example, the urban public continued to flock to performances by female impersonators in defiance of the Qing's bans.

Manchu impositions fell mostly on the peasantry, for the Qing financed their administrative structure through taxes on peasant households. In response the peasants sought new lands to cultivate in border areas, often planting New World crops that grew well in difficult soils. This move introduced an important change in Chinese diets: while rice remained the staple diet of the wealthy, peasants increasingly subsisted on corn and sweet potatoes.

EXPANSION AND TRADE UNDER THE QING Despite public disregard for certain imperial edicts, the Qing dynasty enjoyed a heyday during the eighteenth century. It forged tributary relations with Korea, Vietnam, Burma, and Nepal, and its territorial expansion reached far into central Asia, Tibet, and Mongolia. In particular, the Manchus confronted the Junghars of western Mongolia, who controlled much of central Asia in the mid-seventeenth century and whose predecessors had once captured an early Ming emperor. Wary of a potential alliance between the Junghars and an emerging Russia on its northern frontiers, the Qing dynasty launched successive campaigns and dealt a decisive blow to the Junghars by the mid-eighteenth century.

While officials redoubled their reliance on an agrarian base, trade and commerce flourished. Chinese merchants continued to ply the waters stretching from Southeast Asia to Japan, exchanging textiles, ceramics, and medicine for spices and rice. Although the Qing state vacillated about permitting maritime trade with foreigners in its early years, it sought to regulate external commerce more formally as it consolidated its rule. In 1720, in Canton, a group of merchants formed a monopolistic guild to trade with Europeans seeking coveted Chinese goods and peddling their own wares. Although the guild disbanded in the face of opposition from other merchants, it revived after the Qing restricted European trade to Canton. The **Canton system**, officially established by imperial decree in 1759, required European traders to have guild merchants act as guarantors for their good behavior and payment of fees.

Canton. *Not only were foreigners not allowed to trade with the Chinese outside of Canton, but they were also required to have Chinese guild members act as guarantors of their good behavior and payment of fees.*

China, in sum, negotiated a century of upheaval without dismantling established ways in politics and economics. The peasantry continued to practice popular faiths, cultivate crops, and stay close to fields and villages. Trade with the outside world was marginal to overall commercial life; like the Ming, the Qing cared more about the agrarian than the commercial health of the empire, believing the former to be the foundation of prosperity and tranquility. As long as China's peasantry could keep the dynasty's coffers full, the government was content to squeeze the merchants when it needed funds. Some historians view this practice as a failure to adapt to a changing world order, as it ultimately left China vulnerable to outsiders—especially Europeans. But this view puts the historical cart before the horse. By the mid-eighteenth century, Europe still needed China more than the other way around. For the majority of Chinese, no superior model of belief, politics, or economics was conceivable. Indeed, although the Qing had taken over a crumbling empire in 1644, a century later China was enjoying a new level of prosperity.

Tokugawa Japan

Integration with the Asian trading system exposed Japan to new external pressures, even as the islands grappled with internal turmoil. But the Japanese dealt with these pressures more successfully than the mainland Asian empires (Ottoman, Safavid, Mughal, and Ming), which saw political fragmentation and even the overthrow of ruling dynasties. In Japan, a single ruling family emerged. This dynastic state, the **Tokugawa shogunate**, accomplished something that most of the world's other regimes did not: it regulated foreign intrusion. While Japan played a modest role in the expanding global trade, it remained free of outside exploitation.

UNIFICATION OF JAPAN During the sixteenth century, Japan had suffered from political instability as banditry and civil strife disrupted the countryside. Regional ruling families, called *daimyos,* had commanded private armies of warriors known as samurai. The daimyos sometimes brought order to their domains, but no one family could establish preeminence over others. Although Japan had an emperor, his authority did not extend beyond the court in Kyoto.

Ultimately, several military leaders attempted to unify Japan. One general, who became the supreme minister, arranged marriages among the children of local authorities to solidify political bonds. Also, to coax cooperation from the daimyos, he ordered that their wives and children be kept as semihostages in the residences they were required to maintain in Edo. After the general died, one of the daimyos, Tokugawa Ieyasu, took power for himself. This was a decisive moment. In 1603, Ieyasu assumed the title of shogun (military ruler). He also solved the problem of succession, declaring that rulership would be hereditary and that his family would be the ruling household. This hereditary Tokugawa shogunate lasted until 1867.

Now administrative authority shifted from Kyoto to the site of Ieyasu's domain headquarters: the castle town called Edo (later renamed Tokyo; see Map 13.6). The Tokugawa built Edo out of a small earthen fortification clinging to a coastal bluff. Behind Edo lay a village in a swampy plain. In a monumental work of engineering, the rulers ordered the swamp drained, the forest cleared, many of the hills leveled, canals dredged, bridges built, the seashore extended by landfill, and a new stone castle completed. By the time Ieyasu died, Edo had a population of 150,000.

The Tokugawa shoguns ensured a flow of resources from the working population to the rulers and from the provinces to the capital. Villages paid taxes to the daimyos, who transferred resources to the seat of shogunate authority. No longer engaged in constant warfare, the samurai became administrators. Peace brought prosperity. Agriculture thrived. Improved farming techniques and land reclamation projects enabled the country's population to grow from 10 million in 1550 to 16 million in 1600 and 30 million in 1700.

FOREIGN AFFAIRS AND FOREIGNERS Internal peace and prosperity did not insulate Japan from external challenges. When Japanese rulers tackled foreign affairs, their most pressing concern was the intrusion of Christian missionaries and European traders. Initially, Japanese officials welcomed these foreigners out of an eagerness to acquire muskets, gunpowder, and other new technology. But once the ranks of Christian converts swelled, Japanese authorities realized that Christians were intolerant of other faiths, believed Christ to be superior to any authority, and fought among themselves. Trying to stem the tide, the shoguns prohibited conversion to Christianity and attempted to ban its practice. After a rebellion in which converted peasants rose up in protest against high rents and taxes,

Edo in the Rain. *This facsimile of an ukiyo-e ("floating world") print by Hiroshige (1797–1858) depicts one of several bridges in the bustling city of Edo (later Tokyo), with Mount Fuji in the background.*

MAP 13.6 | Tokugawa Japan, 1603–1867

The Tokugawa shoguns created a strong central state in Japan at this time.

- According to this map, how extensive was their control?
- What foreign states were interested in trade with Japan?
- How did Tokugawa leaders attempt to control relations with foreign states and other entities?

Portuguese Arriving in Japan. *In the 1540s, the Portuguese arrival on the islands of Japan sparked a fascination with the strange costumes and the great ships of these "southern barbarians" (so called because they had approached Japan from the south). Silk-screen paintings depicted Portuguese prowess in exaggerated form, such as in the impossible height of the fore and aft of the vessel pictured here.*

the government suppressed Christianity and drove European missionaries from the country.

Even more troublesome was the lure of trade with Europeans. The Tokugawa knew that trading at various Japanese ports would pull the commercial regions in various directions, away from the capital. When it became clear that European traders preferred the ports of Kyūshū (the southernmost island), the shogunate restricted Europeans to trade only in ports under Edo's direct rule in Honshū. Then, Japanese authorities expelled all European competitors. Only the Protestant (and nonmissionizing) Dutch won permission to remain in Japan, confined to an island near Nagasaki. The Dutch were allowed to unload just one ship each year, under strict supervision by Japanese authorities.

These measures did not close Tokugawa Japan to the outside world, however. Trade with China and Korea flourished, and the shogun received missions from Korea and the Ryūkyū islands. Edo also gathered information about the outside world from the resident Dutch and Chinese (who included monks, physicians, and painters). A few Japanese were permitted to learn Dutch and to study European technology, shipbuilding, and medicine (see Chapter 14). By limiting such encounters, the authorities ensured that foreigners would not threaten Japan's security.

Ruling over three islands, Tokugawa Japan was surrounded by "vassals" that were neither part of the realm nor entirely independent. Most important were the Ryūkyūs in the south and the island of Ezo to the north, which the Japanese maintained as buffers. Such areas helped define a distinct Japanese identity for all peoples living "on the inside." When, beginning in 1697, the Russians approached Japan to open relations, the Japanese instead sought to deal with them through the northern buffer zone. As the Russians tried harder to open Japan to trade, the Japanese annexed and began to colonize Ezo (what would eventually be called Hokkaidō), the country's fourth main island and a strong barrier to foreign penetration. In regulating outside contacts, Japanese rulers suppressed potential sources of upheaval and consolidated a dynasty that lasted well into the nineteenth century.

The rulers of Japan invented an approach to relations with the outside world on Japanese terms. They permitted trade and diplomatic relations with the Dutch, Chinese, and Koreans, but in a controlled fashion, and they generally did not permit such relations with the Russians or Christian missionaries. In this, the Japanese were aided by their island status, which had also protected them from the Mongols.

TRANSFORMATIONS IN EUROPE

Between 1600 and 1750, religious conflict, commercial expansion, and the consolidation of dynastic power transformed Europe. Commercial centers shifted northward, and Spain and Portugal lost ground to England and France. Even farther to the north, the state of Muscovy expanded dramatically to become the sprawling Russian Empire.

Expansion and Dynastic Change in Russia

During this period the Russian Empire expanded to become the world's largest-ever state. It gained positions on the Baltic Sea and the Pacific Ocean, and it established political borders with both the Qing Empire and Japan. These momentous shifts involved the elimination of steppe nomads as an independent force. Culturally, Europeans as well as Russians debated whether Russia belonged more to Europe or to Asia. The answer was both.

MAP 13.7 | Russian Expansion, 1462-1795

The state of Muscovy incorporated vast territories through overland expansion as it grew and became the Russian Empire. It did so in part because of its geographical position and its strategic needs.

- Using the map key, identify how many different expansions the Russian Empire underwent between 1462 and 1795 and in what directions generally.
- With what countries and cultures did the Russian Empire come into contact?
- What drove such dramatic expansion?

MUSCOVY BECOMES THE RUSSIAN EMPIRE The principality of Moscow, or Muscovy, like Japan and China, used territorial expansion and commercial networks to consolidate a powerful state. This was the Russian Empire, the name given to Muscovy by Tsar Peter the Great around 1700. Originally a mixture of Slavs, Finnish tribes, Turkic speakers, and many others, **Muscovy** expanded to become a huge empire that spanned parts of Europe, much of northern Asia, numerous North Pacific islands, and even—for a time—a corner of North America (Alaska).

Like Japan, Russia emerged out of turmoil. Three factors inspired the regime to seize territory: security concerns; the ambitions of private individuals; and religious conviction. Security concerns were foremost, as expansion was inseparable from security. Because the steppe, which stretches deep into Asia, remained a highway for nomadic peoples (especially descendants of the powerful Mongols), Muscovy sought to dominate the areas south and east of Moscow. By marrying the niece of the last Byzantine emperor, the Muscovite grand prince Ivan III (r. 1462–1505) added a religious dimension to his expansionist claims: he could assert that Moscow was the center of the Byzantine faith and heir to the conquered city of Constantinople. Later expansion secured Muscovy's eastern borders by reaching into Siberia. Beginning in the 1590s, Russian authorities built forts and trading posts along Siberian rivers at the same time that privateers, enticed by the fur trade, pushed even farther east. By 1639 the state's borders had reached the Pacific. Thus in just over a century, Muscovy had claimed an empire straddling Eurasia and incorporating peoples of many languages and religions (see Map 13.7).

Much of this expansion occurred despite dynastic chaos that followed the death of Ivan IV in 1584. Ultimately a group of prominent families reestablished central authority and threw their weight behind a new family of rulers. These were the Romanovs, court barons who set about reviving the Kremlin's fortunes. (The Kremlin was a medieval walled fortress where the Muscovite grand princes—later, tsars—resided.) Like the Ottoman and Qing dynasts, Romanov tsars and their aristocratic supporters would retain power into the twentieth century.

ABSOLUTIST GOVERNMENT AND SERFDOM In the seventeenth and eighteenth centuries, the Romanovs created an absolutist system of government. Only the tsar and his retinue had the right to make war, tax, judge, and coin money. The Romanovs also made the nobles serve as state officials. Now Russia became a despotic state that had no political assemblies for nobles or other groups, other than mere consultative bodies like the imperial senate. Indeed, away from Moscow, local aristocrats enjoyed nearly unlimited authority in exchange for loyalty and tribute to the tsar.

During this period, Russia's peasantry bore the burden of maintaining the wealth of the small nobility and the monarchy. Most peasant families gathered into communes, isolated rural worlds where people helped one another deal with the harsh climate, severe landlords, and occasional poor harvests. Communes functioned like extended kin networks in that members reciprocated favors and chores. The typical peasant hut was a single chamber heated by a wood-burning stove with no chimney. Livestock and humans often shared the same quarters. In 1649, peasants were legally bound as serfs to the nobles and the tsar, meaning they had to perform obligatory services and deliver part of their produce to their lords. In fact, the lords essentially controlled all aspects of their serfs' lives.

Nenets Hunters. *Hunters of the Nenets tribe in far North Asia's treeless tundra, show off their warm animal-skin clothing and self-fashioned weapons, as depicted in a 1620 engraving by Theodore de Bry, one of the first Europeans to come into contact with them.*

Catherine the Great. *Catherine the Great styled herself an enlightened despot of the baroque epoch, furthering the Russian Empire's adaptation of European high culture.*

IMPERIAL EXPANSION AND MIGRATION Three factors were key to Russia's becoming an empire: (1) the conquest of Siberia, which brought vast territory and riches in furs; (2) incorporation of the fertile southern steppes, known as Ukraine; and (3) victory in a prolonged war with Sweden. Peter the Great (r. 1682–1725) accomplished the victory in Sweden, after which he founded a new capital at St. Petersburg. Yet even as he triumphed over Sweden he sought to imitate a Swedish-style bureaucracy in Russia. Thereafter Russia developed a formidable military-fiscal state bureaucracy, but the aristocracy, not the civil service, remained predominant.

Under Peter's successors, including the hard-nosed Catherine the Great, Russia added even more territory. Catherine placed her former lover on the Polish throne and subsequently, together with the Austrians and Prussians, carved up the medieval state of Poland. Her victories against the Ottomans allowed Russia to annex Ukraine, the grain-growing "breadbasket" of eastern Europe. By the late eighteenth century, Russia's grasp extended from the Baltic Sea through the heart of Europe, Ukraine, and the Crimea on the Black Sea and into the ancient lands of Armenia and Georgia in the Caucasus Mountains.

The Russian Empire was a harsh but colossal space that induced the movement of peoples within it. Many people migrated eastward, into Siberia. Some were fleeing serfdom; others were being deported for having rejected changes in the state's official Eastern Orthodox religious services. Battling astoundingly harsh temperatures (falling to –40 degrees Centigrade/Fahrenheit) and frigid Arctic winds, these individuals traveled on horseback and trudged on foot to resettle in the east. But the difficulties of clearing forested lands or planting crops in boggy Siberian soils, combined with extraordinarily harsh winters, meant that many settlers died or tried to return. Isolation was a problem, too. There was no established land route back to Moscow until the 1770s, when exiles completed the Great Siberian Post Road through the swamps and peat bogs of western Siberia. The writer Anton Chekhov later called it "the longest and ugliest road in the whole world."

Whereas initially over 90 percent of Siberia's inhabitants were natives, by 1750 the number of immigrants almost matched the native population and soon surpassed it. Although many of the immigrants were runaway serfs, others who were religious or political outcasts would later make Siberia infamous as a land for prisoners instead of a destination of freedom. "The road to Siberia is wide," went the saying, "the way back, narrow."

Economic and Political Fluctuations in Western Europe

During this period European economies became more commercialized, especially after recovering from the Thirty Years' War. As in Asia, developments in distant parts of the world shaped the region's economic upturns and downturns. Compounding these pressures was the continuation of dynastic rivalries and religious conflicts.

THE THIRTY YEARS' WAR For a century after Martin Luther broke with the Catholic Church (see Chapter 12), religious warfare raged in Europe. So did contests over territory, power, and trade. The **Thirty Years' War** (1618–1648) was all three of these—a war between Protestant princes and the Catholic emperor for religious predominance in central Europe; a struggle for regional control among Catholic powers (the Spanish and Austrian Habsburgs and the French); and a bid for independence (from Spain) by the Dutch, who wanted to trade and worship as they liked.

The brutal conflict began as a struggle between Protestants and Catholics within the Habsburg Empire, but it soon became a war for preeminence in Europe. It took the lives of civilians as well as soldiers. Just when it seemed as if Protestantism would vanish from central Europe, the Swedish king made a timely intervention, reenergizing the Protestant cause. In the course of a war fought heavily by ill-paid and poorly fed mercenaries, both sides committed many atrocities against civilians. Most famously, in 1631, Catholic forces besieged and then destroyed the beautiful German town of Magdeburg, killing three-quarters of the civilian inhabitants. In total, fighting, disease, and famine wiped out a third of the German states' urban population and two-fifths of their rural population. The war also depopulated Sweden and Poland. Ultimately the Treaty of Westphalia (1648) stated, in essence, that as there was a rough balance of power between Protestant and Catholic states, they would simply have to put up with each other. The Dutch won their independence, but the war's enormous costs provoked severe discontent in Spain, France, and England. Central Europe was so devastated that it did

The Thirty Years' War. *The mercenary armies of the Thirty Years' War were renowned for pillaging and tormenting the civilians of central Europe. Here, the townsfolk exact revenge on some of these soldiers, hanging, as the engraving's caption claims, "damned and infamous thieves, like bad fruit, from this tree."*

Amsterdam Stock Exchange. *The high concentration of deeply religious merchants in Amsterdam naturally gave way to the world's first stock exchange in the seventeenth century. This diverse gathering of men trading stocks and preparing to participate in auctions, as depicted by renowned painter Emanuel de Witte, was a common sight throughout the Dutch Golden Age.*

not recover in economic or demographic terms for more than a century.

The Thirty Years' War transformed war making. Whereas most medieval struggles had been sieges between nobles leading small armies, centralized states fielding standing armies now waged decisive, grand-scale campaigns. The war also changed the ranks of soldiers: as the conflict ground on, local enlisted men defending their king, country, and faith gave way to hired mercenaries or criminals doing forced service. Even officers, who previously obtained their stripes by purchase or royal decree, now had to earn them. Gunpowder, cannons, and handguns became standardized. By the eighteenth century, Europe's wars featured huge standing armies boasting a professional officer corps, deadly artillery, and long supply lines bringing food and ammunition to the front. The costs—material and human—of war began to soar.

WESTERN EUROPEAN ECONOMIES In spite of the toll that warfare took on economic activity, the European states enjoyed significant commercial expansion. Northern Europe gained more than did the south, however. Spain, for example, started losing ground to its rivals as the costs of defending its empire soared and merchants from northern Europe cut in on its trading networks. The weighty costs of its involvement in the Thirty Years' War dealt the Spanish economy a final, disastrous blow. Other previously robust economies also suffered under the pressures of greater economic connection and competition. Venice, for example, which before the era of transoceanic shipping had been Europe's chief gateway to Asia, saw its economy decline.

As European commercial dynamism shifted northward, the Dutch led the way with innovative commercial practices and a new mercantile elite. They specialized in shipping and in financing regional and long-distance trade. Their famous *fluitschips* carried heavy, bulky cargoes (like Baltic wood) with relatively small crews. Now shipping costs throughout the Atlantic world dropped as Dutch ships transported their own and other countries' goods. Amsterdam's merchants founded an exchange bank, established a rudimentary stock exchange, and pioneered systems of underwriting and insuring cargoes. As Europe's other mercantile centers followed suit, the Dutch share of commercial activity eventually shrank. But their pioneering ways set an early example for trading and financing practices that further integrated the Atlantic economies.

England and France also became commercial powerhouses, establishing aggressive policies to promote national business and drive out competitors. Consider the English Navigation Act of 1651. By stipulating that only English ships could carry goods between the mother country and its colonies, it protected English shippers and merchants—especially from the Dutch. The English

Versailles. *Louis XIV's Versailles, just southwest of Paris, was a hunting lodge that was converted at colossal cost in the 1670s–1680s into a grand royal chateau with expansive grounds. Much envied and imitated across Europe, the palace became the epicenter of a luxurious court life that included entertainment such as plays and musical offerings, state receptions, royal hunts, boating, and gambling. Thousands of nobles at Versailles vied with each other for closer proximity to the king in the performance of court rituals.*

subsequently launched several effective trade wars against Holland. The French, too, followed aggressive mercantilist policies and ultimately joined forces with England to invade Holland.

Economic development was not limited to port towns: the countryside, too, enjoyed breakthroughs in production. Most important was expansion in the production of food. In northwestern Europe investments in water drainage, larger livestock herds, and improved cultivation practices generated much greater yields. Also, a four-field crop rotation involving wheat, clover, barley, and turnips kept nutrients in the soil and provided year-round fodder for livestock. As a result (and as we have seen many times throughout history), increased output supported a growing urban population. By contrast, in Spain and Italy, agricultural change and population growth came more slowly.

Production rose most where the organization of rural property changed. Consider again the transformation that occurred in England. Here, in a movement known as **enclosure**, landowners took control of lands that traditionally had been common property serving local needs. Claiming exclusive rights to these lands, the landowners planted new crops or pastured sheep with the aim of selling the products in distant markets—especially cities. The largest landowners put their farms in the hands of tenants, who hired wage laborers to till, plant, and harvest. Thus, in England, peasant agriculture gave way to farms run by wealthy families who exploited the marketplace to buy what they needed (including labor) and to sell what they produced. In this regard, England led the way in a Europe-wide process of commercializing the countryside.

DYNASTIC MONARCHIES: FRANCE AND ENGLAND

European monarchs had varying success with centralizing state power. In France, Louis XIII (r. 1610–1643) and especially his

Queen Elizabeth of England. *This portrait (c. 1600) depicts an idealized Queen Elizabeth near the end of her long reign. The queen is pictured riding in a procession in the midst of an admiring crowd composed of the most important nobles of the realm.*

chief minister, Cardinal Richelieu, concentrated power in the hands of the king. Under his successor, the Bourbon family established a monarchy in which succession passed to the oldest male in the male line. After 1614, kings refused to convene the Estates-General, a medieval advisory body. Composed of representatives of three groups—the clergy (the First Estate, those who pray), the nobility (the Second Estate, those who fight), and the unprivileged remainder of the population (the Third Estate, those who work)—the Estates-General was an obstacle to the king's full empowerment. Instead of sharing power, the king and his counselors wanted him to rule free of external checks, to create in the words of the age an **absolute monarchy.** The ruler was not to be a tyrant, but his authority was to be complete and thorough, and his state free of bloody disorders. The king's rule would be lawful; but he, not his jurists, would dictate the last legal word. If the king made a mistake, only God could call him to account. Thus the Europeans believed in the "divine right of kings," a political belief not greatly different from imperial China where the emperor was thought to rule with the mandate of heaven.

In absolutist France, privileges and state offices flowed from the king's grace. All patronage networks ultimately linked to the king. The great palace Louis XIV built at Versailles teemed with nobles from all over France seeking favor, dressing according to the king's expensive fashion code, and attending the latest tragedies, comedies, and concerts. Just as the Japanese shogun monitored the daimyos by keeping their families in Edo, Louis XIV kept a watchful eye on the French nobility at Versailles.

The French dynastic monarchy provided a model of absolute rule for other European dynasts, like the Habsburgs of the Holy Roman Empire, the Hohenzollerns of Prussia, and the Romanovs of Muscovy. The king and his ministers controlled all public power, while other social groups, from the nobility to the peasantry, had no formal body to represent their interests. Nonetheless, French absolutist government was not as absolute as the king would have wished. Pockets of stalwart Protestants practiced their religion secretly in the plateau villages of central France. Peasant disturbances continued. Criticism of court life, wars, and religious policies filled anonymous pamphlets, jurists' notebooks, and courtiers' private journals. Members of the nobility also grumbled about their political misfortunes, but since the king would not call the Estates-General, they had no formal way to express their concerns.

England might also have evolved into an absolutist regime, but there were important differences between England and France. Queen Elizabeth (r. 1558–1603) and her successors used many policies similar to those of the French monarchy, such as control of patronage (to grant privileges) and elaborate court festivities. Also, refusing to share her power with a man, the "Virgin Queen" never married and exerted sole control over the church, military, and aristocracy. However, not only did the English system of succession allow women to rule as queens in their own right, but the English Parliament remained an important force. Whereas the French kings did not need the consent of the Estates-General to enact taxes, the English monarchs had to convene Parliament to raise money.

Under Elizabeth's successors, fierce quarrels broke out over taxation, religion, and royal efforts to rule without parliamentary consent. Tensions ran high between Puritans (who preferred a simpler form of worship and more egalitarian church government) and Anglicans (who supported the state-sponsored, hierarchically organized Church of England headed by the king). Social and economic grievances led to civil war in the 1640s and an ultimate victory for the parliamentary army (largely Puritan)—and the beheading of King Charles I. Twelve years of government as a commonwealth without a king followed. During that time the middle and lower classes enjoyed political and religious power, but the commonwealth became a military dictatorship.

In 1660 the monarchy was restored, but without resolving issues of religious tolerance and the king's relation to Parliament. Charles II and his successor, James II, aroused opposition by their autocracy and secret efforts to bring England back into the Catholic fold. The conflict between an aspiring absolutist throne and Parliament's insistence on shared sovereignty and Protestant succession culminated in the Glorious Revolution of 1688–1689. In a bloodless upheaval, James II fled to France and Parliament offered the crown to William of Orange and his wife, Mary (a Protestant). The outcome of the conflict established the principle that English monarchs must rule in conjunction with Parliament. Although the Church of England was reaffirmed as the official state church, Presbyterians and Jews were allowed to practice their religions. Catholic worship, still officially forbidden, was tolerated as long as the Catholics kept quiet. By 1700, then, England's nobility and merchant classes had a guaranteed say in public affairs and assurance that state activity would privilege the propertied classes as well as the ruler.

Events in France and England stimulated much political writing. In England, Thomas Hobbes published *Leviathan* (1651), a defense of the state's absolute power over all competing forces. John Locke published *Two Treatises of Civil Government* (1689), which argued not only for the natural rights to liberty and property but also for the rights of peoples to form a government and then to disband and reform it when it did not live up to its contract. French theorists also proposed new ways of conducting politics and making law. As writers discussed the costs of unchecked state power, they differed over the extent to which elites could check the king. As the eighteenth century unfolded, the question of where sovereignty lay grew more pressing.

MERCANTILIST WARS The rise of new powers in Europe, especially France and England, intensified rivalries for control of the Atlantic system. As conflicts over colonies and sea-lanes replaced earlier religious and territorial struggles, commercial struggles became worldwide wars. Across the globe, European empires constantly skirmished over control of trade and territory. English and Dutch trading companies took aim at Portuguese outposts in Asia and the Americas, and then at each other. Ports in India suffered repeated assaults and counterassaults. In response, European powers built huge navies to protect their colonies and trade routes and to attack their rivals.

Smuggling became rampant. English and French traders, sometimes backed by political authorities, violated the sovereign claims of rival colonies. Curaçao, for instance, became an entrepôt for traders from England and the Low Countries selling illegal goods in South America (see Map 13.1). French and English traders set up shop in southern Brazil to smuggle goods in return for Andean silver. All around the Gulf of Mexico and the Caribbean, merchants sneaked their goods into enemies' colonies.

After 1715, mercantilist wars occurred mainly outside Europe, as empires feuded over colonial possessions. These conflicts were especially bitter in border areas, particularly in the Caribbean and North America. Each round of warfare ratcheted up the scale and cost of fighting.

The **Seven Years' War** (known as the French and Indian War in the United States) marked the culmination of this rivalry among European empires around the globe. Fought from 1756 to 1763, it saw Native Americans, African slaves, Bengali princes, Filipino militiamen, and European foot soldiers dragged into a contest over imperial possessions and control of the seas. Some fleets, like the French at the Battle of Quiberon Bay, were dispatched to the bottom of the ocean. Some fortresses, like Spain's Havana, and Quebec City fell to invaders. The battles in Europe were relatively indecisive (despite being large), except in the hinterlands. After all, what sparked the war was a skirmish of British colonial troops (featuring a lieutenant colonel named George Washington) allied with Seneca warriors against French soldiers in the Ohio Valley (see Map 13.2 for North American references). In India, the war had a decisive outcome, for here the East India Company trader Robert Clive rallied 850 European officers and 2,100 Indian recruits to defeat the French (there were but 40 French artillerymen) and their 50,000 Maratha allies at Plassey. The British seized the upper hand—over everyone—in India. Not only did the British drive off the French from the rich Bengali interior, but they also crippled Indian rulers' resistance against European intruders (see Map 12.4 for India references).

The Seven Years' War changed the balance of power around the world. Britain emerged as the foremost colonial empire. Its rivals, especially France and Spain, took a pounding; France lost its North American colonies, and Spain lost Florida (though it gained the Louisiana Territory west of the Mississippi in a secret deal with France). In India, as well, the French were losers and had to acknowledge British supremacy in the wealthy provinces of Bihar and Bengal. But overwhelmingly, the biggest losers were indigenous peoples everywhere. With the rise of one empire over all others, it was harder for Native Americans to play the Europeans off against each other. Maratha princes faced the same problem. Clearly, as worlds became more entangled, the gaps between winners and losers grew more pronounced.

CONCLUSION

In the 1750s, the world's regions were more economically connected than they had been a century and a half earlier. The process of integrating the resources of previous worlds apart that had begun with Christopher Columbus's voyages intensified during this period. Traders shipped a wider variety of commodities—from Baltic wood to Indian cotton, from New World silver and sugar to Chinese silks and porcelain—over longer distances. People increasingly wore clothes manufactured elsewhere, consumed beverages made from products cultivated in far-off locations, and used imported guns to settle local conflicts.

Everywhere, this integration and the consumer opportunities that it made possible came at a heavy price. Nowhere was it more costly than in the Americas, where colonization and exploitation led to the expulsion of Indians from their lands and the decimation of their numbers. The cost was also very high for the millions of Africans forced across the Atlantic to work New World plantations and for the millions more who did not survive the journey.

Along with sugar, silver was the product from the Americas that most transformed global trading networks and that showed how greater entanglements could both enrich and destabilize. Although Spanish colonizers mined New World silver and shipped it to western Europe and Asia, it was Spain's main competitors in Europe that gained the upper hand in the seventeenth and eighteenth centuries. Nearly one-third of the silver from the New World ended up in China as payment for products like porcelains and silks that consumers still regarded as the world's finest manufactures. But if China's economy remained vibrant, silver did play a part in the fall of one dynasty and the rise of another. For the Ottoman, Mughal, and Safavid empires, the influx of silver created rampant inflation and undermined their previous economic autonomy.

Certain societies coped with increased commercial exchange more successfully than others. The Safavid and Ming dynasties could not withstand the pressures; both collapsed. The Spanish, Ottoman, and Mughal dynasties managed to survive but faced increasing pressure from aggressive rivals. For newcomers to the integrating world, the opportunity to trade helped support new dynasties. Japan, Russia, and England emerged on the world stage. But even in these newer regimes, commerce and competition did not erase conflict. To the contrary, while the world was more together economically than ever before, greater prosperity for some hardly translated into peace for most.

TRACING THE GLOBAL STORYLINES

AFTER YOU READ THIS CHAPTER

FOCUS ON: *The Regional Impact of World Trade*

The Americas

- England, France, and Holland join Spain and Portugal as colonial powers in the Americas.
- The English and French colonies in the Caribbean become the world's major exporters of sugar.

Africa

- The Atlantic slave trade increases to record proportions, creating gender imbalances, impoverishing some regions, and elevating the power of slave-supplying states.

Southeast Asia

- The Dutch East India Company takes over the major islands of Southeast Asia.

Islam

- World trade destabilizes the economies of the Safavid, Ottoman, and Mughal empires.

East Asia

- The Ming dynasty in China loses the mandate of heaven and is replaced by the Qing.
- The Tokugawa shogunate unifies Japan and limits the influence of Europeans in the country.

Europe

- Tsarist Russia expands toward the Baltic Sea and the Pacific Ocean and becomes the largest state in the world.
- Europe recovers from thirty years of political and religious warfare (1618–1648), with Holland, England, and France emerging as economic powerhouses.

Review and research materials on **StudySpace:** wwnorton.com/studyspace

CHRONOLOGY

The Americas

Africa
- Massive expansion of Atlantic slave trade

South Asia
- Aurangzeb's expansion weakens the Mughal dynasty **1658–1707**

East Asia
- Tokugawa shogunate formed in Japan **1603**
- Ming dynasty falls, Qing dynasty founded **1644**

Europe
- Thirty Years' War **1618–1648**
- England, France, Netherlands pursue mercantilist expansion abroad

The Islamic World

Russia
- Romanov dynasty founded **1613**

1600 — 1650

KEY TERMS

absolute monarchy *p. 513*
bullion *p. 500*
Canton system *p. 504*
chartered companies *p. 482*
enclosure *p. 512*
Mamluks *p. 497*
Manchus *p. 502*
mercantilism *p. 482*
monetization *p. 500*
Muscovy *p. 508*
Qing dynasty *p. 503*
Seven Years' War *p. 514*
specie *p. 498*
Thirty Years' War *p. 510*
Tokugawa shogunate *p. 504*

STUDY QUESTIONS

1. **Define** mercantilism, and analyze how mercantilist practices affected all regions of the Atlantic world between 1600 and 1750.
2. **Describe** the plantation complex in the Caribbean. Why was it so valued by Europeans relative to other regions of the Americas?
3. **Analyze** how the Atlantic slave trade reshaped sub-Saharan African societies. Which regions and groups benefited from Africa's growing entanglements in global commerce?
4. **Analyze** how global trade affected the Ottoman and Mughal empires during this era. How did each regime respond to these growing entanglements?
5. **List and describe** major factors that caused the end of the Ming dynasty and the rise of the Qing dynasty in China. How did global trade affect this outcome? How did Qing rulers react to global commerce?
6. **Analyze** to what extent the Tokugawa shogunate succeeded in creating a strong central government in Japan. How did it avoid the problems associated with expanding trade that many other dynasties faced at this time?
7. **Compare and contrast** the expansionist policies of the Russian state with those pursued by the British and French regimes during this period. How were they similar and how were they different?
8. **Analyze** how increased global trade shaped the history of Europe during this period. Why did England tend to be the largest beneficiary of these trends in terms of regional dynastic rivalries? What other social and political groups were strongly affected by Europe's increased global entanglements?
9. **Compare and contrast** the impact of global commerce on European and Asian dynasties. Did any dynasty hold an advantage over others in controlling commercial networks and using them to enrich their societies?

Sugar complex emerges in the Caribbean region **17th century**
French and Dutch merchants establish fur trade in North America **17th century**
British defeat French forces in North America during the Seven Years' War **1754–1761**

Asante state founded **1701**
Expansion of Oyo state **17th century**

British assume control of French interests in South Asia during Seven Years' War **1756–1763**

Seven Years' War **1756–1763**

Koprulu reforms stabilize Ottoman Empire **mid-17th century**
Safavid dynasty collapses **1773**

Expansion into Siberia **17th century**
Peter the Great reigns **1682–1725**

1700 | 1750

BEFORE YOU READ THIS CHAPTER

wwnorton.com/
STUDYSPACE

GLOBAL STORYLINES

- Growing global commerce enriches and shapes cultures worldwide.
- The major regions demonstrate pride in their traditions and celebrate political, economic, and cultural achievements.
- Europeans and peoples of European descent in the Americas argue that their races and cultures are superior to all others.

CHAPTER OUTLINE

FOCUS QUESTIONS

- How did increased wealth and new patterns of exchange affect cultures around the world between 1600 and 1750?
- Which groups of people tended to benefit from the global cultural renaissance of this age and which did not?
- To what extent were Islamic, South Asian, and East Asian leaders open to outside cultural influence?
- How did aboriginal peoples in the Americas and Oceania respond to European cultural imperialism?
- How did the cultural developments affect women in this era?

14

Cultures of Splendor and Power, 1500–1780

In 1664, a sixteen-year-old girl from the provinces of New Spain asked her parents for permission to attend the university in the capital. Although she had mastered Greek logic, taught Latin, and become a proficient mathematician, she had two strikes against her: she was a woman, and her thinking ran against the grain of the Catholic Church. So keen was she to pursue her studies that she proposed to disguise herself as a man. But her parents denied her requests, and instead of attending the university she entered a convent in Mexico City, where she would spend the rest of her life. Fortunately, the convent turned out to be a sanctuary for her. There she studied science and mathematics and composed remarkable poetry. Sor (Sister) Juana Inés de la Cruz was her name, and she was the bard of a new world where people mixed in faraway places, where new wealth created new customs, and where new ideas began to take hold. One of her poems, called "You Men," began: "Silly, you men—so very adept / at wrongly faulting womankind, not seeing you're alone to blame / for faults you plant in woman's mind." Her poetry is an example of how new discoveries and new knowledge challenged old ways. But her life story also reminds us of the fierce resistance to new ways. Sor Juana's poetry enraged church authorities, who forced her to recant her words and who burned her books. Only the intervention of the viceroy's wife prevented officials from torching the nun's complete works before she died of a plague in 1695.

Sor Juana's story attests to the conflicts between new ideas and old orders that occurred once the entanglements of commerce and the consolidation of empires fostered knowledge of foreign ways. On the one hand, global commerce created riches that supported arts, architecture, and scientific ventures. On the other, experimentations in new ways caused discomfort among defenders of the old order and provoked attempts to subdue and silence purveyors of innovation.

This chapter explores how global commerce enriched and reshaped cultures in the centuries after the Americas ceased to be worlds apart from Afro-Eurasia. Profiting from trade in New World commodities, many rulers and merchants displayed their power by commissioning fabulous works of art and majestic palaces and sprawling plazas. These cultural splendors were meant to impress, which they surely did. These efforts also demonstrated the growing connections between distant societies, reflecting how exotic, borrowed influences could blend with domestic traditions. Book production and consumption soared with some publications finding their way around the world. The spread of books and ideas and increasing cultural contact led to experiments in religious toleration and helped foster cultural diversity. Yet even as Europeans, who were the greatest beneficiaries of New World riches, claimed to advance new universal truths, cultural productions around the globe still showed the resilience of local traditions.

TRADE AND CULTURE

It is not surprising that in 1500 the world's most dynamic cultures were in Asia, in areas profiting from the Indian Ocean and China Sea trades. It was in China and the Islamic world that the spice and luxury trades first flourished; here, too, rulers had successfully established political stability and centralized control of taxation, law making, and military force. This often involved recruiting people from diverse backgrounds and promoting new kinds of secular (nonreligious) education. Although older ways did not die out, both trade and empire building contributed to the spread of knowledge about distant people and foreign cultures.

Of course, some rulers and polities were more eager for change than others. Moreover, certain societies—in the Americas and the South Pacific, for example—found that contact, conquest, and commerce undermined indigenous cultural life. Although Europeans and native peoples often exchanged ideas and practices, these transfers were not equal. Native Americans, for example, adapted to European missionizing by creating mixed forms of religious worship—but only because they were under pressure to do so. And as the Europeans swallowed up new territories, it was *their* culture that spread and diversified. Indeed, the Europeans absorbed much from Native Americans and African slaves but offered them little share of sovereignty or wealth in return.

For many groups, the global cultural flourishing of this period owed much to the benefits of burgeoning world trade, which allowed some rulers to consolidate wealth, administration, and military power. These rulers were eager to patronize the arts as a way to legitimize their power and reflect their cultural sophistication. In Europe, monarchs known as **enlightened absolutists** restricted the clergy and nobility and hired loyal bureaucrats who championed the knowledge of the new age. British monarchs, though they were not absolutists (because they shared power with Parliament), followed suit. Mughal emperors, Safavid shahs, and Ottoman sultans glorified their regimes by bringing artists and artisans from all over the world to give an Islamic flavor to their major cities and buildings. Rulers in China and Japan also looked to artists to extol their achievements. And in Africa, the wealth garnered from slave trading underwrote cultural productions of extraordinary merit.

Despite the unifying aspects of world trade, each society retained core aspects of its individuality. Ruling classes disseminated values based on cherished classical texts and long-established moral and religious principles. They used space in new ways to establish and project their power. (See Current Trends in World History: The Political Uses of Space.) They mapped their geographies and wrote their histories according to their traditional visions of the universe. Even as global trade drew their attention outward and in some cases introduced foreign influences, societies celebrated their achievements in politics, economics, and culture with pride in their own heritages.

CULTURE IN THE ISLAMIC WORLD

For centuries, Muslim elites had generously funded cultural development. As the Ottoman, Safavid, and Mughal empires gained greater expanses of territory, they acquired new resources to fund more such pursuits. Rulers supported new schools and building projects, and the elite produced books, artworks, and luxury goods. Cultural life was connected to the politics of empire building, as emperors and elites sought greater prestige by patronizing intellectuals and artists.

Forged under contrasting imperial auspices, Islamic cultural and intellectual life now reflected three distinct worlds. In place of an earlier Islamic cosmopolitanism, unique cultural patterns prevailed within each empire. Although the Ottomans, the Safavids, and the Mughals shared a common faith, each developed a relatively autonomous form of Muslim culture.

The Ottoman Cultural Synthesis

By the sixteenth century, the Ottoman Empire was enjoying a remarkably rich culture that reflected a variety of mixing influences. Its blend of ethnic, religious, and linguistic elements exceeded those of previous Islamic empires. The Ottomans' cultural synthesis accommodated both Sufis (mystics who stressed contemplation and ecstasy through poetry, music, and dance) and ultraorthodox *ulama* (Islamic jurists who stressed tradition and religious law). It also balanced the interests of military men and administrators with those of clerics. Finally, it allowed autonomy to the minority faiths of Christianity and Judaism.

RELIGION AND LAW The Ottoman world achieved cultural unity, above all, by an outstanding intellectual achievement—its system of administrative law. As the empire absorbed diverse cultures and territories, the sultans realized that the *sharia* (Islamic holy law) would not suffice because it was silent on many secular matters. Moreover, the Ottoman state needed comprehensive laws to bridge differences among the many social and legal systems under its rule. Mehmed II, conqueror of Constantinople, began the reform. By recruiting young boys, rather than noblemen, for training as bureaucrats or military men and making them accountable directly to the sultan, he fashioned a professional bureaucracy with unswerving loyalty to the ruler. Mehmed's successor, Suleiman the Magnificent and the Lawgiver, continued this work by compiling a comprehensive legal code. The code addressed subjects' rights and duties, proper clothing, and how Muslims were to relate to non-Muslims. The code also reconciled many differences between administrative and religious law.

EDUCATION A sophisticated educational system was crucial for the empire's religious and intellectual integration and for its cultural achievements. Here, too, the Ottomans tolerated difference. They encouraged three educational systems that produced three streams of talent—civil and military bureaucrats, *ulama*, and Sufi masters. The administrative elite attended hierarchically organized schools that culminated in the palace schools at Topkapi (see Chapter 11). Graduates from these institutions staffed the civil and military bureaucracy all across the empire. In the religious sphere, an equally elaborate system took students from elementary schools (where they learned reading, writing, and numbers) on to higher schools, or *madrasas* (where they learned law, religious sciences, the Quran, and the regular sciences). These graduates became *ulama* who served as judges, experts in religious law, or teachers. Yet another set of schools, *tekkes*, taught the devotional strategies and religious knowledge for students to enter Sufi orders.

Islamic Scientists. *This fifteenth-century Persian miniature shows Islamic scholars working with sophisticated navigational and astronomical instruments and reflects the importance that the educated classes in the Islamic world attached to observing and recording the regularities in the natural world. Indeed, many of Europe's advances in sailing drew upon knowledge from the Muslim world.*

Each set of schools created lasting linkages between the ruling elite and the orthodox religious elite. The *tekkes*, especially, promoted social and religious solidarity and helped integrate Muslim peoples living under Ottoman rule. The value that the Ottomans placed on education and scholarship was evident in the saying that "an hour of learning was worth more than a year of prayer." It was also evident in the important advances that those schooled in Ottoman institutions made in astronomy and physics, as well as in history, geography, and politics.

SCIENCE AND THE ARTS Under the patronage of a reformist-minded grand vizier, Ottoman intellectuals also took an interest in works of European science. Some of these appeared in Turkish translation for the first time in the eighteenth century. The Ottomans' most impressive effort to spread European knowledge occurred when a Hungarian convert to Islam, Ibrahim Muteferrika, set up a printing press in Istanbul in 1729.

Muteferrika published works on science, history, and geography. One included sections on geometry; the works of Copernicus, Galileo, and Descartes; and a plea to the Ottoman elite to learn from Europe. When his patron was killed, however, the *ulama* promptly closed off this promising avenue of contact with western learning.

The Ottomans combined inherited traditions with new elements in art as well. For example, portraiture became popular after the Italian painter Gentile Bellini visited Istanbul and composed a portrait of Mehmed II. In other areas, though, the Ottomans kept their own styles. Consider the magnificent architectural monuments of the sixteenth through eighteenth centuries, including mosques, gardens, tombs, forts, and palaces: these showed scant western influence. Nor were the Ottomans interested in western literature or music. For the most part, they believed that God had given the Islamic world a monopoly on truth and enlightenment and that their military successes proved his favor.

Ottoman Court Women. *This eighteenth-century watercolor found in Topkapi Palace in Istanbul shows various musical instruments being played by court women, who were often called upon to provide entertainment.*

The Ottomans' capacity to celebrate their well-being and prosperity was most elegantly displayed during the so-called Tulip Period, which occurred in the first half of the eighteenth century. The elite had long admired the tulip's bold colors and graceful blooms, and for centuries the flower served as the sultans' symbol. In fact, both Mehmed the Conqueror and Suleiman the Magnificent grew tulips in the most secluded and prestigious courtyards at Topkapi Palace in Istanbul. And many Ottoman warriors heading into battle wore undergarments embroidered with tulips to ensure victory. By the early eighteenth century, estate owners had begun to specialize in growing the bulb; tulip designs appeared on tiles, fabrics, and public buildings, and authorities sponsored elaborate tulip festivals.

Fascination with the tulip represented a widespread delight in worldly things, which Grand Vizier Damat Ibrahim (r. 1718–1730) encouraged. As well as restoring order to the empire, Ibrahim loosened the *ulama*'s controls over social activities and sanctioned the elite's consumption of luxury goods. Commoners, too, now celebrated life's pleasures—in coffeehouses and taverns. Indeed, Ottoman demand for luxury goods grew so extensive (seeking lemons, soap, pepper, metal tools, coffee, and wine) that a well-traveled diplomat looked askance at the supposed wealth of Europe. He wrote, "In most of the provinces [of Europe], poverty is widespread, as a punishment for being infidels. Anyone who travels in these areas must confess that goodness and abundance are reserved for the Ottoman realms." Thus, despite challenges from western Europe and foreboding that their best days were behind them, the Ottomans took some foreign elements into their culture while preserving inherited ways.

Safavid Culture

The Safavid Empire in Persia (modern-day Iran) was not as long-lived as the Ottoman Empire, but it was significant for giving Shiism a home base and a location for displaying Shiite culture. There had been Shiite governments before, such as the Fatimid state in Egypt (see Chapter 9). But once the Mamluks overthrew the Fatimids in the thirteenth century, Shiism became overwhelmingly a religion of opposition to established rulers.

THE SHIITE EMPHASIS The Safavids faced a critical dilemma when they seized power. They had owed their rise to the support of Turkish-speaking tribesmen who followed a populist form of Islam. But in order to hold on to power, the Safavid

The Ottomans and the Tulip. *From the earliest times, the Ottomans admired the beauty of the tulip. (Left) Sultan Mehmed II smelling a tulip, symbol of the Ottoman sultans. (Right) The Ottomans used tulip motifs to decorate tiles in homes and mosques and pottery wares, as on the plate shown here.*

shahs needed to cultivate powerful and conservative elements of Iranian society: Persian-speaking landowners and orthodox *ulama*. Thus they turned away from the more popular Turkish-speaking Islamic brotherhoods with their mystical and Sufi qualities and, instead, built a mixed political and religious system that extolled a Shiite vision of law and society and drew on older Persian imperial traditions. The brilliant culture that emerged during the Safavid period provided a unique blend of Shiism and Persia's distinctive historical identity. It found its highest expression in the city of Isfahan, capital of the Safavid state from its creation in 1598 until the empire's end in 1722.

Just as the Ottomans' great achievement was in blending Sufism and clerical orthodoxy, so the Safavids' triumph was in creating a mixed political and religious system based on Shiism and loyalty to the royal family. Also like the Ottomans, the Safavids used established institutions like the *madrasas*, brotherhood lodges, and the *ulama* to promote Shiite orthodoxy and a Shiite-dominated culture. Even after the Safavids lost power in the eighteenth century, Shiism remained the fundamental religion of the Iranian people.

The most effective architect of a cultural life based on Shiite religious principles and Persian royal absolutism was Shah Abbas I (r. 1587–1629). The location that he chose to display the wealth and royal power of his state, its Persian and Shiite heritages, and its artistic sensibility was the new capital city of Isfahan. For this purpose the shah hired skilled artists and architects to design a city that would dwarf even Delhi and Istanbul, the other showplaces of the Islamic world. The architectural goal was to create an earthly representation of heavenly paradise.

ARCHITECTURE AND OTHER CULTURAL PRODUCTIONS The Safavid shahs were unique among Afro-Eurasian rulers of this era, for they sought to project both absolute authority and accessibility. For example, their dwellings were unlike those of other rulers—such as Topkapi Palace in Istanbul, the Citadel in Cairo, and the Red Forts of the Mughals. Those were enclosed and fortified buildings, designed to enhance rulers' power by concealing them from their subjects. In contrast, the buildings of Isfahan were open to the outside, demonstrating the Safavid rulers' desire to connect with their people.

Isfahan's centerpiece was the great plaza next to the royal palace and the royal mosque at the heart of the capital. The plaza, surrounded by elaborate public and religious buildings, measured 83,000 square meters—only slightly less than Tiananmen Square in Beijing, and seven times bigger than the plaza of San Marco in Venice. A seventeenth-century English visitor was suitably impressed, noting that the plaza was 1,000 paces from north to south and 200 from east to west and far larger than the largest urban squares in London and Paris. He added that it "is without doubt as spacious, as pleasant, and aromatic a market as any in the universe."

Other aspects of intellectual life also reflected the elites' aspirations, wealth, and commitment to Shiite principles. Safavid artists perfected the illustrated book, the outstanding example being *The King's Book of Kings,* which contained 250 miniature illustrations. Here, artists demonstrated their mastery of three-dimensional representation and their ability to harmonize different colors. In areas other than painting, proficient weavers produced highly ornate and beautiful silks and carpets for trade throughout the world; artisans painted tiles in vibrant colors and created mosaics that adorned mosques and other buildings. Moreover, the Safavids developed an elaborate calligraphy that was the envy of artists throughout the Islamic world. (See Primary Source: Islamic Views of the World.) In all these ways—but especially in Shah Abbas's pride and joy, the city

PRIMARY SOURCE

Islamic Views of the World

Although maps give the impression of objectivity and geographic precision, they actually reveal the mapmakers' views of the world (via the way they arrange the world, names of locations, areas placed in the center or at the peripheries, and accompanying text). In most cultures, official maps located their own major administrative and religious sites at the center of the universe and reflected local elites' ideas about how the world was organized.

The two maps shown here are from the Islamic world. The map of al-Idrisi, dating from the twelfth century, was a standard one of the period. Showing the world as Afro-Eurasian peoples knew it at that time, the map features only three landmasses: Africa, Asia, and Europe. The second map, made in Iran around 1700, was unabashedly Islamic: it offers a grid that measures the distances from any location in the Islamic world to the holy city of Mecca.

QUESTIONS FOR ANALYSIS

- What does each map reveal about the worldview of these Islamic societies?
- What do you think each map was used for?

Al-Idrisi map, twelfth century

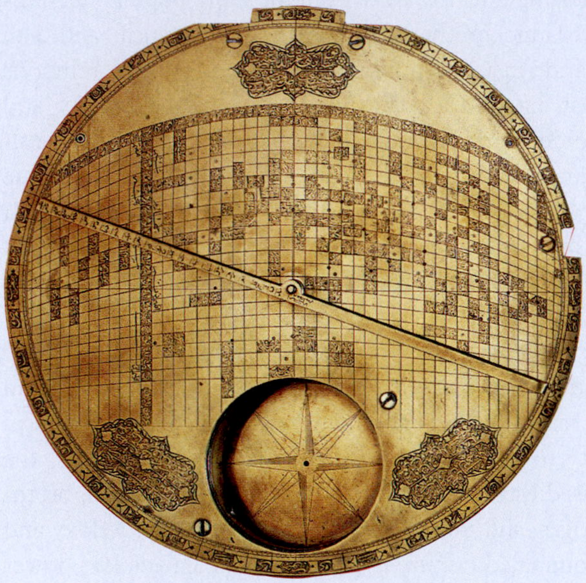

Iranian map, seventeenth century

Sources: (left) Giraudon/Art Resource, NY; (right) Private Collection, courtesy of the owner and D. A. King, contributor; photo by Christie's of London.

of Isfahan—the Safavids gave a Persian and Shiite emphasis to their stunning cultural flourishing.

Power and Culture under the Mughals

Like the Safavids and the Ottomans, the Mughals fostered a courtly high culture. Because they ruled over a large non-Muslim population, the culture that they developed in South Asia was broad and open. So highly did it value art and learning that it welcomed non-Muslims into its circle. Thus, while Islamic traditions dominated the empire's political and judicial systems, Hindus shared with Muslims the flourishing of learning, music, painting, and architecture. In this arena, aesthetic refinement and philosophical sophistication could bridge religious differences.

RELIGION Mughal rulers were flexible toward their realm's diverse peoples, especially in spiritual affairs. Though its primary

Akbar Leading Religious Discussion. *This miniature painting from 1604 shows Akbar receiving Muslim theologians and Jesuits. The Jesuits (in the black robes on the left) hold a page relating, in Persian, the birth of Christ. A lively debate will follow the Jesuits' claims on behalf of Christianity.*

commitment to Islam stood firm, the imperial court also patronized other beliefs, displaying a tolerance that earned it widespread legitimacy. The contrast with Europe, where religious differences drove deep fractures within and between states, was stark.

The promise of an open Islamic high culture found its greatest fulfillment under the emperor Akbar (r. 1556–1605). This skillful military leader was also a popular ruler who allowed common people as well as nobles from all ethnic groups to converse with him at court. Unlike European monarchs, who tried to enforce religious uniformity, Akbar studied comparative religion and hosted regular debates among Hindu, Muslim, Jain, Parsi, and Christian theologians. His quest for universal truths outside the strict *sharia* led him to develop a religion of his own, which incorporated many aspects of Hindu belief and ritual practice (see Chapter 12). Ultimately he introduced at his court a "Divine Faith" (Dīn-i Ilāhī) that was a mix of Quranic, Catholic, and other influences; it emphasized virtues such as piety, prudence, gentleness, liberality, and a yearning for God.

Dīn-i Ilāhī reflected Akbar's desire to strengthen his position against the *ulama* and his interest in philosophical skepticism. Akbar had both a Hindu and a Christian wife (besides a Muslim wife, as well as concubines of many nationalities and religions), and his palace boasted temples to each faith. His tolerance kept a multifaceted spiritual kingdom under one political roof. Akbar's trusted advisor Abulfazl encouraged his cultural pursuits and composed a tribute to the ruler and his predecessors, the *Akbarnamah* (the Book of Akbar). It describes Akbar as receiving kingship as a gift from God because he was a true philosopher and had been born a perfect person in the Sufi sense. The *Akbarnamah* remains one of the major sources of early Mughal history.

ARCHITECTURE AND THE ARTS In architecture, too, the Mughals produced masterpieces that blended styles. This was already evident as builders combined Persian, Indian, and Ottoman elements in tombs and mosques built by Akbar's predecessors. But Akbar enhanced this mixture in the elaborate city he built at Fatehpur Sikri, beginning in 1571. The buildings included residences for nobles (whose loyalty Akbar wanted), gardens, a drinking and gambling zone, and even an experimental school devoted to studying language acquisition in children. Building the huge complex took a decade, much less time than it took for construction of Louis XIV's comparable royal residence—a century later—at Versailles.

Akbar's descendant Shah Jahan was also a lavish patron of architecture and the arts. In 1630, Shah Jahan ordered the building in Agra of a magnificent white marble tomb for his beloved wife, Mumtaz Mahal. Like many other women in the Mughal court, she had been an important political counselor. Designed by an Indian architect of Persian origin, this structure, the **Taj Mahal**, took twenty years and 20,000 workers to build. The 42-acre complex included a main gateway, a garden, minarets, and a mosque. The translucent marble mausoleum lay squarely in the middle of the structure, enclosed by four identical facades and crowned by a majestic central dome rising to 240 feet. The stone inlays of different types and hues, organized in geometrical and floral patterns, and featuring Quranic verses inscribed in Arabic calligraphy gave the surface an appearance of delicacy and lightness. Blending Persian and Islamic design with Indian materials and motifs, this poetry in stone represented the most splendid example of Mughal high culture and the combining of cultural traditions. Like Shah Abbas's great plaza, the Taj Mahal gave a sense of refined grandeur to this empire's power and splendor. (See Current Trends in World History: The Political Uses of Space.)

FOREIGN INFLUENCES VERSUS ISLAMIC CULTURE Under later emperors, Mughal culture remained vibrant although not quite so brilliant. François Bernier, a seventeenth-century

The Taj Mahal. *A symbol of Mughal splendor, the Taj Mahal was a mausoleum that was built of white marble. Often described as poetry in stone, it was constructed under Shah Jahan as an homage to his deceased wife, Mumtaz Mahal (right).*

French traveler, wrote admiringly of the broad philosophical interests of Danishmand Khan, whom the emperor Aurangzeb had appointed as governor of Delhi. According to Bernier, Khan avidly read the works of the French philosophers Gassendi and Descartes and studied Sanskrit treatises to understand different philosophical traditions. But Aurangzeb, a pious Muslim, favored Islamic arts and sciences. He dismissed many of the court's painters and musicians, and in 1669 ordered that all recently built non-Islamic places of worship be torn down. In his court, intellectuals debated whether metaphysics, astronomy, medicine, mathematics, and ethics were of use in the practice of Islam. Women, at least at court, apparently were allowed to pursue the arts, for two of Aurangzeb's daughters were accomplished poets.

Well into the eighteenth century, the Mughal nobility exuded confidence and lived in unrivaled luxury. The presence of foreign scholars and artists enhanced the courtly culture, and the elite eagerly consumed exotic goods from China and Europe. Foreign trade also brought in more silver, advancing the money economy and supporting the nobles' sumptuous lifestyles. In addition, the Mughals assimilated European military technology: they hired Europeans as gunners and military engineers in their armies, employed them to forge guns, and bought guns and cannons from them. However, Mughal appreciation for other European knowledge and technology was limited. Thus, when a representative of the English East India Company presented an edition of Mercator's *Maps of the World* to the emperor in 1617, the emperor returned it a fortnight later with the remark that no one could read or understand it. The Mughals, like the Ottomans, remained supremely confident of their own cultural world.

The Islamic world drew on intellectual currents that spanned the Eurasian–North African landmass, for its centers were in Istanbul, Cairo, Isfahan, and Delhi. From Islam's founding, Muslims had looked to India and China, not to Europe, for inspiration. True, the Crusades had proved that Europeans could be worthy military rivals (see Chapter 10), and the increasing wealth and power of Christian kingdoms enriched by New World colonies made those cultures more imposing. Yet even as Muslims brought a few new European elements into their cultural mix, most still regarded Europeans as rude barbarians. More impressive in the eyes of elites in Persia, India, and the Ottoman Empire were the cultural splendors to be found to the east, not the west.

CULTURE AND POLITICS IN EAST ASIA

Like the Ottomans, Safavids, and Mughals, the Chinese did not need to prove the richness of their scholarly and artistic traditions. China had long been a renowned center of learning, with its emperors and elites supporting artists, poets, musicians, scientists, and teachers. But in late Ming and early Qing China, cultural flourishing owed less to imperial patronage than to a booming internal market. Indeed, a growing population and extensive commercial networks propelled the circulation of ideas as well as goods. As a result, China's cultural sphere expanded and diversified well before similar changes occurred elsewhere.

In Japan, too, prosperity promoted cultural dynamism. Because of its giant neighbor across the sea, the Japanese people had always been aware of outside influences. Like the Chinese government, the Tokugawa shogunate tried to promote Confucian notions of a social hierarchy organized on the basis of social position, age, gender, and kin. It also tried to shield the country from highly egalitarian ideas that would threaten the strict social hierarchy. But the forces that undermined governmental control of knowledge in China proved even stronger in Japan. Here, a decentralized political system enabled different cultural influences to spread, including European ideas and practices. By the eighteenth century, in struggling to define its own identity through these contending currents, the cultural scene in Japan was more lively, open, and varied than its counterpart in China.

China: The Challenge of Expansion and Diversity

While China had become increasingly connected with the outside world in the sixteenth and seventeenth centuries, the sources for its cultural flourishing during the period came primarily from within. Although new opportunities for cultural exchange with foreigners left their mark, it was internal social changes that propelled the circulation of books and ideas.

PUBLISHING AND THE TRANSMISSION OF IDEAS

Broader circulation of ideas had more to do with the decentralization of book production than with technological innovations. After all, woodblock and moveable type printing had been present in China for centuries. Although initially the state had spurred book production by printing Confucian texts, before long the economy's increasing commercialization weakened government controls over what got printed. Even as officials clamped down on unorthodox texts, there was no centralized system of censorship, and unauthorized opinions circulated freely.

By the late Ming era, a burgeoning publishing sector catered to the diverse social, cultural, and religious needs of educated elites and urban populations. European visitors admired the vast collections of printed materials housed in Chinese libraries, describing them as "magnificently built" and "finely adorn'd." In fact, the late Ming was an age of collections of other sorts as well. Members of the increasingly affluent elite acquired objects for display (such as paintings, ceramics, and calligraphy) as a sign of their status and refinement. Connoisseurship of all the arts reached unprecedented levels. Consumers could build collections by purchasing artworks from multiple sources—from roadside peddlers to monks to gentlemen dealers, whose proclaimed love of art masked the commercial orientation of their passions.

Chinese Civil Service Exam. *Lining the sides of this Chinese examination compound were cells in which candidates sat for the examination. Other than three long boards—the highest served as a shelf, the middle one as a desk, and the lowest as a seat—the cell had neither furniture nor a door. Indeed, the cells were little more than spaces partitioned on three sides by brick walls and covered by a roof; the floors were packed dirt. Generations of candidates spent three days and two nights in succession in these cells as they strove to enter officialdom.*

CURRENT TRENDS IN WORLD HISTORY

The Political Uses of Space

The use of space for political purposes is a theme we can trace across world history. It has also allowed us to look at political history in new and different ways through a cultural lens by considering the ways rulers used symbols and space to convey this sense of power. In the early modern period, many kings and emperors opted to build grand palaces to create lavish power centers, from which they could project their influence over their kingdoms; petitioners and potential rivals would have to come to *them* to ask for favors or to complete their business. Monarchs sculpted these environments, creating a series of spaces, each of them open to a smaller and smaller number of the king's favorites. Both palaces and their surrounding grounds were ornate and splendid, were expensive to construct, and involved the best craftsmen and artists available, which often meant borrowing ideas and designs from neighboring cultures. Palace complexes of this type, built in Beijing, in Istanbul, and just outside of Paris, used space to project the rulers' power and to show who was boss.

The **Forbidden City of Beijing** was the earliest of these impressive sites of royal power. (See illustration on p. 430.) Its construction took about four years—from 1416 to 1420—although the actual name "Forbidden City" did not appear until 1576. The entrance of the city was straddled by the Meridian Gate, the tallest structure of the entire complex, which towered over all other buildings at more than 35 meters above the ground. It was from this lofty position that the emperor extended his gaze toward his empire as he oversaw various court ceremonies, including the important annual proclamation of the calendar that governed the entire country's agricultural and ritual activities. Foreign emissaries received by the court were also often allowed to use one of the passageways through the gate, where they were expected to be duly awed. As for the officials' daily audience with the emperor, they had to line up outside the Meridian Gate around 3 A.M. before proceeding to the Hall of Supreme Harmony. It was typical of the entire construction project that this impressive hall with vermilion walls and golden tiles was built at considerable cost. For the columns of the hall, fragrant hardwood had to be found in the tiger-ridden forests of the remote southwest, while the mountain forests of the south and southwest were searched for other timbers that eventually made their way to the capital through the Grand Canal.

The **Topkapi Palace** in Istanbul, capital of the Ottoman Empire, began to take shape in 1458 under Mehmed II and underwent steady expansion over the years. (See illustration on p. 000.) Topkapi projected royal authority in much the same way as the Forbidden City emphasized Chinese emperors' power: governing officials worked enclosed within massive walls, and monarchs rarely went outside their inner domain.

More than two centuries later, in the 1670s and 1680s, the French monarch Louis XIV built the **Palace of Versailles** on the site of a royal hunting lodge eleven miles from Paris, the French capital. (See illustration on p. 512.) This enormously costly complex was built to house Louis's leading clergymen and nobles, who were obliged to visit at least twice a year. Louis hoped that by taking wealthy and powerful men and women away from their local power bases, and by diverting them with entertainments, he could keep them from plotting new forms of religious schism or challenging his right to rule. Going to Versailles also allowed him to escape the pressures and demands of the population of Paris. Many European monarchs—including Russia's Peter the Great—would build palace complexes modeled on Versailles.

If in China, the Ottoman Empire, and France emperors built what were essentially private spaces in which to conduct and dominate state business, Shah Abbas (r. 1587–1629) of the Safavid Empire chose to create a great new public space instead. In the early seventeenth century, Shah

Perhaps more important, books and other luxury goods were now more affordable. For example, a low-quality commentary on the Confucian classics published in 1615 cost only half a tael of silver (a measurement based on the silver's weight). Even a low-level private tutor could earn more than forty taels a year, making it possible to gradually develop a small personal library. Increasingly, publishers offered a mix of wares: guidebooks for patrons of the arts, travelers, or merchants; handbooks for performing rituals, choosing dates for ceremonies, or writing proper letters; almanacs and encyclopedias; morality books; medical manuals.

Especially popular were study aids for the civil service examination. In fact, after the late fifteenth century, when examinees had to submit a highly structured eight-part essay, model essays flooded the market. In 1595, Beijing reeled with scandal over news that the second-place graduate had reproduced verbatim several model essays published by commercial printers. Just over twenty years later, the top graduate plagiarized a winning essay submitted years earlier. Ironically, then, the increased circulation of knowledge led critics to bemoan a decline in real learning; instead of mastering the classics, they charged, examination candidates were simply memorizing the work of others.

Abbas oversaw the construction of the **great plaza at Isfahan**, a structure which reflected his desire to bring trade, government, and religion together under the authority of the supreme political leader. An enormous public mosque, the Shah Abbas Mosque, dominated one end of the plaza, which measured 1,667 feet by 517 feet. At the other end were trading stalls and markets. Along one side sat government offices; the other side offered the exquisite Mosque of Shaykh Lutfollah. If the other rulers of this era devoted their (considerable) income to creating rich *private* spaces, Shah Abbas used the vast open space of the plaza to open up his city to all comers, keeping only the Mosque of Shaykh Lutfollah for his personal use.

The royal use of space says a great deal about how monarchs in this era wished to be seen and remembered, and about how they wanted to rule. While some wanted to retreat from the rest of society, Shah Abbas wanted to create an open space for trade and the exchanging of ideas. World history is full of palaces and plazas (the Piazza San Marco in Venice might be compared to the royal plaza at Isfahan); we can still visit and admire them. But when we do, we should also remember that space, and the architecture that either opens up to the public or sets aside privileged spaces, has always had political as well as cultural functions.

Isfahan. *On the great plaza at Isfahan, markets and government offices operated in close proximity to the public Shah Abbas Mosque, shown here, and the shah's private mosque. This structure represented Shah Abbas's desire to unite control of trade, government, and religion under one leader.*

QUESTIONS FOR ANALYSIS

- Choose one of the places discussed in this feature. How did the architectural layout shape the political power exercised by that space?
- How did private spaces, like the palace at Versailles, differ from public spaces, like the great plaza at Isfahan? What political goals could be accomplished by each?

Explore Further

Babaie, Sussan, *Isfahan and its Palaces: Statecraft, Shi'ism and the Architecture of Conviviality in Early Modern Iran* (2008).

Necipoğlu, Gülru, *Architecture, Ceremonial, and Power: The Topkapi Palace in the Fifteenth and Sixteenth Centuries* (1991).

Examination hopefuls were not the only beneficiaries of the book trade, for elite women also joined China's literary culture. As readers, writers, and editors, these women now began to penetrate what used to be an exclusively male domain. Anthologies of women's poetry were especially popular, not only in the market but when issued in limited circulation to celebrate the refinement of the writer's family. Men of letters soon recognized the market potential of women's writings; some also saw women's less regularized style (usually acquired through family channels rather than state-sponsored schools) as a means to challenge stifling stylistic conformity. On rare occasions, women even served as publishers themselves.

Although elite women enjoyed success in the world of culture, the period brought increasing restrictions on their lives. Remarriage of widows and premarital sex might have met with disapproval in earlier times, but now they were utterly unthinkable for women from "good" families. Ironically, the thriving publishing sector indirectly promoted the stricter morality by printing plays and novels that echoed the government's conservative attitudes. Meanwhile, the practice of footbinding (which elite women first adopted around

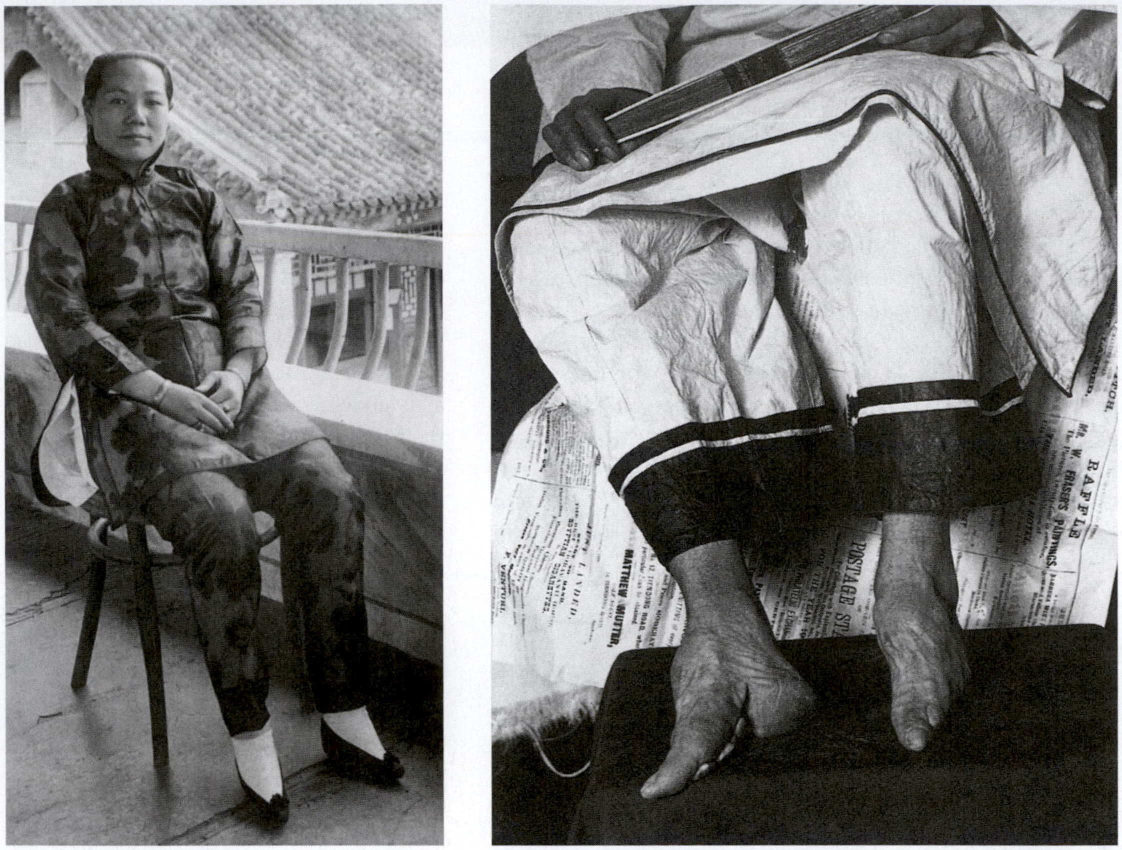

Footbinding. *Two images of bound feet: (left) as an emblem of feminine respectability when wrapped and concealed, as on this well-to-do Chinese woman; (right) as an object of curiosity and condemnation when exposed for the world to see.*

the late Tang-Song period) continued to spread among common people, as small, delicate feet came to signify femininity and respectability.

POPULAR CULTURE AND RELIGION Important as the book trade was, it had only an indirect impact on most men and women in late Ming China. Those who could not read well or at all absorbed cultural values through oral communication, ritual performance, and daily practices. The Ming government tried to control these channels, too. It appointed village elders as guardians of local society, and it instituted "village compacts" to ensure shared responsibility for proper conduct and observation of the laws.

Still, the everyday life of rural and small-town dwellers went on outside these official networks. Apart from toiling in the field, villagers participated in various religious and cultural practices, such as honoring local guardian spirits, patronizing Buddhist and Daoist temples, or watching performances by touring theater groups. Furthermore, villagers often took group pilgrimages to religious sites and attended markets in nearby towns, which drew them in with restaurants, brothels, and other types of entertainment. At the marketplaces the visitors would gather news and gossip in the teahouses or listen to the tales of itinerant storytellers and traveling monks. The open-ended nature of such cultural activities meant that village audiences had opportunities to reinterpret official norms to serve their own purposes and to contest the government's rules. For example, the common people could take officially approved morality tales celebrating the deeds of just and impartial officials and use them to challenge the real-life behavior of government bureaucrats.

Another manifestation of late-Ming cultural flourishing was the fervor associated with popular religions that mingled various cultural traditions. Here, at the grassroots level, there was little distinction among Buddhist, Daoist, and local cults. After all, the Chinese believed in cosmic unity; and although they venerated spiritual forces, they did not consider any of them to be a Supreme Being who favored one sect over another. They believed it was the emperor, rather than any religious group, who held the mandate of heaven. To the Chinese, the enforcement of orthodox values was more a matter of political than of religious control. Unless sects posed an obvious threat, the emperor had no reason to regulate their spiritual practices. This situation promoted religious tolerance and avoided the sectarian warfare that plagued post-Reformation Europe.

TECHNOLOGY AND CARTOGRAPHY Belief in cosmic unity did not prevent the Chinese from devising technologies to master nature's operations in this world. For example, the magnetic compass, gunpowder, and the printing press were all Chinese inventions. Moreover, Chinese technicians had mastered iron casting and produced mechanical clocks centuries before Europeans did.

PRIMARY SOURCE

Chinese Views of the World

The Chinese developed cartographical skills early in their history. A third-century map, no longer in existence, was designed to enable the emperors to "comprehend the four corners of the world without ever having to leave their imperial quarters." The *Huayi tu* (Map of Chinese and Foreign Lands) from 1136 depicted the whole world on stone stele, including 500 place names and textual information on foreign lands. Chinese maps typically devoted more attention to textual explanations with moral and political messages than to locating places accurately. One such map, the Chinese wheel map from the 1760s, is full of textual explanations.

QUESTIONS FOR ANALYSIS

- Why do you think Chinese maps included messages that focused on moral and political themes?
- How are these maps similar to and different from the Islamic maps shown on p. 524?

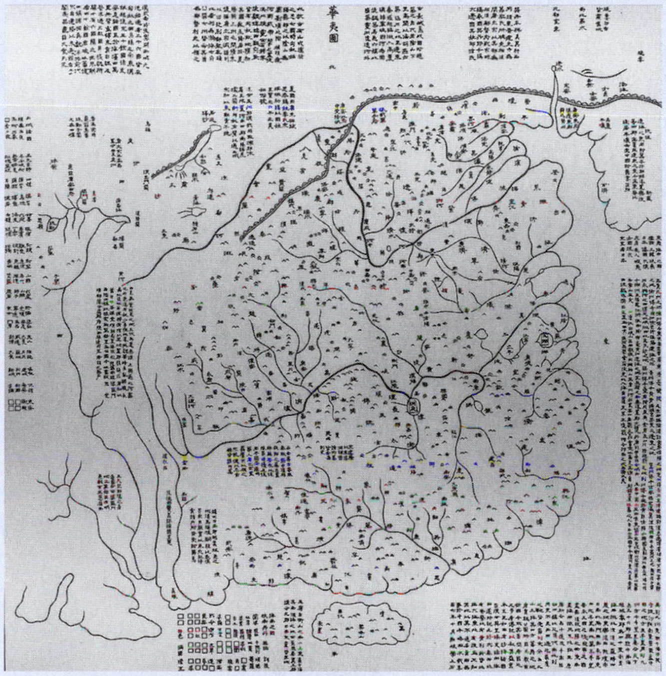

The Huayi tu *map, 1136*

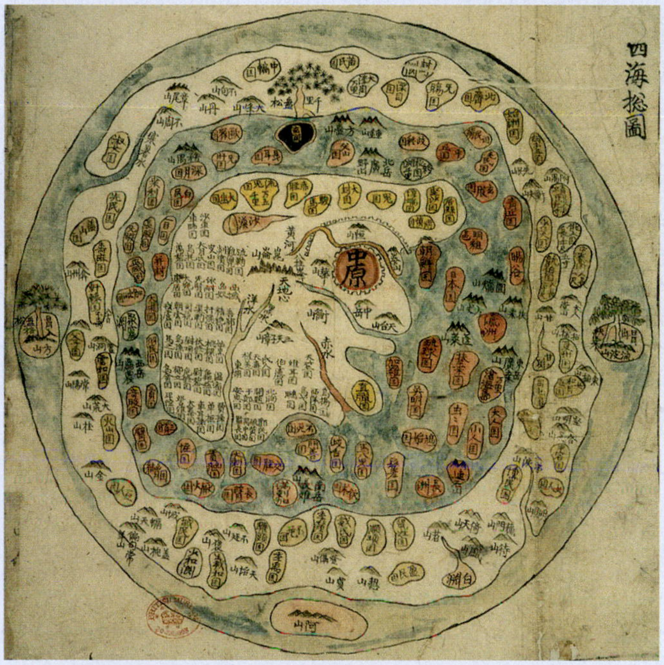

Chinese wheel map, 1760s

Sources: (left) The Needham Research Institute; (right) The British Library, London.

Chinese astronomers also compiled accurate records of eclipses, comets, novae, and meteors. In part, the emperor's needs drove their interest in astronomy and calendrical science. After all, it was his job as the Son of Heaven, and thus mediator between heaven and earth, to determine the best dates for planting, holding festivities, scheduling mourning periods, and convening judicial court sessions. The Chinese believed that the empire's stability depended on correct calculation of these dates.

European missionaries and traders arriving in China were awed by Chinese technological expertise, eloquence, and artistic refinement. Nonetheless, convinced that their sciences were superior, Christian missionaries tried to promote their own knowledge in areas such as astronomy and **cartography** (mapmaking). Possessing sophisticated sciences of their own, the Chinese were selective in appropriating these novel European practices. To be sure, members of the Jesuit order served in the imperial astronomy bureau and, in the early eighteenth century, undertook monumental surveys for the Qing emperor. However, the Europeans' overall cultural impact in China during this period was limited.

In the realm of cartography, the Chinese demonstrated most clearly their understanding of the world. Their maps encompassed elements of history, literature, and art—not just technical detail. It was not that "scientific" techniques were lacking; a map made as early as 1136 reveals that Chinese cartographers could readily draw to scale. Yet, valuing written text over visual and other forms of representation, Chinese elites did not always treat geometric and mathematical precision as the main objective of cartography. Reflecting the elites' worldview, most maps placed the realm of the Chinese emperor, as the ruler of "All under Heaven," at the center, surrounded by foreign countries. Thus the physical scale of China and distances to other lands were distorted. Still, some of the maps cover a vast expanse: one includes an area stretching from Japan to the Atlantic, encompassing Europe and Africa. (See Primary Source: Chinese Views of the World.)

Europeans did not know what to make of the Chinese resistance to their science. In 1583, the Jesuit missionary Matteo Ricci brought European maps to China, hoping to impress the elite with European learning. Challenging their belief that the world was flat, his maps demonstrated that the earth was spherical—and that China was just one country among many others. Yet Chinese critics complained that Ricci treated the Ming Empire as "a small unimportant country." As a concession, he placed China closer to the center of the maps and provided additional textual information. Still, his maps had a negligible impact, as neither the earth's shape nor precise scale was particularly important to most Chinese geographers.

Before the nineteenth century, the Chinese had fairly incomplete knowledge about foreign lands despite a long history of contact. The empire saw itself as superior to all others (a common feature of many cultures). Chinese writers, for example, often identified groups of other people through distinctive and, to them, odd physical features. A Ming geographical publication portrayed the Portuguese as "seven feet tall, having eyes like a cat, a mouth like an oriole, an ash-white face, thick and curly beards like black gauze, and almost red hair." Chinese elites glorified their "white" complexions against the peasants' dark skin; against the black, wavy-haired "devils" of Southeast Asia; and against the Europeans' "ash-white" pallor. Qing authors in the eighteenth century confused France with the Portugal known during Ming times, and they characterized England and Sweden as dependencies of Holland. During this period of cultural flourishing, in short, most Chinese did not feel compelled to revise their view of the world.

Cultural Identity and Tokugawa Japan

Chinese cultural influence had long crossed the Sea of Japan, but under the Tokugawa shogunate there was also interest in European culture. This interest grew via the Dutch presence in Japan and via limited contacts with Russians. At the same time, there was a surge in the study of Japanese traditions and culture. Thus, Tokugawa Japan engaged in a three-cornered conversation among time-honored Chinese ways (transmitted via Korea), European teachings, and distinctly Japanese traditions.

NATIVE ARTS AND POPULAR CULTURE Until the sixteenth and seventeenth centuries, the main patrons of Japanese culture were the imperial court in Kyoto, the hereditary shogunate, religious institutions, and a small upper class. These groups developed an elite culture of theater and stylized painting. Samurai (former warriors turned bureaucrats) and daimyo (regional lords) favored a masked theater, called Nō, and an elegant ritual for making tea and engaging in contemplation. In their gardens, the lords built teahouses with stages for Nō drama. These gave rise to hereditary schools of actors, tea masters, and flower arrangers. The elites also hired commoner-painters to decorate tea utensils and other fine articles and to paint the brilliant interiors and standing screens in grand stone castles. Some upper-class men did their own painting, which conveyed philosophical thoughts. Calligraphy was proof of refinement.

Artist and Geisha at Tea. *The erotic, luxuriant atmosphere of Japan's urban pleasure quarters was captured in a new art form, the ukiyo-e, or "pictures from a floating world." In this image set in Tokyo's celebrated Yoshiwara district, several geisha flutter about a male artist.*

Kabuki Theater. *Kabuki originated among dance troupes in the environs of temples and shrines in Kyoto in the late sixteenth and early seventeenth centuries. As kabuki spread to the urban centers of Japan, the theater designs enabled the actors to enter and exit from many directions and to step out into the audience, lending the skillful, raucous shows great intimacy.*

Alongside the elite culture arose a rougher urban one that artisans and merchants patronized. Urban dwellers could purchase, for example, works of fiction and colorful prints (often risqué) made from carved wood blocks, and they could enjoy the company of female entertainers known as geisha. These women were skilled (*gei*) in playing the three-stringed instrument (*shamisen*), storytelling, and performing; some were also prostitutes. Geisha worked in the cities' pleasure quarters, which were famous for their geisha houses, public baths, brothels, and theaters. Kabuki—a type of theater that combined song, dance, and skillful staging to dramatize conflicts between duty and passion—became wildly popular. This art form featured dazzling acting, brilliant makeup, and sumptuous costumes. In 1629 the shogunate, concerned for public order, banned female actors; thereafter men played women's roles. These male actors sometimes maintained their impersonations offstage, inspiring fashion trends for urban women.

Much popular entertainment chronicled the world of the common people rather than politics or high society. The urbanites' pleasure-oriented culture was known as "the floating world" (*ukiyo*), and the woodblock prints depicting it as *ukiyo-e* (*e* meaning "picture"). Here, the social order was temporarily turned upside down. Those who were usually considered inferior—actors, musicians, courtesans, and others seen as possessing low morals—became idols. Even some upper-class samurai partook of this "lower" culture. But to enter the pleasure quarters they had to leave behind their swords, a mark of rank, since commoners were not allowed to carry such weapons.

Literacy in Japan now surged, especially among men. The most popular novels sold 10,000 to 12,000 copies. In the late eighteenth century, Edo had some sixty booksellers and hundreds of book lenders. In fact, the presence of so many lenders allowed books to spread to a wider public that previously could not afford to buy them. By the late eighteenth century, as more books circulated and some of them criticized the government, officials tried to censor certain publications.

THE INFLUENCE OF CHINA In the realm of higher culture, China loomed large in the Tokugawa world. Japanese scholars wrote imperial histories of Japan in the Chinese style, and Chinese law codes and other books attracted a significant readership. Some Japanese traveled south to Nagasaki to meet Zen Buddhist masters and Chinese residents there. A few Chinese monks even won permission to found monasteries outside Nagasaki and to give lectures and construct temples in Kyoto and Edo.

Although Buddhist temples grew in number, they did not displace the native Japanese practice of venerating ancestors and worshipping gods in nature. Later called Shintō ("the way of the gods"), this practice boasted a network of shrines throughout the country. Shintō developed from time-honored beliefs in spirits, or *kami*, who were associated with places (mountains, rivers, waterfalls, rocks, the moon) and activities (harvest, fertility). Seeking healing or other assistance, adherents appealed to these spirits in nature and daily life through incantations and offerings. Some women under Shintō served as *mikos*, a kind of shaman with special divinatory powers.

Shintō rituals competed with a powerful strain of neo-Confucianism that issued moral and behavioral guidelines. For example, in 1762 "Greater Learning for Females" appeared—an influential text that made Confucian teachings understandable for nonscholars. In particular, it outlined social roles that stressed hierarchy based on age and gender as a way to ensure order. At the same time, merit became important in determining one's place in the social hierarchy. Doing the right thing (propriety) and being virtuous were key.

By the early eighteenth century, neo-Confucian teachings of filial piety and loyalty to superiors had become the official state

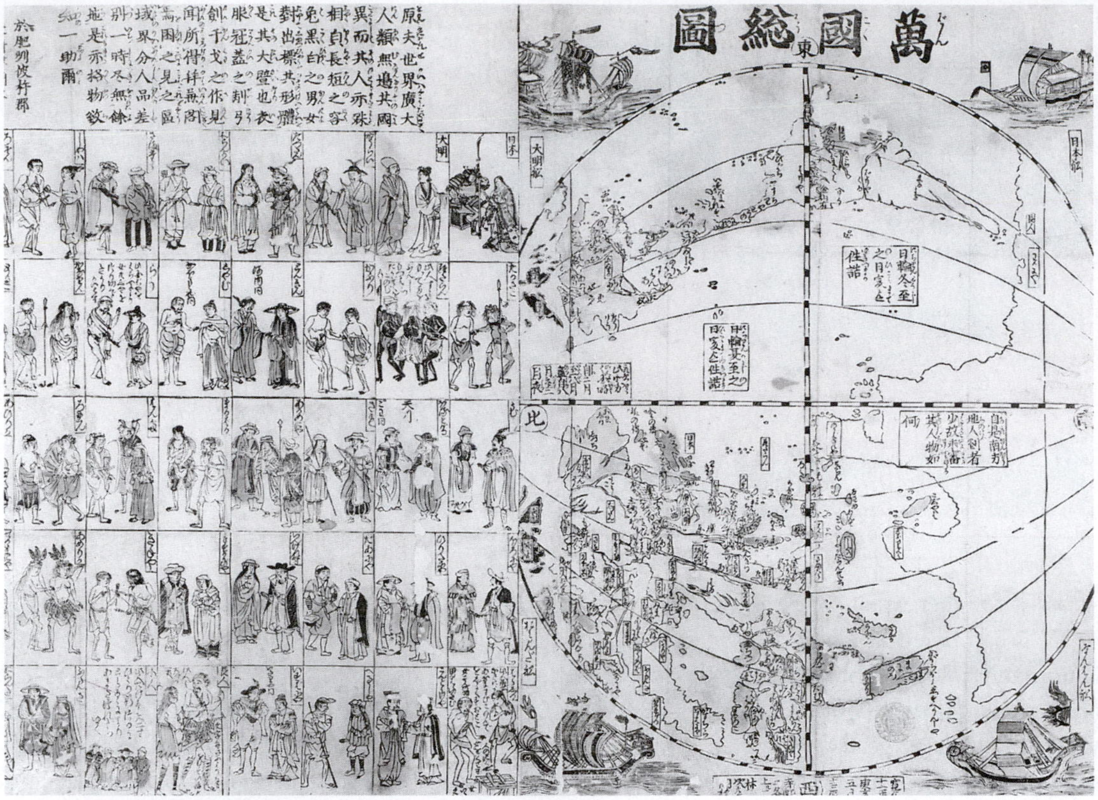

Japanese Map of the World. *Japanese maps underwent a shift in connection with encounters with the Dutch. Here, in a map dated 1671, much information is incorporated about distant lands, both cartographically on the globe and pictorially, to the left, in two-person images representing various peoples of the world in their purported typical costumes.*

creed. This philosophy legitimated the social hierarchy and the absolutism of political authorities, but it also instructed the shogun and the upper class to provide "benevolent administration" for the people's benefit. That meant taking into account petitioners' complaints and requests, whether for improved irrigation and roads or for punishment of unfair officials.

Reacting to a creed adapted from non-native traditions, and desiring to honor their own country's greatness, some thinkers promoted intellectual traditions from Japan's past. These efforts stressed "native learning," Japanese texts, and Japanese uniqueness. In so doing, they formalized a Japanese religious and cultural tradition, and they denounced Confucianism and Buddhism as foreign contaminants. A few thinkers also looked to the uninterrupted imperial line in Kyoto (which did not govern) for validation of Japan's intellectual lineage and cultural superiority. Some who called for restored rule by the emperor faced arrest by the shogun's military men, but others went on to develop Japanese poetry. This art form, which expressed a yearning for a glorious lost age, became popular with both upper and lower classes.

EUROPEAN INFLUENCES Not only did Chinese intellectual influences compete with revived native learning, but by the late seventeenth century Japan was also tapping other sources of knowledge. At this time Portuguese was the common language in East Asia, and even the Dutch used it in communicating with the Japanese. By 1670, however, a guild of Japanese interpreters in Nagasaki who could speak and read Dutch accompanied Dutch merchants on trips to Edo. As European knowledge spread to high circles in Edo, in 1720 the shogunate lifted its ban on foreign books. Thereafter European ideas, called "Dutch learning," circulated more openly. Scientific, geographical, and medical texts appeared in Japanese translations and in some cases displaced Chinese texts. A Japanese-Dutch dictionary appeared in 1745, and the first official school of Dutch learning followed. Students of Dutch or European teachings remained a limited segment of Japanese society, but the demand for translations intensified.

Japan's internal debates about what to borrow from the Europeans and the Chinese illustrate the changes that the world had undergone in recent centuries. A few hundred years earlier, products and ideas generally did not travel beyond coastal regions and had only a limited effect (especially inland) on local cultural practices. By the eighteenth century, though, expanded networks of exchange and new prosperity made the integration of foreign ideas feasible and, sometimes, desirable. The Japanese were especially eager to transform useful new ideas and practices. They did not consider the embracing of outside influences as a mark of inferiority or subordination, particularly when they could put those influences to good use. This was not the case for the great Asian land-based empires, which were eager lenders but hesitant borrowers.

THE ENLIGHTENMENT IN EUROPE

An extraordinary cultural flowering also blossomed in Europe during the seventeenth and eighteenth centuries. Often the **Enlightenment** is defined purely in intellectual terms as the spreading of faith in reason and in universal rights and laws, but this era encompassed broader developments, such as the expansion of literacy, the spread of critical thinking, and the decline of religious persecution. Part of what gave Enlightenment thinkers such influence in Europe and beyond was that they wanted not just to convey new ideas to the elite but also to spread them widely. They hoped to change their contemporaries' worldviews and to transform political and social institutions.

Crucial for the success of this endeavor were widening patronage networks. Previously such networks had involved religious and monarchical supporters of arts and sciences, but they now extended to the lower aristocracy and bureaucratic and commercial elites as well. Equally important were cafés and intellectual salons, public theaters, exchanges of correspondence, and newspaper and book publishing. The male and female thinkers of this period disagreed about many things, but they shared a desire to "spread light" and to speak their minds about how to improve their societies, something that often made them troublesome to religious and political authorities.

Abandoning Christian belief in God's mysterious tampering with natural forces and human events, Enlightenment thinkers wanted to know the world in new ways. They sought universal and objective knowledge that would not reflect any particular religion, political view, class, or gender. Recognizing no territorial boundaries, these scholars struggled to formulate natural laws that would, they presumed, apply everywhere and to all peoples. Most of these thinkers were unaware of the extent to which European, upper-class male perspectives colored their "objective" knowledge.

Origins of the Enlightenment

While the sixteenth century brought new prosperity, the seventeenth century produced civil and religious wars, dynastic conflicts, and famine. These crises devastated central Europe. They bankrupted the Spanish, caused chaos in France, led to the execution of the English king, and saw the Dutch break free from Spanish control. They also contributed to the spread of Protestantism in Europe. At the same time, the crises made some intellectuals wish to turn their backs on religious strife, and to develop useful ways for understanding and improving *this* world. By 1750, too, in some western countries, a larger share of the population was eager to join in these discussions. As literate, middle-class men and women gained confidence in being able to reason for themselves, to understand the world without calling on traditional authorities, and to publicly criticize what they found distasteful or wrong, contemporaries recognized that they were living in an increasingly "enlightened" age.

It helps to pause and consider the development of this confidence, and of Enlightenment knowledge as a whole. First, the Reformation and Counter-Reformation (see Chapter 12) were significant in increasing literacy and diffusing the new science and its premises. Second, greater contacts between Europeans and the wider world after the fourteenth century were key. After all, Europeans had become eager consumers of other peoples' cultural goods. From Native American trapping methods to African slaves' crop cultivation techniques, from Chinese porcelain to New World tobacco and chocolate, contact with others influenced Europe in the seventeenth and eighteenth centuries. Yet the more they learned, the more European intellectuals became critical of other cultures—and more confident that their own culture was unique, superior, and the standard against which to judge all others. (See Primary Source: European Views of the World.)

The New Science

The search for new, testable knowledge began centuries before the Enlightenment, in the efforts of Nicolaus Copernicus (1473–1542) and Galileo Galilei (1564–1642) to understand the behavior of the heavens. These men were both astronomers and mathematicians. Making their own mathematical calculations and observations of the stars and planets, these scholars came to conclusions that contradicted age-old assumptions. By no means was trusting one's own work rather than the accepted authorities easy, or without risk: when Galileo confirmed Copernicus's claims that the earth revolved around the sun, he was put on trial for heresy.

In the seventeenth century, a small but influential group of scholars committed themselves, similarly, to experimentation, calculation, and observation. They adopted a method for "scientific" inquiry laid out by the philosopher Sir Francis Bacon (1561–1626), who claimed that real science entailed the formulation of hypotheses that could be tested in carefully controlled experiments. Bacon believed that traditional authorities could never be trusted; only by conducting experiments could humans begin to comprehend the workings of nature. Bacon was chiefly wary of classical and medieval authorities, but his principle also applied to traditional knowledge that European scientists were encountering in the rest of the world. Confident of their calculations performed according to the new **scientific method**, scientists like Isaac Newton (1642–1727) defined what

PRIMARY SOURCE

European Views of the World

As Europeans became world travelers and traders, they needed accurate information on places and distances so they could get home as well as return to the sites they had visited. Europe's first printed map of the New World, the Waldseemüller map (produced in 1507), portrayed the Americas as a long and narrow strip of land. Asia and Africa dwarf its unexplored landmass. By the mid-seventeenth century, European maps were seemingly more objective, yet they still grouped the rest of the world around the European countries. Moreover, the effort to make world maps that served navigational purposes led to distortions (like the stretching of polar zones in the 1569 Mercator projection) that made Europe seem disproportionately large and central.

QUESTIONS FOR ANALYSIS

- What are the most striking differences between the two maps?
- How are these European maps similar to and different from the Islamic and Chinese ones shown on pp. 524 and 531?

Waldseemüller map, 1507

Mercator projection, 1569

Sources: (top) Courtesy Wychwood Editions; (bottom) Rare Books Division, The News York Public Library, Astor, Lenox and Tilden Foundations.

Galileo. *Worried that the new science would undermine the Christian faith, the Catholic Church put Italian scientist Galileo on trial in 1633 for espousing heretical beliefs and condemned him to house arrest until his death in 1642.*

they believed were universal laws that applied to all matter and motion; they criticized older conceptions of nature (from Aristotelian ideas to folkloric and foreign ones) as absurd and obsolete. Thus, in his *Principia Mathematica* Newton set forth the laws of motion—including the famous law of gravitation, which simultaneously explained falling bodies on earth and planetary motion.

It is no longer fashionable to call these changes a scientific revolution, for European thinking did not change overnight. Only gradually did thinkers come to see the natural world as operating according to inviolable laws that experimenters could figure out. But by the late seventeenth century many rulers had developed a new interest in science's discoveries, and they established royal academies of science to encourage local endeavors. This patronage, of course, had a political function. By incorporating the British Royal Society in 1662, for example, Charles II hoped to show not only that the crown backed scientific progress but also that England's great minds backed the crown. Similar reasoning lay behind Louis XIV's founding of the French Royal Academy of Sciences and building of the fabulously expensive palace complex at Versailles. Like other monarchs, Louis also did his best to subordinate the clergy to the crown. All of France, he meant to say, needed to look to him for cultural, religious, and political guidance.

Gradually, the new science expanded beyond the court to gain popularity among elite circles. Marquise de Chatelet-Lomont built a scientific laboratory in her home and translated Newton's *Principia* into French. Well-to-do landowners formed societies to discuss the latest methods of animal breeding. Military schools increasingly stressed engineering methods and produced graduates with sophisticated technical skills. By about 1750, even artisans and journalists were applying Newtonian mechanics to their practical problems and inventions. In Italy, numerous female natural philosophers emerged, and the genre of scientific literature for "ladies" took hold. In 1763, the mathematician Diamante Medaglia Faini delivered an oration recommending that all women increase their knowledge of science. A consensus emerged among proponents of the new science that useful knowledge came from collecting data and organizing them into universally valid systems, rather than from studying revered classical texts.

By no means, however, did the scientific worldview dominate European thinking. Most people still understood their relationships with God, nature, and fellow humans via Christian doctrines and local customs. Although literacy was increasing, it was far from universal; schools remained church-governed or elite, male institutions. All governments employed censors and punished radical thinkers, peasants still suffered under arbitrary systems of taxation, and judicial regimes were as harsh as during medieval times. Science and rationality certainly did not pervade all spheres of European life by 1700. If that had been so, there would have been no need for the movement we now call the Enlightenment.

Marquise de Chatelet-Lomont. *The Marquise de Chatelet-Lomont (1706–1749) was one of the few in her day to understand Newtonian physics. Her French translation of Newton's* Principia Mathematica *included extensive explanations of the science that informed Newton's thinking. Her lover and admirer Voltaire wrote of her, "She was a great man whose only fault was in being a woman."*

Enlightenment Thinkers

Enlightenment thinkers believed in the power of human reason and the perfectibility of humankind; they rejected the medieval belief in man's sinful nature and helplessness in the face of earthly evils. Such thinkers included the French writers Voltaire (1694–1778) and Denis Diderot (1713–1784) and the Scottish economist Adam Smith (1723–1790). But these writers also called attention to the evils and flaws of human society: Voltaire criticized the torture of criminals, Diderot denounced the despotic tendencies of the French kings Louis XIV and Louis XV, and Smith exposed the inefficiencies of mercantilism.

In general, Enlightenment thinkers trusted nature and individual human reason and distrusted institutions and traditions. "Man is born good," wrote Jean-Jacques Rousseau (1712–1778); "it is society that corrupts him." Rousseau also followed the Englishman John Locke (1632–1704) in insisting on the sovereignty of the people; since all political institutions derived from the original "social contract" made between a people and its ruler, Locke and Rousseau argued, when a government became tyrannical, it violated that contract. In such a case, the people had the right to rebel and create a new contract. If these thinkers showed how traditional political authorities could be challenged, Voltaire repeatedly ridiculed the nobility and clergy for its stupidity, greed, and injustice. Other Enlightenment thinkers, similarly, saw the need for great improvements in human society. They mainly criticized contemporary European conditions, and they often suffered imprisonment or exile for writing about what they considered to be superstitious beliefs and corrupt political structures.

The Enlightenment touched all of Europe, but the extent of its reach varied. In France and Britain, enlightened learning spread widely; in Spain, Poland, and Scandinavia, enlightened circles were small and had little influence on rulers or the general population. Enlightened thought flourished in commercial centers like Amsterdam and Edinburgh and in colonial ports like Philadelphia and Boston. As education and literacy levels rose in these cities, book sales and newspaper circulation surged. By 1770, approximately 3,500 different books and pamphlets were appearing each year in France alone, compared to 1,000 fifty years earlier. By 1776, about 12 million copies of newspapers were circulating in Britain.

POPULAR CULTURE In the emerging marketplace for new books and new ideas, some of the most popular works were not from high intellectuals. They came from the pens of more sensationalist essayists. Pamphlets charging widespread corruption, fraudulent stock speculation, and insider trading circulated widely. Sex, too, sold well. Works like *Venus in the Cloister or the Nun in a Nightgown* racked up as many sales as the now-classic works of the Enlightenment. Bawdy and irreligious, these vulgar best-sellers exploited consumer demand—but they also seized the opportunity to mock authority figures, such as nuns and priests. Some even dared to go after the royal family, portraying Marie Antoinette as having sex with her court confessor. In these cases, pornography—some of it even philosophical—spilled into the literary marketplace for political satire. Such works displayed the seamier side of the Enlightenment, but they also revealed a willingness (on the part of high and low intellectuals alike) to explore modes of thought that defied established beliefs and institutions.

The reading public itself helped generate new cultural institutions and practices. In Britain and Germany, book clubs and coffeehouses sprang up to cater to sober men of business and learning; here, aristocrats and well-to-do commoners could read news sheets or discuss stock prices, political affairs, and technological novelties. The same sort of noncourtly socializing occurred in Parisian salons, where aristocratic women presided. Speaking their minds more openly in these private settings than at court or at public assemblies, women here freely exchanged ideas with men. The number of female readers, and writers, soared, and the relatively new genre of the novel, as well as

Salon of Madame Geoffrin
Much of the important work—and wit—of the Enlightenment was the product of private gatherings known as salons. Often hosted, like the one depicted here, by aristocratic women, these salons also welcomed down-at-the-heels writers and artists, offering everyone, at least in theory, the opportunity to discuss the sciences, the arts, politics, and the idiocies of their fellow humans on an equal basis.

specialized women's journals, appealed especially to them. It is important to note, however, that most funding for intellectuals still came from aristocrats, royal families, and the church. For example, in the German states, Enlightenment thinkers were chiefly university professors, bureaucrats, and pastors. Art collecting boomed—primarily because it gave aristocrats a way to display their good taste, wealth, and distance from the common people. The cultural life of the European Enlightenment was one that remained heavily dominated by the elite.

CHALLENGES TO AUTHORITY AND TRADITION Even though they took the aristocracy's money, many Enlightenment thinkers tried overturn the status distinctions that characterized European society. They emphasized merit rather than birth as the basis for status. In his *Treatise on Human Understanding* (1690), John Locke claimed that man was born with a mind that was a clean slate (*tabula rasa*) and acquired all his ideas through experience. Locke stressed that cultural differences were not the result of unequal natural abilities, but of unequal opportunities to develop one's abilities. Similarly, in *The Wealth of Nations,* Adam Smith remarked that there was little difference (other than education) between a philosopher and a street porter: both were born, he claimed, with the ability to reason, and both were (or should be) free to rise in society according to their talents. Yet, Locke and Smith still believed that a mixed set of social and political institutions was necessary to regulate relationships among ever-imperfect humans. Moreover, they did not believe that women could act as independent, rational individuals in the same way that all men, presumably, could. Although educated women like Mary Wollstonecraft and Olympe de Gouges took up the pen to protest these inequities (see Chapter 15 for further discussion), the Enlightenment did little to change the subordinate status of women in European society.

SEEKING UNIVERSAL LAWS Inspired by the new science, many thinkers sought to discover the "laws" of human behavior, an endeavor linked with criticism of existing governments. Explaining the laws of economic relations was chiefly the work of Adam Smith, whose book *The Wealth of Nations* described universal economic laws. It became one of the most influential and long-lived of enlightened works. Smith claimed that unregulated markets in a laissez-faire economy best suited mankind because they allowed man's "trucking and bartering" nature to express itself fully. (**Laissez-faire** expresses the concept that the economy works best when it is left alone—that is, when the state does not regulate or interfere with the workings of the market.) In Smith's view, the "invisible hand" of the market, rather than government regulations, would lead to prosperity and social peace. Smith was conscious of growing economic gaps between "civilized and thriving" nations and "savage" ones; the latter were so miserably poor that, Smith claimed, they were reduced to infanticide, starvation, and euthanasia. Yet, he believed that until these nations learned to play by what he called nature's laws, they could not expect a happy fate. Smith was just one of many writers who felt that non-Europeans had no other choice but to follow the Enlightenment's "universal" laws.

One of the most controversial areas for applying universal laws was religion. Although few Enlightenment thinkers were

ANALYZING GLOBAL DEVELOPMENTS

How Can We Measure the Impact of an Idea?

The single most important work of the European Enlightenment, which set out to provide an objective compendium of all human knowledge, Denis Diderot's *Encyclopédie* was very French. Of its more than 130 authors, only sixteen were foreign, and, of those sixteen, seven came from the French-speaking city of Geneva, just across the border. All of them were men. Within France, the authors came primarily from the north, especially from Paris. Noble and clerical authors weighed more heavily on the list of authors than in society at large (this had to do with literacy rates, which were much higher among the elite); most of Diderot's authors came from the Third Estate. None of those bourgeois authors had much to do with capitalism, nor did the aristocratic authors have much to do with feudalism. There were large contingents of doctors, lawyers, government officials, and skilled artisans.

We know very little about the production and diffusion of the first edition of the *Encyclopédie*, produced from 1751–1772 under Diderot's direction. The first four editions, in fact, were expensive luxury items, relatively unimportant in terms of diffusion. The great mass of *Encyclopédie*s that circulated in prerevolutionary Europe came from cut-rate quarto and octavo editions published between 1777 and 1782, when the final, revised version, the *Encyclopédie méthodique*, began to appear. For these later editions, thorough records have survived, raising far-reaching questions about how ideas circulated and where during the Enlightenment, at least within Europe. (We know very little about the circulation of the *Encyclopédie* beyond Europe.) Where did the writers come from, where did their ideas go, and how, if at all, did their origins influence the content and ultimate significance of their project? We include a table of key words and their classification in thematic categories from the original edition, to give a sense of its contents and priorities.

Terms	Word Count	Principal Categories
Commerce	5713	Commerce, Geography
Science	2095	[Multiple Categories]
Christ	1821	Theology, Holy Scripture
African	1772	Geography, History, Natural History, Botany
Slavery	238	Natural Law, Ethics, Religion, Ancient History
African slavery (*La traite des nègres*)	15	Commerce
Negro	536	Natural History, Commerce
Saint-Domingue	96	Geography, Botany
China	957	Agriculture, Chemistry, History, Natural History, Geography, Metaphysics, Tapestry
Turk or Turkey	701	Geography, History
Muhammad	356	Theology, History, Philosophy

QUESTIONS FOR ANALYSIS

- What does the diffusion of the *Encyclopédie* within France and across Europe tell us about its influence? How should we evaluate the influence of a book?
- Do you think the *Encyclopédie*'s local origins compromise its universal ambitions?
- How do you think the social origins of the contributors shaped the kinds of topics covered by the *Encyclopédie*?

Source: Darnton, Robert, The Business of Enlightenment: Publishing History of the Encyclopedie, 1775–1800 *(1979).*

atheists (people who do not believe in any god), most of them called for religious toleration. They insisted that the use of reason, not force, was the best way to create a community of believers and morally good people. Their critiques of church authorities and practices were highly controversial. Governments often reacted by censoring books or exiling writers, but the arguments managed to persuade some rulers. Thus, in the late eighteenth century, governments from Denmark to Austria passed acts offering religious minorities some freedom of worship. However, toleration did not mean full civil rights—especially for Catholics in England or Jews anywhere in Europe. Toleration simply meant a loosening of religious uniformity, and the population as a whole often resented even this.

SEEKING UNIVERSAL KNOWLEDGE The Enlightenment produced numerous works that attempted to encompass universal knowledge. Most important was the French *Encyclopedia*, which ultimately comprised twenty-eight volumes containing essays by nearly 200 intellectuals. It was extremely popular among the elite despite its political, religious, and intellectual

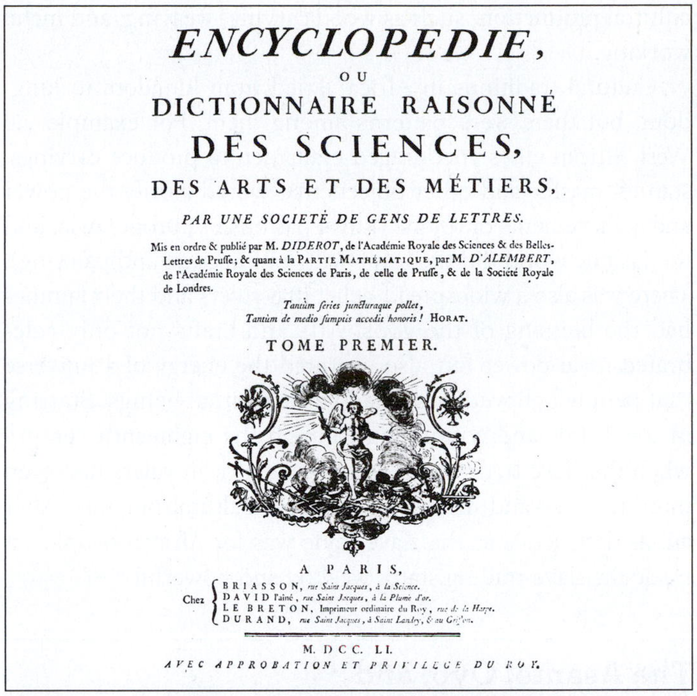

ENCYCLOPEDIE,

OU

DICTIONNAIRE RAISONNÉ

DES SCIENCES,

DES ARTS ET DES MÉTIERS,

PAR UNE SOCIETÉ DE GENS DE LETTRES.

Mis en ordre & publié par M. DIDEROT, de l'Académie Royale des Sciences & des Belles-Lettres de Pruſſe; & quant à la PARTIE MATHÉMATIQUE, par M. D'ALEMBERT, de l'Académie Royale des Sciences de Paris, de celle de Pruſſe, & de la Société Royale de Londres.

Tantùm series juncturaque pollet,
Tantùm de medio ſumptis accedit honoris! HORAT.

TOME PREMIER.

A PARIS,

Chez BRIASSON, *rue Saint Jacques, à la Science.*
DAVID l'aîné, *rue Saint Jacques, à la Plume d'or.*
LE BRETON, Imprimeur ordinaire du Roy, *rue de la Harpe.*
DURAND, *rue Saint Jacques, à Saint Landry, & au Griffon.*

M. DCC. LI.

AVEC APPROBATION ET PRIVILEGE DU ROY.

The ***Encyclopédie.*** *Originally published in 1751, the* Encyclopédie *was the most comprehensive work of learning of the French Enlightenment. The title page (left) features an image of light and reason being dispersed throughout the land. The title itself identifies the work as a dictionary, based on reason, that deals not just with the sciences but also with the arts and occupations. It identifies two of the leading men of letters (*gens de lettres*), Denis Diderot and Jean le Rond d'Alembert, as the primary authors of the work. Contributors to the* Encyclopedia *included craftsmen as well as intellectuals. The detailed illustrations of a pin factory and the processes and machinery employed in pin making shown below are from a plate in the fourth volume of the* Encyclopedia *and demonstrate its emphasis on practical information.*

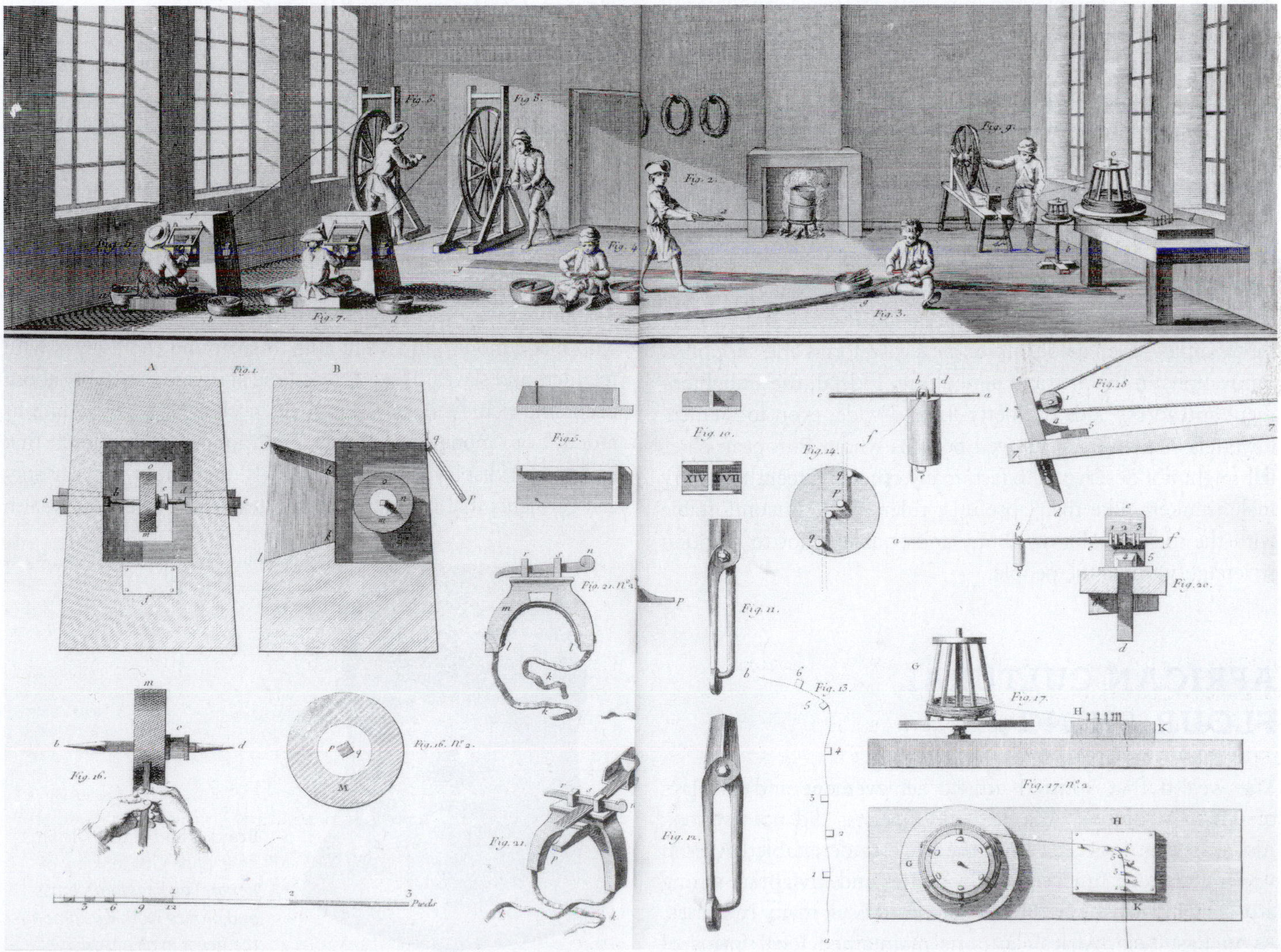

radicalism. Its purpose was "to collect all the knowledge scattered over the face of the earth" and to make it useful to men and women in the present and future. Indeed, the *Encyclopedia* offered a wealth of information about the rest of the world, including more than 2,300 articles on Islam. Here, quite typically, the authors praised Arab culture for preserving and extending Greek and Roman science—and in doing so, preparing the way for scientific advances in Europe. But at the same time the authors portrayed Islam with the same ill will that they applied to other organized religions, condemning Muhammad for promoting a bloodthirsty religion and Muslim culture in general for not rejecting superstition.

Enlightenment thinkers valued commerce and rationality, so they placed all regions that supposedly lacked these ingredients at the bottom of the world's cultures. While praising some cultures like the Chinese for having achieved much in these areas, Enlightenment thinkers were confident that Europe was advancing over the rest of the world in its acquisition of goods and universal knowledge.

Absolutist governments did not entirely reject enlightened ideas. After all, they recognized the virtues of universality (as in a universally applicable system of taxation) and precision (as in a well-drilled army). Also, social mobility allowed more skilled bureaucrats to rise through the ranks, while commerce provided the state with new riches. The idea of collecting knowledge, too, appealed to states that wanted greater control over their subjects. Consider Louis XIV, who was persuaded to establish a census (though he never carried it out) so that he could "know with certitude in what consists his grandeur, his wealth, and his strength." Some enlightened princes—in Prussia and Austria, for example—even made impressive legal reforms and supported innovations in the arts and agriculture. Indeed, the Enlightenment spread the idea of liberty far and wide, even to women, lower-class men, and enslaved peoples whom European elites felt might not deserve it. In fact, many other eighteenth-century male thinkers, like their absolutist rulers, were uncomfortable with the idea of offering liberty and equality (not to mention sovereignty) to *all* the people.

AFRICAN CULTURAL FLOURISHING

The wealth that spurred artistic achievement and displays of power in Europe, Asia, and the Americas did not overlook African states. Proceeds from the slave trade enabled African upper classes to fund cultural activities and invigorate strong artisanal and artistic traditions that dated back many centuries. As in East Asia, African artisans maintained local forms of cultural production, such as wood carving, weaving, and metal working.

Cultural traditions in Africa varied from kingdom to kingdom, but there were patterns among them. For example, all West African elites encouraged craftsmen to produce carvings, statues, masks, and other objects that would glorify the power and achievements of rulers. (Royal patrons in Europe, Asia, and the Islamic world did the same with architecture and painting). There was also a widespread belief that rulers and their families had the blessing of the gods. Arts and crafts not only celebrated royal power but also captured the energy of a universe that people believed was filled with spiritual beings. Starting in the 1500s and continuing through the eighteenth century when the slave trade reached its peak, African rulers had even more reason—and means—to support cultural pursuits. After all, as destructive as the slave trade was for African peoples, it made the slave-trading states wealthy and powerful.

The Asante, Oyo, and Benin Cultural Traditions

The kingdom of Asante, which the charismatic leader and first king (Asantehene) of the large Akan-speaking region in what is present-day Ghana, Osei Tutu (d. 1717) unified, led the way in cultural attainments. The kingdom's access to gold and the revenues that it derived from selling captives undergirded its prosperity, making it the richest state in West Africa, perhaps even in the whole of sub-Saharan Africa. So deeply imbued with a desire to achieve economic success were the citizens of Asante that they accorded the highest respect to entrepreneurs who made money and were able to surround themselves with retainers and slaves. The adages of the age were inevitably about becoming rich: "money is king" or "nothing is as important as money" or "money is what it is all about." Households that had wealth displayed it ostentatiously, beginning to wear special garments that told others that they were persons of wealth

Brass Oba Head. *The brass head of an Oba, or king, of Benin. The kingdom's brass and bronze work was among the finest in all of Africa.*

and power. Those who could command the services of at least 1,000 subjects were entitled to wear a special cloth and to have a horsetail switch carried in front of them. Even more coveted was the right to carry the elephant-tail whip, which carried with it an esteemed title.

Artisans celebrated these traditions through the crafting of magnificent seats or stools coated with gold as symbols of authority; the most ornate were reserved for the head of the Asante federation, the Asantehene, who ruled this far-flung empire from the capital city of Kumasi. By the eighteenth century, these monarchs ventured out from the secluded royal palace only on ceremonial and feast days, when they wore sumptuous silk garments featuring many dazzling colors and geometric patterns, all joined together in interwoven strips. Known as Kente cloth, this fabric could be worn only by the rulers. Kings also had a golden elephant tail carried in front of them, the symbol of the highest level of wealth. Held aloft on these celebratory occasions were maces, spears, staffs, and other symbols of power fashioned from the kingdom's abundant gold supplies. These reminded the common people of the Asantehene's connection to the gods.

Equally resplendent were rulers of the Oyo Empire and Benin, located in the territory that now constitutes Nigeria. Elegant, refined metalwork in the form of West African bronzes reflects these rulers' awesome power and their peoples' highest esteem. The bronze heads of Ife, capital city of the Yoruba Oyo Empire, are among the world's most sophisticated pieces of art. According to one commentator, "little that Italy or Greece or Egypt ever produced could be finer, and the appeal of their beauty is immediate and universal." The Ife heads mark the high point of Yoruba craft and artistic tradition that dates back to the first millennium CE. Artisans fashioned the best known of these works in the thirteenth century (before the slave trade era), but the tradition continued and became more elaborate in the seventeenth and eighteenth centuries.

Bronzes from Benin, too, displayed exquisite craftsmanship. Although historical records have portrayed Benin as one of Africa's most brutal slave-trading regimes, it also produced art of the highest order. Whether Benin's reputation for brutality was deserved or simply part of Europeans' later desire to label African rulers as "savage" in order to justify their conquest of the landmass, it cannot detract from the splendor of its artisans' creations.

HYBRID CULTURES IN THE AMERICAS

In the Americas, mingling between European colonizers and native peoples (as well as African slaves) produced hybrid cultures. But the mixing of cultures grew increasingly unbalanced as Europeans imposed authority over more of the Americas. For Native Americans, the pressure to adapt their cultures to those of the colonists began from the start. Over time, Indians faced mounting pressure as Europeans insisted that their conquests were not simply military endeavors but also spiritual errands. In addition to guns and germs, all of Europe's colonizers brought Bibles, prayer books, and crucifixes. With these, they set out to Christianize and "civilize" Indian and African populations in the Americas. Yet missionary efforts produced uneven and often unpredictable outcomes. Even as Indians and African slaves adopted Christian beliefs and practices, they often retained older religious practices too.

European colonists likewise borrowed from the peoples they subjugated and enslaved. This was especially true in the sixteenth and seventeenth centuries, when the colonists' survival in the New World often depended on adapting. Before long, however, many American settlements had become stable and prosperous, to the extent that colonists preferred not to admit their past dependence on others. New sorts of hierarchies emerged, and elites in Latin America and North America increasingly followed the tastes and fashions of European aristocrats. Yet, even as they imitated Old World ways, these colonials forged identities that separated them from Europe.

Spiritual Encounters

Settlers in the New World had the military and economic power to impose their culture—especially their religion—on indigenous peoples. Although the Jesuits had little impact in China and the Islamic world, Christian missionaries in the Americas had armies and officials to back up their insistence that Native Americans and African slaves abandon their own deities and spirits for Christ.

FORCING CONVERSIONS European missionaries, especially Catholics, used numerous techniques to bring Indians within the Christian fold. Smashing idols, razing temples, and whipping backsliders all belonged to the missionaries' arsenal. Catholic orders (principally Dominicans, Jesuits, and Franciscans) also learned what they could about Indian beliefs and rituals—and then exploited that knowledge to make conversions to Christianity. For example, many missionaries found it useful to demonize local gods, subvert indigenous spiritual leaders, and transform Indian iconography into Christian symbols. But at the same time, the missionaries preserved much linguistic and ethnographic information about Native American communities. In sixteenth-century Mexico, the Dominican friar Bernardino de Sahagún compiled an immense ethnography of Mexican ways and beliefs. In seventeenth-century Canada, French Jesuits

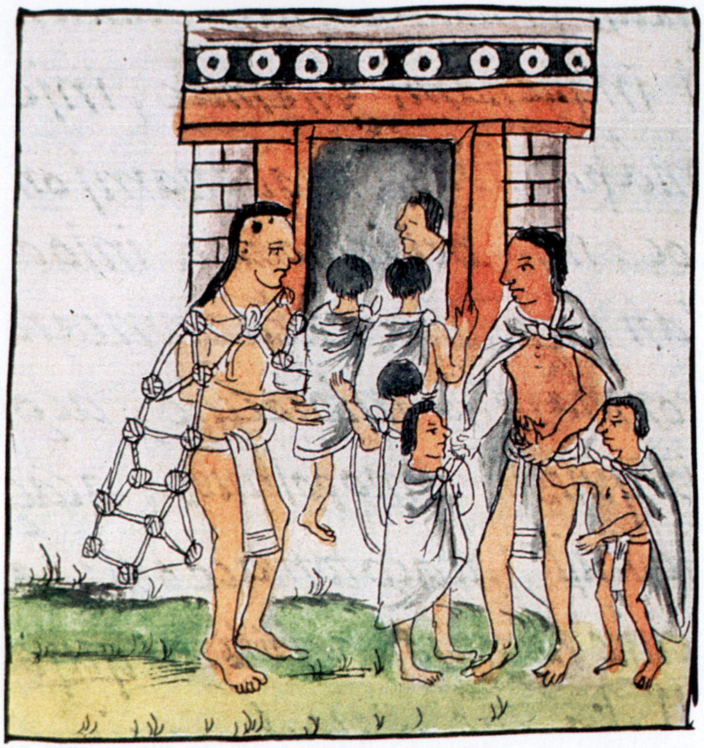

Indians Becoming Christians. *This image is from a colonial chronicle, illustrated and narrated by indigenous scribes who had converted to Christianity. The picture of Indians before the conquest entering a house of prayer is intended to represent the Indians as proto-Christians.*

prepared dictionaries and grammars of the Iroquoian and Algonquian languages and translated Christian hymns into Amerindian tongues.

Neither gentle persuasion nor violent coercion produced the results that missionaries desired. When conversions did occur, the Christian practices that resulted were usually hybrid forms in which indigenous deities and rituals merged with Christian ones. Among Andean mountain people, for example, priestesses of local cults took the Christian name Maria to mask their secret worship of traditional deities. In other cases, indigenous communities turned their backs on Christianity and accused missionaries of bringing disease and death. Those who did convert saw Christian spiritual power as an addition to, not a replacement for, their own religions.

MIXING CULTURES More distressing to missionaries than the blending of beliefs or outright defiance were the Indians' successes in converting captured colonists. Many Indian groups had a tradition of adopting their captives as a way to replace lost kin. It deeply troubled the missionaries that quite a few captured colonists adjusted to their situation, accepted their adoptions, and refused to return to colonial society when given the chance. Moreover, some other Europeans voluntarily chose to live among the Indians. Comparing the records of cultural conversion, one eighteenth-century colonist suggested that "thousands of Europeans are Indians," yet "we have no examples of even one of those Aborigines having from choice become European." (Aborigines are original, native inhabitants of a region, as opposed to invaders, colonizers, or later peoples of mixed ancestry.) While this calculation may be exaggerated, it reflects the fact that Europeans who adopted Indian culture, like Christianized Indians, lived in a mixed cultural world. In fact, their familiarity with both Indian and European ways made them ideal intermediaries for diplomatic arrangements and economic exchanges.

Beyond the attractions of Indian cultures, Europeans mixed with Indians because there were many more men than women among the colonists. Almost all the early European traders, missionaries, and settlers were men (although the British North American settlements saw more women arrive relatively early on). In response to the scarcity of women and as a way to help Amerindians accept the newcomers' culture, the Portuguese crown authorized intermarriage between Portuguese men and local women. These relations often amounted to little more than rape, but longer-lasting relationships developed in places where Indians kept their independence—as among French fur traders and Indian women in Canada, the Great Lakes region, and the Mississippi Valley. Whether by coercion or consent, sexual relations between European men and Indian women resulted in offspring of mixed ancestry. In fact, the mestizos of Spanish colonies and the métis of French outposts soon outnumbered settlers of wholly European descent.

The increasing numbers of African slaves in the Americas complicated the mix of New World cultures even further. Unlike marriages between fur traders and Indian women, in which the women held considerable power because of their connections to Indian trading partners, sexual intercourse between European men and enslaved African women was almost always forced. Children born from such unions swelled the ranks of mixed-ancestry people in the colonial population. Europeans attempted to Christianize slaves, though many slave owners doubted the wisdom of converting persons they regarded as mere property. Protestants had more difficulty than Catholics in accepting that Africans could be both slaves and Christians, and their missionary efforts were less aggressive than the Catholics'.

Sent forth with the pope's blessing, Catholic priests targeted slave populations in the American colonies of Portugal, Spain, and France. Applying many of the same techniques that missionaries used with Indian "heathens," these priests produced similarly mixed results. Often converts blended Islamic or traditional African religions with Catholicism. Converted slaves wove remembered practices and beliefs from their homeland into their American Christianity, transforming both along the way. In northeastern Brazil, for example, slaves combined the Yoruba faiths of their ancestors with Catholic beliefs, and they

Racial Mixing. (Left) *This image shows racial mixing in colonial Mexico—the father is Spanish, the mother Indian, and the child a mestizo. This is a well-to-do family, illustrating how Europeans married into the native aristocracy.* (Right) *Here too we see a racially mixed family. The father is Spanish, the mother black or African, and the child a mulatto. Observe, however, the less aristocratic and markedly less peaceful nature of this family.*

frequently attributed powers of African deities to Christian saints. Sometimes Christian and African faiths were practiced side by side. In Saint-Domingue, slaves and free blacks practiced *vodun* ("spirit" in the Dahomey tongue); in Cuba, *santería* ("cult of saints" in Spanish), a faith of similar origins.

Just as slaveholders feared, Christianity—especially in its hybrid forms—could inspire resistance, even revolt, among slaves. Indeed, a major runaway slave leader in mid-eighteenth-century Surinam was a Christian. Those held in bondage in the English colonies drew inspiration from Christian hymns that promised deliverance, and they embraced as their own the Old Testament story of Moses leading the Israelites out of Egypt. By the late eighteenth century, freed slaves like the Methodist Olaudah Equiano (see Chapter 13) were saying in their own voices that slavery was unjust and incompatible with Christian brotherhood.

Making Americans

The colonization of the Americas brought Europeans, Africans, and Indians into sustained contact, though the nature of the colonies and the character of the contact varied considerably. Where their dominance was most certain, European colonists imposed their ways on subjugated populations and imported what they took to be the chief attributes of the countries and cultures they had left behind. Yet Europeans were not immune to cultural influences from the groups they dispossessed and enslaved, and over time the colonists developed a sense of their own distinctive "American" identities. The cultures and identities of Indians and African slaves also underwent significant transformations, though often what Europeans imposed was only partially and selectively adapted.

THE CREOLE IDENTITY In Spanish America, ethnic and cultural mixing produced a powerful new class, the **creoles**—persons of European descent who were born in the Americas. By the late eighteenth century, creoles increasingly resented the control that **peninsulars**—men and women born in Spain or Portugal but living in the Americas—had over colonial society. Creoles especially chafed under the exclusive privileges given to peninsular rulers, like those that forbade creoles from trading with other colonial ports. Also, they disliked the fact that royal ministers gave most official posts to peninsulars. While the Spanish and Portuguese rulers did occasionally soften their discrimination for fear of angering the creoles, their reforms usually aggravated tensions with peninsulars.

The growing creole identity gained strength from new ideas spreading in the colonies, especially those circulating under the umbrella of the Enlightenment. The French writer Abbé Raynal's *History of the Settlements and Trade of the Europeans in the East and West Indies* (1770), for example, was a favorite text among colonial reading circles in Buenos Aires and Rio de Janeiro. As a history of colonization in the New World, it was unkind to Iberian (Spanish and Portuguese) emperors and conquerors—and often helped creoles justify their dissatisfaction. Other French works were also popular, especially those of Rousseau. So were some English texts, like Adam Smith's *The Wealth of Nations*. Smith's reformist spirit contributed to creole impressions that mercantilist Iberian authorities lagged behind them in political and economic matters.

In many cities of the Spanish and Portuguese empires, reading clubs and salons hosted energetic discussions of fresh ideas. In one university in Peru, Catholic scholars taught their students that Spanish labor drafts and taxes on Andean natives not only violated divine justice but also offended the natural rights of free men. The Spanish crown, recognizing the role of printing presses in spreading troublesome ideas, strictly controlled the number and location of printers in the colonies. In Brazil, royal authorities banned them altogether. Nonetheless books, pamphlets, and simple gossip allowed new notions of science, history, and politics to circulate among literate creoles.

ANGLICIZATION In one important sense, wealthy colonists in British America were similar to the creole elites in Spanish and Portuguese America: they too copied European ways. For example, they constructed "big houses" (in Virginia) modeled on the country estates of English gentlemen, imported opulent furnishings and fashions from the finest British stores, and exercised more control over colonial assemblies. Imitating the English also involved tightening patriarchal authority. In seventeenth-century Virginia, men had vastly outnumbered women, which gave women some power (widows in particular gained greater control over property and more choices when they remarried). During the eighteenth century, however, sex ratios became more equal, and women's property rights diminished as English customs took precedence. Overall, patriarchal authority was evident in family portraits, where husband-patriarchs sat or stood in front of their wives and children.

Intellectually, too, British Americans were linked to Europe. Importing enormous numbers of books and journals, these Americans played a significant role in the Enlightenment as producers and consumers of political pamphlets, scientific treatises, and social critiques. Indeed, drawing on the words of numerous Enlightenment thinkers, American intellectuals created the most famous of enlightened documents: the Declaration of Independence. It announced that all men were endowed with equal rights and were created to pursue worldly happiness. In this way Anglicized Americans showed themselves, like the creole elites of Latin America, to be products of both European and New World encounters.

Chronometer. *In the 1760s, the English clockmaker John Harrison perfected the chronometer, a timepiece mariners could use to reckon longitude while at sea. Although the Royal Scientific Society initially refused to believe that Harrison had solved this long-standing problem, Harrison's instrument made navigation so much safer and more predictable that it became standard equipment on European ships.*

THE MAKING OF A NEO-EUROPEAN CULTURE IN OCEANIA

Not only in Europe and the Americas but also in the South Pacific, an "enlightened" form of cultural expansionism took shape in the eighteenth century. Though in centuries past Hindu, Buddhist, Islamic, and Chinese missionaries and traders had traveled to Malaysia and nearby islands, they had not ventured beyond Timor (see Map 14.1). Europeans began to do so in the years after 1770, turning their sights on **Oceania** (Australia, New Zealand, and the islands of the southwest Pacific). Using their new wealth to fund voyages with scientific and political objectives, Europeans invaded these remaining unexplored areas. The results were mixed: while some islands maintained their autonomy, the biggest prize, Australia, underwent thorough Anglicization.

Until Europeans colonized it in the late eighteenth century, Australia was, like the Americas before Columbus, truly a world apart. Separated by water and sheer distance from other regions, Australia's main features were harsh natural conditions and a sparse population. At the time of the European colonization, the island was home to around 300,000 people, mostly hunter-gatherers. While seafarers from Java, Timor, and particularly the port of Makassar may have ventured into the area in the past, there was little evidence that either Chinese or Muslim merchants had ever strayed that far south.

Europeans had visited Oceania before the eighteenth century. Spices had drawn the Portuguese and Dutch into the South Pacific (see Chapter 13), and the Spanish had plied Pacific waters while traveling between Manila and Acapulco, but they had stopped only in Guam and the Mariana Islands. In the 1670s and 1680s they attempted to conquer these islands, and despite considerable resistance they succeeded by 1700. The Dutch visited Easter Island in 1722, and the French arrived in Tahiti in 1767. Both the Portuguese and the Dutch had seen the northern and western coasts of Australia, but they had found only sand, flies, and Aborigines. Not until the late eighteenth century did

MAP 14.1 | Southeast Asia

Captain Cook's voyages throughout the Pacific Ocean symbolized a new era in European exploration of other societies.

- According to this map, how many voyages did Cook take?
- Where did Cook explore, and what peoples did he encounter?
- According to your reading, how did Cook's endeavors symbolize "scientific" imperialism?

Europeans see Australia's more hospitable eastern coast or find grounds for serious interest in colonization. Now the intrusion into Oceania presented Europeans with a previously unknown region that could serve as a laboratory for studying other peoples and geographical settings.

The Scientific Voyages of Captain Cook

In Oceania and across the South Pacific, Europeans experimented with a scientific form of imperialism. The story of the region's most famous explorer, Captain James Cook (1728–1779), shows how closely related science and imperialist ventures could be, and how unequal cultural exchange could be. Cook's voyages and his encounter with the South Sea Islanders opened up the Pacific, and particularly Australia, to European colonizers.

Captain Cook has become a legendary figure in European cultural history, portrayed as one of the saintly scientists of enlightened progress. His first voyage had two objectives. The Royal Society charged him with the scholarly task of observing the movement of the planet Venus from the Southern Hemisphere, and the British government assigned him the secret mission of finding and claiming "the southern continent" for Britain. Cook set sail in 1768, and his voyage was so fruitful that he subsequently undertook two more scientific-imperial adventures. The extremely popular accounts of his discoveries, and the engravings that accompanied them, opened up the exotic worlds of Tahiti, New Zealand, Australia, and Hawaii to European scrutiny. They also prepared the way for a new, more intensive sort of cultural colonization.

SCIENTIFIC AND CULTURAL ASPECTS Cook was chosen to head the first expedition because of his scientific interests and skills. Although he had little schooling, he had gone to sea early and, through long experience in navigating the uncharted North American waters of Newfoundland, had developed excellent surveying skills. Besides Cook, the Royal Society sent along one of its members who was a botanist; a doctor and student of the renowned Swedish naturalist Carolus Linnaeus (1707–1778); and numerous artists and other scientists. The crew also carried sophisticated instruments and had instructions to keep detailed diaries. This was to be a grand data-collecting journey.

Cook's voyages surpassed even the Royal Society's hopes. The scientists made approximately 3,000 drawings of Pacific plants, birds, landscapes, and peoples never seen in Europe. The men described the region's flora and fauna according to Swedish naturalist Carolus Linnaeus's recently developed system for classifying all natural phenomena, and they gave English names to geographical features.

More than science was at stake, however, for Australia was intended to supply Britain with raw materials. But as in the Americas, extracting those materials required a labor force, and

The Voyages of Captain James Cook. *During his celebrated voyages to the South Pacific, Cook (left) kept meticulous maps and diaries. Although he had little formal education, he became one of the great exemplars of enlightened learning through experience and experiment. (Right) Kangaroos were unknown in the West until Cook and his colleagues encountered (and ate) them on their first visit to Australia. This engraving of the animal (which unlike most animals, plants, and geographical features actually kept the name the Aborigines had given it) from Cook's 1773 travelogue,* A Voyage Round the World in the Years 1768–1771, *lovingly depicts the kangaroo's environs and even emotions.*

the Aborigines of Australia, like the Indians of the Americas, perished in great numbers from imported diseases. Those who survived generally fled to escape control by British masters. Thus, to secure a labor force, plans arose for grand-scale conquest and resettlement by British colonists. On his third voyage, Cook took along an astonishing array of animals and plants with which to turn the South Pacific into a European-style garden. His lieutenant later brought apples, quinces, strawberries, and rosemary to Australia; the seventy sheep imported in 1788 laid the foundations for the region's wool-growing economy. In fact, the domestication of Australia arose from the Europeans' certainty about their superior know-how and a desire to make the entire landmass serve British interests.

In 1788, a British military expedition took official possession of the eastern half of Australia. The intent was, in part, to establish a prison colony far from home. This plan belonged as well to the realm of "enlightened" dreams: that of ridding "civilized" society of all evils by resettling lawbreakers among the "uncivilized." The intent was also to exploit Australia for its timber and flax and to use it as a strategic base against Dutch and French expansion. In the next decades, immigration—free and forced—increased the Anglo-Australian population from an original 1,000 to about 1.2 million by 1860. Importing their customs and their capital, British settlers turned Australia into a frontier version of home, just as they had done in British America. Yet, such large-scale immigration had disastrous consequences for the surviving Aborigines. Like the Native Americans, the original inhabitants of Australia were decimated by diseases and increasingly forced westward by European settlement.

Omai. *Omai, the South Sea Islander brought to England by Captain Cook, was the object of much curiosity in London in the 1780s.*

STUDYING FOREIGNERS In one important way, Cook continued practices of the past. Earlier travelers had developed an efficient way to study foreign peoples and their languages: by taking some of them to Europe, through kidnapping if necessary. On Columbus's first voyage to the New World, he had captured six Amerindians and taken them back to Spain—to show them off as exotic people, and to enable them to learn Spanish so they could serve as intermediaries between the two cultures. Other explorers did the same, seizing local people, taking them to Europe, and putting them on display.

This was not the way that Europeans learned about peoples whom they considered to be civilized—for example, the Chinese and the Arabs. For such "civilized" peoples, texts stood in for living bodies. But exhibiting live individuals continued to be a crude means for studying those whom the Europeans considered uncivilized. Cook himself captured and transported to England a highly skilled Polynesian navigator, Omai. Omai quickly became the talk of London society and symbolized for some people the innocence and beauty that were vanishing as Europe developed complicated machines and stock exchanges. Cook's return of Omai to his home on his third voyage was a sensation of equal proportions, seen as a colossally generous act by the revered British explorer.

The Enlightenment and the Origins of Racial Thought

Cook's description of the South Sea Islanders underscores the place that "race" had come to occupy in Europeans' views of themselves and others. Previously, the word *race* referred to a swift current in a stream or a test of speed, and sometimes it meant a lineage (mainly that of a royal or noble family). By the late seventeenth century, a few writers were expanding the definition to designate a European ethnic lineage, identifying, for example, the indomitable spirit and freedom-loving ethos of the Anglo-Saxon race.

The Frenchman François Bernier, who had traveled in Asia, may have been the first European to attempt to classify the peoples of the world. He used a variety of criteria, including those that were to become standard from the late eighteenth century down to the present, such as skin color, facial features, and hair texture. Bernier published this work in his *New Division of the Earth by the Different Groups or Races Who Inhabit It* (1684). In addition to the Swedish naturalist Carolus Linnaeus, the French scholar Georges Louis LeClerc, the comte de Buffon (1707–1788), and the German anatomist Johann Friedrich Blumenbach (1752–1840) were the first to use racial principles to classify humankind.

CATEGORIZING HUMAN GROUPS In his *Systema Naturae* (1735), Europe's most accomplished naturalist, Carolus Linnaeus, sought to classify all the world's plants and animals by giving each a binomial, or two-worded, name. In subsequent editions of his *Systema* Linnaeus perfected his system, identifying five subspecies of the mammal he called *Homo sapiens,* or "wise man." Linnaeus gave each of the continents a subspecies: there was *Homo europaeus, Homo americanus, Homo afer*, and *Homo asiaticus*. He added a fifth category, *Homo monstrosus,* for "wild" men and "monstrous" types.

Linnaeus's classifications were based on a combination of physical characteristics that included skin color and social qualities. He characterized Europeans as light-skinned and governed by laws; Asians as "sooty" and governed by opinion; indigenous American peoples as copper-skinned and governed by custom; and Africans (whom he consigned to the lowest rung of the human ladder) as ruled by personal whim. Later eighteenth-century natural historians dismissed Linnaeus's fifth category, which contained mythical monstrous races and people with mental and physical disabilities, but the habit of ranking "races" and lumping together physical and cultural characteristics persisted.

THE EUROPEAN BIAS In inventorying the world's peoples and assigning each group a place on the ladder of human achievement, Europeans applied their reverence for classical sculpture. Those who most resembled Greek nudes were considered the most beautiful, as well as the most civilized and suited for world power. In his *Natural History* (1750), the comte de Buffon insisted that classical sculptures had established the proper proportion for the human form. Having divided humans into distinct "races," he determined that white peoples were the most admirable, and Africans the most contemptible.

In these emerging racial hierarchies, South Sea Islanders fell somewhere between Caucasians and Ethiopians. To some, their isolation from European and Asian cultures and their residence in a tropical "paradise" made them seem like direct descendants of Adam and Eve—a virtuous, uncorrupted people who fit the description of the "noble savage" popularized by Jean-Jacques Rousseau. But in succeeding decades Europeans would come to emphasize not the nobility but the savagery of the South Sea Islanders. Declining appreciation for their innocence and simplicity may have begun with the final act in the Cook legend: his killing by the Hawaiians in 1779. The news scandalized Cook's homeland; the king himself, it is said, shed tears. Thereafter Europeans began to write about a "darker side" of South Pacific cultures.

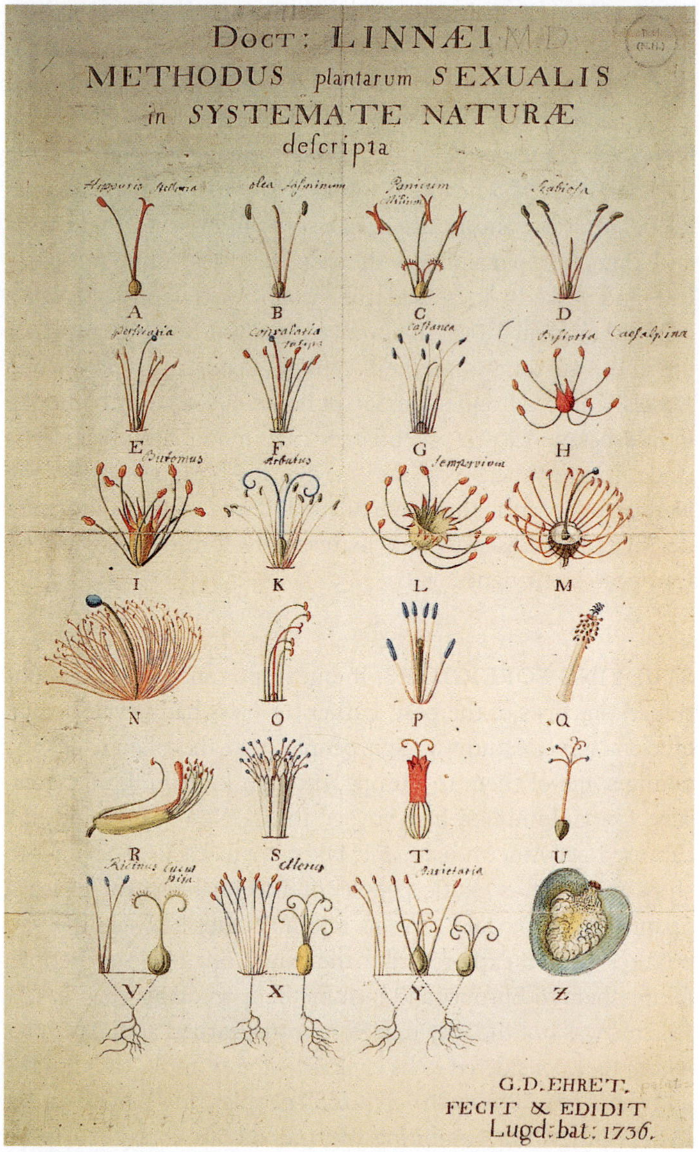

Linnaeus and Classification. *Linnaeus's famous system of plant and animal classifications, which depended on sexual forms (such as the stamen and pistil in plants), was in wide use by the end of the eighteenth century.*

CONCLUSION

New wealth produced by commerce and state building created the conditions for a global cultural renaissance in the sixteenth, seventeenth, and eighteenth centuries. It began in the Chinese and Islamic empires and then stretched into Europe, Africa, and previous worlds apart in the Americas and Oceania. Experiments in religious toleration encouraged cultural exchange; book production and consumption soared; grand new monuments took shape; luxury goods became available for wider enjoyment.

A striking aspect of this cultural renaissance was its unevenness. While elites and sometimes the middle classes benefited, the poor did not. They remained illiterate, undernourished, and often subjected to brutal treatment by rulers and landowners. Elite women in Europe and China increasingly joined literate society, but they gained no new rights. Urban areas also profited more from the new wealth than rural ones, so people seeking refinement flocked to the cities. Some former cultural centers, like the Italian peninsula, lost their luster as new, more commercially and culturally dynamic centers took their place.

Among states, too, cultural inequalities were glaring. Although the Islamic and Chinese worlds confidently retained their own systems of knowing, believing, and representing, the Americas and Oceania increasingly faced European cultural pressures. Here, while hybrid practices became widespread by the late eighteenth century, European beliefs and habits took over as the standards for judging degrees of "civilization." African cultures largely escaped this influence, though their homelands felt the impact of European expansionism because of the slave trade.

From a commercial standpoint, the world was more integrated than ever before. But the exposure and cultural borrowing that global trade promoted largely reconfirmed established ways. The Chinese, for instance, still believed in the superiority of their traditional knowledge and customs. Muslim rulers, confident of the primacy of Islam, allowed others to form subordinate cultural communities within their realm and adopted the Europeans' knowledge only when it served their own imperial purposes.

Only the Europeans were constructing knowledge that they believed was both universal and objective, enabling mortals to master the world of nature and all its inhabitants. This view would prove consequential, as well as controversial, in the centuries to come.

AFTER YOU READ THIS CHAPTER

Review and research on STUDYSPACE: wwnorton.com/studyspace

TRACING THE GLOBAL STORYLINES

FOCUS ON: *The Flourishing of Regional Cultures*

The Islamic World

- The Ottomans' unique cultural synthesis accommodates not only mystical Sufis and ultraorthodox *ulama* but also military men, administrators, and clerics.
- The Safavid state proclaims the triumph of Shiism and Persian influences in the sumptuous new capital, Isfahan.
- Mughal courtly culture values art and learning and welcomes non-Muslim contributions.

East Asia

- China's cultural flourishing, coming from within, is evident in the broad circulation of traditional ideas, publishing, and mapmaking.
- Japan's imperial court at Kyoto develops an elite culture of theater, stylized painting, tea ceremonies, and flower arranging.

Europe

- Cultural flourishing known as the Enlightenment yields a faith in reason and a belief in humans' ability to fathom the laws of nature and human behavior.
- European thinkers articulate a belief in unending human progress.
- Europeans expand into Australia and the South Pacific.

Africa

- Slave-trading states such as Asante, Oyo, and Benin celebrate royal power and wealth through art.

The Americas

- Even as Euro-Americans participate in the Enlightenment, their culture reflects Native American and African influences.

CHRONOLOGY

The Islamic World
- Shah Abbas builds Isfahan **1587–1629**
- Taj Mahal built in Mughal dynasty **1630–1650**

Europe

East Asia
- Growing circulation of books and ideas in China **1600s**
- "Floating worlds" appear in Japanese cities **1600s**

Africa
- Oyo and Asante kingdoms produce vibrant artistic works **1600s**

The Americas
- Hybrid cultures appear **1600s**

1600 | 1650

KEY TERMS

cartography *p. 531*

creoles *p. 545*

enlightened absolutists *p. 520*

Enlightenment *p. 535*

Forbidden City of Beijing *p. 528*

great plaza at Isfahan *p. 529*

laissez-faire *p. 539*

Oceania *p. 546*

Palace of Versailles *p. 528*

peninsulars *p. 545*

scientific method *p. 535*

Taj Mahal *p. 525*

Topkapi Palace *p. 528*

STUDY QUESTIONS

1. **Explain** the processes that brought forth cultural syntheses in the three Islamic dynasties during this era. To what extent did European culture influence each empire?
2. **Describe** Chinese and Japanese cultural achievements during this period. How did foreign influences affect each dynasty?
3. **Define** the term *Enlightenment* as it pertained to Europe. How did Enlightenment ideas shape European attitudes toward other cultures?
4. **Explain** the various factors that contributed to the growth of hybrid cultures in the Americas during this era. How similar and different were these new societies across the Americas?
5. **Analyze** the impact of Enlightenment ideas in the Americas. Did the spread of this philosophy bring communities across the Atlantic together, or did it drive them apart?
6. **Compare and contrast** European exploration of Oceania in the eighteenth century to European exploration of the Americas in the sixteenth century (see Chapter 12). How did European exploration of Oceania transform European attitudes toward non-European groups around the world?
7. **Explain** how global trade changed world cultures at this time.
8. **Analyze** the extent to which dynastic rulers around the world were able to control cultural developments during this period. How did new cultural productions potentially undermine local governments?

Tulip Period in Ottoman Empire **1720s**

Isaac Newton publishes *Principia Mathematica* **1687**

Enlightenment philosophy spreads among educated elites **1700s**

Adam Smith publishes *The Wealth of Nations* **1776**

Voyages of Captain Cook **1768–1779**

Enlightenment philosophy spreads among colonial elites **1700s**

1700 1750 1800

BEFORE YOU READ THIS CHAPTER

wwnorton.com/
StudySpace

GLOBAL STORYLINES

- A new era based on radically new ideas of freedom and the nation-state emerges in Europe and the Americas.
- The watchwords of the age are free inquiry, free markets, free labor, and governments freely chosen by free individuals.
- The worldwide balance of power changes.

CHAPTER OUTLINE

15

Reordering the World, 1750–1850

FOCUS QUESTIONS

- What were the new languages of freedom and how did they alter social, economic, and political relations in the Atlantic world?
- How did the concept of the nation-state challenge traditional political and social arrangements?
- What were the industrious and industrial revolutions and how did they transform the global economy?
- How did transformations in the Atlantic world alter the economic, political, and military balance in the world?

In 1798, the French commander Napoleon Bonaparte invaded Egypt. At the time, Europeans regarded this territory as the cradle of a once-great culture, a land bridge to the Red Sea and trade with Asia, and an outpost of the Ottoman Empire. Occupying the country would allow Napoleon to introduce some of the principles of the French Revolution and to seize control of trade routes to Asia. Napoleon also hoped that by defeating the Ottomans, who ruled over Egypt, he would augment his and France's historic greatness. But events did not go as Napoleon planned, for his troops faced a resentful Egyptian population.

Although Napoleon soon returned to France and his dream of a French Egypt was short-lived, his invasion challenged Ottoman rule and threatened the balance of power in Europe. Indeed, Napoleon's actions in Africa, the Americas, and Europe, combined with the principles of the French Revolution, laid the foundations for a new era—one based on a radically new idea—freedom—which first rang out across western Europe and the Americas. Freedom was expected to manifest itself in personal relationships, economic exchanges, and political action. In Europe and the Americas, though not elsewhere, the era also witnessed the emergence of the nation-state. This new form of political organization derived legitimacy from its inhabitants, often referred to as citizens, who in theory, if not always in practice, shared a common culture, ethnicity, and language.

The demand for freedom had its roots in the Atlantic world, where it destroyed the American colonial domains of Spain, Portugal, Britain, and France and brought new nations to the stage. The impulse for change was a belief that new, unfettered institutions would benefit all. The watchwords of the age were free inquiry, free markets, free labor, and governments freely chosen by free individuals. Yet, freedom in some corners of the globe set the stage for unfreedoms elsewhere and led inexorably to changes in the worldwide balance of power. Even as western European countries lost their New World colonies, they gained economic and military strength, which further challenged Asian and African governments. In China, the ruling Manchus faced European pressure to permit expanded trade. In Egypt and the Ottoman Empire, reform-minded leaders tried to modernize. When the rise of Egypt threatened Europe's strategic interests in the eastern Mediterranean, the European states intervened to rein in that country's ambitions. Underlying much of these political and social upheavals were major changes in the world economy, in which countries began to produce goods less for their own population and more for people living in other places and countries around the globe, intensifying the trend for worlds coming together.

REVOLUTIONARY TRANSFORMATIONS AND NEW LANGUAGES OF FREEDOM

In the eighteenth century, the circulation of goods, people, and ideas created pressures for reform around the Atlantic world. As economies expanded, many people felt that the restrictive mercantilist system prevented them from sharing in the new wealth and power. Similarly, an increasingly literate public called for their states to adopt just practices, including the abolition of torture and the accountability of rulers. Although elites resisted the demands for more freedom to trade and more influence in government, power holders could not stamp out these demands before they became—in several places—full-scale revolutions.

Reformers wanted to establish **popular sovereignty** (power residing in the people themselves) and argued that unregulated economies would produce faster economic growth. In fact, they argued that three important aspects of such economies would yield more just and more efficient societies, ultimately benefiting everyone everywhere in the world. These three aspects were **free trade**, that is, domestic and international trade unencumbered by tariff barriers, quotas, and fees; **free markets**, which would be unregulated; and **free labor**, which meant wage-paying rather than slave labor.

The struggle to create new political and economic relationships gave people the chance to think differently. Two new ideas were especially appealing: **nationalism** (the idea that members of a shared community called a "nation" should have sovereignty within the borders of their state) and **democracy** (the idea that these people, through membership in a nation, should choose their own representatives and be governed by them). The first expression of this new thinking occurred in thirteen of Britain's North American colonies and in France. In both places, the "nation" and the "people" toppled their former rulers.

As democratic and nationalist ideas emerged in the American and French revolutions, questions arose as to how far freedom should be extended. Should women, Native Americans, and slaves be given the rights of citizens? Should people without property be given the vote? Should freedom be extended to non-Europeans? For the most part, European and Euro-American elites answered no. The same elites who wanted a freer world often exploited slaves, denied women equal treatment, restricted colonial economies, and tried to forcibly open Asia's and Africa's markets to European trade and investment. In Africa, another corner of the Atlantic world, idealistic upheavals did not lead to free and sovereign peoples, but to greater enslavement.

POLITICAL REORDERINGS

Late in the eighteenth century, revolutionary ideas spread across the Atlantic world (see Map 15.1) following the trail of Enlightenment ideas about freedom and reason. As more newspapers, pamphlets, and books circulated in European countries and American colonies, readers began to discuss their societies' problems and to believe they had the right to participate in governance.

The slogans of independence, freedom, liberty, and equality seemed to promise an end to oppression, hardship, and inequities. In the North American colonies and in France, revolutions ultimately brought down monarchies and blossomed in republics. The examples of the United States and France soon encouraged others in the Caribbean and Central and South America to reject the rule of monarchs. In all of these revolutionary environments, new institutions—such as written constitutions and permanent parliaments—claimed to represent the people. The claims of popular sovereignty also became rooted in the idea of the nation (people of a common language, common culture, and common history), giving rise to the notion of the **nation-state**.

The North American War of Independence, 1776–1783

By the mid-eighteenth century, Britain's colonies in North America swelled with people and prosperity. Bustling port cities like Charleston, Philadelphia, New York, and Boston saw inflows of African slaves, European migrants, and manufactured goods, while agricultural staples flowed out. A "genteel" class of merchants and landowning planters dominated colonial affairs.

But with settlers arriving from Europe and slaves from Africa, land was a constant source of dispute. Planters struggled with independent farmers (yeomen). Sons and daughters of farmers, often unable to inherit or acquire land near their parents, moved westward, where they came into conflict with Amerindian peoples. To defend their lands, many Indians allied with Britain's rival, France. After losing the Seven Years' War (see Chapter 13), however, France ceded its Canadian colony to Britain. This left many Indians no choice but to turn to Britain to help them resist the aggressive advances of land-hungry colonists. British officials did make some concessions to Indian interests, most visibly by issuing the Proclamation of 1763, which drew a line at the crest of the Appalachians beyond which Indian lands were to be protected from colonial settlement. Still, Britain did not have the troops to police the line, so while the proclamation antagonized some colonists, it did not really secure Indian lands.

The Boston Massacre. *Paul Revere's idealized view of the Boston Massacre of March 5, 1770. In the years after the Seven Years' War, Bostonians grew increasingly disenchanted with British efforts to enforce imperial regulations. When British troops fired on and killed several members of an angry mob in what came to be called the "Boston Massacre," the resulting frenzy stirred revolutionary sentiments among the populace.*

ASSERTING INDEPENDENCE FROM BRITAIN Even as tensions simmered and sometimes boiled over into bloodshed on the western frontier of British North America, the situation of the British in North America still looked very strong in the mid-1760s. At that point, Britain stood supreme in the Atlantic world, with its greatest foes defeated and its empire expanding. Political revolution seemed unimaginable. And yet, a decade later, that is what occurred.

The spark came from King George III, who insisted that colonists help pay for Britain's war with France and for the benefits of being subjects of the British Empire. It seemed only reasonable to King George and his ministers, faced with staggering war debts, that colonists contribute to the crown that protected them. Accordingly, the king's officials imposed taxes on a variety of commodities and tried to end the lucrative smuggling by which colonists had been evading the restrictions that mercantilism was supposed to impose on colonial trade. To the king's surprise and dismay, colonists raised vigorous objections to the new measures and protested having to pay taxes when they lacked political representation in the British Parliament. (See Primary Source: The Other Revolution of 1776.)

In 1775, resistance in the form of petitions and boycotts turned into open warfare between a colonial militia and British troops in Massachusetts. Once blood was spilled, more radical voices came to the fore. Previously, leaders of the resistance to taxation without representation had claimed to revere the British Empire while fearing its corruptions. Now calls for severing the ties to Britain became more prominent. Thomas Paine, a recent immigrant from England, captured the new mood in a pamphlet he published in 1776, arguing that it was "common sense" for people to govern themselves. Later that year, the Continental Congress (in which representatives from thirteen colonies gathered) adapted part of Payne's popular pamphlet for the Declaration of Independence.

Drawing on Enlightenment themes (see Chapter 14), the declaration written by Thomas Jefferson stated the people's natural rights to govern themselves. It also drew inspiration from the writings of the British philosopher John Locke, notably the idea that governments should be based on a **social contract** in which the law binds both ruler and people. Locke had even written that the people had the right to rebel against their government if it broke the contract and infringed on their rights.

With the Declaration of Independence, the rebels announced their right to rid themselves of the English king and form their own government. But neither the Declaration of Independence nor Locke's writings explained how these colonists (now calling themselves Americans) should organize a nonmonarchical

Hudson
Bay
RUSSIA
BRITISH NORTH AMERICA
OREGON
(Claimed by Spain, Russia and Britain)
Quebec
Boston
New York
Philadelphia
Washington, D.C.
LOUISIANA
UNITED STATES
1776
(independence recognized by Great Britain 1783)
Charleston
Santa Fe
MEXICO
1821
FLORIDA
ATLANTIC
OCEAN
Gulf of Mexico
CUBA
PUERTO RICO
Mexico City
BELIZE
JAMAICA
REPUBLIC OF HAITI
1804
GUADELOUPE (Fr.)
MARTINIQUE (Fr.)
UNITED PROVINCES OF CENTRAL AMERICA
1823
Cartagena
Caracas
TRINIDAD (Br.)
PACIFIC
OCEAN
REPUBLIC OF COLOMBIA
1819
GUIANA
Quito
PERU
1821
Lima
BRAZIL
1822
BOLIVIA
1825
PARAGUAY
1811
Rio de Janeiro
CHILE
1818
PROVINCES OF LA PLATA
1816
URUGUAY
1828
Buenos Aires
Montevideo
British possessions
Spanish possessions
French possessions
Portuguese possessions
Dutch possessions
Ottoman possessions
Russian Empire
1776 Date of political independence from European (or Ottoman) colonial rule
0
1000
2000 Miles
0
1000
2000 Kilometers

MAP 15.1 | Revolutions of National Independence in the Atlantic World, 1776–1829

Influenced by Enlightenment thinkers and the French Revolution, colonies gained independence from European powers (and in the case of Greece, from the Ottoman Empire) in the late eighteenth and early nineteenth centuries.

- Which European powers granted independence to their colonial possessions in the Americas during this period? What were the first two colonial territories to become independent in the Americas?
- Given that the second American republic arose from a violent slave revolt, why do you suppose the United States was reluctant to recognize its political independence?
- According to your reading, why did colonies in Spanish and Portuguese America obtain political independence decades after the United States won its independence?

PRIMARY SOURCE

The Other Revolution of 1776

The year 1776 is mainly known as the year American colonists declared their independence from the British Empire. But it also marked the publication of Adam Smith's* An Inquiry into the Nature and Causes of the Wealth of Nations, *the most important book in the history of economic thought. Smith, a Scottish philosopher, felt that constraints on trade (by governments or private monopolies) prevented people from achieving their full potential and thereby impoverished nations. Although he was not opposed to colonies per se, in this selection Smith warns British authorities that mercantilist controls on their colonies are not only unjust but counterproductive. Thus, "free trade" is tied to the fate of Europe's colonies.

The exclusive trade of the mother countries tends to diminish, or, at least, to keep down below what they would otherwise rise to, both the enjoyments and industry of all those nations in general, and of the American colonies in particular. . . . By rendering the colony produce dearer in all other countries, it lessens its consumption, and thereby cramps the industry of the colonies, and both the enjoyments and the industry of all other countries, which both enjoy less when they pay more for what they enjoy, and produce less when they get less for what they produce.

By rendering the produce of all other countries dearer in the colonies, it cramps, in the same manner, the industry of all other countries, and both the enjoyments and the industry of the colonies. It is a clog which, for the supposed benefit of some particular countries, embarrasses the pleasures, and encumbers the industry of all other countries; but of the colonies more than of any other.

It not only excludes, as much as possible, all other countries from one particular market; but it confines, as much as possible, the colonies to one particular market: and the difference is very great between being excluded from one particular market, when all others are open, and being confined to one particular market, when all others are shut up. The surplus produce of the colonies, however, is the original source of all that increase of enjoyments and industry which Europe derives from the discovery and colonization of America; and the exclusive trade of the mother countries tends to render this source much less abundant than it otherwise would be.

QUESTIONS FOR ANALYSIS

- In terms of the American colonies, who is "the mother country"?
- According to Smith, how does exclusive trade between the mother country and the colonists diminish the colonies' development?

Source: Adam Smith, An Inquiry into the Nature and Causes of the Wealth of Nations, *Book 4, edited by Edwin Cannan (Chicago: University of Chicago Press, 1776/1977), pp. 105–106.*

government—or how thirteen weakly connected colonies (now calling themselves states) might prevail against the world's most powerful empire. Nonetheless, the colonies soon became embroiled in a revolution that would turn the world upside down.

During their War of Independence, Americans designed new political arrangements. First, individual states elected delegates to constitutional conventions, where they drafted written constitutions to govern the workings of each state. Second, by eliminating royal authority, the state constitutions gave extensive powers to legislative bodies, whose members "the people" would elect. But who constituted the people? That is, who had voting rights? Not women. Not slaves. Not Indians. Not even adult white men who owned no property.

Despite the limited extent of voting rights, the notion that all men were created equal overturned former social hierarchies. Thus common men no longer automatically deferred to gentlemen of higher rank. Many women claimed that their contributions to the Revolution's cause (by managing farms and shops in their husbands' absence) earned them greater equality in marriage, including property rights. In letters to her husband, John Adams, who was a representative in the Continental Congress and a champion of American independence, Abigail Adams stopped referring to the family farm as "yours" and instead called it "ours." Most revolutionary of all, many slaves sided against the Revolution, for it was the British who offered them freedom—most directly in exchange for military service.

Alas, their hopes for freedom were thwarted when Britain conceded the loss of its rebellious American colonies. That improbable outcome owed to a war in which British armies won most of the major battles but could not finish off the Continental Army under the command of General George Washington. Washington

Abigail Adams. *Abigail Adams was the wife of John Adams, a leader in the movement for American independence and later the second president of the United States. Abigail's letters to her husband testified to the ways in which revolutionary enthusiasm for liberty and equality began to reach into women's minds. In the spring of 1776, Abigail wrote to implore that the men in the Continental Congress "remember the ladies, and be more generous and favorable to them than your ancestors. . . . If particular care and attention is not paid to the Ladies we are determined to foment a Rebellion, and will not hold ourselves bound by any Laws in which we have no voice, or Representation."*

hung on and held his troops together long enough to convince the French that the American cause was not hopeless and that supporting it might be a way to settle a score against the British. This they did, and with the Treaty of Paris (1783) the United States gained its independence.

BUILDING A REPUBLICAN GOVERNMENT With independence, the former colonists had to build a new government. They generally agreed that theirs was not to be a monarchy. But what it *was* to be remained through the 1780s a source of much debate, involving heated words and sometimes heated action.

Amid the political revolution against monarchy, the prospect of a social revolution of women, slaves, and artisans generated a reaction against what American elites called the "excesses of democracy." Their fears increased after farmers in Massachusetts, led by Daniel Shays, interrupted court proceedings in which the state tried to foreclose on their properties for nonpayment of taxes. The farmers who joined in Shays's rebellion in 1786 also denounced illegitimate taxation—this time, by their state's government. Acting in the interests of the fledgling government, Massachusetts militiamen defeated the rebel army. But to save the young nation from falling into "anarchy," propertied men convened the Constitutional Convention in Philadelphia a year later.

This gathering aimed to forge a document that would create a more powerful national government and a more unified nation. After fierce debate, the convention drafted a charter for a **republican government** in which power and rulership would rest with representatives of the people—not a king. When it went before the states for approval, the Constitution was controversial. Its critics, known as Anti-Federalists, feared the growth of a potentially tyrannical national government and insisted on including a Bill of Rights to protect individual liberties from abusive government intrusions. Ultimately the Constitution won ratification, and it was soon amended by the Bill of Rights.

Ratification of the Constitution and the addition of the Bill of Rights did not end arguments about the scope and power of the national government of the United States, although they did quiet the most heated controversies. In an uneasy truce, political leaders agreed not to let the debate over whether to abolish slavery escalate into a cause for disunion. As the frontier pushed westward, however, the question of which new states would or would not allow slavery sparked debates again. Initially, the existence of ample land postponed a confrontation. In 1800, Thomas Jefferson's election as the third president of the United States marked the triumph of a model of sending pioneers out to new lands in order to reduce conflict on old lands. In the same year, however, a Virginia slave named Gabriel Prosser raised an army of slaves to seize the state capital at Richmond and won support from white artisans and laborers for a more inclusive republic. His dream of an egalitarian revolution fell victim to white terror and black betrayal, though: twenty-seven slaves, including Prosser, went to the gallows. With them, for the moment, died the dream of a multiracial republic in which all men were truly created equal.

But the issue of slavery did not go away. Indeed, with ideas of the dignity and rights of free labor gaining popularity in the northern states, the truce by which political leaders tried to keep debates over slavery from escalating into a cause for disunion became even more uneasy.

In a larger Atlantic world context, the American Revolution ushered in a new age based on ideas of freedom. The successful defiance of Europe's most powerful empire and the establishment of a nonmonarchical, republican form of government sent shock waves through the Americas and Europe and even into distant corners of Asia and Africa.

The French Revolution, 1789–1799

Partly inspired by the American Revolution, French men and women soon began to call for liberty too—and the result profoundly shook Europe's dynasties and social hierarchies. Its impact, though, reached well beyond Europe, for the French Revolution, even more than the American, inspired rebels and terrified rulers around the globe.

ORIGINS AND OUTBREAK For decades, enlightened thinkers had attacked France's old regime—the court, the aristocracy, and the church—at the risk of imprisonment or exile. But by the mid-eighteenth century, discontent had spread beyond the educated few. In the countryside, peasants grumbled about having to pay taxes and tithes to the church, whereas nobles and clergy paid almost no taxes. Also, despite improved health and nutrition, peasants still suffered occasional deprivation. A combination of these pressures, as well as a fiscal crisis, unleashed the French Revolution of 1789.

Ironically, the king himself opened the door to revolution. Eager to weaken his rival, England, Louis XVI spent huge sums in support of the American rebels—and thereby overloaded the state's debt. It was not the size of the debt but the French king's inability to raise funds that put him in a bind. To restore his credit, Louis needed to raise taxes on the privileged classes, but to do so he was forced to convene the Estates-General, a medieval advisory body that had not met for over a century. Like the American colonists, French nobles argued that taxation gave them the right of representation. When the king reluctantly agreed to summon the Estates-General in 1788, he still thought he would prevail. After all, the delegates of the clergy (the First Estate) and the aristocracy (the Second Estate) could overrule the delegates representing everyone else (the Third Estate), because each estate voted as one body. This meant that it was possible to outvote the Third Estate.

However, when the delegates assembled, the Third Estate refused to be outvoted. It insisted that those who worked and paid taxes *were* the nation, and it demanded that all delegates sit together in one chamber and vote as individuals. The privileged few, critics claimed, were parasites. As arguments raged, peasants began to attack castles in another indication that "the people" were throwing off old inequalities. Soon delegates of the Third Estate declared themselves to be the "National Assembly," the body that should determine France's future.

On July 14, 1789, a Parisian crowd attacked a medieval armory in search of weapons. Not only did this armory—the Bastille—hold gunpowder, but it was also an infamous prison for political prisoners. The crowd stormed the prison and murdered the commanding officer, then cut off his head and paraded it through the streets of Paris. On this day (Bastille Day), the king made the fateful decision not to call out the army, and the capital city belonged to the crowd. As news spread to the countryside, peasants torched manor houses and destroyed municipal archives containing records of the hated feudal dues. Barely three weeks later, the French National Assembly abolished the feudal privileges of the nobility and the clergy. It also declared a new era of liberty, equality, and fraternity.

REVOLUTIONARY TRANSFORMATIONS The "Declaration of the Rights of Man and Citizen" followed a few weeks later. It echoed the Americans' Declaration of Independence, but in more radical terms. It guaranteed all citizens of the French nation inviolable liberties and gave all men equality under the law. It also proclaimed that "the principle of all sovereignty rests essentially in the nation." Thus, the French Revolution connected more closely the concept of a people with a nation. Both the rhetorical and the real war against feudal privileges threatened to end dynastic and aristocratic rule in Europe.

The "Tennis Court Oath." *Locked out of the chambers of the Estates-General, the deputies of the Third Estate reconvened at a nearby indoor tennis court in June 1789; there they swore an oath not to disband until the king recognized the sovereignty of a national assembly.*

Women March on Versailles. *On October 5, 1789, a group of market women, many of them fishwives (traditionally regarded as leaders of the poor), marched on the Paris city hall to demand bread. Quickly, their numbers grew, and they redirected their march to Versailles, some twelve miles away and the symbol of the entire political order. In response to the women, the king finally appeared on the balcony and agreed to sign the revolutionary decree and return with the women to Paris.*

Relations in social hierarchies changed too, as women felt that the new principles of citizenship should include women's rights. In 1791, a group of women demanded the right to bear arms to defend the revolution, but they stopped short of claiming equal rights for both sexes. In their view, women would become citizens by being good revolutionary wives and mothers, not because of any natural rights. In the same year, Olympe de Gouges composed the "Declaration of the Rights of Woman and Citizen," proposing rights to divorce, hold property in marriage, be educated, and have public careers. The all-male assembly did not take up these issues, believing that a "fraternity" of free *men* composed the nation. (For a statement claiming similar rights for women in Britain, see Primary Source: Mary Wollstonecraft on the Rights of Women.)

As the revolution gained momentum, more nobles and clergy fled the country. In late 1790, all clergy had to take an oath of loyalty to the new state—an action that enraged Catholics. Meanwhile, the revolutionary ranks began to splinter, as men and women argued over the revolution's proper goals. Soon a new National Convention was elected by universal manhood suffrage, meaning that all adult males could vote—the first such election in Europe. In 1792, the first French Republic was proclaimed. But radicalization continued, and by early 1793 Louis XVI had lost his head to the guillotine, and France was at war with many of its neighbors.

THE TERROR After the king's execution, radicals known as Jacobins, who wanted to extend the revolution beyond France's borders, launched the Reign of Terror to purge the nation of its internal enemies. Jacobin leaders, including the lawyer Maximilien Robespierre, oversaw the execution of as many as 40,000 so-called enemies of the people—mostly peasants and laborers.

To spread revolution to other parts of Europe, the radicals instituted the first national draft. By 1794 France's army numbered some 800,000 soldiers, making it the world's largest. Most French officers now came from the middle classes, some even from the lower class. Foot soldiers identified with the French fatherland and demonstrated their solidarity by singing songs like "The Marseillaise."

The revolutionaries understood that to change society they would have to eliminate all symbols of the old regime. So they changed street names to honor revolutionary heroes, destroyed monuments to the royal family, adopted a new flag, eliminated titles, and insisted that everyone be addressed as "Citizen." They were so exhilarated by the new world they were creating that they changed time itself. Now they reckoned time not from the birth of Christ but from the moment the French Republic was proclaimed. Thus September 22, 1792, became day 1 of year 1 of the new age. The radicals also unsuccessfully attempted to replace the Catholic faith, which they accused of corruption and inequality, with a religion of reason.

By mid-1794, enthusiasm for Robespierre's measures had lost popular support, and Robespierre himself went to the guillotine on 9 Thermidor (July 28, 1794). His execution marked the end of the Terror. Several years later, following more political turmoil, a coup d'état brought to power a thirty-year-old general from the recently annexed Mediterranean island of Corsica.

The general, **Napoleon Bonaparte** (1769–1821), put security and order ahead of social reform. True, his regime retained many of the revolutionary changes, especially those associated with more efficient state government, but retreating from the Jacobins' anti-Catholicism, he allowed religion to be freely practiced again in France. Determined not only to reform France but also to prevail over its enemies, he retreated from republican principles. Napoleon first was a member of a three-man consulate;

PRIMARY SOURCE

Mary Wollstonecraft on the Rights of Women

As revolutionaries stressed the rights of "man" across the Atlantic world, Mary Wollstonecraft (1759–1797), an English writer, teacher, editor, and proponent of spreading education, resented her male colleagues' celebration of their newfound liberties. In* A Vindication of the Rights of Woman *(1792), one of the founding works of modern feminism, she argued that the superiority of men was as arbitrary as the divine right of kings. For this, male progressives denounced her. The author is a "hyena in petticoats," noted one critic. In fact, she was arguing that women had the same rights to be reasonable creatures as men and that education should be available equally to both sexes.

I love man as my fellow; but his sceptre, real or usurped, extends not to me, unless the reason of an individual demands my homage; and even then the submission is to reason, and not to man. In fact, the conduct of an accountable being must be regulated by the operations of its own reason; or on what foundation rests the throne of God?

It appears to me necessary to dwell on these obvious truths, because females have been insulated, as it were; and while they have been stripped of the virtues that should clothe humanity, they have been decked with artificial graces that enable them to exercise a short-lived tyranny. Love, in their bosoms, taking the place of every nobler passion, their sole ambition is to be fair, to raise emotion instead of inspiring respect; and this ignoble desire, like the servility in absolute monarchies, destroys all strength of character. Liberty is the mother of virtue, and if women be, by their very constitution, slaves, and not allowed to breathe the sharp invigorating air of freedom, they must ever languish like exotics, and be reckoned beautiful flaws in nature. Let it also be remembered, that they are the only flaw.

As to the argument respecting the subjection in which the sex has ever been held, it retorts on man. The many have always been enthralled by the few; and monsters, who scarcely have shown any discernment of human excellence, have tyrannized over thousands of their fellow-creatures. Why have men of superior endowments submitted to such degradation? For, is it not universally acknowledged that kings, viewed collectively, have ever been inferior, in abilities and virtue, to the same number of men taken from the common mass of mankind—yet have they not, and are they not still treated with a degree of reverence that is an insult to reason? China is not the only country where a living man has been made a God. *Men* have submitted to superior strength to enjoy with impunity the pleasure of the moment; *women* have only done the same, and therefore till it is proved that the courtier, who servilely resigns the birthright of a man, is not a moral agent, it cannot be demonstrated that woman is essentially inferior to man because she has always been subjugated.

QUESTIONS FOR ANALYSIS

- Wollstonecraft compares men to kings and women to slaves. What are her criticisms of kings, and why does she call them "monsters"?
- In what ways are Wollstonecraft's ideas an outgrowth of Enlightenment thinking?
- Do you find Wollstonecraft's arguments compelling? Explain why or why not.

Source: Mary Wollstonecraft, A Vindication of the Rights of Woman, *edited by Miriam Brody (New York: Penguin Books, 1792/1993), pp. 122–23.*

then he became first consul; finally, he proclaimed himself emperor. But he took the title Emperor of the French, not Emperor of France, and prepared a constitution subject to a vote of approval. He also centralized government administration and created a system of rational tax collection. Most important, he created a civil legal code—the "Code Napoleon"—that applied throughout all of France (and the French colonies, including the Louisiana Territory). By designing a law code applicable to the nation as a whole, Napoleon created a model that would be widely imitated by emerging nation-states in Europe and the Americas in the century to come.

Napoleon's Empire, 1799–1815

Determined to extend the reach of French influence, Napoleon had his armies trumpet the principles of liberty, equality, and fraternity wherever they went. Many local populations actually embraced the French, regarding them as liberators from the old order. Although Napoleon thought the entire world would take up his cause, this was not always the case, as he learned in Egypt. After defeating Mamluk troops there in 1798, Napoleon soon faced a rebellious local Egyptian population.

Battle of the Pyramids. *The French army invaded Egypt with grand ambitions and high hopes. Napoleon brought a large cadre of scholars along with his 36,000-man army, intending to win Egyptians to the cause of the French Revolution and to establish a French imperial presence on the banks of the Nile. This idealized portrait of the famous* Battle of the Pyramids, *fought on July 21, 1798, shows Napoleon and his forces crushing the Mamluk military forces.*

In Portugal, Spain, and Russia, French troops also faced fierce popular resistance. Portuguese and Spanish soldiers and peasants formed bands of resisters called guerrillas, and British troops joined them to fight the French in the Peninsular War (1808–1813). In Germany and Italy, as local inhabitants grew tired of hearing that the French occupiers' ways were superior, many looked to their past for inspiration to oppose the French. Now they discovered something they had barely recognized before: *national* traditions and borders. In fact, one of the ironies of Napoleon's attempt to bring all of Europe under French rule was that instead of creating a unified continent, it laid the foundations for nationalist strife.

In Europe, Napoleon extended his empire from the Iberian Peninsula to the Austrian and Prussian borders (see Map 15.2). By 1812, when he invaded Russia, however, his forces were too overstretched and undersupplied to survive the harsh winter. Until this point, divisions among his enemies had aided Napoleon's progress. But after his failed attack on Russia, all the major European powers united against him. Forced to retreat, Napoleon and his army were vanquished in Paris. Subsequently Napoleon escaped exile to lead his troops one last time; but at the Battle of Waterloo in Belgium in 1815, armies from Prussia, Austria, Russia, and Britain crushed his troops as they made their last stand.

In 1815, delegates from the victorious states met at the Congress of Vienna. They agreed to respect one another's borders and to cooperate in preventing future revolutions and war. They restored thrones to monarchs deposed by the French under Napoleon, and they returned France itself to the care of a new Bourbon king. Great Britain and Russia—one a constitutional monarchy (ruled by a prime minister and legislative body, with oversight by a king), the other an autocracy (in which the ruler did not share power with anyone)—cooperated to prevent any future attempts to dominate the continent.

The impact of the French Revolution and Napoleon's conquests, however, was far-reaching. In numerous German states, the changes introduced under French revolutionary occupation remained in place. Napoleon's occupation of the Italian peninsula also sparked underground movements for liberty and for Italian unification, much to the chagrin of Austrian and French monarchs. These upheavals even affected Spain and Portugal's links to their colonies in the Americas. The stage was now set for a century-long struggle between those who wanted to restore society as it was before the French Revolution and those who wanted to guarantee a more liberal order based on individual rights, limited government, and free trade.

Revolutions in the Caribbean and Iberian America

REVOLUTION IN SAINT DOMINGUE (HAITI) The thirteen colonies were not the only ones to secede from European masters. France also saw colonies break away in this age of new freedoms. This was the case in Saint Domingue. Unlike most of British North America, here the revolution came from the

MAP 15.2 | Napoleon's Empire, 1812

Early in the first decade of the nineteenth century, Napoleon controlled almost all of Europe.

- What major states were under French control? What countries were allied to France?
- Compare this map with the European part of Map 15.1, and explain how Napoleon redrew the map of Europe. What major country was not under French control?
- How was Napoleon able to control and build alliances with so many states and kingdoms?

bottom rungs of the social ladder: slaves. In this Caribbean colony, freedom therefore meant not just liberation from Europe, but emancipation from white planters. Saint Domingue therefore added a second, global dimension to the nineteenth-century struggle over personal liberties. It also posed very dramatically the question: how universal were these new rights?

The French Revolution sent shock waves through this highly prized French colony. At the time, the island's black slave population numbered 500,000, compared with 40,000 white French settlers and about 30,000 free "people of color" (individuals of mixed black and white ancestry, as well as freed black slaves). Almost two-thirds of the slaves were relatively recent arrivals, brought to the colony to toil on its renowned sugar plantations. The slave population was an angry majority producing wealth for a rich minority of a different race.

After the events of 1789 in France, white settlers in Saint Domingue sought self-government, while slaves borrowed the revolutionary language to denounce their masters. As civil war erupted, Dominican slaves fought French forces that had arrived to restore order. Finally, in 1793, the National Convention in France abolished slavery. In part, the motive was to declare the universality of liberty, equality, and fraternity within the French nation, which included colonies. In part, it was to restore order to the colony.

Once liberated, the former slaves took control of the island, but their struggles were not over. First they had to fight British and Spanish forces on the island. Then Napoleon took power in France, restored slavery, and sent an army to suppress forces led by Toussaint L'Ouverture, a former slave. But before long a combination of guerrilla fighters and yellow fever decimated the French army. In 1804, General Jean-Jacques Dessalines declared "Haiti" independent (see Current Trends in World History: Two Case Studies of Greed and Environmental Degradation as Evidence that History Matters).

The specter of a free country ruled by former slaves sent shudders across the Western Hemisphere. What if the revolt went viral? All around the Caribbean, news circulated about slave conspiracies. In Florida, fugitive slaves banded together with Seminole Indians to drive European settlers into the sea. The Haitian government contributed money and some troops to insurrectionists in South America. Charleston, South Carolina, went into a panic in 1793 when Dominican slaves were freed. As far away as Albany, New York, slaves were executed for arson. Jamaican rulers went on high alert. A version of martial law was declared in Venezuela. Even Thomas Jefferson, author of the Declaration of Independence and U.S. president at the time, refused to recognize Haiti. Like other American slave owners, he worried that the example of a successful slave uprising might inspire similar revolts in the United States.

Revolution in Saint Domingue. *In 1791, slaves and people of color rose up against white planters. This engraving was based on a German report on the uprising and depicts white fears of slave rebellion as much as the actual events themselves.*

The revolution in Saint Domingue therefore tilted the scales of campaigns for liberty far beyond the island. Fear of the contagion of slave revolt forced some governments to rethink the commitment to slavery altogether. The British government curtailed the expansion of plantation agriculture in Trinidad. One by one, European and American governments began to question the wisdom of importing more African slaves lest they lose control of their colonies. It was not just exalted ideals of liberty that fueled the abolitionist movement, but also the fear of what would happen if slaves rose up violently to claim rights given to other humans. Conservative thinkers like Edmund Burke took note; when he heard that 10,000 British soldiers died fighting Haitian slaves, he declared that fighting against such revolutionaries was like trying to conquer a cemetery! One of the greatest German philosophers of all time, Georg Wilhelm Friedrich Hegel, was an avid reader of the influential political journal *Minerva*. Hegel pored over the news of events in Saint Domingue and the freedom struggle of blacks as he was writing his famous treatise, *The Phenomenology of Mind*. That book would present a powerful image that would guide thinkers for the nineteenth and twentieth centuries: the image of slaves and masters locked in a struggle for mutual recognition and rights. Among those most charged by this image was Karl Marx.

From North America and France, revolutionary enthusiasm spread through Spanish and Portuguese America. But unlike the colonists' war of independence that produced the United States, political upheaval in the rest of the Americas began first of all from subordinated people of color. Then it was fueled by Napoleon's wider, global ambitions (see Map 15.3).

Even before the French Revolution, Andean Indians rebelled against Spanish colonial authority. In a spectacular uprising in the 1780s, they demanded freedom from forced labor and compulsory consumption of Spanish wares. After an army of 40,000 to 60,000 Andean Indians besieged the ancient capital of Cuzco and nearly vanquished Spanish armies, it took Spanish forces many years to eliminate the insurgents.

After this uprising, Iberian-American elites who feared their Indian or slave majorities renewed their loyalty to the Spanish or Portuguese crown. They hesitated to imitate the independence-seeking Anglo-American colonists, lest they unleash a social revolution. Ultimately, however, the French Revolution and Napoleonic wars shattered the ties between Spain and Portugal and their American colonies. Nonetheless, elites limited local power by interpreting "liberty" to apply just to property-owning classes.

CURRENT TRENDS IN WORLD HISTORY

Two Case Studies in Greed and Environmental Degradation

The Caribbean has four large islands, known as the Greater Antilles, each of which has a distinctive history—Cuba, Jamaica, Puerto Rico, and Hispaniola. Our discussion here is about the island of Hispaniola, which Columbus discovered in 1492 and which briefly became the center of Spain's New World empire. Later, in the seventeenth century, the French took over the smaller, western part of the island, and when political independence came to the Caribbean the island evolved into the two present-day states of Haiti and the Dominican Republic. Although both are relatively poor countries, their present economic and social differences are markedly and surprisingly different, especially considering that they share a relatively small island.

Haiti is the poorest country in the Americas. It is 99 percent deforested, suffers from massive soil erosion, and has a government unable to provide even the most basic services of water, electricity, and education to its people. Right next door, the Dominican Republic, with a population roughly the same size as Haiti's, has five times as many cars and trucks, six times as many paved roads, seven times as many college and university graduates, and eight times as many physicians. Its citizens enjoy significantly longer life expectancy and lower infant mortality than their Haitian neighbors. The differences cry out for an explanation, and one can be found only by examining the radically different histories of the two lands.

Two hundred and fifty years ago, Haiti, which was under French colonial rule at that time and known as Saint Domingue, was the richest colony in the Americas, perhaps even the richest colony in the world, accounting for two-thirds of France's worldwide investment. In contrast, Spanish-ruled Santo Domingo, which had ceased to be of interest to the Spanish colonial elites, who had turned their attention to the more populous and resource-rich territories of Mexico and Peru, was a backwater colonial territory. Saint Domingue's extraordinary wealth came from large, white-owned sugar plantations that used a massive and highly coerced slave population. The slaves' lives were short and brutal, lasting on average only fifteen years; hence the wealthy planter class had to replenish their labor supplies from Africa at frequent intervals.

White planters on the island were eager to amass quick fortunes so that they could sell out and return to France. Vastly outnumbered by enslaved Africans at a time when abolitionist sentiments were gaining ground in Europe and even

Toussaint L'Ouverture. *In the 1790s, Toussaint L'Ouverture led the slaves of the French colony of Saint Domingue in the world's largest and most successful slave insurrection. Toussaint embraced the principles of the French Revolution and demanded that universal rights be applied to people of African descent.*

BRAZIL AND CONSTITUTIONAL MONARCHY Brazil was a prized Portuguese colony whose path to independence saw little political turmoil and no social revolution. In 1807, French troops stormed Lisbon, the capital of Portugal, but not before the royals and their associates fled to Rio de Janeiro, then the capital of Brazil. There they made reforms in administration, agriculture, and manufacturing, and they established schools, hospitals, and a library. In fact, the royals' migration prevented the need for colonial claims for autonomy, because with their presence Brazil was now the center of the Portuguese empire. Furthermore, the royal family willingly shared power with the local planter aristocracy, so the economy prospered and slavery expanded.

In 1821, the exiled Portuguese king returned to Lisbon, instructing his son Pedro to preserve the family lineage in Rio de Janeiro. Soon, however, Brazilian elites rejected Portugal altogether. Fearing that colonists might topple the dynasty in Rio de Janeiro and spark regional disputes, in 1822 Pedro declared Brazil an independent empire. Shortly thereafter he established a constitutional monarchy, which would last until the late nineteenth century.

Now Brazilian business elites and bureaucrats cooperated to minimize conflicts, lest a slave revolt erupt. They crushed circulating among slaves in the Americas, the planters' families knew that their prosperity was unlikely to last. They gave little thought to sustainable growth and were not troubled that they were destroying their environment.

Yet, the planters greeted the onset of the French Revolution in 1789 with enthusiasm. They saw an opportunity to assert their independence from France, to engage in wider trading contacts with North America and the rest of the world, and thus to become even richer. They ignored the possibility that the ideals of the French Revolution—especially its slogan of liberty, equality, and fraternity—could inspire the island's free blacks, free mulattoes, and slaves. Indeed, no sooner had the white planters thrown in their lot with the Third Estate in France than a slave rebellion broke out in Saint Domingue. From its beginnings in 1791, it led, after great loss of life to African slaves and French soldiers, to the proclamation of an independent state in Haiti in 1804, ruled by African Americans. Haiti became the Americas' second independent republican government.

Although the revolt brought political independence to its black population, it only intensified the land's environmental deterioration. Not only did sugarcane fields become scorched battlefields, but freed slaves rushed to stake out independent plots on the old plantations and in wooded areas. In both places, the new peasant class energetically cleared the land. The small country became even more deforested, and intensive cultivation increased erosion and soil depletion. Haiti fell into a more vicious cycle of environmental degradation and poverty.

The second case study of greed leading to the destruction of the environment comes from the independent Brazilian state where the ruling elite, having achieved autonomy from Portugal, expanded the agrarian frontier. Landowners oversaw the clearing of ancient hardwood forests so that slaves and squatters could plant coffee trees. The clearing process had begun with sugarcane in the coastal regions, but it accelerated with coffee plantings in the hilly regions of São Paulo. In fact, coffee was a worse threat to Brazil's forests than any other invader in the previous 300 years. Consider that coffee trees thrive on soils that are neither soggy nor overly dry. Therefore planters razed the "virgin" forest, which contained a balanced variety of trees and undergrowth, and Brazil's once-fertile soil suffered rapid depletion by a single-crop industry. Within one generation the clear-cutting led to infertile soils and extensive erosion, which drove planters farther into the frontier to destroy even more forest and plant more coffee groves. The environmental impact was monumental: between 1788 and 1888, when slavery was abolished, Brazil produced about 10 million tons of coffee at the expense of 300 million tons of ancient forest biomass (the accumulated biological material from living organisms).

QUESTIONS FOR ANALYSIS

- Who intensified the deforestation and degradation in each story, and why did they do it?
- Why do you think deforestation increased in intensity after Haitians and Brazilians gained their autonomy/independence?

Explore Further

David Geggus (ed.), *The Impact of the Haitian Revolution in the Atlantic World* (2001).

Diamond, Jared, and James A. Robinson (eds.), *Natural Experiments of History* (2010).

regional uprisings, like the fledgling Republic of the Equator, and a campaign seeking a decentralized federation of southern provinces free from the Rio de Janeiro rulers. Even the largest urban slave revolt in the Americas, led by African Muslims in the state of Bahia, was quashed in a matter of days. By the 1840s, Brazil had achieved a political stability unmatched in the Americas. Its socially controlled transition from colony to nation was unique in Latin America.

MEXICO'S INDEPENDENCE When Napoleon occupied Spain, he sparked a crisis in the Spanish empire. Because the ruling Spanish Bourbons fell captive to Napoleon in 1807, colonial elites in Buenos Aires (Argentina), Caracas (Venezuela), and Mexico City (Mexico) enjoyed self-rule without an emperor. Once the Bourbons returned to power in 1814 after Napoleon was crushed, creoles (American-born Spaniards) resented it when Spain reinstated peninsulars (colonial officials born in Spain) and wanted to free themselves of these officials.

In Mexico, the royal army prevailed as long as there was any hope that the emperor in Madrid could maintain political authority. But from 1810 to 1813 two rural priests, Father Miguel Hidalgo and Father José María Morelos, galvanized

MAP 15.3 | Latin American Nation Building

Creating strong, unified nation-states proved difficult in Latin America. The map highlights this experience in Mexico, the United Provinces of Central America, and the Republic of Colombia. In each case, the governments' territorial and nation-building ambitions failed to some degree.

- During what period did a majority of the colonies in Latin America gain independence?
- Which European countries lost the most in Latin America during this period?
- Why did all these colonies gain their independence during this time?

an insurrection of peasants, Indians, and artisans. They sought an end to abuses by the elite, denounced bad government, and called for redistribution of wealth, return of land to the Indians, and respect for the Virgin of Guadalupe (who later became Mexico's patron saint). The rebellion nearly choked off Mexico City, the colony's capital, which horrified peninsulars and creoles alike and led them to support royal armies that eventually crushed the uprising.

Despite the military victory, Spain's hold on its colony weakened. Like the creoles of South America, those of Mexico identified themselves more as Mexicans and less as Spanish Americans. So when the Spanish king appeared unable to govern effectively abroad and even within Spain, the colonists considered home rule. A critical factor was the army, which remained faithful to the crown. However, when anarchy seemed to spread through Spain in 1820, Mexican generals (with support of the creoles) proclaimed Mexican independence in 1821. Unlike in Brazil, Mexican secession did not lead to stability.

OTHER SOUTH AMERICAN REVOLUTIONS The loosening of Spain's grip on its colonies was more prolonged and militarized than Britain's separation from its American colonies. Venezuela's **Simón Bolívar** (1783–1830), the son of a merchant-planter family who was educated on Enlightenment texts, dreamed of a land governed by reason. He revered Napoleonic France as a model state built on military heroism and constitutional proclamations. So did the Argentine leader General José de San Martín (1778–1850). Men like Bolívar, San Martín, and their many generals waged extended wars of independence against Spanish armies and their allies between 1810 and 1824. In some areas, like present-day Uruguay and Venezuela, the wars left entire provinces depopulated.

What started in South America as a political revolution against Spanish colonial authority escalated into a social struggle among Indians, mestizos, slaves, and whites. The militarized populace threatened the planters and merchants; rural folk battled against aristocratic creoles; Andean Indians fled the mines and occupied great estates. Provinces fought

Latin American Revolutionaries. (Left) *At the center of this Juan O'Gorman mural is the Mexican priest and revolutionary Miguel Hidalgo y Costilla, who led—as O'Gorman portrays—a multiclass and multiethnic movement.* (Right) *Simón Bolívar fought Spanish armies from Venezuela to Bolivia, securing the independence of five countries with the greater goal of transforming the former colonies into modern republics. Among his favorite models were George Washington and Napoleon Bonaparte, whose iconic portrait by Jacques-Louis David inspired this painting of Bolívar.*

their neighbors. Popular armies, having defeated Spanish forces by the 1820s, fought civil wars over the new postcolonial order.

New states and collective identities of nationhood now emerged. However, a narrow elite led these political communities, and their guiding principles were contradictory. Simón Bolívar, for instance, urged his followers to become "American," to overcome their local identities. He wanted the liberated countries to form a Latin American confederation, urging Peru and Bolivia to join Venezuela, Ecuador, and Colombia in the "Gran Colombia." But local identities prevailed, giving way to unstable national republics. Bolívar died surrounded by enemies; San Martín died in exile. The real heirs to independence were local military chieftains, who often forged alliances with landowners. Thus the legacy of the Spanish American revolutions was contradictory: the triumph of wealthy elites under a banner of liberty, yet often at the expense of poorer, ethnic, and mixed populations.

CHANGE AND TRADE IN AFRICA

Africa also was swept up in revolutionary tides, as increased domestic and world trade—including the selling of African slaves—shifted the terms of state building across the continent. The main catalyst for Africa's political shake-up was the rapid growth and then the demise of the Atlantic slave trade.

Abolition of the Slave Trade

Even as it enriched and empowered some Africans and many Europeans, the slave trade became a subject of fierce debate in the late eighteenth century. Some European and American revolutionaries argued that slave labor was inherently less productive than free wage labor and ought to be abolished. At the same time, another group favoring abolition of the slave trade insisted that traffic in slaves was immoral. In London they created committees, often led by Quakers, to lobby Parliament for an end to the slave trade. Quakers in Philadelphia did likewise. Pamphlets, reports, and personal narratives denounced the traffic in people. (See Primary Source: Frederick Douglass Asks, "What to the Slave Is the Fourth of July?")

In response to abolitionist efforts, North Atlantic powers moved to prohibit the slave trade. Denmark acted first in 1803, Great Britain followed in 1807, and the United States joined the campaign in 1808. Over time, the British persuaded the French and other European governments to do likewise. To enforce the ban, Britain posted a naval squadron off the coast of West Africa to prevent any slave trade above the equator and compelled Brazil's emperor to end slave imports. After 1850, Atlantic slave-shipping dropped sharply.

But until the 1860s, slavers continued to buy and ship captives illegally. British squadrons that stopped these smugglers

PRIMARY SOURCE

Frederick Douglass Asks, "What to the Slave Is the Fourth of July?"

Frederick Douglass spent the first twenty years of his life as a slave. After running away in 1838, he toured the northern United States delivering speeches that attacked the institution of slavery. The publication of his autobiography in 1845 cemented his standing as a leading abolitionist. In the excerpt below, taken from an address delivered on July 5, 1852, Douglass contrasts the freedom and natural rights extolled in the Declaration of Independence and celebrated on the Fourth of July with the dehumanizing condition—and lack of freedom—of African American slaves.

Fellow-Citizens—pardon me, and allow me to ask, why am I called upon to speak here to-day? What have I, or those I represent, to do with your national independence? Are the great principles of political freedom and of natural justice, embodied in that Declaration of Independence, extended to us? and am I, therefore, called upon to bring our humble offering to the national altar, and to confess the benefits, and express devout gratitude for the blessings, resulting from your independence to us?. . .

But, such is not the state of the case. I say it with a sad sense of the disparity between us. I am not included within the pale of this glorious anniversary! Your high independence only reveals the immeasurable distance between us. The blessings in which you this day rejoice, are not enjoyed in common. The rich inheritance of justice, liberty, prosperity, and independence, bequeathed by your fathers, is shared by you, not by me. The sunlight that brought life and healing to you, has brought stripes and death to me. This Fourth of July is *yours*, not *mine*. *You* may rejoice, *I* must mourn. . . .

Must I undertake to prove that the slave is a man? That point is conceded already. Nobody doubts it. The slaveholders themselves acknowledge it in the enactment of laws for their government. They acknowledge it when they punish disobedience on the part of the slave. There are seventy-two crimes in the state of Virginia, which, if committed by a black man (no matter how ignorant he be) subject him to the punishment of death; while only two of these same crimes will subject a white man to the like punishment. What is this but the acknowledgment that the slave is a moral, intellectual, and responsible being. The manhood of the slave is conceded. It is admitted in the fact that southern statute books are covered with enactments forbidding, under severe fines and penalties, the teaching of the slave to read or write. When you can point to any such laws, in reference to the beasts of the field, then I may consent to argue the manhood of the slave. When the dogs in your streets, when the fowls of the air, when the cattle on your hills, when the fish of the sea, and the reptiles that crawl, shall be unable to distinguish the slave from a brute, then will I argue with you that the slave is a man!

QUESTIONS FOR ANALYSIS

- What examples does Douglass give of the disparity between slaves and free white Americans?
- How does Douglass suggest that slaves are human beings?
- What is the significance of the last sentence of the speech?

Source: David W. Blight (ed.), Narrative of the Life of Frederick Douglass: An American Slave, Written by Himself *(Boston: Bedford Books, 1993), pp. 141–45.*

took the freed captives to the British base at Sierra Leone and resettled them there. Liberia, too, became a refuge for freed captives and for former slaves returning from the Americas.

New Trade with Africa

Even as the Atlantic slave trade died down, Europeans promoted commerce with Africa. Now they wanted Africans to export raw materials and to purchase European manufactures. What Europeans liked to call "legitimate" trade aimed to raise the Africans' standards of living by substituting trade in produce for trade in slaves. West Africans responded by exporting palm kernels and peanuts. The real bonanza was in vegetable oils to lubricate machinery and make candles and in palm oil to produce soap. Africa's palm and peanut plantations were less devastating to the environment than their predecessors in the West Indies had been. There, planters had felled forests to establish sugar estates (see Chapter 12). In West Africa, where palm products became crucial exports, the palm tree had always grown

Chasing Slave Dhows. *From being the major proponents of the Atlantic slave trade the British became its chief opponents, using their naval forces to suppress those European and African slave traders who attempted to subvert the injunction against slave trading. Here a British vessel chases an East African slaving dhow trying to run slaves from the island of Zanzibar.*

wild. Although intensive cultivation caused some deforestation, the results were not as extreme as in the Caribbean. Regardless of the environmental impact, European merchants argued that by becoming vibrant export societies, Africans would earn the wealth to profitably import European wares.

SUCCESS IN THE AGE OF LEGITIMATE COMMERCE Arising in the age of legitimate commerce, the new trade gave rise to a generation of successful West African merchants. There were many rags-to-riches stories, like that of King Jaja of Opobo (1821–1891). Kidnapped and sold into slavery as a youngster, he started out paddling canoes carrying palm oil to coastal ports. Ultimately becoming the head of a coastal canoe house, as a merchant-prince and chief he founded the port of Opobo and could summon a flotilla of war canoes on command. Another freed slave, a Yoruba, William Lewis, made his way back to Africa and settled in Sierra Leone in 1828. Starting with a few utensils and a small plot of land, he became a successful merchant who sent his son Samuel to England for his education. Samuel eventually became an important political leader in Sierra Leone.

EFFECTS IN AFRICA Just as the slave trade shaped African political communities, its demise brought sharp adjustments. For some, it was a welcome end to the constant drainage of people. For others, it was a disaster because it cut off income necessary to buy European arms and luxury goods. Many West African regimes, like the Yoruba kingdom, collapsed once chieftains could no longer use the slave trade to finance their retinues and armies.

The rise of free labor in the Atlantic world and the dwindling foreign slave trade had an unanticipated and perverse effect in Africa. It strengthened slavery. In some areas, by the mid-nineteenth century, slaves accounted for more than half the population. No longer did they comfortably serve in domestic employment; instead, they toiled on palm oil plantations or, in East Africa, on clove plantations. They also served in the military forces, bore palm oil and ivory to markets as porters, or paddled cargo-carrying canoes along rivers leading to the coast. In 1850, northern Nigeria's ruling class had more slaves than independent Brazil, and almost as many as the United States. No longer the world's supplier of slaves, Africa itself had become the world's largest slaveholding region.

ECONOMIC REORDERING

Behind the political and social upheavals, profound changes were occurring in the world economy. Until the middle of the eighteenth century, global trade touched only the edges of societies, most of which produced for their own subsistence. Surpluses of special goods, from porcelains to silks, entered trade arteries but did not change the cultures that produced them. An exception was the Americas, where especially in the slave societies of the Caribbean, Brazil, and the southern United States, plantations produced goods for export. Yet, this commercial specialization anticipated developments to come, in which communities would be transformed to produce for other societies and less and less for themselves. This gradual, halting, but ineluctable process would gather speed in the eighteenth century and bring the world together in ways that were unimaginable during the age of older European empires.

An Industrious Revolution

Many of these developments took place first in northwestern Europe and British North America. Here, as elsewhere in the world, households had always produced mainly for themselves and made available for marketplaces only meager surpluses of goods and services. But dramatic changes occurred when family members, including wives and children, decided to work harder and longer in order to produce more for the market and purchase more in the market. In these locations, households devoted less time to leisure activities and more time to working, using the additional income from hard work to improve their standards of living. Scholars recently have come to call this change an **industrious revolution**. Beginning in the second half of the seventeenth century, it gained speed in the eighteenth century and laid the foundations for the industrial revolution of the late eighteenth and early nineteenth centuries.

The willingness on the part of families to work more and an eagerness to eat more diverse foods, to wear better clothes, and to consume products that had once been available as luxuries only to the wealthy classes led in turn to a large expansion in trade—both regionally and globally. By the eighteenth century, separate trading spheres described in earlier chapters were merging increasingly into integrated circuits. Sugar and silver were the pioneering products. But by the eighteenth century, other staples joined the long-distance trading business. Tea, for instance, became a beverage of world trade. Its leaves came from China, the sugar to cut its bitterness from the Caribbean, the slaves to harvest the sweetener from Africa, and the ceramics from which to drink a proper cup from the English Midlands.

The significance of growing cross-cultural trade and specialization, and the shift away from a few precious cargoes to basic staples, can be seen in the story of a single commodity: soap. By the 1840s, the American entrepreneur William Colgate was importing palm oil from West Africa, coconut oil from Malabar and Ceylon, and poppy seed oil from South Asia, all to make aromatic bars of soap. A London barber called Andrew Pears added glycerine to his product to give it a clean, transparent look, and his grandson-in-law, Thomas Barratt, launched an aggressive marketing campaign—in 1886 buying a painting from the *Illustrated London News* called "Bubbles" to enhance the image of his family's soap. Colgate and his Atlantic rivals in the toiletry trade like Pears advertised their products as necessities for the prim and proper home. Pears promised African and Indian buyers that his product would actually whiten their skin.

Global trading trickled its way down from elites to ordinary folk. Even ordinary people could purchase imported goods with their earnings. Thus, the poor began to enjoy—some would say became addicted to—coffee, tea, and sugar, and eventually

New Farming Technologies. *Although new technologies only gradually transformed agriculture, the spread of more intensive cultivation led to increased yields.*

even felt the need to use soap. European artisans and farmers purchased tools, furnishings, and home decorations. Slaves and colonial laborers also used their meager earnings to buy imported cotton cloth made in Europe from the raw cotton they themselves had picked several seasons earlier.

The expansion of global trade had important social and political consequences. In many dynastic societies, merchants had long stood high in the social hierarchy, but few extended their business beyond provincial confines. As new goods flowed from ever more distant corners of the globe, immense fortunes grew. To support their enterprise, traders needed new services, in insurance, bookkeeping, and the recording of legal documents. Trade helped nurture the emergence of new classes of professionals—accountants and lawyers. The new cities of the commercial revolution, hubs like Bristol, Bombay, and Buenos Aires, provided the homes and flourishing neighborhoods for a class of men and women known as the **bourgeoisie**.

As Europe moved to the center of this new economic order, one class in particular moved to the top: the trader-financiers. Like the merchandiser, the financier did not have to emerge from the high and mighty of Eurasia's dynasties. Consider Mayer Amschel Rothschild (1744–1812): born the son of a money changer in the Jewish ghetto of Frankfurt, Rothschild progressed from coin dealing to money changing, then from trading textiles to lending funds to kings and governments. By the time of his death he owned the world's biggest banking operation and his five sons were running powerful branches in London, Paris, Vienna, Naples, and Frankfurt.

By extending credit, families like the Rothschilds also enabled traders to ship goods across long distances without having to worry about immediate payment. All these financial changes implied world integration through the flow of goods as well as the flow of money. In the 1820s, sizeable funds amassed in London flowed to Egypt, Mexico, and New York to support trade, public investment, and, of course, speculation.

The Industrial Revolution

Trade and finance repositioned western Europe's relationship with the rest of the world. So did the emergence of manufacturing—a big leap, as in agriculture, in the output, in this case of industrial commodities. The heart of this process was a gradual accumulation and diffusion of technical knowledge. Lots of little inventions, their applications, and their diffusion across the Atlantic world gradually built up a stock of technical knowledge and practice. Historians have traditionally called these changes the **industrial revolution**, a term first used by the British economic historian Arnold Toynbee in the late nineteenth century. Although the term suggests radical and rapid economic change, the reality was much more gradual and less dramatic than originally believed. Yet, the term still has great validity, for the major economic changes that occurred in Britain, northwestern Europe, and North America catapulted these countries ahead of the rest of the world in industrial and agricultural output and standards of living.

Nowhere was this industrial revolution more evident than in Britain. Britain had a few advantages, like large supplies of coal and iron—key materials used in manufactured products. It also had a political and social environment that allowed merchants and industrialists to invest heavily while also expanding their internal and international markets. Among their investments was the application of steam power to textile production—which enabled Britain's manufacturers to produce cheaper goods in larger quantities. Finally, Britain had access to New World lands as sources of financial investment, raw materials, and markets for manufactured goods. These factors' convergence in Britain promoted self-sustaining economic growth.

An example of the new alliance of the inventor and the investor that fueled the industrial revolution was the advent of the steam engine. Such engines burned coal to boil water, and the resulting steam drove mechanized devices. There were several tinkerers working on the device. But the most famous was James Watt (1736–1819) of Scotland, who managed to separate steam condensers from piston cylinders so that pistons could stay hot and run constantly, and who also joined forces with the industrialist Matthew Boulton, who marketed the steam engine and set up a laboratory where Watt could refine his device. The steam engine catalyzed a revolution in transportation. Steam-powered engines also improved sugar refining, pottery making, and other industrial processes, generating more products at lower cost than when workers had made them by hand.

Technical changes made possible the consolidation of textile manufacturing within a single factory. With new machinery, a single textile operator handled many looms and spindles at once and produced bolts of cloth with stunning efficiency. Gone were the hand tools, the family traditions, and the loosely organized and dispersed systems of households putting out cloth for local merchants to carry to markets. The material was also stronger, finer, and more uniform. All the while, the price of cotton cloth almost halved between 1780 and 1850. As England became the world's largest cloth producer, it imported cotton from Brazil, Egypt, India, and the United States.

Most raw cotton for the British cloth industry had come from colonial India until 1793, when the American inventor Eli Whitney (1765–1825) patented a "cotton gin" that separated cotton seeds from fiber. After that, cotton farming spread so quickly in the southern United States that by the 1850s it was producing more than 80 percent of the world's cotton supply. In turn, every black slave in the Americas and many Indians in British India were consumers of cheap, British-produced cotton shirts.

A Cotton Textile Mill in the 1830s. *The region of Lancashire became one of the major industrial hubs for textile production in the world. By the 1830s, mills had made the shift from artisanal work to highly mechanical mass production. Among the great breakthroughs was the discovery that cloth could be printed with designs, such as paisley or calico (as in this image), and marketed to middle-class consumers.*

It is important to note that the industrial revolution did not imply the creation of large-scale industries. The large factory was rare in manufacturing. Indeed, the largest employers at the time were the slave plantations of the Americas that produced the staples for industrial consumption. Small-scale production remained the norm, mass production the exception. Small-scale production simply became more efficient through innovations in techniques and machinery. The silks of Lyon, cutlery of Solingen, calicoes of Alsace, and cottons of Pawtucket, Rhode Island, were all products of small firms in heavily industrialized belts.

Wherever the industrial revolution took hold, it allowed societies to outdistance rivals in manufacturing and elevated them to a new place in the emerging global economic order (see Map 15.4). But why did this revolution cluster mainly in the Atlantic world? This is an important question, because the unequal distribution of global wealth, the gap between the haves and have-nots, really took off in this era of revolutions. In much of Asia and Africa, technical change altered modes of production and business practices, but it was not followed by a continuous cascade of changes. The great mystery was China, the home of astronomical water clocks and gunpowder. Why did China not become the epicenter of the industrial revolution?

There are two reasons. China did not foster experimental science of the kind that allowed Watt to stumble onto the possibility of steam, or Procter and Gamble to invent floating soap. Experimentation, testing, and the links between thinkers and investors were a distinctly Atlantic phenomenon. The Qing, like the Mughal and Ottoman dynasties, swept the great minds into the bureaucracy and reinforced the old agrarian system based on peasant exploitation and tribute. Second, Chinese rulers did not support overseas expansion and trade that helped create the commercial revolution in the Atlantic world. The agrarian dynasties of China and India neither showered favors on local merchants nor effectively shut out interlopers. This made them vulnerable to cheap manufactured imports from European traders backed by their governments extolling the virtues of free trade.

The effects were profound. Historically, Europe had a trade imbalance with partners to the east—furs from Russia, and spices and silks from Asia. It made up for this with silver from the Americas. But the new economic order meant that by the nineteenth century, western Europe not only had manufactures like soap to export to Asia, it also had capital. One of Europe's biggest debtors was none other than the sultan of the Ottoman Empire, whose tax system could not keep up with spending necessary to keep the realm together. More and more, Asian, African, and American governments found themselves borrowing from Europe's financiers just as their people were buying industrial products from Europe and selling their primary products to European consumers and producers.

Working and Living

The industrial revolution brought more demanding work routines—not only in the manufacturing economies of western Europe and North America but also on the farms and plantations of Asia and Africa. Although the European side of the story is better known, cultivators toiled harder and for longer hours throughout the rest of the world.

MAP 15.4 | Industrial Europe around 1850

By 1850 much of western Europe was industrial and urban, with major cities linked to one another through a network of railroads.

- According to this map, what natural resources contributed to the growth of the industrial revolution? What effects did it have on urban population densities?
- Explain how the presence of an extensive railroad system helped to accelerate industrialization.
- According to your reading, why were the effects of the industrial revolution more rapidly apparent in Great Britain and in north-central Europe?

URBAN LIFE AND WORK ROUTINES Increasingly, Europe's workers made their livings in cities. London, Europe's largest city in 1700, saw its population nearly double over the next century to almost 1 million. By the 1820s, population growth was even greater in the industrial hubs of Leeds, Glasgow, Birmingham, Liverpool, and Manchester. By contrast, in the Low Countries (Belgium and the Netherlands) and France, where small-scale, rural-based manufacturing flourished, the shift to cities was less extreme.

For most urban dwellers, cities were not healthy places. Water that powered the mills, along with chemicals used in dyeing, went directly back into waterways that provided drinking water. Overcrowded tenements shared just a few outhouses. Most European cities as late as 1850 had no running water, no garbage pickup, no underground sewer system. The result was widespread disease. (In fact, no European city at this time had as clean a water supply as the largest towns of the ancient Roman Empire once had.)

As families found jobs in factories, their wages bolstered family revenues. Children, wives, and husbands increasingly worked outside the home for cash, though some still made handicrafts inside the home as well. Urban employers experimented with paying according to the tasks performed or the number of goods produced per day. To earn subsistence wages, men, women, and children frequently stayed on the job for twelve or more hours at a time.

Changes in work affected the understanding of time. Whereas most farmers' workloads had followed seasonal rhythms, after 1800 industrial settings imposed a rigid concept of work discipline. To keep the machinery operating, factory and mill owners installed huge clocks and used bells or horns to signify the workday's beginning and end. Employers also measured output per hour and compared workers' performance. Josiah Wedgwood, a maker of teacups and other porcelain, installed a Boulton & Watt steam engine in his manufacturing plant and made his workers use it efficiently. He rang a bell at 5:45 in the morning so employees could start work as day broke. At 8:30 the bell rang for breakfast, at 9:00 to call them back, and at 12:00 for a half-hour lunch; it last tolled when darkness put an end to the workday. Sometimes, though, factory clocks were turned back in the morning and forward at night, falsely extending the exhausted laborers' workday.

Despite higher production, industrialization imposed numbing work routines and paltry wages. Worse, however, was having no work at all. As families abandoned their farmland and depended on wages, being idle meant having no income. Periodic downturns in the economy put wage workers at risk, and many responded by organizing protests. In 1834, the British Parliament centralized the administration of all poor relief and deprived able-bodied workers of any relief unless they joined a workhouse, where working conditions resembled those of a prison.

SOCIAL PROTEST AND EMIGRATION While entrepreneurs accumulated private wealth, the effects of the industrial revolution on working-class families raised widespread concern. In the 1810s in England, groups of jobless craftsmen, called Luddites, smashed the machines that had left them

A Model Textile Mill. *Distressed by the terrible working conditions of nineteenth-century textile mills, Welsh industrialist and reformer Robert Owen sought to create humane factories. From maintaining the orderliness of the factory floor to posting work rules on the walls, Owen's reforms saw significant improvements in the health and morale of his workers. Nonetheless, he would continue to employ children in his factories, like most of his contemporaries.*

ANALYZING GLOBAL DEVELOPMENTS

Town and Countryside, Core and Periphery in the Nineteenth Century

The textile industry was by far the most dynamic sector of the world economy in the nineteenth century. It was dependent on cotton, whose production was labor intensive but required relatively little capital investment and benefited little from economies of scale. In the first half of the century, cotton was primarily produced by slaves in the southern United States. By the late 1850s, the United States accounted for 77 percent of the cotton consumed in Britain, for 90 percent in France, and for about 92 percent in Russia. After the U.S. Civil War and subsequent slave emancipations, sharecroppers continued to produce the crop, though cotton production began to flourish in Brazil, Egypt, West Africa, and India.

Wheat, on the other hand, was the basic staple of European and Mediterranean diets well into the nineteenth century, and it remains vitally important. Before the advent of railroads, most wheat was consumed locally. In the second half of the century, however, vast quantities of wheat came onto world markets as railroads spread through the Midwest of the United States and the plains of Central and Eastern Europe. Grown on large, capital-intensive farms, that wheat—as well as rye, corn, millet, and other grains—fed radically expanding European and American industrial cities and factory towns, linking them to rich agricultural hinterlands and contributing unwittingly to the economic volatility of the nineteenth century. Here we chart the fortunes of two of the most important commodities of the nineteenth-century world—cotton and wheat—against the growth of cities and railroads.

QUESTIONS FOR ANALYSIS

- Which countries appear to be the most dynamic? Pay attention to relative change over time—not only in the biggest cities and most extensive rail networks but also in those growing the fastest.
- How do the growth of railroads and cities vary by country? What does this tell us about the relationship between economic core regions and their peripheries, and about patterns of inequality more generally?
- How did the extension of railroads, and the economic integration they fostered, influence patterns of inequality worldwide?

Population of Major Cities (in thousands)

	1800	1830	1850	1880	1900
Alexandria	15		60	231	320
Delhi		150	152	173	209
Rio de Janeiro	43	125	166	360	523
London	1,117		2,685	4,770	6,586
Paris	576		1,053	2,269	2,714
Moscow	250		365	748	989
New York City	60	161	340	847	1,478
Tokyo	457			824	1,819

Population Estimates (in thousands)

	1800	1825	1850	1875	1900
Egypt	3,854	4,541	4,752	6,961	10,186
India	255,000	257,000	285,000	306,000	
Brazil			7,678	9,930	17,438
England	8,893	12,000	17,928	22,712	32,528
France	27,349	30,462	35,783	36,906	38,451
Russia	35,500	52,300	68,500	90,200	132,900
America	5,297	11,252	23,261	45,073	76,094
Japan	25,622	26,602	27,201	25,037	44,359

Output of Cotton (in thousand metric tons)

	1800	1825	1850	1875	1900
Egypt				132	293
India			12	533	536
America	17	121	484	1,050	2,120

Wheat Production (in thousand metric tons)

	1825	1850	1875	1900
France	4,580	6,600	7,550	8,860
Russia			53	136
America		2,722	8,546	16,302

Length of Open Railway Lines (in kilometers)

	1825	1850	1875	1900
Egypt		1,184	1,410	2,237
India		32	10,527	39,834
Brazil		14	1,801	15,316
England	43	9,797	23,365	30,079
France	17	2,915	19,351	38,109
Russia	27	501	19,029	53,234
America	37	14,518	119,246	311,160
Japan		29	62	6,300

Source: Beckert, S., "Emancipation and Empire: Reconstructing the Worldwide Web of Cotton Production in the Age of the American Civil War," The American Historical Review *109, no. 5 (December 2004): 1405–1438; Mitchell, B.R.,* International Historical Statistics: Africa, Asia, and Oceania, 1750–2005, International Historical Statistics: The Americas, 1750–2005, *and* International Historical Statistics: Europe, 1750–2005 *(London : Palgrave Macmillan, 2007).*

unemployed. In 1849, the English novelist Charlotte Brontë published a novel, *Shirley*, depicting the misfortunes caused by the power loom. Charles Dickens described a mythic Coketown to evoke pity for the working class in his 1854 classic, *Hard Times*. Both Elizabeth Gaskell, in England, and Émile Zola, in France, described the hardships of women whose malnourished children were pressed into the workforce too early. Gaskell and Zola also highlighted the hunger, loneliness, and illness that prostitutes and widows endured. These social advocates sought protective legislation for workers, including curbing child labor, limiting the workday, and, in some countries, legalizing prostitution for the sake of monitoring the prostitutes' health.

Some people, however, could not wait for legislative reform. Thus, the period saw unprecedented emigration, as unemployed workers or peasants abandoned their homes to seek their fortunes in America, Canada, and Australia. During the Irish Potato Famine of 1845–1849, at least 1 million Irish citizens left their country (and a further million or so died) when fungi attacked their subsistence crop. Desperate to escape starvation, they booked cheap passage to North America on ships so notorious for disease and malnutrition that they earned the name "Coffin Ships." Those who did survive faced discrimination in their new land, for many Americans feared the immigrants would drive down wages or create social unrest.

PERSISTENCE AND CHANGE IN AFRO-EURASIA

Western Europe's military might, its technological achievements, and its economic strength represented a threat to the remaining Afro-Eurasian empires. Across the continent, western European merchants and industrialists sought closer economic and (in some cases) political ties. They did so in the name of gaining "free" access to Asian markets and products. In response, Russian and Ottoman rulers modernized their military organizations and hoped to achieve similar economic strides while distancing themselves from the democratic principles of the French Revolution. The remote Chinese empire was largely unaffected by the upheavals in Europe and America—until the first Opium War of the early 1840s forced the Chinese to acknowledge their military weaknesses. Thus, changes in the Atlantic world unleashed new pressures around the globe, though with varying degrees of intensity.

Revamping the Russian Monarchy

Some eastern European dynasties responded to the pressures by strengthening their traditional rulers, through modest reforms and the suppression of domestic opposition. This was how Russian rulers reacted. Tsar Alexander I (r. 1801–1825) was fortunate that Napoleon committed several blunders and lost his formidable army in the Russian snows. Yet the French Revolution and its massive, patriotic armies struck at the heart of Russian political institutions, which rested upon a huge peasant population laboring as serfs.

The tsars could no longer easily justify their absolutism by claiming that enlightened despotism was the most advanced form of government, since a new model, rooted in popular sovereignty and the concept of the nation, had arisen. In December 1825, when Alexander died unexpectedly and childless, there was a question over succession. Some Russian officers launched a patriotic revolt, hoping to convince Alexander's brother Constantine to take the throne (and to guarantee a constitution) in place of a more conservative brother, Nicholas. The Decembrists, as they were called, came primarily from elite families and were familiar with western European life and institutions. A few Decembrists called for a constitutional monarchy to replace Russia's despotism; others favored a tsar-less republic and the abolition of serfdom. But the officers' conspiracy failed to win over conservatives or the peasantry, who still believed in the tsar's divine right to rule. Constantine supported Nicholas's claim to power, so Nicholas (r. 1825–1855) became tsar and brutally suppressed the insurrectionists. For the time being, the influence of the French Revolution was quashed.

Still, Alexander's successors faced a world in which powerful European states had constitutions and national armies of citizens, not subjects. In trying to maintain absolutist rule, Russian tsars portrayed the monarch's family as the ideal historical embodiment of the nation with direct ties to the people. Nicholas himself prevented rebellion by expanding the secret police, enforcing censorship, conducting impressive military exercises, and maintaining serfdom. And in the 1830s he introduced a conservative ideology that stressed religious faith, hierarchy, and obedience. Even some officials and members of society who supported the monarchy wondered whether this would be enough to enable Russia to remain a competitive great power.

Reforming Egypt and the Ottoman Empire

Unlike in Russia, where Napoleon's army had reached Moscow, the Ottoman capital in Istanbul never faced a threat by French troops. Still, Napoleon's invasion of Egypt shook the Ottoman Empire. Even before this trauma, imperial authorities faced the challenge posed by increased trade with Europe—and the greater presence of European merchants and missionaries. In addition, many non-Muslim religious communities in the sultan's empire wanted the European powers to advance their interests. In the

Decembrists in St. Petersburg. *Russians energetically participated in the coalition that defeated Napoleon, but the ideas of the French Revolution greatly appealed to the educated upper classes, including aristocrats of the officer corps. In December 1825, at the death of Tsar Alexander I, some regimental officers staged an uprising of about 3,000 men, demanding a constitution and the end of serfdom. But Nicholas I, the new tsar, called in loyal troops and brutally dispersed the "Decembrists," executing or exiling their leaders.*

wake of Napoleon, who had promised to remake Egyptian society, reformist energies swept from Egypt to the center of the Ottoman domain. (See Primary Source: An Egyptian Intellectual's Reaction to the French Occupation of Egypt.)

REFORMS IN EGYPT In Egypt, far-reaching changes came with **Muhammad Ali**, a skillful, modernizing ruler. After the French withdrawal in 1801, Muhammad Ali (r. 1805–1848) won a chaotic struggle for supreme power in Egypt and aligned himself with influential Egyptian families. Yet he looked to revolutionary France for a model of modern state building. As with Napoleon (and with Simón Bolívar in Latin America), the key to his hold on power was the army. With the help of French advisors, the modernized Egyptian army became the most powerful fighting force in the Middle East.

Muhammad Ali also reformed education and agriculture. He established a school of engineering and opened the first modern medical school in Cairo under the supervision of a French military doctor. And his efforts in the countryside made Egypt one of the world's leading cotton exporters. A summer crop, cotton required steady watering when the Nile's irrigation waters were in short supply. So Muhammad Ali's public works department, advised by European engineers, deepened the irrigation canals and constructed a series of dams across the Nile. These efforts transformed Egypt, making it the most powerful state in the eastern Mediterranean and alarming the Ottoman state and the great powers in Europe.

Muhammad Ali's modernizing reforms, however, disrupted the habits of the peasantry. After all, incorporation into the industrial world economy involved harder work (as English wage workers had discovered), often with little additional pay. Because irrigation improvements permitted year-round cultivation, Egyptian peasants now had to plant and harvest three crops instead of one or two. Moreover, the state controlled the prices of cultivated products, so peasants saw little profit from their extra efforts. Young men also faced conscription into the state's enlarged army, while whole families had to toil, unpaid, on public works projects. In addition, a state-sponsored program of industrialization aimed to put Egypt on a par with Europe: before long, textile and munitions factories employed 200,000 workers. But Egypt had few skilled laborers or cheap sources of energy, so by the time of Muhammad Ali's death in 1849 few of the factories survived.

External forces also limited Muhammad Ali's ambitious plans. At first, his new army enjoyed spectacular success. But Muhammad Ali overplayed his hand when he sent forces into Syria in the 1830s and later when he threatened Anatolia, the heart of the Ottoman state. Fearing that an Egyptian ruler might attempt to overthrow the Ottoman sultan and threaten the balance of power in the eastern Mediterranean region, the European powers compelled Egypt to withdraw from Anatolia and reduce its army.

OTTOMAN REFORMS Under political and economic pressures like those facing Muhammad Ali in Egypt, Ottoman rulers also made reforms. Indeed, military defeats and humiliating treaties with Europe were painful reminders of the sultans' vulnerability. In 1805 Sultan Selim III tried to create a new infantry, trained by western European officers. But before he could bring this force up to fighting strength, the janissaries

PRIMARY SOURCE

An Egyptian Intellectual's Reaction to the French Occupation of Egypt

In the 1798 invasion of Egypt, Napoleon Bonaparte attempted to win rank-and-file Egyptian support against the country's Mamluks, who were the most powerful group in Egypt at the time though the country was still under the authority of the Ottoman sultan. Bonaparte portrayed himself as a liberator and invoked the ideals of the French Revolution, as he had done with great success all over Europe. His Egyptian campaign did not succeed, however, and local opposition was bitter. The chronicler Abd al-Rahman al-Jabarti has left one of the most perceptive accounts of these years.

On Monday news arrived that the French had reached Damanhur and Rosetta [in the Nile Delta]. . . . They printed a large proclamation in Arabic, calling on the people to obey them. . . . In this proclamation were inducements, warnings, all manner of wiliness and stipulations. Some copies were sent from the provinces to Cairo and its text is:

In the name of God, the Merciful, the Compassionate. There is no God but God. He has no son nor has He an associate in His Dominion.

On behalf of the French Republic which is based upon the foundation of liberty and equality, General Bonaparte, Commander-in-Chief of the French armies makes known to all the Egyptian people that for a long time the Sanjaqs [its Mamluk rulers] who lorded it over Egypt have treated the French community basely and contemptuously and have persecuted its merchants with all manner of extortion and violence. Therefore the hour of punishment has now come.

Unfortunately, this group of Mamluks . . . have acted corruptly for ages in the fairest land that is to be found upon the face of the globe. However, the Lord of the Universe, the Almighty, has decreed the end of their power.

O ye Egyptians . . . I have not come to you except for the purpose of restoring your rights from the hands of the oppressors and that I more than the Mamluks serve God. . . .

And tell them also that all people are equal in the eyes of God and the only circumstances which distinguish one from the other are reason, virtue, and knowledge. . . . Formerly, in the lands of Egypt there were great cities, and wide canals and extensive commerce and nothing ruined all this but the avarice and the tyranny of the Mamluks.

[Jabarti then challenged the arguments in the French proclamation and portrayed the French as godless invaders, inspired by false ideals.] They follow this rule: great and small, high and low, male and female are all equal. Sometimes they break this rule according to their whims and inclinations or reasoning. Their women do not veil themselves and have no modesty. . . . Whenever a Frenchman has to perform an act of nature he does so where he happens to be, even in full view of people, and he goes away as he is, without washing his private parts after defecation. . . .

His saying "[all people] are equal in the eyes of God" the Almighty is a lie and stupidity. How can this be when God has made some superior to others as is testified by the dwellers in the Heavens and on Earth?. . .

So those people are opposed to both Christians and Muslims, and do not hold fast to any religion. You see that they are materialists, who deny all God's attributes. . . . May God hurry misfortune and punishment upon them, may He strike their tongues with dumbness, may He scatter their hosts, and disperse them.

QUESTIONS FOR ANALYSIS

- When the proclamation speaks of "the fairest land that is to be found upon the face of the globe," what land is it referring to?
- Why do you think Napoleon's appeals to the ideals of the French Revolution failed with Egyptians?
- Why does al-Jabarti claim that the invaders are godless even though the proclamation clearly suggests otherwise?

Source: Abd al-Rahman al-Jabarti, Napoleon in Egypt: Al-Jabarti's Chronicle of the French Occupation, 1798, *translated by Shmuel Moreh (Princeton, NJ: Markus Wiener Publishing, 1993), pp. 24–29.*

stormed the palace, killed its officers, and deposed Selim in 1807. Over the next few decades, janissary military men and clerical scholars (*ulama*) cobbled together an alliance that continuously thwarted reformers.

Why did reform falter in the Ottoman state before it could be implemented? After all, in France and Spain the old regimes were also inefficient and burdened with debts and military losses. But reform was possible only if the forces of restraint—especially

Muhammad Ali. *The Middle Eastern ruler who most successfully assimilated the educational, technological, and economic advances of nineteenth-century Europe was Muhammad Ali, ruler of Egypt from 1805 until 1848.*

in the military—were weak and the reformers strong. In the Ottoman Empire, the janissary class had grown powerful, providing the main resistance to change. Ottoman authority depended on clerical support, and the Muslim clergy also resisted change. Blocked at the top, Ottoman rulers were hesitant to appeal for popular support in a struggle against anti-reformers. Such an appeal, in the new age of popular sovereignty and national feeling, would be dangerous for an unelected dynast in a multiethnic and multireligious realm.

Mahmud II (r. 1808–1839), who acknowledged Europe's rising power, broke the political deadlock. He shrewdly manipulated his conservative opponents. Convincing some clerics that the janissaries neglected traditions of discipline and piety, and promising that a new corps would pray fervently, the sultan won the *ulama*'s support and in 1826 established a European-style army corps. When the janissaries plotted their inevitable mutiny, Mahmud rallied clerics, students, and subjects. The schemers retreated to their barracks, only to be shelled by the sultan's artillery and then destroyed in flames. Thousands of other janissaries were rounded up and executed.

The sultan could now pursue reform within an autocratic framework. Like Muhammad Ali in Egypt, Mahmud brought in European officers to advise his forces. Here, too, military reform spilled over into nonmilitary areas. The Ottoman modernizers created a medical college, then a school of military sciences. To understand Europe better and to create a first-rate diplomatic corps, the Ottomans schooled their officials in European languages and had European classics translated into Turkish. As Mahmud's successors extended reforms into civilian life, this era—known as the Tanzimat, or Reorganization period—saw legislation that guaranteed equality for all Ottoman subjects, regardless of religion.

The reforms, however, stopped well short of revolutionary change. For one thing, reform relied too much on the personal whim of rulers. Also, the bureaucratic and religious infrastructure remained committed to old ways. Moreover, any effort to reform the rural sector met resistance by the landed interests. Finally, the merchant classes profited from business with a debt-ridden sultan. By preventing the empire's fiscal collapse through financial support to the state, bankers lessened the pressure for reform and removed the spark that had fired the revolutions in Europe. Together, these factors impeded reform in the Ottoman Empire.

Colonial Reordering in India

Europe's most important colonial possession in Asia between 1750 and 1850 was British India. Unlike in North America, the changes that the British fostered in Asia did not lead to political independence. Instead, India was increasingly dominated by the **East India Company**, which the crown had chartered in 1600. The company's control over India's imports and exports in the eighteenth and nineteenth centuries, however, contradicted British claims about their allegiance to a world economic system based on "free trade."

THE EAST INDIA COMPANY'S MONOPOLY Initially the British, through the East India Company, tried to control India's commerce by establishing trading posts along the coast but without taking complete political control. After conquering the state of Bengal in 1757, the company began to fill its coffers and its officials began to amass personal fortunes. Even the British governor of Bengal pocketed a portion of the tax revenues. Such unbridled abuse of power caused the Bengal army, along with forces of the Mughal emperor and of the ruler of Awadh, to revolt. Although the rebels were unsuccessful, British officials left the emperor and most provincial leaders in place—as nominal rulers. Nonetheless, the British secured the right for the East India Company to collect tax revenues in

Indian Resistance to Company Rule. *Tipu Sultan, the Mysore ruler, put up a determined resistance against the British. This painting by Robert Home shows Cornwallis, the East India Company's governor, receiving Tipu's two sons as hostages after defeating him in the 1792 war. The boys remained in British custody for two years. Tipu returned to fighting the British and was killed in the war of 1799.*

Bengal, Bihar, and Orissa and to trade free of duties throughout Mughal territory. In return, the emperor would receive a hefty annual pension. The company went on to annex other territories, bringing much of South Asia under its rule by the early 1800s (see Map 15.5).

To carry out its responsibilities, the East India Company needed to establish a civil administration. Rather than place Britons in these positions, the company enlisted Hindu kings and Muslim princes; they retained royal privileges while losing their autonomy. The emperor himself was now permanently under the thumb of the company's administrators. Yet the company did not depend entirely on local leaders, for it also maintained a large standing army and a centralized bureaucracy. Together, the military force, the bureaucracy, and an array of local leaders enabled the company state to guarantee security and the smooth collection of revenues.

To rule with minimal interference, however, required knowing the conquered society. This led to Orientalist scholarship: English scholar-officials wrote the first modern histories of South Asia, translated Sanskrit and Persian texts, identified philosophical writings, and compiled Hindu and Muslim law books. Through their efforts, the company state presented itself as a force for revitalizing authentic Hinduism and recovering India's literary and cultural treasures. Although the Orientalist scholars admired Sanskrit language and literature, they still supported English colonial rule and did not necessarily agree with local beliefs.

EFFECTS IN INDIA Maintaining a sizeable military and civilian bureaucracy also required taxation. Indeed, taxes on land were the East India Company's largest source of revenue. From 1793 onward, land policies required large and small landowners alike to pay taxes to the company. As a result, large estate owners gained more power and joined with the company in determining who could own property. Whenever smaller proprietors defaulted on their taxes, the company put their properties up for auction, with the firm's own employees and large estate owners often obtaining title.

Company rule and booming trade altered India's urban geography as well. By the early nineteenth century, colonial cities like Calcutta, Madras, and Bombay became the new centers at the expense of older Mughal cities like Agra, Delhi, Murshidabad, and Hyderabad. As the colonial cities attracted British merchants and Indian clerks, artisans, and laborers, their populations surged. Calcutta's reached 350,000 in 1820; Bombay's jumped to 200,000 by 1825. In these cities, Europeans lived close to the company's fort and trading stations, while migrants from the countryside clustered in crowded quarters called "black towns."

Back in Britain, the debts of rural Indians and the conditions of black towns generated little concern. Instead, calls for reform

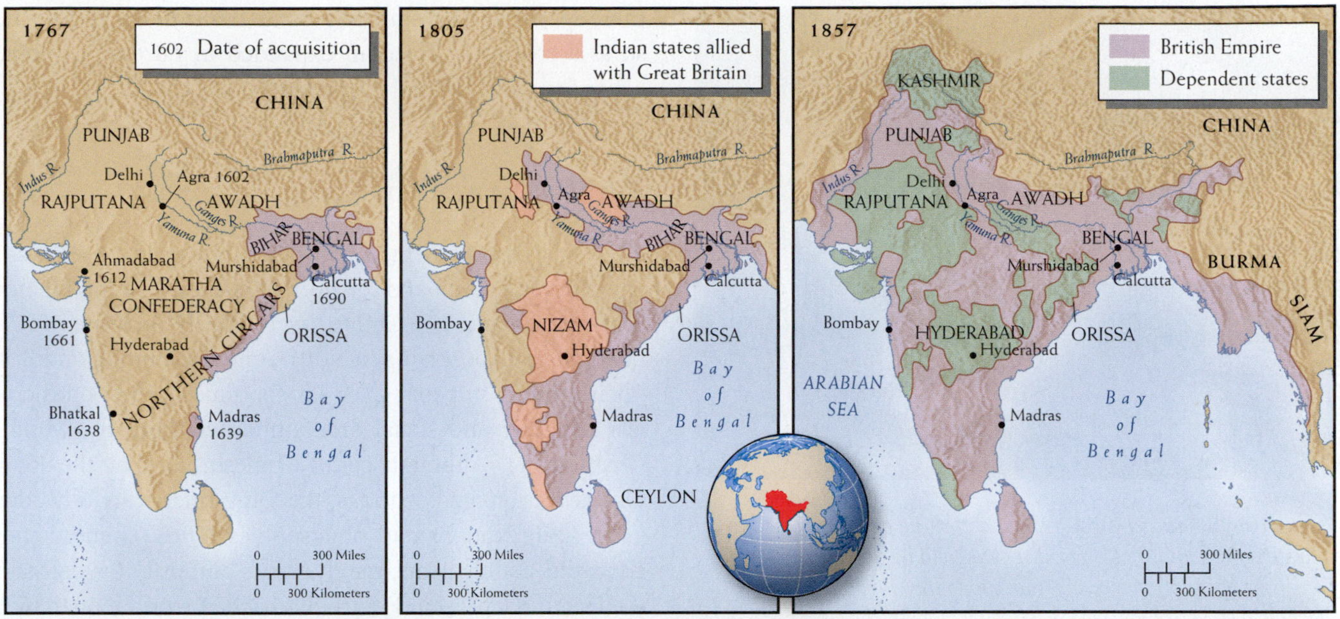

MAP 15.5 | The British in India, 1767–1857

Starting from locations in eastern and northeastern India, the British East India Company extended its authority over much of South Asia prior to the outbreak of the Indian Rebellion of 1857.

- What type of location did the British first acquire in India? How did the company expand into the interior of India and administer these possessions?
- Why did Britain choose a strategy of direct and indirect rule over different areas within the larger region?

focused on the East India Company's monopoly: its sole access to Indian wealth, and its protection of company shareholders and investors. In 1813 the British Parliament, responding to merchants' and traders' demands to participate in the Indian economy, abolished the company's monopoly over trade with India.

India now had to serve the interests of an industrializing Britain, so it became an importer of British textiles and an exporter of raw cotton—a reversal of its traditional pattern of trade. In the past, India had been an important textile manufacturer, exporting fine cotton goods throughout the Indian Ocean and to Europe. But its elites could not resist the appeal of cheap British textiles. As a result, India's own process of industrialization slowed down. In addition, the import of British manufactures caused unfavorable trade balances that changed India from a net importer of gold and silver to an exporter of these precious metals.

Calcutta. *Designated the capital of British India in 1772, Calcutta became vital to the British East India Company's activities as a main exporter of goods as cotton and opium. The wealthy British merchants and Anglo-Indians that Calcutta attracted utterly transformed its landscape, as shown in this 1910 photograph of the Great Eastern Hotel, which was commonly hailed the "Jewel of the East." This street scene of wide paved roads, carriages, and Victorian architecture would be difficult to distinguish from one of turn-of-the-century London, were it not for the Indian figures in traditional dress.*

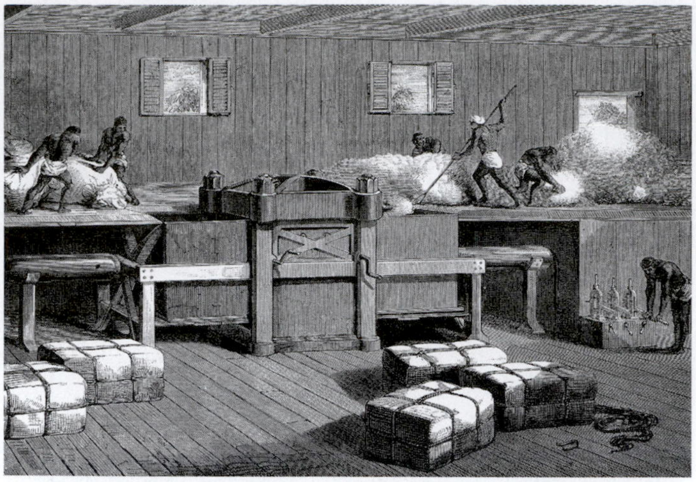

Packing Cotton Bales. *This 1864 engraving of the packing of cotton bales registers the shift in cotton trade between India and Britain: from being an exporter of cotton manufactures up to the eighteenth century, India became a source of raw cotton in the nineteenth century.*

PROMOTING CULTURAL CHANGE The British did more than alter the Indian economy; they also advocated far-reaching changes in Indian culture so that its people would value British goods and culture. In 1817, James Mill, a philosopher and an employee of the East India Company, condemned what he saw as backward social practices and cultural traditions. He and his son, John Stuart Mill, argued that only dictatorial rule could bring good government and economic progress to India, whose people they considered unfit for self-rule or liberalism. (See Primary Source: James Mill on Indian Tradition.)

Evangelicals and liberal reformers also tried to change Hindu and Muslim social practices, through legislation and European-style education. For example, they sought to stop the practice of *sati,* by which women burned to death on the funeral pyres of their dead husbands. Now the mood swung away from the Orientalists' respect for India's classical languages, philosophies, cultures, and texts. In 1835, when the British poet, historian, and Liberal politician Lord Macaulay was making recommendations on educational policies, he urged that English replace Persian as the language of administration and that European education replace Oriental learning. The result, reformers hoped, would be a class that was Indian in blood and color but English in tastes and culture.

This was a new colonial order, but it was not stable. Most wealthy landowners resented the loss of their land and authority. Peasants, thrown to the mercy of the market, moneylenders, and landlords, were in turmoil. Dispossessed artisans stirred up towns and cities. And merchants and industrialists chafed under the British-dominated economy. Even though India was part of a more interconnected world and thereby supported Europe's industrialization, it was doing so as a colony. As freedom expanded in Europe, exploitation expanded in India.

Persistence of the Qing Empire

The Qing dynasty, which had taken power in 1644, was still enjoying prosperity and territorial expansion as the nineteenth century dawned. The Chinese were largely unaware of revolutionary events occurring in North America, France, and Britain. Their sense of imperial splendor continued to rest on the political structure and social order inherited from the Ming (see Chapter 11). Although some Chinese felt that the Manchu Qing were foreign occupiers, the Qing rulers carefully adapted Chinese institutions and philosophies. Thus, Chinese elites at court did not challenge the dynasty's authority (as delegates to the Estates-General in France did to the French monarchy).

EXPANSION OF THE EMPIRE The Qing had a talent for extending the empire's boundaries and settling frontier lands. Before 1750, they conquered Taiwan (the stronghold of remaining Ming forces), pushed westward into central Asia, and annexed Tibet. Qing troops then eliminated the threat of the powerful Junghars in western Mongolia and halted Russian efforts to take southern Siberia in the 1750s. To secure these territorial gains, the Qing encouraged settlement of frontier lands like Xinjiang. New crops from the Americas aided this process—especially corn and sweet potatoes, which grow well in less fertile soils.

Through rising agricultural productivity and population growth, rural life became commercialized and state revenues surged. Furthermore, despite the Chinese ideal for women to stay home while men worked the land, in reality most rural women had toiled at fieldwork for centuries—and now their labor became even more important. In the eighteenth century, rural markets participated in more interregional trade in grain, cotton, tea, and silk. As rural industries proliferated, peasant households became the backbone of early manufactures (as in Europe), especially in textiles.

Like their European counterparts, Chinese peasants were on the move. But migration occurred in Qing China for different reasons. The state-sponsored westward movement into Xinjiang, for example, aimed to secure a recently pacified frontier region through military colonization, after which civilians would follow. So peasants received promises of land, tools, seed, and the loan of silver and a horse—all with the dual objectives of producing enough food grain to supply the troops and relieve pressure on the poor and arid northwestern part of the country. These efforts brought so much land under cultivation by 1840 that the region's ecological and social landscape completely changed.

PRIMARY SOURCE

James Mill on Indian Tradition

James Mill was a Scottish political economist and philosopher who believed that according to the principles of utilitarianism, law and government were essential for maximizing a people's usefulness and happiness. Thus his* History of British India *(1818) criticized India's Hindu and Muslim cultures and attributed their so-called backwardness to the absence of a systematic form of law. Mill's critique was also an attack on earlier British Orientalists, whose close engagement with Indian culture and Indian texts led them to oppose interfering in traditional practices. A year after the book's publication, the East India Company appointed him as an official.

The condition of the women is one of the most remarkable circumstances in the manners of nations. Among rude people, the women are generally degraded; among civilized people they are exalted.

...

Nothing can exceed the habitual contempt which the Hindus entertain for their women. Hardly are they ever mentioned in their laws, or other books, but as wretches of the most base and vicious inclinations, on whose natures no virtuous or useful qualities can be engrafted. "Their husbands," says the sacred code, "should be diligently careful in guarding them: though they well know the disposition with which the lord of creation formed them; Manu allotted to such women a love of their bed, of their seat, and of ornament, impure appetites, wrath, weak flexibility, desire of mischief, and bad conduct."

...

They are held, accordingly, in extreme degradation. They are not accounted worthy to partake of religious rites but in conjunction with their husbands. They are entirely excluded from the sacred books. . . .

...

They [the Hindus] are remarkably prone to flattery; the most prevailing mode of address from the weak to the strong, while men are still ignorant and unreflecting. The Hindus are full of dissimulation and falsehood, the universal concomitants of oppression. The vices of falsehood, indeed, they carry to a height almost unexampled among other races of men. Judicial perjury is more than common; it is almost universal.

...

This religion has produced a practice, which has strongly engaged the curiosity of Europeans; a superstitious care of the life of the inferior animals. A Hindu lives in perpetual terror of killing even an insect; and hardly any crime can equal that of being unintentionally the cause of death to any animal of the more sacred species. This feeble circumstance, however, is counteracted by so many gloomy and malignant principles, that their religion, instead of humanizing the character, must have had no inconsiderable effect in fostering that disposition to revenge, that insensibility to the sufferings of others, and often that active cruelty, which lurks under the smiling exterior of the Hindu.

...

Few nations are surpassed by the Hindus, in the total want of physical purity, in their streets, houses, and persons. Mr. Forster, whose long residence in India, and knowledge of the country, render him an excellent witness, says of the narrow streets of Benares: "In addition to the pernicious effect which must proceed from a confined atmosphere, there is, in the hot season, an intolerable stench arising from the many pieces of stagnated water dispersed in different quarters of the town. The filth also which is indiscriminately thrown into the streets, and there left exposed, (for the Hindus possess but a small portion of general cleanliness) add to the compound of ill smells so offensive to the European inhabitants of this city."

...

The attachment with which the Hindus, in common with all ignorant nations, bear to astrology, is a part of their manners exerting a strong influence upon the train of their actions. "The Hindus of the present age," says a partial observer, "do not undertake any affair of consequence without consulting their astrologers, who are always Brahmans." The belief of witchcraft and sorcery continues universally prevalent.

QUESTIONS FOR ANALYSIS

- What did James Mill hold to be the chief indicator of a civilization's accomplishment?
- In what ways do Mill's views on India reflect a deep disagreement with British Orientalists?

Source: James Mill, The History of British India *(New Delhi: Atlantic Publishers & Distributors, 1990), pp. 279, 281–82, 286–87, 288, 289, 297, 299.*

Rice cultivation. *From hand-sowing seedlings to harvesting the grains in leech-infested waters, the process of rice cultivation was so labor-intensive that multi-generational households cropped up throughout imperial China to yield the necessary manpower.*

Other migrants were on the move by their own initiative. The ever-growing competition for land even drove them into areas where the Qing regime had tried to restrict migration (because of excessive administrative costs), such as Manchuria and Taiwan. As the migrants introduced their own agricultural techniques, they reshaped the environment through land reclamation and irrigation projects and sparked large population increases.

PROBLEMS OF THE EMPIRE Despite their success in expanding the empire, the Qing faced nagging problems. As a ruling minority, they took a conservative approach to innovation. And only late in the eighteenth century did they deal with rapid population growth. On the one hand, the tripling of China's population since 1300 demonstrated the realm's prosperity; on the other, a population of over 300 million severely strained resources—especially soil for growing crops and wood for fuel.

Bureaucrats were understaffed. And as local authorities introduced many new taxes, the common people regarded them as corrupt. In the late eighteenth and early nineteenth centuries, uprisings inspired by mystical beliefs in folk Buddhism, and at times by the idea of restoring the Ming, engulfed northern China.

In spite of the difficulties that beset the Qing, European rulers and upper classes remained eager consumers of Chinese silks, teas, carved jade, tableware, jewelry, paper for covering walls, and ceramics. The Chinese, for their part, had little interest in most European manufactures. In 1793, Emperor Qianlong wrote in response to a request for trade by Britain's king that "as your ambassador can see for himself, we possess all things," adding, "I have no use for your country's manufactures."

By the mid-nineteenth century, however, extraordinary changes had made western European powers stronger than ever before, and the Qing could no longer dismiss their demands. The first clear evidence of an altered balance of power was a British-Chinese war over a narcotic. Indeed, the **Opium War** exposed China's vulnerability in a new era of European ascendancy.

THE OPIUM WAR AND THE "OPENING" OF CHINA Europeans had been selling staples and intoxicants in China for a long time. For example, tobacco, a New World crop, had become widely popular in China by the seventeenth century. Initially, few people would have predicted that tobacco smoking would lead to the widespread use of opium, previously used as a medicine or an aphrodisiac. But before long people in Southeast Asia, Taiwan, and China were smoking crude opium mixed with tobacco. By the late eighteenth century, opium smokers with their long-stemmed pipes were conspicuous at every level of Chinese society.

Although the Qing banned opium imports in 1729, the Chinese continued to smoke the drug and import it illegally. Sensing its economic potential, the East India Company created an opium monopoly in India in 1773. The reason was a rapid growth in the company's purchase of tea. Because the Chinese showed little taste for British goods, the British had been financing their tea imports with exports of silver to China. But by the late eighteenth century, the company's tea purchases had become too large to finance with silver. Fortunately for the company, the Chinese were eager for Indian cotton and opium, and then mostly just opium. Thus the British exported essentially no silver after 1804. Given the drug's importance, the company expanded its cultivation by offering loans to Indian peasants: they agreed to grow opium and sell it to the company's agents at a predetermined price.

The illegal opium traffic could not have flourished without the involvement of corrupt Chinese bureaucrats and a network of local brokers and distributors. Although another official ban in 1799 slowed the flow of opium into China for a while, the volume increased eightfold by 1839. The dramatic increase reflected an influx of private British merchants after the British government revoked the East India Company's monopoly over trade with China.

Opium. (Left) *A common sight in late Qing China were establishments catering specifically to opium smoking. Taken from a volume condemning the practice, this picture shows opium smokers idling their day away.* (Right) *Having established a monopoly in the 1770s over opium cultivation in India, the British greatly expanded their manufacture and export of opium to China to balance their rapidly growing import of Chinese tea and silk. This picture from the 1880s shows an opium warehouse in India where the commodity was stored before being transported to China.*

Opium's impact on the empire's balance of trade was devastating. In a reversal from earlier trends, silver began to flow out of instead of into China. Once silver shortages occurred, the peasants' tax burden grew heavier because they had to pay in silver (see Chapter 13). Consequently, long-simmering unrest in the countryside gained momentum. At the Qing court, some officials wanted to legalize the opium trade so as to eliminate corruption and boost revenues. (After all, as long as opium was an illegal substance, the government could not tax its traffic). Others wanted stiffer prohibitions. In 1838 the emperor sent a special commissioner to Canton, the main center of the trade, to eradicate the influx of opium. In a letter to Queen Victoria of Britain, the commissioner, Lin Zexu, claimed that China exported tea and silk for no other reason than "to share the benefit with the people of the whole world." He asked, therefore, why the British inflicted harm on the Chinese people through opium imports.

Lin demanded that foreigners hand over their opium stocks to the Chinese government (for destruction) and stop the trade. When British merchants in Canton resisted, Lin ordered the arrest of the president of the British Chamber of Commerce. After this man refused to comply, 350 foreigners were blockaded inside their own quarters. Lin ultimately convinced the foreign community to surrender 20,283 chests of opium with an estimated value of $9 million—an enormous sum in those days. But merchants had overstocked in anticipation of the trade's legalization, and the British government representative in Canton promised to compensate them for their losses. For Lin, the surrendering of the opium (which the Chinese flushed out to sea) was proof that the foreigners accepted submission. The Chinese victory, however, was short-lived. War soon broke out.

Though determined, the Chinese were no match for Britain's modern military technology. After a British fleet—including four steam-powered battleships—entered Chinese waters in June 1840, the warships bombarded coastal regions near Canton and sailed upriver for a short way (see Map 15.6). On land, Qing soldiers used spears, clubs, and a few imported matchlock muskets against the modern artillery of British troops, many of whom were Indians supplied with percussion cap rifles. Along the Yangzi River, outgunned Qing forces fought fiercely, as soldiers killed their own wives and children before committing suicide themselves.

FORCING MORE TRADE The Qing ruling elite capitulated, and with the 1842 Treaty of Nanjing, the British acquired the island of Hong Kong and the right to trade in five treaty ports. They also forced the Chinese to repay their costs for the war—and the value of the opium Lin had destroyed. British traders now won the right to trade directly with the Chinese and to live in the treaty ports.

Subsequent treaties guaranteed that the British and other foreign nationals would be tried in their own courts for crimes, rather than in Chinese courts, and would be exempt from Chinese law. Moreover, the British insisted that any privileges granted through treaties with other parties would also apply to them. Other

MAP 15.6 | The Qing Empire and the Opium War

- How many treaty ports were there after the opium war? What was their significance?
- How did the opium war change relations between China and the western powers?

Western nations followed the British example in demanding the same right, and the arrangement thus guaranteed all Europeans and North Americans a privileged position in China.

Still, China did not become a formal colony. To the contrary, in the mid-nineteenth century Europeans and North Americans were trading only on its outskirts. Most Chinese did not encounter the Europeans. Daily life for most people went on as it had before the Opium War. Only the political leaders and urban dwellers were beginning to feel the foreign presence and wondering what steps China might take to acquire European technologies, goods, and learning.

CONCLUSION

During the period 1750–1850, changes in politics, commerce, industry, and technology reverberated throughout the Atlantic world and, to varying degrees, elsewhere around the globe. By 1850, the world was more integrated economically, with Europe increasingly at the center.

In the Americas, colonial ties broke apart. In France, the people toppled the monarchy. Dissidents threatened the same in Russia. Such upheavals introduced a new public vocabulary—the language of the nation—and made the idea of revolution empowering. In the Americas and parts of Europe, nation-states took shape around redefined hierarchies of class, gender, and color. Britain and France emerged from the political crises of the late eighteenth century determined to expand their borders. Their drive forced older empires such as Russia and the Ottoman state to make reforms.

As commerce and industrialization transformed economic and political power, European governments compelled others (including Egypt, India, and China) to expand their trade with European merchants. Ultimately, such countries had to participate in a European-centered economy as exporters of raw materials and importers of European manufactures.

By the 1850s, many of the world's peoples became more industrious, producing less for themselves and more for distant

Trade in Canton. *In this painting, we can see the hongs, the buildings that made up the factories, or establishments, where foreign merchants conducted their business in Canton. From the mid-eighteenth century to 1842, Canton was the only Chinese port open to European trade.*

markets. Through changes in manufacturing, some areas of the world also made more goods than ever before. With its emphasis on free trade, Europe began to force open new markets—even to the point of colonizing them. Gold and silver now flowed out of China and India to pay for European-dominated products like opium and textiles.

However, global reordering did not mean that Europe's rulers had uncontested control over other people, or that the institutions and cultures of Asia and Africa ceased to be dynamic. Some countries became dependent on Europe commercially; others became colonies. China escaped colonial rule but was forced into unfavorable trade relations with the Europeans. In sum, dramatic changes combined to unsettle systems of rulership and to alter the economic and military balance between western Europe and the rest of the world.

AFTER YOU READ THIS CHAPTER

Review and research on **StudySpace**
wwnorton.com/studyspace

TRACING THE GLOBAL STORYLINES

FOCUS ON: The Global Effects of the "New Ideas"

The Atlantic World

- North American colonists revolt against British rule and establish a nonmonarchical, republican form of government.
- Inspired by the American Revolution, the French citizenry abolishes feudalism; proclaims a new era of liberty, equality, and fraternity; and executes opponents of their revolution, notably the king and queen of France.
- Napoleon's French empire extends many principles of the French Revolution throughout Europe.
- Drawing on the ideals of the French Revolution, Haitian slaves throw off French rule, abolish slavery, and create an independent state.
- Napoleon's invasion of Iberia frees Portuguese and Spanish America from colonial rule.
- The British lead a successful campaign to abolish the Atlantic slave trade and promote new sources of trade with Africa.
- An industrial revolution spreads outward from Britain to the rest of the world.
- The Russian monarchy strengthens its power through modest reforms and suppression of rebellion.

Africa, India, and Asia

- In Egypt, a military adventurer, Muhammad Ali, modernizes the country and threatens the political integrity of the Ottoman Empire.
- The British East India Company increasingly dominates the Indian subcontinent.
- The Qing Empire persists despite major European encroachments on its sovereignty.

CHRONOLOGY

The Americas
- The American Revolution **1776–1783**
- The Haitian Revolution **1791–1804**

Europe
- James Watt invents the steam engine **1769**
- The French Revolution **1789–1799**

East Asia

South Asia
- British East India Company rules India **1757–1858**

Africa

Ottoman Empire

1750 | 1775

KEY TERMS

Simón Bolívar *p. 570*
Napoleon Bonaparte *p. 563*
bourgeoisie *p. 575*
democracy *p. 556*
East India Company *p. 583*
free labor *p. 556*
free markets *p. 556*
free trade *p. 556*
industrial revolution *p. 575*
industrious revolution *p. 574*
Muhammad Ali *p. 581*
nationalism *p. 556*
nation-state *p. 556*
Opium War *p. 588*
popular sovereignty *p. 556*
republican government *p. 561*
social contract *p. 557*

STUDY QUESTIONS

1. **Describe** the political and social revolutions that occurred in the Atlantic world between 1750 and 1850. What ideas inspired these changes? How far did revolutionaries extend these changes?
2. **Compare and contrast** the way Latin American peoples achieved independence to the similar process in the United States. How similar were their goals? How well did they achieve these goals?
3. **Explain** Napoleon's role in spreading the ideas of political and social revolution. How did his armies spread the concept of nationalism? How did Napoleon's military pursuits affect political and social ferment in the Americas?
4. **Explain** how the Atlantic world's political and social revolution led to the end of the Atlantic slave trade. What economic, social, and political consequences did this development have on sub-Saharan Africa?
5. **Explain** the relationship between industrialization and the "industrious revolution." Where did the industrial revolution begin? What other parts of the Atlantic world did it spread to during this time?
6. **Explore** how industrialization altered the societies that began to industrialize during this time. What impact did this process have on the environment? How were gender roles and familial relationships altered?
7. **Analyze** how the two intertwined Atlantic revolutions (political and industrial) altered the global balance of power. How did the Russian, Mughal, Ottoman, and Qing dynasties respond to this change?
8. **To what extent** did Great Britain emerge as the leading global power between 1750 and 1850? How did the British state shape political and economic developments around the world during this time?

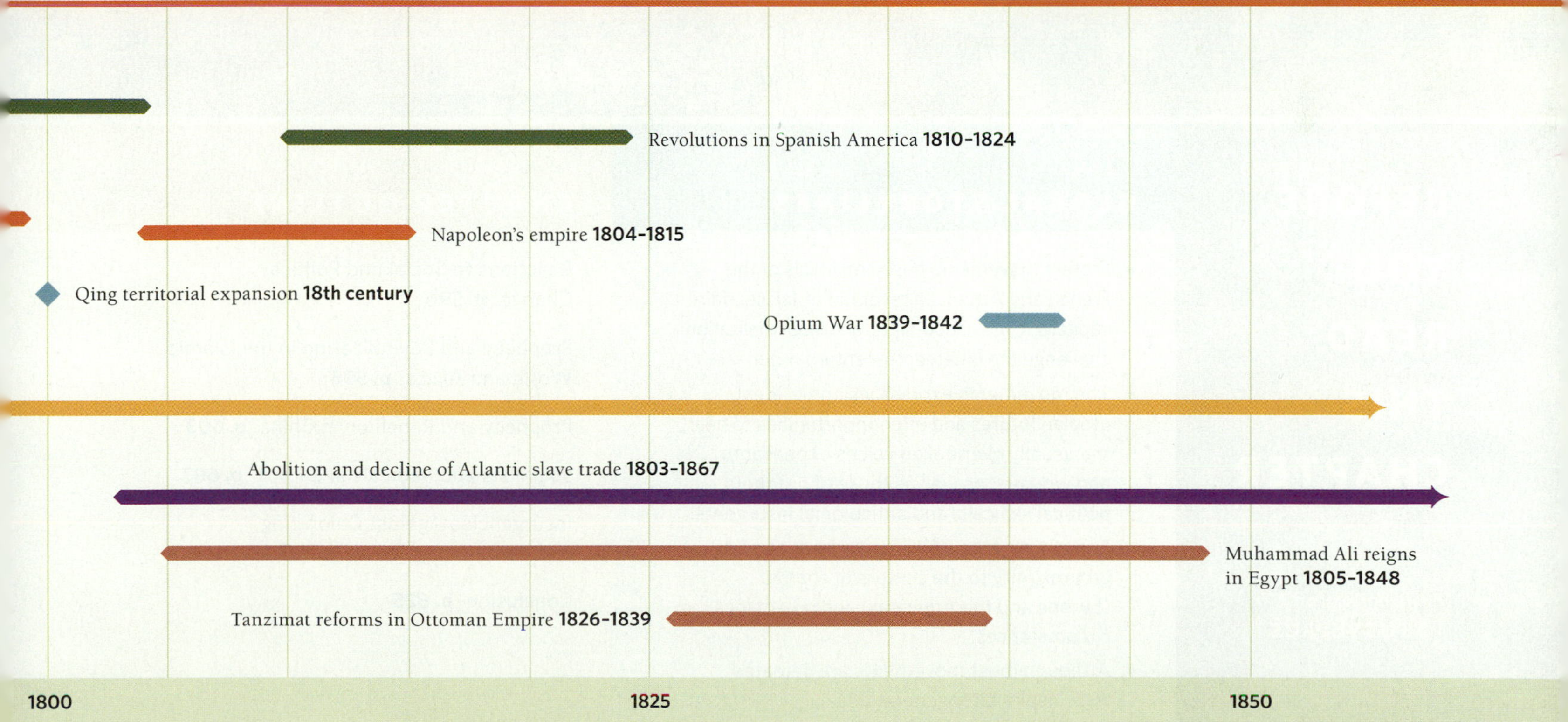

BEFORE YOU READ THIS CHAPTER

wwnorton.com/
STUDYSPACE

GLOBAL STORYLINES

- Protest movements based on ideals of the French and American revolutions, laissez-faire capitalism, the nation-state, and industrialization challenge the nineteenth-century order.
- The movements express visions of ideal, utopian futures and offer opportunities to hear the usually overlooked voices of peasants and workers, as well as those of prophets, political radicals, and anticolonial insurgents.
- The movements differ markedly depending on proximity to the centers of change (Europe and the Americas) and reflect local circumstances.
- Although most movements are defeated, they inspire later generations.

CHAPTER OUTLINE

16

Alternative Visions of the Nineteenth Century

FOCUS QUESTIONS

- Why did alternative visions to capitalism, colonialism, and nation-states emerge in the nineteenth century?
- What traits and goals did these movements share?
- What factors accounted for the differences among them?
- What groups supported these alternative movements?
- What were the legacies of these disparate movements?

By the late nineteenth century, territorial expansion in the United States confined almost all Indians to reservations. Across the American West, many Indians fell into despair. One was a Paiute Indian named Wovoka. But in 1889, he had a vision of a much brighter future. In his dream, the "Supreme Being" told Wovoka that if Indians lived harmoniously, shunned white ways (especially alcohol), and performed the cleansing Ghost Dance, then the buffalo would return and Indians, including the dead, would be reborn to live in eternal happiness.

As word spread of Wovoka's vision, Indians from hundreds of miles around made pilgrimages to the lodge of this new prophet. Many proclaimed him the Indians' messiah or the "Red Man's Christ," an impression fostered by scars on his hands. Especially among the Shoshone, Arapaho, Cheyenne, and Sioux peoples of the northern Plains, Wovoka's message inspired new hope. Soon increasing numbers joined in the ritual Ghost Dance, hoping it would restore the good life that colonialism had extinguished. Among the hopefuls was Sitting Bull, a revered Sioux chief who was himself famous for his visions. Yet, less than two years after

Wovoka's vision, Sitting Bull died at the hands of police forces on a Sioux reservation. A few days later, on December 29, 1890, Sioux Ghost Dancers were massacred at a South Dakota creek called Wounded Knee.

Though it failed, this movement was one of many prophetic crusades that challenged an emerging nineteenth-century order. The ideals of the French and American revolutions, laissez-faire capitalism, the nation-state organization, new technologies, and industrial organizations now provided the dominant answers to age-old questions of who should govern and what beliefs should prevail. But these answers did not stamp out other views. A diverse assortment of political radicals, charismatic prophets, peasant rebels, and anticolonial insurgents put forward striking counterproposals to those that capitalists, colonial modernizers, and nation-state builders had developed. The people making these counterproposals were motivated by the impending loss of their existing worlds and were energized by visions of ideal, utopian futures.

This chapter attends to the voices and visions of those who opposed a nineteenth-century world in which capitalism, colonialism, and nation-states held sway. It puts the spotlight on challengers who shared a dislike of global capitalism and European (and North American) colonialism. Beyond that similarity they differed in significant ways, for the alternatives they proposed reflected the local circumstances in which each of them developed. Although many of the leaders and movements they inspired suffered devastating defeats, like the Ghost Dancers at Wounded Knee, the dreams that aroused their fervor did not always die with them. Some of these alternative visions of the nineteenth century endured to propel the great transformations of the twentieth.

REACTIONS TO SOCIAL AND POLITICAL CHANGE

The transformations of the late eighteenth and early nineteenth centuries had upset polities and economies around the globe. In Europe, the old order had been either swept aside or severely battered by the tide of political and economic revolutions. In North America, the newly independent United States began an expansion westward. Territorial growth led to the dispossession of hundreds of Indian tribes and the acquisition of nearly half of Mexico by conquest. In Latin America, fledgling nation-states that now replaced the Spanish Empire struggled to control their subject populations. And in Asia and Africa, rulers and common people alike confronted the growing might of western military and industrial power. At stake were issues of how to define and rule territories, and what social and cultural visions they would embody.

The alternatives to the dominant trends varied considerably. Some rebels and dissidents called for the revitalization of traditional religions; others wanted to strengthen village and communal bonds; still others imagined a society where there was no private property and where people shared goods equally. The actions of these dissenters depended on their local traditions and the degree of contact they had with the effects of industrial capitalism, European colonialism, and centralizing nation-states.

This era of rapid social change, when differing visions of power and justice vied with one another, offers unique opportunities to hear the voices of the lower orders—the peasants and workers, whose perspectives the elites often ignored or suppressed. While there are few written records that capture the views of the illiterate and the marginalized, we do have traditions of folklore, dreams, rumors, and prophecies. Handed down orally from generation to generation, these resources illuminate the visions of common folk.

The alternative visions that challenged the dominance of colonialism, capitalism, and nation-states differed markedly. In Europe and the Americas, the heartlands of industrial capitalism and the nation-state, radical thinkers dreamed of far-reaching changes. They sought nothing less than an end to private property and a socialist alternative to capitalism. In Africa, the Middle East, and China, regions not yet colonized by Europeans, dynamic religious prophets and charismatic military leaders emerged. Here, men (and sometimes women) revitalized traditional ways, rejuvenated destabilized communities, and reorganized societies in hopes of preventing the spread of unwelcome foreign ideas and institutions. Finally, in South Asia and the Americas, where indigenous groups had come under the domination of Europeans and peoples of European descent, rebellions targeted the authority of the state. Just as Wovoka inspired a revolt against the U.S. government, the Mayans similarly fought to defend their cultural and political autonomy against the power of the Mexican state. So, too, did Indian peasants and old elites join forces in a fierce revolt against their colonial masters in British India.

PROPHECY AND REVITALIZATION IN THE ISLAMIC WORLD AND AFRICA

By the end of the eighteenth century, the Islamic world and non-Islamic Africa had reached a crossroads. The Ottomans, Safavids, and Mughals had extended Muslim trading zones, facilitated cross-cultural communication, and promoted common knowledge over vast territories—but now their era of flowering had ended, and political and military declines had begun.

Although much of this territory had not been colonized and was only partially involved with European-dominated trading networks, a sense of alarm intensified as Christian Europe's power spread. (See Current Trends in World History: Islam: An Enduring Alternative.) In Egypt and the Ottoman Empire, leaders responded by attempting to modernize their states along European lines (see Chapter 15). Farther away from the main trade routes and political centers, however, this sense of alarm also bred religious revitalization movements that sought to recapture the glories of past traditions. Led by prophets who feared that Islam was in trouble, these movements spoke the language of revival and restoration as they sought to replace Muslim monarchs they regarded as corrupt and insufficiently faithful with new theocratic governments.

Prophecy also exerted a strong influence in non-Islamic Africa, where long-distance trade and population growth were upending the social order. Just as Muslim clerics and political leaders sought solutions to unsettling changes by rereading Islamic classics, African communities looked to charismatic leaders who drew strength from their peoples' spiritual and magical traditions. Often uniting disparate groups behind their dynamic visions, prophetic leaders and other "big men" gained power because they were able to resolve local crises—mostly caused by drought, a shortage of arable land, or some other issue related to the harsh environment.

Islamic Revitalization

Movements to revitalize Islam took place on the peripheries—in areas that seemed immune from the potentially threatening repercussions of the world economy. Here, religious leaders rejected westernizing influences (see Map 16.1). Instead, revitalization movements looked back to Islamic traditions and modeled their revolts on the life of Muhammad. But even as they looked to the past, they attempted to establish something new: full-scale theocratic polities. These reformers conceived of the state as the primary instrument of God's will and as the vehicle for purifying Islamic culture.

WAHHABISM One of the most powerful reformist movements arose on the Arabian Peninsula, the birthplace of the Muslim faith. In the Najd region, an area surrounded by mountains and deserts, a religious cleric named Muhammad Ibn abd al-Wahhab (1703–1792) galvanized the population by attacking what he regarded as lax religious practices. His message found a ready response among local inhabitants, who felt threatened by the new commercial activities and fresh intellectual currents swirling around them. Abd al-Wahhab demanded a return to the pure Islam of Muhammad and the early caliphs.

Although Najd was far removed from the currents of the expanding world economy, Abd al-Wahhab himself was not. Having been educated in Iraq, Iran, and the Hijaz (a region on the western end of modern Saudi Arabia, on the Red Sea), he believed that Islam had fallen into a degraded state, particularly in its birthplace. He railed against the polytheistic beliefs that had taken hold of the people, complaining that in defiance of Muhammad's tenets men and women were worshipping trees, stones, and tombs and making sacrifices to false images. Abd al-Wahhab's movement stressed the absolute oneness of Allah (hence his followers were called *Muwahhidin,* or Unitarians) and severely criticized Sufi sects for extolling the lives of saints over the worship of God.

As **Wahhabism** swept across the Arabian Peninsula, the movement posed less of a threat to European power than it did to the Ottomans' hold on the region. Wahhabism gained a powerful political ally in the Najdian House of Saud, whose followers, inspired by the Wahhabis' religious zeal, undertook a militant religious campaign. They sacked the Shiite shrines of Karbala in southern Iraq, and in 1803 they overran the holy cities of Mecca and Medina, damaging the tombs of the saints. Their assault on the Shiite sites reflected their commitment to Sunni Islam, while their destruction of the tombs of Sufi saints stemmed from a belief that monuments to individuals whose beliefs were distant from the mainstream beliefs of Islam desecrated Islam's two holiest cities. Frightened by the Wahhabi challenge, the Ottoman sultan persuaded the provincial ruler of Egypt to send troops to the Arabian Peninsula to suppress the movement. The Egyptians defeated the Saudis, but Wahhabism and the House of Saud continued to represent a pure Islamic faith that attracted clerics and common folk throughout the Muslim world.

USMAN DAN FODIO AND THE FULANI In West Africa, Muslim revolts erupted from Senegal to Nigeria, responding in part to increased trade with the outside world and the circulation of religious ideas from across the Sahara Desert. In this region, the Fulani people were decisive in religious uprisings that sought, like the Wahhabi movement, to re-create a supposedly purer Islamic past. Although the Fulani had originated in the eastern part of present-day Senegal (and retain a powerful presence there today), they moved eastward to escape drought and, over time, set down roots across the savannah lands of West Africa. The majority were cattle-keepers, practicing a pastoral and nomadic way of life. But some were sedentary, and people in this group converted to Islam, read the Islamic classics, and communicated with holy men of North Africa, Egypt, and the Arabian Peninsula. They concluded that West African peoples were violating Islamic beliefs and engaging in irreligious practices.

CURRENT TRENDS IN WORLD HISTORY

Islam: An Enduring Alternative

Many of the alternative movements featured in this chapter derived their impetus from deeply held religious beliefs. Religion played a role in the Indian mutiny and in the visions that spurred the Taiping rebels. In Muslim locations far from the main currents of Western influence, like the Arabian Peninsula and northern Nigeria, it generated revivalist movements. But elsewhere it became a political force, and one that developed a palpably anti-European nature as well as the power to endure long beyond the victory of European invaders. World historians like to study political and social movements like these because they bring into relief the relationship between the colonizer and the colonized and, in the case of these alternative movements, the relationship between peoples living on the peripheries of empires and those living in the center who are part of the ruling elite, including indigenous elites.

This was the case in particular along the old Ottoman periphery, one of the major targets for European colonization. Strikingly, in the first decades of the nineteenth century, in the Ottomans' Balkan domains of Serbia and Greece, Christianity had linked together opponents against the empire. In the decades to follow, as Ottoman power receded, it left behind it Islamic groups who also used religion as the glue that bound together otherwise diverse peoples. The example below highlights the importance of Islam in galvanizing resistance to French imperialism in Algeria. But it would also be possible to cite examples from the Caucasus Mountains, another Ottoman periphery, where Islam linked together Chechen and other groups in opposition to Russian colonization in the 1840s and 1850s; in the early twentieth century, Libyans attempted to oppose Italian colonization by rallying behind the green flag of the prophet. Unquestionably, the more Europeans sought to dominate lands inhabited by Muslims, the more they called forth in reaction Islamic alternatives and politicized forms of Islamic resistance.

In 1830, through a series of mishaps and miscalculations, the French found themselves in possession of the Regency of Algiers, a territory of 60,000 square miles where previously 10,000 Ottoman Turks had ruled over 3 million Arab and Berber tribesmen. The French invasion had been an ill-considered adventure, designed to divert attention from the fact that the backward-looking French king, Charles X, had lost his legitimacy at home. In 1830, Charles was toppled by the so-called July Revolution, but his successor, King Louis Philippe (r. 1830–1848), decided to pursue France's adventure abroad. This was a risky and in the long run costly plan, however, as the French controlled only a few coastal enclaves and the capital city of Algiers; in 1831, the European civilian population was a mere 3,228. Moreover, although the French had driven out the Turks, they had emboldened Arab tribes in the western part of the land to found their own independent state.

In seeking a leader to unite them, the Arab tribes turned to Abd al-Qadir (1807–1883), a charismatic and domineering personality although he was only twenty-five years old. His father, head of the most important Sufi Brotherhood in Algeria, had groomed his son to be a leader, and taught him to despise the Ottoman overlords. Abd al-Qadir and his followers had already committed themselves to overthrowing the Ottomans; but once the French arrived, they were even more determined to rid the area of invaders they regarded as infidels who were intent on seizing their lands and imposing their way

The most powerful of these reform movements flourished in what is today northern Nigeria. Its leader was a Fulani Muslim cleric, **Usman dan Fodio** (1754–1817), who ultimately created a vast Islamic empire. Dan Fodio's movement had all the trappings of the Islamic revolts of this period. It sought inspiration in the life of Muhammad and demanded a return to early Islamic practices. It attacked false belief and heathenism and urged followers to wage holy war (*jihad*) against unbelievers. Usman dan Fodio's adversaries were the old Hausa rulers (city-states that emerged between 1000 and1200), who, in his view, were not sufficiently faithful to Islamic beliefs and practices. So dan Fodio withdrew from his original habitation in Konni and established a new community of believers at Gudu, citing the ancient precedent of Muhammad's withdrawal from Mecca to establish a community of true believers at Medina (see Chapter 9). The practice of withdrawal, called *hijra* in Muhammad's time, was yet another of the prophet's inspirations that religious reformers invoked at this time.

Dan Fodio was a member of the Qadiriyya, one of many Sufi brotherhoods that had helped spread Islam into West Africa. Sufism, the mystical and popular form of Islam, sought an emotional connection with God through a strict regimen of

Abd al-Qadir. *Polish artist Stanislaw Chlebowski painted Abd al-Qadir in 1866 during his exile in Constantinople.*

of life on them. In organizing resistance to the French, it mattered greatly that Abd al-Qadir was also known as a holy man and a scholar, rather than as merely the head of one of the tribes. In preparation for battle he called on his soldiers to follow him in a holy war (*jihad*) against Christian invaders, promising those who joined him in battle that "anyone of you who dies, will die a martyr; those of you who survive will gain glory and live happily." Tribes that might not have fought together, or fought together so long, did so because they were united by their loyalty to a religious as well as a political leader. Abd al-Qadir succeeded in part because he was a forceful personality, but in part, too, because he stood for Islam, a powerful faith that the native Algerians shared, whatever their kinship ties or their loyalties to local leaders.

For fifteen years, Abd al-Qadir's forces held out, only surrendering to a massive French force of 108,000 men in 1847. Although often defeated in pitched battles, Abd al-Qadir used his superior knowledge of the terrain and his ability to wait in ambush for French column to frustrate the French. The French government was finally compelled to send its most accomplished military man, Thomas-Robert Bugeaud, marshal of France, and to provide him with one-third of its entire military force, to finish the job of "pacifying" Algeria.

France's conquest of Algeria marks one of the bloodiest episodes in the history of those two lands. No fewer than 300,000 Algerians perished during these years. Although the French portrayed Abd al-Qadir as a Muslim fanatic, determined to take his people back to a dark age, their message fell on deaf ears. The Algerians extolled him for resisting the French and later made him an iconic figure of the nationalist movement. One of the first acts carried out by the independent Algerian government in 1962 was to tear down the statue of Marshal Bugeaud and replace it with one of Abd al-Qadir. The religiously motivated resistance leader had prevailed over the secular political conquerors after all.

QUESTIONS FOR ANALYSIS

- What impact did Algeria's geographic location have in determining its role in these revolutionary events?
- How did the native Algerians view their former Ottoman rulers compared to the French Europeans? What was the Algerians' ultimate goal?

Explore Further

Clancy-Smith, Julia, *Rebel and Saint: Muslim Notables, Populist Protest, Colonial Encounter (Algeria and Tunisia, 1800–1904)* (1994).

Danziger, Raphael, *Abd al-Qadir: Resistance to the French and Internal Consolidation* (1977).

Ruedy, John, *Modern Algeria: The Origins and Development of a Nation* (2005).

prayers, fasting, and religious exercises to obtain mystical states. Like Wovoka and Sitting Bull in North America, dan Fodio had visions that led him to challenge the West African ruling classes. In one vision, the founder of the Qadiriyya order instructed him to unsheathe the sword of truth against the enemies of Islam.

Dan Fodio won the support of devout Muslims in the area, who agreed that the people were not properly practicing Islam. He also gained the backing of his Fulani tribes and many of the Hausa peasantry, who had suffered under the rule of the Hausa landlord class. The revolt, initiated in 1804, resulted in the overthrow of the Hausa rulers and the creation of a confederation of Islamic emirates, almost all of which were in the hands of the Fulani allies of dan Fodio.

Fulani women of northern Nigeria made critical contributions to the success of the religious revolt. Although dan Fodio and other male leaders of the purification movement expected women to obey the *sharia* (Islamic law), being modest in their dress and their association with men outside the family, they also expected women to support the community's military and religious endeavors. In this effort, they cited women's important role in the first days of Islam. The best known of the Muslim women leaders was Nana Asma'u, daughter of dan

MAP 16.1 | Muslim Revitalization Movements in the Middle East and Africa, and the *Mfecane* Movement in Southern Africa

During the nineteenth century, a series of Muslim revitalization movements took place throughout the Middle East and North Africa.

- According to this map, in how many different areas did the revitalization movements occur?
- Based on their geographic location within their larger regions, did these movements occur in central or peripheral areas?
- Were any of the same factors that led to Islamic revitalization involved in the *Mfecane* developments in southern Africa?

Fodio. Fulani women of the upper ranks acquired an Islamic education, and Asma'u was as astute a reader of Islamic texts as any of the learned men in her society. Like other Muslim Fulani devotees, she accompanied the warriors on their campaigns, encamped with them, prepared food for them, bound up their wounds, and provided daily encouragement. According to many accounts, Asma'u inspired the warriors at their most crucial battle, hurling a burning spear into the midst of the enemy army. Her poem "Song of the Circular Journey" celebrates the triumphs of military forces that trekked thousands of miles to bring a reformed Islam to the area. (For another poem by Asma'u, see Primary Source: A Female Muslim Voice in Africa.)

Usman dan Fodio considered himself a cleric first and a political and military man second. Although his political leadership was decisive in the revolt's success, thereafter he retired to a life of scholarship and writing. He delegated the political and administrative functions of the new empire to his brother and his son. An enduring decentralized state structure, which became known as the Sokoto caliphate in 1809, developed into a stable empire that helped spread Islam through the region. A century later, the faith of a small minority of people living in northern Nigeria had become the religion of the vast majority.

Charismatic Military Men in Non-Islamic Africa

Non-Islamic Africa saw revolts, new states, and prophetic movements arise from the same combination of factors that influenced the rest of the world—particularly long-distance trade and population increase. Local communities here also looked to religious traditions and, as was so often the case in African history, expected "big men" to provide political leadership.

In southern Africa, early in the nineteenth century, a group of political revolts reordered the political map. Collectively known as the ***Mfecane* movement** ("the crushing" in Zulu), its epicenter was a large tract of land lying east of the Drakensberg Mountains, an area where growing populations and land resources existed in a precarious balance (see again Map 16.1). Compounding this pressure, trade with the Portuguese in Mozambique and with other Europeans at Delagoa Bay had disrupted the traditional social order. This set the stage for a political crisis for the northern Nguni (Bantu-speaking) peoples.

Many branches of Bantu-speaking peoples had inhabited the southern part of the African landmass for centuries. At the end of the eighteenth century, however, their political organizations

Shaka and His Zulu Regiments. *Though he is renowned for his reforms and infamous for his brutality, the only existing image of Shaka is this engraving (left) by English trader Henry Francis Fynn, the first white settler in Natal, a British colony near the Zulu kingdom. Nonetheless, Shaka's awesome presence and strength is as obvious to modern viewers as it would have been to his young warriors, who were deeply loyal to him and superbly trained. At right is a Zulu regimental camp; warrior huts were arranged in a circular pattern to surround a courtyard, where the warriors did their drills and practiced close combat.*

PRIMARY SOURCE

A Female Muslim Voice in Africa

The Islamic scholar, writer, and poet Nana Asma'u was the daughter of Usman dan Fodio, the leader of the Fulani revolt in northern Nigeria at the turn of the nineteenth century. Many of her poems conveyed religious inspiration and sought to demonstrate how much her father's revolt was inspired by the life and message of the Prophet Muhammad. She was also deeply attached to her brother, Muhammad Bello, who succeeded their father as head of the Sokoto caliphate. Muhammad Bello looked to his sister to promote traditional Muslim values among the female population in his empire, and she worked to extend education to rural women. Following is an elegy, written in poetic form, that Nana Asma'u composed in praise of her brother, underlining his commitment to an Islamic way of life.

I give thanks to the King of Heaven, the One God. I invoke blessings on the Prophet and set down my poem.

The Lord made Heaven and earth and created all things, sent prophets to enlighten mankind.

Believe in them for your own sake, learn from them and be saved, believe in and act upon their sayings.

I invoke blessings on the Prophet who brought the Book, the Qur'an: he brought the *hadith* to complete the enlightenment.

Muslim scholars have explained knowledge and used it, following in the footsteps of the Prophet.

It is my intention to set down Bello's characteristics and explain his ways.

For I wish to assuage my loneliness, requite my love, find peace of mind through my religion.

These are his characteristics: he was learned in all branches of knowledge and feared God in public and in private.

He obeyed religious injunctions and distanced himself from forbidden things: this is what is known about him.

He concentrated on understanding what is right to know about the Oneness of God.

He preached to people and instructed them about God: he caused them to long for Paradise.

He set an example in his focus on eternal values: he strove to end oppression and sin.

He upheld the *shari'a,* honored it, implemented it aright, that was his way, everyone knows.

And he made his views known to those who visited him: he said to them "Follow the *shari'a,* which is sacred."

He eschewed worldly things and discriminated against anything of ill repute; he was modest and a repository of useful knowledge.

He was exceedingly level-headed and generous, he enjoyed periods of quietude: but was energetic when he put his hand to things.

He was thoughtful, calm, a confident statesman, and quick-witted.

He honored people's status: he could sort out difficulties and advise those who sought his help.

still operated on a small scale, revolving around families and clans and modest chieftaincies. These tiny polities could not cope with the overpopulation and competition for land that now dominated southern Africa. A branch of the Nguni, the Zulus, produced a fierce war leader, Shaka (1787–1828), who created a ruthless warrior state. It drove other populations out of the region and forced a shift from small clan communities to large, centralized monarchies throughout southern and central Africa.

Shaka was the son of a minor chief who emerged victorious in the struggle for cattle-grazing and farming lands that arose during a severe drought. A muscular and physically imposing figure, Shaka was also a violent man who used terror to intimidate his subjects and to overawe his adversaries. His enemies knew that the price of opposition would be a massacre, even of women and children. Nor was he much kinder to his own people. Following the death of his beloved mother, for example, Shaka executed those who were not properly contrite and did not weep profusely. Reportedly, it took 7,000 lives to assuage his grief.

Shaka built a new state around his own military and organizational skills and the fear that his personal ferocity produced. He drilled his men relentlessly in the use of short stabbing spears and in discipline under pressure. Like the Mongols, he had a remarkable ability to incorporate defeated communities into the state and to absorb young men into his ultra-dedicated warrior forces. His army of 40,000 men comprised regiments that lived, studied, and fought together. Forbidden from marrying until they were discharged from the army, Shaka's warriors developed an intense esprit de corps and regarded no sacrifice as too great in the service of the state. So overpowering were these forces that other peoples of the region fled from

He had nothing to do with worldly concerns, but tried to restore to a healthy state things which he could. These were his characteristics.

He never broke promises, but faithfully kept them: he sought out righteous things. Ask and you will hear.

He divorced himself entirely from bribery and was totally scrupulous: He flung back at the givers money offered for titles.

One day Garange [chief of Mafora] sent him a splendid gift, but Bello told the messenger Zitaro to take it back.

He said to the envoy who had brought the bribe, "Have nothing to do with forbidden things."

And furthermore he said, "Tell him that the gift was sent for unlawful purposes; it is wrong to respond to evil intent."

He was able to expedite matters: he facilitated learning, commerce, and defense, and encouraged everything good.

He propagated good relationships between different tribes and between kinsmen. He afforded protection; everyone knows this.

When strangers came he met them, and taught about religious matters, explaining things: he tried to enlighten them.

He lived in a state of preparedness, he had his affairs in order and had an excellent intelligence service.

He had nothing to do with double agents and said it was better to ignore them, for they pervert Islamic principles.

He was a very pleasant companion to friends and acquaintances: he was intelligent, with a lively mind.

He fulfilled promises and took care of affairs, but he did not act hastily.

He shouldered responsibilities and patiently endured adversities.

He was watchful and capable of restoring to good order matters which had gone wrong.

He was resourceful and could undo mischief, no matter how serious, because he was a man of ideas.

He was gracious to important people and was hospitable to all visitors, including non-Muslims.

He drew good people close to him and distanced himself from people of ill repute.

Those are his characteristics. I have recounted a few examples that are sufficient to provide a model for emulation and benefit.

May God forgive him and have mercy on him: May we be united with him in Paradise, the place we aspire to.

For the sake of the Prophet, the Compassionate, who was sent with mercy to mankind.

May God pour blessings on the Prophet and his kinsmen and all other followers.

May God accept this poem. I have concluded it in the year 1254 AH [after *hijra*, the Muslim dating system].

QUESTIONS FOR ANALYSIS

- In what ways does this description convey a sense of proper Muslim values?
- Identify at least ten ways in which Bello was exemplary, according to this poem.
- Why would Nana Asma'u feel compelled to write a poem in praise of her brother?

their home areas, and Shaka claimed their estates for himself and his followers.

Thus did the Zulus under Shaka create a ruthless warrior state that conquered much territory in southern and central Africa, assimilating some peoples and forcing others to fashion their own similarly centralized polities. Shaka's defeated foes adopted many of the Zulu state's military innovations. They did so first to defend themselves and then to take over new land as they fled their old areas. The new states of the Ndebele in what later became Zimbabwe and of the Sotho of South Africa came into existence in the mid-nineteenth century in this way and proved long-lasting.

In turning southern Africa from a region of smaller polities into an area with larger and more powerful ones, Shaka seemed very much a man of the modern, nineteenth-century world. Yet he was, in his own unique way, a familiar kind of African leader. He shared a charismatic and prophetic style with others who emerged during periods of acute social change. He was, in this sense, one of many big men to seek dominance.

PROPHECY AND REBELLION IN CHINA

In the mid-nineteenth century China witnessed an explosive popular rebellion that incorporated Christian beliefs into its long tradition of peasant revolts. Just as European influence began to creep into Africa and the Islamic world, China too was no longer isolated. Even before 1842, European opium traders had conducted a brisk trade with the Chinese through Canton, the only port open to western commerce. After the Opium

War, however, westerners forced Qing rulers to open up a number of other ports to trade. To be sure, the dynasty retained authority over almost the whole realm, and western influence remained confined to a small minority of merchants and missionaries. Nevertheless, foreign gunboats and extraterritorial rights reminded the Chinese of the looming power of the West.

As in the Islamic world and other parts of sub-Saharan Africa, population increases in China—from 250 million in 1644 to around 450 million by the 1850s—were putting considerable pressure on land and other resources. Moreover, the rising consumption of opium, grown in India and brought to China by English traders, was producing further social instability and financial crisis. As banditry and rebellions spread, the Qing dynasts turned to the gentry to maintain order in the countryside. But as the gentry raised its militia to suppress these troublemakers, it whittled away at the authority of the Qing Manchu rulers. Faced with these changes, the Qing dynasty, already weakened by the humiliating Treaty of Nanjing following the Opium War, struggled to maintain control and legitimacy. Searching for an alternative present and future, beginning in 1850 hundreds of thousands of disillusioned peasants joined what became known as the Taiping Rebellion.

MAP 16.2 | The Taiping Rebellion in China, 1851–1864

Note that the Taiping Rebellion started in the southwestern part of the country. The rebels, however, went on to control much of the lower Yangzi region and part of the coastal area.

- What cities did the rebels' march start and end in?
- Why do you think the Taiping rebels were so successful in southern China and not in northern regions?
- How did western powers react to the Taiping Rebellion?
- Would they have been as concerned if the rebellion took place farther to the north or west?

The uprising drew on China's long history of peasant revolts. Traditionally, these rebellions ignited within popular religious sects whose visions were egalitarian or **millenarian** (convinced of the imminent coming of a just and ideal society). Moreover, in contrast to orthodox institutions, here women played important roles. Inspired by Daoists, who revered a past golden age before the world was corrupted by human conventions, or by Buddhist sources, these sects threatened the established order. In times of political breakdown, millenarian sects could transform local revolts into large-scale rebellions. Thus did the Taiping Rebellion, which began as a local movement in southern China, tap into the millenarian tradition and spread rapidly.

The Dream

The story of the rebellion begins with a complex dream that inspired its founding prophet, Hong Xiuquan (1813–1864). A native of Guangdong province in the southernmost part of the country (see Map 16.2), Hong first encountered Christian missionaries in the 1830s. He was then trying, unsuccessfully, to pass the civil service examination, which would have won him entry into the elite and a potential career in the Qing bureaucracy. Disappointed by his poor showing, Hong began to have visions, including a dream in 1837 that led him to form the Society of God Worshippers and the Taiping Heavenly Kingdom (see below).

In this dream, a ceremonial retinue of heavenly guards escorted Hong to heaven. The group included a cock-like figure that he later identified as Leigong, the Duke of Thunder, a familiar figure in Chinese mythology. When Hong reached heaven, his belly was slit open and his internal organs were replaced with new ones. As the operation for his renewal was completed, heavenly texts were unrolled for him to read. The "Heavenly Mother" then met and thoroughly cleansed him. She addressed him as "Son" before bringing him in front of the "Old Father." Although not part of the heavenly bureaucracy, Confucius and women generals from the Song dynasty were also present. Upon meeting Hong, the "Old Father" complained that human beings had been led astray by demons, as demonstrated by the vanity of their shaven heads (a practice the Manchu Qing regime imposed), their consumption of opium, and other forms of debauchery. The "Old Father" even denounced Confucius, who, after being flogged and begging for mercy before Hong's heavenly "Elder Brother," was allowed to stay in heaven but forbidden to teach again. Still, the world was not yet free of demons. So the "Old Father" instructed Hong to leave his heavenly family behind and return to earth to rescue human beings from demons.

How much of this account has been embellished with hindsight scholars will probably never know. What we do know is that Hong, after failing the civil service exam for the third time, suffered a strange "illness" in which he had visions of combating demons. He also began proclaiming himself the Heavenly King. Relatives and neighbors thought he might have gone mad, but Hong gradually returned to his normal state. In 1843, after failing the exam for the fourth time, Hong immersed himself in a Christian tract entitled *Good Words for Exhorting the Age*. Reportedly, reading this tract enabled Hong to realize the full significance of his earlier dream. All the pieces suddenly fell into place. The "Old Father," he concluded, was the Lord Ye-huo-hua (a Chinese rendering of "Jehovah"), the creator of heaven and earth. Accordingly, the cleansing ritual foretold Hong's baptism. The "Elder Brother" was Jesus the Savior, the son of God. He, Hong Xiuquan, was the younger brother of Jesus—God's other son. Just as God had previously sent Jesus to save mankind, Hong thought that God was now sending *him* to rid the world of evil. What was once a dream was now a prophetic vision.

The Rebellion

Unlike earlier sectarian leaders whose plots for rebellion were secret before exploding onto the public arena, Hong chose a more audacious path. Once convinced of his vision, he began

Taiping Rebellion. *The tens of thousands who had joined the "Heavenly King" became such a formidable force that they swiftly conquered and settled in many of the cities they encountered. Depicted in this mid-nineteenth-century painting are Imperial Chinese troops driving the Taiping rebels from their stronghold in Tientsin.*

to preach his doctrines openly, baptizing converts and destroying Confucian idols and ancestral shrines. Such assaults on the establishment testified to his conviction that he was carrying out God's will. Hong's message of revitalization of a troubled land and restoration of the "heavenly kingdom," imagined as a just and egalitarian order, appealed to the subordinate classes caught in the flux of social change. Drawing on a largely rural social base and asserting allegiance to Christianity, the **Taiping** ("Great Peace") **Rebellion** claimed to herald a new era of economic and social justice.

Many early followers came from the margins of local society—those whose anger at social and economic dislocations caused by the Opium War was directed not at the Europeans, but at the Qing government. The Taiping identified the ruling Manchus as the "demons" and as the chief obstacle to realizing God's kingdom on earth. Taiping policies were strict: they prohibited the consumption of alcohol, the smoking of opium, or any indulgence in sensual pleasure. Men and women were segregated for administrative and residential purposes.

PRIMARY SOURCE

The Taiping on the Principles of the Heavenly Nature

In this excerpt from 1854, the Taiping leaders envision a radically new community based on values that challenge those of conventional Chinese society. Inspired by their understanding of Christianity, the Taiping leadership confronted the central role of the family and ancestral worship in Chinese society by urging all its followers to regard themselves as belonging to a single family. It also advocated the segregation of the sexes, despite striving to improve women's lives in some of its other policy proclamations.

We brothers and sisters, enjoying today the greatest mercy of our Heavenly Father, have become as one family and are able to enjoy true blessings; each of us must always be thankful. Speaking in terms of our ordinary human feelings, it is true that each has his own parents and there must be a distinction in family names; it is also true that as each has his own household, there must be a distinction between this boundary and that boundary.

Yet we must know that the ten thousand names derive from the one name, and the one name from one ancestor. Thus our origins are not different. Since our Heavenly Father gave us birth and nourishment, we are of one form though of separate bodies, and we breathe the same air though in different places. This is why we say, "All are brothers within the four seas." Now, basking in the profound mercy of Heaven, we are of one family. . . .

We brothers, our minds having been awakened by our Heavenly Father, joined the camp in the earlier days to support our Sovereign, many bringing parents, wives, uncles, brothers, and whole families. It is a matter of course that we should attend to our parents and look after our wives and children, but when one first creates a new rule, the state must come first and the family last, public interests first and private interests last.

Moreover, as it is advisable to avoid suspicion [of improper conduct] between the inner [female] and the outer [male] and to distinguish between male and female, so men must have male quarters and women must have female quarters; only thus can we be dignified and avoid confusion. There must be no common mixing of the male and female groups, which would cause debauchery and violation of Heaven's commandments. Although to pay respects to parents and to visit wives and children occasionally are in keeping with human nature and not prohibited, yet it is only proper to converse before the door, stand a few steps apart and speak in a loud voice; one must not enter the sisters' camp or permit the mixing of men and women. Only thus, by complying with rules and commands, can we become sons and daughters of Heaven.

QUESTIONS FOR ANALYSIS

- What reasons do the Taiping leaders give for telling their followers "we are of one family"?
- Why do they insist that men and women have separate quarters?

Source: The Principles of the Heavenly Nature, *in* Sources of Chinese Tradition, *2nd ed., Vol. 2, compiled by W. Theodore de Bary and Richard Lufrano (New York: Columbia University Press, 2000), pp. 229–30.*

(See Primary Source: The Taiping on the Principles of the Heavenly Nature.) At the same time, in a drastic departure from dynastic practice, women joined the army in segregated units. These female military units mostly comprised Hakka women. Hakka is an ethnic subgroup within the Han (to which Hong Xiuquan, the founder of the Taiping, belonged) with a distinct identity. An important part of their culture was that Hakka women did not bind their feet.

There were further challenges to established social and cultural norms. For example, women could serve in the Taiping bureaucracy. Also, examinations now focused on a translated version of the Bible and assorted religious and literary compositions by Hong. Finally, all land was to be divided among the families according to family size, with men and women receiving equal shares. Once each family met its own needs for sustenance, the communities would share the remaining surplus. These were all radical departures from Chinese traditions. But the Taiping opposition to the Manchus did not involve the formation of a modern nation-state. The rebellion remained caught between the modern and the traditional.

By 1850, Hong's movement had amassed a following of over 20,000, giving Qing rulers cause for concern. When they sent troops to arrest Hong and other rebel leaders, Taiping forces repelled them and then took their turmoil beyond the southwestern part of the country. In 1851, Hong declared himself Heavenly King of the "Taiping Heavenly Kingdom" (or "Heavenly Kingdom of Great Peace"). By 1853, the rebels had captured major cities. Upon capturing Nanjing, the Taiping cleansed the city of "demons" by systematically killing all the Manchus they could find—men, women, and children. Then they established their own "heavenly" capital in the city.

But the rebels could not sustain their vision. Several factors contributed to the fall of the Heavenly Kingdom: struggles within the leadership, excessively rigid codes of conduct, and the rallying of Manchu and Han elites around the embattled dynasty. Disturbed by the Taiping's repudiation of Confucianism and wanting to protect their property, landowning gentry led militias against the Taiping. Moreover, western governments also opposed the rebellion, claiming that its doctrines represented a perversion of Christianity. Thus did a mercenary army led by foreign officers take part in suppressing the rebellion. Hong himself perished as his heavenly capital fell in 1864. With the Qing victory imminent, few of the perhaps 100,000 rebels in Nanjing surrendered. Their slaughter prepared the stage for a determined attempt by imperial bureaucrats and elite intellectuals to rejuvenate the Qing state. Although the Taiping's millenarian vision vanished, the desire to reconstitute Chinese society and government did not. The rebellion, in that sense, continued to inspire reformers as well as future peasant uprisings.

Like their counterparts in the Islamic world and Africa, the Taiping rebels promised to restore lost harmony. Despite all the differences of cultural and historical background, what Abd al-Wahhab, dan Fodio, Shaka, and Hong had in common was the perception that the present world was unjust. Thus, they sought to reorganize their communities—an endeavor that involved confronting established authorities. In this regard, the language of revitalization used by prophets in Islamic areas and China was crucial, for it provided an alternative vocabulary of political and spiritual legitimacy. Although in non-Islamic Africa the impulse was not religious revitalization, it still was an appeal to tradition—to communal solidarity and to the familiar role of "big men" in stateless societies. By mobilizing masses eager to return to an imagined golden age, these prophets and charismatic leaders gave voice to those dispossessed by global change, while producing new, alternative ways of organizing society and politics.

SOCIALISTS AND RADICALS IN EUROPE

Europe and North America were the core areas of capitalist activity, nation-state building, and colonialism. But there, too, the main currents of thought and activity faced challenges. Prophets of all stripes—political, social, cultural, and religious—voiced antiestablishment values and dreamed of alternative arrangements. Radicals, liberals, utopian socialists, nationalists, abolitionists, and religious mavericks made plans for better worlds to come. They did so in the face of a new era dominated by conservative monarchies. This conservatism was pervasive in central Europe, where reestablished kings and aristocrats revived most of their former power and privileges (see Map 16.3). Restoration of the old regimes had occurred at the Congress of Vienna in 1815, at the end of the French Revolution and Napoleon's conquests (see Chapter 15). However, opposition to this arrangement was widespread, and radical voices confidently predicted the coming of a new day.

Congress of Vienna. *At the Congress of Vienna in 1815, the Austrian prime minister Clemens von Metternich took the lead in drafting a peace settlement that would balance power among the states of Europe.*

Restoration and Resistance

The social and political ferment of the **Restoration period** (1815–1848) owed a great deal to the ambiguous legacies of the French Revolution and the Napoleonic wars. Kings had been toppled and replaced by republics, and then by Napoleon and his relatives; these experiments gave Restoration-era states and radicals many political options to choose from. The revolutionaries' attempt to replace Christianity with reason resulted in the clergy's loss of power and property, but very few Europeans actually gave up their religious beliefs. In the 1820s, the reactionary powers tried to reinstitute religious orthodoxy and clerical power, hoping to use the churches to suppress radical ideas. But in the religious sphere as in the political one, ideas and forces had been unleashed that would be impossible to tame.

Europeans in the Restoration era could draw not only on revolutionary ideas, but also on longer traditions of religious radicalism and reformist thought. Like purification movements in the Islamic world and religious sects in China, fundamentalist beliefs fueled social and political rebellions in Europe.

MAP 16.3 | Civil Unrest and Revolutions in Europe, 1819–1848

Civil unrest and revolutions swept Europe after the Congress of Vienna established a peace settlement at the end of the French Revolution and Napoleon's conquests. Conservative governments had to fight off liberal rebellions and demands for change.

- How many sites of revolutionary activity can you locate on this map?
- What parts of Europe appear to have been politically stable, and what parts rebellious?
- Can you explain the stability of some parts of Europe and the instability of others?

For example, the sixteenth- and seventeenth-century English Puritans and German Anabaptists had sought to remake communities from the ground up. In predicting an apocalyptic end for those who lived under sinful and oppressive rulers, these radical dissenters had established principles of both violent and passive resistance that now found application again.

Radicals could also invoke the early egalitarian image of "Pansophia," an ideal republic of inquisitive Christians united in the search for knowledge of nature as a means of loving God. This idea was promoted by the Czech Protestant John Amos Comenius, who championed education for all as early as the 1620s—at a time, that is, when most believed that learning was a privilege reserved for the elite. Forced into exile by Catholic victories during the Thirty Years' War, Comenius traveled widely in Protestant Europe, inspiring egalitarian movements in many countries. Alternatively, the Europeans could refer to certain Enlightenment thinkers who were confident that mankind was already well on its way to scientific, political, and even biological perfection. Critics of the old regime in the Restoration period appeared in many stripes, but all of them reflected, in one way or another, a combination of recent experience and older traditions.

Self-conscious "reactionaries" also emerged at this time. Their crusade was not just to restore privileges to kings and nobles but also to reverse the religious and democratizing concessions that sovereigns had made during the revolutionary and Napoleonic periods. In Russia, for example, the Slavophiles touted what they regarded as "native" traditions and institutions against the excessively "westernizing" reforms introduced by Peter the Great and continued by his self-styled "enlightened despot" successors. Many Slavophiles were ardent monarchists. Their desire for a strong yet "traditional" Russia brought them into conflict with the conservative, but modernizing, tsarist state.

The liberals, in contrast, wanted their states to carry through the legal and political reforms envisioned in 1789—but not to attempt economic leveling in the manner of the radical Jacobins (see Chapter 15). Liberals were eager to curb the states' restrictions on trade, destroy the churches' stranglehold on education, and give more people the right to vote—all the while preserving the free market, the Christian churches, and the rule of law. Proponents of **liberalism** insisted on the individual's right to think, speak, act, and vote as he or she pleased, so long as no harm came to people or property. Liberals feared that powerful states would become corrupt or tyrannical and held that the proper role of government was to foster civil liberties and promote legal equality.

In sum, the reactionaries wanted a return to the traditionally ordered societies that existed prior to the French Revolution; the liberals wanted reforms that would limit the power of government and the church and promote the rights of individuals and free trade. For the most part, the reactionaries got their way in eastern, central, and southern Europe; in Britain, France, and the Low Countries, liberals had greater sway. But neither group dominated fully, and the rivalry between these two groups continued to define the political landscape until at least the 1840s.

Radical Visions

If reactionaries and liberals offered contrasting solutions to social and political questions, they also had to contend with alternative groups even more determined to effect grand-scale change, the radicals. The term *radicals* refers to those who favored the total reconfiguration of the old regime's state system: going to the root of the problem and continuing the revolution, not reversing it or stopping reform. In general, radicals shared a bitter hatred for the status quo and an insistence on popular sovereignty, but beyond this consensus there was much dissension in their ranks. If some radicals demanded the equalization or abolition of private property, others (like Serbian, Greek, Polish, and Italian nationalists) were primarily interested in throwing off the oppressive overlordship of the Ottoman, Russian, and Austrian empires and creating their own nation-states. It was the radicals' threat of a return to revolutions that ultimately reconciled both liberals and reactionaries to preserving the status quo.

NATIONALISTS In the period before 1848, nationalism was a cause dear to liberals and radicals, and threatening to the conservative balance of power introduced into Europe at the Congress of Vienna in 1815. The age of revolutions had spread the idea of popular sovereignty, but the question remained: who exactly were "the people"? For radicals who longed for liberation from the multiethnic empires, "the people" encompassed all those who shared a common language and what was thought to be a common history, and each "people" deserved its own state.

Each fledgling nationalist movement—whether Polish, Czech, Greek, Italian, or German—had different contours, but they all drew backers from the liberal aristocracy and the well-educated and commercially active middle classes. University students were especially active in these movements. Most nationalist movements were, at first, weak and easily crushed, such as attempted Polish uprisings inside tsarist Russia in 1830–1831 and 1863–1864. The movements' leaders instead pursued educational and cultural programs to arouse and unite their nation for eventual statehood. By contrast, the Greeks, inspired by religious revivalism and enlightened ideas, managed to wrest independence from the Ottoman Turks after nearly a decade of small-scale, yet brutal, warfare.

Invoking both the classical tradition and their membership in the community of Christians, Greek patriots won support among Europeans in their fight against the Muslim Ottoman Empire. However, most of this support had to come in the form of private donations or volunteer soldiers, for European rulers feared that any sympathy they might show for the oppressed Greeks would fan the flames of revolution or separatism at home. Still, the Europeans sent their ships to the Mediterranean and defeated the Ottomans at Navarino in 1827. The Ottomans finally recognized Greek independence in 1829.

In the new state, the Greeks could not resolve differences between those who wanted a small, essentially secular republic and those who wanted to reclaim Istanbul (Constantinople) for Greek Orthodoxy. So they ended up inviting Otto, a Bavarian prince, to be king of Greece. The new Greek state had won its independence from the Ottomans, but it was neither the resurrected Athens nor the revived Byzantium that the revolutionaries had envisioned.

Other nationalist movements were suppressed or at least slowed down with little bloodshed. In places like the German principalities, the Italian states, and the Hungarian parts of the Habsburg Empire, secret societies of young men—students and intellectuals—gathered to plan bright, republican futures. Regrettably for these patriots, however, organizations like Young Italy, founded in 1832 to promote national unification and renewal, had little popular or foreign support. Censorship and a few strategic executions suppressed them. Yet many of these movements would ultimately succeed in the century's second half, when conservatives and liberals alike in western Europe employed nationalist fervor to advance their own great power ambitions. However, in central Europe, nationalism pitted many claimants for the same territories against one another, like the Czechs, Serbs, Slovaks, Poles, and Ruthenians (Ukrainians). They did not understand why they could not have a nation-state too.

SOCIALISTS AND COMMUNISTS Much more threatening to the ruling elite were the radicals who believed that the French Revolution had not gone far enough. They longed for a grander revolution that would sweep away the Restoration's political *and* economic order. Early socialists and communists (the terms were more or less interchangeable at the time) insisted that political reforms offered no effective answer to the more pressing "social question": what was to be done about the inequalities that industrial capitalism was introducing? The socialists worried in particular about two things. One was the growing gap between impoverished workers and newly wealthy employers. The other concern was that the division of labor—that is, the dividing up and simplifying of tasks so that each worker performs most efficiently—might make people into soulless, brainless machines. The socialists believed that the whole free market economy, not just the state, had to be transformed to save the human race from self-destruction. Liberty and equality, they insisted, could not be separated; aristocratic privilege along with capitalism belonged on history's ash heap.

No more than a handful of radical prophets hatched revolutionary plans in the years after 1815, but ordinary workers, artisans, domestic servants, and women employed in textile manufacturing joined them in staging strikes, riots, peasant uprisings, and protest meetings. A few socialists and feminists campaigned for social and political equality of the sexes. In Britain in 1819, Manchester workers at St. Peter's Field demonstrated peacefully for increased representation in Parliament, but panicking guardsmen fired on the crowd, leaving 11 dead and 460 injured in an incident later dubbed the Peterloo Massacre. In 1839 and 1842, nearly half the adult population of Britain signed the People's Charter, which called for universal suffrage for all adult males, the secret ballot, equal electoral districts, and annual parliamentary elections. This mass movement, known as **Chartism**, like most such endeavors, ended in defeat. Parliament rejected the charter in 1839, 1842, and 1848.

FOURIER AND UTOPIAN SOCIALISM Despite their many defeats, the radicals kept trying. Some sense of this age of revolutionary aspirations reveals itself in one European visionary who had big grievances and even bigger plans: Charles Fourier (1772–1837). Fourier's **utopian socialism** was perhaps the most visionary and influential of all Restoration-era alternative movements. He introduced planning, whereas the revolutionaries invoked violence, and he generally rejected the equalizing of conditions, fearing the suppression of diversity. Still, he and like-minded socialists dreamed of transforming states, workplaces, and human relations in a much more thorough way than their religious or political predecessors.

Fired by the egalitarian hopes and the cataclysmic failings of the French Revolution, Fourier believed himself to be the scientific prophet of the new world to come. He was a highly imaginative, self-taught man who earned his keep in the cloth trade,

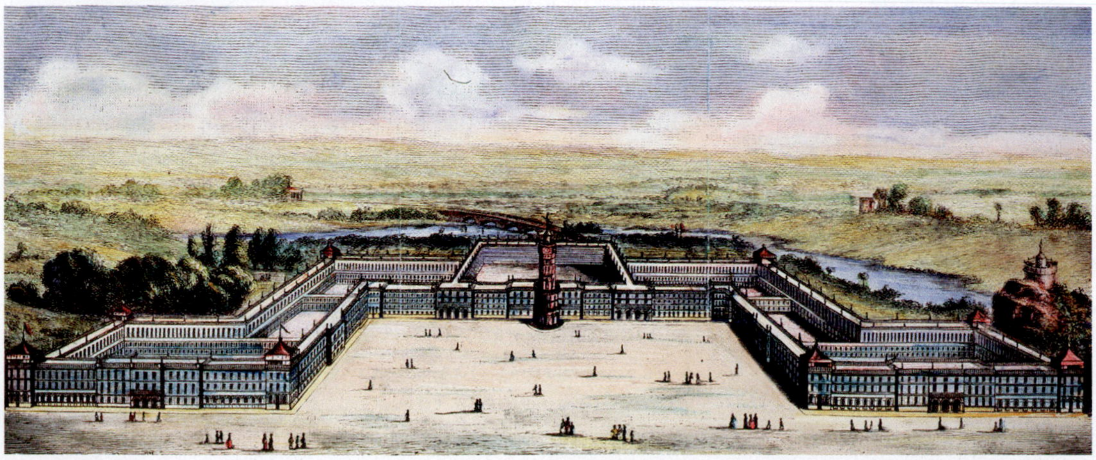

The Phalanx. *The Phalanx, as one of Fourier's German followers envisioned it. In this rendering, the idealized home for the residents of the cooperative social system is represented as a building architecturally similar to the home of the French kings, the Louvre.*

an occupation that gave him an intense hatred for merchants and middlemen. Convinced that the division of labor and repressive moral conventions were destroying mankind's natural talents and passions, Fourier concluded that a revolution grander than that of 1789 was needed. But this utopian transformation of economic, social, and political conditions, he thought, could occur through organization, not through bloodshed. Indeed, by 1808 Fourier believed that the thoroughly corrupt world was on the brink of giving way to a new and harmonious age, of which he was the oracle.

First formulated in 1808, his "system" envisioned the reorganization of human communities into what he called phalanxes. In these harmonious collectives of 1,500 to 1,600 people and 810 personality types, diversity would be preserved, but efficiency maintained; best of all, work would become enjoyable. All members of the phalanx, rich and poor, would work, though not necessarily at the same tasks. All would work in short spurts of no more than two hours, so as to make labor more interesting and sleep, idleness, and overindulgence less attractive. A typical rich man's day would begin at 3:30 A.M. for eating breakfast, reviewing the previous day, and participating in an industrial parade. At 5:30 he would hunt; at 7:00 he would turn to fishing. At 8:00 he would have lunch and read the newspapers (though what news there might be in this world is hard to fathom). At 9:00 he would meet with horticulturists, and at 10:00 he would go to mass. At 10:30 he would meet with a pheasant breeder; later he would tend exotic plants, herd sheep, and attend a concert. Each man would cultivate what he wanted to eat and learn about what he wanted to know. As for unpleasant tasks, they would become less so because they would now occur in more comfortable settings, such as warmed barns and spotless factories. Truly undesirable jobs, like sweeping out stables or cleaning latrines, would fall to young adolescents, who, Fourier argued, actually liked mucking about in filth.

Fourier's phalanxes by no means constituted an Eden in which humankind lived without knowing what it was like to sweat; rather, it was a workers' paradise in which comforts and rewards made working enjoyable. However, this system of production and distribution would run without merchants. Fourier intentionally excluded middlemen like himself from his plan for paradise. He believed that they corrupted civilization and introduced unnaturalness into the division of labor.

Fourier's writings gained popularity in the 1830s, appealing to radicals who supported a variety of causes. In France, women were particularly active in spreading his ideas. Longing for social and moral reforms that would address problems such as prostitution, poverty, illegitimacy, and the exploitation of workers (including women and children), some women saw in **Fourierism** a higher form of Christian communalism. By reshaping the phalanx to accommodate monogamous families and Christian values, women helped to make his work more respectable to middle-class readers. In Russia, Fourier's works fired the imaginations of the young writer Fyodor Dostoevsky. He and fourteen others in the radical circle to which he belonged were sentenced to death for their views (though their executions were called off at the last minute). In 1835–1836, both the young Italian nationalist Giuseppe Mazzini and the Spanish republican Joaquin Abreu published important articles on Fourier's thought. Karl Marx read Fourier with great care, and there are many remnants of utopian thought in his work. In *The German Ideology* Marx describes life in an ideal communist society; in a postrevolutionary world, he predicts that "nobody has one exclusive sphere of activity but each can become accomplished in any branch he wishes, society regulates the general production and thus makes it possible for me to do one thing today and another tomorrow, to hunt in the morning, fish in the afternoon, rear cattle in the evening, [and] criticize after dinner."

MARXISM Karl Marx proved to be the most important Restoration-era radical. University-educated and philosophically radical, Marx (1818–1883) took up a career in journalism. Required to cover legislative debates over property rights and taxation, he was forced to deal with economics. His understanding of *capitalism*, a term he was instrumental in popularizing, deepened through his collaboration with Friedrich Engels (1820–1895). Engels was a German-born radical who, after observing conditions in the factories owned by his wealthy father in Manchester, England, published a hair-raising indictment of industrial wage-labor entitled *The Condition of the Working Class in England*.

Together, Marx and Engels developed what they called "scientific socialism," which they contrasted with the "utopian socialism" of others like Fourier. Scientific socialism was rooted, they argued, in a materialist theory of history: what mattered in history were the production of material goods and the ways in which society was organized into classes of producers and

Karl Marx. *The author (with Friedrich Engels) of* The Communist Manifesto, *Karl Marx argued that the exploitation of wage laborers would trigger a proletarian revolution and would lead to socialism supplanting capitalism.*

PRIMARY SOURCE

"Bourgeoisie and Proletariat": From *The Communist Manifesto*

In January 1848, Karl Marx and Friedrich Engels prepared a party program for the Communist League, a German workingman's association. Published in French as* The Communist Manifesto, *the document foretold the inevitable overthrow of bourgeois-dominated capitalism by the working classes and the transition to socialism and ultimately to communism. The following excerpt demonstrates their certainty that history, driven by economic factors and class conflict, was moving unavoidably toward the revolution of the proletariat. Marx and Engels defined the bourgeoisie as capitalists, owners of the means of production and employers of wage laborers. They defined the proletariat as wage laborers who had to sell their labor to live.

A spectre is haunting Europe—the spectre of Communism. . . .

The history of all hitherto existing society is the history of class struggles. . . .

The modern bourgeois society that has sprouted from the ruins of feudal society has not done away with class antagonisms. It has but established new classes, new conditions of oppression, new forms of struggle in place of the old ones.

Our epoch, the epoch of the bourgeoisie, possesses, however, this distinctive feature: it has simplified the class antagonisms: Society as a whole is more and more splitting up into two great hostile camps, into two great classes directly facing each other: Bourgeoisie and Proletariat. . . .

The bourgeoisie . . . has put an end to all feudal, patriarchal, idyllic relations. It has pitilessly torn asunder the motley feudal ties that bound man to his "natural superiors," and has left remaining no other nexus between man and man than naked self-interest, than callous "cash payment." . . .

The need of a constantly expanding market for its products chases the bourgeoisie over the whole surface of the globe. It must nestle everywhere, settle everywhere, establish connexions everywhere. . . .

The bourgeoisie, by the rapid improvement of all instruments of production, by the immensely facilitated means of communication, draws all, even the most barbarian, nations into civilisation. The cheap prices of its commodities are the heavy artillery with which it batters down all Chinese walls, with which it forces the barbarians' intensely obstinate hatred of foreigners to capitulate. . . .

The weapons with which the bourgeoisie felled feudalism to the ground are now turned against the bourgeoisie itself.

But not only has the bourgeoisie forged the weapons that bring death to itself; it has also called into existence the men who are to wield those weapons—the modern working class—the proletarians. . . . These labourers, who must sell themselves piece-meal, are a commodity, like every other article of commerce, and are consequently exposed to all the vicissitudes of competition, to all the fluctuations of the market. . . .

But with the development of industry the proletariat not only increases in number; it becomes concentrated in greater masses, its strength grows, and it feels that strength more. . . . Thereupon the workers begin to form combinations (Trades Unions) against the bourgeois; they club together in order to keep up the rate of wages; they found permanent associations in order to make provision beforehand for these occasional revolts. Here and there the contest breaks out into riots.

Now and then the workers are victorious, but only for a time. The real fruit of their battles lies, not in the immediate result, but in the ever-expanding union of the workers. . . .

What the bourgeoisie, therefore, produces, above all, is its own grave-diggers. Its fall and the victory of the proletariat are equally inevitable.

QUESTIONS FOR ANALYSIS

- According to Marx and Engels, how does the bourgeoisie draw "all, even the most barbarian, nations into civilization"?
- How does the bourgeoisie contribute to its own downfall?
- Is the new social system supposed to arise automatically, or is human action required to bring it about?

Source: Karl Marx and Friedrich Engels, The Communist Manifesto, *in* The Marx-Engels Reader, 2nd *ed., edited by Robert C. Tucker (New York: Norton, 1978), pp. 473–83, 490–91, 500.*

exploiters. History, they claimed, consisted of successive forms of exploitative production and rebellions against them. Capitalist exploitation of the wage worker was only the latest, and worst, version of class conflict, Marx and Engels contended. In industrialized societies, capitalists owned the means of production (the factories and machinery) and exploited the wage workers. Marx and Engels were confident that the clashes between industrial wage workers—or **proletarians**—and capitalists would end in a colossal transformation of human society and would usher in a new world of true liberty, equality, and fraternity. These beliefs constituted the fundamentals of **Marxism**. For Marx and Engels, history moved through stages: feudalism to capitalism, to socialism, and eventually to communism.

From these fundamentals, Marx and Engels issued a comprehensive critique of post-1815 Europe. They identified a whole class of the exploited—the working class. They believed that more and more people would fall into this class as industrialization proceeded and that the masses would not share in the rising prosperity that capitalists monopolized. Marx and Engels predicted that there would be overproduction and underconsumption, which would lead to lower profits for capitalists and, consequently, to lower wages or unemployment for workers—which would ultimately spark a proletarian revolution. This revolution would result in a "dictatorship of the proletariat" and the end of private property. With the destruction of capitalism, the men claimed, exploitation would cease and the state would wither away.

In 1848, revolutionary fervor ignited uprisings in France, Austria, Russia, Italy, Hungary, and the German states. After hearing that revolution had broken out in France, Marx and Engels published *The Communist Manifesto,* calling on the workers of all nations to unite in overthrowing capitalism. (See Primary Source: "Bourgeoisie and Proletariat": From *The Communist Manifesto*.) But the men were sorely disappointed (not to mention exiled) by the reactionary crackdowns that followed the 1848 revolutions. After 1850, Marx and Engels took up permanent residence in England, where they tried to organize an international workers' movement. In the doldrums of midcentury they turned to science, but they never abandoned the dream of total social reconfiguration. Nor would their many admirers and heirs. The failure of the 1848 revolutions did not doom prophecy itself or diminish commitment to alternative social landscapes.

INSURGENCIES AGAINST COLONIZING AND CENTRALIZING STATES

Outside Europe, for Native Americans and for Britain's colonial subjects in India, the greatest threat to traditional worlds was the colonizing process itself, not industrial capitalism and centralizing states. While European radicals looked back to revolutionary legacies in imagining a transformed society, Native American insurgents and rebels in British India drew on their traditional cultural and political resources to imagine local alternatives to foreign impositions. Like the peoples of China, Africa, and the Middle East, native groups in the Americas and India met the period's challenges with prophecy, charismatic leadership, and rebellion. Everywhere the insurgents spoke in languages of the past, but the new worlds they envisioned bore unmistakable marks of the present as well.

Alternative to the Expanding United States: Native American Prophets

Like other native peoples threatened by imperial expansion, the Indians of North America's Ohio Valley dreamed of a world in which intrusive colonizers disappeared. Taking such dreams as prophecies, in 1805 many Indians flocked to hear the revelations of a Shawnee Indian named Tenskwatawa. Facing a dark present and a darker future, they enthusiastically embraced the Shawnee Prophet's visions, which (like that of the Paiute prophet Wovoka nearly a century later) foretold how invaders would vanish if Indians returned to their customary ways and traditional rites.

EARLY CALLS FOR RESISTANCE AND A RETURN TO TRADITION Tenskwatawa's visions—and the anticolonial uprising they inspired—drew on a long tradition of visionary leaders. From the first encounters with Europeans, Indian seers had periodically encouraged native peoples to purge their worlds of colonial influences and to revitalize indigenous traditions. Often these prophets had aroused their followers not only to engage in cleansing ceremonies but also to cooperate in violent, anticolonial uprisings. In 1680, for example, previously divided Pueblo villagers in New Mexico had united behind the prophet Popé to chase Spanish missionaries, soldiers, and settlers out of that colony. After their victory, Popé's followers destroyed all things European: they torched wheat fields and fruit orchards, slaughtered livestock, and ransacked Catholic churches. For a dozen years the Indians of New Mexico reclaimed control over their lands, but soon divisions within native ranks prepared the way for Spanish reconquest in 1692.

Seventy years later and half a landmass away, the charismatic oratory of the Delaware shaman Neolin encouraged Indians of the Ohio Valley and Great Lakes to take up arms against the British, leading to the capture of several British military posts. Although the British put down the uprising, imperial officials learned a lesson from the conflict: they assumed a less arrogant posture toward Ohio Valley and Great Lakes Indians, and to preserve peace they forbade colonists from trespassing on lands west of the Appalachian Mountains. The British, however, were incapable of restraining the flow of settlers across the mountains, and the problem became much worse for the Indians once the American Revolution ended. With the Ohio Valley transferred to the new United States, American settlers crossed the Appalachians and flooded into Kentucky and Tennessee.

MAP 16.4 | Native American Revolts in the United States and Mexico

The new world order of expanding nation-states and industrial markets strongly affected indigenous peoples in North America.

- According to this map, where did the fiercest resistance to centralizing states and global market pressures occur?
- What regions of the United States were Indians forced to leave?
- According to your reading, to what extent, if any, did the natives' alternative visions create or preserve an alternative to the new emerging order?

Despite the settlers' considerable migration, much of the territory between the Appalachian Mountains and the Mississippi River, which Americans referred to as the "western country," remained an Indian country. North and south of Kentucky and Tennessee, Indian warriors more than held their own against American forces. As in previous anticolonial campaigns, the visions of various prophets bolstered the confidence and unity of Indian warriors, who twice joined together to rout invading American armies. But their confederation failed in a third encounter, in 1794, and their leaders had to surrender lands in what is now the state of Ohio to the United States (see Map 16.4).

TENSKWATAWA: THE SHAWNEE PROPHET The Shawnees, who lost most of their holdings, were among the most bitter—and bitterly divided—of Indian peoples living in the Ohio Valley. Some Shawnee leaders concluded that their people's survival now required that they cooperate with American officials and Christian missionaries. This strategy, they realized, entailed wrenching changes in Shawnee culture. European reformers, after all, insisted that Indian men give up hunting and take up farming, an occupation that the Shawnees and their neighbors had always considered "women's work." Moreover, the Shawnees were pushed to abandon communal traditions in favor of private property rights. Of course, missionaries prodded Indians to quit their "heathen" beliefs and practices and become faithful, "civilized" Christians. For many Shawnees, these demands went too far; worse, they promised no immediate relief from the dispossession and impoverishment that now

PRIMARY SOURCE

Tenskwatawa's Vision

In the first decade of the nineteenth century, the Shawnee Indian leader Tenskwatawa recalled an earlier, happier time for the Indian peoples of the Great Lakes and Ohio Valley. It was a time before the coming of the Europeans. In this oration, Tenskwatawa recounts how contact with the "white men's goods" contaminated and corrupted the Indians. He urges them to spurn the ways of white Americans and return to the pure ways of a precolonial past.

Our Creator put us on this wide, rich land, and told us we were free to go where the game was, where the soil was good for planting. That was our state of true happiness. We did not have to beg for anything. Our Creator had taught us how to find and make everything we needed, from trees and plants and animals and stone. We lived in bark, and we wore only the skins of animals.

Thus were we created. Thus we lived for a long time, proud and happy. We had never eaten pig meat, nor tasted the poison called whiskey, nor worn wool from sheep, nor struck fire or dug earth with steel, nor cooked in iron, nor hunted and fought with loud guns, nor ever had diseases which soured our blood or rotted our organs. We were pure, so we were strong and happy.

For many years we traded furs to the English or the French, for wool blankets and guns and iron things, for steel awls and needles and axes, for mirrors, for pretty things made of beads and silver. And for liquor. This was foolish, but we did not know it. We shut our ears to the Great Good Spirit. We did not want to hear that we were being foolish.

But now those things of the white men have corrupted us, and made us weak and needful. Our men forgot how to hunt without noisy guns. Our women don't want to make fire without steel, or cook without iron, or sew without metal awls and needles, or fish without steel hooks. Some look in those mirrors all the time, and no longer teach their daughters to make leather or render bear oil. We learned to need the white men's goods, and so now a People who never had to beg for anything must beg for everything! . . .

And that is why Our Creator purified me and sent me down to you full of the shining power, to make you what you were before!

No red man must ever drink liquor, or he will go and have the hot lead poured in his mouth! . . .

Do not eat any food that is raised or cooked by a white person. It is not good for us. Eat not their bread made of wheat, for Our Creator gave us corn for our bread. . . .

The Great Good Spirit wants our men to hunt and kill game as in the ancient days, with the silent arrow and the lance and the snare, and no longer with guns.

If we hunt in the old ways, we will not have to depend upon white men, for new guns and powder and lead, or go to them to have broken guns repaired. Remember it is the wish of the Great Good Spirit that we have no more commerce with white men! . . .

. . . Our Creator told me that all red men who refuse to obey these laws are bad people, or witches, and must be put to death. . . .

The Great Good Spirit will appoint a place to be our holy town, and at that place I will call all red men to come and share this shining power. For the People in all tribes are corrupt and miserable! In that holy town we will pray every morning and every night for the earth to be fruitful, and the game and fish to be plentiful again.

QUESTIONS FOR ANALYSIS

- Tenskwatawa mentions many commodities and habits that the Indians had been adopting from white men. Identify at least ten.
- According to Tenskwatawa, how has this dependency reduced a proud people to begging?
- What rules did "Our Creator" give Tenskwatawa to help him make his people "what you were before"?

Source: Words of Tenskwatawa, in Messages and Letters of William Henry Harrison, *edited by Logan Esarey (Indianapolis: Indiana Historical Commission, 1922). Retrieved from http://history.missouristate.edu/FTMiller/EarlyRepublic/tecandtensk.htm*

marked the natives' daily lives. Young men especially grew angry and frustrated.

Among the demoralized was **Tenskwatawa** (1775–1836), whose story of overcoming personal failures through religious visions and embracing a strict moral code has uncanny parallels with that of Hong Xiuquan, the Taiping leader. In his first thirty years, Tenskwatawa could claim few accomplishments. He had failed as a hunter and as a medicine man, had blinded himself in one eye, and had earned a reputation as an obnoxious braggart. All this changed in the spring of 1805, however, after he fell into a trance and experienced a vision, which he vividly recounted to one and all. In this dream, Tenskwatawa encountered a heaven where the virtuous enjoyed the traditional Shawnee way of life and a hell where evildoers suffered punishments. Additional revelations followed, and Tenskwatawa soon stitched these together into a new social gospel that urged disciples to abstain from alcohol and return to traditional customs.

Like other prophets, Tenskwatawa exhorted Indians to reduce their dependence on European trade goods and to sever their connections to Christian missionaries. Thus he urged his audiences to replace imported cloth and metal tools with animal skins and implements fashioned from wood, stone, and bone. Livestock, too, was to be banished, as Indian men again gathered meat by hunting wild animals with bows and arrows, instead of guns and powder. If Indians obeyed these dictates, Tenskwatawa promised, the deer, which "were half a tree's length under the ground," would come back in abundant numbers to the earth's surface. Likewise, he claimed, Indians killed in conflict with colonial intruders would be resurrected, while evil Americans would depart from the country west of the Appalachians. (See Primary Source: Tenskwatawa's Vision.)

Like the Qing's response to Hong's visions, American officials initially dismissed Tenskwatawa as deluded but harmless; their concerns grew, however, as the Shawnee Prophet gathered more followers. These converts came not only from among the Shawnees but also from Delaware, Ottawa, Wyandot, Kickapoo, and Seneca villages. The spread of Tenskwatawa's message raised anew the specter of a pan-Indian confederacy. Hoping to undermine the Shawnee Prophet's claims to supernatural power, territorial governor William Henry Harrison challenged Tenskwatawa to make the sun stand still. But Tenskwatawa one-upped Harrison. Having learned of an impending eclipse from white astronomers, Tenskwatawa assembled his followers on June 16, 1806. Right on schedule, and as if on command, the sky darkened. Claiming credit for the eclipse, Tenskwatawa saw his standing soar, as did the ranks of his disciples. Now aware of the growing threat, American officials tried to bribe Tenskwatawa, hoping that cash payments might dim his vision and quiet his voice. Failing that, they wondered if one of the prophet's Indian adversaries might be encouraged to assassinate him.

In fact, Tenskwatawa had made plenty of enemies among his fellow Indians. His visions, after all, consigned drinkers to hell (where they would be forced to swallow molten metal) and singled out those who cooperated with colonial authorities for punishment in this world and the next. Indeed, Tenskwatawa condemned as witches those Indians who rejected his preaching in favor of the teachings of Christian missionaries and American authorities. (To be sure, Tenskwatawa's damnation of Christianized Indians was somewhat paradoxical, for missionary doctrines obviously influenced his vision of a burning hell for sinners and his crusade against alcohol.)

TECUMSEH AND THE WISH FOR INDIAN UNITY

Although Tenskwatawa's accusations alienated some Indians, his prophecies gave heart to many more. This was particularly the case once his brother, **Tecumseh** (1768–1813), helped circulate the message of Indian renaissance among Indian villages from the Great Lakes to the Gulf Coast. On his journeys after 1805, Tecumseh did more than spread his brother's visions; he also wed them to the idea of a renewed and enlarged Indian confederation. Moving around the Great Lakes and traveling across the southern half of the western country, Tecumseh preached the need for Indian unity. He repeatedly urged Indians to resist any American attempts to get them to sell more land. In response, thousands of followers renounced their ties to colonial ways and prepared to combat the expansion of the United States.

By 1810, Tecumseh had emerged, at least in the eyes of American officials, as even more dangerous than his brother. Impressed by Tecumseh's charismatic organizational talents, William Harrison warned that this new "Indian menace" was forming "an Empire that would rival in glory" that of the Aztecs and the Incas. In 1811, while Tecumseh was traveling among southern tribes, Harrison had his troops attack Tenskwatawa's village, Prophet's Town, on the Tippecanoe River in what is now the state of Indiana. The resulting battle was evenly fought, but the Indians eventually gave ground and American forces burned Prophet's Town. That defeat discredited Tenskwatawa, who had promised his followers protection from destruction at American hands. Spurned by his former disciples, including his brother, Tenskwatawa fled to Canada.

Tecumseh soldiered on. Although he mistrusted the British, he recognized that only a British victory over the Americans in the War of 1812 could check further American expansion. So he aligned himself with the British. Commissioned as a brigadier general in the British army, Tecumseh recruited many Indians to the British cause, though his real aim remained the building of a pan-Indian union. But in 1813, with the war's outcome in doubt and the pan-Indian confederacy still fragile, Tecumseh perished at the Battle of the Thames, north of Lake Erie.

INDIAN REMOVALS The discrediting of Tenskwatawa and the death of Tecumseh damaged the cause of Indian unity; then British betrayal dealt it a fatal blow. Following the war's end in 1814, the British withdrew their support and left the Indians south of the Great Lakes to fend for themselves against land-hungry American settlers and the armies of the United States. By 1815, American citizens outnumbered Indians in the western country by a seven-to-one margin, and this gap dramatically widened in the next few years. Recognizing the hopelessness of military resistance, Indians south of the Great Lakes resigned themselves to relocation. During the 1820s, most of the peoples north of the Ohio River were removed to lands

Visions of American Indian Unification. (Left) *A portrait of Tenskwatawa, the "Shawnee Prophet," whose visions stirred thousands of Indians in the Ohio Valley and Great Lakes to renounce dependence on colonial imports and resist the expansion of the United States.* (Right) *A portrait of his brother, Tecumseh, who succeeded in building a significant pan-Indian confederation, although it unraveled following his death at the Battle of Thames in 1813.*

west of the Mississippi River. During the 1830s, the southern tribes were cleared out, completing what amounted to an ethnic cleansing of Indian peoples from the region between the Appalachians and the Mississippi.

In the midst of these final removals, Tenskwatawa died, though his dream of an alternative to American expansion had faded for his people years earlier. Through the rest of the nineteenth century, however, other Indian prophets emerged, and their visions continued to inspire followers with the hope of an alternative to life under the colonial rule of the United States. But like Wovoka and the Ghost Dancers in 1890, these dreams failed to halt the expansion of the United States and the contraction of Indian lands.

Alternative to the Central State: The Caste War of the Yucatan

As in North America, the Spanish establishment of an expansionist nation-state in Mexico sparked widespread revolts by indigenous peoples. The most protracted was the Mayan revolt in the Yucatan. The revolt started in 1847, and its flames were not finally doused until the full occupation of the Yucatan by Mexican national troops in 1901.

EARLY MAYAN AUTONOMY The strength and endurance of the Mayan revolt stemmed in large measure from the unusual features of the Spanish conquest in southern Mesoamerica. Because this area was not a repository of precious metals or fertile lands, Spain and its rivals focused their efforts elsewhere—on central and northern Mexico and the Caribbean islands. As a result, the Mayan Indians escaped forced recruitment for silver mines or sugar plantations. This does not mean, however, that global processes sidestepped the Mayan Indians. In fact, the production of dyes and foodstuffs for shipment to other regions drew the Yucatan into long-distance trading networks. Nonetheless, cultivation and commerce were much less disruptive to indigenous lives in the Yucatan than elsewhere in the New World.

The dismantling of the Spanish Empire early in the nineteenth century gave way to almost a century of political turmoil in Latin America. In the Yucatan, civil strife brought the region autonomy by default, allowing Mayan ways to survive without much upheaval. Their villages still constituted the chief political domain, ruled by elders; ownership of their land was collective, the property of families and not individuals. Corn, a mere staple to white consumers, continued to enjoy sacred status in Mayan culture.

GROWING PRESSURES FROM THE SUGAR TRADE Local developments, however, encroached on the Mayan world. First, regional elites—mainly white, but often with the support of mestizo populations—bickered for supremacy so long as the central authority of Mexico City remained weak. Weaponry flowed freely through the peninsula, and some belligerents even appealed for Mayan support. At the same time, regional and international trade spurred the spread of sugar estates, which threatened traditional corn cultivation. Over the decades, plantations encroached on Mayan properties. Planters used several devices to lure independent Mayans to work, especially in the harvest. The most important device, debt peonage, involved giving small cash advances to Indian families, which obligated fathers and sons to work for meager wages to pay off the debts. In addition, Mexico's costly wars, culminating in a showdown with the United States in 1846, drove tax collectors and army recruiters into villages in search of revenues and soldiers.

The combination of spiritual, material, and physical threats was explosive. When a small band of Mayans, fed up with rising taxes and ebbing autonomy, used firearms to drive back white intruders in 1847, they sparked a war that took a half-century to complete. The rebels were primarily free Mayans who had not yet been absorbed into the sugar economy. They wanted to dismantle old definitions of Indians as a caste—a status that deprived the Indians of rights to defend their sovereignty on equal legal footing with whites and that also subjected the Indians to special taxes. Thus, local Mayan leaders, like Jacinto Pat and Cecilio Chi, upheld a republican model in the name of formal equality of all political subjects and devotion to a spiritual order that did not distinguish between Christians and non-Christians. "If the Indians revolt," one Mayan rebel explained, "it is because the whites gave them reason; because the whites say they do not believe in Jesus Christ, because they have burned the cornfield."

Caste War of the Yucatan. *The ruthless slaughter of Mayan farmers by Mexican troops is captured in this 1850 painting. The intimacy of the bloodstained straw hats strewn on the road suggests this work was an eyewitness account.*

THE CASTE WAR Horrified, the local white elites reacted to the uprising with vicious repression and dubbed the ensuing conflict a **Caste War**. In their view, the bloody conflict was a struggle between forward-looking liberals and backward-looking Indians. At first, whites and mestizos were no match for the determined Mayans, whose forces seized town after town, demolishing as they did so the whipping posts where Indians had endured public humiliation and punishment. By 1848, Indian armies controlled three-quarters of the peninsula and were poised to take the Yucatan's largest city, Mérida. Fear seized the embattled whites, who appealed for U.S. and British help, offering the peninsula for foreign annexation in return for military rescue from the Mayans.

In the end, fortune, not political savvy, saved the Yucatan's whites. The Mayan farmers, who had taken up arms to defend their world, returned to their farms when planting season came, declaring that "the time has come for us to make our planting, for if we do not we shall have no Grace of God to fill the bellies of our children." Like many ordinary people, the farmers were unaware of international changes that had an impact on their situation. In 1848, the Mexican-American War ended with Washington paying the Mexican government $15 million for giving up its northern provinces. Thereafter, Mexico could spend freely to build up its southern armies. The Mexican government soon fielded a force of 17,000 soldiers and waged a scorched-earth campaign to drive back the depleted Mayan forces.

By 1849, the confrontation had entered a new phase in which Mexican troops engaged in mass repression of the Mayans. Mexican armies set Indian fields and villages ablaze. Slaughtering Indians became a blood sport of barbaric proportions. Between 30 and 40 percent of the Mayan population perished in the war and its repressive aftermath. The white governor even sold captured Indians into slavery to Cuban sugar planters. Indeed, the white formulation of the caste nature of the war eventually became a self-fulfilling prophecy. Entire Mayan cities pulled up stakes and withdrew to isolated districts protected by fortified villages. War between armies degenerated into guerrilla warfare between an occupying Mexican army and mobile bands of Mayan squadrons, inflicting a gruesome toll on the invaders. As years passed, the war ground to a stalemate, especially once the U.S. funds ran out and Mexican soldiers began deserting in droves.

RECLAIMING A MAYAN IDENTITY Warfare prompted a spiritual transformation that reinforced a purely Mayan identity against the invaders' "national" project. Thus, a struggle that began with demands for legal equality and relative cultural autonomy became a crusade for spiritual salvation and the complete cultural separation of the Mayan Indians. A particularly influential group under José María Barrera retreated to a hamlet called Chan Santa Cruz. There, at the site where he found a cross shape carved into a mahogany tree, Barrera had a vision of a divine encounter. Thereafter a swath of Yucatan villages refashioned themselves as moral communities orbiting around Chan Santa Cruz. Leaders created a polity, with soldiers, priests, and tax collectors pledging loyalty to the Speaking Cross. As with the followers of Hong in China's Taiping Rebellion, Indian rebels forged an alternative religion: it blended Christian rituals, faiths, and icons with Mayan legends and beliefs. At the center was a stone temple, Balam Na ("House of God"), 100 feet long and 60 feet wide. Through pious pilgrimages to Balam Na and the secular justice of Indian judges, the Mayans soon governed their autonomous domain in the Yucatan, almost completely cut off from the rest of Mexico.

This alternative to Latin American state formation, however, faced formidable hurdles. For example, disease ravaged the people of the Speaking Cross. Once counting 40,000 inhabitants, the villages dwindled to 10,000 by 1900. Also a new crop, henequen, used to bind bales for North American farms and to stuff the seats of automobiles, began to spread across the Yucatan. In place of the peninsula's mixed agrarian societies, it now became a desiccated region producing a single crop, driving the people to seek refuge farther into the interior. As profits from henequen production rose, white landowners began turning the Yucatan into a giant plantation. But Mayan villagers refused to give up their autonomy and rejected labor recruiters.

Finally, the Mexican oligarchy, having resolved its internal disputes, threw its weight behind the strong-arm ruler General Porfirio Díaz (r. 1876–1911). The general sent one of his veteran commanders, Ignacio Bravo, to do what no other Mexican could accomplish: vanquish Chan Santa Cruz and drive Mayans into the henequen cash economy. When General Bravo finally entered the town, he found the once-imposing temple Balam Na covered in vegetation. Nature was reclaiming the territories of the Speaking Cross. Hunger and arms finally drove the Mayans to work on white Mexican plantations; the alternative vision was vanquished.

The Rebellion of 1857 in India

Like Native Americans, the peoples of nineteenth-century India had a long history of opposition to colonial domination. Armed revolts had occurred since the onset of rule by the English East India Company (see Chapter 15). Nonetheless, the uprising of 1857 was unprecedented in its scale, and it posed a greater threat than had any previous rebellion. Marx, with the hope for revolution dashed in Europe, cast his eyes on the revolt in British India, eagerly following the events and commenting on them in daily columns for the New York *Daily Tribune*. Though led primarily by the old nobility and petty landlords, it was a popular uprising with strong support from the lower orders of Indian society. The rebels appealed to bonds of local and communal solidarity, invoked religious sentiments, and reimagined traditional hierarchies in egalitarian terms. They did this to pose alternatives to British rule and the deepening involvement of India in a network of capitalist relationships.

INDIA UNDER COMPANY RULE When the revolt broke out in 1857, the East India Company's rule in India was a century old. During that time, the company had become an increasingly autocratic power whose reach encompassed the whole region. Mughal rule still existed in name, but the emperor lived in Delhi, all but forgotten and without any effective power. For a while, the existence of several princely states with which the British had entered into alliances prevented the British from

Rebellion of 1857. *Russian painter Vasili Vereshchagin depicts the cruel and unusual method in which British officers executed the Indian rebels—by strapping them to the mouths of cannons. The inhumanity of this practice was not soon forgotten by Europeans; this particular reproduction of the painting comes from* Raubstaat England *("Robber State England"), an anti-British pamphlet published by the Nazis during World War II.*

exercising complete control over all of India. These princely domains enjoyed a measure of fiscal and judicial authority within the British Empire. They also contained landed aristocrats who held the right to shares in the produce and maintained their own militias.

Believing that the princely powers and landed aristocracies were out of date, the company instituted far-reaching changes in administration in the 1840s. These infuriated local peoples and laid the foundations for one of the world's most violent and concerted movements of protest against colonial authority. Lord Dalhousie, upon his appointment as governor-general in 1848, immediately began annexing what had been independent princely domains and stripping native aristocrats of their privileges. Swallowing one princely state after another, the British removed their former allies. The government also decided to collect taxes directly from peasants, displacing the landed nobles as intermediaries. In disarming the landed nobility, the British threw the retainers and militia of the notables into unemployment. Moreover, the company's new systems of land settlement eroded peasant rights and enhanced the power of moneylenders. Meanwhile, the company transferred judicial authority to an administration that was insulated from the Indian social hierarchy.

MAP 16.5 | Indian Rebellion of 1857

The Indian Rebellion of 1857 broke out first among the Indian soldiers of the British army. Other groups soon joined the struggle.

- According to this map, how many centers of rebellion were located in British territory, and how many in dependent states?
- Can you speculate on why the rebellion occurred in the interior of the subcontinent rather than along the coasts?
- In what way was the company's expansion into formerly autonomous areas during the first half of the nineteenth century a factor in the rebellion?

The most prized object for annexation was the kingdom of Awadh in northern India (see Map 16.5). Founded in 1722 by an Iranian adventurer, it was one of the first successor states to have gained a measure of independence from the Mughal ruler in Delhi. With access to the fertile resources of the Ganges Plain, its opulent court in Lucknow was one place where Mughal splendor still survived. In 1765, the company imposed a treaty on Awadh under which the ruler paid an annual tribute for British troops stationed in his territory to "protect" his kingdom from internal and external enemies. The British constantly ratcheted up their demands for tribute and abused their position to monopolize the lucrative trade in cotton,

The Indian Sepoys. *Pictured here are Indian soldiers, or sepoys, who were armed, drilled, and commanded by British officers. The sepoys were drawn from indigenous groups that the British considered to be "martial races." This photograph shows the Sikhs, designated as one such "race."*

indigo, textiles, and other commodities. But the more successful they were in exploiting Awadh, the more they longed to annex it completely. Thus, Dalhousie declared in 1851 that Awadh was "a cherry which will drop into our mouths some day."

TREATY VIOLATIONS AND ANNEXATION In 1856, citing misgovernment and deterioration in law and order, the East India Company violated its treaty obligations and sent its troops to Lucknow to take control of the province. Nawab Wajid Ali Shah, the poet-king of Awadh, whom the British saw as effete and debauched, refused to sign the treaty of abdication. Instead, he came dressed in his mourning robes to meet with the British official charged to take over the province. After pleading unsuccessfully for his legal rights under the treaty, he handed over his turban to the official and then left for Calcutta to argue his case before Dalhousie. There was widespread distress at the treatment he received. Dirges were recited, and religious men rushed to Lucknow to denounce the annexation.

In fact, the annexation of princely domains and the abolition of feudal privileges formed part of the developing practices of European imperialism. To the policy of annexation, Dalhousie added an ambitious program of building railroads, telegraph lines, and a postal network to unify the disjointed territory into a single "network of iron sinew" under British control. Dalhousie saw these infrastructures as key to developing India into a productive colony—a supplier of raw materials for British industry, and a market for its manufactures.

A year after Dalhousie's departure in 1856, India went up in flames. The spark that ignited the simmering discontent into a furious rebellion—the **Rebellion of 1857 (Great Rebellion)**—was the "greased cartridge" controversy. At the end of 1856, the British army, which consisted of hundreds of thousands of Hindu and Muslim recruits (sepoys) commanded by British officers, introduced the new Enfield rifle to replace the old-style musket. To load the rifle, soldiers had to bite the cartridge open. Although manufacturing instructions stated that linseed oil and beeswax be used to grease the cartridge, a rumor circulated that cow and pig fat had been used. But biting into cartridges greased with animal fat meant violating the Hindu and Muslim sepoys' religious traditions. The sepoys became convinced that there was a plot afoot to defile them and to compel their conversion to Christianity. So a wave of rebellion spread among the 270,000 Indian soldiers, who greatly outnumbered the 40,000 British soldiers employed to rule over 200 million Indians.

REBELLION BREAKS OUT The mutiny broke out on May 10, 1857, at the military barracks in Meerut. The previous day, the native soldiers had witnessed eighty-five of their comrades being manacled and shackled in irons and marched off to the prison for refusing to load their rifles. The next day, all three regiments at Meerut mutinied, killed their British officers, and marched thirty miles south to Delhi, where their comrades in regiments there welcomed them joyfully. Together, they "restored" the aging Bahadur Shah as the Mughal emperor, which lent legitimacy to the uprising.

The revolt soon turned from a limited military mutiny into a widespread civil rebellion that involved peasants, artisans, day laborers, and religious leaders. While the insurgents did not eliminate the power of the East India Company, which managed to retain the loyalty of princes and landed aristocrats in some places, they did throw the company into a crisis. Before

PRIMARY SOURCE

The Azamgarh Proclamation

The Indian leaders of the Rebellion of 1857 issued numerous proclamations. The Azamgarh Proclamation, excerpted below, is representative of these petitions. The emperor, Bahadur Shah, issued it in August 1857 on behalf of the mutineers who had seized the garrison town of Azamgarh, sixty miles north of Benares. Like other proclamations, it attacks the British for subverting Indian traditions and calls on its followers to restore the pre-British order—in this case, the Mughal Empire.

It is well known to all, that in this age the people of Hindoostan, both Hindoos and Mohammedans, are being ruined under the tyranny and oppression of the infidel and treacherous English. It is therefore the bounden duty of all the wealthy people of India, especially of those who have any sort of connection with any of the Mohammedan royal families, and are considered the pastors and masters of their people, to stake their lives and property for the well being of the public. . . .

Several of the Hindoo and Mussalman chiefs, who have long since quitted their homes for the preservation of their religion, and have been trying their best to root out the English in India, have presented themselves to me, and taken part in the reigning Indian crusade. . . . Parties anxious to participate in the common cause, but having no means to provide for themselves, shall receive their daily subsistence from me; and be it known to all, that the ancient works, both of the Hindoos and the Mohammedans, the writings of the miracle-workers and the calculations of the astrologers, pundits, and rammals, all agree in asserting that the English will no longer have any footing in India or elsewhere. . . .

Section I—Regarding Zemindars [large landholders, responsible for collecting land taxes for the government]. It is evident, that the British Government in making zemindary settlements have imposed exorbitant *Jumas* [revenue assessments], and have disgraced and ruined several zemindars. . . . Such extortions will have no manner of existence in the Badshahi Government; but on the contrary, the *Jumas* will be light, the dignity and honour of the zemindars safe, and every zemindar will have absolute rule in his own zemindary. . . .

Section II—Regarding Merchants. It is plain that the infidel and treacherous British Government have monopolized the trade of all the fine and valuable merchandise, such as indigo, cloth, and other articles of shipping, leaving only the trade of trifles to the people, and even in this they are not without their share of the profits, which they secure by means of customs and stamp fees, &c. in money suits, so that the people have merely a trade in name. . . . When the Badshahi Government is established, all these aforesaid fraudulent practices shall be dispensed with, and the trade of every article, without exception, both by land and water, shall be open to the native merchants of India. . . .

Section IV—Regarding Artisans. It is evident that the Europeans, by the introduction of English articles into India, have thrown the weavers, the cotton dressers, the carpenters, the blacksmiths, and the shoemakers, &c., out of employ, and have engrossed their occupations, so that every description of native artisan has been reduced to beggary. But under the Badshahi Government the native artisan will exclusively be employed in the services of the kings, the rajahs, and the rich. . . .

Section V—Regarding Pundits, Fakirs and other learned persons. The pundits and fakirs being the guardians of the Hindoo and Mohammedan religions respectively, and the Europeans being the enemies of both the religions, and as at present a war is raging against the English on account of religion, the pundits and fakirs are bound to present themselves to me, and take their share in the holy war.

QUESTIONS FOR ANALYSIS

- What are the main grievances against the English in India?
- How will the emperor's Badshahi Government alleviate these grievous conditions?
- What was the role of religion in the 1857 rebellion?

Source: "Proclamation of Emperor Bahadur Shah," in India in 1857: The Revolt against Foreign Rule, *edited by Ainslie T. Embree (Delhi: Chanakya Publications, 1987), pp. 3–6.*

long, the mutineers in Delhi issued a proclamation declaring that because the British were determined to destroy the religion of both Hindus and Muslims, it was the duty of the wealthy and the privileged to support the rebellion. (See Primary Source: The Azamgarh Proclamation.) To promote Hindu-Muslim unity, rebel leaders asked Muslims to refrain from killing cows in deference to Hindu sentiments.

Triumphant in Delhi, the rebellion spread to other parts of India. In Awadh, proclamations in Hindi, Urdu, and Persian called on Hindus and Muslims to revolt. Troops at the garrison in Lucknow, Awadh's capital, did just that. Seizing control of the town, the rebels urged all classes to unite in expelling the British and succeeded in compelling the colonial forces to retreat.

Although the dispossessed aristocracy and petty landholders led the rebellion, leaders also appeared from the lower classes. Bakht Khan, who had been a junior noncommissioned officer in the British army, became commander-in-chief of the rebel forces in Delhi, replacing one of the Mughal emperor's sons. And Devi Singh, a wealthy peasant, set himself up as a peasant king. Dressed in yellow, the insignia of Hindu royalty, he constituted a government of his own, modeling it on the British administration. While his imitation of company rule showed his respect for the British bureaucracy, he defied British authority by leading an armed peasantry against the hated local moneylenders. The call to popular forces also marked the rebel career of Maulavi Ahmadullah Shah, a Muslim theologian. He stood at the head of the rebel forces in Lucknow, leading an army composed primarily of ordinary soldiers and people from the lower orders. Claiming to be an "Incarnation of the Deity," and thus inspired by divine will, he emerged as a prophetic leader of the common people. He voiced his undying hatred of the British in religious terms, calling on Hindus and Muslims to destroy British rule and warning his followers against betrayal by landed authorities.

PARTICIPATION BY THE PEASANTRY The presence of popular leadership points to the role of lower classes as historical actors. Although feudal chieftains often brought them into the rebellion, the peasantry made it their own. The organizing principle of their uprising was the common experience of oppression. Thus, they destroyed anything that represented the authority of the company: prisons, factories, police posts, railway stations, European bungalows, and law courts. Equally significant, the peasantry attacked native moneylenders and local power-holders who had purchased land at government auctions and were seen as benefiting from company rule.

Vigorous and militant as the popular rebellion was, it was limited in its territorial and ideological horizons. To begin with, the uprisings were local in scale and vision. Peasant rebels attacked the closest seats of administration and sought to settle scores with their most immediate and visible oppressors. They did not carry their action beyond the village or collection of villages. Their loyalties remained intensely local, based on village attachments and religious, caste, and clan ties. Nor did popular militants seek to undo traditional hierarchies of caste and religion.

COUNTERINSURGENCY AND PACIFICATION Convinced that the rebellion was the result of plotting by a few troublemakers, the British carried out their counterinsurgency with brutal vengeance. Villages were torched, and rebels were tied to cannons and blown to bits to teach Indians a lesson in power. Delhi fell in September 1857; Lucknow in March 1858. The British exiled the unfortunate Mughal emperor to Burma, where he died, and murdered his sons. Most of the other rebel leaders were either killed in battle or captured and executed. When, at the same time, the British also moved to annex the state of Jhansi in northern India, its female leader, Lakshmi Bai, mounted a counterattack. After a two-week siege, Jhansi fell to the British, but Lakshmi Bai escaped on horseback, only to die in the fighting for control of a nearby fortress. Her intelligence, bravery, and youth (she was twenty-eight) made her the subject of many popular Indian ballads in the decades to follow.

The Rani of Jhansi. *The Rani of Jhansi, who was deposed by the British, rose up during the revolt of 1857. In subsequent nationalist iconography, as this twentieth-century watercolor illustrates, she is remembered as a heroic rebel, all the more so because of her gender.*

ANALYZING GLOBAL DEVELOPMENTS

Alternative Movements in Asia and Africa

During the nineteenth century, five uprisings of global significance occurred in Africa and Asia. Two of these were carried out on a massive scale (the Taiping Rebellion and the Great Rebellion); the other three involved much smaller numbers. The two large-scale uprisings did not last as long as the three movements in sub-Saharan Africa and the Arabian Peninsula and were put down with great loss of life. In contrast, the political and cultural successes of the Wahhabi revolt in the Arabian Peninsula, Shaka's Zulu state in southern Africa, and the Fulani revolt in northern Nigeria can be seen clearly even to this day.

QUESTIONS FOR ANALYSIS

- Why were Europeans involved in suppressing the larger-scale uprisings in China and India but not the smaller-scale ones in Africa and the Arabian Peninsula?
- Although all five movements suffered stinging military defeats (the Fulani at the hands of the British in 1900, the Zulu state at the hands of the British in 1878, the Wahhabis at the hands of Egyptian troops at the beginning of the nineteenth century, the Taiping rebels at the hands of the Qing rulers, and the Indian rebels by British soldiers), were their long-term consequences markedly different?
- What holds these diverse movements together and allows us to represent them as alternatives to the main developments under way in western Europe and North America, the regions that had become dynamic centers of historical change?

Movement/Leader	Short-Term Consequences	Long-Term Consequences
Smaller-Scale Uprisings		
Fulani Revolt Northern Nigeria (1804–1817)	• Created largest state in sub-Saharan Africa • Occupied two-thirds of present day Nigeria	• Gained independence in 1960 • Fulani elite families who worked with British now rule over present-day Nigeria
Usman dan Fodio (1754–1817)	• British conquered it in early twentieth century	
Shaka's Zulu State	• Created an army of 40,000 warriors	• British conquered Zulu in 1878
Shaka (1787–1828)	• Created Zulu State covering 11,500 sq. miles in South Africa	• Zulu maintained their identity through apartheid • Population of 11 million today
Wahhabi Rebellion Arabian Peninsula (1744–1818)	• Ruled over much of the Arabian Peninsula	• Created the House of Saud, which rules over Saudi Arabia today
Ibn Abd al-Wahhab (1703–1792)	• Defeated by Egyptian army in 1812	• Retains commitment Wahhab principles today
Larger-Scale Uprisings		
Taiping Rebellion (1851–1864)	• Accrued half a million members	• Rebellion caused 20 million deaths by 1853
Hong Xiuquan (1813–1864)	• Leader Hong and rebels ruled over central and southern China from Nanjing for eleven years	• Nearly toppled Qing Dynasty; Mao Zedong viewed it as precursor to peasant-led Communist movement; now viewed as threat to social order due to large-scale violence
Great Rebellion (1857–1858)	• Indian sepoys of East India Company started revolt	• British crown ended company rule after suppressing rebellion brutally
Geographic Leaders, no monolithic figure	• Sepoys pledged support to Mughal emperor • Revolt included sepoys, peasants, small landholders, and religious leaders across north India	• Laid the foundation for later Indian populist and nationalist resistance

Sources: Dalrymple, William, The Last Mughal: The Fall of a Dynasty: Delhi, 1857 *(2007); Hamilton, Carolyn (ed.),* The Mfecane Aftermath: Reconstructive Debates in Southern African History *(1995); Hiskett, Mervyn,* The Sword of Truth: The Life and Times of the Shehu Usman dan Fodio *(1994); Spence, Jonathan,* God's Chinese Son: The Taiping Heavenly Kingdom of Hong Xiuquan *(1996).*

By July 1858, the vicious pacification campaign had achieved its goal. Yet, in August, the British Parliament abolished company rule and the company itself, and transferred responsibility for the governing of India to the crown. In November, Queen Victoria issued a proclamation guaranteeing religious toleration, promising improvements, and allowing Indians to serve in the government. She promised to honor the treaties and agreements with princes and chiefs and to refrain from interfering in religious matters. The insurgents had risen up not as a nation, but as a multitude of communities acting independently, and their determination to find a new order shocked the British and threw them into a panic. Having crushed the uprising, the British resumed the work of transforming India into a modern colonial state and economy. But the desire for radical alternatives and traditions of popular insurgency, though vanquished, did not vanish.

CONCLUSION

The nineteenth century was a time of turmoil and transformation. While powerful forces reconfigured the world as a place for capitalism, colonialism, and nation-states, so too did prophets, charismatic leaders, radicals, peasant rebels, and anticolonial insurgents arise to offer alternatives. Reflecting local circumstances and traditions, the struggles of these men and women for a different future opened up spaces for the ideas and activities of subordinate classes.

Conventional historical accounts either neglect these struggles or fail to view them as a whole. These individuals were not just romantic, last-ditch resisters, as some scholars have argued. Even after defeat, their messages remained alive within their communities. Nor were their actions isolated and atypical events, for when viewed on a global scale they bring to light a world that looks very different from the one that became dominant. To see the Wahhabi movement in the Arabian Peninsula together with the Shawnee Prophet in North America, the utopians and radicals in Europe with the peasant insurgents in British India, and the Taiping rebels with the Mayans in the Yucatan is to glimpse a world of marginalized regions and groups. It was a world that more powerful groups endeavored to suppress but could not erase.

In this world, prophets and rebel leaders usually cultivated power and prestige locally; the emergence of an alternative polity in one region did not impinge on communities and political organizations in others. As much as these individuals had in common, they envisioned widely different kinds of futures. Even Marx, who called the workers of the world to unite, was acutely aware that the call for a proletarian revolution applied only to the industrialized countries of Europe. Other dissenters had even more localized horizons. A world fashioned by movements for alternatives meant a world with multiple centers and different historical paths.

What gave force to a different mapping of the world was the fact that common people were at the center of these alternative visions, and their voices, however muted, gained a place on the historical stage. Egalitarianism in different forms defined efforts to reconstitute alternative worlds. In Islamic regions, the egalitarianism practiced by revitalization movements was evident in their mobilization of all Muslims, not just the elites. Even charismatic military leaders in Africa, for all their use of raw power, used the framework of community to build new polities. The Taiping Rebellion distinguished itself by seeking to establish an equal society of men and women in service of the Heavenly Kingdom. Operating under very different conditions, the European radicals imagined a society free from aristocratic privileges and bourgeois property. Anticolonial rebels and insurgents depended on local solidarities and proposed alternative moral communities. In so doing, these movements compelled ruling elites to adjust the way they governed. The next chapter explores this challenge.

AFTER YOU READ THIS CHAPTER

Review and research on **StudySpace:** wwnorton.com/studyspace

TRACING THE GLOBAL STORYLINES

FOCUS ON: ***Regional Variations in Alternative Visions***

Europe and the Americas—The Heartland of Modernizing Change

- European socialists and radicals envision a world free of exploitation and inequalities, while nationalists work to create new independent nation-states.
- Native American prophets in the United States imagine a world restored to its customary ways and traditional rites.
- Mayans in the Yucatan defy the central Mexican government in a rebellion known as the Caste War.

The Islamic World and Africa

- Revivalist movements in the Arabian Peninsula and West Africa demand a return to traditional Islam.
- A charismatic warrior, Shaka, creates a powerful state in southern Africa.

Semi-colonial China

- An inspired prophetic figure, Hong Xiuquan, leads the Taiping Rebellion against the Qing dynasty and European encroachment on China.

Colonial India

- Indian troops mutiny against the British and attempt to restore Mughal rule.

CHRONOLOGY

The Americas

Tecumseh's Rebellion (North America) **1810–1813**

South Asia

East Asia

Europe

Greek independence **1829**

Fourier's utopian socialism gains popularity **1830s**

Africa and the Middle East

Dan Fodio's movement in West Africa **1804–1809**

Wahhabis wage militant religious campaign in Arabian Peninsula **1813–1815**

Shaka creates Zulu Empire in South Africa **1818–1828**

1800

1820

KEY TERMS

Caste War *p. 618*
Chartism *p. 610*
Usman dan Fodio *p. 598*
Fourierism *p. 611*
liberalism *p. 609*
Marxism *p. 613*
Mfecane movement *p. 601*
millenarian *p. 604*
proletarians *p. 612*
Rebellion of 1857 (Great Rebellion) *p. 621*
Restoration period *p. 607*
Taiping Rebellion *p. 605*
Tecumseh *p. 616*
Tenskwatawa *p. 615*
utopian socialism *p. 610*
Wahhabism *p. 597*

STUDY QUESTIONS

1. **Define** the global order emerging in the nineteenth century in light of the revolutions in the Atlantic world studied in Chapter 15. How did it challenge social relations within societies?
2. **Explain** the goals of Islamic revitalization movements such as Wahhabism in the Arabian Peninsula and dan Fodio's movement in West Africa. How were these regions affected by the new world order? What alternative did Islamic revitalization propose?
3. **Describe** Hong Xiuquan's vision for China during the Taiping Rebellion. How did he propose reordering Chinese society?
4. **Describe** the various alternative visions to the status quo that European radicals proposed in the nineteenth century. What traditions and beliefs did they reflect?
5. **Compare and contrast** the Shawnee rebellion in the United States and the Caste War in Mexico. How did they reflect tensions between Native Americans and European Americans?
6. **Analyze** to what extent the Indian Rebellion of 1857 encouraged a new identity among its followers. What goals did participants in the rebellion share?
7. **Explore** the role of women in promoting alternative visions around the world in the nineteenth century. Which alternative vision movements proposed new roles for women in society?
8. **List** major similarities among the alternative visions explored in this chapter. Why did they all fail to achieve their objectives? Did they have any important legacies?

Ghost Dance movement (North America) **1889–1890**

Caste War (Mexico) **1847–1901**

Indian Great Rebellion **1857–1858**

Taiping Rebellion **1851–1864**

Restoration period **1815–1848**

Revolutions across Europe, Marx and Engels publish The Communist Manifesto **1848**

1840 — 1865

BEFORE YOU READ THIS CHAPTER

wwnorton.com/
STUDYSPACE

GLOBAL STORYLINES

- The advance of nation-state building and imperialism.
- Industrialization, science, and technology elevate states in North America and western Europe over the rest of the world.
- European and American imperialism encounters fierce opposition in Africa and Asia.

CHAPTER OUTLINE

FOCUS QUESTIONS

- How were nations conceptualized and how were nation-states built?
- Why did nationalism often lead to colonization and/or territorial expansion?
- How did colonization and territorial expansion shape the lives of indigenous people?
- How did new developments in industry, science, and technology reorder the relationships among different parts of the world?
- How did developments in technology, finance, and business reshuffle people and resources?

17

Nations and Empires, 1850–1914

In 1895, the Cuban patriot José Martí launched a rebellion against the last Spanish holdings in the Americas. The anti-Spanish struggle continued until 1898, when Spain withdrew from Cuba and Puerto Rico. Martí hoped to bring freedom to a new Cuban nation and equality to all Cubans. But even as he helped secure freedom from the declining Spanish empire, he could not prevent Cuba's military occupation and political domination by the world's newest imperial power, the United States.

Martí's hopes and frustrations found parallels around the world. After 1850, the building of nation-states and the expansion of their empires changed the map of the world, exhilarating some peoples and frustrating others. The communities that benefited most were Europeans and peoples of European descent. During these decades the nation-states of Europe, now locked in intense political and economic rivalry, projected their power across the entire world. Much of the rivalry among European states intensified through disruptions in the European balance of power, caused by the unification of two new states (Italy and Germany). Across the Atlantic, the United States forsook its anticolonial origins and annexed overseas possessions. Yet, imperial expansion did not go unchallenged. It encountered fierce resistance from communities being incorporated into the new empires. In Asia and Africa resisters struggled to repel their invaders, often demanding the right to govern themselves.

The second half of the nineteenth century, as this chapter details, witnessed the simultaneous—and entwined—advance of nationalism and imperialism. These decades also saw the further expansion of the industrial revolution. Taken together, the era's political and economic developments allowed western Europe and the United States to attain greater primacy in world affairs. But tensions inside these nations and their empires, as well as within other states, made the new world order anything but stable.

CONSOLIDATING NATIONS AND CONSTRUCTING EMPIRES

During the second half of the nineteenth century, the idea of building nation-states engulfed the globe. In the previous century a series of wars, ending with the Napoleonic Wars, had made Europeans increasingly conscious of political and cultural borders—and of the power of new bureaucracies. Enlightenment thinkers had emphasized the importance of nations, defined as peoples who shared a common past, territory, culture, and traditions. To many people it seemed natural that once absolutist rulers had fallen, the state should draw its power and legitimacy from those who lived within its borders and that the body of institutions governing each territory should be uniquely concerned with promoting the welfare of that particular people. This seemed such a natural process that little thought was given to how nation-states arose; they were simply supposed to well up from the people's longing for liberty and togetherness.

Building Nationalism

In practice, nations did not usually well up from people's longings for liberty and togetherness. More often than not, ruling elites themselves created nations. They did so by compelling diverse groups of people and regions to accept a unified network of laws, a central administration, time zones, national markets, and a single regional dialect as the "national" language. To overcome strong regional identities, state administrators broadened public education in the national language and imposed universal military service to build a national army. These efforts nurtured the notion of a one-to-one correspondence between a "people" and a nation-state, and they radiated the values and institutions of dominant elites outward to regions throughout each nation-state and beyond their national borders.

The world's major nation-states of the late nineteenth century were not all alike, however. They took many forms. Some had been in existence for years, such as Japan, England, France, Spain, Portugal, and the United States; here, citizens widely embraced their national identities. Two nation-states (Germany and Italy) were entirely new, forged through strategic military conquests. Elsewhere, plans for nation-states like those in central Europe, the Balkans, Poland, and the Ukraine were chiefly the inventions of local elites; their plans displeased Russian, Austrian, and Ottoman monarchs and were of little interest to the multilingual, multiethnic peasantry in these areas. In many parts of the world, intellectuals were the primary agents agitating for new nation-states, often urging new states to break away from existing empires. That secessionist impulse posed a particularly thorny challenge to the rulers of multinational empires like Russia and Austria.

Expanding the Empires

In countries that became nation-states, the processes of nation building and the acquisition of new territories, often called **imperialism**, went hand in hand. Their rulers measured national strength not only by their people's unity and the possession of the most modern means of production but also by the conquest of new territories. Thus Germany, France, the United States, Russia, and Japan rivaled Britain by expanding and modernizing their industries and seizing nearby or far-off territories. By the century's end, gaining new territory had become so important that these states scrambled to colonize peoples from Africa to the Amazon, from California to Korea.

Never before had there been such a rapid reshuffling of peoples and resources. As transportation costs declined, workers left their homelands in search of better opportunities. Japanese moved to Brazil, Indians to South Africa and the Caribbean, Chinese to California, and Italians to New York and Buenos Aires. At the same time, American capitalists invested outside the United States, and British investors financed the construction of railroads in China and India. Raw materials from Africa and Southeast Asia flowed to the manufacturing nations of Europe and the Americas.

Imperial rule facilitated a widespread movement of labor, capital, commodities, and information. As scholars studied previously unknown tribes and races, new schools taught colonized peoples the languages, religions, scientific practices, and cultural traditions of their colonizers. Publications and products from the "mother country" circulated widely among indigenous elites. Yet empire builders did not extend to nonwhite inhabitants of their colonies the same rights as they gave to inhabitants of their own nations; here, nation and empire were incompatible. Not only were colonial subjects prohibited from participating in government, but they were also not considered members of the nation at all. As a result, imperialism produced diametrically opposed reactions: exultation among the colonizers, and bitterness among the colonized.

EXPANSION AND NATION BUILDING IN THE AMERICAS

Once freed from European control, the elites of the Americas set about creating political communities of their own. By the 1850s, they shared a desire both to create widespread loyalty to their political institutions and to expand territorial domains. This required refining the tools of government to include national laws and court systems, standardized money, and national political parties. It also meant finding ways to settle hinterlands that previously belonged to indigenous populations. Having once been European colonies, New World territories became vibrant nation-states based on growing prosperity and industrialization.

Although nation-states took shape throughout the world, the Americas saw the most complete assimilation of new possessions. Instead of treating outlying areas as colonial outposts, American nation-state builders turned them into new provinces. With the help of rifles, railroads, schools, and land surveys, frontiers became staging areas for the expanding populations of North and South American societies. For indigenous peoples, however, such national expansion meant the loss of traditional lands on a vast scale.

Not all national consolidations in the Americas were the same. The United States, Canada, and Brazil, for example, experienced different processes of nation building, territorial expansion, and economic development. Each one incorporated frontier regions into national polities and economies, although they used different techniques for subjugating indigenous peoples and administering their new holdings.

The United States

Military might, fortuitous diplomacy, and the power of numbers enabled the United States to claim territory that spanned the North American continent (see Map 17.1). At its independence, the nation had been a barely united confederation of states. Indian resistance and Spanish and British rivalry hemmed in the "Americans" (as they came to call themselves). At the same time, the disunited states threatened to fracture into northern and southern polities, for questions of slavery versus free labor intruded into national politics. Yet, rallying to the rhetoric of **Manifest Destiny**, which maintained that it was God's will for the United States to "overspread" North America, Americans pushed their boundaries westward. They acquired territories via purchase agreements and treaties with France, Spain, and Britain and via warfare and treaties with diverse Indian nations and Mexico. (See Primary Source: Manifest Destiny.)

As part of the territories taken from Mexico after the Mexican-American War (1846–1848), the United States gained California, where the discovery of gold brought migration on an unprecedented scale. As news of the find spread, hopeful prospectors raced to stake their claims. In the next few years, over 100,000 Americans took to the overland trails and to the seas in quest of California's riches.

The California gold rush, however, was not only a great American migration; it also inspired tens of thousands of individuals from Latin America, Australia, Asia, and Europe to pour into California. What had just a few years earlier been a sparsely populated corner of northwestern Mexico was transformed almost overnight into the most cosmopolitan place on earth. In the 1850s, California was truly where worlds came together.

CIVIL WAR AND STATES' RIGHTS Ironically, California and the territories that the United States took from Mexico also spurred the coming apart of the American nation. The deeply divisive issue was whether these lands would be open to slavery or restricted to free labor. Following the 1860 election of Abraham Lincoln, who pledged to halt the expansion of slavery, the United States divided between North and South and plunged into a gruesome Civil War (1861–1865).

The bloody conflict led to the abolition of slavery, and the struggle to extend voting and citizenship rights to freed slaves qualified the Civil War as a second American Revolution. It gave the nation a new generation of heroes and martyrs such as the assassinated president, Abraham Lincoln. He had promised a new model of freedom for a nation reborn out of bloodshed. Its cornerstone would be the incorporation of freed slaves as citizens of the United States. Alas, the experiments in biracial democracy during the Reconstruction period (1867–1877) were short-lived. In the decades after the Civil War, counterrevolutionary pressure led to the denial of voting rights to African Americans and the restoration of (white) planter rule in the southern states. This pressure was spearheaded by the terrorism of the Ku Klux Klan, a group of former Confederates that sought to reverse freedmen's legal and political gains and to restore planters to power in the South.

Nonetheless, the war brought enduring changes across the United States. The defeat of the South established the preeminence of the national government. After the Civil War, Americans learned to speak of their nation in the singular ("the United States is" in contrast to "the United States are"). With an invigorated nationalism came an enlarged national government.

Even more dizzying were social and economic changes. Within ten years of the war's end, the industrial output of the United States had climbed by 75 percent. Symbolizing

MAP 17.1 | U.S. and Canadian Westward Expansion, 1803–1912

Americans and Canadians expanded westward in the second half of the nineteenth century, aided greatly by railways.

- How many railroad lines ultimately reached the western borders of Canada and the United States?
- By what years were the territorial expansions of Canada and the United States complete? How did territorial expansion strengthen Canadian and American nationalism?
- What were the major events that led to the annexation of the western half of the United States?

PRIMARY SOURCE

Manifest Destiny

In July 1845, the New York newspaper editor John L. O'Sullivan coined the phrase* Manifest Destiny *to explain how the "manifest design of Providence" supported the territorial expansion of the United States. In this excerpt, O'Sullivan outlines the reasons why the United States was justified in annexing Texas and why it must soon do the same in replacing Mexican rule in California. Claims of Manifest Destiny often accompanied American conquest and colonization of new territories.

. . . Texas has been absorbed into the Union in the inevitable fulfilment of the general law which is rolling our population westward; the connexion of which with that ratio of growth in population which is destined within a hundred years to swell our numbers to the enormous population of *two hundred and fifty millions* (if not more), is too evident to leave us in doubt of the manifest design of Providence in regard to the occupation of this continent. It was disintegrated from Mexico in the natural course of events, by a process perfectly legitimate on its own part, blameless on ours; and in which all the censures due to wrong, perfidy and folly, rest on Mexico alone. And possessed as it was by a population which was in truth but a colonial detachment from our own, and which was still bound by myriad ties of the very heart strings to its old relations, domestic and political, their incorporation into the Union was not only inevitable, but the most natural, right and proper thing in the world. . . .

California will, probably, next fall away from the loose adhesion which, in such a country as Mexico, holds a remote province in a slight equivocal kind of dependence on the metropolis. Imbecile and distracted, Mexico never can exert any real governmental authority over such a country. The impotence of the one and the distance of the other, must make the relation one of virtual independence. . . . The Anglo-Saxon foot is already on its borders. Already the advance guard of the irresistible army of Anglo-Saxon emigration has begun to pour down upon it, armed with the plough and the rifle, and marking its trail with schools and colleges, courts and representative halls, mills and meeting-houses. A population will soon be in actual occupation of California, over which it will be idle for Mexico to dream of dominion. They will necessarily become independent.

QUESTIONS FOR ANALYSIS

- What is the main reason O'Sullivan gives for why the United States must expand westward?
- How does O'Sullivan justify the annexation of Texas by the United States?
- In terms of California, in what ways is "the Anglo-Saxon foot already on its borders"?
- Why does O'Sullivan think that the people of Texas and California will want to join the United States?

Source: John L. O'Sullivan, "Manifest Destiny," Democratic Review *(July 1845), pp. 7–10, in Clark C. Spence, ed.,* The American West: A Source Book *(New York: Thomas Y. Crowell Company, 1966), pp. 108–9.*

this growth was the expansion of railroad lines. In 1865, the United States boasted 35,000 miles of track. By 1900, nearly 200,000 miles of track connected the Atlantic to the Pacific and crisscrossed the American territory in between. Increasingly, steam-powered machines replaced human muscle as the engine of production, bringing dramatic improvements in output. Before the Civil War, it took sixty-one hours of labor to produce an acre of wheat; by 1900, new machinery cut the time to a little over three hours. Mechanization boosted production on farms and in factories, and rapid railroad transportation permitted the shipment of more goods at lower prices across greater distances.

ECONOMIC AND INDUSTRIAL DEVELOPMENT Americans made such impressive industrial gains that the United States soon joined Britain and Germany atop the list of economic giants. (The gains were in technical education, inventions, factory routines, marketing, and the mobilization of capital.) A potent instrument of capital accumulation appeared at this time—the **limited-liability joint-stock company**. Firms such as Standard Oil and U.S. Steel mobilized capital from shareholders, who left the running of these enterprises to paid managers. Intermediaries, like J. Pierpont Morgan, the New York financial giant who became the world's wealthiest man, loaned money and brokered big deals on the New York Stock Exchange. So great were the fortunes amassed by leading financiers and industrialists that by 1890 the richest 1 percent of Americans owned nearly 90 percent of the nation's wealth.

African American Gains and Losses. *In the immediate aftermath of the American Civil War, "Radical Republicans" asserted political control by passing laws and constitutional amendments ending slavery, guaranteeing equal rights, and enfranchising freedmen. One result was the election of African Americans* (above) *to the U.S. Congress. During the 1870s, however, white leaders retreated from the commitment to black rights, allowing ex-Confederates to re-assert control over southern politics.* (Right) *The Ku Klux Klan terrorized African Americans in the post-Civil War South. Klan violence reversed many of the legal and political gains made by freedmen and helped restore planters to power in the South.*

As mechanized production churned out ever more goods, farms and factories produced more than Americans needed or could afford to purchase. In the 1890s, overproduction plunged the American economy into a harsh depression. Millions of urban workers lost their jobs; others suffered sharp cuts in wages. Soon radical labor leaders called for the dismantling of the industrial capitalist state, and strikes proliferated. In the countryside, declining prices and excessive railroad freight charges pushed countless farmers toward bankruptcy.

Meanwhile, Americans were continuing their migrations west. Joined by throngs of immigrants from Europe, they were attracted by homestead acts promising nearly free acreage to settlers and by the railroad's real estate promoters. (Railroad corporations had been given enormous land grants as a subsidy for building transcontinental lines.) The migrations sparked another round of wars with Indians, which resulted in their dispossession and concentration on reservations.

By now the United States had become a major world power. It boasted an economy that despite its troubles in the 1890s had expanded rapidly over the last decades of the nineteenth century. It also was a more integrated nation after the Civil War, with an amended constitution that claimed to uphold the equality of all members of the American nation. But there was no agreement on what that equality should involve or how the country would adjust to a new century in which the nation's "destiny" had already been fulfilled.

Canada

Canadians also built a new nation, enjoyed economic success, and followed an expansionist course. Like the United States, Canada had access to a vast frontier prairie for growing agricultural exports. And as in the United States, these lands became the homes and farms of more European immigrants. However, whereas the United States had waged a war to gain independence, Canada's separation from Britain was peaceful. From the 1830s to the 1860s, Britain gradually passed authority to the colony, leaving Canadians to grapple with the task of creating a shared national community.

BUILDING A NATION Sharp internal divisions made that task especially difficult. For one thing, there was a well-established French population. It had remained after the British took control of France's northernmost North American colony in 1763. Wanting to keep their villages, their culture, their religion, and their language intact, these French Canadians did not feel integrated into the emerging Canadian national community. Nor were they eager to join the English-speaking population in settling new areas, lest such migration dilute their French-Canadian presence.

The English-speakers were equally unenthusiastic about creating an independent nation. Fear of being absorbed into the American republic reinforced these Canadians' loyalty to

Oklahoma Land Rush. *This photograph captures the rush of homesteaders to claim lands on the "Cherokee Strip" on September 16, 1893. The opening of land that had previously been restricted to Indians set off several similar rushes in the Oklahoma Territory.*

the British crown and made them content with colonial status. Indeed, when Canada finally gained its independence in 1867, it was by an Act of Parliament in London and not by revolution. But even with nationhood granted, Canadians promised to remain loyal to the British crown and declared themselves a "dominion" within the British Commonwealth.

TERRITORIAL EXPANSION Lacking cultural and linguistic unity, not to mention an imperial overlord, Canadians used territorial expansion to build an integrated state. But their process differed from that of their neighbor to the south. In response to the U.S. purchase of Alaska from Russia and the movement of settlers onto the American plains, Canadian leaders realized that they had to incorporate their own western territories, lest these, too, fall into American hands. Pioneers seemed unwilling to venture to these prairies—it was far, it was cold, and the growing season was cruelly short. So the state lured emigrant farmers from Europe and the United States with subsidized railway rates and the promise of fortunes to be made. It also offered attractive terms to railway companies to connect agrarian hinterlands with Montreal and Toronto (see again Map 17.1), and *not* with commercial cities in the United States.

The Canadian state also faced friction with Indians. Frontier warfare threatened to drive away investors and settlers, who could always find property south of the border instead. To prevent the kind of bloodletting that characterized the United States' westward expansion, the Canadian government signed treaties with Indians to ensure strict separation between natives and newcomers. It also created a special police force, the Royal Canadian Mounted Police, to patrol the territories.

Canadian expansion was hardly bloodless, however. Many Indians and mixed-blood peoples (*métis*) resented the treaties. Moreover, the Canadian government was often less than honest in its dealings. As in the United States, the government's Indian policy in Canada sought to turn Indians into farmers and then incorporate them into Canadian society—regardless of whether they wanted to become farmers or join the nation.

The need to accommodate resident French speakers, defensive expansionism, and a degree of legality in dealing with Indians gave the Canadian government a strong foundation. Indeed, it acquired significant powers to intervene, regulate, and mediate social conflict and relations. (These powers, in fact, were fuller than those of the U.S. government.) But even though the state was relatively strong, the sense of a national identity was comparatively weak. Expansionism helped Canada remain an autonomous state, but it did not solve the question of what it meant to belong to a Canadian nation.

Latin America

Latin American elites also engaged in nation-state building and expanded their territorial borders. But unlike in the United States and Canada, expansion did not always create homesteader frontiers that could help expand democracy and forge national identities. Instead, civil conflict fractured certain countries in the region (see Chapters 15 and 16), although one—Brazil—remained united.

Much of Latin America shared a common social history. Far more than in North America, the richest lands in Latin America went not to small farmers, but to large estate holders producing

Opera House in Manaus. *The turn-of-the-century rubber boom brought immense wealth to the Amazon jungle. As in many boom-and-bust cycles in Latin America, the proceeds flowed to a small elite and diminished when the rubber supply outstripped the demand. But the wealth produced was sufficient to prompt the local elite to build temples of modernity in the midst of the jungle. Pictured here is the Opera House in the rubber capital of Manaus. Like other works built by Latin American elites of the period, this one emulated the original in Paris.*

exports such as sugar, coffee, or beef. The result: privileged elites monopolized power more than in North America's young democracies. Even though territorial expansion and strong economic growth were Latin American hallmarks, these processes sidelined the poor, the Indians, and the blacks.

CONSOLIDATION VERSUS FRAGMENTATION Indian and peasant uprisings were a major worry in new Latin American republics. Fearing insurrections, elites devised governing systems that protected private property and investments while limiting the political rights of the poor and the propertyless. Likewise, the specter of slave revolts, driven home not just by earlier, brutal events in Haiti (see Chapter 15) but also by daily rumors of rebellions, kept elites in a state of alarm. One Argentine writer echoed the concern about giving too much power to the masses, and he described the challenge of nation-state building in Latin America as a struggle between elitist "civilization" and popular "barbarism." Creating strong nations, it seemed to many Latin American elites, required excluding large groups of people from power.

BRAZIL: AN "EXCLUSIVE" NATION-STATE Brazil illustrates the process by which Latin American rulers built nation-states that excluded much of the population from both the "nation" and the "state." Through the nineteenth century, rulers in Rio de Janeiro defused political conflict by allowing planters to retain the reins of power. Moreover, although the Brazilian government officially abolished the slave trade in 1830, it allowed illegal slave imports to continue for another two decades (until British pressure compelled Brazil to enforce the ban).

The end of the slave trade, coupled with slave resistance, began to choke the planters' system by driving up the price of slaves within the region. Sensing that the system of forced labor was unraveling, slaves began to flee the sugar and coffee plantations, and army personnel refused to hunt them down. In the 1880s, even while laws still upheld slave labor, country roads in the state of São Paulo were filled with fugitive slaves looking for relatives or access to land. Finally, in 1888, the Brazilian emperor abolished slavery.

Thereafter, as in the United States, Brazilian elites followed two strategies in creating a new labor force for their estates. They retained some former slaves as gang-workers or sharecroppers, and they also imported new workers—especially from Italy, Spain, and Portugal. These laborers often came as seasonal migrant workers or indentured tenant farmers. Indeed, European and even Japanese migration to Brazil helped planters preserve their holdings in the post-slavery era. In all, 2 million Europeans and some 70,000 Japanese moved to Brazil.

The Brazilian state was deliberately exclusive. The constitution of 1891, which established a federal system and proclaimed Brazil a republic, separated those who could be trusted with power from the rest. After all, with the abolition of slavery, the sudden enfranchisement of millions of freedmen would have threatened to flood the electoral lists with propertyless, potentially uncontrollable voters. As in the United States, politicians responded by slapping severe restrictions on suffrage and by rigging rules to reduce political competition. However, given the greater share of the black population in Brazil, restrictions there excluded a larger share of the potential electorate than in the United States.

BRAZIL: EXPANSION AND ECONOMIC DEVELOPMENT Like Canada and the United States, the Brazilian state extended its reach to distant areas and incorporated them as provinces. The largest land-grab occurred in the Amazon River basin, the world's largest drainage watershed and tropical forest. It had built up over millennia around the meandering tributaries that convey runoffs from the eastern slopes of the Andean mountains all the way to the Atlantic Ocean. It was a massive yet delicate habitat of balanced biomass suspended by towering trees with a canopy of leaves and vines that kept the basin ecologically diverse. Here, the Brazilian state gave giant concessions to local capitalists to extract rubber latex. When combined with sulfur, rubber was a key raw material for tire manufacturing in European and North American bicycle and automobile industries.

Rubber Plantation Workers. *A worker harvests latex, a milky fluid that is secreted from a rubber tree via taps in its trunk (left). The worker must work quickly to collect (right) and process it into dry rubber before it coagulates.*

As Brazil became the world's exclusive exporter of rubber, its planters, merchants, and workers prospered. Rich merchants became lenders and financiers, not only to workers but also to landowners themselves. The mercantile elite of Manaus, the capital of the Amazon region, designed and decorated their city to reflect their new fortunes. Although the streets were still paved with mud, the town's elite built a replica of the Paris Opera House, and Manaus became a regular stopover for European opera singers on the circuit between Buenos Aires and New York. Rubber workers also benefited from the boom. Mostly either Indians or mixed-blood people, they sent their wages home to families elsewhere in the Amazon jungle or on the northeastern coast of Brazil.

But the Brazilian rubber boom soon went bust. One problem was the ecosystem: such a diversified biomass could not tolerate a regimented form of production that emphasized the cultivation of rubber trees at the expense of other vegetation and made the forest vulnerable to nonhuman predators. Leaf blight and ferocious ants destroyed all experiments at creating more sustainable rubber plantations. Moreover, it was expensive to haul the rubber latex out of the jungle all the way to the coast along the slow-moving Amazon River. Another problem was that Brazilian rubber faced severe competition after a British scientist smuggled rubber plant seeds out of Brazil in 1876. Following years of experimentation, British patrons transplanted a blight-resistant hybrid to the British colony of Ceylon (present-day Sri Lanka). As competition led to increased supplies and reduced prices, Brazilian producers went bankrupt. Merchants called in their loans, landowners forfeited their titles, and rubber workers returned to their subsistence economies. Tropical vines crept over the Manaus Opera House, and it gradually fell into disrepair.

Throughout the Americas, nineteenth-century societies worked to adapt obsolete elite models of politics and to satisfy popular demands for inclusion. While the ideal was to construct nation-states that could reconcile differences among their citizens and pave the way for economic prosperity, in fact political autonomy did not bring prosperity, or even the right to vote, to all. As each nation-state expanded its territorial boundaries, many new inhabitants were left out of the political realm.

CONSOLIDATION OF NATION-STATES IN EUROPE

In Europe, no "frontier" existed into which new nations could expand. Instead, nation-states took shape out of older monarchies, and their borders were determined by diplomats or by battles between rival claimants. In the wake of the French Revolution, the idea caught on that "the people" should form the basis for the nation and that nations should be culturally homogenous—but no one could agree on who "the people" should be. Yet, over the course of the nineteenth century, as literacy, the cities, industrial production, and the number and prosperity of property owners expanded, ruling elites had no choice but to share power with a wider group of citizens. These citizens, in turn, increasingly defined themselves as, say, Frenchmen or Germans, rather than as residents of Marseilles or subjects of the King of Bavaria.

Defining "The Nation"

For a very long time, in most places, "the nation" was understood to comprise kings, clergymen, nobles—and occasionally rich merchants or lawyers—and no one else. Although some peoples, such as the English and the Spanish, were already self-conscious about their unique histories, only in the late eighteenth century were the crucial building blocks of European nationalism put in place.

To begin with, intellectuals laid the ideological foundations of the nation. In 1776, Adam Smith had described the wealth of each nation as equivalent to the combined output of all its producers, not the sum in the king's treasury. Then, in 1789, the left-leaning French clergyman Emmanuel Joseph Sieyès had published a widely circulated pamphlet arguing that the nation consisted of all of those who worked to enrich it, and that those who were "parasites" (Sieyès meant the clergy and the aristocracy) did not belong. Sieyès's revolutionary Declaration of the Rights of Man and the Citizen, inspired by the American Declaration of Independence, declared that all men were equal under the law and insisted that "the principle of all sovereignty lies essentially in the nation."

Material and social conditions also prepared the way for nation-states. During the nineteenth century, a huge expansion of literacy and the periodical press made it possible for people all across Europe to read books and newspapers in their own languages. At the same time, the emerging industrial economy brought people into closer contact and made merchants anxious to standardize laws, taxation policies, and weights and measures. States invested huge sums in building roads and then railroads—and these linked provincial towns and bigger cities, laying the foundations for a closer political integration.

But who were the people, and what constituted a viable nation-state? Neither Smith's treatise nor Sieyès's pamphlet could clarify which people belonged inside which nation-state, for belonging to a nation had long been associated with the sharing of cultural or religious traditions. For some people, the nation was a collection of all those who spoke one language; for others, it was all those who lived in the domains of one prince, or who shared a religious heritage. This was a particularly acute problem in multiethnic central and southeastern Europe, where even peasants were often multilingual. But some who shared the same language objected to being lumped into one nation-state. The Irish, for example, spoke English but were predominately Catholics and wanted to be free from Anglican rule.

The Europe-wide revolutions of 1848 (see Chapters 15 and 16) sought to put "the people" in power; in many cases, too, rebels sought to create unified nation-states, each of which would serve one particular cultural and linguistic group. (Examples include the Czechs and Italians, both of whom wanted states independent from the Habsburg Empire.) But the revolutions ran into difficulties defining who "the people" were and how to fashion new nations out of Europe's multiethnic empires. Deep divisions opened among ethnic groups and between middle-class liberals and radicals, some of whom wanted to share out the nation's wealth. Monarchs took advantage of the chaos and restored their regimes. The troubling questions continued to agitate Europe for many years to come. (See Primary Source: What Is a Nation?)

Unification in Germany and Italy

Two of Europe's fledgling nation-states came into being when the dynastic states of Prussia and Piedmont-Sardinia swallowed their smaller, linguistically related neighbors, creating the German and Italian nation-states (see Map 17.2). In both regions, conservative prime ministers—Count Otto von Bismarck of Prussia and Count Camillo di Cavour of Piedmont—exploited radical, and especially liberal, nationalist sentiment to rearrange the map of Europe.

BUILDING UNIFIED STATES The unification of Germany and Italy posed all the familiar problems of who the people were and who should be included in the new nation-states. To begin with, German-speakers were spread all across central and eastern Europe, a result of more than a millennium of eastward colonization. For centuries, they had lived in many different states. Similarly, Italian-speakers had lived separately in city-states and small kingdoms on the Italian peninsula. The historical experiences and economic developments had made Bavarian Germans (Catholic) quite different from Prussian Germans (Protestant); likewise, the Milanese (who lived in a wealthy urban industrial center) shared little with the typical Sardinian peasant. But liberal nationalists had made the case that a shared language and literature overrode all these differences, and emotional appeals by poets, composers, and orators convinced many people that this was indeed the case.

Ultimately, two conservative leaders, Bismarck and Cavour, merged nationalist rhetoric with clever diplomacy to forge united German and Italian polities. Nor did they ignore military might. In a famous address in 1862, Bismarck bellowed: "Not through speeches and majority decisions are the great questions of the day decided—that was the great mistake of 1848 and 1849—but through blood and iron." True to his word, Bismarck accomplished the unification of northern German states by war: with Denmark in 1864, Austria in 1866, and France (over the western provinces of Alsace and Lorraine) in 1870–1871. Italy also was united through a series of small conflicts, many of them engineered to prevent the establishment of more radical republics.

STATES' INTERNAL CONFLICTS These "unified" states rejected democracy. In the new Italy, which was a constitutional monarchy, not a republic, less than 5 percent of the 25 million people could vote. The new German empire (the Reich) did have an assembly elected by all adult males (the Reichstag), but

PRIMARY SOURCE

What Is a Nation?

The French linguist and historian of religion Ernest Renan explored the concept of nationhood in an 1882 essay entitled "What Is a Nation?" Arguing with racial, religious, and language-based interpretations of nationhood, Renan offers an explicitly republican model.

. . . The principle of nations is our principle. But what, then, is a nation? . . . Why is Switzerland, with its three languages, its two religions, and three or four races, a nation, when Tuscany, for example, which is so homogeneous, is not? Why is Austria a state and not a nation? In what does the principle of nations differ from that of races? . . .

Ethnographic considerations have . . . played no part in the formation of modern nations. France is Celtic, Iberic, and Germanic. Germany is Germanic, Celtic, and Slav. Italy is the country in which ethnography finds its greatest difficulties. Here Gauls, Etruscans, Pelasgians, and Greeks are crossed in an unintelligible medley. The British Isles, taken as a whole, exhibit a mixture of Celtic and Germanic blood, the proportions of which are particularly difficult to define.

The truth is that no race is pure, and that to base politics on ethnographic analysis is tantamount to basing it on a chimera. . . .

What we have said about race, applies also to language. Language invites union, without, however, compelling it. The United States and England, as also Spanish America and Spain, speak the same language without forming a single nation. Switzerland, on the contrary, whose foundations are solid because they are based on the assent of the various parties, contains three or four languages. There exists in man a something which is above language: and that is his will. The will of Switzerland to be united, in spite of the variety of these forms of speech, is a much more important fact than a similarity of language, often attained by vexatious measures. . . .

Nor can religion provide a satisfactory basis for a modern nationality. . . . Nowadays . . . everyone believes and practices religion in his own way according to his capacities and wishes. State religion has ceased to exist; and a man can be a Frenchman, an Englishman, or a German, and at the same time a Catholic, a Protestant, or a Jew, or practice no form of worship at all.

A nation is a soul, a spiritual principle. Two things, which are really only one, go to make up this soul or spiritual principle. One of these things lies in the past, the other in the present. The one is the possession in common of a rich heritage of memories; and the other is actual agreement, the desire to live together, and the will to continue to make the most of the joint inheritance. . . . The nation, like the individual, is the fruit of a long past spent in toil, sacrifice, and devotion. . . . To share the glories of the past, and a common will in the present; to have done great deeds together, and to desire to do more— . . . These are things which are understood, in spite of differences in race and language.

. . . The existence of a nation is . . . a daily plebiscite. . . . A province means to us its inhabitants; and if anyone has a right to be consulted in the matter, it is the inhabitant. It is never to the true interest of a nation to annex or keep a country against its will. The people's wish is after all the only justifiable criterion, to which we must always come back.

QUESTIONS FOR ANALYSIS

- According to Renan, what are the two key ingredients needed to create a nation-state?
- What arguments does Renan offer against basing nationhood on a common race, religion, or language?

Source: Ernest Renan, "What Is a Nation?" in The Nationalism Reader, *edited by Omar Dahbour and Micheline R. Ishay (Atlantic Highlands, NJ: Humanities Press, 1995), pp. 143–55.*

it was ruled by a combination of aristocrats and bureaucrats under a monarch. Liberals dominated in many localities, but only the emperor (the kaiser) could depose the prime minister. In fact, Bismarck continued to dominate Prussian politics for twenty-eight years, until fired in 1890 by Kaiser Wilhelm II, who was even more authoritarian and bellicose.

The new states were not internally cohesive. In Italy, Piedmontese liberals in the north hoped that centralized rule would transform southern Italy into a prosperous, commercial, and industrial region like their own. But southern notables, who owned large agricultural estates, had little interest in northern customs. While the northern provinces industrialized and developed commercial links with Switzerland and France, the southern ones remained agrarian and largely isolated from modernizing processes. In Germany, many non-Germans—Poles in Silesia, French in Alsace and Lorraine, Danes in the provinces of

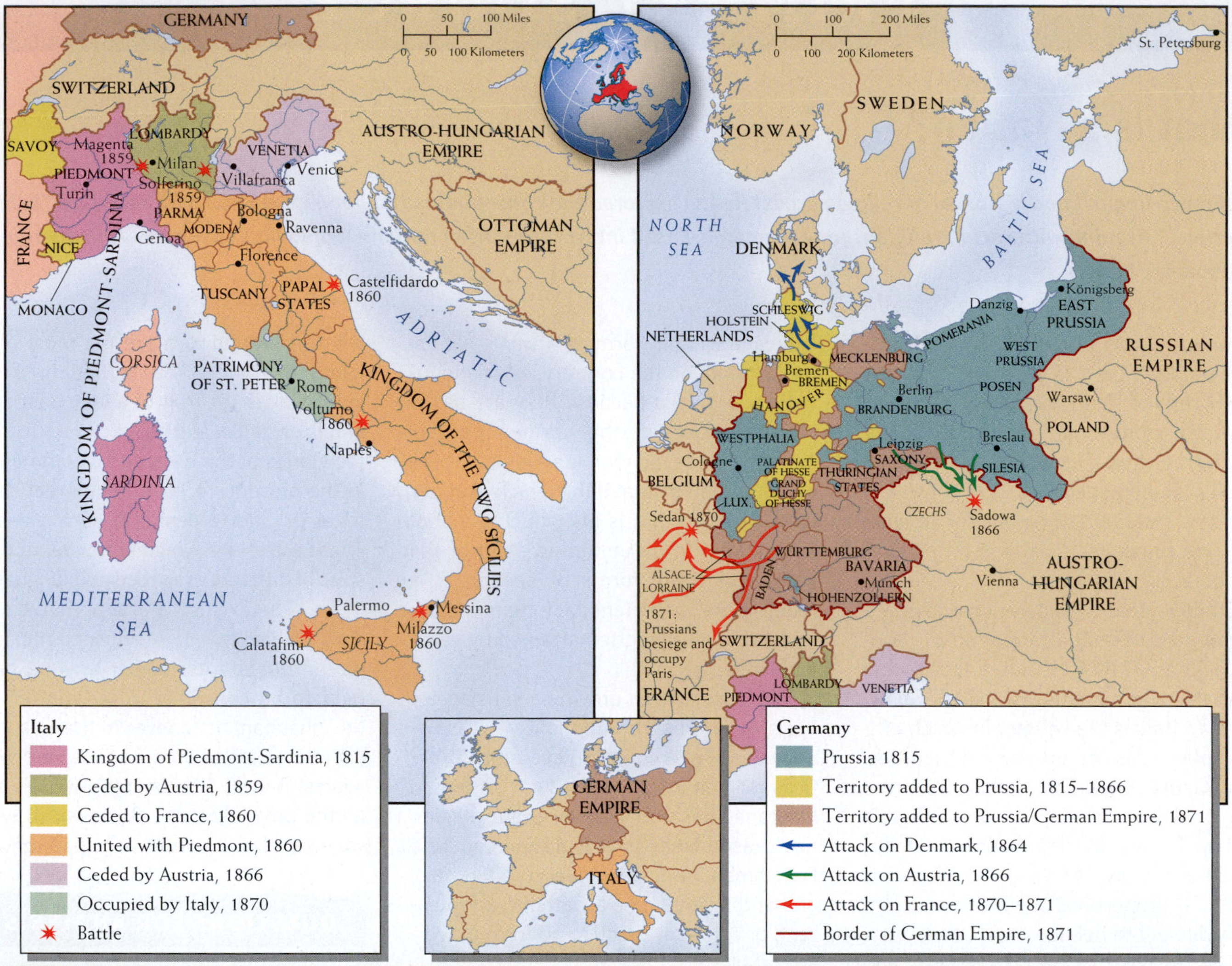

MAP 17.2 | Italian Unification and German Unification, 1815–1871

Italian unification and German unification altered the political map of Europe.

- What were the names of the two original states that grew to become Italy and Germany? Who were the big losers in these territorial transfers?
- According to your reading, what problems did the new Italian and German states face in creating strong national communities?

Schleswig-Holstein—became "national minorities" whose rights remained in question. In the 1870s, Bismarck branded both Catholics and socialists as traitors to the new state; both retaliated by forming powerful political movements. By the 1890s, unification had yielded brisk economic growth, especially for the Germans, but conflict between regions and political groups continued.

Berlin, the capital of Prussia, now became the capital of the German Reich. Although Kaiser Wilhelm II remarked in 1892 that "the glory of Paris robs Berliners of their sleep," Berlin was on the rise. Its population of 1 million people in 1875 had doubled by 1910. The overall German population boomed as well, and the French, whose birthrates were dropping, worried about swelling battalions of well-drilled German soldiers.

Nation Building and Ethnic Conflict in the Austro-Hungarian Empire

Bismarck's wars of unification came at the expense of Habsburg supremacy in central Europe and of French territory and influence in the west. Following Germany's swift victory over the Austrian army in 1866, the Hungarian nobles who controlled the eastern Habsburg Empire forced the weakened dynasts to grant them home rule. In the Compromise of 1867, the Habsburgs agreed that their state would officially be known as the Austro-Hungarian Empire. But this move did not solve Austria-Hungary's nationality problems. In both the Hungarian and the Austrian halves of the dual state, Czechs, Poles, and other Slavs now began to clamor for their own power-sharing "compromise" or autonomous national homelands.

In 1871, the Habsburg emperor seemed prepared to accommodate the Czechs and put them politically on a par with the Hungarians. But the emperor's Hungarian partners scuttled the deal. After this point, interethnic conflict increased over divisive issues such as whether the Czech (or Italian, Serbo-Croatian, Polish, Ukrainian, etc.) language could be used instead of German in regional administrative and educational settings and whether bureaucrats should have to be able to speak more than one language. Moreover, by the 1880s, a wave of impoverished eastern European Jews and non-Jewish Slavs migrating from the countryside entered Austria-Hungary's larger cities, stimulating anti-Semitic feeling and racist political pressure groups. Still, loyalty to the emperor was widespread and multinationalism flourished in the imperial bureaucracy, in the army officers' corps (whose members had to speak both German and the languages of the soldiers under their command), in the upper administration of the Catholic Church, and in the highly cosmopolitan cities.

Domestic Discontents in France and Britain

Although already unified as nation-states, Britain and France, too, faced major difficulties. For the French, dealing with military defeat at the hands of the Germans was the primary national concern in the decades leading up to World War I. For the British, issues of Irish separatism, the rise of the working class, and feminists' demands troubled the political arena.

DESTABILIZATION IN FRANCE Bismarck launched the Franco-Prussian War of 1870–1871 in order to complete the unification of Germany; he did not intend to destabilize France. But the sound drubbing the French troops received, and the capture of Napoleon III early in the conflict, proved embarrassing and upsetting. Even more catastrophic for France was the German siege of Paris, which lasted for more than three months. Unprepared, Parisians had no food stocks and were compelled to eat all sorts of things, including two zoo elephants. Under terrible conditions and without effective leadership, the French capital resisted until January 1871, when the government signed a humiliating peace treaty—in the Hall of Mirrors at Versailles, formerly the residence of France's powerful "Sun King." The Germans left in place a weak provisional French government. Furious Parisians vented their rage and established a socialist commune proclaiming the city a utopia for workers. The leftist commune lasted until the provisional government's predominantly peasant army stormed Paris a few months later. At least 25,000 Parisians died in the bloody mop-up that followed.

A "Third Republic" took the place of Napoleon III's empire, but its conservative leaders were wary of the socialists and workers. They also were determined to revenge themselves for their humiliation in 1871. For the French, the years to follow would bring two unsettling developments: increasingly sharp conflict between classes over the shape of the republic, and rising anti-German nationalism. Some of this antagonism also radiated outward to target French colonial subjects, who now experienced more virulent forms of racism.

IRISH NATIONALISM IN GREAT BRITAIN Although the English had long thought of themselves as a nation, the idea that all Britons belonged in the same state was much more problematic. Great Britain—composed of England, Wales, Scotland, and Ireland—was home to people whose historical experiences, religious backgrounds, and economic opportunities were very different. In the nineteenth century, British leaders wrestled in particular with lower-class agitation and demands for independence from Irish nationalists. England responded to these pressures by extending political rights to all men but not women. Thereafter, free trade and progress became the priorities of a middle class flush with new wealth generated by industry and empire. The long reign of Queen Victoria (r. 1837–1901), as well as England's prosperity, overseas conquests, and world power, increasingly bound both workers and owners to the nation.

Yet Ireland remained England's Achilles' heel. Although in 1836 Irish Catholics finally became equal to Protestants before the law, the two communities' political and economic conditions remained very uneven. The English were widely condemned for their failure to relieve Irish suffering during the potato famine of 1846–1849 (see Chapter 15); even though millions of poor Irish and Scottish workers made their way to England, seeking either passage to North America or work in the English mill towns, they did not assimilate easily and often got the lowliest jobs. All of this, on top of 300 years of repressive English domination, spawned a mass movement for Irish home rule.

Born in opposition to the old monarchical regimes, European nationalism by the end of the nineteenth century had become a means used by liberal and conservative leaders alike to unite "the people" behind them. In most places, aside from Russia, "the people" essentially meant all adult males—and that group had won the right to vote in national elections (though most states still had monarchs as well). The new nation-states had been shaped by increasing literacy and urbanization, but also by warfare.

INDUSTRY, SCIENCE, AND TECHNOLOGY

A powerful combination of industry, science, and technology shaped the emerging nation-states in North America and western Europe. It also reordered the relationships among different parts of the world. One critical factor was that after 1850 western Europe and North America experienced a new phase of industrial development—essentially a second industrial revolution. Japan, too, joined the ranks of industrializing nations as its state-led program of industrial development started to pay dividends. These changes transformed the global economy and intensified rivalries among industrial societies. For example, Britain now had to contend with competition from the United States and Germany.

New Materials, Technologies, and Business Practices

New materials and new technologies were vital in late-nineteenth-century economic development. For example, **steel**, which was more malleable and stronger than iron, became essential for industries like shipbuilding and railways. The world output of steel shot up from half a million tons in 1870 to 28 million tons in 1900. The miracle of steel was celebrated through the construction of the Eiffel Tower (completed in 1889) in Paris, an aggressively modern monument that loomed over the picturesque cityscape and was double the height of any other building in the world at the time. Steel was part of a bundle of innovations that included chemicals, oil, pharmaceuticals, and mass transportation vehicles like trolleys and automobiles.

The late nineteenth century witnessed major technological changes with the arrival of new organic sources of power (like oil) and new ways to get old organic sources (like coal) to processing plants. These changes freed manufacturers from having to locate their plants close to their fuel sources. Not only did the most important new source of energy—electricity—permit factories to arise in areas with plenty of skilled workers, but it also slashed production costs. Scientific research, too, boosted industrial development. German companies led the way in creating laboratories where university-trained chemists and physicists conducted research to serve industrial production. The United States likewise wedded scientific research with capitalist enterprise: universities and corporate laboratories produced swelling ranks of engineers and scientists, as well as patents.

The breakthroughs of the second industrial revolution ushered in new business practices, especially mass production and the giant integrated firm. No longer would modest investments

Eiffel Tower. *This 1890 photograph of an illuminated Eiffel Tower encapsulates the fact and spirit of early twentieth-century technological innovation, from the architectural breakthrough of the tower itself to the harnessing of electricity to truly render Paris its namesake—The City of Light.*

suffice, as they had in Britain a century earlier. Now large banks were the major providers of funds. In Europe, limited-liability joint-stock companies were as wildly successful in raising capital on stock markets as they were in the United States. Companies like Standard Oil, U.S. Steel, and Siemens mobilized capital from a large number of investors, called shareholders. The scale of these firms was awesome. U.S. Steel alone produced over half the world's steel ingots, castings, rails, and heavy structural shapes—and nearly half of all its steel plates and sheets, which were vital in the construction of buildings, railroads, ships, and the like.

Integration of the World Economy

Not only did industrial change concentrate power in North Atlantic societies, but it also reinforced their power on the world economic stage. Of course, Europe and the United States increased their exports in new products; but at the same time, they grew eager to control the importation of tropical commodities such as cocoa and coffee. While the North Atlantic societies were still largely self-sufficient in coal, iron, cotton, wool, and wheat (the major commodities of the first industrial revolution), the second industrial revolution bred a need for rubber, copper,

Railroad Workers. *The construction of railroad lines across the United States was dangerous work, much of it done by immigrant laborers, including large numbers of Chinese, such as those in this photograph taken in 1886.*

oil, and bauxite (an ore used to make aluminum), which were not available domestically. Equally important, large pools of money became available for investing overseas. London may have lost its industrial leadership, but it retained dominance over the world's financial operations. By 1913, the British had the huge sum of £4 billion invested overseas—funds that generated an annual income of £200 million, or one-tenth of Britain's national income.

MOVEMENTS OF LABOR AND TECHNOLOGY Because the more integrated world economy needed workers for fields, factories, and mines, vast movements of the laboring population took place. Indians moved thousands of miles to work on sugar plantations in the Caribbean, Mauritius, and Fiji, and to build railroads in East Africa. Chinese workers constructed railroads in the western United States and toiled on sugar plantations in Cuba. The Irish, Poles, Jews, Italians, and Greeks flocked to North America to fill its burgeoning factories. Italians also moved to Argentina to harvest wheat and corn.

New technologies of warfare, transportation, and communication eased global economic integration—and strengthened European domination. With steam-powered gunboats and breech-loading rifles, Europeans opened new territories for trade and conquest. At home and in their colonial possessions, imperial powers constructed networks of railroads that carried people and goods from hinterlands to the coasts. From there, steamships bore them across the seas. Completion of the Suez Canal in 1869 shortened ship voyages between Europe and Asia and lowered the costs of interregional trade. Information moved even faster than cargoes, thanks to the laying of telegraph cables under the oceans, supplemented by overland telegraph lines.

CHARLES DARWIN AND NATURAL SELECTION Although machines were the most visible evidence that humans could master the universe, perhaps the most momentous shift in the conception of nature derived from the travels of one British scientist: **Charles Darwin** (1809–1882). Longing to see exotic fauna, in 1831 he signed on for a four-year voyage on a surveying vessel bound for Latin America and the South Seas. As the ship's naturalist, Darwin collected large quantities of specimens and recorded observations daily. After returning to England, he became convinced that the species of organic life had evolved under the uniform pressure of natural laws, not by means of a special, one-time creation as described in the Bible.

Suez Canal. *The Suez Canal opened to world shipping in 1869 and reduced the time it took to sail between Europe and Asian ports. Although the French and the Egyptians supplied most of the money and the construction plans and Egyptians were the main workforce, British shipping dominated canal traffic from the outset.*

Charles Darwin. *Darwin testing the speed of a tortoise in the Galapagos Islands. It was during his visit to these islands that Darwin developed many of the ideas that he would put forth in his 1859* Origin of Species.

Darwin's theory, articulated in his *Origin of Species* (1859), laid out the principles of **natural selection**. Inevitably, he claimed, populations grew faster than the food supply; this condition created a "struggle for existence" among species. In later work he showed how the passing on of individual traits was also determined by what he called sexual selection—according to which the "best" mates are chosen for their strength, beauty, or talents. The outcome: the "fittest" survived to reproduce, while the less adaptable did not. The "economy of nature" was, Darwin confessed, a painful reality: people would rather behold "nature's face bright with gladness" than recognize that some animals must be others' prey and that shortages are, ultimately, part of nature's "miraculous efficiency." Although Darwin's book dealt exclusively with animals (and mostly with birds), his readers immediately wondered what his theory implied for humans. (See Primary Source: *The Origin of Species*.)

A passionate debate began among scientists and laymen, clerics and anthropologists. Some read Darwin's doctrine of the "survival of the fittest" to mean that it was natural for the strong nations to dominate the weak, or justifiable to allow disabled persons to die—something Darwin explicitly refuted. As more groups (mis)interpreted Darwin's theory to suit their own objectives, a set of beliefs known as Social Darwinism legitimated the suffering of the underclasses in industrial society: it was unnatural, Social Darwinists claimed, to tamper with natural selection. In subsequent years Europeans would repeatedly suggest that they had evolved more than Africans and Asians. Extending Darwinian ideas far beyond the scientist's intent, some Europeans came to believe that therefore nature itself gave them the right to rule others.

GLOBAL EXPANSIONISM AND AN AGE OF IMPERIALISM

Increasing rivalries among nations and social tensions within them produced an expansionist wave late in the nineteenth century. Although Africa became the primary focus of interest, a frenzy of territorial conquest overtook Asia as well. The period witnessed the French occupation of Vietnam, Cambodia, and Laos, and the British expansion in Malaya (present-day Malaysia). In China's territories, competition by foreign powers to establish spheres of influence heated up in the 1890s. And in India, imperial ambitions provoked the British to conquer Burma (present-day Myanmar). Moreover, Britain and Russia competed for preeminence from their respective outposts in Afghanistan and central Asia. In the Americas, expansion usually involved the incorporation of new territories as provinces, making them integral parts of the nation.

In Asia and Africa, however, European imperialism turned far-flung territories into colonial possessions. Here, inhabitants were usually designated as subjects of the empire without the rights and privileges of citizens. Britain's imperial regime in India provided lessons to a generation of European colonial officials in Africa and other parts of Asia on how to build this kind of empire.

PRIMARY SOURCE

The Origin of Species

Charles Darwin's* Origin of Species *(1859) was the product of his many years of studying animals and plants. In addressing the question "How and why are new species created?" the book described the process of natural selection, according to which nature creates overabundance so that the "fittest" species survive and adapt themselves to their environments. Although Darwin's book said nothing about human beings, his contemporaries speculated on his theory's implications for the evolution of human beings.

Again, it may be asked, how is it that varieties, which I have called incipient species, become ultimately converted into good and distinct species, which in most cases obviously differ from each other far more than do the varieties of the same species? How do those groups of species, which constitute what are called distinct genera, and which differ from each other more than do the species of the same genus, arise? All these results . . . follow inevitably from the struggle for life. Owing to this struggle for life, any variation, however slight and from whatever cause proceeding, if it be in any degree profitable to an individual of any species, in its infinitely complex relations to other organic beings and to external nature, will tend to the preservation of that individual, and will generally be inherited by its offspring. The offspring, also, will thus have a better chance of surviving, for, of the many individuals of any species which are periodically born, but a small number can survive. I have called this principle, by which each slight variation, if useful, is preserved, by the term of Natural Selection, in order to mark its relation to man's power of selection. We have seen that man by selection can certainly produce great results, and can adapt organic beings to his own uses, through the accumulation of slight but useful variations, given to him by the hand of Nature. But Natural Selection, as we shall hereafter see, is a power incessantly ready for action, and is as immeasurably superior to man's feeble efforts, as the works of Nature are to those of Art.

We will now discuss in a little more detail the struggle for existence. . . . I should premise that I use the term Struggle for Existence in a large and metaphorical sense, including dependence of one being on another, and including (which is more important) not only the life of the individual, but success in leaving progeny. Two canine animals in a time of dearth, may be truly said to struggle with each other which shall get food and live. But a plant on the edge of a desert is said to struggle for life against the drought, though more properly it should be said to be dependent on the moisture. . . .

A struggle for existence inevitably follows from the high rate at which all organic beings tend to increase. Every being, which during its natural lifetime produces several eggs or seeds, must suffer destruction during some period of its life, and during some season or occasional year, otherwise, on the principle of geometrical increase, its numbers would quickly become so inordinately great that no country could support the product. Hence, as more individuals are produced than can possibly survive, there must in every case be a struggle for existence, either one individual with another of the same species, or with the individuals of distinct species, or with the physical conditions of life. . . . Although some species may be now increasing, more or less rapidly, in numbers, all cannot do so, for the world would not hold them.

It may be said that natural selection is daily and hourly scrutinising, throughout the world, every variation, even the slightest; rejecting that which is bad, preserving and adding up all that is good; silently and insensibly working, whenever and wherever opportunity offers, at the improvement of each organic being in relation to its organic and inorganic conditions of life. We see nothing of these slow changes in progress, until the hand of time has marked the long lapses of ages, and then so imperfect is our view into long past geological ages, that we only see that the forms of life are now different from what they formerly were.

QUESTIONS FOR ANALYSIS

- How does Darwin explain the divergence of species?
- Why does Darwin think struggle is inevitable for all living beings?

Source: Charles Darwin, The Origin of Species, *Chapters 3 and 4.*

India and the Imperial Model

Britain's successful colonial rule in India provided a model for others, but its methods of rule also were responses to popular discontent. Having suppressed the Indian Rebellion of 1857 (see Chapter 16), authorities revamped the colonial administration. Indians were not to be appeased—and certainly not brought into British public life. But they did have to be governed, and the economy had to be revived. So, after replacing East India Company rule by crown government in 1858, the British set out

Sinews of the Raj. (Top) *During the second half of the nineteenth century, the British built an extensive system of railroads to develop India as a profitable colony and to maintain military security. This engraving shows the East India Railway around 1863.* (Bottom) *The British allowed several native princes to remain in power as long as they accepted imperial paramountcy. This photograph shows a road-building project in one such princely state. Officials of the Muslim princely ruler and British advisers supervise the workers.*

to make India into a more secure and productive colony. This period of British sovereignty was known as the **Raj** ("rule").

The most urgent tasks facing the British in India were those of modernizing its transportation and communication systems and transforming the country into an integrated colonial state. These changes had begun under the governor-general of the East India Company, Lord Dalhousie, who oversaw the development of India's modern infrastructure. When he left office in 1856, he boasted that he had harnessed India to the "great engines of social improvement—I mean Railways, uniform Postage, and the Electric Telegraph." A year later, northern India exploded in the 1857 rebellion. But the rebellion also demonstrated the military value of railroads and telegraphs, for these modern systems were useful tools for rushing British troops to severely affected regions. After the British suppressed the revolt, they took up the construction of public works with renewed vigor. Railways were a key element in this project, attracting approximately £150 million of British capital. (Though it came from British investors, Indian taxpayers paid off the debt through their taxes.) The first railway line opened in 1853, and by 1910 India had 30,627 miles of track in operation—the fourth largest railway system in the world.

Construction of other public works followed. Engineers built dams across rivers to tame their force and to irrigate lands; workers installed a grid of telegraph lines that opened communication between distant parts of the region. These public works served imperial and economic purposes: India was to become a consumer of British manufactures and a supplier of primary staples such as cotton, tea, wheat, vegetable oil seeds, and jute (used for making rope or burlap sacking). The control of India's massive rivers allowed farmers to cultivate the rich floodplains, transforming them into lucrative cotton-producing provinces.

On the hillsides of the island of Ceylon and the northeastern plains of India, the British established vast plantations to grow tea—which was then marketed in England as a healthier alternative to Chinese green tea. India also became an important consumer of British manufactures, especially textiles, in an ironic turnaround to its centuries-old tradition of exporting its own cotton and silk textiles.

India recorded a consistent surplus in its foreign trade through the export of agricultural goods and raw materials. But what India gained from its trade to the world it lost to Britain, its colonial master, because it had to pay for interest on railroad loans, salaries to colonial officers (even when they went on furlough in Britain), and the maintenance of imperial troops outside India. In reality, India ended up balancing Britain's huge trade deficits with the rest of the world, especially the Americas.

Nonetheless, administrative programs made India into a unified territory and enabled its inhabitants to regard themselves as "Indians." These were the first steps to becoming a "nation"—like Italy and the United States. But there were profound differences. Indians lacked a single national language, and they were not citizens of their political community who enjoyed sovereignty. Rather, they were colonial subjects ruled by outsiders.

Dutch Colonial Rule in Indonesia

The Dutch, like the British, joined the parade of governments trying to modernize and integrate their colonies economically without welcoming colonial peoples into the life of the nation at home. Decades before the British government took control of India away from the East India Company, Holland had terminated the rule of the Dutch East India Company over Indonesia. Beginning in the 1830s, the Dutch government took administrative responsibility over Indonesian affairs. Holland's new colonial officials envisioned a more regulated colonial economy than that of their British counterparts in India. For example, they ordered Indonesian villagers to allocate one-third of their land for cultivating coffee beans, an important export. In return, the colonial government paid a set price (well below world market prices) and placed a ceiling on rents owed to landowners.

These policies had dreadful local consequences. For example, increased production of the export crops of coffee beans, sugar, and tobacco meant reduced food production for the local population. By the 1840s and 1850s, famine spread across Java; over 300,000 Indonesians perished from starvation. Surviving villagers voiced growing discontent, prompting harsh crackdowns by colonial forces. Back in Holland, the embarrassing spectacle of colonial oppression prompted calls for reform. Thus in the 1860s the Dutch government introduced what it called an ethical policy for governing Asian colonies: it reduced governmental exploitation and encouraged Dutch settlement of the islands and more private enterprise. For Indonesians, however, the replacement of government agents with private merchants made little difference. In some areas, islanders put up fierce resistance. On the sprawling island of Sumatra, for instance, armed villagers fought off Dutch invaders. After decades of warfare, Sumatra was finally subdued in 1904. The shipping of Indonesian staples continued to enrich the Dutch.

Colonizing Africa

No region felt the impact of European colonialism more powerfully than Africa. In 1880, the only two large European colonial possessions there were French Algeria and two British-ruled South African states, the Cape Colony and Natal. But within a mere thirty years, seven European states had carved almost all of Africa into colonial possessions (see Map 17.4).

A major moment in initiating the European scramble for African colonies occurred in 1882 when the British invaded and occupied Egypt. This action provoked the French, who had regarded Egypt as their special sphere of influence ever since Napoleon's 1798 invasion. Indeed, Britain's move not only intensified the two powers' rivalry to seize additional territories in Africa, but it also alarmed the other European states, fearful that they might be left behind. As these powers joined the

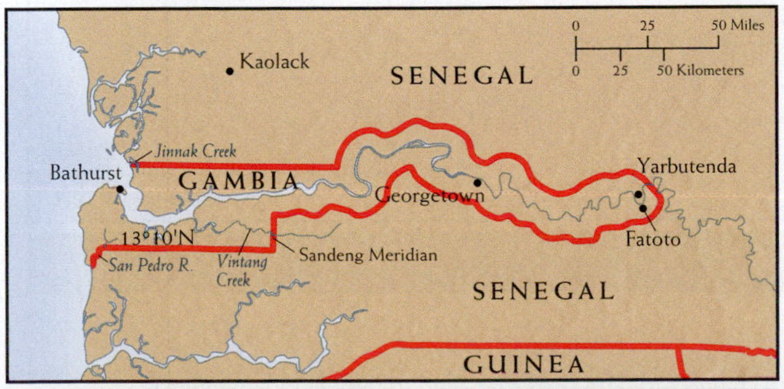

MAP 17.3A | Senegal and Gambia

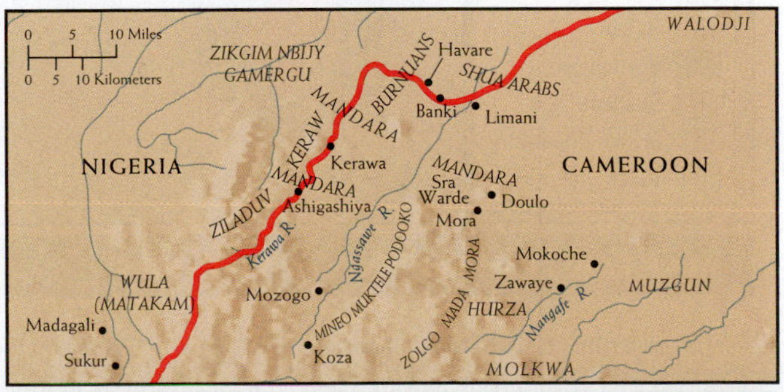

MAP 17.3B | Mandara Peoples

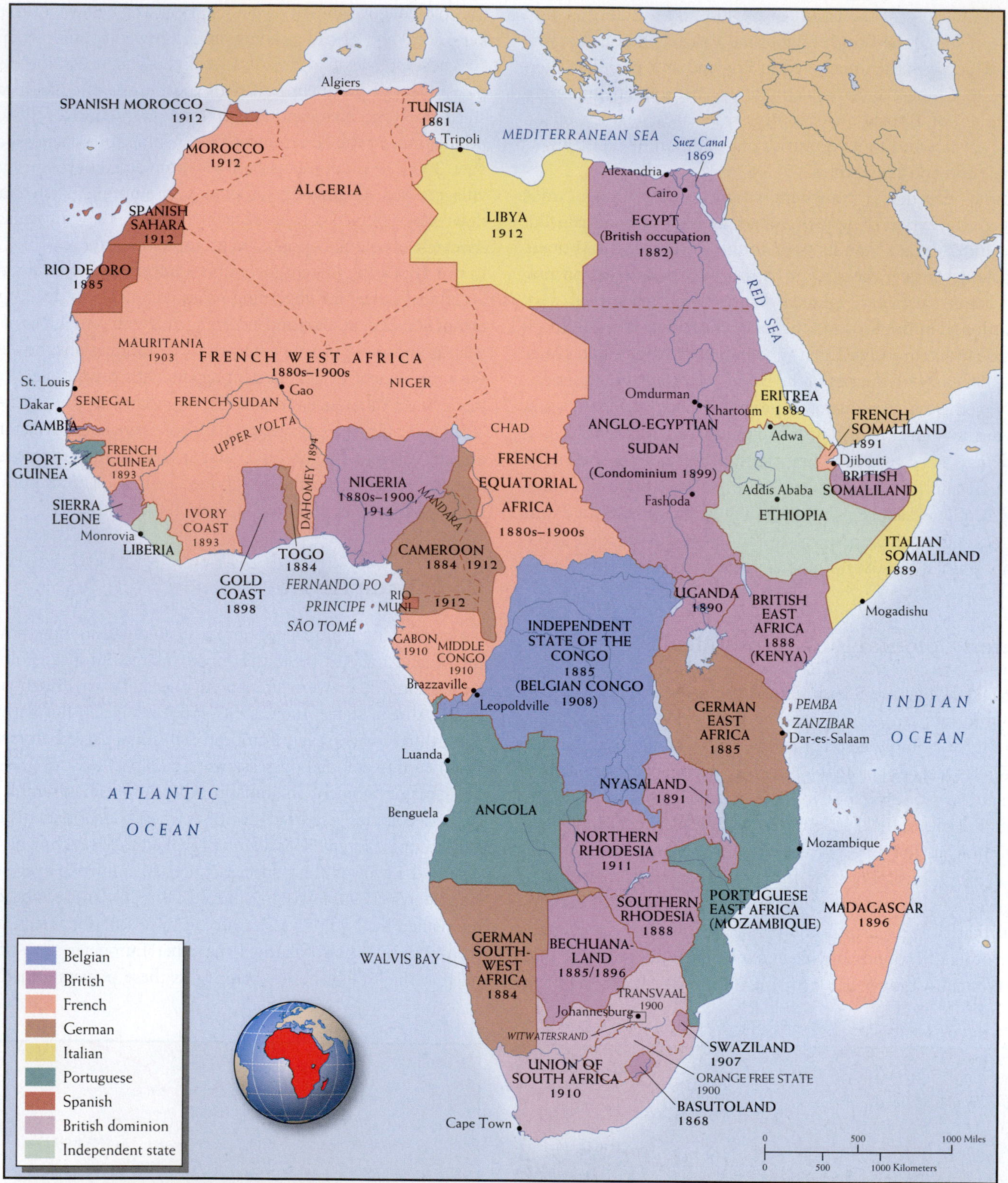

MAP 17.4 | Partition of Africa, 1880–1914

The partition of Africa took place between the early 1880s and the outbreak of World War I.

- Which two European powers gained the most territory in Africa? Which two African states managed to remain independent?
- What kind of economic and political gain did European powers realize through the colonization of Africa? Did any of the European states fully realize their ambitions in Africa?

scramble, Portugal called for an international conference to discuss claims to Africa. Meeting in Berlin between 1884 and 1885, delegates from Germany, Portugal, Britain, France, Belgium, Spain, Italy, the United States, and the Ottoman Empire agreed to carve up Africa and to recognize the acquisitions of any European power that had achieved occupation on the ground.

PARTITIONING THE AFRICAN LANDMASS The consequences for Africa were devastating. Nearly 70 percent of the newly drawn borders failed to correspond to older demarcations of ethnicity, language, culture, and commerce—for Europeans knew little of the landmass beyond its coast and rivers. They based their new colonial boundaries on European trading centers rather than on the location of African population groups. In West Africa, for example, the Yoruba were split between the French in Dahomey and the British in southwestern Nigeria. In fact, Nigeria became an administrative nightmare, as the British attempted to integrate the politically centralized Muslim populations of the north with the city-state Yoruba dwellers and small tribes of the Ibos of the south.

Several motives led the European powers into their frenzied partition of Africa. Although European businesses were primarily interested in Egypt and South Africa, where their investments were lucrative, small-scale traders and investors harbored fantasies of great treasures locked in the vast uncharted interior. Politicians, publicists, and the reading public also took an interest. The writings of explorers like David Livingstone (1813–1873), a Scottish doctor and missionary, and Henry Morton Stanley (1841–1904), an adventurer in the pay of the *New York Herald*, excited readers with accounts of Africa as a continent of unlimited economic potential.

There was also the lure of building personal fortunes and reputations. In eastern Africa, Carl Peters (1856–1918) aspired to found a vast German colony, and he brought German East Africa into existence, although his ruthlessness eventually caused the German Parliament to force him to give up control of "his" state.

Europeans in Africa. (Left) *Henry Morton Stanley was one of the most famous of the nineteenth-century explorers in Africa. He first made his reputation when he located the British missionary-explorer David Livingstone, feared dead, in the interior of Africa, uttering the famous words, "Dr. Livingstone, I presume." Stanley worked on behalf of King Leopold, establishing the Belgian king's claims to territories in the Congo and often using superior weaponry to cow African opponents.* (Right) *The ardent British imperialist Cecil Rhodes endeavored to bring as much of Africa as he could under British colonial rule. He had an ambition to create a swath of British-controlled territory that would stretch from the Cape in South Africa to Cairo in Egypt, as this cartoon shows.*

CURRENT TRENDS IN WORLD HISTORY

Africa's Newest Hunters and Gatherers: Greed, Environmental Degradation, and Resistance

As we have noted, Africa was the birthplace of hunting and gathering (see Chapter 1). Ironically, although the European colonizers justified their partition of Africa on the grounds of bringing civilization to a benighted people, in fact, in their quest to enrich themselves, the first generation of colonizers despoiled the continent, enslaved and killed huge numbers of people, and returned parts of the continent to a hunting and gathering mode of production. The most driven and greediest of these figures was Leopold II, king of the Belgians, who was determined, in spite of sweet-sounding rhetoric, to do whatever it took to line his pockets and make himself a formidable figure in European politics. King Leopold's story—and others like it—fascinates world historians because it conveys in the starkest detail the nature of the relationship between the rulers and the ruled. It also provides a strong point of comparison for the different models of ruling that each European power instituted in their colonies.

Even before ascending the throne in 1865, Leopold cast about for ways to become more than the constitutional monarch of a small, recently established, and neutral state. A voracious reader on colonialism, he was struck forcibly by one book: *How the Dutch Ruled Java*, published in 1861. By demonstrating how the Dutch colonial state had expropriated money from the East Indies (called Indonesia today) to spend on projects at home, the book fired his imagination. Could he not do the same? Could he not stake out a colony, take money from it to swell his own exchequer, and use some of it on public works at home—to beautify the cities of Belgium the way Paris had been beautified in the 1850s and 1860s?

Fixing his gaze on central Africa, in the 1880s Leopold manipulated the other European states into recognizing him as the sovereign head of a "Congo Free State," in which he lead a European effort to "civilize" (and especially to exploit) the Congo River basin. Leopold hired the world-famous explorer Henry Stanley to "pacify" the country and ready it for economic development.

But how to make these lands pay off? They were almost entirely unexplored and unsurveyed, and though in time they would yield some of the richest mineral deposits in the world, these prospects were unknown to Leopold and his administrators at first. What the rain forests of Africa had was wild products, especially rubber and ivory. But how to get Africans, who at that point hardly participated in

King Leopold. *Despite the inhumane ways in which he funded his vast array of public buildings, Leopold is sometimes called, not unaffectionately, the "Builder King" by Belgians today.*

The most determined of the African empire builders was Leopold II (r. 1865–1909), king of the Belgians. (See Current Trends in World History: Africa's Newest Hunters and Gatherers: Greed, Environmental Degradation, and Resistance.) In southern Africa, the British champion of imperialism Cecil Rhodes (1853–1902) brought the Rhodesias, Nyasaland, Bechuanaland, the Transvaal, and the Orange Free State into the British Empire. He was delighted that the Rhodesias bore his name.

Other Europeans saw Africa as a grand opportunity for converting souls to Christianity. In fact, Europe's civilizing mission was an important motive in the scramble for African territory. In Uganda, northern Nigeria, and central Africa, missionaries went ahead of European armies, begging the European statesmen to follow their lead.

AFRICAN RESISTANCE Contrary to European assumptions, Africans did not welcome European "civilization." Resistance, however, was largely futile. Africans faced two unappealing options: they could capitulate to the Europeans and negotiate to limit the loss of their autonomy, or they could fight to preserve their sovereignty. Only a few chose the course of moderation. Lat Dior, a Muslim warlord in Senegal, refused to let the French build a railway through his kingdom. "As long as I live, be well assured," he wrote the French commandant, "I shall oppose with all my might the construction of this railway. I will always answer no, no, and I will never make you any other reply. Even were I to go to rest, my horse, *Malay*, would give you the same answer." Conflict was inevitable, and Lat Dior lost his life in a battle with the French in 1886.

world trade, to tap wild rubber vines and hunt elephants? The solution here and elsewhere in similar African environments was to create large standing armies (known in Leopold's state as the Force Publique), fix quotas for districts to procure, and compel villagers to bring in baskets of rubber and elephant tusks.

For Leopold the results were little short of astonishing. He extracted vast sums from the Congo, spending lavishly on himself and on Belgium. He sank millions of francs into making the seaside city of Ostend one of the finest resorts in the world. At Tervuren, while a choir sang the new Congo anthem, Leopold laid the foundation stone of a world college for overseas colonial administration. In Brussels he spent over $5 million renovating royal palaces and constructing parks, avenues, casinos, and racecourses.

For the Congolese, Leopold's state was nothing more than a reign of terror. Forced to roam farther and farther from their home villages in search of rubber and elephants to keep pace with ever-escalating quotas, villagers suffered an immense loss of life. Perhaps as many as 10 million Africans perished in a population that had been roughly 20 million before Leopold's agents arrived.

Henry Stanley in the Congo. *Stanley was given the nickname "Bula Matari," meaning "Breaker of Stones," by the native Congolese.*

Leopold's brutality did not go unobserved, however. Already in 1899, the writer Joseph Conrad took the Congo as his model of rapacious European imperialism in his novella *Heart of Darkness*. African villagers rebelled, though unsuccessfully, and, by the first decade of the twentieth century, rumors and then detailed reports painted a stark picture of terror and environment degradation. In 1908, just a year before his death, Leopold was compelled, against his wishes, to turn the administration of the Congo over to the Belgian parliament.

QUESTIONS FOR ANALYSIS

- Why do you think King Leopold was able to rule over the Congo for as many years as he did unchecked by his own government? By the other governments in Europe?
- While the Congo story is arguably the most brutal of all stories of colonial exploitation and resistance, which other episodes in world history does it remind you of and why?

Explore Further

Herbst, Jeffrey, *States and Power in Africa: Comparative Lessons in Authority and Control* (2000).

Hochschild, Adam, *King Leopold's Ghost* (New York, 1998).

Only Menelik II of Ethiopia repulsed the Europeans, for he knew how to play rivals off one another. By doing so, he procured weapons from the French, British, Russians, and Italians. He also had a united, loyal, and well-equipped army. In 1896, his troops routed Italian forces at the Battle of Adwa, after which Adwa became a celebrated moment in African history. Its memory inspired many of Africa's later nationalist leaders.

Most resisters were ignorant of the disparity in military technology between Africans and Europeans—especially the killing power of European breech-loading weapons and the Maxim machine gun. In addition, the European armies had better tactics and a more sustained appetite for battle. Africa's armies fought during the nonagricultural season, engaging in open battles so as to achieve quick and decisive results and then returning to their farms. Such military traditions were effective in fighting neighbors, but not well-equipped invaders.

Some African forces did adapt their military techniques to the European challenge. For example, Samori Touré (1830–1900) proved a stubborn foe for the French, employing guerrilla warfare and avoiding full-scale battles in the savannah lands of West Africa. From 1882 until 1898, Touré eluded the French. Dividing his 35,000-man army, Touré had one part take over territories not yet conquered by the French and there reestablish a fully autonomous domain. A smaller contingent conducted a scorched-earth campaign in the regions from which it was retreating, leaving the French with parched and wasted new possessions. But these tactics only delayed the inevitable. The French finally defeated and captured Touré and sent him into exile in Gabon, where he died in 1900.

Battle of Adwa. *Portrait of King Menelik, who defeated the Italian forces at the battle of Adwa in 1896, thus saving his country from European colonization.*

COLONIAL ADMINISTRATIONS IN AFRICA Once the euphoria of partition and conquest had worn off, power fell to "men on the spot"—military adventurers, settlers, and entrepreneurs whose main goal was to get rich quick. As these individuals established near-fiefdoms in some areas, Africans (like Native Americans on the other side of the Atlantic) found themselves confined to territories where they could barely provide for themselves. To uphold such an invasive system at minimal expense, Europeans created permanent standing armies by equipping their African supporters, whom they either bribed or compelled to join their side. Such armies bullied local communities into doing the colonial authorities' bidding.

Eventually, these rough-and-ready systems led to violent revolts from aggrieved Africans, and in their aftermath the colonial rulers had to create more efficient and rational administrations. As in India, colonial powers in Africa laid the foundations for future nation-state organizations. Once information trickling out of Africa revealed that the imperial governments were not realizing their goal of bringing "civilization" to the "uncivilized," each European power implemented a new form of colonial rule, stripping the strongman conquerors of their absolute powers.

However much the colonial systems of the European states differed, all had three similar goals. First, the colony was to pay for its own administration. Second, administrators on the spot had to preserve the peace; nothing brought swifter criticism from the mother country than a colonial rebellion. Third, colonial rule was to attract other European groups, such as missionaries, settlers, and merchants. Missionaries came to convert "heathens" to Christianity, convinced that they were battling with Islam for the soul of the continent. Settlers went only to those parts of Africa that had climatic conditions similar to those in Europe. They poured into Algeria and South Africa but only trickled into Kenya, Southern Rhodesia, Angola, and Mozambique, attracted by advertising at home that stressed comfortable living conditions and promised that these areas would someday become white man's territories. Moreover, colonial governments' promises to construct railroads, roads, and deep-water facilities persuaded European merchants and investors to take out bigger commercial stakes in Africa.

Eventually, stabilized colonies began to deliver on their economic promise. Whereas early imperialism in Africa had relied on the export of ivory and wild rubber, after these resources became depleted the colonies pursued other exports. From the rain forests came cocoa, coffee, palm oil, and palm kernels. From the highlands of East Africa came tea, coffee, sisal (used in cord and twine), and pyrethrum (a flower used to make insecticide). Another important commodity was long-staple, high-quality cotton, grown in Egypt and the Anglo-Egyptian Sudan. Indeed, tropical commodities from all across Africa (as from India and Latin America) flowed to industrializing societies.

Thus, European colonial administrators saw Africa as fitting into the world economy in the same way that British administrators viewed India—as an exporter of raw materials and an importer of manufactures. They expected Africa to profit from this role. But, in truth, African workers gained little from participating in colonial commerce, while the price they paid in disruption to traditional social and economic patterns was substantial.

Such disruptions were particularly acute in southern Africa, where mining operations lured African men thousands of miles from their homes. Meanwhile, women had to take care of subsistence and cash crop production in the home villages. By the turn of the century the gold mines of Witwatersrand in South Africa required a workforce of 100,000, drawing miners from as far away as Mozambique, the Rhodesias, and Nyasaland, as well as from South Africa itself. Because work below ground was hazardous and health services were inadequate, workers often tried to flee. But armed guards and barbed-wired compounds kept them in the mines. Companies made enormous profits for their European shareholders, while the workers toiled in dangerous conditions and barely eked out a living wage.

To observers, the European empires in Africa seemed solid and durable, but in fact, European colonial rule there was fragile. For all of British Africa, the only all-British force was 5,000 men garrisoned in Egypt. Elsewhere, European officers depended on

ANALYZING GLOBAL DEVELOPMENTS

Imperialism and the African Trade Revolution

The colonial period initiated a trade revolution in Africa, which, as we have seen, had been a supplier of human labor to the Americas from the fifteenth century until the middle of the nineteenth century (see Chapter 13). Even as the Europeans endeavored to eradicate the African institution of slavery and slave trading within the continent, they also promoted the reintegration of African economies into the world economy through the export of important, often new cash crops like cocoa from West Africa, significant minerals like gold and diamonds from South Africa, and the import of European manufactures. To this end, the colonial powers financed railways and deepened harbors. Already by the outbreak of World War I, West Africa had become the leading exporter of cocoa, South Africa the leading exporter of diamonds and gold, and Egypt, along with the United States, the leading exporter of high-quality cotton.

QUESTIONS FOR ANALYSIS

- Is there a correlation between the increase in the number of railroads built and the amount of natural resources taken out of Africa? If so, how can you tell?
- During what period were the largest increases in the construction of the railroads and the exportation of cocoa and gold?
- Do you think the general trend towards increasing production continued well into the twentieth century, or do you think this was the high point? Please explain your answer.

Length of Railway Line Opened (in kilometers)

Year	Africa
1880	4,579
1885	6,813
1890	9,202
1895	11,962
1900	16,319
1905	25,574
1910	37,768
1915	47,624

Cocoa Exports from the Gold Coast and Nigeria (in tons)

Year	Gold Coast	Nigeria
1900	536	202
1905	5,090	470
1910	22,600	2,932
1915	77,300	9,105
1920	125,000	17,155

Union of South Africa Gold Mines (in ounces)

Year	Total Output	Estimated % of World Output
1897	2,744	24%
1907	6,451	32.4%
1913	8,799	39.3%
1916	9,297	42.3%
1921	8,129	50.9%

Sources: Mitchell, B. R., International Historical Statistics: Africa, Asia, and Oceania, 1750–2005 (2007); *Hill, Polly,* The Gold Coast Cocoa Farmer: A Preliminary Survey (1965); *Berry, Sara,* Cocoa, Custom and Socio-Economic Change in Western Nigeria (1975); *Frankel, S. Herbert,* Capital Investment in Africa: Its Course and Effects (1938).

African military and police forces. And prior to 1914, the number of British administrative officers available for the whole of northern Nigeria was less than 500. These were hardly strong foundations for statehood. It would not take much to destabilize the European order in Africa.

The American Empire

The United States, like Europe, was drawn into the mania of overseas expansion and empire building. Echoing the rhetoric of Manifest Destiny from the 1840s, the expansionists of the 1890s claimed that Americans still had a divine mission to spread their superior civilization and their Christian faith around the globe. However, America's new imperialists followed the European model of colonialism from Asia and Africa: colonies were to provide harbors for American vessels, supply raw materials to American industries, and purchase the surplus production of American farms and factories. These new territorial acquisitions were not intended for American settlement or statehood. Nor were their inhabitants to become American citizens, for non-white foreigners were considered unfit for incorporation into the American nation.

The pressure to expand came to a head in the late 1890s, when the United States declared war on Spain and invaded the Philippines, Puerto Rico, and Cuba. From 1895, Cuban patriots had been slowly pushing back Spanish troops and occupying

Diamond Mine. *The discovery of diamonds and gold in South Africa in the late nineteenth century led to the investment of large amounts of overseas capital, the mobilization of severely exploited African mine workers, and the Boer War of 1899 to 1902, which resulted in the incorporation of the Afrikaner states of the Transvaal and the Orange Free State into the Union of South Africa.*

sugar plantations—some of which belonged to American planters. Fearing social revolution off the shores of Florida, the American expansionists presented themselves as the saviors of Spanish colonials yearning for freedom, while at the same time safeguarding property for foreign interests in the Spanish-American War (1898). After defeating Spanish regulars in Cuba, American forces began disarming Cuban rebels and returning lands to their owners.

Although the Americans claimed that they were intervening to promote freedom in Spain's colonies, they quickly forgot their promises. The United States annexed Puerto Rico after minimal protest, but Cubans and Filipinos resisted becoming colonial subjects. Bitterness ran particularly high among Filipinos, to whom American leaders had promised independence if they joined in the war against Spain. Betrayed, Filipino rebels launched a war for independence in the name of a Filipino nation. In two years of fighting, over 5,000 Americans and perhaps 200,000 Filipinos perished. The outcome: the Philippines became a colony of the United States.

Colonies in the Philippines and Cuba laid the foundations for a revised model of U.S. expansionism. The earlier pattern had been to turn Indian lands into privately owned farmsteads and to extend the Atlantic market across the continent. But now, in this new era, the nation's largest corporations (with government support) aggressively intervened in the affairs of neighbors near and far. Following the Spanish-American War,

Uncle Sam Leading Cuba. *In the years before the Spanish-American War, cartoonists who wished to see the United States intervene on behalf of Cuba in the islanders' struggle for independence from Spain typically depicted Cuba as a white woman in distress. By contrast, in this and other cartoons following the Spanish-American War, Cubans were drawn as black, and usually as infants or boys unable to care for themselves and in need of the benevolent paternal rule of the United States.*

The Women of Algiers in Their Apartment. *An oil painting by Eugène Delacroix (1798–1863) of Algerian women being attended by a black servant. European painters in the nineteenth century often used images of women to portray Arab Muslim society.*

the United States repeatedly sent troops to many Caribbean and Central American countries. The Americans preferred to turn these regimes into dependent client states, rather than making them part of the United States itself (as with Alaska and Hawaii) or converting them into formal colonies (as the Europeans had done in Africa and Asia). The entire world was an object for the powerful states to shape to their needs.

Imperialism and Culture

At least since the Crusades, Europeans had regularly written and thought about others. These images and ideas had grown more numerous and varied as commerce and colonialism in Asia and the Atlantic world increased; they served various purposes, including those of informing, entertaining, flattering, and criticizing European culture. As Europeans began to exert more control over various parts of the world, they found it easier to force open closed cultures and to carry away treasures. As Europeans and Americans grew more and more confident that they were the knowers and the collectors, they became convinced that their arts and sciences were superior—and curiosity often turned to disdain. Exerting full imperial control then gave new legitimacy to ideas of European and American cultural superiority, and such ideas made imperialism seem natural and just. In time, Europeans presumed that the only true modern civilization was their own; other peoples might have reigned over great empires in antiquity, but had since fallen into decadence and decline. In literature and painting, for example, a new genre known as **Orientalism** portrayed nonwestern peoples as exotic, sensuous, and economically backward. Rather than depicting Egyptian dock workers or middle-class Algerian women, these paintings featured snake charmers and inhabitants of the harem, thereby suggesting that the whole region was inhabited by people of these types, in contrast to a uniformly progressive Europe, inhabited by industrial workers and men of science.

Darwinism, and even Darwin himself, in his 1873 *The Descent of Man*, ratified this view of "lower" and "higher" races, the former stuck in the past and the latter anointed by God (or in Darwin's case, by Nature itself) to define and dictate civilization's future. Europeans' relationship to others might now be one of condescending sympathy or of ruthless exploitation, but the bottom line was that it was up to white Europeans and Americans to create modern culture; the darker people, the cultural Darwinians argued, were not nearly as fully "evolved" as the Europeans, and could not hope to catch up (or to offer a viable alternative model for poetry or painting, for example). At best, they could be taught European languages, sciences, and religions, and perhaps be made to evolve more quickly. It is telling that French colonial subjects who did well at French schools were known as "evolués," "the evolved ones."

The Civilizing Mission. *This advertisement for Pears' Soap shamelessly tapped into the idea of Europeans bringing civilization to the people of their colonies. It said that use of Pears' Soap would teach the virtues of cleanliness to the "natives" and implied that it would even lighten their skin.*

CELEBRATING IMPERIALISM Especially in middle- and upper-class circles, Europeans celebrated their imperial triumphs. After the invention of photographic film and the Eastman Kodak camera in 1888, imperial images surfaced in popular forms such as postcards and advertisements. Imperial themes also decorated packaging materials; tins of coffee, tea, tobacco, and chocolates featured pictures highlighting the commodities' colonial origins. Cigarettes often had names like "Admiral," "Royal Navy," "Fighter," and "Grand Fleet." Some of this served as propaganda, produced by investors in imperial commodities or by colonial pressure groups.

Propaganda promoted imperialism abroad but also inspired changes at home. For example, champions of empire argued that if the British population did not grow fast enough to fill the world's sparsely settled regions, then the population of other nations would. Population was power, and the number of healthy children provided an accurate measure of global influence. "Empire cannot be built on rickety and flat-chested citizens," warned a British member of Parliament in 1905. In addition, writers for young audiences often invoked colonial settings and themes. Whereas girls' literature stressed domestic service, child rearing, and nurturing, boys' readings depicted exotic locales, devious Orientals and savage Africans, and daring colonial exploits.

It should be noted, however, that empire, and imperial culture, did not affect, or interest, all Europeans equally. In general, the extension and upkeep of colonies directly involved only a small minority of Europeans, and those who saw "orientalist" paintings saw many other types of paintings too, including those of scantily clad Greeks and Romans. Nor were all students of Asian languages complicit in imperialist exploitation; some were truly curious about other peoples' histories and cultures, and laid the foundations for studies of world history today. But even they were beneficiaries of imperialism, which made the world's cultures newly accessible to Europeans, for the purposes of both exploiting others and learning more about them.

PRESSURES OF EXPANSION IN JAPAN, RUSSIA, AND CHINA

The challenge of integrating political communities and extending territorial borders was a problem not just for western Europe and the United States. Other societies also aimed to overcome domestic

Perry Arrives in Japan. *A Japanese woodblock print portraying the uninvited arrival into Edo (Tokyo) Bay on August 7, 1853, of a tall American ship, which was commanded by Matthew Perry. This arrival marked the end of Japan's ability to fully control the terms of its interactions with foreigners.*

Economic Transformation of Japan. *During the Meiji period, the government transformed the economy by building railroads, laying telegraph lines, founding a postal system, and encouraging the formation of giant firms known as* zaibatsu, *which were family organizations consisting of factories, import-export businesses, and banks. Here we see a raw-silk-reeling factory that was run by one of the* zaibatsu.

dissent and establish larger domains. Japan, Russia, and China provide three contrasting models; their differing forms of expansion eventually led them to fight over possessions in East Asia.

Japan's Transformation and Expansion

Starting in the 1860s, Japanese rulers tried to recast their country less as an old dynasty and more like a modern nation-state. Since the early seventeenth century, the Tokugawa Shogunate had kept outsiders within strict limits and thwarted internal unrest. But after an American naval officer, Commodore Matthew Perry, entered Edo Bay in 1853 with a fleet of steam-powered ships, other Americans, Russians, Dutch, and British followed in his wake. These outsiders forced the Tokugawa rulers to sign humiliating treaties that opened Japanese ports, slapped limits on Japanese tariffs, and exempted foreigners from Japanese laws. Younger Japanese, especially among the military (samurai) elites, felt that Japan should respond by adopting, not rejecting, western practices. They respected the power demonstrated by the intruding ships and weaponry; yet in adapting Western technology, they expected to remain true to their own culture.

In 1868, a group of reformers toppled the Tokugawa Shogunate and promised to return Japan to its mythic greatness. Then Emperor Mutsuhito—the Meiji ("Enlightened Rule") Emperor—became the symbol of a new Japan. His reign (1868–1912) was called the **Meiji Restoration**. By founding schools, initiating a propaganda campaign, and revamping the army to create a single "national" fighting force, the Meiji government promoted a political community that stressed linguistic and ethnic homogeneity, as well as superiority compared to others. In this way the Meiji leaders overcame age-old regional divisions, subdued local political authorities, and mobilized the country to face the threat from powerful Europeans.

ECONOMIC DEVELOPMENT One of the Meiji period's remarkable achievements was the nation's economic transformation. After 1871, when the government banned the feudal system and allowed peasants to become small landowners, farmers improved their agrarian techniques and saw their standard of living rise. Some business practices that underlay the economic transformation had taken shape under the Tokugawa Shogunate, but the Meiji government was far more activist in terms of internal modernization. For example, stressing the slogan "rich country, strong army," the energetic new government unified the currency around the yen, created a postal system, introduced tax reforms, laid telegraph lines, formed compulsory foreign trade associations, launched savings and export campaigns, established an advanced civil service system, began to build railroads, and hired thousands of foreign consultants. In 1889, the Meiji government introduced a constitution (based largely on the German model). The following year, 450,000 people—about 1 percent of the population—elected Japan's first parliament, the Imperial Diet.

As the government sold valuable enterprises to the people it knew best, it created private economic dynasties. The new large companies (such as Sumitomo, Yasuda, Mitsubishi, and Mitsui) were family organizations. Fathers, sons, cousins, and uncles

Map 17.5 | Japanese Expansion, 1870–1910

Under the Meiji Restoration, the Japanese state built a strong national identity and competed with foreign powers for imperial advantage in East Asia.

- According to the map, what were the first areas that the Japanese Empire acquired as it started to expand?
- What two empires' spheres of influence were affected by Japan's aggressive attempts at expansion?
- What were the new Japanese state's objectives? How were they similar to or different from European expansionism of the same period?

ran different parts of large integrated corporations—some in charge of banks, some running the trade wing, some overseeing factories. Women played a crucial role, not just as custodians of the home but also as cultivators of important family alliances, especially among potential marriage partners. In contrast to American limited-liability firms, which issued shares on stock markets to anonymous buyers, Japan's version of large-scale managerial capitalism was a personal affair.

EXPANSIONISM AND CONFLICT WITH NEIGHBORS

As in many other emerging nation-states, expansion in Japan was a tempting prospect. It offered the promise of more markets for selling goods and obtaining staples, and it was a way to burnish the image of national superiority and greatness. Japanese ventures abroad were initially spectacularly successful. The Meiji moved first to take over the kingdom of the Ryūkyūs, southwest of Japan (see Map 17.5). A small show of force, only 160 Japanese soldiers, was enough to establish the new Okinawa Prefecture there in 1879. The Japanese regarded the people of the Ryūkyūs as an ethnic minority and refused to incorporate them into the nation-state on equal terms. In contrast with the British in India or the Americans in Puerto Rico, the Japanese conquerors refused to train a native Ryūkyūs governing class. Meiji intellectuals insisted that the "backward" Okinawans were unfit for local self-rule and representation.

In 1876, the Japanese fixed upon Korea, which put their plans on a collision course with China's sphere of influence. In a formal treaty, the Japanese recognized Korea as an independent state, opened Korea to trade, and won extraterritorial rights. As a result, the Chinese worried that soon the Japanese would try to take over Korea. These fears were well founded, for Japanese designs on Korea eventually sparked the Sino-Japanese War of 1894–1895, in which the Chinese suffered a humiliating defeat.

The Sino-Japanese War accelerated Japan's rapid transformation to a nation-state and a colonial power with no peer in Asia. Having lost the war, China ceded the province of Taiwan to the Japanese. Japan also annexed Korea in 1910 and converted Taiwan and Korea into the twin jewels of its young empire. The colonial administration built transportation networks and established educational and health institutions—while keeping the colonized people out of top managerial and technical positions. Like the British in India, the Japanese regarded their colonial subjects as racially inferior and unworthy of the privileges of citizenship. And like other imperial powers, the Japanese expected their possessions to serve the metropolitan center. Densely populated and short of land, Japan wanted these colonies to become granaries, sending rice to the mother country. Moreover, the Meiji regime exploited Taiwanese sugar exports to relieve a Japanese economy heavily dependent on imports. Indeed, by serving as staple-exporting regions, Korea and Taiwan were a source of foreign exchange that helped defray Japan's trade deficits. They had grown huge as a result of massive imports to build up new industries.

Russian Transformation and Expansion

Russia expanded out of a sense of mission and a need to defend against other countries expanding along its immense border. Facing an emerging Germany, a British presence in the Middle East and Persia, a consolidating China, and an ascendant Japan, Russia knew it would have to enlarge its territorial domain. So it established a number of expansionist fronts simultaneously: southwest to the Black Sea, south into the Caucasus and Turkestan, and east into Manchuria (see Map 17.6). Success depended on annexing territories and establishing protectorates over vulnerable conquered peoples.

Looking west and south, Russia invaded the Ottoman territories of Moldavia (present-day Moldova) and Walachia (present-day Romania) in 1853. The invasion provoked opposition from Britain and France, who joined with the Ottomans to defeat Russia in the Crimean War (1853–1856). By exposing Russia's lack of modern weapons and its problems in supplying troops without a railway system, the defeat spurred a course of aggressive modernization and expansion.

MODERNIZATION AND INTERNAL REFORM In the 1860s, Tsar Alexander II launched a wave of "Great Reforms" to make Russia more competitive. Autocratic rule continued, but officials reintegrated the society. In 1861, for example, a decree emancipated peasants from serfdom. Other changes included a sharp reduction in the duration of military service, a program of education for the conscripts, and the beginnings of a mass school system to teach children reading, writing, and Russian culture. Starting in the 1890s, as railroads and factories expanded, so did the steel, coal, and petroleum industries. But while the reforms strengthened the state, they did not enhance the lives of common people. Workers in Russia were brutally exploited, even by the standards of the industrial revolution. Also, large landowners had kept most of the empire's fertile land, and the peasants had to pay substantial redemption fees for the poorer-quality plots they received.

The reforms revealed a fundamental problem: the rulers were eager to reform society, but not the basis of government (autocracy). This caused liberals, conservatives, and malcontents alike to question the state-led modernizing mission. Before long, in the press, courtrooms, and streets, men and women denounced the regime. Revolutionaries engaged in terror and assassination. In 1881, a terrorist bomb blew the tsar to pieces. In the 1890s, following another famine, the radical doctrines of Marxism (see Chapter 16) gained popularity in Russia. Even aristocratic intellectuals, such as the author of *War and Peace,* Count Leo Tolstoy, lamented their despotic government.

TERRITORIAL EXPANSION Yet the critics of internal reform did not hold back the Russian expansionists, who believed they had to take over certain lands to keep them out of rivals' hands.

Map 17.6 | Russian Expansion, 1801–1914

The Russian state continued to expand in the nineteenth century.

- According to this map, what lands did Russia acquire during the period 1796–1855? What lands did it acquire next?
- Compare this map on Russian expansion with Map 13.7 (p. 508). How did the direction of Russia's expansion change in the nineteenth century? Which states did the expanding Russian Empire more resemble in this era, western Europe (such as Great Britain) or American states (such as the United States)?

So they conquered the highland people of the Caucasus Mountains to prevent Ottomans and Persians from encroaching on Russia's southern flank. And they battled the British over areas between Turkestan and British India, such as Persia (Iran) and Afghanistan. Although some Russians moved to these lands, they never became a majority there. The new provinces were multiethnic, multireligious communities that were only partially integrated into the Russian state. (See Primary Source: Two Faces of Empire.)

Perhaps the most impressive Russian expansion occurred in East Asia, where the underpopulated Amur River basin boasted rich lands, mineral deposits, and access to the Pacific Ocean. The Chinese also wanted to colonize this area, which lay just north of Manchuria. After twenty years of struggle, Russia claimed the land north and south of the Amur River and in 1860 founded Vladivostok, a port on the Pacific Ocean whose name signified "Rule the East." Deciding to focus on these areas in Asia, the Russian government sold its one territory in North America (Alaska) to the United States. Then, to link the capital (Moscow) and the western part of the country to its East Asian spoils, the government began construction of the Trans-Siberian Railroad. When it was completed in 1903, the new railroad bridged the east and the west. Russia then began to eye the Korean peninsula, on which Japan, too, had set its sights.

GOVERNING A DIVERSE NATION Russia was a huge empire whose rulers were only partially effective at integrating its diverse parts into a political community. In 1897, during the first complete population census, ethnographers struggled over what to call all the empire's peoples: nations or tribes. In the end, authorities chose the term *nationalities,* recognizing 104

PRIMARY SOURCE

Two Faces of Empire

Russification (forced assimilation) was one of the Russian Empire's responses to the challenge of the nation-state idea. In 1863 the tsar prohibited publication of the Bible in the Little Russian (Ukrainian) language, alienating many otherwise loyal Slavic subjects. By contrast, most non-Christians, such as the Muslims of newly annexed Turkestan (central Asia), were exempted from Russification because they were considered "aliens" who should be ruled separately. The excerpts below present an 1876 edict prohibiting the use of Ukrainian, and a celebration of colonialism by a member of the Russian governor-general's office in Turkestan.

RUSSIFICATION IN UKRAINE

In order to halt what is, from the state's point of view, the dangerous activity of the Ukrainophiles, it is appropriate to take the following measures immediately: 1. To prohibit the import into the empire of any books published abroad in the Little Russian dialect [Ukrainian], without the special permission of the Chief Press Administration. 2. To prohibit the printing inside of the empire of any original works or translations in this dialect, with the exception of historical documents. . . . 3. Equally to prohibit any dramatic productions, musical lyrics and public lectures (which at present have the charter of Ukrainophile demonstrations) in this dialect. . . . 6. To strengthen supervision by the local educational administration so as not to allow any subjects in primary schools be taught in the Little Russian dialect. . . . 7. To clear the libraries of all primary and secondary schools in the Little Russian provinces of books and pamphlets prohibited by paragraph 2. . . . 8. . . . To demand from the heads of these districts a list of teachers with a note as to their reliability in relation to Ukrainophile tendencies. Those noted as unreliable or doubtful should be transferred to Great Russian provinces.

COLONIALISM IN TURKESTAN

Our battalion arrived in Tashkent four years after Turkestan had been annexed to the empire. Tashkent at that time looked more like a military settlement than the chief city of the region, that is the capital of Russian Central Asia. The majority of the inhabitants were soldiers, either resting after some campaign or else about to go out on a new expedition. Civilians and women were a rarity. Now, thirty-six years later, looking proudly at the path we have followed, I can see the colossal results achieved by the Russian government, always humane to the vanquished, but insistently pursuing its civilising mission. Of course, there have been many mistakes, there have been abuses, but this has not halted the rational and expedient intentions of the government. We went into a region which had a population alien to us. . . . They had for many centuries been accustomed to submitting humbly to the barbaric and cruel despotism of their rulers, but they nevertheless came to terms with their position because their rulers were of their own faith. . . . The fanatical mullahs began rumours amongst the mass of the population that, instead of true believer khans, they were to be ruled by heathens who would convert them to Christianity, put crosses around their necks, send them to be soldiers, introduce their own laws, revoke the Sharia [the fundamental law of Islam] and make their wives and daughters uncover their faces.

. . . Frequent outbursts, uprisings and disorders took place and repression followed. But at the same time the natives saw that the very first steps of the first Governor-General proved the complete falseness of the mullahs. . . . It was announced solemnly everywhere to the local population, that as subjects of the Russian monarch, the population would keep its faith, its national customs, its courts and its judges, that all taxes demanded by the previous collectors were illegal and burdensome in the extreme and would be revoked, and that instead just taxes would be imposed, and that the position of women would remain inviolable. All this of course soon calmed the population and an industrious people settled down to a peaceful life.

QUESTIONS FOR ANALYSIS

- Based on the "Russification in Ukraine" document, explain how important the arts and education can be in maintaining a people's identity—and in subverting a foreign power's authority.
- According to the "Colonialism in Turkestan" document, what steps did the Russians take to calm the Muslims' fears of colonial domination?

Source: Martin McCauley and Peter Waldron, The Emergence of the Modern Russian State, 1855–1881 *(Totowa, NJ: Barnes and Noble Books, 1988), pp. 209, 211–12.*

of them, speaking 146 languages and dialects. Ethnic Russians accounted for slightly more than half the population.

Counting and categorizing peoples formed part of the state's attempts to figure out how to govern this diverse realm. As the United States did, Russia made conquered regions into full parts of the empire. But unlike the United States, Russia was suspicious of decentralized federalism, fearing it would lead groups to demand secession. Moreover, the tsars were terrified

The Trans-Siberian Railroad. *Russia's decision to build a railway across Siberia to the Pacific Ocean derived from a desire to expand the empire's power in East Asia and to forestall British advances in Asia. The colossal undertaking, which claimed the lives of thousands of workers, reached completion just as Russia clashed militarily with Japan. The new railroad ferried Russian troops over long distances to battles, such as the one at Mukden, in Manchuria, which was then the largest land battle in the history of warfare.*

by the idea of popular sovereignty. Preferring the tried-and-true method of centralized autocracy, they divided most of the empire into governorships ruled by appointed civilian or military governors who were supposed to function like local tsars or autocrats.

Unlike the United States, which displaced or slaughtered native populations during its expansion across an entire continent, Russia mostly assimilated the new peoples. In this daunting task, the state's approach ranged from outright repression (of Poles and Jews) to favoritism (toward Baltic Germans and Finns), although the beneficiaries of favoritism often later lost favor if they became too strong. Further, unlike the United States, which managed to pacify borders with its weaker neighbors, Russia faced the constant suspicions of Persians and Ottomans and the menace of British troops in Afghanistan. (The troops were there to prevent Russia from cutting off the overland route to India.) In East Asia, a clash with expansionist Japan loomed on the horizon.

Such expansionism was a constant fiscal drain and a heavy burden on the population. To promote the image of a great Russian Empire, rulers leaned more heavily on the rural poor and pursued intensive modernization, but that generated instability. For the time being, Moscow's main threat did not come from within Russia's borders. It came from the outside.

China under Pressure

While the Russians and Japanese scrambled to copy European models of industrialism and imperialism, the Qing were slower to mobilize against threats from the west. Even as the European powers were dividing up China into spheres of influence, Qing officials were much more worried about internal revolts and threats from their northern borders. Into the 1850s and 1860s, many Qing officials still regarded the increasing European incursions and demands as a lesser danger by comparison.

ADOPTING WESTERN LEARNING AND SKILLS A growing number of Chinese officials, however, recognized the superior armaments and technology of rival powers and were deeply troubled by the threat posed by European military might. Starting in the 1860s, reformist bureaucrats sought to adopt elements of western learning and technological skills—but with the intention of keeping the core Chinese culture intact.

This so-called **Self-Strengthening movement** included a variety of new ventures: arsenals, shipyards, coal mines, a steamship company to contest the foreign domination of coastal shipping, and schools for learning foreign ways and languages. Most interesting was the dispatch abroad of about 120 schoolboys under the charge of Yung Wing. The first Chinese graduate of an American college (Yale University, 1854), Yung believed that western education would greatly benefit Chinese students, so he took his charges to Connecticut in the 1870s to attend school and live with American families. Conservatives at the Qing court were soon dismayed by reports of the students' interest in Christianity and aptitude for baseball. In 1881, after the U.S. government refused to admit the boys into military academies, they summoned the students home.

Yung Wing's abortive educational mission was not the only setback for the Self-Strengthening movement, for skepticism about western technology was rife among conservative officials. Some insisted that the introduction of machinery would lead to unemployment; others worried that railways would facilitate western military maneuvers and lead to an invasion; still others complained that the crisscrossing tracks disturbed the harmony between humans and nature. The first short railway track ever laid in China was torn up in 1877 shortly after being built, and the country had only 288 kilometers of track prior to 1895.

Although they did not acknowledge the railroad's usefulness, the Chinese did adopt other new technologies to access a wider range of information. For example, by the early 1890s there were about a dozen Chinese-language newspapers (as distinct from the foreign-language press) published in major cities, with the largest ones having a circulation of 10,000 to 15,000. To avoid government intervention, these papers sidestepped political controversy; instead, they featured commercial news and literary contributions. In 1882, the newspaper *Shenbao* made use of a new telegraph line to publish dispatches within China.

INTERNAL REFORM EFFORTS China's defeat by Japan in the Sino-Japanese War (1894–1895), sparked by quarrels over Korea, prompted the first serious attempt at reform by the Qing. Known as the Hundred Days' Reform, the episode lasted only from June to September 1898. The force behind it was a thirty-seven-year-old scholar named Kang Youwei and his twenty-two-year-old student Liang Qichao. Citing rulers such as Peter the Great of Russia and the Meiji Emperor of Japan as their inspiration, the reformers urged Chinese leaders to develop a railway network, a state banking system, a modern postal service, and institutions to foster the development of agriculture, industry, and commerce.

The reformers' opportunity to accelerate change came in the summer of 1898 when the twenty-seven-year-old Guangxu emperor decided to implement many of their ideas, including changes in the venerable civil service examination system. But the effort was short-lived, for conservative officials rallied behind Guangxu's aunt, the Empress Dowager Cixi, who emerged from retirement to overturn the reforms. The young emperor was put under house arrest. Kang and Liang fled for their lives and went into exile. It would take still more military defeats to finally jolt the Qing court into action, but by then it was too late to save the regime.

The reforms of the Self-Strengthening movement were too modest and poorly implemented. Very few Chinese acquired new skills. Despite talk of modernizing, the civil service examination remained based on Confucian classics and still opened the only doors to government service. Governing elites were not yet ready to reinvent the principles of their political community, and they adhered instead to the traditional dynastic structure.

By the late nineteenth century, the success of the Qing regime in expanding its territories a century earlier seemed like a distant memory, as various powers repeatedly forced it to make economic and territorial concessions. Unlike Japan or Russia, however, the Qing government resisted any comprehensive social reforms (until after the turn of the twentieth century), and its policies left the country vulnerable to both external aggression and internal instability.

CONCLUSION

Between 1850 and 1914, most of the world's people lived not in nation-states but in landed empires or in the colonies of nation-states. But as reformers sought a new political framework in response to popular upheavals and economic changes, the nation-state became a desirable form of governance.

Although the ideal of "a people" united by territory, history, and culture grew increasingly popular worldwide, it was not easy to make it a reality. Official histories, national heroes, novels, poetry, and music helped, but central to the process of nation formation were the actions of bureaucrats. Asserting sovereignty over what it claimed as national territory, the state "nationalized" diverse populations by creating a unified system of law, education, military service, and government.

Colonization beyond borders was another part of nation building in many societies. In these efforts, territorial conquests took place under the banner of nationalist endeavors. In Europe, the Americas, Japan, and to some extent Russia, the intertwined processes of nation building and territorial expansion were most effective. The Amazon River basin, Okinawa, and especially the North American West became important provinces of integrated nation-states, populated with settlers who produced for national and international markets.

However, the integrating impulses of emerging nations did not wipe out local differences, mute class antagonisms, or eliminate gender inequalities. Even as Europeans and Americans came to see themselves as chosen—by God or by natural selection—to rule the rest, they suffered deep divisions. Not everyone identified with the nation-state or the empire, or agreed on what it meant to belong or to conquer. But by the century's end, racist advocates and colonial lobbyists seem to have convinced many that their interests and destinies were bound up with their nations' unity, prosperity, and global clout.

Ironically, nation building had an unintended consequence, for self-determination could also apply to racial or ethnic minorities at home and in the colonies. Armed with the rhetoric of progress and uplift, colonial authorities tried to subjugate distant people, but colonial subjects themselves often asserted the language of "nation" and accused imperial overlords of betraying their own lofty principles. As the twentieth century opened, Filipino and Cuban rebels used Thomas Jefferson's Declaration of Independence to oppose American invaders, Koreans defined themselves as a nation crushed under Japanese heels, and Indian nationalists made colonial governors feel shame for violating English standards of "fair play."

AFTER YOU READ THIS CHAPTER

Review and research on STUDYSPACE wwnorton.com/StudySpace

TRACING THE GLOBAL STORYLINES

FOCUS ON: ***Nationalism, Imperialism, and Scientific/Technological Innovations***

The Americas and Europe: Consolidating Nations

- Residents of the United States claim territory across the North American continent after fighting a bloody civil war to preserve the union and abolish slavery.
- Canadians also build a new nation and expand across the continent.
- Brazilians create a prosperous nation-state that excludes much of the population from the privileges of belonging to the "nation" and the "state."
- The dynastic states of Prussia and Sardinia-Piedmont create German and Italian nation-states at the expense of France and the Austrian Empire.

Industry, Science, and Technology on a Global Scale

- Continued industrialization, coupled with scientific research, transforms the global economy.
- New technologies of warfare, transportation, and communication ease global economic integration.
- Charles Darwin's *Origin of Species* overturns previous conceptions of nature, arguing that present-day life forms evolved from simpler ones over long periods.

Empires

- After suppressing the Indian Mutiny, the British reorganize their rule in India.
- The Dutch take over administrative responsibilities in Indonesia from the Dutch East India Company.
- Seven European powers partition the entire African continent (except for Ethiopia and Liberia) despite intense African resistance.
- Americans win the Spanish-American War, annex Puerto Rico, and establish colonial rule over the Philippines.
- The expansionist aims of Japan, Russia, and China lead to clashes over possessions in East Asia, with Russia gaining much territory and Japan defeating the Chinese.
- Colonial rule spurs nationalist sentiments among the colonized.

CHRONOLOGY

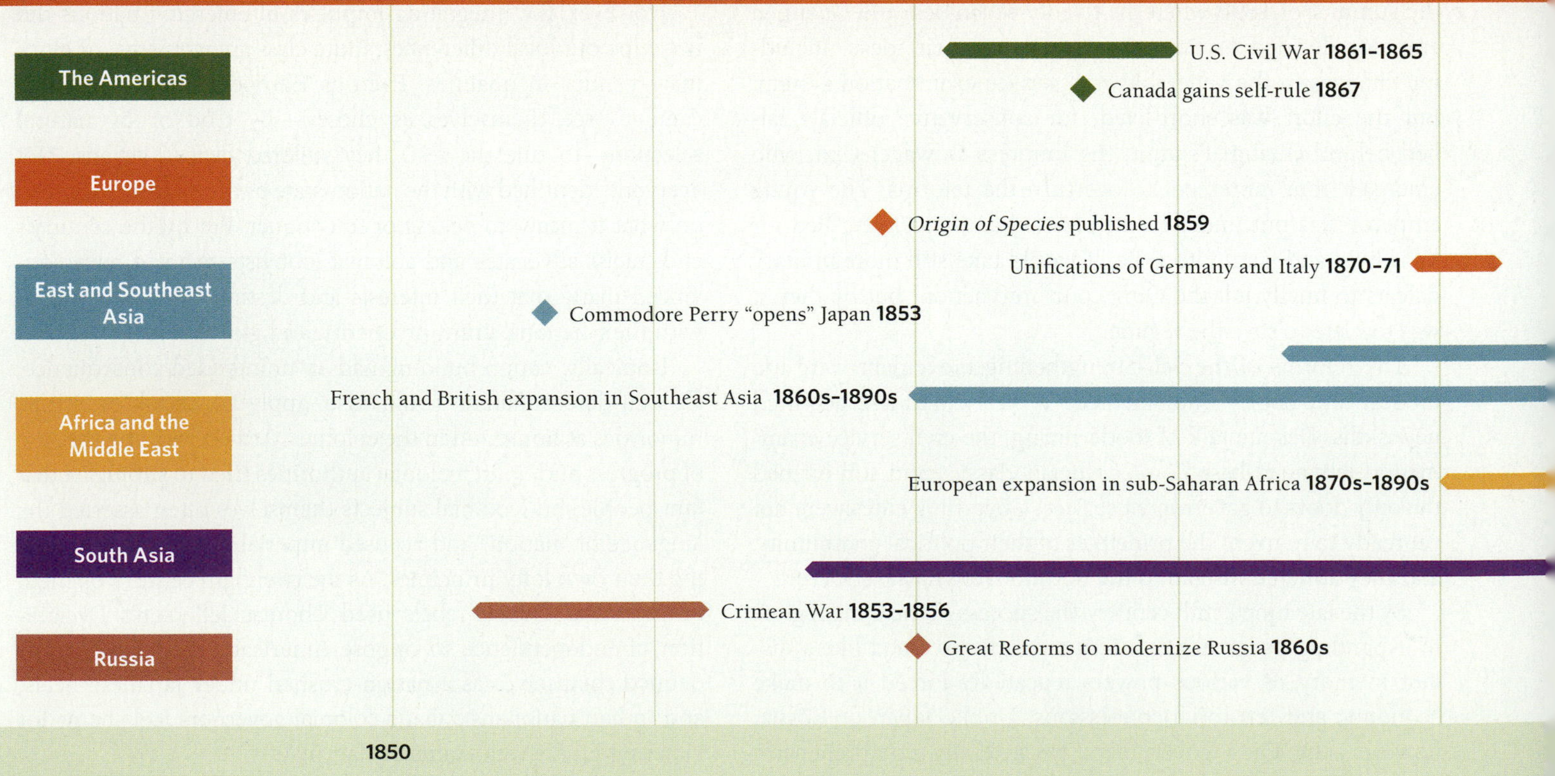

KEY TERMS

Charles Darwin *p. 643*

imperialism *p. 630*

limited-liability joint-stock company *p. 633*

Manifest Destiny *p. 631*

Meiji Restoration *p. 657*

natural selection *p. 644*

Orientalism *p. 655*

Raj *p. 646*

Self-Strengthening movement *p. 662*

steel *p. 642*

STUDY QUESTIONS

1. **Explain** the process of nation building that occurred in the nineteenth century. What polities initiated these efforts, and what different strategies were involved?
2. **Identify** where strong nation-states emerged during this period. How did the nation-state idea challenge certain polities and other organized groups?
3. **Define** imperialism. Why did state-directed efforts at nation building often lead to imperialist efforts and other forms of territorial expansion?
4. **List and explain** several major sources of the new wave of imperialism that occurred in the second half of the nineteenth century. To what extent did these ideas find support among the populations of imperialist states?
5. **Analyze** to what extent different colonized societies resisted imperialist efforts. How successful were their actions?
6. **Describe** the policies that imperial powers used to govern their overseas colonies. What were the goals of imperial administrations, and how successful were they in achieving them?
7. **Analyze** the cultural impact of imperialist ambitions on imperialist nations themselves. How did colonization and territorial expansion shape notions of race and ethnicity there?
8. **Analyze** how the spread of nationalism and imperialism shaped state behavior in China, Russia, and Japan. To what extent did each state adapt to these new patterns?
9. **Explain** how nation-state building, territorial expansion, and imperialism reshaped the global economy. How would you describe the relationship between industrial regions and the rest of the world's societies?

Brazil abolishes slavery **1888**

Spanish-American War **1898**

Meiji Era in Japan **1868–1912**

Sino-Japanese War **1894–1895**

British occupation of Egypt **1882**

British Raj **1858–1947**

Construction of Trans-Siberian Railroad **1890s**

1900

BEFORE YOU READ THIS CHAPTER

wwnorton.com/
STUDYSPACE

GLOBAL STORYLINES

- Numerous factors lead to global anxieties: vast population movements, deep-seated poverty, failure of nation-states to achieve important goals, and hatred of colonial domination.
- The tumult challenges Europeans' faith in "progress."
- Turmoil promotes new scientific thinking and artistic expression, known as cultural modernism.

CHAPTER OUTLINE

18

An Unsettled World, 1890–1914

FOCUS QUESTIONS

- What developments produced global anxieties and insecurities at the beginning of the twentieth century?
- What was modernism and how did it challenge traditional ways of thinking across the globe?
- How did states respond to growing economic and political inequities?
- How did new conceptions of race, nation, and class challenge the political status quo during this era?
- How did shifting economic and political structures affect women?

In 1905 a young African man, Kinjikitile Ngwale, began to move among various ethnic groups in German East Africa, spreading a message of opposition to German colonial authorities. In the tradition of visionary prophets (see Chapter 16), Kinjikitile claimed that by anointing his followers with blessed water (*maji* in Swahili), he could protect them from European bullets and drive the Germans from East Africa. Kinjikitile's reputation spread rapidly, drawing followers from across 100,000 square miles of territory. Although German officials soon executed Kinjikitile, they could not prevent a broad uprising, called the Maji-Maji Revolt. The Germans brutally suppressed the revolt, killing between 200,000 and 300,000 Africans.

At the very moment when the movement of goods, ideas, and armies was linking together the world's peoples in unprecedented—and for groups like the Maji-Maji, disastrous—ways, events like the one described above revealed that many of the world's citizens were deeply dissatisfied with global inequalities in wealth and power. In Asia, Africa, and Latin America, anticolonial critics and exploited classes protested European domination and organized increasingly powerful and violent forms of opposition. But dissatisfaction was not restricted to the non-European world. At home in Europe and America, faith in capitalism, industrialization, and the idea of progress endured, but was challenged by internal critics, especially women, wage workers, and frustrated nationalists, who felt deprived of the full benefits of industrializing nation-states. Strikes, political assassination, and the rise of increasingly powerful popular political movements threatened the status quo; competition between empires increasingly touched off armed conflicts. The rising intensity of these conflicts unsettled the world, even as new forms of communication, investment, and transportation linked it, increasingly, together.

This chapter tackles the anxieties and insecurities that unsettled the world around the turn of the twentieth century. It ties them in particular to several key factors: (1) the uprooting of millions of people from countryside to city and from one continent to another, (2) discontent with the poverty that many suffered even as economic production leaped upward, (3) frustration with the incomplete expansion of rights within nation-states and the incomplete realization of national aspirations, and, (4) in Asia and Africa, resentment of and resistance to European domination. Around the globe, this tumult caused a questioning of old ideas that led to a flowering of new thinking and fresh artistic expression under the label of "modernism." Championed by some and despised by others, modernism *meant* to be unsettling—to represent the world in shocking new ways—and thus tells us a great deal, then, about the conflicts and crises that defined this era.

PROGRESS, UPHEAVAL, AND MOVEMENT

The decades leading up to 1914 were a time of unprecedented possibility for some, and social disruption and economic frustration for others. They were also years of anxiety worldwide. Rapid economic progress brought challenges to the established order and the people in power. In Europe and the United States, radicals and middle-class reformers agitated for political and social change. In areas colonized by European countries and the United States, resentment focused on either colonial rulers or indigenous elites. Even in nations such as China, which had not been formally colonized but which faced repeated intrusions, popular discontent targeted domination by Europeans. In China, Mexico, and Russia, angry peasants and workers allied with frustrated reformers to topple autocratic regimes.

In the late nineteenth century, whole new industries fueled economic growth, especially in the industrial countries and in territories that exported vital raw materials to Europe and the United States. But industrial capitalism also spurred inequalities within industrial countries and, especially, between the world's industrial and nonindustrial regions. It also brought unwelcome changes in how and where people worked and lived. Rural folk flocked into the cities, hoping to escape the poverty that encumbered most people in the countryside. In the cities, even though public building projects produced sewer systems, museums, parks, and libraries, the poor had little access to them. Anxieties intensified when economic downturns left thousands out of work. This led, in some cases, to organized opposition to authoritarian regimes or to the free market system.

In Europe and North America, as industrialization expanded, a generation of younger artists, writers, and scientists known as **modernists** broke with older conventions and sought new ways of seeing and describing the world. In Asia, Africa, and South America as well, many modernists were energized by the idea of moving beyond traditional forms of art, literature, music, and science. But the modernist generation's exuberance worried those who were not ready to give up their cultural traditions and institutions. In the colonized world, and in areas threatened by colonial domination, "modernism" seemed to some to mean full-on "westernization" and with it, the loss of cultural autonomy. The acceleration of cultural change, like that of economic advances, sparked new conflicts and new anxieties both within states and across the globe.

Peoples in Motion

If the world was being *unsettled* by political, economic, and cultural changes, it was also being *resettled* by mass emigration (see Map 18.1). Consider what historian Alfred Crosby called the "Caucasian tsunami": the emigration of throngs of Europeans to North America, Australia, Argentina, Africa, and Cuba. The "tsunami" began after the Napoleonic wars and gathered momentum in the 1840s, when the Irish fled their starving communities to seek better lives in North America. After 1870, the flow of Europeans became a torrent. The United States was the favored destination, with European migrants exceeding by sixfold the number of Europeans who migrated to Argentina (the second-place receiving country) between 1871 and 1920. The high point occurred between 1901 and 1910, when over 6 million Europeans entered the United States. This was nothing less than a demographic revolution.

EMIGRATION, IMMIGRATION, INTERNAL MIGRATION

Europeans were not the only peoples on the move. Between the 1840s and the 1940s, 29 million South Asians migrated into the Malay Peninsula and Burma (British colonies), the Dutch

Indies (Indonesia), East Africa, and the Caribbean. Most were recruited to labor on plantations, railways, and mines in British-controlled territories. Merchants followed laborers, making the South Asian migrant populations more diverse. Meanwhile, the Chinese, too, emigrated in significant numbers. Between 1845 and 1900, forces such as population pressure, a shortage of cultivable land, and social turmoil drove 800,000 Chinese to seek new homes in North and South America, New Zealand, Hawaii, and the West Indies. Close to four times as many settled in Southeast Asia.

At the same time, industrial changes caused millions to migrate *within* their own countries or to neighboring ones, seeking employment in the burgeoning cities or other opportunities in frontier regions. In North America, hundreds of thousands headed west, while millions relocated from the countryside to the cities. In Asia, about 10 million Russians went east to Siberia and central Asia, and 2 million Koreans moved northwest to Manchuria. In Africa, small numbers of South Africans moved north into Northern and Southern Rhodesia in search of arable land and precious metals. Across the world, gold rushes, silver rushes, copper rushes, and a diamond rush took people across landmasses and across oceans. Mostly men, these emigrants were hell-bent on profit and often willing to destroy the land in order to extract precious commodities as quickly as possible.

People traveled with varying credentials and goals. Some went as colonial officials or soldiers; some as missionaries or big-game hunters—most of these folks did not plan to stay. Merchants and traders were more likely to settle in for the long term. Several million East Asians (mostly Chinese) went to the Philippines and South Africa, California and Cuba, British Columbia and Singapore, Guyana and Trinidad, replacing freed slaves on plantations or doing construction. Japanese laborers migrated to Peru to mine guano for fertilizer and to Hawaii to harvest sugar.

Migrants took big risks. Travel was often hazardous, and leaving behind native cultures and kin groups was painful. Many experienced conflicts with resident populations, as did Chinese migrants who ventured into Taiwan and other frontier regions. In the cities, tensions mounted as migrant workers faced low wages, poor working and living conditions, and barriers to higher-paying positions. In China, women without male relatives to protect them sometimes suffered abuse or exploitation. And yet, the economic rewards were substantial enough that the risks of sending the men abroad seemed worth taking.

Until 1914, governments imposed almost no controls on immigration or emigration. The Qing government tried to restrict emigration into the Manchus' northeastern homelands, but it failed. The United States allowed entry to anyone who was not a prostitute, a convict, or a "lunatic"; but in 1882, racist reactions spurred legislation that barred entry to almost all Chinese. Travel within Europe required no passports or work permits; foreign-born criminals were subject to deportation, but that was the extent of immigration policy. In fact, there generally was no reason to have an immigration policy, because immigration seemed doubly good: emigrants allowed large productivity gains in the countries they *left* (because low-productivity populations departed), and immigrants fueled economic growth in the countries they *entered*. This was especially true in North America, where funds were flowing for building railroads and other infrastructure, and where a growing population meant growing consumer markets. Overall, immigration to the New World prompted enormous leaps in productivity.

URBAN LIFE AND CHANGING IDENTITIES Cities boomed, with both positive and negative repercussions. Tokyo's population climbed from 500,000 in 1863 to 1,750,000 in 1908, and London's passed 6.5 million. Major cities faced housing shortages, despite governments' massive rebuilding and beautification projects. This was the era in which city planning came into its own—to widen and regularize thoroughfares for train and streetcar traffic, and to make crowded city life attractive to new inhabitants. City governments in Paris, New York, Cairo, Buenos Aires, and Brussels spent lavishly on opera houses, libraries, sewers, and parks, hoping to ward off disease and crime and to impress others with their modernity. Still, modern amenities did not yet make much difference for the vast majority of city dwellers, who labored long (if they could find steady work) for low wages and lived in overcrowded and unsanitary conditions.

Life in the metropolis at the turn of the century was different from city life in the mid-1800s. Workplaces were farther away from residences, and different social classes lived in separate districts. The lives of western women in particular were transformed. They had long worked as domestic servants, textile workers, or agricultural laborers, but now some took positions as shop girls, secretaries, or—thanks to educational opportunities—teachers; a few became doctors, although their practices were largely limited to treating other women. Increasing female literacy and the falling price of books and magazines gave western women access to new models of acceptable behavior. In cities it became respectable, even fashionable, for women to be seen on the boulevards. The availability in some places of ready-made clothes and packaged goods offered relief from household drudgery (provided one could afford them). Yet, for most women, leisure time and luxury consumption were still dreams more than realities.

Personal and national identities now came under scrutiny, not just in cities but in entire nations. In response to political

NORTH SEA
DENMARK
Copenhagen
Glasgow
BRITAIN
Bradford
Leeds
Manchester and Liverpool
Sheffield
Birmingham
Bristol
London
NETHERLANDS
Amsterdam
Rotterdam
Antwerp
BELGIUM
Brussels
Hamburg
GERMANY
Berlin
Wuppertal
Cologne
Leipzig
Dresden
Frankfurt
LUX.
Paris
FRANCE
Nuremberg
Munich
AUSTRIA-HUNGARY
SWITZ.
Lyons
Bordeaux
Turin
Milan
ITALY
Marseilles
0 200 400 Miles
0 200 400 Kilometers
CANADA
BRITISH COLUMBIA
Pittsburgh
Cleveland
Montreal
Detroit
Buffalo
Chicago
UNITED STATES
Boston
New York
Philadelphia
Baltimore
Washington, D.C.
Cincinnati
St. Louis
San Francisco
CALIFORNIA
New Orleans
32 million (1620–1914)
7.4 million (1530–1914)
12 million (1530–1860)
ATLANTIC OCEAN
CUBA
MEXICO
Mexico City
CENTRAL AMERICA
TRINIDAD
VENEZUELA
COLOMBIA
GUYANA
ECUADOR
BRAZIL
PERU
BOLIVIA
PARAGUAY
CHILE
Rio de Janeiro
ARGENTINA
URUGUAY
Santiago
Buenos Aires
Montevideo
PACIFIC OCEAN
IRELAND
Belfast
Dublin
Inset area
PORTUGAL
Lisbon
Barcelona
Madrid
SPAIN
SPANISH MOROCCO
MOROCCO
ALGERIA
SPANISH SAHARA
FRENCH WEST AFRICA
GAMBIA
PORT. GUINEA
SIERRA LEONE
LIBERIA
TOGO
SP. GUINEA
GOLD COAST
Boundary in 1900
Percentage Population Increase 1700–1900
0–49%
50–99%
100–249%
250–1000%
Over 1000%
City Population in 1900
250,000–500,000
500,000–1,000,000
Over 1,000,000
Major Population Movements 1500–1914
Migration originating from:
Europe, Scandinavia, and western Russia
Asia
Africa
0 1000 2000 Miles
0 1000 2000 Kilometers

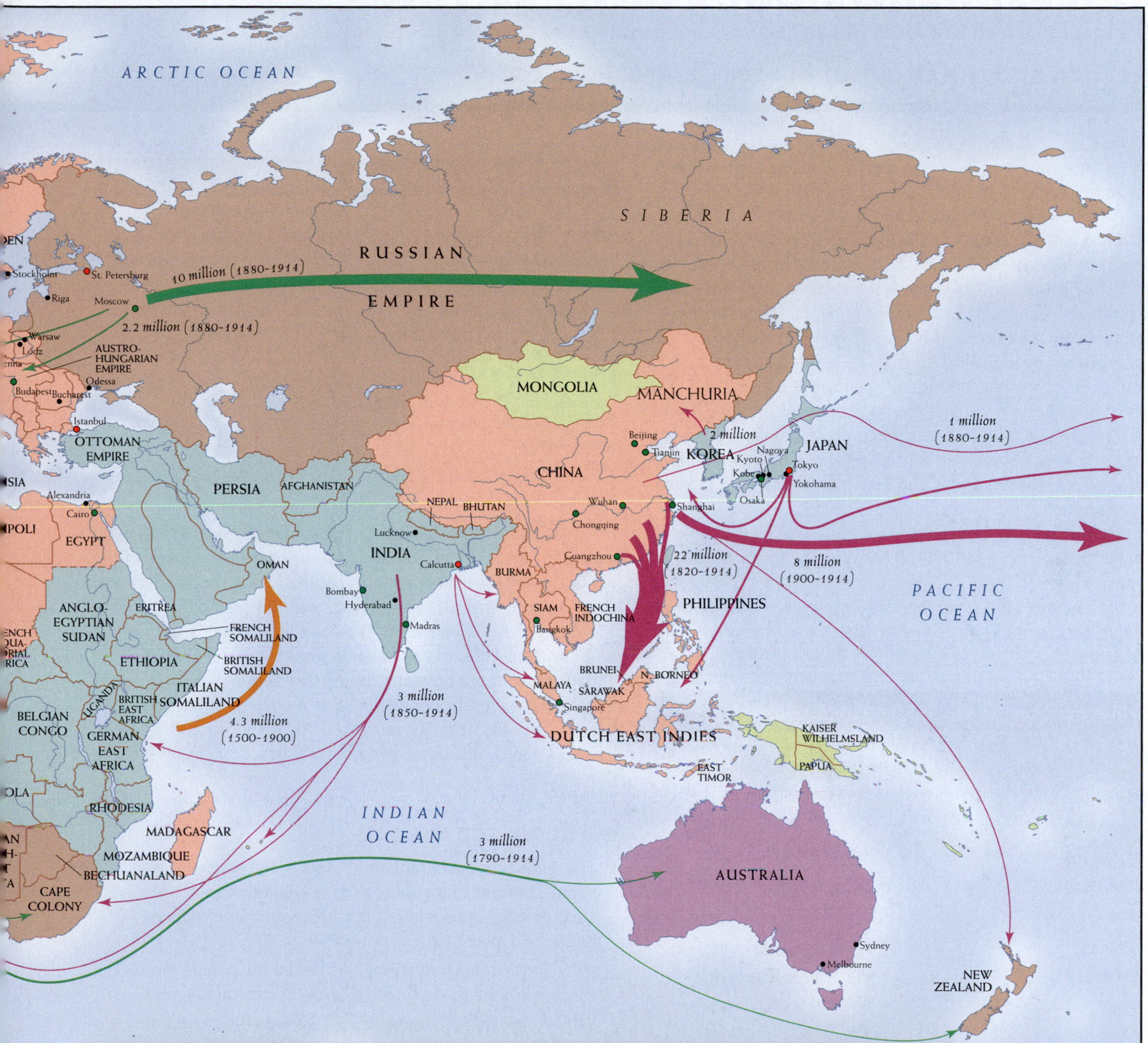

MAP 18.1 | Nineteenth-Century Migration

The nineteenth century witnessed a demographic revolution in terms of migration, urbanization patterns, and population growth. The world's population also rose from roughly 625 million in 1700 to 1.65 billion in 1900 (a two-and-a-half-fold increase).

- To what areas did most of the migrants from Europe go? What about the migrants from China, India, and Africa?
- What four areas saw the greatest population increase by 1900?
- How were migration flows and urbanization connected?
- What factor most accounted for this demographic trend, internal growth or external migration?

ANALYZING GLOBAL DEVELOPMENTS

Migration and the Origin of Border Control Policies

The movement of large numbers of people within and across regions—namely, the spread of the Mongols, the Atlantic world slave trade, and nineteenth-century migrations from Europe and Asia to the Americas—is not a new phenomenon in world history. What is relatively more recent to world history is the effort over the last 150 years to increase border control and identity documentation of people(s) on the move. Historian Adam McKeown in a recent work has demonstrated that the origins of the effort to regulate and document border control go back to late-nineteenth-century America and the efforts to substantially restrict the number of Asian immigrants trying to enter the United States. In contrast, earlier arguments held that modern day border control grew out of long-standing sovereignty practices of states and countries dating back to even earlier centuries.

In the first table below, we see a comparison of the rates of population growth from 1850–1950 between the major regions of the world.

In the second table, we see more concretely the number of people on the move in terms of their points of origin and destinations.

World Population Growth, 1850–1950 (in millions)

	1850 Population	1950 Population	Average Annual Growth (%)
Receiving			
Americas	59	325	1.72
North Asia	22	104	1.57
Southeast Asia	42	177	1.45
Sending			
Europe	265	515	0.67
South Asia	230	445	0.66
China	420	520	0.21
Africa	81	205	0.93
World	1,200	2,500	0.74

Global Long-Distance Migration, 1840–1940

Destination	Origins	Migrants (millions)	Auxiliary Origins
Americas	Europe	55–58	2.5 million from India, China, Japan, Africa
Southeast Asia, Indian Ocean Rim, Australasia	India South China	48–52	5 million from Africa, Europe, Northeast Asia, Middle East
Manchuria, Siberia, Central Asia, Japan	Northeast Asia Russia	46–51	

This data was compiled from port and customs statistics at significant entry points to major countries. What we see in the data is that the receiving nation's populations grew by a factor of 4.0-5.5 during this 100-year period, and that their overall growth was more than twice that of the "sending" regions during this time. Not only was the population growth rate of the receiving nations much more dramatic during this period, but the redistribution of the world's population was equally dramatic. In 1850, 10 percent of the world's population lived in the "receiving" areas; by 1950, nearly 25 percent of the world's population lived in those areas.

QUESTIONS FOR ANALYSIS

- The number of immigrants from Asia to the Americas was only about 3 percent of the total. Why do you think such a relatively small number of people would cause a dramatic change in border and identification control?
- Why do you think that during this period the populations in the sending areas also continued to grow at substantial rates?
- Why do you think so many people were on the move from South China and India to other parts of the Indian Ocean world? From northeast Asia to East Asia and Inner Asia?

Sources: Colin McEvedy and Richard Jones, Atlas of World Population History *(1978); Adam McKeown, "Global Migration, 1846–1940,"* Journal of World History *15 (2004); McKeown,* Melancholy Order: Asian Migration and the Globalization of Borders *(2008).*

and economic upheaval, social disruption, massive migration, and modern thinking, western notions of race became key in defining identities and justifying inequalities. Seeking to unify nations internally, many writers, artists, and political leaders created mythic histories that aimed to give diverse groups a common story of nationhood. Such inventions were crucial in nation building, but they also fueled conflict among nations that in 1914 erupted in the Great War—an event that would generate another huge wave of emigration, much of it involuntary.

Urban Transportation. (Left) *Streetcars in Tokyo, Japan's capital, are watched over by sword-bearing patrolmen in 1905, during the Russo-Japanese War. The first electric streetcar began running in Japan in 1895. Note the elevated electricity lines, which dated to the 1880s.* (Right) *Heavy traffic in London, in about 1910, points to an urban population on the move. Note the many kinds of transportation—motor buses as well as horse-drawn wagons; the railings in the foreground mark the entrance to the Underground, or subway.*

DISCONTENT WITH IMPERIALISM

In the decades before the Great War, opposition to European domination in Asia and Africa gathered strength. During the nineteenth century, as Europeans touted imperialism as a "civilizing mission," local prophets had voiced alternative visions contesting European supremacy (see Chapter 16). Although these movements were quashed, opposition did not stop. While imperialists consolidated their hold, suppression of unrest in the colonies required ever more force and bloodshed. As the cycle of resistance and repression escalated, many Europeans back home questioned the harsh means of controlling their colonies. By 1914, these questions were intensifying as colonial subjects across Asia and Africa challenged imperial domination. In China, too, where Europeans were scrambling for trading opportunities without actually establishing formal colonial power, local populations were resisting foreign influences.

Unrest in Africa

Africa witnessed many anticolonial uprisings in the first decades of colonial rule (see Map 18.2). Violent conflicts embroiled not only the Belgians and the Germans, who ruled autocratically, but also the British, whose colonial system left traditional African rulers in place. These uprisings made Europeans uneasy: why were Africans resisting regimes that had huge advantages in firepower and transport and that were bringing medical skills, literacy, and other fruits of European civilization? Some Europeans concluded that Africans were too stubborn or unsophisticated to appreciate Europe's generosity. Others, shocked by colonial cruelty, called for reform. A few radicals even demanded an end to imperialism.

African opposition was too spirited to ignore. Across the continent, organized armies and unorganized villagers rose up to challenge the European conquest. The resistance of villagers in the central highlands of British East Africa (Kenya) was so intense that the British mounted savage punitive expeditions to bring the area back under their control. Nonetheless, Africans continued to revolt against imperial authority—especially in areas where colonial rulers imposed forced labor, increased taxes, and appropriated land.

THE ANGLO-BOER WAR The continent's most devastating anticolonial uprising occurred in South Africa. This unique struggle pitted two white communities against each other: the British in the Cape Colony and Natal against the Afrikaners,

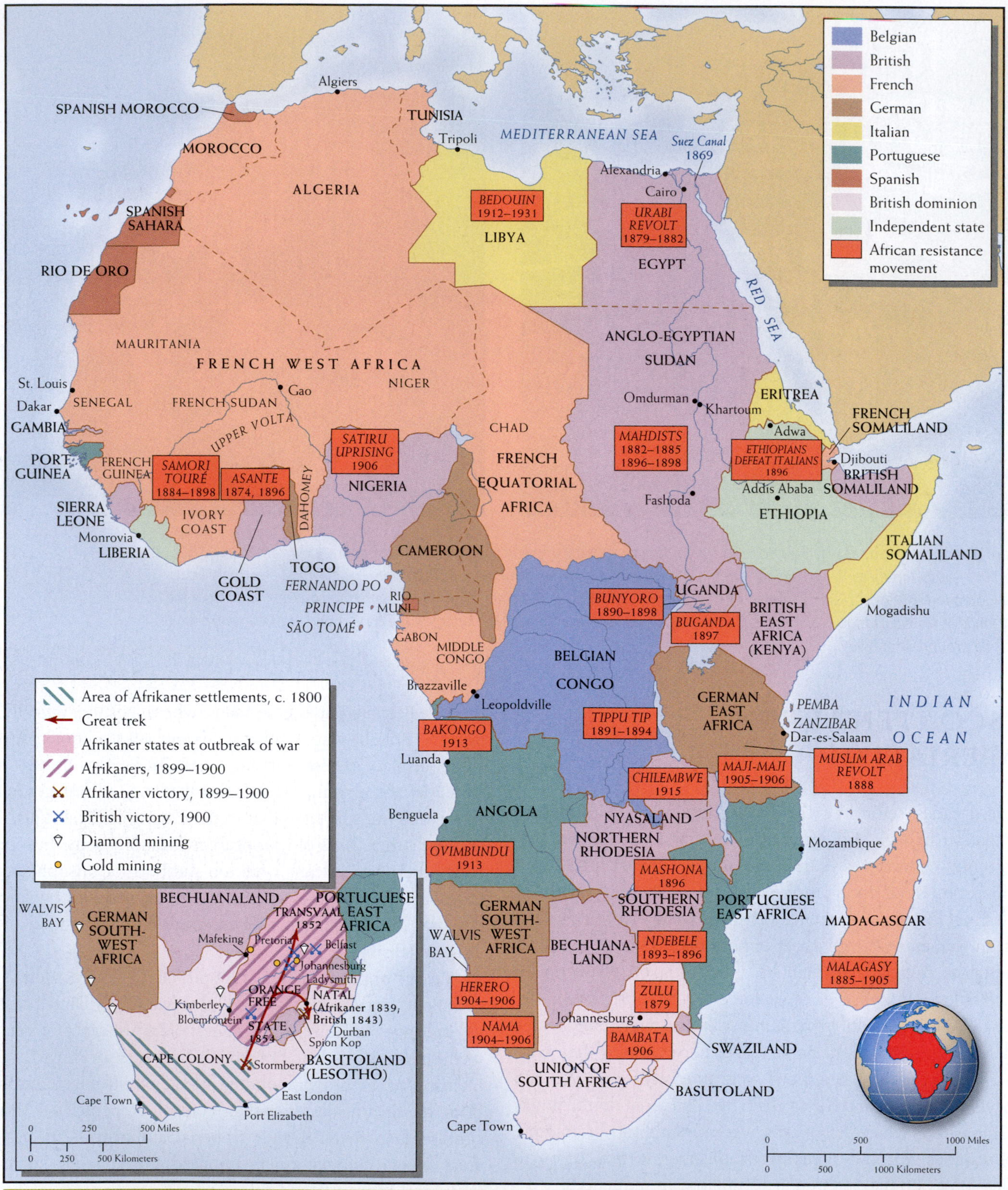

MAP 18.2 | Uprisings and Wars in Africa

The European partition and conquest of Africa were violent affairs.

- How many separate African resistance movements can you count on this map? • Where was resistance the most prolonged? • According to your reading, why were Ethiopians, who sustained their autonomy, able to do what other African opponents of European armies were not?

descendants of original Dutch settlers who lived in the Transvaal and the Orange Free State (see Map 18.2 inset). Although two white regimes were the main adversaries, the **Anglo-Boer War** (1899–1902) involved the area's 4 million black inhabitants as fully as its 1 million whites. Its horrors also traumatized the British at home, who regarded themselves as Europe's most enlightened and efficient colonial rulers.

The war's origins lay in the discovery of gold in the Transvaal in the mid-1880s. As the area rapidly became Africa's richest state, the prospect that Afrikaner republics might become the powerhouse in southern Africa was more than British imperialists could accept. Joseph Chamberlain, colonial secretary in London, and Cecil Rhodes, the leading politician in the Cape Colony, found allies in the British population living in the Afrikaner republics. Lacking voting rights and experiencing other forms of discrimination, these outsiders protested the Afrikaner governments' policies and pressed the British government to intervene. For their part, Afrikaner leaders emphasized the rights of a free people to resist.

Fearing that war was inevitable, the president of the Transvaal launched a preemptive strike against the British. In late 1899, Afrikaner forces crossed into South Africa. Fighting a relentless guerrilla campaign, Afrikaners waged a war that would last three years and cost Britain 20,000 soldiers and £200 million. Britain's frustrated attempts to respond to the Afrikaner insurgency and to cut its soldiers off from the local civilian population led the British to institute a terrifying innovation: the concentration camp. At one moment in the war, at least 155,000 captured men, women, and children were held in camps surrounded by barbed wire. Nor were the camps restricted to Afrikaners. The British also rounded up Africans whom they feared would side with the "anticolonial" Dutch descendants. The suffering and loss in these camps were appalling; by the war's end, 28,000 Afrikaner women and children, as well as 14,000 black Africans, had perished there. Thanks to a new sort of international actor, the war correspondent, newspaper reports and photographs brought the misery of the Anglo-Boer War, including reports of its atrocities, back to Europe. The British were scandalized by how long it had taken for the "empire on which the sun never sets" to subdue such a ragtag opponent, but they did, eventually, win the war, bringing the Transvaal and the Orange Free State—with their vast gold reserves—under their control.

OTHER STRUGGLES IN COLONIZED AFRICA The revulsion that the Anglo-Boer War sent through western public opinion deepened after Germany's activities in Africa also went

The Anglo-Boer War. *The British sent a large contingent of troops to South Africa to deal with the resistance of the two Boer republics—the Orange Free State and the Transvaal. The loss of life and the cruelties inflicted on soldiers and civilians alike during the war, which lasted from 1899 to 1902, did much to undermine the British people's views of their imperial mission. Transvaal and the Orange Free State fought valiantly to keep from becoming part of the British Empire. In the end, they lost.*

Extermination of the Herero. *The Germans carried out a campaign of near-extermination against the Herero population in German Southwest Africa in 1904–5. Nearly 90 percent of the Herero were killed. In this 1906 photograph, a German soldier stands guard over Herero women and children in a prison camp.*

brutally wrong. Germany had established colonies in Southwest Africa (present-day Namibia), Cameroon, and Togo in 1884 and in East Africa in 1885. In German Southwest Africa, the Herero and San people resisted German settlers' attempts to seize their native pasture lands, and in German East Africa (modern-day Tanzania), the Muslim Arab peoples rebelled. Between 1904 and 1906, fighting in German Southwest Africa escalated to such an extent that the German commander issued a genocidal extermination order against the Herero population. Equally troubling was the Maji-Maji Revolt in German East Africa of 1905–1906, described at the beginning of this chapter.

Apologists for imperial violence tried to dampen public outcries. Journalists portrayed the Maji-Maji rebels as fanatics in the thrall of a demonic African witch doctor, Kinjikitile Ngwale, and the Afrikaners as uncouth ruffians who deserved what they got. According to defenders, the unjustifiable horrors of Leopold's Belgian Congo (see Chapter 17) were an exception, created by a dissolute and reckless monarch who had no scruples when it came to enhancing his own wealth and political power. Apologists from all the European powers argued that these incidents did not represent the reality of empire—at least not *their* nation's empire. Thus, the British denounced the Belgians to highlight their own benevolence, while the French spread gory images of German repression to underscore their own success at uplifting Africans. Portraying Africans as either accepting subjects or childlike primitives, the European powers sought to redouble their coercive efforts and, in many cases, the number of officials and soldiers stationed in the colonies.

The Boxer Uprising in China

At the turn of the century, forces from within and without also unsettled China. Although China's turmoil differed from Africa's, it, too, arose from concern about European intrusions. As the population swelled to over half a billion and outstripped the country's resources, problems of landlessness, poverty, and peasant discontent (constants in China's modern history) led many to mourn the decay of political authority. In response, in 1898 the Qing emperor tried to modernize industry, agriculture, commerce, education, and the military. But opponents blocked the emperor's designs. Before long the emperor faced house arrest in the palace, while the Empress Dowager Cixi, whom conservatives supported, actually ruled.

EXTERNAL FACTORS The breakdown of dynastic authority originated largely with foreign pressure. For one thing, China's defeat in the Sino-Japanese War of 1894–1895 (see Chapter 17) was deeply humiliating. Although Japan, which acquired Taiwan as its first major colony, was the immediate beneficiary of the war, Britain, France, Germany, and Russia quickly scrambled for additional concessions from China. They demanded that the Qing government grant them specific areas within China as their respective "spheres of influence" (see Map 18.3). The United States argued instead for maintaining an "open door" policy that would keep access available to all traders. But the Americans also wanted the Qing to accept western norms of political and economic exchange and to acknowledge the superiority

Cixi's Allies. *The Empress Dowager Cixi emerged as the most powerful figure in the Qing court in the last decades of the dynasty, from the 1860s until her death in 1908. Highly able, she approved many of the early reforms of the Self-Strengthening movement, but her commitment to the preservation of the Manchu Qing dynasty made her suspicious of more fundamental and wide-ranging changes. Here she is shown surrounded by court eunuchs; Cixi relied upon them, especially as her relationships with orthodox officials were often ambivalent.*

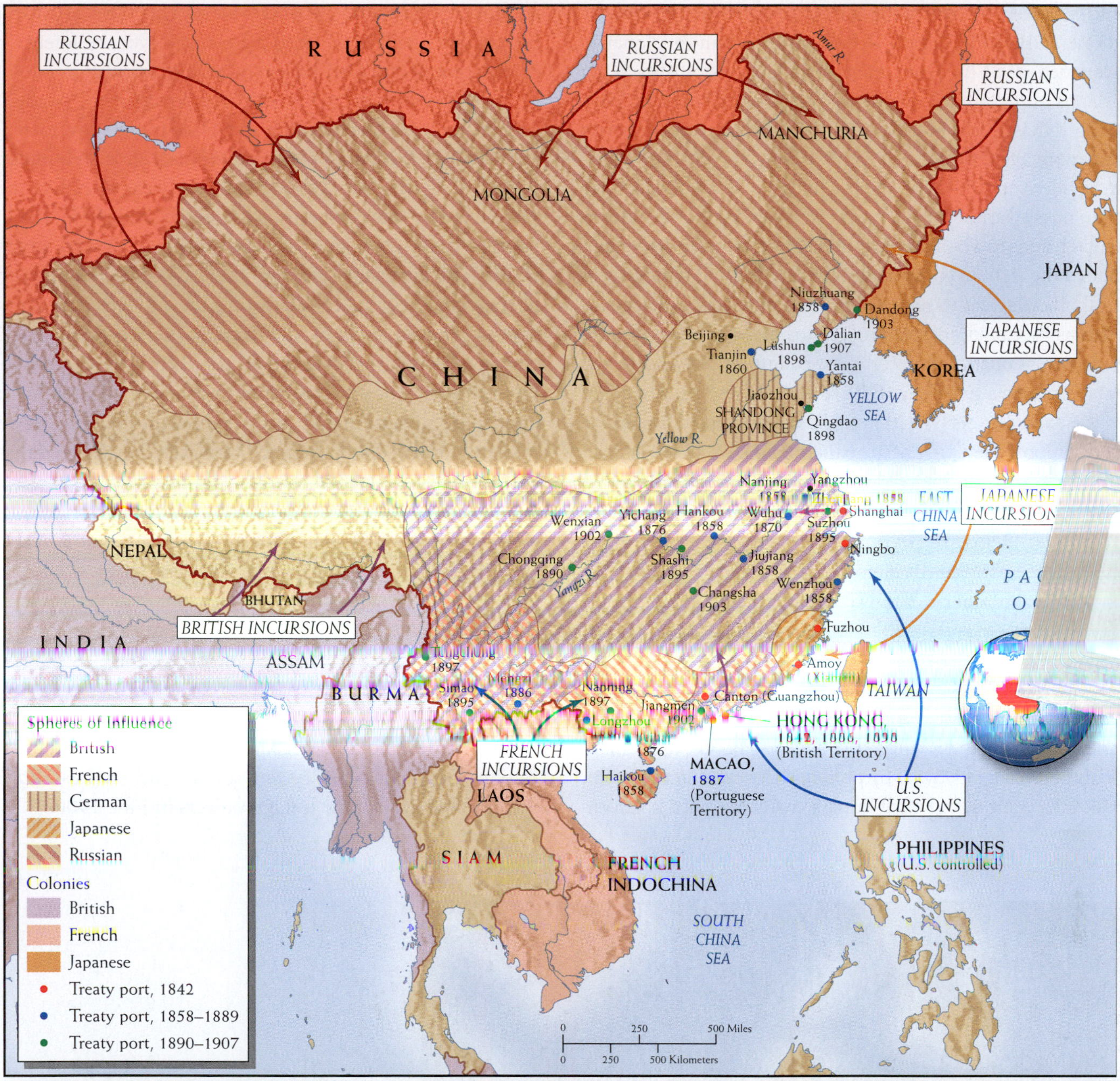

MAP 18.3 | Foreign Spheres of Influence in China, 1842–1907

While technically independent, the Qing dynasty could not prevent foreign penetration and domination of its economy during the nineteenth century.

• Which five powers established spheres of influence in China? • At what time was the greatest number of treaty ports established? According to your reading, what did the foreign powers hope to achieve within their spheres of influence? • What kinds of local opposition did the foreign influence inspire?

of Christian civilization. In response, some Chinese elites developed an anti-European stance while advocating the use of European ideas and technology to strengthen China itself.

The most explosive reaction to these pressures, the **Boxer Uprising**, started within the peasantry. Like colonized peoples in Africa, the Boxers violently resisted European meddling in their communities. And like the Taiping Rebellion decades earlier (see Chapter 16), the story of the Boxers was tied to missionary activities. Whereas in earlier centuries Jesuit missionaries had sought to convert the court and the elites, by the mid-nineteenth century the missionary goal was to convert commoners. After the Taiping Rebellion, Christian missionaries had streamed into China, impatient to make new converts in the hinterlands and confident of their governments' backing. With the Qing dynasty in a weakened state, Christian missionaries became more aggressive.

An incident in 1897, in which Chinese residents killed two German missionaries in the northern province of Shandong, brought tensions to a boil. In retribution, the German government demanded the right to construct three cathedrals, to remove hostile local officials, and to seize the northeastern port of Jiaozhou. As tensions mounted, martial arts groups in the region began to attack the missionaries and converts, calling for an end to the Christians' privileges. In early 1899, several of these groups united under the name Boxers United in Righteousness and adopted the slogan, "Support the Qing, destroy the foreign." Like the African followers of Kinjikitile, the Boxers believed that divine protection made them immune to all earthly weapons: "We requested the gods to attach themselves to our bodies. When they had done so, we became Spirit Boxers, after which we were invulnerable to swords and spears, our courage was enhanced, and in fighting we were unafraid to die and dared to charge straight ahead."

INTERNAL FACTORS The Boxer movement flourished especially where natural disasters and harsh economic conditions spread hardships. Shandong province had suffered floods throughout much of the decade, followed by prolonged drought in the winter of 1898. Idle, restless, and often hungry, many peasants, boatmen, and peddlers turned to the Boxers for support. They also liked the Boxers' message that the gods were angry over the foreign presence in general and Christian activities in particular.

As these activists, many of them young men, swelled the Boxers' ranks, women also found a place in the movement. The so-called Red Lanterns were mostly teenage girls and unmarried women who announced their loyalty by wearing red garments. Although the Red Lanterns were segregated from the male Boxers—they worshipped at their own altars and practiced martial arts at separate boxing grounds—they were important to the movement in counteracting the influence of Christian women. Indeed, one of the Boxers' greatest fears was that cunning Christian women would use their guile to weaken the Boxers' spirits. The rebels believed that their invulnerability came from spirit possession and that the inherent polluting power of women threatened their "magic." However, they claimed that the "purity" of the Red Lanterns could counter this threat. The Red Lanterns were supposedly capable of incredible feats: they could walk on water or fly through the air. Belief in their magical powers provided critical assistance for the uprising.

As the movement gained momentum, the Qing vacillated between viewing the Boxers as a threat to order and embracing them as a force to check foreign intrusion. Early in 1900, Qing troops clashed with the Boxers in an escalating cycle of violence. By spring, however, the Qing could no longer control the tens of thousands of Boxers roaming the vicinities of Beijing and Tianjin. Embracing the Boxers' cause, the empress dowager declared war against the foreign powers in June 1900.

The Boxer Uprising in China. *The Boxer Uprising was eventually suppressed by a foreign army made up of Japanese, European, and American troops that arrived in Beijing in August 1900. The picture here shows fighting between the foreign troops and the combined forces of Qing soldiers and the Boxers. After a period of vacillation, the Qing court, against the advice of some of its officials, finally threw its support behind the quixotic struggle of the Boxers against the foreign presence, laying the ground for the military intervention of the imperialist powers.*

FOREIGN INVOLVEMENT AND AFTERMATH Acting without any discernible plan or leadership, the Boxers went after Christian and foreign symbols and persons. They harassed and sometimes killed Chinese Christians in parts of northern China, destroyed railroad tracks and telegraph lines, and attacked owners of foreign objects such as lamps and clocks. In Beijing, the Boxers besieged foreign embassy compounds where diplomats and their families cowered in fear. The Boxers also reduced the Southern Cathedral to ruins and then besieged the Northern Cathedral, where more than 3,000 Catholics and 40 French and Italian marines had sought refuge. Those inside were rescued only with the arrival of a foreign expeditionary force.

In August 1900, a foreign army of 20,000 troops crushed the Boxers. About half came from Japan; the rest came primarily from Russia, Britain, Germany, France, and the United States. Thereafter, the victors forced the Chinese to sign the punitive Boxer Protocol. Among other punishments, it required the regime to pay an exorbitant compensation in gold (about twice the empire's annual income) for damages to foreign life and property. The protocol also authorized western powers to station troops in Beijing. Furthermore, although the defeat prompted the Qing to make a last-ditch effort at reform, it dealt another blow to the dynasty's standing both internally and externally.

Even in defeat, the Boxers' anti-western uprising showed how much had changed in China since the Taiping Rebellion. Although the Boxers were primarily peasants, even they had felt the unsettledness generated by European inroads into China. Indeed, the Europeans' commercial and spiritual reach, once confined to elites and port cities, had extended across much of China. Whereas the Taiping Rebellion had mobilized millions against the Qing, the Boxers remained loyal to the dynasty and focused their wrath on foreigners and Chinese Christians. The Boxer Rebellion, like the Maji-Maji Revolt in East Africa, revealed the widespread political opposition to westernization and the willingness of local disaffected populations to resist western programs.

WORLDWIDE INSECURITIES

Protests against European intrusion in Africa and China were distant movements that most Europeans could disregard. News of unrest in the colonies and in China generally did not lead them to question their ways. Instead, it reinforced their belief in the inferiority of other cultures. In Africa, for example, unrest in a rival's empire was taken as a sign of poor management. Anxiety here reflected the difficulty of the "civilizing mission," although a few did begin to question imperial ethics. At the same time, however, conflicts closer to home tore at European and North American confidence. These included rivalries among western powers, the booms and busts of expanding industrial economies, new types of class conflict, challenges about the proper roles of women, and problems of uncontrolled urbanization (see again Map 18.1).

Imperial Rivalries at Home

The rise of a European-centered world deepened rivalries within Europe and promoted instability there. Numerous factors fostered conflict, including France's smoldering resentment at its defeat in the Franco-Prussian War (see Chapter 17), but tension increased as the European states competed for raw materials and colonial footholds. Even as these powers built up their supply of weapons, as well as ships and railroads to transport troops, not everyone supported the buildup. Many Europeans, for example, disapproved of spending on massive steam-powered warships. Others warned that the arms race would end in a devastating war.

Intra-European rivalry had powerful effects on Germany and Russia. In fact, the unifications of Germany and Italy at the expense of France and the Austrian Empire had smashed the old balance of power in Europe. New alliances began to crystallize after 1890, as German–French hostility persisted and German–Russian friendship broke down. This left Germany surrounded by foes: Britain and France to the west, Russia to the east. As ethnic nationalism spread among the Arabs, Turks, Czechs, and southern Slavs, the multinational Ottoman and Habsburg empires began to fragment; the Balkans in particular became a hotbed of interethnic violence. Roiled by internal conflicts, the two venerable empires looked likely to collapse, leaving power vacuums in central and southeastern Europe. Sensing conflict on the horizon, Britain, Germany, France, and Russia entered into a massive arms race.

FINANCIAL, INDUSTRIAL, AND TECHNOLOGICAL INSECURITIES Economic developments helped make powers "great," but they could also unsettle societies. Indeed, pride about wealth and growth coincided with laments about changes in national and international economies. To begin with, Americans and Europeans recognized that the small-scale, laissez-faire capitalism championed by Adam Smith (see Chapter 14) was giving way to an economic order dominated by huge, heavily capitalized firms. Gone, it seemed, was Smith's vision of many small producers in vigorous competition with one another, all benefiting from efficient—but not exploitative—divisions of labor.

Instead of smooth progress, the economy of the West in the nineteenth century bounced between booms and busts: long-term business cycles of rapid growth followed by counter-cycles of stagnation. Late in the century, the pace of economic change accelerated. Large-scale steel production, railroad building, and textile manufacturing expanded at breakneck speed, while

Labor Disputes. *The late nineteenth century witnessed a surge in industrial strife, worker strikes, and violent suppression of labor movements.* (Left) *One of the deadliest confrontations in the United States occurred in May 1892, when a strike against the Carnegie Steel Company escalated into a gunfight, which left ten dead and many more wounded. Here, a group of striking workers keeps watch over the steel mill in Homestead, Pennsylvania.* (Right) *Striking dock workers rally in London's Trafalgar Square, 1911. By this time, residents of European cities were used to seeing crowds of protesters pressing for improved working conditions or political reform.*

waves of bank closures, bankruptcies, and agricultural crises ruined many small property owners, including farmers. By the century's end, European and North American economies were dominated as never before by a few large-scale firms.

GLOBAL FINANCIAL AND INDUSTRIAL INTEGRATION

These were years of heady international financial integration. More and more countries joined the world system of borrowing and lending; more and more countries were linked financially because their national currencies were all backed by gold. At the hub of this world system were the banks of London, which since the Napoleonic wars had been a major source of capital for international borrowers.

The rise of giant banks and huge industrial corporations caused alarm, for it seemed to signal an end to free markets and competitive capitalism. In the United States, an entire generation of journalists cut their teeth exposing the skullduggery (shady dealings) of financial and industrial giants. These "muckrakers" portrayed the captains of finance like J. P. Morgan and John D. Rockefeller as bent on amassing private power at the expense of working families and public authorities. In Europe, too, critics lamented a similar trend in which lack of competition created greater disparities of wealth between the owners of firms and the workforce.

Rather than longing for the return of truly free markets, many critics sought reforms that would protect people from economic instability. Indeed, starting in the 1890s, the reaction against economic competition gathered steam. Producers, big and small, grew unhappy with supply and demand mechanisms. To cope with an unruly market, farmers created cooperatives. For their part, big industrialists fashioned monopolies, or cartels, in the name of improving efficiency, correcting failures in the market, and heightening profits. At the same time, government officials and academic specialists worried that modern economies were inherently unstable, prone to overproduce, and vulnerable to bankruptcy and crisis. The solution, many economists thought, was for the state to manage the market's inefficiencies.

FINANCIAL CRISES Banking especially seemed in need of closer government supervision. Many industrial societies already had central banks, and London's Bank of England had long since overseen local and international money markets. But public institutions did not yet have the resources to protect all investments during times of economic crisis. Between 1890 and 1893, fully 550 American banks collapsed, and only the intervention of J. P. Morgan prevented the depletion of the nation's gold reserves.

The road to regulation, however, was hardly smooth. In 1907, a more serious crisis threatened, caused by a panic on Wall Street that led to a run on the banks. Once again, it fell to J. P. Morgan to rescue the American dollar from financial panic—by compelling financier after financier to commit unprecedented funds (eventually $35 million) to protect banks and trusts against depositors' panic. Morgan himself lost $21 million and emerged from the bank panic convinced that some sort of public oversight was needed. By 1913, the U.S. Congress ratified the Federal Reserve Act, creating boards to monitor the supply and demand of the nation's money.

The crisis of 1907 showed how national financial matters could quickly become international affairs. The sell-off of the shares of banks and trusts in the United States also led American investors to withdraw their funds from other countries that relied on American capital. As a result, Canada, for instance, suffered a bank crisis of its own. Countries like Egypt and Mexico, far apart geographically yet linked through international capital, also suffered either withdrawal of investors' funds or a suspension of new investments and a string of bankruptcies. Although the head of Mexico's government, General Porfirio Díaz, tried to regain investors' confidence and their funds, Mexico fell into a severe recession as U.S. capital dried up. In turn, Mexicans lost faith in their own economic—and political—system. Unemployed and suffering new hardships, many Mexicans flocked to Díaz's political opponents, who eventually raised the flag of rebellion in 1910. A year later, the entire regime collapsed in revolution (see below).

INDUSTRIALIZATION AND THE MODERN ECONOMY Just as financial circuits linked nations as never before, so did industrialization. Backed by big banks, industrialists could afford to extend their enterprises physically and geographically. So heavy industries now came to new places. In Russia, for example, industrial activity quickened. With loans from European (especially French, Belgian, and British) investors, Russia built railways, telegraph lines, and factories and developed coal, iron, steel, and petroleum industries. By 1900, Russia was producing half of the world's oil and a considerable amount of steel. Yet industrial development remained uneven: southern Europe and the American South continued to lag behind northern regions. The gap was even more pronounced in colonial territories, which contained few industrial enterprises aside from railroad building and mining.

By 1914, the factory and the railroad had become global symbols of the modern economy—and of its positive and negative effects. Everywhere, the coming of the railroad to one's town or village was a big event: for some, it represented an exhilarating leap into the modern world; for others, a terrifying abandonment of the past. Ocean liners, automobiles, and airplanes, likewise, could be both dazzling and disorienting. The older conservative elite found technological development more worrisome than did urban liberals, who increasingly set state policies.

For ordinary people, the new economy brought benefits and drawbacks. Factories produced cheaper goods, but they belched clouds of black smoke. Railways offered faster transport, but they ruined small towns unlucky enough to be left off the branch line. Machines (when operating properly) were more efficient than human and animal labor, but workers who used them felt reduced to machines themselves. Indeed, the American Frederick Winslow Taylor proposed a system of "scientific management" to make human bodies perform more like machines, maximizing the efficiency of workers' movements. But workers did not want to be managed or to cede control of the pace of production to employers. Labor's resistance to "Taylorization" led to numerous strikes. For strikers, as for conservatives, the course of progress had taken an unsettling turn.

The "Woman Question"

Complicating the situation was turmoil about the politics of domesticity, or the "woman question." In the West, female activists demanded that women be given more rights as citizens, and more radical voices called for fundamental changes to the family and the larger society. At the same time, imperial architects claimed that colonial rule was bringing great improvements to women in Asia and Africa. But the "woman question" was no more easily settled there than elsewhere.

WOMEN'S ISSUES IN THE WEST In western countries, for most of the nineteenth century, a belief in "separate spheres" had supposedly confined women to domestic matters, while leaving men in charge of public life and economic undertakings. (In practice, only women from middle- and upper-class families avoided working outside the home for wages.) Men did not mind having women work for their charities or churches, or educate their daughters at home. But most men as well as most women continued to think that higher education and public activism were not suitable for "ladies"—and, if possible, these "ladies" too should not have to labor outside the home or acquire a profession. But as economic developments created new jobs for women and greater access to education, women who craved new opportunities increasingly did find work as teachers, secretaries, typists, department store clerks, social workers, and telephone operators. These jobs offered greater economic and social independence, at least for a few.

Changes in women's social status did not, however, translate into electoral reform at the national level. By midcentury, several women's suffrage movements had appeared, but these campaigns bore little immediate fruit. In 1868, women received the right to vote in local elections in Britain. Within a few years, Finland, Sweden, and some American states allowed single, property-owning women the right to cast ballots—again, only

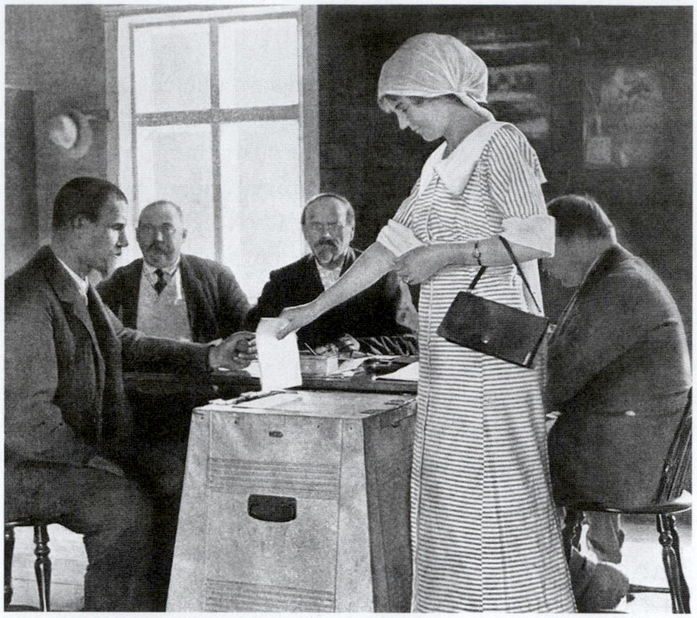

Woman Suffrage in Finland. *The British and then the French introduced the concept of citizenship with universal rhetoric, but in practice the category of citizen was generally restricted to property-holding males. Finland granted its women the right to vote in 1906, earlier than most countries. In this photograph, a Finnish woman casts her ballot in the election of 1906.*

in local elections. Women obtained the right to vote in national elections in New Zealand in 1893, in Australia in 1902, in Finland in 1906, and in Norway in 1913. Despite these gains, male alarmists portrayed women's suffrage and women's rights as the beginning of civilization's end.

Quietly, and without conferring with one another, many women began to take charge of their lives in another way, and that was to assert control over reproduction. Although in numerous countries the use of contraceptive devices was illegal, women still found ways to limit the number of children they bore. The French birthrate fell so precipitously in the second half of the nineteenth century that commentators began to worry about France's "degeneration." Early in the twentieth century, the birthrate in America was half of what it had been a century before. As women well knew, having fewer children was one way to raise the class status of the rest of the household, and to leave more income for the smaller family's education, housing, and leisure activities.

VARYING VIEWS ON FEMINISM Most middle-class women in Europe and the Americas were not seeking to make women equal to men. Indeed, many bourgeois women recoiled from the close relationships between socialism and feminism, and feared that too much equality would make women abominably "mannish." But there were radical women in Europe and America, as well as elsewhere, some of whom, like the Polish-German communist Rosa Luxemburg, became powerful philosophers and political organizers in their own right.

Radical women met stiff repression wherever they challenged the established order. This was especially true outside Europe and the Americas, where the feminist movement was not strong and where women's education and entry into the professions lagged far behind those of men. In 1903, China's Qiu Jin (1875–1907) left her husband and headed to Japan to study. There she befriended other radicals and made a name for herself by dressing in men's clothing, carrying a sword, and trying her hand at bomb making. Returning to China in 1906, she founded the *Chinese Women's Journal* (*Zhongguo nübao*) and wrote articles urging women to fight for their rights and to leave home if necessary. (See Primary Source: A Chinese Feminist Condemns Injustices to Women.) Qing authorities executed Qiu Jin after she participated in a failed attempt to topple the dynasty.

WOMEN'S STATUS IN COLONIES In the colonial world, the woman question was a contentious issue—but it was mainly argued among men. European authorities liked to boast that colonial rule improved women's status. Citing examples of traditional societies' subordination of women, they criticized as barbaric the veiling of women in Islamic societies, the binding of women's feet in China, widow burning (*sati*) in India, and female genital mutilation in Africa. Europeans believed that prohibiting such acts was a justification for colonial intervention.

And yet, for women in Africa, the Middle East, and India, colonialism added to their burdens. As male workers headed into the export economy, formerly shared agricultural work fell exclusively on women's shoulders. In Africa, for example, the opening of vast gold and diamond mines drew thousands of men away to work in the mines, leaving women to fend for themselves. Similarly, the rise of European-owned agricultural estates in Kenya and Southern Rhodesia depleted surrounding villages of male family members, who went to work on the estates. In these circumstances, women kept the local, food-producing economy afloat.

Nor did colonial "civilizing" rhetoric improve women's political or cultural circumstances. In fact, European missionaries preached a message of domesticity to Asian and African families, emphasizing that women's place was in the home raising children and that women's education should be different from men's. Thus males overwhelmingly dominated the new schools that Europeans built. Moreover, customary law in colonial Africa, as interpreted by chiefs who collaborated with colonial officials, favored men. As a result, African women often lost landholding and other rights that they had enjoyed before the Europeans' arrival. (See Primary Source: Industrialization and Women's Freedom in Egypt.)

PRIMARY SOURCE

A Chinese Feminist Condemns Injustices to Women

Although a small minority, Chinese feminists of the early twentieth century were vocal in condemning the injustices inflicted on women in China. In this essay from 1904, directed to her countrywomen, Qiu Jin compares the treatment of Chinese women to slavery. She also displays a strong nationalistic streak as she ties the future of Chinese women to the fate of the Chinese nation.

Alas! The greatest injustice in this world must be the injustice suffered by our female population of two hundred million. If a girl is lucky enough to have a good father, then her childhood is at least tolerable. But if by chance her father is an ill-tempered and unreasonable man, he may curse her birth: "What rotten luck: another useless thing." Some men go as far as killing baby girls while most hold the opinion that "girls are eventually someone else's property" and treat them with coldness and disdain. In a few years, without thinking about whether it is right or wrong, he forcibly binds his daughter's soft, white feet with white cloth so that even in her sleep she cannot find comfort and relief until the flesh becomes rotten and the bones broken. What is all this misery for? Is it just so that on the girl's wedding day friends and neighbors will compliment him, saying, "Your daughter's feet are really small"? Is that what the pain is for?

But that is not the worst of it. When the time for marriage comes, a girl's future life is placed in the hands of a couple of shameless matchmakers and a family seeking rich and powerful in-laws. A match can be made without anyone ever inquiring whether the prospective bridegroom is honest, kind, or educated. On the day of the marriage the girl is forced into a red and green bridal sedan chair, and all this time she is not allowed to breathe one word about her future. . . .

When Heaven created people it never intended such injustice because if the world is without women, how can men be born? Why is there no justice for women? We constantly hear men say, "The human mind is just and we must treat people with fairness and equality." Then why do they greet women like black slaves from Africa?

How did inequality and injustice reach this state? . . .

I hope that we all shall put aside the past and work hard for the future. Let us all put aside our former selves and be resurrected as complete human beings. Those of you who are old, do not call yourselves old and useless. If your husbands want to open schools, don't stop them; if your good sons want to study abroad, don't hold them back. Those among us who are middle-aged, don't hold back your husbands lest they lose their ambition and spirit and fail in their work. After your sons are born, send them to schools. You must do the same for your daughters and, whatever you do, don't bind their feet. As for you young girls among us, go to school if you can. If not, read and study at home. Those of you who are rich, persuade your husbands to open schools, build factories, and contribute to charitable organizations. Those of you who are poor, work hard and help your husbands. Don't be lazy, don't eat idle rice. These are what I hope for you. You must know that when a country is near destruction, women cannot rely on the men any more because they aren't even able to protect themselves. If we don't take heart now and shape up, it will be too late when China is destroyed.

Sisters, we must follow through on these ideas!

QUESTIONS FOR ANALYSIS

- Identify at least three ways in which Chinese women suffer injustice, according to Qiu Jin.
- In what way does the Qiu Jin's comparison of Chinese women to "black slaves from Africa" reveal a growing global awareness within the Chinese population?
- Why is nationalism an important part of Qiu Jin's message?

Source: Qiu Jin, "An Address to Two Hundred Million Fellow Countrywomen." Reprinted with the permission of The Free Press, a division of Simon & Schuster, Inc., from Chinese Civilization: A Sourcebook, *Second Edition, revised and expanded by Patricia Buckley Ebrey.*

Class Conflict in a New Key

Capitalism's volatility shook confidence in free market economies and sharpened conflicts between classes; the tone of political debates was transformed as new, more strident voices called for radical change. Although living conditions for European and North American workers improved over time, widening inequalities in income and the slow pace of reform led to frustration. Most workers remained committed to peaceful agitation, but some radicals turned to violence. Often, especially in eastern Europe and Russia, the closed character of political systems fueled frustration—and radicalism. This was also the case in

PRIMARY SOURCE

Industrialization and Women's Freedom in Egypt

In this selection, taken from a 1909 lecture in Cairo open only to women, an educated upper-class Egyptian woman insists that female confinement is unnatural and absurd. She demands a place for women in the workplace. The writer, Bahithat al-Badiya, criticizes the effect of traditional religious practices on women's freedom and blames men for not allowing women to enter the professions and enjoy the freedoms that men take for granted.

Men say when we become educated we shall push them out of work and abandon the role for which God created us. But isn't it rather men who have pushed women out of work? Before, women used to spin and to weave cloth for clothes for themselves and their children, but men invented machines for spinning and weaving and put women out of work. . . . Since male inventors and workers have taken away a lot of our work should we waste our time in idleness or seek other work to occupy us? Of course, we should do the latter. . . . Obviously, I am not urging women to neglect their home and children to go out and become lawyers or judges or railway engineers. But if any of us wish to work in such professions our personal freedom should not be infringed. . . .

Men say to us categorically, "You women have been created for the house and we have been created to be bread-winners." Is this a God-given dictate? How are we to know this since no holy book has spelled it out? Political economy calls for a division of labor but if women enter the learned professions it does not upset the system. The division of labor is merely a human creation. . . . If men say to us that we have been created weak we say to them, "No it is you who made us weak through the path you made us follow." After long centuries of enslavement by men, our minds rusted and our bodies weakened. . . .

Men criticize the way we dress in the street. They have a point because we have exceeded the bounds of custom and propriety. . . . [But] veiling should not prevent us from breathing fresh air or going out to buy what we need if no one can buy it for us. It must not prevent us from gaining an education nor cause our health to deteriorate. When we have finished our work and feel restless and if our house does not have a spacious garden why shouldn't we go to the outskirts of the city and take the fresh air that God has created for everyone and not just put in boxes exclusively for men.

QUESTIONS FOR ANALYSIS

- How has al-Badiya's Muslim faith influenced her views on the role of women in society? Find two places in the reading where these influences are apparent.
- How have western influences affected her views on the role of women in society? Find at least two places in the reading where these influences are evident.

Source: Bahithat al-Badiya, "A Public Lecture for Women Only in the Club of the Umma Party," from "Industrialization and Women's Freedom in Egypt," in Opening the Gates: A Century of Arab Feminist Writing, *edited by Margot Badran and Miriam Cooke. Copyright © 1990. Reprinted with permission of Indiana University Press.*

Latin America, where even the middle classes were largely shut out of politics until new parties offered fresh opportunities for political expression. In Argentina, for example, urban workers found outlets for protest within movements known as **syndicalism** (the organization of workplace associations that included unskilled laborers), socialism, and **anarchism** (the belief that society should be a free association of members, not subject to government, laws, or police).

STRIKES AND REVOLTS In the Americas and in Europe, radicals adopted numerous tactics for asserting the interests of the working class. In Europe, the franchise was gradually expanded in hopes that the lower classes would prefer voting to revolution—and indeed, most of the new political parties that catered to workers had no desire to overthrow the state. But conservatives feared them anyway, especially as they gained electoral clout. The Labour Party, founded in Britain in 1900, quickly boasted a large share of the vote. By 1912, the German Social Democratic Party was the largest party in the Reichstag. But it was not the legally sanctioned parties that sparked violent street protests and strikes in the century's last decades. A whole array of syndicalists, anarchists, radical royalists, and revolutionary socialists sprang up in this period, making work stoppages everyday affairs.

Although the United States did not have similarly radical factions or successful labor parties, American workers were also organizing. The labor movement's power burst forth dramatically in 1894 when the American Railway Union launched a strike that spread across the nation. Spawned by wage cuts and firings following an economic downturn, the Pullman Strike (directed against the maker of railway sleeping cars, George Pullman) involved approximately 3 million workers. The strike's conclusion, however, revealed the enduring power of the status quo. After hiring replacement workers to break the strike, Pullman requested federal troops to protect his operation. When the troops arrived, infuriated strikers reacted with violence—which led to a further crackdown by the government against the union. After its leaders were jailed, the strike collapsed.

A few upheavals from below did succeed, at least briefly. In 1905, in the wake of the Russo-Japanese War (in which the Russians lost to the Japanese), revolt briefly shook the tsarist state and yielded a fledgling form of representative government. The revolutionaries tried some new forms, most notably workers' soviets, which were groups of delegates representing particular industries. Ultimately, however, the army put down both urban and rural unrest. Autocracy was reestablished. Both liberals and radicals were excluded from power.

REVOLUTION IN MEXICO Perhaps the most successful turn-of-the-century revolution occurred in Mexico. A peasant uprising, it thoroughly transformed the country. Fueled by the unequal distribution of land and by disgruntled workers, the **Mexican Revolution** erupted in 1910 when political elites split over the succession of General Porfirio Díaz after decades of his strong-arm rule. Dissidents balked when Díaz refused to step down, and peasants and workers rallied to the call to arms.

What destroyed the Díaz regime and its powerful army was the swelling flood of peasants, farmers, cattlemen, and rural workers who were desperate for a change in the social order. From the north (led by the charismatic Pancho Villa) to the south (under the legendary Emiliano Zapata), rural folk helped topple the Díaz regime. In the name of providing land for farmers and ending oligarchic rule, peasant armies defeated Díaz's troops and then proceeded to destroy many large estates. The fighting lasted for ten brutal years, during which almost 10 percent of the country's population perished.

Thereafter, political leaders had to accept popular demands for democracy, respect for the sovereignty of peasant communities, and land reform. As a result the Constitution of 1917 incorporated widespread reform, and by 1920 an emerging generation of politicians recognized the power of a militarized peasantry and initiated deep-seated changes in Mexico's social structure. These leaders also realized that their new regime had to appeal ideologically to common folk. Revolutionaries gave trade unions sweeping rights to organize, paving the way for nationalizing the country's mines and oil industries. But perhaps the radicals' most lasting legacy was the creation of rural

The Mexican Revolution. (Left) *By 1915, Mexican peasants, workers, and farmers had destroyed much of the old elitist system. This was the first popular, peasant revolution of the twentieth century. Among the most famous leaders were Pancho Villa and Emiliano Zapata. They are pictured here in the presidential office in the capital. Villa took the president's chair jokingly. Zapata, carrying the broad hat typical of his people, refused to wear military gear and glowered at the camera suspiciously.* (Right) *By the 1920s, Mexican artists and writers were putting recent events into images and words. Pictured here is one of the muralist Diego Rivera's paintings of the Mexican Revolution. Notice the nationalist interpretation: Porfirio Díaz's troops defend foreign oil companies and white aristocrats against middle-class and peasant (and darker-skinned) reformers who call for a "social revolution." Observe also the absence of women in this epic mural.*

CURRENT TRENDS IN WORLD HISTORY

Industrialization and Its Antidotes: Conservation and Regulation

As the impact of industrialization spread during the late nineteenth century, a few individuals, including those who championed rapid economic development, recognized that this progress brought unwanted consequences. A new awareness dawned—that while industrialization allowed production to increase dramatically, it also resulted in the depletion of natural resources and the degradation of the quality of life for humans. Awakened to the ecological costs of economic progress, these environmentalist pioneers tried to reverse a trend of humankind's growing tendency to pollute the environment, overgraze marginal areas, and exploit resources to their exhaustion.

One of the first world leaders to take seriously industrialization's threats to the environment—and to national character—was President Theodore Roosevelt. A man who delighted in hunting, riding, and testing himself against the elements, Roosevelt worried that as the United States became an increasingly industrialized and urbanized society, the American people would lose the courage, fitness, and "rugged individualism" that the taming of wildernesses had supposedly imbued in them. He was especially struck by George Perkins Marsh's 1864 *Man and Nature,* which explored the ways in which the depletion of forests and other natural resources had determined the rise and fall of civilizations around the ancient Mediterranean. If the United States failed to curb its destruction of woodlands, Marsh suggested, it faced a collapse similar to that of Greece and Rome. Although several "national" parks and forests had been founded before Roosevelt became U.S. president in 1901, he was extremely active in pushing forward legislation to conserve more land, especially in the West. By offering visitors the opportunity to experience wilderness conditions, the national parks were to provide a partial antidote to what Roosevelt saw as the effeminizing tendencies of modern society.

But Roosevelt had other objects in view, too, in pressing the state to take a more activist role in the economy. Noting that on the European continent, "progressives" and urban-based reformers were augmenting the reach and power of the state to combat economic inequalities and to build infrastructures that benefited all, Roosevelt pushed for a departure from the laissez-faire principles that had dominated American political-economic discourse in the last decades of the nineteenth century. With European state-funded projects like the straightening of the Rhine River in mind, Roosevelt argued that the state should itself tackle projects that were too large to be built by private enterprises.

In yet another area, Roosevelt created a national regulatory solution to a problem that the market could not solve by itself. In the decade or so before he came into office, newspaper reporters had exposed hundreds of schemes by sellers of home remedies such as Mrs. Winslow's Soothing Syrup to get rich by promising consumers that their "patent" medicines would cure any disease. In truth, many of these "medicines" contained alcohol, cocaine, or just cod-liver oil; some were harmful, others were simply useless. Other investigators, such as the novelist Upton Sinclair, exposed horrors in the meatpacking industry. Sinclair's realist novel *The Jungle* (1906), for example, contained

communes for Mexico's peasantry, especially for indigenous people or villagers who had taken on collective ways. These communal village holdings, called *ejidos*, sought to re-enliven a precolonial way of life. The revolution thus spawned a set of new national myths, based on the heroism of rural peoples, Mexican nationalism, and a celebration of the Aztec past.

PRESERVING ESTABLISHED ORDERS Although the Mexican Revolution succeeded in toppling the old elite, elsewhere in Latin America the ruling establishment remained united against assaults from below. Already in 1897, the Brazilian army had mercilessly suppressed a peasant movement in the northeastern part of the country. Moreover, in Cuba, the Spanish and then the American armies crushed tenant farmers' efforts to reclaim land from sugar estates. In Guatemala, Mayan Indians lost land to coffee barons.

Much the same occurred in Europe and the United States, where the preservation of established orders did not rest on repression alone. Here, too, elites grudgingly agreed to gradual change. Indeed, by the century's end, left-wing agitators, muckraking reporters, and middle-class reformers began to win meaningful social improvements. Unable to suppress the socialist movement, Otto von Bismarck, the German chancellor, defused the appeal of socialism by enacting social welfare measures in 1883–1884 (as did France in 1904 and England in 1906). He enacted legislation insuring workers against illness, accidents, and old age and establishing maximum working hours. In the United States, it took lurid journalistic accounts reports of extremely unsanitary workplace conditions and of workers falling into fat-rendering machines and being canned along with the beef. In the same year that Sinclair's hugely influential novel appeared, Roosevelt oversaw the creation of the Food and Drug Administration and the passage of the Pure Food and Drug Act. The FDA's charge was to implement this act and to look after public health—something that did not concern profit-hungry corporations—by regulating food and medicines against contamination. In the wake of the banking panic of 1907 too, Americans came to accept that they needed banking regulations as well, and in 1913 Congress enacted the Federal Reserve Act.

Americans were not alone in beginning to temper capitalism with regulation and industrialization with conservation. Europeans at last began to enact legislation to protect workers from dangerous workplaces, and to create large green spaces in cities so that the industrialized world might have "lungs" with which to breathe. In Argentina, many were drawn to mountainous regions to escape becoming too "soft" in urban surroundings, and a conservation movement began that would hit its stride in the 1930s. Although such developments only slightly moderated the industrialized world's contributions to environmental degradation and the exploitation of mass consumers, they did signal the reality that some, at least, had begun to recognize that progress, too, had its price.

Patent Medicines. *Like Mrs. Winslow's Soothing Syrup, Hamlin's Wizard Oil claimed to cure anything from headaches to cancer, in humans and animals alike.*

QUESTIONS FOR ANALYSIS

- Who benefited from Roosevelt's national parks and the Pure Food and Drug Act? Who may have suffered from these regulations?
- Roosevelt considered courage, fitness, and "rugged individualism" vital to the American identity. Why did he choose these traits specifically, and are these traits as vital today? Explain.

Explore Further

Brinkley, Douglas, *Wilderness Warrior: Theodore Roosevelt and the Crusade to Save America* (2010).

Morris, Edmund, *Theodore Rex* (2002).

of unsanitary practices in Chicago slaughterhouses, a series of bank failures (see above, under Financial Crises), and anxieties about the ill effects of the "closing of the frontier" in the American West to spur the federal government into action. (See Current Trends in World History: Industrialization's Antidotes: Conservation and Regulation.) In 1906, President Theodore Roosevelt signed a Meat Inspection Act that provided for government supervision of meatpacking operations. In other cases (banking, steel production, railroads), the federal government's enhanced supervisory authority served corporate interests as well.

These consumer and family protection measures reflected a broader reform movement, one dedicated to creating a more efficient society and correcting the undesirable consequences of urbanization and industrialization. At local and state levels, **progressive reformers** attacked corrupt city governments that had allegedly fallen into the hands of immigrant-dominated "political machines." The progressives also attacked other vices, such as gambling, drinking, and prostitution—all associated with industrialized, urban settings. The creation of city parks preoccupied urban planners, who hoped parks' green spaces would offer healthier forms of entertainment than houses of prostitution, gambling dens, and bars. In Europe and the United States, thousands of associations took shape against capitalism's excesses. From Scandinavia to California, the proponents of old-age pensions and public ownership of utilities put pressure on lawmakers, and they occasionally succeeded in changing state policies. Intervening in the market and supporting the poor, the aged, the unemployed, and the sick in ways never dreamed of in classical liberal philosophy, progressive reform movements laid the foundations for the modern welfare state.

CULTURAL MODERNISM

The intellectuals, artists, and scientists of the fin de siècle wrestled with uncertainty, increasing social tensions, and the acceleration of the pace of change just as did revolutionaries and reformers. What we call modernism—the sense of having broken with tradition—came to prominence in many fields, from physics to architecture, from painting to the social sciences. The movement largely originated from the experimental thinking shaped by turn-of-the-century anxieties and opportunities. Emblematic of the new ideas was the work of Pablo Picasso (1881–1973), a Spanish painter who spent much of his life in Paris: inspired by seeing African masks in Paris's ethnographic museum, Picasso broke with the Renaissance style of representation in producing his *Les Demoiselles d'Avignon* (1907). Shocking in its form, this painting also depicted a series of nude prostitutes, who confront the viewer and seem to say, "Go ahead and look at me and here see what really lies beneath your civilized exterior." No wonder modernism remained, throughout its existence, controversial: it meant to break the rules, and sometimes to terrorize the rule makers.

Pablo Picasso. *The Franco-Spanish artist Pablo Picasso was one of the first to incorporate "primitive" artistic forms into his work, as displayed in his breakthrough canvas,* Les Demoiselles d'Avignon *(The Courtesans of Avignon, 1907), which was inspired by the artist's study of African sculpture and masks.*

Modernist movements were notably international, but sometimes also elitist. Egyptian social scientists read the works of European thinkers, while French and German painters flocked to museums to inspect artifacts from Africa and Oceania. But increasingly it took expertise to understand or appreciate modern art, like that of Picasso, or modern music, which abandoned the comfort of harmonic and diatonic sound (the eight-tone scale standard in classical western music at the time). Many artists demonstrated their cutting-edge originality by spurning sales figures for loftier ambitions. "Art for art's sake" became their motto; their aim was to speak to posterity. Modern science grew to depend more and more on laboratory work, or on high-level mathematical training—though it proved possible for a patent-office clerk, Albert Einstein (1879–1955), to publish papers on special relativity (showing that measurements are not absolute, but depend on the position of the measurer) in the first years of the twentieth century; there were at the time only a small handful of readers able to read and understand Einstein's physics, and even fewer able to appreciate the transformative potential of his ideas.

If modernism in arts and sciences did not appeal to all, it did, gradually, transform cultural production across the globe, and as it did so, it replaced the certainties of the Renaissance and the Enlightenment with the unsettledness of the new age. It is telling that Picasso broke with Renaissance conventions of representation at just about the same time that Einstein introduced special relativity to physics. No longer confident about European "laws," and increasingly critical of urban and industrial "progress," artists and scientists struggled to make sense of a world in which older beliefs and traditional faiths had given way. What would come next, however, no one could say.

Popular Culture Comes of Age

Changes in elite culture were crucial, but by the fin de siècle, too, the world of popular culture had expanded enormously. The change derived mainly from new urban settings, technological innovations, and increased leisure time. As education (especially in America and Europe) became nearly universal, there were many more readers and museumgoers. At the same time, cultural works now found their way down to nonelite members of society. Middle-class art lovers who could not afford original paintings eagerly purchased lithographs and mass-produced engravings; millions who could not attend operas and formal dress balls attended dance halls and vaudeville shows (entertainment by singers, dancers, and comedians). People flocked to hear lectures given by travelers, often accompanied by slide shows. For the first time, sports attracted mass followings. Soccer in Europe, baseball in the United States, and cricket in India had wildly devoted middle- and working-class fans. Thus did a truly **popular culture** emerge, delivering affordable and accessible forms of art and entertainment to "the masses."

By the century's close, the press constituted a major form of popular entertainment and information. This was partly because publishers were offering different wares to different classes of readers and partly because many more people could read, especially in Europe and the Americas. The "yellow press" was full of stories of murder and sensationalism that appealed to the urban masses. By now, the English *Daily Mail* and the French *Petit Parisien* boasted circulations of over 1 million. In the United States, urban dwellers, many of whom were immigrants, avidly read newspapers—some in English, others in their native languages. Here, too, banner headlines, sensational stories, and simple language drew in readers with little education or poor English skills. Books, too, proliferated and fell in price; penny novels about cowboys, murder, and romance became the rage.

Díaz and the Liberal Party. *In this 1910 print, the Mexican satirist José Guadalupe Posada portrays the leaders of the popular Liberal Party as being literally under the feet of the elitist followers of General Porfirio Díaz.*

By now the kind of culture one consumed had become a reflection of one's real (or desired) status in society, a central part of one's identity. For many Latin American workers, for example, reading one's own newspaper or comic strip was part of the business of being a worker. Argentina's socialist newspaper, *La Vanguardia*, was one of Buenos Aires's most prominent periodicals, read and debated at work and in the cafés of working-class neighborhoods. Anyone seen reading the bourgeois paper, *La Prensa*, faced heckling and ridicule by proletarian peers.

As the community of cultural consumers broadened, and as ideas from across the globe flooded in, writers, artists, and scholars struggled to adapt. Their attempts to confront the brave new world in the making resulted in the remarkable innovations that characterize modernism—the breaking with tradition.

Modernism in European Culture

In intellectual and artistic terms, Europe at the turn of the twentieth century experienced perhaps its richest age since the Renaissance. A desire to understand social and imperial maladies laid the foundations for the twentieth century's social sciences. The French scholar Emile Durkheim (1858–1917), for example, pioneered the field of sociology by studying a characteristic affliction of his age—suicide. In 1895, the French social psychologist Gustave Le Bon (1841–1931) wrote a treatise on crowd behavior that became a classic in Europe and beyond; he equated the unconscious volatility of crowds with the irrationality of women and "primitives." Le Bon's work became wildly popular, appealing even to Benito Mussolini in Italy and Vladimir Lenin in Russia.

Artists' work reflected their ambivalence about the modern, as represented by the railroad, the big city, and the factory. While the impressionists and realists of the mid-nineteenth century had largely celebrated progress, the painters and novelists of the century's end took a darker view. They turned away from enlightened clarity and descriptive prose, searching for more instinctual truths. Now the primitive came to symbolize both Europe's lost innocence and the forces that reason could not control, such as sexual drives, religious fervor, or brute strength. The painter who led the way in incorporating these themes into modern art was Paul Gauguin (1848–1903), who left Europe for Tahiti in 1891, and there found new forms

Impressionism. *These two paintings, Claude Monet's* The Gare Saint-Lazare (left) *and Camille Pissarro's* Sunset over the Boieldieu Bridge at Rouen (right), *exemplify the impressionists' celebration of nineteenth-century progress.*

of contentment and new ways of representing the world that he believed were less artificial than those practiced in Europe. In paintings such as *Where Do We Come From? What Are We? Where Are We Going?* (1897), Gauguin posed humankind's great questions, and intimated that the Polynesians—despite European contempt for their religious rituals and lack of "progress"—might have more answers than did his "civilized" compatriots back home.

However, the arts alone did not undermine older views of the world. Even science, in which the Enlightenment had placed so much faith, worked a disenchanting magic on the midcentury bourgeois worldview. After the century's turn, pioneering physicists and mathematicians like Einstein took apart the Enlightenment's conviction that man could achieve full knowledge of, and control over, nature. In his later work, Einstein drew on the previously ridiculed work of the Indian physicist Satyendra Nath Bose (1894–1974), who understood light to be a gas composed of particles. These particles were too tiny to be distinguished by any microscope, but their existence could be hypothesized through the application of statistics. The work of Einstein, Bose, and other scholars of their generation laid the foundations for today's quantum physics.

Paul Gauguin, *Where Do We Come From? What Are We? Where Are We Going?* *In this large-scale painting, Gauguin used Tahitian rather than European biblical figures to pose some of humanity's deepest questions about the meaning of life, the relationship between humans and gods, and our destinies after death.*

Sigmund Freud, at Work in His Study in Vienna. *Freud surrounded himself not only with books but also with Egyptian figurines and African masks, expressions of universal artistic prowess—and irrational psychological drives.*

In this modernist form of science, probabilities took the place of certainties. Although most scientists continued to collect data feeling certain that they could plumb nature's depths, some of their colleagues began to question the arrogance of this view.

From the time of the Enlightenment, Europeans had prided themselves on their "reason." To be rational was to be civilized; respectable, middle-class nineteenth-century men were thought to embody these virtues. But in the late nineteenth century, faith in rationality began to falter. Perhaps reason was *not* man's highest attainment, said some; perhaps reason was too hard for man to sustain, said others. Friedrich Nietzsche (1844–1900) claimed that conventional European attempts to assert The Truth—including science and Judeo-Christian moral codes—were nothing more than life-destroying quests for power; individuals would do better to dispense with the old forms and invent new forms of truth to live by. Sigmund Freud (1856–1939) began to excavate layers of the human subconscious, where irrational desires and fears lay buried. For Freud, human nature was not as simple as it had seemed to Enlightenment thinkers. Instead, he asserted, humans were driven by sexual longings and childhood traumas, some revealed only as neuroses, in dreams, or during extensive psychoanalysis. Neither Nietzsche nor Freud was well loved among liberal elites. But in the new century, Nietzsche would become the prophet for many antiliberal, antirational causes, from nudism to Nazism; and Freud's dark vision would become central to the twentieth century's understanding of the self.

Cultural Modernism in China

As in Europe, Chinese artists and scientists at the turn of the century were active experimenters and innovators, reflecting critically upon their own traditions as well as selectively importing western ideas. As in the West, Chinese writers and artists now had wider audiences for their work; by the late nineteenth century, more than 170 presses in China were serving a potential readership of 2 to 4 million concentrated mostly in the urban areas. These cities were more economically vibrant and culturally fluid than the hinterlands. Not only was there an expanding body of readers, but newly rich beneficiaries of the treaty-port economy now patronized the arts. These new opportunities made for increased cultural diversity. Indeed, some scholars have described the late Qing period as a time of competing cultural *modernities,* in contrast to the post-Qing era, which pursued a single, western-oriented *modernity*.

In art as in literature, late Qing intellectuals integrated indigenous and foreign styles into their explorations of topics such as the self, sexuality, and China's future. In the late nineteenth century, for example, painters from the lower Yangzi region congregated in Shanghai. Collectively known as the **Shanghai School**, these classically trained painters appropriated western technical novelties into their artistic practice. Consider the self-portrait of the artist Ren Xiong (1820–1857): bareheaded and legs apart, he

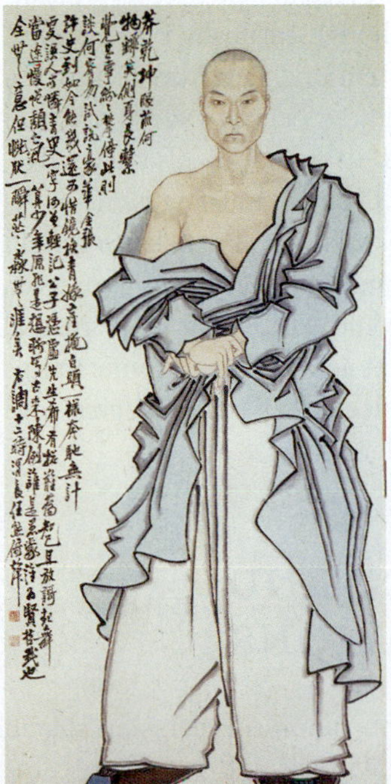

Ren Xiong, Self-Portrait. *This famous self-portrait of Ren Xiong was most likely produced in the 1850s. Ren Xiong was probably familiar with the new practice of portrait photography in the treaty ports. Although his self-portrait reproduced some old conventions of Chinese scholarly art, such as the unity of the visual image with a lengthy self-composed inscription, it is also clear that, through its rather unconventional pose and image, Ren Xiong had pointed to the establishment of a new kind of subject position characteristic of the trend of cultural modernism in China during this period.*

stands upright and stares straight at the viewer. Ren Xiong's work reflected the influence of photography, a new visual medium. Similarly, experimental writers drew on modern science, sometimes in order to explore the question of China's future relations with the West. The novel *New Era* (1908), for example, put its opening scenes in the year 1999, by which time, as the story envisioned, China would be a supreme world power and a constitutional monarchy. Depicting China at war with western powers, *New Era* celebrated military strength but also introduced inventions such as electricity-repellent clothing and bulletproof satin. More visionary still was the *The Stone of Goddess Nüwa* (1905), whose male author imagined a technologically advanced feminist utopia. Its female residents studied subjects ranging from the arts to physics, drove electric cars, and ate purified liquid food extracts. Their mission was to save China by eliminating corrupt male officials. Such works, combining the fanciful with the critical, offered a new and provocative vision of China.

Yet the integration of western science into Chinese culture was an intellectual challenge. Did being modern mean giving up China's scholarly traditions and values? The nineteenth century had seen Christian missionaries use their scientific knowledge to attract followers. For example, John Fryer, an English missionary and translator, founded *The Science Journal* (*Gezhi huibian*) in 1876. Other publications in the same period included *The Universal Gazette* (*Wanguo gongbao*). Recognizing the usefulness of western science, many Chinese scholars helped missionaries promote it—although they considered it mostly as a way to acquire national wealth and power, rather than as a way of understanding the world.

It is not surprising that the Chinese scholars took this stance, for western visitors to China also presented science as a means to material betterment. Thus, although steamships, telegraphs, and railroads captured public attention, there was little interest in changing fundamental Chinese beliefs. Indeed, even as Chinese intellectuals recognized new modes of knowledge, many of the elite insisted that Chinese learning remain the principal source of all knowledge. What kind of balance should exist between western thought and Chinese learning, or even whether the ancient classics should keep their fundamental role, was an issue that would haunt generations to come. In this respect, the Chinese dilemma reflected a worldwide challenge to accepting the impulses of modernism.

RETHINKING RACE AND REIMAGINING NATIONS

Ironically, at this time of huge population transfers and shared technological modernization, individuals and nations became passionate defenders of the idea that identities were deeply rooted and unchangeable. Although physical characteristics had always played *some* role in identifying persons, by the late nineteenth century the Linnaean classifications (see Chapter 14) had become the means for ranking the worth of whole nations.

Race now defined who could belong to the nation and enjoy its rights and privileges; by the century's close, racial roots had also become a crucial part of cultural identity. This was the era of ethnographic museums, folkloric collectors, national essence movements, and racial genealogies. People wanted to know who they (and their neighbors) were—especially in terms of *biological* ancestry. Now the idea of inheritance took on new weight, in both cultural and biological forms. Doctors, officials, and novelists described the genetic inheritance of madness, alcoholism, criminality, and even homosexuality; nationalists spoke of the uniqueness of the Slavic soul, the German mind, and the Hispanic race. They spoke of Hindu spirituality and of Islamic principles, as if there were no variations or conflicts within these categories. The preoccupation with race reflected a worldwide longing for fixed roots in an age that seemed to be burning all its bridges to the past.

Nationalist and racial ideas were different in different parts of the world. In Europe and America, debates about race and national purity reflected several concerns: fear of losing individuality in a technological world, rising tensions among states, and fear of being overrun by the brown, black, and yellow peoples beyond the borders of "civilization." By contrast, in India these ideas were part of the anticolonial debate, and they helped to mobilize people politically. This was also the case in China, Latin America, and the Islamic world, where discussions of identity went hand in hand with opposition to western domination and corrupt indigenous elites. Especially in the colonial world, racial identity was primarily a question about the community's coherence and endurance, not about the races of humankind in general.

These new impulses produced a variety of national movements, from China's anti-Qing campaign to India's Swadeshi movement (see below). At the same time, pan-ethnic movements looked beyond the nation-state, envisioning communities based on ethnicity. Behind these movements was the notion that political communities should be built on racial purity or unsullied indigenous traditions. These views indicated just how unsettled the world was by the century's end and how urgent the questions of identity and belonging had become.

Nation and Race in North America and Europe

In the United States, the changing mood was striking. Americans greeted the end of the century with a combination of chest-beating pride and shoulder-slumping pessimism. In the early 1890s, for example, Americans flocked to extravagant commemorations of the four hundredth anniversary of Christopher Columbus's discovery. The largest was the Columbian Exposition in Chicago. Such events displayed the most modern machinery and celebrated the nation's marvelous destiny. Yet, at the same time, Americans feared for their future. They especially worried that America had exhausted its supposedly infinite supply of new land and resources—as evidenced by the disappearance of the buffalo, the erosion of soils, and the depletion of timber stands by aggressive logging companies. Conservationists' alarm grew more intense with the Census Bureau's 1890 announcement that the American frontier had "closed."

RESTRICTING IMMIGRATION Some white Americans may have worried that the closing of the "frontier" spelled the end of American pioneer individualism. But most did not agonize about what the African American intellectual W. E. B. Du Bois (1868–1963) predicted would be "the problem of the twentieth century"—that is, "the problem of the color line." Rather, white Americans were busily drawing new color lines, initiating new forms of racial discrimination where old forms (like slavery) had broken down. In the American West, animosity toward Chinese workers led to the 1882 Exclusion Act, which prohibited almost all immigration from China. In the American South, where most of the nation's 7 million African Americans resided, a system of "Jim Crow" laws upheld racial segregation and inequality.

The Columbian Exposition. *More than 27 million people attended the Columbian Exposition in Chicago in 1893. Like many of the era's world's fairs, this one celebrated technological progress, including the spread of electricity, as evidenced by the General Electric Tower of Light.*

White Americans grew even more anxious as throngs of "swarthy" immigrants entered the United States. These people came primarily from southern and eastern Europe, but to the champions of "Anglo-Saxonism" they were not "white." Even more threatening were darker peoples who were colonial subjects in the Philippines, Puerto Rico, and Cuba. Talk of the end of white America fueled support for more restrictive immigration policies.

Across the North Atlantic, European elites engaged in similar discussions. For them, the final divvying up of Africa was in many respects equivalent to the closing of the American frontier. The Germans and Italians, in particular, complained about the lack of new territories on which to plant their flags. The French and British began to worry about how to preserve their empires, especially in light of the anticolonial sentiments seething in their colonies.

FACING NEW SOCIAL ISSUES Like Americans, Europeans also expressed concerns about trends at home. For example, intellectuals suggested that mechanization deprived men of their vitality. At the same time, Darwinist theory provoked new anxieties about inherited diseases, racial mixing, and the dying out of white "civilizers." Sexual relations between European colonizers and indigenous women—and their mixed offspring—had almost always been a part of European expansionism, but as racial identities hardened, such relations now seemed to threaten the moral fiber of the whole nation. Talk of virility arose, partly provoked by doctors' and scientists' involvement in treating social problems. Before long, English and American schoolboys were encouraged to play sports, to avoid becoming too weak to defend the nation. In addition, medical attention focused on homosexuality, regarding it as a disease and a threat to Anglo-Saxon civilization. In France, the falling birthrate seemed to signal a period of decadence characterized by weak, sickly men and irrational women.

Some people tied decadence to debates about whether Jews—defined by religious practice or, increasingly, by ethnicity—could be fully assimilated into European society. Even though Jews had gained rights as citizens in most European nations by the late nineteenth century, powerful prejudices persisted. In the 1880s and 1890s, violent pogroms, often involving police complicity, targeted the large Jewish populations in the Russian Empire's western territories and pushed the persecuted farther westward. These emigrants' presence, in turn, stirred up fear and resentment, especially in Austria, Germany, and France. Reactionaries began to talk about the "pollution" of the European races by mixing with Semites and to circulate rumors about Jewish bankers' conspiratorial powers. Perhaps because nothing else seemed stable and enduring, wealthy white male Europeans (like their American counterparts) promoted programs of racial purity to shore up the civilizations they saw coming apart at the seams.

Race-Mixing and the Problem of Nationhood in Latin America

In Latin America, debates about identity chiefly addressed ethnic intermixing and the legacy of a system of government that, unlike much of the North Atlantic world, excluded rather than included the populace. After all, social hierarchies reaching back to the sixteenth century ranked white Iberians at the top, creole elites in the middle, and indigenous and African populations at the bottom. Thus, the higher on the social ladder, the more likely the people were to be white.

CONTESTED MIXTURES It is important to note that "mixing" did not lead to a shared heritage. Nor did it necessarily lead to homogeneity. In fact, the "racial" order did not stick, since some Iberians occupied the lower ranks, while a few people of color did manage to ascend the social ladder. Moreover, starting in the 1880s, the racial hierarchy saw further disruption by the deluge of poor European immigrants; they were flooding into prospering Latin American countrysides or into booming cities like Buenos Aires in Argentina and São Paulo in Brazil. Latin American societies, then, did not easily become homogeneous "nations." Indeed, many Latin American observers wondered whether national identities could survive these transformations at all.

In an age of acute nationalism, the mixed racial composition of Latin Americans generated special anxieties. In the 1870s in Mexico, it was common to view Indians as obstacles to change. One demographer, Antonio García Cubas, considered indigenous people "decadent and degenerate." According to him, their presence deprived the republic of the right kind of citizens. In Cuba and Brazil, observers made the same claims about blacks. According to many modernizers, Latin America's own people were holding it back. The solution, argued some writers, was to attract white immigrants and to establish educational programs that would uplift Indians, blacks, and people of mixed descent. Thus, many intellectuals joined the crusade to modernize and westernize their populations. In the effort to "whiten" their republics, many Latin American governments made especially strong pitches for northern European migrants, despite the mounting evidence that they often made lousy farmers and did not work well with others. So, even by 1900, some of the shine of "pure" white races was rubbing off, not least because European migrants did not live up to the propagandists' expectations.

Diego Rivera's *History of Mexico.* *This is one of the most famous works of Mexican art, a portrait of the history of Mexico by the radical nationalist painter Diego Rivera. In this chapter, and in previous chapters, we have shown parts of this mural. In stepping back to view the whole work, which is in the National Palace in Mexico City, we can see how Rivera envisioned the history of his people generally. Completed in 1935, this work seeks to show a people fighting constantly against outside aggressors, from their glorious preconquest days (lower center), winding like a grand epic through the conquest, colonial exploitation, the revolution for independence, nineteenth-century invasions from France and the United States, to the popular 1910 Revolution. It culminates in an image of Karl Marx, framed by a "scientific sun"—pointing to a future of progress and prosperity for all, as if restoring a modern Tenochtitlán of the Aztecs. This work captured many Mexicans' efforts to return to the indigenous roots of the nation and to fuse them with modern scientific ideas.*

PROMOTING NATIONHOOD BY CELEBRATING THE PAST For their part, Latin American leaders began to exalt bygone glories as a way to promote national selfhood. Inventing successful myths could make a government seem more legitimate—as the heir to a rightful struggle of the past. Thus in Mexico, General Díaz placed the bell that Father Hidalgo had tolled on September 16, 1810, to mark the beginning of the war against Spain (see Chapter 15), in the National Palace in Mexico City. In the month of that centennial in 1910, grand processions wound through the capital. Many of the parades celebrated Aztec grandeur, thereby creating a mythic arc from the greatness of the Aztec past to the triumphal story of Mexican independence—and to the benevolence and progress of the Díaz regime. As the government glorified the Aztecs with pageants, statues, and pavilions, however, it continued to ignore modern Aztec descendants, who lived in squalor.

Some thinkers now began to celebrate ancient heritages as a basis for modern national identities. For example, in Mexico and eventually in the Andes, the pre-Spanish past became a crucial foundation stone of the nation-state. The young Mexican writer José Vasconcelos (1882–1959) grew disenchanted with the brutal rule of Díaz and his westernizing ambitions. Nonetheless, he endorsed Díaz's celebration of the Indian past, for he believed that Mexicans were capable of a superior form of civilization. He insisted that if they had fewer material concerns, their combined Aztec and Spanish Catholic origins could create a spiritual realm of even higher achievement. In Vasconcelos's view, Mexico's greatness flowed not in spite of, but because of, its mixed nature.

Sun Yat-sen and the Making of a Chinese Nation

Just as Latin American thought celebrated an authentic past, so did Chinese writers emphasize the power and depth of Chinese culture—in contrast to the Qing Empire's failing political and social strength. Here, writers used race to emphasize the superiority of the Han Chinese. Here, too, the pace of change generated a desire to trace one's roots back to secure foundations. Moreover, traditions were reinvented in the hope of saving the Chinese soul threatened by modernity.

In China, as elsewhere, scholars and political mobilizers took up the challenge of redefining identities. By the century's end, prominent members of both groups had abandoned their commitment to preserving the old order but were not ready to fully adopt western practices. Their attempts at combining traditions and values from home and abroad gave rise to the modern Chinese intelligentsia and modern Chinese nationalism.

PROMOTING HAN NATIONALISM Symbolizing the challenge of nation building were the endeavors of **Sun Yat-sen** (1866–1925), who was part of an emerging generation of critics of the old regime. Like his European counterparts, Sun dreamed of a political community reshaped along national lines. Born into a modest rural household in southern China, he studied medicine in the British colony of Hong Kong and then turned to politics during the Sino-Japanese War. When the Qing government rejected his offer of service to the Chinese cause, he became convinced that China's rulers were out of touch with the times. Subsequently he established an organization based in Hawaii to advocate the Qing downfall and the cause of republicanism. The cornerstone of his message was Chinese—specifically, Han—nationalism.

Sun blasted the feeble rule by outsiders, the Manchus, and trumpeted a sovereign political community of "true" Chinese. No ruler, he argued, could enjoy legitimacy without the nation's consent. He envisioned a new China free of Manchu rule, building a democratic form of government and an economic system based on equalized land rights. In this fashion, Sun claimed, China would join the world of nation-states and have the power to defend its borders.

Sun's nationalism did not catch on immediately in China itself, partly because the Qing regime persecuted all dissenters. His ideas fared better among the hundreds of thousands of Chinese who had emigrated in the second half of the nineteenth century. Often facing discrimination in their adopted homelands, these overseas communities applauded Sun's racial nationalism and democratic ideas. In addition, Chinese students studying abroad found inspiration in his message.

REPLACING THE QING AND RECONSTITUTING A NATION Sun's nationalist and republican call resonated more powerfully as the Qing Empire grew weaker early in the twentieth century. Military defeat at the hands of the Japanese was especially humiliating, coming from those whom the Chinese had historically considered a "lowly" folk. Realizing that reforms were necessary, the Manchu court began overhauling the administrative system and the military in the aftermath of the Boxer Uprising. Yet these changes came too late. The old elites grumbled, and the new class of urban merchants, entrepreneurs, and professionals (who often benefited from business with westerners) regarded the government as outmoded. Peasants and laborers resented the high cost of the reforms, which seemed to help only the rulers.

A mutiny, sparked in part by the government's nationalization of railroads and its low compensation to native Chinese investors, broke out in the city of Wuchang in central China in 1911. As it spread to other parts of the country, Sun Yat-sen hurried home from traveling in the United States. Few people rallied to the emperor's cause, and the Qing dynasty collapsed—an abrupt end to a dynastic tradition of more than 2,000 years. In the provinces, coalitions of gentry, merchants, and military leaders ran the government.

Sun Yat-sen. *Through the medium of clothing, these two images of Sun Yat-sen, the man generally known as the "father of the Chinese nation," epitomize the evolving cultural ambiguities of China in the late nineteenth and early twentieth centuries.* (Left) *As a young man studying medicine in the British colony of Hong Kong in the late 1880s, Sun and his friends dressed in the conventional Qing garb of Chinese gentlemen.* (Right) *Two decades later, in early 1912, Sun and the officials of the new republic appeared in public in full western-style jackets and ties. Clothing, like so many parts of the cultural arena in China during this period, had become a contested ground in the battle to forge a new nation's identity.*

China would soon be reconstituted, and Sun's ideas, especially those regarding race, would play a central role. The original flag of the republic, for example, consisted of five colors representing the citizenry's major racial groups: red for the Han, yellow for the Manchus, blue for the Mongols, white for the Tibetans, and black for the Muslims. But Sun had reservations about this multiracial flag, believing there should be only one Chinese race. The existence of different groups in China, he argued, was the result of incomplete assimilation—a problem that the modern nation now had to confront.

Nationalism and Invented Traditions in India

British imperial rule persisted in India, but the turn of the century saw cracks in its stranglehold. Four strands had woven the territory together: the consolidation of colonial administration, the establishment of railways and telegraphs, the growth of western education and ideas, and the development of colonial capitalism. Now it was possible to speak of India as a single unit. And it was also possible for anticolonial thinkers to imagine seizing and ruling India by themselves. Thus a new form of resistance emerged, different from peasant rebellions of the past. Now, dissenters talked of Indians as "a people" who had both a national past and national traditions.

A MODERNIZING ELITE Leaders of the nationalist opposition were western-educated intellectuals from colonial cities and towns. Although a tiny minority of the Indian population, they gained influence through their access to the official world and their familiarity with European knowledge and history. This elite group used their knowledge to develop modern cultural forms. For example, they turned colloquial languages (such as Hindi, Urdu, Bengali, Tamil, and Malayalam) into standardized, literary forms for writing novels and dramas. Now the publication of journals, magazines, newspapers, pamphlets, novels, and dramas surged, facilitating communication throughout British India.

Along with print culture came a growing public sphere where intellectuals debated social and political matters. By 1885, voluntary associations in big cities had united to establish a political party, the Indian National Congress. Lawyers, prominent merchants, and local notables dominated its early leadership. The congress demanded greater representation of Indians in administrative and legislative bodies, criticized the government's economic policies, and encouraged India's industrialization.

Underlying this political nationalism, embodied by the Indian National Congress, was cultural nationalism. The nationalists claimed that Indians might not be a single race but were at least a unified people, because of their unique culture and common colonial history. Indeed, nationalism in India (unlike in Europe) developed with an acute awareness of Indians as colonial subjects. The critical question was: could India be a modern nation *and* hold on to its Indian identity?

BUILDING A MODERN IDENTITY ON REWRITTEN TRADITIONS The recovery of traditions became a way to establish a modern Indian identity without acknowledging the recent subjugation by British colonizers. So Indian intellectuals (like those in Latin America) turned to the past and rewrote the histories of ancient empires and kingdoms. In this way, Indian intellectuals promoted the idea of the nation-state even though the region had no integrated, national history prior to colonization.

To portray Indians as a people with a unifying religious creed, intellectuals reconfigured Hinduism so that it resembled western religion. This was no easy task, for traditional Hinduism did not have a supreme textual authority, a monotheistic God, an organized church, or an established creed. Nonetheless, nationalist Hindu intellectuals combined various philosophical texts, cultural beliefs, social practices, and Hindu traditions into a mix that they labeled the authentic Hindu religion. Other Indian revivalists, too, explored the roots of a national culture. Some researched ancient Indian contributions to astronomy, mathematics, algebra, chemistry, and medicine and called for a national science. In the fine arts, intellectuals constructed an imaginary line of continuity to the glorious past to promote a specifically Indian art and aesthetics (sense of beauty).

Modern Indian Art. *Painter Abanindranath Tagore's 1902* The Passing of Shah Jahan *incorporates elements typical to Western art, like perspective and foreshortening, while it retains the palette, patterns, and figures of prominence that reach back to India's glorious past.*

While fashioning hybrid forms, revivalists also narrowed the definition of Indian traditions. As Hindu intellectuals looked back, they identified Hindu traditions and the pre-Islamic past as the only sources of India's culture. Other contributors to the region's mosaic past were forgotten; the Muslim past, in particular, had no prominent role. However, the Muslims and other religious, ethnic, and linguistic groups also attempted to mobilize their communities for modern, secular purposes. The Indian National Muslim League, for example, which formed in 1906, advanced the *political* interests of Muslims, not the Islamic religion.

HINDU REVIVALISM Hindu revivalism became a powerful political force in the late nineteenth century, when the nationalist challenge to the colonial regime took a militant turn. New leaders rejected constitutionalism and called for militant agitation. The British decision to partition Bengal in 1905 into two provinces—one predominantly Muslim, the other Hindu—drew militants into the streets to urge the boycott of British goods. Rabindranath Tagore, a famous Bengali poet and future Nobel laureate, composed stirring nationalist poetry. Activists formed voluntary organizations, called Swadeshi ("one's own country") Samities ("societies"), that championed indigenous enterprises for manufacturing soap, cloth, medicine, iron, and paper, as well as schools for imparting nationalist education. Although few of these ventures succeeded, the efforts reflected the nationalist desire to assert Indians' autonomy as a people.

Rabindranath Tagore. *The Bengali writer, philosopher, and teacher Rabindranath Tagore became the poet laureate of the Swadeshi Movement in Bengal in 1903–1908. The first Asian Nobel laureate, he became disenchanted with nationalism, viewing it as narrow and not universalistic. The photo shows Tagore reading to a group of his students in 1929.*

The Swadeshi movement swept aside the moderate leadership of the Indian National Congress and installed a radical leadership that broadened the nationalist agitation. Although the people did not topple the colonial regime, Indian mass mobilization was enough to alarm the British rulers, who turned to force to keep the colony intact. When the movement slipped into a campaign of terrorism in 1908, the government responded by imprisoning militant leaders. However, the colonial administrators also annulled their partition of Bengal in 1911.

Late-nineteenth-century Indian nationalism posed a different kind of challenge to the British than the suppressed 1857 rebellion. Back then, insurgents had wanted to preserve local identities against the encroaching modern state and colonial economy. Now, in contrast, nationalist leaders imagined a modern national community. Invoking religious and ethnic symbols, they formed modern political associations to operate in a national public arena. Unlike the insurgents of 1857, they did not seek a radical alternative to the colonial order; instead, they fought for the political rights of Indians as a secular, national community. In these new nationalists, British rulers discovered an enemy not so different from themselves.

The Birth of the Turkish Nation. *Sultan Abdul Hamid II bestows a constitution on the Turkish people.*

The Pan Movements

India and China were not the only places where activists dreamed of founding new states. Across the globe, groups had begun to imagine new communities based on ethnicity or, in some cases, religion. **Pan movements** (from the Greek *pan,* "all") sought to link people across state boundaries. The grand aspiration of all these movements—which included pan-Asianism, pan-Islamism, pan-Africanism, pan-Slavism, pan-Turkism, pan-Arabism, pan-Germanism, and Zionism—was the rearrangement of borders in order to unite dispersed communities. But such remappings posed a threat to rulers of the Russian, Austrian, and Ottoman empires, as well as to overseers of the British and the French colonial empires.

PAN-ISLAMISM Within the Muslim world, intellectuals and political leaders begged their coreligionists to put aside sectarian and political differences so that they could unite under the banner of Islam in opposition to European incursions. The leading spokesman for pan-Islamism was the well-traveled Jamal al-Din al-Afghani (1839–1897). Born in Iran and given a Shiite upbringing, he nonetheless called on Muslims worldwide to overcome their Sunni and Shiite differences so that they could work together against the West. During a sojourn in Egypt, he joined with a young Egyptian reformer, Muhammad Abduh (1849–1905), to inspire an Islamic protest against Europe. Later, Afghani and Abduh (then living in Paris) published a pan-Islamic newspaper. Afghani subsequently made his way to Istanbul, where he supported the pan-Islamic ambitions of Sultan Abdul Hamid II, who promoted the defense of Islam as a way to thwart European schemes to divide up the Ottoman Empire.

The pan-Islamic appeal only added to Muslims' confusion as they confronted the West. Indeed, Arab Muslims living as Ottoman subjects had many calls on their loyalties. Should they support the Ottoman Empire to resist European encroachments? Or should they embrace the Islamism of Afghani? Most decided to work within the fledgling nation-states of the Islamic world, looking to a Syrian or Lebanese identity as the way to deal with the West and gain autonomy. But Afghani and his disciples had struck a chord in Muslim culture, and their Islamic message has long retained a powerful appeal. (See Primary Source: A Muslim Philosopher Describes Why Islam Has Become Weak.)

PAN-GERMANISM AND PAN-SLAVISM Pan-Germanism found followers across central Europe, where it often competed with a pan-Slavic movement that sought to unite all Slavs against their Austrian, German, and Ottoman overlords. This area had traditionally been ruled by German-speaking elites, who owned the land farmed by Poles, Czechs, Russians, and other Slavs. German elites began to feel increasingly uneasy as

PRIMARY SOURCE

A Muslim Philosopher Describes Why Islam has become Weak

Jamal al-Din al-Afghani is one of the most perplexing and mysterious figures in modern Islamic history. Born in Iran and raised in its Shiite tradition, he claimed Afghani birth and traveled widely in the Sunni world. His early sojourn in India, almost immediately after the Rebellion of 1857, left him with an undying hatred of the British and a conviction to unite the Islamic world. Although he believed that Islam was capable of reform, he devoted most of his energies to convincing the intellectual and political leaders in Arab and Ottoman-ruled lands to put aside their many differences and draw on their shared commitment to Islam in order to ward off Europe's ambitions in their region.

At the height of his influence in Egypt between 1871 and 1879, he gathered around him young men of leadership potential, though he would soon be exiled for his radical ideas and watch Egypt fall under British colonial power.

The undated document below was probably written toward the end of Afghani's career, which he spent in the court of Abdul Hamid II, sultan of the Ottoman Empire (r. 1876–1909), who also shared Afghani's vision of Islamic unity. It contrasts past Muslim greatness with present-day decline, and encourages united resistance to western dominance; these are themes that have reverberated throughout the Islamic world ever since.

"God changes not what is in a people, until they change what is in themselves." (13:11)

"That is because God would never change His favour that He conferred on a people until they change what was within themselves." (8:55)

These are verses of the Honourable Qur'an, the Admonitory Book which leads to the Right Path, and which calls [men] to the true religion. . . The Qur'an is the Book of God which He has sent down for the guidance [of mankind] and what is necessary for his life in this world and the world to come. It is a cure for the disease of straying [from the right path] and a remedy for the disease of ignorance. . . .

God roused the Islamic *umma* with a small number of people and gave them the highest rank to the point that the Muslims trod upon the lofty mountains and shook them with awe. . . . Their astonishing advent frightened every soul and their extraordinary progress amazed every intellect. The inhabitants of the world bit their fingers in astonishment at the unbelievable progress which these people achieved in a short period of time. They wondered . . . how the brave nations of the world had fallen helpless in facing them; and how the powerful states had been worn out under the hoofs of their horses. . . .

Let us now take a look at the present situation of the Muslims and compare it with their past and clarify their progress vis à vis their decline. The Muslim population in the world today is more than . . . two thousand times as large as the Muslim population at the time of their conquest of the territories of the world. The Islamic state extended from the shore of the Atlantic Ocean in West Africa to the heart of China. All these areas were independent and prosperous lands located in the best regions of the earth. . . .

In spite of this, the Islamic states today are unfortunately pillaged and their property stolen; their territory is occupied by foreigners and their wealth in the possession of others. There is no day in which foreigners do not grab a part of the Islamic lands, and there is no night in which foreigners do not make a group of Muslims obey their rule. They disgrace the Muslims and dissipate their pride. . . . Sometimes they call them savages and sometimes regard them as hard-hearted and cruel and finally consider them insane animals. What a disaster! What an affliction! . . .

What should be done then? Where can we find the cause? Where can we look for the reason and whom should we ask? [There is no answer to these questions] except to say that: "God changes not what is in a people, until they change what is in themselves."(13:11)

QUESTIONS FOR ANALYSIS

- What is Afghani suggesting about the quality of his fellow Muslims when he points to the origins of the Islamic *umma*?
- Explain why Afghani uses the land mass of the Islamic state as a measure of the devoutness of the Muslims within it.
- Following the fall of Egypt to British rule, Afghani argued that *jihad* obligated every individual to defend the remaining Muslim land from European domination. What is *jihad*? Do you think the introspective self-reform that Afghani calls for is at odds with *jihad*?

Source: Sayid Jamāl al-Dīn al Afghānī and Abdul-Hādī Hā'irī, "Afghānī on the Decline of Islam," in Die Welt des Islams, *New Series, vol. 13, no. 1/2 (1971): 121–125.*

PRIMARY SOURCE

A Pan-German Leader Rails against the Rising Power of the Slavs and the Jews in the Austro-Hungarian Empire

Georg von Schönerer was a right-wing radical and member of the Austrian House of Deputies. A German of Austrian descent, he was one of the first to object vehemently to the rising aspirations of the Slavic peoples of the Austro-Hungarian Empire for rights equal to those of the German population. For Schönerer, any sharing of cultural or political power with the Slavs or Jews was a threat to the dominance of ethnic Germans in the Empire. Claiming (falsely) that Jews were taking all of the good jobs in the empire, controlling the press, and manipulating financial markets, he aimed not just at keeping them out of the economy, but, as he states below, at eliminating Jewish influence "in all areas of the administration, law making, and public life as a whole."

Schönerer delivered the following speech on April 28, 1887, before the Austrian House of Deputies. His attempt to push through anti-Semitic legislation a month later was unsuccessful, but he continued to campaign for such pan-German causes for the rest of his life. Although they never met in person, Schönerer would become a hero to another Austrian pan-German and anti-Semite, Adolf Hitler.

This I must say in advance: we can only lament, that some Germans have set out on a false path and most sincerely believe that if the foreigner, whether he be a Jew, or a Negro, or a Chinese, or a Singhalese, learns to speak German and declares himself without a religion, or allows himself to be baptized Christian, then he can be welcomed with friendship as a German brother. . . . Today I have . . . set myself the task . . . of discussing the social question together first of all with respect to the Jewish nation. Now as a few days ago the highest imperial court has supported the community's right to free expression of its opinion, I must also hope that that I, as a representative of the people in the Parliament also will not have this right taken away from me today (bravo, bravo, on the far left). . . I must also today most decidedly take the opportunity to announce, from our German-national standpoint, the division of Bohemia that has been advocated and perhaps even planned by various parties. Such a division must, in our view, necessarily lead to the division of other territories, such as Carinthia or Steiermark or other partially linguistically-mixed regions, and materially damage not only the solidarity of all the Germans in Austria, but also the united character of the formerly German federal states of Austria. Thus together with my party members in the German national party and in agreement with those who are most closely sympathetic with our views outside this House, I have requested again to present our program publicly, and particularly to today present important parts of it which bear on the so vital reforms in the social and economic sector.

This proposed, and we believe, authentic, racially organic reform legislation, is also . . . of great significance for our national struggles. The foundations, however, of this social political reformist measures especially lie, in our view, *first in protections to be created against the falsification of public opinion by the press; and secondly, in the pushing out of Jewish influence in all areas of the administration, law making, and public life as a whole.*

Above all, I must, in the name of the German Nationals, stress the fact that we are proud to be members of a great people (*Volk*) and that as such we feel a holy duty to stand up for the welfare and the power, for the securing of national identity and for the protection of the national life of the German community in Austria at all times and incessantly. We Germans in Austria are certainly obliged to maintain ourselves in between the expanded power-positions of the Slavs, remembering that our German brothers in the Empire have repeatedly fought and bled for our nation against the enemy [the French] in the West. . . . We will also never forget, especially in the light of the unremitting, threatening influx of Slavdom into ancient German-language territory, that the German lands of Austria have for a long time formed part of Germany, and we see it as our national duty, to enduringly strengthen the existing alliances between Germany and Austria with legal and economic laws, in order that the existing union organically and permanently grows together.

QUESTIONS FOR ANALYSIS

- According to Schönerer, what characteristics must a person possess in order to be properly deemed a German?
- Why does Schönerer consider this pan-German cause a "holy duty"? What other "holy duties" have you encountered in this book that ultimately resulted in violent conflict?
- Outline the political, economic, and cultural changes that Schönerer proposes in this speech.

Source: Fünf Reden der Reichsratabgeordneten Georg Ritter von Schönerer (Horn: Ferdinand Berger, 1891), pp. 89–90. Translated by Suzanne Marchand.

Slavic nationalisms (spurred by the midcentury revivals of traditional Czech, Polish, Serbian, and Ukrainian languages and cultures) became more popular. Even more threatening was the fact that the Slavic populations were growing faster than the German. As pogroms in the Russian Empire's borderlands in the 1880s, as well as economic opportunities, drove crowds of eastern European Jews westward, German resentment toward these newcomers also increased.

What made pan-Germanism a movement, however, was the intervention of a former liberal, Georg von Schönerer (1842–1921). In 1882, Schönerer, outraged by the Habsburg Empire's failure to favor Germans, founded the League of German Nationalists. It comprised students, artisans, teachers, and small businessmen in the interests of uniting German Austrians with the Germans in Bismarck's Empire. Schönerer detested the Jews, defining them by their "racial characteristics" rather than by their religious practices. After his election to the Austrian upper house, he attempted to pass anti-Jewish legislation modeled on the American Chinese Exclusion Act of 1882. Although Schönerer's plans were too radical for most German Austrians, his anti-Semitism found echoes in a milder form by Viennese mayor Karl Lueger in the late 1890s and in a stronger form by Adolf Hitler after 1933. (See Primary Source: A Pan-German Leader Rails against the Rising Power of the Slavs and the Jews in the Austro-Hungarian Empire.)

The rhetoric of pan-Germanism motivated central Europeans to think of themselves as members of a German *race*, their identities determined by blood rather than defined by state boundaries. This, too, was the lesson of pan-Slavism. Both movements led fanatics to take actions that were dangerous to existing states. The organization of networks of radical southern Slavs, for example, unsettled Serbia and Herzegovina (annexed by the Austrians in 1908). Indeed, it was a Serbian proponent of plans to carve an independent Slav state out of Austrian territory in the Balkans who assassinated the heir to the Habsburg throne in June 1914. By August, the whole of Europe had descended into mass warfare, bringing much of the rest of the world directly or indirectly into the conflict as well. Eventually, the war would fulfill the pan-Slav, pan-German, and anti-Ottoman Muslim nationalist longing to tear down the Ottoman and Habsburg empires.

CONCLUSION

Ever since the Enlightenment, Europeans had put their faith in "progress." Through the nineteenth century, educated elites took pride in their booming industries, bustling cities, and burgeoning colonial empires. Yet by the century's end, urbanization and industrialization seemed more disrupting than uplifting, more disorienting than reassuring. Moreover, colonized people's resistance to the "civilizing mission" fueled doubts about the course of progress.

Especially unsettling to the ruling elite was the realization that "the people" not only were against them but also were developing ways to unseat them. In colonial settings, nationalists learned how to mobilize large populations. In Europe, socialist and right-wing leaders challenged liberal political power. By contrast, old elites, whose politics relied on closed-door negotiations between "rational" gentlemen, were unprepared to deal with modern ideas and identities.

Nor were the elites able to control the scope of change, for the expansion of empires had drawn ever more people into an unbalanced global economy. Everywhere, disparities in wealth appeared—especially in Africa, Asia, and Latin America. Moreover, the size and power of industrial operations threatened small firms and made individuals seem insignificant. Even some cities seemed too big and too dangerous. All these social and economic challenges stretched the capacities of gentlemanly politics.

Yet anxieties stimulated creative energy. Western artists borrowed nonwestern images and vocabularies; nonwestern intellectuals looked to the West for inspiration, even as they formulated anti-western ideas. The upheavals of modern experience propelled scholars to study the past and to fabricate utopian visions of the future.

Revivals and dislocations, as well as cultural and political movements, influenced the reformulating of identities. However, this was an incomplete process. For even as these changes unsettled the European-centered world, they intensified rivalries among Europe's powers themselves. Thus, this order was unstable at its center—Europe itself. And in the massive conflict that destroyed this era's faith in progress, Europe would ravage itself. The Great War would yield an age of even more rapid change—and even more violent consequences.

TRACING THE GLOBAL STORYLINES

AFTER YOU READ THIS CHAPTER

Review and research **STUDYSPACE:** wwnorton.com/studyspace

FOCUS ON: *Sources of Global Anxieties and Expressions of Cultural Modernism*

Global Trends

- Mass migrations and unprecedented urban expansion challenge national identities.

Africa and China: Anti-Colonialism

- The Anglo-Boer War and violent uprisings against colonial rule in Africa call Europe's imperializing mission into question.
- The Chinese rise up against European encroachments in the Boxer Rebellion.

Europe and North America: Mounting Tensions

- Intense political rivalries, financial insecurities and crises, rapid industrialization, feminism, and class conflict roil Europe and spread to the rest of the world.

Mexico: Resentment toward Elites

- The most widespread revolution from below takes place in Mexico.

Cultural Modernism

- Popular culture comes of age.
- Elite culture explores new forms in painting, architecture, music, literature, and science in order to break with the past and differentiate itself more dramatically from popular culture.
- New ideas of race emerge, as does a renewed emphasis on the nation-state and nationalism.

CHRONOLOGY

The Americas
- Jim Crow laws (United States) **1890s**

Europe

South Asia
- Indian National Congress founded **1885**

East Asia

Russia

Africa

1870 | 1880 | 1890

KEY TERMS

anarchism *p. 684*

Anglo-Boer War *p. 675*

Boxer Uprising *p. 677*

Mexican Revolution *p. 685*

modernists *p. 668*

pan movements *p. 698*

popular culture *p. 689*

progressive reformers *p. 687*

Shanghai School *p. 691*

Sun Yat-sen *p. 695*

syndicalism *p. 684*

STUDY QUESTIONS

1. **Explain** why westerners used the term *progress* to describe the world at the end of the nineteenth and beginning of the twentieth centuries. What did they believe were the sources of this progress?
2. **List and explain** various examples of worldwide anxieties that challenged the idea of progress during this time. Which groups protested the status quo?
3. **Describe** the armed uprisings against western imperialism in Africa and China during this era. How similar were these movements to other alternative visions to the new world order explored in Chapter 16?
4. **Compare and contrast** revolutionary and reform movements in Latin America and China during this era. How were their goals and methods similar and different?
5. **Analyze** how anxieties about progress shaped cultural developments around the world. What was cultural modernism, and how did it challenge traditional assumptions about art and science?
6. **Define** the term *popular culture*. Why did it become so powerful during this time, and how did it shape individuals' identity?
7. **Analyze** to what extent new ideas of race and nation created tension within and between states. What new forms of nationalism emerged during this time?

Labor unrest **1880s–1910s**

Progressive reforms (United States) **1900–1920**

Mexican Revolution **1910–1920**

Labor unrest **1880s–1910s**

Social welfare laws enacted in many states **1880s–1910**

Picasso unveils *Les Demoiselles d'Avignon* **1907**

Indian National Muslim League founded **1906**

Boxer Uprising **1899–1900**

Chinese Republican Revolution **1911**

Russo-Japanese War **1904–1905**

Revolts in Russian Empire **1905**

South African War **1899–1902**

Herrero Revolt **1904–1906**

Maji-Maji Revolt **1905–1906**

1900 1910 1920

BEFORE YOU READ THIS CHAPTER

wwnorton.com/ STUDYSPACE

GLOBAL STORYLINES

- The Great War (World War I) engulfs the entire globe, exhausts Europe, and promotes production and consumption on a mass scale.
- The harsh terms of the peace settlement unbalance the global economy and lead directly to the Great Depression.
- Three strikingly different visions for building a better world arise: liberal democratic, authoritarian, and anticolonial.

CHAPTER OUTLINE

19

Of Masses and Visions of the Modern, 1910–1939

FOCUS QUESTIONS

- How did World War I disrupt societies around the world?
- How did the war usher in the age of "mass society"?
- How did authoritarian, liberal, and anticolonial visions propose to reorder their societies during the 1920s and 1930s?

The last guns of the Great War (World War I) fell silent not on the bloody battlefields of Europe, but in a remote corner of East Africa. It took a full day for news of the armistice to reach that region where African soldiers, under British and German officers, were battling for control of German East Africa. Here, 10,000 German-led African soldiers used guerrilla tactics to thwart the efforts of over 300,000 British-led African soldiers. Thousands of African troops died in these battles, beyond the spotlight of international opinion. Thus did this world conflagration come to a close outside Europe.

Raging from August 1914 to November 1918, World War I shook the foundations of the European-centered world. Although most major battles occurred on European soil, multitudes of American, African, and Asian soldiers were ferried across oceans to join the killing and maiming there. Campaigns also bloodied the soil in Turkey, Egypt, Syria, and sub-Saharan Africa. This was the first modern war involving whole societies. Its impact was thoroughly global. In addition to involving countless soldiers from Europe's colonies, its aftermath fostered notions of freedom and self-determination and a growing disillusionment with

European rule in these locations. Elsewhere, nations grappled with competing visions for building a viable, modern society.

This chapter deals with the Great War and its global impact. First, because the war was fought on a worldwide scale and to utter exhaustion in Europe, it required the resources of a large part of the world. Therefore it prompted production and consumption on a mass scale. These in turn became defining features of economic modernity. Wartime leaders used new media such as radio and film to promote national loyalties and to discredit enemies—and thereby helped to spread a mass culture. Second, the harsh terms of the peace settlement unbalanced the global economy and led directly to the Great Depression. Third, political turmoil surrounding the war inflamed disputes over how to manage mass societies and build a better world. To this end, three strikingly different visions arose: liberal democratic, authoritarian, and anticolonial. These ideologies competed for preeminence in the decades leading up to World War II.

THE QUEST FOR THE MODERN

When people spoke of "being modern" in the 1920s and 1930s, they disagreed on what it meant. Most agreed, however, that in economic terms modernity involved mass production and mass consumption. In the West, for example, the automobile, the gramophone (a record player), the cinema, and the radio reflected the benefits of economic and cultural modernism. In terms of political issues, being modern meant the involvement of the masses in politics. Everywhere people favored strong leadership to reinvigorate their societies; some wanted more democracy to replace monarchical and colonial rule. Following the Great Depression in the 1930s, even more intense debates arose. These debates led to bitter divisions on how to build modern societies.

The first political vision of modernism—the *liberal democratic* one—confronted economic failings without sacrificing market economies or parliamentary democracy. It did so through widened participation in governance but also gave greater power to state regulatory bureaucracies. However, after the Great Depression spread hard times and unemployment, this predominantly American and western European model linking capitalism and democracy no longer seemed so promising. Around the world, people considered alternatives that might better deliver the promises of modernity. Although many rejected the parliamentary or liberal perspective, the system survived in the United States, parts of western Europe, and several Latin American nations.

For many observers, liberal democracies failed to match the astonishing dynamism of a second perspective—*authoritarianism.* Authoritarian regimes rejected parliamentary rule, subordinated the individual to the state, managed and often owned most aspects of the production process, used censorship and terror to enforce loyalty, and exalted an all-powerful leader. Authoritarianism was evident in both right-wing dictatorships (Fascist Italy, Nazi Germany, dictatorial Spain and Portugal, and militaristic Japan) and a left-wing dictatorship (the Soviet Union).

The third vision—*anticolonial*—also questioned the liberal democratic order, primarily because of its connection to colonialism. However, most anticolonialists did not reject parliaments or private enterprise. Resentful of European rulers who preached democracy but practiced despotism, anticolonial leaders sought to oust their colonial rulers and then find their own path to modernity. They generally favored mixing western ideas with indigenous traditions.

THE GREAT WAR

Few events were more decisive in drawing men and women worldwide into national and international politics than the **Great War**. For over four years, millions of soldiers from Europe, as well as from its dominions and colonies, killed and mutilated one another. Such carnage damaged European claims to civilized superiority and encouraged colonial subjects to break from imperial masters. Among Europeans, too, the war's effects shook the hierarchies of prewar society. Above all, the war made clear how much the power of the state now depended on the support of the people.

The war's causes were complex. The bedrock cause was the combustible rivalry between Great Britain and Germany. Through most of the nineteenth century, Britain had been the preeminent power. By the century's end, however, German industrial output had surpassed Britain's, and Germany had begun building a navy. For the British, who controlled the world's seas, the German navy was an affront; for the Germans, it was a logical step in their expanding ambitions. This Anglo-German antagonism drew in the other powers in rival alliances. Germany joined Austria-Hungary to form the **Central Powers**; Britain affiliated itself with France and Russia in the Triple Entente (called the **Allied Powers** later, after Italy joined).

Well armed and secretly pledged to defend their partners, the rivals lacked only a spark to ignite open hostilities. That came in August 1914, when the heir to the Habsburg throne was assassinated in Sarajevo, the capital of Austrian Bosnia. The assassin hoped to trigger an independence movement that would detach South-Slav territories from the Austro-Hungarian Empire (see Chapter 18) and unite them with independent Serbia. But as the Ottoman Empire was pushed out of the Balkans, Russia and Austria-Hungary competed for influence and territory there.

Russia backed the Serbs against Austria-Hungary, and the British, French, and Germans were drawn into the conflict in support of their partners. The world war that followed dragged in Europe's colonies, too.

The Fighting

The declarations of war drew cries of jubilation from those who anticipated a short triumphal conflict for their side. Dreams of glory inspired tens of thousands of men to enlist. But the fighting did not go as expected.

BATTLE FRONTS, STALEMATE, AND CARNAGE Despite hopes for a swift resolution, the war became infamous for its duration and horrors. The initial German offensive, which intended to thrust through neutral Belgium, stalled thirty miles outside Paris at the battle of the Marne in September 1914 (see Map 19.1). A stalemate ensued. Instead of a quick war, vast land armies dug trenches along the Western Front—from the English Channel through Belgium and France to the Alps—installing barbed wire and setting up machine-gun posts. The troops became immobilized. Anything but glorious, life in the trenches mixed boredom, dampness, dirt, vermin, and disease, punctuated by the terror of being ordered to "go over the top" to attack the enemy's entrenched position. Doing so meant running across a "no man's land" in which machine guns mowed down almost all attackers.

On the other side of Europe, Russian troops advanced into East Prussia and Austria-Hungary along the Eastern Front. Although the Russians defeated Austro-Hungarian troops in Galicia (between present-day Poland and Ukraine) and scored initial victories in eastern Germany, they suffered devastating reversals in East Prussia once the Germans threw in well-trained divisions that were better armed and better provisioned than the Russian troops.

By 1915, the war had ground to a gruesome standstill. Along the Western Front, neither the Allies nor the Central Powers could advance. On the Eastern Front, the Russians had been driven back and had lost much of Poland. At Ypres in 1915, the Germans tried to break the stalemate by introducing poison gas, but a countermove of equipping soldiers with gas masks nullified that advantage. In July 1916, the British launched an offensive along the Somme River in northeastern France. By November, when the futile attack halted, approximately 600,000 British and French and 500,000 Germans had perished. Yet the battle lines had hardly budged. Attempts to win by opening other fronts—in Turkey, the Middle East, and Africa—failed and added to the war's carnage (see Map 19.2).

The death toll forced governments to call up more men than ever before. More than 70 million men worldwide fought in the war, including almost all of Europe's young adult males. From 1914 to 1918, 13 million served in the German army. In Russia, more than 15 million men took up arms. The British Empire mobilized nearly 9 million soldiers, and the British nation's 5.25 million troops constituted almost half the prewar population

Trenches in World War I. *The anticipated war of mobility turned out to be an illusion; instead, armies dug trenches and filled them with foot soldiers and machine guns. To advance entailed walking into a hail of machine-gun fire. Life in the trenches meant cold, dampness, rats, disease, and boredom.*

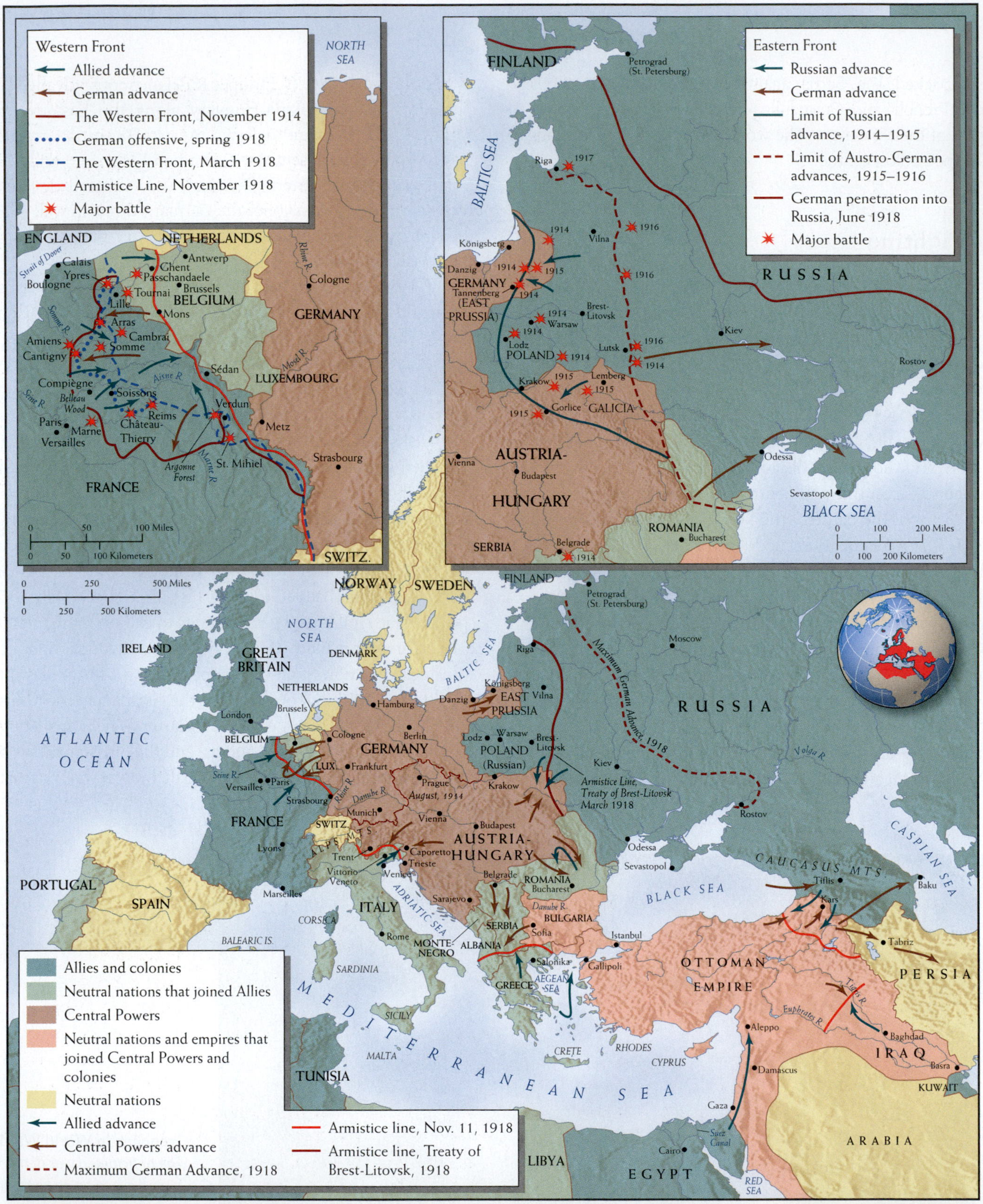

MAP 19.1 | World War I: The European and Middle Eastern Theaters

Most of the fighting in World War I, despite its designation as a world war, occurred in Europe. Although millions of soldiers fought on both sides, the territorial advances were relatively small.

- Look at the maps above, and identify all the countries where Allies and Central Powers made advances. Which countries had to fight a two-front war? • Did the armies of the Central Powers or the Allies gain the most territory during the war? • According to your reading, how did this factor affect the war's outcome?

of men age fifteen to forty-nine. In France, around 8 million served, nearly 80 percent of the same prewar age-group population. For those who fought, the personal outcomes were mainly unhappy. Over half of the men who were mobilized died, were wounded or taken prisoner, or were reported missing in action.

Mass mobilization also undermined traditional gender boundaries. Tens of thousands of women served at or near the front as doctors, nurses, and technicians. Even more women mobilized on the "home front," taking on previously male occupations—especially in munitions plants. But women could also turn against the state. Particularly in central Europe and Russia, the war's demands for soldiers and supplies left farms untended and caused food shortages. Bread riots and peaceful protests by women, traumatized by loss and desperate to feed their children, put states on notice that their citizens expected compensation for their sacrifices. Indeed, civilian pressure forced many states to make promises they would have to fulfill after the war, in the form of welfare provisions, expanded suffrage, and pensions for widows and the wounded.

In the four years of war, military deaths exceeded 9 million. Another 21 million soldiers were wounded. Vast numbers of survivors bore artificial limbs. Naval blockades and aerial bombardments had aggravated civilian food shortages and left people susceptible to epidemics, like influenza. As demobilizing soldiers spread disease into their communities, influenza claimed 50 million people worldwide.

EMPIRE AND WAR The war's horrors reached across the world's regions (see again Map 19.2). The sprawling Ottoman Empire sided with the Central Powers, battling British- and Russian-led forces in Egypt, Iraq, Anatolia, and the Caucasus. In 1915–1916, Ottoman forces massacred or deported 1.3 million Armenians, who were accused en masse of collaborating with the Russians. Many analysts regard these attacks as the world's first genocide, the intentional elimination of a whole people. To increase their forces, the British and the French conscripted colonial subjects: India provided 1 million soldiers; over 1 million Africans fought in Africa and Europe for their colonial masters, and another 3 million transported war supplies. Even the sparsely populated British dominions of Australia, New Zealand, and Canada dispatched over a million loyal young men to fight for the empire.

Despair and disillusionment at the prolonged, bloody war turned into revolt and revolution. In British-ruled Nyasaland, a mission-educated African, John Chilembwe, directed his compatriots to refuse British military demands and to stand up for "Africa for the Africans." Although the British suppressed the insurrection and executed the rebel leader, Chilembwe's death did not stop the growing desire to undo bonds to the mother country.

Controlling the mobilized masses proved even more difficult in Europe. In 1916, after the second winter of deprivation,

Women's War Effort. *With armies conscripting nearly every able-bodied man, women filled their places in factories, especially in those that manufactured war materials, such as the French plant pictured here in 1916.*

antiwar demonstrations broke out. The next year, strikes roiled Germany, France, Britain, Italy, and Russia. Meanwhile, in trying to break the battlefield stalemate, Allied commanders introduced devastating new weapons such as the tank. Neither civilian protest nor new armaments could stop the war's devastation, though. As a result, Europe's postwar leaders reaped a bitter harvest of anger, sorrow, and despair.

THE RUSSIAN REVOLUTION The war destroyed entire empires. The first to go was Romanov Russia. In February 1917, Tsar Nicholas II stepped down under pressure from his generals. They wanted to quash the mass unrest in the capital, which, they believed, threatened the war effort along the Eastern Front. Some members of the Russian parliament formed a provisional government; at the same time, grassroots councils (soviets) sprang up in factories, garrisons, and towns. The irony of Russia's February Revolution, which brought an end to the monarchy, was that the military and civilian elites wanted to restore order, and implement a more "bourgeois" parliamentary form of government, not encourage a revolution. With the tsar removed, millions of peasants seized land, soldiers and sailors abandoned the front, and borderland nationalities declared autonomy from the crumbling Russian Empire.

In October 1917, left-wing socialists calling themselves **Bolsheviks** seized power. Led by Vladimir Lenin and Leon Trotsky, the Bolsheviks drew support among radicalized soldiers, sailors, and factory workers organized in the soviets. Arresting provisional government members and claiming power in the name

GREENLAND
CANADA
UNITED STATES
ATLANTIC OCEAN
PACIFIC OCEAN
FINLAND
NORWAY
SWEDEN
BALTIC SEA
DENMARK
UNITED KINGDOM
GERMANY
POLAND
AUSTRIA-HUNGARY
FRANCE
ROMANIA
SERBIA
BLACK SEA
BULGARIA
ITALY
SPAIN
PORTUGAL
MONTENEGRO
ALBANIA
OTTOMAN EMPIRE
GREECE
TUNISIA
MOROCCO
ALGERIA
LIBYA
EGYPT
RIO DE ORO
BRITISH HONDURAS
BAHAMAS
CUBA
JAMAICA
WEST INDIES
HONDURAS
NICARAGUA
COSTA RICA
PANAMA
COLOMBIA
VENEZUELA
BRITISH GUIANA
DUTCH GUIANA
FRENCH GUIANA
ECUADOR
BRAZIL
PERU
BOLIVIA
PARAGUAY
CHILE
ARGENTINA
URUGUAY
ANGLO-EGYPTIAN SUDAN
GAMBIA
GUINEA
SIERRA LEONE
NIGERIA
GOLD COAST
TOGO
CAMEROON
UGANDA
BRITISH EAST AFRICA
GERMAN EAST AFRICA
NORTHERN RHODESIA
SOUTHERN RHODESIA
GERMAN SOUTH-WEST AFRICA
SOUTH AFRICA
Allied Powers, colonies and allies
Central Powers and colonies
Neutral nations throughout the war
Troop movements
0 1000 2000 Miles
0 1000 2000 Kilometers

MAP 19.2 | World War I: The Global Theater

This map illustrates the ways in which World War I was a truly global conflict.

- Which states outside Europe became involved?
- Other than Europe, which continent experienced the most warfare?
- Which parts of the world were spared the fighting, and why?

of the soviets, the Bolsheviks proclaimed a socialist revolution to overtake the February "bourgeois" revolution. Several months later, Soviet Russia signed the Treaty of Brest-Litovsk, acknowledging German victory on the Eastern Front as the Russian army collapsed. For protection, the Bolshevik leadership relocated the capital to Moscow and set up a so-called dictatorship of the proletariat. Lenin insisted on accepting the peace treaty and the loss of vast territories to safeguard the socialist revolution.

THE FALL OF THE CENTRAL POWERS On April 2, 1917, the United States declared war on Germany. This occurred after German submarines sank several American merchant ships and after a secret telegram came to light in which German officials sought Mexican support by promising to help Mexico regain territories it had lost to the United States in 1848.

With U.S. troops added to the fray, the balance of military power in Europe changed. The Allies turned the tide at the Second Battle of the Marne in July 1918 and forced the Germans to retreat into Belgium. German troops then began to surrender en masse, and some announced a soldiers' strike as hunger and influenza became unbearable. Before long, Germany tottered on the edge of civil war as the Allied blockade caused food shortages. Faced with defeat and civil strife, the Central Powers fell in succession. Although most of Austria-Hungary's troops remained at the front, German generals agreed to an armistice in November 1918. After Kaiser Wilhelm II slipped into exile, the German empire became a republic. The last Habsburg emperor also abdicated, and Austria-Hungary dissolved into several new states. With the collapse of the Ottoman Empire, the war claimed a fourth dynasty among its casualties.

The Peace Settlement and the Impact of the War

To decide the fate of vanquished empires and the future of the modern world, the victors convened five peace conferences, one for each of the Central Powers. Most important was the conference to negotiate peace with Germany, held at Versailles, France, in January 1919. Delegates drew many of their ideas from American President Woodrow Wilson's "Fourteen Points," a blueprint he had devised for making peace in Europe. Wilson especially insisted that postwar borders be redrawn by following the principle of "self-determination of nations" and that an international **League of Nations** be set up to negotiate further quarrels. Such high-minded ideas were appealing, but once delegates got down to the business of carving up Europe and doling out Germany's colonies, negotiations became tense and difficult. Over the objections of the Americans and British, the French insisted on a punitive treaty that assigned Germany sole blame for the war and forced it to pay reparations.

Applying the principle of self-determination was much more difficult in practice than Wilson had understood. Suddenly, 60 million people in central and eastern Europe now emerged as

The Russian Revolution. (Left) *The July 1917 demonstrations in Petrograd were among the largest in the Russian Empire during that turbulent year of war and revolution. In this photo, marchers carry banners, "Down with the Ministers-Capitalists" and "All Power to the Soviets of Worker, Soldier and Peasant Deputies."* (Right) *Vladimir Lenin died just six years and three months after the October 1917 revolution, but he lived on in his writings and images, such as in this painting by Pavel Kuznetsov. Artists and propagandists helped make Lenin a ubiquitous icon of the new Soviet order.*

MAP 19.3 | **Outcomes of World War I in Europe, North Africa, and Some of the Middle East**

The political map of Europe and the Middle East changed greatly after the peace treaty of 1919.

- Comparing this map with Map 19.1, which shows the European and Middle Eastern theaters of war, identify the European countries that came into existence after the war. What happened to the Ottoman Empire, and what powers gained control over many territories of the Ottoman state?
- What states emerged from the Austro-Hungarian Empire?

inhabitants of new nation-states (see Map 19.3). The patchwork nature of the old multiethnic empires here meant that as many as 25 million now lived in states in which they were ethnic minorities and vulnerable to persecution in the tumultuous years after the armistice. The limits of self-determination were even more telling in terms of non-Europeans' rights, for the peacemakers were not prepared to extend self-determination beyond Europe.

ANALYZING GLOBAL DEVELOPMENTS

Measuring Casualties in World War I

You would think that tabulating historical data would be a fairly easy thing to do. At different points in this text, however, we have seen that it takes painstaking efforts on the part of historians and demographers to first figure out the best way to collect the data and second to then accurately categorize and count it. Figuring out the number of Africans that left on slave ships and where they embarked and disembarked during the Atlantic slave trade is a great example of this kind of work. Historian Jay Winter and others have worked tirelessly for thirty years to come up with accurate death tolls for the soldiers and civilians in World War I. In a landmark book, *The Great War and the British People*, Winter used a range of archival sources from government agencies' data and mortality rate tables from major insurance companies to estimate and calculate the number of deaths among people in Britain and Ireland. While the carnage in World War I seems beyond measure, Winter, in one paradoxical finding, demonstrated that death rates among civilians actually went down during that war in Britain and Ireland. He suggests that the best explanation for this development was the efforts of the state to mobilize the civilian population and provide health insurance, and, most important, to improve nutrition.

The table below builds on Winter's early efforts and shows the best estimates for the military death tolls across all the major participants in World War I.

QUESTIONS FOR ANALYSIS

- Based on data provided in the table, did the mobilization for the war have a greater impact on the societies of the Central Powers or the Allied Powers? Please justify your answer.
- While the number of people mobilized was a factor of 1.5 greater in the Central Powers, why do you think the dead, wounded, and missing/POW rates were nearly twice as high as those of the Allied Powers?
- The United State played a major role in World War I, but why were the number of its dead, wounded, and missing/POW so low compared to that of the other major combatants?

Military participation and military losses in World War I

Allied Powers	Mobilized	Dead	Wounded	POW/Missing	Total	% Casualties
Russia	15,798,000	1,800,000	4,950,000	2,500,000	9,250,000	59
France	7,891,000	1,375,800	4,266,000	537,000	6,178,800	78
GB, incl. empire	8,904,467	908,371	2,090,212	191,652	3,190,235	36
Italy	5,615,000	578,000	947,000	600,000	2,125,000	38
United States	4,273,000	114,000	234,000	4,526	352,526	8
Japan	800,000	300	907	3	1,210	0
Romania	1,000,000	250,706	120,000	80,000	450,706	45
Serbia	750,000	278,000	133,148	15,958	427,106	57
Belgium	365,000	38,716	44,686	34,659	118,061	32
Greece	353,000	26,000	21,000	1,000	48,000	14
Portugal	100,000	7,222	13,751	12,318	33,291	33
Montenegro	50,000	3,000	10,000	7,000	20,000	40
Total	**45,899,467**	**5,380,115**	**12,380,704**	**3,984,116**	**22,194,935**	**46**
Central Powers						
Germany	13,200,000	2,037,000	4,216,058	1,152,800	7,405,858	56
Austria-Hungary	900,000	1,100,000	3,620,000	2,200,000	6,920,000	77
Turkey	2,998,000	804,000	400,000	250,000	1,454,000	48
Bulgaria	400,000	87,500	152,390	27,029	266,919	67
Total	**25,598,000**	**4,028,500**	**8,388,448**	**3,629,829**	**16,046,777**	**63**
Grand Total	**71,497,467**	**9,408,615**	**21,219,152**	**7,613,945**	**38,241,712**	**53**

Sources: John Horne (ed.), A Companion to World War I *(2010); Tucker Spencer (ed.),* The European Powers in the First World War: An Encyclopedia *(1996); J. M. Winter,* The Great War and the British People *(1985).*

Instead of granting independence to the inhabitants of Germany's former colonies in Africa, the treaty parceled them out to the French, the British, the Belgians, and the South Africans. They were assigned as mandates under the oversight of the League of Nations. The same was true of the Arab provinces of the Ottoman Empire (Syria, Lebanon, Palestine, Jordan, and Iraq), which were turned over to the British and the French.

Whatever idealism survived the peacemaking process absorbed another blow when the U.S. Senate, reflecting a resurgence of isolationism, turned down the Treaty of Versailles and kept the United States out of the League of Nations. Russia, too, was outside the league. For Britain, France, Japan, and the United States, keeping communist "Red" Russia isolated became a postwar priority.

Demobilization hit societies hard, especially working women; when soldiers hobbled home, women faced layoffs from their wartime jobs. Still, they did not retreat entirely. Within a few years, women gained the vote in Russia, Britain, Germany, and the United States. France held out until 1944, partly because the left feared that French women were under the thumb of the conservative Catholic Church. Nonetheless, in all these nations women claimed new privileges. Young, unmarried women went out in public unescorted, dressed as they saw fit, and maintained their own apartments. Such behavior shocked cultural conservatives, but young women and men alike were determined to enjoy the new, modern world.

MASS SOCIETY: CULTURE, PRODUCTION, AND CONSUMPTION

The war also contributed to another modern phenomenon: the making of mass societies. Even before World War I mobilized entire societies to produce and to fight, parliamentary regimes had begun to democratize, in many cases granting non–property holders and women the right to vote. Authoritarian regimes, meanwhile, had begun to mobilize the people via rallies and mass organizations. And new technologies, such as radio, were helping to create mass cultures that spanned geographic and class divides.

Mass Culture

Indicative of the modern world were new forms of mass communication and entertainment. These were partially wartime products. In an effort to mobilize populations for total war, leaders had disseminated propaganda as never before—through public lectures, theatrical productions, musical compositions, and (censored) newspapers. Indeed, the war's impact had politicized cultural activities while broadening the audience for nationally oriented information and entertainment. Together with new media, the war was instrumental in fostering mass culture.

Postwar **mass culture** was distinctive. First, it differed from elite culture (opera, classical music, paintings, literature) because it reflected the tastes of the working and the middle classes, who now had more time and money to spend on entertainment. Second, mass culture relied on new technologies, especially film and radio, which could reach an entire nation's population and consolidate their sense of being a single state.

RADIO Radio entered its golden age after World War I. Invented early in the twentieth century, it made little impact until the 1920s, when powerful transmitters permitted stations to reach much larger audiences—often with nationally syndicated programs. Radio "broadcasts" gave listeners a sense of intimacy with newscasters and stars, addressing consumers as personal friends and drawing them into the lives of serial heroes. Special programs targeted children and women, making radio listening something for the whole family. Even the illiterate could enjoy the programs, such as *The Lone Ranger*. By the late 1920s, nearly two-thirds of homes in the United States had at least one radio. Britain achieved similar radio saturation a decade later.

Radio also was a way to mobilize the masses, especially in authoritarian regimes. For example, the Italian dictator Benito Mussolini pioneered the radio address to the nation. Later, Soviet and Nazi propagandists used this format with great regularity and effect. In Japan, too, radio became a tool to promote the right-wing government's goals. But even dictatorships could not exert total control over mass culture. Although the Nazis regarded jazz as racially inferior music and the Soviets regarded it as "bourgeois," neither could prevent young or old from tuning in to foreign radio broadcasts, smuggling gramophone records over the borders, or creating their own jazz bands.

FILM AND ADVERTISING Film, too, had profound effects. For traditionalists, Hollywood by the 1920s signified vulgarity and decadence because the silver screen prominently displayed modern sexual habits. And like radio, film served political purposes. Here, again, antiliberal governments took the lead. German filmmaker Leni Riefenstahl's movie of the Nazi Nuremberg rally of 1934, *Triumph of the Will,* is a key example of propagandistic cinema. Nazi-era films were comedies, musicals, melodramas, detective films, and adventure epics—sometimes framed by racial stereotypes and political goals. Soviet film studios also produced Hollywood-style musicals alongside didactic pictures about Socialist triumphs.

In market economies, radio and film grew into big businesses, and with expanded product advertising they promoted other enterprises as well. Especially in the United States, advertising became a major industry, with radio commercials shaping national consumer tastes. Increasingly, too, American-produced entertainment,

Triumph of the Will. *The shooting of* Triumph of the Will, *perhaps the greatest propaganda film ever, directed by Leni Riefenstahl. The film, later denounced, won gold medals in Venice in 1935 and at the World's Fair in 1937.*

radio programs, and cinematic epics reached an international audience. Thanks to new media, America and the world began to share mass-produced images and fantasies.

Mass Production and Mass Consumption

The same factors that promoted mass culture also enhanced production and consumption on a mass scale. In fact, World War I paid perverse tribute to the power of industry, for machine technologies produced war materials with abundant and devastating effect.

Never before had armies had so much firepower at their disposal. Whereas in 1809 Napoleon's artillery had discharged 90,000 shells over two days during the largest battle waged in Europe to that point, by 1916 German guns were firing 100,000 rounds of shells per hour over the full twelve hours of the Battle of Verdun. To sustain military production, millions of men and women worked in factories at home and in the colonies. Producing huge quantities of identical guns, gas masks, bandage rolls, and boots, these factories reflected the modern world's demands for greater volume, faster speed, reduced cost, and standardized output—key characteristics of **mass production**.

The war reshuffled the world's economic balance of power, boosting the United States as an economic powerhouse. As its share of world industrial production climbed above one-third in 1929 (roughly equal to that of Britain, Germany, and Russia combined), people around the globe regarded the United States as a "working vision of modernity" in which not only production but also consumption boomed.

THE AUTOMOBILE ASSEMBLY LINE The most outstanding example of the relationship between mass production and consumption in the United States was the motor car. It symbolized the machine age and the American road to modernization. Before World War I, the automobile had been a rich man's toy. Then came Henry Ford, who founded the Ford Motor Company in 1903. Five years later, he began production of the Model T, a car that at $850 was within the reach of middle-class consumers. Soon popular demand outstripped supply. Seeking to make more cars faster and cheaper, Ford used mechanized conveyors to send the auto frame along a track, or assembly line, where each worker performed one simplified, repetitious task. By standardizing the manufacturing process, subdividing work, and substituting machinery for manual labor, Ford's assembly line brought a new efficiency to the mass production of automobiles.

By the 1920s, a finished car rolled off Ford's assembly line every ten seconds. Although workers complained about becoming "cogs" in a depersonalized labor process, the system boosted output and reduced costs. The effects reverberated throughout the nation's economy. Ford's factory near Detroit employed 68,000 workers—the largest factory in the world. In addition, millions of cars required millions of tons of steel alloys, as well as vast amounts of glass, rubber, textiles, and petroleum. Cars also needed roads to drive on and service stations to keep them running. Altogether, nearly 4 million jobs related directly or indirectly to the automobile—an impressive total in a labor force of 45 million workers.

After World War I, automobile ownership became more common among Americans. By the 1920s, assembly-line production had dropped the Model T's price to $290. Ford further expanded the market for cars by paying his own workers $5 per day—approximately twice the average manufacturing wage in the United States. He understood that without **mass consumption**, increased purchasing power in the middle classes, and appetite for goods there could be no mass production. Whereas in 1920 Americans owned 8 million motor cars, a decade later they owned 23 million. The automobile's rapid spread seemed to demonstrate that mass production worked. (See Primary Source: Bruce Barton's Gospel of Mass Production.)

THE GREAT DEPRESSION Not all was easy listening or smooth motoring in countries where mass societies were taking root. During the 1920s, many producers of foodstuffs, coal, and ores

Car Assembly Line. *Mass production was made possible by the invention of the electric motor in the 1880s, and it enacted three principles: the standardization of core aspects of products, the subdivision of work on assembly lines, and the replacement of manual labor by machinery as well as by reorganizing flow among shops. The greatest successes occurred in the auto plants of Henry Ford, shown here in 1930. With each worker along the line assigned a single task, millions of automobiles rolled off the Ford assembly line, and millions of Americans became owners of automobiles.*

faced sagging prices because of overproduction. As staple prices declined in proportion to manufactured goods, farmers throughout the United States, Canada, Australia, and Latin America lamented their dwindling fortunes compared to those of their urban cousins.

On October 24, 1929—Black Tuesday—the American stock market collapsed, plunging not only the American economy but also international financial and trading systems into crisis. This event led the world into the **Great Depression**. Its causes went back to the Great War, which had left European nations in deep debt as they struggled to rebuild their economies and pay off war debts. To restore stability, Europeans borrowed heavily from the United States. When wobbly governments and small investors defaulted on their loans, the U.S. Federal Reserve reacted by raising interest rates. Starting in central Europe, financial institutions began to collapse. As banks fell, other lenders scrambled to call in their loans. Companies, governments, and private borrowers were soon floating in a sea of debt. The panic then spread to the world's stock markets, which led to the Wall Street crash of 1929, which spurred more bank closures.

Financial turmoil produced a major contraction of world trade. Striving to protect workers and investors from the influx of cheap foreign goods, governments raised tariff barriers against imports. After the United States enacted protective tariffs, other governments abandoned free trade in favor of protectionism.

Stock Traders after the Crash. *On October 24, 1929, the American stock market crashed. Here traders are pictured congregating in the financial district of New York City, on what came to be known as "Black Tuesday." As stock values plummeted, panic gripped Wall Street and soon spread across the nation. The market crash was followed by even more devastating bank runs as the Great Depression overtook the world.*

PRIMARY SOURCE

Bruce Barton's Gospel of Mass Production

In 1925, the journalist (and, later, advertising executive) Bruce Barton published* The Man Nobody Knows, *which became a best-seller. In the book, Barton interpreted the life and teachings of Jesus as a gospel for success in modern business. In the excerpt below, Barton uses Henry Ford, whose Model T automobile reigned as the era's marvel of mass production, to show the profitable connections between religion and commerce.

"If you're forever thinking about saving your life," Jesus said, "you'll lose it; but the man who loses his life shall find it."

Because he said it and he was a religious teacher, because it's printed in the Bible, the world has dismissed it as high minded ethics but not hard headed sense. But look again! . . .

What did Henry Ford mean, one spring morning, when he tipped a kitchen chair back against the whitewashed wall of his tractor plant and talked about his career?

"Have you ever noticed that the man who starts out in life with a determination to make money, never makes very much?" he asked. It was rather a startling question; and without waiting for my comment he went on to answer it: "He may gather together a competence, of course, a few tens of thousands or even hundreds of thousands, but he'll never amass a really great fortune. But let a man start out in life to build something better and sell it cheaper than it has ever been built or sold before—let him have *that* determination, and, give his whole self to it—and the money will roll in so fast that it will bury him if he doesn't look out.

"When we were building our original model, do you suppose that it was money we were thinking about? Of course we expected that it would be profitable, if it succeeded, but that wasn't in the front of our minds. We wanted to make a car so cheap that every family in the United States could afford to have one. So we worked morning, noon and night, until our muscles ached and our nerves were so ragged that it seemed as if we just couldn't stand it to hear anyone mention the word automobile again. One night, when we were almost at the breaking point I said to the boys, 'Well, there's one consolation,' I said, 'Nobody can take this business away from us unless he's willing to work harder than we've worked.' And so far," he concluded with a whimsical smile, "nobody has been willing to do that."

QUESTIONS FOR ANALYSIS

- What are the key ingredients to success, according to Ford?
- What was foremost on Ford's mind when he set out to build "our original model"?
- How do the lessons from the Bible and Henry Ford relate to each other? Do you think the indirect analogy is effective? Explain why or why not.

Source: Bruce Barton, The Man Nobody Knows: A Discovery of the Real Jesus, *in Loren Baritz, ed.,* The Culture of the Twenties *(Indianapolis: Bobbs-Merrill, 1925), pp. 241–42.*

Manufacturers cut back production, laid off millions of workers, and often went out of business. By 1935, world trade had shrunk to one-third of its 1929 level. Primary producers felt the harshest effects, for their international markets shut down almost completely. World prices for Argentine beef, Chilean nitrates, and Indonesian sugar all dropped sharply. The combination of shrinking markets and drastic shortages of credit forced industries and farms worldwide into bankruptcy.

The Great Depression soon spawned rethinking of the tenet that markets should govern themselves, the core of laissez-faire liberalism (see Chapter 14). By the late 1930s, the exuberant embrace of private mass production had ceded to a new conviction: state intervention to regulate the economy was critical to prevent disaster. In 1936, the British economist John Maynard Keynes published a landmark treatise, *The General Theory of Employment, Interest, and Money*. He argued that the market could not always adjust to its own failures and that sometimes the state had to stimulate it by increasing the money supply and creating jobs. Although the "Keynesian Revolution" took years to transform economic policy and to produce the welfare state, many governments were determining that capitalism had to be saved from itself. This unsettling realization called into question political liberalism.

MASS POLITICS: COMPETING VISIONS FOR BUILDING MODERN STATES

World War I heightened the prewar unsettling of class, gender, and colonial relations, further challenging the liberal vision of technological progress, free markets, and societies guided by the educated few. On battlefronts and home fronts, countless workers, peasants, women, and colonial subjects had sacrificed and now expected to share in the fruits of peace. Many, even in victorious nations, lost confidence in traditional authorities who had failed to prevent the cataclysm and allowed it to go on so long.

Politics, no longer contained in genteel chambers, shifted to the street. Everywhere except in the United States, variants of socialism gained throngs of new adherents. In the Soviet Union, the Bolsheviks began to construct a society whose rules defied capitalist principles. Elsewhere, mass movements sought to replace imperiled liberal democratic states, as in Germany, Italy, and Spain. Even liberal democratic empires such as Britain and France faced challenges to square their rule over colonial subjects with their rhetoric of freedom. And a hybrid political order, mixing democratic and authoritarian institutions, emerged in Latin America. Meanwhile, the Great Depression further undermined capitalism and parliaments. (See Current Trends in World History: Population Movements: Filling Up the Empty Spaces and Spreading Capitalism).

Authoritarian solutions to problems like mass unemployment grew increasingly popular, especially as the communist Soviet Union, Nazi Germany, fascist Italy, dictatorial Portugal and Spain, and militaristic Japan projected images of national strength and pride. Outside Europe, anticolonial movements gathered steam; here, liberal models could not cope with the scale and diversity of the new politics. Thus, by the late 1930s, the states that retained democracy and capitalism in some form appeared weak and vulnerable. Dictators seemed to be riding the wave of the future, and colonies were threatening to go their own separate ways.

Liberal Democracy under Pressure

In Europe of the 1920s, anxiety about modernization increased. Reacting to the war's carnage, elite Europeans looked longingly for supposedly pristine worlds that their own corrupting civilization had not destroyed. This trend found expression in the arts. For example, Josephine Baker, an African American dancer who performed nude, wild dances on the Parisian stage, enjoyed colossal popularity. So did Oswald Spengler's *The Decline of the West* (1919), a best-seller whose title seemed to capture the trajectory of liberal modernity.

The demands of fighting a total war had offered European states the opportunity to experiment with illiberal policies. Indeed, the war brought both the suspension of parliamentary rule and an effort by governments to manage industry and distribution. States on both sides of the conflict jailed many individuals who opposed the war. Governments regulated both production and, through rationing, consumption. Above all, the war revolutionized the size and scope of the state.

BRITISH AND FRENCH RESPONSES TO ECONOMIC CRISES At the war's end, liberal democratic elites wished to return to free-market policies, but women, veterans, and workers insisted that the states for which they had fought address their needs—for jobs, housing, and compensation for war wounds. Recurrent economic crises, especially the Great Depression, forced most liberal democrats to rethink their ideas. By 1930, even Britain had given up on free trade, and other countries were seeking economic self-sufficiency.

Britain and France retained their parliamentary systems, but even here, old-fashioned liberal democracy was on the run. Strife rippled across the British Empire, and in the home isles Britain gave independence to what became the Republic of Ireland in 1922. Britain's working-class Labour Party came to power twice between 1923 and 1931; but either alone or in coalition with Liberals and Conservatives, Labour could not lift the country

Josephine Baker. *The African-American entertainer Josephine Baker was a sensation on the stage in interwar Paris. Many of her shows exoticized or even caricatured her African descent.*

CURRENT TRENDS IN WORLD HISTORY

Population Movements: Filling Up the Empty Spaces and Spreading Capitalism

As we have seen in Chapters 12 and 13, the European discovery of the Americas resulted in a vast movement of peoples across the Atlantic Ocean from Europe and Africa into the western hemisphere. These population movements, among the largest in world history to that point, pale when measured against the long-distance migrations that occurred in the hundred years between 1840 and 1940. During these years, 150 million individuals of European and Asian descent filled up the less populated parts of the world, moving from Europe, South Asia, and China into the Americas, Southeast Asia, and northern Asia in unprecedented numbers and spreading a capitalist mode of production wherever they moved. A great many of the migrants went as laborers in the factories and on the plains of the Americas and on the rubber, sugar, tea, and coffee plantations springing up in the Dutch East Indies and East and southern Africa. They were as essential to the expansion of the capitalist system in these regions as the 12 million African captives transported to the Americas during the Atlantic slave trade were for the economic expansion of the Americas. Although the new watchword in economic relations was free labor, not all of the men and women who moved were in fact free workers. Indentured servitude—that is, agreeing to work for a certain number of years, usually between three and seven, in return for transportation to the region, food, housing, and clothing—was widely used with Chinese and Indian workers.

A good example of the movement and use of semi-coerced or indentured workers in less-developing regions comes from East Africa. There, the British and Germans were engaged in a furious political rivalry to extend their control over territories, and British officials believed that constructing a railway from the coast of East Africa at the port of Mombasa to Kisumu at Lake Victoria would enhance their territorial ambitions in East Africa. They also concluded that they would be unable to recruit a sufficient supply of African workers to accomplish the task. Not surprisingly, they looked to the government of India to assist them in providing the necessary work force.

The British government of India did more than help them. In all, it made available nearly 35,000 indentured South Asian workers on three-year contracts for the construction of what was known as the Uganda Railway, the track for which, covering a distance of 582 miles, was completed in a mere five years from 1896 to 1901. The work was arduous, the living conditions in the work camps were horrific, yet the British official overseeing the construction concluded that had it not been for this work force, it is doubtful if the project could have been completed

out of its economic crisis. In 1926, 162 million working days were lost to strikes. Still, despite hard times, the British retained their commitment to parliamentarianism and capitalism.

Disorder was even more pronounced in France, which had lost 10 percent of its young men and seen the destruction of vast territory. In 1932–1933, six government coalitions came and went over the course of just nineteen months. Against the threat of a rightist coup, a coalition of the moderate and radical left, including the French communist party, formed the Popular Front government (1936–1939). It introduced the right of collective bargaining, a forty-hour workweek, two-week paid vacations, and minimum wages.

THE AMERICAN NEW DEAL In the United States, too, markets and liberalism faced challenges. When the Great Depression shattered the nation's fortunes, pressure intensified to create a more secure political and economic system.

In contrast to postwar Europe, where labor parties and socialist movements were surging, the 1920s saw a conservative tide engulf American politics. Calling for a "return to normalcy" (a retreat from the government activism that had characterized the presidencies of Theodore Roosevelt and Woodrow Wilson), Warren Harding won the presidency in 1920 with a resounding 60 percent of the popular vote. Four years later, Calvin Coolidge scored an even greater landslide; his remark that the "business of America is business" reflected his dislike of government interference in free enterprise. With the election of Herbert Hoover in 1928, Republicans continued their string of presidential triumphs.

Largely left behind was the nation's African American population. In the rural American South, "Jim Crow" laws enforced social segregation, economic inequality, and political disenfranchisement. Like rural whites, millions of blacks quit the countryside and moved to northern cities such as New York and Chicago. Here they found some relief from the legal barriers that had limited their opportunities and rights, but discrimination continued to hold them down and to restrict their residences to urban ghettos. Still, within black neighborhoods, most famously New York City's Harlem, a vibrant cultural scene blossomed. The New Negro Movement, or Harlem Renaissance,

Ugandan Railway. *Indian workers cut rock for the Uganda Railway in this 1905 photograph, taken in British East Africa.*

QUESTIONS FOR ANALYSIS

- Why do you think that in some cases, like the building of the Uganda Railway, governments had to be involved in forcibly moving workers to where they were needed rather than letting market forces draw the workers to where work was available?
- What do you see as some of the similarities and differences between the way that the African slaves were treated versus the forced or indentured servants during this period?

in under twenty years. The building of the Uganda Railway is one of many examples where we see significant numbers of people moving to new places and regions, sometimes by their own choosing and sometimes not, to play an important role in the expansion of the capitalist system and the rivalries between colonial powers.

Explore Further

McKeown, Adam, *Melancholy Order: Asian Migration and the Globalization of Border* (2008).

showcased black novelists, poets, painters, and musicians, many of whom used their art to protest racial subordination.

With the Great Depression came deeper challenges to liberal modernity. By the end of 1930, more than 4 million American workers had lost their jobs. As President Hoover insisted that citizens' thrift and self-reliance, not government handouts, would restore prosperity, the economic situation worsened. By 1933, industrial production had dropped by a staggering 50 percent since 1929. The hard times were even worse in the countryside, where farm income plummeted by two-thirds between 1929 and 1932.

In the 1932 presidential election, a Democrat, Franklin Delano Roosevelt, won by a landslide. He promptly launched what came to be called the **New Deal**, a set of programs and regulations that dramatically expanded the scope of the American national government and its role in the nation's economic life. In his first hundred days in office, Roosevelt obtained legislation to provide relief for the jobless and to rebuild the shattered economy. Among his administration's experiments were the Federal Deposit Insurance Corporation to guarantee bank deposits up to $5,000, the Securities and Exchange Commission to monitor the stock market, and the Federal Emergency Relief Administration to help states and local governments assist the needy. Subsequently, in 1935, the Works Progress Administration put nearly 3 million people to work building roads, bridges, airports, and post offices. In addition, the Social Security Act inaugurated old-age pensions supported by the federal government.

Never before had the U.S. federal government expended so much on social welfare programs or intervened so directly in the national economy. Yet the Depression lingered, and before long unemployment again climbed—from 7 million in 1937 to 11 million in 1938.

The persistence of hard times opened the New Deal to attacks from both the left and the right. Emboldened labor leaders, resurgent radicals, and populist demagogues claimed that the New Deal was not addressing the problems of the poor and the unemployed. But Roosevelt continued on a moderate course. The New Deal did not substantially redistribute national income. Likewise, although Roosevelt's administration established public agencies to build dams and to oversee the

"Jim Crow." *"Jim Crow" laws mandated the segregation of races in the American South, with African Americans forced to use separate, and usually unequal, facilities, including schools, hotels, and theaters, such as this one in Mississippi.*

irrigation of arid lands and the electrification of rural districts, these were exceptions. Privately owned enterprises continued to dominate American society. Roosevelt's aim was not to destroy capitalism, but to save it. In this regard the New Deal succeeded, for it staved off authoritarian solutions to modern problems.

Authoritarianism and Mass Mobilization

Like the liberal systems they challenged, authoritarian regimes came in various stripes. On the right arose dictatorships in Italy, Germany, and Japan. Although differing in important respects, all disliked the left-wing dictatorship of the Soviet Union. The Soviets had no liking for the Fascists. Yet all the postwar dictatorships were forged principally in opposition to the liberal democracies. In place of liberal inertia, these regimes touted their success in mobilizing the masses to create dynamic yet orderly societies. They also had charismatic leaders, who personified the power and unity of the societies over which they ruled.

Although rejecting liberal democracy, post–World War I dictators insisted that they had their people's support. True, they treated their people as a mass conscript army that needed firm leadership to build new societies and guarantee well-being. But their demands, the leaders maintained, would yield robust economies, restore order, and renew pride. In addition, dictators gained support by embracing public welfare programs. They also vowed to deliver on all of modernity's promises (prosperity, national pride, technology) without having to endure any of its costs (class divisions, unemployment, urban-industrial squalor, moral breakdown). For a time, many of the globe's inhabitants believed them.

THE SOVIET UNION AND SOCIALISM The most dramatic blow against liberal capitalism occurred in Russia when the highly radical Bolshevik Party seized power. The coup aroused opposition inside and outside the country. Fearing the spread of socialist revolution, Britain, France, Japan, and the United States sent armies to Russia to contain Bolshevism. But after executing the tsar and his family, the Bolsheviks rallied support by defending the homeland against its invaders. They also mobilized people to fight (and win) a civil war (1918–1921) in the name of defending the revolution. The conflict pitted an array of disunified forces (former tsarist supporters but also some social democrats and independent peasant armies) against the Bolsheviks and their supporters (many soldiers, sailors, workers, and state functionaries).

In the all-out mobilization against those whom they labeled the Whites, or counterrevolutionaries, the Bolsheviks, calling themselves the Reds, began to rebuild state institutions. Amid this turmoil, the need to requisition grain from the peasantry as well as the extensive military operations weighed heavily on the population and interfered with the harvest. From 1921 to 1923, Russia suffered a severe famine in which some 7 to 10 million people died from hunger and disease.

To revive the economy, the Bolsheviks grudgingly legalized private trade and private property. In 1924, with the country

Stalin. *Joseph Stalin posing at the Allies' "Big Three" conference in Yalta, on Soviet soil, February 1945. Much had changed since Stalin became leader of the communist party of the Soviet Union in 1922.*

still recovering from civil war, the undisputed leader of the revolution, Lenin, died. No one had done more to shape the institutions of the revolutionary regime, including creating expectations for a single ruler. After eliminating his rivals, **Joseph Stalin** (1878–1953) emerged as the new leader of the communist party and the country, which soon became the Union of Soviet Socialist Republics (U.S.S.R.), or Soviet Union.

THE SOVIETS BUILD SOCIALISM Since socialism as a fully developed social and political order did not exist anywhere in the 1920s, no one was sure how it would actually work. Stalin resolved this dilemma by defining Soviet or revolutionary socialism in opposition to capitalism. Since capitalism had "bourgeois" parliaments serving the interests of the rich, socialism, as elaborated by Stalinist leaders, would have soviets (councils) of worker and peasant deputies. Since capitalism had unregulated markets, which led to inefficiency and unemployment, socialism would have economic planning and full employment. And since capitalism relied on the "exploitation" of private ownership, socialism would outlaw private trade and private property. In short, socialism would eradicate capitalism and then invent socialist forms in housing, culture, values, dress, and even modes of reasoning.

The efforts to build a noncapitalist society required class war, and these began in the heavily populated countryside. Peasants already lived in village communes, leasing the land together while working it individually (as households). Stalin wanted to combine the farms into larger units owned and worked collectively, and run by regime loyalists. Tens of thousands of urban activists and Red Army soldiers led a drive to establish these collective farms and to compel farmers to sell all their grain and livestock at state-run collection points for whatever price the state was willing to pay (often very little).

In protest, many peasants burned their crops, killed their livestock, and destroyed their farm machinery. The government responded by deporting these protesters, along with many bystanders, to remote areas. Villages had to fill quotas for deportation; often those selected were people who had slept with someone's wife rather than those whose cows produced the most milk. Thus, "class warfare" reflected personal animosities, greed, and ambition. Meanwhile harvests again declined, and a second famine claimed millions more lives. Grudgingly, the regime conceded household plots to the collectivized peasants. Here they could grow their own food and take some of their produce to approved markets. But few escaped the collectives, which depended on the state for seed, fertilizers, and machinery.

Collectivized Agriculture. *Soviet plans for the socialist village envisioned the formation of large collectives supplied with advanced machinery, thereby transforming peasant labor into an industrial process. The realities behind the images of smiling farmers—such as in this poster, exhorting "Give first priority to gathering the Soviet harvest!"—were low productivity, enormous waste, and often broken-down machinery.*

MAP 19.4 | The Soviet Union

The Union of Soviet Socialist Republics (U.S.S.R.) came into being after World War I.

- How did its boundaries compare with those of the older Russian Empire, as shown in Map 17.6 (p. 660)?
- What does the large number of Soviet republics suggest about the ethnic diversity within the Soviet Union?
- According to your reading, how did Soviet leaders govern non-Russian minorities within the new state?

The late 1920s saw the beginning of a frenzied Five-Year Plan to "catch and overtake" the leading capitalist countries. Now millions of enthusiasts (as well as deported peasants) set about building a socialist urban utopia founded on advanced technology, almost all of it purchased from the Depression-mired capitalist countries. More than 10 million people helped build or rebuild hundreds of factories, hospitals, and schools. Huge hydroelectric dams, automobile and tractor factories, and heavy machine-building plants symbolized the promise of Soviet-style modernity, which eliminated unemployment during the capitalist Great Depression.

Soviet authorities also started building socialism in the borderlands. In 1922, the U.S.S.R. joined the independent states of Ukraine, Belorussia (Belarus), and the Transcaucasian Federation with Soviet Russia to form a single federal state. The U.S.S.R. also soon included several new republics, such as those in central Asia; eventually there were fifteen (see Map 19.4), all of which acquired their own institutions—but under centralized rule from Moscow. In the 1930s, collectivization and mass arrests devastated the peasants and nomads as well as the officials of the republics, but industrialization and urbanization strengthened local elites.

MASS TERROR AND STALIN'S DICTATORSHIP The Soviet political system became more despotic as the state expanded. Police power grew the most, partly from forcing peasants into collectives and organizing mass deportations. As the party's ranks swelled, ongoing loyalty verifications also led to the removal of party members, even when they professed absolute loyalty. From 1936 to 1938, trials of supposedly treasonous "enemies of the people" resulted in the execution of around 750,000 people and the arrest or deportation of several million more. They were sent to forced labor camps, collectively known as the Gulag. Such purges decimated the loyal Soviet elite—party officials, state officials, intelligentsia, army officers, and even members of the police who had enforced the terror.

Behind this mass terror loomed fear, a sense of omnipresent conspiracies, and the Soviet leader's overpowering personal dictatorship. Although Stalin initiated mass terror against the elite, his motives remain unclear. Neither he nor the regime was under threat, and the leaders' loyalty was not in doubt. What is clear is that the political police, given sizeable arrest quotas, often exceeded them. In addition, millions of ordinary people helped implement the terror. Some reluctantly turned in neighbors; some did so to try to save themselves; many showed fanatical zeal in fingering "enemies." In the end, the terror manifested highly petty motives as well as a desire to participate in the violent crusade of building socialism in a hostile world, full of internal and external enemies.

ITALIAN FASCISM Long before the Soviets had created a new anticapitalist model, the political situation in capitalist societies had begun to change. Two key factors were disillusionment with the costs of the Great War and fear that a communist takeover like that in Russia could occur in western Europe. In Italy, for example, mass strikes, occupations of factories, and peasant land seizures swept the country in 1919 and 1920. Amid this disorder, rightists seized power. Their leader was **Benito Mussolini** (1883–1945), a former socialist journalist.

In 1919, Mussolini sought to organize disaffected veterans into a mass political movement called **fascism**. His early programs mixed nationalism with social radicalism and revealed a yearning to sweep away all the institutions discredited by the war. Fascist supporters demanded the annexation of "Italian" lands in the Alps and on the Dalmatian coast and called for female suffrage, an eight-hour workday, a share of factory control for workers, a tax on capital, land redistribution, and a constituent assembly—in short, a populist program.

Fascists attracted numerous followers. Their violence-prone shock troops wore black shirts and loose trousers tucked into high black leather boots and saluted with a dagger thrust into the air. In 1920, the squads received money from landowners and factory owners to beat up socialist leaders, after which Italian fascism became fully identified with the right. Still, the fascists saw themselves as champions of the little guy, of peasants and workers, as well as of war veterans, students, and white-collar types.

Mussolini. *Benito Mussolini liked to puff out his chest, particularly when appearing in public. Il Duce pioneered the leader's radio address to the people, and he encouraged fascist versions of the mass spectacles that also became common in Soviet Russia.*

In 1922, Mussolini announced a march on Rome. The march was a bluff, yet it intimidated the king, who opposed fascist ruffians but feared bloodshed. So he withheld use of the army against the lightly armed marchers. When the Italian government resigned in protest, the monarch invited Mussolini to become prime minister, despite the fact that fascists had won only a small minority of seats in the 1921 elections.

The 1924 elections, in which fascists won 65 percent of the vote, took place in an atmosphere of intimidation and fraud. Mussolini dealt with other challenges by mobilizing the squads and police for crackdowns on the liberal and socialist opposition. Soon a series of decrees transformed Italy from a constitutional monarchy into a dictatorship. Within two years, all parties except that of the fascists had been dissolved.

Mussolini's dictatorship made deals with big business and the church, thus falling short of a total social revolution. Nonetheless, it was skilled at using parades, films, radio, and visions of recapturing Roman imperial grandeur to boost support during the troubled times of the Depression. The cult of the leader, *Il Duce*, also provided cohesion. As the first antiliberal, anti-socialist alternative, Italian fascism served as a model for other countries.

GERMAN NAZISM In Germany, too, fear of Bolshevism and anger over the war's outcome propelled the right to power. Here, the dictator was **Adolf Hitler** (1889–1945). After a small nationalist workers' organization took shape in Munich, dedicated to winning workers over from socialism, the army high command ordered a young demobilized corporal to infiltrate the group. That corporal, Hitler, soon dominated the nationalist workers' movement, whose name he changed to the National Socialist German Workers' Party (*National-Sozialistische Arbeits-Partei*, or **Nazis**).

Unlike Mussolini, the young Hitler was never a socialist. The first Nazi Party platform, set forth in 1920, combined nationalism with anticapitalism and anti-Semitism. It also called for the renunciation of the Treaty of Versailles. It was an assertion of Germany's grievances against the world and of the small man's grievances against the rich. At first, Hitler and the Nazis were unsuccessful, and Hitler himself was arrested. He was sentenced to five years in prison for treason, but served less than a year. While in prison he wrote an autobiographical and fanatically anti-Semitic treatise called *Mein Kampf* (My Struggle, 1925), which subsequently became wildly popular among Nazis.

The Weimar Republic enjoyed a period of stability after hyperinflation was curtailed by the intervention of American bankers, and in the 1926 elections the Nazi Party received only 2.6 percent of the votes. It only gained popularity after the

Hitler. *Adolf Hitler and his advisors mastered the staging of mass rallies. These rallies and marches projected an image of dynamism and collective will, which Hitler claimed to embody.*

collapse of the American stock market in 1929, when short-term loans were called in. As more and more people lost their jobs, farms, and small businesses, Germans considered radical alternatives. In this atmosphere, fearing popular support of the communist and socialist parties and convinced that he could control Hitler, Germany's president appointed Hitler chancellor (prime minister) in 1933. Initially, Hitler pledged that traditional conservatives would dominate the government. Thus, like Mussolini, Hitler came to power peacefully and legally.

Hitler's first step as chancellor was to heighten fear of a communist conspiracy to take power. The burning of the Reichstag building in Berlin the following month provided the opportunity. The Nazis blamed the fire on the communists, immediately suspended civil liberties "as a defensive measure against the communists," and forced the left-wing press out of business. The latter move robbed opponents of the ability to criticize the regime publicly. Hitler then proposed legislation that would enable him to promulgate laws on his authority as chancellor without the parliament's approval.

Within a month Hitler was free from the control of parliament and the conservative elites. Soon the government seized the offices, banks, and newspapers of trade unions and arrested their leaders. The socialist and communist parties were outlawed; others were dissolved. By July 1933, the Nazis were the only legal party and Hitler was dictator of Germany. He aggressively curbed dissent and banned strikes, jailing political opponents and building the first concentration camps (initially to house political prisoners) when the jails overflowed.

He also unleashed a campaign of persecution against the Jews, believing that assimilated Jews controlled the banks and that eastern Jewish emigrants carried disease. Like many other right-wing Germans, Hitler also believed that a Jewish-socialist conspiracy had stabbed the German army in the back, causing its surrender in World War I, and that intermarriage with Jews was destroying the supposed purity of the Aryan race (which included northern, white, Europeans). Hitler and the Nazis did not believe that religious practice defined Jewishness; instead, they held, it was transmitted biologically from parents to children. Once he became dictator, Hitler instituted legal measures that excluded Jews from the civil service and the professions, forced them to sell their property, deprived them of citizenship, and forbade them to marry or have sex with Aryans. Hitler also encouraged the use of terror against Jews, destroying their businesses, homes, and marriages with non-Jews, frightening them into leaving Germany, and ultimately eliminating all traces of Jewish life and culture in Nazi-dominated central Europe.

Although some Germans opposed Hitler's illiberal activism, the Nazis won popular support for restoring order and reviving the economy. In 1935, defying the Treaty of Versailles, Hitler began a vast rearmament program that absorbed the unemployed. Now economic despair and national disgrace turned into fierce pride and impressive national power. The state also financed public works including reforestation and swamp drainage projects; organized leisure, entertainment, travel, and vacations; and built highways and public housing. Anti-Semitism

PRIMARY SOURCE

Cult of the Dynamic Leader

Nazi political theorists offered no apologies for dictatorship. On the contrary, they bragged about it as the best way of mobilizing the masses and directing the state. The Führer, or Leader, stood above the Nazi Party and all government institutions and embodied the supposed will of the German nation. He also decided who belonged, or did not belong, to the nation. The following excerpt, taken from the writings of Ernst Rudolf Huber, Germany's major constitutional expert of the 1930s, elaborated on the awesome powers being conferred on Hitler as Führer.

The office of Führer has developed out of the National Socialist movement. In its origins it is not a State office. This fact must never be forgotten if one wishes to understand the current political and legal position of the Führer. The office of Führer has grown out of the movement into the Reich, firstly through the Führer taking over the authority of the Reich Chancellor and then through his taking over the position of Head of State. Primary importance must be accorded to the position of "Führer of the movement"; it has absorbed the two highest functions of the political leadership of the Reich and thereby created the new office of "Führer of the Nation and of the Reich."...

The position of Führer combines in itself all sovereign power of the Reich; all public power in the State as in the movement is derived from the Führer power. If we wish to define political power in the Third Reich correctly, we must not speak of "State power" but of "Führer power." For it is not the State as an impersonal entity which is the source of political power but rather political power is given to the Führer as the executor of the nation's common will. Führer power is comprehensive and total; it unites within itself all means of creative political activity; it embraces all spheres of national life; it includes all national comrades who are bound to the Führer in loyalty and obedience. Führer power is not restricted by safeguards and controls, by autonomous protected spheres, and by vested individual rights, but rather it is free and independent, exclusive and unlimited.

QUESTIONS FOR ANALYSIS

- How did the office of Führer arise, according to Huber?
- What are the source and scope of "Führer power"?

Source: Ernst Rudolf Huber, "Führergewalt," from Nazism 1919–1945: A Documentary Reader; Volume 2: State, Economy, and Society, 1933–1939, *pp. 198–99, edited by J. Noakes and G. Pridham. Reprinted by permission of University of Exeter Press.*

mixed with full employment and social welfare programs that privileged racially approved groups.

Germany reemerged as a great power with expansionist aspirations. Hitler called his state the Third Reich (the first being the Holy Roman Empire, or Reich, and the second the Reich created by Bismarck in 1871). He claimed that, like the Holy Roman Empire, his empire would last 1,000 years. Hitler also harbored grand aspirations to impose racial purity and German power in Europe and perhaps beyond. (See Primary Source: Cult of the Dynamic Leader.)

DICTATORSHIPS IN SPAIN AND PORTUGAL As authoritarian regimes spread across Europe, the military took over and instituted dictatorships in Spain and Portugal. Their effort to seize power in Spain provoked a brutal civil war from 1936 to 1939, which left 250,000 dead.

The Spanish civil war was, from the start, an international war. When the Spanish republican government introduced reforms to break the hold of the church and landlords on the state, the military intervened and all of Europe's major powers got involved. The military's attack against the republic at first failed, but with the help of German and Italian weapons (above all, airplanes), Generalissimo Francisco Franco gained the upper hand. Meanwhile, Britain and France dithered and only Stalin's Russia supported the republican government, allowing Franco to establish a dictatorship.

MILITARIST JAPAN Unlike authoritarian regimes, Japan did not suffer wounded power and pride during World War I. In fact, because wartime disruptions reduced European and American competition, Japanese products found new markets in Asia. Japan expanded production, exporting munitions, textiles, and consumer goods to Asian and western markets. During the war, the Japanese gross national product (GNP) grew 40 percent, and the country built the world's third largest navy. After a devastating earthquake and fire in 1923, Tokyo was rebuilt with steel and reinforced concrete, symbolizing the new, modern Japan.

MAP 19.5 | **The Japanese Empire in Asia, 1933**

Hoping to become a great imperial power like the European states, Japan established numerous colonies and spheres of influence early in the twentieth century.

- What were the main territorial components of the Japanese Empire?
- How far did the Japanese succeed in extending their political influence throughout East Asia?
- According to your reading, what problems did the desire to extend Japanese influence in China present to Japanese leaders?

Hirohito. *A portrait of Crown Prince Hirohito of Japan in 1925, the year before he ascended the Japanese throne. Hirohito presided over Japan's war in Asia, beginning with the 1931 seizure of Manchuria and culminating in the 1945 surrender, but he remained emperor for another four decades. When he died in 1989, his wartime responsibility was still a difficult subject for many.*

Manchurian Incident. *Taken from among the throng of Japanese troops, this September 1931 photograph documents the Japanese invasion of Manchuria after the bombing of the South Manchurian Railroad, later known as the Manchurian Incident.*

Initially, post–World War I Japan seemed headed down the liberal democratic road. When Japan's Meiji Emperor died in 1912, his third son succeeded him and oversaw the rise of mass political parties. Suffrage expanded in 1925, increasing the electorate roughly fourfold. But along with democratization came repressive measures. Although the Meiji Constitution remained in effect, a new Peace Preservation Law specified up to ten years' hard labor for any member of an organization advocating change in the political system or abolition of private property. The law served as a club against the mass leftist parties.

Japan veered still further from the liberal democratic road after Emperor Hirohito came to power in 1926. In Japan, as in Germany, the Great Depression spurred the eventual shift to dictatorship. Japan's trade with the outside world had more than tripled between 1913 and 1929, but after 1929 China and the United States imposed barriers on Japanese exports in preference for domestic products. These measures contributed to a 50 percent decline in Japanese exports. Unemployment surged.

Such turmoil invited calls for stronger leadership, which military commanders were eager to provide. Already beyond civilian control, in 1927 and 1928 the army flexed its muscles by twice forcing prime ministers out of office. New "patriotic societies" used violence to intimidate political opponents. Violence culminated in the assassination of Japan's prime minister, accompanied by an uprising of young naval officers and army cadets. Their coup failed, but it further eclipsed the power of political parties.

It was in the Japanese Empire that militarism and expansionism received a boost. In 1931, a group of army officers arranged an explosion on the Japanese-owned South Manchurian Railroad as a pretext for taking over Manchuria. In 1932, adding Manchuria to its Korean and Taiwanese colonies (see Map 19.5), Japan oversaw the proclamation of the puppet state of Manchukuo. In 1933, the Japanese army seized the Chinese province of Jehol to use as a buffer zone between China proper and Manchukuo. Later, they annexed it to the Empire of Manchukuo. Meanwhile, at home, "patriots" continued a campaign of terror against uncooperative businessmen and critics of the military. As in Italy and Germany, the state in Japan took on a sacred aura. This occurred through the promotion of an official religion, Shinto, and of Emperor Hirohito's divinity. By 1940, the clique at the top had merged all political parties into the Imperial Rule Assistance Association, ending even the semblance of parliamentary rule.

COMMON FEATURES OF AUTHORITARIAN REGIMES

Despite important differences, the major authoritarian regimes of this period—communist Soviet Union, fascist Italy, Nazi Germany, and militarist Japan—shared many traits. All rejected parliamentary rule and sought to revive their countries' power through authoritarianism, violence, and a cult of the leader.

All claimed that modern economies required state direction. In Japan, the government fostered huge business conglomerates; in Italy, it encouraged big business to form cartels. The German state also regarded the private sector as the vehicle of economic growth, but it expected entrepreneurs to support the Nazis' racial, antidemocratic, and expansionist aims. The most thorough form of economic coordination occurred in the Soviet Union, which adopted American-style mass production while eliminating private enterprise. Instead, the Soviet state owned and managed all the country's industry. Here, as elsewhere, state-organized labor forces replaced independent labor unions.

Another common feature involved using mass organizations for state purposes. Russia, Italy, and Germany had single mass parties; Japan had various rightist groups until the 1940 merger. All promoted dynamic youth movements, such as the Hitler Youth and the Union of German Girls, the Soviet Communist Youth League, and the Italian squads marching to the anthem "Giovinezza" (Youth).

Hitler Youth. *Like the communists in the Soviet Union, the Nazis organized and indoctrinated boys and girls in the hopes of making them strong supporters of the regime. Pictured here are members of the Hitler Youth, about 1939.*

Three of the states adopted extensive social welfare policies. The Nazis emphasized full employment, built public housing, and provided assistance to needy Aryan families. The Italian National Agency for Maternity and Infancy provided services for unwed mothers and infant care. Soviet programs addressed maternity, disability, sickness, and old age. In fact, the Soviet state viewed welfare assistance as an ongoing program that distinguished socialism from capitalism. Although Japan did not enact innovative social welfare legislation, its Home Affairs Ministry enlisted helpmates among civic groups, seeking to raise savings rates and improve childrearing practices.

A fourth common feature was ambivalence about women in public roles—the Soviet Union excepted. But even that state eventually promoted higher rates of reproduction, rewarding mothers who had many children and restricting abortion. State officials were eager to honor new mothers as a way to repair the loss of so many young men during the Great War. Yet, many more women were also entering professional careers, and some were becoming their families' primary wage earners. In Italy, fascist authorities had to accept the existence of *la maschietta*—the new woman, or flapper, who wore short skirts, bobbed her hair, smoked cigarettes, and engaged in freer sex. In Japan, the *mogā* or *modan gāru* ("modern girl") phenomenon provoked considerable negative comment, but authorities could not suppress it. The Soviets demonstrated the most contradictory behavior. In 1918, they declared men and women equal, legalized (and subsidized) abortion, and eased divorce laws. However, by 1935–1936 new laws made divorce nearly impossible, drove abortion underground, and rewarded "hero mothers" of multiple children. Nonetheless, the rapidly industrializing Soviets had the highest percentage of women in the paid workforce.

Finally, all the dictatorships used violence and terror against their own citizens, colonial subjects, and "foreigners" living within their state borders. These tools served as levers for remaking the sociopolitical order. The Italians and the Japanese were not shy about arresting political opponents, particularly in their colonies. However, it was the Nazis and especially the Soviets who filled concentration and labor camps with alleged enemies of the state, whether Jews or supposed counterrevolutionaries.

Still, brutal as these regimes were, their successes in mastering the masses drew envious glances even from those trying to stay on the liberal democratic road. They also attracted imitators. British and French fascists and communists, though they never came to power, formed national parties and proclaimed support for foreign models. Certain politicians, intellectuals, and labor organizers in South and North America admired Hitler, Lenin, and Stalin. Many also hoped to use the methods of mass mobilization and mass violence for their own ends. This was particularly true of anticolonial movements.

The Hybrid Nature of Latin American Corporatism

Latin American nations felt the same pressures that produced liberal democratic and authoritarian responses in Europe,

Russia, and Japan. However, the Latin American leaders devised solutions that combined democratic and authoritarian elements.

ECONOMIC TURMOIL Latin American countries had stayed out of the fighting in World War I, but their export economies had suffered. As trade plummeted, popular confidence in oligarchic regimes fell, and radical agitation surged. During the war years, trade unionists in the port of Buenos Aires took control of the city's docks, and the women of São Paulo's needle trades inspired Brazil's first general strike. Bolivian tin miners, inspired by events in Russia, proclaimed a full-blown socialist revolution.

The Great Depression brought even sharper challenges from workers' groups. More than in any other region, the Depression battered Latin America's trading and financial systems because they were most dependent on the exports of basic staples, from sugar to wheat, and faced stiff protection or evaporating demand for their commodities. The region, in fact, suffered a double whammy because it had borrowed so much money to invest in infrastructure and expansion. When world money markets went belly-up, creditors called in their loans from Latin America. This move drove borrowers to default. In response, Latin American governments—with enthusiastic backing from the middle classes, nationalist intellectuals, and urban workers—turned to their domestic rather than foreign markets as the main engine of growth. Here, too, the state took on a more interventionist role in market activity.

After the war, Latin American elites confronted the mass age by establishing mass parties and encouraging interest groups to associate with them. Collective bodies such as chambers of commerce, trade unions, peasant associations, and organizations for minorities like blacks and Indians all operated with state sponsorship. This form of modern politics, often labeled corporatist, used social groups to bridge the gap between ruling elites and the general population.

CORPORATIST POLITICS IN BRAZIL Corporatist politics took hold especially in Brazil, where the old republic collapsed in 1930. In its place, a coalition led by the skilled politician Getúlio Vargas (1883–1954) cultivated a strong following by enacting socially popular reforms.

Dubbing himself the "father of the poor," Vargas encouraged workers to organize, erected monuments to national heroes, and supported the building of schools and the paving of roads. He made special efforts to appeal to Brazilian blacks, who had been excluded from public life since the abolition of slavery. Thus he legalized many previously forbidden Afro-Brazilian practices, such as the ritual *candomblé* dance, whose African and martial overtones seemed threatening to white elites. Vargas also supported samba schools, organizations that not only taught popular dances but also raised funds for public works. Moreover, Vargas addressed maternity and housing policies and enfranchised women (although they had to be able to read, as did male voters). Although he condemned the old elites for betraying the country to serve the interests of foreign consumers and investors, he also arranged foreign funding and technical transfers to build steel mills and factories. However, he took this step to create domestic industry so that Brazil would not be so dependent on imports.

Ruling as a patriarch enabled Vargas to squelch dissent and build new lines of loyalty. When he revamped the constitution in 1937, he banned competitive political parties and created forms of national representation along corporatist lines. Each social

Getúlio Vargas. *This cartoon of Vargas, governor of the southern state of Rio Grande do Sul, portrays him as a country bumpkin even as he leads the overthrowing of Brazil's Old Republic.*

Samba dancers. *The dance started in the shanty towns of Rio de Janeiro and eventually became popular throughout the world, thanks to films, photographs, and long-playing records that featured samba music.*

sector or class would be represented by its function in society (for example, as workers, industrialists, or educators), and each would pledge allegiance to the all-powerful state. Although his opponents complained about losing their democratic rights, Vargas also created rights for previously excluded groups like trade unions, who now could use their corporatist representatives to press for demands. To bolster the system, he employed a small army of modern propagandists using billboards, loudspeakers, and radio to broadcast the benevolence of "Father" Vargas.

Anticolonial Visions of Modern Life

Debates over liberal democratic versus authoritarian models engaged the world's colonial and semicolonial regions as well. But here there was a larger concern: what to do about colonial authority? Throughout Asia, most educated members of these communities wanted to roll back the European and American imperial presence. Some Asians even accepted Japanese imperialism as an antidote, under the slogan "Asia for the Asians." In Africa, however, where the European colonial presence was more recent, intellectuals still questioned the real meaning of colonial rule: were the British and the French sincerely committed to African improvement, or were they obstacles to African peoples' well-being?

World War I crippled Europe but gave it more colonies than ever before. Ottoman territories, in particular, wound up in Allied hands. Great Britain emerged with an empire that straddled one-quarter of the earth. Rechristened as the British Commonwealth of Nations, Britain conferred dominion status on white-settler colonies in Canada, Australia, and New Zealand. This meant independence in internal and external affairs in exchange for continuing loyalty to the crown. But no such privileges went to possessions in Africa and India, where nonwhite peoples were the vast majority. Here the British fell back on an old line: nonwhite peoples were not yet ready for self-government.

In Africa as well as Asia, then, the search for the modern encompassed demands for power sharing or full political independence. Anticolonialism was the preeminent vision. To overcome the contradictions of European democratic liberalism, educated Asians and Africans proposed various incarnations of nationalism.

Behind the Asian and African nationalist movements were profound disagreements about how best to govern nations once they gained independence and how to define citizenship. For many intellectuals, the democratic ethos of the imperial powers was appealing. Others liked the radical authoritarianism of fascism and communism, with their promises of rapid change to modernity. Whatever their political preferences, most literate colonials also regarded their own religious and cultural traditions as sources for political mobilization. Thus Muslim, Hindu, Chinese, and African values became vehicles for galvanizing the rank and file. The colonial figures involved in political and intellectual movements insisted that the societies they sought to establish were going to be modern *and* at the same time retain their indigenous characteristics.

AFRICAN STIRRINGS Africa contained the most recent territories to come under the Europeans' control, so anticolonial nationalist movements there were quite young. The region's fate remained very much in the hands of Europeans. After 1918, however, African peoples probed more deeply for the meaning of Europe's imperial presence.

In some parts of Africa, environmental degradation contributed to resentment. In the peanut belt of Senegal, for example, African cultivators pushed into more arid regions, cutting down trees and eventually exhausting the soil. Across the continent, in Kenya, where African peoples were confined to specific locations so as to make land available to European settlers, Africans began to overgraze and overcultivate their lands. A severe problem occurred among the Kamba people living near Nairobi. Their herds had become so large that the government attempted to implement a forcible campaign of culling. Refusing to cooperate, the Kamba joined the chorus of African protesters against British authority.

There was some room (but not much) for voicing African interests under colonialism. The French had long held to a vision of assimilating their colonial peoples into French culture. In France's primary West African colony, Senegal, four coastal cities had traditionally elected one delegate (of mixed African and European ancestry) to the French National Assembly. This practice lasted until 1914, when Blaise Diagne (1872–1934), an African candidate, ran for office and won, invoking his African origins and garnering the African vote. While the British allowed Africans to elect delegates to municipal bodies, they refused to permit colonial representatives to sit in Parliament.

Blaise Diagne. *Diagne was the first African elected to the French National Assembly. He won the election to the French Parliament in 1914, beating white and mixed-race candidates by appealing to the majority black African population that lived in the four communes of Senegal.*

PRIMARY SOURCE

Facing Mount Kenya

Jomo Kenyatta, one of Kenya's leading nationalists, wrote a moving account of his own Kikuyu community in* Facing Mount Kenya *(1937). The book demonstrated the cohesion and strong tribal bonds of precolonial Kikuyu society, as well as the destructive elements of the colonial assault on African traditions. The excerpt below is from the conclusion.

And it is the culture which he inherits that gives a man his human dignity as well as his material prosperity. It teaches him his mental and moral values and makes him feel it worth while to work and fight for liberty.

But a culture has no meaning apart from the social organisation of life on which it is built. When the European comes to the Gikuyu country and robs the people of their land, he is taking away not only their livelihood, but the material symbol that holds family and tribe together. In doing this he gives one blow which cuts away the foundations from the whole of Gikuyu life, social, moral, and economic. When he explains, to his own satisfaction and after the most superficial glance at the issues involved, that he is doing this for the sake of the Africans, to "civilise" them, "teach them the disciplinary value of regular work," and "give them the benefit of European progressive ideas," he is adding insult to injury, and need expect to convince no one but himself.

There certainly are some progressive ideas among the Europeans. They include the ideas of material prosperity, of medicine, and hygiene, and literacy which enables people to take part in world culture. But so far the Europeans who visit Africa have not been conspicuously zealous in imparting these parts of their inheritance to the Africans, and seem to think that the only way to do it is by police discipline and armed force. They speak as if it was somehow beneficial to an African to work for them instead of for himself, and to make sure that he will receive this benefit they do their best to take away his land and leave him with no alternative. Along with his land they rob him of his government, condemn his religious ideas, and ignore his fundamental conceptions of justice and morals, all in the name of civilisation and progress.

If Africans were left in peace on their own lands, Europeans would have to offer them the benefits of white civilisation in real earnest before they could obtain the African labour which they want so much. They would have to offer the African a way of life which was really superior to the one his fathers lived before him, and a share in the prosperity given them by their command of science. They would have to let the African choose what parts of European culture would be beneficially transplanted, and how they could be adapted. He would probably not choose the gas bomb or the armed police force, but he might ask for some other things of which he does not get so much today. As it is, by driving him off his ancestral lands, the Europeans have robbed him of the material foundations of his culture, and reduced him to a state of serfdom incompatible with human happiness. The African is conditioned, by the cultural and social institutions of centuries, to a freedom of which Europe has little conception, and it is not in his nature to accept serfdom for ever. He realises that he must fight unceasingly for his own complete emancipation; for without this he is doomed to remain the prey of rival imperialisms, which in every successive year will drive their fangs more deeply into his vitality and strength.

QUESTIONS FOR ANALYSIS

- According to Kenyatta, why is it so devastating when European imperialists rob African people of their land?
- Why do you think the Europeans were not zealous in imparting "progressive ideas" to the Africans?
- Why does Kenyatta think the Africans would not choose to adopt "the gas bomb or the armed police force" from European culture?

Source: Excerpt from Facing Mount Kenya: The Tribal Life of the Gikuyu *by Jomo Kenyatta, published by Vintage Books, a division of Random House, Inc. Used by permission of Alfred A. Knopf, a division of Random House, Inc.*

Committed to democracy at home, the European powers were steadfastly against it in their colonies.

Excluded from representative bodies, Africans experimented with various forms of protest. For example, in southeastern Nigeria in 1929, Ibo and Ibibio women responded to a new tax by breaking off contact with the local colonial chiefs. Moving beyond boycotts of local officials, women burned down chiefs' huts, as well as European and Lebanese trading establishments, to protest their exploitation.

Opposition was still not widespread in Africa, for protests ran up against not only colonial administrators but also western-educated African elites. These individuals often built western-style homes, drove automobiles, wore western clothing, and consumed western foods. Yet, even this privileged group began to reconsider its relationship to colonial authorities. In Kenya, immediately after World War I, a small contingent of mission-educated Africans called on the British to provide more and better schools and to return lands they claimed European settlers had stolen. Although they enlisted the support of liberal missionaries, their pleas fell on deaf ears and their leader was arrested. Although defeated in this instance, the young nationalists drew important lessons from their confrontation with the authorities. They now viewed colonialism in a more combative light. Their new spokesperson, Jomo Kenyatta (1898–1978), invoked their precolonial Kikuyu traditions as a basis for resisting colonialism. (See Primary Source: Facing Mount Kenya.)

IMAGINING AN INDIAN NATION As Africans explored the use of modern politics against Europeans, opposition in India took on a more advanced form. The war and its aftermath brought full-blown challenges to British rule. Indeed, the Indian nationalist challenge provided inspiration for other anticolonial movements.

For over a century, Indians had heard British authorities extol the virtues of parliamentary government, yet they were excluded from participation. In 1919, the British did slightly enlarge the franchise in India and allowed more local self-government, but these moves did not satisfy Indians' nationalist longings. During the 1920s and 1930s, the nationalists, led by **Mohandas Karamchand (Mahatma) Gandhi** (1869–1948), laid the foundations for an alternative, anticolonial movement.

GANDHI AND NONVIOLENT RESISTANCE Gandhi had studied law in England and had worked in South Africa on behalf of Indian immigrants before returning to India in 1915. Thereafter, he assumed leadership in local struggles. He also spelled out the moral and political philosophy of *satyagraha*, or **nonviolent resistance**, which he had developed while in South Africa. His message to Indians was simple: Develop your own resources and inner strength and control the instincts and activities that encourage participation in colonial economy and government, and you shall achieve *swaraj* ("self-rule"). Faced with Indian self-reliance and self-control pursued nonviolently, Gandhi claimed, the British eventually would have to leave. (See Primary Source: India and Self-Government.)

A crucial event in rising opposition to British rule was a massacre in 1919 of Indian civilians protesting British policies in the Punjab. The incident, in which a British general ordered soldiers to fire on the protesters, left 379 Indian civilians dead and more than 1,200 wounded. As news of the massacre spread, many Indians were infuriated—especially when they learned that British authorities were not punishing the general.

This and other conflicts spurred the nationalists to oppose cooperation with government officials, to boycott goods made in Britain, to refuse to send their children to British schools, and to withhold taxes. Gandhi added his voice, calling for an all-India *satyagraha*. He also formed an alliance with Muslim leaders and began turning the Indian National Congress from an elite organization of lawyers and merchants into a mass organization open to anyone who paid dues, even the illiterate and poor.

When the Depression struck India in 1930, Gandhi singled out salt as a testing ground for his ideas on civil disobedience. Every Indian used salt, whose production was a heavily taxed government monopoly. Thus, salt symbolized the Indians' subjugation to an alien government. To break the colonial government's

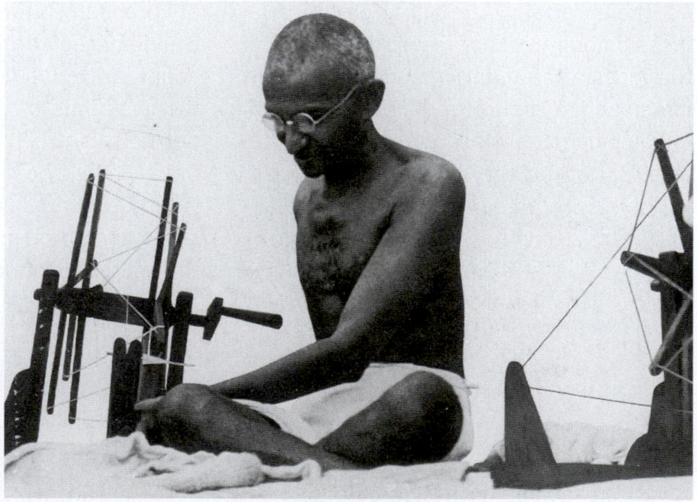

Gandhi and the Road to Independence. (Left) *Gandhi launched a civil disobedience movement in 1930 by violating the British government's tax on salt. Calling it "the most inhuman poll tax the ingenuity of man can devise," Gandhi, accompanied by his followers, set out on a month-long march on foot covering 240 miles to Dandi on the Gujarat coast. The picture shows Gandhi arriving at the sea, where he and his followers broke the law by scooping up handfuls of salt.* (Right) *Gandhi believed that India had been colonized by becoming enslaved to modern industrial civilization. Indians would achieve independence, he argued, when they became self-reliant. Thus, he made the spinning wheel a symbol of* swaraj *and handspun cloth the virtual uniform of the nation.*

PRIMARY SOURCE

India and Self-Government

The following excerpt is from Mohandas (Mahatma) Gandhi's* Hind Swaraj*, a pamphlet that he wrote in 1909 to explain why India needed self-government. Gandhi wrote it as a dialogue between a newspaper editor and a reader. Taking the role of the editor, he criticized modernity as represented by modern western civilization, which was based on industry and materialism. In contrast, Gandhi's imagined civilization of India derived from religion and harmonious village life. According to Gandhi, India demanded modern nationhood (or self-rule, swaraj) so that it could restore the best elements of its age-old civilization.

READER: . . . I would now like to know your views on Swaraj. . . .

EDITOR [GANDHI]: It is quite possible that we do not attach the same meaning to the term. You and I and all Indians are impatient to obtain Swaraj, but we are certainly not decided as to what it is. . . .

Why do we want to drive away the English?

READER: Because India has become impoverished by their Government. They take away our money from year to year. The most important posts are reserved for themselves. We are kept in a state of slavery. They behave insolently towards us, and disregard our feelings.

EDITOR: Supposing we get self-government similar to what the Canadians and the South Africans have, will it be good enough?

READER: . . .We must own our navy, our army, and we must have our own splendour, and then will India's voice ring through the world.

EDITOR: . . . In effect it means this: that we want English rule without the Englishman. You want the tiger's nature, but not the tiger; that is to say, you would make India English, and, when it becomes English, it will be called not Hindustan but Englistan. This is not the Swaraj that I want.

READER: Then from your statement I deduce that the Government of England is not desirable and not worth copying by us.

EDITOR: . . . If India copies England, it is my firm conviction that she will be ruined.

READER: To what do you ascribe this state of England?

EDITOR: It is not due to any peculiar fault of the English people, but the condition is due to modern civilisation. It is a civilisation only in name. Under it the nations of Europe are becoming degraded and ruined day by day.

READER: . . . I should like to know your views about the condition of our country.

EDITOR: . . . India is being ground down not under the English heel but under that of modern civilisation. It is groaning under the monster's terrible weight. . . . India is becoming irreligious. Here I am not thinking of the Hindu, the Mahomedan, or the Zoroastrian religion, but of that religion which underlies all religions. We are turning away from God.

READER: You have denounced railways, lawyers and doctors. I can see that you will discard all machinery. What, then, is civilisation?

READER: . . . The tendency of Indian civilisation is to elevate the moral being, that of the Western civilisation is to propagate immorality. The latter is godless, the former is based on a belief in God. So understanding and so believing, it behooves every lover of India to cling to the old Indian civilisation even as a child clings to its mother's breast.

READER: . . . What, then, . . . would you suggest for freeing India?

EDITOR: . . . Those alone who have been affected by Western civilisation have become enslaved. . . . If we become free, India is free. And in this thought you have a definition of Swaraj. It is Swaraj when we learn to rule ourselves.

QUESTIONS FOR ANALYSIS

- What are Gandhi's complaints about English colonial rule?
- Why does Gandhi reject modern civilization?
- According to Gandhi, what are the best aspects of "the old Indian civilisation"?

Source: M. K. Gandhi, Hind Swaraj and Other Writings, *edited by Anthony J. Parel (Cambridge: Cambridge University Press, 1997), pp. 26–91.*

monopoly, Gandhi began a 240-mile march from western India to the coast to gather sea salt for free. Accompanying him were seventy-one followers representing different regions and religions of India. News wire services and mass circulation newspapers worldwide reported on the drama of the sixty-one-year-old Gandhi, wooden staff in hand, dressed in coarse homespun garments, leading the march. Thousands of people gathering en route were moved by the sight of the frail apostle of nonviolence encouraging them to embrace independence from colonial rule. The air thickened with tension as observers speculated on the British reaction to Gandhi's arrival at the sea. After nearly three weeks of walking, Gandhi waded into the surf, picked up a lump of natural salt, held it high, confessed that he had broken the salt law, and invited every Indian to do the same.

Inspired by Gandhi's example, millions of Indians joined strikes, boycotted foreign goods, and substituted indigenous hand-woven cloth for imported textiles. Many Indian officials in the colonial administration resigned in solidarity. The colonizers were taken aback by the mass mobilization. Yet, British denunciations of Gandhi only added to his personal aura and to the anticolonial crusade. By insisting that Indians follow their conscience (always through nonviolent protest), by exciting the masses through his defiance of colonial power, and by using symbols like homespun cloth to counter foreign, machine-spun textiles, Gandhi instilled in the people a sense of pride, resourcefulness, and Indian national awareness.

A DIVIDED ANTICOLONIAL MOVEMENT Unlike the charismatic authoritarians who dominated Italy, Germany, and Russia, Gandhi did not aspire to dictatorial power. Moreover, his program met opposition from within, for many in the Indian National Congress Party did not share his vision of community as the source of public life. Cambridge-educated Jawaharlal Nehru (1889–1964), for example, believed that only by embracing science and technology could India develop as a modern nation.

Even less enamored were radical activists who wanted a revolution, not peaceful protest. In the countryside, these radicals sought to organize peasants to overthrow colonial domination. Other activists galvanized the growing industrial proletariat by organizing trade unions. Their stress on class conflict ran against Gandhi's ideals of national unity.

Religion, too, threatened to fracture Gandhi's hope for anticolonial unity. The Hindu-Muslim alliance crafted by nationalists in the early 1920s splintered over who represented them and how to ensure their political rights. The gulf widened after the Government of India Act of 1935 conceded substantial provincial autonomy and enlarged the franchise. The Muslim community found an impressive leader in Muhammad Ali Jinnah, who set about making the Muslim League the sole representative organization of the Muslim community. In 1940, the Muslim League passed a resolution demanding independent Muslim states in provinces where they constituted a majority, on the grounds that Muslims were not a religious minority of the Indian nation, but a nation themselves.

Hindus also sought a political role on the basis of religious identity. Movements to revitalize Hinduism began organizing Hindus as a religious nation. Indeed, the influence of Hindu culture on Indian nationalism was broad. Hindu symbols and a Hindu ethos colored the fabric of Indian nationalism woven by Gandhi and the Indian National Congress Party.

A further challenge came from women. Long-standing efforts to "uplift" women now escalated into a demand for women's rights, including suffrage. Following the formation of the All India Women's Conference in 1927, activists took up issues relating to women workers, health, employment, education, and literacy and demanded legislative seats for women. The Indian National Congress Party, however, elevated its nationalist agenda above women's demands, just as it had done in dealing with the lower castes and the relations between Hindus and Muslims.

In 1937, the British belatedly granted India provincial assemblies, a bicameral (having two chambers or bodies) national legislature, and a self-governing executive. By then, however, India's people were deeply politicized. The Congress Party, which inspired the masses to overthrow British rule, struggled to contain the different ideologies and new political institutions, such as labor unions, peasant associations, religious parties, and

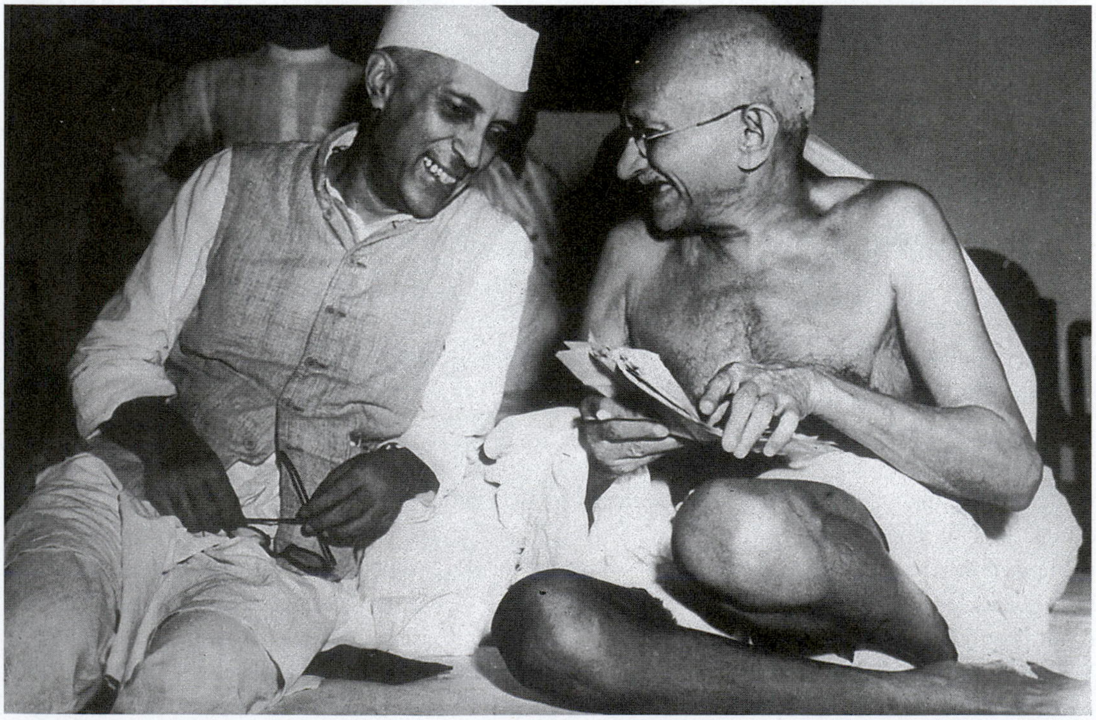

Gandhi and Nehru Sharing a Light Moment. *Despite their divergent views on modernity, Gandhi was personally close to Nehru, who was his chosen political heir.*

communal organizations. Seeking a path to economic modernization, Gandhi, on one side, envisioned independent India as an updated collection of village republics organized around the benevolent authority of male-dominated households. Nehru, on another side, hoped for a socioeconomic transformation powered by science and state-sponsored planning. Both believed that India's traditions of collective welfare and humane religious and philosophical practices set it apart from the modern West. By the outbreak of World War II, India was well on its way toward political independence, but British policies and India's divisions foretold a violent end to imperial rule (see Chapter 20).

CHINESE NATIONALISM Unlike India and Africa, China was never formally colonized. But foreign powers' "concession areas" on Chinese soil compromised its sovereignty. Indeed, foreign nationals living in China enjoyed many privileges, including immunity from Chinese law. Furthermore, unequal treaties imposed on the Qing government had robbed China of its customs and tariff autonomy. Thus, the Chinese nationalists' vision of a modern alternative echoed that of the Indian nationalists: ridding the nation of foreign domination was the initial condition of national fulfillment. For many, the 1911 Revolution (as the fall of the Qing dynasty came to be known; see Chapter 18) symbolized the first step toward transforming a crumbling agrarian empire into a modern nation.

Despite high hopes, the new republic could not establish legitimacy. For one thing, factional and regional conflicts made the government little more than a loose alliance of gentry, merchants, and military leaders. Its intellectual inspiration came from the ideas of the nationalist leader Sun Yat-sen. In 1912, after the Qing emperor stepped down, a military strongman, Yuan Shikai, forced Sun Yat-sen to concede the presidency to him. Although Sun had organized his followers into a political party, the Guomindang, Yuan dismissed all efforts to further democracy and dissolved the parliament. Only Yuan's death in 1916 ended his attempt to establish a new personal dynasty.

The republic endured another blow when the Treaty of Versailles awarded Germany's old concession rights in the Shandong peninsula to Japan. On May 4, 1919, thousands of Chinese students demonstrated in Beijing. As the protests spread to other cities, students appealed to workers and merchants to join their ranks. In what became known as the May Fourth movement, workers went on strike and merchants closed shops. Across the country, the Chinese boycotted Japanese goods.

As the Guomindang, still led by Sun Yat-sen, tried to rejuvenate itself, it looked to students and workers as well as the Russian Revolution for inspiration. In 1923, Sun reached an agreement with the Russians and admitted Chinese communists to the Guomindang as individual members. Under the banner of anti-imperialism, the reorganized party sponsored mass organizations of workers' unions, peasant leagues, and women's associations.

In 1926, amid a renewed tide of antiforeign agitation, **Chiang Kai-shek** (1887–1975) seized control of the party following Sun's death. Chiang launched a partially successful military campaign to reunify the country and established a new national government with its capital in Nanjing. However, he broke with the Soviets and the Chinese communists, whom he viewed as more threat than ally. Furthermore, instead of repudiating foreign treaty rights and concessions, Chiang's regime modified its anti-imperialism platform and sought to revise the concessions through diplomacy.

Still, Chiang acknowledged that China needed to change in order to succeed as a modern nation. He believed that the Chinese masses had to be mobilized. The New Life movement, launched with a torchlight parade in 1934 in Nanchang, exemplified his aspiration for a new Chinese national consciousness. Drawing on diverse ideas (from Confucian precepts to Social Darwinism) and fascist practices such as the militarization of everyday life in the name of sacrificing for the nation, the New Life movement aimed to instill discipline and moral purpose into a unified citizenry. It promoted dress codes for women, condemned casual sexual liaisons, and campaigned against spitting, urinating, or smoking in public.

PEASANT POPULISM IN CHINA: WHITE WOLF For many Guomindang leaders, the peasant population represented a backward class. Thus, the leadership failed to tap into the revolutionary potential of the countryside, which was alive with grassroots movements such as that of White Wolf.

From late 1913 to 1914, Chinese newspapers circulated reports about a roving band of armed men led by a mysterious figure known as White Wolf. This figure terrified members of the elite with his almost magical power. It is unlikely that the band, rumored to have close to a million followers, had more than 20,000 members even at its height. But the mythology surrounding White Wolf was so widespread that the movement's impact reverberated well beyond its physical presence.

Popular myth depicted White Wolf as a Chinese Robin Hood with the mission to restore order. The band's objective was to rid the country of the injustices of Yuan Shikai's government.

Chiang Kai-shek. *Riding the current of anti-imperialism, Chiang Kai-shek, shown here in 1924 in military dress, led the Guomindang on a military campaign in 1926–1928 and seized power, establishing a new national government based in Nanjing.*

Raiding major trade routes and market towns, White Wolf's followers gained a reputation for robbing the rich and aiding the poor. It was said that once the band captured a town, "cash and notes were flung out to the poor." Such stories won the White Wolf army many followers in rural China, where local peasants joined temporarily as fighters and then returned home when the band moved on.

Although the White Wolf army lacked the power to restore order to the countryside, its presence reflected the changes that had come to China. The army struck areas where inhabitants were feeling the effects of the new market forces. In the northwestern province of Shaanxi (Shensi), for example, where the band made its most famous march, markets that formerly flourished with trade in Chinese cotton now awaited camels carrying cotton bales shipped from Fall River, Massachusetts. The fact that the Guomindang never managed to bridge the differences between themselves and a rural-based movement such as that of White Wolf showed the limits of their nationalist vision. The challenge fell to the Chinese communists, who had fled to the countryside to escape Chiang's persecution. They learned that the rural population could indeed become a mass political force—a lesson that served them well during the subsequent war and Japanese occupation in the 1930s and 1940s.

A POST-IMPERIAL TURKISH NATION Of all the postwar anticolonial movements, none was more successful or more committed to European models than that of **Mustafa Kemal Ataturk** (1881–1938), who helped forge the modern Turkish nation-state. Until 1914, the Ottoman Empire was a colonial power in its own right. But having fought on the losing German side, it saw its realm shrink to a part of Anatolia under the Treaty of Sèvres, which ended the war between the Allies and the Ottoman Empire.

Some of its former territories, such as those in southern Europe, became independent states; others, such as those in the Middle East, came under British and French administration as mandates of the League of Nations. Fearing that the rest of the empire would be colonized, Ottoman military leaders, many of whom had resisted Turkish nationalism, now embraced the cause. What made modern Turkish nationalism so successful was its ability to convert the mainstay of the old regime, the army, to the goal of creating a Turkish nation-state. These men, in turn, mobilized the masses and launched a state-led drive for modernity.

In 1920, an Ottoman army officer and military hero named Mustafa Kemal harnessed this groundswell of Turkish nationalism into opposition to Greek troops who had been sent to enforce the peace treaty. Rallying his own troops to defend the fledgling Turkish nation, Kemal reconquered most of Anatolia and the area around Istanbul and secured international recognition for the new state in 1923 at the Treaty of Lausanne. Thereafter, a vast, forcible exchange of populations occurred. Approximately 1.2 million Greek Christians left Turkey to settle in Greece, and 400,000 Muslims relocated from Greece to Turkey.

Ataturk. *In the 1920s, Mustafa Kemal, known as Ataturk, introduced the Latin alphabet for the Turkish language as part of his campaign to modernize and secularize Turkey. He underscored his commitment to change by being photographed while giving instruction in the use of the new alphabet.*

With the Ottoman Empire gone, Kemal and his followers moved to build a state based on Turkish national consciousness. First they deposed the sultan. Then they abolished the Ottoman caliphate and proclaimed Turkey a republic, whose supreme authority would be an elected House of Assembly. Later, after Kemal insisted that the people adopt European-style surnames, the assembly conferred on Kemal the mythic name Ataturk, "father of the Turks."

In forging a Turkish nation, Kemal looked to construct a European-style secular state and to eliminate Islam's hold over civil and political affairs. The Turkish elite replaced Muslim religious law with the Swiss civil code, instituted the western (Christian) calendar, and abolished the once-powerful dervish religious orders. They also suppressed Arabic and Persian words from Turkish, substituted Roman script for Arabic letters, forbade polygamy, made wearing the fez (a brimless cap) a crime, and instructed Turks to wear European-style hats. The veil, though not outlawed, was denounced as a relic. In 1934, the government enfranchised Turkish women, granted them property rights in marriage and inheritance, and allowed them to enter the professions. Schools, too, were taken out of the hands of Muslim clerics, placed under state control, and, along with military service, became the chief instrument for making the masses conscious of belonging to a Turkish nation. Yet, many villagers did not accept

Ataturk's non-Islamic nationalism, remaining devoted to Islam and resentful of the prohibitions against dervish dancing.

In imitating Europe, Kemal borrowed many of its antidemocratic models. Inspired by the Soviets, he inaugurated a five-year plan for the economy emphasizing centralized coordination. During the 1930s, Turkish nationalists also drew on Nazi examples by advocating racial theories that posited central Asian Turks as the founders of all civilization. In another authoritarian move, Kemal occasionally rigged parliamentary elections, while using the police and judiciary to silence his critics. The Kemalist revolution in Turkey was the most far-reaching and enduring transformation that had occurred outside Europe and the Americas up to that point. It offered an important model for the founding of secular, authoritarian states in the Islamic world.

NATIONALISM AND THE RISE OF THE MUSLIM BROTHERHOOD IN EGYPT Elsewhere in the Middle East, where France and Britain expanded their holdings at the Ottomans' expense, anticolonial movements borrowed from European models while putting their own stamp on nation-making and modernization campaigns. In Egypt, British occupation predated the fall of the Ottoman Empire, but here, too, World War I energized the forces of anticolonial nationalism.

When the war ended, Sa'd Zaghlul (1857–1927), an educated Egyptian patriot, pressed for an Egyptian delegation to be invited to the peace conference at Versailles. He hoped to present Egypt's case for national independence. Instead, British officials arrested and exiled him and his most vocal supporters. When news of this action came out, the country burst into revolt. Rural rebels broke away from the central government, proclaiming local republics. Villagers tore up railway lines and telegraph wires, the symbols of British authority.

After defusing the conflict, British authorities tried to mollify Egyptian sensibilities. In 1922, Britain proclaimed Egypt independent, though it retained the right to station British troops on Egyptian soil. Ostensibly, this provision would protect traffic through the Suez Canal and foreign populations residing in Egypt, but it also enabled the British to continue to influence Egyptian politics. Two years later, elections placed Zaghlul's nationalist party, the Wafd, in office. But the British prevented the Wafd from exercising real power.

This subversion of independence and democracy provided an opening for antiliberal variants of anticolonialism. During the Depression years, a fascist group, Young Egypt, garnered wide appeal. Much more influential and destined to have an enduring influence throughout the Arab world was an Islamic group, the Muslim Brotherhood, which attacked liberal democracy as a facade for middle-class, business, and landowning interests. The Muslim Brotherhood was anticolonial and anti-British, but its members considered mere political independence insufficient. Egyptians, they argued, must also renounce the lure of the West (whether liberal capitalism or godless communism) and return to a purified form of Islam. For the Muslim Brotherhood, Islam offered a complete way of life. A "return to Islam" through the nation-state created yet another model of modernity for colonial and semicolonial peoples.

CONCLUSION

The Great War and its aftermath accelerated the trend toward mass society and the debate over how to organize it. Because mass society meant production and consumption on a staggering scale, satisfying the populace became a pressing concern for rulers worldwide. Competing programs vied for ascendancy in the new, broader, public domain.

Most programs fell into one of three categories: liberal democratic, authoritarian, or anticolonial. Liberal democracy defined the political and economic systems in western Europe and the Americas. Resting on faith in free enterprise and representative democracy (with a restricted franchise), liberal regimes had already been unsettled before the Great War. Turn-of-the-century reforms broadened electorates and brought government oversight and regulation into private economic activity. But during the Great Depression, dissatisfaction again deepened. Only far-reaching reforms, introducing greater regulation and more aggressive government intervention to provide for the citizenry's welfare, saved capitalist economies and democratic political systems from collapse.

Still, through the 1930s, liberal democracy was in retreat. Authoritarianism seemed better positioned to satisfy the masses while representing the dynamism of modernity. While authoritarians differed about the faults of capitalism, they joined in the condemnation of electoral democracy. Authoritarians mobilized the masses to put the interests of the nation above the individual. That mobilization often involved brutal repression, yet it seemed also to restore pride and purpose to the masses.

Meanwhile, the colonial and semicolonial world searched for ways to escape from European domination. In Asia and Africa, anticolonial leaders sought to eliminate foreign rule while turning colonies into nations and subjects into citizens. Some looked to the liberal democratic West for models of nation building, but others rejected liberalism because it was associated with colonial rule. Instead, socialism, fascism, and a return to religious traditions offered more promising paths.

The two decades after the end of World War I brought great political upheavals and deep economic dislocations. At times, the competition among liberal democracy, authoritarianism (both right and left), and anticolonial nationalism grew heated. Yet the traumas were tame compared to what followed with the outbreak in 1939 of World War II.

AFTER YOU READ THIS CHAPTER

Review and research materials on **StudySpace:** wwnorton.com/studyspace

TRACING THE GLOBAL STORYLINES

FOCUS ON: *World War I and Its Aftermath*

The great war

- The war destroys empires, starting with the Bolshevik Revolution against the tsarist regime in Russia, followed by the defeat and dissolution of the German, Austro-Hungarian, and Ottoman empires.
- Mass mobilization sees almost 70 million men join the fighting, undermines traditional gender boundaries, and forces states to recognize their peoples' demands for compensation afterward.
- Mass culture spreads as leaders use the new media of radio and film to promote national loyalties and discredit enemies.

The aftermath

- Liberal democracies in France, Britain, and the United States survive the Great Depression by enacting far-reaching changes in their political systems and free market economies.
- Authoritarian (communist and fascist) dictatorships with many political similarities emerge in the Soviet Union, Italy, Germany, Spain, and Portugal.
- Latin American leaders devise hybrid solutions that combine democratic and authoritarian elements.
- Peoples living under colonial rule in Asia and Africa mobilize traditional values to oppose imperial rulers.
- Key individuals emerge in the struggle to define newly independent nations: Kenyatta, Gandhi, Chiang Kai-shek, and Ataturk.

CHRONOLOGY

The Americas
- U.S. enters World War I **1917**

Europe
- World War I **1914–1918**
- Mussolini takes over Italy **1922**

Soviet Union
- Bolshevik Revolution **1917**
- Russian civil war **1918–1921**

East Asia

South Asia

Middle East
- Mustafa Kemal creates modern Turkish nation-state **1923**

1910

KEY TERMS

Allied Powers p. 706

Mustafa Kemal Ataturk p. 738

Bolsheviks p. 709

Central Powers p. 706

Chiang Kai-shek p. 737

fascism p. 725

Mohandas Karamchand (Mahatma) Gandhi p. 734

Great Depression p. 717

Great War (World War I) p. 706

Adolf Hitler p. 725

League of Nations p. 712

mass consumption p. 716

mass culture p. 715

mass production p. 716

Benito Mussolini p. 725

Nazis p. 725

New Deal p. 721

nonviolent resistance p. 734

Joseph Stalin p. 723

STUDY QUESTIONS

1. **List and explain** the numerous ways in which World War I changed the world. How did it usher in a new age for diverse societies?
2. **Define** the terms *mass culture, mass production,* and *mass consumption*. How did World War I help to diffuse these concepts across the world's cultures?
3. **Analyze** how the Great Depression challenged political establishments after World War I. How were the two events linked? What values and assumptions did the Great Depression challenge?
4. **Explain** competing visions of modernity that emerged across the globe during the period covered in this chapter. How were they similar and how were they different?
5. **Compare and contrast** the liberal democratic and authoritarian visions of modernity as epitomized by various states in the 1930s. What features did they have in common?
6. **List and explain** various anticolonial visions of modern life that emerged in the first half of the twentieth century. To what extent did they reflect borrowed developments versus native traditions and ideas?
7. **Describe** how Latin American societies adjusted to modern ideas at this time. How did visions of modernity affect states and societies in that region of the world?

Great Depression begins **1929**

Vargas becomes leader of Brazil **1930**

New Deal reforms (United States) **1933–1941**

Hitler takes over Germany **1933**

Popular Front rules France **1936–1939**

Collectivization and Five Year Plans instituted **1929–1935**

Political purges **1936–1938**

Chiang Kai-shek becomes leader of China **1928**

Japan annexes Manchuria **1932**

Gandhi's March to the Sea **1930**

Muslim Brotherhood founded in Egypt **1928**

1940

BEFORE YOU READ THIS CHAPTER

GLOBAL STORYLINES

- World War II shatters the European-centered order and lays the groundwork for a world divided into three camps: an American-led liberal democratic order; a communist world led by the Soviet Union; and newly independent, decolonized states in Asia, Africa, and Latin America.
- War and postwar reconstruction enhance the reach and functions of the modern nation-state.
- Allies during World War II, the United States and the Soviet Union engage in an ideological cold war, each touting the superiority of its views on how best to organize societies, while decolonized states in Asia, Africa, and Latin America struggle to find a "third way" but find themselves caught between rival superpowers.

CHAPTER OUTLINE

FOCUS QUESTIONS

- How did World War II contribute to the creation of the three-world order after 1945?
- What major similarities and differences existed between the three worlds in terms of goals and aspirations?
- How did cold war rivalries shape developments in the third world?
- What successes and failures did each world experience from 1945 to 1975?
- What major fissures developed in the three-world order by 1975?

20

The Three-World Order, 1940–1975

In February 1945, the three leaders of the World War II Allies—President Franklin Delano Roosevelt of the United States, Prime Minister Winston Churchill of Great Britain, and Premier Joseph Stalin of the Soviet Union—met to prepare for the postwar world. By then, Germany, Italy, and Japan were losing the war. But the world's reordering was a source of deep contention, for the three leaders had profoundly different visions. Roosevelt, who envisioned independent nation-states kept at peace by an international body, had no interest in restoring the old European empires. Churchill, however, resisted liquidation of the British Empire. Stalin's negotiations left no doubt that he intended to secure influence in eastern Europe and Asia and to weaken Germany so that it could never again menace the Soviet Union.

When the fighting finally stopped, it was clear that the European-centered order, shocked by World War I, had been shattered by World War II. Empires either lay in ruins or faced dismantling by colonial independence movements. The nation-state had emerged as the prevailing political organization. Moreover, the state's reach had expanded as it took on new functions related to postwar reconstruction. Meanwhile, with the weakening of Great Britain, France, and Germany, a new three-world order emerged.

This chapter explores the development of the three-world order in the wake of World War II. Heading the "First World" was the United States, which with its allies championed capitalism and democracy as the best way to bring unprecedented prosperity in the decades after 1945. Leading the "Second World" was the Soviet Union, the crucial ally of the United States during World War II, which became its chief adversary in the protracted cold war that followed. As leader of the communist bloc, the Soviet Union contested capitalist societies' claims and trumpeted socialism's accomplishments. Caught in between (and sometimes literally caught in the crossfire when the cold war turned hot) were formerly colonized and semicolonized people. Lumped together as the "Third World," these nations emerged from the war eager to seek their own ways forward.

COMPETING BLOCS

The roots of the world's division into three blocs lay in the breakup of Europe's empires and the demise of European world leadership. The destruction of Europe and the defeat of Japan left a power vacuum, which the United States and the Soviet Union rushed to fill. Both believed that their respective systems—capitalism and communism—had universal application. They were now **superpowers** because of the size of their economies and arsenals, the transcontinental reach of their political influence, and the fact that each embodied a model of civilization applicable to the whole world. As their spheres of influence expanded, they engaged in a bitter ideological rivalry known as the **cold war** because no direct military conflict occurred between the superpowers, both of which after 1949 possessed the atomic bomb.

While the capitalist and communist blocs embarked on a cold war, conflicts in the Third World got very hot. In Asia and Africa, anticolonial leaders intensified their campaigns for independence. Winning popular support by mobilizing deep-seated desires for justice and autonomy, they swept away foreign rulers and asserted their claims for national independence. Latin American countries, too, sought progress and nationhood. But newfound political freedom did not easily translate into economic development or social equity. Moreover, as the two superpowers looked for allies and client states, they militarized rival states and factions within the Third World.

Each superpower also faced internal problems. Even as the United States maintained that its booming industrial economy, abundant consumer goods, liberal democracy, and vibrant popular culture were proof of capitalism's superiority, the nation also wrestled with racism and became involved in unpopular wars to stop the spread of communism—most notably in Vietnam. The Soviet Union celebrated its own economic prowess and social welfare policies, but it continued to imprison and persecute reformers and dissenters and to operate a command economy, oriented to heavy industrial products and armaments. By the 1960s, the USSR's use of military force to crush socialist reform efforts within the Soviet bloc was undermining communism's allure.

By the 1960s and the early 1970s, tensions were simmering in the three-world order. The United States and the Soviet Union faced discontent within their societies and opposition within their respective blocs. At the same time, the rising economic might of Japan and the other Pacific economies, the emerging clout of oil-rich states, and the specter of radical revolution in Africa, Asia, and Latin America suggested a shift in the balance of wealth and power away from the First and Second worlds.

WORLD WAR II AND ITS AFTERMATH

World War II grew out of unresolved problems connected to the Great War. World War I had not been, as many had prophesied, "the war to end all wars." It became instead merely the *First* World War after the *Second* World War began in 1939. Especially influential were the resentments bred by the harsh provisions and controversial state boundaries set out in the treaties signed at the war's end.

World War II also resulted from the aggressive ambitions and racial theories of Germany and Japan. Both states sought to impose racial hierarchy (master and inferior races) through conquest and coerced labor. By the late 1930s, German and Japanese ambitions to become colonial powers brought these conservative dictatorships (which along with Italy constituted the **Axis powers**) into conflict with France, Britain, the Soviet Union, and eventually the United States (the **Allied powers**).

Even more than its predecessor, World War II was truly a world conflict, and a devastatingly total one. Fighting occurred in Europe, Africa, and Asia, the Atlantic and the Pacific, and the Northern and Southern hemispheres. Warring nations mobilized millions of people, including the colonized, into armed forces and placed enormous demands on civilians. Noncombatants in places such as India and Greece, Yugoslavia and Korea, Poland and the Philippines suffered terrible hardships, including famines, reprisal killings, and deportations in the course of this war without mercy. Moreover, as aerial bombardment of cities caused colossal civilian casualties, the total war erased the old distinction between soldiers and civilians. Women—as victims and as collaborators, as volunteers and as forced laborers, as workers behind the scenes and as witnesses to the conflict—were involved as never before. They, together with children, the infirm, and the elderly, also swelled the

MAP 20.1 | World War II: The European Theater

The Axis armies enjoyed great success during the early stages of World War II.

- Which states were within the Axis territory when World War II began in September 1939? What were the territorial boundaries when the Axis powers reached their greatest extent?
- When did the military balance begin to turn against Germany and Italy?

enormous population of refugees seeking safety in the midst of worldwide chaos.

World War II also completed the decline of European world dominance that World War I had set in motion. The unspeakable acts of barbarism perpetrated during the Second World War, including the Nazi genocides directed against Jews and others, robbed Europe of its lingering claims as a superior civilization. In the war's wake, anticolonial movements demanded national self-determination from battered and morally bankrupted European powers.

The War in Europe

Although Hitler had annexed Austria and parts of Czechoslovakia in 1938, World War II officially began in Europe in September 1939, with Germany's invasion of Poland and the British and French decision to oppose it. Before it was all over in 1945, much of Europe, including Germany, had been leveled.

BLITZKRIEG AND RESISTANCE Hitler's early success was staggering. His troops overran Poland, France, Norway, Denmark, Luxembourg, Belgium, and Holland. In 1940 he signed the Tripartite Pact with Italy and Japan, formalizing an alliance among the Axis powers. Within less than two years, the Germans controlled virtually all of Europe from the English Channel to the Soviet border (see Map 20.1). Only Britain escaped Axis control, although Nazi bombers pulverized British cities. In the east, Germany signed a nonaggression pact with the Soviet Union in 1939, after which the two powers once again partitioned Poland, murdering and deporting thousands. But in 1941 the German army broke its pact and invaded the Soviet Union with 170 divisions, 3,000 tanks, and 3.2 million men—an invasion force of a size unmatched before or since. Here, as elsewhere, the Germans fought a *blitzkrieg* ("lightning war") of tank-led assaults followed by motorized infantrymen and then foot soldiers. Already by October 1941, the Germans had reached the outskirts of Moscow. The Soviet Union seemed on the verge of a monumental defeat.

The Nazi war was not just a grab for land and raw materials; it was also a crusade for a new order based on race. Nazi racial occupation policies created massive social, economic, and political upheavals throughout Europe. Hitler established puppet governments that complied with deportation orders against Jews and dissidents. His new order made Europe a giant police state and spawned both collaborators and resistance fighters of many types. Among the resistance movements were both nationalists (who opposed German domination) and communists (who wanted to defeat both fascism and capitalism), who would fight among themselves even after the war was won.

In the east, the tide turned against the Germans and their collaborators after the ferocious battles of Stalingrad in 1942–1943 and Kursk in 1943. Once the Soviet army blunted the initial German assault, it launched a massive counteroffensive. This move initiated the defeat of the German war effort on the Eastern Front, but full retreat took another two years as the Soviets drove Hitler's army slowly westward. Before 1944 the Soviets bore the brunt of the fighting, causing more than 85 percent of all German casualties, although the British attacked the Nazis in the air and on the sea and, along with American troops, stopped a German advance across North Africa into Egypt. The spectacular D-Day landing of western Allied forces in Normandy on June 6, 1944 (when the Germans had a mere 15 divisions in France, against more than 300 on the Eastern Front), brought the Germans face to face with American and British troops also determined to fight their way to Germany. On April 30, 1945, as Soviet and Anglo-American forces converged on Berlin, Hitler committed suicide. Days later, Germany surrendered unconditionally. Still, what the postwar European map would look like remained unclear.

THE BITTER COSTS OF WAR The war in Europe had devastating human and material costs. This was particularly the case in eastern Europe, where German forces leveled more than 70,000 Soviet villages, obliterated one-third of the Soviet Union's wealth, and inflicted 7 million Soviet military deaths (by contrast, the Germans lost 3.5 million soldiers) and at least 20 million civilian deaths. German bombing of British cities, such as London, inflicted a heavy toll on civilians and buildings, as did Allied bombing of war plants and Axis cities like Dresden

The Devastation of War. (Left) *In the Battle of Britain, Nazi warplanes strafed British cities in an effort to break British morale. But the devastating bombing raids, such as this one in Coventry in November 1940, helped rally the British, who refused to give in.* (Right) *In November 1942, Nazi troops entered Stalingrad, some 2,000 miles from Berlin. Hitler wanted to capture the city not only to exploit the surrounding wheat fields and the oil of the Caucasus but also for its very name. With handheld flamethrowers and sometimes just their fists, Soviet troops drove out the Germans in February 1943.*

MAP 20.2 | World War II: The Pacific Theater

Like Germany and Italy, Japan experienced stunning military successes in the war's early years.

- In what directions did the Japanese direct their military offensives? Analyzing this map, why do you think the Japanese were so concerned about an American presence in East Asia, when the United States was so geographically distant? According to your reading, how did the Allied strategies to defeat the Japanese Empire shape postwar relations in the region?

and Tokyo. Urban casualties were perhaps greatest in Leningrad, a city that was surrounded and besieged for nine hundred days; 900,000 people lost their lives during this struggle. By the war's end, Poland had lost 6 million people and Great Britain had lost 400,000. Tens of millions in the east and west were left homeless.

Europe's Jews paid an especially high price. Hitler had long talked of "freeing" Europe of all Jews. At the war's outset, the Nazis herded Jews into ghettos and labor camps and then seized their property. As the German army moved eastward, more and more Jews came under their control. At first the Nazi bureaucrats

ANALYZING GLOBAL DEVELOPMENTS

World War II Casualties

World War II was the most destructive armed conflict in recorded history. It mobilized more than 120 million military personnel; more than 20 million died. The death toll of civilian populations was substantially greater. Civilian deaths directly caused by the war, including genocide, bombing, starvation, and disease, were estimated to range from 30 million to 55 million. Historians now put the total at roughly 60 million dead, including the 6 million Jews killed in the Holocaust, more than double the number killed in World War I.

A total reordering of the globe was at stake from the outset of World War II. The war was a struggle not only for the control of resources and territory, as World War I had been, but it was also fought to decide which peoples would control the world's resources and which peoples would be destroyed, because the aggressors decided that they were undesirable.

QUESTIONS FOR ANALYSIS

- Compare and contrast the casualties for World Wars I and II. (See the Analyzing Global Developments feature in Chapter 19.)
- Which countries endured the greatest loss of life in World War II and why? Which of the major participants in the war endured the fewest casualties and why?
- Contrast civilian and military casualties in World War II and explain why civilian casualty rates were so much higher than military losses?
- Many historians regard World War I as a greater turning point in European and western history than World War II, with its extraordinarily high loss of life. Why do you think historians would hold to this view? What is your view of the relative global importance of the two wars?

World War II Casualties

Nation	Population in 1939	Max. No. Mobilized	Military Deaths	Missing in Action	Civilian Deaths Due to War	Estimated Total Deaths
Belgium	8,386,000	800,000	22,651	55,513	76,000	88,000
Brazil	40,289,000	200,000		4,222		1,000
British Commonwealth		4,683,000	400,000	369,267	92,673	466,000
Australia	6,968,000	680,000	37,467	39,803		24,000
Canada	11,267,000	780,000	42,666	53,174		38,000
India	311,820,000	2,150,000	48,674	64,354		1,500,000
New Zealand	1,628,500	157,000	13,081	19,314		10,000
South Africa	10,160,000	140,000	8,681	14,363		7,000
UK	47,760,000	4,683,000	403,195	369,267	92,673	357,000
China	517,568,000	5,000,000	2,220,000	14,685,593		10,000,000
Czechoslovakia	15,300,000 (1938)	180,000	10,000	8,017	215,000	225,000

World War II Casualties (*continued*)						
Nation	**Population in 1939**	**Max. No. Mobilized**	**Military Deaths**	**Missing in Action**	**Civilian Deaths Due to War**	**Estimated Total Deaths**
Denmark	3,795,000	15,000	6,400	2,000	2,000	4,000
France	40,000,000	5,000,000	245,000	390,000	350,000	563,000
Greece	7,221,900	414,000	88,300	42,290	325,000	413,000
Netherlands	8,729,000	500,000	7,900	2,860	200,000	208,000
Norway	2,944,900	25,000	3,000	364	7,000	10,000
Poland	34,775,700	1,000,000	597,320	766,606	56,75,000	5,800,000
Philippines	16,000,300	105,000	127,000		91,000	118,000
United States	131,028,000	16,353,659	292,000	671,801	6,000	298,000
USSR	108,377,000	12,500,000	8,700,000	14,685,593		27,000,000
Yugoslavia	5,510,100	500,000	305,000	425,000	1,200,000	1,505,000
Bulgaria	6,458,000	450,000	18,500	21,878	10,000	20,000
Finland	3,700,000	250,000	82,000	50,000	2,000	84,000
Germany	69,622,500	9,200,000	325,000	7,250,000	780,000	4,200,000
Hungary	9,129,000	350,000	200,000	89,313	290,000	490,000
Italy	44,394,000	4,000,000	380,000	225,000	152,941	395,000
Japan	71,380,000	6,095,000	1,740,955	326,000	672,000	2,700,000
Romania	19,933,800	600,000	300,000		200,000	500,000
Indonesia	69,435,000					4,000,000

Total WWII Deaths: 60 million (including 6 million Jews)

Sources: Alan Axelrod (ed.), Encyclopedia of World War II, *vol. 1 (2007); John Dower,* War without Mercy *(1986); Geoffrey Hosking,* Rulers and Victims: The Russians in the Soviet Union *(2006).*

contemplated deportation but then ruled out transporting "subhumans" as too costly, and so settled for starving them and crowding them together in unsanitary ghettoes. By the summer of 1941, special troops operating behind the army on the Eastern Front had begun mass shootings of communists and Jewish civilians, and by fall 1941, Hitler and the S.S. (the *Schutzstaffel*, or special security forces) were building a series of killing centers. The largest concentration camp was Auschwitz-Birkenau in Poland. Cattle cars shipped Jews from all over Europe to the extermination sites in the east, where Nazis used the latest technology to kill men, women, and children. The deliberate racial extermination of the Jews, known as the **Holocaust**, claimed around 6 million European Jews. About half of this number died in the gas chambers of concentration camps; the others perished in face-to-face executions or from starvation, disease, or exhaustion. The Nazis also turned their mass killing apparatus against gypsies, homosexuals, communists, and Slavs, with deportations to the death camps continuing to the very end of the war.

The Pacific War

Like the war in Europe, the conflict in the Pacific transformed the military and political landscape (see Map 20.2). The war broke out when Japan's ambitions to dominate Asia targeted American interests and might.

JAPAN'S EFFORTS TO EXPAND Japan's expansionist aims became clear when its military invaded and occupied Manchuria in 1931 and then launched an offensive against the rest of China in 1937. Although the Japanese did not achieve China's complete submission, the invaders exacted a terrible toll on the population. Most infamous was the so-called rape of Nanjing, in which Japanese aggressors slaughtered at least 100,000 civilians and raped thousands of women in the Chinese city between December 1937 and February 1938.

Meanwhile, events in Europe opened opportunities for further Japanese expansion in Asia. Germany's swift occupation of western Europe left defeated nations' colonies at the mercy of Japanese forces. After concluding a pact with Germany in 1940, the Japanese occupied French Indochina in 1941 and made demands on the Dutch East Indies for oil and rubber. Now the chief obstacle to further expansion in the Pacific was the United States, which already had imperial interests in places like China and the Philippines, as well as other Pacific islands. Hoping to strike the United States before it was prepared for war, the Japanese launched a surprise air attack on the American naval base at Pearl Harbor in Hawaii on December 7, 1941. As the United States entered the war, Germany and Italy also declared war on America.

Japanese Aggression. *The brutal Battle of Shanghai (August–November 1937) marked the beginning of what turned out to be World War II in Asia. Claiming to be "protecting" China from European imperialists and expecting a relatively easy victory, the Japanese instead met with stiff resistance from the Chinese troops under Chiang Kai-shek. Here we see Japanese marines parading through the streets of the city after they finally broke through Chinese defenses. About a quarter of a million Chinese soldiers, close to 60 percent of Chiang's best troops, were killed or wounded in the campaign, a blow from which Chiang's regime never recovered. The Japanese sustained more than 40,000 casualties.*

Now Japan's expansion shifted into high gear. During 1942, its military racked up victory after victory over the tottering western armies. With French Indochina already under their control, the Japanese turned against the American colony of the Philippines and against the Dutch East Indies, both of which fell in 1942. By coordinating their army, naval, and air force units and using tactical surprise, the Japanese seized a huge swath of territory that included British-ruled Hong Kong, Singapore, Malaya, and Burma, while threatening the British Empire's hold on India as well.

Japan justified its aggression on the grounds that it was anticolonial and pan-Asian; Japan promised to drive out the European imperialists and to build a new order reflecting "Asia for Asians." In practice, however, the Japanese made terrible demands on fellow Asians for resources, developed myths of Japanese racial purity and supremacy, and treated Chinese and Koreans with brutality. During the war, Japan put up to 4 million Koreans to work for its empire, forcibly imported another 700,000 Korean men as laborers, and pressed up to 200,000 young women into service as prostitutes for Japanese soldiers. (In a similar move, the Nazi war effort in Europe involved forcing 12 million foreign laborers—including 2 million prisoners of war—to settle and work in Germany.)

ALLIED ADVANCES AND THE ATOMIC BOMB Like the Germans in their war against Russia, the Japanese could not

The Aftermath of the Atomic Bomb. (Left) *A view of Nagasaki less than half a mile from "ground zero" after the atomic bomb was dropped in August 1945. A few reinforced concrete buildings still stand.* (Right) *Thousands of people were immediately crushed or burned to death in the blast. Many died later from horrendous burns and radiation poisoning.*

sustain their military successes against the United States. By mid-1943, U.S. forces had put the Japanese on the defensive. Fighting from island to island, American troops recaptured the Philippines, and a combined force of British, American, and Chinese troops returned Burma to Britain. The Allies then moved toward the Japanese mainland. By summer 1945, American bombers had all but devastated the major cities of Japan. Yet Japan did not surrender.

Anticipating that an invasion of Japan would cost hundreds of thousands of American lives, U.S. president Harry Truman unleashed the Americans' secret weapon. It was the work of a team of scientists who were predominantly European refugees. On August 6, 1945, an American plane dropped an atomic bomb on the city of Hiroshima, killing or maiming over 100,000 people, and poisoning the air, soil, and groundwater for decades to come. Three days later, the Americans dropped a second atomic bomb on Nagasaki. Within days, Emperor Hirohito announced Japan's surrender.

THE BEGINNING OF THE COLD WAR

World War II left much of Europe in ruins. Charred embers lay where great cities had once stood. Major bridges lay crumbled at the bottom of rivers; railway lines were twisted scrap; sunken ships blocked harbors. Scarcity and hunger were widespread. Millions had died; tens of millions more were wounded, displaced, widowed, and orphaned. "What is Europe now?" mused British prime minister Winston Churchill. "A rubble heap, a charnel house, a breeding ground of pestilence and hate."

Rebuilding Europe

The task of political rebuilding was daunting, for the old order had been discredited. By contrast, communism gained new appeal because its credo promised a clean slate. Many eastern

Postwar Planning at Yalta. *The "Big Three" allies confer about the end of the war at the Black Sea resort of Yalta in February 1945. On the left is British prime minister Winston Churchill; at the center is American president Franklin Roosevelt; and on the right is Soviet premier Joseph Stalin.*

Europeans, following the horrors of fascism and not knowing the extent of Stalin's crimes, looked to the Soviets for answers. Even many of those opposed to the Soviets saw some form of socialism as a way to create powerful, modern, egalitarian societies in Europe.

Europe's leftward tilt alarmed U.S. policymakers. They feared that the Soviets would use their ideological influence and the territory taken over by the Red Army to spread communism. They also worried that Stalin might seize Europe's overseas possessions and create communist regimes outside Europe. But no one wished to fight another "hot" war. As President Truman began advocating a policy of containment to prevent the further advance of communism, an American journalist popularized the term *cold war* in 1946 to describe the new struggle.

Truman's containment policy was tested when the Soviets attempted to seize control of Berlin. Like the rest of Germany, Berlin had been partitioned into British, French, American, and Soviet zones of occupation; but the city itself was an island lying within the Soviet zone. In 1948, the Soviets attempted to cut the city off from western access by blocking western routes to the capital. The Allies responded with the Berlin Airlift, which involved transporting supplies in planes to western Berlin to keep the population from capitulating to the Soviets. This crisis lasted for almost a year, until Stalin allowed trucks to roll through the eastern zone in May 1949.

In that same year, occupied Germany was split into two hostile states: the democratic Federal Republic of Germany in the west, and the communist German Democratic Republic in the east. In 1961, leaders in the German Democratic Republic built a wall around West Berlin to insulate the east from capitalist propaganda and to halt a flood of émigrés fleeing communism. The **Berlin Wall** became the great symbol of a divided Europe and of the cold war. U.S. policymakers wanted to shore up democratic governments in Europe, so Truman promised American military and economic aid. Containing the spread of communism meant securing a capitalist future for western Europe, a job that fell to Truman's secretary of state, General George C. Marshall. He launched the Marshall Plan, an ambitious program that provided over $13 billion in grants and credits to reconstruct Europe and facilitate an economic revival. U.S. policymakers hoped the aid would dim communism's appeal by fostering economic prosperity, muting class tensions, and integrating western European nations into an alliance of capitalist democracies.

Stalin saw the Marshall Plan as a threat to the Soviet Union. He felt the same about the formation in 1949 of the **North Atlantic Treaty Organization (NATO)**, a military alliance between countries in western Europe and North America. He believed that the Soviet Union, having sacrificed millions of people to the war against fascism, deserved to be dominant in eastern Europe. Soviet troops had occupied eastern European nations at the war's end, and both communists and leftist members of other parties formed Soviet-backed coalition governments there. By tricking their moderate leftist allies and repressing their critics and opponents, the communists established dictatorships in Bulgaria, Romania, Hungary, and

The Berlin Airlift. *In summer 1948, a new currency was issued for the united occupation zones of West Germany. It began to circulate in Berlin at more favorable exchange rates than the eastern zone's currency, and Berlin seemed poised to become an outpost of the West inside the Soviet occupation zone. The Soviets responded by blocking western traffic into Berlin; the West countered with an airlift, forcing the Soviets to back down in May 1949 but hastening the division of Germany into two countries.*

MAP 20.3 | NATO and Warsaw Pact Countries

The cold war divided Europe into two competing blocs: those joined with the United States in the North Atlantic Treaty Organization (NATO) and those linked to the Soviet Union under the Warsaw Pact.

- Which nations had borders with nations belonging to the opposite bloc?
- Comparing this map with Map 20.1, explain how combat patterns in World War II shaped the dividing line between the two blocs.
- According to the map, where would you expect cold war tensions to be the most intense?

Czechoslovakia in 1948. In 1955, the Soviets formally allied themselves with these communist nations in the **Warsaw Pact**, a military alliance of their own (see Map 20.3). The tense confrontations between NATO and the Warsaw Pact in Europe and in other parts of the world in the 1950s and 1960s brought the world to the brink of an atomic World War III.

War in The Nuclear Age: The Korean War

The dropping of the atomic bombs on Japan in 1945 changed military affairs forever. Spurred by the onset of the cold war, the Soviets worked hard to catch up to the Americans, and in 1949 tested their first nuclear bomb. Thereafter, each side rushed to stockpile nuclear weapons and update its military technologies. By 1960, the explosive power of these weapons had increased so greatly that nuclear war might lead to the world's destruction without a soldier firing a single shot. This sobering realization changed the rules of the game. Each side now possessed the power to inflict total destruction on the other, a circumstance that inhibited direct confrontations but sparked smaller conflicts in parts of Asia, such as Korea, where the postwar settlement was murky.

In 1950, North Korean troops backed by the Soviet Union invaded U.S.-backed South Korea, setting off the **Korean War** (see Map 20.4). Claiming this violated the Charter of the United Nations, which had been established in 1945 to safeguard world peace and protect human rights, President Truman ordered American troops to drive back the North Koreans. The U.N. Security Council, thanks to a Soviet boycott, also sent troops from fifteen nations to restore peace. Within a year, the invaders had been routed and were near collapse. When U.N. troops advanced to the Chinese border, however, Stalin maneuvered his communist Chinese allies into rescuing the communist regime in North Korea and driving the South Korean and U.N. forces back to the old boundary. Across the Korean isthmus, communist and American-led U.N. troops waged a seesaw war. The fighting continued until 1953, when an armistice divided the country at roughly the same spot as at the start of the war. Nothing had been gained. Losses, however, included 33,000 Americans, at least 250,000 Chinese, and up to 3 million Koreans.

Atom Bomb Anxiety. *Schoolchildren taking shelter under their desks during an A-bomb drill in Brooklyn, New York, 1951. The Soviets had exploded their first test bomb in 1949. Underground bomb shelters were built in many American urban areas as places in which to survive a doomsday attack.*

The Korean War energized America's anticommunist commitments and spurred a rapid increase in NATO forces. U.S. policy shifted because Japan now was seen as a bulwark against communism. Although Japan renounced war in its postwar constitution, a 1951 treaty with the United States stipulated that the Japanese could rearm for self-defense and that American troops could be stationed in Japan. Moreover, the United States resolved to rebuild Japanese economic power. Like West Germany, Japan went from being the enemy in World War II to being a valued ally during the cold war.

DECOLONIZATION

The unsettling of all empires during the war inspired colonial peoples to reconsider their political futures. Rid of the Japanese, the liberated Asian territories had no desire to restore colonial or quasi-colonial rule. Africa, too, felt increasing pressure for decolonization. A weakened Europe emboldened anticolonial leaders to dismantle the European order and create a world of their own.

The process of **decolonization** and nation building followed three patterns: civil war, negotiated independence, and incomplete decolonization. The first occurred principally in China, where the ousting of Japanese occupiers led to a civil war that ended in a communist triumph. Here, national independence was associated with a socialist revolution. The second pattern, involving negotiated independence, played out in India and much of Africa. Algeria and South Africa illustrate the third pattern, in which the presence of sizeable European settler populations complicated the path from colony to nation.

The Chinese Revolution

The communist movement in China had its origins in post–World War I hostility toward the western powers. In this period, communists had vowed to free China from colonialism,

MAP 20.4 | The Korean War

The Korean War was an early confrontation between the capitalist and communist blocs during the cold war era.

- What were the dates of each side's farthest advance into the other side's territory?
- Why was this peninsula strategically important?
- According to your reading, how did the outcome of the war shape political affairs in East Asia for the next several decades?

The Long March. *In China, the Long March of 1934–1935 has been commemorated by the ruling communists as one of the most heroic episodes in the party's history. This picture shows communist partisans crossing the snow-covered mountains in the western province of Sichuan in 1935. Despite their efforts, the ranks of the party were decimated by the end of the 6,000-mile journey from the southeastern to the northwestern part of the country—fewer than one in eight reached their destination.*

but had been outgunned by Chiang Kai-shek's Nationalist regime and had been driven from China's cities; they retreated into the interior, where they founded base camps. In 1934, under attack by Chiang's forces, the communists, led by **Mao Zedong** (1893–1976), abandoned their bases and undertook an arduous 6,000-mile journey through rugged terrain of northwestern China (see Map 20.5). In the course of this great escape, glorified in communist lore as the Long March, fewer than 10,000 of the approximately 80,000 people who started the journey reached their destination. Fortunately for the communists, the Japanese invasion in 1937 diverted Nationalist troops and offered Mao and the survivors a chance to regroup.

The Japanese forces not only inflicted irreparable damage on the Nationalist military; they also further debilitated the capacity of Chiang's regime to govern areas that had not fallen to the invaders. Nationalist soldiers and citizens alike were often left to fend for themselves and became increasingly demoralized and disaffected. When the Japanese invaders seized China's major cities but were unable to control the countryside, the communists expanded their support among the vast peasantry. Mao's followers cultivated popular support by advocating the lowering of taxes, cooperative farming, and policies aimed at women, such as the outlawing of arranged marriages and the legalization of divorce. Like many anticolonial reformers, Mao regarded women's emancipation as a key component in building a new nation, since he considered their oppression to be both unjust and an obstacle to progress.

The communist expansion in the rural areas during World War II swelled its membership from 40,000 in 1937 to over a million in 1945. After Japan's surrender, China's civil war between Nationalists and communists resumed. But communist forces now had the numbers, the guns (mostly supplied by the Soviet Union), and the popular support to assault Nationalist strongholds. By contrast, although the Nationalist government had weapons and financing from the United States, as well as control of the cities, it had not recovered from its defeat at the hands of the Japanese. No match for the invigorated communists, the Nationalists fled to establish a rival Chinese state on the island of Taiwan.

In 1949, Mao proclaimed that China had "stood up" to the world and had experienced a "great people's revolution." Subsequently, many of his ventures proved disastrous failures (see later in this chapter), but China's model of an ongoing people's revolution provided much hope in the Third World. (See Primary Source: Mao Zedong on "New Democracy.")

Negotiated Independence in India and Africa

In India and most of colonial Africa, gaining independence involved little bloodshed, although the aftermaths were often extremely violent. The British, realizing that they could no longer rule India without coercion, bowed to the inevitable and withdrew. Much the same happened in Africa, even though British and French colonial officials knew that African territories were much less ready for independence than India.

INDIA Unlike China, India achieved political independence without an insurrection. But it did veer dangerously close to civil war. As anticolonial elites in the Indian National Congress Party negotiated a peaceful transfer of power from British rule, they disagreed about what kind of state an independent India should have. Should it, as Gandhi wished, be a nonmodern utopia of self-governing village communities, or should it emulate western and Soviet models with the goal of establishing a modern nation-state? Even more pressing was the question of relations between a Hindu majority and the Muslim minority.

MAP 20.5 | The Long March, 1934–1935

During the Long March, which took place during the struggle for power between the Guomindang (Nationalists) and the communists within China, communist forces traveled over 6,000 miles to save their lives and their movement.

- What route did the communist forces take?
- Why did the communists take this particular route?
- How did this movement affect the outcome of this internal struggle in the long run?

The Founding of the People's Republic of China. (Left) *Mao Zedong standing atop the reviewing stand at Tiananmen Square declares the founding of the People's Republic of China on October 1, 1949. Although most Chinese knew little about the communist party, many had high hopes for a new, independent, and liberated China.* (Right) *With flags flying, the crowd celebrates the dawn of a new era.*

For the most part, the congress leadership retained tight control over the mass movement that it had mobilized in the 1920s and 1930s. Even Gandhi hesitated to leave the initiative to the common people, believing that they had not yet assimilated the doctrine of nonviolence. Accordingly, Gandhi and the leadership worked hard to convince the British that they, the middle-class leaders, spoke for the nation. At the same time, the threat of a mass peasant uprising with radical aims (as was occurring in China) encouraged the British to transfer power quickly.

As negotiations moved forward, Hindu-Muslim unity deteriorated. Whose culture would define the new nation? The Indian nationalism that had existed in the late nineteenth century reflected the culture of the Hindu majority. Yet this movement masked the multiplicity of regional, linguistic, caste, and class differences *within* the Hindu community, just as Muslim movements that arose in reaction to Hindu-dominated Indian nationalism overlooked divisions within their own ranks. Now the prospect of defining "India" created a grand contest between newly self-conscious communities. Riots broke out between Hindus and Muslims in 1946, which increased the mutual distrust between congress and Muslim League leaders. The leader of the Muslim League demanded that British India be partitioned into separate Hindu and Muslim states if there were no constitutional guarantees for Muslims. The specter of civil war haunted the proceedings, as outgoing colonial rulers decided to divide the subcontinent into two states: India and Pakistan.

On August 14, 1947, Pakistan gained independence from Britain; a day later, India did the same. The euphoria of decolonization, however, drowned in a frenzy of brutality. Shortly after independence, up to 1 million Hindus and Muslims killed one another. Fearing further violence, 12 million Hindus and Muslims left their homes to relocate in the new countries

Jawaharlal Nehru. *Nehru, the leader of independent India, sought to create a "mixed economy" of private and public sectors with democracy to chart an independent path for India. The photo shows him at a public meeting in 1952.*

PRIMARY SOURCE

Mao Zedong on "New Democracy"

Many twentieth-century Chinese political and intellectual leaders, including the communists, believed that the rejuvenation of China required changing its culture. The key question was what to embrace and what to discard. Here we find Mao in 1940 explaining the New-Democratic culture—nationalistic, scientific, and mass-based—that he regarded as a transitional stage to communism. He cautions against the wholesale importation of western values and practices, including Marxism, and emphasizes instead the specific conditions of the Chinese revolution.

New-Democratic culture is national. It opposes imperialist oppression and upholds the dignity and independence of the Chinese nation. . . . China should absorb on a large scale the progressive cultures of foreign countries as an ingredient for her own culture; in the past we did not do enough work of this kind. We must absorb whatever we today find useful, not only from the present socialist or New-Democratic cultures of other nations, but also from the older cultures of foreign countries, such as those of the various capitalist countries in the age of enlightenment. However, we must treat these foreign materials as we do our food, which should be chewed in the mouth, submitted to the working of the stomach and intestines, mixed with saliva, gastric juice, and intestinal secretions, and then separated into essence to be absorbed and waste matter to be discarded—only thus can food benefit our body; we should never swallow anything raw or absorb it uncritically.

So-called wholesale Westernization is a mistaken viewpoint. China has suffered a great deal in the past from the formalist absorption of foreign things. Likewise, in applying Marxism to China, Chinese Communists must fully and properly unite the universal truth of Marxism with the specific practice of the Chinese revolution; that is to say, the truth of Marxism must be integrated with the characteristics of the nation and given a definite national form before it can be useful; it must not be applied subjectively as a mere formula. . . .

Communists may form an anti-imperialist and anti-feudal united front for political action with certain idealists and even with religious followers, but we can never approve of their idealism or religious doctrines. A splendid ancient culture was created during the long period of China's feudal society. To clarify the process of development of this ancient culture, to throw away its feudal dross, and to absorb its democratic essence is a necessary condition for the development of our new national culture and for the increase of our national self confidence; but we should never absorb anything and everything uncritically.

QUESTIONS FOR ANALYSIS

- How does Mao expect to integrate Marxism with the Chinese revolution?
- What does Mao think of China's "splendid ancient culture"? In this regard, how does he differ from previous rulers of China?

Source: Mao Zedong, Selected Works, *in* Sources of Chinese Tradition, *2nd ed., vol. 2, edited by Wm. Theodore de Bary and Richard Lufrano (New York: Columbia University Press, 2000), pp. 422–23.*

where they would be in the majority. Distraught by the rampage, Gandhi fasted, refusing sustenance until the killings stopped. The violence abated. This was perhaps Gandhi's finest hour. But animosity and fanaticism remained. Less than six months later, a Hindu zealot shot Gandhi dead as he walked to a prayer meeting.

Had Gandhi lived, he would not have approved of the direction independent India took. He had already voiced disapproval of industrialization and of equipping the Indian state with army and police forces. But India's first prime minister and leader of the Indian National Congress Party, Jawaharlal Nehru, and other leaders in the congress were committed to state-directed modernization. Inspired by Soviet-style planned development, on the one hand, and by western democratic institutions, on the other, Nehru sought a "socialistic pattern of society" based on a mixed economy of public and private sectors. Declaring that he wanted to give India the "garb of modernity," Nehru asked Indians to consider hydroelectric dams and steel plants the temples of modern India. He made his watchwords education and economic development, believing that these would loosen the hold of religion on Muslims and encourage them to join the national mainstream. He also hoped that the diminished role of religious traditions would improve women's condition. Such a vision allowed Nehru, until his death in 1964, to guide Indian modernization along a third path. (See Primary Source: Nehru on Building a Modern Nation.)

PRIMARY SOURCE

Nehru on Building a Modern Nation

The following excerpt, written by Jawaharlal Nehru in 1940, documents the centrality of planning in the desire to build a modern nation. Although the idea of planning derived from the Soviet experience, Nehru did not want India to adopt communism. He saw planned development as a scientific instrument for achieving rapid economic growth and fundamental social changes. Planning would avoid the excesses and inequalities of capitalism and provide a "third way"—equally distanced from both communism and capitalism.

The octopus of war grips and strangles the world and the energy of mankind is more and more directed to destroying what man has built up with infinite patience and labour. Yet it is clear that war by itself cannot solve any problem. It is by conscious, constructive and planned effort alone that national and international problems can be solved. In India many people thought, with reason, that it was premature to plan, so long as we did not have the power to give effect to our planning. The political and economic freedom of India was a prerequisite to any planning, and till this was achieved our national and international policy would continue to be governed, as heretofore, in the interests of the City of London and other vested interests. And yet we started, wisely I think, a National Planning Committee and we are trying, even in these days of world conflict and war, to draw up a picture of planned society in the free India of the future.

Our immediate problem is to attack the appalling poverty and unemployment of India and to raise the standards of our people. That means vastly greater production which must be allied to juster and more equitable distribution, so that the increased wealth may spread out among the people. That means a rapid growth of industry, scientific agriculture and the social services, all co-ordinated together, under more or less state control, and directed towards the betterment of the people as a whole. The resources of India are vast and if wisely used should yield rich results in the near future.

We do not believe in a rigid autarchy, but we do want to make India self-sufficient in regard to her needs as far as this is possible. We want to develop international trade, importing articles which we cannot easily produce and exporting such articles as the rest of the world wants from us. We do not propose to submit to the economic imperialism of any other country or to impose our own on others. We believe that nations of the world can co-operate together in building a world economy which is advantageous for all and in this work we shall gladly co-operate. But this economy cannot be based on the individual profit motive, nor can it subsist within the framework of an imperialist system. It means a new world order, both politically and economically, and free nations cooperating together for their own as well as the larger good.

QUESTIONS FOR ANALYSIS

- According to Nehru, what are the key problems that India faces?
- How does Nehru's vision of India compare to Gandhi's (see Chapter 19, p. 735)?

Source: Jawaharlal Nehru, "A Note to the Members of the National Planning Committee," May 1, 1940, in Jawaharlal Nehru: An Anthology, *edited by Sarvepalli Gopal (Delhi: Oxford University Press, 1980), pp. 306–7.*

AFRICA FOR AFRICANS Shortly after Indian independence, most African states also gained their sovereignty. Except for southern Africa, where minority white rule persisted, the old colonial states ceded to indigenous rulers. One reason for this rapid decolonization was the fact that nationalist movements had made gains during the interwar period. These years had taught a generation of nationalists to seek wider support for their political parties. World War II, then, swelled the ranks of anticolonial political parties, as many African soldiers expected tangible rewards for serving in imperial armies.

The postwar years also saw throngs of Africans flock to the cities in search of a better life. As expanding educational systems produced a wave of primary and secondary school graduates, these educated young people and other new urban dwellers became disgruntled when attractive employment opportunities were not forthcoming. The three groups—former servicemen, the urban unemployed or underemployed, and the educated—led the nationalist agitation that began in the late 1940s and early 1950s (see Map 20.6).

Faced with rising nationalist demands, and too much in debt themselves to invest more in pacifying the discontented, European powers agreed to decolonize. The new world powers, the Soviet Union and the United States, for their own reasons, also favored decolonization. Thus decolonization in most

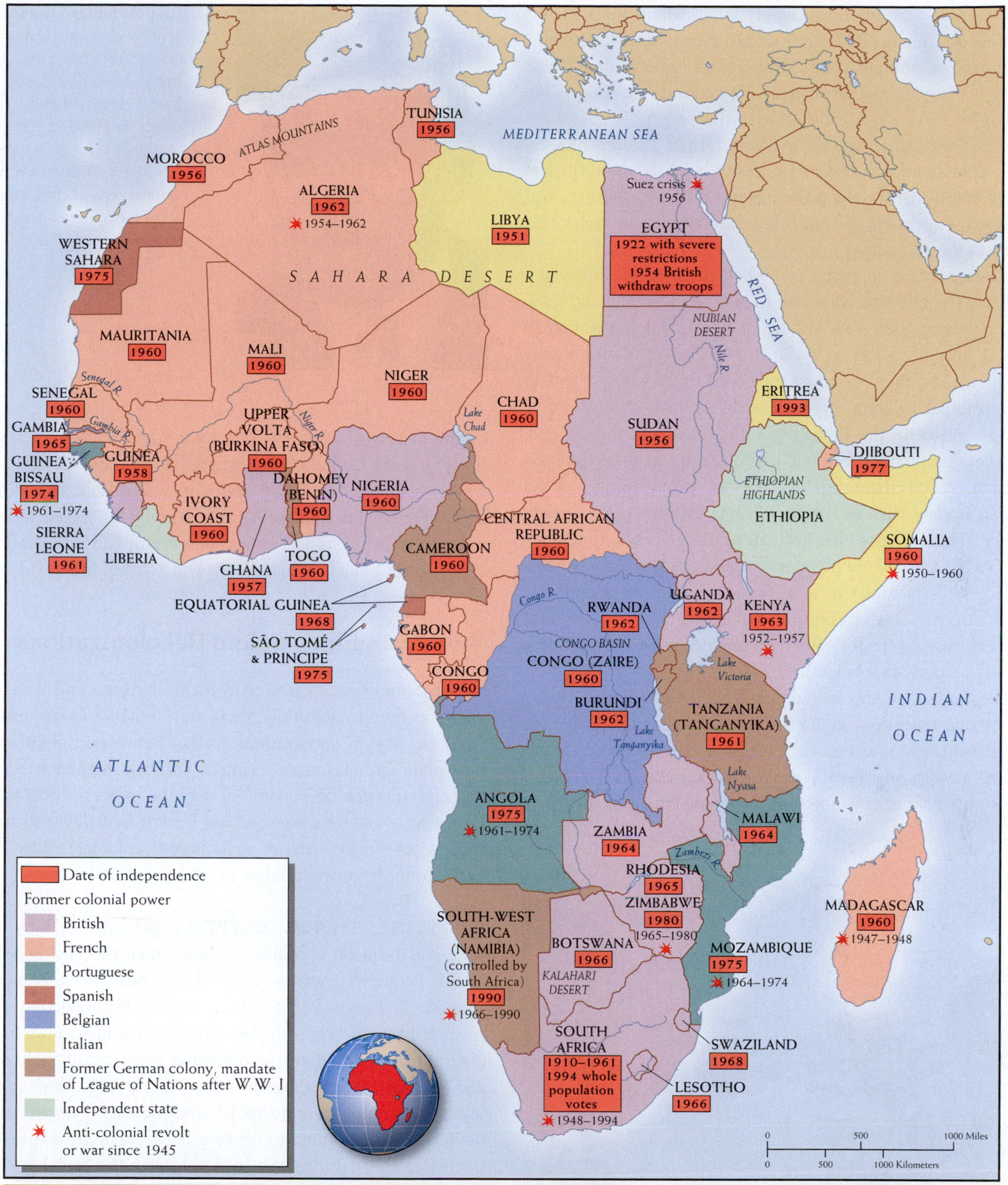

MAP 20.6 | Decolonization in Africa

African decolonization occurred after World War II, largely in the 1950s, 1960s, and 1970s.

- Find at least four areas that won independence in the 1950s, and identify which former colonial power had ruled each area.
- What areas took longer to gain independence?
- According to your reading, what problems and tensions contributed to this uneven process across Africa?

of Africa was a rapid and relatively sedate affair. In 1957, the Gold Coast (renamed Ghana) under Prime Minister Kwame Nkrumah became tropical Africa's first independent state. Other British colonial territories followed in rapid succession, so that by 1963 all of British-ruled Africa except for Southern Rhodesia was independent. In these former colonial possessions, charismatic nationalist leaders became the authorities to whom the British ceded power. Many of the new rulers had obtained western educations but were committed to returning Africa to the Africans.

Decolonization in much of French-ruled Africa followed a similarly smooth path, although the French were initially resistant. Believing their own culture to be unrivaled, the French treated decolonization as assimilation: instead of negotiating independence, they tried first to accord fuller voting rights to their colonial subjects, even allowing Africans and Asians to send delegates to the French National Assembly. In the end, however, the French electorate had no desire to share the privileges of French citizenship with overseas populations. Nor did African leaders wish to submerge their identities in a Greater France. Thus, France dissolved its political ties with French West Africa and French Equatorial Africa in 1960, having given protectorates in Morocco and Tunisia their independence in 1956. Algeria, always considered an integral part of France overseas, was a different matter. Its independence did not come quickly or easily (see below).

The leaders of African independence believed that Africa's precolonial traditions would enable the region to move from colonialism right into a special African form of socialism, escaping the ravages of capitalism. Without rejecting western culture completely, they vaunted the so-called African personality, exemplified by the idea of "Negritude" developed by Senegal's first president, Léopold Sédar Senghor. Negritude, they claimed, was steeped in communal solidarities and able to embrace social justice and equality, while rejecting the naked individualism that Africans felt lay at the core of European culture. (See Primary Source: Senghor's View of Political Independence.)

Léopold Sédar Senghor. *Senghor combined sharp intellect with political savvy. An accomplished poet and essayist and one of the founders of the Negritude movement among Francophone intellectuals, he became Senegal's first president when the country gained full independence in 1960.*

Kwame Nkrumah. *West Africa's leading nationalist Kwame Nkrumah mobilized the peoples of the Gold Coast and, through electoral successes, convinced the British to confer independence on the Gold Coast, which was renamed Ghana in 1957.*

Violent and Incomplete Decolonizations

Although transfers of power in most of Africa and Asia ultimately occurred peacefully, there were notable exceptions. In Palestine, Algeria, and southern Africa, the presence of European immigrant groups created violent conflicts that aborted any peaceful transfer of power—or left the process incomplete. In Vietnam, the process was also violent and delayed, partly because of France's desire to reimpose colonial control and partly from the power politics of cold war competition.

PALESTINE, ISRAEL, EGYPT In Palestine, Arabs and Jews had been on a collision course since the end of World War I. Before that war, a group of European Jews, known as Zionists, had argued that only an exodus from existing states to their place of origin in Palestine could lead to Jewish self-determination. **Zionism** combined a yearning to realize the ancient biblical injunction to return to the holy lands with a fear of anti-Semitism and anguish over increasing Jewish assimilation. Zionists wanted to create a Jewish state, and they won a crucial victory during World War I when the British government, under the Balfour Declaration, promised a homeland for the Jews in Palestine. But when the British awarded themselves Palestine as a mandate after 1918, they also guaranteed the rights of indigenous Palestinians, and sought to mediate between an increasing number of Zionist settlers and their Arab and Christian neighbors.

PRIMARY SOURCE

Senghor's View of Political Independence

One of the most striking visions of African independence as a "third way" came from the pen of Léopold Sédar Senghor, a Senegalese nationalist leader who became the first president of Senegal. The first excerpt, drawn from an essay published in 1959, differentiates the socialism of Africa from Marxism. The second excerpt, taken from a speech delivered in 1961, develops the idea of "Negritude," or black civilization, markedly different from but not inferior to European cultural forms.

AFRICAN SOCIALISM

In the respective programs of our former parties, all of us used to proclaim our attachment to socialism. This was a good thing, but it was not enough. Most of the time, we were satisfied with stereotyped formulas and vague aspirations, which we called scientific socialism—as if socialism did not mean a return to original sources. Above all, we need to make an effort to rethink the basic texts in the light of the Negro African realities. . . .

Can we integrate Negro African cultural values, especially religious values, into socialism? We must answer that question once and for all with an unequivocal "Yes.". . .

We are not Communists for a practical reason. The anxiety for human dignity, the need for freedom—man's freedom, the freedoms of collectivities—which animate Marx's thought and provide its revolutionary ferment—this anxiety and this need are unknown to Communism, whose major deviation is Stalinism. The "dictatorship of the proletariat," which was to be only temporary, becomes the dictatorship of the part and state by perpetuating itself. . . .

The paradox of socialistic construction in Communist countries—in the Soviet Union at least—is that it increasingly resembles capitalistic construction in the United States, the American way of life, with high salaries, refrigerators, washing machines, and television sets. And it has less art and freedom of thought. Nevertheless, we shall not be won over by a regime of liberal capitalism and free enterprise. We cannot close our eyes to segregation, although the government combats it; nor can we accept the elevation of material success to a way of life.

We stand for a middle course, for a *democratic socialism* which goes so far as to integrate spiritual values, a socialism which ties in with the old ethical current of the French socialists. . . . In so far as they are idealists, they fulfill the requirements of the Negro African soul, the requirements of men of all races and countries. . . .

A third revolution is taking place, as a reaction against capitalistic and Communistic materialism—one that will integrate moral, if not religious, values with the political and economic contributions of the two great revolutions. In this revolution, the colored peoples, including the Negro African, must play their part; they must bring their contribution to the construction of the new planetary civilization.

"WHAT IS NEGRITUDE?"

Assimilation was a failure; we could assimilate mathematics or the French language, but we could never strip off our black skins or root out black souls. And so we set out on a fervent quest for the "holy grail": our collective soul. And we came upon it. . . .

Negritude is the *whole complex of civilized values—cultural, economic, social, and political—which characterize the black peoples,* or, more precisely, the Negro-African world. All these values are essentially informed by intuitive reason, because this sentient reason, the reason which comes to grips, expresses itself emotionally, through that self-surrender, that coalescence of subject and object; through myths, by which I mean the archetypal images of the collective soul; and, above all, through primordial rhythms, synchronized with those of the cosmos. In other words, the sense of communion, the gift of mythmaking, the gift of rhythm, such are the essential elements of Negritude, which you will find indelibly stamped on all the works and activities of the black man.

QUESTIONS FOR ANALYSIS

- What is African socialism for Senghor?
- In what way, according to Senghor, does Negritude express Negro Africans' "collective soul"?

Source: Léopold Sédar Senghor, excerpts from African Socialism *(New York: American Society of African Culture, 1959), trans. Mercer Cook. Reprinted by permission of Moorland-Spingarn Research Center, Howard University, Washington, DC.*

As more Jews settled in Palestine, buying up land and seeking to increase their political influence, tensions rose between Zionists and Palestinian Arabs; both grew dissatisfied with British rule. Arabs resented the presence of Jews, who did not conceal their intention to create their own independent state and continued to buy land and displace farmers who had lived on the land for generations. The Zionists became especially enraged: when Hitler began persecuting the Jews of Europe, the British, authorities, mindful of Arab opposition and the Arab states' strategic oil wealth, vacillated over supporting Zionist

The Creation of the State of Israel. *Standing beneath a portrait of Theodore Herzl, the founder of the Zionist movement, David Ben Gurion, the first Israeli prime minister, proclaimed independence for the state of Israel in May 1948.*

demands for greater immigration. After World War II, the pressure to allow more immigration increased as hundreds of thousands of concentration camp survivors clamored for entry into Palestine, and Zionist militants began using force to attempt to gain control of the state.

In 1947, after the British announced that they would leave negotiations over the area's fate to the United Nations, that body voted to partition Palestine into Arab and Jewish territories. The Arab states rejected the partition, and the Zionist Agency only reluctantly accepted it. When the British withdrew their troops in 1948, a Jewish provisional government proclaimed the establishment of the state of Israel. Although the Jews were delighted to have an independent state, they were unhappy about its small size, its indefensible borders, and the fact that it did not include all the lands that had belonged to ancient Israel. For their part, the Palestinians were shocked at the partition, and they looked to their better-armed Arab neighbors to regain the territories set aside for the new state of Israel.

The ensuing **Arab-Israeli War** of 1948–1949 shattered the legitimacy of Arab ruling elites. Arab states entered the war poorly prepared to take on the well-run and enthusiastically supported Israeli Defense Force. By the time the United Nations finally negotiated a truce, Israel had extended its boundaries and more than 1 million Palestinians had become refugees in surrounding Arab countries.

Embittered by this defeat, a group of young officers in the Egyptian army plotted to overthrow a regime that they felt had not yet shed its colonial subordination. Although Egypt had acquired legal independence from Britain in 1936, the plotters believed that incompetent leaders were squandering the nation's sovereignty. One of the officers, Gamal Abdel Nasser, became the head of a secret organization of junior military officers—the Free Officers Movement. These men had ties with communists and other dissident groups, including the Muslim Brotherhood, which favored a return to Islamic rule. They launched a successful coup in 1952, forcing the king to abdicate and leave the country. Then they enacted a land reform scheme that deprived large estate owners of lands in excess of 200 acres and redistributed these lands to the landless and smallholders, who instantly became ardent supporters of the new regime. The new regime also dissolved the parliament, banned political parties (including the communists and the Muslim Brotherhood), and stripped the old elite of its wealth.

In 1956, Nasser moved to nationalize the Suez Canal Company (an Egyptian company, mainly run by French businessmen and experts), inciting the Israelis, the British, and the French to invade Egypt and seize territory along the Suez Canal. Opposition by the United States and the Soviet Union forced them to withdraw, providing Nasser with a spectacular diplomatic triumph. As Egyptian forces reclaimed the canal, Nasser's reputation as leader of the Arab world soared. He became the chief symbol of a pan-Arab nationalism that swept across the Middle East and North Africa and especially through the camps of Palestinian refugees.

THE ALGERIAN WAR OF INDEPENDENCE The appeal of Arab nationalism was particularly strong in Algeria, where

The Anglo-Egyptian Treaty. *The photo shows Egyptian president Nasser signing the Anglo-Egyptian Treaty with the British minister of state in 1954. The agreement ended the stationing of British troops on Egyptian soil and called for the withdrawal of British troops stationed at the Suez Canal military base. But shortly after the last British soldiers left Egypt in early 1956, Britain invaded the country in a vain effort to block Nasser's nationalization of the Suez Canal Company and to remove the Egyptian leader from power.*

a sizeable French settler population (the *colons*) stood in the way of a complete and peaceful decolonization. Indeed, French leaders claimed that Algeria was an integral part of France, an overseas department that was legally no different from Brittany or Normandy. Although the *colons* were a minority, they held the best land and lived in wealthy residential quarters in the major cities. Also, although all residents of Algeria were supposedly entitled to the same rights as the French citizenry, in fact the *colons* reserved these advantages to themselves.

As elsewhere, anticolonial nationalism in Algeria gathered force after World War II. When the French military responded with harsh countermeasures, the independence movement gained strength. The Front de Libération Nationale (FLN), the leading nationalist party, used violence to provoke its opponents and to make the local population choose between supporting the nationalist cause or the *colons*. The full-fledged revolt that erupted in 1954 pitted FLN troops and guerrillas against thousands of French troops. Atrocities and terrorist acts occurred on both sides.

The war dragged on for eight years, at a cost of perhaps 300,000 lives. At home, French society was torn asunder, for many French citizens had accepted the myth that Algeria was not a colonial territory but part of France itself. The *colons* insisted that they had emigrated to Algeria in response to their government's promises and that yielding power to the nationalists would be a betrayal. After an insurrection led by *colons* and army officers brought down the French government in 1958, the new French president, Charles de Gaulle, negotiated a peace accord.

Shortly after handing over power to FLN leaders, more than 300,000 *colons* left Algeria. By late 1962, over nine-tenths of the European population had departed. At independence, then, Algeria had a population mix no different from that of the other North African countries.

EASTERN AND SOUTHERN AFRICA The bloody conflict in Algeria highlights a harsh reality of African decolonization: the presence of European settlers prevented the smooth transfer of power. Even in British-ruled Kenya, where the European settler population had never been large, a violent war of independence broke out between European settlers and African nationalists. Employing secrecy and intimidation, the Kikuyu peoples, Kenya's largest ethnic group, organized a revolt. This uprising, which began in 1952, forced the British to fly in troops to suppress it, but ultimately the British government conceded independence to Kenya in 1963. Decolonization proved even more difficult in the southern third of the continent, where Portuguese Angola, Portuguese Mozambique, and British Southern Rhodesia (present-day Zimbabwe) did not gain independence until the 1970s.

Mau Mau Rebellion. *A large segment of the Kikuyu population rose up against the British colonial occupation of Kenya. This revolt, which began in 1952, was finally suppressed by British arms and Kikuyu "loyalists." Nonetheless, the Mau Mau Revolt led to Kenya's independence from British rule.*

Women played vital roles in these decolonization struggles. In Egypt, for example, the leading nationalists were all men, but they gained crucial support from educated and modernizing women, many of whom organized impressive demonstrations on their behalf. The wife of Sa'd Zaghlul, Egypt's most dynamic nationalist figure after World War I, gained a large following and a reputation as mother of the nation. Moreover, during Kenya's battle against British colonial rule, women supplied the fighters with food, medical resources, and information about the British. Those who were caught ended up in concentration camps and suffered brutal treatment from their prison guards. Yet, once independence was achieved, most women reverted to their traditional subordinate status.

South Africa, which held the continent's largest and wealthiest settler population (a mixture of Afrikaans-and English-speaking peoples of European descent), defied black majority rule longer than other African states. After winning the elections of 1948, the Afrikaner-dominated National Party enacted an extreme form of racial segregation known as **apartheid**. Under apartheid, laws stripped Africans, Indians, and colored persons (those of mixed descent) of their few political rights. Racial mixing of any kind was forbidden, and schools were strictly segregated. The Group Areas Act, passed in 1950, divided the country into separate racial and tribal areas and required Africans to live in their own racial areas, called homelands. Pass laws prohibited Africans from traveling outside their homelands without special work or travel passes.

The ruling party tolerated no protest. Nelson Mandela, one of the leaders of the African National Congress (ANC) who campaigned for an end to discriminatory legislation, was repeatedly harassed, detained, and tried by the government, even though he urged peaceful resistance. After the Sharpeville massacre in 1960, in which police killed demonstrators who were peacefully protesting the pass laws, Mandela and the ANC decided to oppose the apartheid regime with violence. Subsequently the government announced a state of emergency, banned the ANC, and arrested those of its leaders who had not fled the country or gone underground. A South African court sentenced Mandela to life imprisonment. Other black leaders were tortured or beaten to death. Here, too, women kept resistance flames burning. The most dynamic of these individuals was Winnie Mandela, wife of the imprisoned Nelson Mandela. Unlike many of the ANC leaders, who opposed the regime from exile, she remained behind and openly and courageously spoke out against the apartheid government. Despite such human rights violations, the whites retained external support. Through the 1950s and 1960s, western powers (especially the United States) saw South Africa as a bulwark against the spread of communism in Africa.

Apartheid Protest. *In Johannesburg, South Africans march in the street to protest the new restrictions on African citizens, soon to be known worldwide as apartheid, implemented by the white minority government of Daniel Malan. During the Malan administration (1948–1954), informal discrimination was systematically made law, and all electoral, housing, civil, and employment rights of African citizens were dismantled.*

VIETNAM The same concern to contain communism also drew the United States into support for a regime in South Vietnam. Vietnam had come under French rule in the 1880s, and by the 1920s approximately 40,000 Europeans were living among and ruling over roughly 19 million Vietnamese. To promote an export economy of rice, mining, and rubber, the colonial rulers granted vast land concessions to French companies and local collaborators, while leaving large numbers of peasants landless.

The colonial system also generated a new intelligentsia. Primarily schooled in French and Franco-Vietnamese schools, educated Vietnamese worked as clerks, shopkeepers, teachers, and petty officials. Yet they had few opportunities for advancement in the French-dominated colonial system. Thus, discontented, they turned from the traditional ideology of Confucianism to modern nationalism. Vietnamese intellectuals overseas, notably Ho Chi Minh, took the lead in imagining a new Vietnamese nation-state.

Ho had left Vietnam at an early age and found his way to London and Paris. During the interwar period he read the writings of Marx, Engels, and Lenin, and he discovered not only an ideology for opposing French exploitation but also a vision for transforming the common people into a political force. He was

Ho Chi Minh. *Ho Chi Minh's formation of the League for the Independence of Vietnam, or Viet Minh, in 1941 set the stage for Ho's rise at the end of World War II. Here he attends a youth rally in October 1955, just over a year after the victory of his forces at Dien Bien Phu, which resulted in the ousting of the French from Vietnam.*

a founding member of the French communist party and subsequently founded the Indochinese communist party. After the Japanese occupied Indochina, he traveled to China, embraced the idea of an agrarian revolution, and established the Viet Minh, a liberation force, in 1941. Back in Vietnam, the communist-led Viet Minh became a powerful nationalist organization as it mobilized the peasantry.

When the French tried to restore their rule in Vietnam after Japan's defeat in 1945, Ho appealed to the United States (for whom he had been an intelligence agent during the war) for diplomatic and moral support. His appeals fell on deaf ears, but the Viet Minh declared independence anyway. War with France followed (1946–1954), featuring guerrilla tactics to undermine French positions. The Viet Minh were most successful in the north, but even in the south their campaign bled the French. Finally, in 1954, the anticolonial forces won a decisive military victory. At the Geneva Peace Conference, Vietnam (like Korea) was divided into two zones. Ho controlled the north, while a government with French and American support took charge in the south.

Although the French departed, decolonization in Vietnam was incomplete. North Vietnam supported the Viet Cong—communist guerrillas—who combined anti-imperialist nationalism with a land reform program that appealed greatly to the peasants. Determined to contain the spread of communism in Southeast Asia, the United States began smuggling arms to the regime in the south. During the early 1960s, U.S. involvement escalated. In 1965, large numbers of American troops entered the country to fight on behalf of South Vietnam, while communist North Vietnam turned to the Soviet Union for supplies. Over the next several years, the United States sent some 500,000 soldiers to fight the **Vietnam War**, but peasant support enabled the Viet Cong to continue fierce guerrilla fighting. Even the bombing of villages and the deployment of counterinsurgency forces failed to prevent the spread of communism in Southeast Asia.

Faced with antiwar opposition at home and ferocious resistance from the Vietnamese, the U.S. government adopted the policy of "Vietnamization"—that is, placing the responsibility of fighting the communists on the South Vietnamese puppet government. Vietnamization was a convenient fiction spun to enable the United States to withdraw without losing face. In 1975, just two years after the final withdrawal of American troops, the South Vietnamese government collapsed.

THREE WORLDS

World War II made the Soviet Union and the United States into superpowers. Possessing nuclear weapons, superior armies, and industrial might, they vied for global influence. As decolonization spread, the two cold war belligerents offered new leaders their models for modernization. On one side, the United States, together with its western European allies and Japan, had developed democratic forms of governance and a dynamic capitalist economy that produced immense quantities of affordable consumer goods. The Soviet Union, on the other side, trumpeted the communist party's egalitarian ideology and its rapid transition from being "backward" to highly industrialized. Both the First World and the Second World expected the decolonized Third World to adopt their models.

The decolonized, however, had their own ideas. With the communist takeover in 1949, China had shrugged off semicolonial status, but Mao soon broke from Soviet direction. Other decolonized nations in Asia and Africa had underdeveloped economies and could not leap into capitalist or communist industrial development. Moreover, in some places decolonization remained incomplete, and civilians were not allowed even a "cold" peace.

The First World

As the cold war spread in the early 1950s, western Europe and North America became known as the **First World**, or "the free world." Later on, Japan joined this group. Following the principles of liberal modernism, First World states sought to organize the world on the basis of capitalism and democracy. Yet, in struggling against communism, the free world sometimes aligned with Third World dictators, thereby sacrificing its commitment to freedom and democracy for the sake of propping up pro-western regimes.

WESTERN EUROPE The reconstruction of western Europe after World War II was a spectacular success. By the late 1950s, most nations' economies there were thriving, thanks in part to massive American economic assistance. Improvements in agriculture were particularly impressive. With increased mechanization and the use of pesticides, fewer farmers were feeding more people. In 1950, for example, each French farmer had produced enough food for seven people; by 1962, one farmer could feed forty. And as industrial production boomed and wages rose, goods that had been luxuries before the war—refrigerators, telephones, automobiles, indoor plumbing—became commonplace. Prosperity and the dismantling of national military establishments allowed governments to expand social welfare systems, such that by the late 1950s education and health care were within the reach of virtually all citizens.

Western Europe's economic recovery blunted the appeal of socialist and communist programs. Moreover, the cold war slowed down efforts to punish fascists, Nazis, and collaborators. Although war crimes trials brought the conviction of a number of prominent Nazis, the fear was that a complete de-Nazification would deprive Germany of political and economic leaders, leaving it susceptible to communist subversion.

THE UNITED STATES While Europe lay in ruins, the United States enjoyed economic expansion and a rising standard of living. Americans could afford more consumer goods than ever before—almost always U.S. manufactures. Home ownership became more common, especially in the burgeoning suburbs. Stimulating suburban development was a baby boom that reversed more than a century of declining birth rates. Indeed, in contrast to the gloomy 1930s, in the 1950s Americans enjoyed unprecedented prosperity.

Yet, even as suburbanites basked in the affluence that they credited to free enterprise, anxieties about the future of the free world abounded. Following the Soviet Union's explosion of an atomic bomb, the communist revolution in China, and the outbreak of the Korean War, fear of the communist threat prompted increasingly harsh rhetoric. In fact, anticommunist hysteria led the Republican senator from Wisconsin, Joseph McCarthy, to initiate a campaign to uncover closet communists in the State Department and in Hollywood. Televised congressional hearings broadcast his views to the entire nation. Although by late 1954 the tide had turned against him, McCarthyism persisted in American foreign policy. Now almost all elected officials, not wanting to seem "soft" on communism, voted to spend more money on American armies and armaments.

Postwar American prosperity did not benefit all citizens equally. During the prosperous 1950s, nearly a quarter of the American population lived in poverty. But many African

Levittown. *In the decades after World War II, the American population shifted from the cities to the suburbs. To satisfy the demand for single-family homes, private developers, assisted by government policies, built thousands of new communities on the outskirts of urban centers. Places like Long Island's Levittown (pictured here), made affordable by the use of standard designs and construction, enabled many middle-class Americans to own their own homes.*

Anticommunism. *As the Cold War heated up, anticommunist fervor swept the United States. Leading the charge against the "communist conspiracy" was Wisconsin senator Joseph McCarthy, pictured here with his aide, the attorney Roy Cohn.*

Civil Rights Movement. *The 1955 arrest of Rosa Parks* (left), *for refusing to relinquish her seat on a Montgomery, Alabama, bus, led to a boycott that brought Martin Luther King, Jr. to prominence and galvanized the challenge to legal racial segregation in the American South.* (Right) *Borrowing from Gandhi's tactics of nonviolent civil disobedience, protesters staged "sit-ins" across the southern United States in the 1950s and early 1960s, as in this photograph of black and white students seated together at a segregated lunch counter in Jackson, Mississippi.*

Americans, a group disproportionately trapped below the poverty line, participated in a powerful movement for equal rights and the end of racial segregation. The National Association for the Advancement of Colored People (NAACP) won court victories that mandated the desegregation of schools. Boycotts, too, became a weapon of the growing **civil rights movement**, with **Martin Luther King, Jr.** (1929–1968) leading a successful strike against injustices in the bus system of Montgomery, Alabama. Here and in subsequent campaigns against white supremacy, King borrowed his most effective weapon—the commitment to nonviolent protest and the appeal to conscience—from Gandhi. As the civil rights movement spread, the federal government gradually supported programs for racial equality.

THE JAPANESE "MIRACLE" An impressive triumph for the western liberal capitalist vision was the emergence of Japan as a postwar economic powerhouse. The war had ended with Japan's unconditional surrender in 1945, its dreams of dominating East Asia dashed, and its homeland devastated. But after 1945, in an attempt to incorporate Japan into the First World, American military protection, investment, and transfers of technology helped to rebuild Japanese society. The Japanese government guided this economic development through directed investment, partnerships with private firms, and protectionist policies. To promote an export-driven economy, the government encouraged its citizens to save, not spend. By the mid-1970s, Japan, formerly a dictatorship, was a politically stable civilian regime with a thriving economy.

The Second World

The scourge of World War II and the shadow of the cold war fell heavily on the Soviet Union, which with its satellites in eastern and central Europe as well as Mongolia and North Korea constituted the **Second World**. Having suffered more deaths and more damage than any other industrialized nation, the Soviet Union was determined to insulate itself from future aggression from the West. That meant turning eastern Europe into a bloc of communist buffer states.

THE APPEAL OF THE SOVIET MODEL The Soviet model's egalitarian ideology and success with rapid industrialization made it seem a worthy alternative to capitalism. Here, there was no private property and thus, in Marxist terms, no exploitation. Workers "owned" the factories and worked for themselves. The Soviet state promised full employment, boasting that a state-run economy would be immune from upturns and downturns in business cycles. Freedom from exploitation, combined with security, was contrasted with the capitalist model of owners hoarding profits and suddenly firing loyal workers when they were not needed.

Soviet Model. *The rapid infrastructural development under Stalin was certainly a great feat, though at the great loss of human life. Displayed in this German poster is a map of new canals constructed in this period as part of Stalin's Five Year Plan.*

The Soviet system touted protections for workers, inexpensive mass transit, paid maternity leave, free health care, and universally available education. Whereas under the tsarist regime less than one-third of the Russian Empire's population had been literate, by the 1950s the literacy rate soared above 80 percent. True, Soviet policies did not provide material abundance of the sort that First World nations were enjoying. But if consumer goods were often scarce, they were always cheap. Likewise, while it sometimes took ten years to obtain a small apartment through waiting lists at work, when one's turn finally came the apartment carried low annual rent and could be passed on to one's children.

Critical to the Soviet system's attractiveness was the fact that few among the population knew how their counterparts lived in the capitalist world. Government censors skewed news about the First World and suppressed unfavorable information about the Soviet Union and the communist bloc. Yet, even when people learned about the prosperity of western Europe and the United States (usually from western films and radio), they still contended that the Soviet Union was the more just society. Theirs, they believed, was a land with no racial or class divisions at all. If members of the Soviet elite lived in privileged circumstances, their luxurious lifestyles were well concealed. Indeed, socialism's internal critics did not typically seek to overthrow the system and restore capitalism. Rather, they wanted the Soviet regime to introduce reforms that would create "socialism with a human face."

REPRESSION OF DISSENT Few outside the Soviet sphere knew just how inhuman Soviet communism was, and few within knew the extent of the brutality. After the war, the leadership tightened its grip. Surviving soldiers who had been prisoners of war in Germany and civilians who had survived being slave laborers for the Germans were sent to special screening camps, simply because they had been abroad; many disappeared. By the time of Stalin's death in 1953, the vast gulag (labor camp complex) confined several million people, who dug for gold and uranium and survived on hunks of bread and gruel.

Stalin's successors had to face hard questions: What to do with so many prisoners? How to explain the existence of the labor camp system? This problem became acute when strikes rocked the camps. In 1956, the new party leader, Nikita Khrushchev, delivered a speech at a closed session of the Communist Party Congress in which he attempted to separate Stalin's crimes from true communism. The speech was never published in the Soviet Union, but party members distributed

The Gulag. *The Soviet labor camp system was an integral part of the Soviet economy. At any given time, around 3 million prisoners labored in camps, like this one in Perm, Siberia, felling timber, building railroads, or digging for gold. Several million more were forced into exile in isolated locales. During World War II, the gulag population fell drastically, as inmates were sent to certain death at the front or perished from starvation. Between the war's end and Khrushchev's destalinization in the 1950s, the gulag system reached its peak, with German and Japanese POWs, the deportation of entire nations, and the Soviet internment of its own returnees from German camps.*

it to party organizations abroad. The crimes that Khrushchev revealed came as a terrible shock.

Repercussions were far-reaching. Eastern European leaders interpreted Khrushchev's speech as an endorsement for political liberation and economic experimentation. Right away, Polish intellectuals began a drive to break free from the communist ideological straitjacket. Soon Polish workers organized a general strike in Poznań—first over bread and wages, then against Soviet occupation. Emboldened by these events, Hungarian intellectuals and students held demonstrations demanding an uncensored press, free elections with genuine alternative parties, and the withdrawal of Soviet troops. The Hungarian Party leader, Imre Nagy, endorsed the campaign for reform and threatened to withdraw from the Warsaw Pact.

But the seeming liberalization promised by Khrushchev's speech proved short-lived. Rather than let eastern Europeans stray, the Soviet leadership crushed dissent. In Poland, the security police massacred strikers. In Hungary, tanks from the Soviet Union and other Warsaw Pact members invaded and installed a new government that aimed to smash all "counterrevolutionary" activities; Nagy was kidnapped, then murdered. After the revolts, Hungary and Poland did win some economic and cultural autonomy; but unquestionably, the Second World remained very much the dominion of the Soviet Union.

Despite its repressive policies, the Soviet Union was undeniably a superpower. In fact, its status surged after the launching of Sputnik, the first satellite, into space in 1957. Students from Third World countries flocked to the Soviets' excellent education system for training as engineers, scientists, army commanders, and revolutionaries. The updated 1961 communist party program predicted euphorically that within twenty years the Soviet Union would surpass the United States and eclipse the First World, but reckless industrialization left terrible scars both on the population and on the landscape. (See Current Trends in World History: Soviet Ecocide.)

The Third World

In the 1950s, French intellectuals coined the term **Third World** (*tiers monde*) to describe those countries that, like the "third estate" in the 1789 French Revolution, represented the majority of the population but were oppressed. By the early 1960s, the term characterized a large bloc of countries in Asia, Africa, and Latin America. All had experienced colonial domination and now aimed to create more just societies than those of the First and Second worlds. Their leaders believed that they could build strong democratic societies, like those in the West, and promote rapid economic development, as the Soviet Union had done. All this could occur, they felt, without the empty materialism of western capitalism or the state oppression of communist regimes.

The early 1960s were years of heady optimism in the Third World. Ghanaian prime minister Kwame Nkrumah trumpeted pan-Africanism as a way to reach a par with the rest of the world. Egyptian president Gamal Abdel Nasser boasted that his

Hungarian Revolt. *Khrushchev's secret 1956 speech denouncing Stalin's crimes unintentionally destabilized the communist bloc. Tanks of the Soviet-led Warsaw Pact crossed into Hungary to put down a revolt that year, restoring the Soviet-style system but damaging Soviet prestige. Some American officials and especially American-supported radio had encouraged the Hungarians to rise up but then did nothing to support them, damaging U.S. prestige. The upshot was a turn to "national communism" in the Soviet satellites as a way to promote stability and loyalty.*

CURRENT TRENDS IN WORLD HISTORY

Soviet Ecocide

Before the twentieth century, the spread of peasant agriculture, settlement in the steppe and forest zones, and the hunting of fur-bearing forest animals brought profound changes in the Russian environment, including soil degradation, deforestation, and depopulation of species. But the environmental impact of Soviet-era industrialization was staggering. No other industrial civilization poisoned its land, air, water, and people so systematically and over so long a time. Scholars have deemed the Soviet environmental catastrophe an "ecocide."

Soviet economic planners and propagandists celebrated the plumes of purple and orange smoke in their skies as evidence of their huge quantities of industrial production. Pollution-control devices remained unheard of well after their 1950s introduction in Europe and the United States; even when installed in Soviet factories, they were rarely turned on so as not to depress output. Sulfur dioxide, hydrogen sulfide, and solid phenols in water, the food supply, and the air caused epidemic levels of respiratory and intestinal ailments, blood diseases, and birth defects. The giant steel plant at Magnitogorsk, once the pride of Stalin's industrial leap, became a zone of atmospheric and soil devastation 120 miles long and 40 miles wide; inside, chronic bronchitis, asthma, and cancers attacked the population.

In agriculture, the Soviet Union continued to use the fertilizer DDT long after its 1972 banning in the U.S. Despite the socialist country's overall development, in the 1970s Soviet life expectancy began to decline and infant mortality to rise. By 1989, Soviet men lived an average of 63.9 years from birth, down from 66.1 in 1965. Infant mortality by the late 1980s rose to 25.4 per 1,000—roughly the same as in Malaysia, a developing country, and Harlem, NY. Alcoholism also contributed mightily to adverse health trends.

The April 1986 Chernobyl nuclear disaster exposed 20 million people in Ukraine and Belarus to excess radiation. Although there was no bomb concussion, the accident spewed more radioactive material into the atmosphere than had been released in the atomic bombs over Hiroshima and Nagasaki. The Chernobyl cleanup claimed around 7,000 lives. Soviet Uzbekistan, with twice the population of Soviet Belarus, was served by only one-third the hospitals.

Few symbols of Soviet ecocide surpassed the Aral Sea. Because of dams built for wasteful power plants and excess irrigation for cotton production, the Aral's volume shrank by two-thirds and gave way to huge white, lifeless salt marshes. Soviet cosmonauts looking down from space in 1975 were astonished to see immense storms of dust and salt over Central Asia. Toxic salt rain wreaked enormous damage on human and animal lungs.

From the 1950s, Lake Baikal, the largest fresh body of water, and once among

democratic socialism was neither western nor Soviet and that Egypt would remain neutral in the cold war struggle. Indian prime minister Jawaharlal Nehru blended democratic politics and vigorous state planning to promote India's quest for political independence and economic autonomy.

LIMITS TO AUTONOMY Charting a third way proved difficult. Both the Soviets and the Americans saw the Third World as "underdeveloped," and Americans especially wanted to ensure that market structures and private property underlay modernization. The western powers looked to two new instruments of global capitalism, the World Bank and the International Monetary Fund (IMF), to provide crucial economic guidance in the Third World. The World Bank funded loans for projects to lift poor societies out of poverty (such as providing electricity in India and building roads in Indonesia), while the IMF supported the new governments' monetary systems when they experienced economic woes (as in Ghana, Nigeria, and Egypt). Yet both institutions also intruded on these states' autonomy.

Another force that threatened Third World economic autonomy was the multinational corporation. In the rush to acquire advanced technology, Africans, Asians, and Latin Americans struck deals with multinationals to import their know-how. Owned primarily by American, European, and Japanese entrepreneurs, firms such as United Fruit, Firestone, and Volkswagen expanded cash cropping and plantation activities and established manufacturing branches worldwide. But such corporations impeded the growth of indigenous firms. Although the world's nations were more economically interdependent, the West still made the decisions—and reaped most of the profits.

Whether dealing with the West or the Soviet Union, Third World leaders had limited options because neither side welcomed neutral parties. To create more client states, the Soviet Union backed communist insurgencies around the globe, while the United States supported almost all leaders who declared their anticommunism. Indeed, to contain communist expansion, the United States formed a number of military alliances. Following the 1949 creation of NATO, similar regional arrangements

Aral Sea catastrophe. *What was once one of the largest lakes in the world shrank to less than 10 percent of its original size, due to the aggressive Soviet construction of irrigation canals in the sixties to bolster cotton production. Here a shipping vessel is moored in the field of the former Aral Sea, in present-day Kazakhstan.*

the cleanest, suffered the construction of factories on its perimeter, especially a cellulose cord plant (for tires on Soviet bombers) and pulp plant (for paper). The threat to Baikal, as well as the Aral Sea catastrophe, sparked grassroots environmental groups in an otherwise tightly controlled Soviet society. Scientists led the way in breaking censorship taboos, and people from all walks of life turned up at unsanctioned meetings and signed their names to petitions to stop the damage and protect the environment.

QUESTIONS FOR ANALYSIS

- Why do you think environmental degradation was so much more severe in the Soviet Union compared to western powers?
- Why do you think environmental awareness developed much sooner in the United States than in the Soviet Union?

Explore Further

Feshbach Murray, and Alfred Friendly, Jr. *Ecocide in the USSR: Health and Nation under Siege* (1992).

Wiener, Douglas R. *A Little Corner of Freedom: Russian Nature Protection from Stalin to Gorbachev* (2002).

took shape in Southeast Asia (SEATO) and in the Middle East (the Baghdad Pact). These organizations brought many Third World nations into American-led alliances and allowed the United States to establish military bases in foreign territories. The Soviet Union countered by positioning its own forces in other Third World countries.

Nowhere was the militarization of Third World countries more threatening to economic development than in Africa. Whereas in the colonial era African states had spent little on military forces, this trend ended abruptly once the states became independent and were drawn into the cold war. Civil wars, like the one that splintered Nigeria between 1967 and 1970, were opportunities for the great powers to wield influence. When the West refused to sell weapons to the Nigerian government so it could suppress the breakaway eastern province of Biafra, the Soviets supplied MIG aircraft and other vital weapons. A similar situation occurred in Egypt, a strategic region to both superpowers. After the founding of Israel, Egypt's new military rulers insisted that their country never again be caught militarily unprepared. Aware of the West's support for Israel, the Egyptians turned to the Soviet bloc. The resulting arms race between Egypt and Israel left the region bristling with modern weaponry.

Thus, Third World nations now confronted a situation that has been called **neocolonialism**. How were they to apply liberal or socialist models to their own situations? How were they to deal with economic relations that seemed to reduce their autonomy and limit their development? And how might they escape being puppets of the West or the Soviet Union? No wonder Third World nations grew frustrated about prospects for an alternative way to modernity.

By the mid-1960s, as the euphoria of decolonization evaporated and new states became mired in debt and dependency, many Third World nations fell into dictatorship and authoritarian rule. Although some dictators still spoke about forging a third way, they did so mainly to justify their own corrupt regimes. They had forgotten the democratic commitments that were promised at independence. Most also had been drawn into the cold war, the better to extract arms and assistance from one of the superpowers.

REVOLUTIONARIES AND RADICALS Against the background of blasted expectations, Third World radicalism emerged as a powerful force. Revolutionary movements in the late 1950s and the 1960s sought to transform their societies. But while some radicals seized power, they, too, had trouble cracking the existing world order.

Third World revolutionaries drew on the pioneering writings of Frantz Fanon (1925–1961). While serving as a psychiatrist in French Algeria, Fanon (who was born in a French Caribbean colony) became aware of the psychological damage of European racism. He subsequently joined the Algerian Revolution and became a radical theorist of liberation. His 1961 book *The Wretched of the Earth* urged Third World peoples to achieve catharsis through violence against their European oppressors. The book also scathingly criticized those Third World nationalists who wished merely to replace European masters without making radical social changes.

THE MAOIST MODEL While Fanon moved people with his writings, others did so by building radical political organizations and undertaking revolutionary social experiments. One model was Mao Zedong. In 1958, Mao introduced the Great Leap Forward—an audacious attempt to unleash the people's energy. Mao's program organized China into 24,000 social and economic units, called communes. Peasants took up industrial production in their own backyards. The campaign aimed to catapult China past the developed countries, but the communes failed to feed the people and the industrial goods were inferior. Thus China took an economic leap backward. As many as 45 million people may have subsequently perished from famine and malnutrition, forcing the government to abandon the experiment. The Great Leap also exacted a devastating environmental cost from the country. The drive for a dramatic—and unrealistic—increase in steel production, for example, led to widespread deforestation, as farmers everywhere made a mad dash to cut down trees for fuel for their backyard furnaces. In some areas, up to 80 percent of forest land disappeared, leading to severe problems of soil erosion and water loss.

Fearing that China's revolution was losing spirit, in 1966 Mao launched the Great Proletarian Cultural Revolution. This time Mao turned against his associates in the communist party and appealed to China's young people. They enthusiastically responded. Organized into "Red Guards," over 10 million of them journeyed to Beijing to participate in huge rallies. Chanting, crying, screaming, and waving the little red book of Mao's quotations, they pledged to cleanse the party of its corrupt elements and to thoroughly remake Chinese society.

With help from the army, the Red Guards set out to rid society of the "four olds"—old customs, old habits, old culture,

The Cultural Revolution in China. (Left) *Young women were an important part of the Red Guards during the Cultural Revolution. Here female Red Guards, armed with their "little red books," march in the front row of a parade in the capital city of Beijing under a sign that reads "Rise."* (Right) *In their campaign to cleanse the country of undesirable elements, the Red Guards often turned to public denunciation as a way to rally the crowd. Here a senior provincial party official is made to stand on a chair wearing a dunce's cap, while the young detractors chant slogans and wave their fists in the air.*

and old ideas. They ransacked homes, libraries, museums, and temples. They destroyed classical texts, artworks, and monuments. With its rhetoric of struggle against American imperialism and Soviet revisionism, the Cultural Revolution also targeted anything foreign. Knowledge of a foreign language was enough to compromise a person's revolutionary credentials. The Red Guards attacked government officials, party cadres, or just plain strangers in an escalating cycle of violence. Even family members and friends were pressured to denounce one another; all had to prove themselves faithful followers of Chairman Mao. As chaos mounted, in late 1967 the army moved in to quell the disorder and reestablish control. To forestall further disruption, the government created an entire "lost generation" when, between 1967 and 1976, it deprived some 17 million Red Guards and students of their formal education and relocated them to the countryside "to learn from the peasants."

Given the costs of the Great Leap Forward and the Cultural Revolution, many of Mao's revolutionary policies were hard to celebrate. But radicals in much of the Third World were unaware of these costs and found the style of rapid and massive—if deeply undemocratic—uplift of the populace attractive. At least rhetorically, such policies aimed to transform poor countries within a generation.

LATIN AMERICAN REVOLUTION Most Third World radicals did not go as far as Mao, but they still dreamed of overturning the social order. In Latin America, such dreams excited those who wished to throw off the influence of U.S.-owned multinational corporations and local elites.

Reform programs in Latin America addressed numerous concerns. Economic nationalists urged greater protection for domestic industries and sought to curb the multinationals. Liberal reformers wanted to democratize political systems and redistribute land, lest discontent erupt into full-blown revolutions like China's. But when liberals and nationalists joined forces, as in Guatemala in the 1950s, their reforms met resistance from local conservatives and from the United States. In Guatemala, the banana-producing American multinational United Fruit Company (which was the largest landowner and controlled the country's railroads and its major port) opposed land reform. Still, the progressive and nationalist regime of Jacobo Arbenz persevered with plans for agrarian reform and proposed taking over uncultivated land owned by United Fruit. Despite Arbenz's intention of compensating the company for its land, the U.S. Central Intelligence Agency (CIA) plotted with sectors of the Guatemalan army to put an end to reform, culminating in a coup d'état. Through moves such as this, the United States warned other governments that Washington would not tolerate assaults on its national interests in what it deemed its backyard.

In Cuba, the failure to address political, social, and economic concerns spurred a revolution. Since the Spanish-American War of 1898, Cuba had been ruled by governments better known for their compliance with U.S. interests than with popular sentiment. In 1933, during the crisis resulting from the Great Depression, Sergeant Fulgencio Batista emerged as a strongman, and in 1952 he led a military coup that deposed a corrupt civilian government and made him dictator. Under the Batista dictatorship, sugar planters, casino operators, and North American investors prospered, but middle- and working-class Cubans did not. The latter demanded a voice in politics and a new moral bond between the people and their government. In 1953, a group composed heavily of university students launched a botched assault on a military garrison. One of the leaders, a law student named **Fidel Castro**, gave a stirring speech at the rebels' trial, which made him a national hero. After his release from prison in 1955, he fled to Mexico. Several years later, he returned and started organizing guerrilla raids.

Batista's fortunes nose-dived when the U.S. Congress suspended military supplies and aid in response to newspaper reports about his thuggery. Deprived of American support, his regime crumbled in 1958. Entire regiments of his army defected to the rebels. On New Year's Day 1959, Batista announced that he was leaving Cuba. Within days, guerrillas, including Fidel Castro, seized the capital.

Castro then set about consolidating power, elbowing aside rivals and wresting control of the economy from the wealthy

Fidel Castro and Cuba's National Liberation. *The Cuban Revolution of 1958–1959 was a powerful model for many national liberation movements elsewhere in the world. No sooner did Cuban rebels force a break with the United States in 1959 than they discovered that they needed outside support to survive. The Soviet Union, eager to lay a toehold for communism close to the United States, began to provide economic and military subsidies to their Caribbean ally. Here Castro grasps the hand of Nikita Khrushchev atop the Lenin Mausoleum for the May Day parade in 1963.*

elite, who fled to exile. As his policies grew increasingly radical, American leaders began to plot his demise. When Castro announced a massive redistribution of land and the nationalization of foreign oil refineries, the United States ended all aid and sealed off the American market to Cuban sugar. Then, in 1961, the CIA mounted an invasion by Cuban exiles, landing at the Bay of Pigs. The invasion not only failed to overthrow Castro but further radicalized his ambitions for Cuba. He now declared himself a socialist and aligned himself with the Soviet Union. It was over Cuba and its radicalizing revolution that the world came closest to nuclear Armageddon in the Cuban Missile Crisis of 1962. To deter further U.S. attacks, Castro appealed to the Soviet Union to install nuclear weapons in Cuba—a mere ninety miles off the coast of Florida. When U.S. intelligence detected the weapons, President John F. Kennedy ordered a blockade of Cuba just as weapons-bearing Soviet ships were heading toward Havana. For several weeks, the world was paralyzed with anxiety as Kennedy, Khrushchev, and Castro matched threats. In the end, Kennedy succeeded in getting the Soviets to withdraw their nuclear missiles from Cuba.

Che Guevara. *Ernesto "Che" Guevara, shown here addressing a conference in Uruguay in 1961 at which he denounced U.S. interventions in Latin America, was a chief lieutenant to Cuba's Fidel Castro and a fierce champion of Third World radicalism.*

The Cuban Revolution was a turning point in the making of the Third World. By rejecting the power of capitalist industrial societies, Castro and his followers promoted revolution, not reform, as a way to achieve Third World liberation. The symbol of this new spirit was Castro's closest lieutenant, Ernesto "Che" Guevara (1928–1967). "El Che" grew up in Argentina and traveled widely around Latin America as a student. Shortly after receiving his medical degree in 1953, he arrived in Guatemala in time to witness the CIA-backed overthrow of the progressive Arbenz government. Thereafter, Guevara became increasingly bitter about American influences in Latin America. He joined Castro's forces and helped topple the pro-American regime of Fulgencio Batista in Cuba in 1958. After 1959, he held several posts in the Cuban government but grew restive for more action. Latin America, he felt, should challenge the world power of the United States. Soon his casual military uniform, his patchy beard, his cigar, and his moral energy became legendary symbols of revolt.

The idea of revolution as a way to overcome underdevelopment and to free Third World societies spread beyond Latin America. Che became Castro's envoy to world meetings and summits of Third World state leaders, where he celebrated the Cuban road to freedom. Returning to Latin America, Che set up his center of operations in highland Bolivia in 1966, among South America's most downtrodden Indians. "We have to create another Vietnam in the Americas with its center in Bolivia," he proclaimed. Guevara did not, however, know the local Indian language, and he had little logistical support. He and his two-dozen fighters launched their region-wide war in absolute isolation. Thus, it took little time for the Bolivian army and CIA operators to capture the rebels. After a brief interrogation, Bolivian officers ordered that the guerrilla commander be killed on the spot.

If radicals could make a revolution ninety miles off the coast of the United States, what did this spell for the rest of the hemisphere? To combat the germ of revolution, the Kennedy administration sent American advisers throughout Latin America to dole out aid, explain how to reform local land systems, and demonstrate the benefits of liberal capitalism. But to most Latin American radicals, these were inadequate Band-Aids. Instead, inspired by the Cuban Revolution, peasants in Colombia and Venezuela seized estates; workers in Argentina occupied factories. And in Chile, a leftist alliance led by President Salvador Allende triumphed at the ballot box in 1970.

Reacting to revolutionary insurgency, the United States and its allies in the region bolstered their own counterinsurgency program. Working with American advisers, Latin American militaries were trained to root out radicalism. They learned that gaining the support of indigent civilians was the key to defeating the guerrillas. Even Salvador Allende's democratically elected socialist government in Chile was not spared; the CIA and U.S. policymakers aided General Augusto Pinochet's military coup against the regime in 1973 and looked the other way while political opponents were butchered. By 1975, rebel forces had been liquidated in Argentina, Uruguay, Brazil, Mexico, Bolivia, and Venezuela. Elsewhere, they hunkered down in isolated hamlets. Where civilian governments failed to keep stability, militaries took over—not just to topple weak governments, but to rule directly.

Latin American Human Rights. *By the early 1980s, human rights movements were gaining strength all over Latin America, even in Chile under the repressive General Pinochet. Here, a crowd of 400,000 demonstrates against his rule in November 1983.*

TENSIONS IN THE THREE-WORLD ORDER

Third World radicalism did not alter the balance of global wealth and power, but it exposed vulnerabilities in the three-world order. So did the continuation of the Vietnam War, which opened fissures within the First World. As antiwar and civil rights movements mushroomed, the United States experienced social unrest on a scale not seen since the Great Depression. In the Second World, too, dissent challenged the Soviet Union's hold on world communism. Satellite states in eastern Europe sought more flexible orbits, while Mao's China charted a course at odds with Soviet designs. Finally, in the 1970s, the rising fortunes of oil-producing nations and of Japan introduced new problems in the relations within and among worlds.

Tensions in the First World

Although the First World enjoyed great prosperity in the decades after World War II, a variety of issues created friction within these societies and between allies. In the United States, the problem of racial discrimination became a source of greater internal strain and international embarrassment. In western Europe, the expansion of the welfare states that preserved free enterprise while limiting the excesses of capitalism eased, though hardly eliminated, the pressure from economic inequality. In both hemispheres, the demands of women and minorities contributed to postwar tensions.

WOMEN'S ISSUES, CIVIL RIGHTS, AND ENVIRONMENTAL CONCERNS One source of dissension was the "woman question," which became more acute as women made gains after World War II. In Italy, France, and Belgium, women obtained the right to vote. Throughout Europe, as women filled new jobs in the service sector, the female workforce grew to comprise not just single servant or factory girls but mature women in offices, stores, hospitals, and schoolrooms. Although women made gains in employment outside the home, they still awaited a decrease in domestic responsibilities. This fault line would create long-lasting conflict in western societies.

There were other sources of tension. During the 1960s, students in Europe protested the deployment of nuclear weapons in their countries, as well as the rigid social and educational institutions that preserved power and high culture for the elite few. Protests reached their apex in Paris in 1968, when workers joined students in a general strike and clashed violently with police. Sons and daughters criticized their parents, and radicals attacked colonial governments for their oppressive and racist policies.

In these same years, American society lost some of the confidence and much of the contentment that had characterized the previous decade. Prosperity no longer translated into complacency. First there was the assassination of President Kennedy in 1963, and then violent race riots in major cities. In 1964, resistance to the civil rights movement turned lethal in Mississippi with the murders of three civil rights workers and the bombing and burning of two-dozen African American churches.

Under Kennedy's successor, Lyndon Johnson, the federal government promoted a bold plan to ensure civil rights and

Urban Riots. *Racial tensions boiled over in a number of American cities during the 1960s. This photograph of a man being taken into custody was snapped on July 23, 1967, the first day of what turned out to be five days of rioting in Detroit. The unrest left 43 people dead, 467 injured, and more than 2,000 buildings burned down.*

end poverty. The Civil Rights Act of 1964 banned segregation in public facilities and outlawed racial discrimination in employment, and the Voting Rights Act of 1965 gave millions of previously disenfranchised African Americans an opportunity to exercise equal political rights. The Johnson administration also supported programs targeting social security, health, education, and assistance to the poor. Aided by impressive economic growth, the War on Poverty nearly halved the U.S. poverty rate. But legacies of racism and inequality were not easy to overcome. In spite of Supreme Court decisions, most schools remained racially homogeneous not only in the South but across the United States, as "white flight" to the suburbs left inner-city neighborhoods and schools to minorities. Especially in Atlanta, Philadelphia, Detroit, Miami, and St. Louis, African Americans' frustration over discrimination and lack of jobs led to violence. Militant voices, like those of Malcolm X and the Black Panthers, became prominent. Instead of integration, these radicals advocated black separatism; instead of Americanism, they espoused pan-Africanism.

African American struggles inspired Native Americans, Mexican Americans, homosexuals, and women to initiate their own campaigns for equality and empowerment. Women now questioned a life built around taking care of home and family. In fact, the introduction of the birth control pill in 1960 and the publication of Betty Friedan's *The Feminine Mystique* in 1963 stand as watershed moments in American women's history. Because oral contraception allowed women to limit childbearing and to have sex with less fear of pregnancy, the resulting freedom helped unleash a **sexual revolution**. Moreover, Friedan blasted the myth of middle-class domestic contentment, describing the idealized 1950s suburban home as a "comfortable concentration camp" from which women must escape. Despite rising numbers of married women and college-educated women in the workforce, their compensation and opportunity for advancement lagged far behind those of men. (See Primary Source: Betty Friedan on "The Problem That Has No Name.")

Feminism. *Betty Friedan, author of* The Feminine Mystique, *leads a 1970 march in New York City on the fiftieth anniversary of the passing of the Nineteenth Amendment, which granted American women the right to vote.*

PRIMARY SOURCE

Betty Friedan on "The Problem That Has No Name"

In 1963, Betty Friedan published* The Feminine Mystique, *which challenged the idea that women found fulfillment solely by getting married, keeping house, and raising children. Friedan's book contributed to the rise of the women's movement in the United States. In this excerpt, Friedan writes about "the problem" that afflicted suburban housewives—a problem that, she suggested, was widely shared but as yet had "no name."

The problem lay buried, unspoken, for many years in the minds of American women. It was a strange stirring, a sense of dissatisfaction, a yearning that women suffered in the middle of the twentieth century in the United States. Each suburban wife struggled with it alone. As she made the beds, shopped for groceries, matched slipcover material, ate peanut butter sandwiches with her children, chauffeured Cub Scouts and Brownies, lay beside her husband at night—she was afraid to ask even of herself the silent question—"Is this all?"

For over fifteen years there was no word of this yearning in the millions of words written about women, for women, in all the columns, books, and articles by experts telling women their role was to seek fulfillment as wives and mothers. Over and over women heard in voices of tradition and of Freudian sophistication that they could desire no greater destiny than to glory in their own femininity. Experts told them how to catch a man and keep him, how to breastfeed children and handle their toilet training, how to cope with sibling rivalry and adolescent rebellion; how to buy a dishwasher, bake bread, cook gourmet snails, and build a swimming pool with their own hands; how to dress, look, and act more feminine and make marriage more exciting; how to keep their husbands from dying young and their sons from growing into delinquents. They were taught to pity the neurotic, unfeminine, unhappy women who wanted to be poets or physicists or presidents. They learned that truly feminine women do not want careers, higher education, political rights—the independence and the opportunities that the old-fashioned feminists fought for. Some women, in their forties and fifties, still remembered painfully giving up those dreams, but most of the younger women no longer even thought about them. A thousand expert voices applauded their femininity, their adjustment, their new maturity. All they had to do was devote their lives from earliest girlhood to finding a husband and bearing children.

By the end of the 1950s, the average marriage age of women in America dropped to 20, and was still dropping, into the teens. Fourteen million girls were engaged by 17. The proportion of women attending college in comparison with men dropped from 47 per cent in 1920 to 35 per cent in 1958. A century earlier, women had fought for higher education; now girls went to college to get a husband. By the mid-fifties, 60 per cent dropped out of college to marry, or because they were afraid too much education would be a marriage bar. Colleges built dormitories for "married students," but the students were almost always husbands. A new degree was instituted for the wives - "Ph.T." (Putting Husband through). . . .

The suburban housewife—she was the dream image of the young American women and the envy, it was said, of women all over the world. The American housewife—freed by science and labor-saving appliances from the drudgery, the dangers of childbirth, and the illnesses of her grandmother. She was healthy, beautiful, educated, concerned only about her husband, her children, her home. She had found true feminine fulfillment. As a housewife and mother, she was respected as a full and equal partner to man in his world. She was free to choose automobiles, clothes, appliances, supermarkets; she had everything that women ever dreamed of. . . .

If a woman had a problem in the 1950s and 1960s, she knew that something must be wrong with her marriage, or with herself. Other women were satisfied with their lives, she thought. What kind of a woman was she if she did not feel this mysterious fulfillment waxing the kitchen floor? She was so ashamed to admit her dissatisfaction that she never knew how many other women shared it. If she tried to tell her husband, he didn't understand what she was talking about. She did not really understand it herself. . . .

If I am right, the problem that has no name stirring in the minds of so many American women today is not a matter of loss of femininity or too much education, or the demands of domesticity. It is far more important than anyone recognizes. It is the key to these other new and old problems which have been torturing women and their husbands and children, and puzzling their doctors and educators for years. It may well be the key to our future as a nation and a culture. We can no longer ignore that voice within women that says, "I want something more than my husband and my children and my home."

QUESTIONS FOR ANALYSIS

- What criticisms do you think were leveled at Friedan's book when it appeared in 1963?
- What criticisms have emerged in subsequent decades?

A year before Friedan authored her challenge to the subordination of women, Rachel Carson published *The Silent Spring*, a book that was equally revolutionary in its attack against long-held practices. In particular, Carson's book took on the use of synthetic pesticides such as dichlorodiphenyltrichloroethane (DDT), which she said caused cancer, devastated wildlife, and destroyed natural ecosystems. Although chemical manufacturers responded that pesticides had vastly multiplied agricultural yields, *The Silent Spring* stirred opposition that ultimately led to the banning of DDT in the United States in 1972. More broadly, Carson's book spurred the development of an environmental movement that questioned many of the ideas about economic progress and material prosperity upon which the "American Dream" had rested.

PROTESTS AGAINST THE VIETNAM WAR The civil rights and women's movements led many white college students to question the ideals of American society, but what spurred them to massive resistance was escalation of the Vietnam War. As the United States increased troop levels there in the 1960s, it conscripted more men. Tens of thousands of young Americans fled the country to escape the draft. Upwards of 250,000 simply did not register; another 100,000 burned their draft cards. After President Richard Nixon sent American troops into Cambodia in 1970 to root out North Vietnamese soldiers, students at over 500 campuses occupied buildings and closed down universities. At Kent State University in Ohio, National Guardsmen attempting to stop the protests killed four students. The United States withdrew from Vietnam in 1973, but not before the divisions created by the war had strained the country almost to the breaking point.

Tensions in World Communism

The unity of the communist world also came under increasing pressure. As early as 1948, Yugoslavia had broken free of the Soviet yoke and embarked on its own road to building socialism. Other satellites within the Soviet bloc had more trouble freeing themselves. In 1956, Poland and Hungary were forced back in line. Twelve years later, Czechoslovakia experienced the **Prague Spring**, in which communist authorities experimented with creating a democratic and pluralist socialist world. Workers and students rallied behind the reformist government of Alexander Dubček, calling for more freedom of expression, more autonomy for workers and consumers, and more debate within the ruling party. Once again, Soviet tanks crushed what they branded a "counterrevolutionary" movement. As the tanks rolled into Prague, the Czech capital, one desperate student doused himself with gasoline and lit a match—his public suicide a gesture of defiance against communist rule.

Thereafter, the Prague Spring served as a symbol for dissenters, who were divided between those who still wanted to reform socialism and those who wanted to overturn it. Underground reading groups proliferated throughout eastern Europe, and many Russians renewed their faith in Orthodox Christianity, their prerevolutionary religion. Many dissidents were exiled from the Soviet Union. Most famous by the early 1970s was the Russian novelist Alexander Solzhenitsyn. His masterwork, *The Gulag Archipelago,* repudiated the notion that socialism could be reformed by a turn away from Stalin's policies. Yet very few people in the Soviet Union could obtain copies of Solzhenitsyn's exposé, which had been published abroad and was a best-seller in the West. In 1974 the author himself was expelled from the USSR.

Still, there were important changes within the Second World. During the 1950s and 1960s, "national communism" became the rule throughout eastern Europe, even in countries that experienced Soviet invasions. National variations also arose within the Soviet Union, where Moscow conceded some autonomy to the communist party machines of its fifteen republics—in exchange for fundamental loyalty. Dissidents were still persecuted, but by the 1970s, many fewer were murdered outright, and the population of the gulags declined. Shared antipathy for the United States created a Sino-Soviet alliance in the years just after the Chinese Revolution of 1949. By the late 1950s, the Soviet Union had contributed massive military and economic aid to China. But the Chinese increasingly sought to define their own brand of Marxism and criticized Khrushchev's efforts to reduce tensions with the United States and the West. Preferring to accentuate confrontation, the Chinese built their own nuclear weapons and began to tout themselves as a peasant-socialist alternative to the Soviet model of development, especially for Third World countries. The fissure raised China's profile throughout Asia and even in eastern Europe. Indeed, Romania achieved a measure of autonomy in foreign policy by playing off China and the Soviet Union. Albania declared its allegiance to China. African nations, interested in Soviet aid, increased their demands with subtle hints that they might consider deepening ties with China instead. Clearly, the Second World was no monolith.

Tensions in the Third World

In contrast to the First and Second worlds, the Third World was never unified by economic, military, or political alliances. Despite a common history of domination and the shared search for a "third way," the cold war polarized Third World nations. It pushed them to choose between alignment with the First World or the Second. Nonetheless, radicalism nourished new hopes for unifying and empowering the Third World.

One effort at collaboration was the formation in 1960 of a cartel of oil exporters. The Organization of Petroleum Exporting Countries (OPEC)—which included Algeria, Ecuador, Gabon, Indonesia, Iran, Iraq, Kuwait, Libya, Nigeria, Qatar, Saudi Arabia, the United Arab Emirates, and Venezuela—had little impact in raising oil revenues through the 1960s, even though several members nationalized their oil fields. But after the fourth major Arab-Israeli war broke out in 1973, OPEC's Arab members decided to pressure Israel's First World allies by halting oil exports to them. Overnight, the embargo lifted oil prices more than threefold, a bonanza that enriched all oil producers and led to an oil crisis in the West. To many, the bulging treasuries of OPEC nations seemed like the Third World's revenge. Here were Saudi Arabian princes, Venezuelan magnates, and Indonesian ministers dictating world prices to industrial consumers.

But the realignment was not thorough. Third World producers of raw materials such as coffee and rubber tried unsuccessfully to duplicate OPEC's model, and OPEC itself had trouble controlling the world's oil market. During the 1970s, discoveries in the North Sea, Mexico, and Canada reduced pressures on the large oil-consuming states to be more fuel efficient. With supply up, prices fell. To compensate for lost revenue, various OPEC states raised their own production, putting further downward pressure on prices.

Nor did oil revenues help overcome poverty and dependency in the Third World as a whole. To the contrary, most revenue surpluses from OPEC simply flowed back to First World banks or boosted real-estate holdings in Europe and the United States. Some of it was in turn reloaned to the world's poorest countries in Africa, Asia, and Latin America, at high interest rates, to pay for more expensive imports—including oil! The biggest bonanza went to multinational petroleum firms whose control over production, refining, and distribution yielded enormous profits.

For all the talk in the mid-1970s of changing the balance of international economic relations between the world's rich and poor countries, fundamental inequalities persisted. Those nations that appeared to break out of the cycle of poverty, like South Korea and Taiwan, did not achieve success through international markets. Rather, these states regulated markets, nurtured new industries, educated the populace, and required multinationals to work collaboratively with local firms. These were exceptions that proved the general rule: the international economy reinforced existing structures.

CONCLUSION

The three-world order arose on the ruins of European empires and their Japanese counterpart. First, the Soviet Union and the United States became superpowers. Second, World War II affirmed the nation-state rather than the empire as the primary form for organizing communities. Third, in spite of the rhetoric of individualism and the free market, the war and postwar reconstruction enhanced the reach and functions of the modern state. In the Third World, too, leaders of new nations saw the state as the primary instrument for promoting economic development.

The organization of the world into three blocs lasted into the mid-1970s. This arrangement fostered the economic recovery of western Europe and Japan from the wounds inflicted by war. These nations' recovery grew out of a cold war alliance with the United States, where anticommunist hysteria accompanied an economic boom. The cold war also cast a shadow over the citizens of the Soviet Union and eastern Europe. Gulags and political surveillance became widespread, while the Soviets and their satellite regimes mobilized resources for military purposes. The Third World, squeezed by its inability to reduce poverty, on the one hand, and superpower rivalry, on the other, struggled to pursue a "third way." While some states maintained democratic institutions and promoted economic development, many tumbled into dictatorships and authoritarian regimes, and often suffered irreparable environmental damage.

In this context Third World revolutionaries sought radical social and political transformation, seeking paths different from both western capitalism and Soviet communism. Though not successful, they energized considerable tensions in the three-world order. These tensions intensified in the late 1960s and early 1970s as Vietnamese communists defeated the United States, an oil crisis struck the West, and protests escalated in the First and Second worlds. Thirty years after the war's end, the world order forged after 1945 was beginning to give way.

AFTER YOU READ THIS CHAPTER

Review and research materials on **STUDYSPACE:** wwnorton.com/studyspace

TRACING THE GLOBAL STORYLINES

FOCUS ON: *World War II and a New Global Order*

World War II

- World War II grows out of unresolved problems connected to World War I, especially the aggressive plans of Germany and Japan to expand their political and economic influence.
- The war brings unheard-of human and material costs and ushers in an age of nuclear weapons.
- At war's end, the United States, fearing the spread of communism and Soviet influence, rebuilds war-torn Europe and Japan and creates military and political alliances to contain Soviet expansionist ambitions.

A new global order

- The Soviet Union and the United States become superpowers.
- Japan emerges as an economic powerhouse and a U.S. ally.
- A weakened Europe cannot resist demands for independence from Asian and African nationalists.
- Chinese communists engineer a revolution, while Indian nationalists and many African leaders achieve independence through negotiations.
- Elsewhere, decolonization is violent (Palestine, Israel, Egypt, Algeria, and Kenya) or incomplete (southern Africa).
- Actions by Latin American reformers and revolutionary insurgents spark counterinsurgency efforts by the United States and its regional allies.
- An insecure three-world order emerges after most Asian and African states achieve independence.

CHRONOLOGY

The Americas
- United States emerges as a global superpower **1945**

Europe
- World War II **1939–1945**
- NATO formed **1949**

Soviet Union
- Soviet Union emerges as a global superpower, creates client states in Eastern Europe **1945**

Africa

Middle East
- Decolonization **1940s and 1950s**
- The United Nations partitions Palestine **1948**

South Asia
- British Raj ends, India and Pakistan declare independence **1947**

East Asia
- World War II **1937–1945**
- Communist victory in Chinese civil war **1949**
- Korean War **1950–1953**
- Vietnamese fight for independence **1950–1975**

1935 | 1940 | 1945 | 1950

KEY TERMS

Allied powers *p. 744*
apartheid *p. 766*
Arab-Israeli War *p. 764*
Axis powers *p. 744*
Berlin Wall *p. 752*
Fidel Castro *p. 775*
civil rights movement *p. 769*
cold war *p. 744*
decolonization *p. 754*
First World *p. 767*
Holocaust *p. 750*
Martin Luther King, Jr. *p. 769*
Korean War *p. 754*
Mao Zedong *p. 756*
neocolonialism *p. 773*
North Atlantic Treaty Organization (NATO) *p. 752*
Prague Spring *p. 780*
Second World *p. 769*
sexual revolution *p. 778*
superpowers *p. 744*
Third World *p. 771*
Vietnam War *p. 767*
Warsaw Pact *p. 754*
Zionism *p. 762*

STUDY QUESTIONS

1. **Analyze** how World War II was a truly global war and why it led to the end of a European-dominated world. How did the war challenge the ideological justifications for imperialism?
2. **Define** the term *cold war*. How did the task of rebuilding Europe and Asia after World War II lead to this intense global rivalry between the Soviet Union and the United States?
3. **Describe** the other process that dominated world affairs during these years—decolonization. What forms did it take?
4. **Compare and contrast** the three worlds of the postwar order. What was each world attempting to achieve? How successful was each one in achieving these goals?
5. **List and explain** tensions among the three worlds of the postwar era. How did cold war rivalries affect the Third World?
6. **List and explain** various successes and failures in the three competing worlds as they struggled to create "modern societies." What problems did the Third World face?
7. **Evaluate** the impact of Third World revolutionaries and radicals in transforming their societies. How successful were Mao and Castro in challenging the international status quo?
8. **Assess** the impact of nuclear weapons on state rivalries and relations after World War II. How did the proliferation of these weapons affect Soviet-American relations?
9. What tensions emerged between 1945 and 1975 to challenge the three-world order? What challenges did they present for various states?

- U.S. civil rights movement **1950s and 1960s**
- Ascendance of Fidel Castro in Cuba **1959**
- Warsaw Pact formed **1955**
- Prague Spring **1968**
- Stalin dies **1953**
- Soviets launch Sputnik **1957**
- Decolonization **1950s–1970s**
- South African state bans the ANC **1960**
- Arab OPEC oil boycott of Israeli allies **1973**
- Mao's Great Leap Forward in China **1958–1961**
- China's Cultural Revolution **1966**
- Japanese economic "miracle" **1950s–1970s**

1955 | 1960 | 1965 | 1970 | 1975

BEFORE YOU READ THIS CHAPTER

wwnorton.com/
StudySpace

GLOBAL STORYLINES

- A new architecture of power organized around electoral systems and market economies after the collapse of the three-world order creates large disparities between those who participate in the networks of globalization and those who do not.
- The United States emerges as the most influential society in the world, with its cultures and institutions spreading to most corners of the globe, while the world also comes to America and shapes its texture.
- Transnational forces like migration, investment networks, and trade begin to operate independently of the nation-state via international organizations like the United Nations and the International Monetary Fund, which erode the power of the nation-state.

CHAPTER OUTLINE

21

Globalization, 1970–2000

FOCUS QUESTIONS

- What forces drove global integration at the end of the twentieth century?
- What were the characteristics of globalization?
- What possibilities and disparities did globalization create for many?
- How did globalization shape personal identities?

Consider the following comparison. In the thirteenth century, few people could imagine moving beyond their local regions. Venetian explorer Marco Polo, who traveled through China, and Arab scholar Ibn Battuta, who traversed the Islamic world, were rare exceptions. In contrast, by the late twentieth century people traversed in a matter of hours the distances that it took Marco Polo and Ibn Battuta years to cover. Many others staying at home could "travel" the world via the Internet, books, newspapers, and televisions.

But not all travelers moved about so comfortably. Many migrants—desperate to escape political chaos, religious persecution, or poverty—slipped across borders in the dark of night, traveled as human cargo inside containers, or used their own feet to flee their homelands. Billions of others still had no access to the global age's technological wonders and economic opportunities. Thus, while **globalization** (the development of integrated worldwide cultural and economic structures) created possibilities for some, it also caused deeper disparities.

Moreover, consider two different settings: a fishing village in the Amazon River basin, and cosmopolitan Los Angeles. Picture an elderly

Amazonian fisherman trying to teach his children their parents' tongue, Cocama-Cocamilla, but to no avail. All his children speak Spanish instead. "I tried to teach them. It's like paddling against the current." Seven centuries ago, over 500 languages rang throughout the Amazon River basin. As of 2000, only 57 languages survived there. Evidently, one effect of globalization is to reduce diversity. But it can also increase local diversity. For example, Los Angeles, once the emblem of white, suburban America, became a cacophonous city with over 100 languages spoken in its public schools.

This chapter observes the impact of globalization in several ways: (1) the movement of families and groups, as well as goods and ideas, across boundaries that once divided religious, ethnic, and national communities; (2) the role of international financial organizations in addressing world financial issues; (3) the power of multinational corporations in transforming local markets into international ones; and (4) unexpected effects such as galvanizing discontent, sparking a revival of traditional religions (to counter secular and materialist influences), and driving deeper divisions among and within the world's regions—even while bringing them closer together.

GLOBAL INTEGRATION

The full impact of globalization remains unknown. Clearly, though, by the late twentieth century the forces driving global integration—and inequality—were no longer the political empires of old. By the mid-twentieth century, the European empires had lost their sway. The cold war and decolonization movements that had produced the three-world order had also lost their salience. Power structures in the First World, under such stress in the 1970s, did not crack. But those in the Second World did. Thus did the cold war end with the implosion of the Soviet bloc. The Third World also splintered, with some areas becoming highly advanced and others falling into deep poverty; the term **developing world** obscured these differences. Now a new architecture of power organized the world into a unified marketplace with unhindered flows of capital, commerce, culture, and labor. By 2000, most societies had endorsed electoral systems and adopted some form of market economy.

Because the United States promoted these changes, globalization has looked to some like Americanization. The United States unquestionably stood as the world's most influential society, with its music, food, principles of representative government, and free markets spreading worldwide. Yet the process did not run one way. The world also came to America and shaped its society: people living in the United States, their inventions, sports stars, and musical inspirations increasingly came from elsewhere.

Nor was the United States immune from transnational forces challenging the power of the nation-state itself. In the United States, as elsewhere, globalization functioned through networks of investment, trade, and migration that operated relatively independently of nation-states. In the process, globalization shook entrenched forms of political and social identification, from religious to military authority. Members of societies now often identified more with local, subnational, or international movements or cultures, rather than with nation-states. To be sure, nation-states remained essential for establishing democratic institutions and protecting human rights, but supranational institutions like the European Union and the International Monetary Fund (see later discussion) often impinged on their autonomy.

REMOVING OBSTACLES TO GLOBALIZATION

In the mid-1970s, political practices and institutions associated with the three-world order started to deteriorate. By the late 1980s, the communist Second World was disintegrating. The collapse of the Soviet Union brought the cold war to an end. At the same time, the capitalist First World gave up its last colonial possessions, and the remnants of white settler supremacy disintegrated. But as this occurred, the formerly colonized Third World's dream of a "third way" also vanished. As empires withdrew, they revealed a world integrated by ties other than forced loyalties to imperial masters.

Ending the Cold War

A world divided between two hostile factions limited the prospects for a global exchange of peoples, ideas, and resources. There was widespread exchange within the rival blocs—that is, among socialist countries and among capitalist countries—but for other countries the pressure from the Soviet Union and the United States to align with a superpower imposed limits to interaction, even with neighboring nations. A few countries, like Egypt, managed to switch sides (from the Soviets to the Americans), opening up some new global links while closing off others. Pushing against the cold war superpower framework, however, were strong nationalist aspirations and religious movements, which the cold war order tried to control, or in some cases inflame, at great cost.

MOUNTING COSTS The many regional conflicts of the cold war era (Vietnam, Afghanistan, Nicaragua) were costly for countries caught in the ideological crossfire. Vietnam became

a battleground for Russian, Chinese, and American ambitions. This war spilled over into Laos and Cambodia, dragging them to ruin along with Vietnam. China attracted several client states in the competition for influence in the Third World and within the communist bloc. In Afghanistan, Moscow propped up a puppet regime, only to fall into a bloody war against Islamic and tribal guerrillas financed and armed by the United States, Saudi Arabia, and Pakistan. In Central America, U.S. president Ronald Reagan and his advisers opposed the victory of the left-leaning Nicaraguan Sandinista coalition in 1979. During the 1980s the U.S. government pumped millions of dollars to the Contras (right-wing opponents of the left-wing Sandinistas) and lent military and monetary assistance to other Central American anti-communist forces. Thus, for much of the world, the cold war was a real confrontation with tremendously high costs for local powers.

Rivalry was costly to the superpowers, too, for the 1970s and 1980s saw the largest peacetime accumulation of arms in history. Despite myriad treaties and summits, the United States and the Soviet Union stockpiled nuclear and conventional weaponry. Furthermore, in 1983 Reagan unveiled the Strategic Defense Initiative ("Star Wars"), a plan to use satellites and space missiles to insulate the United States from incoming nuclear bombs. For both sides, military spending sprees brought economic troubles. The U.S. national debt increased; Soviet life expectancy began to decline and infant mortality to rise.

Cracks on either side of the conflict appeared in the 1970s. The intelligence organizations of both the Soviet Union and the United States produced secret memos questioning whether the Soviet bloc could sustain its global position. As stalemate in Afghanistan undermined the image of the mighty Soviet armed forces, mothers of Soviet soldiers protested their government's involvements abroad. The eastern European satellites became dependent on western European loans and consumer goods. At the same time, the western alliance itself faced internal tensions. In Europe and North America, the antinuclear movement rallied millions to the streets. Western industrialists worried about competition from Japan, which had been plowing money into rapid industrialization rather than arms. Political leaders also grappled with distressingly high unemployment rates. Thus, both sides shared a common crisis: fatigue from the cold war, and an economic challenge from East Asia.

THE SOVIET BLOC COLLAPSES In the end, the Soviet bloc collapsed (see Map 21.1). Even though planned economies employed the entire Soviet population, they failed to fill stores with sufficient consumer goods. Socialist health care and benefits lagged behind those of the capitalist welfare states. Authoritarian political structures relied on deception and coercion rather than elections and civic activism. Although the communist party had promised to beat capitalism by building socialism on the way to achieving full communism, the latter paradise was nowhere on the horizon. The gap between socialism and capitalism was growing.

One catalyst in socialism's undoing was Poland. A critical event was the naming of a Polish archbishop as pope in 1978. The first non-Italian pope in 455 years, John Paul opposed the Soviet form of socialism. In 1979, he made a pilgrimage to his native Poland, holding enormous outdoor masses; in 1980, he supported mass strikes at the Gdansk shipyard, which led to the formation of the Soviet bloc's first independent trade union, Solidarity. As communist party members in Poland defected to its side, the union became a society-wide movement; it aimed not to reform socialism (as in Czechoslovakia in 1968; see Chapter 20) but to overcome it. A crackdown by the Polish military and police put most of Solidarity's leadership in prison and drove the movement underground, but Soviet intelligence officials secretly worried that Solidarity could not be easily eradicated.

The most consequential factor in the collapse of the Soviet superpower was Mikhail Gorbachev, who became general secretary of the Soviet communist party in 1985 and launched an effort to reform the Soviet system. Under this effort (*perestroika*, "reconstruction"), Gorbachev permitted contested elections for communist party posts, relaxed censorship, sanctioned civic associations, legalized small nonstate businesses, granted autonomy to state firms, and encouraged the republics to be responsible for their own affairs within the Soviet Union. These reforms were linked with dramatic arms control initiatives to

Lech Walesa. *A Polish electrician from the Lenin Shipyard in the Baltic port city of Gdansk, Walesa spearheaded the formation of Solidarity, a mass independent trade union of workers who battled the communist regime that ruled in their name. He later was elected president of post-communist Poland.*

MAP 21.1 | Collapse of the Communist Bloc in Europe

The Soviet Union's domination of eastern Europe ended precipitously in 1989. The political map of eastern and central Europe took on a different shape under European integration.

- What significant event in many communist countries signaled the collapse of communism?
- In what part of eastern and central Europe did the most political instability and conflict occur?
- According to your reading, why did the end of communist rule cause the reshuffling of political boundaries in the region?

ease the superpower burden on the Soviet Union. Gorbachev then began withdrawing troops from Afghanistan and informed eastern European leaders that they could not count on Moscow's armed intervention to prop up their regimes.

Having set out to improve socialism, however, Gorbachev instead destabilized it. Civic groups called not for reform of the system, but for its liquidation. Eastern Europe declared its intention to leave the Soviet orbit, and some of the union republics

began to push for independence. In response, disgruntled factions within the communist party and the Soviet military tried to preserve the destabilized old order by staging a coup attempt in 1991. However, the former communist party boss of Moscow and elected president of the Russian republic, Boris Yeltsin, rallied the opposition and faced down the hard-liners. Under Yeltsin, Russia, like Ukraine and the other republics of the Soviet Union, became a refuge for beleaguered Soviet elites. Thereafter they abandoned the cause of the Soviet Union and socialism and divided up state property among themselves.

When communist regimes collapsed, the European and Asian political maps changed dramatically. Old states disappeared, and new ones emerged. In Asia, although the division between North and South Korea remained, Vietnam was united and, along with China, welcomed western capitalism under communist party rule. In Europe, East Germany ceased to exist; West Germany absorbed its remnants after the Berlin Wall came down in 1989. (See Primary Source: Tidal Pull of the West: East Germany Disappears.) Soon thereafter the Soviet empire dissolved into independent states (see Map 21.2). But the end of Soviet-style socialism was not entirely peaceful. The worst carnage occurred in the former Yugoslavia, which suffered wars of dissolution as leaders exploited ethnic fears. Serbs and Croats, in particular, engaged in savage struggles over territories in the Balkans.

By historical standards the cold war had been relatively brief, spanning four decades. But communism had played a major role in the military conflicts and the headlong modernization of Russia and China, and it exercised important influence on India. However, it could not keep up the cold war *and* deliver the good life to its adherents *and* survive in a more competitive world economy.

The Berlin Wall. *The breaching of the Berlin Wall in November 1989 spelled the end of the Soviet bloc. Decades of debate over whether communism could be reformed turned out to be moot. In the face of competition from the richer, consumer-oriented West, communism collapsed.*

Africa and the End of White Rule

Although the aftermath of World War II saw the dismantling of most of Europe's empires, remnants of colonial rule remained in southern Africa (see Map 20.6 on p. 759). Here, whites clung to centuries-old notions of their racial superiority over non-Europeans. Final decolonization meant that self-rule would return to all of Africa.

THE LAST HOLDOUTS The last fortresses under direct European control were the Portuguese colonies of southern and western Africa. However, by the mid-1970s efforts to suppress African nationalist movements had exhausted Portugal's resources. Demoralized Portuguese officers now pushed aside their nation's dictatorship and began the Portuguese experiment with democracy. As African nationalist demands led to a hurried Portuguese withdrawal from Guinea-Bissau, Angola, and Mozambique, formal European colonialism in Africa came to an end.

But white rule still prevailed elsewhere in Africa. In Rhodesia, a white minority resisted all international pressure to allow black rule. In the end, independent African neighbors helped support a liberation guerrilla movement under Robert Mugabe. Surrounded, Rhodesian whites finally capitulated. Mugabe swept to power with massive electoral support in 1979. The new constitutional government renamed the country Zimbabwe, erasing from Africa's map the name of the long-deceased British expansionist Cecil Rhodes (see Chapter 17).

SOUTH AFRICA AND NELSON MANDELA The final outpost of white rule was South Africa, where a European minority was larger, richer, and more entrenched than elsewhere in the region—and highly invulnerable to outside pressures. Although powerful international firms operated there, they were reluctant to risk their investments by boycotting the racist regime. In addition, the U.S. government regarded South Africa's large army as a useful tool to fight Soviet allies elsewhere in southern Africa. In any case the ruling Afrikaner-led National Party used ruthless tactics against internal critics. Yet, in the countryside and cities, defiance of white rule was growing. Africans lobbed rocks and crude bombs (Molotov cocktails) at tanks and organized mass strikes in the multinational-owned mines.

At the same time, pressures from abroad were mounting. The International Olympic Committee banned South African athletes starting in 1970. American students insisted that their universities divest themselves of companies with investments in South Africa. As international pressures grew, foreign governments—even that of the United States, once South Africa's staunchest ally—applied economic sanctions against South Africa. A swelling worldwide chorus demanded that **Nelson Mandela**, the imprisoned leader of the African National Congress (ANC), be freed. The white political elite eventually realized that it was better to negotiate new arrangements than to endure international ostracism and

PRIMARY SOURCE

Tidal Pull of the West: East Germany Disappears

After Soviet premier Mikhail Gorbachev instituted a series of reforms to save socialism, dissenters in eastern Europe saw their chance to throw off Russian dominance. The Berlin Wall (erected in 1961) was the most visible symbol of Soviet oppression. Here journalist Ann Tusa recalls the November 1989 press conference that accidentally led to the opening of the Berlin Wall. As both the wall and East Germany fell, Russia kept its nearly 400,000 troops that were on East German soil confined to their barracks.

At about 7 o'clock on the evening of November 9, 1989, some 300 journalists from all over the world are crammed into a room in East Berlin for a routine press conference. . . . For the first time since the foundation of a separate Communist East German state in 1946, the German Democratic Republic, there have been massive demonstrations against the regime. . . .

East Germans, who have not known a free election since 1933, have been voting with their feet. From January to October 1989, some 200,000 people had left their country. By early November the figure was up to 250,000—and that was out of a total population of 16.7 million. At first, many East Germans went out on "holiday visas" to Iron Curtain countries [European states under Soviet domination], then claimed asylum in West German embassies in Warsaw, Budapest or Prague. Thousands more have driven or walked round the East German frontiers looking for an undefended crossing or a guard with a blind eye, wriggled across, then headed for Austria and a refugee camp. . . .

The November 9 press conference is handled by Günter Schabowski. . . . This evening he feeds the press a startling hint that there might soon be free elections. Good story. Everyone wants to go out and file it. But then Schabowski turns up a sheet from the bottom of the pile of papers on his table. "This will be interesting for you." And in a style that suggests it is all news to him, slowly reads aloud: "Today the decision was taken to make it possible for all citizens to leave the country through the official border crossing points. All citizens of the GDR can now be issued with visas for the purposes of travel or visiting relatives in the West. This order is to take effect at once. . . ."

The news is broadcast on an East German television bulletin at 7:30 P.M. The station's switchboard is immediately jammed with callers. "Is it true? I can't believe it." They always believed West German television, though, and it is soon flashing the announcement. A few East and West Berliners go to the Wall to see what is happening. . . . Then at 10:30 a discussion program on Sender Freies Berlin, the West Berlin television station, is interrupted by a live broadcast from the Wall. No preamble, just shots of a small crowd milling round a checkpoint, then a man runs toward the camera: "They've opened the crossing at Bornholmer Strasse." After that the news spreads like wildfire, by radio, television, telephone, shouts in the street. The trickle across the Wall swells to a flood. That weekend 2 million East Germans are reckoned to have stood in West Berlin. One reaction is common to them all: "We've seen the West on TV, of course. But this is real."

. . . The fatal piece of paper had been hurriedly swept up as he left for the press conference. It had never been intended for publication. It was a draft based on a recent Politburo decision: unable to control the tide of refugees, thrashing around for ways to quiet the demonstrators on the streets, they had decided that in their own good time they would ease travel restrictions, having first made arrangements for a limited issue of visas under carefully controlled circumstances.

QUESTIONS FOR ANALYSIS

- The Berlin Wall (and other border defenses) kept East Germans and West Germans apart for twenty-eight years. How did some East Germans try to circumvent the barriers during that time?
- Why didn't the 400,000 Soviet troops in East Germany intervene during the collapse of the Berlin Wall?
- What does this piece tell us about the state of mind of the East German government at this time?

years of internal warfare against a majority population. In 1990, President F. W. de Klerk (of the National Party) released Mandela from prison and legalized the ANC and the communist party of South Africa. Ensuing negotiations produced South Africa's first free, mass elections in 1994. These brought an overwhelming victory to the ANC, with Nelson Mandela elected as president. Majority rule had finally come to South Africa, and for the first time in centuries Africans ruled over all of Africa.

In Nelson Mandela, South Africa's white rulers found a man of exceptional integrity and political savvy. He had spent more than two decades in prison, much of it at hard labor. But he looked beyond past injustices to ease the transition

MAP 21.2 | The Breakup of the Soviet Union

The Soviet Union broke apart in 1991. Compare this map with Map 17.6 (see p. 660), which illustrates Russian expansion in the nineteenth century.

- Which parts of the old Russian Empire remained under Russian rule, and which territories established their own states?
- In what areas did large migrations accompany the breakup, and for what reasons?
- According to your reading, how did the breakup of the Soviet Union change Russia's status in Europe and Asia?

to full democracy. Besides, he was aware that, with the country veering toward civil war, only a negotiated change would preserve South Africa's industries, wealth, and educational system.

Still, the leaders of independent Africa faced immense problems in building stable political communities. Although they set out to destroy the vestiges of colonial political structures and to erect African-based public institutions, local contests for

The End of Apartheid. *Nelson Mandela, running for president in 1994 as the candidate of the African National Congress, here casts a ballot in the first all-races election in South Africa. This election ended apartheid and saw the African National Congress take control of the Republic of South Africa.*

political power impeded this process. Ethnic and religious rivalries, held in check during the colonial period, now blazed forth. Civil wars erupted in many countries (most violently in Nigeria, Sudan, and Zaire), and military leaders were drawn into politics. Coups d'état were common. Nigeria, for instance, had six military coups between 1966 and 1999. The ruling elements increasingly maintained power by using the state's resources to reward their clients and to punish their enemies. By the 1990s, the continent was aflame with civil strife—armed conflicts that started with the cold war and lasted well after it ended.

UNLEASHING GLOBALIZATION

As obstacles to international integration began to dissolve, capital, commodities, people, and culture crossed borders with ever-greater freedom. Even though trade, foreign investment, migration, and cultural borrowing had long been hallmarks of modern history, the global age changed their scale. At the same time, never had there been such unequal access to the fruits of globalization. Several factors contributed to increasing integration and to new power arrangements: international banking, expanded international trade, population migrations, and technical breakthroughs in communications.

Finance and Trade

The increased international flow of goods and capital was well under way in the 1970s, but the end of the cold war removed many impediments to globalization. During the 1990s, even the strongest nation-states felt the effects of economic globalization.

GLOBAL FINANCIAL TRANSFERS AND DEREGULATED MARKETS Major transformations occurred in the world's financial system in the 1970s. America's budget and trade deficits prompted President Richard Nixon to take the dollar off the gold standard, an action that enabled the yen, the lira, the pound, the franc, and other national currencies to cut their ties to the American dollar. Now international financiers enjoyed greater freedom from national regulators and found fresh business opportunities. A new system of informal money management across borders replaced an older system of formal management within borders. Where formal management of world financial relations existed, it fell increasingly under international authorities such as the World Bank and the International Monetary Fund.

The primary agents of the heightened global financial activity were banks. Based mainly in London, New York, and Tokyo, big, highly diversified financial banks became conduits for mobile capital looking for lucrative ventures. Revenues from oil producers provided a large infusion of cash into the global economy in the 1970s. At the same time, banks joined forces to issue mammoth loans to developing nations.

International financial firms found academic allies who outlined the economic rules for a global economic environment. These intellectuals were primarily North American–trained economists whose new framework minimized the welfare concerns of the Keynesian approach (see Chapter 19). Instead, these economists emphasized unfettered markets and profit motivations as the cornerstone of capitalist economic development. Employed in banks and ministries worldwide, they argued that the old regulatory policies of nation-states prevented rather than promoted economic growth. Working as advisers in many governments (especially under Margaret Thatcher in Britain and Ronald Reagan in the United States), these economists guided public policy to deregulate market life.

No international financial organization was more influential than the **International Monetary Fund (IMF)**. During the 1980s it emerged as a central player, especially in response to the so-called debt crisis in Third World and eastern-bloc countries. Throughout the 1970s, European, Japanese, and North American banks had loaned money on very easy terms to cash-strapped Third World and eastern-bloc borrowers. But what was once good business soon turned sour. In 1982, a wave of defaults threatened to overrun Latin America in particular. Throughout the 1980s, international banks and the IMF kept heavily indebted customers solvent. The IMF offered short-term loans to governments on condition that recipients adopt new fiscal ways and compel civilian populations to tighten their belts. Latin Americans pioneered the process of merging their domestic markets with international ones. Trade barriers crumbled, state enterprises became private firms, and foreign investors called the former debtors "emerging markets." Eastern Europe

and Asia followed suit in the 1990s, and emerging-market mania buoyed a boom in international finance.

EFFECTS OF INTEGRATED NETWORKS New technologies and institutions enabled many more financial investors and traders to participate in the integrated networks of world finance. The Internet and online trading accelerated the mobility—and volatility—of capital across borders. Volatility soon created problems, however. In the 1990s, currency devaluations in Mexico, in Russia, and across East Asia shocked financiers. When the Mexican economy went into paralysis in 1994, the crisis was so extreme that not even the IMF could bail it out; the U.S. Treasury had to issue the largest international loan in history to pull Mexico out of its economic tailspin. Despite acting as the lender in that instance, the United States emerged in the new financial order as the world's largest borrower. Early in the new millennium, its net foreign debt soared past $2 trillion—a 700 percent increase since the early 1990s. Much of this debt was owed to Asian, especially Chinese, bankers.

Globalization increased commercial, as well as financial, interdependence. The total value of world trade increased nearly tenfold between 1973 and 1998, and trade in Asia grew even faster. In 1960, trade accounted for 24 percent of the world gross domestic product (GDP; the total value of all goods and services produced in a country in a single year). By 1995, that share had almost doubled. Where an American would once have worn American-made clothes (Levi's), driven an American car (a Ford), and watched an American television (Zenith), such was rarely the case by century's end. Increasingly, consumers bought foreign goods and services and sold a greater share of their own output abroad. This pattern had always been true of smaller regions like Central America and southern Africa. But in the 1980s it intensified, with Hong Kong and Singapore prospering through expanding world trade.

International trade also shifted the international division of labor. After World War II, Europeans and North Americans dominated manufacturing, while Third World countries supplied raw materials. But by the 1990s this was no longer the case. Brazil became a major airplane maker, South Korea exported millions of automobiles, and China emerged as the world's largest source of textiles, footwear, and electronics.

The most remarkable global shift involved East Asian industry and commerce. Manufactured goods, including high-technology products, now issued from the eastern fringe of Afro-Eurasia as often as from its western fringe. Japan blazed the Asian trail: between 1965 and 1990, its share of world trade doubled to almost 10 percent. China, too, flexed its economic muscle. When Deng Xiaoping took power in 1978, China was already a growing economy. Under Deng, China started to become an economic powerhouse. For the next two decades, China chalked up astounding 10 percent annual growth rates, swelling its share of world GDP from 5 percent to 12 percent.

Globalization. *In the past, Americans mostly bought products, such as cars, that were manufactured domestically. Now, Americans often buy products made abroad.*

For East Asia as a whole, the share of world exports doubled in the same period, with smaller countries like Singapore, Taiwan, South Korea, and Hong Kong becoming mini-powerhouses. By the early 1990s, these countries and Japan were major investors abroad. Overall, East Asia's share of world production rose from 13.6 percent to 25.3 percent between 1965 and 1989. By contrast, over the same period, the U.S. and European shares decreased.

REGIONAL TRADE BLOCS AND GROWING DISPARITIES Industrialization of previously less developed countries, combined with lower trade barriers, increased the pressures of world competition on national economies. Some areas responded by creating regional blocs. In North America, much trade and finance flowed back and forth across the U.S.-Canadian border. By the 1980s, fearing competition from inexpensive Asian manufactures, the two countries admitted Mexico into the trading bloc to encourage plants to locate within the region. They negotiated a North American Free Trade Agreement (NAFTA) in 1992.

Meanwhile, the most complete regional integration occurred in Europe. Indeed, Europeans slashed trade barriers and

harmonized their commercial policies toward the rest of the world. In 1993, the Maastricht Treaty established the **European Union (EU)** under its current name, and what had been conceived as a trading and financial bloc began to evolve into a political union as well. In hopes of establishing permanent peace and prosperity, European states agreed to give up aspects of their sovereignty and allowed European-wide legislative and judicial bodies (the European Parliament and the Court of Justice of the European Union) to make binding political and legal decisions. In 2002, a number of the European Union states deepened their economic interdependence by adopting a single currency, the euro. A few nations—most notably the United Kingdom—did not want to give up control of their own currency. By 2012, the European Union had twenty-seven members, and the Eurozone seventeen members. Trade integration and interdependence coincided with a transformation in traded commodities. Pharmaceuticals, computers, software, and services from insurance to banking became key exports and imports. High technology, in particular, now occupied an ever-greater share of the manufacturing and exports of the world's richest countries.

Competition and the shift to producing sophisticated goods affected world incomes. For "rich" countries as a whole, about half of total GDP reflected the production and distribution of such goods and services, giving those countries a competitive advantage. In general, where global incomes were lower and people were less educated, the share of knowledge as a contributor to wealth was also lower. Poor nations remained, with few exceptions, locked in the production of low-tech goods and the export of raw materials. Increasingly, technology and knowledge now divided the world into affluent, technically sophisticated countries and poor, technically underdeveloped regions.

Migration

Migration, a constant feature of world history, became more pronounced in the twentieth century (see Map 21.3). Although after 1970 fewer Europeans were on the move, many more Asians, Africans, and Latin Americans were. By 2000, there were 120 million migrants scattered across 152 countries, up from 75 million in 1965. Most left poorer countries for richer destinations.

PATTERNS OF MIGRATION Migratory flows often followed the contours of existing political relations. Where North America and Europe had had colonies or dependencies, their political withdrawal left tracks for migrants to follow. Indians and Pakistanis moved to Britain. Dominicans, Haitians, and Mexicans went to the United States. Algerians and Vietnamese moved to France. And where emerging rich societies cultivated close diplomatic ties, these relations opened migratory gates. This was true of Germany's relationship with Turkey, of Japan's with South Korea, and of Canada's with Hong Kong. In most cases, economic factors propelled migrants across national borders.

International migration was often an extension of regional and national migration from poorer, rural areas to urban centers. In Nigeria, for example, rural-urban migration intensified after 1970. In 1900, Nigeria's capital at the time, Lagos, had a population of 41,847. At the century's end, Lagos had more than 10 million people, with predictions that it would double by 2025. The key to Lagos's boom in the 1970s was the existence of large oil reserves inside the country and the high prices that oil fetched in international markets. When the Organization of Petroleum Exporting Countries (OPEC) sent oil prices soaring, money poured into Nigeria. The government kept most of it in its largest city. That, in turn, spurred people to move to Lagos. This rural-urban migration increased Lagos's population by 14 percent per year in the 1970s and 1980s. No government—least of all a new, weakly supported one like Nigeria's—could cope with such a huge influx. Electricity supplies failed regularly. There were never enough schools, teachers, or textbooks. But the city burst with the vitality of new arrivals, prompting one immigrant to exclaim: "It's a terrible place; I want to go there!"

The search for opportunities also pushed people to move from less developed to more developed nations. Although many corporations relocated their manufacturing plants in poorer countries, where unskilled labor was abundant and government regulations were few, these jobs remained less attractive than even the lowest-wage positions available in richer nations. Thus, the possibility for better wages—and the hope for better lives—inspired millions to leave their homelands.

TEMPORARY MIGRANTS Some migrants moved for temporary sojourns. At least that was the original intent. In the 1950s and 1960s, southern Europeans moved northward; but when Spain, Portugal, Greece, and Italy also became wealthy societies, not only did the exodus decline, but these countries became magnets for Middle Eastern, North African, and (more recently) eastern European migrants. However, Europeans' strong identification with their nations did not permit the easy integration of foreigners. Nor did European states support the permanent settlement of immigrants. Most migrants from Asia and Africa went initially to Europe in search of temporary jobs as guest workers. With time they settled in their host countries, often living in urban slums (for example, Pakistanis in Britain's city of Leeds, and Algerians in impoverished suburbs of Paris).

In Japan, too, immigrants were not easily incorporated. Tokyo's policy in the 1970s resembled the European guest worker program. Discouraging permanent settlement and immigration, Japan encouraged mainly itinerant workers to move to the country, yet its economy required increasing numbers of these sojourners. Indeed, Japan's deep reluctance to integrate migrants led to dire labor shortages.

Lagos, Nigeria. *During the twentieth century, Lagos was one of the fastest-growing and most crowded cities in Africa.*

After Japan, the economic tigers of Hong Kong, Taiwan, and Malaysia all became hosts for temporary migrants. So millions of guest workers moved there, but ultimately the migrants sank deeper roots, especially once their children entered schools. This presented a challenge to host societies that were accustomed to thinking of their national communities as ethnically homogeneous. At times, discrimination led to violent conflicts among recent immigrants, long-time residents, and the state's security forces. Governments also grappled with the challenge of extending citizenship rights to and culturally assimilating newcomers who wanted to dress according to religious custom, as in the case of Muslims in France (10 percent of that country's population).

DEMOGRAPHIC CHANGES IN THE UNITED STATES One society that had fewer problems integrating migrants, and that attracted the lion's share of international migrants, was the United States. Long a magnet for Europeans, the United States enacted an immigration reform in 1965 that opened its gates to the world's migrants. By 2000, 27 million immigrants lived there, accounting for almost 10 percent of the population—double the share in 1970.

The profile of migration also changed. In 1970, there were more Canadians or Germans living in the United States than Mexicans. Over the next thirty years, the Mexican influx rose tenfold and by 2000 accounted for almost one-third of immigrants in the United States. The numbers migrating from Asia also surged, accounting for over 40 percent of all immigrants to the United States in the 1990s, with the flow of legal and illegal immigrants from Mexico and Central America having an especially dramatic impact on the border states. A backlash developed against the new immigration. Opponents called for tighter policing of the border between the United States and Mexico and campaigned for laws that cut off public benefits from those who had come into the United States illegally. Several states passed "English only" statutes aimed at forcing immigrants, both legal and illegal, to "Americanize."

RESIDENT NONCITIZENS AND REFUGEES Arguments in Los Angeles over schools and health care for resident noncitizens became part of a global debate. In Argentina, up to 500,000 undocumented Peruvians, Bolivians, and Paraguayans also lived without rights as citizens. Even more staggering, between 3 and 8 million migrants moved from Mozambique, Zimbabwe, and Lesotho to South Africa. In some Middle Eastern countries, like Saudi Arabia and Kuwait, foreign-born workers constituted over 70 percent of the workforce. In general, migrants were only partially accommodated, while many were fully excluded from host societies. Thus, even though population movements flowed across political, kinship, and market networks, demographic reshuffling heightened national concerns about the ethnic makeup of political communities.

Finally, forced migrations remained a hallmark of the modern world. In contrast to earlier centuries' forced migration of slaves from Africa, recent involuntary flows involved refugees fleeing civil war and torture. Many suffered for weeks, months, or years in refugee camps on the periphery of violence. The greatest concentration of refugees occurred in the world's poorest region—Africa. Those Africans unable to reach wealthier areas were often

CANADA
UNITED STATES
MEXICO
BELIZE
GUATEMALA
NICARAGUA
CUBA
HAITI
COLOMBIA
BRAZIL
ARGENTINA
GREAT BRITAIN
SPAIN
MOROCCO
ALGERIA
IVORY COAST
ATLANTIC OCEAN
PACIFIC OCEAN
East Europeans 1918–1919
East Europeans 1918–1919
Russian Jews to USA 1980s and 1990s
European Jews to USA 1930s
West Indians to Britain
Spaniards to Mexico 1936
Jamaicans, Haitians, and Dominicans to USA 1990–
1950–
1960–
1960–1980
1980
1970–
Foreign-born people as percentage of total population (latest available year)
Less than 1.5%
1.5%–2.9%
3.0%–7.5%
More than 7.5%
Data not available
Migration
0 1000 2000 Miles
0 1000 2000 Kilometers

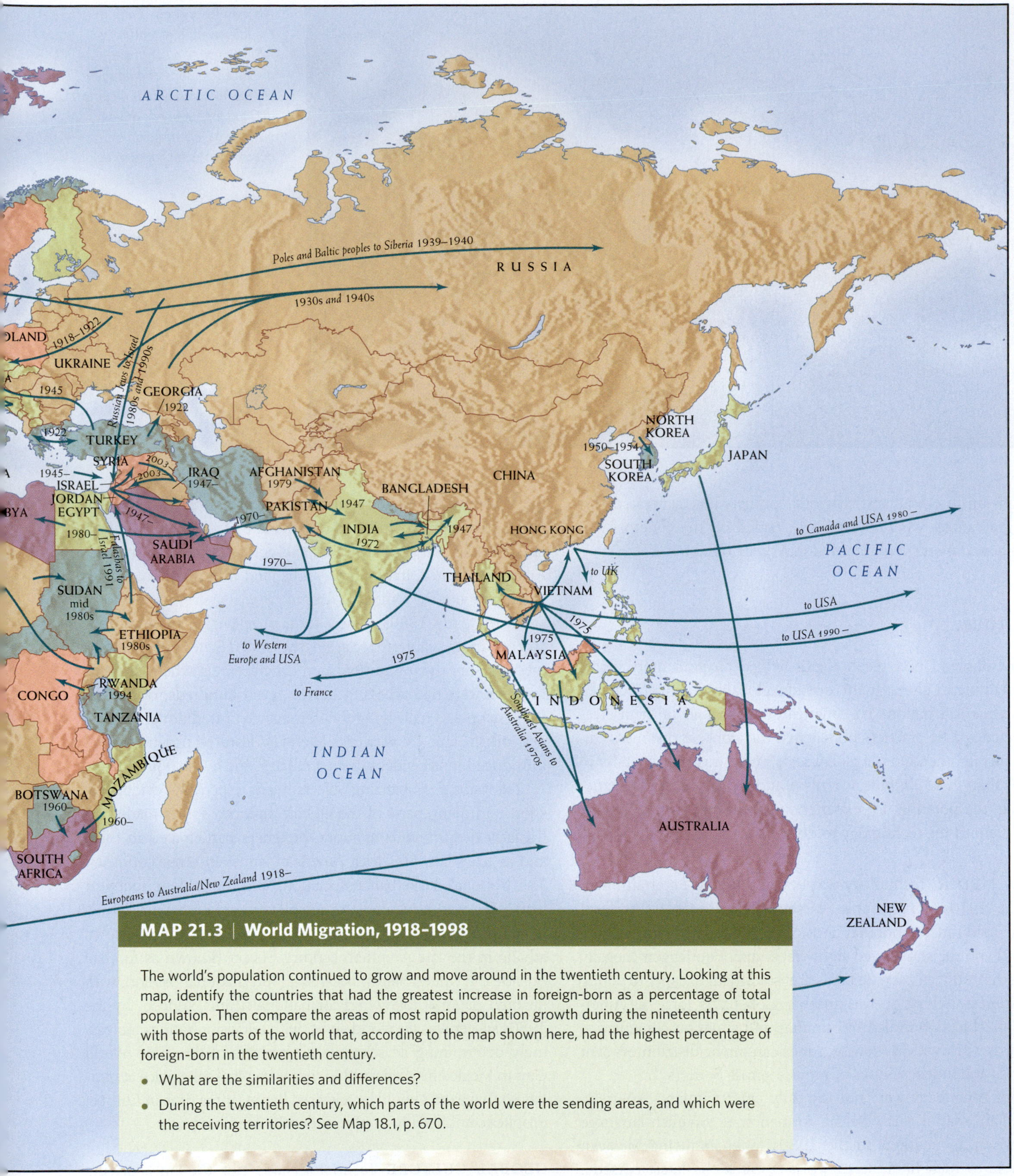

MAP 21.3 | World Migration, 1918–1998

The world's population continued to grow and move around in the twentieth century. Looking at this map, identify the countries that had the greatest increase in foreign-born as a percentage of total population. Then compare the areas of most rapid population growth during the nineteenth century with those parts of the world that, according to the map shown here, had the highest percentage of foreign-born in the twentieth century.

- What are the similarities and differences?
- During the twentieth century, which parts of the world were the sending areas, and which were the receiving territories? See Map 18.1, p. 670.

African Refugees. *During the late twentieth century, Africa became a continent of displaced persons and refugee camps. Pictured here is a camp in Chad for Sudanese driven out of the Darfur region by government-sponsored raids.*

caught up in ethnic and religious conflicts that generated vast refugee camps, where survival depended on the generosity of host governments and international contributions.

Culture

Migrations and new technologies helped create a more global entertainment culture. In this domain, globalization often equated with Americanization. Yet American entertainments themselves reflected artistic practices from across the globe, as one mass culture met another. On the global scale, there was less diversity in 2000 than in 1300; but in terms of individuals' everyday experience, the potential for experiencing cultural diversity (if one could afford the technology to do so) increased.

NEW MEDIA Technology was key in diffusing entertainment. In the 1970s, for example, cassette tapes became the dominant medium for popular music, sidelining the long-playing record and the short-lived eight-track tape. Bootleggers illegally mass-reproduced cassette tapes and sold them cheaply to young consumers. Television was another globalizing force, as American producers bundled old dramas and situation comedies to stations worldwide. Likewise, American movie distributors sent movies and videocassettes of movies across borders.

But Americans were not the only entertainment exporters. Brazilian soap operas began to penetrate Spanish-language American TV markets in the 1980s, often inducing Mexican viewers to rush home from work to catch the latest episode. Latin American television shows and music were distributed in the United States in areas with large Spanish-speaking populations. Bombay also produced its fair share of programs for viewers of British television. Movies and actors from New Zealand, Australia, France, Italy, China, India, and Iran found audiences in Europe and the United States.

In the early 1980s, a new form of television programming spread rapidly: cable. Once again, the United States pioneered the medium, but the innovation soon caught on elsewhere. Increasingly, viewers had access to dozens, even hundreds, of specialized channels, challenging the dominance of traditional national networks. Cable TV networks like MTV featured pop music and introduced music videos, both a musical and a visual product.

Television's globalizing effects were especially evident in sports. In many parts of the globe, American sports made particularly deep inroads as more foreigners participated in them and as television broadcast American games in other countries. The National Basketball Association (and the athletic footwear firm Nike) was particularly successful in international marketing; in the process, it made Michael Jordan the world's best-known athlete in the late twentieth century. Soccer (known as football outside the United States) became an international passion, with devoted national followings for national teams. Indeed, by the 1980s soccer was *the* world sport, with television ratings increasingly determining its schedule. Organizers of the 1986 World Cup in Mexico insisted that big soccer matches take place at midday so that games could be televised live at prime time in Europe, despite teams' having to play under the scorching sun.

GLOBAL CULTURE Technology was not the only driving force of world cultures, for migration and exchange were also

Bob Marley. *In the 1970s, young Europeans and North Americans began to listen to music from the Third World. Among the most popular was Jamaican-based reggae, and its most renowned artist, Bob Marley. Marley's music combined rock and roll with African rhythms and lyrics about freedom and redemption for the downtrodden of the world.*

important. For example, as people moved around they brought their own musical tastes and borrowed others. Reggae, born in the 1960s among Jamaica's Rastafarians, became a hit sensation in London and Toronto, where large West Indian communities had migrated. Reggae lyrics and realist imagery invoked a black countercultural sensibility and a redemptive call for a return to African roots. Soon, Bob Marley and the Wailers, reggae's flagship band, played to audiences worldwide. In northeast Brazil, where African culture emerged from decades of disdain, Bob Marley became a folk hero. In Soweto, South Africa, populated by black workers, he was a symbol of resistance.

Reggae propelled a shift in black American music. In broadcasting reggae, DJs merged sounds and chant lyrics over a beat, a "talkover" form that soon characterized rap music as well. This was a disruptive concept in the late 1970s, but within ten years rap had become a club favorite—and a nonconventional provocation. Rap lyrics emulated reggae realism by focusing on black problems, but they also opened a new domain of controversies involving gang worldviews. On the world stage, Latino rappers stressed multicultural themes, often in "Spanglish." Asian rap stressed the genre as a vehicle for cross-cultural sharing.

The effects of migration on global music were also evident in Latin American transformations of North American genres. Latin music came into its own thanks to Latin American migrants to the United States. In New York and New Jersey, Puerto Ricans and Dominicans popularized boogaloo, salsa, and merengue. In Los Angeles, Mexican *corridos* (ballads) became pop hits.

What reinforced cross-cultural borrowing was not just the medium of production and distribution of entertainment across borders, but also the message. Increasingly, world popular culture was youth culture—especially its message of generational opposition. Consider Egypt's popular TV serial *The School of Troublemakers*, which carried a resolutely antiestablishment message: it showed schoolboys challenging their teachers' authority and then reveling in the chaos that resulted. In Argentina, rock and roll was crucial to the counterculture during the military dictatorship of the 1970s and 1980s. Charlie García urged Buenos Aires audiences to defy authorities by daring to dream of a different order. Indeed, in countries where repressive regimes quashed public cultures, pop culture was usually counterculture.

The same globalizing effects influenced sports. Consider the staple of American identity, baseball, whose major league teams took on a more global cast. Beginning in the 1960s, the number

Baseball Goes International. *The 1980s and 1990s saw an influx of ballplayers from Latin America and quite a few from Asia as well. (Left) Boston Red Sox slugger David Ortiz hails from the Dominican Republic. (Right) New York Yankees superstar Ichiro Suzuki is from Japan.*

CURRENT TRENDS IN WORLD HISTORY

Urbanization as a Global Phenomenon: Transforming Bombay to Mumbai

The city has played a pivotal role in world history since it first emerged thousands of years ago along the Tigris and Euphrates Rivers in Mesopotamia (modern day Iraq). People have since flocked to cities for the social and economic advantages that these locations offered. By the end of the twentieth century, the proportion of people living in cities, usually defined as having populations over 5,000 or 10,000, exceeded 50 percent in the wealthiest countries and was approaching that proportion in the less developed countries as well.

Of the burgeoning cities in the Southern Hemisphere, one of the most dynamic is Mumbai in India. Acquired in the sixteenth century by the Portuguese, who then transferred its control to the British East India Company, Bombay (as it was named at that time) developed as a port city for colonial commerce. It profited from the cotton trade, developed a vibrant textile industry, attracted migrants, and acquired a cosmopolitan image. After India's independence in 1947, Bombay was renamed Mumbai in 1996, though it still epitomized the modern face of the nation, and its heterogeneous population symbolized the Indian melting pot.

Beginning in the 1980s, however, the nature of the city's relationship with the world economy started to change. The cotton textile industry, Bombay's economic backbone, went into a decline. Industrial employment fell sharply. Moreover, the share of informal household enterprises, small shops, petty subcontractors, and casual laborers rose, along with banking and insurance. Economic liberalization removed hurdles against foreign businesses and brought the city directly into the global economy.

Today Mumbai occupies a strategic place in transnational geography. This is evident in the increasing presence of financial institutions, trading organizations, insurance companies, telecommunications corporations, and information technology enterprises with worldwide operations. Even the city's vibrant film industry addresses a global, not just national, audience; rather appropriately, Bombay cinema has acquired the nickname "Bollywood."

The city, however, still attracts a large number of poor migrants who live in slums or call the pavements their home. The gap between Mumbai's rich and poor has grown alarmingly. Millions who eke out a miserable living stand in stark contrast to a tiny elite enriched by the global economy.

Globalization has also affected its residents' identity. In the 1990s, the political party in power was the Shiv Sena,

of Latin Americans playing in North American professional leagues grew steadily. Notable in the 1980s was the Mexican pitcher Fernando Valenzuela, whose exploits as a member of the Los Angeles Dodgers made him a hero to that city's Mexican population and in his native land as well. The Dodgers also took the lead in reaching for Asian talent. In the 1990s, as Los Angeles experienced a growing Asian immigrant population, the Dodgers signed the Japanese pitcher Hideo Nomo. Meanwhile, in the Dominican Republic, baseball fans were riveted by their favorite players in the big leagues: slugger Sammy Sosa and ace pitcher Pedro Martínez.

LOCAL CULTURE World cultures may have become more integrated and homogeneous, but they did not completely replace national and local cultures. Indeed, technology and migration often reinforced the appeal of "national" cultural icons, as national celebrities gained popularity among immigrant groups abroad. Inexpensive new technology introduced these stars to more and more people. In Egypt, the most popular singer of the Nasser years was Umm Kalthum, who became the favorite of the middle classes via radio. In 1975 she was given a state funeral, the likes of which had rarely been seen. Egypt's more liberal policies under Nasser's successor, President Anwar al-Sadat, created new national pop stars. Some, like Muhammad Abd al-Wahhab, blended western and eastern musical themes. Educated in Quranic schools, he fused Quranic vocals and chants with western synthesizers and beats to become a national sensation.

As the market for world cultures grew increasingly competitive, there was more room for acceptable performance. Among the breakthroughs that occurred since the 1970s was the triumph of black performers (Bob Marley, Whitney Houston), black athletes (Pelé, Michael Jordan), and black writers (Toni Morrison, Chinua Achebe). Competition also shattered some sexual biases. Female performers like Madonna became popular icons. So did gay performers, starting with the Village People, whose campy multicultural anthem "YMCA" created a place for a new generation of homosexual or bisexual artists. Of course, beyond Europe and North America, flirting with sexual conventions had its limits. In the Middle East, female video artists continued to wear veils—but they still swung their hips.

Because globalization introduced world consumers to a set of common icons—athletic, musical, and performing—it

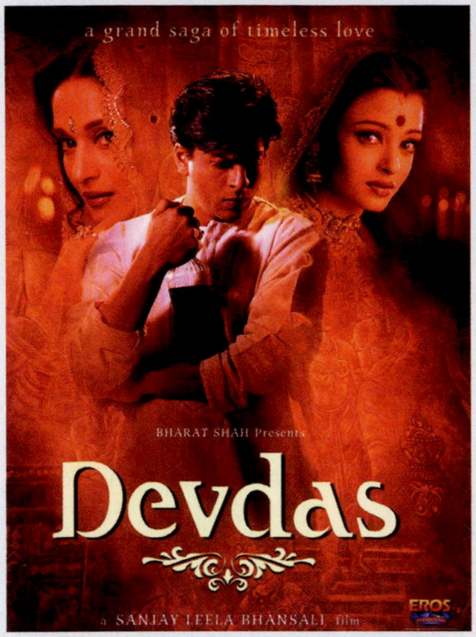

Bollywood. *Bombay cinema, or Bollywood, has an increasing global presence. This is the poster for* Devdas, *a three-hour romance that won awards in India and around the world.*

a nativist regional party named after a seventeenth-century Maratha chieftain who opposed the Mughal Empire. As the industrial economy and trade unions gave way to the service sector and unorganized labor, the Shiv Sena utilized the social and political fluidity produced by globalization to win support for its nativist ideology. Mumbai's cosmopolitan image went up in smoke in 1992–1993, when the Shiv Sena led pogroms against the city's Muslim residents. In response, a Muslim underworld don engineered a series of bomb blasts in March 1993. Since then the city has experienced episodes of violence, none more gruesome than the terrorist attacks on two luxury hotels, a crowded railway station, and a Jewish center in November 2006. Ironically, the terrorists chose to attack Mumbai for its reputation as a cosmopolitan city.

Mumbai today illustrates the uneven effects of globalization. The society is sharply divided, economic disparities are great, and the city's politics is a cauldron of conflicting identities. These are the local forms in which this vast and influential city experiences globalization.

QUESTIONS FOR ANALYSIS

- What similarities and differences emerge when you compare the vignette of Los Angeles in the chapter introduction to Mumbai here?
- How does Mumbai fit into the larger theme of worlds together and worlds apart?

Explore Further

Mehta, Suketu, *Maximum City: Bombay Lost and Found* (2005).

Prakash, Gyan, *Mumbai Fables* (2010).

promoted a more homogeneous world culture. Mass culture from the United States became an especially important purveyor of products worldwide, even as local cultures became more diverse. Relatively homogeneous national cultures, often dominated by men representing the ethnic majority, gave way to a wide variety of entertainers and artists who broke loose of confining local cultures.

Communications

Migration, markets, and mass entertainment were not the only forms that now enjoy global networks; even more important was a revolution in communications. By the 1970s, satellites relayed telecommunications into living rooms worldwide. Television brought the world home—but it was not interactive. Starting in the 1970s and early 1980s, however, engineers based primarily in California's Santa Clara Valley (so-called **Silicon Valley**) tinkered with the idea of computers for personal use. (Computers had served government and corporate needs since the 1940s.) At first these big, underpowered machines had little memory, but with the invention of the silicon chip, the computer weighed less and gained enormous memory capacity. On the heels of this hardware revolution, a software revolution enabled people to process words, run businesses, play games, and eventually communicate with one another via computer terminals.

Computer technology galvanized interactive communications. In the late 1980s, while working in Switzerland, the British physicist Tim Berners-Lee devised a means to pool data stored on various computers. Whereas previous electronic links had existed only between major universities and research stations, Berners-Lee made data more accessible by creating the World Wide Web. With each use and each connection, and as people entered more data, however, the Web grew unmanageably crowded. The early 1990s saw the first commercial browsers used in navigating the so-called Internet. Within a few years, the computer revolution had achieved a fully interactive form of communications and storage with the clarity and resolution of a television. Suddenly people were communicating across global networks more easily than with neighbors and more inexpensively than with local phone calls.

The change created a new generation of wealth. CEOs of top companies like General Motors, Royal Dutch Shell, and Merck had less net worth than Michael Dell (hardware maker), Bill Gates (software maker), and Jeff Bezos (creator of Amazon.com). Shares of Internet firms, known as dot-coms, swept the world's stock markets. Money from these companies flowed globally as they established offices worldwide. Software and Internet technologies developed enormous economies of scale and thus became prone to monopolization. Monoliths emerged by taking over small companies.

Hardware, software, and the Internet were not purely American innovations. Within a few years of their invention, personal computers were being made in Mexico and computer chips mass-produced in Taiwan. The brains behind the Internet were likely to be students from Indian institutes of technology. Originally engineering schools, these institutes trained a whole generation of pioneering computing engineers, many of whom resettled in California's Silicon Valley. By 1996, Indians held half of the 55,000 temporary work visas issued by the U.S. government for high-tech employees. Roughly half of Silicon Valley start-up companies in the late 1990s were the brainchildren of Indian entrepreneurs.

While this revolution provided new means to share and sell information, it also reinforced hierarchies between haves and have-nots. Great swathes of the world's population living outside big cities had no access to the Internet. According to World Bank calculations, in the late 1990s countries with low-income economies had, on average, 26 phone lines per 1,000 people; countries with high-income economies had 550 lines per 1,000 people. The biggest losers were the billions living in rural areas or towns neglected by state and private communications providers.

The have-nots were poor not just from lack of capital but from lack of access to knowledge and new media. The result: a widening gap between rich and poor. In 1870, the average American made nine times what the average African earned; by 1990, an American earned forty-five times the income of someone in Chad or Ethiopia. From 1990, as globalization intensified, world inequities became massive. Paradoxically, globalization both integrated the world's peoples more tightly and intensified disparities among them. (See Current Trends in World History: Urbanization as a Global Phenomenon.)

CHARACTERISTICS OF THE NEW GLOBAL ORDER

By 2000, globalization had promoted recognizable social and economic characteristics. Populations expanded dramatically, requiring greater industrial and agricultural output from all parts of the world. Families changed, and life spans increased. Decent education and good health determined one's status in society as never before. In general, while providing access to an unimaginable array of goods and services, globalization also deepened world inequalities.

The Demography of Globalization

It took 160 years (1800–1960) for the world's population to increase from 1 billion to 3 billion; over the next 40 years (1960–2000) it jumped from 3 billion to over 6 billion. Behind this steepening curve were two important developments: a decline in mortality, especially among children, and a rise in life expectancy.

Population growth was hardly equal worldwide (see Map 21.4). In Europe, population growth peaked around 1900, and it moved upward only gradually from 400 million to 730 million during the twentieth century, with little growth after the 1970s. North America's population quadrupled over the same period, mainly because of immigration. The population booms in the twentieth century occurred in Asia (400 percent), Africa (550 percent), and Latin America (700 percent). China and India each passed the billion-person mark. Increases were greatest in the cities. By the 1980s, the world's largest cities were Asian, African, and Latin American. Greater Tokyo-Yokohama had 30 million inhabitants, while Mexico City had 20 million, São Paulo, 17 million; Cairo, 16 million; Calcutta, 15 million; and Jakarta, 12 million.

Population growth slowed most dramatically in richer societies. For some, like Italy, the growth rate declined to zero. More recently enriched societies like Korea, Taiwan, and Hong Kong also had fewer births. Societies that did not see their birthrates decline by the same rate (much of Africa, southern Asia, and impoverished parts of Latin America) had difficulty raising income levels. But even among poor nations, birthrates declined after the 1970s.

The most remarkable turnaround occurred in China, where the government instituted a "one-child family" policy with rewards for compliance and penalties for transgression. Inducements included cash subsidies, preferential access to nurseries and kindergartens, priority in medical care, and the promise of favored treatment in housing, education, and employment. The policy also prompted an imbalance in sex ratio at birth. The bias in favor of sons (long a feature of China's patrilineal system, which emphasized descent through the male line), together with the availability of ultrasound scanners, promoted the widespread—albeit illegal—practice of prenatal sex selection.

In general, however, declining family size resulted from choice. In rich countries, more women deferred having children as education, career prospects, and birth control devices provided incentives and methods to postpone starting a family.

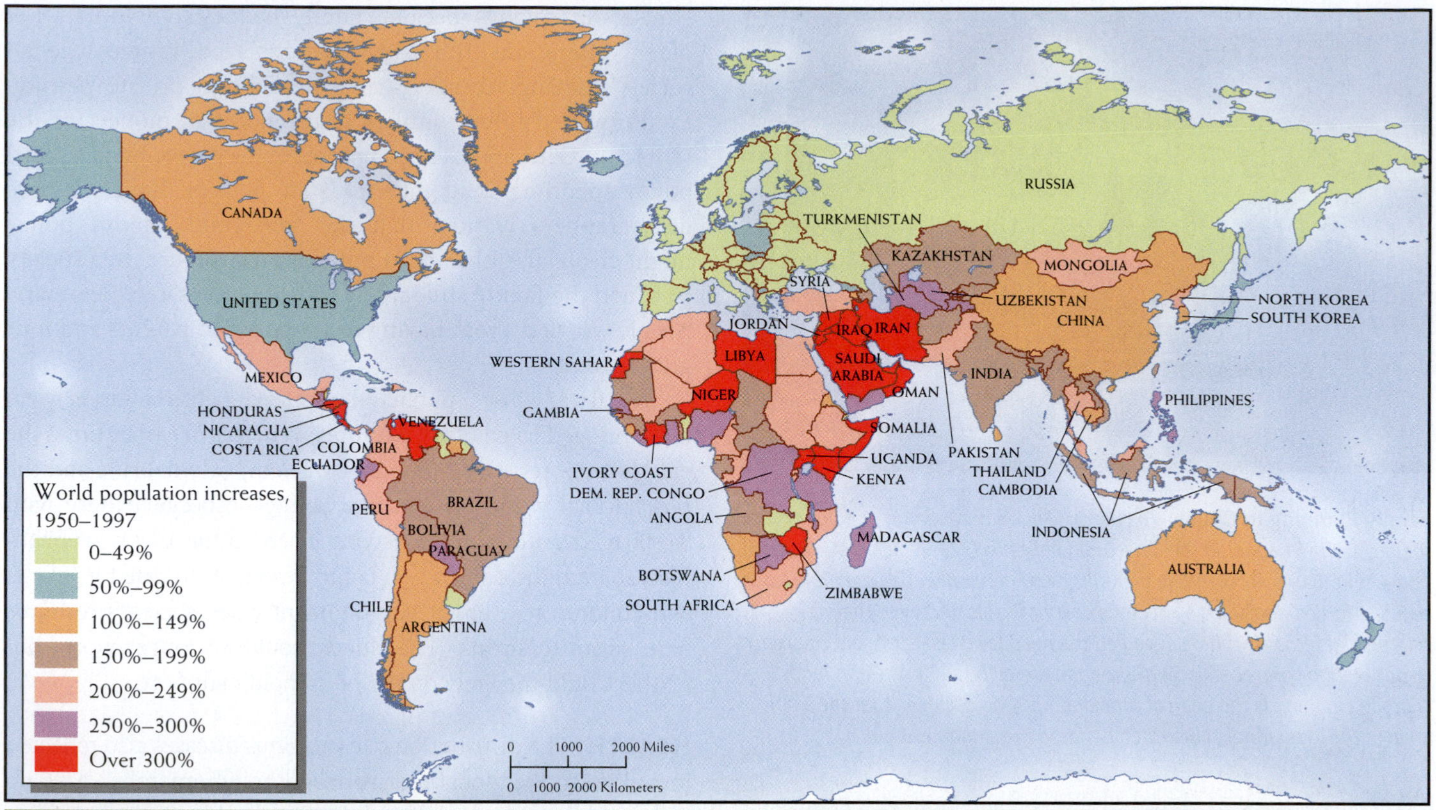

MAP 21.4 | World Population Increases, 1950–1997

The world's population more than doubled between 1950 and 1997, rising from approximately 2.5 billion to nearly 6 billion.

- Which countries had the largest population increases over these five decades? Why do you suppose these countries experienced such high population increases?
- According to your reading, why did western Europe and Russia have the lowest population increases?

In addition, love became a precondition to marriage and family formation in societies that had traditionally emphasized arranged marriages.

FAMILIES The legal definition of families became more fluid in this period. Here again, the change reflected women's choices and the relationship between love and marriage. First, couples chose to end their marriages at unprecedented rates. In the United States, for example, the divorce rate doubled between 1970 and 1998; by the century's end, one in two marriages ended in divorce. In Belgium and Britain late in the twentieth century, fewer than half of all marriages survived. China's divorce rate soared too. In Beijing, by century's end it approached 25 percent—double the 1990 rate. As of 2000, women initiated more than 70 percent of divorces.

As marriages became shorter-lived, new forms of childrearing proliferated. In the United States, out-of-wedlock childbirths constituted one-third of all births in the late 1990s, with only about half of American children living in households with both parents (compared with nearly three-quarters of children in the early 1970s). Europeans, too, including the supposedly more traditional Italians and Greeks, abandoned nuclear family conventions. In those European countries where divorce remained difficult, more couples lived together without getting married.

AGING Longer life spans also affected family fortunes, as more infants survived childhood and lived to be old. Also, along with other industrialized nations, the U.S. population "grayed" considerably. Fewer children and longer-living adults caused a marked increase in the median age of the American population: whereas in 1970 half of all Americans were twenty-eight or under, by 1990 the median age had risen to thirty-four. Likewise, the percentage of Americans over age sixty-five grew from 8 percent in 1950 to 13 percent in 1990. In western Europe and Japan, graying rates were even more marked. Japan's birthrate plummeted, and the citizenry aged at such a rate that the country began to depopulate. From a population of 127 million in 2000, estimates forecast a decline to 105 million by 2050.

Family Planning in China. *To control China's burgeoning population, the government enacted the One-Child Policy in 1979, which restricts each household to one child. While the policy was generally effective, numerous cases of forced abortions by zealous party officials and overwhelming numbers of female orphans revealed the need for a less stringent approach to population control. This 1996 propaganda billboard in Wuhan reads: "Family planning is the need of mankind." It is no accident that the single child in the ideal family illustrated beneath the slogan is a girl.*

The aging population presented new challenges for families. For centuries, being a parent meant providing for children until they could be self-sufficient. Old age, the years of relatively unproductive labor, was brief. Communities and households absorbed the cost of caring for the elderly. Household savings became family bequests to future, not older, generations. But as populations aged, retirees needed society's savings to survive. So public and private pension funds swelled to accumulate future pools of money for the retired. In Germany, over 30 percent of the government's social policy spending went into the state pension fund. Chinese demographers warned that the "one-child family" policy might create an unbalanced population structure. In a society in which the family still largely provided the safety net, many people worried about having to support two parents and four grandparents.

In Africa, where publicly supported pension funds were rare, the aged faced bleaker futures. Whereas in earlier times the elderly were respected founts of wisdom, colonial rule and the postcolonial world elevated the young—especially those with western educations and lifestyles. Then, in the 1970s, as birthrates soared, the demand on family resources to care for infants and children rose at the very moment when society's resource base began to shrink. The elderly could no longer work, but neither could they rely on the household's support.

HEALTH The distribution of contagious diseases also reflected inequities in the globalized world. Although microbes have no respect for borders, the effects of public health regulations, antibiotics, and vaccination campaigns reduced the spread of contagions. By the late twentieth century, not only did nutrition and healthy habits count (as they always had), but access to medicines did too.

Wedding Ceremonies. *(Left) The union of bride and groom is symbolized in this Northern Indian Hindu ceremony by the knot between their clothes. (Right) South Korean martial artist Kim Jong-bok holds his bride, actress Song Hee-jung, during their 2005 wedding ceremony, held on the Tokto islets off the Korean peninsula to protest Japan's claim of the territory.*

What used to be universal afflictions in previous centuries (such as the Black Death) now just affected certain peoples. Water treatment and proper sewerage, for example, had banished cholera from most urban centers by the mid-twentieth century. More recently, however, its deadly grip again reached across Asia and into the eastern Mediterranean, parts of Latin America, and much of sub-Saharan Africa. From the 1970s, Africa suffered frequent outbreaks. The crucial cause of the re-spread of cholera was urban developers' failure to keep sanitation systems growing apace with the demand for water. Thus, diseases proliferated where urban squalor was most acute—in cities with the greatest post-1970s population growth.

In the 1970s, entirely new diseases began to devastate the world's population. Consider **AIDS (Acquired Immuno Deficiency Syndrome)**, which in its first two decades killed 12 million people. Transmitted through contact with the semen or blood of an infected person, AIDS compromises the ability of the infected person's immune system to ward off disease. First detected in 1981, AIDS was initially stigmatized as a "gay cancer" (it appeared primarily in homosexual men) and received little attention. But as it spread to heterosexuals and public awareness about it increased, a new campaign urged the practice of safe sex, control of blood supplies, and restrictions on sharing hypodermic needles. In Europe and North America, where the campaigns intensified and new drugs kept the virus under control, AIDS rates stabilized.

New treatments were very expensive, however, leaving the poor and disadvantaged still vulnerable to infection. By 2000, 33 million people had AIDS (the vast majority in poor countries) and even more were infected with HIV, the human immunodeficiency virus that causes AIDS (see Map 21.5). At least two-thirds of those with AIDS lived in Africa below the Sahara. In India, 7 million carried the virus; in China, the figure topped 1 million.

Other factors behind the geographic and demographic prevalence of AIDS were schooling and literacy. Better education led to safer sexual practices. Worldwide, more educated men and women showed higher use of condoms. One Tanzanian survey showed that 20 percent of women with four to five years of education insisted that their sexual partners use condoms, whereas only 6 percent of women with no education insisted on using condoms during sex with a casual partner.

EDUCATION Access to decent education increasingly separated the haves from the have-nots. Moreover, because educational opportunities usually favored men, schooling shaped differences between males and females. In sub-Saharan Africa and in India, for example, literacy rates were, respectively, 63 and 64 percent for men and only 39 and 40 percent for women as of 2000. In the Arab world, the gap between men and women decreased somewhat by the end of the twentieth century. Yet low levels of literacy overall and the depressed levels for women continued to impede each region's efforts to combat poverty. (See Primary Source: Education and Inequality: Why Gender Matters.)

Gender bias also remained in rich societies. For decades, however, women and girls pressed for equal access, with some astounding results. In the United States, by the late 1980s, more

AIDS Treatment and Education. (Left) *At the Thirteenth International AIDS Conference in Durban, South Africa, in July 2000, AIDS activists express their displeasure at the high prices and unavailability of life-saving drugs for most of those in the Third World who are affected by AIDS.* (Right) *African governments did not tackle the problem of AIDS in their severely affected continent with the energy that it warrants. Pictured here, however, a doctor seeks to impress on the youth of a local community how they should conduct their social and sexual lives in light of the AIDS crisis.*

ANALYZING GLOBAL DEVELOPMENTS

Globalization: One World or Many?

People, funds, commodities and information move around the world with lightning speed. This rapid mobility has contributed to radical changes in population growth rates from one country to the next and one continent to the next, and it has led to significant changes in the rate of economic growth worldwide. But do these kinds of changes dictate a growing uniformity in the world? In other words, is globalization creating a single world community? The following two tables reveal some striking demographic differences, by continent and country, with respect to rapid or not-so-rapid population growth rates, the age distribution of populations, and the Gross National Product per person.

QUESTIONS FOR ANALYSIS

- Which of the continents is the fastest growing in terms of population and why would this be the case?
- Although this table does not provide data on the AIDS epidemic (see Map E.5 for that data), we know that Africa has been the most severely impacted continent. What impact is AIDS having on Africa population growth rates? Why do you think that its effects are so muted?
- Two of the countries in this table, Russia and Japan, have negative population growth rates. What are the reasons that would account for these differences and what sorts of problems do you think that these countries are likely to encounter?
- Japan and Germany are the only countries in this table that have a smaller percentage of the population under the age of fifteen than over the age of sixty-five. On the other hand, the countries of sub-Saharan Africa have the largest proportion of their populations under the age of fifteen. What is the cause for these developments and what problems are these countries likely to encounter as they move forward?
- Does this data suggest that the world is becoming more unified or integrated?

Table 1. Ten Most Populous Countries, 2012 and 2050

2012	Population in Millions	2050	Population in Millions
China	1,350	India	1,691
India	1,260	China	1,311
United States	314	United States	423
Indonesia	241	Nigeria	402
Brazil	194	Pakistan	314
Pakistan	180	Indonesia	309
Nigeria	170	Bangladesh	226
Bangladesh	153	Brazil	213
Russia	143	Democratic Republic of Congo	194
Japan	128	Ethiopia	166

than half of all college degrees went to women (up from 38 percent in 1960). More dramatic was the proportion of women earning postgraduate degrees (up from 3 percent to 35 percent). Chinese women made even greater strides, although roadblocks persisted. Ironically, with China's recent market reforms women's access to basic education regressed, as families, particularly in rural areas, reverted to spending their limited resources on educating sons. Thus, in 2000, up to 70 percent of China's 140 million illiterates were female.

WORK Although more women held jobs outside the home, they lacked full equity at work. Limited by job discrimination and burdens of child-rearing, women's participation in the workforce reached a fairly stable level by the 1980s. However, in Russia and Mexico, middle-class women pursuing professional careers often encountered informal obstacles and found themselves channeled into feminized professions such as nursing, teaching, and marketing. The percentage of women at the top of the corporate pyramid was considerably smaller than their

Table 2. World Population References for 2012 and Projection for 2050

Continents and Selected Countries	Population, 2012 (millions)	Rate of Natural Increase (%)	Projected Population, 2050 (millions)	Percent of Population under age 15	Percent of Population over age 65	GNP per capita (US $)
World	**7,058**	**+1.2**	**9,624**	**26**	**8**	**10,760**
AFRICA	1,072	+2.5	2,339	41	3	2,630
Egypt	82.3	+2.0	135.6	32	4	5,760
Nigeria	170.1	+2.6	402.4	44	3	1,910
South Africa	51.1	+0.9	57.2	31	5	2,240
Democratic Republic of Congo	69.1	+2.8	194.2	46	3	320
THE AMERICAS	948	+1.0	1,212	25	9	23,870
United States	349	+0.5	471	20	13	47,310
Brazil	194.3	+1.0	213.4	24	7	11,000
Mexico	116.1	+1.5	143.9	29	6	14,400
Haiti	10.3	+1.8	14.2	36	4	1,180
ASIA	4,260	+1.1	5,284	25	7	6,860
China	1,350.4	+0.5	1,310.7	16	9	7,640
India	1,259.7	+1.5	1,691.1	31	5	3,430
Japan	127.6	−0.2	119.8	13	24	34,610
Indonesia	241.0	+1.3	309.4	27	6	4,200
EUROPE	740	0.0	732	16	16	27,080
United Kingdom	63.2	0.4	79.6	18	17	35,840
France	63.6	0.4	78.4	19	17	34,750
Germany	81.8	−0.2	71.5	13	21	38,100
Russia	143.2	−0.1	127.8	15	13	19,240

Source: Population Reference Bureau, 2012: World Population Data Sheet, Washington D.C., pp. 2, 6, 7, 8, and 9.

proportion in the labor force or their college graduation rates. In 1995, the Chinese government claimed that Chinese women had made better advances than their U.S. counterparts: there were more Chinese women (10 percent) than American women (3 percent) in senior managerial posts. Still, Chinese women graduates complained of discrimination in the job market. In 2000, some 60 percent of China's unemployed were women, and the number was growing. Women worldwide had difficulties breaking through the "glass ceiling"—a seemingly invisible barrier to women's advancement. Consequently, while income disparities between men and women narrowed, a significant gap persisted.

Working outside the home led to problems inside the home. Who would take care of the children? Jamaican and Filipino women migrated by the thousands in the 1970s and 1980s to Canada and Australia to work as nannies to raise money to send back home, where they had often left their own children. In South Africa and Brazil, local women served as domestic

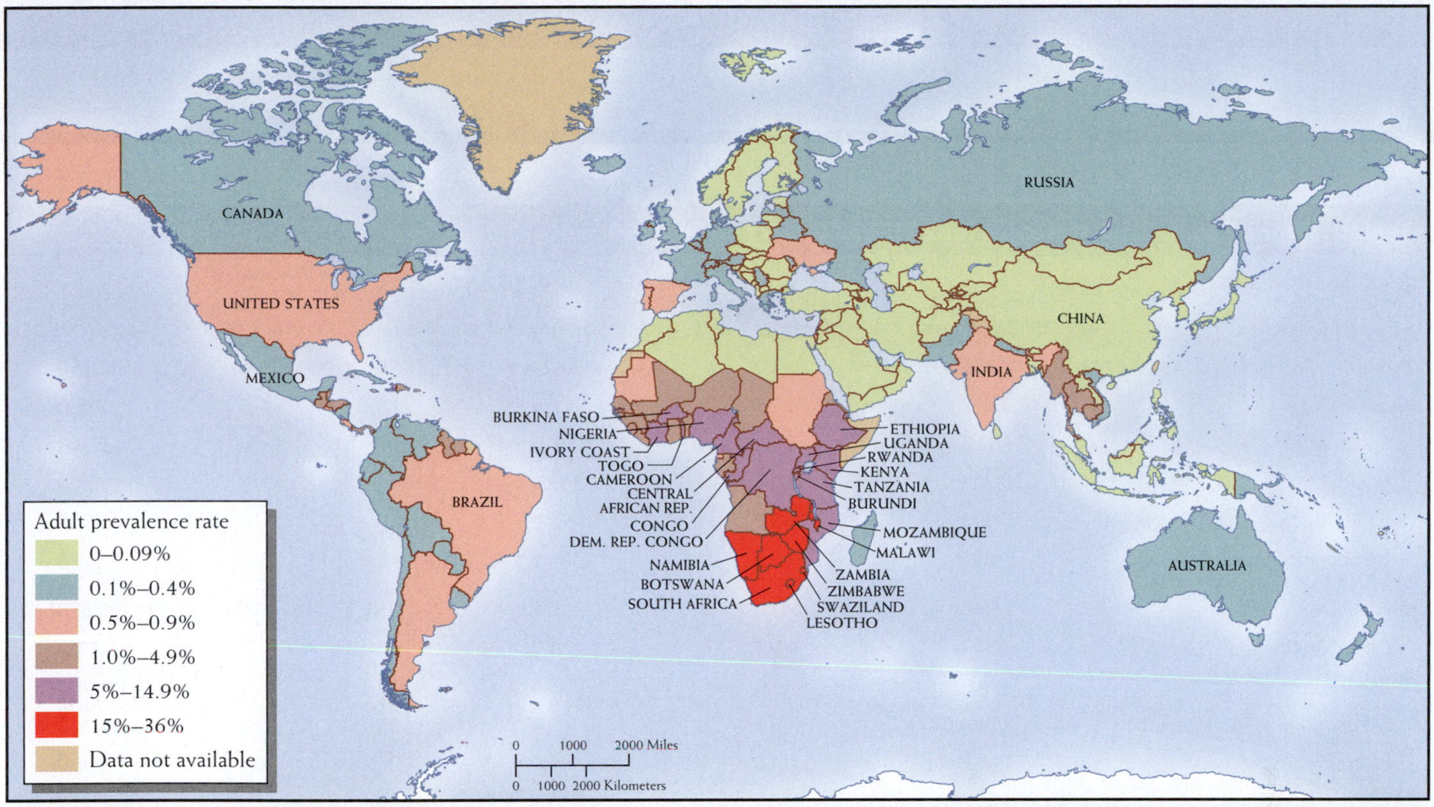

MAP 21.5 | HIV Infection across the World, 1999

HIV, which leads to AIDS, spread across the whole world, providing further evidence of global interconnectedness. The outbreak began in Africa.

- Where in Africa have the highest rates of HIV infection occurred? Which countries *outside* the African continent have had the highest rates of infection, and why is this so?
- Why have Egypt, North Africa, and much of the rest of the Islamic world, despite their close connections with Africa below the Sahara, thus far been little affected?

servants and nannies. They were doing the jobs that once belonged to middle- and upper-class homemakers, women who now wanted the same rights as men: to parent *and* to work.

FEMINISM The deeply ingrained inequality between men and women prompted calls for change. **Feminist movements** arose mainly in Europe and in North America in the 1960s and then become global in the 1970s. In 1975, the first truly international women's forum took place in Mexico City. But becoming global did not necessarily imply overturning local customs. What feminists called for was not the abolition of gender differences,

African Women and Education. *Though women's education lagged behind that of men in Africa, a number of women, like Stella Kenyi, pictured here, graduated from African high schools and attended universities at home or abroad. Kenyi taught business skills to men and women in Sudan after completing an undergraduate degree at Davidson College in North Carolina.*

PRIMARY SOURCE

Education and Inequality: Why Gender Matters

In the 1970s, aid agencies recognized that reducing world poverty means improving educational opportunities. So international organizations urged national governments to plow resources into schools. The results were stunning. But a disparity appeared: the beneficiaries were mainly boys. Thus, beginning in the 1980s, aid organizations became especially active in trying to channel educational opportunities to girls. In the World Bank study excerpted here, researchers found that development among the poor improves not just with better education, but especially with better education for girls.

Evaluations of recent initiatives that subsidize the costs of schooling indicate that demand-side interventions can increase girls' enrollments and close gender gaps in education. A school stipend program established in Bangladesh in 1982 subsidizes various school expenses for girls who enroll in secondary school. In the first program evaluation girls' enrollment rate in the pilot areas rose from 27 percent, similar to the national average, to 44 percent over five years, more than twice the national average. . . . After girls' tuition was eliminated nationwide in 1992 and the stipend program was expanded to all rural areas, girls' enrollment rate climbed to 48 percent at the national level. There have also been gains in the number of girls appearing for exams and in women's enrollments at intermediate colleges. . . . While boys' enrollment rates also rose during this period, they did not rise as quickly as girls'.

Two recent programs in Balochistan, Pakistan, illustrate the potential benefits of reducing costs and improving physical access. Before the projects there were questions about whether girls' low enrollments were due to cultural barriers that cause parents to hold their daughters out of school or to inadequate supply of appropriate schools. Program evaluations suggest that improved physical access, subsidized costs, and culturally appropriate design can sharply increase girls' enrollments.

The first program, in Quetta, the capital of Balochistan, uses a subsidy tied to girls' enrollment to support the creation of schools in poor urban neighborhoods by local NGOs. The schools admit boys as long as they make up less than half of total enrollments. In rural Balochistan the second program has been expanding the supply of local, single-sex primary schools for girls by encouraging parental involvement in establishing the schools and by subsidizing the recruitment of female teachers from the local community. The results: girls' enrollments rose 33 percent in Quetta and 22 percent in rural areas. Interestingly, both programs appear to have also expanded boys' enrollments, suggesting that increasing girls' educational opportunities may have spillover benefits for boys.

QUESTIONS FOR ANALYSIS

- What does this excerpt reveal about the ways that organizations like the World Bank promote change in developing countries?
- Why do you think there was a spillover effect for boys that coincided with these programs?

Source: Reproduced with permission of the World Bank from "Using Subsidies to Close Gender Gaps in Education," World Development Report 2000–2001, *p. 122, Box 7.2. Copyright 2000 by World Bank. Permission conveyed through Copyright Clearance Center, Inc.*

but equal treatment—equal pay and equal opportunities for obtaining jobs and advancement.

Women took increasingly active stances against discrimination in government and in the workplace. Indeed, as economic integration intensified with regional trade pacts (usually negotiated by men in the interest of male-owned and male-run firms), women struggled to ensure that globalization did not cut them out of new opportunities. For instance, after Argentina, Uruguay, Paraguay, and Brazil negotiated the Mercosur free trade pact, traffic across South American borders soared. But as trade grew, so did government efforts to monitor illegal commerce and foster approved trade along new highways and bridges. Women were responsible for one kind of illicit commerce, because for generations they had transported goods across the river separating Argentina and Paraguay. When customs officers tried to stop this practice in the mid-1990s, Argentine and Paraguayan women locked arms to occupy the new bridge that male truckers used to ship Mercosur products, protesting the restrictions on their age-old enterprise.

The rising tide of global feminism culminated in a conference in Beijing in 1995. Government delegates from more than 180 countries attended the Fourth World Conference on

Forum on Women. *Women representing different cultures of the world hold a "peace torch" during the opening ceremony of the Non-Governmental Organizations Forum for Women in Beijing in 1995.*

Women to produce "a platform for action" regarding women's rights in politics, business, education, and health. Alongside the official conference was a parallel conference for nearly 30,000 representatives at the NGO Forum for Women. These grassroots activists represented 2,000 nongovernmental organizations from every corner of the globe. Representatives planned strategies and coordinated programs on how to improve women's living and working conditions. What emerged from the conference were associations and groups that pledged to lobby for the rights of women and girls worldwide.

Production and Consumption in the Global Economy

The growing world population, the desire for more education and better health, the entry of women into paid employment, and the promise of rising standards of living spurred unprecedented production and consumption of the world's resources. The most immediate challenge was how to feed so many people while developing sustainable practices that do not use up limited natural resources.

AGRICULTURAL PRODUCTION Changing agrarian practices made a huge difference in increasing food production. Starting in the 1950s, chemistry increased outputs dramatically. The "green revolution," largely involving nonfarm inputs such as chemical fertilizers, herbicides, and pesticides, produced dramatically larger harvests. Then, in the 1970s, biologists began offering genetically engineered crops that multiplied yields at an even faster rate.

But these breakthroughs were not evenly distributed. American farmers, the biggest innovators, were the greatest beneficiaries. For example, by century's end they produced approximately one-ninth of the world's wheat and two-fifths of its corn. From this output, American exports accounted for about one-third of the world's international wheat trade and four-fifths of all corn exports. At the heart of the innovation was political power, for farmers had the clout to force officials to maintain roads, subsidize credit and prices, and mop up surplus supply. But Asian rice farmers made impressive innovations, too. In Taiwan and Korea, chemical and biological breakthroughs allowed rice yields to jump by 53 and 132 percent, respectively, between 1965 and 1985. And as Indian wheat farmers deployed chemical fertilizers, new seed varieties, and irrigation systems to double their output, the Ganges River basin supported an ever-larger urban population. The most miraculous transformation occurred in China. Beginning in the late 1970s, the Chinese government broke up some of the old collective farms and restored the individual household as the basic economic unit in rural areas. Thereafter, agricultural output surged by roughly 9 percent per year between 1978 and 1986.

Other agricultural producers also replied to world demand, but sometimes their added production was disruptive. While biology and chemistry allowed some farmers to get more out of their land, others simply opened up new lands to cultivation. Lacking access to credit, seed, and good land, small farmers had to go where land was cheap. In Java, farmers cleared sloping woodland to make way for coffee plantings. In southern Colombia, peasants moved into semitropical woodlands to cultivate coca bushes (the source of cocaine) at profits that other cultivators could never realize.

The most notorious frontier expansion occurred in the Amazon River basin. Populations flocked to the Amazon frontier, largely from impoverished areas in northeastern Brazil. They cleared (by fire) cheap land, staked their claims, and, like nineteenth-century American homesteaders, tried to climb the social ladder by cultivating crops and raising livestock. But the promise of bounty failed: the soils were poor and easily eroded, and land titles provided little security, especially once large speculators moved into the area. So the frontiersmen moved farther inland to repeat the cycle. By the 1980s, migrants to the Amazon River basin had burned away much of the jungle, contaminated the biosphere (the environment in which life exists), reduced the stock of diverse plant and animal life, and fostered social conflict in the Brazilian hinterland.

Nor were breadbaskets always able to feed exploding populations. This was especially true in Africa from the 1970s onward, when domestic food production could not keep pace with population growth (see Map 21.6). Food shortages thereafter increased in frequency and duration, wiping out

Saving the Amazon. *The rise of an international environmental movement in the 1970s led to alliances with local indigenous and environmental leaders, especially in the Amazon.* (Left) *One of the most prominent advocates of the rights of indigenous people and the need to protect imperiled jungles was the British musician Sting. Here he is pictured alongside one of the Amazon's foremost Indian leaders, Bep Koroti Paiakan.* (Right) *Farmers and ranchers cut and burned the Amazon at a ferocious rate in pursuit of frontier lands. In these remote regions, it was hard for local authorities to enforce conservation laws.*

large numbers of sub-Saharan peoples. The protruding ribs on African children became a clichéd image of the region.

What explained Africa's famines? As the Indian Nobel Prize–winning economist Amartya Sen observed, famines—and their increasing frequency—are not natural disasters; they are man-made. Food shortages in Africa stemmed largely from governments that ignored the rural sector and its politically unorganized farmers. Unable to persuade their governments to raise prices for their crops, the farmers lacked incentives to expand production. Food shortages were also by-products of global inequities. African countries, earmarking hefty chunks of their economies to agrarian exports to repay debts incurred in the 1970s, could not produce enough foodstuffs domestically and thus became food importers.

NATURAL RESOURCES While American farmers now produced a large share of the world's food, Americans also consumed a high proportion of its natural resources. By 2000, they were using water at a per-capita rate three times the world's average. Indeed, extensive irrigation was crucial to California's agricultural sector, the most productive and profitable in the world. Gathering more water also allowed a desert metropolis like Los Angeles to grow.

Energy consumption presented a similar story, although America's enormous appetite for fossil fuels generated a domestic debate about reliance on foreign sources and pollution of the environment. In the United States and Canada, attempts to curb energy consumption saw little success, and the United States grew more dependent on imported oil. In the late 1990s, North American demand for fuel-guzzling sport utility vehicles intensified oil imports. Dependence on foreign sources locked oil importers into recurring clashes with oil exporters. In the 1970s, OPEC raised the price of crude oil (see Chapter 20). The cartel weakened in the 1980s, partly because new oil fields opened elsewhere in the world and partly because internal struggles divided the exporters.

The harshest conflict over oil occurred in the mid-1980s between Iran and Iraq, followed by the 1990 Iraqi invasion of Kuwait. Iraq was poised to become dominant in the area and thus to control oil policies. The conquest of Kuwait would have given Iraq control over about 7 percent of world oil supplies and nearly 20 percent of the world's known reserves. Only Iraq's neighbors Saudi Arabia and Iran would have been larger oil exporters, and Iraq would have been in a position to menace both. As the situation threatened to unsettle the regional balance of power, the U.S. government moved to restore it. Rallying a coalition of other nations, the Americans and their allies launched a military invasion called Operation Desert Storm. The ensuing Gulf War, which ended with Iraq's expulsion from Kuwait, restored an order in which the global distribution of power favored oil consumers over producers and preserved a regional balance of power.

ENVIRONMENTAL EFFECTS The consumption of water, oil, and other natural resources became matters of international concern late in the twentieth century. So did pollution control and the disposal of waste products. Part of this internationalization reflected the recognition that individual nations could not

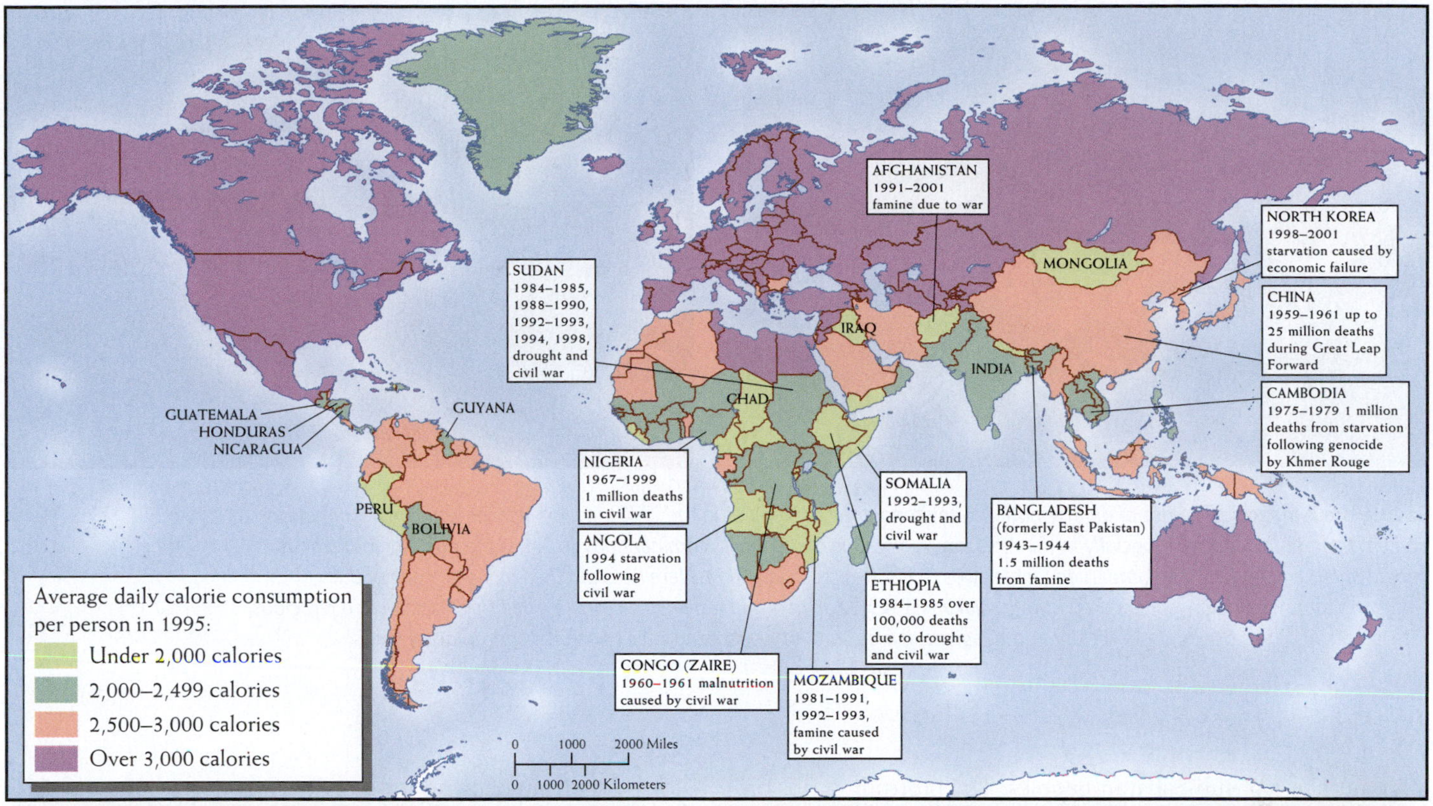

MAP 21.6 | Food Consumption and Famine since the 1940s

There is perhaps no better indicator of the division of the world into rich and poor, haves and have-nots, than this map on food consumption and famine.

- Which parts of the world have had the most difficulty in feeding their populations? What have been some of the causes of famine and malnourishment in these regions?
- How much have they been due to human agency, and how much to climate and other matters over which human beings have little control?

solve environmental issues on their own. Air and water, after all, do not stop flowing at political boundaries.

As Canadians saw their northern lakes fill up with acid rain (precipitation laced with sulfur, mainly from coal-fired plants), they urged their southern neighbor to curb emissions. Thus, reciprocal agreements between Canada and the United States took shape in the 1980s. Europeans, also beset by acidification, likewise negotiated regional environmental treaties. But some polluters simply moved overseas to poorer and less powerful nations. As the West cleaned up its environment, the rest of the world paid the price.

Other problems crossed man-made borders as well. These included the greenhouse effect and **global warming** (release into the air of human-made carbons that contribute to rising temperatures worldwide), ocean pollution, and declining biological diversity. International meetings addressed these threats inconclusively. After all, it was difficult to enforce an international solution on all national authorities when the forces of globalization compelled some of them to rely on energy-intensive industries, which generated massive emissions, in order to produce exports to pay off their debts. In 1992, the world's governments flocked to the first Earth Summit in Rio de Janeiro. But eco-friendly fanfare yielded only ineffective accords. Several years later, world leaders again met (in Kyoto, Japan) to draft a plan to enforce compliance. Even the grumblers agreed that it was necessary to reverse the emission of gases that led to global warming. However, when the administration of George W. Bush came to power in Washington in 2001, it revoked U.S. support for the Kyoto Treaty, which led others to defect as well. As a result, global climate change did not gain a global accord.

The relationship between power and resources was especially stark in dealing with contaminants. Increasing numbers of automobiles, emitting carbon fumes, caused serious air pollution in cities like Los Angeles, Tokyo, Mexico City, and Jakarta. But where environmentalists acquired political

Kyoto Protocol. *That America would no longer participate in the Kyoto Protocol was especially infuriating to the global audience, as America is the largest emitter of carbon dioxide and other major greenhouse gases. Here, Greenpeace environmental activists look on as one of their cohorts, dressed as Bush, brandishes a flaming globe in a dramatic protest outside of the US embassy in Mexico City.*

power, they forced regulators to curb emissions. Starting in the late 1960s, Japanese local governments slapped pollution controls on coal plants. Japan pioneered what one historian has called an "environmental miracle," spreading its regulations to many contaminating activities. By 1978, Japanese cars discharged only 10 percent as much pollution as in 1968. In 1987, Japan banned leaded gas altogether. But controls on fossil fuel emissions depended on power and wealth, for it was hard to impose restrictions in societies where high energy use seemed a necessity of economic life. Even the Japanese pioneers of clean fuel were polluters in other spheres. With increasing controls at home, Japanese industrialists went abroad to unload hazardous waste. U.S. industrialists did the same, sending hazardous waste to Mexico. Argentina and Canada sent their nuclear waste not abroad, but to poor provinces desperate for jobs.

Environmental problems gained new urgency after the meltdown of a Soviet nuclear reactor in Chernobyl in 1986. Initially, communist authorities tried to cover up the disaster; but when the fallout reached Sweden, they had to accept responsibility. The delayed response was disastrous for Ukraine and Belarussia (present-day Belarus). Being relatively powerless under a centralized authoritarian regime, they had no political voice to cry out for help in addressing the contamination. As Chernobyl and global warming demonstrated, environmental concerns did not observe boundary lines. Yet at the end of the twentieth century, global guidelines for regulating the impact of human activities on the environment had eluded the world's leaders.

CITIZENSHIP IN THE GLOBAL WORLD

Globalization distributed its benefits unequally. In general, people with access to better education and more opportunities profited from the border-crossing freedoms that the new order permitted. For most of the world's population, however, the new power structure was not so kind. Finding little opportunity in the globalized world, disadvantaged groups often invoked older religious and nationalist ideals. As globalization fostered human rights, environmental and labor standards, and women's rights worldwide, critics claimed that the language of international rights and standards was promoting neocolonial power in the form of a new "civilizing mission."

In particular, globalization posed massive problems for the nation-state. Since the nineteenth century, nation-states were supposed to be key in defining the rights of citizens. But now the rapid movement of ideas, goods, capital, and people across national boundaries undercut the authority of even the most powerful nations. Accordingly, other political spheres emerged to define and defend citizens. After the 1970s, people realized that international organizations often had more influence over their lives than did their own national governments. These organizations became increasingly important in shaping the meaning of citizenship. This was true especially in the Third World, where nation-states struggled hardest to accommodate globalization.

Supranational Organizations

Various organizations with international responsibilities took shape after World War II for the purpose of facilitating global activities. Although these **supranational organizations** often successfully managed crisis situations, they also impinged on the autonomy of all but the most powerful states.

The most prominent supranational organizations were the World Bank and the International Monetary Fund, which provided vital economic assistance to poorer nations. Indeed, these bodies financed and offered technical information for some of the largest development programs in the Third World. The **World Bank** made available funds for the Volta River Project in Ghana to create an electrical power grid, as well as a system of national parks in the Philippines to help indigenous people manage rain forests, coral reefs, and other threatened ecological zones. Nonetheless, the World Bank required that recipient governments implement far-reaching economic reforms, which were often unpopular. Not infrequently, World Bank– and IMF-imposed programs required local governments to abolish subsidies for essential foodstuffs, leading to riots and charges that these international groups were agents of a new kind of imperialism.

Another set of supranational bodies, **nongovernmental organizations (NGOs)**, also stepped forward late in the twentieth century. Many championed human rights or highlighted environmental problems. Others, like the International Committee of the Red Cross, once dedicated to war relief, became more active in peacetime, sheltering the homeless or providing food for famine victims. What united NGOs was not so much their goals but the way they pursued them: autonomously from state power. NGOs created a layer of international forces that rivaled the political power of nation-states.

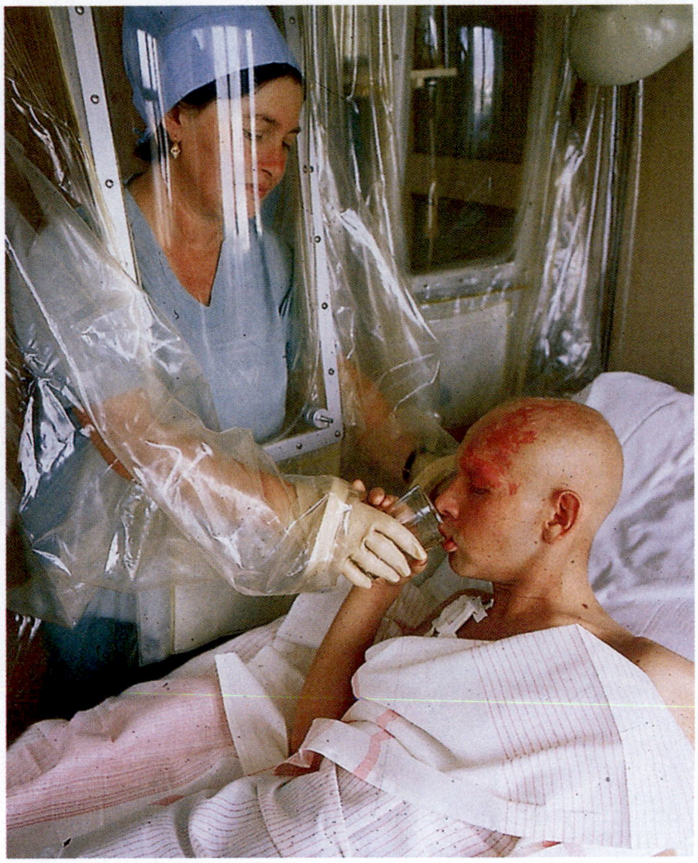

Chernobyl and Protest. *Among the victims of the 1986 explosion at the Chernobyl power plant, history's worst nuclear meltdown, were firefighters, such as the man pictured here, sent in to put out the blaze. Chernobyl turned Mikhail Gorbachev's* glasnost, *or openness, into more than a slogan, and it became a rallying cry for the populace, which hoped for political change and improvements in daily life.*

International NGOs reached a new level of influence in the 1970s because most nation-states at that time were still not democracies. Of the 121 countries in 1980, only 37 were democracies, accounting for only 35 percent of the world population. People found it difficult to rely on authoritarians to uphold their rights as citizens. Indeed, the United Nations itself was a latecomer to enforcing human rights provisions, largely because its own members were the self-same authoritarians.

NGOs, then, took the lead in trying to make the language of human rights stick. The brutality of military regimes in Latin America inspired the emerging network of international human rights organizations to take action. After the overthrow of Chile's Salvador Allende in 1973, solidarity groups proliferated to protest the military junta's harsh repression. When the Argentine military began killing tens of thousands of innocent civilians in 1976 and news of their torture techniques leaked out, human rights movements again took action. Prominent among them was Amnesty International. Formed in 1961 to defend prisoners of conscience (detained for their beliefs, color, sex, ethnic origin, language, or religion), Amnesty International catalogued human rights violations worldwide. The organization became one of the most influential human rights organizations in the world. Moreover, even American foundations recognized NGOs' importance. The biggest one, the Ford Foundation, initiated support for human rights groups and research. By 2000, an extensive network of associations was informing the public, lobbying governments, and pressuring U.N. member nations to live up to commitments to respect the rights of citizens.

Violence

International organizations and NGOs could play only a limited role in preserving peace and strengthening human rights. The end of the cold war left entire regions in such turmoil that

even the most effective humanitarian agencies could not prevent mass killings.

Consider the Balkans in the 1990s. In the territorial remains of Yugoslavia, groups of Serbs, Croats, Bosnians, ethnic Albanians, and others fought for control. Former neighbors, fueled by opportunistic leaders' rhetoric, no longer saw themselves as citizens of pluralistic political communities. Instead, demagogues trumpeted the superiority of ethnically defined states. Serbians took up arms against their Croat neighbors, and vice versa. When international agencies moved in to try to bolster public authority, they failed as Yugoslavia's ethnic mosaic imploded into civil war. The Dayton Accords of 1995 ended the bloodshed by partitioning Bosnia and assigning several international organizations to maintain peace. But in 1999 Serbian president Slobodan Milosevic sent troops to suppress unrest in the province of Kosovo; only NATO air strikes on Serbia's capital, Belgrade, convinced Milosevic to back down. Subsequently Milosevic was found guilty of war crimes and crimes against humanity.

The most gruesome political violence occurred in Africa, where nation-states capable of upholding the rule of law for all citizens were weakest. Here, tension often erupted in conflict between ethnic groups. The failure of African agriculture to sustain growing populations, as well as unequal access to resources like education, made ethnic rivalries worse. Droughts, famine, and corruption ignited the rivalries into riots and killings—even into bitter civil war and the breakdown of centralized authority.

Rwanda reflected Africa's horrifying experience with political violence. Friction grew between the majority Hutus (agrarian people, often very poor) and the minority Tutsis (herders, often with better education and more wealth) after the two peoples had intermarried and lived side by side for many generations. Some resentful Hutus blamed the Tutsis for all their woes. As tensions mounted, the United Nations dispatched peacekeeping troops. Moderate Hutus urged peaceful coexistence, only to be shouted down by government forces in command of radio stations and a mass propaganda machine. Although alerted to the impending problem, U.N. forces, fearing a clash and uncertain of their mandate, failed to prevent the violence.

The failure on the part of the international community, including the United States, which did not have troops on the ground and which had no clear policy toward Rwanda, gave the Hutu government a green light to wipe out opponents. In one hundred days of carnage in 1994, Hutu militias massacred 800,000 Tutsis and moderate Hutus. This was not, as many proclaimed, the militarization of ancient ethnic rivalries, for many Hutus were butchered as they tried to defend Tutsi friends, relatives, and neighbors. Meanwhile, the ensuing refugee crisis destabilized neighboring countries. The civil war in Rwanda sent riptides across eastern and central Africa, creating a whole new generation of conflicts.

Bosnia in the Midst of War. *Despite extensive destruction and perpetual sniper fire, the multiethnic population of Sarajevo refused to abandon their city. With the help of U.N. soldiers and aid workers, they kept alive the hope for the peaceful coexistence of Muslims, Serbs, and Croats in Bosnia.*

Some societies, however, tried to put political violence behind them. In Argentina, El Salvador, Guatemala, and South Africa, the transition to democracy compelled elected rulers to establish inquiries into past rulers' human rights abuses. These **truth commissions** were vital for creating a new aura of legitimacy for democracies and for promising to uphold the rights of individuals. In South Africa, many blacks backed the new president, Nelson Mandela, but also demanded a reckoning with the punitive experience of the apartheid past. To avoid a backlash against the former white rulers, the South African leadership opted to record the past events rather than avenge them. Truth, the new leaders argued, would be powerful enough to heal old wounds. The Truth and Reconciliation Commission, chaired by Nobel Peace Prize winner and longtime opponent of apartheid Bishop Desmond Tutu, called on all who had been involved in political crimes, whites as well as blacks, to come before its

Rwandan Refugees. *Perhaps as many as 800,000 Tutsis were killed in 1994 as the Hutus turned against the local Tutsi population while Rwanda was being invaded by a Tutsi-led army from Uganda. Not surprisingly, the massacre led to an enormous refugee crisis.*

tribunal and speak the truth. Although the truth alone did not fully settle old scores, a more open discussion of basic liberties fostered new bonds between public authority and citizens.

Religious Foundations of Politics

Secular concerns for human rights and international peace were not the only foundations for politics after the cold war. In many regions, people wanted religion to define the moral fabric of political communities. Very often, religion provided a way to re-imagine the nation-state, just as globalization was undermining national autonomy.

HINDU NATIONALISM In India, Hindu nationalism offered a communal identity for a country being rapidly transformed by globalization. In the 1980s, India freed market forces, privatized state firms, and withdrew from its role as welfare provider. Economic reforms under the ruling Congress Party sparked economic growth, thereby creating Asia's largest, best-educated, and most affluent middle class. But because these changes also widened the gap between rich and poor, lower classes and castes formed political parties to challenge the traditional elites. With established hierarchies and loyalties eroding, Hindu nationalists argued that religion could now fill the role once occupied by a secular state. Claiming that the ideology of Hindutva ("Hinduness") would bring the help that secular nationalism had failed to give, Hindu militants trumpeted the idea of India as a nation of Hindus (the majority), with minorities relegated to a lesser status.

The chief beneficiary of the politics established by economic liberalization was a Hindu nationalist party, the Bhartiya Janata Party (BJP), or Indian People's Party. It was the political arm of an alliance of Hindu organizations devoted to establishing India as a Hindu state. By the late 1980s, the BJP and other like-minded parties were advancing an anti-minority (chiefly anti-Muslim) ideology. Claiming that the state had systematically appeased the minorities and trampled on the rights of the majority, they urged Hindus to overthrow "pseudo secularism." This communal ideology was a winning formula, and by 1998 a BJP coalition came to power. Hindu nationalists sought to transform the secular nation-state into a moral community, but without challenging the economic forces of globalization.

ISLAMIC CONSERVATISM In some cases, religion provided a way to resist seemingly American-dominated globalization. One of the most spirited challenges arose in the Islamic Middle East. Here, many people believed that modernizing and westernizing programs were leading their societies toward rampant materialism and unchecked individualism. Critics included traditional clerics and young western-educated elites whose job prospects seemed bleak and who felt that the promise of modernization had failed. Having criticized modernizing processes since the nineteenth century, Islamic conservatives

Ayatollah Khomeini. *After fifteen years of exile in France due to his outspoken opposition to the shah, Ayatollah Khomeini returned to Tehran in 1979 to the ardent welcome of his supporters.*

flourished once more in the 1970s, as global markets and social dislocations undermined the moral foundations of secular leadership.

The most revolutionary Islamic movement arose in Iran, where clerics forced the shah from power in 1979. The revolt pitted a cadre of religious officials possessing only pamphlets, tracts, and tapes against the military arsenal and the vast intelligence apparatus of the Iranian state. Shah Mohammad Reza Pahlavi had enjoyed U.S. technical and military support since the Americans had helped place him on the throne in 1953. His bloated army and police force, as well as his brutally effective intelligence service, had crushed all challenges to his authority. The shah also had benefited from oil revenues, which soared after 1973. Yet the uneven distribution of income, the oppressive police state, and the royal family's ostentatious lifestyle fueled widespread discontent. As discontent rose, so did repression. And as repression intensified, so did the feeling that the government had abandoned the people.

The most vociferous critique came from the mullahs (Muslim scholars or religious teachers), who found in the **Ayatollah Ruhollah Khomeini** a courageous leader. Khomeini used his traditional Islamic education and his training in Muslim ethics to accuse the shah's government of gross violations of Islamic norms. He also identified the shah's ally, America, as the great Satan. With opposition mounting, the shah fled the country in 1979. In his wake, Khomeini established a theocratic state ruled by a council of Islamic clerics. Although some Iranians grumbled about aspects of this return to Islam (women's reduced status, leaders' arbitrariness, ruptured relations with the West, and the failure to institute democratic procedures), they prided themselves on having inspired a revolution based on principles other than those drawn from the West.

RELIGIOUS CONSERVATISM IN THE UNITED STATES

The search for moral foundations of politics in the global age reached beyond nonwestern societies. Indeed, in the United States, religion became a potent force after the 1970s as the membership and activism of conservative, fundamentalist Prot-

American Hostage Crisis in Iran. *The United States was stunned in 1979 by Iran's Islamic Revolution, which overthrew the shah and brought the exiled cleric Ayatollah Ruhollah Khomeini to power. After radical students captured the U.S. embassy, as well as fifty-three hostages, an American rescue raid failed, leading to celebration by Iranians, as shown here.*

estant churches eclipsed mainline denominations. Insisting on literal interpretation of the Bible, Protestant fundamentalists railed against secularizing trends in American society. This traditionalist crusade took up a broad range of cultural and political issues. Religious conservatives (predominantly evangelical Protestants, but including some Catholics and Orthodox Jews) attacked many of the social changes that had emerged from liberation movements of the 1960s. Shifting sexual and familial relations were sore points, but the religious conservatives especially targeted public leaders who, they felt, had abandoned the moral purpose of authority by legalizing abortion and supporting secular values.

Acceptance of and Resistance to Democracy

New sources of power and new social movements drastically changed politics in the global age. Increasingly, international organizations were decisive in defining the conditions of democratic citizenship.

Perhaps most remarkable was how much democracy spread toward the end of the twentieth century. In South Africa, Russia, and Guatemala, elections now decided politicians' fate. In this sense, the world's societies embraced the idea that people have a right to choose their own representatives. Nevertheless, democracy did not triumph everywhere. An important holdout was China. Mao died in 1976, and within a few years his successor, Deng Xiaoping, opened the nation's economy to market forces. But Deng and other Chinese communist party leaders resisted multiparty competition. Instead of capitalism and western-style democracy, they maintained that China should follow its own path to modernity.

By the late 1980s, economic reforms had produced spectacular increases in production and rising standards of living for most of China's people. But the widening gap between rich and poor, together with increasing public awareness of corruption within the party and the government, triggered popular discontent. Worker strikes and slowdowns, peasant unrest, and student activism spread. On April 22, 1989, some 100,000 people gathered in **Tiananmen Square** at the heart of Beijing in silent defiance of a government ban on assembling. The following month brought a greater show of defiance when television cameras and world journalists converged on China to cover the historic visit of Soviet leader Mikhail Gorbachev. Several hundred students, flanked by thousands of supporters, began a hunger strike at the square to demand democratic reform. Tiananmen Square was now their stage and the world their audience. Within days, the strike spread to other cities. In Beijing, where well over a million people filled the city center, a carnivalesque atmosphere prevailed as the students sang and danced to rock songs and folk ballads.

The regime responded by declaring martial law. Two huge protest demonstrations followed, and residents erected barricades to defend the city against government troops. As the protest's momentum waned, a twenty-eight-foot icon, partly inspired by the Statue of Liberty, was unveiled at the square, capturing the imagination of the crowd and the attention of the cameras. But by then the government had assembled troops to crush the movement. In a night of terror that began at dusk on June 3, the People's Liberation Army turned their guns against the people. Most students in the square negotiated a

Tiananmen Square. *This white plaster and styrofoam statue, inspired in part by the Statue of Liberty and dubbed the Goddess of Democracy, was created by students in Beijing in the spring of 1989. It was brought to Tiananmen Square and unveiled at the end of May in an attempt to reinvigorate the democracy movement and the spirits of the protesters. For five days it captured worldwide attention, until it was toppled by a tank on June 4 and crushed as the Chinese People's Liberation Army cleared the square of its democracy advocates.*

safe passage; those who lost their lives—estimates vary from 2,000 to 7,000—were the nameless people who wielded Molotov cocktails, sticks, or bricks in a futile attempt to repel the troops.

The Chinese government weathered the storm. It continued to suppress unofficial social organizations; to control access to information, including that obtained over the Internet; and to crack down on dissidents. But it could not completely control the forces of globalization. Some organizations, like the quasi-religious group Falun Gong, eluded authorities and even used the Internet to enlist international support. At the dawn of the twenty-first century, signs of change were apparent. A visible urban entrepreneurial class had emerged, whose top echelon conducted its global businesses over nearly ubiquitous cellular phones. Rural dwellers paid what little they had to be smuggled abroad, at great risk and often with lethal consequences, so that they could make a better living in America or Europe. Within China, tens of millions of people lived a transient existence, with tens of thousands daily leaving the countryside for the cities. There they often suffered economic and social exploitation, as well as police and other government abuse. Existing at the margins of the new prosperity, they, too, served as reminders of the uneven effects of globalization.

In Mexico, democracy finally triumphed, as the single party that had dominated the country for seventy-one years fell after the election of Vicente Fox in 2000. Until that time, Mexican rulers had combined patronage and rigged elections to stay in office. By the 1980s, corruption and abuse permeated the system. The abuse of democratic rights fell hardest on poor communities, especially those with large numbers of indigenous people.

Consider the state of Chiapas. An impoverished area with many Mayan descendants, Chiapas had trouble coping with social and economic change in the 1980s. The president stripped Indians of their right to communal land and let the ruling party run Chiapas like a fiefdom. By the early 1990s, the province was demanding material betterment, cultural recognition of Indian rights, and local democracy. When one group of rebels, the Zapatistas, rose up in Mexico City against the government in 1994, the government prepared to crush the insurgents. (See Primary Source: Indigenous People in Mexico Speak Out.) But no one anticipated how supranational forces would play a role in helping local democracy: Cable News Network (CNN) broadcast the clash worldwide, and the rebel leader created a Web site that drew thousands of "hits." Thereafter, international news media flooded Chiapas, filming Indians waving flags and pronouncing victory. Leaders in Mexico City, deeply embarrassed, asked local church authorities to negotiate peace and spearhead a commission to hear the villagers' concerns. In 2000, national elections toppled the ruling party (including its representatives in Chiapas), and Mexico dismantled its one-party ruling system.

Mexico, South Africa, and China were powerful examples of how men and women in every corner of the earth yearned

Protests in Mexico. (Left) *After generations of oppression and exclusion, peasants of Chiapas, in southern Mexico, called for democracy and respect for their right to land. When Mexican authorities refused to bend, peasants took up arms. While they knew that they posed no military threat to the Mexican army, the Zapatista rebels used the world media and international organizations to embarrass the national political establishment into allowing reforms.* (Right) *Among the great Mexican muralists of the twentieth century, David Alfaro Siqueiros most advocated class struggle. In this 1957 mural image,* The People in Arms, *Siqueiros portrays Mexican peasants as they pick up arms in 1910 to fight for a new order. Paintings such as these provided inspiration for movements such as the Chiapas Rebellion.*

PRIMARY SOURCE

Indigenous People in Mexico Speak Out

In late 1993, peasants of Chiapas rejected the false promises of the Mexican national government. Mostly Indians living in a jungle region, they had seen their land rights taken away and had tired of living under oppressive authorities. On January 1, 1994, they took up arms against the government, calling for a restoration of the principles of the Mexican Revolution: land for the hungry, democracy, and an end to centuries of neglect and oppression of Indians across the Americas. They formed the Zapatista Army for National Liberation (EZLN), mounted a brilliant public relations campaign, and enlisted massive international support. Here is an excerpt from their declaration of war against the Mexican government.

We are a product of 500 years of struggle: first against slavery, during the War of Independence against Spain led by the insurgents; afterward to avoid being absorbed by American imperialism; then to promulgate our constitution and expel the French Empire from our soil; and later the Porfirista dictatorship denied us just application of the Reform laws, and the people rebelled, forming their own leaders; . . . we have nothing, absolutely nothing, not even a decent roof over our heads, no land, no work, no health care, no food, or education; without the right to freely and democratically elect our authorities; without independence from foreigners, without peace or justice for ourselves and our children.

But TODAY WE SAY, ENOUGH! We are the heirs of those who truly forged our nationality. We the dispossessed are millions, and we call on our brothers to join in this call as the only path in order not to die of hunger in the face of the insatiable ambition of a dictatorship for more than 70 years led by a clique of traitors who represent the most conservative and sell-out groups in the country. They are the same as those who opposed Hidalgo and Morelos, who betrayed Vicente Guerrero, the same as those who sold over half our territory to the foreign invader, the same as those who brought a European prince to rule us, the same as those who formed the dictatorship of the Porfirista "scientists," the same as those who opposed the Oil Expropriation, the same as those who massacred the railroad workers in 1958 and the students in 1968, the same as those who today take everything from us, absolutely everything.

To prevent this, and as our last hope, after having tried everything to put into practice the legality based on our Magna Carta, we resort to it, to our Constitution, to apply Constitutional Article 39, which says:

"National sovereignty resides essentially and originally in the people. All public power emanates from the people and is instituted for the people's benefit. The people have, at all times, the unalienable right to alter or modify the form of their government."

Therefore, according to our Constitution, we issue this statement to the Mexican federal army, the basic pillar of the Mexican dictatorship that we suffer . . .

In conformity with this Declaration of War, we ask the other branches of the Nation's government to meet to restore the legality and the stability of the Nation by deposing the dictator. . . .

PEOPLE OF MEXICO: We, upright and free men and women, are conscious that the war we declare is a last resort, but it is just. The dictators have been applying an undeclared genocidal war against our people for many years. Therefore we ask for your decided participation in support of this plan of the Mexican people in their struggle for work, land, housing, food, health care, education, independence, liberty, democracy, justice, and peace.

QUESTIONS FOR ANALYSIS

- In what other periods in this book have we encountered the ancestors of the Chiapas peasants?
- What does this declaration of war suggest about current and past Mexican governments?

Source: General Council of the EZLN, Declaración de la Selva Lacandona, 1993 (www.ezln.org, January 1, 1994).

to choose their own leaders. In 1994, millions of previously disenfranchised South Africans lined up for hours to cast a vote for their new black African president, Nelson Mandela. In 2000, the Mexican electorate turned out the ruling party, while in China the ruling communist party had to call in the army to prevent regime change and democratic reforms.

CONCLUSION

In the thirteenth century (as long before), a few travelers like Ibn Battuta and Marco Polo ventured over long distances to trade, to explore, and to convert souls; yet communications technology was rudimentary, making long-distance mobility and exchange

expensive, rare, and perilous. The world was much more a series of communities set apart than a world bound together by culture, capital, and communication networks.

By the late twentieth century, that balance had changed. Food, entertainment, clothing, and even family life were becoming more similar worldwide. To be sure, some local differences remained. In 2000, the local lived on, and in some cases was revived, through challenges to the authority of nation-states. No longer did the nation-state or any single level of community life define collective identities. At the same time, worldwide purveyors of cultural and commercial resources offered local communities the same kinds of products, from aspirin to Nike shoes. Exchanges across local and national boundaries became easier. For the first time, many of the world's peoples felt they belonged to a global culture.

New technologies, new methods of production and investment, and the greater importance of personal health and education for human betterment created new possibilities and greater inequalities. Indeed, the disparities between haves and have-nots in 2000 were astonishing. For as humanity harnessed new technologies to accelerate exchanges across and within cultures, an ever-larger gulf separated those who participated in global networks from those who languished on the margins. This disparity produced divergent political and cultural forms, despite the collapse of the three-world order. Thus, as the world became more integrated, it also grew apart along ever-deeper lines.

AFTER YOU READ THIS CHAPTER

Review and research on **StudySpace:** wwnorton.com/StudySpace

TRACING THE GLOBAL STORYLINES

FOCUS ON: ***Globalization***

Removing obstacles to globalization

- Communism's fall and the end of the cold war improve prospects for global exchange of peoples, ideas, and resources.
- Final decolonization in Angola and Mozambique and the end of apartheid in South Africa return self-rule throughout Africa.

Unleashing globalization

- Financial deregulation and the end of gold and silver standards allow money to move freely across borders but lead to a Third World debt crisis.
- Widespread migrations occur as people in Africa, Asia, and Latin America move to Europe and America, following the tracks of their former colonizers.
- Revolutions in culture and communications spread American culture worldwide, but also make cultural diversity more possible for those who can afford it.

The new global order

- Globalization leads to dramatic population expansion, requiring greater agricultural and industrial output.
- Family structure changes, life spans increase, and more goods are available, yet inequalities deepen as decent education and good health determine social status as never before.
- As globalization erodes the power of the nation-state, greater violence occurs between and within states. Nongovernmental organizations (NGOs) and religion become resources for dealing with violence and inequality and for reimagining the nation-state.

CHRONOLOGY

The Americas
- United States announces Strategic Defense Initiative (SDI) **1983**

Europe

Soviet Union
- Gorbachev assumes power **1985**
- Chernobyl nuclear accident **1986**

Africa

The Middle East
- Khomeini establishes theocratic state in Iran **1979**

Asia

East Asia

1975

KEY TERMS

AIDS (Acquired Immuno Deficiency Syndrome) p. 805

developing world p. 786

European Union (EU) p. 794

feminist movements p. 808

globalization p. 785

global warming p. 812

International Monetary Fund (IMF) p. 792

Ayatollah Ruhollah Khomeini p. 817

Nelson Mandela p. 789

nongovernmental organizations (NGOs) p. 814

Silicon Valley p. 801

supranational organizations p. 814

Tiananmen Square p. 818

truth commissions p. 815

World Bank p. 814

STUDY QUESTIONS

1. **To what extent** did the three-world order discussed in Chapter 20 not exist by 1975? What architecture of power was replacing it?
2. **What** led to the end of the cold war? How did U.S. containment policies contribute to the Soviet Union's demise?
3. **Describe** the process through which apartheid was dismantled in South Africa. Why was the process relatively nonviolent?
4. **Analyze** how globalization transformed popular culture. To what extent does global popular culture reflect American culture?
5. **Explain** how globalization transformed world demography. What patterns emerged in terms of international migration?
6. **Discuss** how globalization affected women. How did new patterns in trade, production, and finance help or hinder opportunities for women worldwide?
7. **Explain** trends in agricultural production and natural resource consumption over the last several decades. Who produced the goods, and who consumed them?
8. **Analyze** how globalization affected the world's environment. How effectively has the global community addressed new environmental concerns?
9. **Explain** how globalization altered people's sense of identity. How did globalization challenge national identity and the idea of the nation-state?

- North American Free Trade Association approved **1992**
- Chiapas Rebellion in Mexico **1994**
- Eastern European communist regimes collapse **1989**
- Yugoslavia dissolves, ethnic cleansing ensues **1989–1995**
- European Union formed **1991**
- Soviet war in Afghanistan **1979–1989**
- Dissolution of the Soviet Union **1991**
- Mandela released from prison **1990**
- Free elections in South Africa **1994**
- Ethnic cleansing in Rwanda **1998**
- First Gulf War **1991**
- BJP Party heads government in India **1998**
- Deng Xiaoping reforms China **1978–1992**
- Chinese state cracks down on Tiananmen Square protesters **1989**

2000

THE TRUE ADMINISTRATION OF JUSTICE IS THE FIRMEST PILLAR OF
orations
PEOPLE too"
?!
JOBS NOT CUTS
99:1
JOBS, JUSTICE AND EDUCATION

Epilogue

2001–The Present

On December 31, 1999, people worldwide celebrated the beginning of a new millennium. With the cold war over, optimists hoped for an end to the history of ideological conflict that had bloodied the twentieth century. They looked forward to an era of peace and prosperity. But in the first decade of the new millennium, it became painfully clear that while the global economy and technologies had brought the world together as never before, divergent ideals could still blow things apart. People across the world grappled with common challenges while also experiencing possibilities and problems specific to their region.

GLOBAL CHALLENGES

Barely nine months into the twenty-first century, terrorist violence shattered the exuberance that had welcomed the new millennium. On September 11, 2001, nineteen hijackers commandeered four airplanes.

The hijackers slammed two of the planes into the World Trade Center in New York City and a third into the Pentagon Building (home of the U.S. Department of Defense) in Washington, D.C. The fourth hijacked plane was deterred from its intended target—the White House or the Capitol—by the courageous actions of its passengers and crashed in a field in southwestern Pennsylvania. Television captured the event live for global viewers, recording the horrifying images of the Trade Center's twin towers engulfed in flames, then crumbling into a heap of ash and twisted metal.

War on Terror

The terrorist attack of 9/11 created revulsion across the world. "We are all New Yorkers" was heard in far corners of the globe. In the United States, grief unified the nation. Anger focused on Osama bin Laden and al-Qaeda, the militant Islamist group that had organized the attack. The militants claimed that it was a response to America's imperialist policies in the Middle East and retribution for American troops' presence in Saudi Arabia (during the first Iraq War). Many Americans likened 9/11 to the Japanese bombing of Pearl Harbor sixty years earlier. George W. Bush, who had become president after a close and disputed election the year before, gained broad public support for his tough talk about bringing terrorists to justice and for his insistence that the events of September 11 had introduced a divide between the "pre-9/11 world" and the "post-9/11" one. Domestically, Bush pushed for security measures to curb future terrorist violence, protect freedom, and secure the American homeland.

Internationally, President Bush declared a "global war on terror." With the nearly unanimous backing of the American people, as well as strong support from many nations, Bush unsuccessfully sent American forces to Afghanistan to hunt down bin Laden, destroy al-Qaeda training camps, and topple the Taliban government that had provided a haven for the terrorists. Expanding the battlefront of the war on terror, in 2003 the Bush administration ordered an invasion of Iraq, falsely charging its brutal dictator, Saddam Hussein, with abetting the terrorist assault of 9/11 and producing weapons of mass destruction. As in Afghanistan, the initial offensive went well: the United States and a military coalition representing Britain, Spain, Italy, and several eastern European nations quickly overthrew Hussein's regime. But defeating the Iraqi army and finding Hussein proved easier than restoring order to the country, improving living standards, and persuading the population to rally around the American vision of a democratic polity.

Moreover, the failure to find weapons of mass destruction or to uncover indisputable links between Hussein and al-Qaeda, together with mounting American losses from an ongoing insurgency, left many U.S. citizens questioning the wisdom of this war. Although Bush won reelection in 2004, the national and global unity so evident right after September 11 seemed increasingly distant—as was the sense that the new century

9/11. (Left) *The North Tower already aflame, this photograph captures a second hijacked jet, an instant before it crashed into the South Tower of New York's World Trade Center on September 11, 2001.* (Right) *Firefighters search for survivors in the smoldering ruins.*

would be one of peace and prosperity under an American-led world order.

In Afghanistan, the situation shifted noticeably. U.S.-led coalition forces started to find themselves in a quagmire like the one that the Soviets had fallen into two decades earlier (see Chapter 21). Early successes to maintain stability became more challenging as local warlords exercised personal power toward achieving their own goals and as the revitalized Taliban received support from neighboring Pakistan.

While the campaigns in Iraq and Afghanistan faltered, the United States doubled down on its terrorist manhunts. Meanwhile, the American image internationally suffered with the exposés of its programs of extensive surveillance, including those of U.S. citizens, the use of coercive interrogation techniques, "rendition" of suspected militants to sites where they could be tortured to extract information, the inhumane treatment of Iraqi prisoners at the Abu Ghraib prison, and the harsh and indefinite detention of suspected terrorists at Guantanamo. The domestic support for the Bush administration also eroded.

Helped by the growing chorus of disapproval of the Iraq war, Barack Obama secured the presidency in 2008 and the Democratic Party took over both houses of Congress. Following his campaign promise, President Obama announced plans to end the Iraq war and refocus attention on Afghanistan. With an increased military presence, the Americans assaulted Taliban strongholds in the countryside and carried the terrorist manhunt across the border into Pakistan by sharply escalating unmanned drone strikes. On May 2, 2011, the U.S. forces carried out a daring operation in Pakistan, killing Osama bin Laden. The Democratic president ended the Iraq occupation in 2011, and announced that American troops would withdraw from Afghanistan in 2014.

Islamic Militancy

In spite of the war on terror, Islamic militancy has gained a strong foothold in many parts of the world. Elections in Iraq under American occupation were won by sectarian and regionalist parties. The major Shiite religious party won heavily in Shiite areas, while the Kurdish party swept the northern, predominantly Kurdish, region of Iraq. The Sunni population, living in the center of the country, supported its own religious party. Secular parties had no success at all. Similarly, in the 2006 elections in Palestine, Hamas, the radical Islamist party and avowed foe of Israel, triumphed over Fatah, the party of the once-dominant Palestine Liberation Organization. In Afghanistan, American and NATO troops have weakened al-Qaeda, but the Taliban remains a formidable force. In Pakistan, militant groups, long supported and used by the military in its proxy wars in Kashmir and Afghanistan, have proliferated, with some even turning against the regime itself in order to impose their radical agenda.

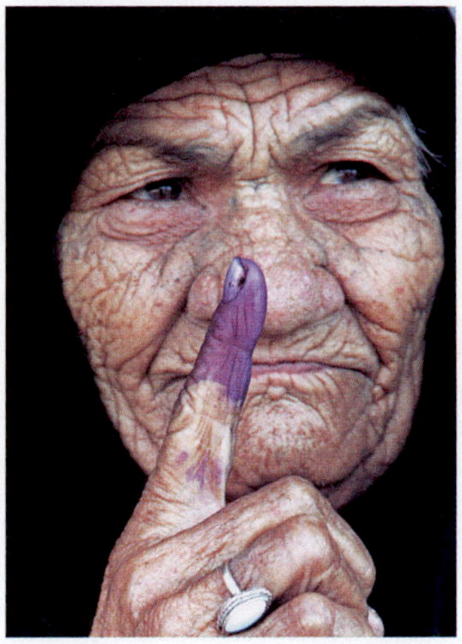

Iraqi Elections. *Iraqis voted on December 15, 2005, while the country was under American and allied military occupation. Voters' fingers were stained after voting so that they could not vote twice; many walked away from the polling booths showing their stained fingers with pride.*

The power of a revivified Islam reaches far beyond the Middle East and South Asia. Among the many Muslim communities of northern Nigeria, for instance, one state after another has embraced the *sharia* as its legal guide and moral compass. In 2012, militant Islamists took control of northern Mali, imposing a strict version of Islamic law. Radical Islam has found pockets of appeal even among the Muslim communities in Europe.

At the most general level, the appeal of radical Islam is connected to globalization. Confronting a world transformed and woven ever so tightly by economic, political, and cultural forces larger than the nation, the radical Islamists offer a return to the fundamental elements of the Muslim faith as a global alternative to what they consider as modern, western, and un-Islamic influences.

Local conditions have conspired to lend traction to this global vision. In the Arab world, with the exception of oil-rich Persian Gulf states, which are awash in petroleum dollars, poverty and economic insecurity are widespread. The long domination of the region by oppressive and dictatorial regimes has bred discontent that, in the absence of democratic institutions, finds an outlet in radical Islam. The continuing plight of Palestinians is a source of fury against Israel and its principal ally, the United States. Although the U.S. government claimed that the invasion of Iraq aimed to free Iraqis from the tyrannical rule of Saddam Hussein and bring democratic governance to the region, the occupation bred new resentments against the Americans. Drone attacks in Pakistan, claiming many innocent lives, serve to produce recruits for radical Islamists. Many in the Asian and African world see the recent actions of the United States and western powers through the memory of their previous colonial and imperial history. This is also true in Europe itself, where its Muslims citizens see their exclusion, discrimination, and attacks on identity as a continuation of the colonial past.

The Global Economic Crisis

If the global political environment was a specter of uncertainty, there was no uncertainty about another crisis: the nosedive of the world economy beginning in 2007. The problem began in the financial sector, the most globally interlinked of all. Investors from around the world poured their money into riskier and riskier investments—many of which were so complex that not even the regulators in charge of monitoring the financial sector could understand them.

One of the most enticing of these risky bets was real estate in the United States, whose bubble burst, leading to a plunge in property values. This meant not only that banks and financial agencies were stuck with increasingly worthless assets but also that millions of homeowners went belly-up. Massive defaults on loans ripped through the world financial system and led to a seizure of credit. By the summer of 2008, there was a worldwide panic. The elaborate banking system collapsed with a series of high-profile failures like Northern Rock (in Britain), Lehman Brothers (in the United States), and several European institutions. As credit dried up and consumers stopped spending, factories shut down and stores went bankrupt. Between 2000 and 2007, the United States had accounted for fully one-third of the world's consumption. So, when the financial crisis blew a massive hole in American wallets, it dragged much of the rest of the world down, too. Germany and Japan each saw their gross domestic product sink by 15 percent; Mexico's and Russia's dropped by almost one-quarter in the first half of 2009. Ireland, Spain, Italy, Portugal, and Greece were hit by a severe debt crisis; although these states have been helped by bailouts and loans offered by the European Union, each government has been compelled to make deep cuts in state spending in order to show that they are worthy to remain within the Eurozone. Layoffs, higher taxes, and reduced consumption have resulted in the contraction of these economies and in skyrocketing unemployment; in early 2013, overall unemployment in Greece and Spain exceeded 25 percent; for young people eighteen to twenty-five, the rates topped 55 percent. The world had not seen a contraction of production, employment, and trade of this magnitude since the 1930s (see Chapter 19). Times have changed, and lessons have been learned; in the 1930s, countries often tried to solve their economic problems through strategies that hurt their neighbors. By contrast, nowadays the degree of global interdependence is so great that governments generally avoid protectionism; there is now talk—although it is very premature—of a more coordinated global monitoring system of world finance. But states still do try to protect their own economies. The Chinese, for example, have refused to allow the appreciation of their currency; this keeps Chinese exports cheap and stems the influx of foreign goods. The United States has simply borrowed more money in order to inject "stimulus" spending into the economy. The bailouts offered by the European Union have stabilized the situation for the present but compelled debtor states such as Greece and Spain to impose austerity measures and suffer high unemployment.

Global Financial Crisis. *When the major investment firm Lehman Brothers declared bankruptcy in September 2008, the world's increasingly integrated financial system teetered on the brink of collapse. Although massive government interventions kept the system afloat, they did not prevent severe downturns and sharply rising unemployment rates.*

The financial crisis has brought signs of gathering discontent. To forestall a change in government, desperate Argentine leaders nationalized the private pension system for revenues in 2008, and in 2009 they made a grab at the Central Bank's reserves. In Europe, where, at last, economic and political integration had seemed to promise an end to conflict between states, the crisis has created new tensions. In Greece, radical new parties have arisen to protest austerity measures or to take out frustrations on immigrants, and many blame the richer nations, especially the Germans, for having profited from the creation of the Eurozone at the expense of the poorer nations. For the first time in decades, vehement nationalist slogans have come into wide circulation, and some pundits have predicted that the Eurozone—and perhaps even the European Union—in its current form will not last.

Global Stirrings

The turmoil of war, militancy, and economic crisis was part of a broader set of changes at the global level. The very same ongoing integration of the world economy that globalized the economic crisis also produced fresh wealth across the world. Brazil, Russia, China, India, Vietnam, Indonesia, and South Africa all became more prosperous than they were even just a decade ago. Capital, technology, and media brought the world together ever more closely. The movement of ideas and images across national

Occupy Wall Street. *Inspired by other stirrings around the world, this largely national movement was fueled by methods as novel as social media and as traditional as a sit-in. Here an Occupy Wall Street rally joins a labor union demonstration outside the New York County Courthouse in 2011.*

borders accelerated. Social media like Facebook provided new lines of communication and connections, particularly among the young. New aspirations for employment, prosperity, consumption, and political expression appeared. While these varied across the different regions of the world, as we shall see in the following sections, we can also identify certain emergent global patterns.

Juan Evo Morales came to power in Bolivia as the first president of Indian descent in 2005—and was reelected in 2009—on the basis of his activism as leader of peasants and working people. Thousands took to the streets in the Orange Revolution in Ukraine during 2004 and 2005, protesting electoral fraud and corruption. An upsurge against Vladimir Putin erupted in Russia in 2011, culminating in the dramatic protest staged in 2012 by Pussy Riot, a feminist punk rock band. The Arab Spring swept across the Middle East in 2011, offering new expressions of political transformation in sharp contrast to Islamic militancy. An anticorruption movement broke out in India in 2011, mobilizing people demanding transparency and accountability in politics. Barack Obama swept to power in 2008 as the first African American president. Even though his campaign of hope and change crashed at the shores of the economic crisis, he was reelected in 2012.

The global economic and political stirrings were full of paradoxes and contradictions. The growth of prosperity and wealth around the world was highly unequal and accompanied by an unprecedented rise in the power and influence of corporations and financial institutions. Even as a global middle class came into being, inequality deepened. This sparked protests, none more powerfully and dramatically than by Occupy Wall Street (OWS), a movement that started in September 2011 in New York and was organized by a Canadian anarchist group called Adbusters. It highlighted growing social and economic inequality and challenged the power of banks and corporations.

OWS was one among a wide range of emergent political upheavals around the world. Each one had a character specific to the region. Yet together they represent a new phenomenon. Almost all of them took shape outside conventional politics and ideological agendas. Expressing antiestablishment ideals and using social media to mobilize, the young took the lead in these new popular upsurges. We do not know if they will endure or what shapes they will take, but these global stirrings represent something new on the horizon.

Global Warming

Global warming is just one of numerous environmental issues that have gained prominence in the new millennium. As the world population continues to grow and as more areas industrialize, the pressure on vital natural resources (especially oil and water) has inspired calls for greater conservation and more environmentally sustainable economic development. But the U.S.

Hurricane Katrina. *As the hurricane dissipated in the tail end of August 2005, the U.S. Coast Guard surveyed the affected areas by aircraft and conducted damage assessment of what would be the costliest natural disaster in American history. This Coast Guard photograph captures New Orleans immediately after the passing of Katrina.*

government's resistance to global regulations, as well as a rising demand for resources (especially by China and India), has made the future of the earth's environment uncertain.

Despite difficulties in achieving a consensus on actions, there is growing recognition that the planet needs healing. Thus, when the Group of Eight (G8), a forum of leaders from Canada, France, Germany, Italy, Japan, Russia, the United Kingdom, and the United States, met in 2007, a key topic was global warming. It acknowledged that humankind is contributing to, if not causing, the increase in temperatures and that climate change will bring catastrophic storms, severe droughts, famine, and flooding. Hurricane Katrina in 2005, for example, left much of New Orleans and the Mississippi Gulf Coast in ruins. Hurricane Sandy had similar catastrophic effects on the shorelines of New Jersey and New York in 2013. As always, the impact of these changes may be uneven, but if the warnings are correct, global warming will reshape the lives of everyone on the planet. Indeed, global warming affirms just how integrated the world has become and how actions across national frontiers are required to nurse the planet.

THE UNITED STATES, THE EUROPEAN UNION, AND JAPAN

The global political and economic crisis had a deep impact on the United States. Americans moved from supporting Bush to electing Barack Obama, tiring of the wars in Iraq and Afghanistan. But the protection of citizens from terrorist attacks emerged as a continuing concern, posing a challenge to balance security against freedom. The recession following the economic crisis resulted in soaring foreclosures, dwindling tax revenues, and millions thrown out of work.

As the Obama administration sought to cope with the economic crisis while introducing health-care reform, it encountered a conservative backlash in the shape of the Tea Party movement. Consisting largely of older whites, the conservative activists espoused the ideals of small government and market freedom, helping to administer a stinging defeat to the Democrats in the 2010 congressional elections. From the opposite side of the ideological spectrum arose the Occupy Wall Street movement in 2011. Claiming to speak on behalf of the 99 percent against the 1 percent of people, the Occupy activists, consisting largely of young people, railed against the banks and financial institutions that the bailout had helped. Although the movement ran out of steam by the end of the year, it succeeded in inserting the growing inequality into political discussions. Partially helped by the focus on inequality brought about by the Occupy movement, Obama won reelection and his party fared better in the 2012 elections.

A Changing Western Europe

The American invasion of Iraq created fractures in the alliance between the United States and western Europe. During the 1990s, the collapse of the Soviet Union and the development of the European Union (EU) had caused some rumblings about the future of NATO, but disagreements remained muted prior to the American military's entrance into Iraq. In fact, in the immediate wake of September 11, European allies rallied behind the United States. But before and after the invasion of Iraq, leaders in France and Germany sharply criticized U.S. foreign policy.

Notwithstanding the internal divisions, what was striking from a historical standpoint was the region's continuing integration. By 2010, the European Union had widened its membership to twenty-seven countries, including ten nations that formerly had been part of the Soviet bloc. True, this unification faced some reversals, most notably when voters in France and the Netherlands rejected the EU constitution. Still, viewed against the backdrop of twentieth-century total wars and attempts at ethnic cleansing, it is remarkable that member states could bind themselves together in a union to which each relinquished significant degrees of sovereignty.

Demographic Issues

Looking forward, the greater threat to European integration—and to Europe's future peace and prosperity—remains the interlocking issues of aging and immigration. Roughly speaking, to maintain its population of 500 million people, each female in the European Union would have to bear a mean of 2 children, but women in the union now average only 1.5 offspring. Adding to the demographic and labor pressures is the aging of the population. With the percentage of elderly Europeans rising rapidly, sustaining the present workers-to-retirees ratio and paying for the region's burgeoning number of pensioners will require the European Union to attract around 15 million immigrants annually.

Although this number has not been reached, European populations have been boosted by millions of immigrants, many of them Muslims. As of 2010, Europe was home to 38 million Muslims, of whom 25 million (roughly 5 percent of the total population) resided within the European Union. Islam now represents the fastest-growing religion in Europe. In France, the figure has topped 10 percent. These immigrants often live in impoverished circumstances, and in many countries their status as guest workers (see Chapter 21) denies them the full benefits of citizenship. Their presence in Europe's larger cities threatens those who still equate Europe with Christendom and challenges those who believe that European integration requires complete assimilation of all inhabitants.

Europe is not alone in confronting the problems of an aging population and the integration of immigrants. As its baby boom generation ages, the United States faces a similar imbalance between retirees and workers that endangers its Social Security system. Likewise, the flood of immigrants, particularly from Asia and Latin America, continues to shift the nation's ethnic composition. According to U.S. Census Bureau projections, in 2010 people of Latin American descent in the United States will number nearly 48 million (about 15.5 percent of the population). The presence of so many Spanish-speakers troubles those who think the United States should remain an English-only country, and the degree to which immigrants should be required to assimilate remains a contentious issue. More heated still are debates about illegal immigration. (For a global look at population growth and life expectancies, see Maps E.1 and E.2.) It took an overwhelming turnout of Latino and Hispanic voters in the 2012 U.S. presidential election in support of incumbent Democratic Party candidate Barack Obama to bring Republicans and Democrats to the bargaining table to pass immigration reforms.

In many respects, the twin dilemmas of aging and immigration press hardest today on Japan. Like Europeans and North Americans, the Japanese are marrying later and having fewer children. Japan's female population now averages barely 1.37 children, compared with nearly 3.7 in 1950. At the same time, Japanese life expectancy has reached eighty-five, the highest in the world, which further tilts the nation's age pyramid. In 1970 the elderly (those over age sixty-five) represented around 7 percent of the population; in 2005 they reached 20 percent and are expected to hit 40 percent by 2050. Analysts surmise that Japan's population peaked at around 128 million and might decline to perhaps 90 million by 2050. Such a downturn bodes ill for Japan's dynamic economy, which is currently the world's second largest (although China's economy is poised to overtake it).

As in Europe and North America, Japan relies on immigrants to fill out its labor force. In the 1960s, the nation's booming economy experienced labor shortages, but neither the government nor major corporations chose to invite in foreign laborers. They preferred automation or recruitment of workers of Japanese descent from abroad. By the 1980s, however, deepening labor shortages and the yen's rising value led to an expanded dependence on immigrant workers. Recent estimates put the number of foreign nationals in Japan at nearly 2 million, or around 1.5 percent of the total population. Most of them hail from the Korean peninsula, the Philippines, Indochina, Brazil, and Iran.

Anti-Immigrant Sentiments

In Europe, where unemployment rates remain higher than in Japan or North America, the political reaction against immigration has been sharpest. Far right groups have demanded that immigration be halted or "foreigners" expelled. Support levels vary in each country, but across Europe the far right's electoral base appears to be around 15 percent; in some countries it is above 25 percent. The Freedom Party in Austria and the Northern League and National Alliance in Italy regularly place cabinet representatives in coalition governments. Ultra-right forces such as France's National Front, Denmark's People's Party, and the League of Polish Families sometimes pressure governing coalitions to slow EU integration and immigration, especially from Muslim countries.

In recent years, anti-immigrant sentiments in general and anti-Muslim ones in particular have risen in the wake of violent episodes. In Holland, the precipitant was the grisly murder of filmmaker Theo Van Gogh by Mohammed Bouyeri in 2004. Bouyeri claimed he was fulfilling his duty as a Muslim by killing Van Gogh, who had made a film about the abuse of Muslim women. Following the assassination, many in Holland questioned the nation's traditional tolerance of diversity and expressed concern that Muslims were too alien in their values to ever fit in Dutch society. Such questions about the assimilation (and assimilability) of Muslims arose again in 2006 after the publication of anti-Islamic cartoons in a Dutch newspaper generated violent demonstrations across Europe and throughout the Muslim world.

France confronted similar dilemmas after rioting rocked the mostly Muslim suburbs of Paris in 2005. This unrest highlighted the desperate plight of unemployed and alienated immigrants, but it also fed fears about Muslims' loyalties and led some politicians to take a harder line against foreigners. Nicolas Sarkozy, who was interior minister at the time, ordered the deportation of immigrants convicted of rioting, while Jean-Marie Le Pen, leader of the far right National Front, demanded that even naturalized rioters be stripped of their citizenship. In the 2007 race

French turban ban. *During French President Sarkozy's state visit to India in 2010, Indian Sikh students held a demonstration in New Delhi calling for the lifting of the French ban on the turban, a religious practice that dates back to the eighteenth century.*

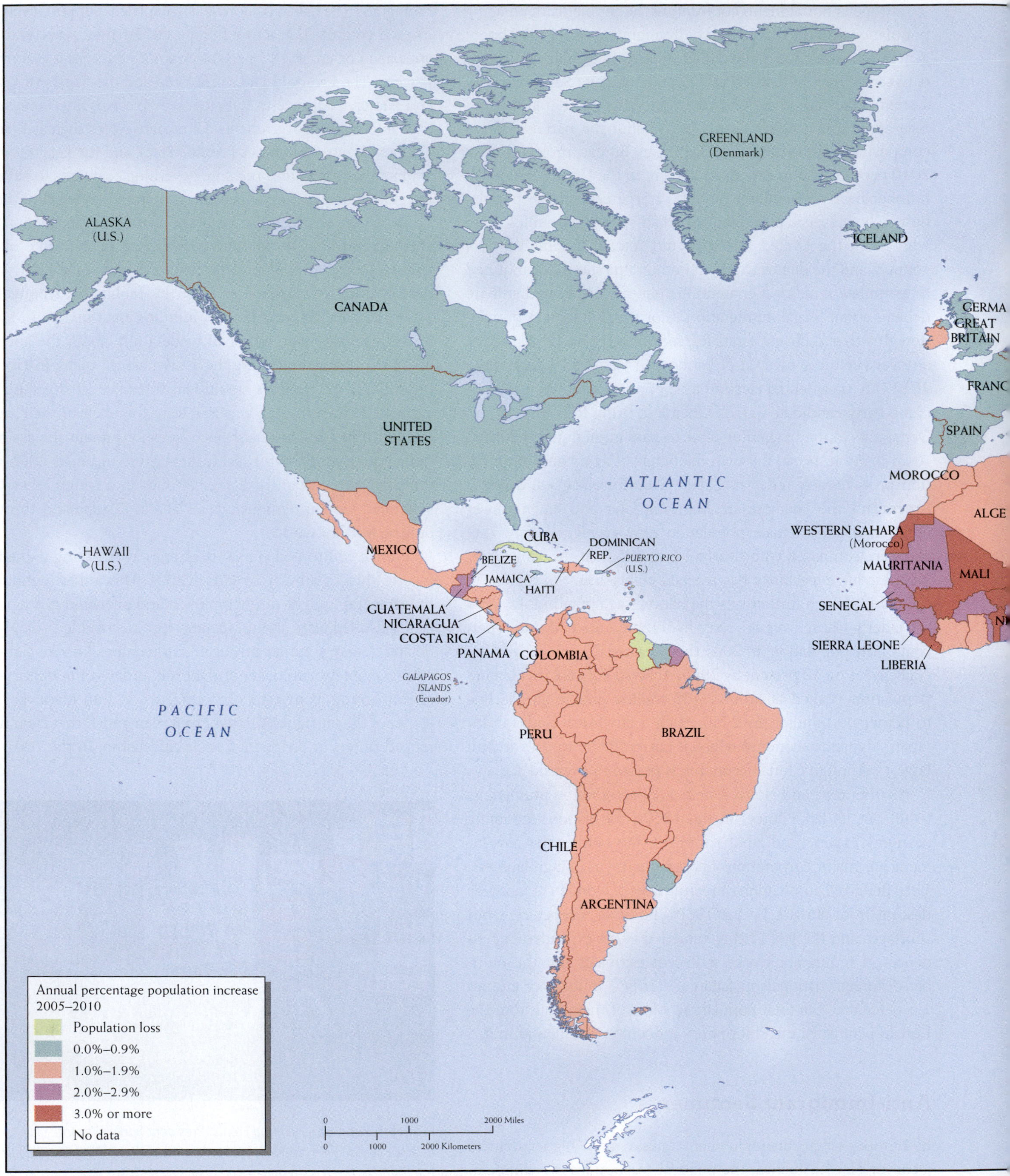
GREENLAND
(Denmark)
ICELAND
ALASKA
(U.S.)
CANADA
UNITED
STATES
GERMA
GREAT
BRITAIN
FRANC
SPAIN
MOROCCO
ALGE
WESTERN SAHARA
(Morocco)
MAURITANIA
MALI
SENEGAL
SIERRA LEONE
LIBERIA
ATLANTIC
OCEAN
HAWAII
(U.S.)
MEXICO
CUBA
DOMINICAN
REP.
PUERTO RICO
(U.S.)
BELIZE
JAMAICA
HAITI
GUATEMALA
NICARAGUA
COSTA RICA
PANAMA
COLOMBIA
GALAPAGOS
ISLANDS
(Ecuador)
PACIFIC
OCEAN
PERU
BRAZIL
CHILE
ARGENTINA
Annual percentage population increase
2005–2010
Population loss
0.0%–0.9%
1.0%–1.9%
2.0%–2.9%
3.0% or more
No data
0
1000
2000 Miles
0
1000
2000 Kilometers

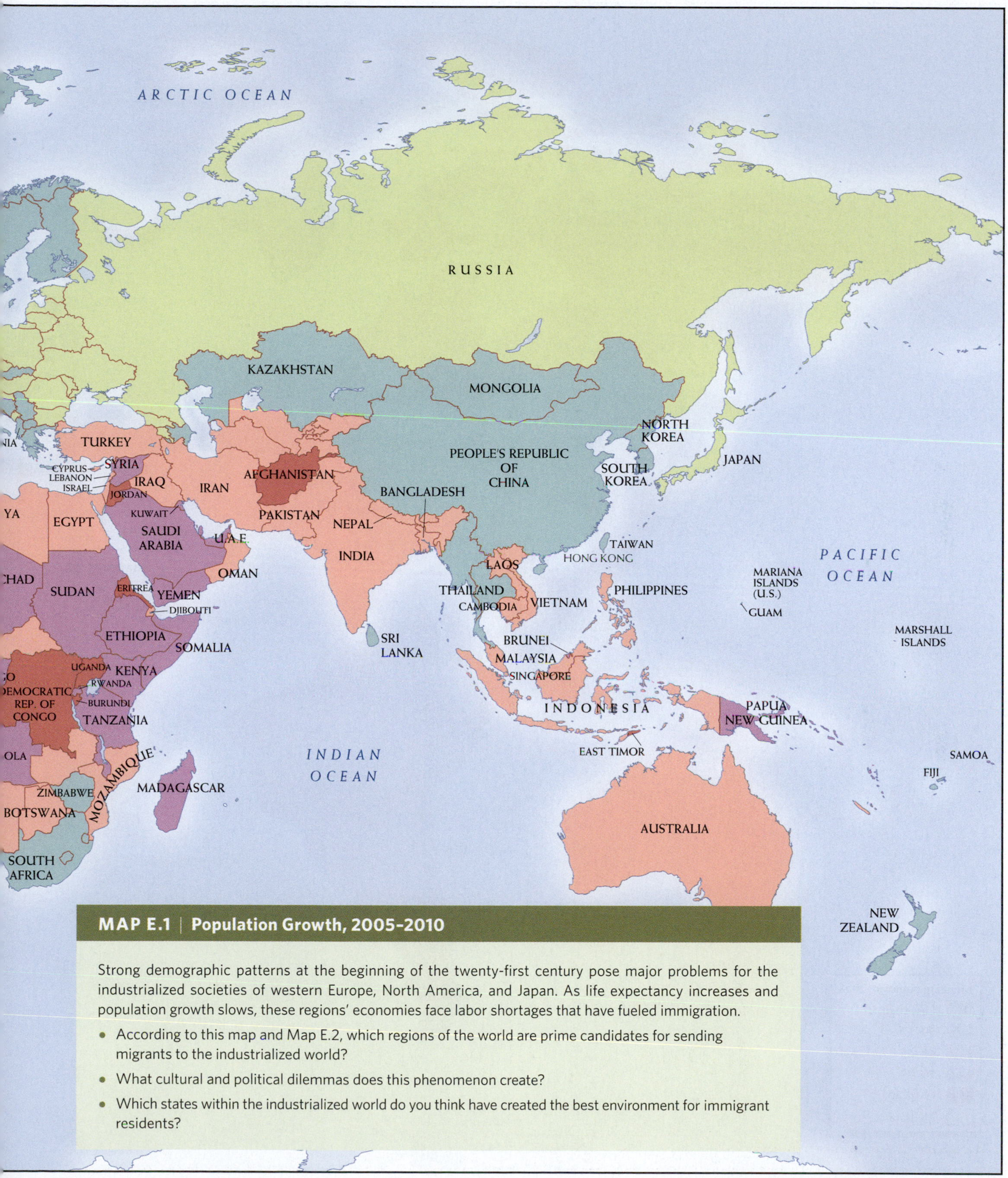

MAP E.1 | Population Growth, 2005–2010

Strong demographic patterns at the beginning of the twenty-first century pose major problems for the industrialized societies of western Europe, North America, and Japan. As life expectancy increases and population growth slows, these regions' economies face labor shortages that have fueled immigration.

- According to this map and Map E.2, which regions of the world are prime candidates for sending migrants to the industrialized world?
- What cultural and political dilemmas does this phenomenon create?
- Which states within the industrialized world do you think have created the best environment for immigrant residents?

GREENLAND
(Denmark)
ALASKA
(U.S.)
CANADA
ICELAND
GERMA
GREAT
BRITAIN
FRANC
SPAIN
UNITED
STATES
ATLANTIC
OCEAN
MOROCCO
ALGE
WESTERN SAHARA
(Morocco)
MAURITANIA
MALI
SENEGAL
SIERRA LEONE
LIBERIA
HAWAII
(U.S.)
MEXICO
CUBA
DOMINICAN
REP.
PUERTO RICO
(U.S.)
BELIZE
JAMAICA
HAITI
GUATEMALA
NICARAGUA
COSTA RICA
PANAMA
COLOMBIA
GALAPAGOS
ISLANDS
(Ecuador)
PACIFIC
OCEAN
PERU
BRAZIL
CHILE
ARGENTINA
Life expectancies, 2008
Less than 50
50–59
60–69
70–79
Over 80
No data
0
1000
2000 Miles
0
1000
2000 Kilometers

MAP E.2 | Life Expectancies in Global Perspective, 2008

The increased attention to public health, medicine, nutrition, and education since as early as the nineteenth century has contributed to prolonging life expectancy around the world, as have the many scientific breakthroughs and technological advancements of the twentieth and twenty-first centuries.

- According to Map E.1 and this map, which regions experienced population increase but has lower life expectancy? Population decrease and high life expectancy? Explain.
- Which countries do not match the life expectancy trends of their geographical regions? Why?
- Looking at the World Satellite Map, do you note any correlations between a region's life expectancy and its physical environment? Why or why not?

for the French presidency, Sarkozy defeated Le Pen (as well as the first French woman to run for the seat, Ségolène Royal).

But the question of how to include the 4 to 5 million Muslims in the republic continued to roil the country. In 2004 the French government passed a law forbidding the wearing of "conspicuous religious symbols" in French public primary and secondary schools. Although the law did not specify what such symbols were, it clearly targeted Muslim girls, many of whom wore head scarves, or *hijabs*. Many French officials believed these scarves undermined the basic secular norms that were at the heart of French culture. Anti-Muslim sentiment was also on the rise in Switzerland. In 2009, 57 percent of voters there approved a plebiscite that banned minarets (the towers over mosques).

Still more alarming to the Europeans' sense of well-being were several deadly terrorist bombings. In 2004, a series of bombings of commuter trains in Madrid killed 191 people and wounded more than 2,000; in 2005, terrorists struck London's subways, leaving 52 dead and 700 injured. In both cases, authorities pinned responsibility on al-Qaeda. But investigators also alleged that the operations were the work of Muslims who had resided in Spain or Britain for some time, which sparked doubts about the integration of all immigrants into European society.

In just a few years, the mood of the world's most advanced industrial societies has shifted decisively. The triumphant atmosphere that ushered in the new millennium has given way to a pessimistic outlook. Whereas in 2000 talk of the blessings of global integration dominated the political and economic scene, prognosticators now warn about the dangers emanating from disaffected members of their societies and from radicals, especially Islamic radicals, willing and able to unleash terror anywhere in the world.

RUSSIA, CHINA, AND INDIA

Fueling anti-immigrant fires in Europe, Japan, and North America is the increasing number of jobs being "outsourced." In the past, businesses had turned to immigrants to fill low-wage positions (and to keep all wages down). But at the end of the twentieth and the beginning of the twenty-first centuries, it has become more economical to relocate manufacturing to places where cheap labor is already available. To compete successfully in the global market, businesses need to be agile, to take advantage of differences in prevailing wages.

Economic Globalization and Political Effects

In the new millennium, business mobility is not limited to low-skilled and low-wage jobs. The *New York Times* columnist Thomas Friedman observed in a best-selling book that "the world" has become "flat." In other words, technological advances—particularly in computers and communication—have truly brought the world together by virtually erasing distances and enabling all sorts of enterprises to operate from almost any point on the globe. No longer do educated workers have to leave India and China for employment in Europe or North America, because it is increasingly cost-effective for corporations to shift certain operations to those countries. The playing field has been leveled in the globalized market economy, although countries with vast labor reserves such as China, India, and Russia still have a long way to go to achieve the per capita income levels enjoyed in the older capitalist societies like the United States, Europe, and Japan.

Child Labor. *Girls in a Javanese village work in a factory transferring bundles of cotton yarn to bobbins to be used in handlooms.*

Certainly, Russia, China, and India had healthy economic growth in the first years of the new century. With the price of oil regularly topping $60 per barrel and spiking at $140 per barrel in 2008, Russia enjoyed windfall energy revenues that boosted budget and trade surpluses and expanded personal incomes. Between 1999 and 2008, Russia's gross domestic product climbed at an average rate of more than 7 percent per year—an impressive achievement after the steep economic decline that followed the Soviet Union's dissolution in 1991.

At the same time that Russia's economy is opening to the world, however, its political system seems to be closing in on itself. In addressing the anarchy of the Yeltsin era (see Chapter 21), President Putin presided over the repossession of television stations from billionaires and the reassignment of other private properties to the state (or to his colleagues from the former KGB). He also eliminated elections for regional executives and restricted non-governmental organizations receiving foreign financing. In short, Russia's economy is now more firmly connected to the capitalist world, but its political system remains dominated by the executive branch. This situation has dashed hopes for the eventual consolidation of a real legislature and an independent judiciary that the Gorbachev-Yeltsin era seemed to promise.

The Chinese have followed a similar path, encouraging market economic reforms while quashing the possibilities for political liberalization. Their economic strategies seem to be successful. Over the last three decades, China's economy has grown at a breathtaking rate of over 9 percent annually, a spectacular ascent that shows no sign of abating. Consumer goods made in China dominate so many markets that it is virtually impossible, as several newspaper reporters have found, to supply an American family's needs on a "China-free" diet. As of 2010, China's economy was the third largest in the world, and projections—if current growth rates can be sustained—suggest that China will have the world's largest economy by midcentury (although its per capita income will still lag behind that of the United States).

In many ways, China's fortunes illustrate both the promises and the pitfalls of the economic reforms undertaken by many developing countries—what used to be called the Third World—in the era of globalization. On the one hand, despite the continued monopoly of political power by the Chinese communist party at home, China's entry into the World Trade Organization (WTO) in 2001 signified its full integration into the global capitalist economy. On the other hand, the reforms have caused political, social, and environmental problems that defy easy solutions. The disparity between the relatively prosperous coastal areas and the poor interior of the country—a problem that the communist government pledged to redress after it came to power in 1949—has once again become a glaring challenge.

At the same time, the gap between rich and poor in China's more economically developed urban areas has widened at an alarming rate. Government statistics indicate that the richest 10 percent of households own 45 percent of private urban wealth, while the poorest tenth command less than 1.4 percent of the wealth in the cities. Also, at home and abroad, there are concerns about the environmental impact of China's economic development. China's homes and factories, for instance, use 40 percent more coal than those in the United States, and Chinese city dwellers suffer from some of the world's worst smog and least healthy air quality.

As its energy consumption and economy have soared, so has China's global standing. In the period after 1949, China was the eager junior partner to the Soviet Union, slavishly imitating the Stalinist developmental model until the Sino-Soviet split of the 1960s (see Chapter 20). Subsequently, Richard Nixon and Henry Kissinger's courting of Mao in 1972 opened up a global option for China that Mao's successors have exploited. China's shift in foreign policy orientation from an alliance with the Soviet Union to a partnership with the United States has arguably been the most important geopolitical realignment in the contemporary world.

Moreover, China has become the number one trading partner with almost every country in Asia, displacing the United States. It has even become the top trading partner with Brazil as well as many countries in Africa. China has also replaced the United States as the number one customer for Saudi Arabian oil. China-India economic relations have strengthened, too. In parallel, the Chinese government has invested heavily in building an ocean-going navy. Although China faces numerous challenges, from environmental degradation to an aging population, it has regained the enormous global weight it held for centuries up to the eighteenth century. In fact, commentators have begun to speculate that China's authoritarian capitalism could be a model for other countries seeking rapid economic development without political liberalization.

Chinese Environmental Concerns. *Despite its prosperity, Hong Kong, like other major Chinese cities, suffers from severe air pollution, which threatens its future as a hub of international commerce. This picture shows part of the city's waterfront shrouded in smog.*

Internal Divisions, External Rivalries

Like China, India seems to be one of the success stories of economic globalization, yet internal divisions and external rivalries threaten to undo many benefits. After coming to power in 1998, a coalition led by the Bharatiya Janata Party (BJP), the Hindu nationalist party, embraced market liberalization. Over the next five years, the government opened India to the global market economy with spectacular economic results. Growth rates topped 7 percent annually, and India's stock market boomed. India is now a favorite destination for the flow of international capital, particularly in the information technology sector. Bangalore, Hyderabad, Mumbai, and Delhi have prospered as hot spots in the global economy.

At the same time that the BJP-led government promoted market reforms, it also championed *Hindutva* (Hinduness) as the bedrock of Indian identity. Nowhere were the effects of this twin strategy of economic liberalism and Hindu nationalism more visible than in the western state of Gujarat. Home to merchant communities for centuries, Gujarat has been in the forefront of capitalist manufactures and commerce. While aggressively participating in the global economy, the state has also been a fertile ground for Hindu nationalism.

The dark side of that nationalism erupted in February 2002 after sixty Hindus perished in a fire that consumed a train compartment. Although the circumstances of the fire remain disputed, a rumor immediately spread, authenticated by the BJP government in Gujarat, that Muslims and a "foreign hand" were responsible. For the next few months, Hindu mobs went on a rampage, burning Muslim homes and hacking the residents to death. Newspapers reported that government leaders and the police force assisted in this carnage or looked the other way as over 2,000 Muslims lost their lives. In the provincial elections of December 2002, the BJP aggressively projected itself as a Hindu nationalist and pro-business party. This strategy paid rich dividends, and the BJP was reelected to power with a commanding majority. It repeated its impressive electoral feat once again in the 2012 elections.

Yet another dark side is in fact related to market-led growth. In an effort to boost capitalist economy, the government has declared an open season on land acquisition for real estate development, industrial parks, and mining, leading to the eviction of farmers and forest dwellers. The displaced people have responded with Maoist insurgencies. The flood of corporate money has also corrupted politics, with scandal after scandal dominating the newspaper headlines. In 2011 an outburst of revulsion against politicians led to a movement against corruption.

The ongoing tension with neighboring Pakistan is yet another problem faced by India. Flexing its nationalist muscle, the Indian government exploded a nuclear device in 1998. Pakistan responded by exploding its own bombs, casting an ominous shadow over the two nations' unresolved conflict over Kashmir. In that contested province, terrorist violence repeatedly disturbed the peace and brought the nuclear-armed neighbors close to a potentially devastating war. The tension between the two countries escalated in 2008 when a small band of terrorists from Pakistan carried out raids in Mumbai, slaughtering many civilians and security personnel before being subdued.

Hindu-Muslim Tensions. *In 2002, Gujarat was consumed by sectarian riots, set off by a train fire in which fifty-nine Hindu pilgrims died. Although an Indian government investigation concluded that the fire was accidental, the incident sparked an orgy of violence by Hindu mobs against Muslims. Shown here is an angry right-wing Hindu party activist.*

Presently, India and Pakistan appear to have taken a step away from that brink, in part because national elections in 2004 returned a coalition headed by the Congress Party to power in India. Led by the Italian-born Sonia Gandhi (wife of the deceased Rajiv Gandhi, Nehru's grandson), the coalition included diverse caste, regional, and ideological interests. Its victory represented a setback to the Hindu nationalist effort to define India's identity in singular terms—at least for the time being. In 2009 the Congress Party again won national elections, and its leader, Manmohan Singh, became prime minister of a coalition government for the second time.

Projecting recent trends into the future, many observers forecast a rearrangement of the world's economic order, with China and India especially moving to the fore during the twenty-first century. Yet China, India, and Russia, like other parts of the world, have not escaped from the past. These societies, too, struggle with widening internal divisions and potentially devastating external rivalries. The impulse toward greater global integration conflicts with the desire to preserve local, regional, and national autonomy. (For a global look at hunger and disparities in income, see Maps E.3 and E.4.)

THE MIDDLE EAST, AFRICA, AND LATIN AMERICA

Although anxieties about terrorism and immigration add to the worries of the West, North American, European, and Japanese societies still boast the world's largest economies and longest life expectancies. Likewise, Russia, China, and India have benefited from bulging trade surpluses and rising per capita incomes. Elsewhere, however, it is harder to find signs of enduring peace or general prosperity.

The Arab Spring

In the 2011 report issued by the Eurasia Group, a multinational organization that assesses countries at risk for political instability, not a single Arab country appeared on their extensive lists. Their predictions were completely off target. The trigger for what became known as the Arab Spring occurred on December 17, 2010, with a seemingly futile act of an insignificant twenty-six-year-old Tunisian vegetable vendor and father of eight who set himself on fire outside a provincial office to protest constant police harassment. This singular act aroused the entire population of Tunisia against the ruling elite. Not only had the police confiscated Mohammed Bouazizi's vegetable stand, and not for the first time, but a policewoman had slapped him in the face. In explaining his decision to take his life, his sister exclaimed, "[I]n Sidi Bouzidi [where he resided] those with no connections and no money for bribes are humiliated and insulted and not allowed to live." As the story circulated through the country, large numbers poured out into the streets, demanding an end to the long-term dictatorship of Zine al-Abidine Ben Ali, who had taken over from Habib Bourguiba, Tunisia's president from independence in 1956 until 1978. Ben Ali was an easy target for reproach. Not only had he ruled with an iron fist, but his second wife, Leila Trabelsi, was a notoriously corrupt person, a former hairdresser who lived in splendor and spent lavishly on herself and her prominent European and Arab guests. Ben Ali's promises to change his behavior convinced no one. The catchword of the protesters was *degage*, "get out." With the army refusing to suppress the dissenters and the security police overwhelmed, Ben Ali took the only way open to him. He departed for Saudi Arabia on January 14, 2011.

Young Egyptian radicals watched events in Tunisia with growing interest. After all, if the Tunisians could get rid of their dictator, why not the Egyptians? On January 25, 2011, ironically a holiday to honor Egypt's police forces, by now an object of people's hatred, Egyptians of all backgrounds and ages—Copts and Muslims, workers and professionals—assembled in Cairo's major plaza, Midan al-Tahrir, or Liberation Square, to let Egypt's president, Hosni Mubarak, in office since 1981, know that he was no longer wanted. Their watchword, *irhal,* meaning "scram" in Arabic, expressed the protesters' utter contempt for him and his rule. His efforts to offer concessions by promising that he would not be a candidate for the presidency in the elections that were to take place at the end of the year had the same effect that Ben Ali's promised reforms had. On February 11, 2011, just three weeks after the first mass demonstration, Hosni Mubarak left office, turning the reins of power over to the Supreme Command of the Armed Forces, a small group of officers whom the president had chosen to lead Egypt's army.

The ouster of Ben Ali and Mubarak sent shock waves of excitement throughout the Arab world. Decades of pent-up rage could no longer be contained. An outpouring of protests occurred in all of the Arab world's major cities. The demands were consistent—the end of repression, the establishment of democratic institutions, and the ousting of rulers who had stayed in power too long and who did not represent the will of the people. The results were astonishing. Monarchs in Jordan and Morocco promised new constitutions; they said that going forward they would rule, not reign. Bahraini Shiites exacted a new constitution from their Sunni king, and Ali Saleh, ruler of Yemen since 1978, fled the country. Even Muammar Qaddafi, the Libyan strongman, in power since ousting King Idris in 1969, felt the sting of protest, though his ouster and eventual execution on October 20, 2011, in the city of Sirte, owed as much to NATO air power as it did to the rebel army that rose up to unseat him.

Although much of the world had misunderstood the causes of these uprisings, they were not hard to discern after the fact. In the first place, Arab populations, 60 percent of whom were under thirty years of age and had known no other rulers, resented the fact that the wave of democratic reforms that had swept through Russia, much of eastern and central Europe, and large parts of sub-Saharan Africa had passed them by. They saw no reason why they, too, should not have leaders who represented their wishes rather than rigged elections and fraudulent referendums that supported the wishes of the ruling elites. The young came to be known as the generation in waiting—waiting for jobs that never seemed to appear; waiting to have enough money to move out of their parents' homes; and waiting to get married and start families. The fact that Hafez al-Assad had passed power to his son, Bashar al-Assad, and Hosni Mubarak was grooming his son, Gamal, heightened the rage. Although the

GREENLAND
(Denmark)
ICELAND
ALASKA
(U.S.)
CANADA
UNITED
STATES
GERMA
GREAT
BRITAIN
FRANC
SPAIN
MOROCCO
ALGE
ATLANTIC
OCEAN
BERMUDA
(Br.)
WESTERN SAHARA
(Morocco)
MAURITANIA
MALI
SENEGAL
SIERRA LEONE
LIBERIA
HAWAII
(U.S.)
MEXICO
CUBA
DOMINICAN
REP.
PUERTO RICO
(U.S.)
BELIZE
JAMAICA
HAITI
GUATEMALA
NICARAGUA
COSTA RICA
PANAMA
COLOMBIA
GALAPAGOS
ISLANDS
(Ecuador)
PACIFIC
OCEAN
PERU
BRAZIL
CHILE
ARGENTINA
Hunger
<2.5%, extremely low
2.5%–4.0%, very low
5.0%–19.0%, moderately low
20.0%–34.0%, moderately high
>35.0%, very high
No data
0
1000
2000 Miles
0
1000
2000 Kilometers

MAP E.3 | Hunger Is a Global Problem

Despite much optimism, globalization has not yet shown the ability to meet the basic human needs of the entire world population.

- According to this map, in which regions is hunger very high?
- Comparing this map with Map E.4, identify at least twelve countries where hunger is very high *and* per capita income is low ($825 or less). What other characteristics do these regions share?

GREENLAND
(Denmark)
ICELAND
ALASKA
(U.S.)
CANADA
GERM
GREAT
BRITAIN
FRAN
SPAIN
UNITED
STATES
ATLANTIC
OCEAN
BERMUDA
(Br.)
MOROCCO
ALG
WESTERN SAHARA
(Morocco)
MAURITANIA
MALI
BAHAMAS
CUBA
DOMINICAN
REP.
PUERTO RICO
(U.S.)
HAWAII
(U.S.)
MEXICO
BELIZE
JAMAICA
HAITI
GUATEMALA
NICARAGUA
COSTA RICA
PANAMA
COLOMBIA
SENEGAL
SIERRA LEONE
LIBERIA
CÔTE
D'IVOIRE
GHANA
BEN
TOGO
CAMER
GALAPAGOS
ISLANDS
(Ecuador)
PACIFIC
OCEAN
PERU
BRAZIL
CHILE
ARGENTINA
World income, 2007
$10,066 or more, high
$3,256–$10,065, upper middle
$826–$3,255, lower middle
$825 or less, low
No data
0
1000
2000 Miles
0
1000
2000 Kilometers

MAP E.4 | Rich and Poor Countries: The World by Income, 2007

Wealth and income derived from globalization have not been shared equally among the world population.

- Using this map, identify the regions with the highest per capita income and those with the lowest. What factors do you think account for this disparity? What historical antecedents helped to create this disparity?
- According to your reading, why have India and China, despite recent economic growth, failed to catch up with the United States, western European countries, and Japan in terms of per capita income?

Arab Spring. *Day and night, Cairo's Tahrir Square swarmed with Egyptians of all ages to protest the ongoing military rule after the ousting of Mubarak. Here protestors burn the midnight oil to decry the dissolution of Parliament by Egypt's Supreme Constitutional Court, a move to consolidate power in the hands of military generals. Note the man documenting the heated demonstration with his video camera* (bottom left), *whose footage would likely have found its way to the wide array of social media sites for discussion and further dissemination.*

uprisings often took names that suggested peaceful protest—the Jasmine Revolution in Tunisia followed by the White Revolution in Egypt—in reality these outbursts reflected deep-seated and long-standing fury at rulers who were repressive, corrupt, and unresponsive to their people.

Of high importance was the fact that the dictatorships and monarchies had lost control over the media. CNN was the first global station to intrude on the regimes' control of the news, but even more important, because it was homegrown, was the Qatari television station and newspaper, Aljazeera, founded in 1995. It became an open forum for all kinds of opinions, including those that found fault with existing governments. One of its most dramatic and widely quoted programs featured an intense discussion about whether the Arab populations did not have the right like those in the West to criticize their leaders. In addition, mobile phones, Facebook, Twitter, and other social media all helped dissenters communicate with one another and enabled groups to organize large assemblies outside the purview of the state.

The early results led euphoric protesters to believe that they could create new and more open societies. Dictators were ousted, free elections were held, and new constitutions were promised. But the progress was hard to sustain. In Bahrain, where the king promised a more democratic constitution and appeared willing to make concessions to his Shiite subjects, violence in the capital persuaded the Saudi army to intervene and suppress the protest movement. In Tunisia, a moderate Muslim Brotherhood party, al-Nahda, won control of parliament. While it affirmed its commitment to respect the rights of all, liberals and secularists worried about a return to strict *sharia* law. Egypt, too, held elections that were won by the Muslim Brotherhood party, Justice and Development, but nullified by the courts. It also elected a Muslim Brotherhood president, Muhammad Morsi, who was unseated after a year for his unchecked expansion of powers; Egyptian judge Adly Mansour now serves as interim president. Strict Muslims, in the meantime, continue to work for a full implementation of sharia law while many fear that outcome.

By far, the most lethal outcome of the Arab Spring has occurred in Syria where protesters, seeking the ouster of President Bashar al-Assad, have formed a free Syrian army, gained international recognition for their movement, and led protests that have resulted in violent confrontation with Assad's forces. To date, more than 60,000 Syrians have lost their lives in the conflict, and while most commentators believe that Assad's days are numbered, few know what kind of a regime will emerge once he has been driven from the country. Still, the Arab world looks entirely different from its autocratic and repressive appearance of 2010. The ideals enunciated by the protesters—open societies, representative of the people, promoting economic progress—have transformed the region.

Poverty, Disease, Genocide

The new millennium did not begin auspiciously for the peoples of Africa. The region remained the poorest in the world and suffered the uncontrolled and uncontrollable spread of HIV/AIDS. Of the thirty-eight sub-Saharan African countries surveyed in the World Bank *Annual Development Report* for 2009, all but seven were low-income countries. The poorest of the poor (Burundi, the Republic of the Congo, and Liberia) reported per capita incomes of $150 or less. Botswana, which enjoyed the second-highest per capita income level at $6,120 (behind only mineral-rich Gabon), was so devastated by HIV/AIDS that life expectancy, once the highest in Africa at close to seventy years, had tumbled to fifty-one years in 2007 and was one of the lowest in the world. (For a global look at HIV incidence, see Map E.5.)

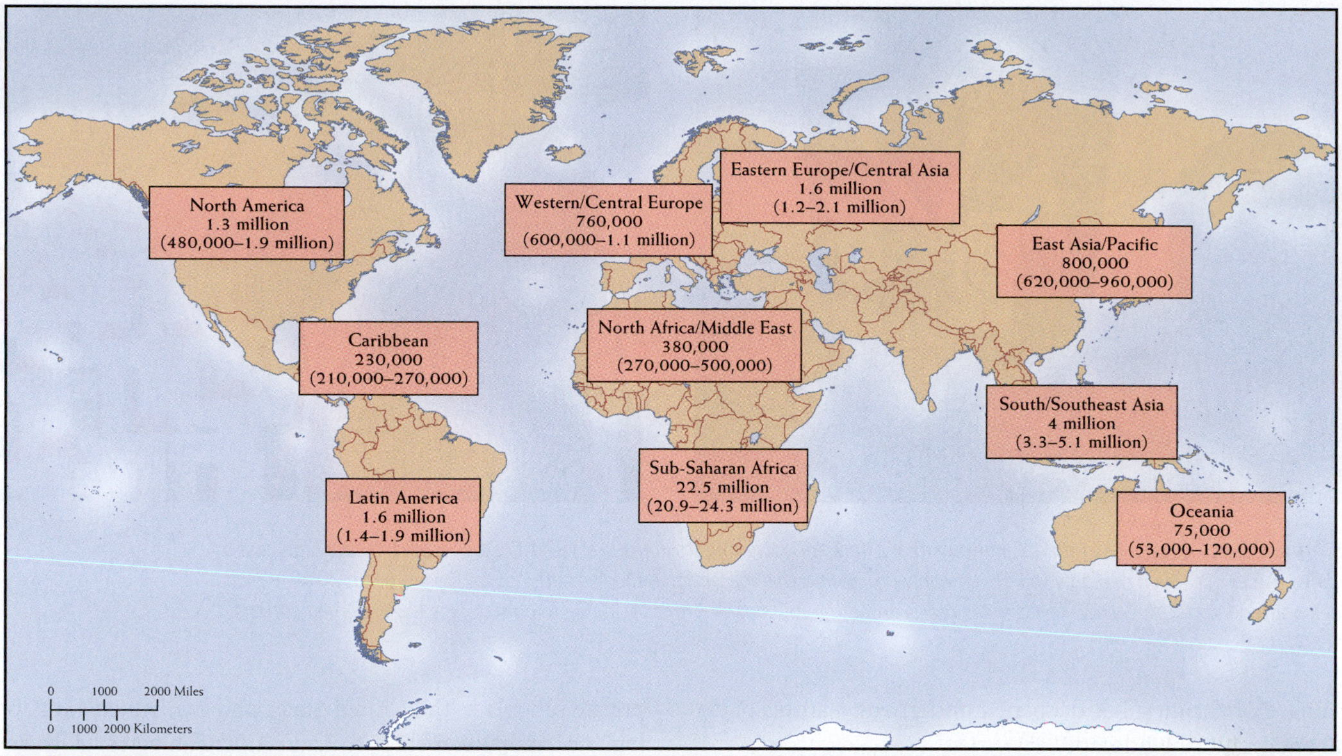

MAP E.5 | The Number of HIV-Positive People Worldwide, 2007

The spread of HIV threatens the development of human capital in the twenty-first century.

- According to this map, which region has the highest amount of HIV infection?
- Using Maps E.3 and E.4 as reference, what connections do you see between poverty and HIV prevalence?
- How does the spread of HIV compromise economic development in poorer regions of the world?

There are a few promising signs. Ghana embraced parliamentary and presidential elections. Civil strife ended in Mozambique and Angola. South Africa convened a Truth and Reconciliation Commission to put the trauma of apartheid behind it and to stay on the course of parliamentary democracy while addressing the gross disparities of income between whites and blacks that were legacies of the twentieth century.

But these have been exceptions to the rule in which political instability wrought misery and devastation. Three of West Africa's countries (Liberia, Sierra Leone, and the Ivory Coast) were torn asunder because of ethnic and personal rivalries and required foreign interventions. Nigeria finally rid itself of unwanted military dictatorial control and moved to a civil, parliamentary system. But Nigeria's democratically elected presidents have barely been able to hold the country together. The northern, mostly Muslim territories continue to fear and resent the southern, mainly Christian communities.

In 2003, just when Africa's longest-running civil war, pitting the animist and Christian southern Sudanese against the northern Muslim peoples, had been resolved and led to the creation of a new state carved out of Sudan and known as South Sudan, a new dispute broke out in western Sudan. In the region of Darfur the state allowed local horse-riding, nomadic tribesmen to carry out ethnic cleansing campaigns against settled agriculturalists. This has led to perhaps the worst case of displaced peoples in the early twenty-first century. Over 2 million refugees fled government terror and civil war to huddle in vast, miserable camps. As in Rwanda in the 1990s (see Chapter 21), genocide has once more visited Africa. But there is some hope. In the West African country of Liberia, after years of pitiless civil war, the belligerents agreed to put down their guns in 2004. In 2005, remarkable elections swept Ellen Johnson-Sirleaf into office to become Africa's first woman president.

Deepening Inequalities

Compared with sub-Saharan Africa, Latin America's situation is not so bleak. Globalization has had profound effects on Latin America, but it has not created an entirely new age. In some areas, globalization has changed the way Latin Americans see their worlds and their place in the wider world. In other

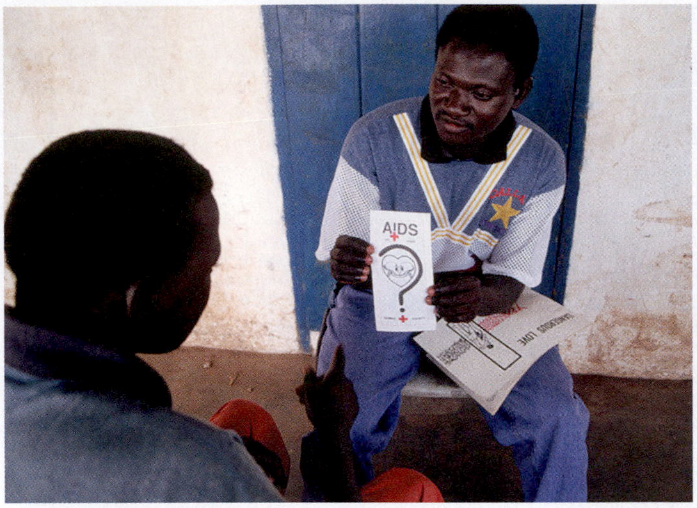

AIDS Awareness. (Left) *A Gambian health worker offers AIDS awareness literature.* (Right) *Due, in part, to the high cost of medicines, AIDS has taken a deadly toll on Africans, prompting this memorial in the Netherlands on December 1, 2009, which was designated World AIDS Day. The crosses represented the millions of Africans unable to gain access to AIDS medications.*

domains, globalization has deepened underlying features of the social and political landscape.

Across the region, the divide between haves and have-nots has widened what has historically been the world's most unequal region. The very rich in Buenos Aires live like the very rich in Boston; magnates of Mexico City drive the same cars, eat the same food, read the same books, and vacation in the same spots as their social cousins from Moscow. They send their children to private schools in the United States and the United Kingdom to join a cosmopolitan elite. To Latin American elites, globalization has been a boon to their wealth and has facilitated integration into the international circulation of goods, ideas, and people. Many, in fact, identify less and less with a particular place in the world.

Liberia's President. *Ellen Johnson-Sirleaf after her inauguration at the Capitol Building in Monrovia, on January 16, 2006. Johnson-Sirleaf is Africa's first elected woman president; she enjoys strong U.S. support and has vowed to fight graft and rebuild her country after years of war.*

Some of the same features hold for the social bottom. Being disadvantaged and poor in southern Mexico looks a lot like being on the losing end in southern Africa: people cling to tiny parcels of land, migrate long distances for seasonal jobs, and fight against insensitive authorities for their basic needs. Globalization has offered few opportunities to make it at home. Old factories have closed in Rosario, Argentina, when faced with competition from Japan; maize farmers in Mexico have to contend with imports from Iowa. In many cases, thanks to globalization, the main solution to the problem is to leave—to move to the city or across borders in search of opportunities elsewhere.

Latin Americans have responded to these challenges in many ways. One sweeping trend is for voters to elect left-wing governments. Most of these are not like the rebel firebrands of the 1960s. Instead, in Brazil, Chile, Argentina, and Uruguay, left-wing governments offer policies designed to soften the blows of globalization and meet basic needs for land, schools, and decent housing. Here the same pressures of globalization that contribute to leftist electoral triumphs limit what these fledgling governments can do. Elsewhere, a more nationalist and populist brand of politics has emerged, one that decries globalization altogether. Rather than softening its effects, leaders here promise to reverse them. In Venezuela, Ecuador, and Bolivia, presidents criticize imperialism and challenge American influence. Their message is that Latin America is better off being a world apart; being together, especially if it means cozying up to

São Paulo, Brazil. *An aerial view of one of São Paulo's biggest slums, Favela Morumbi; Favela Morumbi borders one of the city's richest neighborhoods, also called Morumbi.*

the United States, implies a future of subservience and impoverishment. But as many of these leaders also stifle criticism at home, being apart does not ensure empowerment and prosperity for all, either.

The appeal of anti-globalist politics is not limited to Latin America, or even to the underdeveloped world. In the most advanced industrial societies, as well as in rapidly rising nations like China and India, programs to check globalization or buffer people from its destabilizing effects have found receptive audiences. Still, opposition to deeper global integration continues to be greatest in the poorest parts of the world, where globalization's benefits are least apparent and its costs are often lethal.

Historians are better at interpreting the past than at forecasting the future, but what seems certain is that economic, cultural, political, and environmental developments will continue to encourage exchange and interaction, fostering the integration of peoples and cultures in the new millennium. But cultural and religious diversity, local political institutions and prerogatives, economic competition, and environmental particularities will also persist. And so will the dynamic tensions that both link our worlds together and keep our worlds apart.

Anti-Globalization. *Anti-globalization activists target annual summits of the leaders of the eight most industrialized countries. This one, in Germany in June 2007, saw riot police drive back protesters. Notice the New York Yankees baseball cap on one of the protesters.*

FURTHER READINGS

CHAPTER 10

Allsen, Thomas, *Commodity and Exchange in the Mongol Empire: A Cultural History of Islamic Textiles* (1997). A study that uses golden brocade, the textile most treasured by Mongol rulers, as a lens through which to analyze the vast commercial networks facilitated by the Mongol conquests and control.

———, *Culture and Conquest in Mongol Eurasia* (2001). A work that emphasizes the cultural and scientific exchanges that took place across Afro-Eurasia as a result of the Mongol conquest.Bartlett, Robert, *The Making of Europe: Conquest, Colonization and Cultural Change, 950–1350* (1993). The modes of cultural, political, and demographic expansion of feudal Europe along its frontiers, especially in eastern Europe.

Bay, Edna G., *Wives of the Leopards: Gender, Politics, and Culture in the Kingdom of Dahomey* (1998). A work that stresses the role of women in an important West African society and dips into the early history of this area.

Beach, D. N., *Shona and Zimbabwe, 900–1850: An Outline of Shona History* (1980). A good place to start for exploring the history of Great Zimbabwe.

Brooks, George E., *Landlords and Strangers: Ecology, Society, and Trade in Western Africa, 1000–1630* (1993). A survey assembled from primary sources of early West African history that stresses transregional connections.

Buzurg ibn Shahriyar of Ramhormuz, *The Book of the Wonders of India: Mainland, Sea and Islands,* ed. and trans. G. S. P. Freeman-Greenville (1981). A collection of stories told by sailors, both true and fantastic; they help us imagine the lives of sailors of the era.

Chappell, Sally A. Kitt, *Cahokia: Mirror of the Cosmos* (2002). A thorough and vivid account of the "mound people"; it explores not just what we know of Cahokia but how we know it.

Christian, David, *A Short History of Russia, Central Asia, and Mongolia,* vol. 1, *Inner Eurasia from Prehistory to the Mongol Empire* (1998). Essential reading for students interested in interconnections across the Afro-Eurasian landmass.

Curtin, Philip, *Cross-Cultural Trade in World History* (1984). A groundbreaking book on intercultural trade with a primary focus on Africa, especially the cross-Saharan trade and Swahili coastal trade.

Dawson, Christopher, *Mission to Asia* (1980). Accounts of China and the Mongol Empire brought back by Catholic missionaries and diplomats after 1240 CE.

Foltz, Richard C., *Religions of the Silk Road: Overland Trade and Cultural Exchange from Antiquity to the Fifteenth Century* (1999). A study of the populations and the cities of the Silk Road as transmitters of culture across long distances.

Franklin, Simon, and Jonathan Shepherd, *The Emergence of Rus: 750–1200* (1996). The formation of medieval Russia between the Baltic and Black seas.

Gibb, Hamilton A. R., *Saladin: Studies in Islamic History,* ed. Yusuf Ibish (1974). A sympathetic portrait of one of Islam's leading political and military figures.

Goitein, S. D., *Letters of Medieval Jewish Traders* (1973). The classic study of medieval Jewish trading communities based on the commercial papers deposited in the Cairo Geniza (a synagogue storeroom) during the tenth and eleventh centuries; it explores not only commercial activities but also the personal lives of the traders around the Indian Ocean basin.

———, *A Mediterranean Society: An Abridgment in One Volume,* rev. and ed. Jacob Lassner (1999). A portrait of the Jewish merchant community with ties across the Afro-Eurasian landmass, based largely on the documents from the Cairo Geniza (of which Goitein was the primary researcher and interpreter).

———, "New Light on the Beginnings of the Karim Merchant," *Journal of Social and Economic History of the Orient* 1 (1958). Goitein's description of Egyptian trade.

Harris, Joseph E., *The African Presence in Asia: Consequences of the East African Slave Trade* (1971). One of the few books that looks broadly at the impact of Africans and African slavery on the societies of Asia.

Hartwell, Robert, "Demographic, Political, and Social Transformations of China, 750–1550," *Harvard Journal of Asiatic Studies* 42 (1982): 365–442. A pioneering study of the demographic changes that overtook China during the Tang and Song dynasties, which are described in light of political reform movements and social changes in this crucial era.

Historical Relations across the Indian Ocean: Report and Papers of the Meeting of Experts Organized by UNESCO at Port Louis, Mauritius, from 15 to 19 July, 1974 (1980). Excellent essays on the connections of Africa with Asia across the Indian Ocean.

Hitti, Philip, *An Arab-Syrian Gentleman and Warrior in the Period of the Crusades: Memoirs of* Usāmah *ibn-Munqidh* (1929). The Crusaders seen through Muslim eyes.

Hodgson, Natasha, *Women, Crusading, and the Holy Land in Historical Narrative* (2007). A book dealing with the Crusades and focusing on the place of women in them.

Holt, P. M., *The Age of the Crusades: The Near East from the Eleventh Century to 1517* (1984). The Crusades period as seen from the eastern Mediterranean and through the lens of a leading British scholar of the area.

Hymes, Robert, and Conrad Schirokauer (eds.), *Ordering the World: Approaches to State and Society in Sung Dynasty China* (1993). A collection of essays that traces the intellectual, social, and political movements that shaped the Song state and its elites.

Ibn Battuta, *The Travels of Ibn Battuta,* trans. H. A. R. Gibb (2002). A readable translation of the classic book, originally published in 1929.

Ibn Fadlan, Ahmad, *Ibn Fadlan's Journey to Russia: A Tenth Century Traveler from Baghdad to the Volga River,* trans. with commentary by Richard Frye (2005). A coherent summary of the observations of an envoy who traveled from Baghdad to Russia.

Irwin, Robert, *The Middle East in the Middle Ages: The Early Mamluk Sultanate, 1250–1582* (1986). Egypt under Mamluk rule.

Jeppie, Shamil, and Diagne, Souleymane Bachir, editors, *The Meanings of Timbuktu* (2008). New materials on the ancient Muslim city of Timbuktu by scholars who have been preserving its manuscripts and writing about its historical importance.

Lancaster, Lewis, Kikun Suh, and Chai-shin Yu (eds.), *Buddhism in Koryo: A Royal Religion* (1996). A description of Buddhism at its height in the Koryo period, when the religion made significant contributions to the development of Korean culture.

Levtzion, Nehemia, and Randall L. Pouwels (eds.), *The History of Islam in Africa* (2000). A useful general survey of the place of Islam in African history.

Lewis, Bernard (trans.), *Islam: From the Prophet Muhammad to the Capture of Constantinople* (1974). Vol. 2: *Religion and Society.* A fine collection of original sources that portray various aspects of classical Islamic society.

Lopez, Robert S., *The Commercial Revolution of the Middle Ages, 950–1350* (1976). An account focusing on the development around the Mediterranean of commercial practices such as the use of currency, accounting, and credit.

Lyons, Malcolm C. & D. E. P. Jackson, *Saladin: The Politics of the Holy War,* Cambridge (1984: reprint 2001). The fundamental revisionist work on one of the more important historical figures of the time.

Maalouf, Amin, *The Crusades through Muslim Eyes,* trans. Jon Rothschild (1984). The European Crusaders as seen by the Muslim world.

Marcus, Harold G., *A History of Ethiopia* (2002). An authoritative overview of the history of this great culture.

Mass, Jeffrey, *Yoritomo and the Founding of the First Bakufu: The Origins of Dual Government in Japan* (1999). A revisionist account of how the Kamakura military leader Minamoto Yoritomo established the "dual polity" of court and warrior government in Japan.

McDermott, Joseph, *A Social History of the Chinese Book: Books and Literati Culture in Late Imperial China* (2006). The history of the book in China since the Song dynasty, with comparisons to the book's role in other civilizations, particularly the European.

McIntosh, Roderik, *The Peoples of the Middle Niger: The Island of Gold* (1988). A historical survey of an area often omitted from other textbooks.

Moore, Jerry D., *Cultural Landscapes in the Ancient Andes: Archaeologies of Place* (2005). The most recent and up-to-date analysis of findings based on recent archaeological evidence, emphasizing the importance of local cultures and diversity in the Andes.

Niane, D. T. (ed.), *Africa from the Twelfth to the Sixteenth Century,* vol. 4 of *General History of Africa* (1984). The general UNESCO history of Africa's volume on four centuries of African history. This work features the scholarship of Africans.

Oliver, Roland (ed.), *From c. 1050 to c. 1600,* vol. 3 of *The Cambridge History of Africa,* ed. J. D. Fage and Roland Oliver (1977). Another general survey of African history. This volume draws heavily on the work of British scholars.

Peters, Edward, *The First Crusade* (1971). The Crusaders as seen through their own eyes.

Petry, Carl F. (ed.), *Islamic Egypt, 640–1517,* vol. 1 of *The Cambridge History of Egypt,* ed. M. W. Daly (1998). A solid overview of the history of Islamic Egypt up to the Ottoman conquest.

Polo, Marco, *The Travels of Marco Polo,* ed. Manuel Komroff (1926). A solid translation of Marco Polo's famous account.

Popovic, Alexandre, *The Revolt of African Slaves in Iraq in the 3rd/9th Century,* trans. Leon King (1999). The account of a massive revolt against their slave masters by African slaves taken to labor in Iraq's mines and fields.

Scott, Robert, *Gothic Enterprise: A Guide to Understanding the Medieval Cathedral* (2003). The meaning and social function of religious building in medieval cities in northern Europe.

Shaffer, Lynda Norene, *Maritime Southeast Asia to 1500* (1996). A history of the peoples of the southeast fringe of the Eastern Hemisphere, up to the time that they became connected to the global commercial networks of the world.

Shimada, Izumi, "Evolution of Andean Diversity: Regional Formations (500 BCE–CE 600)," in Frank Salomon and Stuart Schwartz (eds.), *South America,* vol. 3 of *The Cambridge History of the Native Peoples of the Americas* (1999), part 1, pp. 350–517. A splendid overview that contrasts the varieties of lowland and highland cultures.

Steinberg, David Joel, et al., *In Search of Southeast Asia: A Modern History* (1987). An account of the emergence of the modern Southeast Asian polities of Cambodia, Burma, Thailand, and Indonesia.

Tyerman, Christopher, *God's War: A New History of the Crusades* (2006). The balance of religious and nonreligious motivations in the Crusades.

Waley, Daniel, *The Italian City-Republics,* 3rd ed. (1988). The structures and culture of the new cities of medieval Italy.

Watson, Andrew, *Agricultural Innovation in the Early Islamic World: The Diffusion of Crops and Farming Techniques, 700–1100* (1983). An impressive study of the spread of new crops throughout the Muslim world.

CHAPTER 11

Bois, Guy, *The Crisis of Feudalism: Economy and Society in Eastern Normandy, c. 1300–1550* (1984). A good case study of a French region that illustrates the turmoil in fourteenth-century Europe.

Brook, Timothy, *Praying for Power: Buddhism and the Formation of Gentry Society in Late Ming China* (1994). An analysis of the role of a significant religious force in the political and social developments of the Ming.

Dardess, John, *A Ming Society: T'ai-ho County, Kiangsi, Fourteenth to Seventeenth Centuries* (1996). A work that covers the different changes and developments of a single locality in China through the centuries.

Dols, Michael W., *The Black Death in the Middle East* (1977). One of the few scholarly works to examine the Black Death outside Europe.

Dreyer, Edward, *Early Ming China: A Political History, 1355–1435* (1982). A useful account of the early years of the Ming dynasty.

Finkel, Caroline, *Osman's Dream: The Story of the Ottoman Empire, 1300–1923* (2005). The most authoritative overview of Ottoman history.

Hale, John, *The Civilization of Europe in the Renaissance* (1994). A beautifully crafted account of the politics, economics, and culture of the Renaissance period in western Europe.

Hodgson, Marshall, *The Venture of Islam: Conscience and History in a World*

Civilization, vol. 3 (1974). A good volume on the workings of the Ottoman state.

Itzkowitz, Norman, *Ottoman Empire and Islamic Tradition* (1972). Another good book on the Ottoman state.

Jackson, Peter, *The Delhi Sultanate* (1999). A meticulous, highly specialized, political and military history.

Jackson, Peter, and Lawrence Lockhart (eds.), *The Cambridge History of Iran,* vol. 6 (1986). A volume that deals with the Timurid and Safavid periods in Iran.

Jones, E. L., *The European Miracle* (1981). A provocative work on the economic and social recovery from the Black Death.

Kafadar, Cemal, *Between Two Worlds: The Construction of the Ottoman State* (1995). A thorough reconsideration of the origins of one of the world's great land empires.

Karamustafa, Ahmed, *God's Unruly Friends: Dervish Groups in the Islamic Later Middle Period, 1200–1550* (1994). A book that describes the unorthodox Islamic activities that were occurring in the Islamic world prior to and alongside the establishment of the Ottoman and Safavid empires.

Levathes, Louise, *When China Ruled the Seas: The Treasure Fleet of the Dragon Throne, 1405–33* (1994). A book that provides a lively account of the Zheng He expeditions.

Lowry, Heath W., *The Nature of the Early Ottoman State* (2003). New perspectives on the rise of the Ottomans to prominence.

McNeill, William, *Plagues and Peoples* (1976). A pathbreaking work with a highly useful chapter on the spread of the Black Death throughout the Afro-Eurasian landmass.

Morgan, David, *Medieval Persia, 1040–1797* (1988). Contains an informative discussion of the Safavid state.

Peirce, Leslie, *The Imperial Harem: Women and Sovereignty in the Ottoman Empire* (1993). A work that describes the powerful place that imperial women had in political affairs.

Pirenne, Henri, *Economic and Social History of Medieval Europe* (1937). A classic study of the economic and social recovery from the Black Death.

Reid, James J., *Tribalism and Society in Islamic Iran, 1500–1629* (1983). A useful account of how the Mongols and other nomadic steppe peoples influenced Iran in the era when the Safavids were establishing their authority.

Singman, Jeffrey L. (ed.), *Daily Life in Medieval Europe* (1999). An introductory description of the social and material world experienced by Europeans of different walks of life.

Tuchman, Barbara W., *A Distant Mirror: The Calamitous Fourteenth Century* (1978). A book that shows, in a vigorous way, how war, famine, and pestilence devastated Europeans in the fourteenth century.

Wittek, Paul, *The Rise of the Ottoman Empire* (1958). A work that contains vital insights on the emergence of the Ottoman state amid the political chaos in Anatolia.

CHAPTER 12

Axtell, James, *Beyond 1492: Encounters in Colonial North America* (1992). A wonderfully informed speculation about Indian reactions to Europeans.

Brady, Thomas A., et al. (eds.), *Handbook of European History 1400–1600: Late Middle Ages, Renaissance, and Reformation, Structures and Assertions* (1996). A good synthetic survey of recent literature and historiographical debates.

Brook, Timothy, *Vermeer's Hat: The Seventeenth Century and the Dawn of the Global World* (2008). An interesting look at the connections forged across the globe through the works of a well-known European artist.

Cass, Victoria, *Dangerous Women: Warriors, Grannies, and Geishas of the Ming* (1999). An original study of Chinese female archetypes in memoirs, miscellanies, short stories, and novels.

Chaudhuri, K. N., *Trade and Civilisation in the Indian Ocean: An Economic History from the Rise of Islam to 1750* (1985). An excellent, comprehensive work that deals with the Indian Ocean economy and the appearance of European merchants there from the sixteenth century onward.

Clendinnen, Inga, *Aztecs: An Interpretation* (1991). Brilliantly reconstructs the culture of Tenochtitlán in the years before its conquest.

Crosby, Alfred W., *The Columbian Exchange: Biological and Cultural Consequences of 1492* (1972). A provocative discussion of the ecological consequences that followed the European "discovery" of the Americas.

———, *Ecological Imperialism: The Biological Expansion of Europe, 900–1900* (1986). Another important work on the ecological consequences of European expansion.

Curtin, Philip, *Cross-Cultural Trade in World History* (1984). A work stressing the role of trade and commerce in establishing cross-cultural contacts.

Febvre, Lucien, *The Problem of Unbelief in the Sixteenth Century: The Religion of Rabelais* (1982). A tour de force of intellectual history by the man who moved the study of the Reformation away from great men to the broader question of religious revival and mentalities.

Flynn, Dennis, and Arturo Giráldez (eds.), *Metals and Monies in an Emerging Global Economy* (1997). Contains several articles relating to silver and the Asian trade.

Frank, Andre Gunder, *ReOrient: Global Economy in the Asian Age* (1998). A reassessment of the role of Asia in the economic development of the world from around 1400 onward.

Gruzinski, Serge, *The Conquest of Mexico* (1993). An important work on the conquest of Mexico.

Habib, Irfan, *The Agrarian System of Mughal India* (1963). One of the best studies on the subject.

Hall, Richard Seymour, *Empires of the Monsoon: A History of the Indian Ocean and Its Invaders* (1996). A very engaging journalistic account with fabulous details.

Hodgson, Marshall, *The Venture of Islam,* vols. 2 and 3 (1974). A magisterial work that includes the Indian subcontinent in its careful study of the political and cultural history of the whole Islamic world.

Hulme, Peter, *Colonial Encounters: Europe and the Native Caribbean, 1492–1797* (1986). Presents an interesting interpretation of the encounters of Europeans and Native Americans.

Lach, Donald F., *Asia in the Making of Europe,* 5 books in 3 vols. (1965–). Perhaps the single most comprehensive and innovative guide to the European voyages of discovery.

Lockhart, James, and Stuart Schwartz, *Early Latin America* (1983). One of the finest studies of European expansion in the late fifteenth century.

McCann, James, *Maize and Grace: Africa's Encounter with a New World Crop, 1500–2000* (Cambridge, MA, 2005).

Melville, Elinor G. K., *A Plague of Sheep: Environmental Consequences of the Conquest of Mexico* (1994). A history of the transformation of a valley in Mexico from the Aztec period to the era of Spanish rule.

Mignolo, Walter D., *The Darker Side of the Renaissance: Literacy, Territoriality, and*

Colonization (1995). Uses literary theory and literary images to present provocative interpretations of the encounter of Europeans and Native Americans.

Pagden, Anthony, *European Encounters with the New World* (1993). A complex look at the deep and lasting imprint of the New World on its conquerors.

Parker, Geoffrey, *The Military Revolution: Military Innovation and the Rise of the West, 1500–1800* (1996). Traces the changes in technology and tactics in the early modern period and discusses the political significance of this "revolution."

Pelikan, Jaroslav, *Reformation of Church and Dogma (1300–1700)* (1988). An important overview of major religious controversies.

Phillips, William D., and Carla Rahn Phillips, *The World of Christopher Columbus* (1992). One of the finest studies of European expansion in the late fifteenth century.

Russell-Wood, A. J. R., *The Portuguese Empire, 1415–1808* (1992). An important survey of early Portuguese exploration.

Von Glahn, Richard, *Fountain of Fortune: Money and Monetary Policy in China, 1000–1700* (1996). Includes an excellent analysis of the history of silver in Ming China.

CHAPTER 13

Alam, Muzaffar, *The Crisis of Empire in Mughal North India* (1993). Represents the best of the new scholarly interpretations on the subject.

Bay, Edna, *Wives of the Leopard: Gender, Politics, and Culture in the Kingdom of Dahomey* (1998). A useful treatment of gender issues in Dahomey.

Blackburn, Robin, *The Making of New World Slavery: From the Baroque to the Modern, 1492–1800* (1997). A good place to begin when studying African slavery and the Atlantic slave trade, it compares the early expansion of the plantation systems across the Atlantic and throughout the Americas.

Calloway, Colin G., *One Vast Winter Count: The Native American West before Lewis and Clark* (2003). A sweeping survey of North American Indian histories prior to the nineteenth century.

Crossley, Pamela, *A Translucent Mirror: History and Identity in Qing Imperial Ideology* (1999). The author deals with the formation of identities such as "Manchu" and "Chinese" during the Qing period.

Eltis, David and Richardson, David, *Atlas of the Transatlantic Slave Trade* (New Haven, 2010). This work contains the most up-to-date data on the Atlantic slave trade, the numbers transported, where the captives came from, and where they landed.

Flynn, Dennis O., and Arturo Giraldez (eds.), *Metals and Money in an Emerging World Economy* (1997). A collection of articles about the place of silver in the world economy.

Forsyth, James, *A History of the Peoples of Siberia: Russia's North Asian Colony 1581–1990* (1992). A narrative overview of a violent history reminiscent of the western expansion of the United States.

Glahn, Richard von, *Fountains of Fortune: Money and Monetary Policy in China, 1000–1700* (1996). A discussion of the place of silver in the Chinese economy.

Halperin, Charles J., *Russia and the Golden Horde: The Mongol Impact on Medieval Russian History* (1985). A book on the rise of Muscovy, forebear of the Russian Empire, from within the Mongol realm.

Hämäläinen, Pekka, *The Comanche Empire* (2008). A book that inverts the conventional history of empires in North America by arguing that the Comanches were the most successful expansionist power in the middle of the continent during the eighteenth century.

Hattox, Ralph S., *Coffee and Coffeehouses: The Origins of a Social Beverage in the Medieval Near East* (1985). This work shows how widespread and popular coffee consumption and coffeehouses were around the world.

Huang, Ray, *1587, A Year of No Significance: The Ming Dynasty in Decline* (1981). An insightful analysis of the problems confronting the late Ming.

Lensen, George, *The Russian Push Toward Japan: Russo-Japanese Relations 1697–1875* (1959). A discussion of why and how Japan established its first border with another state and how Russia pursued its ambitions in the Pacific.

Lockhart, James, *The Nahuas After the Conquest* (1992). A landmark study of the social reorganization of Mesoamerican societies under Spanish rule.

Lovejoy, Paul, *Transformations in Slavery: A History of Slavery in Africa* (1983). An excellent discussion of African slavery.

Nakane, Chie, and Shinzaburo Oishi (eds.), *Tokugawa Japan: The Social and Economic Antecedents of Modern Japan* (1990). First-rate essays on Japanese village society, urban life, literacy, and culture.

Pamuk, Sevket, *A Monetary History of the Ottoman Empire* (2000). A discussion of the place of silver in the Ottoman Empire.

Parker, Geoffrey (ed.), *The Thirty Years' War* (1997). The standard account of the conflict and its outcomes.

Perdue, Peter C., *China Marches West: The Qing Conquest of Central Asia* (2005). This volume chronicles the expansion of the Qing Empire to its northwest, drawing comparisons to other colonial empires and their legacies.

Platonov, S. F., *Ivan the Terrible* (1986). Covers the controversies over Russia's infamous tsar.

Rawski, Evelyn, *The Last Emperors: A Social History of Qing Imperial Institutions* (1998). This volume explores the mechanisms and processes through which the Qing court negotiated its Manchu identity.

Reid, Anthony, *Charting the Shape of Early Modern Southeast Asia* (1999). A collection of articles by a leading historian of Southeast Asia.

Spence, Jonathan, and John Wills (eds.), *From Ming to Ch'ing: Conquest, Region, and Continuity in Seventeenth-Century China* (1979). Covers the various aspects of a tumultuous period of dynastic transition.

Taylor, Alan, *American Colonies: The Settling of North America* (2001). Brings together British, French, and Spanish colonial histories and shows how the fortunes of each were entangled with one another and with those of diverse Native American peoples.

Thornton, John, *Africa and Africans in the Making of the Atlantic World, 1400–1800* (1998). A wonderful discussion of how African slaves played a large role in the formation of the Atlantic world.

Thornton, John K., *The Kongolese Saint Anthony: Dona Beatriz Kimpa Vita and the Antonian Movement, 1684–1706* (1998). An excellent monograph on religious movements in the Kongo.

Toby, Ronald P., *State and Diplomacy in Early Modern Japan: Asia in the Development of the Tokugawa Bakufu* (1984). The author shows that the Japanese, far from being isolated from the outside world, engaged in vigorous and successful diplomacy.

Vilar, Pierre, *A History of Gold and Money* (1991). An excellent study of the development of the early silver and gold economies.

CHAPTER 14

Axtell, James, *The Invasion of America: The Contest of Cultures in Colonial North America* (1985). Discusses the strategies of Christian missionaries in converting the Indians, as well as the success of Indians in converting Europeans.

Babaie, Sussan, *Isfahan and Its Palaces: Statecraft, Shi'ism and the Architecture of Conviviality in Early Modern Iran* (2008). An overview of the city of Isfahan, as the capital of the Safavid state.

Barmé, Geremie, R., *The Forbidden City* (2008). A concise introduction to the history of one of the most important physical emblems of Chinese imperial power.

Berlin, Ira, *Many Thousands Gone: The First Two Centuries of Slavery in North America* (1998). Surveys the development of African-American culture in colonial North America.

Brook, Timothy, *The Confusions of Pleasure: Commerce and Culture in Ming China* (1999). An insightful survey of Ming society.

Clunas, Craig, *Superfluous Things: Material Culture and Social Status in Early Modern China* (1991). A good account of the late Ming elite's growing passion for material things.

Collcutt, Martin, Marius Jansen, and Isao Kumakura, *A Cultural Atlas of Japan* (1988). A sweeping look at the many different forms of Japanese cultural expression over the centuries, including the flourishing urban culture of Edo.

Darnton, Robert, *The Business of the Enlightenment: A Publishing History of the Encyclopédie, 1775–1800* (1979). The classic study of Europe's first great compendium of knowledge.

Dash, Mike, *Tulipomania: The Story of the World's Most Coveted Flower and the Extraordinary Passions It Aroused* (1999). A global perspective on and lively account of the spread of the tulip around the world as a flower signifying both beauty and status.

Elman, Benjamin A., *On Their Own Terms: Science in China, 1550–1900* (2005). A study of the development of "native" Chinese science and how the process interacted with the introduction of western science to China over the course of three and a half centuries.

Eze, Emmanuel Chukwudi (ed.), *Race and the Enlightenment: A Reader* (1997). Readings examining the idea of race in the context of the Enlightenment.

Fleischer, Cornell, *Bureaucrat and Intellectual in the Ottoman Empire: The Historian Mustafa Ali (1540–1600)* (1986). Offers good insight into the world of culture and intellectual vitality in the Ottoman Empire.

Grafton, Anthony, April Shelford, and Nancy Siraisi, *New Worlds, Ancient Texts: The Power of Tradition and the Shock of Discovery* (1995). A concise discussion of the impact of the New World on European thought.

Gutierrez, Ramon, *When Jesus Came, the Corn Mothers Went Away: Marriage, Sexuality, and Power in New Mexico, 1500–1846* (1991). A provocative dissection of the spiritual dimensions of European colonialism in the Americas.

Harley, J. B., and David Woodward (eds.), *The History of Cartography.* Vol. 2, Book 2: *Cartography in the Traditional East and Southeast Asian Societies* (1994). An authoritative treatment of the subject.

Horton, Robin, *Patterns of Thought in Africa and the West: Essays on Magic, Religion, and Science* (1993). Reflections on African patterns of thought and attitudes toward nature, which can help us understand African-American religious beliefs and resistance movements.

Keene, Donald, *The Japanese Discovery of Europe: Honda Toshiaki and Other Discoverers, 1720–1798* (1952). A study of the ways Japan managed to incorporate knowledge from the outside world with the development of national traditions.

Ko, Dorothy, *Teachers of the Inner Chambers: Women and Culture in Seventeenth-Century China* (1994). Explores the lives of elite women in late Ming and early Qing China.

Lewis, Bernard, *Race and Color in Islam* (1979). Examines the Islamic attitude toward race and color.Morgan, Philip D., *Slave Counterpoint: Black Culture in the Eighteenth-Century Chesapeake and Lowcountry* (1998). Describes the development of African-American culture in colonial North America.

Munck, Thomas, *The Enlightenment: A Comparative Social History, 1721–1794* (2000). A wonderful survey, with unusual examples from the periphery, especially from Scandinavia and the Habsburg Empire.

Necipoglu, Gulru, *Architecture, Ceremonial, and Power: The Topkapi Palace in the Fifteenth and Sixteenth Centuries* (1991). A magnificently illustrated book that shows the enormous artistic talent that the Ottoman rulers poured into their imperial structure.

Publishing and the Print Culture in Late Imperial China (Special Issue). *Late Imperial China,* Vol. 17:1 (June 1996). Contains a collection of important articles with a foreword by the French cultural historian Roger Chartier.

Qaisar, Ahsan Jan, *The Indian Response to European Technology,* AD *1498–1707* (1998). A meticulous, scholarly work on this little-studied subject.

Rizvi, Athar Abbas, *The Wonder That Was India.* Vol. 2: *A Survey of the History and Culture of the Indian Sub-continent from the Coming of the Muslims to the British Conquest, 1200–1700* (1987). A deeply learned work in intellectual history.

Smith, Bernard, *European Vision and the South Pacific* (1985). An excellent cultural history of Cook's voyages.

Smith, Richard J., *Chinese Maps: Images of "All under Heaven"* (1996). Provides a good introduction to the history of cartography in China.

Welch, Anthony, *Shah Abbas and the Arts of Isfahan* (1973). Describes the astonishing architectural and artistic renaissance of the city of Isfahan under the Safavid ruler Shah Abbas.

Whitfield, Peter, *The Image of the World: Twenty Centuries of World Maps* (1994). A good introduction to the history of cartography in different parts of the world.

Wilks, Ivor, *Forests of Gold: Essays on the Akan and the Kingdom of Asante* (Athens, OH, 1993). A study that focuses on the Asante's drive for wealth.

Zilfi, Madeline C., *The Politics of Piety: The Ottoman Ulema in the Post-Classical Age (1600–1800)* (1988). Explores the cultural flourishing that took place within the Islamic world in this period.

CHAPTER 15

Allen, Robert C., *The British Industrial Revolution in Global Perspective* (2009). The most recent and authoritative study of the industrial revolution in Britain and its implications around the world.

Anderson, Fred, *Crucible of War: The Seven Years' War and the Fate of Empire in British North America, 1754–1766* (2000). The best synthesis of the "great war for empire" that set the stage for the American Revolution.

Bayly, C. A., *Indian Society and the Making of the British Empire* (1998). A useful work on the early history of the British conquest of India.

Blackburn, Robin, *The Overthrow of Colonial Slavery*, 1776–1848 (1988). Places the abolition of the Atlantic slave trade and colonial slavery in a large historical context.

Cambridge History of Egypt: Modern Egypt from 1517 to the End of the Twentieth Century, Vol. 2 (1998). Volume 2 contains authoritative essays on all aspects of modern Egyptian history, including the impact of the French invasion and the rule of Muhammad Ali.

Chaudhuri, K. N., *The Trading World of Asia and the East India Company, 1660–1760* (1978). An authoritative economic history of the East India Company's operations.

Crafts, N. F. R., *British Economic Growth during the Industrial Revolution* (1985). A pioneering study that emphasizes a long-term, more gradual process of adaptation to new institutional and social circumstances.

de Vries, Jan, *Industrious Revolution: Consumer Behavior and the Household Economy, 1650 to the Present* (2008). A book on the lead-up to the industrial revolution, written by the leading economic historian who coined the term industrious revolution.

Diamond, Jared, and James A. Robinson (eds.), *Natural Experiments of History* (2010). This book consists of eight comparative studies drawn from history, archeology, economics, economic history, geography, and political science, covering a spectrum of approaches, ranging from a non-quantitative narrative style to quantitative statistical analyses.

Doyle, William, *The Oxford History of the French Revolution* (1990). A highly detailed discussion of the course of events.

Drescher, Seymour, *Abolition: A History of Slavery and Anti-Slavery* (2009). A recent and authoritative overview of slavery and its opponents.

Elvin, Mark, *The Retreat of the Elephants: An Environmental History of China* (2004). A study of the different ways in which China's natural environment was shaped.

Fick, Carolyn E., *The Making of Haiti: The Saint Domingue Revolution from Below* (1990). Provides a detailed account of the factors that led to the great slave rebellion on the island of Haiti at the end of the eighteenth century.

Findley, Carter, *Bureaucratic Reform in the Ottoman Empire: The Sublime Porte, 1789–1922* (1980). A useful guide to Ottoman reform efforts in the nineteenth century.

Geggus, David (ed.), *The Impact of the Haitian Revolution in the Atlantic World* (2001). A lively effort to disentangle the effects of the Haitian Revolution from those of the French Revolution.

Hevia, James, *Cherishing Men from Afar: Qing Guest Ritual and the Macartney Embassy of 1793* (1995). Offers a definitive interpretation of the nature of Sino-British conflict in the Qing period.

Hobsbawm, Eric, *Nations and Nationalism since 1780* (1990). An important overview of the rise of the nation-state and nationalism around the world.

Howe, Daniel Walker, *What Hath God Wrought: The Transformation of America, 1815–1848* (2007). A Pulitzer Prize–winning interpretation of how new technologies and new ideas reshaped the economy, society, culture, and politics of the United States in the first half of the nineteenth century.

Hunt, Lynn, *Politics, Culture and Class in the French Revolution* (1984). Examines the influence of sociocultural shifts as causes and consequences of the French Revolution, emphasizing the symbols and practice of politics invented during the revolution.

Inikori, Joseph, *Africans and the Industrial Revolution in England* (2002). Demonstrates the important role that Africa and Africans played in facilitating the industrial revolution.

Isset, Christopher Mills, *State, Peasant, and Merchant in Qing Manchuria, 1644–1862* (2007). A study of the relationships between the sociopolitical structures and peasant lives in a key region during the Qing.

James, C. L. R., *The Black Jacobins: Toussaint L'Ouverture and the San Domingo Revolution* (1938). A classic chronicle of the only successful slave revolt in history and provides a critical portrait of their leader, Toussaint L'Ouverture.

Jones, E. L., *Growth Recurring* (1988). Discusses the controversy over why the industrial revolution took place in Europe, stressing the unique ecological setting that encouraged long-term investment.

Kinsbruner, Jay, *Independence in Spanish America* (1994). A fine study of the Latin American revolutions that argues that the struggle was as much a civil war as a fight for national independence.

Landers, Jane, *Atlantic Creoles in the Age of Revolutions* (2011). A collection of fascinating and unique portraits of Atlantic World creoles who managed to move freely and purposefully through French, Spanish, and English colonies, and through Indian territory, in the unstable century between 1750 and 1850.

Mokyr, Joel, *Enlightened Economy: An Economic History of Britain, 1700–1850* (2009). Perspectives on the evolution of the British economy in the era that produced the industrial revolution.

———, *The Lever of Riches* (1990). An important study of the causes of the industrial revolution that emphasizes the role of small technological and organizational breakthroughs.

Naquin, Susan, and Evelyn Rawski, *Chinese Society in the Eighteenth Century* (1987). A survey of mid-Qing society.

Neal, Larry, *The Rise of Financial Capitalism* (1990). An important study of the making of financial markets.

Nikitenko, Aleksandr, *Up from Serfdom: My Childhood and Youth in Russia, 1804–1824* (2001). One of the very few recorded life stories of a Russian serf.

Pomeranz, Kenneth, *The Great Divergence: Europe, China, and the Making of the Modern World Economy* (2000). Offers explanations of why Europe and not some other place in the world, like parts of China or India, forged ahead economically in the nineteenth century.

Rudé, George, *Europe in the Eighteenth Century* (1972). Emphasizes the rise of a new class, the bourgeoisie, against the old aristocracy, as a cause of the French Revolution.

Wakeman, Frederic, Jr., "The Canton Trade and the Opium War," in John K. Fairbank (ed.), *The Cambridge History of China*, Vol. 10 (1978), pp. 163–212. The standard account of the episode.

Wong, R. Bin, *China Transformed: Historical Change and the Limits of European Experience* (2000). Draws attention to the relative autonomy of merchant capitalists in relation to dynastic states in Europe compared to China.

Wood, Gordon S., *Empire of Liberty: A History of the Early Republic, 1789–1815* (2009). An excellent synthesis of the history of the United States in the tumultuous years between the ratification of the Constitution and the War of 1812.

Wortman, Richard, *Scenarios of Power: Myth and Ceremony in Russian Monarchy*, 2 vols. (1995–2000). Examines how dynastic Russia confronted the challenges of the revolutionary epoch.

CHAPTER 16

Anderson, David M., *Revealing Prophets: Prophets in Eastern African History* (1995). Good discussion of the prophets in eastern Africa.

Beecher, Jonathan, *The Utopian Vision of Charles Fourier* (1983). A fine biography of this important thinker.

Boyd, Jean, *The Caliph's Sister: Nana Asma'u, 1793–1865, Teacher, Poet, and Islamic Leader* (1988). A study of the most powerful female Muslim leader in the Fulani religious revolt.

Clancy-Smith, Julia, *Rebel and Saint: Muslim Notables, Populist Protest, Colonial Encounter (Algeria and Tunisia, 1800–1904)* (1994). Examines Islamic protest movements against western encroachments in North Africa.

Clogg, Richard, *A Concise History of Greece* (1997). A good introduction to the history of Greece in its European context.

Dalrymple, William, *The Last Mughal: The Fall of a Dynasty: Delhi, 1857* (2007). A deeply researched and riveting account of Delhi during the 1857 revolt.

Danziger, Raphael, *Abd al-Qadir: Resistance to the French and Internal Consolidation* (1977). Still the indispensable work on this important Algerian Muslim leader.

Dowd, Gregory E., *A Spirited Resistance: The North American Indian Struggle for Unity, 1745–1815* (1992). Emphasizes the importance of prophets like Tenskwatawa in the building of pan-Indian confederations in the era between the Seven Years' War and the War of 1812.

Guha, Ranajit, *Elementary Aspects of Peasant Insurgency in Colonial India* (1983). Not specifically on the Indian Rebellion of 1857 but includes it in its pioneering "subalternist" interpretation of South Asian history.

Hamilton, Carolyn (ed.), *The Mfecane Aftermath: Reconstructive Debates in Southern African History* (1995). Debates on Shaka's *Mfecane* movement and its impact on southern Africa.

Hiskett, Mervyn, *The Sword of Truth: The Life and Times of the Shehu Usman dan Fodio* (1994). An authoritative study of the Fulani revolt in northern Nigeria.

Johnson, Douglas H., *Nuer Prophets: A History of Prophecy from the Upper Nile in the Nineteenth and Twentieth Centuries* (1994). Deals with African prophetic and charismatic movements in eastern Africa.

Keddie, Nikki, *An Islamic Response to Imperialism: Political and Religious Writings of Sayyid Jamal ad-Din "al-Afghani" (1968)*. Definitive information on the Afghani's life and influence, coupled with a translation of one of his most important essays.

Michael, Franz, and Chung-li Chang, *The Taiping Rebellion: History and Documents*, 3 vols. (1966–1971). The basic source for the history of the Taiping.

Mukherjee, Rudrangshu, *Awadh in Revolt 1857–58* (1984). A careful case study of the Indian Rebellion.

Omer-Cooper, J. D., *The Zulu Aftermath: A Nineteenth-Century Revolution in Bantu Africa* (1966). A good place to start in studying Shaka's *Mfecane* movement, which greatly rearranged the political and ethnic makeup of southern Africa.

Ostler, Jeffrey, *The Plains Sioux and U.S. Colonialism from Lewis and Clark to Wounded Knee* (2004). Uses the lens of colonial theory to track relations between the Sioux and the United States, offering fresh insights about the Ghost Dance movement.

Peires, J. B. (ed.), *Before and After Shaka* (1981). Discusses elements in the debate over Shaka's *Mfecane* movement.

Pilbeam, Pamela, *French Socialists Before Marx: Workers, Women and the Social Question in France* (2001). Describes the development of a variety of socialist ideas in early nineteenth-century France.

Reed, Nelson, *The Caste War of Yucatan* (1964). A classic narrative of the Caste War of the Yucatan.

Restall, Matthew, *The Maya World* (1997). Describes in economic and social terms the origins of the Yucatan upheaval in southern Mexico.

Ruedy, John, *Modern Algeria: The Origins and Development of a Nation* (2005). Still the best overview of the modern political history of Algeria.

Rugeley, Terry, *Rebellion Now and Forever: Mayans, Hispanics, and Caste War Violence in Yucatán, 1800–1880* (2009). Explains the combination of economic and cultural pressures that drove the Mayans in the Yucatan to revolt in the Caste War.

Spence, Jonathan, *God's Chinese Son: The Taiping Heavenly Kingdom of Hong Xiuquan* (1996). A fascinating portrayal of the Taiping through the prism of its founder.

Wagner, Rudolf, *Reenacting the Heavenly Vision: The Role of Religion in the Taiping Rebellion* (1982). A brief but insightful analysis of the religious elements in the Taiping's doctrines.

White, Richard, *The Middle Ground: Indians, Empires, and Republics in the Great Lakes Region, 1650–1815* (1991). A pathbreaking exploration of intercultural relations in North America that offers a provocative interpretation of the visions of Tenskwatawa and the efforts of Tecumseh to resist the expansion of the United States.

CHAPTER 17

Berry, Sara, *Cocoa, Custom and Socio-Economic Change in Western Nigeria*, Clarendon Press, 1975), Innovative study based on interviews with local farmers that suggests that farmer enterprise and micro-economic theory better explain the spectacular growth in cocoa production than grand economic theory.

Cain, P. A., and A. G. Hopkins, *British Imperialism: Innovation and Expansion, 1688–1914* (1993). An excellent discussion of British imperialism, especially British expansion into Africa.

Cronon, William, *Nature's Metropolis: Chicago and the Great West* (1991). Makes connections among territorial expansion, industrialization, and urban development.

Davis, John, *Conflict and Control: Law and Order in Nineteenth-Century Italy* (1988). A superb study of the north-south and other rifts after Italian political unification.

Frankel, S. Herbert, *Capital Investment in Africa: Its Course and Effects*, Oxford University Press (1938). A careful study based on a mass of detailed figures and statistics on the general economic development of states in sub-Saharan Africa.

Friesen, Gerald, *The Canadian Prairies* (1984). The most comprehensive account of Canadian westward expansion.

Gluck, Carol, *Japan's Modern Myths: Ideology in the Late Meiji Period* (1985). A study of how states fashion useful historical traditions to consolidate and legitimize their rule.

Headrick, Daniel R., *The Tools of Empire: Technology and European Imperialism in the Nineteenth Century* (1981). A useful general study of the relationship between imperialism and technology.

Herbst, Jeffrey, *States and Power in Africa: Comparative Lessons in Authority and Control* (2000). An overview of the impact of colonial rule on contemporary African states.

Hill, Polly, *The Gold Coast Cocoa Farmer: A Preliminary Survey*, Oxford University Press (1965).

Hine, Robert V., and John Mack Faragher, *The American West: A New Interpretive History* (2000). Presents an excellent synthesis of the conquests by which the United States expanded from the Atlantic to the Pacific.

Hobsbawm, Eric J., *Nations and Nationalism since 1780: Programme, Myth, Reality* (1993). An insightful survey of the origins and development of nationalist thought throughout Europe.

Hochschild, Adam, *King Leopold's Ghost* (1998). A full-scale, eminently readable study of Europe's most egregiously destructive colonial regime in Africa.

Lee, Leo Ou-fan, and Andrew Nathan, "The Beginnings of Mass Culture: Journalism and Fiction in the Late Ch'ing and Beyond," in David Johnson, Andrew Nathan, and Evelyn Rawski (eds.), *Popular Culture in Late Imperial China* (1985), pp. 360–95. An important article on the emergence of a mass-media market in late-nineteenth- and early-twentieth-century China.

Lieven, Dominic, *Empire: The Russian Empire and Its Rivals* (2000). A comparison of the British, Ottoman, Habsburg, and Russian empires.

Mackenzie, John M., *Propaganda and Empire* (1984). Contains a series of useful chapters showing the importance of the empire to Britain.

Mamdani, Mahmood, *Citizen and State: Contemporary Africa and the Legacy of Late Colonialism* (1996). A survey of the impact of European colonial powers on African political systems.

McClintock, Anne, *Imperial Leather: Race, Gender and Sexuality in the Colonial Contest* (1995). A study of the imperial relationship between Victorian Britain and South Africa from the point of view of cultural studies.

McNeil, William, *Europe's Steppe Frontier: 1500–1800* (1964). An excellent study of the definitive victory of Russia's agricultural empire over grazing nomads and independent frontier people.

Mitchell, B. R., *International Historical Statistics: Africa, Asia, and Oceania, 1750–2005* Palgrave Macmillan. (2007). This comparative volume provides data from over two centuries for all principal areas of economic and social activity in both Eastern and Western Europe.

Montgomery, David, *The Fall of the House of Labor: The Workplace, the State, and American Labor Activism, 1865–1925* (1987). An excellent discussion of changes in work in the late nineteenth century.

Myers, Ramon, and Mark Peattie (eds.), *The Japanese Colonial Empire, 1895–1945* (1984). A collection of essays exploring different aspects of Japanese colonialism.

Needell, Jeffrey, *A Tropical Belle Epoque: Elite Culture and Society in Turn of the Century Rio de Janeiro* (1987). Shows the strength of the Brazilian elites at the turn of the century.

Pan, Lynn (ed.), *The Encyclopedia of Chinese Overseas* (1999). A comprehensive coverage of the history of the Chinese diaspora.

Porter, Bernard, *The Absent-Minded Imperialists: What the British Really Thought about Empire* (2004). A careful dissection of the ways in which empire changed the British—and did not.

Stengers, Jean, *Combien le Congo a-t-il coûté à la Belgique* (1957). A detailed financial accounting of how much Leopold put into the Congo and how much he took out, underscoring just how ruthlessly he exploited this possession.

Topik, Steven, *The Political Economy of the Brazilian State, 1889–1930* (1987). An excellent discussion of the Brazilian state, and especially of its elites.

Walker, Mack, *German Home Towns: Community, State, and the General State, 1648–1871* (1971, 1998). A brilliant, street-level analysis of the Holy Roman Empire (the First Reich) and the run-up to the German unification of 1871 (the Second Reich).

Wasserman, Mark, *Everyday Life and Politics in Nineteenth-Century Mexico* (2000). Wonderfully captures the way in which people coped with social and economic dislocation in late-nineteenth-century Mexico.

Weeks, Theodore R., *Nation and State in Late Imperial Russia: Nationalism and Russification on the Western Frontier, 1863–1914* (1996). A good discussion of the Russian Empire's responses to the concept of the nation-state.

White, Richard, *Railroaded: The Transcontinentals and the Making of Modern America* (2011). A seering exposé of the corruptions and a startling critique of the economic and environmental costs associated with the expansion of railroad lines across Canada, the United States, and Mexico.

Yung Wing, *My Life in China and America* (1909). The autobiography of the first Chinese graduate of an American university.

CHAPTER 18

Bayly, C. A., *The Birth of the Modern World, 1780–1914: Global Connections and Comparisons* (2004). A general study of the key political, economic, social, and cultural features of the modern era in world history.

Bergère, Marie-Claire, *Sun Yat-sen* (1998). Originally published in French in 1994, this is a judicious biography of the man generally known as the father of the modern Chinese nation.

Chatterjee, Partha, *The Nation and Its Fragments* (1993). One of the most important works on Indian nationalism by a leading scholar of "Subaltern Studies."

Conrad, Joseph, *Heart of Darkness* (1899). First published in a magazine in 1899, this novella contained a searing critique of King Leopold's oppressive and exploitative policies in the Congo and was part of a growing concern for the effects that European empires were having around the world, especially in Africa.

Esherick, Joseph, "How the Qing became China," in Joseph W. Esherick, Hasan Kayali, and Eric Van Young, eds., *Empire to Nation: Historical Perspectives on the Making of the Modern World* (2006). A study of the processes through which the Qing Empire became the nation-state of China.

______, *The Origins of the Boxer Uprising* (1987). The definitive account of the episode.

Everdell, William R., *The First Moderns: Profiles in the Origins of Twentieth-Century Thought* (1997). A rich account of the many faces of modernism, focusing particularly on science and art.

Finnane, Antonia, *Changing Clothes in China: Fashion, History, Nation* (2008). An exploration of changing Chinese identities from the perspective of clothing.

Gay, Peter, *The Cultivation of Hatred* (1994). A provocative discussion of the violent passions of the immediate pre–Great War era.

Gilmartin, Christina, Gail Hershatter, Lisa Rofel, and Tyrene White (eds.), *Engendering China: Women, Culture, and the State* (1994). Analyzes politics and society in modern China from the perspective of gender.

Hochschild, Adam, *King Leopold's Ghost: A Story of Greed, Terror, and Heroism in Colonial Africa* (1998). A well-written account of the violent colonial history of the Belgian Congo under King Leopold in the late nineteenth century.

Katz, Friedrich, *The Life and Times of Pancho Villa* (1998). An exploration of the Mexican Revolution that shows how Villa's armies destroyed the forces of Díaz and his followers.

Keddie, Nikki, *An Islamic Response to Imperialism: Political and Religious Writings of Sayyid Jamal ad-Din "al-Afghani" (1968).* Definitive information on the Afghani's life and influence, coupled with a translation of one of his most important essays.

Kern, Stephen, *The Culture of Time and Space 1880–1918* (1986). A useful study of the enormous changes in the experience of time and space in the age of late industrialism in Europe and America.

Kuhn, Philip, *Chinese among Others: Emigration in Modern Times* (2008). An overview of the history of Chinese migration.

McKeown, Adam, *Melancholy Order: Asian Migration and the Globalization of Borders* (2008). An examination of global migration patterns since the mid-nineteenth century and how regulations designed to restrict Asian migration to other parts of the world led to the modern regime of migration control.

Meade, Teresa, *"Civilizing" Rio: Reform and Resistance in a Brazilian City, 1889–1930* (1997). A wonderful study of cultural and class conflict in Brazil.

Pick, Daniel, *Faces of Degeneration: A European Disorder, c. 1848–c. 1918* (1993). A study of Europe's fear of social and biological decline, particularly focusing on France and Italy.

Pretorius, Fransjohn (ed.), *Scorched Earth* (2001). A study of the Anglo-Boer War in terms of its environmental impacts.

Sarkar, Sumit, *The Swadeshi Movement in Bengal* (1973). A comprehensive study of an early militant movement against British rule.

Schorske, Carl E. *Fin-de-Siècle Vienna: Politics and Culture* (1980). The classic treatment of the birth of modern ideas and political movements in turn-of-the-century Austria.

Trachtenberg, Alan, *The Incorporation of America: Culture and Society in the Gilded Age* (1982). A provocative synthesis of changes in the American economy, society, and culture in the last decades of the nineteenth century.

Wang, David Der-wei, *Fin-de-Siècle Splendor: Repressed Modernities of Late Qing Fiction, 1849–1911* (1997). A fine work that attempts to locate the "modern" within the writings of the late Qing period.

Warren, Louis, *Buffalo Bill's America: William Cody and the Wild West Show* (2005). A superb portrait of William F. Cody, the person; of Buffalo Bill, the persona Cody (and others) created; and of the popular culture his Wild West shows brought to audiences in Europe and North America.

Warwick, Peter, *Black People and the South African War, 1899–1902* (1983). An important study that reminds readers of the crucial involvement of black South Africans in this bloody conflict.

Womack, John, Jr., *Zapata and the Mexican Revolution* (1968). A major work on the Mexican Revolution that discusses peasant struggles in the state of Morelos in great detail.

CHAPTER 19

Bloxham, Donald, *The Great Game of Genocide: Imperialism, Nationalism, and the Destruction of the Ottoman Armenians* (2005). The definitive work on the Armenian genocide, set in a wide historical context.

Brown, Judith, *Gandhi: Prisoner of Hope* (1990). A biography of Gandhi as a political activist.

De Grazia, Victoria, and Ellen Furlough (eds.), *The Sex of Things: Gender and Consumption in Historical Perspective* (1996). Path-breaking essays on how gender affects consumption.

Dumenil, Lynn, *The Modern Temper: America in the 1920s* (1995). A general discussion of American culture in the decade after World War I.

Fainsod, Merle, *Smolensk under Soviet Rule* (1989). The most accessible and sophisticated interpretation of the Stalin revolution in the village.

Friedman, Edward, *Backward toward Revolution: The Chinese Revolutionary Party* (1974). An insightful look at the failure of liberalism in early republican China through the prism of the short-lived Chinese Revolutionary Party.

Gelvin, James, *Divided Loyalties: Nationalism and Mass Politics in Syria at the Close of Empire* (1998). Offers important insights into the development of nationalism in the Arab world.

Horne, John (ed.), *A Companion to World War I* (2010). A collection of articles written by leading scholars of World War I; the most comprehensive and up-to-date work on this war.

———, *State, Society, and Mobilization during the First World War* (1997). Essays on what it took to wage total war among all the belligerents.

Johnson, G. Wesley, *The Emergence of Black Politics in Senegal* (1971). A useful examination of the stirrings of African nationalism in Senegal.

Kennedy, David M., *Freedom from Fear: The American People in Depression and War, 1929–1945* (1999). A wonderful narrative of turbulent years.

Kershaw, Ian, *Hitler*, 2 vols. (1998–2000). A masterpiece combining biography and context.

Kimble, David, *A Political History of Ghana* (1963). An excellent discussion of the beginnings of African nationalism in Ghana.

Kotkin, Stephen, *Magnetic Mountain: Stalinism as a Civilization* (1995). Recaptures the atmosphere of a time when everything seemed possible, even creating a new world.

LeMahieu, D. L., *A Culture for Democracy: Mass Communication and the Cultivated Mind in Britain between the Wars* (1988). One of the great works on mass culture.

Lyttelton, Adrian, *The Seizure of Power: Fascism in Italy, 1919–1929* (1961). Still the classic account.

Marchand, Roland, *Advertising the American Dream: Making Way for Modernity, 1920–1945* (1985). An excellent discussion of the force of mass production and mass consumption.

Mazower, Mark, *Dark Continent: Europe's Twentieth Century* (1999). A wide-ranging overview of Europe's tempestuous twentieth century.

McKeown, Adam, *Melancholy Order: Asian Migration and the Globalization of Border* (2008). A major study of the vast movement of peoples around the globe between the middle of the nineteenth and twentieth centuries.

Morrow, John H., Jr., *The Great War: An Imperial History* (2004). Places World War I in the context of European imperialism.

Nottingham, John, and Carl Rosberg, *The Myth of "Mau Mau": Nationalism in Kenya* (1966). Dispels the myths in describing the roots of nationalism in Kenya.

Taylor, Jay, *The Generalissimo: Chiang Kai-shek and the Struggle for Modern China* (2009). The first serious biographical study of Chiang Kai-shek in English, although its reliance on Chiang's own diary as a source does raise some questions of historical interpretation.

Thorp, Rosemary (ed.), *Latin America in the 1930s* (1984). An important collection of essays on Latin America's response to the shakeup of the interwar years.

Tsin, Michael, *Nation, Governance, and Modernity in China: Canton, 1900–1927* (1999). An analysis of the vision and social dynamics behind the Guomindang-led revolution of the 1920s.

Vianna, Hermano, *The Mystery of Samba* (1999). Discusses the history of samba, emphasizing its African heritage as well as its persistent popular content.

Wakeman, Frederic, Jr., *Policing Shanghai, 1927–1937* (1995). An excellent account of Guomindang rule in China's largest city during the Nanjing decade.

Winter, J. M., *The Experience of World War* (1988). A comprehensive presentation of the many sides of the twentieth century.

Young, Louise, *Japan's Total Empire: Manchuria and the Culture of Wartime Imperialism* (1998). An innovative case study of Japanese imperialism and mass culture with broad implications.

CHAPTER 20

Aburish, Said K., *Nasser: The Last Arab* (2004). A recent and impressive look at Egypt's most powerful political leader in the 1950s and 1960s.

Anderson, Jon Lee, *Che Guevara: A Revolutionary Life* (1997). A sweeping study of the radicalization of Latin American nationalism.

Bayly, Christopher, and Tim Harper, *Forgotten Armies: Britain's Asian Empire and the War with Japan* (2004). A brilliant social and military history of the Second World War as fought and lived in South and Southeast Asia.

Chatterjee, Partha, *Nationalist Thought and the Colonial World: A Derivative Discourse?* (1986). An influential interpretation of the ideological and political nature of Indian nationalism and the struggle for a postcolonial nation-state.

Crampton, R. J., *Eastern Europe in the Twentieth Century and After* (2nd ed., 1997). Comprehensive overview covering all Soviet-bloc countries.

Dikötter, Frank, *Mao's Great Famine: The History of China's Most Devastating Catastrophe, 1958–1962* (2010). A recent detailed account of one of the greatest man-made disasters in twentieth-century history.

Dower, John W., *Embracing Defeat: Japan in the Wake of World War II* (1999). A prize-winning study of the transformation of one of the war's vanquished.

Elkins, Caroline, *Imperial Reckoning: The Untold Story of Britain's Gulag in Kenya* (2005). Pulitzer Prize–winning study of the brutal war to suppress the nationalist uprising in Kenya in the 1950s that ultimately led to independence for that country.

Feshbach Murray, and Alfred Friendly, Jr. (1992). *Ecocide in the USSR: Health and Nation under Siege*. A crucial study of ecological disasters in the Soviet Union.

Gao Yuan, *Born Red: A Chronicle of the Cultural Revolution* (1987). A gripping personal account of the Cultural Revolution by a former Red Guard.

Gordon, Andrew (ed.), *Postwar Japan as History* (1993). Essays covering a wide range of topics on postwar Japan.

Hargreaves, John D., *Decolonization in Africa* (1996). A good place to start when exploring the history of African decolonization.

Hasan, Mushirul (ed.), *India's Partition: Process, Strategy and Mobilization* (1993). A useful anthology of scholarly articles, short stories, and primary documents on the partition of India.

Iriye, Akira, *Power and Culture: The Japanese-American War, 1941–1945* (1981). A discussion that goes beyond the military confrontation in Asia.

Jackson, Kenneth T., *Crabgrass Frontier: The Suburbanization of the United States* (1985). An insightful and influential consideration of the movement of the American population from cities to suburbs.

Jalal, Ayesha, *The Sole Spokesman: Jinnah, the Muslim League and the Demand for Pakistan* (1985). A study of the high politics leading to the violent partition of British India.

Keep, John L. H., *Last of the Empires: A History of the Soviet Union 1945–1991* (1995). A detailed overview of the core of the "Second World."

Morris, Benny, *Righteous Victims: A History of the Zionist-Arab Conflict, 1881–1999* (2000). On the Arab-Israeli War of 1948.

Patterson, James T., *Grand Expectations: The United States, 1945–1974* (1996). Synthesizes the American experience in the postwar decades.

Patterson, Thomas, *Contesting Castro* (1994). The best study of the tension between the United States and Cuba. Culminating in the Cuban Revolution, it explores the deep American misunderstanding of Cuban national aspirations.

Roberts, Geoffrey, *Stalin's Wars: From World War to Cold War, 1939–1953* (2007). A reassessment of Stalin's wartime leadership that conveys the vast scale of what took place.

Ruedy, John, *Modern Algeria: The Origins and Development of a Nation* (1992). Gives the history of the Algerian nationalist movements and provides an overview of the Algerian war for independence.

Saich, Tony, and Hans van de Ven (eds.), *New Perspectives on the Chinese Communist Revolution* (1995). A collection of essays reexamining different aspects of the Chinese communist movement.

Schram, Stuart, *The Thought of Mao Tse-tung* (1989). Standard work on the subject.

Tignor, Robert L., *W. Arthur Lewis and the Birth of Development Economics* (2006). An intellectual biography of the Nobel Prize–winning, West Indian–born economist, who proposed formulas to promote the economic development of less developed societies and then sought to implement them in Africa and the West Indies.

Wiener, Douglas R. (2002). *A Little Corner of Freedom: Russian Nature Protection from Stalin to Gorbachev*. A groundbreaking book about Russian environmentalism.

Zubkova, Elena, *Russia after the War: Hopes, Illusions, and Disappointments, 1945–1957* (1998). Uses formerly secret archives to catalogue the devastation and difficult reconstruction of one of the war's victors.

CHAPTER 21

Collier, Paul, *The Bottom Billion: Why the Poorest Countries Fail and What Can Be Done About It* (2007). Shows that despite the world's advancing prosperity, more than a billion people have been left behind in abject poverty.

Davis, Deborah (ed.), *The Consumer Revolution in Urban China* (2000). A look at the different aspects of the recent, profound social transformation of urban China.

Davis, Mike, *City of Quartz: Excavating the Future in Los Angeles* (1990). Offers provocative reflections on the recent history, current condition, and possible future of Los Angeles.

Dutton, Michael, *Streetlife China* (1999). A fascinating portrayal of the survival tactics of those inhabiting the margins of society in modern China.

Eichengreen, Barry, *Globalizing Capital: A History of the International Monetary System* (1996). An insightful analysis of how international capital markets changed in the period from 1945 to 1980.

Gourevitch, Philip, *We Wish to Inform You That Tomorrow We Will Be Killed with Our Families: Stories from Rwanda* (1999). A volume that reveals the hatreds that culminated in the Rwanda genocide.

Guillermoprieto, Alma, *Looking for History: Dispatches from Latin America* (2001). A collection of articles by the most important journalist reporting on Latin American affairs.

Han Minzhu (ed.), *Cries for Democracy: Writings and Speeches from the 1989 Chinese Democracy Movement* (1990). A collection of documents from the events leading up to the incident in Tiananmen Square on June 4, 1989.

Herbst, Jeffrey, *States and Power in Africa: Comparative Lessons in Authority and Control* (2000). Explores the political dilemmas facing modern African polities.

Honig, Emily, and Gail Hershatter, *Personal Voices: Chinese Women in the 1980's* (1988). A record of Chinese women during a period of rapid social change.

Huang, Yasheng, *Capitalism with Chinese Characteristics: Entrepreneurship and the State* (2008). A sharp, unsentimental inside look at China's market economy and its future prospects.

Klitgaard, Robert, *Tropical Gangsters* (1990). On the intimate connections between corrupt native elites and international aid agencies.

Kotkin, Stephen, *Armageddon Averted: The Soviet Collapse, 1970–2000* (2001). Places the surprise fall of the Soviet Union in the context of the great shifts in the post–World War II order.

Mamdani, Mahmood, *When Victims Become Killers: Colonialism, Nativism, and the Genocide in Rwanda* (2001). Discusses the genocide in Rwanda in light of the legacy of colonialism.

Mehta, Suketu, *Maximum City: Bombay Lost and Found* (2005). Examines one of the great, and contradictory, cities in the era of globalization.

Mottahedeh, Roy, *The Mantle of the Prophet: Religion and Politics in Iran* (2nd ed., 2008). Perhaps the best book on the 1979 Iranian Revolution and its aftermath.

Nathan, Andrew, and Perry Link, *The Tiananmen Papers* (2002). An inside look at the divisions within the Chinese elite in connection with the 1989 crackdown.

Portes, Alejandro, and Rubén G. Rumbaut, *Immigrant America* (2nd ed., 1996). A good comparative study of how immigration has transformed the United States.

Prakash, Gyan, *Mumbai Fables* (2010). A spirited account of the rise of India's most modern city, a center of intellectual, commercial, and political vitality.

Prunier, Gerald, *Africa's World War: Congo, the Rwandan Genocide, and the Making of a Continental Catastrophe* (2009). A chilling discussion of the spillover effects of the Rwandan genocide on central, eastern, and southern Africa.

Reinhart, Carmen, and Kenneth Rogoff, *This Time Is Different: Eight Centuries of Financial Folly* (2009). Explains the latest financial crash using historical perspective.

Van Der Wee, Hermann, *Prosperity and Upheaval: The World Economy, 1945–1980* (1986). Describes very well the transformation and problems of the world economy, particularly from the 1960s onward.

Westad, Odd Arne, *The Global Cold War: Third World Interventions and the Making of our Times* (2007). A genuinely global perspective on the cold war and its consequences.

Winn, Peter, *Americas: The Changing Face of Latin America and the Caribbean* (1992). A useful portrayal of Latin America since the 1970s.

GLOSSARY

Abd al-Rahman III Islamic ruler in Spain who held a countercaliphate and reigned from 912 to 961 CE.

aborigines Original, native inhabitants of a region, as opposed to invaders, colonizers, or later peoples of mixed ancestry.

absolute monarchy Form of government where one body, usually the monarch, controls the right to tax, judge, make war, and coin money. The term *enlightened absolutists* was often used to refer to state monarchies in seventeenth- and eighteenth-century Europe.

acid rain Precipitation containing large amounts of sulfur, mainly from coal-fired plants.

adaptation Ability to alter behavior and to innovate, finding new ways of doing things.

African National Congress (ANC) Multiracial organization founded in 1912 in an effort to end racial discrimination in South Africa.

Afrikaners Descendants of the original Dutch settlers of South Africa; formerly referred to as Boers.

Agones Athletic contests in ancient Greece.

Ahmosis Egyptian ruler in the southern part of the country who ruled from 1550 to 1525 BCE; Ahmosis used Hyksos weaponry—horse chariots in particular—to defeat the Hyksos themselves.

Ahura Mazda Supreme God of the Persians believed to have created the world and all that is good and to have appointed earthly kings.

AIDS (Acquired Immuno Deficiency Syndrome) Virus that compromises the ability of the infected person's immune system to ward off disease. First detected in 1981, AIDS was initially stigmatized as a "gay cancer," but as it spread to heterosexuals, public awareness about it increased. In its first two decades, AIDS killed 12 million people.

Akbarnamah Mughal intellectual Abul-fazl's *Book of Akbar*, which attempted to reconcile the traditional Sufi interest in the inner life within the worldly context of a great empire.

Alaric II Visigothic king who issued a simplified code of innovative imperial law.

Alexander the Great (356–323 BCE) Leader who used novel tactics and new kinds of armed forces to conquer the Persian Empire, which extended from Egypt and the Mediterranean Sea to the interior of what is now Afghanistan and as far as the Indus River valley. Alexander's conquests broke down barriers between the Mediterranean world and Southwest Asia and transferred massive amounts of wealth and power to the Mediterranean, transforming it into a more unified world of economic and cultural exchange.

Alexandria Port city in Egypt named after Alexander the Great. Alexandria was a model city in the Hellenistic world. It was built up by a multiethnic population from around the Mediterranean world.

Al-Khwarizmi Scientist and mathematician who lived from 780 to 850 CE and is known for having modified Indian digits into Arabic numerals.

Allied powers Name given to the alliance between Britain, France, Russia, and Italy, who fought against Germany and Austria-Hungary (the Central powers) in World War I. In World War II the name was used for the alliance between Britain, France, and America, who fought against the Axis powers (Germany, Italy, and Japan).

allomothering System by which mothers relied on other women, including their own mothers, daughters, sisters, and friends, to help in the nurturing and protecting of children.

alluvium Area of land created by river deposits.

American Railway Union Workers' union that initiated the Pullman Strike of 1894, which led to violence and ended in the leaders' arrest.

Amnesty International Non-governmental organization formed to defend "prisoners of conscience"—those detained for their beliefs, race, sex, ethnic origin, language, or religion.

Amorites Name that Mesopotamian urbanites called the transhumant herders from the Arabian desert. Around 2300 BCE, the Amorites, along with the Elamites, were at the center of newly formed dynasties in southern Mesopotamia.

Amun Once insignificant Egyptian god elevated to higher status by Amenemhet (1991–1962 BCE). *Amun* means "hidden" in Ancient Egyptian; the name was meant to convey the god's omnipresence.

Analects Texts that included the teachings and cultural ideals of Confucius.

anarchism Belief that society should be a free association of its members, not subject to government, laws, or police.

Anatolia Now mainly the area known as modern Turkey; in the sixth millennium BCE, people from Anatolia, Greece, and the Levant took to boats and populated the Aegean. Their small villages endured almost unchanged for two millennia.

ancestral worship Religious practice in which the living honor their dead ancestors through performative rituals, under the belief that the dead intervene with their powers on behalf of the living.

Angkor Wat Magnificent Khmer Vaishnavite temple that crowned the royal palace in Angkor. It had statues representing the Hindu pantheon of gods.

Anglo-Boer War (1899–1902) Anticolonial struggle in South Africa between the British and the Afrikaners over the gold-rich Transvaal. In response to the Afrikaners' guerrilla tactics and in order to contain the local population, the British instituted the first concentration camps. Ultimately, Britain won the conflict.

animal domestication Gradual process that occurred simultaneously with or just before the domestication of plants, depending on the region.

annals Historical records. Notable annals are the cuneiform inscriptions that record successful Assyrian military campaigns.

Anti-Federalists Critics of the U.S. Constitution who sought to defend the people against the power of the federal government and insisted on a bill of rights to protect individual liberties from government intrusion.

apartheid Racial segregation policy of the Afrikaner-dominated South African government. Legislated in 1948 by the Afrikaner National Party, it had existed in South Africa for many years.

Arab-Israeli War of 1948–1949 Conflict between Israeli and Arab armies that arose in the wake of a U.N. vote to partition Palestine into Arab and Jewish territories. The war shattered the legitimacy of Arab ruling elites.

Aramaic Dialect of a Semitic language spoken in Southwest Asia; it became the lingua franca of the Persian Empire.

Aristotle (384–322 BCE) Philosopher who studied under Plato but came to different conclusions about nature and politics. Aristotle believed in collecting observations about nature and discerning patterns to ascertain how things worked.

Aryans Nomadic charioteers who spoke Indo-European languages and entered South Asia in 1500 BCE. The early Aryan settlers were herders.

Asante state State located in present-day Ghana, founded by the Asantes at the end of the seventeenth century. It grew in power in the next century because of its access to gold and its involvement in the slave trade.

ascetic One who rejects material possessions and physical pleasures.

Asiatic Society Cultural organization founded by British Orientalists who supported native culture but still believed in colonial rule.

A´soka Emperor of the Mauryan dynasty from 268 to 231 BCE; he was a great conqueror and unifier of India. He is said to have embraced Buddhism toward the end of his life.

Assur One of two cities on the upper reaches of the Tigris River that were the heart of Assyria proper (the other was Nineveh).

A´svaghosa First known Sanskrit writer. He may have lived from 80 to 150 CE and may have composed a biography of the Buddha.

Ataturk, Mustafa Kemal (1881–1938) Ottoman army officer and military hero who helped forge the modern Turkish nation-state. He and his followers deposed the sultan, declared Turkey a republic, and constructed a European-like secular state, eliminating Islam's hold over civil and political affairs.

Atlantic system New system of trade and expansion that linked Europe, Africa, and the Americas. It emerged in the wake of European voyages across the Atlantic Ocean.

Atma Vedic term signifying the eternal self, represented by the trinity of deities.

Atman In the Upanishads, an eternal being who exists everywhere. The atman never perishes but is reborn or transmigrates into another life.

Attila Sole ruler of all Hunnish tribes from 433 to 453 CE. Harsh and much feared, he formed the first empire to oppose Rome in northern Europe.

Augustus Title meaning "Revered One," assumed in 27 BCE by the Roman ruler Octavian (63–14 BCE). This was one of many titles he assumed; others included *imperator*, *princeps*, and *Caesar*.

australopithecines Hominid species that appeared 3 million years ago and, unlike other animals, walked on two legs. Their brain capacity was a little less than one-third of a modern human's or about the size of the brain capacity of today's African apes. Although not humans, they carried the genetic and biological material out of which modern humans would later emerge.

Austro-Hungarian Empire Dual monarchy established by the Habsburg family in 1867; it collapsed at the end of World War I.

authoritarianism Centralized and dictatorial form of government, proclaimed by its adherents to be superior to parliamentary democracy and especially effective at mobilizing the masses. This idea was widely accepted in parts of the world during the 1930s.

Avesta Compilation of holy works transmitted orally by priests for millennia and eventually recorded in the sixth century BCE.

Axis powers The three aggressor states in World War II: Germany, Japan, and Italy.

Aztec Empire Mesoamerican empire that originated with a league of three Mexica cities in 1430 and gradually expanded through the Central Valley of Mexico, uniting numerous small, independent states under a single monarch who ruled with the help of counselors, military leaders, and priests. By the late fifteenth century, the Aztec realm may have embraced 25 million people. In 1521, they were defeated by the conquistador Hernán Cortés.

baby boom Post–World War II upswing in U.S. birth rates; it reversed a century of decline.

bactrian camel Two-humped animal domesticated in central Asia around 2500 BCE. The bactrian camel was heartier than the one-humped dromedary and became the animal of choice for the harsh and varied climates typical of Silk Road trade.

Baghdad Capital of the Islamic Empire under the Abbasid dynasty, founded in 762 CE (in modern-day Iraq). In the medieval period, it was a center of administration, scholarship, and cultural growth for what came to be known as the Golden Age of Islamic science.

Baghdad Pact (1955) Middle Eastern military alliance between countries friendly with America who were also willing to align themselves with the western countries against the Soviet Union.

Balam Na Stone temple and place of pilgrimage for the Mayan people of Mexico's Yucatan peninsula.

Balfour Declaration Letter (November 2, 1917) by Lord Arthur J. Balfour, British foreign secretary, that promised a homeland for the Jews in Palestine.

Bamboo Annals Shang stories and foundation myths that were written on bamboo strips and later collected.

Bantu Language first spoken by people who lived in the southeastern area of modern Nigeria around 1000 CE.

Bantu migrations Waves of rapid population movement from West Africa into eastern and southern Africa during the first millennium ce that brought advanced agricultural practices to these regions and absorbed most of the preexisting hunting-and-gathering populations.

barbarian Derogatory term used to describe pastoral nomads, painting them as enemies of civilization; the term *barbarian* used to have a more neutral meaning than it does today.

barbarian invasions Violent migration of people in the late fourth and fifth centuries into Roman territory. These migrants had long been used as non-Roman soldiers.

basilicas Early church buildings, based on old royal audience halls.

Battle of Adwa (1896) Battle in which the Ethiopians defeated Italian colonial forces; it inspired many of Africa's later national leaders.

Battle of Wounded Knee (1890) Bloody massacre of Sioux Ghost Dancers by U.S. armed forces.

Bay of Pigs (1961) Unsuccessful invasion of Cuba by Cuban exiles supported by the U.S. government. The invaders intended to incite an insurrection in Cuba and overthrow the communist regime of Fidel Castro.

Bedouins Nomadic pastoralists in the deserts of the Middle East.

Beer Hall Putsch (1923) Nazi intrusion into a meeting of Bavarian leaders in a Munich beer hall; the Nazis were attempting to force support for their cause; Adolf Hitler was imprisoned for a year after the incident.

Beghards (1500s) Eccentric European group whose members claimed to be in a state of grace that allowed them to do as they pleased—from adultery, free love, and nudity to murder; also called Brethren of Free Speech.

bell beaker Ancient drinking vessel, an artifact from Europe, so named because its shape resembles an inverted bell.

Berenice of Egypt Egyptian "queen" who helped rule over the Kingdom of the Nile from 320 to 280 BCE.

Beringia Prehistoric thousand-mile-long land bridge that linked Siberia and North America (which had not been populated by hominids). About 18,000 years ago, *Homo sapiens* edged into this landmass.

Berlin Airlift (1948) Supply of vital necessities to West Berlin by air transport primarily under U.S. auspices. It was initiated in response to a land and water blockade of the city instituted by the Soviet Union in the hope that the Allies would be forced to abandon West Berlin.

Berlin Wall Wall built by the communists in Berlin in 1961 to prevent citizens of East Germany from fleeing to West Germany; torn down in 1989.

bhakti Religious practice that grew out of Hinduism and emphasizes personal devotion to gods.

Bhakti Hinduism Popular form of Hinduism that emerged in the seventh century. The religion stresses devotion (*bhakti*) to God and uses vernacular languages (not Sanskrit) spoken by the common people.

big men Leaders of the extended household communities that formed village settlements in African rain forests.

big whites French plantation owners in Saint Domingue (present-day Haiti) who created one of the wealthiest slave societies.

Bilad al-Sudan Arabic for "the land of the blacks"; it consisted of the land lying south of the Sahara.

bilharzia Debilitating water-borne illness. It was widespread in Egypt, where it infected peasants who worked in the irrigation canals.

Bill of Rights First ten amendments to the U.S. Constitution; ratified in 1791.

bipedalism Walking on two legs, thereby freeing hands and arms to carry objects such as weapons and tools; one of several traits that distinguished hominids.

Black Death Great epidemic of the bubonic plague that ravaged Europe, East Asia, and North Africa in the fourteenth century, killing large numbers, including perhaps as many as one-third of the European population.

Black Jacobins Nickname for the rebels in Saint Domingue, including Toussaint L'Ouverture, a former slave who led the slaves of this French colony in the world's largest and most successful slave insurrection.

Black Panthers Radical African American group in the 1960s and 1970s; they advocated black separatism and pan-Africanism.

black shirts Fascist troops of Mussolini's regime; the squads received money from Italian landowners to attack socialist leaders.

Black Tuesday (October 29, 1929) Historic day when the U.S. stock market crashed, plunging the United States and international trading systems into crisis and leading the world into the "Great Depression."

Blitzkrieg "Lightning war"; type of warfare in which the Germans, during World War II, used coordinated aerial bombing campaigns along with tanks and infantrymen in motorized vehicles.

Bodhisattvas In Mahayan Buddhism, enlightened demigods who were ready to reach *nirvana* but delayed so that they might help others attain it.

Bolívar, Simón (1783–1830) Venezuelan leader who urged his followers to become "American," to overcome their local identities. He wanted the liberated countries to form a Latin American confederation, urging Peru and Bolivia to join Venezuela, Ecuador, and Colombia in the "Gran Colombia."

Bolsheviks Former members of the Russian Social Democratic Party who advocated the destruction of capitalist political and economic institutions and started the Russian Revolution. In 1918 the Bolsheviks changed their name to the Russian Communist Party.

Bonaparte, Napoleon (1769–1821) General who rose to power in a post-Revolutionary coup d'état, eventually proclaiming himself emperor of France. He placed security and order ahead of social reform and created a civil legal code. Napoleon expanded his empire through military action, but after his disastrous Russian campaign, the united European powers defeated Napoleon and forced him into exile. He escaped and reassumed command of his army but was later defeated at the Battle of Waterloo.

Book of the Dead Ancient Egyptian funerary text that contains drawings and paintings as well as spells describing how to prepare the jewelry and amulets that were buried with a person in preparation for the afterlife.

bourgeoisie The middle class. In Europe, they sought to be recognized not by birth or title, but by capital and property.

Boxer Protocol Written agreement between the victors of the Boxer Uprising and the Qing Empire in 1901 that placed western troops in Beijing and required the regime to pay exorbitant damages for foreign life and property.

Boxer Uprising (1899–1900) Chinese peasant movement that opposed foreign influence, especially that of Christian missionaries; it was put down after the Boxers were defeated by an army composed mostly of Japanese, Russians, British, French, and Americans.

Brahma One of three major deities that form a trinity in Vedic religion. Brahma signifies birth. *See also* Vishnu *and* Siva.

Brahmans Vedic priests who performed rituals and communicated with the gods. Brahmans provided guidance on how to live in balance with the forces of nature as represented by the various deities. The codification of Vedic principles into codes of law took place at the hands of the Brahmans. They memorized Vedic works and compiled commentaries on them. They also developed their own set of rules and rituals, which developed into a full-scale theology. Originally memorized and passed on orally, these may have been written down sometime after the beginning of the Common Era. Brahmanism was reborn as Hinduism sometime during the first half of the first millennium CE.

British Commonwealth of Nations Union formed in 1926 that conferred "dominion status" on Britain's white settler colonies in Canada, Australia, and New Zealand.

British East India Company *See* East India Company.

bronze Alloy of copper and tin brought into Europe from Anatolia; used to make hard-edged weapons.

brown shirts Troops of German men who advanced the Nazi cause by holding street marches, mass rallies, and confrontations and by beating Jews and anyone who opposed the Nazis.

bubonic plague Acute infectious disease caused by a bacterium that is transmitted to humans by fleas from infected rats. It ravaged Europe and parts of Asia in the fourteenth century. Sometimes referred to as the "Black Death."

Buddha (Siddhartha Gautama; 563–483 BCE) Indian ascetic who founded Buddhism.

Buddhism Major South Asian religion that aims to end human suffering through the renunciation of desire. Buddhists believe that removing the illusion of a separate identity would lead to a state of contentment (nirvana). These beliefs challenged the traditional Brahmanic teachings of the time and provided the peoples of South Asia with an alternative to established traditions.

bullion Uncoined gold or silver.

Cahokia Commercial center for regional and long-distance trade in North America. Its hinterlands produced staples for urban consumers. In return, its crafts were exported inland by porters and to North American markets in canoes. *See also* Mound people.

Calaveras Allegorical skeleton drawings by the Mexican printmaker and artist José Guadalupe Posada. The works drew on popular themes of betrayal, death, and festivity.

caliphate Institution that arose as the successor to Muhammad's leadership and became both the political and religious head of the Islamic community. Although the caliphs exercised political authority over the Muslim community and were the head of the religious community, the *ummah,* they did not inherit Muhammad's prophetic powers and were not authorities in religious doctrine.

Candomblé Yoruba-based religion in northern Brazil; it interwove African practices and beliefs with Christianity.

Canton system System officially established by imperial decree in 1759 that required European traders to have Chinese guild merchants act as guarantors for their good behavior and payment of fees.

caravan cities Set of networks at long-distance trade locations where groups of merchants could assemble during their journeys. Several of these developed into full-fledged cities, especially in the deserts of Arabia.

caravans Companies of men who transported and traded goods along overland routes in North Africa and central Asia; large caravans consisted of 600–1,000 camels and as many as 400 men.

caravansarais Inns along major trade routes that accommodated large numbers of traders, their animals, and their wares.

caravel Sailing vessel suited for nosing in and out of estuaries and navigating in waters with unpredictable currents and winds.

carrack Ship used on open bodies of water, such as the Mediterranean.

Carthage City in what is modern-day Tunisia; emblematic of the trading aspirations and activities of merchants in the Mediterranean. Pottery and other archaeological remains demonstrate that trading contacts with Carthage were as far-flung as Italy, Greece, France, Iberia, and West Africa.

cartography Mapmaking.

caste system Hierarchical system of organizing people and distributing labor.

Caste War of Yucatan (1847–1901) Conflict between Mayan Indians and the Mexican state over Indian autonomy and legal equality, which resulted in the Mexican takeover of the Yucatan peninsula.

Castro, Fidel (1926–) Cuban communist leader whose forces overthrew Batista's corrupt regime in early January 1959. Castro became increasingly radical as he consolidated power, announcing a massive redistribution of land and the nationalization of foreign oil refineries; he declared himself a socialist and aligned himself with the Soviet Union in the wake of the 1961 CIA-backed Bay of Pigs invasion.

Çatal Hüyük Site in Anatolia discovered in 1958. It was a dense honeycomb of settlements filled with rooms whose walls were covered with paintings of wild bulls, hunters, and pregnant women. Çatal Hüyük symbolizes an early transition into urban dwelling and dates to the eighth millennium BCE.

Cathedra Bishop's seat, or throne, in a church.

Catholic Church Unifying institution for Christians in western Europe after the collapse of the Roman Empire. Rome became the spiritual capital of western Europe and the bishops of Rome emerged as popes, the supreme head of the church, who possessed great moral authority.

Cato the Elder (234–149 BCE) Roman statesman, often seen as emblematic of the transition from a Greek to a Roman world. Cato the Elder wrote a manual for the new economy of slave plantation agriculture, invested in shipping and trading, learned Greek rhetoric, and added the genre of history to Latin literature.

Caudillos South American local military chieftains.

cave drawings Images on cave walls. The subjects are most often large game, although a few are images of humans. Other elements are impressions made by hands dipped in paint and pressed on a wall or abstract symbols and shapes.

Celali revolts (1595–1610) Peasant and artisan uprisings against the Ottoman state.

Central powers Defined in World War I as Germany and Austria-Hungary.

Chan Chan City founded between 850 and 900 CE by the Moche people in what is now modern-day Peru. It had a core population of 30,000 inhabitants.

Chan Santa Cruz Separate Mayan community formed as part of a crusade for spiritual salvation and the complete cultural separation of the Mayan Indians; means "little holy cross."

Chandra Gupta II King who reigned in South Asia from 320 to 335 CE. He shared his name with Chandragupta, the founder of the Mauryan Empire.

Chandravamsha One of two main lineages (the lunar one) of Vedic society, each with its own creation myth, ancestors, language, and rituals. Each lineage included many clans. *See* Suryavamsha.

chapatis Flat, unleavened Indian bread.

chariots Horse-driven carriages brought by the pastoral nomadic warriors from the steppes that became the favored mode of transportation for an urban aristocratic warrior class and for other men of power in agriculture-based societies. Control of chariot forces was the foundation of the new balance of power across Afro-Eurasia during the second millennium BCE.

charismatic Person who uses personal strengths or virtues, often laced with a divine aura, to command followers.

Charlemagne Emperor of the West and heir to Rome from 764 to 814 CE.

chartered companies Firms that were awarded monopoly trading rights over vast areas by European monarchs (e.g., Virginia Company, Dutch East India Company).

Chartism (1834–1848) Mass democratic movement to pass the Peoples' Charter in Britain, granting male suffrage, secret ballot, equal electoral districts, and annual parliaments, and absolving the requirement of property ownership for members of the parliament.

chattel slavery Form of slavery that sold people as property, the rise of which coincided with the expansion of city-states. Chattel slavery was eschewed by the Spartans, who also rejected the innovation of coin money.

Chavín A people who lived in what is now northern Peru from 1400 to 200 BCE. They were united more by culture and faith than by a unified political system.

Chernobyl (1986) Site in the Soviet Union (in Ukraine) of the meltdown of a nuclear reactor.

Chiang Kai-shek (1887–1975) Leader of the Guomindang following Sun Yat-sen's death who mobilized the Chinese masses through the New Life movement. In 1949 he lost the Chinese Revolution to the communists and moved his regime to Taiwan.

Chimu Empire South America's first empire; it developed during the first century of the second millennium in the Moche Valley on the Pacific coast.

chinampas Floating gardens used by Aztecs in the 1300s and 1400s to grow crops.

China's Sorrow Name for the Yellow River, which, when it changed course or flooded, could cause mass death and waves of migration.

chinoiserie Chinese silks, teas, tableware, jewelry, and paper; popular among Europeans in the seventeenth and eighteenth centuries.

Christendom Entire portion of the world in which Christianity prevailed.

Christianity Religion that originated at the height of the Roman Empire and in a direct confrontation with Roman imperial authority: the trial of Yeshua ben Yosef (Joshua son of Joseph; we know him today by the Greek form of his name, Jesus). Jesus was condemned for sedition and crucified. His followers believed that he was resurrected and that his teachings were not that of a man, but a god who had walked among human beings. At first, the Roman Empire refused to recognize Christianity and persecuted its followers, but in the fourth century ce Christianity was officially recognized as the Roman state religion.

Church of England Established form of Christianity in England dating from the sixteenth century.

city Highly populated concentration of economic, religious, and political power. The first cities appeared in river basins, which could produce a surplus of agriculture. The abundance of food freed most city inhabitants from the need to produce their own food, which allowed them to work in specialized professions.

city-state Political organization based on the authority of a single, large city that controls outlying territories.

Civil Rights Act (1964) U.S. legislation that banned segregation in public facilities, outlawed racial discrimination in employment, and marked an important step in correcting legal inequality.

civil rights movement Powerful movement for equal rights and the end of racial segregation in the United States that began in the 1950s with court victories against school segregation and nonviolent boycotts.

civil service examinations The world's first written civil service examination system, instituted by the Tang dynasty to recruit officials and bureaucrats. Open to most males, the exams tested a candidate's literary skills and knowledge of the Confucian classics. They helped to unite the Chinese state by making knowledge of a specific language and Confucian classics the only route to power.

Civil War, American (1861–1865) Conflict between the northern and southern states of America; this struggle led to the abolition of slavery in the United States.

clan A social group comprising many households, claiming descent from a common ancestor.

clandestine presses Small printing operations that published banned texts in the early modern era, especially in Switzerland and the Netherlands.

Clovis people Early humans in America who used basic chipped blades and pointed spears in pursuing prey. They extended the hunting traditions they had learned in Afro-Eurasia, such as establishing campsites and moving with their herds. They were known as "Clovis people" because the arrowhead point that they used was first found by archaeologists at a site near Clovis, New Mexico.

codex Early form of book, with separate pages bound together; it replaced the scroll as the main medium for written texts. The codex emerged around 300 CE.

cognitive skills Skills such as thought, memory, problem-solving, and—ultimately—language. Hominids were able to use these skills and their hands to create new adaptations, like tools, which helped them obtain food and avoid predators.

Cohong Chinese merchant guild that traded with Europeans under the Qing dynasty.

coins Form of money that replaced goods, which previously had been bartered for services and other products. Originally used mainly to hire mercenary soldiers, coins became the commonplace method of payment linking buyers and producers throughout the Mediterranean.

cold war (1945–1990) Ideological conflict in which the Soviet Union and eastern Europe opposed the United States and western Europe.

colonies Regions under the political control of another country.

Colons French settler population in Algeria.

Colosseum Huge amphitheater completed by Titus and dedicated in 80 CE. Originally begun by Flavian, the structure is named after a colossal statue of Nero that formerly stood beside it.

Columbian exchange Movements between Afro-Eurasia and the Americas of previously unknown plants, animals, people, diseases, and products that followed in the wake of Columbus's voyages.

commanderies Provinces. Shi Huangdi (First August Emperor) divided China into commanderies (*jun*) to enable the Qin dynasty to rule the massive state effectively. The thirty-six commanderies were then subdivided into counties (*xian*).

Communist Manifesto Pamphlet published by Karl Marx and Friedrich Engels in 1848 at a time when political revolutions were sweeping Europe. It called on the workers of all nations to unite in overthrowing capitalism.

compass Navigation instrument invented by the Chinese and used to determine directions with a magnetized needle, which always points to the North cardinal direction on the compass rose.

Compromise of 1867 Agreement between the Habsburgs and the peoples living in Hungarian parts of the empire that the Habsburg state would be officially known as the Austro-Hungarian Empire.

concession areas Territories, usually ports, where Chinese emperors allowed European merchants to trade and European people to settle.

Confucian ideals The ideals of honoring tradition, emphasizing the responsibility of the emperor, and respect for the lessons of history, promoted by Confucius, which the Han dynasty made the official doctrine of the empire by 50 BCE.

Confucianism Ethics, beliefs, and practices stipulated by the Chinese philosopher Kong Qiu, or Confucius, which served as a guide for Chinese society up to modern times.

Confucius (551–479 BCE) Influential teacher, thinker, and leader in China who developed a set of principles for ethical living. He believed that coercive laws and punishment would not be needed to maintain order in society if men following his ethics ruled. He taught his philosophy to anyone who was intelligent and willing to work, which allowed men to gain entry into the ruling through education.

cong tube Ritual object crafted by the Liangzhu. A cong tube was made of jade and was used in divination practices.

Congo Independent State Large colonial state in Africa created by Leopold II, king of Belgium, during the 1880s, and ruled by him alone. After rumors of mass slaughter and enslavement, the Belgian parliament took the land and formed a Belgian colony.

Congress of Vienna (1814–1815) International conference to reorganize Europe after the downfall of Napoleon. European monarchies agreed to respect each other's borders and to cooperate in guarding against future revolutions and war.

conquistadors Spanish military leaders who led the conquest of the New World in the sixteenth century.

Constantine Roman emperor who converted to Christianity in 312 CE. In 313, he issued a proclamation that gave Christians new freedoms in the empire. He also founded Constantinople (at first called "New Rome").

Constantinople Capital city, formerly known as Byzantium, which was founded as the New Rome by Constantine the Great.

Constitutional Convention (1787) Meeting to formulate the Constitution of the United States of America.

Contra rebels Opponents of the Sandinistas in Nicaragua; they were armed and financed by the United States and other anticommunist countries (1980).

Conversion of Constantine A significant political and religious turning point in the Roman Empire. Before the decisive battle for Rome in 312 CE, Constantine supposedly had a dream in which he was told to place a sign with the opening letters of Christ's name on his soldiers' shields. Constantine won the ensuing battle; he soon issued a proclamation giving privileges to Christian bishops. The edict spread Christianity through the institutions and across the byways of the Roman Empire.

Conversos Jewish and Muslim converts to Christianity in the Iberian Peninsula and the New World.

Coptic Form of Christianity practiced in Egypt. It was doctrinally different from Christianity elsewhere, and Coptic Christians had their own views of Christology, or the nature of Christ.

Corn Laws Laws that imposed tariffs on grain imported to Great Britain, intended to protect British farming interests. The Corn Laws were abolished in 1846 as part of a British movement in favor of free trade.

cosmology Branch of metaphysics devoted to understanding the order of the universe.

Council of Nicaea Church council convened in 325 CE by Constantine and presided over by him as well. At this council, a Christian creed was articulated and made into a formula that expressed the philosophical and technical elements of Christian belief.

Counter-Reformation Movement to counter the spread of the Reformation; initiated by the Catholic Church at the Council of Trent in 1545. The Catholic Church enacted reforms to attack clerical corruption and it placed a greater emphasis on individual spirituality. During this time, the Jesuits were founded to help revive the Catholic Church.

coup d'état Overthrow of established state by a group of conspirators, usually from the military.

creed Formal statement of faith or expression of a belief system. A Christian creed or "credo" was formulated by the Council of Nicaea in 325 CE.

creoles Persons of full-blooded European descent who were born in the Spanish American colonies.

Crimean War (1853–1856) War waged by Russia against Great Britain and France. Spurred by Russia's encroachment on Ottoman territories, the conflict revealed Russia's military weakness when Russian forces fell to British and French troops.

crossbow Innovative weapon used at the end of the Warring States period that allowed archers to shoot their enemies with accuracy, even from a distance.

Crusades Wave of attacks launched in the late eleventh century by western Europeans. The First Crusade began in 1095, when Pope Urban II appealed to the warrior nobility of France to free Jerusalem from Muslim rule. Four subsequent Crusades were fought over the next two centuries.

Cuban Missile Crisis (1962) Diplomatic standoff between the United States and the Soviet Union that was provoked by the Soviet Union's attempt to base nuclear missiles in Cuba; it brought the world close to a nuclear war.

cult Religious movement, often based on the worship of a particular god or goddess.

cultigen Organism that has diverged from its ancestors through domestication or cultivation.

cuneiform Wedge-shaped form of writing. As people combined rebus symbols with other visual marks that contained meaning, they became able to record and transmit messages over long distances by using abstract symbols or signs to denote concepts; such signs later came to represent syllables, which could be joined into words. By impressing these signs into wet clay with the cut end of a reed, scribes engaged in cuneiform.

Cyrus the Great Founder of the Persian Empire. This sixth-century ruler (559–529 BCE) conquered the Medes and unified the Iranian kingdoms.

Daimyo Ruling lords who commanded private armies in pre-Meiji Japan.

dan Fodio, Usman (1754–1817) Fulani Muslim cleric whose visions led him to challenge the Hausa ruling classes, whom he believed were insufficiently faithful to Islamic beliefs and practices. His ideas gained support among those who had suffered under the Hausa landlords. In 1804, his supporters and allies overthrew the Hausa in what is today northern Nigeria.

Daoism School of thought developed at the end of the Warring States period that focused on the importance of following the Dao, or the natural way of the cosmos. Daoism emphasized the need to accept the world as it was rather than trying to change it through politics or the government. Unlike Confucianism, Daoism scorned rigid rituals and social hierarchies.

Dar al-Islam Arabic for "the House of Islam"; it describes a sense of common identity.

Darius I (521–486 BCE) Leader who put the emerging unified Persian Empire onto solid footing after Cyrus's death.

Darwin, Charles (1809–1882) British scientist who became convinced that the species of organic life had evolved under the uniform pressure of natural laws, not by means of a special, one-time creation as described in the Bible.

D-Day (June 6, 1944) Day of the Allied invasion of Normandy under General Dwight Eisenhower to liberate western Europe from German occupation.

Dear Boy Nickname of an early human remain discovered in 1931 by a team of archaeologists named the Leakeys. They discovered an almost totally intact skull. Other objects discovered with Dear Boy demonstrated that by the time of Dear Boy, early humans had begun to fashion tools and to use them for butchering animals and possibly for hunting and killing smaller animals.

Decembrists Russian army officers who were influenced by events in revolutionary France and formed secret societies that espoused liberal governance. They were put down by Nicholas I in December 1825.

Declaration of Independence U.S. document stating the theory of government on which America was founded.

Declaration of the Rights of Man and Citizen (1789) French charter of liberties formulated by the National Assembly that marked the end of dynastic and aristocratic rule. The seventeen articles later became the preamble to the new constitution, which the assembly finished in 1791.

decolonization End of empire and emergence of new independent nation-states in Asia and Africa as a result of the defeat of Japan in World War II and weakened European influence after the war.

Delhi Sultanate (1206–1526) Turkish regime of Northern India. The regime strengthened the cultural diversity and tolerance that were a hallmark of the Indian social order, which allowed it to bring about political integration without enforcing cultural homogeneity.

democracy The idea that people, through membership in a nation, should choose their own representatives and be governed by them.

Democritus Thinker in ancient Greece who lived from 470 to 360 BCE; he deduced the existence of the atom and postulated that there was such a thing as an indivisible particle.

demotic writing The second of two basic forms of ancient Egyptian writing. Demotic was a cursive script written with ink on papyrus, on pottery, or on other absorbent objects. It was the most common and practical form of writing in Egypt and was used for administrative record keeping and in private or pseudo-private forms like letters and works of literature. *See also* Hieroglyphs.

developing world Term applied to countries collectively called the Third World during the cold war and seeking to develop viable nation-states and prosperous economies.

Devshirme System of taking non-Muslim children in place of taxes in order to educate them in Ottoman Muslim ways and prepare them for service in the sultan's bureaucracy.

dhamma Moral code espoused by A´soka in the Kalinga edict, which was meant to apply to all—Buddhists, Brahmans, and Greeks alike.

***dhimma* system** Ottoman law that permitted followers of religions other than Islam, such as Armenian Christians, Greek Orthodox Christians, and Jews, to choose their own religious leaders and to settle internal disputes within their religious communities as long as they accepted Islam's political dominion.

dhows Ships used by Arab seafarers; the dhow's large sails were rigged to maximize the capture of wind.

Dien Bien Phu (1954) Defining battle in the war between French colonialists and the Viet Minh that secured North Vietnam for Ho Chi Minh and his army and left the south to form its own government to be supported by France and the United States.

Din-I-llahi "House of worship" in which the Mughal emperor Akbar engaged in religious debate with Hindu, Muslim, Jain, Parsi, and Christian theologians.

Diogenes Greek philosopher who lived from 412 to 323 BCE and who espoused a doctrine of self-sufficiency and freedom from social laws and customs. He rejected cultural norms as out of tune with nature and therefore false.

Directory Temporary military committee that took over the affairs of the state of France in 1795 from the radicals and held control until the coup of Napoleon Bonaparte.

divination The interpretation of rituals used to communicate the wishes of gods or royal ancestors to foretell future events. Divination was used to legitimize royal authority and demand tribute.

Djoser Ancient Egyptian king who reigned from 2630 to 2611 BCE. He was the second king of the Third Dynasty and celebrated the Sed festival in his tomb complex at Saqqara.

domestication Bringing a wild animal or plant under human control.

Dominion in the British Commonwealth Canadian promise to keep up the country's fealty to the British crown, even after its independence in 1867. Later applied to Australia and New Zealand.

Dong Zhongshu Emperor Wu's chief minister, who advocated a more powerful view of Confucius by promoting texts that focused on Confucius as a man who possessed aspects of divinity.

double-outrigger canoes Vessels used by early Austronesians to cross the Taiwan Straits and colonize islands in the Pacific. These sturdy canoes could cover over 120 miles per day.

Duma Russian parliament.

Dutch learning Broad term for European teachings that were strictly regulated by the shoguns inside Japan.

dynastic cycle Political narrative in which influential families vied for supremacy. Upon gaining power, they legitimated their authority by claiming to be the heirs of previous grand dynasts and by preserving or revitalizing the ancestors' virtuous governing ways. This continuity conferred divine support.

dynasty Hereditary ruling family that passed control from one generation to the next.

Earth Summit (1992) Meeting in Rio de Janeiro between many of the world's governments in an effort to address international environmental problems.

East India Company (1600–1858) British charter company created to outperform Portuguese and Spanish traders in the Far East; in the eighteenth century the company became, in effect, the ruler of a large part of India.

Eastern Front Battlefront between Berlin and Moscow during World War I and World War II.

Edict of Nantes (1598) Edict issued by Henry IV to end the French Wars of Religion. The edict declared France a Catholic country but tolerated some Protestant worship.

Egyptian Middle Kingdom Period of Egyptian history lasting from about 2040 to1640 BCE, characterized by a consolidation of power and building activity in Upper Egypt.

Eiffel Tower Steel monument completed in 1889 for the Paris Exposition. It was twice the height of any other building at the time.

eight-legged essay Highly structured essay form with eight parts, required on Chinese civil service examinations.

Ekklesia Church or early gathering committed to leaders chosen by God and fellow believers.

Ekpe Powerful slave trade institution that organized the supply and purchase of slaves inland from the Gulf of Guinea in West Africa.

Elamites A people with their capital in the upland valley of modern Fars who became a cohesive polity that incorporated transhumant people of the Zagros Mountains. A group of Elamites who migrated south and west into Mesopotamia helped conquer the Third Dynasty of Ur in 2400 BCE.

empire Group of states or different ethnic groups under a single sovereign power.

Enabling Act (1933) Emergency act passed by the Reichstag (German parliament) that helped transform Hitler from Germany's chancellor, or prime minister, into a dictator following the suspicious burning of the Reichstag building and a suspension of civil liberties.

enclosure A movement in which landowners took control of lands that traditionally had been common property serving local needs.

Encomenderos Commanders of the labor services of the colonized peoples in Spanish America.

Encomiendas Grants from European Spanish governors to control the labor services of colonized people.

Endeavor Ship of Captain James Cook, whose celebrated voyages to the South Pacific in the late eighteenth century supplied Europe with information about the plants, birds, landscapes, and people of this uncharted territory.

Engels, Friedrich (1820–1895) German social and political philosopher who collaborated with Karl Marx on many publications, including *The Communist Manifesto*.

English Navigation Act of 1651 Act stipulating that only English ships could carry goods between the mother country and its colonies.

English Peasants' Revolt (1381) Uprising of serfs and free farm workers that began as a protest against a tax levied to raise money for a war on France. The revolt was suppressed but led to the gradual emergence of a free peasantry as labor shortages made it impossible to keep peasants bound to the soil.

enlightened absolutists Seventeenth- and eighteenth-century monarchs who claimed to rule rationally and in the best interests of their subjects and who hired loyal bureaucrats to implement the knowledge of the new age.

Enlightenment Intellectual movement in eighteenth-century Europe stressing natural laws and reason as the basis of authority.

entrepôts Trading stations at the borders between communities, which made exchange possible among many different partners. Long-distance traders could also replenish their supplies at these stations.

Epicurus Greek philosopher who espoused emphasis on the self. He lived from 341 to 279 BCE and founded a school in Athens called The Garden. He stressed the importance of sensation, teaching that pleasurable sensations were good and painful sensations bad. Members of his school sought to find peace and relaxation by avoiding unpleasantness or suffering.

Estates-General French quasi-parliamentary body called in 1789 to deal with the financial problems that afflicted France. It had not met since 1614.

Etruscans A dominant people on the Italian peninsula until the fourth century BCE. The Etruscan states were part of the foundation of the Roman Empire.

eunuchs Loyal and well-paid men who were surgically castrated as youths and remained in service to the caliph or emperor. Both Abbasid and Tang rulers relied for protection on a cadre of eunuchs.

Eurasia The combined area of Europe and Asia.

European Union (EU) International body organized after World War II as an attempt at reconciliation between Germany and the rest of Europe. It initially aimed to forge closer industrial cooperation. Eventually, through various treaties, many European states relinquished some of their sovereignty, and the cooperation became a full-fledged union with a single currency, the euro, and with a somewhat less powerful common European parliament.

evolution Process by which the different species of the world—its plants and animals—made changes in response to their environment that enabled them to survive and increase in numbers.

Exclusion Act of 1882 U.S. congressional act prohibiting nearly all immigration from China to the United States; fueled by animosity toward Chinese workers in the American West.

Ezo Present-day Hokkaido, Japan's fourth main island.

fascism Mass political movement founded by Benito Mussolini that emphasized nationalism, militarism, and the omnipotence of the state.

Fascists Radical right-wing group of disaffected veterans that formed around Mussolini in 1919 and a few years later came to power in Rome.

Fatehpur Sikri Mughal emperor Akbar's temporary capital near Agra.

Fatimids Shiite dynasty that ruled parts of the Islamic Empire beginning in the tenth century CE. They were based in Egypt and founded the city of Cairo.

February Revolution (1917) The first of two uprisings of the Russian Revolution, which led to the end of the Romanov dynasty.

Federal Deposit Insurance Corporation (FDIC) Organization created in 1933 to guarantee all bank deposits up to $5,000 as part of the New Deal in the United States.

Federal Republic of Germany (1949–1990) Country formed of the areas occupied by the Allies after World War II. Also known as West Germany, this country experienced rapid demilitarization, democratization, and integration into the world economy.

Federal Reserve Act (1913) U.S. legislation that created a series of boards to monitor the supply and demand of the nation's money.

Federalists Supporters of the ratification of the U.S. Constitution, which was written to replace the Articles of Confederation.

feminist movements Movements that called for equal treatment for men and women—equal pay and equal opportunities for obtaining jobs and advancement. Feminism arose mainly in Europe and in North America in the 1960s and then became global in the 1970s.

Ferangi Arabic word meaning "Frank" that was used to describe Crusaders.

Fertile Crescent Site of the world's first agricultural revolution; an area in Southwest Asia, bounded by the Mediterranean Sea in the west and the Zagros Mountains in the east.

feudalism System instituted in medieval Europe after the collapse of the Carolingian Empire (814 CE) whereby each peasant was under the authority of a lord.

fiefdoms Medieval economic and political units.

First World Term invented during the cold war to refer to western Europe and North America (also known as the "free world" or the West); Japan later joined this group. Following the principles of liberal modernism, First World states sought to organize the world on the basis of capitalism and democracy.

Five Pillars of Islam The five tenets, or main aspects, of Islamic practice: testification or bearing witness that there is no God other than God (Allah, in Arabic) and that Muhammad is the messenger of God; praying five times a day; fasting from sunup to sundown every day during Ramadan (a month on the Islamic calendar); giving alms; and making a pilgrimage to Mecca.

Five-Year Plan Soviet effort launched under Stalin in 1928 to replace the market with a state-owned and state-managed economy, to promote rapid economic development over a five-year period of time and thereby "catch and overtake" the leading capitalist countries. The First Five-Year Plan was followed by the Second Five-Year Plan (1933–1937), and so on, until the collapse of the Soviet Union in 1991.

Flagellants European social group that came into existence during the bubonic plague in the fourteenth century; they believed that the plague was the wrath of God.

floating population Poor migrant workers in China who supplied labor under Emperor Wu.

Fluitschips Dutch shipping vessels that could carry heavy bulky cargo with relatively small crews.

flying cash Letters of exchange—early predecessors of paper cash instead of coins—first developed by guilds in the northwestern Shanxi. By the thirteenth century, paper money had eclipsed coins.

Fondûqs Complexes in caravan cities that included hostels, storage houses, offices, and temples.

Forbidden City of Beijing Palace city of the Ming and Qing dynasties.

Force Publique Colonial army used to maintain order in the Belgian Congo; during the early stages of King Leopold's rule, it was responsible for bullying local communities.

Fourierism Form of utopian socialism based on the ideas of Charles Fourier (1772–1837). Fourier envisioned communes where work was made enjoyable and systems of production and distribution were run without merchants. His ideas appealed to middle-class readers, especially women, as a higher form of Christian communalism.

free labor Wage-paying rather than slave labor.

free markets Unregulated markets.

Free Officers Movement Secret organization of Egyptian junior military officers who came to power in a coup d'état in 1952, forced King Faruq to abdicate, and consolidated their own control through dissolving the parliament, banning opposing parties, and rewriting the constitution.

free trade Domestic and international trade unencumbered by tariff barriers, quotas, and fees.

Front de Libération Nationale (FLN) Algerian anticolonial, nationalist party that waged an eight-year war against French troops, beginning in 1854, that forced nearly all of the 1,000,000 colonists to leave.

Fulani Muslim group in West Africa that carried out religious revolts at the end of the eighteenth and the beginning of the nineteenth centuries in an effort to return to the pure Islam of the past.

fur trade Trading of animal pelts (especially beaver skins) by Indians for European goods in North America.

Gandhi, Mohandhas Karamchand (Mahatma) (1869–1948) Indian leader who led a nonviolent struggle for India's independence from Britain.

garrison towns Stations for soldiers originally established in strategic locations to protect territorial acquisition. Eventually, they became towns. Alexander the Great's garrison towns evolved into cities that served as centers from which Hellenistic culture was spread to his easternmost territories.

garrisons Military bases inside cities; often used for political purposes, such as protecting rulers and putting down domestic revolts or enforcing colonial rule.

gauchos Argentine, Brazilian, and Uruguayan cowboys who wanted a decentralized federation, with autonomy for their provinces and respect for their way of life.

Gdansk shipyard Site of mass strikes in Poland that led in 1980 to the formation of the first independent trade union, Solidarity, in the communist bloc.

gendered relations A relatively recent development that implies roles emerged only with the appearance of modern humans and perhaps Neanderthals. When humans began to think imaginatively and in complex symbolic ways and give voice to their insights, perhaps around 150,000 years ago, gender categories began to crystallize.

genealogy History of the descent of a person or family from a distant ancestor.

Geneva Peace Conference (1954) International conference to restore peace in Korea and Indochina. The chief participants were the United States, the Soviet Union, Great Britain, France, the People's Republic of China, North Korea, South Korea, Vietnam, the Viet Minh party, Laos, and Cambodia. The conference resulted in the division of North and South Vietnam.

Genoa One of two Italian cities (the other was Venice) that linked Europe, Africa, and Asia as nodes of commerce in 1300 CE. Genoese ships linked the Mediterranean to the coast of Flanders through consistent routes along the Atlantic coasts of Spain, Portugal, and France.

German Democratic Republic Nation founded from the Soviet zone of occupation of Germany after World War II; also known as East Germany.

German Social Democratic Party Founded in 1875, the most powerful Socialist party in Europe before 1917.

Ghana The most celebrated medieval political kingdom in West Africa.

Ghost Dance American Indian ritual performed in the nineteenth century in the hope of restoring the world to precolonial conditions.

Gilgamesh Heroic narrative written in the Babylonian dialect of Semitic Akkadian. This story and others like it were meant to circulate and unify the kingdom.

Girondins Liberal revolutionary group that supported the creation of a constitutional monarchy during the early stages of the French Revolution.

global warming Release into the air of human-made carbons that contribute to rising temperatures worldwide.

globalization Development of integrated worldwide cultural and economic structures.

Gold Coast Name that European mariners and merchants gave to that part of West Africa from which gold was exported. This area was conquered by the British in the nineteenth century and became a British colony; upon independence, it became Ghana.

Goths One of the groups of "barbarian" migrants into Roman territory in the fourth century.

government schools Schools founded by the Han dynasty to provide an adequate number of officials to fill positions in the administrative bureaucracy. The Imperial University had 30,000 members by the second century BCE.

Gracchus brothers Two tribunes, the brothers Tiberius and Gaius Gracchus, who in 133 and 123–21 BCE attempted to institute land reforms that would guarantee all of Rome's poor citizens a basic amount of land that would qualify them for army service. Both men were assassinated.

Grand Canal Created in 486 BCE, a thousand-mile-long connector between the Yellow and Yangzi rivers, linking the north and south, respectively.

grand unity Guiding political idea embraced by Qin rulers and ministers, with an eye toward joining the states of the Central Plain into one empire and centralizing administration.

"Greased cartridge" controversy Controversy spawned by the rumor that cow and pig fat had been used to grease the shotguns of the sepoys in the British army in India. Believing that this was a British attempt to defile their religion and speed their conversion to Christianity, the sepoys mutinied against the British officers.

Great Depression Worldwide depression following the U.S. stock market crash on October 29, 1929.

great divide The division between economically developed nations and less developed nations.

Great East Asia Co-Prosperity Sphere Term used by the Japanese during the 1930s and 1940s to refer to Hong Kong, Singapore, Malaya, Burma, and other states that they seized during their run for expansion.

Great Flood One of many traditional Mesopotamian stories that were transmitted orally from one generation to another before being recorded. The Sumerian King List refers to this crucial event in Sumerian memory and identity. The Great Flood was assigned responsibility for Uruk's demise to the gods.

Great Game Competition over areas such as Turkistan, Persia (present-day Iran), and Afghanistan. The British (in India) and the Russians believed that controlling these areas was crucial to preventing their enemies' expansion.

Great League of Peace and Power Iroquois Indian alliance that united previously warring communities.

Great Leap Forward (1958–1961) Plan devised by Mao Zedong to achieve rapid agricultural and industrial growth in China. The plan failed miserably and more than 20 million people died.

great plaza at Isfahan The center of Safavid power in the seventeenth century created by Shah Abbas (r. 1587–1629) to represent the unification of trade, government, and religion under one supreme political authority.

Great Proletarian Cultural Revolution (1966–1976) Mass mobilization of urban Chinese youth inaugurated by Mao Zedong in an attempt to reinvigorate the Chinese revolution and to prevent the development of a bureaucratized Soviet style of communism; with this movement, Mao turned against his long-time associates in the communist party.

Great Trek Afrikaner migration to the interiors of Africa after the British abolished slavery in the empire in 1833.

Great War (August 1914–November 1918) A total war involving the armies of Britain, France, and Russia (the Allies) against those of Germany, Austria-Hungary, and the Ottoman Empire (the Central Powers). Italy joined the Allies in 1915, and the United States joined them in 1917, helping tip the balance in favor of the Allies, who also drew upon the populations and material of their colonial possessions. Also known as World War I.

Greek Orthodoxy Enduring form of Christianity that used the framework of the "Roman" state inherited from Constantine and Justinian to protect itself from Roman Catholicism and Muslim forces. The Greek Orthodox capital was Constantinople and its spiritual empire included the Russian peoples, Baltic Slavs, and peoples living in southwest Asia.

Greenbacks Members of the American political party of the late nineteenth century that worked to advance the interest of farmers by promoting cheap money.

griots Counselors and other officials to the royal family in African kingships. They were also responsible for the preservation and transmission of oral histories and repositories of knowledge.

Group Areas Act (1950) Act that divided South Africa into separate racial and tribal areas and required Africans to live in their own separate communities, including the "homelands."

guerrillas Portuguese and Spanish peasant bands who resisted the revolutionary and expansionist efforts of Napoleon; after the French word *guerre*.

guest workers Migrants looking for temporary employment abroad.

Gulag Administrative name for the vast system of forced labor camps under the Soviet regime; it originated in a small monastery near the Arctic Circle and spread throughout the Soviet Union and to other Soviet-style socialist countries. Penal labor was required of both ordinary criminals (rapists, murderers, thieves) and those accused of political crimes (counterrevolution, anti-Soviet agitation).

Gulf War (1991) Armed conflict between Iraq and a coalition of thirty-two nations, including the United States, Britain, Egypt, France, and Saudi Arabia. It was started by Iraq's invasion of Kuwait, which it had long claimed, on August 2, 1990.

gunpowder Explosive powder. By 1040, the first gunpowder recipes were being written down. Over the next 200 years, Song entrepreneurs invented several incendiary devices and techniques for controlling explosions.

gunpowder empires Muslim empires of the Ottomans, Safavids, and Mughals that used cannonry and gunpowder to advance their military causes.

Guomindang Nationalist party of China, founded just before World War I by Sun Yat-sen and later led by Chiang Kai-shek.

Habsburg Empire Ruling house of Austria, which once ruled both Spain and central Europe but came to settle in lands along the Danube River; it played a prominent role in European affairs for many centuries. In 1867, the Habsburg Empire was reorganized into the Austro-Hungarian Dual Monarchy, and in 1918 it collapsed.

Hadith Sayings attributed to the Prophet Muhammad and his early converts. Used to guide the behavior of Muslim peoples.

Hagia Sophia Enormous and impressive church sponsored by Justinian and built starting in 532 CE. At the time, it was the largest church in the world.

Hajj Pilgrimage to Mecca; an obligation for Muslims.

Hammurapi's Code Legal code created by Hammurapi, the most famous of the Mesopotamian rulers, who reigned from 1792 to 1750 BCE. Hammurapi sought to create social order by centralizing state authority and creating a grand legal structure that embodied paternal justice. The code was quite stratified, dividing society into three classes: free men, dependent men, and slaves, each with distinct rights and responsibilities.

Han agrarian ideal Guiding principle for the free peasantry that made up the base of Han society. In this system, peasants were honored for their labors, while merchants were subjected to a range of controls, including regulations on luxury consumption, and were belittled for not engaging in physical labor.

Han Chinese Inhabitants of China proper who considered others to be outsiders. They felt that they were the only authentic Chinese.

Han Fei Chinese state minister who lived from 280 to 223 BCE; he was a proponent and follower of Xunzi.

Han military Like its Roman counterpart, a ruthless military machine that expanded the empire and created stable conditions that permitted the safe transit of goods by caravans. Emperor Wu heavily influenced the transformation of the military forces and reinstituted a policy that made military service compulsory.

Hangzhou City and former provincial seaport that became the political center of the Chinese people in their ongoing struggles with northern steppe nomads. It was also one of China's gateways to the rest of the world by way of the South China Sea.

Hannibal Great Roman general from Carthage whose campaigns in the third century BCE swept from Spain toward the Italian peninsula. He crossed the Pyrenees and the Alps mountain ranges with war elephants. He was unable, however, to defeat the Romans in 217 BCE.

Harappa One of two cities that, by 2500 BCE, began to take the place of villages throughout the Indus River valley (the other was Mohenjo Daro). Each covered an area of about 250 acres and probably housed 35,000 residents.

harem Secluded women's quarters in Muslim households.

Harlem Renaissance Cultural movement in the 1920s that was based in Harlem, a part of New York City with a large African American population. The movement gave voice to black novelists, poets, painters, and musicians, many of whom used their art to protest racism; also referred to as the "New Negro movement."

harnesses Tools made from wood, bone, bronze, and iron for steering and controlling chariot horses. Harnesses discovered by archaeologists reveal the evolution of headgear from simple mouth bits to full bridles with headpiece, mouthpiece, and reins.

Hatshepsut Leader known as ancient Egypt's most powerful woman ruler. Hatshepsut served as regent for her young son, Thutmosis III, whose reign began in 1479 BCE. She remained co-regent until her death.

Haussmannization Redevelopment and beautification of urban centers; named after the city planner who "modernized" mid-nineteenth-century Paris.

Hegira "Emigration" of Muhammad and his followers out of a hostile Mecca to Yathrib, a city that was later called Medina. The year in which this journey took place, 622 CE, is also year 1 of the Islamic calendar.

Heian period Period from 794 to 1185, during which began the pattern of regents ruling Japan in the name of the sacred emperor.

Hellenism Process by which the individuality of the cultures of the earlier Greek city-states gave way to a uniform culture that stressed the common identity of all who embraced Greek ways. This culture emphasized the common denominators of language, style, and politics to which anyone, anywhere in the Afro-Eurasian world, could have access.

hieroglyphs One of two basic forms of Egyptian writing that were used in conjunction throughout antiquity. Hieroglyphs are pictorial symbols; the term derives from a Greek word meaning "sacred carving"—they were employed exclusively in temple, royal, and divine contexts. *See also* Demotic writing.

Hijra Tradition of Islam, whereby one withdraws from one's community to create another, more holy, one. The practice is based on the Prophet Muhammad's withdrawal from the city of Mecca to Medina in 622 CE.

Hinayana (Lesser Vehicle) Buddhism Form of Buddhism that accepted the divinity of Buddha himself but not of demigods, or bodhisattvas.

Hinduism A refashioning of the ancient Brahmanic Vedic religion, bringing it in accord with rural life and agrarian values. It emerged as the dominant faith in Indian society in the third century CE. Believers became vegetarians and adopted rituals of self-sacrifice. Three major deities—Brahma, Vishnu, and Siva—formed a trinity representing the three phases of the universe (birth, existence, and destruction, respectively) and the three expressions of the eternal self, or *atma*.

Hindu revivalism Movement to reconfigure traditional Hinduism to be less diverse and more amenable to producing a narrowed version of Indian tradition.

Hiroshima Japanese port devastated by an atomic bomb on August 6, 1945.

Hitler, Adolf (1889–1945) German dictator and leader of the Nazi Party who seized power in Germany after its economic collapse in the Great Depression. Hitler and his Nazi regime started World War II in Europe and systematically murdered Jews and other non-Aryan groups in the name of racial purity.

Hittites One of the five great territorial states. The Hittites campaigned throughout Anatolia, then went east to northern Syria, though they eventually faced weaknesses in their own homeland. Their heyday was marked by the reign of the king Supiliulimua (1380 to 1345 BCE), who preserved the Hittites' influence on the balance of power in the region between Mesopotamia and the Nile.

Holocaust Deliberate racial extermination of the Jews by the Nazis that claimed around 6 million European Jews.

Holy Roman Empire Enormous realm that encompassed much of Europe and aspired to be the Christian successor state to the Roman Empire. In the time of the Habsburg dynasts, the empire was a loose confederation of principalities that obeyed an emperor elected by elite lower-level sovereigns. Despite its size, the empire never effectively centralized power; it was split into Austrian and Spanish factions when Charles V abdicated to his sons in 1556.

Holy Russia Name applied to Muscovy and then to the Russian Empire by Slavic Eastern Orthodox clerics who were appalled by the Muslim conquest in 1453 of Constantinople (the capital of Byzantium and of Eastern Christianity) and who were hopeful that Russia would become the new protector of the faith.

home charges Fees India was forced to pay to Britain as its colonial master; these fees included interest on railroad loans, salaries to colonial officers, and the maintenance of imperial troops outside India.

hominids Humanlike beings who walked erect and preceded modern humans.

Homo A word used by scientists to differentiate between pre-human and "true human" species.

Homo caudatus "Tailed man," believed by some European Enlightenment thinkers to be an early species of humankind.

Homo erectus Species that emerged about 1.5 million years ago and had a large brain and walked truly upright. *Homo erectus* means "Standing man."

Homo habilis Scientific term for "Skillful man." Toolmaking ability truly made *Homo habilis* the forerunners, though very distant, of modern humans.

Homo sapiens The first humans; they emerged in a small region of Africa about 200,000 years ago and migrated out of Africa about 100,000 years ago. They had bigger brains and greater dexterity than previous hominid species, whom they eventually eclipsed.

homogeneity Uniformity of the languages, customs, and religion of a particular people or place. It can also be demonstrated by a consistent calendar, set of laws, administrative practices, and rituals.

horses Animals used by full-scale nomadic communities to dominate the steppe lands in western Afro-Eurasia by the second millennium BCE. Horse-riding nomads moved their large herds across immense tracts of land within zones defined by rivers, mountains, and other natural geographical features. In the arid zones of central Eurasia, the nomadic economies made horses a crucial component of survival.

Huguenots French Protestants who endured severe persecution in the sixteenth and seventeenth centuries.

humanism The Renaissance aspiration to know more about the human experience beyond what the Christian scriptures offered by reaching back into ancient Greek and Roman texts.

Hundred Days' Reform (1898) Abortive modernizing reform program of the Qing government of China.

hunting and gathering Lifestyle in which food is acquired through hunting animals, fishing, and foraging for wild berries, nuts, fruit, and grains, rather than planting crops, vines, or trees. As late as 1500, as much as 15 percent of the world's population still lived by this method.

Hyksos A western Semitic-speaking people whose name means "Rulers of Foreign Lands"; they overthrew the unstable Thirteenth Dynasty in Egypt around 1640 BCE. The Hyksos had mastered the art of horse chariots, and with those chariots and their superior bronze axes and composite bows (made of wood, horn, and sinew), they were able to defeat the pharaoh's foot soldiers.

Ibn Sina Philosopher and physician who lived from 980 to 1037 CE. He was also schooled in the Quran, geometry, literature, and Indian and Euclidian mathematics.

ideology Dominant set of ideas of a widespread culture or movement.

Il Duce Term designating the fascist Italian leader Benito Mussolini.

Iliad Epic Greek poem about the Trojan War, composed several centuries after the events it describes. It was based on oral tales passed down for generations.

Il-khanate Mongol-founded dynasty in thirteenth-century Persia.

Imam Muslim religious leader and politico-religious descendant of Ali; believed by some to have a special relationship with Allah.

imperialism Acquisition of new territories by a state and the incorporation of these territories into a political system as subordinate colonies.

Imperium Latin word used to express Romans' power and command over their subjects. It is the basis of the English words *empire* and *imperialism*.

Inca Empire Empire of Quecha-speaking rulers in the Andean valley of Cuzco that encompassed a population of 4 to 6 million. The Incas lacked a clear inheritance system, causing an internal split that Pizarro's forces exploited in 1533.

Indian Institutes of Technology (IIT) Institutions originally designed as engineering schools to expand knowledge and to modernize India, which produced a whole generation of pioneering computer engineers, many of whom moved to the United States.

Indian National Congress Formed in 1885, a political party deeply committed to constitutional methods, industrialization, and cultural nationalism.

Indian National Muslim League Founded in 1906, an organization dedicated to advancing the political interests of Muslims in India.

Indo-Greek Fusion of Indian and Greek culture in the area under the control of the Bactrians, in the northwestern region of India, around 200 BCE.

Indu What we would today call India. Called "Indu" by Xuanzang, a Chinese Buddhist pilgrim who visited the area in the 630s and 640s CE.

indulgences Church-sponsored fund-raising mechanism that gave certification that one's sins had been forgiven in return for money.

industrial revolution Gradual accumulation and diffusion of old and new technical knowledge that led to major economic changes in Britain, northwestern Europe, and North America, catapulting these countries ahead of the rest of the world in manufacturing and agricultural output and standards of living.

industrious revolution Dramatic economic change in which households that had traditionally produced for themselves decided to work harder and longer hours in order to produce more for the market, which enabled them to increase their income and standard of living. Areas that underwent the industrious revolution shifted from peasant farming to specialized production for the market.

innovation Creation of a new method that allowed humans to make better adaptations to their environment such as the making of new tools.

Inquisition Tribunal of the Roman Catholic Church that enforced religious orthodoxy during the Protestant Reformation.

internal and external alchemy In Daoist ritual, use of trance and meditation or chemicals and drugs, respectively, to cause transformations in the self.

International Monetary Fund (IMF) Agency founded in 1944 to help restore financial order in Europe and the rest of the world, to revive international trade, and to support the financial concerns of Third World governments.

invisible hand As described in Adam Smith's *The Wealth of Nations*, the idea that the operations of a free market produce economic efficiency and economic benefits for all.

iron Malleable metal found in combined forms almost everywhere in the world; it became the most important and widely used metal in world history after the Bronze Age.

Iron Curtain Term popularized by Winston Churchill after World War II to refer to a rift, or an iron curtain, that divided western Europe, under American influence, from eastern Europe, under the domination of the Soviet Union.

irrigation Technological advance whereby water delivery systems and water sluices in floodplains or riverine areas were channeled or redirected and used to nourish soil.

Islam A religion that dates to 610 CE, when Muhammad believed God came to him in a vision. Islam ("submission"—in this case, to the will of God) requires its followers to act righteously, to submit themselves to the one and only true God, and to care for the less fortunate. Muhammad's most insistent message was the oneness of God, a belief that has remained central to the Islamic faith ever since.

Jacobins Radical French political group that came into existence during the French Revolution and executed the French king and sought to remake French culture.

Jacquerie (1358) French peasant revolt in defiance of feudal restrictions.

jade The most important precious substance in East Asia. Jade was associated with goodness, purity, luck, and virtue, and was carved into such items as ceremonial knives, blade handles, religious objects, and elaborate jewelry.

Jagat Seths Enormous trading and banking empire in eastern India.

Jainism Along with Buddhism, one of the two systems of thought developed in the seventh century BCE that set themselves up against Brahmanism. Its founder, Vardhamana Mahavira, taught that the universe obeys its own everlasting rules that no god or other supernatural being could affect. The purpose of life was to purify one's soul in order to attain a state of permanent bliss, which could be accomplished through self-denial and the avoidance of harming other creatures.

Janissaries Corps of infantry soldiers recruited as children from the Christian provinces of the Ottoman Empire and brought up with intense loyalty to the Ottoman state and its sultan. The Ottoman sultan used these forces to clip local autonomy and to serve as his personal bodyguards.

Jati Social groups as defined by Hinduism's caste system.

Jesuits Religious order founded by Ignatius Loyola to counter the inroads of the Protestant Reformation; the Jesuits, or the Society of Jesus, were active in politics, education, and missionary work.

jihad Literally, "striving" or "struggle." This word also connotes military efforts or "striving in the way of God." It also came to mean spiritual struggles against temptation or inner demons, especially in Sufi, or mystical, usage.

Jih-pen Chinese for "Japan."

Jim Crow laws Laws that codified racial segregation and inequality in the southern part of the United States after the Civil War.

Jizya Special tax that non-Muslims were forced to pay to their Islamic rulers in return for which they were given security and property and granted cultural autonomy.

jong Large ocean-going vessels, built by Southeast Asians, which plied the regional trade routes from the fifteenth century to the early sixteenth century.

Judah The southern kingdom of David, which had been an Assyrian vassal until 612 BCE, when it became a vassal of Assyria's successor, Babylon, against whom the people of Judah rebelled, resulting in the destruction of Jerusalem in the sixth century BCE.

Julius Caesar Formidable Roman general who lived from 100 to 44 BCE. He was also a man of letters, a great orator, and a ruthless military man who boasted that his campaigns had led to the deaths of over a million people.

junks Trusty seafaring vessels used in the South China Seas after 1000 CE. These helped make shipping by sea less dangerous.

Justinian Roman or Byzantine emperor who ascended to the throne in 527 CE. In addition to his many building projects and military expeditions, he issued a new law code.

Kabuki Theater performance that combined song, dance, and skillful staging to dramatize conflicts between duty and passion in Tokogawa, Japan.

Kamikaze Japanese for "divine winds" or typhoons; such a storm saved Japan from a Mongol attack.

Kanun Highly detailed system of Ottoman administrative law that jurists developed to deal with matters not treated in the religious law of Islam.

Karim Loose confederation of shippers banding together to protect convoys.

karma Literally "fate" or "action," in Confucian thought; this is a universal principle of cause and effect.

Kassites Nomads who entered Mesopotamia from the eastern Zagros Mountains and the Iranian plateau as early as 2000 BCE. They gradually integrated into Babylonian society by officiating at temples. By 1745 BCE, they had asserted order over the region, and they controlled southern Mesopotamia for the next 350 years, creating one of the territorial states.

Keynesian Revolution Post-Depression economic ideas developed by the British economist John Maynard Keynes, wherein the state took a greater role in managing the economy, stimulating it by increasing the money supply and creating jobs.

KGB Soviet political police and spy agency, formed as the Cheka not long after the Bolshevik coup in October 1917. Grew to more than 750,000 operatives with military rank by the 1980s.

khan Ruler who was acclaimed at an assembly of elites and supposedly descended from Chinggis Khan on the male line; those not descended from Chinggis continually faced challenges to their legitimacy.

Khanate Major political unit of the vast Mongol empire. There were four Khanates, including the Yuan Empire in China, forged by Chinggis Khan's grandson Kubilai.

Kharijites Radical sect from the early days of Islam. The Kharijites seceded from the "party of Ali" (who themselves came to be known as the Shiites) because of disagreements over succession to the role of the caliph. They were known for their strict militant piety.

Khmers A people who created the most powerful empire in Southwest Asia between the tenth and thirteenth centuries in what is modern-day Cambodia.

Khomeini, Ayatollah Ruhollah (1902–1989) Iranian religious leader who used his traditional Islamic education and his training in Muslim ethics to accuse the shah's government of gross violations of Islamic norms. He also identified the shah's ally, America, as the great Satan. The shah fled the country in 1979; in his wake, Khomeini established a theocratic state ruled by a council of Islamic clerics.

Khufu A pyramid, among those put up in the Fourth Dynasty in ancient Egypt (2575–2465 BCE), which is the largest stone structure in the world. It is in an area called Giza, just outside modern-day Cairo.

Khusro I Anoshirwan Sasanian emperor who reigned from 530 to 579 CE.

He was a model ruler and was seen as the personification of justice.

Kiev City that became one of the greatest cities of Europe after the eleventh century. It was built to be a small-scale Constantinople on the Dnieper.

Kikuyu Kenya's largest ethnic group; organizers of a revolt against the British in the 1950s.

King, Martin Luther, Jr. (1929–1968) Civil rights leader who borrowed his most effective weapon—the commitment to nonviolent protest and the appeal to conscience—from Gandhi.

Kingdom of Awadh One of the most prized lands for annexation and the fertile, opulent, and traditional vestige of Mughal rule in India.

Kingdom of Jerusalem What Crusaders set out to liberate when they launched their attack.

Kizilbash Mystical, Turkish-speaking tribesmen who facilitated the Safavid rise to power.

Knossos Area in Crete where, during the second millennium BCE, a primary palace town existed.

Koine Greek Common form of Greek that became the international spoken and written language in the Hellenistic world. This was a simpler everyday form of the ancient Greek language.

Koprulu reforms Reforms named after two grand viziers who revitalized the Ottoman Empire in the seventeenth century through administrative and budget trimming as well as by rebuilding the military.

Korean War (1950–1953) Cold war conflict between Soviet-backed North Korea and U.S.- and UN-backed South Korea. The two sides seesawed back and forth over the same boundaries until 1953, when an armistice divided the country at roughly the same spot as at the start of the war. Nothing had been gained. Losses, however, included 33,000 Americans, at least 250,000 Chinese, and up to 3 million Koreans.

Koryo dynasty Leading dynasty of the northern-based Koryo kingdom in Korea. It is from this dynasty that the name "Korea" derives.

Kremlin Once synonymous with the Soviet government; refers to Moscow's walled city center.

Kshatriyas Originally the warrior caste in Vedic society, the dominant clan members and ruling caste who controlled the land.

Ku Klux Klan Racist organization that first emerged in the U.S. South after the Civil War and then gained national strength as a radically traditionalist movement during the 1920s.

Kubilai Khan (1215–1294) Mongol leader who seized southern China after 1260 and founded the Yuan dynasty.

kulak Originally a pejorative word used to designate better-off peasants, the term used in the late 1920s and early 1930s to refer to any peasant, rich or poor, perceived as an opponent of the Soviet regime. Russian for "fist."

Kumarajiva Renowned Buddhist scholar and missionary who lived from 344 to 413 CE. He was brought to China by Chinese regional forces from Kucha, modern-day Xinjiang.

Kushans Northern nomadic group that migrated into South Asia in 50 CE. They unified the tribes of the region and set up the Kushan dynasty. The Kushans' empire embraced a large and diverse territory and played a critical role in the formation of the Silk Road.

Labour Party Founded in Britain in 1900, the party that represented workers and was based on socialist principles.

laissez-faire The concept that the economy works best when it is left alone—that is, when the state does not regulate or interfere with the workings of the market.

"Land under the Yoke of Ashur" Lands not in Assyria proper, but under its authority; they had to pay the Assyrian Empire exorbitant amounts of tribute.

language System of communication reflecting cognitive abilities. Natural language is generally defined as words arranged in particular sequences to convey meaning and is unique to modern humans.

language families Related tongues with a common ancestral origin; language families contain languages that diverged from one another but share grammatical features and root vocabularies. More than a hundred language families exist.

Laozi Also known as Master Lao; perhaps a contemporary of Confucius and the person after whom Daoism is named. His thought was elaborated upon by generations of thinkers.

Latifundia Broad estates that produced goods for big urban markets, including wheat, grapes, olives, cattle, and sheep.

Laws of Manu Part of the handiwork of Brahman priests; a representative code of law that incorporated social sanctions and practices and provided guidance for living within the caste system.

League of Nations Organization founded after World War I to solve international disputes through arbitration; it was dissolved in 1946 and its assets were transferred to the United Nations.

Legalism Also called Statism, a system of thought about how to live an ordered life. It was developed by Master Xun, or Xunzi (310–237 BCE). It is based on the principle that people, being inherently inclined toward evil, require authoritarian control to regulate their behavior.

Lenin, Nikolai (1870–1924) Leader of the Bolshevik Revolution in Russia and the first leader of the Soviet Union.

Liangzhu Culture spanning centuries from the fourth to the third millennium BCE that represented the last new Stone Age culture in the Yangzi River delta. One of the Ten Thousand States, it was highly stratified and is known for its jade objects.

liberalism Political and social theory that advocates representative government, free trade, and freedom of speech and religion.

limited-liability joint-stock company Company that mobilized capital from a large number of investors, called shareholders, who were not to be held personally liable for financial losses incurred by the company.

Linear A and B Two linear scripts first discovered on Crete in 1900. On the island of Crete and on the mainland areas of Greece, documents of the palace-centered societies were written on clay tablets in these two scripts. Linear A script, apparently written in Minoan, has not yet been deciphered. Linear B was first deciphered in the early 1950s.

"Little Europes" Urban landscapes between 1100 and 1200 CE composed of castles, churches, and towns in what are today Poland, the Czech Republic, Hungary, and the Baltic States.

Liu Bang Chinese emperor from 206 to 195 BCE; after declaring himself the prince of his home area of Han, in 202 BCE, Liu declared himself the first Han emperor.

llamas Animals similar in utility and function to camels in Afro-Eurasia. Llamas could carry heavy loads for long distances.

Long March (1934–1935) Trek of over 10,000 kilometers by Mao Zedong and his communist followers to establish a new base of operations in northwestern China.

Longshan peoples Peoples who lived in small agricultural and riverine villages in East Asia at the end of the third millennium BCE. They set the stage for the Shang in terms of a centralized state, urban life, and a cohesive culture.

lord Privileged landowner who exercised authority over the people who lived on his land.

lost generation The 17 million former members of the Red Guard and other Chinese youth who were denied education from the late 1960s to the mid-1970s as part of the Chinese government's attempt to prevent political disruptions.

Louisiana Purchase (1803) American purchase of French territory from Napoleon, including much of the present-day United States between the Mississippi River and the Rocky Mountains.

Lucy Relatively intact skeleton of a young adult female australopithecine unearthed in the valley of the Awash River in 1974 by an archaeological team working at a site in present-day Hadar, Ethiopia. The researchers nicknamed the skeleton Lucy. She stood just over three feet tall and walked upright at least some of the time. Her skull contained a brain within the ape size range. Also, her jaw and teeth were humanlike. Lucy's skeleton was relatively complete and was the oldest hominid skeleton ever discovered.

Luftwaffe German air force.

Maastricht Treaty (1991) Treaty that formed the European Union, a fully integrated trading and financial bloc with its own bureaucracy and elected representatives.

Ma'at Term used in ancient Egypt to refer to stability or order, the achievement of which was the primary task of Egypt's ruling kings, the pharaohs.

Maccabees Leaders of a riot in Jerusalem in 166 BCE; the riot was a response to a Roman edict outlawing the practice of Judaism.

Madhyamika (Middle Way) Buddhism Chinese branch of Mahayana Buddhism established by Kumarajiva (344–413 CE) that used irony and paradox to show that reason was limited.

madrassas Higher schools of Muslim education that taught law, the Quran, religious sciences, and the regular sciences.

Mahayana (Greater Vehicle) Buddhism School of Buddhist theology that believed that the Buddha was a deity, unlike previous groups that had considered him a wise human being.

Mahdi The "chosen one" in Islam whose appearance was supposed to foretell the end of the world and the final day of reckoning for all people.

maize Grains, the crops that the settled agrarian communities across the Americas cultivated, along with legumes (beans) and tubers (potatoes).

Maji-Maji Revolt (early 1900s) Swahili insurrection against German colonialists; inspired by the belief that those who were anointed with specially blessed water (*maji*) would be immune to bullets. It resulted in 200,000–300,000 African deaths.

Mamluks (Arabic for "owned" or "possessed") Military men who ruled Egypt as an independent regime from 1250 until the Ottoman conquest in 1517.

Manaus Opera House Opera house built in the interior of Brazil in a lucrative rubber-growing area at the turn of the twentieth century.

Manchukuo Japanese puppet state in Manchuria in the 1930s.

Manchus Descendants of the Jurchens who helped the Ming army recapture Beijing in 1644 after its seizure by the outlaw Li Zicheng. The Manchus numbered around 1 million but controlled a domain that included perhaps 250 million people. Their rule lasted more than 250 years and became known as the Qing dynasty.

mandate of heaven Ideology established by Zhou dynasts to communicate the moral transfer of power. Originally a pact between the Zhou people and their supreme god, it evolved in the first century BCE into Chinese political doctrine.

Mande A people who lived in the area between the bend in the Senegal River and the bend in the Niger River east to west and from the Senegal River and Bandama River north to south. Also known as the Mandinka. Their civilization emerged around 1100.

Mandela, Nelson (1918–) Leader of the African National Congress (ANC) who was imprisoned for more than two decades by the apartheid regime in South Africa for his political beliefs; worldwide protests led to his release in 1990. In 1994 Mandela won the presidency in South Africa's first free mass elections.

Manifest Destiny Belief that it was God's will for the American people to expand their territory and political processes across the North American continent.

Mao Zedong (1893–1976) Chinese communist leader who rose to power during the Long March (1934). In 1949, he defeated the Nationalists and established a communist regime in China. Although many of Mao's efforts to transform China, such as the industrialization program of 1958 (known as the Great Leap Forward) and the Cultural Revolution of 1966, failed and brought great suffering to the people, he did instill a new spirit of independence in China and a sense of purpose after many decades of political and economic failure.

maroon community Sanctuary for runaway slaves in the Americas.

Marshall Plan Economic aid package given by the United States to Europe after World War II in hopes of a rapid period of reconstruction and economic gain, thereby securing the countries that received the aid from a communist takeover.

martyrs People executed by the Roman authorities for persisting in their Christian beliefs and refusing to submit to pagan ritual or belief.

Marx, Karl (1818–1883) German philosopher and economist who created Marxism and believed that a revolution of the working classes would overthrow the capitalist order and create a classless society.

Marxism Form of scientific socialism created by Karl Marx and Friedrich Engels that was rooted in a materialist theory of history: what mattered in history were the production of material goods and the ways in which society was organized into classes of producers and exploiters.

mass consumption Increased purchasing power in the early-twentieth-century prosperous and mainly middle-class societies, stemming from mass production.

mass culture Distinctive form of popular culture that arose in the wake of World War I. It reflected the tastes of the working and the middle classes, who now had more time and money to spend on entertainment, and relied on new technologies, especially film and radio, which could reach an entire nation's population and consolidate their sense of being a single state.

mass production System in which factories were set up to produce huge quantities of identical products, reflecting the early-twentieth-century world's demands for greater volume, faster speed, reduced cost, and standardized output.

Mastaba Word meaning "bench" in Arabic; it refers to a huge flat structure identical to earlier royal tombs of ancient Egypt.

Mau-Mau Revolt (1952–1957) Uprising orchestrated by a Kenyan guerrilla movement; this conflict forced the British to grant independence to the black majority in Kenya.

Mauryan Empire Dynasty extended by the Mauryans from 321 to 184 BCE, from the Indus Valley to the northwest areas of South Asia, in a region previously controlled by Persia. It was the first large-scale empire in South Asia and was to become the model for future Indian empires.

Mawali Non-Arab "clients" to Arab tribes in the early Islamic Empire. Because tribal patronage was so much a part of the Arabian cultural system, non-Arabs who converted to Islam affiliated themselves with a tribe and became clients of that tribe.

Maxim gun European weaponry that was capable of firing many bullets per second; it was used against Africans in the conquest of the continent.

Mayans Civilization that ruled over large stretches of Mesoamerica; it was composed of a series of kingdoms, each built around ritual centers rather than cities. The Mayans engaged neighboring peoples in warfare and trade and expanded borders through tributary relationships. They were not defined by a great ruler or one capital city, but by their shared religious beliefs.

McCarthyism Campaign by Republican senator Joseph McCarthy in the late 1940s and early 1950s to uncover closet communists, particularly in the State Department and in Hollywood.

Meat Inspection Act (1906) Legislation that provided for government supervision of meat-packing operations; it was part of a broader "Progressive" reform movement dedicated to correcting the negative consequences of urbanization and industrialization in the United States.

Mecca Arabian city in which Muhammad was born. Mecca was a trading center and pilgrimage destination in the pre-Islamic and Islamic periods. Exiled in 622 CE because of resistance to his message, Muhammad returned to Mecca in 630 CE and claimed the city for Islam.

Medes Rivals of the Assyrians and the Persians. The Medes inhabited the area from the Zagros Mountains to the modern city of Tehran; known as expert horsemen and archers, they were eventually defeated by the Persians.

megaliths Literally, "great stone"; the word *megalith* is used when describing structures such as Stonehenge. These massive structures are the result of cooperative planning and work.

Megarons Large buildings found in Troy (level II) that are the predecessors of the classic Greek temple.

Meiji Empire Empire created under the leadership of Mutsuhito, emperor of Japan from 1868 until 1912. During the Meiji period Japan became a world industrial and naval power.

Meiji Restoration Reign of the Meiji emperor, which was characterized by a new nationalist identity, economic advances, and political transformation.

Mencius Disciple of Confucius who lived from 372 to 289 BCE.

mercantilism Economic theory that drove European empire builders. In this economic system, the world had a fixed amount of wealth, which meant one country's wealth came at the expense of another's. Mercantilism assumed that colonies existed for the sole purpose of enriching the country that controlled the colony.

Mercosur Free-trade pact between the governments of Argentina, Brazil, Paraguay, and Uruguay.

meritocracy Rule by persons of talent.

Meroe Ancient kingdom in what is today Sudan. It flourished for nearly a thousand years, from the fifth century BCE to the fifth century CE.

mestizos Mixed-blood offspring of Spanish settlers and native Indians.

métis Mixed-blood offspring of French settlers and native Indians.

Mexican Revolution (1910) Conflict fueled by the unequal distribution of land and by disgruntled workers; it erupted when political elites split over the succession of General Porfirio Díaz after decades of his rule. The fight lasted over ten years and cost one million lives, but it resulted in a widespread reform and a new constitution.

***Mfecane* movement** African political revolts in the first half of the nineteenth century that were caused by the expansionist methods of King Shaka of the Zulu people.

microsocieties Small-scale communities that had little interaction with others. These communities were the norm for peoples living in the Americas and islanders in the Pacific and Aegean from 2000 to 1200 BCE.

migration Long-distance travel for the purpose of resettlement. In the case of early man, the need to move was usually a response to an environmental shift, such as climate change during the Ice Age.

millenarian Convinced of the imminent coming of a just and ideal society.

millenarian movement Broad, popular upheaval calling for the restoration of a bygone moral age, often led by charismatic spiritual prophets.

Millets Minority religious communities of the Ottoman Empire.

minaret Slender tower within a mosque from which Muslims are called to prayer.

Minbar Pulpit inside a mosque from which Muslim religious speakers broadcast their message to the faithful.

Minoans A people who built a large number of elaborate, independent palace centers on Crete, at Knossos, and elsewhere around 2000 BCE. Named after the legendary King Minos, said to have ruled Crete at the time, they sailed throughout the Mediterranean and by 1600 BCE had planted colonies on many Aegean islands, which in turn became trading and mining centers.

mission civilisatrice Term French colonizers used to refer to France's form of "rationalized" colonial rule, which attempted to bring "civilization" to the "uncivilized."

mitochondrial DNA Form of DNA found outside the nucleus of cells, where it serves as cells' microscopic power packs. Examining mitochondrial DNA enables researchers to measure the genetic variation among living objects, including human beings.

Moche A people who extended their power and increased their wealth at the height of the Chimu Empire over several valleys in what is now modern-day Peru.

Model T First automobile, manufactured by the Ford Motor Company of Henry Ford, to be priced reasonably enough to be sold to the masses.

modernists A generation of exuberant young artists, writers, and scientists in the late nineteenth century who broke with older conventions and sought new ways of seeing and describing the world.

Mohism School of thought in ancient China, named after Mo Di, or Mozi, who lived from 479 to 438 BCE. It emphasized one's obligation to society as a whole, not just to one's immediate family or social circle.

monarchy Political system in which one individual holds supreme power and passes that power on to his or her next of kin.

monasticism Christian way of life that originated in Egypt and was practiced as early as 300 CE in the Mediterranean. The word itself contains the meaning of a person "living alone" without marriage or family.

monetization An economic shift from a barter-based economy to one dependent on coin.

Mongols Combination of nomadic forest and prairie peoples who lived by hunting and livestock herding and were expert horsemen. Beginning in 1206, the Mongols launched a series of conquests that brought far-flung parts of the world together under their rule. By incorporating conquered peoples and adapting some of their customs, the Mongols created a unified empire that stretched from the Pacific Ocean to the shores of the eastern Mediterranean and the southern steppes of Eurasia.

Moors Term employed by Europeans in the medieval period to refer to Muslim occupants of North Africa, the western Sahara, and the Iberian Peninsula.

mosque Place of worship for the people of Islam.

"Mound people" Name for the people of Cahokia, since its landscape was dominated by earthen monuments in the shapes of mounds. The mounds were carefully maintained and were the loci from which Cahokians paid respect to spiritual forces. *See also* Cahokia.

Mu Chinese ruler (956–918 BCE) who put forth a formal bureaucratic system of governance, appointing officials, supervisors and military captains to whom he was not related. He also instituted a formal legal code.

muckrakers Journalists who aimed to expose political and commercial corruption in late-nineteenth- and early-twentieth-century America.

Muftis Experts on Muslim religious law.

Mughal Empire One of Islam's greatest regimes. Established in 1526, it was a vigorous, centralized state whose political authority encompassed most of modern-day India. During the sixteenth century, it had a population of between 100 and 150 million.

Muhammad (570–632 CE) Prophet and founder of the Islamic faith. Born in Mecca in Saudi Arabia and orphaned when young, Muhammad lived under the protection of his uncle. His career as a prophet began around 610 CE, with his first experience of spiritual revelation.

Muhammad Ali Ruler of Egypt between 1805 and 1848. He initiated a set of modernizing reforms that sought to make Egypt competitive with the great powers.

mullahs Religious leaders in Iran who in the 1970s led a movement opposing Shah Reza Pahlavi and denounced American materialism and secularism.

multinational corporations Corporations based in many different countries that have global investment, trading, and distribution goals.

Muscovy The principality of Moscow. Originally a mixture of Slavs, Finnish tribes, Turkic speakers, and many others, Muscovy used territorial expansion and commercial networks to consolidate a powerful state and expanded to become the Russian Empire, a huge realm that spanned parts of Europe, much of northern Asia, numerous North Pacific islands, and even—for a time—a corner of North America (Alaska).

Muslim Brotherhood Egyptian organization founded in 1938 by Hassan al-Banna. It attacked liberal democracy as a cover for middle-class, business, and landowning interests and fought for a return to a purified Islam.

Muslim League National Muslim party of India.

Mussolini, Benito (1883–1945) Italian dictator and founder of the fascist movement in Italy. During World War II, he allied Italy with Germany and Japan.

Muwahhidin Term meaning "unitarians"; these were followers of the Wahhabi movement that emerged in the Arabian Peninsula in the eighteenth century.

Mycenaeans Mainland competitors of the Minoans; they took over Crete around 1400 BCE. Migrating to Greece from central Europe, they brought their Indo-European language, horse chariots, and metalworking skills, which they used to dominate until 1200 BCE.

Nagasaki Second Japanese city to be hit by an atomic bomb near the end of World War II.

Napoleonic Code Legal code drafted by Napoleon in 1804; it distilled different legal traditions to create one uniform law. The code confirmed the abolition of feudal privileges of all kinds and set the conditions for exercising property rights.

National Assembly of France Governing body of France that succeeded the Estates-General in 1789 during the French Revolution. It was composed of, and defined by, the delegates of the Third Estate.

National Association for the Advancement of Colored People (NAACP) Founded in 1910, the U.S. civil rights organization dedicated to ending inequality and segregation for black Americans.

National Recovery Administration (NRA) New Deal agency created in 1933 to prepare codes of fair administration and to plan for public works. It was later declared unconstitutional.

nationalism The idea that members of a shared community called a "nation" should have sovereignty within the borders of their state.

nation-state Form of political organization that derived legitimacy from its inhabitants, often referred to as citizens, who in theory, if not always in practice, shared a common language, common culture, and common history.

native learning Japanese movement to promote nativist intellectual traditions and the celebration of Japanese texts.

native paramountcy British form of "rationalized" colonial rule, which attempted to bring "civilization" to the "uncivilized" by proclaiming that when the interests of European settlers in Africa clashed with those of the African population, the latter should take precedence.

natural rights Belief that emerged in eighteenth-century western Europe and North America that rights fundamental to human nature were discernible to reason and should be affirmed in human-made law.

natural selection Charles Darwin's theory that populations grew faster than the food supply, creating a "struggle for existence" among species. In later work he showed how the passing on of individual traits was also determined by what he called sexual selection—according to which the "best" mates are chosen for their strength, beauty, or talents. The outcome: the "fittest" survived to reproduce, while the less adaptable did not.

Nazis (National Socialist German Workers Party) German organization dedicated to winning workers over from socialism to nationalism; the first Nazi Party platform combined nationalism with anticapitalism and anti-Semitism.

Neanderthals Members of an early wave of hominids from Africa who settled in western Afro-Eurasia, in an area reaching from present-day Uzbekistan and Iraq to Spain, approximately 150,000 years ago.

needle compass Crucial instrument made available to navigators after 1000 CE that helped guide sailors on the high seas. It was a Chinese invention.

negritos Hunter-gatherer inhabitants of the East Asian coastal islands who migrated there around 28,000 BCE but by 2000 BCE had been replaced by new migrants.

Negritude Statement of the virtues of the black identity and the validation of African culture and the African past, even in a westernizing world. This idea was shaped by African and African American intellectuals like Senegal's first president, Léopold Sédar Senghor.

Nehemiah Jewish eunuch of the Persian court who was given permission to rebuild the fortification walls around the city of Jerusalem from 440 to 437 BCE.

Neo-Assyrian Empire Afro-Eurasian empire that dominated around 950 BCE. The Neo-Assyrians extended their control over resources and people beyond their own borders, and their empire lasted for three centuries.

neocolonialism Contemporary geopolitical policy or practice in which a politically, economically, and often militarily superior nation asserts control over a country that remains nominally sovereign.

Nestorian Christians Denomination of Christians whose beliefs about Christ differed from those of the official Byzantine church. Named after Nestorius, former bishop of Constantinople, they emphasized the human aspects of Jesus.

New Deal President Franklin Delano Roosevelt's package of government reforms that were enacted during the 1930s to provide jobs for the unemployed, social welfare programs for the poor, and security to the financial markets.

New Economic Policy Enacted decrees of the Bolsheviks between 1921 and 1927 that grudgingly sanctioned private trade and private property.

New Negro movement *See* Harlem Renaissance.

New World Term applied to the Americas that reflected the Europeans' view that anything previously unknown to them was "new," even if it had existed and supported societies long before European explorers arrived on its shores.

Nirvana Literally, nonexistence; nirvana is the state of complete liberation from the concerns of worldly life, as in Buddhist thought.

No–drama Masked theater favored by Japanese bureaucrats and regional lords during the Tokugawa period.

Noble Eightfold Path Buddhist concept of a way of life by which people may rid themselves of individual desire to achieve nirvana. The path consists of wisdom, ethical behavior, and mental discipline.

Nok culture Spectacular culture that arose in what is today Nigeria, in the sixth century BCE. Iron smelting occurred there around 600 BCE. Thus the Nok people made the transition from stone to iron materials.

nomads People who move across vast distances without settling permanently in a particular place. Often pastoralists, nomads and transhumant herders introduced new forms of chariot-based warfare that transformed the Afro-Eurasian world.

nongovernmental organizations (NGOs) Term used to refer to private organizations like the Red Cross that play a large role in international affairs.

nonviolent resistance *(Satyagraha)* Moral and political philosophy of resistance developed by Indian National Congress leader Mohandas Gandhi. Gandhi believed that if Indians pursued self-reliance and self-control in a nonviolent way, the British would eventually have to leave.

North American Free Trade Agreement (NAFTA) Treaty negotiated in the early 1990s to promote free trade between Canada, the United States, and Mexico.

North Atlantic Treaty Organization (NATO) International organization set up in1949 to provide for the defense of western European countries and the United States from the perceived Soviet threat.

Northern Wei dynasty Regime founded in 386 CE by the Tuoba, a people originally from Inner Mongolia, that lasted one and a half centuries. The rulers of this dynasty adopted many practices of the earlier Chinese Han regime. At the same time, they struggled to consolidate authority over their own nomadic people. Ultimately, several decades of intense internal conflict led to the dynasty's downfall.

northwest passage Long-sought marine passageway between the Atlantic and Pacific oceans.

Oceania Collective name for the lands of Australia and New Zealand and the islands of the southwest Pacific Ocean.

Odyssey Composed in the eighth century BCE, an epic tale of the journey of Odysseus, who traveled the Mediterranean back to his home in Ithaca after the siege of Troy.

Oikos The word for "small family unit" in ancient Greece, similar to the *familia* in Rome. Its structure, with men as heads of household over women and children, embodied the fundamental power structure in Greek city-states.

oligarchy Clique of privileged rulers.

Olmecs A people who emerged around 1500 BCE and lived in Mesoamerica. The name means those who "lived in the land of the rubber." Olmec society was composed of decentralized villages. Its members spoke the same language and worshipped the same gods.

Open Door Policy Policy proposed by American Secretary of State John Hay that would give all foreign nations equal access to trade with China. As European imperial powers carved out spheres of trade in late-nineteenth-century China, American leaders worried that the United States would be excluded from trade with China. To prevent this, Hay proposed the Open Door Policy.

Opium War (1839–1842) War fought between the British and Qing China over British trade in opium; resulted in the granting to the British the right to trade in five different ports and the ceding of Hong Kong to the British.

oracle bones Animal bones used by Shang diviners. Diviners applied intense heat to the shoulder bones of cattle or to turtle shells, which caused them to crack. The diviners would then interpret the cracks as signs from the ancestors regarding royal plans and actions.

Organization of Petroleum Exporting Countries (OPEC) International association established in 1960 to coordinate price and supply policies of oil-producing states.

Orientalism Genre of literature and painting that portrayed the nonwestern peoples of North Africa and Asia as exotic, sensuous, and economically backward with respect to Europeans.

orientalists Western scholars who specialized in the study of the East.

Orrorin tugenensis Predecessor to hominids that first appeared 6 million years ago.

Ottoman Empire Rulers of Anatolia, the Arab world, and much of southern and eastern Europe in the early sixteenth century. They transformed themselves from nomadic warrior bands who roamed the borderlands between Islamic and Christian worlds in Anatolia into sovereigns of a vast, bureaucratic empire. The Ottomans embraced a Sunni view of Islam. They adapted traditional Byzantine governmental practices but tried new ways of integrating the diverse peoples of their empire.

Pacific War (1879–1883) War between Chile and the alliance of Bolivia and Peru.

Pagani Pejorative word used by Christians to designate pagans.

palace Official residence of the ruler, his family, and his entourage. The palace was both a social institution and a set of buildings. It first appeared around 2500 BCE, about a millennium later than the Mesopotamian temple, and quickly joined the temple as a defining landmark of city life. Eventually, it became a source of power rivaling the temple, and palace and temple life often blurred, as did the boundary between the sacred and the secular.

Palace of Versailles The palace complex, eleven miles away from the French capital of Paris, built by Louis XIV in the 1670s and 1680s to house and entertain his leading clergymen and nobles, with the hopes of diverting them from plotting against him.

Palmyra Roman trading depot in modern-day Syria; part of a network of trading cities that connected various regions of Afro-Eurasia.

pan movements Groups that sought to link people across state boundaries in new communities based on ethnicity or, in some cases, religion (e.g., pan-Germanism, pan-Islamism, pan-Slavism).

Pansophia Ideal republic of inquisitive Christians united in the search for knowledge of nature as a means of loving God.

papacy The institution of the pope; the Catholic spiritual leader in Rome.

papal Of, relating to, or issued by a pope.

Parthians Horse-riding people who pushed southward around the middle of the second century BCE and wiped out the Greek kingdoms in Iran. They then extended their power all the way to the Mediterranean, where they ran up against the Roman Empire in Anatolia and Mesopotamia.

pastoral nomadic communities Groups of people that moved their domesticated animals from place to place to meet the animals' demanding grazing requirements. Around 3500 BCE, western Afro-Eurasia witnessed the growth and spread of pastoral nomadic communities.

pastoralism Herding and breeding of sheep and goats or other animals as a primary means of subsistence.

Paterfamilias Latin for "Father of the family," which itself was the foundation of the Roman social order.

Patria Latin, meaning "fatherland."

patrons In the Roman system of patronage, men and women of wealth and high social status who protected dependents or "clients" of a lower class.

Pax Mongolica Term that refers to the political and especially the commercial stability that the vast Mongol Empire provided for the travelers and merchants of Eurasia during the thirteenth and fourteenth centuries.

Pax Romana Latin for "Roman Peace"; refers to the period between 25 BCE and 235 CE during which conditions in the Roman Empire were settled and peaceful.

Pax Sinica Period of peace (149–87 BCE) during which agriculture, commerce, and industry flourished in East Asia under the rule of the Han.

Peace Preservation Act (1925) Act instituted in Japan that specified up to ten years' hard labor for any member of an organization advocating a basic change in the political system or the abolition of private property.

Pearl Harbor American naval base in Hawaii on which the Japanese launched a surprise attack on December 7, 1941, bringing the United States into World War II.

Peloponnesian War War fought between 431 and 404 BCE between two of Greece's most powerful city-states, Athens and Sparta.

Peninsular War (1808–1814) Conflict in which the Portuguese and Spanish populations, supported by the British, resisted the French invasion under Napoleon of the Iberian Peninsula.

peninsulars Spaniards who, although born in Spain, resided in the Spanish colonial territories. They regarded themselves as superior to Spaniards born in the colonies (Creoles).

Peoples' Charter Document calling for universal suffrage for adult males, the secret ballot, electoral districts, and annual parliamentary elections. It was signed by over 3 million British between 1839 and 1842.

periplus Book that reflected sailing knowledge; in such books captains would record landing spots and ports. The word *periplus* literally means "sailing around."

Persepolis Darius I's capital city in the highlands of Fars; a ceremonial center and expression of imperial identity as well as an important administrative hub.

Peterloo Massacre (1819) The killing of 11 and wounding of 460 following a peaceful demonstration for political reform by workers in Manchester, England.

Petra City in modern-day Jordan that was the Nabataean capital. It profited greatly by supplying provisions and water to travelers and traders. Many of its houses and shrines were cut into the rocky mountains. *Petra* means "rock."

phalanx Military formation used by Philip II of Macedonia, whereby heavily armored infantry were closely arrayed in battle formation.

Philip II of Macedonia Father of Alexander the Great, under whose rule Macedonia developed into a large ethnic and territorial state. After unifying Macedonia, Philip went on to conquer neighboring states.

philosophia Literally "love of wisdom"; this system of thought originally included speculation on the nature of the cosmos, the environment, and human existence. It eventually came to include thought about the nature of humans and life in society.

Phoenicians Known as the Canaanites in the Bible, an ethnic group in the Levant under Assyrian rule in the seventh century BCE; they provided ships and sailors for battles in the Mediterranean. The word *Phoenician* refers to the purple dye they manufactured and widely traded, along with other commercial goods and services, throughout the Mediterranean. While part of wider Mesopotamian culture, their major contribution was the alphabet, first introduced in the second millennium BCE, which made far-reaching communication possible.

phonemes Primary and distinctive sounds that are characteristic of human language.

piety Strong sense of religious duty and devoutness, often inspiring extraordinary actions.

plant domestication Process of growing plants, harvesting their seeds, and saving some of the seeds for planting in subsequent growing cycles, resulting in a steady food supply. This process occurred as far back as 5000 BCE, when plants began to naturally retain their seeds. Plant domestication was practiced first in the southern Levant and spread from there into the rest of Southwest Asia.

Plato (427–347 BCE) Disciple of the great philosopher Socrates; his works are the only record we have of Socrates' teaching. He was also the author of formative philosophical works on ethics and politics.

plebs In Rome, term that referred to the "common people." Their interests were protected by officials called tribunes.

Pochteca Archaic term for merchants of the Mexicos.

polities Politically organized communities or states.

polyglot communities Societies composed of diverse linguistic and ethnic groups.

popular culture Affordable and accessible forms of art and entertainment available to people at all levels of society.

popular sovereignty The idea that the power of the state resides in the people.

populists Members of a political movement that supported U.S. farmers in late-nineteenth-century America. The term is often used generically to refer to political groups who appeal to the majority of the population.

potassium-argon dating Major dating technique based on the changing chemical structure of objects over time, since over time potassium decays into argon. This method makes possible the dating of objects up to a million years old.

potato famine (1840s) Severe famine in Ireland that led to the rise of radical political movements and the migration of large numbers of Irish to the United States.

potter's wheel Fast wheel that enabled people to mass-produce vessels in many different shapes. This advance, invented at the city of Uruk, enabled potters to make significant technical breakthroughs.

pottery Vessels made of mud and later clay that were used for storing and transporting food. The development of pottery was a major breakthrough.

Prague Spring (1968) Program of liberalization under a new communist party in Czechoslovakia that strove to create a democratic and pluralist socialism.

predestination Belief of many sixteenth- and seventeenth-century Protestant groups that God had foreordained the lives of individuals, including their bad and good deeds.

primitivism Western art movement of the late-nineteenth and early-twentieth centuries that drew upon the so-called primitive art forms of Africa, Oceania, and pre-Columbian America.

progressive reformers Members of the U.S. reform movement in the early twentieth century that aimed to eliminate political corruption, improve working conditions, and regulate the power of large industrial and financial enterprises.

proletarians Industrial wage workers.

prophets Charismatic freelance religious men of power who found themselves in opposition to the formal power of the kings, bureaucrats, and priests.

Prophet's Town Indian village that was burned down by American forces in the early nineteenth century.

Protestant Reformation Religious movement initiated by sixteenth-century monk Martin Luther, who openly criticized the corruption in the Catholic Church and voiced his belief that Christians could speak directly to God. His doctrines gained wide support, and those who followed this new view of the Christianity rejected the authority of the papacy and the Catholic clergy, broke away from the Catholic Church, and called themselves "Protestants."

Protestantism Division of Christianity that emerged in western Europe from the Protestant Reformation.

Proto-Indo-European The parent of all the languages in the Indo-European family, which includes, among many others, English, German, Norwegian, Portuguese, French, Russian, Persian, Hindi, and Bengali.

Pullman Strike (1894) American Railway Union strike in response to wage cuts and firings.

puppet states Governments with little power in the international arena that follow the dictates of their more powerful neighbors or patrons.

Puritans Seventeenth-century reform group of the Church of England; also known as dissenters or nonconformists.

Qadiriyya Sufi order that facilitated the spread of Islam into West Africa.

Qadis Judges in the Ottoman Empire.

qanats Underground water channels, vital for irrigation, which were used in Persia. Little evaporation occurred when water was being moved through qanats.

Qing dynasty (1644–1911) Minority Manchu rule over China that incorporated new territories, experienced substantial population growth, and sustained significant economic growth.

Questions of King Milinda (Milindapunha) Name of a second-century BCE text espousing the teachings of Buddhism as set forth by Menander, a Yavana king. It featured a discussion between the king and a sophisticated Buddhist sage named Nagasena.

Quetzalcoatl Ancient deity and legendary ruler of Native American peoples living in Mexico.

Quran The scripture of the Islamic faith. Originally a verbal recitation, the Quran was eventually compiled into a book in the order in which we have it today. According to traditional Islamic interpretation, the Quran was revealed to Muhammad by the angel Gabriel over a period of twenty-three years.

radicals Widely used term in nineteenth-century Europe that referred to those individuals and political organizations that favored the total reconfiguration of Europe's old state system.

radiocarbon isotope C^{14} Isotope contained by all living things, which plants acquire directly from the atmosphere and animals acquire indirectly when they consume plants or other animals. When living things die, the C^{14} isotope they contain begins to decay into a stable nonradioactive element, C^{12}. The rate of decay is regular and measurable, making it possible to ascertain the date of fossils that leave organic remains for ages of up to 40,000 years.

Raj British crown's administration of India following the end of the East India Company's rule after the Rebellion of 1857.

raja "King" in the Kshatriya period in South Asia; could also refer to the head of a family, but indicated the person who had control of land and resources in South Asian city-states.

Ramadan Ninth month of the Muslim year, during which all Muslims must fast during daylight hours.

Rape of Nanjing Attack against the Chinese in which the Japanese slaughtered at least 100,000 civilians and raped thousands of women between December 1937 and February 1938.

Rashtriya Swayamsevak Sangh (RSS) (1925) Campaign to organize Hindus as a militant, modern community in India; translated in English as "National Volunteer Organization."

Rebellion of 1857 (Great Rebellion) Indian uprising against the East India Company to bring religious purification, an egalitarian society, and local and communal solidarity without the interference of British rule.

rebus Probably originating in Uruk, a representation that transfers meaning from the name of a thing to the sound of that name. For example, a picture of a bee can represent the sound "b." Such pictures opened the door to writing: a technology of symbols that uses marks to represent specific discrete sounds.

Reconquista Spanish reconquest of territories lost to the Islamic Empire, beginning with Toledo in 1061.

Red Guards Chinese students who were the shock troopers in the early phases of Mao's Cultural Revolution in 1966–1968.

Red Lanterns Female supporters of the Chinese Boxers who rebelled against foreign intrusions in China at the turn of the twentieth century. Most were teenage girls and unmarried women and dressed in red garments.

Red Turban Movement Diverse religious movement in China during the fourteenth century that spread the belief that the world was drawing to an end as Mongol rule was collapsing.

Reds Bolsheviks.

Reich German empire composed of Denmark, Austria, and parts of western France.

Reichstag The German parliament.

Reign of Terror Campaign at the height of the French Revolution in the early 1790s that used violence, including systematic execution of opponents of the revolution, to purge France of its enemies and to extend the revolution beyond its borders; radicals executed as many as 40,000 persons who were judged enemies of the state.

Renaissance Term meaning "rebirth" that historians use to characterize the expanded cultural production of European nations between 1430 and 1550. Emphasized a break from the church-centered medieval world and a new concept of humankind as the center of the world.

republican government Government in which power and rulership rest with representatives of the people—not a king.

Res publica Literally "public thing"; this referred to the Roman republic, in which policy and rules of behavior were determined by the Senate and by popular assemblies of the citizens.

Restoration period (1815–1848) European movement after the defeat of Napoleon to restore Europe to its pre-French revolutionary status and to quash radical movements.

Rift Valley Area of northeastern Africa where some of the most important early human archaeological discoveries of fossils were found, especially one of an intact skull that is 1.8 million years old.

river basin Area drained by a river, including all its tributaries. River basins were rich in fertile soil, water for irrigation, and plant and animal life, which made them attractive for human habitation. Cultivators were able to produce surplus agriculture to support the first cities.

riverine Term denoting an area whose inhabitants depended on irrigation for their well-being and whose populations are settled near great rivers. Egypt was, in a sense, the most riverine of all these cultures, in that it had no hinterland of plains as did Mesopotamia and the Indus valley. Away from the banks of the Nile, there is only largely uninhabitable desert.

Roman army Military force of the Roman Empire. The Romans devised a military draft that could draw from a huge population. In their encounter with Hannibal, they lost up to 80,000 men in three separate encounters and still won the war.

Roman Catholicism Branch of Christianity established by 1000 CE in western Europe and led by the Roman papacy. In contrast to ancient Greek Orthodoxy, Western Catholics believed that their church was destined to expand everywhere, and they set about converting the pagan tribes of northern Europe. Western Catholics contemptuously called the East Romans "Greeks" and condemned them for their "Byzantine" cunning.

Roman law Roman legal system, under which disputes were brought to the public courts and decisions were made by judges and sometimes by large juries. Rome's legal system featured written law and institutions for settling legal disputes.

roving bandits Large bands of dispossessed and marginalized peasants who vented their anger at tax collectors in the waning years of the Ming dynasty.

Royal Road A 1,600-mile road from Sardis in Anatolia to Susa in Iran; used by messengers, traders, the army, and those taking tribute to the king.

Russification Programs to assimilate people of over 146 dialects into the Russian Empire.

S.S. *(Schutzstaffel)* Hitler's security police force.

Sack of Constantinople Rampage in 1204 by the Frankish armies on the capital city of Constantinople.

sacred kingships Institutions that marked the centralized politics of West Africa. The inhabitants of these kingships believed that their kings were descendants of the gods.

Sahel region Area of sub-Saharan Africa with wetter and more temperate locations, especially in the upland massifs and their foothills, villages, and towns.

St. Bartholomew's Day Massacre (1572) Roman Catholic massacre of French Protestants in Paris.

St. Patrick Former slave brought to Ireland from Briton who later became a missionary, or the "Apostle of Ireland." He died in 470 CE.

Salt March (1930) A 240-mile trek to the sea in India, led by Mohandas Gandhi, to gather salt for free, thus breaking the British colonial monopoly on salt.

Samurai Japanese warriors who made up the private armies of Japanese daimyos.

Sandinista coalition Left-leaning Nicaraguan coalition of the 1970s and 1980s.

Santería African-based religion, blended with Christian influences, that was first practiced by slaves in Cuba.

Sargon the Great King of Akkad, a city-state near modern Baghdad. Reigning from 2334 to 2279 BCE, Sargon helped bring the competitive era of city-states to an end and sponsored monumental works of architecture, art, and literature.

Sasanian Empire Empire that succeeded the Parthians in the mid-220s ce in Inner Eurasia. The Sasanian Empire controlled the trade crossroads of Afro-Eurasia and possessed a strong armored cavalry, which made them a powerful rival to Rome. The Sasanians were also tolerant of Judaism and Christianity, which allowed Christians to flourish.

Sati Hindu practice whereby a woman was burned to death on the pyre of her dead husband.

satrap Governor of a province in the Persian Empire. Each satrap was a relative or intimate associate of the king.

Satyagraha *See* nonviolent resistance.

scientific method Method of inquiry based on experimentation in nature. Many of its principles were first laid out by the philosopher Sir Francis Bacon (1561–1626), who claimed that real science entailed the formulation of hypotheses that could be tested in carefully controlled experiments.

Scramble for Africa European rush to colonize parts of Africa at the end of the nineteenth century.

scribes Those who wield writing tools; from the very beginning they were at the top of the social ladder, under the major power brokers.

Scythian ethos Warrior ethos that embodied the extremes of aggressive mounted-horse culture, c. 1000 BCE. In part the Scythian ethos was the result of the constant struggle between settlers, hunter-gatherers, and nomads on the northern frontier of Europe.

Sea Peoples Migrants from north of the Mediterranean who invaded the cities of Egypt and the Levant in the second millennium BCE. Once settled along the coast of the Levant, they became known as the Philistines and considerably disrupted the settlements of the Canaanites.

SEATO (Southeast Asia Treaty Organization) Military alliance of pro-American, anticommunist states in Southeast Asia in 1954.

Second World Term invented during the cold war to refer to the communist countries, as opposed to the West (or First World) and the former colonies (or Third World).

second-generation societies Societies that expanded old ideas and methods by incorporating new aspects of culture and grafting them onto, or using them in combination with, established norms.

Seleucus Nikator Successor of Alexander the Great who lived from 358 to 281 BCE. He controlled Mesopotamia, Syria, Persia, and parts of the Punjab.

Self-Strengthening movement In the latter half of the nineteenth century, a movement of reformist Chinese bureaucrats that attempted to adopt western elements of learning and technological skill while retaining their core Chinese culture.

Semu Term meaning "outsiders" or non-Chinese people—Mongols, Tanguts, Khitan, Jurchen, Muslims, Tibetans, Persians, Turks, Nestorians, Jews, and Armenians—who became a new ruling elite over a Han majority population in the late thirteenth century.

sepoys Hindu and Muslim recruits of the East India Company's military force.

serfs Peasants who farmed the land and paid fees to be protected and governed by lords under a system of rule called feudalism.

settled agriculture Application of human labor and tools to a fixed plot of land for more than one growing cycle. It entails the changeover from a hunting and gathering lifestyle to one based on agriculture, which requires staying in one place until the soil has been exhausted.

Seven Years' War (1756–1763) World-wide war that ended when Prussia defeated Austria, establishing itself as a European power, and when Britain gained control of India and many of France's colonies through the Treaty of Paris.

sexual revolution Increased freedom in sexual behavior, resulting in part from the advances in contraception, notably the introduction of oral contraception in 1960, which allowed men and women to limit childbearing and to have sex with less fear of pregnancy.

shah Traditional title of Persian rulers.

shamans Certain humans whose powers supposedly enabled them to commune with the supernatural and to transform themselves wholly or partly into beasts.

Shamisen Three-stringed instrument, often played by Japanese geisha.

Shandingdong Man A *Homo sapiens* whose fossil remains and relics can be dated to about 18,000 years ago. His physical characteristics were closer to those of modern humans, and he had a similar brain size.

Shang state Dynasty in northeastern China that ruled from 1600 to 1045 BCE. Though not as well defined by borders as the territorial states in the southwest of Asia, it did have a ruling lineage. Four fundamental elements of the Shang state were a metal industry based on copper, pottery making, standardized architectural forms and walled towns, and divination using animal bones.

Shanghai School Late-nineteenth-century style of painting characterized by an emphasis on spontaneous brushwork, feeling, and the incorporation of western influences into classical Chinese pieces.

sharecropping System of farming in which tenant farmers rented land and gave over a share of their crops to the land's owners. Sometimes seen as a cheap way for the state to conduct agricultural affairs, sharecropping often resulted in the impoverishment and marginalization of the underclass.

sharia Literally, "the way"; now used to indicate the philosophy and rulings of Islamic law.

Sharpeville Massacre (1960) Massacre of sixty-nine black Africans when police fired upon a rally against the recently passed laws requiring nonwhite South Africans to carry identity papers.

Shawnees Native American tribe that inhabited the Ohio valley during the eighteenth century.

Shays's Rebellion (1786) Uprising of armed farmers that broke out when the Massachusetts state government refused to offer them economic relief.

Shiism One of the two main branches of Islam, practiced in the Safavid Empire. Although always a minority sect in the Islamic world, Shiism contains several subsects, each of which has slightly different interpretations of theology and politics.

Shiites Group of supporters of Ali, Muhammad's cousin and son-in-law, who wanted him to be the first caliph and believed that members of the Prophet's family deserved to rule. The leaders of the Shiite community are known as "Imam," which means "leaders."

Shinto Japan's official religion; it promoted the state and the emperor's divinity. The term means "the way of the gods."

shoguns Japanese military commanders. From 1192 to 1333, the Kamakura shoguns served as military "protectors" of the ruler in the city of Heian.

Shotoku Prince in the early Japanese Yamoto state (574–622 CE) who is credited with having introduced Buddhism to Japan.

shudras Literally "small ones"; workers and slaves from outside the Vedic lineage.

Siddhartha Gautama Another name for the Buddha; the most prominent opponent of the Brahman way of life; he lived from 563 to 483 BCE.

Sikhism Islamic-inspired religion that calls on its followers to renounce the caste system and to treat all believers as equal before God.

Silicon Valley Valley between the California cities of San Francisco and San Jose, known for its innovative computer and high-technology industries.

silk Luxury textile that became a vastly popular export from China (via the Silk Road) to the cities of the Roman world.

Silk Road Trade route linking China with central Asia and the Mediterranean; it extended over 5,000 miles, land and sea included, and was so named because of the quantities of silk that were traded along it. The Silk Road was a major factor in the development of civilizations in China, Egypt, Persia, India, and even Europe.

Silla One of three independent Korean states that may have emerged as early as the third century BCE. These states lasted until 668 CE, when Silla took control over the entire peninsula.

Silver Islands Term used by European merchants in the sixteenth century to refer to Japan, because of its substantial trade in silver with China.

Sino-Japanese War (1894–1895) Conflict over the control of Korea in which China was forced to cede the province of Taiwan to Japan.

Sipahi Urdu for "soldier."

Siva The third of three Vedic deities, signifying destruction. *See also* Brahma *and* Vishnu.

slave plantations System whereby labor was used for the cultivation of crops wholly for the sake of producing surplus that was then used for profit; slave plantations were a crucial part of the growth of the Mediterranean economy.

small seal script Unified script that was used to the exclusion of other scripts under the Qin, with the aim of centralizing administration; its use led to a less complicated style of clerical writing than had been in use under the Han.

social contract The idea, drawn from the writings of British philosopher John Locke, that the law should bind both ruler and people.

Social Darwinism Belief that Charles Darwin's theory of evolution was applicable to humans and justified the right of the ruling classes or countries to dominate the weak.

social hierarchies Distinctions between the privileged and the less privileged.

Social Security Act (1935) New Deal act that instituted old-age pensions and insurance for the unemployed.

socialism Political ideology that calls for a classless society with collective ownership of all property.

Socrates (469–399 BCE) Philosopher in Athens who encouraged people to reflect on ethics and morality. He stressed the importance of honor and integrity as opposed to wealth and power. Plato was his student.

Sogdians A people who lived in central Asia's commercial centers and maintained the stability and accessibility of the Silk Road. They were crucial to the interconnectedness of the Afro-Eurasian landmass.

Solidarity The communist bloc's first independent trade union, it was established in Poland at the Gdansk shipyard.

Song dynasty Chinese dynasty that took over the mandate of heaven for three centuries starting in 976 CE. It ruled an era of many economic and political successes, but it eventually lost northern China to nomadic tribes.

Song porcelain Type of porcelain perfected during the Song period that was light, durable, and quite beautiful.

South African War (1899–1902) Conflict between the British and Dutch colonists of South Africa which resulted in bringing two Afrikaner republics under the control of the British. Often called the Boer War.

Soviet bloc International alliance that included the east European countries of the Warsaw Pact as well as the Soviet Union but also came to include Cuba.

Spanish-American War (1898) War between the United States and Spain in Cuba, Puerto Rico, and the Philippines. It ended with a treaty in which the United States took over the Philippines, Guam, and Puerto Rico; Cuba won partial independence.

speciation The formation of different species.

specie Money in coin.

species Group of animals or plants possessing one or more distinctive characteristics.

spiritual ferment Process that occurred after 300 CE in which religion touched more areas of society and culture than before and touched them in different, more demanding ways.

Spring and Autumn period Period between the eighth and fifth centuries BCE, during which China was ruled by the feudal system. Considered an anarchic and turbulent time, there were 148 different tributary states in this period.

Stalin, Joseph (1879–1953) Leader of the communist party and the Soviet Union; sought to create "socialism in one country."

steel A metal more malleable and stronger than iron that became essential for industries like shipbuilding and railways.

stoicism Widespread philosophical movement initiated by Zeno (334–262 BCE). Zeno and his followers sought to understand the role of people in relation to the cosmos. For the Stoics, everything was grounded in nature. Being in love with nature and living a good life required being in control of one's passions and thus indifferent to pleasure or pain.

Strait of Malacca Seagoing gateway to Southeast and East Asia.

Strategic Defense Initiative ("Star Wars") Master plan, championed by U.S. president Ronald Reagan in the 1980s, that envisions the deployment of satellites and space missiles to protect the United States from incoming nuclear bombs.

stupa Dome monument marking the burial site of relics of the Buddha.

Suez Canal Channel built in 1869 across the Isthmus of Suez to connect the Mediterranean Sea with the Red Sea and to lower the costs of international trade.

Sufi brotherhoods Mystics within Islam who were responsible for the expansion of Islam into many regions of the world.

Sufism Emotional and mystical form of Islam that appealed to the common people.

sultan Islamic political leader. In the Ottoman Empire, the sultan combined a warrior ethos with an unwavering devotion to Islam.

Sumerian King List Text that recounts the making of political dynasties. Recorded around 2000 BCE, it organizes the reigns of kings by dynasty, one city at a time.

Sumerian pantheon The Sumerian gods, each of whom had a home in a particular floodplain city. In the Sumerian belief system, both gods and the natural forces they controlled had to be revered.

Sumerian temples Homes of the gods and symbols of Sumerian imperial identity. Sumerian temples also represented the gods' ability to hoard wealth at sites where people exchanged goods and services. In addition, temples distinguished the urban from the rural world.

Sun Yat-sen (1866–1925) Chinese revolutionary and founder of the Nationalist Party in China.

Sunnis Orthodox Muslims. The majority sect of Islam, Sunnis originally supported the succession of Abu Bakr over Ali and supported the rule of consensus rather than family lineage for the succession to the Islamic caliphate. *See also* Shiism.

superior man In the Confucian view, a person of perfected moral character, fit to be a leader.

superpowers Label applied to the United States and the Soviet Union after World War II because of their size, their possession of the atomic bomb, and the fact that each embodied a model of civilization (capitalism or communism) applicable to the whole world.

supranational organizations International organizations such as NGOs, the World Bank, and the IMF.

survival of the fittest Charles Darwin's belief that as animal populations grew and resources became scarce, a struggle for existence arose, the outcome of which was that only the "fittest" survived.

Suryavamsha The second lineage of two (the solar) in Vedic society. *See* Chandravamsha.

Swadeshi movement Voluntary organizations in India that championed the creation of indigenous manufacturing enterprises and schools of nationalist thought, in order to gain autonomy from Britain.

syndicalism Organization of workplace associations that included unskilled labor.

tabula rasa Term used by John Locke to describe the human mind before it begins to acquire ideas from experience; French for "clean slate."

Taiping Heavenly Kingdom (Heavenly Kingdom of Great Peace) Religious sect established by the Chinese prophet Hong Xiuquan in the mid-nineteenth century. Hong Xiuquan believed that he was Jesus's younger brother. The group struggled to rid the world of evil and "restore" the heavenly kingdom, imagined as a just and egalitarian order.

Taiping Rebellion Rebellion by followers of Hong Xiuquan and the Taiping Heavenly Kingdom against the Qing government over the economic and social turmoil caused by the Opium War. Despite raising an army of 100,000 rebels, the rebellion was crushed.

Taj Mahal Royal palace of the Mughal Empire, built by Shah Jahan in the seventeenth century in homage to his wife, Mumtaz.

Tale of Genji Japanese work written by Lady Murasaki that gives vivid accounts of Heian court life; Japan's first novel (early eleventh century).

talking cures Psychological practice developed by Sigmund Freud whereby the symptoms of neurotic and traumatized patients would decrease after regular periods of thoughtful discussion.

Talmud Huge volumes of oral commentary on Jewish law eventually compiled in two versions, the Palestinian and the Babylonian, in the fifth and sixth centuries BCE.

Talmud of Jerusalem Codified written volumes of the traditions of Judaism; produced by the rabbis of Galilee around 400 CE.

Tang dynasty (608–907 CE) Regime that promoted a cosmopolitan culture, turning China into the hub of East Asia cultural integration, while expanding the borders of their empire. In order to govern such a diverse empire, the Tang established a political culture and civil service based on Confucian teachings. Candidates for the civil service were required to take examinations, the first of their kind in the world.

Tanzimat Reorganization period of the Ottoman Empire in the mid-nineteenth century; modernizing reforms affected the military, trade, foreign relations, and civilian life.

tappers Rubber workers in Brazil, mostly either Indian or mixed-blood people.

Tarascans Mesoamerican society of the 1400s; rivals to and sometimes subjects of the Aztecs.

Tatish Ruler of Chan Santa Cruz during the Mexican Caste War. The term means "father."

Tecumseh (1768–1813) Shawnee who circulated Tenskwatawa's message of Indian renaissance among Indian villages from the Great Lakes to the Gulf Coast. He preached the need for Indian unity, insisting that Indians resist any American attempts to get them to sell more land. In response, thousands of followers renounced their ties to colonial ways and prepared to combat the expansion of the United States.

Tekkes Schools that taught devotional strategies and the religious knowledge for students to enter Sufi orders and become masters of the brotherhood.

temple Building where believers worshipped their gods and goddesses and where some peoples believed the deities had earthly residence.

Tenskwatawa (1768–1834) Shawnee prophet who urged disciples to abstain from alcohol and return to traditional customs, reducing dependence on European trade goods and severing connections to Christian missionaries. His message spread to other tribes, raising the specter of a pan-Indian confederacy.

Teotihuacán City-state in a large, mountainous valley in present-day Mexico; the first major community to emerge after the Olmecs.

territorial state Political form that emerged in the riverine cities of Mesopotamia, which was overwhelmed by the displacement of nomadic peoples. These states were kingdoms organized around charismatic rulers who headed large households; each had a defined physical border.

Third Estate The French people minus the clergy and the aristocracy; this term was popularized in the late eighteenth century and used to exalt the power of the bourgeoisie during the French Revolution.

Third Reich The German state from 1933 to 1945 under Adolf Hitler.

Third World Nations of the world, mostly in Asia, Latin America, and Africa, that were not highly industrialized like First World nations or tied to the Soviet Bloc (the Second World).

Thirty Years' War (1618–1648) Conflict begun between Protestants and Catholics in Germany that escalated into a general European war fought against the unity and power of the Holy Roman Empire.

Tiananmen Square Largest public square in the world and site of the pro-democracy movement in 1989 that resulted in the killing of as many as a thousand protesters by the Chinese army.

Tiers monde Term meaning "Third World," coined by French intellectuals to describe countries seeking a "third way" between Soviet communism and western capitalism.

Tiglath Pileser III Assyrian ruler from 745 to 728 BCE. This leader instituted reforms that changed the administrative and social structure of the empire to make it more efficient and introduced a standing army.

Tiwanaku Another name for Tihuanaco, the first great Andean polity, on the shores of Lake Titicaca.

Tlaxcalans Mesoamerican society of the 1400s; these people were enemies of the powerful Aztec Empire.

Tokugawa shogunate Hereditary military administration founded in 1603 that ruled Japan while keeping the emperor as a figurehead; it was toppled in 1868 by reformers who felt that Japan should adopt, not reject, Western influences.

Toltecs A Mesoamerican people who, by 1000 CE, had filled the political vacuum created by the decline of the city of Teotihuacán.

tomb culture Warlike group from northeast Asia who arrived by sea in the middle of the third century ce and imposed their military and social power on southern Japan. These conquerors are known today as the "Tomb culture" because of their elevated necropolises near present-day Osaka.

Topkapi Palace Political headquarters of the Ottoman Empire, located in Istanbul.

total war All-out war involving civilian populations as well as military forces, often used in reference to World War II.

transhumant migrants Nomads who entered settled territories in the second millennium BCE and moved their herds seasonally when resources became scarce.

Trans-Siberian Railroad Railroad built over very difficult terrain between 1891 and 1903 and subsequently expanded; it created an overland bridge for troops, peasant settlers, and commodities to move between Europe and the Pacific.

Treaty of Brest-Litovsk (1918) Separate peace between imperial Germany and the new Bolshevik regime in Russia. The treaty acknowledged the German victory on the Eastern Front and withdrew Russia from the war.

Treaty of Nanjing (1842) Treaty between China and Britain following the Opium War; it called for indemnities, the opening of new ports, and the cession of Hong Kong to the British.

Treaty of Tordesillas (1494) Treaty in which the pope decreed that the non-European world would be divided into spheres of trade and missionary responsibility between Spain and Portugal.

trickle trade Method by which a good is passed from one village to another, as in the case of obsidian among farming villages; the practice began around 7000 BCE. Also called "down the line trade."

Tripartite Pact (1940) Pact that stated that Germany, Italy, and Japan would act together in all future military ventures.

Triple Entente Alliance developed before World War I that eventually included Britain, France, and Russia.

Troy Important site founded around 3000 BCE in Anatolia, to the far west. Troy is legendary as the site of the war that was launched by the Greeks (the Achaeans) and that was recounted by Homer in the *Iliad*.

Truman Doctrine (1947) Declaration promising U.S. economic and military intervention, whenever and wherever needed, for the sake of preventing communist expansion.

Truth and Reconciliation Commission Quasi-judicial body established after the overthrow of the apartheid system in South Africa and the election of Nelson Mandela as the country's first black president in 1994. The commission was to gather evidence about crimes committed during the apartheid years. Those who showed remorse for their actions could appeal for clemency. The South African leaders believed that an airing of the grievances from this period would promote racial harmony and reconciliation.

truth commissions Elected officials' inquiries into human rights abuses by previous regimes. In Argentina, El Salvador, Guatemala, and South Africa, these commissions were vital for creating a new aura of legitimacy for democracies and for promising to uphold the rights of individuals.

tsar/czar Russian word derived from the Latin *Caesar* to refer to the Russian ruler of Kiev, and eventually to all rulers in Russia.

Tula Toltec capital city; a commercial hub and political and ceremonial center.

Uitlanders British populations living in Afrikaner republics; they were denied voting rights and subject to other forms of discrimination in the late nineteenth century. The term means "outsiders."

ulama Arabic word that means "learned ones" or "scholars"; used for those who devoted themselves to knowledge of Islamic sciences.

Umayyads Family who founded the first dynasty in Islam. They established family rule and dynastic succession to the role of caliph. The first Umayyad caliph established Damascus as his capital and was named Mu'awiya ibn Abi Sufyan.

Umma Arabic word for "community"; used to refer to the "Islamic politu" or "Islamic community."

Universal Declaration of Human Rights (1948) U.N. declaration that laid out the rights to which all human beings are entitled.

universitas Term used from the end of the twelfth century to denote scholars who came together, first in Paris. The term is borrowed from the merchant communities, where it denoted the equivalent of the modern "union."

Untouchables Caste in the Indian system whose jobs, usually in the more unsanitary aspects of urban life, rendered them "ritually and spiritually" impure.

Upanishads Vedic wisdom literature collected in the first half of the first millennium BCE. It took the form of dialogues between disciples and a sage.

urban-rural divide Division between those living in cities and those living in rural areas. One of history's most durable worldwide distinctions, the urban-rural divide eventually encompassed the globe. Where cities arose, communities adopted lifestyles based on the mass production of goods and on specialized labor. Those living in the countryside remained close to nature, cultivating the land or tending livestock. They diversified their labor and exchanged their grains and animal products for necessities available in urban centers.

utopian socialism The most visionary of all Restoration-era movements. Utopian socialists like Charles Fourier dreamed of transforming states, workplaces, and human relations and proposed plans to do so.

Vaishyas Householders or lesser clan members in Vedic society who worked the land and tended livestock.

Vardhamana Mahavira Advocate of Jainism who lived from 540 to 468 BCE; he emphasized interpretation of the Upanishads to govern and guide daily life.

Varna Caste system established by the Vedas in 600 BCE.

vassal states Subordinate states that had to pay tribute in luxury goods, raw materials, and manpower as part of a broad confederation of polities under the kings' protection.

Vedas Rhymes, hymns, and explanatory texts composed by Aryan priests; the Vedas became their most holy scripture and part of their religious rituals. They were initially passed down orally, in Sanskrit. Brahmans, priests of Vedic culture, incorporated the texts into ritual and society. The Vedas are considered the final authority of Hinduism.

Vedic people People who came from the steppes of Inner Asia around 1500 BCE and entered the fertile lowlands of the Indus River basin, gradually moving as far south as the Deccan plateau. They called themselves Aryan, which means "respected ones," and spoke Sanskrit, an Indo-European language.

veiling Practice of modest dress required of respectable women in the Assyrian Empire, introduced by Assyrian authorities in the thirteenth century BCE.

Venus figures Representations of the goddess of fertility drawn on the Chauvet

Cave in southeastern France. Discovered in 1994, they are probably about 35,000 years old.

Versailles Conference (1919) Peace conference between the victors of World War I; resulted in the Treaty of Versailles, which forced Germany to pay reparations and to give up its colonies to the victors.

Viet Cong Vietnamese communist group committed to overthrowing the government of South Vietnam and reunifying North and South Vietnam.

Viet Minh Group founded in 1941 by Ho Chi Minh to oppose the Japanese occupation of Indochina; it later fought the French colonial forces for independence. Also known as the Vietnamese Independent League.

Vietnam War (1965–1975) Conflict that resulted from concern over the spread of communism in Southeast Asia. The United States intervened on the side of South Vietnam in its struggle against peasant-supported Viet Cong guerrilla forces, who wanted to reunite Vietnam under a communist regime. Faced with antiwar opposition at home and ferocious resistance from the Vietnamese, American troops withdrew in 1973; the puppet South Vietnamese government collapsed two years later.

Vikings A people from Scandinavia who replaced the Franks as the dominant warrior class in northern Europe in the ninth century. They used their superior ships to loot other seagoing peoples and sailed up the rivers of central Russia to establish a trade route that connected Scandinavia and the Baltic with Constantinople and Baghdad. The Vikings established settlements in Iceland and Greenland and, briefly, North America.

Vishnu The second of three Vedic deities, signifying existence. *See also* Brahma *and* Siva.

viziers Bureaucrats of the Ottoman Empire.

Vodun Mixed religion of African and Christian customs practiced by slaves and free blacks in the colony of Saint Domingue.

Voting Rights Act (1965) Law that granted universal suffrage in the United States.

Wafd Nationalist party that came into existence during a rebellion in Egypt in 1919 and held power sporadically after Egypt was granted limited independence from Britain in 1922.

Wahhabism Early-eighteenth-century reform movement organized by Muhammad Ibn abd al-Wahhab, who preached the absolute oneness of Allah and a return to the pure Islam of Muhammad.

Wang Mang Han minister who usurped the throne in 9 CE because he believed that the Han had lost the mandate of heaven. He ruled until 23 CE.

war ethos Strong social commitment to a continuous state of war. The Roman army constantly drafted men and engaged in annual spring military campaigns. Soldiers were taught to embrace a sense of honor that did not allow them to accept defeat and commended those who repeatedly threw themselves into battle.

War of 1812 Conflict between Britain and the United States arising from U.S. grievances over oppressive British maritime practices in the Napoleonic Wars.

War on Poverty President Lyndon Johnson's push for an increased range of social programs and increased spending on social security, health, education, and assistance for the disabled.

Warring States period Period extending from the fifth century BCE to 221 BCE, when the regional warring states were unified by the Qin dynasty.

Warsaw Pact (1955–1991) Military alliance between the Soviet Union and other communist states that was established in response to the creation of the NATO alliance.

Weimar Republic (1919–1933) Constitutional Republic of Germany that was subverted by Hitler soon after he became chancellor.

Western Front Military front that stretched from the English Channel through Belgium and France to the Alps during World War I.

White and Blue Niles The two main branches of the Nile, rising out of central Africa and Ethiopia. They come together at the present-day capital city of Sudan, Khartoum.

White Lotus Rebellion Series of uprisings in northern China (1790–1800s) inspired by mystical beliefs in folk Buddhism and, at times, the idea of restoring the Ming dynasty.

White Wolf Mysterious militia leader, depicted in popular myth as a Chinese Robin Hood whose mission was to rid the country of the injustices of Yuan Shikai's government in the early years of the Chinese Republic (1910s).

Whites "Counterrevolutionaries" of the Bolshevik Revolution (1918–1921) who fought the Bolsheviks (the "Reds"); included former supporters of the tsar, Social Democrats, and large independent peasant armies.

witnessing Dying for one's faith, or becoming a martyr.

Wokou Supposedly Japanese pirates, many of whom were actually Chinese subjects of the Ming dynasty.

Works Progress Administration (WPA) New Deal program instituted in 1935 that put nearly 3 million people to work building roads, bridges, airports, and post offices.

World Bank International agency established in 1944 to provide economic assistance to war-torn and poor countries. Its formal title is the International Bank for Reconstruction and Development.

World War II (1939–1945) Worldwide war that began in September 1939 in Europe, and even earlier in Asia, and pitted Britain, the United States, and the Soviet Union (the Allies) against Nazi Germany, Japan, and Italy (the Axis).

Wu or Wudi Chinese leader known as the "Martial Emperor" because of his many military campaigns during the Han dynasty. He reigned from 141 to 87 BCE.

Wu Zhao Chinese empress who lived from 626 to 706 CE. She began as a concubine in the court of Li Shimin and became the mother of his son's child. She eventually gained power equal to that of the emperor, and named herself regent when she finagled a place for one of her own sons after their father's death.

Xiongnu The most powerful and intrusive of the nomadic peoples; originally pastoralists from the eastern part of the Asian steppe in what is modern-day Mongolia. They appeared along the frontier with China in the late Zhou dynasty and by the third century BCE had become the most powerful of all the pastoral communities in that area.

Xunzi Confucian moralist whose ideas were influential to Qin rulers. He lived from 310 to 237 BCE and believed that rational statecraft was more reliable than fickle human nature and that strict laws and severe punishments could create stability in society.

Yalta Accords Results of the meeting between President Roosevelt, Prime Minister Churchill, and Premier Stalin that occurred in the Crimea in 1945 to plan for the postwar order.

Yavana kings Sanskrit name for Greek rulers, derived from the Greek name for the area of western Asia Minor called Ionia, a term that then extended to anyone who spoke Greek or came from the Mediterranean.

yellow press Newspapers that sought a mass circulation by featuring sensationalist reporting.

Yellow Turbans One of several local Chinese religious movements that emerged across the empire, especially under Wang Mang's officials, who considered him a usurper. The Yellow Turbans, so called because of the yellow scarves they wore around their heads, were Daoist millenarians.

Yin City that became the capital of the Shang in 1350 BCE, ushering in a golden age.

Young Egypt Antiliberal, fascist group that gained a large following in Egypt during the 1930s.

Young Italy Nationalist organization made up of young students and intellectuals, devoted to the unification and renewal of the Italian state.

Yuan dynasty Dynasty established by the Mongols after the defeat of the Song. The Yuan dynasty was strong from 1280 to 1368; its capital was at Dadu, or modern-day Beijing.

Yuan Mongols Mongol rulers of China who were overthrown by the Ming dynasty in 1368.

Yuezhi A Turkic nomadic people who roamed on pastoral lands to the west of the Xiongnu territory of central Mongolia. They had friendly relationships with the farming societies in China, but the Yuezhi detested the Xiongnu and had frequent armed clashes with them.

Zaibatsu Large-scale, family-owned corporations in Japan consisting of factories, import-export businesses, and banks that dominated the Japanese economy until 1945.

Zamindars Archaic tax system of the Mughal Empire where decentralized lords collected tribute for the emperor.

Zapatistas Group of indigenous rebels that rose up against the Mexican government in 1994 and drew inspiration from an earlier Mexican rebel, Emiliano Zapata.

Zheng King during the Qin era who defeated what was left of the Warring States between 230 and 221 BCE. He assumed the mandate of heaven from the Zhou and declared himself First August Emperor, to distinguish himself from other kings.

Zheng He (1371–1433) Ming naval leader who established tributary relations with Southeast Asia, Indian Ocean ports, the Persian Gulf, and the east coast of Africa.

Zhong Shang Administrative central complex of the Shang.

Zhongguo Term originating in the ancient period and subsequently used to emphasize the central cultural and geographical location of China in the world; means "Middle Kingdom."

ziggurat By the end of the third millennium BCE, the elevated platform base of a Sumerian temple had transformed into a stepped platform called a *ziggurat*.

Zionism Political movement advocating the reestablishment of a Jewish homeland in Palestine.

Zoroaster Sometimes known as Zarathustra, thought to have been a teacher around 1000 BCE in eastern Iran and credited with having solidified the region's religious beliefs into a unified system that moved away from animistic nomadic beliefs. The main source for his teachings is a compilation called the Avesta.

Zoroastrianism Religion based on the teachings of Zoroaster that became the dominant religion of the Persian Empire.

Zulus African tribe that, under Shaka, created a ruthless warrior state in southern Africa in the early 1800s.

CREDITS

CHAPTER 10

Photo Credits Page 358: HIP/Art Resource, NY; p. 360: Nik Wheeler/Corbis; p. 361: Granger Collection; p. 363: Wikimedia Commons; p. 367 (left): Werner Forman/Art Resource, NY; p. 367 (right): HIP/Art Resource, NY; p. 368 (left): Colin Hoskins/ Cordaiy Photo Library/Corbis; p. 368 (right): The Art Gallery Collection/Alamy; p. 369: Peter Guttman/Corbis; p. 374: Macduff Everton/Corbis; p. 375: Keren Su/Corbis; p. 376: © The Metropolitan Museum of Art. Image source: Art Resource, NY; p. 379 (top): Wikimedia Commons; p. 379 (bottom): Granger Collection; p. 382 (top): akg-images/Werner Forman; p. 382 (bottom): Christophe Loviny/Corbis; p. 385 (top): Erich Lessing/Art Resource, NY; p. 385 (bottom): Hubert Stadler/Corbis; p. 386: akg-images/ Volker Kreidler; p. 388: The Art Archive; p. 389 (left): Charles & Josette Lenars/Corbis; p. 389 (right): Kevin Schafer/Corbis; p. 391: Snark/Art Resource, NY; p. 394 (left): Otto Lang/ Corbis; p. 394 (right): Michael S. Lewis/Corbis; p. 395: akg-images; p. 399: Granger Collection; p. 401: Bettmann/Corbis.

Text Credits Page 366: From *Sundiata: An Epic of Old Mali*, translated by D. T. Niane, pp. 40–41. Copyright © 1965 Longman Group. Reprinted with permission; p. 371: Goitein, S.D. (trans.); *Letters of Medieval Jewish Traders*. © 1973 Princeton University Press, 2001 renewed PUP Reprinted by permission of Princeton University Press; p. 381: From *Sources of Japanese Tradition*, Volume 1, pp. 177–79. Compiled by Ryu¯saku Tsunoda, Wm. Theodore de Bary, and Donald Keene Copyright © 1964 Columbia University Press. Reprinted with permission of the publisher.

CHAPTER 11

Photo Credits Page 404: Snark/Art Resource; p. 406: The Granger Collection, New York; p. 414: Album/Art Resource, NY; p. 415: Yann Arthus-Bertrand/ Corbis; p. 416: Stapleton Collection, UK/ Bridgeman Art Library International Ltd.; p. 417: Library of the Topkapi Palace Museum folio 31b, photograph courtesy of Talat Halman; p. 419: © 2007 The British Library; p. 423: Bibliotheque Nationale de France, Paris/Art Resource, NY; p. 427 (left): Scala/Ministero per i Beni e le Attività culturali/Art Resource; p. 427 (right): Scala/Ministero per i Beni e le Attività culturali/Art Resource; p. 429: Giraudon/Art Resource, NY; p. 430: The Granger Collection, New York; p. 431: The Art Archive; p. 432: Réunion des Musées Nationaux/Art Resource, NY; p. 435: The Jan Adkins Studio.

Text Credits Page 412: Ahmet Karamustafa, "Dervish Groups I the Ottoman Empire 1450–1550" from *God's Unruly Friends: Dervish Groups in the Islamic Later Middle Period*, pp. 6–7, Oneworld Publications, Oxford, 2006. Reprinted with the permission of Oneworld Publications; p. 420: "Nanak's Teachings in India" from *Sources of Indian Tradition*, ed. William T. de Bary, © 1958 Columbia University Press. Reprinted with the permission of the publisher; p. 422: Robertus de Avesbury, "The Flagellants in England" from *The Black Death*, Rosemary Horrox, trans./ed., pp. 153–154. Copyright © Rosemary Horrox 1994. Reprinted with permission of Manchester University Press; p. 433 Lily Hwa, "Proclamations of the Hong Wu Emperor." Reprinted with the permission of The Free Press, a Division of Simon & Schuster, Inc., from *Chinese Civilization: A Sourcebook, Second Edition*, revised & expanded by Patricia Buckley Ebrey. Copyright © 1993 by Patricia Buckley Ebrey. All rights reserved.

CHAPTER 12

Photo Credits Page 440: Courtesy Wychwood Editions; p. 442: Reunion des Musees Nationaux/ Art Resource, NY; p. 444 akg-images/Cameraphoto; p. 445 (top): Biblioteca Estense, Modena, Italy/ Scala/ Art Resource, NY; p. 445 (bottom): Science Museum, London/The Bridgeman Art Library; p. 450: Bildarchiv Preussischer Kulturbesitz/Art Resource, NY; p. 451: Granger Collection; p. 452 (left): Granger Collection; p. 452 (right): The Art Archive/Government Palace Tlaxcala Mexico/ Mireille Vautier; p. 453 (left): Schalkwijk/Art Resource, NY © 2013 Banco de Mexico Diego Rivera Frida Kahlo Museums Trust, Mexico, D.F./Artists Rights Society (ARS), New York; p. 453 (right): Granger Collection; p. 455: The Art Archive/ Archaeological Museum. Lima/Dagli Orti; p. 457 (top): The Granger Collection, New York; p. 457 (bottom): Granger Collection; p. 459: © François Guenet/Art Resource; p. 462: Rare Books Division, New York Public Library, Astor; Lenox and Tilden Foundations; p. 464: akg-images; p. 467: Musee d'Archeologie et d'Histoire, Lausanne, Switzerland/Giraudon/The Bridgeman Art Library; p. 468: Reunion des Musees Nationaux/ Art Resource, NY; p. 473: The Art Archive/Maritime Museum Kronborg Castle Denmark/Gianni Dagli Orti.

Text Credits Page 461: Padden, R.C., editor, "Claudia the Witch," pp. 117–121, from *Tales of Potosi*. © 1975 by Brown University Press. Reprinted by permission of University Press of New England, Lebanon, NH and the author; p. 471: T'ien-Tsê Chang, *Sino-Portuguese Trade From 1514 to 1644: A Synthesis of Portuguese and Chinese Sources* (Leyden: E.J. Brill, 1934), pp. 51–52. Reprinted by permission of Koninklijke Brill NV.

CHAPTER 13

Photo Credits Page 476: Reunion de Musees Nationaux/ Art Resource; p. 478 (left): British Museum/Superstock; p. 478

(right): © The Trustees of the Chester Beatty Library, Dublin/The Bridgeman Art Library; p. 483: Granger Collection; p. 485: MPI/Getty Images; p. 486: MPI/Getty Images; p. 488: The Granger Collection, NY; p. 492 (left): © 1989 North Wind Picture Archives; p. 492 (right): Private Collection/ © Michael Graham-Stewart/ The Bridgeman Art Library; p. 494: The Newberry Library, Chicago; p. 496: Mary Evans Picture Library/The Image Works; p. 497: The Art Archive/Museum der Stadt Wien/Dagli Orti; p. 498 (left): British Library/The Image Works; p. 498 (right): © The Trustees of the Chester Beatty Library, Dublin/The Bridgeman Art Library; p. 500: © The Metropolitan Museum of Art/ Art Resource, NY; p. 503: Granger Collection; p. 504: Sotheby's/ akg-images; p. 505: The Art Archive; p. 507: Reunion de Musees Nationaux/ Art Resource; p. 509 (top): Granger Collection; p. 509 (bottom): Chris Hellier/Corbis; p. 510: Wikimedia Commons; p. 511: bpk, Berlin/Art Resource; p. 512: Chateau de Versailles, France/ Bridgeman Art Library; p. 513: Private Collection/ The Bridgeman Art Library.

Text Credits Page 501: Huang Liu-Hung, "Elimination of Authorized Silversmiths" from *A Complete Book Concerning Happiness and Benevolence*, translated and edited by Djang Chu, pp. 190–191. © 1984 The Arizona Board of Regents. Reprinted by permission of the University of Arizona Press.

CHAPTER 14

Photo Credits Page 518: Scala/Art Resource, NY; p. 521: Topkapi Palace Museum, Istanbul; p. 522: Réunion des Musées Nationaux/Art Resource, NY; p. 523 (left): Topkapi Palace Museum, Istanbul; p. 523 (right): Victoria & Albert Museum, London/ Art Resource, NY; p. 524 (left): Giraudon/ Art Resource; p. 524 (right): Private Collection, courtesy of the owner and D.A. King; photo by Christie's of London; p. 525: Reproduced by the kind permission of the trustees of the Chester Beatty Library and Gallery of Oriental Art, Dublin; p. 526 (left): Scala/Art Resource, NY; p. 526 (right): Granger Collection; p. 527: from World Civilizations (Addison Wesley Longman, 2001); p. 529: Werner Forman/Art Resource, NY; p. 530 (left): Underwood & Underwood/Corbis; p. 530 (right): Underwood & Underwood/Corbis; p. 531 (left): Underwood & Underwood/ Corbis; p. 531 (right): The British Library, London; p. 532: The British Library, London/ The Bridgeman Art Library; p. 533: Reunion de Musees Nationaux/ Art Resource, NY; p. 534: The Fotomas Index; p. 536 (top): Wikimedia Commons; p. 536 (bottom): Euriskodata CDrom/Wikimedia Commons; p. 537: Bridgeman Art Library; p. 538: Bridgeman Art Library; p. 539: Musee des Beaux-Arts, Rouen/Superstock; p. 541 (top): Private Collection/ The Bridgeman Art Library; p. 541 (bottom): Private Collection/ The Bridgeman Art Library; p. 542: Image copyright © The Metropolitan Museum of Art/Art Resource, NY; p. 544: Bridgeman Art Library; p. 545 (left): Museo de America, Madrid; p. 545 (right): Museo de America, Madrid; p. 546: National Maritime Museum, London; p. 548 (left): HIP/ Art Resource, NY; p. 548 (right): Granger Collection; p. 549: The Art Archive/Castle Howard/Eileen Tweedy; p. 550: Natural History Museum, London/ The Bridgeman Art Library.

CHAPTER 15

Photo Credits Page 554: Lauros-Giraudon/ The Bridgeman Art Library; p. 557: Library of Congress; p. 561: Granger Collection; p. 562: Hulton Archive/Getty Images; p. 563: Musee de la Ville de Paris, Musee Carnavalet/ Giraudon/ Art Resource, NY; p. 565: Lauros-Giraudon/ The Bridgeman Art Library; p. 567: North Wind Picture Archives; p. 568: Granger Collection; p. 571 (left): The Art Archive /Museo Nacional de Historia, Castillo de Chapultepec, Mexico City/Dagli Orti; p. 571 (right): Granger Collection; p. 573: Private Collection/ The Bridgeman Art Library; p. 574: Granger Collection; p. 576: Granger Collection; p. 578: Granger Collection; p. 581: Novotsi/ The Bridgeman Art Library; p. 583: Corbis; p. 584: Courtesy of the director, National Army Museum, London; p. 585: Wikimedia Commons; p. 586: Granger Collection; p. 588: The Art Archive; p. 589 (left): The British Library, London/ The Bridgeman Art Library; p. 589 (right): North Wind Picture Archives; p. 591: Roy Miles Fine Paintings/ The Bridgeman Art Library.

Text Credits Page 582: Abd al-Rahman al-Jabarti, From *Napoleon in Egypt: al-Jabarti's Chronicle of the French Occupation*, 1798, translated by Shmuel Moreh, pp. 24–29. (Princeton: Markus Wiener Publishing, 1993).

CHAPTER 16

Photo Credits Page 594: Harvard-Yenching Library, Harvard University; p. 599: Wikimedia Commons; p. 601 (left): The British Library, London; p. 601 (right): National Archives, Zimbabwe; p. 605: Granger Collection; p. 607: Corbis; p. 610: Granger Collection; p. 611: Alamy; p. 617 (left): Granger Collection; p. 617 (right): Granger Collection; p. 618: Wikimedia Commons; p. 619: Wikimedia Commons; p. 621: Getty Images; p. 623: Victoria & Albert Museum/Art Resource, NY.

Text Credits Page 602: "Gikku Bello" from *One Woman's Jihad* by Beverly Mack & Jean Boyd. Copyright © 2000 by Beverly B. Mack and Jean Boyd. Reprinted with permission of Indiana University Press; p. 606: From "The Principles of the Heavenly Nature," in *Sources of Chinese Tradition,* 2nd Edition, Volume 2, pp. 229–30. Compiled by Wm. Theodore de Bary and Richard Lufrano. Copyright © 2000 Columbia University Press. Reprinted with permission of the publisher; p. 612: Karl Marx and Friedrich Engels, from "The Communist Manifesto," in *The Marx-Engels Reader,* 2nd ed., pp. 473–83, 490–91, 500. Edited by Robert C. Tucker.

CHAPTER 17

Photo Credits Page 628: Granger Collection; p. 634 (left): Granger Collection; p. 634 (right): The Granger Collection, New York/The Granger Collection; p. 635: Granger Collection; p. 636: Time & Life Pictures/Getty Images; p. 637 (left): Hulton/Getty Images; p. 637 (right): Hulton/Getty Images; p. 642: Universal History Archive/UIG; p. 643 (top): Peter Newark American Pictures/The Bridgeman Art Library; p. 643 (bottom): Hulton/ Getty Images; p. 644: Bettmann/Corbis; p. 646 (top): Illustrated London News/ Mary Evans Picture Library; p. 646 (bottom): Private Collection (uncredited photo), from Judith Gutman's "Through Indian Eyes, Oxford University Press; p. 649 (left): Hulton /Getty Images; p. 649 (right): Private Collection/ The Bridgeman Art Library; p. 650: Roger-Viollet, Paris/The Bridgeman Art Library; p. 651: Wikimedia Commons; p. 652: The Art Archive; p. 654 (top): Illustrated London News, 1872/ Mary Evans Picture Library; p. 654 (bottom): North Wind Picture Archives; p. 655: Erich Lessing/Art Resource, NY; p. 656 (top): North Wind Picture Archives; p. 656 (bottom): The Art Archive; p. 657: Granger; p. 662: Sovfoto/ Eastfoto.

CHAPTER 18

Photo Credits Page 666: SuperStock; p. 673 (left): SuperStock; p. 673 (right): Hulton Archive/Getty Images; p. 675 (left): Corbis; p. 675 (right): ullstein bild/The Granger Collection; p. 676: Empress Dowager Cixi and the imperial eunuchs, 1903–1905. Photographer: Hsun-ling Tz-u-hi, Empress Dowager of China, 1835–1908, Photographs, negative 261. Freer Gallery of Art and the Arthur M. Sackler Gallery Archives, Smithsonian Institution, Washington, D.C.; p. 678: SuperStock; p. 680 (left): akg-images; p. 680 (right): Hulton-Deutsch Collection/Corbis; p. 682: Bettmann/ Corbis; p. 685 (left): Culver Pictures/Art Archive; p. 685 (right): Sean Sprague/ Mexicolore/ The Bridgeman Art Library; p. 687: Wikimedia Commons; p. 688: © Estate of Pablo Picasso/ Artists Rights Society (ARS), New York. Digital Image (c) The Museum of Modern Art/Licensed by Scala/Art Resource, NY; p. 689: Snark/Art Resource, NY; p. 690 (left): © National Gallery, London/Art Resource, NY; p. 690 (right): Erich Lessing/Art Resource, NY; p. 690 (bottom): Album/Art Resource, NY; p. 691 (top): Sigmund Freud Copyrights/ Mary Evans Picture Library; p. 691 (bottom): The Palace Museum, Beijing; p. 693: Corbis; p. 694: Schalkwijk/Art Resource, NY © 2013 Banco de Mexico Diego Rivera Frida Kahlo Museums Trust, Mexico, D.F./Artists Rights Society (ARS), New York; p. 696 (left): Wikimedia Commons; p. 696 (right): © SZ Photo/AV Photo/The Bridgeman Art Library; p. 697 (left): Wikimedia Commons; p. 697 (right): E.O. Hoppe/ Corbis; p. 698: Domenica del Corriere/Dagli Orti/ The Art Archive.

Text Credits Page 683: Qui Jin, "An Address to Two Hundred Million Fellow Countrywomen." Reprinted with the permission of The Free Press, a Division of Simon & Schuster, Inc., from *Chinese Civilization: A Sourcebook, Second Edition*, revised & expanded by Patricia Buckley Ebrey. Copyright © 1993 by Patricia Buckley Ebrey. All rights reserved; p. 684: Margot Badran & Miriam Cooke (eds.), "Industrialization and Women's Freedom in Egypt" from *Opening the Gates: An Anthology of Arab Feminist Writing*. Copyright © 1990. Reprinted with permission of Indiana University Press; p. 699: Sayid Jamal al-Din al Afghani and Abdul-Hadi Ha'iri, "Afghani on the Decline of Islam," in *Die Welt des Islams*, New Series, Vol. 13, No. 1/2 (1971): 121–125. Reprinted by permission of Koninklijke Brill NV; p. 700: Franziska von Reventlow, "Viragines oder Hetaere" in *Autobiographisches, Novellen, Schriften, Selbtzeugnisse*, edited by Else Reventlow, translated by Suzanne Marchand. Reprinted with the permission of Suzanne Marchand.

CHAPTER 19

Photo Credits Page 704: The Illustrated London News Picture Library, London, UK/The Bridgeman Art Library; p. 707: The Imperial War Museum; p. 709: Hulton-Deutsch Collection/Corbis; p. 712 (left): Sovfoto/ Eastfoto; p. 712 (right): SuperStock; p. 716: Corbis; p. 717 (top): Ullstein bild/Granger Collection; p. 717 (bottom): Hulton/Getty Images; p. 719: SF Palm/Stageimage/ The Image Works; p. 721: The Granger Collection, New York/ The Granger Collection; p. 722: Library of Congress; p. 723 (left): Hulton Archive/Getty Images; p. 723 (right): The Granger Collection, New York/The Granger Collection; p. 725: The Illustrated London News Picture Library; p. 726: Mary Evans Picture Library; p. 729 (left): Bettmann/Corbis; p. 729 (right): Getty Images; p. 730: Heinrich Hoffmann/Time & Life Pictures/Getty Images; p. 731 (left): The Art Archive; p. 731 (right): Genevieve Naylor/Corbis; p. 732: Granger Collection; p. 734 (left): The Illustrated London News Picture Library; p. 734 (right): Private Collection/ The Bridgeman Art Library; p. 736: Dinodia Picture Agency, Bombay; p. 737: Modern China Rare Photography Library, Sun Yat-Sen and the Guomindang Party (The Commercial Press, Ltd. 1994); p. 738: Getty Images.

Text Credits Page 727: Ernest R. Huber, "Fuhrergewalt," *Nazism 1919–1945: A Documentary Reader, Vol. 2: State, Economy and Society 1933–1939*, edited by J. Noakes and G. Pridham, pp. 198–199. Reprinted by permission of University of Exeter Press; p. 733: From *Facing Mt. Kenya* by Jomo Kenyatta, published by Vintage Books, a division of Random House, Inc. and Secker & Warburg. Used by permission of Alfred A. Knopf, a division of Random House, Inc. and The Random House Group Ltd.; p. 735: M. K. Gandhi, from *Hind Swaraj and Other Writings*, edited by Anthony J. Parel, pp. 26–91. Copyright © 1997 Cambridge University Press. Reprinted with permission.

CHAPTER 20

Photo Credits Page 742: F.D.R. Library; p. 746 (left): The Illustrated London News Picture Library; p. 746 (right): Sovfoto/ Eastfoto; p. 748: Hulton/Getty Images; p. 749 (left): Official U.S. Air Force Photo/ Cody Images; p. 749 (right): Yosuke Yamahata/ Cody Images; p. 749 (bottom): F.D.R. Library; p. 750: NATO Photo/ TRH Pictures/Cody Images; p. 752: Bettmann/Corbis; p. 754: Granger Collection; p. 756 (left): Henri Cartier-Bresson/ Magnum Photos; p. 756 (right): Xinhua News Agency; p. 756 (bottom): Bettmann/ Corbis; p. 760 (top): Bettmann/ Corbis; p. 760 (bottom): Bettmann/ Corbis; p. 762: Hulton-Deutsch Collection/ Getty Images; p. 763 (top): Hulton-Deutsch Collection/ Corbis; p. 763 (bottom): Stroud/Express/Getty Images; p. 764: FPG/ Getty Images; p. 765: Hulton-Deutsch Collection/ Corbis; p. 766 (left): Bettmann/ Corbis; p. 766 (right): Bettmann/ Corbis; p. 767 (left): AP Photo; p. 767 (right): Fred Blackwell/State Historical Society of Wisconsin Visual Materials Archive; p. 768 (top): akg-images; p. 768 (bottom): Sovfoto; p. 769: Hulton-Deutsch Collection/Corbis; p. 771: Wikimedia Commons; p. 772 (left): Roger-Viollet/The Image Works; p. 772 (right): Li Zhensheng/ Contact Press Images; p. 773: Itar-Tass/ Sovfoto; p. 774: AP

Photo; p. 775: Bettmann/ Corbis; p. 776 (top): AP Photo; p. 776 (bottom): JP Laffont/Sygma/Corbis.

Text Credits Page 763: Léopold Sédar Senghor, excerpts from *African Socialism* (New York: American Society of African Culture, 1959), trans. Mercer Cook. Reprinted by permission of Moorland-Spingarn Research Center, Howard University, Washington, DC; p. 779: "The Problem That Has No Name" from *The Feminine Mystique* by Betty Friedan. Copyright © 1983, 1974, 1973, 1963 by Betty Friedan. Used by permission of W.W. Norton & Company, Inc. and Victor Gollancz, an imprint of The Orion Publishing Group Ltd.

CHAPTER 21

Photo Credits Page 784: AP Photo; p. 787: Hulton Archive/ Getty Images; p. 789: Robert Maass/Corbis; p. 792: Peter Magubane/ Time Life Pictures/Getty Images; p. 793: AP Photo; p. 795: George Esiri/Reuters/Corbis; p. 798: Uriel Sinai/Getty Images; p. 799 (top): Jeff Albertson/ Corbis; p. 799 (left): Getty Images; p. 799 (right): © Seth Wenig/ /AP; p. 801: Mary Evans/ EROS INTERNATIONAL /Ronald Grant/Everett Collection; p. 804 (top): Serge Attal/ TimePix/Getty Images; p. 804 (left): Copyright © 2007 by Robert Frerck and Odyssey Productions, Inc.; p. 804 (right): Lee Jae-Won/Reuters/Corbis; p. 805 (left): Gisele Wulfsohn/ Panos Pictures; p. 805 (right): © Chris Johnson/ Panos Pictures; p. 808: Vanessa Vick/Redux; p. 810: AP Photo; p. 811 (left): Susan I. Cunningham/ Panos Pictures; p. 811 (right): Douglas Engle/Corbis; p. 813: ASSOCIATED PRESS; p. 814: Sovfoto/ Eastfoto; p. 815: Tom Stoddart/Getty Images; p. 816: Peter Turnley/ Corbis; p. 817 (top): © Jacques Haillot/Corbis; p. 817 (bottom): Bettmann/ Corbis; p. 818: AP Photo; p. 819 (left): Clive Shirley/ Panos Pictures; p. 819 (right): Schalkwijk/Art Resource, NY, (c) 2013 Artists Rights Society (ARS), New York/SOMAAP, Mexico City.

Text Credits Page 790: Ann Tusa, "A Fatal Error" in *Media Studies Journal*, Fall 1999, pp. 26–29. Copyright © 1999. Reprinted by permission of *Media Studies Journal*; p. 809: Reproduced with permission of the World Bank from "Using subsidies to close gender gaps in education," *World Development Report 2000–2001*, p. 122, Box 7.2. Copyright 2000 by World Bank. Permission conveyed through Copyright Clearance Center, Inc.

EPILOGUE

Photo Credits Page 824: ASSOCIATED PRESS; p. 826 (left): AP Photo; p. 826 (right): Matt McDermott; p. 827: Ali Haider/ epa/Corbis; p. 828: AP Photo; p. 829 (top): ASSOCIATED PRESS; p. 829 (bottom): AP Photo/U.S. Coast Guard, Petty Officer 2nd Class Kyle Niemi; p. 831: AP Photo/ Mustafa Quraishi; p. 836: Dean Conger/ Corbis; p. 837: Timothy O'Rourke/ Bloomberg News/Landov; p. 838: Sebastian D'Souza/AFP/Getty Images; p. 844: ASSOCIATED PRESS; p. 846 (left): Liba Taylor/ Corbis; p. 846 (right): Herman Wouters/Hollandse Hoogte/Redux; p. 846 (bottom): Jason Reed/Reuters/Landov; p. 847 (top): AP Photo; p. 847 (bottom): Alexander Hassenstein/Getty Images.

INDEX

Italic page references indicate maps, illustrations, or chronology entries.